ırn

20

the last date below

Microsoft® SharePoint Products and Technologies Resource Kit

Bill English with the Microsoft SharePoint Teams

PUBLISHED BY
Microsoft Press
A Division of Microsoft Corporation
One Microsoft Way
Redmond, Washington 98052-6399

Library of Congress Cataloging-in-Publication Data pending.

Printed and bound in the United States of America.

2 3 4 5 6 7 8 9   QWT   8 7 6 5 4

Distributed in Canada by H.B. Fenn and Company Ltd.

A CIP catalogue record for this book is available from the British Library.

Microsoft Press books are available through booksellers and distributors worldwide. For further information about international editions, contact your local Microsoft Corporation office or contact Microsoft Press International directly at fax (425) 936-7329. Visit our Web site at www.microsoft.com/learning/. Send comments to *rkinput@microsoft.com*.

Active Directory, BizTalk, FrontPage, InfoPath, IntelliSense, JScript, Microsoft, Microsoft Press, MSDN, Outlook, PowerPoint, SharePoint, Visio, Visual Basic, Visual Studio, Win32, Windows, Windows NT, and Windows Server are either registered trademarks or trademarks of Microsoft Corporation in the United States and/or other countries. Other product and company names mentioned herein may be the trademarks of their respective owners.

The example companies, organizations, products, domain names, e-mail addresses, logos, people, places, and events depicted herein are fictitious. No association with any real company, organization, product, domain name, e-mail address, logo, person, place, or event is intended or should be inferred.

This book expresses the author's views and opinions. The information contained in this book is provided without any express, statutory, or implied warranties. Neither the authors, Microsoft Corporation, nor its resellers or distributors will be held liable for any damages caused or alleged to be caused either directly or indirectly by this book.

Acquisitions Editor: Hilary Long
Project Editor: Valerie Woolley
Technical Editors: Mark Harrison and Gary A. Bushey
Development Editor: Maureen Zimmerman
Principal Compositor: Elizabeth Hansford
Indexer: Pamona Corporation

Body Part No. X10-46136

Contents at a Glance

Contents

What do you think of this book?
We want to hear from you!

Microsoft is interested in hearing your feedback about this publication so we can
continually improve our books and learning resources for you. To participate in a brief
online survey, please visit: *www.microsoft.com/learning/booksurvey/*

Part II   SharePoint Products and Technologies Architecture

4   **Windows SharePoint Services Architecture**   **95**

Part IV   Deployment Scenarios

11   Deploying a Single Server and a Small Server Farm   273

12   Deploying Medium and Large Server Farms   281

34   The SharePoint Portal Server Object Model   941

35   Building Applications Using Windows SharePoint Services Data   951

**36   Building Applications for Microsoft Office SharePoint   987
Portal Server 2003**

40   Microsoft Outlook 2003 Integration with SharePoint   1067
Products and Technologies

Part XI   Upgrading and Migrating to SharePoint Products and Technologies

41   Integrating Exchange Server 2003 with SharePoint   1089
Products and Technologies

Acknowledgments

Principle Author
Bill English

Contributing Authors
Jason Ballard, Todd Bleeker, Margriet Bruggeman, Nikander Bruggeman, Penny Coventry, James Edelen, Olga Londer, Rebecca Monson, Sue Mosher, Bogdin Odulinski, Bud Ratliff, Kim Simmons, Chad Solomonson, and David Sterling

Microsoft Press
Acquisitions Editor: Martin DelRe
Acquisitions Editor: Hilary Long
Project Editor: Valerie Woolley
Development Editor: Maureen Zimmerman
Copyeditors: Roger LeBlanc and Lisa Pawlewicz
Technical Editors: Mark Harrison and Gary A. Bushey

Product Team User Assistance
Emily Schroeder, Crystal Thomas, Maria Hristova, Jo Sawyer, and Hannah Love

Product Team Manager
Adam Rosenblatt

Product Team Reviewers
Brad Stevenson, Eric Heino, Michael Herman, Dustin Friesenhahn, Sissie Hsiao, Anne Archambault, Dmitriy Meyerzon, Bill Griffin, David Taylor, Dan McPherson, Reza Dianat, Scott Fynn, Steve Gruman, Dan Hamersley, Jimi Ibbitt, Frank Poloney, Louise Reneau, Clint Covington, Howard Crow, Andrew Datars, Suraj Poozhiyil, Venky Veeraraghavan, Julie Madhusoodanan, Markus Klein, Brenda Carter, Jorgen Bergstrom, Bob Lee, Scott Kendall, KC Lemson, Suraj Poozhiyil, Fitzmaurice Lindhorst, Maurice Prather, Bryan Jeffries, David Vierzba, Greg Foltz, Lana Fly, Noah Chen, Les Smith, Edson Reyes, Shaofeng Zhu, David Mead, Andrew Miller, Michael Herzfeld, Scott Rubie, Douglas Tsang, Ryan Phillips, Syeb Muneeb-ul-Haq, Kimmo Forss, Troy Starr, Dominik Paiha, Alfredo Almada-Mireles, Anne Reese, Anthony Petro, Bryant Fong, Christopher Hall, Dean Justus, Edson Reyes, Frank Delia, Gabe Bratton, Geno White, Alex Hankin, Iyaz Allah Baksh, James Scott, James Sturns, Ken Bullock, Kerry Landen, Kristen Heller, Mark Grossbard, Michael Herman, Naganandhini Kohareswaran, Nigel Bridport, Pam Kessey, Raymond Hung, Rob Giesel, Robin Luft-Kite, Sheng Zhou, Shunri Guo, Stephen Young, Steve Peshka, Thomas Rizzo, Titus Miron, Todd Young, Jason Ma, Xuhao He, Vijay Krishna, Troy Star, Greg Foltz,

Shawn Baden, Mike Brotherton, Paul Bishop, Sarah Minahan, Dan Cui, Kappu Jaykumar, Daren Miller, Keith Bankston, Anuraag Tiwari, Rodrigo Lode, Jared McElwee, Lana Fly, Michael Magondo, Bob Samer, Tom Constantino, Neelima Jain, Tamara Williams, Syed Munee-ul-Haq, Kasey Quanrud, Vivek Srinivasan, Osama Hamden, Mike VandeKerkhof, Sarah Stewart, and Jesse Bedford

PAG Document Writers and Editors

Dan Hamersley, Frank Poloney, Louise Reneau, Steve Gruman, Reza Dianat, Jimi Ibbitt, Scott Fynn, Alix Mae Hughes, Todd Young, Ben Moebius, Brian Hitchcock, Carola Klass, William Jones, Robert Marcus, Garry Gross, Jill Going, Ronen Yacobi, and Scott St. Jean

Resource Kit Tools Editors

Margriet and Nikander Bruggeman

Tools Contributors

Daniel Witriol, Robert Silver, Chris Marshall, Naganandhini Kohareswaran, Daniel James, Maurice Prather, James Edelen, Thomas Rizzo and Renaud Comte.

Acknowledgments

The book that you now hold in your hands is the result of the collective effort of many, many people from July 2003 to April 2004. Even though my name is on the cover, believe me when I say that without the efforts of everyone listed in this acknowledgments section, you would not be holding a resource kit right now.

This is the ninth book project I've worked on in the last three and a half years and it has been, by far, the most comprehensive and most enjoyable (no offense to my other co-authors on the other books!). In addition, it has been the most humbling and rewarding project too. Getting out 1800 pages of content on a new, exciting software product that is (quite literally) changing how we do business is a rare opportunity and I've thoroughly enjoyed it. There are several people in particular who I'd like to acknowledge individually because they played such a pivotal role in either envisioning or seeing this project through to completion.

I'd like to start by thanking Martin DelRe from Microsoft Press, who initially approached me in June of 2003 about doing this book project. He had the vision and energy to get this ball rolling, both with an author like myself and with the product team. In addition, he navigated the book through the Microsoft Press approval process and gained the necessary signatures to get this project in motion. Martin, thanks for all your work on the front end of this project. I'll be forever grateful to you for your vision and assistance in getting this project off the ground.

Secondly, I'd like to thank Neil Salkind from StudioB, my agent, who did an excellent job in helping me work with all the co-authors and with Microsoft Press to ensure the contracts were in place to make this a reality. He also offered me some great advice at key points during this project and I'm grateful for his assistance. As usual, Neil, you did an outstanding job.

I'd also like to thank my co-authors for turning in some really great chapters. There were more than a few times, when I was reading through their chapters, that I'd think "Wow, I like this!" or "Man, this is good stuff!". It has been a real treat to work with all of you and I'd like to tip my hat to you for writing some very good content.

The product team had significant input into both the outline and the content. In fact, each chapter in the book was reviewed by at least one member of either (and often both) the SharePoint Portal Server team and/or the Windows SharePoint Services team. In addition, each team had their own editors who reviewed the chapters for terminology and overall flow. More than a few mistakes and technical inaccuracies were caught and more than a few of the product team members made themselves available for personal interviews to help us understand the technology in areas where it wasn't well documented. These members answered e-mails and endured (at times) our endless stream of questions with grace and patience. Other product team members were "looped in" to answer specific questions and their cooperation was deeply appreciated. To each of you on the product teams, thank you for your input and assistance.

On the SharePoint Portal Server team, I'd like to thank Adam Rosenblatt for his willingness to look at this project and navigate it through the product team hierarchy for their approval and support. Without Adam's help and support, this resource kit would not be a reality today. Thanks, Adam, for working with Microsoft Press and for supporting this project the way you did.

Also, I've communicated with Emily Schroeder, Crystal Thomas, Hannah Love and Maria Hristova on a (nearly) daily basis for the last six months. I think they're glad they're not receiving more e-mails from me! But they were the product team point people who ensured the chapters were passed through the product team members in a timely fashion and as well as making sure the terminology was correct. Their help and input was invaluable and much of what you see is a direct result of their efforts. To all four of you, thank you so much for adding high value to the final product.

At Microsoft Press, Valerie Woolley was our main project editor and she was tasked with worrying about whether this book was going to be finished on time <grin> and keeping me going with my authors. Hilary Long ensured that the production schedule was on time to get the book into print as fast as possible. Both were gracious in working with the common life events that tend to push deadlines out. Thanks for your patience and professionalism. I've enjoyed working with you two and hope to do it again on another book.

Back here in Minnesota, my wife Kathy has really put up with more than a wife should. Writing (and editing) a book is time consuming and she's endured me working evenings and weekends–more than I should have. Kathy, thanks for being a great wife, friend and life-long companion. And to David and Anna, my two children, you two give me more joy and meaning in my life than you know right now. And I'm looking forward to teaching you guys how to ski and tube this summer!

I'd also like to thank several friends of mine whom I've grown to love: Mark and Marcia Schneider, Jay and Dawn Herman, Dave and Merle McGauvran and Rolf and Sandy Engwall. Your friendship, prayers and support have enabled me to keep going when things were tough last year. Life's greatest fulfillments are found in personal relationships and I've been blessed by God to have you all in my life.

Contacting the Author

I've always made it a policy to have an "open door" to those who purchase books that I've worked on. This one is no exception. If you'd like to contact me, you are welcome to do so by e-mailing me at benglish@mindsharp.com or by visiting my company's web site at www.mindsharp.com. My (virtual) door is always open and while I might not respond as quickly as I'd like (I do travel quite a bit), I will try to respond within 72 hours of receiving your e-mail.

Sincerely,
Bill English
MCSE, MCSA, MCT, MVP
Nowthen, Minnesota
April 2004

Introduction

Welcome to Microsoft Office SharePoint Portal Server 2003 and Windows SharePoint Services!

These two products are changing the way we do business, and the *Microsoft SharePoint Products and Technologies Resource Kit* will give you the guidance and information you'll need to design, deploy, customize, and troubleshoot both products. There is really something in this kit for everyone.

The kit is divided into 11 parts. Part 1 will introduce you to SharePoint Products and Technologies and offer you a method of learning about the product at a high level. Part 2 will dive into the architecture of both SharePoint Portal Server and Windows SharePoint Services. Parts 3 and 4 will be of high interest to administrators because it is the Planning and Deployment section. In that section, we cover capacity planning issues, server farm deployment scenarios, and monitoring your servers for operational health.

In Parts 5 and 6 of the kit, we've focused on administration of both a Windows SharePoint Services site and a SharePoint Portal Server portal site. These sections are full of day-to-day administration activities and instructions on how to perform them. Managing users and performing site collection administration activities are just two of the many topics covered in this section.

Part 7 is dedicated to using SharePoint Products and Technologies from an information management perspective. In this section, we'll focus on using documents and working with the built-in information components, and then we'll spend two chapters on the Gatherer service plus the search and indexing features. We'll also cover the personalization features of SharePoint Portal Server, including audiences and My Site.

Part 8 discusses how to secure SharePoint Products and Technologies. We've written a chapter on information security policies, another one on firewalls, and a third chapter on the Single Sign-On service. We also have a chapter on using SSL to secure extranet connections.

Part 9 focuses on maintaining a SharePoint Portal Server deployment, so we'll focus on backup and restore strategies and the usage analysis tools that ship with SharePoint Portal Server 2003.

Part 10 focuses on customizations and development topics, such as using Microsoft FrontPage 2003 to customize a Windows SharePoint Services site, discussion of the object models, and using Microsoft Visual Studio .NET to create new Web Parts.

Finally, Part 11 dives into other product integration points with SharePoint Products and Technologies, so we look at using InfoPath, developing from within an Office 2003 application for a Windows SharePoint Services site and Exchange/Outlook integration points. The final chapter discusses how to migrate from a Share-Point Portal Server 2001 installation to a SharePoint Portal Server 2003 deployment.

The *Microsoft SharePoint Products and Technologies Resource Kit* has a wide audience. First, it is intended to be used by those who will be designing and architecting a new deployment of SharePoint Products and Technologies. These people will use this book to learn about capacity planning, server farm models, integration with Microsoft Active Directory, and other high-level concepts. Second, administrators will use this kit to learn how to administrate a portal site or services site. In addition, administrators will use this kit to learn how to maintain their servers and their sites. Developers will be interested in the chapters about developing applications for Windows SharePoint Services, the object model, and the other customization chapters. We hope that this kit will be a handy reference for many learning about and running SharePoint Products and Technologies.

Thank you for purchasing this resource kit. We all hope that you will find this kit to be something you come back to time and again as you learn about and work with SharePoint Products and Technologies.

About the Companion CD-ROM

The CD accompanying the *Microsoft SharePoint Products and Technologies Resource Kit* contains additional information and software components, including the following:

- **eBook**   You can view an electronic version of this book on screen using Adobe Acrobat Reader. For more information, see the Readme.txt file included in the root folder of the companion CD.

- **Tools**   You'll find more than a dozen tools, including SPSAdmin Tools, Share-Point Database Explorer, and Web Part Toolkit—just to name a few.

- **Appendixes**   Appendix A, "List of Gatherer Service Error Messages," and Appendix B, "Upgrading SharePoint Team Services to Windows SharePoint Services," are also located on the CD-ROM.

System Requrements

The following table lists the system requirements for running Microsoft SharePoint Products and Technologies.

Component	Requirement
Computer and processor	PC with an Intel Pentium–compatible 700-MHz processor CD-ROM drive or DVD drive
Memory	512 MB of RAM
Hard disk	575 MB of available hard-disk space
Operating system	Server requires one of the following: Microsoft Windows Server 2003 Standard Edition, Windows Server 2003 Enterprise, Windows Server 2003 Datacenter, Windows Server 2003 Web Edition, plus the latest service pack. For additional requirements, also see the entry below for "Other."
Other	Running SharePoint Portal Server 2003 on Windows Server 2003 Web Edition requires Microsoft SQL Server 2000 to be installed on a separate computer. For a complete set of system requirements, visit *http://www.microsoft.com/office/preview/sharepoint/sysreq.asp*.

Technical Support

Every effort has been made to ensure the accuracy of this book and the contents of the companion CD-ROM. Microsoft Press provides corrections for books through the World Wide Web at *http://www.microsoft.com/learning/support*.

To connect directly with the Microsoft Learning Knowledge Base and enter a query regarding an issue you might have, go to *http://www.microsoft.com/learning/support/search.asp*.

If you have comments, questions, or ideas regarding this book or the companion CD-ROM, please send them to Microsoft Press using either of the following methods:

E-mail   rkinput@microsoft.com

Postal Mail   Microsoft Press
Attn: Editor, *Microsoft SharePoint Products and Technologies Resource Kit*
One Microsoft Way
Redmond, WA 98052

Please note that product support is not offered through the preceding addresses.

Part I

Introduction to SharePoint Products and Technologies

Chapter 1

Introduction to Microsoft SharePoint Products and Technologies

SharePoint Team Services 1.0 from Microsoft and Microsoft SharePoint Portal Server 2001 were the original versions of Microsoft SharePoint Products and Technologies, released in 2001. SharePoint Team Services addressed the Web-based sharing and communication needs of teams and team websites, and SharePoint Portal Server 2001 addressed the document collaboration, Web portal, and enterprise search requirements of a portal solution. To deliver these features, Microsoft used the best available (but different) technology platforms to build SharePoint Team Services and SharePoint Portal Server 2001.

Based on customer feedback and the experience of developing the 2001 version of SharePoint Products and Technologies, Microsoft designed the next generation of SharePoint Products and Technologies to use a common set of Microsoft Windows Server 2003 services named Microsoft Windows SharePoint Services. This set of services takes advantage of the performance, stability, and security features of the Microsoft .NET Framework. You can use Windows SharePoint Services to create and maintain many team sites. The following applications are based on Windows SharePoint Services:

- SharePoint Portal Server 2003

- Document Workspace sites in Microsoft Office 2003

- Meeting Workspace sites in Office 2003

- Third-party developed solutions and Microsoft customer-developed solutions

SharePoint Portal Server 2003 is a server product that adds features you can use to build and manage integrated, large-scale portal solutions on top of Windows SharePoint Services.

Windows SharePoint Services is a collection of services for Microsoft Windows Server 2003 that you can use to share information, collaborate with other users on documents, and create lists and Web Part pages. You can also use Windows SharePoint Services as a development platform to create collaboration applications and information-sharing applications.

SharePoint Portal Server 2003 is a scalable, enterprise portal server that is built on Windows SharePoint Services. You can use SharePoint Portal Server 2003 to aggregate Windows SharePoint Services sites, information, and applications in your organization to a single portal. In addition to the features of Windows SharePoint Services, SharePoint Portal Server 2003 includes the following features:

- News and topics

- My Site, with personal views and with public views

- Information that can be targeted to specific audiences

- Index functionality and search functionality across file shares, across Web servers, across Microsoft Exchange Public Folders, across Lotus Notes, and across Windows SharePoint Services sites

- Alerts that notify you when changes are made to relevant information, documents, or programs

- Single sign-on functionality for enterprise application integration

- Integration with Microsoft BizTalk Server

Comparison of Features in Windows SharePoint Services and SharePoint Portal Server 2003

Table 1-1 compares the features of Windows SharePoint Services and SharePoint Portal Server 2003.

Table 1-1   Feature Comparisons Between Microsoft Office SharePoint Portal Server 2003 and Windows SharePoint Services

Feature	Windows SharePoint Services	SharePoint Portal Server 2003
Alerts	Yes	Yes
Browser-based customization	Yes	Yes
Discussion boards	Yes	Yes
Document libraries	Yes	Yes
Document Workspace	Yes	Yes
Meeting Workspace	Yes	Yes
Lists	Yes	Yes
BizTalk integration	No	Yes
Microsoft FrontPage 2003 integration	Yes	Yes
Microsoft InfoPath 2003 integration	Yes	Yes
Surveys	Yes	Yes
Templates	Yes	Yes
Web Part pages	Yes	Yes
Automatic categorization	No	Yes
Audiences	No	Yes
Topic areas	No	Yes
News	No	Yes
Personal sites	No	Yes
Shared services	No	Yes
Single sign-on	No	Yes
Site directory	No	Yes
User profiles	No	Yes

By using the combined collaboration features of Windows SharePoint Services and of SharePoint Portal Server 2003, users in your organization can create, manage, and build collaborative websites and make them available throughout the organization.

To understand the differences in purpose between SharePoint Portal Server 2003 and Windows SharePoint Services, think of them this way:

■ SharePoint Portal Server 2003 is designed to aggregate information, create a taxonomy, target content to users, and create personal portals (My Site) for individual users.

■ Windows SharePoint Services is designed to the place where collaboration takes place as it relates to content development and team interactions.

Main Design Goals for SharePoint Products and Technologies

The overall design goal for SharePoint Products and Technologies was to unify and integrate Windows SharePoint Services as a technology platform on which to build products such as SharePoint Portal Server 2003. This goal of unification and integration was divided into four areas:

■ Consistent SharePoint Products and Technologies experience for users, developers, and IT professionals

■ Consistency and integration with the .NET Framework

■ Integrated storage strategy

■ Trustworthy Computing Initiative: security and reliability

Consistent Experience for Users, Developers, and IT Professionals

Solution developers who use SharePoint Products and Technologies now need to know only one user-interface technology (ASP.NET Web pages and controls), one data storage technology (Microsoft SQL Server), and one SharePoint Products and Technologies object model to create advanced sharing solutions. Developers can use their choice of .NET Framework development and database tools to develop, test, and tune their SharePoint Products and Technologies solutions.

Similarly, network administrators can take advantage of their existing knowledge by using well-known tools and procedures based on Windows Server 2003 and SQL Server to deploy and manage SharePoint Products and Technologies.

Consistency and Integration with the .NET Framework

The strategy of using the .NET Framework, Web services, Microsoft Visual Studio .NET, and Windows Server 2003 to build SharePoint Products and Technologies is part of Microsoft's technology strategy for connecting people, information, applications, and devices. The first advantage of using the .NET Framework in building SharePoint Products and Technologies is that it is the most scalable, flexible, and secure foundation for building, deploying, and managing enterprise Web applications. SharePoint Products and Technologies workspaces and portal sites share these attributes as a result of this integration with the .NET Framework. Additionally, integrating SharePoint Products and Technologies with information from virtually any enterprise application is easy with the support for Web services included in the .NET Framework.

Integrated Storage Strategy

The long-term strategy for storage technology at Microsoft is for SQL Server technology to become the single repository for absolutely everything. Except for the full-text search indices created by Microsoft Search technologies and certain pages that are stored in the files system on front-end Web servers as a performance enhancement, all content, configuration information, and other SharePoint Products and Technologies data is stored in SQL Server databases. Using a single, consistent, integrated data storage platform creates significant advantages for IT professionals and developers by increasing their productivity and reducing their day-to-day development, deployment, and management costs.

Trustworthy Computing Initiative: Security and Reliability

The secure, reliable operation of everyday computer systems is at the heart of the Trustworthy Computing Initiative at Microsoft. All new Microsoft products, including SharePoint Products and Technologies, adhere to these Trustworthy Computing initiatives. Developers at Microsoft have extensive software security training and apply their knowledge by performing security audits of each Microsoft software component that they are responsible for. Furthermore, the development teams for SharePoint Products and Technologies groups took advantage of the built-in security and reliability of Windows Server 2003 and the .NET Framework when they designed, implemented, and tested the new version of SharePoint Products and Technologies.

Architecture and Design Decisions

SharePoint Portal Server 2003 and Windows SharePoint Services require advanced planning to be successfully deployed. We'll discuss several planning issues in depth, including taxonomy planning (in Chapter 8, "Planning Your Information Structure Using Microsoft Office SharePoint Portal Server 2003") and writing information security policies (in Chapter 24, "Information Security Policies for SharePoint Products and Technologies"). In this section, we'll outline some high-level decisions that need to be addressed as part of your SharePoint Products and Technologies deployment.

Integrated Storage

SharePoint Team Services used a hybrid model of Web server, file system, Windows registry, and SQL Server–based storage to manage documents, lists, views, and configuration information. SharePoint Portal Server 2001 used a document store based on the Microsoft Web Storage System (the same storage technology used by Microsoft Exchange Server) for most data storage requirements. Both of these solutions required content to be stored on the same server that hosted the Web portal. This requirement limited the range of deployment scenarios and scalability.

These storage solutions served the 2001 version of SharePoint Products and Technologies well. However, these storage solutions did not support the additional requirements for administration, management, performance, scalability, and functionality that were needed in the next generation of SharePoint Products and Technologies. For example, backup and restore operations are difficult to implement and manage when the relevant data is spread out among many storage systems on the server.

Windows SharePoint Services stores all documents, lists, views, and configuration information in SQL Server content stores. Because of this, Windows SharePoint Services offers true enterprise scalability.

SharePoint Portal Server 2003 uses the same SQL Server content store architecture as Windows SharePoint Services. SharePoint Portal Server 2003 also supports the option of installing backward-compatible document libraries (Web Storage System–based) for document storage. The backward-compatible document libraries are compatible with SharePoint Portal Server 2001 document approval and routing, and they support multiple document profiles for each document library folder. With the backward-compatible document libraries, you can use a phased strategy to migrate to SharePoint Portal Server 2003.

Note   SharePoint Portal Server 2003 requires a SQL Server content store for managing ASP.NET portal Web pages, lists, views, and configuration information. Windows SharePoint Services and SharePoint Portal Server 2003 both use SQL Server content stores and require SQL Server or Microsoft SQL Server Desktop Engine (MSDE). SQL Server is a separately licensed product that is not included with Windows SharePoint Services or SharePoint Portal Server. MSDE is included with Windows SharePoint Services and with SharePoint Portal Server 2003. For a discussion on the differences in use between MSDE and SQL, please see the two installation chapters in this resource kit: Chapter 2, "Installing Windows SharePoint Services," and Chapter 3, "Installing Microsoft Office SharePoint Portal Server 2003."

ASP.NET Web Part Pages and Web Parts

SharePoint Products and Technologies now uses Web Part Pages and Web Parts based on the .NET Framework and ASP.NET. SharePoint Team Services and Share-Point Portal Server 2001 used separate technologies to create and display (render) SharePoint sites in a Web browser. Web pages in SharePoint Team Services were based on Microsoft FrontPage and Office Web Server technologies, and Web portal pages in SharePoint Portal Server 2001 were based on Web Storage System, dash-board, and Web Part technologies.

This version of SharePoint Products and Technologies uses ASP.NET Web Part Pages to create and display SharePoint sites in a Web browser. You can easily inte-grate Web Parts with Web services, Office, and BizTalk Server to provide powerful solutions for work sharing, enterprise applications, and portal sites.

Common Collaboration Management Services

SharePoint Portal Server 2001 was designed to provide document version tracking and check-in and check-out document collaboration functions. However, SharePoint Team Services was the solution that large numbers of teams used every day to cre-ate, review, approve, and manage their Office documents; to plan and hold meet-ings; and to track project tasks. Document version tracking and document check-in and check-out are now included in Windows SharePoint Services, where users need them the most and where all SharePoint Products and Technologies solutions can take advantage of these document collaboration functions.

Document collaboration is one of the most valuable end-user features in Win-dows SharePoint Services, and it is the area in which Microsoft made the most changes. The following list shows the main differences between the document col-laboration functions in SharePoint Portal Server 2001 and the document collabora-tion functions in Windows SharePoint Services:

- In SharePoint Portal Server 2001, the document libraries based on the Web Storage System supported multiple document profiles for each document library folder. In Windows SharePoint Services, the SQL Server content store supports one set of properties (the equivalent of one document profile) for each document library. Because of this, you might want to store the properties of the most common document profile in the area where it would normally belong, and then store the documents that use secondary document profiles in a subarea, using one set of properties for each secondary document profile.

- SharePoint Portal Server 2001 provided both serial and parallel routing and approval processes. Windows SharePoint Services now provides a simpler, one-step moderator approval process.

- SharePoint Portal Server 2001 provided support for document version tracking using major and minor version numbers. Windows SharePoint Services and SharePoint Portal Server 2003 use major version numbers only.

- SharePoint Portal Server 2001 supported access control at the folder level and subfolder level (and user and group exclusions at the file level). Windows SharePoint Services and SharePoint Portal Server 2003 support access control at the site level and the document library level.

Site Creation and Management Services

To improve support for very large numbers of SharePoint sites in this version of SharePoint Products and Technologies, Windows SharePoint Services now provides common site creation and management features, such as site templates and self-service creation of Windows SharePoint Services sites. SharePoint Portal Server 2003 adds the following deployment and management features for large organizations: a site directory that provides an easy-to-use site registration system, enterprise application integration (EAI) solutions with single sign-on support for third-party applications, dynamically configurable site maps, large-scale server topology management, and the ability to share multiple index and search servers.

Integrated Search Solution

For full-text content indexing and searching, SharePoint Team Services used the Microsoft Windows Indexing Service, an early version of Microsoft Search technologies included in Microsoft Windows 2000. When SharePoint Portal Server 2001 was released, it included an updated enterprise version of Microsoft Search technologies.

Windows SharePoint Services uses the full-text searching features from the latest version of SQL Server. SharePoint Portal Server 2003 uses the latest version of Microsoft Search services and includes the ability to crawl external content.

Personalization and Audience-Targeted Information and Applications

To help individual users find and use the information and tools they need, a portal solution must support targeted delivery of content, information, and application functionality. A portal solution includes targeting information and applications to individuals, teams, divisions, and entire organizations. It also includes effective support for personalized content and support for group-based portal page content.

Windows SharePoint Services provides personalization by offering shared and personal views of team sites. SharePoint Portal Server 2003 uses audiences to extend this service. Audiences are dynamic groups of users that share one or more common properties (for example, business function, department, or team membership). The properties that determine audience membership can reside in an enterprise directory such as Microsoft Active Directory or any other SQL Server–based database. Audiences are used to determine which Web Parts appear on a particular Web page, and they can also act as a filter for the information displayed in those Web Parts.

SharePoint Portal Server 2003 also supports creating and managing personal sites (My Site) that can become a personal storage and sharing location.

Subscriptions and Alerts

In SharePoint Team Services and SharePoint Portal Server 2001, you could use subscriptions to receive messages when your shared documents were changed. The name of the subscriptions feature has now changed to alerts. Windows SharePoint Services and SharePoint Portal Server 2003 both continue to support alerts. Windows SharePoint Services supports alerts on lists and individual items in lists, and SharePoint Portal Server 2003 builds on this functionality by adding support for alerts on people, areas, searches, and news alerts.

Simple Single-Server Configurations and Highly Scalable Server Farm Configurations

SharePoint Team Services and SharePoint Portal Server 2001 were deployed as single-server solutions or as groups of servers, but little support was available for creating and deploying highly scalable server farms. Windows SharePoint Services is specifically designed to vastly improve performance for each server and to support deployment in highly scalable server farms using multiple stateless front-end servers connected to one or more back-end content servers.

Important Features and Terminology Used in SharePoint Products and Technologies

In addition to understanding the technical design of SharePoint Products and Technologies, you also need to understand the new and changed terminology introduced in SharePoint Products and Technologies.

SharePoint Sites and Site Collections

The terminology used to name the components in SharePoint Products and Technologies varies depending on whether you are an end user, a developer, a Windows administrator, or a SharePoint Products and Technologies administrator. For SharePoint Products and Technologies end users, the terminology used in the SharePoint Products and Technologies Web interface is consistent with the long-term goals and direction for SharePoint Products and Technologies. Some of the terminology for developers is more consistent with the older SharePoint Team Services object model. The terminology for Windows administrators and SharePoint Products and Technologies administrators is a mixture of SharePoint Team Services terminology and Windows SharePoint Services terminology. Microsoft plans to increase the consistency of the terminology for developers and administrators in future versions of SharePoint Products and Technologies.

In SharePoint Team Services, the term for the top-level content directory of a Web server is *root Web site*. In a multihosting environment, each virtual Web server that is configured on the Web server contains one top-level (root Web) site. Additionally, the term for a site within a root website in SharePoint Team Services is *subweb*. Subweb is a term adopted from Microsoft FrontPage websites (the original technology on which SharePoint Team Services was built). You can create multiple subwebs in a root Web site, and you can create subwebs within other subwebs.

In SharePoint Portal Server 2001, the term for the top-level content directory of a Web server is *workspace*. The term for a site within a workspace is *subdashboard*. You can create additional subdashboards and personal dashboards for subprojects and individual users.

In the latest version of SharePoint Products and Technologies, the term *site* (in the SDK, the term *site* is called *myweb*) replaces the previous terms. There are two types of SharePoint sites you can use to divide site content into distinct, separately manageable sites: top-level websites and subsites. A top-level SharePoint site is the parent site of all sites in a site collection. Top-level websites can contain multiple subsites, and subsites can also contain multiple subsites, continuing for as many levels as your users require. You can use this hierarchy to create a main subsite for your entire team and create individual subsites or shared sites for side projects. Top-level websites and subsites permit different levels of control over site features and settings.

Single-Server Scenario

SharePoint Products and Technologies supports both vertical, single-server solutions and horizontal, server farm solutions. This section describes a single-server configuration.

One of the minimum system requirements for Windows SharePoint Services is the Windows Server 2003 operating system. Additionally, you must install and configure Internet Information Services (IIS) and ASP.NET before you install Windows SharePoint Services. When you install Windows SharePoint Services, it creates and configures a virtual server named SharePoint Central Administration. Additionally, if you install Windows SharePoint Services in a single-server configuration, it automatically extends the existing default website that was created when you installed IIS.

Windows IIS websites are also referred to as IIS virtual Web servers, virtual servers, or v-servers. In addition to the two default IIS virtual servers that are created when you install Windows SharePoint Services, you can configure as many as nine end-user virtual servers with separate application pools or 99 end-user virtual servers with a shared application pool on a single Windows Server 2003–based computer. Each IIS virtual server can host multiple SQL Server content stores. (For a discussion of application pools, please consult the Internet Information Services 6.0 Resource Kit, Microsoft Press 2003.)

Each SQL Server content store for SharePoint Portal Server 2003 can contain only one portal site collection. Each SQL Server content store for Windows SharePoint Services can contain as many as 50,000 site collections, even if the site collection is hosted under a SharePoint Portal Server 2003 portal site. These numbers point to a design that will result in fewer portals but many more team sites in most deployments.

A site collection is a set of websites that share a common GUID and namespace and have the same owner and administration settings and that reside on the same virtual server. Each site collection contains a top-level website and can contain one or more subsites. A site collection serves as the administrative unit for assigning users to site groups and for granting security rights to site groups. For more information about site administration, see the next section. You can nest a site within another site. The term for the nested site is *subsite*. Each site (and subsite) uses the same SQL Server content database as its parent site.

In SharePoint Portal Server 2003, the term *site collection* is the equivalent of the older term *site* in SharePoint Team Services. In the new version of SharePoint Products and Technologies, the term *site* or *SharePoint site* is the equivalent to the older term *subweb* in SharePoint Team Services. Be careful to avoid confusing the overlapping terminology. Table 1-2 outlines the new terms for SharePoint Products and Technologies.

Table 1-2   New Terms for SharePoint Products and Technologies

SharePoint Products and Technologies terms	SharePoint Products and Technologies object model terms	SharePoint Team Services terms
Windows IIS Web site	SPVirtualServer	Windows IIS virtual server
Site collection	SPSite	Site
Top-level Web site	SPWeb	Root Web site
Subsite	SPWeb	Child Web site
Site (including top-level sites and subsites)	SPWeb	Subweb (including root Web sites and child Web sites)
Subsite collection	SPWebCollection	Subweb collection
Site group	SPRole	Role
Cross-site group	SPGroup	n/a
Cross-site group collection	SPGroupCollection	n/a
Rights mapping for a principle	SPPermission	n/a
Access control list	SPPermissionCollection	Access control list
Security principle	SPUser	n/a
Security principle collection	SPUserCollection	n/a
Area	Area	Category (SharePoint Portal Server 2001)

> **Note** If you are a developer, note that the SharePoint Products and Technologies object model uses the (sometimes overlapping) names from SharePoint Team Services for many of the new SharePoint Products and Technologies components. Use the preceding table to cross-reference terms from the old and new naming conventions.

Server Farm Scenario

In a server farm scenario, the terminology remains the same, and the requirement that all SharePoint sites use the same SQL Server configuration database as the top-level website remains the same. However, you can use multiple stateless front-end Web servers to support a large number of user connections and to render ASP.NET Web pages. Logically located behind these front-end Web servers, a SharePoint Products and Technologies configuration can use many back-end database servers.

You can use multiple content database servers to support multiple site collections and to provide fault-tolerant failover. Optionally, you can use separate database servers to store the configuration database for server farm configuration maps and site collection-to-content database maps.

Portal Sites

One of the minimum system requirements for SharePoint Portal Server 2003 is Windows SharePoint Services. When you install SharePoint Portal Server 2003, Setup automatically installs Windows SharePoint Services if it is not already installed.

You can configure only one portal site for each end-user IIS virtual Web server. The portal site corresponds to the SharePoint Products and Technologies top-level website for both the virtual server and the site collection rooted at the virtual server.

Security

The new security features in SharePoint Products and Technologies is described in this section. Included is an introduction to groups, authorization, and authentication.

Site Groups and Rights

SharePoint Products and Technologies uses a security model based on site groups and rights. Site groups are groups of users with related security requirements. Security rights are assigned to each security group. You can customize the rights assigned to these site groups or add new site groups to combine different sets of rights. By default, Windows SharePoint Services includes the following five site groups:

- **Administrator.** Members have complete control over a website. They can configure settings, manage users and site groups, and view usage analysis data.

- **Web Designer.** Members can use a SharePoint Products and Technologies–compatible Web page editor, such as Microsoft Office FrontPage 2003, to customize the website.

- **Contributor.** Members can interact with Web Parts, lists, and document libraries. Additionally, they can create and manage personal views and cross-site groups and personalize Web Part pages.

- **Reader.** Members can view items in lists and document libraries, view pages on the site, and create a site using Self-Service Site Creation.

- **Guest.** This group is designed to be combined with specific permissions for specifics lists so that guest users can have access to a specific list without having access to the entire site. You cannot customize or delete the Guest site group.

If you use one of the SharePoint Products and Technologies upgrade tools to create the SharePoint Products and Technologies installation, the upgrade tool inspects the permissions granted to each role in SharePoint Team Services or SharePoint Portal Server 2001 and uses the permissions granted to each role to assign users to corresponding SharePoint Products and Technologies site groups. For a complete list of SharePoint Products and Technologies security rights, see Table 1-3.

Table 1-3   SharePoint Products and Technologies Security Rights

Right	Description	Default site groups
Add and Customize Pages	Permission to create ASP.NET, ASP, and HTML pages for a website	Web Designer, Administrator
Add Items	Permission to add items to lists or documents to document libraries	Contributor, Web Designer, Administrator
Add/Remove Personal Web Parts	Permission to add and remove Web Parts to personalize Web Part Pages	Contributor, Web Designer, Administrator
Apply Style Sheets	Permission to apply a style sheet to the entire website	Web Designer, Administrator
Apply Themes and Borders	Permission to apply a theme or border to an entire website	Web Designer, Administrator
Browse Directories	Permission to browse the directory structure of a website	Contributor, Web Designer, Administrator
Cancel Check-Out	Permission to cancel the check-out action performed by another user	Web Designer, Administrator
Create Cross-Site Groups	Permission to create or delete cross-site groups, or to change membership of a cross-site group	Contributor, Web Designer, Administrator

Table 1-3   SharePoint Products and Technologies Security Rights   *(continued)*

Right	Description	Default site groups
Create Sites and Work-spaces	Permission to create a new subsite or workspace, such as a Document Workspace or Meeting Workspace	Reader, Contributor, Web Designer, Administrator
Delete Items	Permission to delete list items and documents from the website	Contributor, Web Designer, Administrator
Edit Items	Permission to edit existing list items and documents in the website	Contributor, Web Designer, Administrator
Manage Lists	Permission to create, edit, or delete lists and change their settings	Web Designer, Administrator
Manage List Permis-sions	Permission to change permissions for a list or document library	Administrator
Manage Personal Views	Permission to create, edit, or delete personal views on lists	Contributor, Web Designer, Administrator
Manage Site Groups	Permission to create, delete, and edit site groups, both by changing the rights assigned to the site group and by changing which users are members of the site group	Administrator
Manage Web Site	Permission to perform administration tasks for a particular site or subsite	Administrator
Update Personal Web Parts	Permission to update Web Parts to display personalized information	Contributor, Web Designer, Administrator
Use Self-Service Site Creation	Permission to use the Self-Service Site Creation tool to create a top-level website	Reader, Contributor, Web Designer, Administrator
View Items	Permission to view items in lists, documents in document libraries, and Web discussion comments	Reader, Contributor, Web Designer, Administrator
View Pages	Permission to browse pages in the website	Reader, Contributor, Web Designer, Administrator
View Usage Data	Permission to view reports on website usage	Administrator

Cross-Site Groups, Local Groups, and Domain Groups

Cross-site groups, local groups, and domain groups can be members of site groups. Cross-site groups are collections of users who can be managed as a single group across multiple SharePoint Products and Technologies sites. Cross-site groups are configured in SharePoint Products and Technologies, and they can be members of a site group.

Domain groups and local groups can also be members of site groups. However, cross-site groups and site groups cannot be members of local groups or domain groups.

Authentication

Authentication is the process of verifying the identity of a user or a process. IIS handles authentication for SharePoint Products and Technologies. To be authenticated, you need a local user account or a domain user account (if working in a networked domain). In most cases, a domain account is a better choice than a local account.

You can configure authentication (in a Windows SharePoint Services–only installation) to operate in either pre-existing account mode or account creation mode. In pre-existing account mode (also known as *Domain Mode*), SharePoint Products and Technologies does not automatically create new user accounts. In account creation mode, Windows SharePoint Services can automatically create new user accounts in Active Directory. Account creation mode is a feature you must select when you install Windows SharePoint Services. This feature is not available in SharePoint Portal Server 2003 because the default is Domain Mode.

Note   If you use account creation mode, make sure that IIS is configured to use basic authentication. SharePoint Products and Technologies no longer supports IIS digest authentication.

Authorization

SharePoint Products and Technologies stores all security metadata (groups and rights) in SQL Server content stores. User security metadata for SharePoint Products and Technologies is not stored in IIS or anywhere else in Windows. After IIS uses a local computer account or an Active Directory account to authenticate a user, SharePoint Products and Technologies compares the rights assigned to the user by IIS with the access control information for the SharePoint site to determine which SharePoint site resources the user is permitted to use.

Note   Active Directory is not required for Windows SharePoint Services or SharePoint Portal Server 2003 to operate. However, without Active Directory, SharePoint Portal Server cannot prepopulate and synchronize the SharePoint Portal Server profile database with the list of users from Active Directory, and users' personal sites are not registered for cross-farm synchronization in a multiserver configuration. For best results, deploy SharePoint Products and Technologies in an Active Directory environment.

Site Administration

Members of the Administrator site group for a top-level website can control settings and features for the top-level website and any subsites. For example, an administrator of a top-level website can perform any of the following tasks:

- Add, delete, or change user permissions
- View usage statistics
- Change regional settings
- Manage Web Part catalogs and template catalogs
- Manage Web document discussions and alerts
- Change the name, description, theme, and home-page organization of the site
- Configure settings (for example, regional settings) for the top-level website and all subsites
- Update e-mail settings for the top-level website and all subsites
- Configure Web Parts settings for the top-level website and all subsites

A member of the Administrator site group for a subsite can control settings and features only for that particular subsite, and the administrator of a site under that subsite can control settings and features for only that particular second-level subsite. For example, an administrator of a subsite can perform any of the following tasks:

- Add, delete, or change user permissions
- View usage statistics
- Change regional settings
- Manage Web Part catalogs and template catalogs
- Manage Web document discussions and subscriptions
- Change the name, description, theme, and home-page organization for the subsite

Document and Content Storage

SharePoint Products and Technologies supports two types of content stores. The primary store is the SQL Server content store. Based on SQL Server technology, the SQL Server content store provides a single, consistent data storage solution for document content, list content, and metadata. You can use common Windows and SQL Server management tools and development tools to easily manage, tune, back up, and enhance SQL Server content stores.

When you install SharePoint Portal Server 2003, you have the option of installing the backward-compatible document store. The backward-compatible document store is the Web Storage System–based document store used in SharePoint Portal Server 2001. The backward-compatible document store is provided for users who require features from SharePoint Portal Server 2001, such as complex document routing and approval, folder-level security, minor-level version numbers, and multiple document profiles for each folder.

The primary interfaces for the document collaboration features in SharePoint Products and Technologies are document libraries, which you can add to any SharePoint site. A document library consists of the virtual folder where the files are stored, the files themselves, and the user-definable descriptive information (metadata) associated with each item in the document library.

Organizing Documents and Other Content

You can configure each SharePoint site with a document library and a corresponding list component. The list component can display customizable views of the metadata for each document.

With SharePoint Portal Server 2003, you can associate documents and other content in a site with one or more *areas*. Areas provide an alternative way to navigate and search content in a SharePoint Portal Server 2003 portal site. Areas are similar to categories in SharePoint Portal Server 2001.

In a SharePoint Products and Technologies configuration that uses only SQL Server content stores, major version numbers are used to track document revisions (minor version numbers are not supported). A single-step moderator approval mechanism is used to approve documents.

Search Configuration and Usage

Windows SharePoint Services keeps all content in SQL Server content stores, and it uses the Microsoft Search full-text indexing and searching technology from SQL Server. Because of this, Windows SharePoint Services can only index and search content in SQL Server content stores.

SharePoint Portal Server 2003 uses the latest version of Microsoft Search technology to index both local and external document collections and websites. It supports all the advanced indexing and searching features from SharePoint Portal Server 2001, with improved performance, scalability, and extensibility. SharePoint Portal Server 2003 can now index and search millions of documents, and it can support load-balanced queries across multiple catalog servers.

Summary

Windows SharePoint Services and SharePoint Portal Server 2003 provide easy-to-use sharing tools for your organization. You can use Windows SharePoint Services to create and maintain many team sites, and you can use SharePoint Portal Server 2003 to build and manage integrated, large-scale portal solutions.

To achieve this significant increase in capability, performance, stability, and security, the overall architecture of SharePoint Products and Technologies includes many significant changes. The most important of these changes are the use of the .NET Framework, Windows Server 2003, and SQL Server for content storage.

To benefit most from the latest version of SharePoint Products and Technologies, you must be familiar with the changes and new features in SharePoint Products and Technologies, and you must be familiar with the new, consistent terminology for SharePoint Products and Technologies. This knowledge can greatly increase your understanding of both basic and advanced SharePoint Products and Technologies concepts.

In this chapter, we have introduced—at a very high level—Microsoft SharePoint Products and Technologies. The following chapters will further specify and illustrate how to use SharePoint Portal Server 2003 and Windows SharePoint Services.

Chapter 2

Installing Windows SharePoint Services

This chapter provides all information required to install Microsoft **Windows Share-Point Services** in several scenarios. We will cover the following subjects:

- Prerequisites for installing Microsoft Windows SharePoint Services

- Installing with Microsoft SQL Server 2000 Desktop Engine (Windows) (**WMSDE**)

- Installing with SQL Server 2000

- Upgrading from WMSDE to SQL Server 2000

- Integrating an existing Windows SharePoint Services Installation into a Share-Point Portal Server 2003 **portal site**

- Installing Windows SharePoint Services into a **server farm**

- Uninstalling Windows SharePoint Services

Prerequisites

Before installing Windows SharePoint Services, you should review the requirements and prerequisites for the product to prevent rework. This section describes the hardware and software requirements for installing Windows SharePoint Services and then delves into several common application coresidency and configuration issues.

Hardware and Software Requirements

Before you install Microsoft Windows SharePoint Services on your Web server, make sure that you have installed the required hardware and software, as described in Table 2-1.

Table 2-1   Windows SharePoint Services Requirements

Item	Minimum Requirement	Recommended Requirement
Server Requirements		
Operating System	Microsoft Windows Server 2003 (any version)	Windows Server 2003 (any version) with all Service Packs and hotfixes applied
CPU	1 CPU running at 550 MHz	2 CPUs running at 1 GHz+ (server farm installation)
RAM	512	1 GB+
Disk Space	500 MB	~500 MB+ per site
File System	NTFS	NTFS
Internet Information Services	6.0 in Worker Process Isolation Mode with Microsoft ASP.NET enabled	6.0 in Worker Process Isolation Mode with Microsoft ASP.NET enabled
Database	WMSDE or SQL Server 2000 with Service Pack 3	SQL Server 2000 (in a single server or server farm configuration) with the most current service packs and patches applied
Browser	Microsoft Internet Explorer 5.01 with Service Pack 2 Internet Explorer 5.5 with Service Pack 2 Internet Explorer 6 Netscape Navigator 6.2 or later	Internet Explorer 6 with the latest Service Pack and hotfixes applied

Table 2-1   Windows SharePoint Services Requirements   *(continued)*

Item	Minimum Requirement	Recommended Requirement
Client Requirements		
Browser	Internet Explorer 5.01 with Service Pack 2	Internet Explorer 6 with the latest Service Pack and hotfixes applied
	Internet Explorer 5.5 with Service Pack 2	
	Internet Explorer 6	
	Netscape Navigator 6.2 or later	
	Internet Explorer 5.2 for Macintosh or later	
Office System	Microsoft Office 2000	Microsoft Office System 2003

Note   Disk space requirements depend largely on the site's content and function. If, for example, the site's function is to simply list activities for a team, not much space will be needed. By contrast, if the site stores all the Microsoft PowerPoint presentations for a sales team, the space requirements would be much larger. Be sure to interview your users, plan according to your unique needs, and build in room to grow.

Extract Windows SharePoint Services Installation Files

If you've downloaded the Windows SharePoint Services 2.0 files, you can execute the Stsv2.exe file to start the Microsoft Windows SharePoint Services Setup program; but, to use any command-line installation options (such as the /datadir or /remotesql=yes properties) to install Windows SharePoint Services, you will need to extract the setup files by using a decompression utility such as WinZip or PKZip. You can also simply type **stsv2.exe /c /t:c:\temp** at the command line to extract the files to the c:\temp directory (or another directory of your choosing). Should you extract the files, use the Setupsts.exe file to install the product.

Install Microsoft Internet Information Services (IIS) 6.0

For Windows SharePoint Services to install, IIS 6.0 must be installed in Worker Process Isolation Mode, and ASP.NET must be installed. You can use the Manage Your Server Wizard to configure the W2K3 box as an application server, which installs all necessary components for Windows SharePoint Services. Alternatively, you can install the IIS and ASP.NET components from Add/Remove Programs.

> **Warning**   Avoid installing FrontPage Server Extensions (FPSE) from Microsoft because this is not a supported configuration when installing Windows SharePoint Services. If you must run FPSE, be aware that you should install it into another virtual server, and that Windows SharePoint Services will not automatically extend the Default Web Site.

Windows SharePoint Services Database Options

Microsoft SQL Server 2000 Desktop Engine (Windows) (WMSDE) is installed whenever you install Windows SharePoint Services under the following conditions:

- When installing without specifying the Remotesql flag in the command line
- When installing from a command line using the remotesql=no flag
- When selecting the Typical Installation install option in the setup dialog boxes

If you are using the command-line interface to install Windows SharePoint Services or a script to run the installation, you can specify a separate server to use for your database. See Table 2-2 for an overview of the ways in which Windows SharePoint Services installations use either WMSDE or SQL Server databases.

Table 2-2   Database Installation Configurations for Windows SharePoint Services

Installation Scenario	Database Used
No database on server	WMSDE locally, or connect to a SQL Server on another machine
SharePoint Team Services 1.0 installed	MSDE 1.0 upgraded to WMSDE
SQL Server installed on local machine, and default installation run	WMSDE
SQL Server installed on local machine, and Server Farm option chosen	SQL Server
SQL Server installed on local server, and Setupsts.exe run with the remotesql=yes property	SQL Server on the local or a remote machine
SQL Server installed on remote server, and Setupsts.exe run with the remotesql=yes property	SQL Server installed on remote server

Application Coresidency and Configuration Considerations

Interactions between Windows SharePoint Services and other technologies can result in problems. This section outlines some of the issues and workarounds available to operate Windows SharePoint Services most effectively in your environment. For more information about problems, be sure to check *http://support.microsoft.com* for the latest Microsoft Knowledge Base articles. See Table 2-3 for an overview of the applications with which Windows SharePoint Services has issues.

Table 2-3   Windows SharePoint Services Application Compatibility

Application	Limitation
Existing Web applications	Installation disables existing Web applications and extends the default website unless another virtual server is specified.
Exchange 2003	If Exchange is installed in a front-end/back-end configuration, Microsoft Outlook Web Access (OWA) requests might be incorrectly handled and fail.
Microsoft Office XP or Office 2000	Cannot use multiple upload features or other features that depend on the new features in Office 2003.
Microsoft FrontPage	You can use FrontPage 2003 to modify Windows SharePoint Services sites; earlier versions of FrontPage are not compatible.
FrontPage Server Extensions (FPSE)	If the default website's virtual server is extended with FPSE 2002, Windows SharePoint Services will not automatically extend or upgrade it when installed using the Typical Installation option.
Microsoft Class Server	Class server can use only the default virtual server, so Windows SharePoint Services must be installed to a different virtual server.

Installing Windows SharePoint Services with Existing Web Applications

Windows SharePoint Services should not be installed on a server that is already running another Web application. Any preexisting Web applications on the server will be disabled during installation. For information about running Windows SharePoint Services with another Web application, refer to Microsoft Knowledge Base Article 823265 at *http://support.microsoft.com/?kbid=823265*.

Exchange 2003 and Windows SharePoint Services

When Windows SharePoint Services is installed on a computer that is running Microsoft Exchange Server, the deployment causes Kerberos authentication to be disabled in Internet Information Services and can result in incorrect handling of OWA requests to an Exchange Server.

> **More Info**   For information about running Windows SharePoint Services using Kerberos authentication, refer to Microsoft Knowledge Base Article 832769 at *http://support.microsoft.com/?kbid=832769*.

When an IIS virtual server is extended with Windows SharePoint Services, the virtual server is configured to use Integrated Windows authentication (formerly named *NTLM*, or Microsoft Windows NT Challenge/Response authentication). By configuring Integrated Windows authentication on the virtual server, the Windows SharePoint Services virtual server can run as a domain account, and you do not have to configure a service principal name (SPN) in Active Directory directory services (which benefits you by reducing administrative overhead).

This type of authentication prevents appropriate authentication for OWA in environments where front-end servers run Exchange 2003 and separate back-end servers run Exchange 2003, Windows Server 2003, and Windows SharePoint Services.

> **Note**   Windows Small Business Server 2003 is not affected by this problem because it is by default a single-server setup with OWA and the Exchange 2003 information store on the same server.

If your environment requires Kerberos authentication, follow these two steps to configure Kerberos authentication on the virtual server:

1. Enable Kerberos in the IIS Metabase.

2. Configure a Service Principal Name for the Domain User Account.

Using Windows SharePoint Services and Project Server 2003 on the Same Server

Although Project Server 2003 can be installed on either Windows 2000 (Service Pack 3 or later) or Windows Server 2003, the product was designed specifically to work with Windows SharePoint Services, which can run only on Windows Server 2003. Windows SharePoint Services provides collaboration options such as sharing documents for Project Server. When you install both solutions on the same server, you should install Windows SharePoint Services first, and then install Project Server 2003. This installation order helps to simplify the configuration of your site.

Installing Windows SharePoint Services on a Single Machine with WMSDE

When you install Windows SharePoint Services using the default commands, the WMDSE database installs. WMDSE can be installed only on the same server as Windows SharePoint Services and is most appropriate for smaller environments that will host fewer than 1000 websites. You should also not consider using WMSDE if you are using very large amounts of data.

The version of WMSDE installed with Windows SharePoint Services is different from the standard MSDE database, which limited the number of possible concurrent connections to five and the size of the database to 2 GB. The WMDSE has neither of those limitations built in. Be aware, however, that remote users still cannot connect to the WMSDE database, which prevents its use on a remote server, in a server farm scenario, or in a clustered environment.

Avoiding Installation Issues

Avoid the following two common mistakes when installing Windows SharePoint Services with WMSDE:

- Unintentionally damaging the default website

- Introducing an error that relates to a virtual server running FrontPage 2002 Server Extensions

Before installing Windows SharePoint Services, ensure that all your existing websites have been backed up because an install of Windows SharePoint Services extends the default website in IIS. If you already have a website running in the default website, Windows SharePoint Services will extend that site, which could have unpredictable results depending on how that site is configured.

If you want to specify the location other than the default website to install the WMSDE database, use the /datadir= option with the Setupsts.exe command-line tool. The syntax is as follows:

```
setupsts.exe /datadir="path\\"
```

For example, to install the WMSDE database to the d:\program files\wmsde-data\ directory, type the following command:

```
setupsts.exe /datadir="d:\program files\wmsdedata\\"
```

You can avoid another issue by verifying that FrontPage 2002 Server Extensions from Microsoft are not running on the virtual server on port 80. (If you upgraded from Windows 2000 to Windows Server 2003, FrontPage 2002 Server Extensions were installed by default to port 80.) If FrontPage 2002 Server Extensions are running on the default virtual server, the virtual server will *not* be extended when you install Windows SharePoint Services.

> **More Info**   To understand this issue in more detail, see "Virtual Server Is Running FrontPage 2002 Server Extensions' Message When You Run Windows SharePoint Services Setup or When You Try to Extend the Virtual Server with Windows SharePoint" at *http://support.microsoft.com/?kbid=823378*.

To install Windows SharePoint Services with WMSDE

1. Double-click **Stsv2.exe** (if you are running the compressed package from the Web) or **Setupsts.exe** (if you're running setup from the CD or have extracted the compressed package from the Web) to begin the installation.

2. On the End-User License Agreement (EULA) page, read the EULA, select the **I Accept The Terms In The License Agreement** check box, and then click **Next**.

3. On the Type Of Installation page, select the **Typical Installation** option button and then click **Next**.

4. On the Summary page, review your selections and then click **Install**. The installation process for Windows SharePoint Services will take place.

5. After the installation completes, your default browser will start and open to the Team website at *http://localhost/default.aspx*, as shown in Figure 2-1.

Figure 2-1   A view of the Windows SharePoint Services Base site

You can also install Windows SharePoint Services with WMSDE from a command line using the following command: `setupsts.exe /qr`. You will see all the dialogs, but you will not have to choose all the default options. For more command-line setup options, see Installing Windows SharePoint Services from a Command Line later in this chapter.

Installing Windows SharePoint Services with SQL 2000

In situations requiring more than 1000 websites or more than 4 GB of data, use SQL Server. Windows SharePoint Services and SQL Server can be installed on the same machine or separate servers. You can even install Windows SharePoint Services into a server farm with multiple Windows SharePoint Services installations. These scenarios will be covered in the following section.

When installing Windows SharePoint Services, at a minimum the SQL Server 2000 database requires SQL Server 2000 Service Pack 3 (SP3). Unlike the WMSDE installation, once the installation completes you will need to configure both SQL Server and the appropriate website.

More Info   When you install SQL Server on a Windows Server 2003 computer, you will receive a message stating that the program is not supported on Windows Server 2003. You can click the Continue button to install the program, and then apply the latest SQL Server service pack from *http://www.microsoft.com/sql/downloads*.

Installing Windows SharePoint Services with SQL Server on the Same Computer

In this section, you will install Windows SharePoint Services to work with SQL Server. You will install SQL Server, and then configure it to use Windows Authentication. Finally, you will install and configure Windows SharePoint Services to use the SQL Server database for administration and content.

Note   If you are upgrading from a WMSDE installation of Windows SharePoint Services, see the "Upgrading from WMSDE to SQL Server" section later in this chapter.

To install Windows SharePoint Services with SQL Server, install SQL Server on the appropriate machine and then follow the steps in the next procedure.

> **Note**   Before you begin, be sure to review the prerequisites for installing Windows SharePoint Services outlined at the beginning of this chapter. For example, you want to ensure that your server has IIS 6.0 running in process isolation mode, and that you have ASP.NET installed. Take the time to read through these prerequisites to prevent problems.

To install Windows SharePoint Services with SQL Server

1. Start the installation by opening the **Stsv2.exe** file, or double-clicking **Setupsts.exe**, or typing **setupSTS.exe remotesql=yes** from a command line and then pressing **Enter**.

> **Note**   You can automate the Windows SharePoint Services setup installation. From a command line, start the **SetupSTS** program using the remotesql=yes property. For example, if you extracted your installation files into the c:\Temp\WSS directory, type **c:\temp\WSS\SetupSTS.exe remotesql=yes /qr** from a command prompt, and then click **OK**. The program installs without intervention and without loading WMSDE. Finally, configure the SQL Server connections.

2. On the End-User License Agreement (EULA) page, read the EULA, select the **I Accept The Terms In The License Agreement** check box, and then click **Next**.

3. On the Type Of Installation page, select the **Server Farm** option button and then click **Next**.

4. On the Summary page, review your selections and then click **Install**. The installation process for Windows SharePoint Services will take place.

> **Note**   Once the installation appears to complete, scripts run to restart the IIS services on your machine. Be patient if you experience pauses of one to two minutes.

5. After the installation completes, your default browser will start and open to the Configure Administrative Virtual Server page at *http://localhost:22030 /configadminvs.aspx*, as shown in Figure 2-2.

> **Note**   The administrative port (shown as *22030* in this example) will be different on each machine and different for each install. The Administration port number is randomly assigned during the install by setup. In a server farm scenario, you will need to change this port number on each server in the farm to allow Central Administration to work correctly from a single console to all servers in the farm.

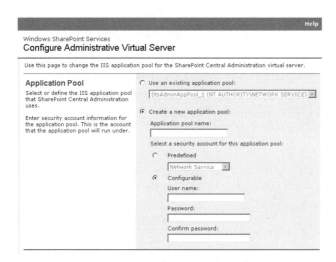

Figure 2-2   Configuring the Administrative Virtual Server Properties

6. By default, the **Configure A New Application Pool** option button is selected. Type a name for the new application pool.

> **Best Practices**   Although you can install Windows SharePoint Services into an existing application pool, your database security is at risk because other Web applications in the same pool can modify Windows SharePoint Services databases. To protect your databases, install Windows SharePoint Services in its own application pool.

7. Choose the security account you want to use for the application pool. You can choose the **Predefined** option button and select the drop-down to choose between **Network Service**, **Local Service**, or **Local System**, or you can choose the **Configurable** option button and type in the *User Name*, *Password*, and *Confirm Password* fields. Click **OK** to continue.

> **Best Practices**   It is best to use the predefined security accounts because they most likely already have the required rights to create and modify databases. If you set a network account for your SQL Server services, use this option.

> **Tip**   You can change these options later by using the Internet Information Services (IIS) Manager, expanding the **Application Pools** node, right-clicking the application pool, selecting **Properties**, and then clicking the **Identity** tab.

8. The Application Pool Changed page will appear and prompt you to restart the IIS Services. *Do not click OK yet*. Minimize this window until you have completed configuring your SQL Server security.

To configure SQL Server security

1. Open **Enterprise Manager**, and navigate to your SQL Server. Expand the **Security** node, right-click the **Logins** property, and then click the **New Login** option. If the account you will use already appears in the Logins pane, right-click the account and then click **Properties**.

2. If you have not already created Microsoft Windows NT accounts as SQL Server service accounts using the **Active Directory Users And Computers** console, you must do so before you can assign the account-appropriate permissions. For more information about how to create secure accounts, see the SQL Server

Security Checklist at *http://www.microsoft.com/technet/prodtechnol/sql/maintain/security/sp3sec/SP3SEC04.ASP.*

3. In the **SQL Server Login Properties** dialog box, type the name of the account you will use in the **Name** field using the ***DomainName\UserName*** convention (for example, **NT AUTHORITY\NETWORK SERVICE**).

4. Click the **Server Roles** tab, and then select the **Security Administrators** option and the **Database Creators** option from the **Server Role** list. Click **OK** to close this window, and then close **Enterprise Manager**.

To create or connect to the SQL Server

1. Click the **Start** button, and then select **Run**. In the **Open** box, type **iisreset** and then press **Enter**. The IIS Services will restart.

2. Restore the Application Pool Changed Web page you minimized in step 8 of the "To install Windows SharePoint Services with SQL Server" section, and then click **OK**. The Set Configuration Database page will appear.

3. In the **Database Server** box, type the name of your SQL Server.

4. In the **SQL Server Database Name** box, type the name of the database you will use.

5. In the **Database Connection Type** section, select the **Use Windows Authentication (Recommended Security Level)** option button.

> **Note**   Although it is possible to connect using SQL Authentication, the environment is much less secure. If you must use SQL Authentication, be certain that you configure the SQL Account with a complex password.

Only if you have previously created the database to which you are connecting should you select the **Connect To Existing Configuration Database** check box.

> **Note**   If you receive an error message that states "[DBNETLIB][Connection-Open (Connect()).]SQL Server does not exist or access denied. (Error code: 17)" make certain that you have the correct name for your server and database, and ensure that the account you specified has Security Administrators and Database Creators roles assigned in SQL Server.

6. In the **Active Directory Account Creation** section, the default selection is **Users Already Have Domain Accounts**, **Do Not Create Active Directory Accounts**. If you need to allow users who do not already have domain accounts created to use your Windows SharePoint Services site, refer to the "Separate Active Directory Directory Service Organization Unit Deployment" section of the Microsoft Windows SharePoint Services Administrator's Guide located on the companion CD-ROM.

7. Click **OK**. The Windows SharePoint Services Central Administration page now appears.

You have set up the administrative database for your Windows SharePoint Services installation.

To extend a virtual server and connect to SQL Server

1. On the SharePoint Central Administration page, click the **Extend Or Upgrade Virtual Server** option.

2. On the Virtual Server List page, click the name of the virtual server that you want to extend. The Extend Virtual Server page will appear. If you want to create a new virtual server, use the **Internet Information Services (IIS) Manager** or create a new site from the command prompt by using the IIsWeb.vbs script included with IIS 6.0.

> **More Info**   For more information about the tools that come with IIS 6.0, see the IIS 6.0 Services SDK Documentation.

3. On the Extend Virtual Server page, select the **Extend And Create A Content Database** option in the **Provisioning Options** section, as shown in Figure 2-3.

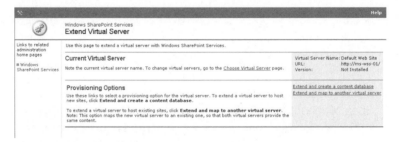

Figure 2-3   Extend and create a content database

4. In the **Application Pools** section, select **Create A New Application Pool** and type the application pool name, the user name, and the password.

> **Note**   Although you can choose the **Use An Existing Application Pool**, you improve your security and stability by running each virtual server in its own application pool. Virtual servers could share application pools in cases where several virtual servers relate to similar functions, or if there will be so many different application pools that performance will be degraded.

5. In the **List owner** section, type the user name for your site owner in the **Account Name** box (using the *DomainName\UserName* convention), and type the e-mail address for that account in the **E-Mail Address** box.

6. In the **Database Information** section, you will either select an existing content database or create a new one. If you create a new database, be sure to use a new database name to avoid overwriting existing content.

7. Specify a URL in the **Custom URL Path** box if you want to do so.

8. In the **Quota Settings** section, select a template in the **Select A Quota Template** box. (If you are not using quotas, there is of course no need to set this property.)

9. Select the language you will use from the **Site Languages** section.

10. Click **OK** to commit the changes. Once the virtual server extension completes, the browser will display a confirmation page. Click **OK** to return to the Virtual Server Settings page; otherwise, to view your extended site, click the link on the Virtual Server Successfully Extended page, and then choose a template for your site.

You now have installed Windows SharePoint Services with SQL Server located on the same machine. To learn more about configuring Windows SharePoint Services, refer to Chapter 16, "Administering Windows SharePoint Services."

The process for installing Windows SharePoint Services with a remote SQL Server is the same as installing a SQL Server on the same machine as described earlier, but you will specify the name of the remote SQL Server in the configuration options.

Upgrading from WMSDE to SQL Server

If you find that your WMSDE installation no longer can meet the number of websites you host, you can either upgrade or migrate WMSDE to use the more scalable and robust SQL Server product. If you want to maintain the SQL Server on the same server as Windows SharePoint Services 2.0, you can upgrade the WMSDE database itself to SQL Server. If you need to run SQL Server on another computer, you will need to migrate your data. Both scenarios are outlined in the following sections.

Backing Up Your WMSDE Server

Before you perform any upgrade, you should first back up your server. In the case of an upgrade from WMSDE to SQL Server on the same machine, the backup serves as insurance in case anything goes awry. If you are migrating to a remote SQL Server, the backup can be used to restore the Windows SharePoint Services 2.0 data to your remote SQL Server machine.

To back up your Windows SharePoint Services sites using the Stsadm.exe tool, follow these steps:

1. Use Stsadm.exe to list all the sites currently running on your server by typing **stsadm.exe -o enumsites -url** *YourURL* at a command line (where *YourURL* is the path to your Windows SharePoint Services virtual server that lists your site collections).

2. Once you've chosen the site you want to back up, type **stsadm.exe -o backup -url http://***server_name/site* **-filename** *backup***.dat** where *backup* is the name of the backup file you're creating.

> **Note** These steps do not back up the entire SQL Server database; rather, they back up the Windows SharePoint Services sites contained within the database. To actually back up the SQL Server database, the user must use Enterprise Manager, or osql.exe.

Upgrading WMSDE to SQL Server on the Same Server

If your SQL Server is installed on the same computer as Windows SharePoint Services 2.0, follow these steps:

1. Insert or connect to the SQL Server 2000 installation CD, clicking Autorun.exe if the installation splash screen does not appear. Click the **SQL Server 2000 Components** link.

2. Click the **Install Database Server** link, and then click **Next**.

3. Select **Local Computer** in the **Computer Name** box, and then click **Next**.

4. On the Installation Selection page, select **Upgrade, Remove, Or Add Components To An Existing Instance Of SQL Server**, and then click **Next**.

5. On the Instance Name page, clear the **Default** check box, select **SharePoint** from the **Instance Name** drop-down list, and then click **Next**.

6. On the Existing Installation page, the **Upgrade** option should be selected by default. If it is not, select it. Click **Next**.

7. On the Upgrade page, the **Yes, Upgrade My Programs** check box should be selected by default. If it is not, select it. Click **Next**.

8. On the Licensing Options page, select the appropriate licensing options, and then click **Next**.

9. On the Select Components page, click **Server Components** options. You will require the Enterprise Manager and Query Analyzer from Management Tools.

10. Choose any other components you require, and then click **Next**.

11. On the Start Copying Files page, click **Next**, and then **Finish**. The upgrade process will take place.

12. Download the latest SQL Server service pack from *http://www.microsoft.com /sql/downloads*, and then install it on the computer.

Once you've completed the upgrade, you can manage your database from the Enterprise Manager. Your SharePoint sites should work normally.

Migrating WMSDE to a Remote SQL Server or Server Farm

If you are moving to a larger environment with one or many front-end Web servers and one or many back-end database servers, the process is more complicated. To switch from WMSDE to SQL Server and move to a server farm, you must perform steps using the Internet Information Services (IIS), Windows SharePoint Services, and SQL Server administration tools. You must also take your sites offline for a while. It is recommended that you perform these steps at a time when usage of your sites is generally low, and also that you notify users that their site will be offline for a time.

> **Note** Ensure you have backed up the database as described in the "Backing Up Your WMSDE Server" section earlier in the chapter.

The following process assumes that you will continue to use the original Web server computer as either a stand-alone server or part of a server farm and that you are moving the databases to a new back-end database server running SQL Server.

The following steps describe how to move from a single-server WMSDE installation to a server farm with SQL Server:

■ Install the SQL Server client tools on the original server running WMSDE and SQL Server 2000 SP3. The client tools are used to back up and restore the content and configuration databases. The version of WMSDE that is installed with Windows SharePoint Services does not enable remote connections from SQL Server client tools.

- Prepare the destination database server by installing SQL Server 2000 Service SP3 or later.

- Using the IIS Manager, stop any virtual servers that are hosting SharePoint sites so that users cannot access the sites.

- Disconnect the content databases from the virtual server, and remove Windows SharePoint Services from the virtual server. In case you decide to reinstall Windows Sharepoint Services and want to reconnect to the database, don't delete the content database when prompted to do so.

- Decide which domain accounts to use for the SharePoint Central Administration virtual server and the content virtual servers, and then, using the Windows SharePoint Services administration pages, update the SharePoint Central Administration virtual server to use the domain account.

> **Note**   You can use the same account for both SharePoint Central Administration and the other virtual servers, or, for more granular security, you can choose to use different accounts.

- Register the instance of WMSDE in SQL Server Enterprise Manager, and then back up the content and configuration databases.

- Copy the backup files to the destination server, and restore the content and configuration databases.

- In SQL Server, change the database ownership and permissions for the configuration and content databases.

- Reconnect to the configuration database.

- Extend the content virtual server, and add the restored content databases to the virtual server.

- Update the default content database server for future content database creation.

Installing Windows SharePoint Services from a Command Line

To install Windows SharePoint Services from a command line, you can use the following conventions.

When you install Microsoft Windows SharePoint Services, you can use command-line properties and setup options to control how it is installed. For example, to install Windows SharePoint Services to work with a remote installation of Microsoft SQL Server, you run Setupsts.exe with the remotesql=yes option to avoid installing Microsoft SQL Server 2000 Desktop Engine (Windows) (WMSDE). Then, after the installation, you can specify the SQL Server connection information and extend your servers.

Setupsts.exe Command-Line Installation Properties

Table 2-4 lists and explains the properties you can use with the command-line Setup program (Setupsts.exe) for Windows SharePoint Services.

Table 2-4   Setupsts.exe Command-Line Properties

Property	Description
remotesql=yes/no	An optional property that specifies whether or not WMSDE is installed with Windows SharePoint Services. The default value is No. Set this property to Yes if you are going to use an existing or remote installation of Microsoft SQL Server with Windows SharePoint Services.
fulluninstall=yes/no	Specifies whether or not to remove Windows SharePoint Services from extended virtual servers when performing an uninstall. The default value is Yes. It is recommended that you use the Add or Remove Programs control panel to uninstall Windows SharePoint Services.
provision=yes/no	Specifies whether or not to provision the administrative virtual server, extend the default virtual server, and create a top-level website during installation. The default value is Yes. Set this property to No if you want to provision virtual servers later using the Stsadm.exe command-line tool, located in C:\Program Files\Common Files\Microsoft Shared\web server extensions\60\BIN.

Note   The remotesql=yes property also installs Windows SharePoint Services without provisioning the default virtual server, but it does provision the administration virtual server.

SetupSTS-Supported Command-Line Switches

Not all the standard setup options for Microsoft Windows Installer programs are supported by Windows SharePoint Services. For example, you cannot create an administrative installation point for Windows SharePoint Services (performed for other programs by including the /a option). Table 2-5 lists and describes the setup options supported by Windows SharePoint Services.

Table 2-5   Setupsts.exe Command-Line Switches

Option	Description
l <path to log file>	Logs setup messages to the specified file.
q or qn	Runs Setupsts.exe in quiet mode (unattended setup with no user intervention).
qb	Runs Setupsts.exe in basic mode (limited user intervention). Includes a progress bar.
qf	Runs Setupsts.exe in full mode (user must fill in options during setup). This is the default option.
qr	Runs Setupsts.exe in reduced mode. Displays reduced user interface (UI) during installation.
qn+	Runs Setupsts.exe in quiet mode (unattended setup with no user intervention). Displays a Setup Complete dialog box at the end of the installation.
qb+	Runs Setupsts.exe in basic mode (limited user intervention). Includes a progress bar and a Setup Complete dialog box at the end of the installation. If you cancel the installation, the dialog box is not displayed.
qb-	Runs Setupsts.exe in basic mode (limited user intervention). Does not display a Setup Complete dialog box.
x	Uninstalls Windows SharePoint Services.
-	Suppresses all modal dialog boxes. Used only with the /b option.
+	Adds a completion message to the /n option or the /b option.

Installing Windows SharePoint Services into a Server Farm

Windows SharePoint Services is fully scalable, installing and operating extremely well in a server farm configuration; however, the increased complexity produces more potential errors. When you install Windows SharePoint Services into a server farm, be sure to think through your configuration and implement it carefully.

Server Farm with Multiple Host Names Deployment

You can install and configure Microsoft Windows SharePoint Services to allow your server farm to host several sites on the same virtual server using the same IP address but use multiple site names and separate content. This configuration is known as a server farm serving multiple host names. In this configuration, you have a single IP address (192.168.2.1, for example), but this same IP address can point to the following individual sites:

- Mary.WoodgroveBank.com

- John.WoodgroveBank.com

- ProjectTeam.WoodgroveBank.com

- Information.WoodgroveBank.com

Each of these sites has its own content, its own set of users, and a different site owner. Each site can use unique Windows SharePoint Services features and share the same virtual server using the same IP address. The Web servers and configuration database make the appropriate content available depending on the URL requested.

This section describes the steps you need to take to configure the servers in your server farm to serve multiple host names with Windows SharePoint Services.

Preparing the Servers

Before you can install and configure Windows SharePoint Services in your server farm, you must be sure you meet the hardware and software requirements and plan out your server farm configuration. The following sections help you determine the configuration to use.

Hardware and Software Requirements

To be able to set up Windows SharePoint Services in a server farm configuration, you must meet the criteria described in more detail in the "Prerequisites" section at the beginning of this chapter.

Installing and Configuring Windows SharePoint Services

After you have prepared the back-end database and front-end Web servers, you can install and configure Windows SharePoint Services on the front-end Web servers. To install and configure Windows SharePoint Services on your front-end Web servers, perform the following steps:

- **Install Windows SharePoint Services.**   You must install Windows Share-Point Services on each front-end Web server. Using the remote SQL Server option (setupsts.exe remotesql=yes) allows you to install Windows SharePoint Services without also installing WMSDE.

- **Create the administration virtual server and configuration database.**   You need to create the configuration database when you configure the first front-end Web server. For subsequent front-end servers, simply connect to the database.

- **Create and extend a virtual server.**   Before you can create sites, you must create a virtual server to contain them in IIS. You can create multiple virtual servers with different IP addresses or host all your sites using the same IP address and virtual server.

- **Create sites.**   Creating sites for users is the final step. You can also enable Self-Service Site Creation so that users can create their own sites. For more information, see Configuring Self-Service Site Creation in the *Windows Share-Point Services Administrator's Guide*.

To perform these steps for a server farm, we recommend you use the command-line administration tool, Stsadm.exe.

Install Windows SharePoint Services with the Remote SQL Server Option

Install Windows SharePoint Services with SQL Server, as described earlier in this chapter. After setup, the HTML Administration pages open so that you can configure the administration virtual server and configuration database. For a server farm environment, you must use the command-line administration tool to create the configuration database rather than HTML Administration. The host header (-hh) parameter is available only from the command line.

> **Note** The host header (-hh) parameter is a one-time-only configuration choice that you only need to use when creating the configuration database for a server farm. This parameter puts Windows SharePoint Services in the scalable hosting mode and only host-named sites should be created in this configuration.

To create the administration virtual server and configuration database

1. Open a command prompt window, and navigate to the \Program Files\Common Files\Microsoft Shared\Web Server Extensions\60\bin folder.

2. Run the following command to create the administration virtual server:

```
stsadm.exe -o setadminport -port <port> -admapcreatenew
  -admapidname <id for application pool>
  -admapidtype <configurableid/NetworkService/LocalService/LocalSystem>
  -admapidlogin <user account for the application pool>
  -admapidpwd <password>
```

> **Note** Remember that you can use any unused port between 1023 and 32,767.

3. Run the following command to create the configuration database:

```
stsadm.exe -o setconfigdb -ds <database server name>
  -du <database user> -dp <password> -dn sts_config -hh
```

> **Note** If you are using Windows authentication, you do not need to specify the -du parameter or the -dp parameter.

To connect to the configuration database from subsequent front-end Web servers, use the Set Configuration Database page in HTML Administration, or use the following syntax:

```
stsadm.exe -o setconfigdb -ds <database server name>
  -du <database user> -dp <password> -dn sts_config -connect
```

> **Note**   If you are using Windows authentication, you do not need to specify the -du parameter or the -dp parameter.

With the administration virtual server and configuration database in place, you can create the virtual server to provide sites for your users. Each front-end Web server needs at least one virtual server for websites. If you do not want to use the existing default website, you can create a new virtual server by using the following steps.

To create a virtual server

1. Click **Start**, point to **All Programs**, point to **Administrative Tools**, and then click **Internet Information Services (IIS) Manager**.

2. Click the plus sign (+) next to the server name to which you will add a virtual server.

3. Right-click the **Web Sites** folder, click **New**, and then click **Web site**.

4. Click **Next**.

5. In the **Description** box, type the description of your virtual server and then click **Next**.

6. In the **Enter the IP address to use for this Web site** box, select the IP address you want to use or use the default (**All Unassigned**).

7. In the TCP port, this website should use the **(Default: 80)** box; type the port number to assign to the virtual server. You do not need to assign a host header because the hosting is handled through Windows SharePoint Services.

8. Click **Next**.

9. In the **Path** box, type or browse to the path on your hard disk where the site content will reside.

10. If you do not want to allow anonymous access to your virtual server, clear the **Allow anonymous access to this Web site** check box.

11. Click **Next**.

12. On the **Permissions** panel, select the permissions to use and then click **Next**.

> **Tip** The default permissions, **Read** and **Run Scripts** (such as ASP), are recommended. The **Execute** (such as ISAPI applications or CGI) permission will be added automatically to the appropriate folders by Windows Share-Point Services.

13. Click **Finish**.

For more information about creating virtual servers, see the Adding Sites topic in the Help system for Internet Information Services.

Now that the virtual server has been created, you can extend it with Windows SharePoint Services. You can use either the command line or the HTML Administration pages to extend the virtual server.

To extend the virtual server from the command line

1. Open a command prompt window, and navigate to the \Program Files\Common Files\Microsoft Shared\Web Server Extensions\60\bin folder.

2. Run the following command to extend the virtual server:

```
stsadm -o extendvs -url http://servername
-ds <database server name> [-du <database user> -dp <password>]
-dn <database name> -ownerlogin <DOMAIN\user>
-owneremail <email address> -ownername <display name>
-donotcreatesite -apcreatenew -apidname <application pool name>
-apidtype <configurableid/NetworkService/LocalService/LocalSystem>
-apidlogin <app pool user account> -apidpwd <app pool password>
```

Be sure to use the -donotcreatesite parameter when you extend the virtual server. Without this parameter, a site is automatically created when you extend the virtual server, and the site will not be affiliated with a host name.

Notice that the -du and -dp parameters are not needed if you are using Windows authentication to connect to SQL Server. It is recommended that you create a new application pool to use for your virtual servers so that they run in separate processes from the administrative virtual server. Use the same application pool for each server farm virtual server on each front-end Web server. This application pool should use a domain account, but it does not need to have database creation rights in SQL Server. The administration virtual server account will create any databases required.

To extend the virtual server using the HTML Administration pages

1. On the SharePoint Central Administration page, click **Extend or upgrade virtual server**.

2. On the Virtual Server List page, click the name of the virtual server to extend.

3. On the Extend Virtual Server page, in the **Provisioning Options** section, select **Extend and create a content database**.

4. In the **Application Pool** section, select either **Use an existing application pool** or **Create a new application pool**.

> **Note** It is recommended that you create a new application pool for each virtual server so that they run in separate processes. This application pool should use a domain account, but it does not need to have database creation rights in SQL Server. The administration virtual server account will create any databases required.

5. If you selected **Use an existing application pool**, select the application pool to use. If you selected **Create a new application pool**, type the new application pool name, user name, and password to use.

6. In the **Site Owner** section, in the **Account name** box, type the user name for the site owner (in the format *DOMAIN\username* if the user name is part of a Windows domain group).

7. In the **E-mail address** box, type the e-mail address that corresponds to the account.

8. In the **Database Information** section, select the **Use default content database server** check box or type the database server name and database name to use for a new content database.

9. If you want to specify a path for the URL, in the **Custom URL path** box, type the path to use.

10. If you are using quotas, select a template in the **Select a quota template** box of the **Quota Settings** section.

11. In the **Site Language** section, select the language to use.

12. Click **OK**.

Creating Sites

After following the preceding steps, you are ready to create sites for your users. This is the last step in the process for setting up your server farm. After this step, you can start adding users and managing the sites.

If you are setting up the multiple host names model for your server farm, you need to create the mapping for the sites you will create for users. Each host name and host header name will need an entry in DNS for each virtual server that will host your sites. Without these entries, name resolution will fail and you will not be able to access your sites.

To create a new site, perform the following actions:

1. Open a command prompt window, and navigate to the \Program Files\Common Files\Microsoft Shared\Web Server Extensions\60\bin folder.

2. Run the following command to create a site:

```
stsadm.exe -o createsite -url http://site1.WoodgroveBank.com
  -ownerlogin <DOMAIN\user> -owneremail <email address>
  [-ownername <display name> -lcid <lcid>
  -sitetemplate <site template> -title <title>
  -description <description>]
```

3. Repeat this step for every site you want to create.

> **Note** Should you need to remove the original top-level website for the virtual server, use the following command-line syntax:
>
> ```
> stsadm.exe -o -deletesite -url http://servername
> ```
>
> If you are setting up any of the other hosting models for your server farm, you can simply create the sites.

To create a site

1. Open a command prompt window, and navigate to the \Program Files\Common Files\Microsoft Shared\Web Server Extensions\60\bin folder.

2. Run the following command to create a site:

```
stsadm.exe -o createsite -url <url>
-ownerlogin <DOMAIN\user> -owneremail <email address>
-ownername <display name>
```

3. Repeat this step for every site you want to create.

Uninstalling Windows SharePoint Services

If you need to uninstall Windows SharePoint Services, you can choose from several options that remove the Windows SharePoint Services installation from a particular virtual server.

There are different degrees to which you can uninstall Microsoft Windows SharePoint Services. Depending on your needs, you can choose from the following options:

- Remove Windows SharePoint Services from a virtual server and preserve the site content.

- Remove Windows SharePoint Services from a virtual server and delete the site content.

  You can choose to remove Windows SharePoint Services and delete the site content in the database. Use this method to remove a virtual server permanently, but continue using Windows SharePoint Services on other virtual servers. For example, use this method if you are finished with a project and no longer need the associated websites.

> **Caution**   When you use this method, you cannot reconnect to the site content later. If you choose to delete the content databases, you are permanently deleting the site content and cannot recover the site data except from a backup.

Uninstall Windows SharePoint Services Completely from a Server

You can choose to uninstall Windows SharePoint Services by using the Add/Remove Programs control panel. This method does not delete site content. You can reinstall and reconnect to the site content. Use this method to repair an installation or to remove a Web front-end server from a server farm.

All these methods leave the virtual server or server in a clean state, ready to be used for other websites or applications; however, each method affects the content and configuration databases in a different way. Table 2-6 explains what happens when you use each of these remove or uninstall methods.

Table 2-6   Windows SharePoint Services Uninstall Scenarios

Method	What Happens to the Databases	Actions During Removal
Remove and preserve content	The content databases associated with the virtual server remain untouched. You can reconnect to the site content.	The Windows SharePoint Services ISAPI filter is uninstalled, and the virtual directories for Windows SharePoint Services are removed from the virtual server.
	The entry for the virtual server remains in the configuration database.	Any physical directories created by Windows SharePoint Services under the physical home directory of the virtual server are removed.
		The Port section in the registry for the virtual server is removed. This means that any managed paths and any URL mapping are removed.
Remove and delete content	The content databases are deleted. You cannot reconnect to the site content.	The Windows SharePoint Services ISAPI filter is uninstalled, and the virtual directories for Windows SharePoint Services are removed from the virtual server.
	The entry for the virtual server is removed from the configuration database.	Any physical directories created by Windows SharePoint Services under the physical home directory of the virtual server are removed.
		The Port section in the registry for the virtual server is removed. This means that any managed paths and any URL mapping are removed.
Uninstall	The content and configuration databases associated with the server remain untouched. You can reinstall Windows SharePoint Services later and reconnect to databases. If you do not want to reconnect, you can delete the databases by using the Microsoft SQL Server or Microsoft SQL Server Desktop Engine (Windows) 2000 (WMSDE) database administration tools.	Windows SharePoint Services is removed from any virtual servers.
		The Windows SharePoint Services administration virtual server is removed.
		The Windows SharePoint Services DLL files are removed from the installation directory.

Removing Windows SharePoint Services from a Virtual Server

You can choose to remove Windows SharePoint Services but keep the site content in the content database. This allows you to extend the virtual server again later and reconnect to the site content. If you leave the content databases intact, you can reconnect to them, from the same virtual server or from a different virtual server, and continue hosting the site content using the same URL. Use this method to temporarily remove and then restore a virtual server, or to change which virtual servers are hosting which content in a server farm setting.

You can remove Windows SharePoint Services from a virtual server by using HTML Administration or the command-line administration tool. Both of these tools allow you to either preserve or delete content when you remove Windows SharePoint Services.

Removing Windows SharePoint Services from a Virtual Server by Using HTML Administration

To remove Windows SharePoint Services from a virtual server by using HTML Administration, use the Remove Windows SharePoint Services from Virtual Server page.

1. Click **Start**, point to **All Programs**, point to **Administrative Tools**, and then click **SharePoint Central Administration**.

2. On the Central Administration page, under Virtual Server Configuration, click **Configure Virtual Server Settings**.

3. On the Virtual Server List page, select the virtual server you want to configure.

4. On the Virtual Server Settings page, under **Virtual Server Management**, click **Remove Windows SharePoint Services From Virtual Server**.

5. On the Remove Windows SharePoint Services From Virtual Server page, select one of the following:

   ■ **Remove without deleting content databases.**   This removes only the Windows SharePoint Services folders from the virtual server—the content database remains intact, so you can reconnect to it later using the same virtual server or a different one.

   ■ **Remove and delete content databases.**   This both removes the Windows SharePoint Services folders from the virtual server and deletes the content database. You will not be able to reconstruct the sites previously stored on that virtual server unless you have a backup.

Figure 2-4 illustrates the options available for removing Windows SharePoint Services.

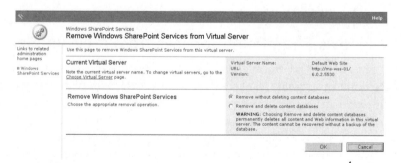

Figure 2-4   Options for removing Windows SharePoint Services

6. Click **OK**.

Removing Windows SharePoint Services from a Virtual Server by Using the Command Line

You can use the unextendvs operation with the Stsadm.exe command-line utility to remove Windows SharePoint Services from a virtual server. The unextendvs operation takes the -url parameter and the optional -deletecontent parameter. When you use unextendvs without the -deletecontent parameter, it leaves the content databases in place so that you can reconnect to the content for a virtual server. When you include the -deletecontent parameter, the content databases are removed and the virtual server is removed from the configuration database.

For example, to remove Windows SharePoint Services from a virtual server but preserve the content databases, use the unextendvs operation with syntax as shown in the following example:

```
stsadm -o unextendvs -url http://servername
```

To remove Windows SharePoint Services from a virtual server and remove the content databases permanently, use the unextendvs operation with syntax as shown in the following example:

```
stsadm -o unextendvs -url http://servername -deletecontent
```

When you use the unextendvs operation with the -deletecontent parameter, you cannot reconnect to the site content later.

Uninstalling Windows SharePoint Services from the Server Computer

If you want to remove Windows SharePoint Services from a server computer entirely, you can uninstall by using the Add Or Remove Programs control panel. Uninstalling Windows SharePoint Services does not remove any chained products that were installed, such as WMSDE. You must uninstall these programs separately.

You must be an administrator on the server computer to uninstall Windows SharePoint Services.

When you use the Add or Remove Programs control panel to remove Windows SharePoint Services from a server, it calls a command-line operation, stsadm -o uninstall, to perform the task. The uninstall operation does not remove any chained products that were installed. The uninstall operation takes the optional -deletecontent parameter. When uninstall is used without the -deletecontent parameter, it leaves the content and configuration databases in place so that Windows SharePoint Services can be reinstalled, and so that you can reconnect to the databases and continue hosting sites. When the -deletecontent parameter is used, the content and configuration databases are removed, and you cannot recover the site content.

Summary

This chapter discussed the prerequisites required for installing Windows SharePoint Services and then outlined how to install Windows SharePoint Services using either WMDSE or SQL Server. It also described the steps necessary to install Windows SharePoint Services into a server farm and concluded by discussing how to uninstall Windows SharePoint Services using several different methods. In the next chapter, we will discuss how to install SharePoint Portal Server 2003.

Chapter 3

Installing Microsoft Office SharePoint Portal Server 2003

Microsoft Office SharePoint Portal Server 2003 can be installed in a variety of ways with a wide selection of both mandatory and optional components. In this chapter, we will cover the following subjects:

- Prerequisites for installing SharePoint Portal Server 2003

- Installing SharePoint Portal Server 2003

- Upgrading from **Microsoft SQL Server Desktop Engine (MSDE)** to **SQL Server 2000**

- Installing the **backward-compatible document library**

- Installing SharePoint Portal Server into a non–Active Directory environment

- Uninstalling SharePoint Portal Server 2003

Prerequisites

SharePoint Portal Server 2003 requires **Internet Information Server (IIS) 6.0**, which requires Microsoft Windows Server 2003. SharePoint Portal Server 2003 caches content in RAM, so while the minimum requirements for RAM are moderate (512 MB), if you use more RAM you'll experience better performance.

Hardware and Software Requirements

Table 3-1 details the minimum and recommended installation requirements for SharePoint Portal Server 2003.

Table 3-1   Hardware and Software Requirements for SharePoint Portal Server 2003

Item	Minimum Requirement	Recommended Requirement
Server Requirements		
Operating System	Windows Server 2003 (any version), although the Web Edition does not support local installation of SQL Server or MSDE.	Windows Server 2003 Standard and Enterprise Editions with all Service Packs and hotfixes applied.
CPU	Intel Pentium III 700 MHZ or higher.	Intel Pentium 4 1GHz or higher.
RAM	512 MB RAM.	512 MB of RAM, with an additional 256 MB for every 512 MB of content that will be used at a given time.
Disk Space (Pre-Installation)	300 MB free disk space on boot partition, 200 MB free disk space in the Program Files installation directory, and 75 MB free disk space in the Data Files installation directory.	500 MB plus the amount of RAM installed of free space on the boot partition, and 1GB of free disk space in the Data Files installation directory.
Disk Space (Post Installation)	Minimum 700 MB free disk space in the Data Files installation directory, and 2.0 GB free disk space in the Database (SQL 2000 or MSDE 2000) directory.	Minimum 1 GB free disk space in the Data Files installation directory, and 2.0 GB or more free disk space in the Database (SQL 2000 or MSDE 2000) directory.
Disk Configuration	Separate drives to store boot partition, pagefile, transaction logs, and databases.	Mirrored drive for boot and system partition, mirrored drive for transaction logs, RAID 5 configuration for databases, and single disk drive for pagefile.
File System	Any partition that will host SharePoint Portal Server data must be formatted with NTFS.	NTFS.

Table 3-1 Hardware and Software Requirements for SharePoint Portal Server 2003 *(continued)*

Item	Minimum Requirement	Recommended Requirement
Database	Microsoft SQL Server Desktop Engine (MSDE) or SQL Server 2000 is compatible on all versions of Windows Server 2003 except when using Web Edition—in this case, SQL Server 2000 must be installed on a remote server and the SQL Server Desktop Engine cannot be used.	SQL Server 2000 with the most current Service Packs and hotfixes applied.
Browser	Microsoft Internet Explorer 5.01 and later for Windows; Internet Explorer 5.2 and above for Mac OS X; Netscape Navigator 6.2 and above for Microsoft Windows, Mac, and UNIX. Only Internet Explorer 5.5 and later allow management of a portal site.	Internet Explorer 6.0 for Windows with the latest service packs and patches installed.
Client Requirements		
Browser	Microsoft Internet Explorer 5.01 or 5.5 with Service Pack 2 and Patch from Knowledge Base 324929; Internet Explorer 6 with Knowledge Base 324929; Netscape Navigator 6.2 or later for Mac, UNIX, or Windows; Internet Explorer 5.2 for Macintosh or later.	Microsoft Internet Explorer 6 with the latest Service Pack and hotfixes applied.

Windows Server Web Edition and SharePoint Portal Server

While it is possible to install SharePoint Portal Server 2003 on Microsoft **Windows Server 2003, Web Edition**, there are many limitations that make the use of Web Edition undesirable. For example, Windows Server 2003, Web Edition, cannot extend its RAM beyond 2 GB, which severely limits the amount of content that the SharePoint Portal Server 2003 installation could serve. In addition, you have a limit of only two CPUs, which means that if you're using application pools, you severely limit your ability to map specific pools to different processors. Most importantly, however, is that you are unable to join an Active Directory domain or install either MSDE or SQL Server, making the only supported configuration a workgroup installation with a remote installation of SQL Server. Again, installing SharePoint Portal Server 2003 on Windows Server 2003, Web Edition, is not a recommended configuration.

Internet Information Services (IIS 6.0)

SharePoint Portal Server, like Microsoft Windows SharePoint Services, relies on IIS 6.0. In Chapter 2, "Installing Windows SharePoint Services," we discussed the requirements needed to use IIS 6.0, including ASP.NET and Worker Process Isolation Mode. SharePoint Portal Server 2003 depends directly on the IIS 6.0 architecture for new technology components such as **Application Pools**, which are a group of Web applications that can be configured centrally and set to share the same worker process.

> **More Info**   For more information on Internet Information Services 6.0 architecture, refer to the IIS product documentation at *http://www.microsoft.com /technet/treeview/default.asp?url=/technet/prodtechnol/windowsserver2003 /proddocs/standard/iiswelcome.asp.*

Backward-Compatible Document Libraries and Server Farm Limitations

For small, medium, and large **server farm** deployments, the backward-compatible document library and SQL Server 2000 cannot be installed on the same computer. For more information on configuring the backward-compatible document library for use in a server farm, refer to Chapter 11, "Deploying a Single Server and a Small Server Farm."

Product Language

While SharePoint Portal Server 2003 ships in multiple languages, it supports only one language per installation (whether a single server or a server farm). If you have a server farm, all SharePoint Portal Server 2003 installations need to be the same language version, and all portal sites in the farm must use the same language. Don't feel overly limited by this setup, however, as the portal sites can link to any type of content. If, for example, you have a multinational company that must support sites in Japanese, English, and Spanish, you can link to websites, Windows SharePoint Services sites (which support multiple language packs), or other SharePoint Portal Server sites that use any one of those languages. One common configuration calls for downloading and installing the language packs for Windows SharePoint Services, and creating websites on the same server that use different languages. You could have SharePoint Portal Server installed in Spanish, but then create a Windows SharePoint Services website in Japanese and another in English. You then control the clients routed to each website through **user profiles** or by configuring **audiences**, which allow all members in a particular group, or all browsers with the default language settings for their language, to be routed to the appropriate language site.

You could, for example, create a SharePoint Portal Server site that accommodates a user whose preferred language is English and a user whose preferred language is Italian. Both users have an area on the portal site that provides content and navigation bars in his or her preferred language. This user experience is provided by creating one portal area (called the *TOP* area) and two subareas (English and Italiano). Security features are used to grant access to a specific subarea to a specific user only; in that subarea, **Web Parts** and navigation bars are customized to provide, as much as possible, content in the user's preferred language.

The content itself is in a Windows SharePoint Services site which, using the language template feature, is completely in the user's preferred language. These sites are connected, one for each language, to each area; portal listings are used to target the site content to the specific area.

Audiences are used to duplicate Web Parts in the TOP area to provide the (translated) Web Part to the right user. Audiences are also used to target portal listings so that users can add links to content on SharePoint sites to the TOP area.

Finally, two search scopes are defined to provide users with the ability to search content in their area (and sites) only.

To set up this solution, follow these steps:

1. Create a global group for the primary language of your user community, and add the appropriate users. For example, your English users would have a group called EnglishLanguage, and your Japanese users would have a group called JapaneseLanguage. Follow this pattern for all the languages used in your environment.

2. Add the users as readers in the portal site by navigating to the Site Settings page and clicking the **Manage Users** link in the **General Settings** section.

3. Specify the content that will be displayed for each language group by creating audiences for each language-specific global group you've created. Complete this task by clicking the **Manage Audiences** link on the **User Profile, Audiences, And Personal Sites** section of the Site Settings page.

4. Verify that the appropriate users have appropriate membership by clicking the **View Audiences** link on the Manage Audiences page, clicking the arrow that appears next to your audience's description, and then clicking the **View Membership** link.

5. Create a top-level area that will contain all other language-specific subareas, and then create a subarea for each language by using the **Actions** list on the portal page, and clicking **Create Subarea**.

6. Customize the top-level area and each language subarea by creating Web Parts and configuring them to be viewable based on language-specific global groups.

More Info   There is not room to describe all the steps required to perform this customization in this book. For more detailed step-by-step instructions on configuring SharePoint Portal Server 2003 with multiple languages, see "Using Microsoft SharePoint Products and Technologies in Multilingual Scenarios," at *http://www.microsoft.com/technet/prodtechnol/office/sps2003 /maintain/spmultil.mspx.*

7. From the Sites page, create a site for each language using the **Create Site** link from the **Actions** list.

Define the search scopes for each language site by navigating to the Site Settings page for the portal site, clicking the **Configure Search And Indexing** link, and then configuring scopes for each language-specific area.

Firewalls

Windows SharePoint Services supports connectivity through firewalls. Depending on your configuration, for external users to connect to the SharePoint server you must ensure that the standard HTTP ports 80 and 443 on the firewall are open. When using a firewall, you must configure SharePoint sites with **Basic authentication** because **Integrated Windows authentication** cannot pass through a firewall.

Note   For detailed information about how to best configure SharePoint Portal Server with Microsoft ISA Server 2000, see "Announcing the ISA Server 2000 SharePoint Portal Server Deployment Kit," by Martin Grasdal and Thomas Shinder, at *http://www.isaserver.org/articles/sharepointkit.html.*

Application Coresidency and Installation Considerations

SharePoint Portal Server 2003 cannot be installed on just any server, because there are Microsoft products that will interfere with SharePoint Portal Server and affect its operation. For instance, installing Windows SharePoint Services prior to installing SharePoint Portal Server causes conflicts. The following products also can cause issues with SharePoint Portal Server 2003:

- **Microsoft SharePoint Portal Server 2001**
- **Exchange Server** (any version)

- **Microsoft Site Server** (any version)
- **Office Server Extensions**
- **Microsoft FrontPage Server Extensions (FPSE)**

Uninstall the conflicting products before installing SharePoint Portal Server 2003. In some cases, you can make the conflicting products work together (such as FPSE); see Technet for more detailed information.

Ensure the Account Performing the Installation Has Authority

When preparing for an installation of SharePoint Portal Server 2003, you must ensure that the account with which you log on to the server has either local administrator or Domain Admin privileges before continuing. In addition, the account that you'll specify for SQL Server during setup will also need to be a member of the Power Users group (if installing on a Member Server) or the Built-In Administrators group (if installing on a Domain Controller).

Third-Party Database Interoperability

Microsoft SQL Server 2000 is the only database product that SharePoint Portal Server can use to store the SharePoint Portal Server configuration and content databases; however, it can connect to almost any third-party database products to store Web Part information.

Using the Database Engine Option on a Domain Controller

The Microsoft SQL Server Database Engine (MSDE) option is not available when installing SharePoint Portal Server on a domain controller. If you are to install SharePoint Portal Server on a domain controller, you must either first install SQL Server 2000 Service Pack 3 on the domain controller itself or use a remote server running SQL Server 2000. If you require MSDE as the database repository, configure the server running Windows Server 2003 as a member server of a domain.

> **More Info**   Best practices are to not run applications such as SharePoint Portal Server 2003 on domain controllers. Following best practices in this regard prevents performance issues that can result from processes competing for resources and provides more in-depth security.

Installing SharePoint Portal Server

Installing SharePoint Portal Server 2003 is fairly intuitive. If you're performing a simple installation, you can choose the default settings and have your environment up and running quickly. If you have to install SharePoint Portal Server on a domain controller—or if you're installing in a larger, more complex environment—a few decision points will require a bit more explanation. A common example is deciding when to use a SQL Server database instead of the default MSDE database.

When installing SharePoint Portal Server, many of the first installation steps are the same whether you plan to install with MSDE or with SQL Server. If you are implementing a fairly simple SharePoint Portal Server environment (one that won't use over 2 GB of information in the portal site and has both SharePoint Portal Server and the database on the same machine), MSDE will probably be your best choice (unless, of course, you need to cluster your SQL databases, in which case SQL Server is required). One advantage of an MSDE scenario is that you don't have to purchase SQL Server licenses. If, however, you need to install SharePoint Portal Server on a domain controller (DC), you *must* use SQL Server: MSDE is not supported on DCs. See Table 3-2 for guidelines on when to use MSDE or SQL Server.

Table 3-2   Database Type Guidelines

Condition	Preferred Database Type
If you require more than 2 GB of storage	SQL Server
If you are installing SharePoint Portal Server on a single server with fewer than 1000 sites	MSDE
If you require database to be located on a server other than the server running SharePoint Portal Server	SQL Server
If you do not have access to SQL Server, but want to work with SharePoint Portal Server	MSDE
If you plan to scale out into a server farm scenario or use any type of multiple-server implementation	SQL Server, because the MSDE database does not accept remote connections
If you're on a tight budget	MSDE
If you need a single-server deployment—for example, when you need to deploy a single server for application testing, for development, or as a proof-of-concept server	MSDE
If you require the ability to cluster your databases	SQL Server 2000 Enterprise Edition

Please note that no database connector exists for databases other than MSDE or SQL Server (such as Oracle or Sybase) for SharePoint Portal Server–specific information. Therefore, such information—including document content, area configurations, user profiles, and other information generated or hosted by SharePoint Portal Server or Windows SharePoint Services—*must* be held in either a SQL Server 2000 or

MSDE database. If you need to access data that resides in third-party databases, such as Oracle, you can build Web Parts that specifically reference this data—the SQL Server/MSDE limitation only prevents provisioning third-party databases from holding SharePoint Portal Server–specific information.

There are some differences in installation when you use SQL Server instead of the default option, MSDE. Table 3-3 explains which of the following sections apply to either an MSDE or SQL Server configuration.

Table 3-3   Sections Describing the SharePoint Portal Server Installation

Installation Section	Used By
Installing SharePoint Portal Server	MSDE and SQL Server
Configure Account Settings and Application Pool Identity	SQL Server
Configure Database Settings	SQL Server
Configuring Account and Proxy Settings	MSDE and SQL Server
Configure Server Topology	SQL Server
Create a Portal Site	MSDE and SQL Server

To install SharePoint Portal Server 2003, follow these steps:

1. Insert the SharePoint Portal Server CD into your CD-ROM drive.

> **Tip**   If the installation does not start, click Setup.exe or Autorun.exe located within the SPS2003 folder of your installation CD to begin setup.

2. If your CD-ROM supports Autorun, click the **Install Microsoft Office Share-Point Portal Server 2003 Components** link.

3. On the Install Microsoft Office SharePoint Portal Server 2003 page, review the requirements, and then click **Next**.

4. The installation requires stopping the IIS services before continuing. Click **OK** to have the services stopped and to continue with the installation.

> **Note**   The services stopped are the World Wide Web Publishing Service, Simple Mail Transfer Protocol (SMTP), HTTP SSL, and IIS Admin services. During the installation process, setup resets IIS. There will be a momentary loss of service on the Web server.

5. Setup installs Windows SharePoint Services, and then the Welcome To The Microsoft Office SharePoint Portal Server 2003 Setup Wizard page appears.

6. On the Welcome To The Microsoft Office SharePoint Portal Server 2003 Setup Wizard page, click **Next**.

7. On the End-User License Agreement page, select the **I Accept All Of The Terms In The License Agreement** check box, and then click **Next**.

8. On the Product Key page, type the product key in the spaces provided and then click **Next**.

9. On the Installation Type And File Location page, if you will be installing with MSDE, click **Install with database engine** as shown in Figure 3-1. Otherwise, to install with SQL Server, click **Install without database engine**. To specify file locations for programs and data, click **Browse**, specify a location, and then click **OK**. Click **Next** to continue.

> **Note**   If the file locations you specified do not exist, you will be prompted to create them. On the message that appears, click **Yes** to create the location, or click **No** to choose another location.

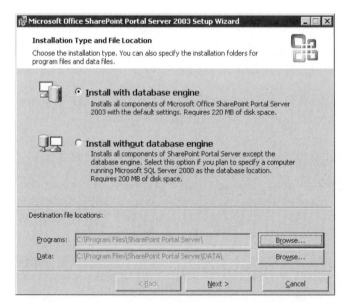

Figure 3-1   Choosing the database engine option and setting the default installation paths

10. If installing without the database engine, you will be prompted to provide the following information as illustrated in Figure 3-2. On the Microsoft Office Share-Point Portal Server 2003 page requesting account information, in the **Account Name** box, type the user account name (format *DOMAIN\user_name*) to be used for administrative operations that create, modify, or grant access to the configuration or portal site databases. In the **Password** and **Confirm Password** boxes, type the password for the account and then click **Next** to continue.

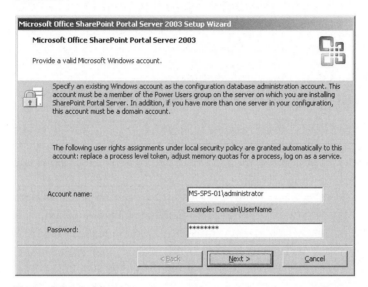

Figure 3-2 Configuring an account for administrative operations on the portal site databases

Tip The account must be a member of the Power Users group on this server. The account must have the Database Creators and Security Administrators server roles on this SQL Server instance. In addition, the account must be a domain account if you have more than one server in your configuration.

To reduce the risk of unwanted administrative access to your servers, specifying an account that is a member of the local Administrators group on the server on which you are installing SharePoint Portal Server is not recommended.

11. On the Install Microsoft Office SharePoint Portal Server 2003 page, click **Next**.

Note   It might take up to one minute for the **Next** button to become active.

12. On the Completing The Microsoft Office SharePoint Portal Server 2003 Setup Wizard page, click **Finish**.

Configure Account Settings and Application Pool Identity

Configuring account settings and application pool identity is specific to SQL Server installations. The following two accounts have to be defined on this page:

- **Default content access account**
- **Portal site application pool identity account**

The default content access account is required to read and crawl content sources, such as websites (intranet and Internet) and network resources that are contained within content indexes. The account creates a full-text index of content located outside of the portal.

The portal site application pool identity account is used by the default application pool (MSSharePointPortalAppPool) created by SharePoint Portal Server to contain all portal sites. This account must be a domain account, unless you are installing the single server with a SQL Server configuration, in which case you can use a local account. It must also be a member of the db_owner database role in SQL Server on the configuration database. It's best to use a domain account regardless of your configuration, as it will allow you to extend your configuration should your SharePoint Portal Server environment grow.

Caution   If using Internet Explorer for the first time on the server, you might be prompted by the Internet Explorer Enhanced Security Configuration message. Select the **In the future, do not show this message** check box, and then click **OK** to continue.

1. On the Configure Server Farm Account Settings page (shown in Figure 3-3), in the **Default Content Access Account** section, select the **Specify account** check box. In the **User name** box, type the account name in the format *DOMAIN\user_name*. In the **Password** and **Confirm Password** boxes, type the password for the account.

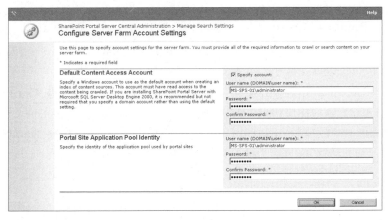

Figure 3-3 Configuring the default content access account and portal site application pool identity during the installation

2. In the **Portal Site Application Pool Identity** section, in the **User name** box, type the account name in the format *DOMAIN\user_name*. In the **Password** and **Confirm Password** boxes, type the password for the account.

3. Click **OK** to continue to the next page.

Configure Database Settings

The configure database settings section is specific to SQL Server installations, so MSDE users can move on to the next section. You will either create a new database or connect to an existing configuration database and then provide the necessary database information (SQL Server name and database name) to continue. The options for configuring the SQL Server database repository are shown in Figure 3-4.

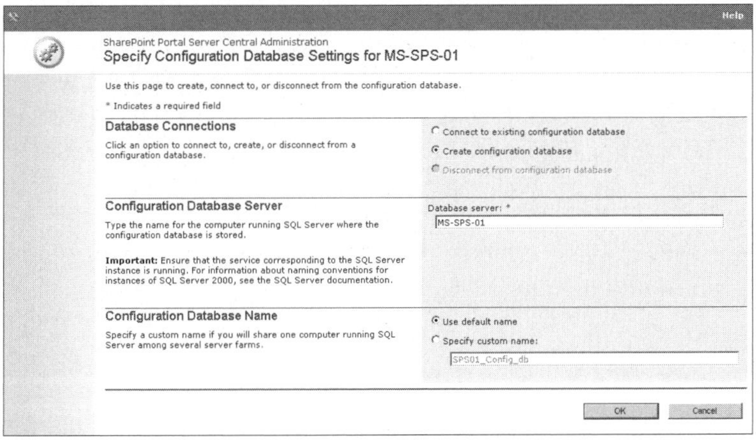

Figure 3-4 Configuring the SQL Server database settings

1. On the Specify Configuration Database Settings For *server_name* page, in the **Database Connections** section, do one of the following:

    ■ If no configuration database exists, click **Create configuration database**.

    ■ If a configuration database already exists, click **Connect to existing configuration database**.

2. In the **Configuration Database Server** section, in the **Database server** box, type the name of the computer running SQL Server.

> **Note** If you have a named SQL Server instance, specify both the name of the computer running SQL Server and the SQL Server instance name in the format *server_name\SQL_instance_name*.

3. In the **Configuration Database Name** section, do one of the following:

    ■ If you want to use the default database name that is displayed, click **Use default name**.

    ■ If you want to specify a name for the database, click **Specify custom name**, and then in the **Custom name** box, type a name for the database.

4. Click **OK** to continue to the next page.

Configure Account and Proxy Settings

When you configure server farm account settings during installation, the Web pages will vary depending on whether you are installing with or without the database engine. Regardless, the emphasis of this page is for you to specify how you want to crawl content sources (websites, network resources, and servers) that will be included in content indexes. The account, also known as the default content access account, requires read access to the content being crawled for crawls to return successful results.

If configuring SharePoint Portal Server with MSDE, you will be prompted to provide the contact e-mail address, default content access account, and proxy server settings as illustrated in Figure 3-5.

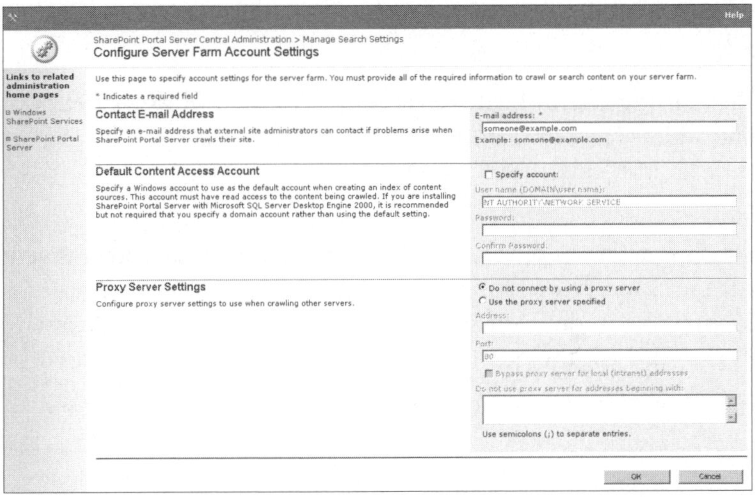

Figure 3-5   Configuring account settings when using MSDE as the database

If configuring SharePoint Portal Server with SQL Server, you will be prompted for the same information with an MSDE install without the need to specify the default content access account. Figure 3-6 illustrates the page shown when configuring with SQL Server.

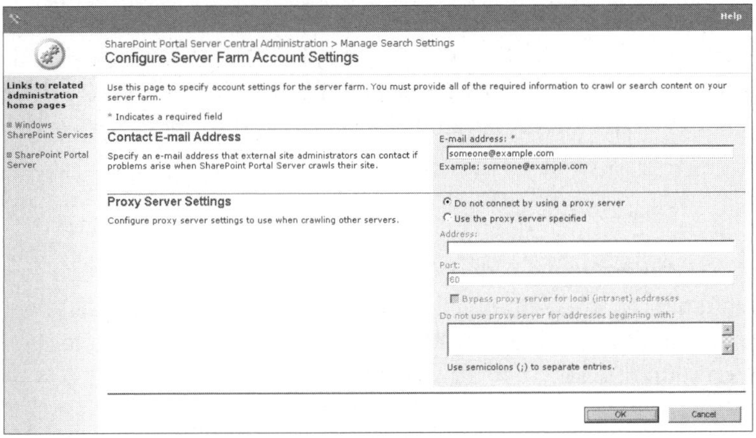

Figure 3-6   Configuring account settings when using a SQL Server database

On the Configure Server Farm Account Settings page, complete the following steps:

1. In the **Contact E-mail Address** section, in the **E-mail address** box, type the e-mail address that an external site administrator can use to contact the administrator if problems occur when SharePoint Portal Server crawls the external site.

2. If installing with SQL Server, in the **Default Content Access Account** section, select the **Specify account** check box, and in the **User name** box, type the account name in the format *DOMAIN\user_name*. In the **Password** box, type the password for the account, and in the **Confirm Password** box, type the password again.

> **Note**   To allow for better auditing and extensibility, specify a domain account with read access to the content being crawled. If necessary, you can leave the default setting (NT AUTHORITY\NETWORK SERVICE), which has more rights to data than is necessary to perform this task.

1. In the **Proxy Server Settings** section, do one of the following:

   ▪ Click **Do not connect by using a proxy server**.

   ▪ Click **Use the proxy server specified**, and then specify the proxy server address, port number, and option to bypass proxy server for local (intranet) addresses.

> **Note**   If you are using a proxy server, the account that you use to access the Internet must have permissions on the proxy server to create a content index of sites on the Internet. Without permissions, you can crawl only content on your intranet.

2. Click **OK** to continue with the installation.

Configure Server Topology

Configuring the **server topology** is specific to SQL Server installations and involves determining what database server settings and components should run on each of the servers configured in a server farm configuration. The various database settings include:

- Configuration database server

- Content database server

- Component settings database server

- Single Sign-On credentials

- Global e-mail server

The various configurable components include: Web, search, index, and job. To configure the server topology, complete the following steps:

1. On the Configure Server Topology page, review the current settings and then click **Change Components** as shown in Figure 3-7.

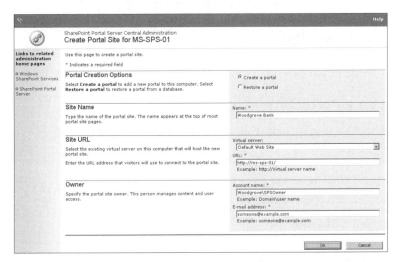

Figure 3-7   Reviewing the server topology configuration during installation

2. On the Change Component Assignments page, in the **Component Assignment** section, select a check box to assign a component to a server as illustrated in Figure 3-8.

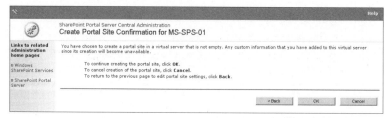

Figure 3-8   Changing the component assignments for the server topology

> **Tip**   You can assign more than one component to each server.

3. In the **Job Server Component** section, in the **Job server** list, select a job server.

4. If you have installed the server component for backward-compatible document libraries, in the **Document Library Server Component (Optional)** section, in the **Document library server** box, type the name of the server to run the document library server component.

5. Click **OK**.

6. On the Configure Server Topology page, click **Close**.

Create a Portal Site

The final step to installing SharePoint Portal Server is creating the portal site. To create a portal site, you will need to provide the following information:

■ Site name

■ Virtual server name to host portal

■ Site URL name

■ Owner account

■ Owner e-mail address

As noted below, some steps differ slightly depending on whether you are creating a portal using MSDE or SQL Server as the database repository.

1. If installing with SQL Server, on the SharePoint Portal Server Central Administration For *server_name* page, in the **Portal Site and Virtual Server Configuration** section, click **Create a portal site**.

2. On the Create Portal Site For *server_name* page, in the **Portal Creation Options** section, click **Create a portal** as shown in Figure 3-9.

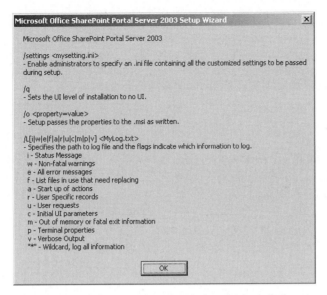

Figure 3-9   Creating a portal site during the installation

3. In the **Site Name** section, in the **Name** box, type a name for the portal site.

4. In the **Site URL** section, do the following:

    ■ In the **Virtual server** list, select the virtual server for this portal site.

    ■ In the **URL** box, type the URL that users will use to connect to the portal site.

> **Note**   By default, this URL is *http://server_name/*. If you are not creating the portal site on the Default Web Site but on another virtual server, the URL includes the port number—for example, *http://server_name:port_number/*.

5. In the **Owner** section, do the following:

    ■ In the **Account name** box, type the account name for the portal site owner in the format *DOMAIN\user_name*.

> **Note**   This account must be a domain account. This account is added to the Administrator site group for the portal site.

    ■ In the **E-mail address** box, type the e-mail address for the portal site owner.

6. Click **OK** to continue to the next page.

7. On the Create Portal Site Confirmation For Server *server_name* page, click **OK** to begin creating the portal site as shown in Figure 3-10.

Figure 3-10   Confirming the creation of the portal site

The Operation Status page appears. This operation might take a few minutes to complete.

At the end of a successful portal site creation, the Operation Successful page appears. On this page, you will find links to launch the portal site, launch the Administration page, or further configure the portal site.

Automated Installations

If you need to configure a large number of SharePoint Portal Server servers across an enterprise or want to ensure consistency of installations, you can automate the installation of SharePoint Portal Server by using either the command line or Setup.exe with an INI file.

Using the Command Line for Installation

You can use the command line to run setup for SharePoint Portal Server by performing these actions:

1. Log on to the computer running Microsoft Windows Server 2003 as a local or domain administrator.

2. Open command prompt.

3. Insert the SharePoint Portal Server CD into your CD-ROM drive.

4. Type **cd** and then press **Enter**.

5. Navigate to the drive letter for the CD-ROM drive.

6. For help with the setup command line parameters, type **setup /?**, and then press **Enter**.

7. Do one of the following:

    ■ To install SharePoint Portal Server with the database engine, type **setup /q /o INSTALLMODE=1 PIDKEY=*CD_key*** and then press **Enter**.

    ■ To install SharePoint Portal Server without the database engine, type **setup /q /o INSTALLMODE=0 ACCOUNTNAME=DOMAIN\user_name ACCOUNTPASSWORD=password PIDKEY=CD_key** and then press **Enter**.

> **Note**   Ensure that the CD_key has no dashes in it; otherwise, setup might fail.
>
> It is recommended that you turn on verbose logging by adding the following parameter to either of the above: /L*V path_to_log_file.

To monitor progress, open **Task Manager** and view MasterSetupApp running in the Applications tab.

Table 3-4 shows the parameters available with the command-line setup, and Figure 3-11 displays the command-line switches available when running setup.exe.

Table 3-4   Parameters Available with Command-Line Setup

Parameter	Description
PIDKEY=CD_key	CD_key is the key for the product. This is required to set up SharePoint Portal Server from the command line.
SPSROOT=path_for_files	Path_for_files is the file path that defines the installation location for the program files for SharePoint Portal Server.
SPSSEARCHDATA=path_for_search_files	Path_for_search_files is the file path that defines the installation location for the content index files.

Table 3-4   Parameters Available with Command-Line Setup *(continued)*

Parameter	Description
INSTALLMODE=[0,1]	To install SharePoint Portal Server with the database engine, install mode is 1. To install SharePoint Portal Server without the database engine, install mode is 0. This is required to set up SharePoint Portal Server from the command line.
ACCOUNTNAME=DOMAIN\account_name	DOMAIN\account_name is the account name for the application pool for the installation without the database engine. This is required if install mode is 0.
ACCOUNTPASSWORD=password	Password is the password for the account name for the application pool. This is required if install mode is 0.
/settings <.ini file>	Automates installation through the use of settings documented in an INI file.
/q	Sets the user interface during installation to none ("quiet mode").
/o	Required when passing values for PIDKEY, SPSROOT, SPSSEARCHDATA, INSTALLMODE, ACCOUNTNAME, or ACCOUNTPASSWORD.
/L[i|w|e|f|a|r|u|c|m|p|v] <log_file.txt>	Specifies the path to the log file. The optional flags indicate the information to log.
i	Log status messages.
w	Log nonfatal warnings.
e	Log all error messages.
f	List files in use that need replacing.
a	Log start up of actions.
r	Log user-specific records.
u	Log user requests.
c	Log initial user interface parameters.
m	Log out-of-memory or fatal exit information.
p	Log terminal properties.
v	Log verbose output.
*	Log all information.

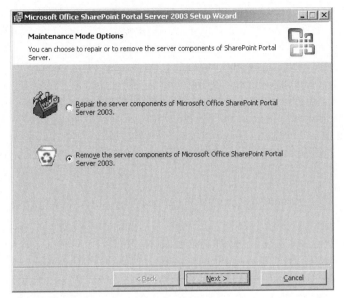

Figure 3-11   Command-line switches used with SharePoint Portal Server's setup.exe

Creating Sites from the Command Line

If you are an administrator of the server computer, you can also create sites by using the Stsadm.exe command-line tool. To create a top-level website, use the createsite operation.

> **Note**   You can also use the createsiteinnewdb operation to create a top-level website and a new content database at the same time.

The createsite operation takes the following required parameters: url, ownerlogin, and owneremail. It also takes the following optional parameters: ownername, lcid, sitetemplate, title, description, and quota. For example, to create a top-level website called site1 on *http://server_name/sites*, you would use syntax similar to the following:

```
stsadm.exe -o createsite -url http://server_name/sites/site1
 -ownerlogin <DOMAIN\user> -owneremail <someone@example.com>
 -ownername <display name>
```

Using the Setup.ini File for Installation

If you are installing a large number of servers or want to customize your installation, you can run SharePoint Portal Server setup in unattended mode by using an .ini file. When you install SharePoint Portal Server by using an .ini file, no dialog boxes or error messages that require user intervention are displayed unless there is no entry in the .ini for a setting. This setup lets you install identical configurations of Share-Point Portal Server on multiple computers in a consistent, automated fashion.

> **Note**   You will not be able to set up remote database installations using the .ini file, as the account name and password listed are valid only for the MSI session being executed for the SharePoint Portal Server installation, and they will not extend to create the Administrative Virtual Server or Application Pool. To automate remote database installations, use the command line.

A Setup.ini file for SharePoint Portal Server 2003 is provided on the root directory of the SharePoint Portal Server CD. A Setup.ini file is also provided for the client components for backward-compatible document libraries. However, you must create the Setup.ini file for the (server) component for backward-compatible document libraries. Instructions to do this are provided later in this section.

You can use the Setup.ini file to do the following:

- Install additional applications (other than SharePoint Portal Server) that use Microsoft Windows Installer.

- Specify different command-line arguments for different applications. For example, if you install additional applications, you can specify that one application installs with no user interface while another application installs with full user interface.

By default, Setup.ini contains the following code:

```
[MSI]
ProductName=Microsoft(R) Windows(R) SharePoint(TM) Services
ProductRelativeLocation=WSS\STS.MSI
[MSI]
ProductName=SharePoint Portal Server
ProductRelativeLocation=SPS\SPS.MSI
[MSI]
ProductName=Microsoft SQL Server Desktop Engine
ProductRelativeLocation=SPS\SQLRUN16.MSI
```

ProductRelativeLocation is the path to the directory that contains the Setup.exe file.

You can include the parameters shown in Table 3-5 in the Setup.ini file.

Table 3-5   Parameters in the Setup.ini File

Parameter	Description
PIDKEY=CD_key	CD_key is the key for the product.
SPSROOT=path_for_files	Path_for_files is the file path that defines the installation location for the program files for SharePoint Portal Server.
SPSSEARCHDATA=path_for_search_files	Path_for_search_files is the file path that defines the installation location for the content index files.
INSTALLMODE=[0,1]	To install SharePoint Portal Server with the database engine, install mode is 1. To install SharePoint Portal Server without the database engine, install mode is 0. This is required to set up SharePoint Portal Server from the command line.
ACCOUNTNAME=DOMAIN\account_name	DOMAIN\account_name is the account name for the application pool for the installation without the database engine. This is required if install mode is 0.
ACCOUNTPASSWORD=password	Password is the password for the account name for the application pool. This is required if install mode is 0. Warning: When you put the password in the Setup.ini file, the password is in plain text.
INSTALLLOCATION=path_to_directory	Path_to_directory is the file path that defines the installation location for additional MSIs that you include in the Setup.ini file.

Tip   Preface the parameters with Arg= and a space, as shown in this example:

```
[MSI]
ProductName=Microsoft(R) Windows(R) SharePoint(TM) Services
ProductRelativeLocation=WSS\STS.MSI
[MSI]
ProductName=SharePoint Portal Server
ProductRelativeLocation=SPS\SPS.MSI
Arg= INSTALLMODE=0 PIDKEY=CD_key ACCOUNTNAME=Domain\user_name ACCOUNTPASS
WORD=password
[MSI]
ProductName=Microsoft SQL Server Desktop Engine
ProductRelativeLocation=SPS\SQLRUN16.MSI
```

You can use ProductLocation instead of ProductRelativeLocation for additional applications.

Using Setup.ini to Install SharePoint Portal Server and an Additional Application

In the following example, the relative location is the path to the directory that contains Setup.exe, so AnotherProduct.msi will be located in a folder called *Other* in the same directory as Setup.exe:

```
[MSI]
ProductName=Microsoft(R) Windows(R) SharePoint(TM) Services
ProductRelativeLocation=WSS\STS.MSI
[MSI]
ProductName=SharePoint Portal Server
ProductRelativeLocation=SPS\SPS.MSI
[MSI]
ProductName=Microsoft SQL Server Desktop Engine
ProductRelativeLocation=SPS\SQLRUN16.MSI
[MSI]
ProductName=Another_Product
ProductRelativeLocation=Other\AnotherProduct.MSI
```

Passing in different arguments to each application   In the following example, two additional applications are installed, in different locations:

```
[MSI]
ProductName=Microsoft(R) Windows(R) SharePoint(TM) Services
ProductRelativeLocation=WSS\STS.MSI
[MSI]
ProductName=SharePoint Portal Server
ProductRelativeLocation=SPS\SPS.MSI
Args= INSTALLMODE=1
[MSI]
ProductName=Microsoft SQL Server Desktop Engine
ProductRelativeLocation=SPS\SQLRUN16.MSI
[MSI]
ProductName=Another_Product
ProductLocation=G:\AnotherProduct.MSI
Args= INSTALLMODE=3 INSTALLLOCATION="C:\Program Files\Another_Product_Location"
[MSI]
ProductName= Another_Product_2
ProductRelativeLocation=Other\AnotherProduct2.MSI
Args= INSTALLLOCATION=C:\AnotherProduct2
```

Installing SharePoint Portal Server with the Database Engine, with No User Interface Displayed and Verbose Logging

In this example, SharePoint Portal Server will be installed to a folder called SharePoint on drive C, and the log files will be written to drive C using verbose logging. The SharePoint Portal Server CD is in drive F.

1. Copy Setup.ini from the SharePoint Portal Server CD to C:\SharePoint.

2. Modify Setup.ini as shown:

```
[MSI]
ProductName=Microsoft(R) Windows(R) SharePoint(TM) Services
ProductRelativeLocation=WSS\STS.MSI
[MSI]
ProductName=SharePoint Portal Server
ProductRelativeLocation=SPS\SPS.MSI
Args= INSTALLMODE=1 PIDKEY=CD_key
[MSI]
ProductName=Microsoft SQL Server Desktop Engine
ProductRelativeLocation=SPS\SQLRUN16.MSI
```

3. Open a command prompt and navigate to **drive F**.

4. Type **setup /q /settings c:\setup.ini /L*V c:\log.txt** and press **Enter**.

Using the .ini File to Install the Component for Backward-Compatible Document Libraries

To use an .ini file to install the server component for backward-compatible document libraries, you must first create an .ini file that contains the default installation settings that you want to use, such as the installation directory. After you create the .ini file, you can edit it by using a text editor. By editing the .ini file, you specify additional options and gain more control over your installation.

To create the .ini file used for unattended setup, you must run the Microsoft Office SharePoint Portal Server 2003 Setup Wizard. However, instead of installing SharePoint Portal Server, the wizard stores the settings that you specify in the .ini file.

Double-byte character set (DBCS) or high-ASCII characters cannot be used in installation paths when performing an unattended installation. Using these characters results in a failed installation. In addition, no path in the .ini file should be longer than 140 characters.

Follow these steps to install the component for backward-compatible document libraries by using an .ini file:

1. Log on to the computer running Microsoft Windows Server 2003 as a local or domain administrator.

2. Perform the following steps to ensure that the proxy server settings for Internet access are specified correctly:

   a. Click **Start**, point to **Control Panel**, and then click **Internet Options**.

   b. In the **Internet Properties** dialog box, click the **Connections** tab.

   c. Click **LAN Settings**.

    d. In the **Local Area Network (LAN) Settings** dialog box, in the **Automatic configuration** section, ensure that both check boxes are cleared.

    e. If you use a proxy server, complete step 6 through step 11. Otherwise, go to step 12.

    f. In the Proxy server section, select the **Use a proxy server for your LAN (These settings will not apply to dial-up or VPN connections)** check box.

    g. Select the **Bypass proxy server for local addresses** check box.

    h. In the **Address** box, type a valid proxy server address.

    i. In the **Port** box, type the port number for the proxy server.

    j. Click **Advanced**.

    k. In the **Proxy Settings** dialog box, select the **Use the same proxy server for all protocols** check box, and then click **OK**.

    l. Click **OK** to close the Local Area Network (LAN) Settings dialog box.

    m. Click **OK** to close the Internet Options dialog box.

3. Insert the SharePoint Portal Server CD into your CD-ROM drive.

4. Create an .ini file:

    a. On the taskbar, click **Start**, and then click **Run**.

    b. In **Open**, type *path_to_server_setup_file* **setup /CreateUnattend path** *filename***.ini** where *filename* is the name of the .ini file that you want to create. For example, if the setup file is in the Setup directory on drive D and you want to create sample.ini on the E drive, type **D:\Setup\setup /CreateUnattend E:\sample.ini**.

    c. Click **OK**.

    d. Follow the instructions that appear in the setup wizard. All settings that you choose are included in the .ini file that you create.

5. Edit the .ini file:

    f. In a text editor, such as Microsoft WordPad, open *filename*.ini where *filename* is the name of the .ini file that you created.

    g. Modify parameters in the file for the settings that you want SharePoint Portal Server setup to use.

    h. If you plan to use an unattended installation file on servers with varying storage configurations, ensure that hard-coded paths are valid for each server configuration before starting the installation. An example of a hard-coded path reference is "C:\." You can force the installer to automatically choose the correct default path by removing an entry line completely.

i. You can modify the following path in the section starting with [gfn_mid microsoft web storage system]:

```
InstallDirectory=C:\Program Files\Common Files\Microsoft Shared\Web Storage Sy
stem
```

The following restrictions apply:

The path cannot be at the root of a hard drive (for example, do not change the path to "F:\").

The entire path consists of only low-ASCII characters (no High-ASCII or DBCS characters).

The path is no longer than 65 characters.

6. You can also modify the following paths in the section starting with [gfn_mid microsoft sharepoint portal server]:

```
InstallDirectory="C:\Program Files\SharePoint Portal Server"
Web Storage System Database Directory="C:\Program Files\SharePoint Portal Serv
er\DMData\Web Storage System"
Web Storage System Streaming Database Directory="C:\Program Files\SharePoint P
ortal Server\DMData\Web Storage System"
Web Storage System Database Log Directory="C:\Program Files\SharePoint Portal
Server\DMData\Web Storage System"
```

7. Run setup:

h. On the taskbar, from the server on which you want to run setup, click **Start**, and then click **Run**.

i. In **Open**, type *installation path***setup /UnattendFile path** *filename*.**ini** where *filename* is the name of the .ini file that you created.

For example, if the SharePoint Portal Server CD is in drive F, you would type **F:\Optional\Server\setup /q /settings c:\setup.ini**

j. Click **OK**.

Migrating from WMSDE to SQL Server

When you install Windows SharePoint Services on a single server choosing the default settings, your installation will use Microsoft SQL Server 2000 Desktop Engine (Windows) (WMSDE) for your databases. This is fine in a small-scale environment, when you are hosting just a few websites, but if your server suddenly gets popular and you need to start hosting hundreds of sites, you might run into performance and storage problems or require a clustered database for high availability. If you find yourself in one of these situations, you can scale out by switching to Microsoft SQL Server 2000 Service Pack 3 (SP3) as your database back end. For step-by-step information on migrating from WMSDE to SQL Server 2000, refer to the "Upgrading from WMSDE to SQL Server" section in Chapter 2.

Installing the Component for Backward-Compatible Document Libraries

Backward-compatible document libraries allow you to access the same store (the extensible storage engine Web storage system) that was available in SharePoint Portal Server 2001. If you don't have a previous version of SharePoint Portal Server, you will not need to install this feature. If, however, you need to retain the old store system or if you'd like to use the workflow features that come with this database, you can install the optional component for backward-compatible document libraries on either a computer that has SharePoint Portal Server 2003 installed or on a computer without SharePoint Portal Server installed.

Install the Component for Backward-Compatible Document Libraries

Before you can install the component for backward-compatible document libraries, ensure that the proxy server settings for Internet access are specified correctly by referring to steps provided earlier in the chapter. Then follow these steps:

1. Insert the SharePoint Portal Server CD into your CD-ROM drive.

2. Click **Install optional components**.

3. On the installation page for optional components, click **Install server and client components for backward-compatible document libraries** as shown in Figure 3-12.

Figure 3-12   Installing the backward-compatible document library components

4. On the Welcome To The Document Library Setup Wizard page, click **Next**.

5. On the License Agreement page, read the license agreement. If you agree with the terms of the agreement, click **I agree**, and then click **Next**.

6. On the Product Identification page, type the product key in the spaces provided and then click **Next**.

7. On the Document library component of Microsoft Office SharePoint Portal Server 2003 Setup page, specify the location on the server disk where you want to install the program and data files for the document library component.

   If you are installing the optional components on a server that already has SharePoint Portal Server installed, you cannot choose the location for the program files. If you are installing the optional components on a server that does not have SharePoint Portal Server installed, you can choose the location for the program files.

   SharePoint Portal Server also installs additional required files on the operating system drive. Click Disk Information for information about the amount of disk space required and the amount remaining. If there are existing files in the installation paths, setup removes these files.

> **More Info**   The path must meet the following restrictions: can contain no more than 80 characters; the path name can contain only characters in the lower ASCII range; and, the path cannot point to a root directory.

8. Click **Next**. A message that lists services that will be stopped appears.

9. Click **OK** to stop the services and continue.

   The Component Progress page appears.

10. On the Completing the Document Library Setup Wizard page, click **Finish**. You might be prompted to restart your computer.

After the setup wizard completes, perform the following steps to make the optional **document library** component functional:

1. Change component assignments for the server farm.

2. Create a document library.

3. Manage security for a backward-compatible document library.

Installing the Client Components for Backward-Compatible Document Libraries

The client components are extensions to Microsoft Windows Explorer and Microsoft Office applications. There is no individual client application. These extensions integrate SharePoint Portal Server 2003 commands with Windows Explorer and Office applications. Users can also access document libraries (Web Storage System–based) from the portal site without installing the client components, but they will not experience the integration with Windows Explorer and Office applications.

You can install the client components by running setup either from the server or from the SharePoint Portal Server CD. By default, the setup wizard installs client installation files to the following location on the server: %SystemDrive%\Program Files\SharePoint Portal Server\ClientDrop\Languages*Language*, where *Language* corresponds to the language of the client. The following steps outline the procedures for installing the client components:

1. Insert the SharePoint Portal Server CD into your CD-ROM drive.

2. Click **Install optional components**.

3. On the installation page for optional components, click **Install client components for backward-compatible document libraries**.

4. On the Welcome To Client Components Setup Wizard page, click **Next**.
   The Install Client Components page appears. This page shows the progress of the installation.

5. On the Completing The Client Components Setup Wizard page, click **Finish**.

After you have installed the client components, you must add a Web folder that points to the document library. The address of the document library is *http://server_name/document_library_name*.

> **More Info**   The steps for adding a Web folder vary, depending on your operating system. See your operating system Help for detailed instructions. For example, in Microsoft Windows 2000 Professional or Microsoft Windows XP Professional, go to **My Network Places** and use the **Add Network Place Wizard** to add a Web folder. In Microsoft Windows 98, go to **Web Folders** in My Computer and use **Add Web Folder** to add a Web folder.

Repairing the Client Components for Backward-Compatible Document Libraries

You can repair the client components for **backward-compatible document libraries** (Web Storage System–based) of Microsoft Office SharePoint Portal Server 2003 by using Add Or Remove Programs in Control Panel. You can also use the command line to repair client components.

Repair the Client Components for Backward-Compatible Document Libraries by Using Control Panel

Using Control Panel, complete the following steps to successfully repair an install of the client components:

1. Open **Add or Remove Programs**.

2. In the **Add or Remove Programs** dialog box, click **Client Components for Microsoft Office SharePoint Portal Server 2003**.

3. Click **Change**.

4. On the Welcome To The Client Components Setup Wizard page, click **Next**.

5. On the Maintenance Mode Options page, click **Repair the client components of the document management component of SharePoint Portal Server**, and then click **Next**.

6. On the Ready To Repair The Program page, click **Install**.

    The Install Client Components progress page appears, and Windows repairs the client components.

7. On the Completing The Client Components Setup Wizard page, click **Finish**.

Repair the Client Components for Backward-Compatible Document Libraries from the Command Line

Another method of repairing the client components is to use the command line. The following steps will repair an installation from the command line.

1. Open a command prompt window.

2. Type "*path*\setup" /f "*path*\SPSClient.msi", where *path* is the path to the Setup.exe and SPSClient.msi files.

> **Tip**   Include the switch /f to repair the client components.

For example, to repair the client components, where Setup.exe and SPSClient.msi are in E:\Client Files, you would type **E:\Client Files\setup" /f "E:\Client Files\SPSClient.msi".**

> **Note**   If you have removed one or more of the installation prerequisites, you cannot repair the client components unless you disable the prerequisite check. You can disable the prerequisite check by adding DISABLEPRE-REQ=1 to the command line. To disable the prerequisite check in the preceding example, you would type **E:\Client Files\setup" /f "E:\Client Files\SPSClient.msi" DISABLEPREREQ=1.**

Installing SharePoint Portal Server into a Non–Active Directory Environment

Active Directory is not required for Windows SharePoint Services or SharePoint Portal Server 2003. However, without Active Directory, you cannot prepopulate and synchronize the SharePoint Portal Server profile database with the list of users from Active Directory, and users' personal sites are not registered for cross-farm synchronization in a multiserver configuration.

SharePoint Portal Server is supported only on servers that are members of a Microsoft Windows NT 4.0, Windows 2000, or Windows Server 2003 domain. Installing and operating a SharePoint Portal Server computer is supported if your server is a member of a domain or a member of a workgroup. (Domain installations are more easily administered, however.) All servers in a server farm must be members of the same domain.

For best results, deploy SharePoint Products and Technologies in an Active Directory environment.

Uninstalling SharePoint Portal Server 2003

SharePoint Portal Server 2003 can be uninstalled by using Add/Remove Programs. Removing SharePoint Portal Server does not remove the following items from your server:

- Windows SharePoint Services
- Microsoft SQL Server Desktop Engine (if installed)
- Microsoft SQL Server (if installed locally)
- Component for backward-compatible document libraries.

Microsoft recommends you remove the applications in this order:

1. SharePoint Portal Server
2. Windows SharePoint Services
3. SQL Server Desktop Engine (if installed)
4. SQL Server (if installed locally)

Warning Most files and subfolders located in installation folders will be removed. All Microsoft SQL Server databases will be detached, but not removed, from the database server. When you remove SharePoint Portal Server, all user data is left in the database files. These files are also left behind if you remove SQL Server Desktop Engine or Microsoft SQL Server.

Uninstall SharePoint Portal Server

In the case that you will need to uninstall SharePoint Portal Server, perform two steps: first uninstall SharePoint Portal Server, and then proceed to uninstalling Windows SharePoint Services. The steps for uninstalling SharePoint Portal Server are as follows:

1. Click **Start**, point to **Control Panel**, and then click **Add or Remove Programs**.

2. In the **Add or Remove Programs** dialog box, click **Microsoft Office Share-Point Portal Server 2003**.

3. Click **Change**.

4. On the Welcome To The Microsoft Office SharePoint Portal Server 2003 Setup Wizard page, click **Next**.

5. On the **Maintenance Mode Options** page, click **Remove the server components of Microsoft Office SharePoint Portal Server 2003** as illustrated in Figure 3-13, and then click **Next**.

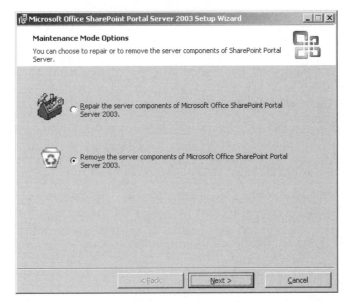

Figure 3-13   Maintenance Mode options for SharePoint Portal Server

6. In the confirmation message box, click **Yes** to remove SharePoint Portal Server, as shown in Figure 3-14.

Figure 3-14   Warning message informing how the uninstall will handle files and SQL databases

7. Click **OK** to allow Setup to stop the necessary services and continue with the removal of SharePoint Portal Server. The removal of SharePoint Portal Server will take a few minutes.

8. Click **OK** to complete the removal of SharePoint Portal Server.

You can now use Add Or Remove Programs to remove Windows SharePoint Services and SQL Server Desktop Engine or SQL Server (if installed). For more information on uninstalling Windows SharePoint Service, refer to Chapter 2.

Optionally, after you have removed SharePoint Portal Server, Windows SharePoint Services, and SQL Server Desktop Engine (if installed), you can also remove the following items if applicable:

1. If your installation of SharePoint Portal Server used SQL Server Desktop Engine, delete the folder \Program Files\Microsoft SQL Server\MSSQL$SHAREPOINT on the operating system drive.

2. If your installation of SharePoint Portal Server used Microsoft SQL Server, remove the following databases associated with SharePoint Portal Server:

   - *site_name_PROF*

   - *site_name_SERV*

   - *site_name_SITE*

   - SharePoint Portal Server configuration database. By default, this database is named *SPS_Config_db*.

   - Remove all jobs for the SQL Server instance of SharePoint Portal Server. All relevant jobs are named *site_name_SERV Subscription Cleanup*.

3. Remove any application pools that were created by SharePoint Portal Server.

Repairing SharePoint Portal Server

You can repair the installation of SharePoint Portal Server 2003 by selecting the Change option in the Add Or Remove Programs dialog box, and then choosing Repair on the Maintenance Mode Options page.

The Repair option is beneficial when you need to repair or restore the Share-Point Portal Server binary files. A repair does not modify or fix the indexes or databases in use by SharePoint Portal Server.

Troubleshooting SharePoint Portal Server Installations

There have been documented issues with installing SharePoint Portal Server. This section will outline the major problems that have been discovered to date.

For further information, refer to the Microsoft Support website at *http://support.microsoft.com*.

"Error 502" Error Message When Trying to Access SharePoint Central Administration Pages

This message occurs when you run SharePoint Portal Server Setup to install Share-Point Portal Server 2003 and MSDE on the server, and then click Finish on the Completing The Microsoft Office SharePoint Portal Server 2003 Setup Wizard page. The symptom is that the Configure Server Farm Account Settings page of SharePoint Central Administration is not displayed in your Web browser window. Instead, you receive an Error 502 message.

This problem can occur if a proxy server is configured in Internet Explorer but the Bypass Proxy Server For Local Addresses option is not enabled. SharePoint Portal Server Setup does not look to see whether proxy server settings in Internet Explorer are configured correctly on the server. The problem can also occur in situations when you install Windows Server 2003 from a Remote Installation Services (RIS) server by using a RIS image that uses the default proxy server settings for Internet Explorer in which the Bypass Proxy Server For Local Addresses option is not enabled.

To work around this problem, enable the Bypass Proxy Server For Local Addresses option in the proxy server settings of Internet Explorer. To do so, follow these steps:

1. Start **Internet Explorer**.

2. On the **Tools** menu, click **Internet Options**.

3. Click the **Connections** tab, and then under **Local Area Network (LAN) Settings**, click **LAN Settings**.

4. Under **Proxy server**, select the **Bypass proxy server for local addresses** check box, and then click **OK**.

5. Click **OK**.

The Configure Server Farm Account Settings Page Does Not Appear

When you run Setup to install SharePoint Portal Server 2003 you might find that the Configure Server Farm Account Settings page is not displayed and the SharePoint Central Administration Site is not configured correctly; this problem occurs after you complete these steps:

1. Specify the user account that you want to use as the Configuration Database Administration Account on the SharePoint Portal Server page that requests account information.

2. Click **Next** on the Install Microsoft Office SharePoint Portal Server 2003 page.

3. Click **Finish** on the Completing The Microsoft Office SharePoint Portal Server 2003 Setup Wizard page.

Additionally, you might experience the following symptoms:

- When you view SharePoint Portal Server 2003–related settings in Microsoft Internet Information Services (IIS) Manager, the following symptoms occur:

  - When you expand websites and view the entry for the SharePoint Central Administration site in the right pane, the State of the site appears as **Stopped**.

  - When you right-click the **SharePoint Central Administration Site**, click **Properties**, and then click the **Home Directory** tab, the value that is displayed in the **Application pool** box is **<Invalid App Pool>**.

  - When you expand **Application Pools**, the CentralAdminAppPool Application Pool is not listed.

  - If you create a new application pool named CentralAdminAppPool and you start SharePoint Central Administration, you are repeatedly prompted to enter your user name and password. After you are prompted to enter your user name and password several times, you receive the following error message: "You do not have permission to view this page."

- An error message that is similar to the following message is logged to the Spsadm.log file:

```
0000059E UNK 00000000 00000600 Service account name is 'SPSUser'. 0000059E UNK
 00000000 00000600 An exception occurred while setting the administration cred
entials. Microsoft.SharePoint.Portal.Topology.p: Error occurred while stopping
 services. See the event log for details. ---
> System.ComponentModel.Win32Exception: The account name is invalid or does no
t exist, or the password is invalid for the account name specified at Microsof
t.SharePoint.Portal.Topology.y.a(q A_0, String A_1, String A_2) ...
```

■ An error message that is similar to the following message is logged to the W3wp.log file:

```
000002CE UNK 00000000 00000980 Url Path: "/sps/FarmDatabase.aspx"
0000031C UNK 00000000 00000980 ShipAssert 0000 Microsoft.SharePoint.Library.SP
RequestInternalClass.RenderFormDigest(String bstrUrl), Unhandled exception cau
ght during execution of Microsoft.SharePoint.Portal.PageBase::ErrorHandler().
Exception information: Exception information: Microsoft.SharePoint.SPException
: Cannot complete this action. Please try again. ---
> System.Runtime.InteropServices.COMException (0x80004005): Cannot complete th
is action. Please try again. at Microsoft.SharePoint.Library.SPRequestInternal
Class.RenderFormDigest(String bstrUrl) at Microsoft.SharePoint.Library.a.k(Str
ing A_0) --- End of inner exception stack trace ---
```

■ The following event is logged to the application event log:

```
Event Type: Warning
Source: W3SVC
Category: None
Event ID: 1048
Description:
The application '/
' belonging to site 'SiteName' has an invalid AppPoolId 'CentralAdminAppPool'
set. Therefore, the application will be ignored.
```

This issue occurs if the user account that you configured as the Configuration Database Administration Account in the Account Name box of the Microsoft Office SharePoint Portal Server 2003 page is specified incorrectly. This issue can occur if either one of the following conditions is true:

■ You configure a local user account as the Configuration Database Administration Account, but you do not specify the user account by using the Server-Name\UserAccount format.

■ You configure a domain user account as the Configuration Database Administration Account, but you do not specify the user account by using the Domain\UserAccount format.

To resolve this issue, remove and then reinstall SharePoint Portal Server 2003 on the server. Make sure that you specify the user account that you want to use as the Configuration Database Administration Account by using either the Server-Name\UserAccount format or the Domain\UserAccount format (as appropriate to your situation). The user account must also be a member of the Power Users group on the server.

Summary

This chapter outlined the steps to install SharePoint Portal Server 2003 in several scenarios. It began by explaining the prerequisite requirements for a SharePoint Portal Server 2003 installation, and then continued by outlining how to install SharePoint Portal Server 2003 with MSDE or SQL Server 2000. The second half of the chapter touched on installing the components for the backward-compatible document library, and how to work with SharePoint Portal Server in a non–Active Directory environment. Finally, we concluded the chapter by explaining how to uninstall and repair a SharePoint Portal Server 2003 installation.

Part II

SharePoint Products and Technologies Architecture

Chapter 4

Windows SharePoint Services Architecture

Microsoft Windows SharePoint Services is the underlying technology on which SharePoint Products and Technologies run. Understanding the architecture of Windows SharePoint Services, both logical and physical, aids an administrator's understanding of not only how the product should be configured, but also which settings have far-reaching effects and which have little impact. This chapter discusses the components of Windows SharePoint Services and how these components interact with each other. This includes how Windows SharePoint Services affect Microsoft Windows Server 2003 services that it runs on and uses.

Although SharePoint Products and Technologies have changed dramatically from version 1.0, some of the underlying architecture remains the same. Windows SharePoint Services handles page requests much the same way that SharePoint Team Services does. In fact, one of the biggest architectural differences between Windows SharePoint Services and SharePoint Team Services is in the way that Windows SharePoint Services stores data and configuration information.

In SharePoint Team Services v1.0, the configuration and site content information was spread out between the local file system, the registry, the Internet Information Server (IIS) metabase, and SQL Server databases. In Windows SharePoint Services, all data is stored in Microsoft SQL Server 2000 or Windows Microsoft SQL Server 2000 Desktop Engine (WMSDE) databases. This includes all site content, documents, product information, and configuration settings.

> **Note**   The WMSDE database that ships with Windows SharePoint Services does not have a 2-GB limit. The standard MSDE database that can be installed with Microsoft Office SharePoint Portal Server 2003 does have a 2-GB storage limit.

Architectural Components

The result of Windows SharePoint Services storing all information in databases is a complete split between front-end and back-end components. The front-end components in Windows SharePoint Services are Web servers that host the individual sites and process client requests. Front-end Web servers are referred to as *stateless* because they contain no website content or configuration information. To complete a client request, the front-end server connects to a back-end database to retrieve the needed data so that it can build and send the Web page to the client. Figure 4-1 shows the relationship between front-end Web servers and back-end database servers.

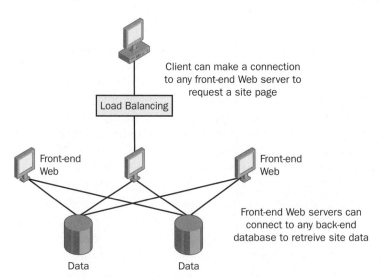

Figure 4-1   The logical architecture of Windows SharePoint Services includes a client requesting pages from front-end Web servers, which in turn get all data from back-end databases

> **Note**   The split between front-end and back-end components in Windows SharePoint Services is a logical one. Physically, the front-end and back-end components can exist on the same server or on separate servers.

Improvements over SharePoint Team Services

By separating front-end and back-end components, Windows SharePoint Services has some dramatic improvements in key areas over SharePoint Team Services. Each of the improvements in the following list affects configuration decisions:

- **Backup.**   Consolidating all site content and configuration information into one type of storage simplifies the backup process.

- **Scalability.**   Windows SharePoint Services can be scaled down to a single server that contains both front-end and back-end components, or it can be scaled up to several front-end Web servers accepting requests and gathering data from multiple back-end database servers.

- **Availability.**   Multiple front-end Web servers can host the same site content, allowing others to take over if one fails. Also back-end databases can be clustered for automatic failover.

- **Integrity of data.**   Consolidating all the settings and data into one location and one format protects the data.

- **Customization.**   Administrators with only an introductory understanding of Web development, using an HTML editor, can customize the many templates and properties available in Windows SharePoint Services. For in-depth customizations, a developer needs to know only ASP.NET Web pages and form controls. For back-end customizations, a programming knowledge of SQL Server is needed.

Front-End Web Servers

The front-end Web servers in Windows SharePoint Services use the Web services provided by Internet Information Services (IIS) in Windows Server 2003. The purpose of these front-end Web servers is just to service requests from clients. They are considered stateless because they install only the minimum files and settings needed to be able to connect to the correct back-end database and retrieve requested site pages and content.

Back-End Databases

Whether a separate SQL Server or WMSDE is used, the back-end server in Windows SharePoint Services creates and uses back-end databases. The purpose of having two database types is to separate the site data from the configuration information. A database that contains site data is called a *content database*, while product information and settings are contained in what is called a *configuration database*. There can be a single content database in a small environment, but in a large environment there can be hundreds or even thousands of content databases. No matter how many content databases exist in a Windows SharePoint Services farm, there is only one configuration database.

Configuration Database

In a Windows SharePoint Services environment, there can be multiple front-end Web servers that contain several websites whose content is stored in one of a number of back-end content databases. To keep the front-end Web servers stateless, a centralized database is needed to keep track of which content database holds the data for a specific site. When a front-end Web server receives a request for a page from a site, the first connection it must make is to this configuration database. For performance reasons, this information is cached on the front-end Web server for subsequent requests and the cached information is used by the front-end Web server thereafter.

Content Database

Content databases provide content to the front-end Web servers when it is requested. All site content—including site documents, list data, Web Part properties, as well as user names and rights—are stored in content databases. You can create as many content databases as needed to support the websites on your servers. This can range from just one to thousands, depending on the number of users.

Physical Configurations

With the split of front-end and back-end services, administrators now have the flexibility to configure Windows SharePoint Services in several ways. By providing any configuration from a single server to a server farm, Windows SharePoint Services can scale to suit small to large organizations.

An organization with fewer users can start with a single-server installation of Windows SharePoint Services. This means that both the front-end and back-end components are installed on the same physical server. In this configuration, WMSDE can be used for the back-end databases instead of SQL Server. If the number of users in an organization grows enough to require a physical separation of front-end and back-end components, the WMSDE databases can be migrated to SQL Server. To do this requires several steps and the use of IIS, Windows SharePoint Services, and SQL Server administration tools, but it can be done.

A server farm in Windows SharePoint Services can have identically configured front-end Web servers that all connect to the same configuration database. Load-balancing software such as Network Load Balancing (NLB) or load-balancing hardware can ensure that client requests are evenly distributed among the front-end Web servers. This not only distributes the load among several front-end Web servers, but it also allows them to provide failover for each other.

IIS Services Used by Windows SharePoint Services

Windows SharePoint Services works only with a specific set of software. This software includes Windows 2003 as the operating system with IIS and ASP.NET installed on the front-end servers. Back-end components require a separate installation of SQL Server 2000 or WMSDE. WMSDE is included as part of Windows SharePoint Services.

Windows SharePoint Services relies on several services that are provided by IIS for its Web services. Figure 4-2 shows the architecture of how IIS handles Web requests before Windows SharePoint Services is installed.

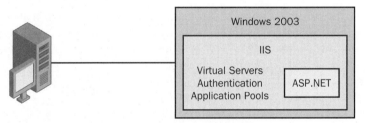

Figure 4-2   Figure displaying required software and underlying services needed by Windows SharePoint Services front-end Web servers

Virtual Servers

IIS uses virtual servers to give websites administrative, security, and resource boundaries. The default virtual server installed by IIS is named Default Web Site and is located at the \inetpub\wwwroot folder. Windows SharePoint Services uses virtual servers provided by IIS to host its websites.

Application Pools

Application pools were introduced as part of IIS 6. Each application pool is an isolated set of worker processes in which Web applications are run. This means that different application pools use separate processor and memory resources. An application pool is also a security boundary because each application pool requires its own set of credentials on the server. Windows SharePoint Services uses IIS application pools for handling resource allocation in its websites.

Authentication

IIS performs **authentication** to validate user accounts that try to access its Web services. Authentication works on a per-virtual-server basis in IIS and in Windows SharePoint Services. Windows SharePoint Services lets IIS handle authentication on the front-end Web server—so much so that changes to authentication must occur in IIS administrative tools as well as in Windows SharePoint Services administrative tools. See Chapter 6, "Security Architecture for SharePoint Products and Technologies," for full details on the authentication in websites.

ASP.NET

When IIS installs, it has only a minimum configuration and does not install many of the features that it includes. This is for security reasons. Because many Windows SharePoint Services components are built on ASP.NET, the Application Server component for ASP.NET must also be installed in IIS before beginning an installation of Windows SharePoint Services.

Changes Made by Windows SharePoint Services

Although some IIS services, such as application pools and authentication, are used without modification, other IIS services, such as virtual servers and request handling, are altered to work with the architecture of Windows SharePoint Services. Figure 4-3 shows the components added and changed in a Windows SharePoint Services installation.

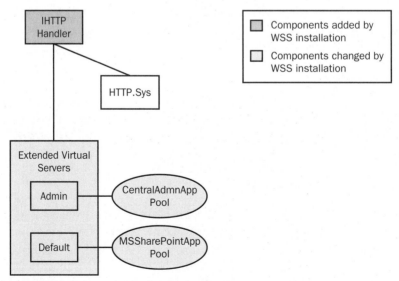

Figure 4-3   Illustrates changes to services after the installation of Windows SharePoint Services

Request Handler

By default, IIS handles all incoming HTTP requests with a kernel-mode driver called HTTP.sys. The only purpose of this file is to read and route incoming requests. Windows SharePoint Services installs its own handler. This handler is an **Internet Server Application Program Interface** (ISAPI) filter called *the IHTTP handler*. The IHTTP handler handles all ASP.NET page requests. All other requests, such as HTML pages that don't contain ASP.NET code, are handled by HTTP.sys. This process is described in more detail later in this chapter in the "Handling Site Page Requests" section.

Extending Virtual Servers

For Windows SharePoint Services to be able to use a virtual server, it must be extended. Extending a virtual server allows it to connect to the configuration database that will in turn direct it to the appropriate content database for site content. If Windows SharePoint Services is installed on a single server with WMSDE using the simple installation method, the default IIS virtual server is extended automatically. In any other case, you must extend each virtual server manually through Windows SharePoint Services administration tools.

Although you can extend a virtual server through Windows SharePoint Services administration tools, you cannot create a virtual server using these tools. You must first create the virtual server through IIS administration tools before extending it in Windows SharePoint Services. To extend a virtual server, you must be logged on as a member of the Administrators group on the local computer or as a user that has the rights to administer both Windows SharePoint Services and IIS.

Application Pools in Windows SharePoint Services

When you extend a virtual server in Windows SharePoint Services, you also choose which application pool it will use. Windows SharePoint Services uses the application pool that is used by IIS for its default website. During the installation of Windows SharePoint Services, one additional application pool is created for the virtual server that contains the Windows SharePoint Services administrative site. The application pool created for the administrative site is called **CentralAdminAppPool**.

Resource Allocation in Application Pools

In Windows SharePoint Services, you can configure a set of virtual servers to share an application pool or you can place each virtual server in a separate application pool. Sharing an application pool means sharing memory space and processor resources. This means that if one of the virtual servers fails, all the virtual servers could fail. Also, the virtual servers could potentially access each other's data.

Setting up separate application pools for virtual servers requires a lot of memory resources. Each virtual server that is assigned its own application pool needs about 150 MB of memory.

Management

The Windows SharePoint Services administrative website has a Web page that is just for management of the **default IIS** application pool. If you choose to create and assign new application pools to new or existing virtual servers, you can do so using Windows SharePoint Services administrative tools. However, you will have to perform other administrative tasks through IIS administrative tools.

There is a difference between an application *pool* and an application pool *identity*. An application pool *identity* is a user account that is used as the security context for an application pool. The account designated as the application pool identity is used to connect the front-end Web server to the back-end databases. The application pool created during the installation of Windows SharePoint Services is given an application pool identity during installation.

By default, the account designated as the application pool identity for the CentralAdminAppPool is the configuration database administration account that is set at the end of setup. This account should be changed only if the password for the CentralAdminAppPool application pool expires or is reset.

The application pool identity for the default website in IIS is set in Windows SharePoint Services when it is extended. In most cases, this account must be a domain account. However, if you are installing the single server with SQL Server configuration, this account can be a local account. This account must also be a member of the db_owner database role in SQL Server on the configuration database.

Virtual Servers vs. Site Collections

If you need to create more websites in a Windows SharePoint Services environment, should you create and extend more virtual servers or should you create more site collections and sites on existing virtual servers? The answer depends on the purpose of the added websites.

Anyone who has experience with SharePoint Team Services v1.0 might notice that Windows SharePoint Services supports far fewer virtual servers per physical Web server than does SharePoint Team Services v1.0. Windows SharePoint Services supports approximately 10 virtual servers per physical Web server, while SharePoint Team Services v1.0 supports approximately 1000. The reason is the architectural change that affects how website space is allocated in Windows SharePoint Services.

In SharePoint Team Services v1.0, there was only one root website per virtual server. In Windows SharePoint Services, you can have multiple top-level sites, each with child subsites. Each of these sets of top-level sites and subsites is referred to as a *site collection* because they share a common GUID and namespace. Because of site collections, the number of sites supported in Windows SharePoint Services is much more than the number of sites that SharePoint Team Services v1.0 can support. When more websites are needed, you have the choice of creating more virtual servers or creating more site collections in existing virtual servers.

Whether you should add more site collections or create new virtual servers depends on a few factors. A virtual server has separate security and administrative boundaries from other virtual servers and can have separate resource boundaries as well. Because site collections are contained within one virtual server, they share these boundaries.

When deciding to go with virtual servers or site collections, you need to ask the following questions:

- **Does the new site have different authentication needs than existing sites?**   The answer to this question is "yes" if you have a need for an internal site as well as an external site in your organization. In that case, the new site should be in a separate virtual server from other sites because all sites in one virtual server must use the same types of authentication. If the answer is "no," the same virtual server can be used.

- **Is there a completely different group of users for the new site with distinct security needs?**   Distinct security needs for a particular group of users might be necessary if you are hosting sites from different organizations or the data in the new site is of a sensitive nature with high security requirements. Each virtual can be given a separate application pool, while site collections that reside in the same virtual server use the same application pool. Because application pools share memory space and worker processes, the data from all sites within a virtual server could be compromised if any one of the websites in a virtual server is compromised.

- **Does the new site have higher availability requirements?**   All sites in a virtual server share the same application pool memory space and worker processes. Because of this, one failed website can cause the others to fail as well.

Web Part Pages

Web Part Pages in Windows SharePoint Services are designed to take disparate information and consolidate it into one location. The elements—Web Parts—that make up a Web Part Page in Windows SharePoint Services affect how the page is processed and displayed. Web Parts are grouped on the Web Part Page into containers called **Web Part zones**. Each of these components has an important part in the behavior of Windows SharePoint Services site pages.

Physically, Web Part Pages are ASP.NET files (.aspx) that can be modified in an HTML editor, such as Microsoft Office FrontPage 2003, that works with Windows SharePoint Services. There are eight templates that come with Windows SharePoint Services that can be used to create a Web Part Page. Each of these templates contains a different set of Web Part zones to which Web Parts can be added.

Web Parts

Web Parts are derived from ASP.NET Server Controls, but are designed so that they are more easily customized than a standard ASP.NET control. Unlike standard ASP.NET Server Controls, Web Parts remove the properties from the code of the control. The code and properties of a Web Part are separated to allow users to be able to manipulate the properties without getting into the code. The code of a Web Part resides in an assembly file that is an ASP.NET dynamic-link library (DLL), while the properties are loaded into the content database of a site.

When a Web Part is installed, the **assembly file** is often placed in the \bin subdirectory of the virtual server that is hosting the site. The path for this directory on a default website in IIS is \inetpub\wwwroot\bin. The other location available for assembly files is the Global Assembly Cache (GAC). By default, this is the \%systemroot%\assembly directory.

Files stored in the \bin directory are only partially trusted, meaning that these files cannot automatically save data to the content database or work with the Web Part object model. Saving a Web Part assembly file to the GAC not only allows the Web Part to do these things, it also makes the Web Part available to all virtual servers on a front-end Web server.

Some Web Parts also include additional files, called *resource files*, which are needed for the Web Part to display correctly. Any included resource files are also stored locally on the site server. Resource files can range from images to language files, depending on the purpose of the Web Part. Resource files can be placed in the inetpub\wwwroot\wpresources directory, but only if the Web Part assembly file is in the \bin directory. If the assembly file is located in the GAC, the resource files must be placed in the *<local drive>*:\program files\common files\microsoft sharepoint\web server extensions\wpresources directory. Any file that is URL addressable should be considered a resource file and placed in the appropriate \wpresources directory.

Web Part Zones

Web Part zones are containers on a Web Part Page that allow a designer to organize and control the behavior of Web Parts. A Web Part zone is part of a system that allows Web Parts to act differently than typical ASP.NET Server Controls. Placing a Web Part within a Web Part zone allows the Web Part to take advantage of the architecture of Window SharePoint Services, while placing a Web Part outside of a Web Part zone does not.

Static Web Parts

A Web Part zone typically contains one or two Web Parts. However, Web Parts do not have to be placed into a zone on the Web Part Page. Web Parts that are placed outside of a Web Part zone are called *static Web Parts* because they are treated and act just like a standard Web control. A static Web Part and its properties are stored within the Web Part Page (.aspx) file. Because of this, a user cannot interact with a static Web Part or modify it within a browser.

Dynamic Web Parts

Web Parts that are contained within a Web Part zone are called *dynamic Web Parts*. This is because unlike with standard Web control or static Web Parts, users can modify the properties of a dynamic Web Part. Web Part zones allow a Web Part to participate in Windows SharePoint Services by connecting the Web Part to a Windows SharePoint Services content database. The properties of a dynamic Web Part are saved to a content database so that users can access the properties and manipulate these properties.

Customization and Personalization for Web Parts

The two views of Web Parts that are used in Windows SharePoint Services are shared or personal. A shared view is a version of the Web Part that is seen by all users. A personal view is created when a user changes the view to Personal. The user can then make changes to one or more of the properties of the Web Part that are only for that user to see. The architecture of a Web Part allows users to save their changes and allows Windows SharePoint Services to keep track of each personal version of a Web Part.

Customization vs. Personalization

Personalization occurs when a user creates a Personal View of a Web Part, while customization happens when a user makes a change to a Web Part that affects the Shared View that is seen by all users. A user must have the rights to design a page in order to change the Shared View of a page. By default, Windows SharePoint Services displays pages in Shared View. Once a user switches to a Personal View of the page and makes a change, the page defaults to Personal View when displayed. A Web Part page can be designed to default to Personal View if the meta tag WebPartPage DefaultviewPersonal is included in the .aspx code.

Personalization

Once a user switches to the Personal View of a page, personalization is as simple as adjusting a property in the display of a Web Part on a site page. It can also include adding a Web Part to a page. The added Web Part can be viewed only by the user who personalized the Web Part. The properties of a dynamic Web Part are stored in a Windows SharePoint Services content database. Once a user makes a change to a property, that change is stored as a personal version of the Web Part. Only properties that are changed from Shared View are stored separately in the database. Windows SharePoint Services reconciles the differences and applies the properties for the Personal View when the Web Part is rendered for that user.

Controlling Personalization

Web Part zones can be used to control whether a Web Part's properties can be changed. By manipulating the properties of a Web Part zone, a designer can choose to disallow modifications to the Web Parts contained in the zone. They can even choose to allow customization for a Shared View but disallow personalization in Personal View. The properties of a Web Part zone cannot be modified through a browser; they can be modified only with an HTML editor that works with Windows SharePoint Services.

Regardless of the number of times the properties of a Web Part are modified, the code in the assembly file never needs to change. All the different versions of a Web Part reference and use the same assembly file.

Exporting Web Parts

Web Parts are designed so that they can be easily shared among users. A user can export a Personal View or a Shared View of a Web Part by selecting the Export command from the Web Part menu. When this command is selected, the entire Web Part is not actually exported. Instead, only the properties of the Web Part are exported.

When a Web Part is installed, the properties are contained in a description file that has a .dwp extension. A user creates a new version of a description file by exporting a Web Part. When the Export command is selected from the Web Part menu, the current state of the properties are read from the content database and saved to a description file.

Users who import a Web Part are actually importing only the description file, not the assembly file or any auxiliary files. When a user imports a .dwp, a new Web Part is created and the properties specified in the .dwp are applied to this new Web Part. Then Windows SharePoint Services will save the settings back to the database and persist them for the next time the user browses to the page. The description file is read, and the customized properties are loaded into the database as a Personal View. If the assembly file does not exist locally on the front-end Web server to which the Web Part is imported, the import will fail.

Description Files

Once a **description file** is created, it can be edited and elements can be added to it. Any changes made to the description file are personalizations that override the default properties of the Web Part. The description file for a different type of Web Part can contain different elements that apply only to that type of Web Part. The only required elements in a description file are the Assembly and Typename elements. However, to display a default name and description for the Web Part after it is imported, you should also include the Title and Description elements. The following example shows a description file for an image Web Part:

```
<?xml version="1.0" encoding="utf-8"?>
<WebPart xmlns:xsd="http://www.w3.org/2001/XMLSchema"
    xmlns:xsi="http://www.w3.org/2001/XMLSchema-instance"
  <Title>Image Web Part</Title>
  <FrameType>Default</FrameType>
  <Description>Use to display pictures and photos.</Description>
  <IsIncluded>true</IsIncluded>
  <ZoneID>LeftColumn</ZoneID>
  <PartOrder>1</PartOrder>
  <FrameState>Normal</FrameState>
  <Height />
  <Width />
  <AllowRemove>true</AllowRemove>
  <AllowZoneChange>true</AllowZoneChange>
  <AllowMinimize>true</AllowMinimize>
  <IsVisible>true</IsVisible>
  <DetailLink />
  <HelpLink />
  <Dir>Default</Dir>
  <PartImageSmall />
  <MissingAssembly />
  <PartImageLarge>_layouts/images/msimagel.gif</PartImageLarge>
  <IsIncludedFilter />
  <Assembly>Microsoft.SharePoint, Version=11.0.0.0, Culture=neutral,
    PublicKeyToken=71e9bce111e9429c</Assembly>
  <TypeName>
    Microsoft.SharePoint.WebPartPages.ImageWebPart
  </TypeName>
</WebPart>
```

A description file opens and closes with a Web Part element. If an element is listed with no value, the default value applies. The Assembly element contains the name of the assembly file for the Web Part. If the assembly file is not present on the local front-end Web server, the Web Part will not load.

Handling Site Page Requests

When a user tries to connect to a Windows SharePoint Services site, the request goes through several specific steps before the pages can be displayed in the requesting client's browser. Figure 4-4 illustrates the steps that a request goes through before it can be returned to the client. Windows SharePoint Services handles page requests in three ways. Pages are handled as either static HTML pages, .aspx pages rendered in direct mode, or .aspx pages rendered in safe mode.

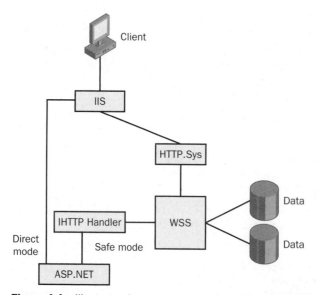

Figure 4-4 Illustrates how page requests are handled in Windows SharePoint Services

Routing Page Requests

Windows SharePoint Services works with the IIS architecture, but it adds several components. The component that handles page requests for IIS, HTTP.sys, is still the first component to handle requests in Windows SharePoint Services. HTTP.sys is not changed when Windows SharePoint Services installs, and it performs the same functions for Windows SharePoint Services that it performs for IIS. HTTP.sys listens for incoming HTTP requests, resolves the URLs to the correct virtual server on the front-end Web server, and authenticates the requesting user.

After HTTP.sys is done with the request, it is passed to an ISAPI filter installed by Windows SharePoint Services. The purpose of this ISAPI filter (Stsfltr.dll) is to pass all other page requests to the correct handler or infrastructure. Stsfltr.dll passes all static HTML pages to an IIS ISAPI extension. .Aspx pages are passed either directly to the ASP.NET infrastructure or to the IHTTP handler. Stsfltr.dll also handles inclusions and exclusions.

Rendering .ASPX Pages

During installation, Windows SharePoint Services defines the association between types of resources and the handlers for each. This set of mappings is defined in the <httpHandlers> section of the Web.config file that is discussed later in this chapter. One of the handlers defined in this section is the IHTTP handler, which is registered to handle all .aspx requests. The IHTTP handler either passes the ASP.NET page directly to ASP.NET (direct mode) or runs the page in safe mode.

Direct Mode

Normally when ASP.NET pages are run, the page is read and then compiled into a DLL file that is saved to the Web server. Because a compiled DLL runs much faster than an .aspx page, the DLL can be used instead of having to parse the page each time it is requested. In Windows SharePoint Services, handling ASP.NET pages in this manner is called *direct mode*. Only the ASP.NET pages that are in the _layouts directory of the front-end Web server run in direct mode. The _layouts directory contains fixed application pages used by Windows SharePoint Services, such as the Create List, Create Field, and Site Settings pages. This directory is considered to be outside the website. All other ASP.NET pages, including Web Part Pages, run in safe mode.

Safe Mode

ASP.NET pages that are considered to be inside a website are run in safe mode. In safe mode, .Aspx pages are not allowed to compile code into a DLL. Also, only controls on the page that are on the safe controls list are run. The safe controls list is included in the Web.config file. All Web Part Pages run in safe mode.

Templates

Windows SharePoint Services comes with templates that are used to create sites and site pages. Templates can apply to an entire site or to different parts of a site, such as Web Part Pages, meeting workspaces, lists, areas, and quotas. By default, templates are stored in the Program Files\Common Files\Microsoft Shared\Web Server Extensions\60\templates directory on the local file system of the front-end Web server. The use of templates saves database space and increases performance in Windows SharePoint Services.

Saving Database Space

The content database of a site includes a documents table that contains a record for each page created in a site. Considering the number of sites and pages that Windows SharePoint Services can support, the number of records in this table can be quite large. Even though the number of records is large, Windows SharePoint Services keep the overall size of the table low by keeping each record in the table relatively empty by default. When a page is created by using a template, the record in the content database for that page contains only the location of the template used to create the page. The record does not contain any customization data for the page.

The customization of each site's page occurs only during the rendering process. During this process, a navigation control looks to the URL of the page and finds the name of the site. The control uses the site name to find customization information in the content database and makes these customization changes before the page displays. In essence, each page that is based on the same template is the same, but users do not realize this because of customizations made during the rendering process.

Increasing Performance

The use of templates also allows ASP.NET pages to run as they were designed. Normally, an ASP.NET page is read and then saved to a DLL file on the local computer. Subsequent requests for that page are handled by running the DLL off the local file system. In Windows SharePoint Services, this is called direct mode. Site pages that are based on templates run in direct mode. A DLL only needs to be created for each template instead of for each site's version of the page. It would not be practical to have a DLL read into memory for each site's version of a page.

The Effects of Customization

The performance enhancements in the architecture of templates and site pages based on templates are lost once a site page is customized. Once the code of a site page is edited and saved, it can no longer use the template to load.

Once this occurs, Windows SharePoint Services changes the site page's record in the documents table of the site content database. It replaces the location of the template in the site pages record with a copy of the entire page. Also, because only templates can run in direct mode, from that point on the page must be run in safe mode.

The Web.Config File

The **Web.config** file is an XML-based text file that contains configuration information for ASP.NET services. There are multiple Web.config files in Windows SharePoint Services. In a Windows SharePoint Services deployment, Web.config files are contained in the following folders within the file system:

- Local_Drive:\Inetpub\wwwroot—This Web.config file defines configuration settings for all virtual servers that are on the server. This file is created when a virtual server is extended.

- Local_Drive:\Inetpub\wwwroot\wpresources—This Web.config file defines configuration settings for Web Parts. This file is created when a virtual server is extended.

- Local_Drive:\Program Files\Common Files\Microsoft Shared\Web Server Extensions\wpresources—This folder is used to store Web Part file resources for assemblies that are placed in the Global Assembly Cache (GAC). The purpose of this Web.config file is to places restrictions on files placed in this folder.

- Local_Drive:\Program Files\Common Files\Microsoft Shared\Web Server Extensions\60\CONFIG—This Web.config file along with other .config files define configuration settings for extending other virtual servers.

- Local_Drive:\Program Files\Common Files\Microsoft Shared\Web Server Extensions\60\ISAPI —This web.config file defines configuration settings for the /_vti_bin virtual directory. This folder holds Web services used by Windows SharePoint Services.

- Local_Drive:\Program Files\Common Files\Microsoft Shared\Web Server Extensions\60\TEMPLATE\LAYOUTS—This Web.config file defines configuration settings for the _layouts virtual directory. The _layouts directory is used to hold trusted application pages that should run in direct mode. Anything placed in the _layouts directory is accessible by all virtual servers on a front-end Web server.

- Local_Drive:\Program Files\Common Files\Microsoft Shared\Web Server Extensions\60\TEMPLATE\ADMIN\Locale_ID—This Web.config file defines configuration settings for pages used in the virtual server that contains the SharePoint Central Administration site.

The \60\CONFIG folder contains .config and .xml files that are used together to create the Web.config file for a virtual server when it is extended with Windows SharePoint Services. Before copying the Web.config file from the \60\CONFIG folder to the root folder of the virtual server, Windows SharePoint Services searches the \60\CONFIG folder for any .xml file with a name in the format Webconfig.*.xml and merges its contents with the Web.config file before writing the resulting Web.config file to the root path of the virtual server. The actions defined in the .xml file are applied to the configuration settings of the virtual server. A major advantage to using an .xml file to supplement the Web.config file is that customizations are not lost when Windows SharePoint Services is upgraded and the Web.config file is overwritten.

Summary

Windows SharePoint Services introduces major improvements over SharePoint Team Services v1.0. One of the main architectural changes is the consolidation of all data and product information into database technologies. The result of this is a complete split of front-end and back-end components that allows for flexibility in the scaling of a Windows SharePoint Services deployment.

The site architecture of Windows SharePoint Services relies on underlying technologies, while adding to them with its own infrastructure. IIS, ASP.NET, and Windows Server 2003 all provide services that Windows SharePoint Services uses and builds upon. The infrastructure provided by Windows SharePoint Services processes client requests and renders pages for clients to view.

Chapter 5

SharePoint Portal Server Architecture

Microsoft Windows SharePoint Services and Microsoft Office SharePoint Portal Server 2003 share the same underlying technologies. This is a change from the first version of SharePoint Portal Server. Microsoft SharePoint Portal Server 2001 did not share underlying technology with SharePoint Team Services from Microsoft. In this version of Microsoft SharePoint Products and Technologies, SharePoint Portal Server, as the server product, works with and builds upon the architecture of Windows SharePoint Services. This chapter does not cover the feature differences between SharePoint Portal Server and Windows SharePoint Services. Instead, it focuses on the architectural differences that are found in SharePoint Portal Server and explains the architecture of services that are particular to SharePoint Portal Server.

Note When referring to both products as a single unit, we'll use the term SharePoint Products and Technologies.

Building on Windows SharePoint Services

Windows SharePoint Services is required when installing SharePoint Portal Server. SharePoint Portal Server can install over an existing Windows SharePoint Services installation, or if Windows SharePoint Services is not yet installed, SharePoint Portal Server installs Windows SharePoint Services first as part of the installation process.

Additional Services

SharePoint Portal Server includes services that are not offered in Windows SharePoint Services. These services can be viewed in the Services application in Control Panel and include the Administration service, the SharePoint Portal Alert service, the Microsoft SharePoint Portal Server Search service, and the Microsoft Single Sign-On service.

> **Note** During installation, all services that SharePoint Portal Server can provide are installed regardless of which services you choose to install. The services are then enabled or disabled based on which services the administrator chooses to provide to users.

Administration Service

SharePoint Portal Server installs an administration service, called SharePoint Portal Administration, that appears as **SPSAdmin** in the Services application in Control Panel. SPSAdmin can stop and start services that SharePoint Portal Server needs, including **SPSSearch**. It can also add or delete catalogs and can add or delete search applications as needed.

SPSAdmin is a service that was written to maintain the configuration of each server in a SharePoint Portal Server deployment. Essentially, this service runs on each server in the farm and is responsible for checking the configuration database every 30 seconds to ensure that the local server is performing its assigned roles.

In the SharePoint Portal Server Central Administration/Component Selection area, each server in the farm must be assigned at least one role to perform in the farm. When a role is assigned to a server in the farm, it is recorded in the configuration database. The SharePoint Portal Administration service checks this database every 30 seconds to ensure that the server is performing its assigned role or roles. If the service discovers that there is a modification in the server's roles, the service will "turn on" or "turn off" those portions of the server's code to either stop performing a role or to start performing a role.

For example, let's assume that there are six front-end Web servers in a large farm. Now let's assume that server1, a front-end Web server, is a search server. This server has a failure and is no longer available. The site administrator gives the role of search server to server2 and removes the role of search server from server1. Because the SharePoint Portal Administration service works locally on each server, each of the five servers that are still online will poll the configuration database and discover that the Search role has been moved to a different server. When server1 comes back online, the local SharePoint Portal Administration service on server1 will also discover the change and will stop the search service on server1 automatically after polling the configuration database.

Note that when you turn off the search service, the server is pulled out of rotation for queries and the new server won't have any catalogs until the next index propagation. For indexing servers, all catalogs are removed when the server is turned off, and a new server is created with no catalogs

SharePoint Portal Alert Service

The purpose of the SharePoint Portal Alert service is to notify a user, when the user requests it, that there is a change to a designated item, document, list, or document library on the website. Alerts are managed by the job server.

Microsoft SharePoint Portal Server Search Service

Windows SharePoint Services can perform SQL text queries, but only on content that resides in a site from which the search query was invoked. Because SharePoint Portal Server has Microsoft SharePoint Portal Server Search service, it can index and perform searches on content that is external as well as internal to the portal site. Additionally, it can perform searches across servers and portals. Microsoft SharePoint Portal Server Search service is listed in the Services application as SharePointPSSearch. For more information on the indexing capabilities of SharePoint Portal Server, see Chapter 21, "The Architecture of the Gatherer."

Microsoft Single Sign-On Service

Third-party enterprise applications such as PeopleSoft, SAP, Siebel, and Lotus Notes use authentication that is different from Microsoft Windows operating systems and SharePoint Portal Server. The **Single Sign-On service** is provided so that disparate authentication databases, such as Active Directory and a third-party application database, can map credentials from authenticated Windows users to enable a single sign-on environment. The Microsoft Single Sign-On service appears as SSOSrv in the Services application in Control Panel.

Changes to Front-End Components

SharePoint Portal Server has the same front-end/back-end split of components that Windows SharePoint Services has. Because SharePoint Portal Server has additional services that it can provide, it also has more front-end server roles and has more back-end database types than does Windows SharePoint Services. Figure 5-1 shows the components that are available in a SharePoint Portal Server deployment.

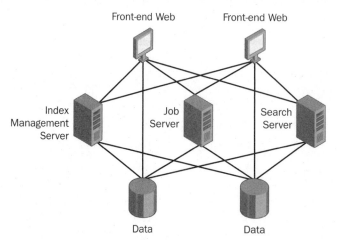

Front-end Web   Front-end Web

Index   Job   Search
Management   Server   Server
Server

Data   Data

Figure 5-1   Architecture of SharePoint Portal Server includes front-end Web servers, search servers, a job server, index servers, and back-end databases

Note   The split between front-end and back-end components in SharePoint Portal Server is a logical one. Physically, the front-end and back-end components can exist on the same server or on separate servers. In fact, in a single-server deployment, all the server farm roles are performed on a single server.

Front-End Servers

Windows SharePoint Services has only one role for front-end Web servers. These servers host sites and process search requests. SharePoint Portal Server includes the ability to separate front-end roles for Web servers and also includes separate roles for index management servers, search servers, and a job server. One or more servers can fill each role, except for the job server, depending on the number of users that are supported. There is only one job server per portal site, regardless of how small or large the environment is.

Job Server

The purpose of a job server is to manage the additional services that are supported in SharePoint Portal Server that are not available in Windows SharePoint Services. This includes the following additional services:

- Hosting the Single Sign-On pages

- Importing user profiles

- Performing audience calculations

- Crawling and indexing portal site content

- Hosting the Alerts service

Index Management Server

Windows SharePoint Services combines the services of hosting site pages, crawling content, and processing search queries from clients into one front-end Web server. SharePoint Portal Server allows these services to be performed separately. An index management server is dedicated to building and updating indexes, which includes crawling content and breaking down the crawled information through the indexing process.

Only one index server can crawl a content source. If you need better performance on crawls, you cannot get it by adding another index management server. To improve crawl performance, you must upgrade the server that is assigned to a particular content source. Index management servers and the indexing process are covered thoroughly in Chapter 21.

Changes to Back-End Database Components

Windows SharePoint Services installs one configuration database and one or more content databases for use with its sites. Even though SharePoint Portal Server installs over Windows SharePoint Services, it does not use any Windows SharePoint Services databases in their original installed state. When a portal site is created in SharePoint Portal Server, an additional three databases are created that are not in a Windows SharePoint Services deployment. A fourth database is created if the Single Sign-On service is used. SharePoint Portal Server also makes changes to the configuration database that is installed by Windows SharePoint Services.

In addition to changing existing databases, SharePoint Portal Server also changes how the front-end Web servers connect to the databases. Windows SharePoint Services front-end Web servers can use Microsoft SQL Server authentication or Windows authentication to connect to back-end databases, but SharePoint Portal Server front-end Web servers can use only Windows authentication. Also, Windows SharePoint Services front-end Web servers use OLE DB to connect to back-end databases. For most connections, SharePoint Portal Server front-end servers use ADO.Net instead. Only the Microsoft SharePoint Portal Search service uses OLE DB to connect to back-end databases.

Configuration Database

SharePoint Portal Server uses a configuration database in the same manner as Windows SharePoint Services. However, during installation SharePoint Portal Server adds extensions to the configuration database that is installed by Windows SharePoint Services. These extensions include adding a new schema and modifying tables by adding new stored procedures. This means that Windows SharePoint Services cannot connect to a SharePoint Portal Server configuration database and vice versa.

Additional Databases

SharePoint Portal Server ignores the content databases that Windows SharePoint Services installs. Instead, SharePoint Portal Server creates a different location for content databases. In addition, SharePoint Portal Server creates supplementary databases to support the services that a portal site can provide. These databases have a hyphenated name that begins with the name given to the portal and ends with a suffix that identifies the type of database. Table 5-1 has a list of the additional databases created in SharePoint Portal Server.

Table 5-1   Additional Databases in SharePoint Portal Server

Database Name	Purpose
*Portalname*_prof	Contains the profile database that holds user profiles and audiences.
*Portalname*_serv	Stores information for services, such as search and alerts, that are provided by a portal site. Also called the component settings database.
*Portalname*_site	Contains site content information and works like the content database in Windows SharePoint Services.

In addition to these three databases, a fourth database is created when the Single Sign-On service is configured. This database stores credential information for the Single Sign-On service. It does not start with the name of the portal because only one is created per server farm and instead can be named by the administrator.

Physical Configurations

Like Windows SharePoint Services, SharePoint Portal Server can be scaled from a single server to a large farm of servers. The difference in these configurations is the physical separations of the available components. As servers are added to a SharePoint Portal Server deployment, each server becomes more specialized in the services it provides.

Single Server

In a single-server configuration, all components (both front-end and back-end) are on a single server. This configuration can use a separate installation of SQL Server or use SQL Server 2000 Desktop Engine for the back-end databases.

Server Farms

Server farms are created in a SharePoint Portal Server environment when components are placed on separate servers. Server farms can range from small to large, depending on the needs of the environment.

The components that are considered front-end are the Web server hosting the portal site, the index server crawling the content and creating the index, the search server that processes client search requests, and the job server that coordinates available services. A small server farm keeps the front-end components on the same server while separating the back-end databases onto one or more servers. Medium server farms separate the indexing functions and the job server from the front-end Web servers and search services. A large farm can handle up to four index management servers, one of which must be a job server, and four search servers, which are separate from the Web front-end servers. To find out more about deploying server farms, see the chapters in Part 4, "Deployment Scenarios."

Personal Sites vs. My Site

Personal sites and the My Site feature are separate features that are both available only in SharePoint Portal Server. Although the names of these two features are often used as synonyms for each other, they are not the same. Site administrators need a good understanding of the architectural differences between the two features to understand differences in the behavior of each.

Personal sites are Windows SharePoint Services sites that are created for individual users. Every user who has the Create Personal Site right can have a personal site. By default, the location of a user's personal site is *portalname*/personal/*username*, where *portalname* is the name of the portal and *username* is the name of the individual user.

My Site is a single page located in the SharePoint Portal Server site. By default, the path for this page is *portalname*/My Site/default.asp, where *portalname* is the name of the portal. Every user who accesses the My Site URL downloads the same page. However, users often don't realize this because some of the information on the page is personalized based on the user's profile information and information from the user's personal site.

So the difference between My Site and personal sites is that My Site is the portal page through which all users must pass to get to their own personal site. A user links to his personal site through the My Site page. It is hard to recognize that the My Site portal page is the same for everyone because it has personalization features. My Site is personalized based on a user's profile information, and it includes links to document libraries and lists that the user has created on her personal site.

The major architectural difference is that the My Site page is owned and controlled by the site owner, while a personal site is owned and controlled by the user. This means that a user can customize the contents and views of her personal site; however, when a user tries to personalize the My Site page, the choices are limited.

User Profiles and Audiences

SharePoint Portal Server includes a way to integrate user profile information into site pages and to target content to a group of users. User profiles and audiences are contained in the ***portalname***_prof database (where ***portalname*** is the name of the portal).

Populating the User Profile Database

The profile database is a list of user account property information. This information is obtained by importing information from a directory that contains user accounts or it is obtained manually by typing in account information. By default, SharePoint Portal Server can import a list of domain users from Active Directory, but code can be written against the SharePoint Portal Server object model that can be used to import information from other directory services or applications. User profile information is stored in a single table in the ***portalname***_prof database. Updates to the database can be scheduled on a regular basis and can be incremental or full.

Creating Audiences

Audiences are also contained in the user profile database, but they are contained in a separate table from the one that contains user profiles. Creating an audience involves creating rules and then compiling the audience. Rules define what user accounts should be included or excluded from the audience. Rules created for any audience are stored in a separate table in the ***portalname***_prof database.

When an audience is compiled, the rules are used as a filter against the complete list of user profiles. Because not all account information is imported into the user profile database, Active Directory is also queried during an audience compilation. Accounts that fit the rule are copied and placed in a separate table that holds the members of the audience. This table contains the members of all audiences for a portal and is separate from the table that stores the rules. The table that contains audience members is not updated, and remains static until the audience is recompiled.

Enabling and Configuring Single Sign-On Service

Like all services in SharePoint Portal Server, Single Sign-On installs automatically, but it is not enabled. Enabling the service requires an administrator to be physically at the server that is designated as the job server for the portal site. The administrator must specify a SQL Server in the server farm on which a credential database is created.

A developer can develop Web Parts that are Single Sign-On–aware and use **enterprise application** definitions to pull information from enterprise applications and display it on pages within a portal site. The purpose of an **enterprise-application definition** is to provide the connection from the enterprise application to the Single Sign-On Web Part on a portal site page. Figure 5-2 shows the relationship between Single Sign-On Web Parts, enterprise-application definitions, the enterprise application, and the credentials database.

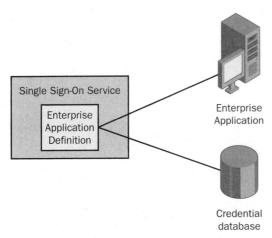

Figure 5-2 SharePoint Portal Server connects users to enterprise applications using the Single Sign-On service and enterprise application definitions

Authentication with Single Sign-On

Authentication with the Single Sign-On service can be set up to work with groups or with individual users. In either case, enterprise application definitions are used to map credentials used by SharePoint Portal Server to credentials used in an enterprise application.

With group authentication, the individual user is associated with a managed group account. In this case, the user does not need to know an individual set of credentials. Instead, an enterprise application definition is configured by an administrator to provide the credentials needed. The enterprise-application definition maps the credentials used in SharePoint Portal Server to the enterprise application without users needing to provide alternate credentials.

Individual authentication is used when users know and manage their own credentials for the enterprise application. In this case, the enterprise-application definitions map the user's SharePoint Portal Server credentials to individual credentials needed by the enterprise application that are stored in the credential database. If a user's credentials are not yet in the Single Sign-On credential database, the Web Part redirects the user to the Single Sign-On logon form used to enter his credentials. Once the credentials are stored in the credentials database, the mapping should happen automatically so that user intervention is no longer needed.

Shared Services

In SharePoint Portal Server, by default, each portal site is configured as a separate entity from other portal sites. As a separate entity, a portal site individually supports and provides needed resources for all services. If the portal sites within a server farm belong to the same organization and support the same set of users, the use of **shared services** can allow the portal sites to consolidate and save resources.

Shared services centralizes the work required to provide services to one portal site by creating a parent/child relationship between the portal sites. When shared services is implemented, the portal site that provides the services becomes the parent while all other portal sites become children. Because the parent portal site provides services, the child portal sites are left with only site information—such as pages, areas, and lists—to support. The following lists how services change when shared service is implemented:

- **Search and index.** With shared services, crawling and index creation are consolidated in the parent portal site. Search requests from child portal sites are processed by the parent portal site.

- **Alerts.** With shared services, alerts are managed and tracked in a single alert store in the parent portal site.

- **Personal sites.** With shared services, personal sites are created only in the parent portal site and can be viewed and accessed from the child portal sites. The My Site portal page is also located in the parent portal site.

- **User profiles.** With shared services, a single user profile database is configured in the parent portal site and is accessed by the child portal sites.

- **Audiences.** With shared services, audiences are compiled and stored only in the parent portal site.

- **Single Sign-On service.** With shared services, only one Single Sign-On credentials database is created. This database is located and administered only in the parent portal site.

Shared services is an all-or-nothing configuration at the server-farm level. This means that if one portal site in a server farm is using shared services, all portal sites in that farm are using shared services. Once a portal site in a farm is designated as the parent, all other portal sites in the farm automatically become child portal sites. It is also a one-way decision, meaning that once you decide to turn on shared services, you can't turn it off later.

Database Access in Shared Services

When shared services is implemented, child portal sites look to the parent's configuration database for shared services data. Although some data is still needed from the original databases used by the child sites after shared services is configured, most information is retrieved from the parent site's databases. By default, each portal site has two user accounts that are used to access databases. These accounts are called the configuration database administration account and the application pool account for the portal site.

The configuration database administration account is the account used by the **CentralAdminAppPool** application pool to access the configuration database and all other databases for a portal site. It is recommended that all servers in a server farm use the same account for the configuration database administration account. Once shared services is implemented, this recommendation becomes a requirement. The **MSSharePointPortalAppPool** is used by the portal site to access the Share-Point Portal Server databases. Although child portal sites must have access to the parent configuration and content databases for added security, that access can be limited to read-only.

Summary

Because SharePoint Portal Server 2003 is built on Windows SharePoint Services, much of the underlying architecture is the same. Both handle page requests and .aspx pages in the same manner. The main architectural differences lie in the way the additional services provided by SharePoint Portal Server are handled. As the server product in Microsoft SharePoint Products and Technologies, SharePoint Portal Server 2003 has additional services that support a larger and more diverse set of users. To accommodate this, additional database types and additional front-end roles are included in SharePoint Portal Server that are not included in Windows SharePoint Services.

Chapter 6

Security Architecture for SharePoint Products and Technologies

Microsoft SharePoint Products and Technologies security is layered on top of, and depends on, the security of underlying products and technologies such as ASP.NET, Internet Information Services (IIS), SQL Server 2000, and Windows Server 2003. Needless to say, communication security and firewall configuration are vital as well. As with any Web application, your SharePoint site is only as secure as its weakest link; security is a concern across all components of your SharePoint Products and Technologies deployment. Because SharePoint Products and Technologies security spans many technologies, you need to have an understanding of security in these technologies to make all parts of your SharePoint Products and Technologies deployment work together in a secure fashion.

It is vital to implement a layered approach to security, often referred to as *defense-in-depth*. Use of defense-in-depth means that security is addressed at a number of levels, including organizational security policies, Windows Server 2003 configuration, IIS configuration, ASP.NET configuration, SharePoint Product and Technologies configuration, communication security, firewall configuration, and so on.

SharePoint Products and Technologies make use of a number of technologies that reduce the risk of security being compromised. These technologies include:

- Authentication that uses Windows principals and therefore can make use of strong authentication methods, password policies, account lockout policies, and encryption

- Authorization that is based on the permissions model to ensure a high degree of granular control over access to contents of a site

- Code access security in .NET Framework that allows you to control code access to protected resources and operations

- Security techniques such as Secure Sockets Layer (SSL) and IPSec that allow you to protect your communications inside and outside the firewall

- Firewall protection of external sites

In this chapter, we will focus on authentication, authorization, code access security, and communication security in SharePoint Products and Technologies. Research has shown that early design of authentication and authorization eliminates a high percentage of vulnerabilities. Code access security allows code to be trusted to varying degrees, depending on where the code originates from and on other aspects of the code's identity. Communication security is an integral part of securing your deployment to protect data passed between users and your site, and between the servers in your deployment. For discussion on security policies for SharePoint Products and Technologies refer to Chapter 24, "Information Security Policies for SharePoint Products and Technologies."

Authentication

Authentication is the process of positively identifying the users of your site. Authentication ensures that the users are who they claim to be. Authenticated clients are referred to as *principals*.

In SharePoint Products and Technologies, authentication is based on Windows security accounts.

For SharePoint sites, ASP.NET is configured to use Windows authentication. In web.config files, the authentication section is as follows:

```
<system.web>
    <authentication mode="Windows" >
</system.web>
```

With Windows authentication mode, ASP.NET relies on IIS to perform the required authentication of a client. IIS authenticates the requesting user against Windows security accounts. After IIS authenticates a client, it passes a user identity to ASP.NET. (See Figure 6-1.)

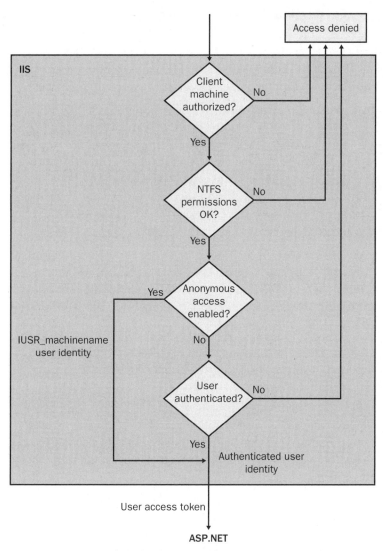

Figure 6-1   Passing user identity in Windows authentication mode

You can use a variety of IIS authentication schemes for SharePoint Products and Technologies user authentication, as follows:

- **Basic.**   Basic authentication is part of the HTTP 1.1 protocol that is supported by virtually all browsers. With SharePoint Products and Technologies, it can be used in the extranet environment. The credentials are transmitted unencrypted. You should use basic authentication only over SSL; otherwise, basic authentication is not secure.

- **Integrated Windows.** Integrated Windows authentication is a secure authentication method that is most suitable for your intranet SharePoint sites. It does not work over proxy servers. It is implemented as either Kerberos or NTLM. Kerberos requires Windows 2000 or later operating systems on the client and server computers.

- **Client Certificates Mapping.**   Clients require X.509 certificates. This is an optional authentication mechanism that can be used when SSL is enabled between the client and the server. For example, it can be used on the extranets when your security policy requires two-level authentication—a system in which clients are required to provide something they have (a certificate) and users are asked to provide something they know (authentication credentials). For configuration details, refer to Chapter 27, "Securing an Extranet Using SSL and Certificates."

- **Anonymous.**   Anonymous authentication allows anonymous access to the website. The default user identity used for anonymous access is IUSR_*machinename*. When IIS receives an anonymous request, it impersonates the IUSR_*machinename* account. In this case, the identity passed to ASP.NET is IUSR_*machinename*.

User access in SharePoint Products and Technologies is based on Windows security principals such as individual user accounts and security group accounts (DOMAIN\user and DOMAIN\security group).

> **Note**   You cannot use distribution lists to control access to content in Windows SharePoint Services because distribution lists are not Windows security principals.

In addition to authenticating users for the SharePoint sites access, SharePoint Portal Server provides a single sign-on (SSO) functionality that allows you to authenticate users to a portal site, and then to retrieve a user's stored credentials for other user-aware enterprise business applications from an SSO database when required. The SSO functionality is implemented by the Microsoft Single Sign-On service (SSOSrv). SSOSrv provides storage and mapping of credentials such as account names and passwords so that the portal-based applications can retrieve information from the third-party applications and back-end systems. This prevents users from having to authenticate themselves again when the portal-based applications need to obtain information from other business applications and systems. For details on how you can enable and configure SSO in SharePoint Portal Server, refer to Chapter 26, "Single Sign-On in SharePoint Portal Server 2003."

Authorization

Authorization defines which resources and operations the authenticated user is allowed to access. In Windows SharePoint Services and SharePoint Portal Server, access to sites is controlled through a role-based membership system by which each user is associated directly or indirectly with a permission that controls the specific actions that the user can perform. This membership system is based on *site groups*. Using a site group is a way to configure rights for users based on the kinds of tasks they perform.

Site groups specify what rights the users have on a site. The rights determine what specific actions the users can perform on the site. Although the concepts of using site groups are the same in Windows SharePoint Services and SharePoint Portal Server, because of the additional feature set in the SharePoint Portal Server there are differences in the user rights and corresponding permissions, as well as the default site groups. Because of these differences, we will look into authorization in Windows SharePoint Services and SharePoint Portal Server separately.

Authorization in Windows SharePoint Services

In this section, we will look into user authorization to access Windows SharePoint Services sites as well as administrative tasks related to setting up authorization. Windows SharePoint Services uses site groups to manage site-wide security. Rights specify the actions that users can perform; in essence, each site group is a collection of rights.

If you want all users to be able to browse your site, you can enable anonymous access to the site. Anonymous access is disabled by default.

> **Note**   With anonymous access enabled, users can browse the site without authentication, but they cannot perform any administrative tasks on the site. The administration pages require authentication.

To run custom code that uses the Windows SharePoint Services object model, users must have the appropriate permissions assigned to them, just as when they interact with a site or list through the user interface.

To be authorized to perform administrative tasks that affect settings for all websites and virtual servers on the server computer, a user must be a member of the local administrators group on the server machine or a member of the SharePoint administrators group.

Site Groups

Windows SharePoint Services includes 21 rights, which are used in the five default user site groups. The five default user rights groups are Guest, Reader, Contributor, Web Designer, and Administrator. Table 6-1 shows user rights that are included in each site group by default.

The rights assigned to the Guest and Administrator site groups cannot be changed. However, you can customize the rights available in Reader, Contributor, and Web Designer site groups to include only the rights you want.

You can add new site groups to combine different sets of rights, edit the rights assigned to a site group, or delete an unused site group.

You cannot assign users directly to the Guest site group, rather users who are given access to lists or document libraries by way of per-list permissions are automatically added to the Guest site group. The Guest site group cannot be customized or deleted.

You can manage site groups and permissions by using HTML administration pages or the command-line administration tool Stsadm.exe. For a detailed description of specific tasks, refer to Chapter 16, "Windows SharePoint Services Site Administration."

You can also use the Windows SharePoint Services object model to perform the management tasks in code. For details, refer to the SharePoint Products and Technologies Software Development Kit (SDK) at *http://msdn.microsoft.com/library /default.asp?url=/library/en-us/spptsdk/html/SPSDKWelcome.asp*.

Table 6-1   Default Windows SharePoint Services Site Groups and their Rights

Site group name	User rights included by default
Guest	None
Reader	Use Self-Service Site Creation View Pages View Items
Contributor	All rights included in the Reader site group, plus: ■ Add Items ■ Add/Remove Private Web Parts ■ Browse Directories ■ Create Cross-Site Groups ■ Delete Items ■ Edit Items ■ Manage Personal Views ■ Update Personal Web Parts

Table 6-1 **Default Windows SharePoint Services Site Groups and their Rights** *(continued)*

Site group name	User rights included by default
Web Designer	All rights included in the Contributor site group, plus: ■ Add and Customize Pages ■ Apply Themes and Borders ■ Apply Style Sheets ■ Cancel Check-out ■ Manage Lists
Administrator	All rights included in the Web Designer site group, plus: ■ Create Subsites ■ Manage List Permissions ■ Manage Site Groups ■ View Usage Data

In addition to defining the site groups, you can define your own cross-site groups. Cross-site groups consist of users and can be assigned to a site group on any website in a site collection. There are no cross-site groups defined by default.

Site groups are defined per website. Subsites can either use the same permissions as the parent website (inheriting both the site groups and users available on the parent website) or use unique permissions. When you create a subsite, you can choose whether to inherit the permissions from the parent website or to create unique permissions for your subsite.

You can specify unique permissions on a per-list basis. Unlike for sites, you can add users together with specified permissions directly to a list, in which case the users are automatically assigned to the Guest site group on the current site if the site is unique and does not inherit permissions from a parent site. If the current site inherits permissions, the users are added to the Guest site group on the most recent unique ancestor site.

The users are granted permissions to a site or list through direct or indirect membership in a site group. They can be added directly to a site group or added to a cross-site group that is a member of a site group, or they can be members of a Windows domain group that is added to a site group. In addition, an individual user can be directly added to a list in association with a specified permission. Figure 6-2 shows the means by which users are granted permissions to a site or a list.

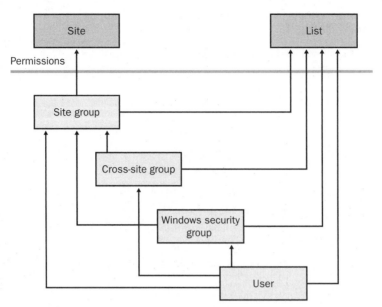

Figure 6-2   Granting user permissions to a site or list in Windows SharePoint Services

Most user rights are dependent on other user rights. For example, you must be able to view items before you can edit items. If a right is deleted from a site group, any rights dependent on that right are also deleted. For detailed information about dependencies on user rights, refer to Table 6-2.

Note   In the Windows SharePoint Services object model, unlike the user interface, rights are not dependent on other rights. To run custom code that uses types and members in the SharePoint Products and Technologies object model, users and groups must be assigned the appropriate permissions, just as when interacting with a site or list by using the user interface. However, in this case there are no dependencies: rights can be assigned individually without including dependent rights, and they can be assigned to users and groups in any combination.

Table 6-2   Windows SharePoint Services Rights Dependencies

Right	Permissions	Groups included by default	Dependent rights
Add and Customize Pages	Create ASP.NET, ASP, and HTML pages for a website	Web Designer, Administrator	Browse Directories, View Pages
Add Items	Add items to lists or add documents to document libraries	Contributor, Web Designer, Administrator	View Items, View Pages
Add/Remove Private Web Parts	Add and remove Web Parts to personalize Web Part Pages	Contributor, Web Designer, Administrator	Update Personal Web Parts, View Items, View Pages
Apply Style Sheets	Apply a style sheet to the entire website	Web Designer, Administrator	View Pages
Apply Themes and Borders	Apply a theme or border to an entire website	Web Designer, Administrator	View Pages
Browse Directories	Browse the directory structure of a website	Contributor, Web Designer, Administrator	View Pages
Cancel Check-Out	Cancel the check-out action performed by another user	Web Designer, Administrator	View Pages
Create Cross-Site Groups	Create or delete cross-site groups, or change membership of a cross-site group	Contributor, Web Designer, Administrator	View Pages
Create Subsites	Create a new subsite or workspace site, such as a Document Workspace site or Meeting Workspace site	Reader, Contributor, Web Designer, Administrator	View Pages
Delete Items	Delete list items and documents from the website	Contributor, Web Designer, Administrator	View Items, View Pages
Edit Items	Edit existing list items and documents in the website	Contributor, Web Designer, Administrator	View Items, View Pages
Manage Lists	Create, edit, or delete lists and change their settings	Web Designer, Administrator	View Items, View Pages, Manage Personal Views
Manage List Permissions	Change permissions for a list or document library	Administrator	Manage Lists, View Items, View Pages, Manage Personal Views

Table 6-2 Windows SharePoint Services Rights Dependencies *(continued)*

Right	Permissions	Groups included by default	Dependent rights
Manage Personal Views	Create, edit, or delete personal views on lists	Contributor, Web Designer, Administrator	View Items, View Pages
Manage Site Groups	Create, delete, and edit site groups, both by changing the rights assigned to the site group and by changing which users are members of the site group	Administrator	View Pages
Manage Web Site	Perform administration tasks for a particular site or subsite	Administrator	View Pages
Update Personal Web Parts	Update Web Parts to display personalized information	Contributor, Web Designer, Administrator	View Items, View Pages
Use Self-Service Site Creation	Use the Self-Service Site Creation tool to create a top-level website.	Reader, Contributor, Web Designer, Administrator	View Pages
View Items	View items in lists, documents in document libraries, and Web discussion comments	Reader, Contributor, Web Designer, Administrator	View Pages
View Pages	Browse pages in the website	Reader, Contributor, Web Designer, Administrator	None
View Usage Data	View reports on website usage	Administrator	View Pages

Site Creation Rights

Site creation rights (Use Self-Service Site Creation and Create Subsites) control whether users can create top-level websites, subsites, or workspaces.

Members of the Administrator site group can create subsites from their websites. However, Self-Service Site Creation is different: it is a feature that is enabled by administrators and allows users to create their own top-level websites. Users do not need administrator permissions on the server or virtual server, only permissions on the website where Self-Service Site Creation is hosted. By default, the Use Self-Service

Site Creation right is included in all site groups except the Guest site group, and it gives users access to the signup page and the ability to use Self-Service Site Creation.

> **Note**   The Self-Service Site Creation right is available only on a top-level website in a site collection.

Self-Service Site Creation allows users to create and manage their own top-level websites automatically. Self-Service Site Creation is disabled by default—you must turn on the feature to use it. You enable Self-Service Site Creation for a single virtual server at a time from the Configure Self-Service Site Creation page for the virtual server that you want to enable. If you want to use it on all virtual servers in your server farm, you must enable it for every virtual server individually.

> **Note**   You can use either HTML administration pages or the command-line tools enablessc.exe and disablessc.exe to turn on and configure Self-Service Site Creation. Either method allows you to turn on or turn off Self-Service Site Creation and specify the type of information to require when creating a site. For details, refer to Chapter 15, "Configuring Windows SharePoint Services."

Anonymous Access

Anonymous access allows users to view pages anonymously or to contribute anonymously to lists and surveys. When you enable anonymous access in Windows SharePoint Services, you are enabling access to your site for the IIS anonymous account IUSR_*machinename.*

Anonymous access is disabled by default and is controlled at the site level. To enable anonymous access, you must first verify that IIS is configured to allow anonymous access, and then enable anonymous access for your website by using the Site Settings. Anonymous access for specific lists is controlled using the per-list permissions. If anonymous access is disabled for your site, it cannot be enabled for a particular list in the site.

You can also grant access to "all authenticated users" to allow all members of your domain to access a website without having to enable anonymous access.

> **More Info**   For detailed description of configuration steps for enabling anonymous access, refer to Chapter 16.

Performing Administration Tasks

Users assigned to the Administrator site group are administrators only for a particular website. To perform any administrative tasks that affect settings for all websites and virtual servers on the server computer, a user must be an administrator for the server computer (also known as a *local administrator*) or a member of the SharePoint administrators group, rather than a member of the Administrator site group for the site.

The virtual server administration pages can be accessed only by local computer administrators or the members of the SharePoint administrators group. This is configured using URL authorization in the web.config file for the Central Administration pages that is located in the folder *<Local Drive>*:\Program Files\Common Files\Microsoft Shared\web server extensions\60\TEMPLATE\ADMIN\1033. The <authorization> element is defined as follows:

```
<authorization>
  <allow roles="BUILTIN\Administrators" />
  <allow users="Domain\SharePoint Administrators account name" />
  <deny users="*" />
</authorization>
```

The SharePoint administrators group is a Windows domain group that has administrative access to Windows SharePoint Services in addition to the local administrators group. Members of this local administrators group configure the name of a Windows group to become the SharePoint Administrators group using Central Administration pages. The name specified in Central Administration pages is the name in web.config file; when you change the SharePoint administrators group, the name is changed in the <authorization> element in web.config file.

You can add users to the SharePoint administrators groups, rather than to the local administrators group, to separate administrative access to Windows SharePoint Services from administrative access to the local server computer. Members of both the SharePoint administrators group and the local administrators group have rights to view and manage all sites created on their servers.

> **Note**   The SharePoint administrators group members do not have access to the IIS metabase, so they cannot perform the following actions for Windows SharePoint Services: extend virtual servers, manage paths, change the SharePoint administrators group, change the configuration database settings, and use the Stsadm.exe command-line tool. They can perform any other administrative action using the HTML Administration pages or the Windows SharePoint Services object model.

Authorization in SharePoint Portal Server

In this section, we will look into user authorization access to SharePoint Portal Server sites, backward-compatible document libraries, and search results.

Similar to Windows SharePoint Services, SharePoint Portal Server uses site groups to manage site-wide security. Each user is a member of at least one site group, and access to portal sites is controlled through a site group membership system. After you create a portal site, you can give users access to it by assigning them to site groups. A user who is not assigned to a site group won't be able to access the portal site.

In addition to providing authorization based on the site groups membership, SharePoint Portal Server provides role-based security for backward-compatible document libraries.

Site Groups

SharePoint Portal Server uses six default site groups to group users with a specific set of customizable rights. You can also create a custom site group for a specific area or list and assign a specific set of rights to it. You can edit the rights assigned to a site group, create a new site group, or delete an unused site group.

The six default SharePoint Server groups are as follows:

- Reader site group allows users to search, view, and browse content in the site.

- Member site group allows users to submit listings and create personal sites.

- Contributor site group allows users to submit content to areas in the site to which they are granted rights.

- Web Designer site group allows users to change layout and settings on a Web page to which they are granted rights.

- Administrator site group allows users full control of the website.

- Content Manager site group allows users to manage all settings and content in an area to which they are granted rights.

You can use site groups to control general access to the portal site as well as to control access to specific areas in the portal site.

Although the site groups in SharePoint Portal Server and Windows SharePoint Services are similar in many respects, there are a number of differences:

- There are two default site groups in SharePoint Portal Server that are not available with Windows SharePoint Services: Member and Content Manager. Both site groups allow users access to the features that are defined only in the SharePoint Portal Server: Member site group allows you to create personal sites, and Content Manager allows you to manage areas for grouping content by user-defined criteria.

- There is no default Guest site group in SharePoint Portal Server. This is because the Guest group is used automatically in Windows SharePoint Services when you assign per-list permissions.

- The user rights and the corresponding permissions differ between SharePoint Portal Server and the Windows SharePoint Services. This is because of the differences in the functionality and feature set of these two products. Some rights are the same—for example, View Pages. However, the rights that relate to managing areas, alerts, user profiles, audiences, and search are distinctly different because these features are present only in SharePoint Portal Server.

The SharePoint Portal Server user rights and corresponding permissions are listed in Table 6-3.

Table 6-3   SharePoint Portal Server User Rights and Corresponding Permissions

Right	Permissions
Add and Customize Pages	Add, change, or delete HTML pages or Web Part Pages, and edit the portal site by using a Windows SharePoint Services–compatible editor
Add Items	Add items to lists, add documents to SharePoint document libraries, add Web Discussion comments
Add/Remove Personal Web Parts	Add or remove Web Parts on a personalized Web Part Page
Apply Style Sheets	Apply a style sheet (.CSS file) to an area or the portal site
Browse Directories	Browse directories in an area
Cancel Check-Out	Check in a document without saving the current changes
Create Area	Create an area on the portal site
Create Personal Site	Create a personal SharePoint site
Create Sites	Create SharePoint sites by using Self-Service Site Creation
Delete Items	Delete items from a list, documents from a document library, and Web discussion comments in documents
Edit Items	Edit items in lists, edit documents in SharePoint document libraries, and customize Web Part Pages in SharePoint document libraries
Manage Alerts	Change alert settings for the portal site and manage alerts for users
Manage Area	Delete or edit the properties for an area on the portal site
Manage Area Permissions	Add, remove, or change user rights for an area
Manage Audiences	Add, change, or delete audiences
Manage Personal Views	Create, change, and delete personal views of lists
Manage Portal Site	Specify portal site properties and manage site settings

Table 6-3 **SharePoint Portal Server User Rights and Corresponding Permissions** *(continued)*

Right	Permissions
Manage Search	Add, change, or delete index and search settings in the portal site
Manage User Profiles	Add, change, or delete user profile information and properties
Search	Search the portal site and all related content
Update Personal Web Parts	Update Web Parts to display personalized information
Use Personal Features	Use alerts and personal sites
View Area	View an area and its contents
View Pages	View pages in an area

As in Windows SharePoint Services, users are granted permissions to a portal site through direct or indirect membership in a site group. However, the difference in assigning rights is that cross-site groups are not supported in SharePoint Portal Server; cross-site groups are supported only in Windows SharePoint Services. In SharePoint Portal Server, users can be added directly to a site group or they can be members of a Windows domain group that is added to a site group. Figure 6-3 shows the means by which users are granted permissions to a portal site.

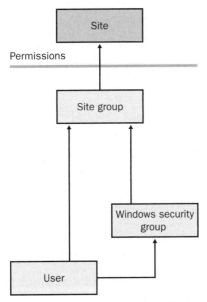

Figure 6-3 Granting user permissions to a portal site

You can adjust access to areas of the portal site by assigning users to a site group for a specific area. You can customize security for each area in the portal by adding, editing, or removing users or site groups.

By default, security settings on a parent area will be applied automatically to all its subareas. Adding users or groups to a specific area will break the inheritance of security settings: if you customize the security on a subarea, the subarea will no longer inherit changes made to the parent area.

Site Creation Rights

Site creation rights (Create Sites and Create Personal Site) control whether users can create portal sites and personal sites.

The Create Sites right allows users to create portal sites by using Self-Service Site Creation. As in Windows SharePoint Services, the Self-Service Site Creation is disabled by default in SharePoint Portal Server—you must turn on the feature to use it. By default, the new sites are created using the default content database; you can configure the alternate content database. For details, refer to Chapter 18, "Managing SharePoint Portal Server 2003."

The Create Personal Sites right allows users to create a personal site by clicking My Site on the title bar on the portal home page. Site administrators control the location and site naming format for the personal sites on the portal by using the Manage Personal Sites page.

Anonymous Access

Anonymous access allows users to view pages on your portal site anonymously or to perform searches anonymously. When you enable anonymous access in SharePoint Portal Server, you are enabling access to your site for the IIS anonymous account IUSR_*machinename*.

Anonymous access is disabled by default and is controlled at the portal-site level. To enable anonymous access, you must first verify that IIS is configured to allow anonymous access, and then enable anonymous access for your portal site by using SharePoint Portal Server Central Administration pages.

If you need to retain the ability to authenticate users as well as provide anonymous access, you can create a new virtual server, extend this virtual server, and then enable anonymous access for this virtual server by using SharePoint Portal Server Central Administration. In this case, users who access the original portal site will require authentication while users who access the new virtual server will have anonymous access.

Note   To create and extend a virtual server, you must be a member of the local administrators group. To enable anonymous access or manage anonymous access settings, you must be an Administrator on the portal site, a member of the SharePoint Administrators group, or a member of the local administrators group.

After you have enabled anonymous access for your portal site, you can allow anonymous users to access and view pages and to perform searches on your portal site. If anonymous access is disabled for your site, it cannot be enabled for viewing areas or performing searches.

> **More Info**   For detailed instruction on configuration steps for setting up anonymous access for a portal site, refer to Chapter 18, "Managing Share-Point Portal Server 2003."

Performing Administration Tasks

SharePoint Portal Server is built on Windows SharePoint Services, so it comes as no surprise that as far as performing administration tasks are concerned, the permissions remain essentially the same:

- To perform any administrative tasks that affect settings for all portal sites and virtual servers on the server computer, a user must be an administrator for the server computer or a member of the SharePoint administrators group.

- Users assigned to the Administrator site group are administrators only for a particular portal site.

Security for Backward-Compatible Document Libraries

It is a frequent requirement to restrict access to information in the backward-compatible document library (Web Storage System–based). In some cases, it is required to restrict the viewing of a document to users who edit or approve it, until it is ready for a larger audience.

In the backward-compatible document library, SharePoint Portal Server roles add actions such as check-in, check-out, publish, and approve to traditional file-access permissions such as Read, Write, and Change. There are three fixed roles; each role identifies a specific set of permissions, as follows:

- Coordinators handle management tasks.

- Authors add and update files.

- Readers have read-only access to published documents.

Access permissions for the three roles are fixed and cannot be modified. Share-Point Portal Server also offers the option of denying users access to specific documents. Roles are usually specified at the folder level, although you can add coordinators at the document-library level for management tasks.

Search Results

SharePoint Portal Server recognizes security policies in use on your organization's servers, file shares, and databases during searches. This authorization is important, as it prevents users from finding documents to which they have no access when they perform searches in the portal site. For detailed discussion on the search architecture, functionality, and configuration, refer to Chapter 21, "The Architecture of the Gatherer," and Chapter 22, "Managing External Content in Microsoft Office SharePoint Portal Server 2003."

Code Access Security

SharePoint Products and Technologies Services use code access security to control access to protected resources. Code access security is a security mechanism that lets you assign to a SharePoint Products and Technologies application a configurable level of trust that corresponds to a predefined set of permissions. Code access security allows code to be trusted to varying degrees, depending on where the code originates and on other aspects of the code's identity. Code access security provides the following functionality:

- Defines permissions and permission sets that represent the right to access various system resources

- Enables administrators to configure security policy by associating sets of permissions with groups of code (code groups)

- Enables code to request the permissions it requires to run, as well as the permissions that would be useful to have, and specifies which permissions the code must never have

- Grants permissions to each assembly that is loaded, based on the permissions requested by the code and on the operations permitted by security policy

- Enables code to demand that its callers have specific permissions

- Enables code to demand that its callers possess a digital signature, thus allowing only callers from a particular organization or site to call the protected code

- Enforces restrictions on code at run time by comparing the granted permissions of every caller on the call stack to the permissions that callers must have

To determine whether code is authorized to access a resource or perform an operation, the runtime's security system walks the call stack, comparing the granted permissions of each caller to the permission being demanded. If any caller in the call stack does not have the demanded permission, a security exception is thrown and access is refused.

To allow the administrator to switch levels of trust assigned to an application, in addition to the ASP.NET default security policy files Windows SharePoint Services provides two policy files of its own: Windows SharePoint Services Minimal (WSS_Minimal) and Windows SharePoint Services Medium (WSS_Medium). When a virtual server is extended to host Windows SharePoint Services, the WSS_Minimal policy is applied to it by default.

SharePoint Products and Technologies Code Access Security Policies

The WSS_Minimal and WSS_Medium policy files are located by default in the folder *<Local Drive>*:\Program Files\Common Files\Microsoft Shared\Web Server Extensions\60\config\. The files are named wss_minimaltrust.config and wss_mediumtrust.config, respectively. Permissions in WSS_Minimal and WSS_Medium policy files are listed in Table 6-4.

Table 6-4   Permissions Defined in WSS_Minimal and WSS_Medium Policies

Permission	WSS_Medium	WSS_Minimal
AspNetHostingPermission	Medium	Minimal
Environment	Read: TEMP, TMP, OS, USERNAME, COMPUTERNAME	
FileIO	Read, Write, Append, PathDiscovery:Application Directory	
IsolatedStorage	AssemblyIsolationByUser, UserQuota specified	
Security	Execution, Assertion, ControlPrincipal, ControlThread, RemotingConfiguration	Execution
WebPermission	Connect to origin host (if configured)	
DNS	Unrestricted or all subpermissions granted	
SqlClientPermission	Unrestricted or all subpermissions granted	
SharePointPermission	SharePointPermission.ObjectModel	
WebPartPermission	WebPartPermission.Connections	WebPartPermission.Connections

Both WSS_Minimal and WSS_Medium policies extend ASP.NET default policy files. These policies grant Full trust to assemblies in the global assembly cache (GAC) and $CodeGen, but they only partially trust the assemblies installed in the /bin directory of the virtual server.

In addition to the default set of permissions defined by ASP.NET and the common language runtime, SharePoint Products and Technologies has defined two custom permissions, SharePointPermission and WebPartPermission, as part of the Microsoft.SharePoint.Security namespace located in the Microsoft.SharePoint.Security.dll. All code that tries to access the SharePoint Products and Technologies class libraries needs the SharePointPermission with the ObjectModel property set to true. For a full list of SharePointPermission and WebPartPermission attributes, refer to the "Microsoft Windows SharePoint Services and Code Access Security" whitepaper located at *http://msdn.microsoft.com/library/default.asp?url=/library/en-us/odc_sp2003_ta/ html /sharepoint_wsscodeaccesssecurity.asp.*

Based on the requirements and the trust associated with assemblies installed in the /bin directory of the virtual server extended with SharePoint Products and Technologies, administrators can choose to change the permissions associated with these assemblies. An easy approach is to change the policy applied to the virtual server by changing the trust level attribute in the web.config file of the specific virtual server. The default levels of trust, listed in permissions order, are as follows:

- Full

- High (This is an ASP.NET default level, so the SharePointPermission and WebPartPermission will not be granted.)

- WSS_Medium

- Medium (This is an ASP.NET default level, so the SharePointPermission and WebPartPermission will not be granted.)

- Low (This is an ASP.NET default level, so the SharePointPermission and WebPartPermission will not be granted.)

- WSS_Minimal

- Minimal (This is an ASP.NET default level, so the SharePointPermission and WebPartPermission will not be granted.)

If your code tries to perform an action or access a resource that is protected by the common language runtime, the default permissions might be insufficient and your code might need one or more of the default ASP.NET permissions.

> **Note**   If you want to use the classes and members in the Microsoft.Share-Point.Portal.SingleSignOn namespace, your code will need an additional permission, SingleSignonPermission.Access. Refer to Chapter 26 for detailed instructions.

There are several ways to make sure your code has the required permissions to access the SharePoint Products and Technologies class libraries, as follows:

- Create a custom security policy and assign the SharePointPermission with the ObjectModel property set to true to the specific assembly or set of assemblies. Refer to Chapter 39, "Using Microsoft Office InfoPath with SharePoint Products and Technologies," for detailed instructions.

- Install the assembly in the global assembly cache, as the code in it always has Full trust. Although installing your Web Part assembly in the GAC is a viable option, it is recommended that you install Web Part assemblies in the /bin directory for a more secure deployment. For the full list of pros and cons of installing an assembly into the GAC, refer to *http://msdn.microsoft.com /library /default.asp?url=/library/en-us/odc_sp2003_ta/html /sharepoint_wsscodeaccesssecurity.asp*.

- Raise the trust level for the virtual server extended with SharePoint Products and Technologies by changing the trust level attribute in the web.config file. For example, to change the policy level of a virtual server from WSS_Minimal to WSS_Medium, perform the following steps:

  1. Open the web.config file of the virtual server in a text editor such as Notepad.

  2. Search for `<trust level="WSS_Minimal" originUrl="" />`.

  3. Change the level to the following: `<trust level="WSS_Medium" originUrl="" />`

  4. Save the web.config file.

  5. Reset Internet Information Services (IIS) by using iisreset in the command prompt.

Communication Security

Secure communication between the components of a SharePoint Products and Technologies deployment is a vital element of an in-depth security architecture. In SharePoint Products and Technologies deployments, it's important to apply secure communication techniques for both inside and outside the firewall. Secure communication provides privacy and integrity of data.

Privacy ensures that data remains private and confidential, and that it cannot be viewed by eavesdroppers armed with network-monitoring software. Privacy is usually provided by means of encryption.

Integrity ensures that data is protected from accidental or deliberate (malicious) modification while in transit. Secure communication channels must provide integrity of data. Integrity is usually provided by using Message Authentication Codes (MACs).

To provide security of communication, you can use the following technologies:

- **Secure Sockets Layer/Transport Layer Security (SSL/TLS).**   Secure Sockets Layer (SSL) is a public key–based security protocol that comprises a set of cryptographic technologies that provides authentication, confidentiality, and data integrity. It is most commonly used to secure the channel between a browser and a Web server. However, it can also be used to secure communications to and from a database server running Microsoft SQL Server 2000.

- **Internet Protocol Security (IPSec).**   IPSec provides a transport-level secure communication solution and can be used to secure the data sent between two computers. IPSec is a transport-layer mechanism through which you can ensure the confidentiality and integrity of TCP/IP-based communications between computers. IPSec is completely transparent to applications because encryption, integrity, and authentication services are implemented at the transport level.

In this section, we will look into communication security for SharePoint Products and Technologies, including the following topics:

- Communication with Microsoft SQL Server

- Communication between index and search servers in the SharePoint Portal Server server farm deployments

- Using firewalls to protect SharePoint sites

- Using SSL for extranet sites

Communication with Microsoft SQL Server

In SharePoint Products and Technologies deployments, connections between the front-end Web server and the computer running SQL Server are not encrypted. It is recommended that you implement Secure Sockets Layer (SSL) or otherwise encrypt server-to-server communications—for example, by using IPSec.

If you decide to use SSL to secure communication with SQL Server 2000, you need to perform the following steps:

1. On a computer running SQL Server, obtain and install a server certificate.

2. The certificate authority (CA) that issued the certificate must be trusted by connecting clients. To achieve this, on the client computers, such as front-end Web servers, install the certificate of the issuing CA.

3. On the computer running SQL Server, use Server Network Utility to configure whether to force all clients to use SSL or to allow clients to choose whether or not to use SSL.

> **More Info** For more information, refer to Microsoft Knowledge Base article 276553, "HOW TO: Enable SSL Encryption for SQL Server 2000 with Certificate Server" at *http://support.microsoft.com/default.aspx?scid=276553*.

If you decide to use IPsec to secure communication with SQL Server 2000, you need to perform the following steps:

1. Create an IP Security policy on the database server computer.

2. Export the IPSec policy that you have created, and copy it to the front-end server computer.

3. On both the database server and the remote server computers, assign the IPSec policy. An IPSec policy must be assigned before it becomes active.

> **More Info** For more information about IPSec, refer to TechNet at *http://www.microsoft.com/technet/prodtechnol/windows2000serv/howto/ipsecwt.mspx*.

Communication Between Index and Search Servers

In a server farm running SharePoint Portal Server, when indexes are propagated from an index management server to a search server, the transmission is not encrypted and therefore might not be secure. It is recommended that you implement IPSec to secure the communication between the index server and the search servers.

To use IPsec to secure the propagation of indexes, do the following:

1. Create an IP Security policy on the index management server computer.

2. Export the IPSec policy to each of the search server computers.

3. On index server and search server computers, assign the IPSec policy to activate it.

Using Firewalls to Protect the SharePoint Sites

When a SharePoint site provides services across an extranet or is accessible from the Internet by the general public, it is essential that external access to the site occurs through a firewall. The firewall inspects all incoming and outgoing traffic, and then allows or disallows the traffic based on the preconfigured policies.

On a simple level, firewalls perform packet filtering: when traffic comes to the firewall, it compares the data in the IP header with the preconfigured rules to determine whether to allow or deny access. However, to protect SharePoint Portal Server deployments from external attacks, it is also necessary to check and verify the payload inside the HTTP header. Microsoft Internet Security and Acceleration (ISA) Server 2000 firewall is an application-layer firewall that, in addition to packet filtering, provides the ability to examine the content contained in the application-level protocols such as HTTP. Refer to Chapter 25, "Firewall Considerations for SharePoint Portal Server Deployments," for detailed information on the ISA server configuration for making your SharePoint sites available to external users without compromising the security of your internal network.

Using SSL for Extranet Deployments

In the Web environment, SSL is commonly used between Web browsers and front-end Web servers to create a secure communication channel. In SharePoint Products and Technologies deployments, SSL provides a secure way of establishing an encrypted communication link with users who connect to the SharePoint sites from outside the firewall.

For a detailed discussion of SSL and instructions on how to enable it in your environment, refer to Chapter 27, "Securing an Extranet Using SSL and Certificates."

Summary

In this chapter, we looked at the security mechanisms SharePoint Products and Technologies uses to provide secure access for users and reduce the threat of security compromise. User authentication is built on underlying technologies such as IIS and ASP.NET and uses Windows security principals, while access authorization is based on a site group membership that associates each user directly or indirectly with a permission that controls the specific actions that the user can perform. Code access security allows you to configure granular access for the SharePoint Products and Technologies application code. Communication security is vital for making sure that the data is transmitted securely both inside and outside the firewall. Because SharePoint Products and Technologies security is layered on top of the security of many underlying technologies, it is important to implement a defense-in-depth approach that addresses security across all components of your SharePoint Products and Technologies deployment.

Chapter 7

Architecting SharePoint Products and Technologies for Operating System Topologies

Specific Requirements for Server and Client

The latest versions of Microsoft SharePoint Products and Technologies have specific requirements for software and for domain membership. Both Microsoft Office Share-Point Portal Server and Microsoft Windows SharePoint Services must be installed on Microsoft Windows Server 2003, and most, but not all, configurations require that the server running either of these applications be a member of a domain. Of course, all features are available if the domain is a Windows Server 2003 domain, but what if a network environment does not have a Windows Server 2003 domain? In a Microsoft Windows NT domain environment, SharePoint Products and Technologies have much of the same functionality.

Server Requirements

Although all configurations of Windows SharePoint Services must be installed on a Windows Server 2003 server, not all configurations require a domain. Single-server Windows SharePoint Services installations can be installed on servers that are not members of a domain. In all other configurations, all servers—such as those in a server farm—must be members of the same domain.

SharePoint Portal Server requires domain membership for all servers in all configurations. Installing and operating a computer running SharePoint Portal Server is not supported if the server is a member of a workgroup. However, any domain type can work. This means that SharePoint Portal Server is supported on Windows Server 2003 servers that are members of a Microsoft Windows NT 4.0, Windows 2000, or Windows Server 2003 domain.

Client Requirements

Regardless of the type of client that connects to SharePoint Products and Technologies, the features that are available are the same. However, these features can be implemented differently based on the capabilities of the different browsers. Any Windows, Macintosh, or UNIX client can use the available features, provided the client runs the following software:

- Microsoft Internet Explorer 5.01 with Service Pack 2

- Internet Explorer 5.5 with Service Pack 2

- Internet Explorer 6

- Internet Explorer 5.2 or later for Macintosh

- Netscape Navigator version 6.2 or later

A client program such as Microsoft Office 2003 is not necessary for browsing but is required if the user contributes to documents on a website. For example, if a Word document exists on a site and a user would like to edit that document, Microsoft Word 2003 is required to edit the document directly from the site.

Authentication

Authentication is the process used to validate the user account that is attempting to gain access to a website or network resource. Authentication for Windows SharePoint Services websites is handled by Internet Information Services (IIS). Windows SharePoint Services uses the authentication method you specify for a virtual server in IIS to control authentication for all top-level websites and subsites of that virtual server. Windows SharePoint Services works with the following authentication methods in IIS:

- Anonymous authentication

- Basic authentication

- Integrated Windows authentication

- Certificate authentication (using Secure Sockets Layer)

All these methods are available regardless of the type of domain to which the front-end servers belong.

Administrative Rights

Two sets of users are allowed to perform administrative functions for Windows SharePoint Services: members of the administrators group for the local server computer and members of the SharePoint administrators group. The SharePoint administrators group is a domain group that is registered with Windows SharePoint Services. The SharePoint administrative group is not created by default. The user who installs Windows SharePoint Services can create this group during installation, and it can contain a domain group, local user, or domain user.

Members of this domain group can perform Central Administration tasks without having to be given administrator rights to the local server computer. This is particularly useful in a server farm, because you can grant rights across the server farm rather than individually for each computer in the server farm. This is also useful for applications that call the administrative object model for Windows SharePoint Services. If the application process can be configured to run as a member of the SharePoint administrators group, it can create new sites, modify quota values for sites, and so on.

There are some operations that members of the local administrator's group can perform that members of the SharePoint administrator's group cannot perform. These tasks include:

- Configuring the SharePoint Central Administration virtual server

- Enabling full-text search

- Extending virtual servers in Windows SharePoint Services

- Managing content databases (i.e., changing properties, etc.)

- Managing paths (inclusions/exclusions)

- Running the stsadm.exe command-line utility

- Setting the configuration database properties

- Setting the default content database server

- Setting the SharePoint Administration Group

- Removing Windows SharePoint Services from a virtual server

User Account Mode

When you install Windows SharePoint Services, you must choose which mode you want to use to allow users access to Windows SharePoint Services sites. Windows SharePoint Services can work with two modes: *domain account mode* and *Active Directory account creation mode*. Domain account mode is used inside organizations to grant access to users that have existing Windows domain accounts. Active Directory account creation mode can be used by Internet service providers to create unique accounts for customers using the Active Directory directory service.

In domain account mode, you use existing domain user accounts. If you choose Active Directory account creation mode, you are choosing to have accounts automatically created in the Active Directory organizational unit you specify. In either mode, you use the same methods to manage users of a site. You add them to the site by using their existing domain or Active Directory accounts, and then assign them to site groups to give them the rights they need to use the site.

The choice between user account modes is a one-time-only choice because it affects how the configuration database for your server or server farm is created. You cannot change user account modes after creating the configuration database, and this step is one of the first choices made during installation when using Microsoft SQL Server. If Windows Microsoft SQL Server 2000 Desktop Engine (WMSDE) is used, the account creation mode is set to domain account mode and cannot be changed.

In a Windows 2000 or Windows Server 2003 domain, Windows SharePoint Services can use Active Directory account creation mode. In a Windows NT domain, the domain account mode is needed.

Controlling Access to Sites

Windows SharePoint Services provides the ability to control site access through the use of site groups. Site groups let you specify which of your users can perform specific actions in your site. For example, a user who is a member of the Contributor site group can add content to Windows SharePoint Services lists, such as the Task list, or a document library.

Because SharePoint Portal Server is designed to work in an Active Directory environment, some functionality for administrative tasks is unavailable. When adding a user to the portal site by clicking Add Users on the Manage Users page, the Select Users And Groups – Web Page Dialog dialog box should appear. However, this feature does not work with Windows NT domains. This dialog box searches for and adds users to the site. As a work-around try the following steps:

1. On the Site Settings page, in the **General Settings** section, click **Manage users**.

2. On the Manage Users page, click **Add Users**.

3. In the **Step 1: Choose Users** section, type the name of the user or users to add in the **Users** box.

    (Enter names in the format *DomainName\UserName*. For more than one user, separate each user name with a semicolon character [;].)

4. In the **Step 2: Choose Permissions** section, select the check boxes next to the site groups to which the users are to be added, and then click **Next**.

5. In the **Step 3: Confirm Users** section, verify the e-mail address, user name, and display name information of the user or users.

6. In the **Step 4: Send E-mail** section, select the **Send the following e-mail to let these users know they've been added** check box to notify users. Type a message to include, if needed.

7. Click **Finish**.

Active Directory–Dependent Features

Some features available in SharePoint Portal Server are dependent on Active Directory. Although most features can still be used in a Windows NT environment, they will need to be configured manually. The features that work with Active Directory include user profiles and audience compilation.

The user profiles feature in SharePoint Portal Server populates a database of user profiles by importing the profiles from Active Directory. Without an Active Directory environment, the accounts must be typed into the user profiles database. This can be done in the Manage User Profile page in the Central Administration site. Also, when an audience is compiled in an Active Directory environment, rules are used as filters against the profile database to create a subset of users. Because not all profile information is imported into the SharePoint Portal Server profile database, Active Directory is checked during an audience compilation if any additional information is needed. Without Active Directory the information is limited to what is manually entered into the user profiles database.

Active Directory Application Mode

The new Active Directory Application Mode (ADAM) lets you run Active Directory as an application in your Windows Server 2003 domains. An application can use Active Directory Application Mode to store "private" directory data (data that is relevant only to the application) in a local directory service, perhaps on the same server as the application, without requiring any additional configuration to the network operating system (NOS) directory. ADAM can support directory-enabled applications running in Microsoft Windows NT 4.0 domains. Because ADAM works with the Windows-integrated security infrastructure, it can also authenticate users from Windows NT 4.0 domains.

Currently SharePoint Products and Technologies does not integrate with Active Directory Application Mode. This is because ADAM does not provide actual logon tokens, but instead provides only LDAP names. SharePoint Portal Products and Technologies requires logon tokens for authentication.

Summary

Upgrading your domains and forests to Windows Server 2003 domains and forests with Active Directory is the optimal way of getting the maximum functionality out of Windows Server 2003. However, not all network environments have a Windows Server 2003 domain. SharePoint Products and Technologies can be installed into a Windows NT domain with the loss of only some features. Many features still work, but require a manual configuration to function with Active Directory.

Part III

Planning and Deployment

Chapter 8

Planning Your Information Structure Using Microsoft Office SharePoint Portal Server 2003

Microsoft Office SharePoint Portal Server 2003 has several compelling features and tools that make it an ideal solution for implementing your information management system. Managing information well is critical to any organization's success. Poor information management leads to inefficient collaboration, ineffective decision-making processes, and lost business opportunities.

SharePoint Portal Server 2003 does not automatically organize your information into an overall **taxonomy** for you. Instead, you'll need to plan and implement your own taxonomy. (A *taxonomy* is a method of organizing or categorizing information and information resources.) Because each environment is unique, you should take the planning process seriously and understand that *installing* SharePoint Portal Server 2003 is not the same thing as *implementing* it.

In this chapter, we'll outline the key decision areas that must be addressed before a product server is ever built—specifically, during the architecting and planning phases. You shouldn't be surprised to learn that the key decision areas are built on the information management features of this product.

Key Information Management Features of SharePoint Portal Server 2003

The key information management features of SharePoint Portal Server 2003 include the following:

- Search and indexing
- Document collaboration
- Best Bets and keywords
- Areas and Topics
- Personal sites (personal site)
- Audience targeting
- User profiles
- Site collections
- Site directory area

The purpose of this chapter is not to discuss how to implement or administer each of these features. Instead, the focus of this chapter is on *planning* for the implementation for each of these features and showing how they relate to the overall information management picture.

Where to Start

When beginning the planning process for a new information management system, you'll need to start by answering two basic questions:

- What information does your organization need to have and use to be successful?
- Where is that information right now?

It might seem a bit silly, but most IT professionals bypass these two questions and immediately get to work on building an information management system without ever considering where their information currently resides. Because most organizations don't have an overall structure to their information, they don't have a good understanding of *where* their business-critical information currently resides and, surprisingly, *what* that information really is (and isn't). When asked, most project managers and system administrators will acknowledge that the organization's current information resides in a plethora of disconnected data islands, including the following:

- People's minds
- E-mail
- Public folders
- File servers

- Local hard drives

- Databases

- Web pages and websites

- Filing cabinets

- Applications

- Document management systems

- Credenzas

- Users' home directories

These data islands cannot be connected unless they are first identified and inventoried for the data that they host. Only after an organization knows where its information resides and what that information is can it really begin the process of detailing how that information will be accessed using SharePoint Portal Server 2003, how it will be structured, and how information growth will be accommodated.

This is not an easy process. Much of this work will need to be accomplished at the team or departmental levels. And this process can become time consuming, requiring thoughtful analysis and methodical discovery of where employees go to get the information they need to perform their jobs and what that information is.

Many administrators who are asked to play the role of an information architect jump ahead and begin the planning process by looking at the organizational chart. They quickly conclude that they should have site collections for each department, a child portal site for each division, and perhaps an overall portal site for the entire organization. These hastily determined structures are nearly always modified from their original configuration because the decisions used to construct them lack any real basis.

Even though SharePoint Products and Technologies is very flexible and can support both the technical needs of an organization as well as its cultural needs, it's not wise to jump ahead of the planning process and start near the end. As you read through this chapter, you'll begin to understand what is meant by this, but for now, the following example will suffice.

You might start the process by quickly looking at your organizational chart and concluding that you'll need one document library for each collaboration team in your organization. However, upon closer inspection, you'll need a different document library for each unique combination of user permission assignment, document profile matrix, approval group, and site placement. Unless you know which documents you want to host in a portal site, which ones you want to host in a team site, and who should access these documents, it will be difficult to know how many document libraries to create and where to create them.

Perhaps your organization will allow the end users to create their own sites and document libraries. And certainly, SharePoint Portal Server 2003 and Windows SharePoint Services support this. But it is best—at least for capacity-planning purposes—to have at least a rough idea of what your document library matrix will look like.

As part of the architecting and planning processes, an organization is well advised to determine where their information currently resides and what that information is. Once you have that information, the planning processes presented in this chapter for using SharePoint Portal Server 2003 to implement a new structure for your information will be of more value to you.

> **Note**   It is important to understand that many of the planning processes we discuss in this chapter are ongoing processes an organization will perform well into the future. SharePoint Portal Server 2003 can be implemented without doing much of this work, but most system administrators and architects who have skipped the planning processes have found that their implementations were much less effective and successful than those who did perform the planning processes. Even with good planning, however, most organizations will need to return to the concepts presented in this chapter multiple times as they hone their organization-wide taxonomy.

Key Decision Areas for SharePoint Portal Server 2003

There are several key decision areas that you'll want to address as part of your pre-implementation planning process. We'll discuss these areas in this section.

Planning Search

This section describes the components of the SharePoint Portal Server search functionality. It provides guidelines on planning a customized version of each search component for your solution.

Overview of Search Functionality

There are four components that contribute to the SharePoint Portal Server search functionality:

- Content sources
- Content indexes
- Source groups
- Search scopes

Content Sources
A content source is a location where content is stored. A content source specifies the starting place for crawling a file system, a portal site, a SharePoint site, an Exchange Public Folder, a Lotus Notes database or a website. The content can be located in a

different portal site on the same server, on another server within your intranet, or on the Internet.

SharePoint Portal Server builds a content index by crawling the locations specified by the content sources and storing the results—such as Web pages and files. For some content source types such as file shares and SharePoint sites, the content index also stores the appropriate security credentials on the crawled content. This enables the search results to show only items to which a user has access by enforcing the security settings on each document as the result set is built.

You need to consider what information will and will not be hosted in SharePoint Portal Server. For example, documents that will remain on a file server will need to be crawled if those documents are to appear in the search result set. Knowing that you have those documents and where they currently reside allows you to make an informed decision about whether the documents should be moved into a SharePoint document library or crawled and left in their current location.

Generally speaking, older documents that will not change need not be placed in a SharePoint document library *if* the only method needed to find those documents is the Search method. However, if users will need to browse the taxonomy hierarchy to find older documents, you'll need to move the documents into a SharePoint document library or at least link to them using a links list.

Content Indexes

A content index is a flat text file that holds the data from crawled content in a content source. Updating a content index requires crawling the locations specified by the content sources and storing the results on the job server. Propagating a content index consists of copying the index from the index server to the search servers. A portal site search returns results from the content indexes stored on the search servers.

Every portal site includes content indexes that allow users to search for documents inside or outside the portal site. After content is included in an index, the content appears in search results on that portal site.

Source Groups

Source groups, topics, and areas are the elements of search scopes. Search scopes allow you to define the breadth and depth of searches within portal sites and across portal sites. These assignable components can create very flexible searches.

A source group is a list consisting of one or more content sources. Source groups are one of the elements used to define search scopes. Source groups are created and managed at the shared services level (if you are using shared services) and can be assigned in any combination to a portal site search scope. These characteristics allow you to easily define search scopes across portal site boundaries. For example, if you want your marketing portal site users to be able to search content on the sales portal site, you can create a search scope consisting of a source group that encompasses all sales portal site data and a source group that encompasses all marketing portal site data.

Search Scopes

A search scope is a list of one or more source groups, in combination with any specified areas and topics located on the portal site on which they are defined. Search scopes allow users to narrow their searches based on the topics, areas, and content sources of items on the portal site.

Search scopes can be limited by topics and areas, or by groups of content sources. Source groups outside the portal site can be grouped, and you can limit your search scope to exclude or include particular source groups.

Search scopes are defined by a portal site administrator and are exposed only to the portal site on which they are created. For example, a search scope created on the Human Resources portal site named "this portal site" might consist of a source group containing content sources that define all content on the HR file server. This scope would be available only on the HR portal site.

> **Note**   You can use search scopes from remote portal sites to give your overall search scope taxonomy consistency throughout the portal sites in your organization. This is an advanced topic that is covered in Chapter 22, "Managing External Content in Microsoft Office SharePoint Portal Server 2003."

Search scopes appear to all users in a drop-down list next to the portal site search box. These search scopes are typically limited to specific topics and source groups that are important and common enough to make them useful to users in the organization as a separate searchable scope.

Planning Content Indexes

SharePoint Portal Server 2003 comes with two content indexes. You can create as many as you need. However, keep in mind that each search query has to be run on each index and the results aggregated before they are returned to the user. The result is that the more indexes you have, the longer search results take to generate. Also, the more index files you have, the greater the possibility is that ranking in the result set will be skewed. This is because that ranking is determined on a per-index file basis and there is no support for single-set ranking when the result set is generated from multiple index files. The advantages of having more (and thus smaller) index files is that propagation between an Index and Search server in a server farm scenario is much faster than copying a few very large index files from the Index to the Search server.

> **Note** Advanced Search Administration mode should be enabled so that you can create and manage additional indexes. In addition, when you create content sources, you can specify the index in which the content source will appear and the source group.

When planning content indexes, consider the following factors:

- **Number of documents.** If the number of documents is very large, you should consider breaking the content sources into many content sources with smaller scopes. Doing this will make the size of the indexes more manageable.

- **Security.** The default content access is used as the security context through which all content sources are crawled. This account needs only Read access, regardless of which content source it is crawling. You can use nearly any account, but one must be specified as the Default Content Access Account. The account should have appropriate access for other internal resources such as site directories, portal site contents, and shared folders, which are part of the personal site.

  For shared folders, you should use an access account that is a member of the SharePoint Portal Server administrator group. This level of access allows for crawling all types of content and its properties in portal sites and site directories.

  To provide different accounts for crawling content, you must use include and exclude rules. You should add rules and include paths that you want to be crawled with different access accounts. These rules are applied to all content sources bound to a content index that creates additional crawling. To avoid duplicate or additional crawling, you need to assign rules only to specific content sources.

- **Scheduling.** Creating separate content indexes allows you to use more flexible scheduling that is based on the nature of content in each content source. Some content sources change quickly and need more updates, while other content sources are less volatile and require fewer updates.

- **Propagation.** Having smaller content indexes provides faster propagation of content indexes to search servers. However, there is a drawback. When a user initiates a search, the search engine has to run that query against each index and then aggregate the results. The more indexes you have, the longer it takes.

  In addition, if you're in a federated search environment, you need to remember that the number of indexes you have and the size of each will affect how fast these indexes can be propagated or copied from the indexing servers to the search servers.

Finally, you should remember that if ranking documents in the result set is important, you should build your index/source group/content source/search scope topology in such a way that most queries query only one index file at a time. Ranking is performed on a per-index file basis, and there is no method supported to group results from multiple index files and have the result set reranked as a single unit. Another solution is to make sure that your index files are statistically equivalent with the same approximate size and number of documents.

■   **Backup and restore.**   Smaller content indexes also provide more flexibility when backing up and restoring.

> **Note**   SharePoint Portal Server does not allow spaces in content index names. Spaces are supported in source group names. Also, note that Non_Portal_Content and Portal_Content exist by default.

Planning Search Scopes

Search scopes should be planned with the end user in mind. By this, we mean that the Scopes should reflect the most natural way that people will want to search for information. A good search-scope matrix will allow educated users the ability to tightly define the portion of the overall index they want to search, giving them a more lean, yet still meaningful result set. A best practice is to ask representatives from each interested party, department, division, or team to help you create a search-scope matrix that will enhance the users' experience in the portal site by allowing them to search for targeted information.

You'll also need to consider using a hierarchical approach to your scope matrix. For example, let's suppose you have a research department with three teams: Chemicals, Data Modeling, and Quality. Each team produces documents of importance to the larger enterprise. In such a scenario, you might find yourself creating four search scopes: chemicals, data modeling, quality, and research. The fourth scope, research, would encompass the documents from all three teams. By using a hierarchical approach, you can give the portal site user flexibility in defining the portion of the overall index that needs to be searched.

In many cases, building the scope matrix will be more art than technology, meaning that the search-scope matrix will be built over time in response to constructive feedback. In some environments, you might have to place a small icon near the Search Web Part that will take the user to a Web page that outlines the various search scopes in the matrix and the information that will be searched via each scope.

If you'll be using multiple portal sites, you can create a consistent search-scope experience across all the portal sites by propagating each scope to the other portal site or sites. If you're planning to have multiple portal sites, you should also plan to propagate your scopes across all your portal sites unless you have a specific reason for not doing this.

> **Note**   If you want to see changes to a search-scope definition immediately, you must reset Internet Information Services (IIS) by using the IISRESET command. This should be done only during the setup process and not when the system is live in production.

Planning Content Sources

When operating a corporate portal site with multiple divisional portal sites, you should, at a minimum, configure content sources as follows:

- One content source for the corporate portal site.

- One content source for each divisional portal site.

- One content source for the people in your organization. This content source is set up by default. It returns matches based on entries in the profile database as well as content from a user's personal site.

- One content source for each divisional Windows SharePoint Services virtual server in your organization.

You'll also need to remember the old adage "garbage in, garbage out." The tighter and more defined your content sources are, the leaner and more meaningful the data in the result set will be. For example, if you need to crawl five documents on a given website that hosts 200 documents, it would not be a best practice to crawl the entire website. Your index would end up with 195 unneeded documents. In a situation like this, you might consider creating one content source to crawl all five documents or even five content sources, one for each document, depending on their location in the directory structure and if they are shared via the same share or different shares.

The point here is to remember that what you crawl gets placed in your index and you should crawl only information that is required to be in your index. This gets back to our earlier discussion about *where* your information is and what it consists of. Knowing this will help you build a tight list of content sources that will, in turn, give you a tight index that will return highly meaningful results to your users when they issue a query in the Search Web Part. Good planning is paramount to a successful deployment.

Planning Source Groups

As a starting point, you should define your source groups as follows:

- Use one source group for each index. Doing this allows you to broadly define search scopes for each portal site. For example, if your organization chose to hold all its indexed content in a single content index, the source group assigned to that index would allow you to easily define a search scope on all content managed by that index.

- Use one source group for each content source. Doing this allows you to more narrowly define search scopes for each portal site. For example, defining a separate content source for the corporate portal site and one for each divisional portal site would allow you to easily define a search scope on the portal site content that each source group crawls.

> **Note** SharePoint Portal Server does not allow spaces in content index names. Spaces are supported in source group names.
>
> When you select the content source as SharePoint Portal Server Site Directory, define the address of the portal site for the content source (for example, *http://sales/**), and then save definitions of content source parameters, the address of the content source automatically changes—for example, it changes to *sps://sales/site$$$site/scope=**.
>
> There is no way to directly crawl the virtual server of another team site. If you want to have certain site collections indexed, you have two options. The first is to add the site collection to another site directory manually. The second option—which is less optimal—is to add a separate content source for each site collection. The first option is the preferred and recommended approach.

Planning Deltas Between Source Groups and Content Indexes

A best practice is to create a source group for each content index so that you'll have maximum flexibility in creating the search scopes. To use the example from the preceding sections, you'd create a content source to each document group for each team (chemicals, data modeling, and quality). You would assign each content source to its own source group, such as Chemicals Source Group, Data Modeling Source Group, and Quality Source Group. Then, for the research search scope, you'd select all three source groups to offer portal site users the ability to search documents across the research department.

Propagating Content Indexes

Index propagation occurs only when the Search application and the Index application are run on two different servers in a medium or large server farm. Propagation happens automatically at the end of every successful update (or crawl). Before propagation can be successful, the following conditions must be met:

- You have configured a search service account for the server farm. This account must have local administrator permissions on the search (destination) server.

- The destination server is on a trusted domain.

- There is sufficient disk space available on the destination server. For each propagated index, allow for more than twice its size in disk space to accommodate both the current index and the propagating index.

- SMB (Server Message Block) traffic must be enabled between the two servers, and if there is a firewall between them, the appropriate ports must be opened too. These ports include the common Netbios and RPC (Remote Procedure Call) ports.

Propagation is considered successful if the index is successfully copied to any one search server. If you have a scenario where propagation is successful to one or more, but not all, search servers, the search servers to which propagation failed is taken off line, an error is logged in the event log, and the error appears on the propagation status page.

> **Note**   If propagation fails because of lack of disk space on the destination server, SharePoint Portal Server 2003 logs an error in the Application Log of the Windows Server 2003 Event Viewer (event log) of both the destination search server and the index management server.
>
>   The contents of a new index are not accessible on the search server until propagation has been completed. The index is not accessible if propagation fails, even if a previous propagation was successful.

Updating Content Indexes

The four methods for updating content indexes are as follows:

- Full
- Incremental
- Incremental (inclusive)
- Adaptive

The method used to update the index can have a significant effect on performance. The following topics describe these four methods.

Full Update

During a full update, SharePoint Portal Server updates all content in a content index. A full update of a content source includes adding new content, modifying changed content, refreshing the content index for existing unchanged content, and removing deleted content from the content index. This is the most time-consuming and resource-intensive type of update, and it should be done only in the following situations:

- If you create a new rule that affects only one content source.

- If files are renamed in a specific content source.

- If it is the first crawl of a content source.

- If you include or exclude a new file type.

- If permissions are changed on documents in the content source. While all updates pick up permission changes, only the full updates pick up changes to membership in local groups. This is why it is recommended that you not use local groups to secure content that SharePoint Portal Server crawls.

- If there is a power outage. In this case, SharePoint will want to run full indexes to reset the index. It might be faster to reset the index files and clean them out before running a full index. (Resetting the index files is discussed in Chapter 22.)

- If you change the noise word file.

- If there is an area name change.

- If you reset the content index.

Given all these changes that will force you to rerun a full index, it is best that you plan for them so that the full indexes can be run without overloading either the indexing server or the content source's server.

Incremental Update

An incremental update of a content source includes only changed content. SharePoint Portal Server does not remove deleted content from the content index and does not recrawl unchanged content. For this reason, performing an incremental update is faster than performing a full update.

You can perform an incremental update if you know that content has changed but you do not want to perform a full update and you don't mind having some deleted content continue to appear in your index. A periodic incremental update creates the index without using the time or resources required for a full update, which enables you to perform a full update less frequently.

Incremental (Inclusive)

SharePoint Portal Server 2003 introduces another type of update known as the incremental (inclusive) update. This update is similar to the incremental update except that it includes deleted content. The incremental (inclusive) update also detects deleted entries in the Microsoft Windows SharePoint Services document libraries and lists. The incremental update detects modified or new documents and list items only.

The incremental update is the least expensive update if it is used with Windows SharePoint Services sites. The incremental (inclusive) update is more resource intensive than the regular incremental update and should therefore be run less often if performance is a top priority for you.

Adaptive Update

An adaptive update, like the incremental update, crawls only the content that, statistically speaking, is most likely to have changed since the last adaptive update. Because adaptive updates are likely to miss at least some content changes, these updates will crawl all the content in a content source every two weeks.

Unlike the incremental update, the adaptive update increases its efficiency every time it is run based on a statistical analysis of the historical information on what content has and has not changed. The time required for an adaptive update varies and is based on the different types of content sources and the protocol handler.

The recommended approach is to run adaptive updates daily for large source groups and more often for smaller source groups. Avoid running full updates whenever possible. However, how you choose to configure your index updates is dependent on your search requirements. If your organization is search intensive and requires immediate updates to the search indexes as new content is added or removed, you might need to schedule updates to occur more frequently. You must balance the search requirements with the time it takes to perform an update and propagate content indexes.

There is also a scheduling factor to consider too. Updates are both processor and RAM intensive. You'll want to ensure that you're scheduling your updates to occur when your servers running SharePoint Portal Server and Windows SharePoint Services are not being backed up, scanned for viruses, or performing any other routine that consumes large processor resources, RAM resources, or both. In addition, you shouldn't crawl content sources during their nightly routines either. Therefore, a best practice is to create a schedule matrix and schedule the crawling of content sources when those sources are being used the least.

Planning Alerts

Alerts provide notification when information of interest is added or updated on the portal site and associated content sources. You can define areas of interest and identify how and when you want to be notified. You can add an alert to track new matches to a search query, changes to content in an area, or a new site added to the Site Directory.

When configuring alerts, keep in mind that alerts for SharePoint Portal Server 2003 and Windows SharePoint Services are managed separately. There are three key differences between SharePoint Portal Server alerts and Windows SharePoint Services alerts:

■ SharePoint Portal Server alerts are managed by the user on the My Alerts page, which is located on the user's personal site. Windows SharePoint Services alerts are managed through the Manage My Alerts link on the Site Settings page of each site.

■ SharePoint Portal Server alert notifications can be delivered to the user's e-mail inbox, to the user's My Alerts Summary Web Part on the personal site, or to both. Windows SharePoint Services alert notifications can be delivered only through e-mail.

■ SharePoint Portal Server users can set alerts on more items than Windows SharePoint Services users can.

SharePoint Portal Server can track alerts for the following items:

■ Search queries

■ Documents

■ Areas

■ New listings and listings in general, such as listings for people, news, new list items, and so forth

■ Sites added to the Site Directory

■ SharePoint lists and libraries

■ List items (requires modification of a site path rule)

■ Portal site users

Windows SharePoint Services can track alerts on the following items within a site:

■ Lists

■ List items

■ Document libraries

■ Documents

When shared services are enabled, management of alert settings is possible only through the Central Administration interface. Through this interface, you can set quotas for alerts per user and for all portal sites. You can define and adjust the default numbers based on the following criteria:

- The number of users

- How many alerts each user can have

- How many alert results you want to be returned per alert

You can adjust these defaults based on the number of users and the alerts per user setting to determine the maximum settings for alerts at the site level. For example, if your company has 20,000 users and you are setting a limit of 10 search alerts per user and 20 other alerts per user, your maximum number of alerts for *all portal sites* is calculated as follows:

*20,000 * 10 = 200,000 (maximum number of search alerts for all sites)*

*20,000 * 20 = 400,000 (maximum number of other alerts for all sites)*

If you're using shared services, these are the maximum numbers allowed for all divisional portal sites and the corporate portal site combined. They are not per site or per portal site.

> **Note**   Alerts on portal sites and Windows SharePoint Services sites are not consolidated.

Planning Topics and Areas

There are basically two ways to find information in the portal site: browse and search. Topics and areas give portal site users the ability to browse for information. Portal site users will use the Search Web Part to find information, a topic that is covered in Chapter 22.

A Topic is a specialized area that hosts specific Web Parts and Portal Listings that expose links to site collections and other URL-addressable content. Topics usually contain highlights of other areas or frequently used content, and they might or might not be limited to a single subject.

Areas are sites templated to host static information and to provide a method of structuring (or categorizing) your information and information sources. Similar in some respects to Topics, areas enable you to organize and structure your data in any manner that makes sense to your organization so that users can browse the area or Topic hierarchy to find the information they are looking for.

There are seven types of area templates and Portal Listings. We'll briefly describe each one here:

1. **TOC (Table of Contents) Category template.**   This is the home page of the Topics area hierarchy. It is used to view three levels of topics in your organization. It is the tree view of the Topics areas.

2. **Topic Category template.**   This is the template used to create an individual Topic area.

3. **News Category template.**   This is the template used to create individual News areas.

4. **News Home Category template.**   This template "rolls up" news items from News areas under the News Home. If there are subareas—such as Public News, Corporate News, and Competitor News—you would see each of the latest items from those three areas in the News Home area. There is also a targeted Web Part named *News for You*, which allows you to target news items to audiences.

5. **Community Category template.**   This template is designed to create an online community for any purpose you might have, such as an event or a social or business concern.

6. **Shared Page template.**   Found under the Page tab of any area when you click on Change Settings. You can select **Inherit the Parent Template**, which allows you to create multiple areas using the same template that hosts different content.

7. **Sites Directory template.**   This template is used to organize site collections that are created as part of your overall collaborative effort.

When planning out your topics and areas, you need to gain the insight and recommendations from each interested party who will be using the portal site. *How* people *think* about information will heavily influence how they will want to browse for information.

For example, let's suppose you're on a marketing team charged with next year's advertising campaign. You develop a marketing budget for the campaign. Now, who would have a legitimate business interest in seeing that budget? Well, several groups come immediately to mind: Accounting, Executives, Sales, Marketing, Content Development, and others. The sales team will quite likely want to browse for this budget differently than the accountants. Because you can't possibly read the minds of your portal site users, a best practice is to glean from them *what they think is the most logical way to structure the data they most commonly use* and then to use those discussions with the different groups, teams, and departments to build an area and Topic hierarchy that makes sense.

Because areas are more flexible than Topics in how static information is presented, you might find yourself using Topics to structure your data and then using areas to present static information that might or might not be time limited. Areas can be used to structure data too. An area's flexibility comes from the fact that different area templates are available when creating a new area. Each template offers different ready-to-use functionality and Web Part designs. The flexibility of SharePoint Portal Server also means that planning is an up-front activity that you cannot ignore.

Here are some recommendations when considering areas:

- Use the area templates to present static, time-limited information. For example, if your company has an annual summer party, use the Community Category template to disseminate information about the party and use the date functions in the area's properties to automatically remove the area from the portal site after the party has taken place.

- Use the Topic Category template to create additional Topic areas and create a taxonomy based on the subject or topics of your information. But remember that you can use the Topic areas to create a taxonomy based on nearly any method of structuring data. For example, you can use the topic areas to create a taxonomy by

    - Subject

    - Customer

    - Project

    - Security level

    - Author

    - Department

    - Location

    - Or any other method of organizing your data that makes sense in your unique environment

- Use the Sites Directory template to create a new or additional Site Directory.

- Do not create too many top-level areas. If you do, your users will be forced to scroll sideways and this will diminish their positive experience in the portal site.

- Base your area (and Topic) hierarchies on static information, not information that changes often or rapidly. For example, don't create an area for each customer because some of your customers won't be with you a year from now and new ones will continually appear. In this example, a best practice would be to create a generic Customers area and then organize your customers according to some other criteria within the Customers area.

Topics enable users to locate information faster by organizing content into logical groups. The following are some recommendations for planning Topics:

- The tree of Topics should not be too deep—usually not more than three levels.

- Select topics that users are likely to look for.

- Find appropriate topics, especially for the top-level Topics, and retain those Topics for a long period of time rather than changing them frequently.

- If you have too many Topics, select those that are pertinent to the most users, or organize the Topics into two levels.

- Provide Topics that are unique to each portal site.

If you have duplicate Topics, qualify them with appropriate prefixes to avoid confusion. For example, if you want to create a topic named Contacts for each division, create IT–Contacts, HR–Contacts, and so forth. Alternatively, you can create a topic named Contacts, with subtopics such as IT, HR, and so forth.

Another example is the Location Topic, which is provided by default when you create a portal site. In this solution, all locations of organizations in the Corporate Portal site are listed under the Location Topic. Remove the Location Topic from other portal sites, or replace it with other topics that are unique and more relevant to a division.

After defining your Topic structure, you can add content (such as documents, list items, and persons) to each Topic and sub-Topic. Each Topic or sub-Topic can have its own document library to which documents are uploaded. You can assign specific groups to manage each of these Topics and sub-Topics by using the Manage Security option, which is on the list of actions in the Topic area. By the same token, you can restrict areas to certain users by using the same security option. By simply assigning permissions at the area level, you can restrict access to areas in the portal and essentially customize the look and feel of the portal through the use of permissions.

Planning Keywords and Keyword Best Bets

Keywords mark specific content as relevant to a particular word included in a search so that the specific content appears more prominently in search results. Users with the Create Area right can create keywords for common searches. The Create Area right is included by default in the Web Designer, Administrator, and Content Manager site groups. For organizational purposes, you can nest related keywords. For example, the keyword *operating system* could contain the keywords *Windows 2000* and *Windows XP*.

Users with the Manage Area right can add keyword Best Bets for each keyword to identify items most relevant to that keyword. The Manage Area right is included by default in the Web Designer, Administrator, and Content Manager site groups. Keyword Best Bets are specific to individual keywords. Any Best Bets that you associate with nested keywords will not return Best Bets for keywords up or down the chain of nesting.

Best Bets are not limited to documents—you can also define people as Best Bets. For example, you can assign a person who is a subject matter expert in an area as the Best Bet. This facilitates person-to-person communication and knowledge transfer in organizations.

When a user types a keyword or synonym for a keyword in the search box, its keyword Best Bets are shown with the highest relevance in search results. These items are also identified with a distinctive icon as keyword Best Bets.

Keyword Control with SharePoint Portal Server 2003

SharePoint Portal Server 2003 allows keywords to be created at the portal site level and documents to be assigned as Best Bets to each keyword. For example, with a keyword such as *SharePoint*, a user on the IT portal site with the Manage Area right can assign a document with technical content as the Best Bet for that keyword. Then, when IT users search on that keyword through their IT division search scope, they get the best technical content for it. Likewise, a user with the Manage Area right on the Sales portal site can create the same SharePoint keyword and assign documents as Best Bets that are more suited to the needs of the Sales division. In all cases, if the user chooses the ***all sources*** search scopes to search for the keyword, the search returns all documents assigned as Best Bets to that keyword.

Refining Keywords

You can reorganize keywords over time based on users' needs. For example, you can refine the keyword definitions based on the most frequently searched keywords. You can filter the IIS log using a third-party utility to get a better understanding of what users are looking for. For example, you can filter to learn the ten most frequently searched keywords in each portal site, and assign Best Bets based on this analysis.

Planning User Profiles

When administrators new to SharePoint hear about importing user profiles from Active Directory into SharePoint, they usually cringe at the thought of having to manage another directory similar to Active Directory. So let's put your mind at ease: importing user profiles from Active Directory into SharePoint Portal Server 2003 does not create another directory for you to manage. All we're doing is grabbing the rich directory information out of Active Directory and using that information in different ways in SharePoint Portal Server to provide the following features and benefits:

- Searching for and connecting with people within your organization
- Generating a personal site in the portal site for individual users
- Providing better search results
- Targeting content to audiences

Importing User Profiles

You can import user profile information directly from Microsoft Active Directory directory services or enter it manually. You can also customize the properties of the user profile to meet the needs of your organization or to map it to Active Directory properties.

If you have already invested in an infrastructure based on Active Directory or any **LDAP (Lightweight Directory Access Protocol)**-compliant directory, you can import user information stored in the directories. With Active Directory, use the Import Profile to import the user information to the SharePoint Portal Server. Importing user profiles requires a domain account. To use the incremental import feature from Active Directory on a Windows Server 2000–based computer, a domain administrator account is required.

> **Note**   While you can import directory information from any LDAP-compliant database, only Active Directory is supported by Microsoft.

You can import user profiles from the same domain that SharePoint Portal Server is installed on or from any trusted domain. You can also configure and customize your connection to Active Directory to import users based on specific criteria as a script in an LDAP query. (For example, you can create a script that selects all the users that belong to a specific organizational unit [OU], or only users whose e-mail address property is not empty.)

If you're using other platforms, you can add users manually or write your own connector by using the object model. You can add more properties to the user profile if you need to extend the information that you want to be displayed about a user. However, any such updates will not be propagated, nor will they update Active Directory.

Updating User Profiles

After the first import from the directory, you can schedule incremental updates based on the frequency of users being added to Active Directory. In most cases, scheduling incremental updates daily and full updates weekly is sufficient.

> **Tip**   Removing a user from Active Directory and fully updating the user profile does not remove a user profile from the profile database. Nevertheless, a user who is removed from Active Directory is not able to access the SharePoint Portal Server because users are authenticated through Internet Information Services, which authenticates users through Active Directory.

Planning Audiences

Audiences allow organizations to target content to users based on any property in Active Directory or by group membership. Hence, you can build an audience based on who is a member of a Windows Server 2003 security or distribution group. Moreover, you can create an audience based on any property assigned to the user account in Active Directory. For example, you can create an audience based on the Department field in the user account so that those who are assigned to the Accounting Department become members of the Accounting Audience.

Audience Rules

Audiences are created based on a set of rules that you define, based on:

- Windows security group, distribution list, or organizational hierarchy
- User profile public property
- Organizational hierarchy
- Distribution lists

A rule is a simple query based on properties of user profiles or the membership of users in security groups and distribution groups. If you have already created security groups or distribution groups in Active Directory, you can create audiences based on those groups. For example, you can define a rule for an audience group that reports to or under a specific manager (using the format of *domain\managerUserName*). You can also create an audience that belongs to a specific department if you have assigned a value to the Department field of user profiles.

Compiling Audiences

After you create or make changes to an audience, you must compile it for use. Compiling an audience group is simply a matter of executing queries to find users who meet the criteria defined in rules.

Audiences can be compiled at will, or they can be compiled by using a schedule that you create. Any changes to security or distribution group membership, security or distribution member properties, or user profile public properties will not be reflected in the audience until it has been recompiled.

To a point, you can customize the appearance of the portal site by using audiences and permissions. But the real purpose in using audiences is to target information to an individual user based on the audience rules. When planning for audiences, you're basically asking the question, "Who needs to see which information?" and then seeing whether audiences (as opposed to permissions or sites) is the best way to quarantine the information to those users.

Targeting vs. Alerts

Targeting and alerts provide an efficient way of pushing and pulling information. The distinction between the two can be summed up as follows:

- Using alerts, users can choose to be notified about certain types of content.

- Using targeting, administrators or managers can push specific content to users and employees.

Targeting and Access Control

In some cases, you can control who can access specific content through access rights and managing security, but you should be aware of differences between managing security and targeting content and try to use each task as intended:

- **Access control lists (ACLs), rights, and permissions.**   Are used to manage security and to limit access to resources. Users' ACLs are verified each time they navigate and access the content or perform actions on the portal sites.

- **Audience Targeting.** The filtering of content delivery. Targeting content is based on audiences, not on ACLs, and even Active Directory distribution groups can be used for audiences. For example, all users have access to the Links For You Web Part on the home page of a corporate portal site, but the content of the Web Part can vary for different users based on the items that are targeted to different audiences.

Targeting Links to Personal Sites

The SharePoint Portal Server administrator can target links to a user or a group of users that will be shown on the Links For You Web Part on a user's personal site. This feature, called Manage Targeted Links On Personal Site, is available only on the portal site that provides shared services.

Planning Personal Sites

The My Site feature of SharePoint Portal Server 2003 enables each employee in the corporate portal site to create and manage a personal site. Personal sites provide a mechanism for person-to-person collaboration. Each personal site has two interfaces:

- The public interface, which is accessible to all users. The owner of the site decides what information to share.

- The private interface, which contains information available only to the owner of the site.

When shared services are enabled in the corporate portal site, this portal site will host personal sites by default and all personal site links in the other portal sites will redirect users to http://corp/Mysite or the portal site that is selected to host My Sites in a shared services deployment.

Prerequisites for Personal Sites

User profiles must be part of the planning for personal sites. To create a personal site, each user needs a user profile and the required permissions. To enable users to create personal sites, the portal site administrator must add users to the prebuilt member site group of the portal site. Audience groups must be created for targeting links and content.

Web Parts in Personal Sites

Some Web Parts are added to personal sites when they are created. Other Web Parts can be added after the site has been created. Web Parts perform three main functions:

- Viewing and managing information that a user has selected. One example is My Alerts Summary, which shows a list of alerts that a user has subscribed to. Another is My Links Summary, which presents a list of links that a user has added.

- Providing content and links that are targeted to the user by the portal site administrator or others. Examples of this are Links For You and News For You.

- Providing content from the system. An example of this is Your Recent Documents, which shows a list of links to documents that have been recently uploaded or modified by the user.

> **Note**   Users can add Web Parts only to their private view. For consistency, all public views of the personal site look the same unless the user adds subsites and workspaces, which can be customized.

Changes made to the properties of a user profile through the portal site interface will not be reflected in Active Directory.

Disabling Personal Sites

The ability to create personal sites is enabled by default. There is no specific switch to turn it off. Rather, access to creating personal sites is controlled through portal site security. Disabling personal site creation is a matter of setting permissions on the various groups that have access to the portal site.

Planning Windows SharePoint Services Team Sites

The corporate portal site addresses the needs of all employees for accessing corporate-wide information, divisional portal sites provide information for department levels, and Windows SharePoint Services sites offer collaboration sites for workgroups and teams. There are different options for deploying team sites. We recommend (although this is not required) creating a separate virtual server for each SharePoint team site collection and for each divisional portal site. This configuration provides the maximum amount of flexibility for granular database backups because each Windows SharePoint Services Virtual Server has its own content database. This configuration also makes it easier to scale out and host Windows SharePoint Services on its own front-end Web servers. If you aren't required to have a one-to-one relationship between your content databases and your site collections, you can host up to 50,000 site collections in a single virtual server.

For the purpose of distributing the load, multiple team site collections can use their own content database and all site collections can use the server farm configuration database. A separate site collection is assigned for hosting team sites with cross-divisional usage or work groups that do not have a portal site.

This model of site collections deployment provides the highest level of flexibility for scaling out. This model can be migrated to a separate server farm that has its own SQL Server cluster. It also provides a scale-out option for many team sites and allows more resources to be allocated for the corporate portal site, shared services, and the divisional portal site in the existing server farm. Partitioning and associating site collections for divisional portal sites provides the following benefits:

- More flexibility to scale out

- Better load distribution on content databases

- Easier navigation on divisional portal sites and SharePoint sites

- Integration of SharePoint site search scopes within the divisional portal site

- More flexibility with delegation of ownership and administrative tasks

- More flexibility with backup and restore of individual site collections

The drawback of this model is that it requires more memory because it hosts each site collection in a separate virtual server.

Configuring SQL Server 2000 Search on Windows SharePoint Services Sites

You must enable the search feature before your site members can use it. If you want to enable SQL Server 2000 searching, you must install the full-text searching feature for SQL Server 2000, and then enable searching in Windows SharePoint Services.

Note that this is not the same as using the Search Web Part in the portal site. The Search Web Part queries the full-text index produced by MSSearch.exe. MSSearch.exe is a different search engine than SQL Server 2000 Search. Moreover, you should be aware that indexes produced by these two different engines cannot be combined or propagated between portal sites and Windows SharePoint Services sites.

Enabling Searching for SQL Server 2000

To use the search feature with Windows SharePoint Services and SQL Server 2000, you must have full-text searching installed on your SQL Server computer. Full-text searching is usually installed by default, but if it is not installed on your server, you can install it using the SQL Server Setup tools. When configuring the search feature on a Windows SharePoint Services site, a link to searching content on the site's associated portal site automatically appears on the Windows SharePoint Services search results page.

Providing the search feature to team sites allows for a granular search scope. However, keep the following points in mind:

- Windows SharePoint Services team site search is provided by SQL 2000 full-text search. Enabling it creates an additional load on the SQL Server.

- Configuring search on Windows SharePoint Services team sites does not supplant configuring SharePoint Portal Server–based search and indexing. They are two entirely separate search engines.

The following topics discuss other considerations for planning Windows SharePoint Services sites:

- Sites storage management
- Site collection ownership and administration
- Sites archiving and autodeletion

Sites Storage Management

Each division will use SharePoint sites in a different way. Some divisions will create and use more SharePoint sites than others. To support different usage patterns, create a separate quota template for each division (instead of a default quota template), with an estimate of disk storage allocated at the site collections. You should also create a separate quota template for each site collection and adjust the quota based on usage of team sites in each organization.

Quotas give the administrator a high level of control over disk storage and content database size for team sites. When these quotas are reached, an e-mail message will notify the administrator to adjust the size or quota. You can write an SQL query script to increase quotas by using a simple update statement.

Site Collection Ownership and Administration

For each site collection, assign two owners to manage sites and to be responsible for users' requests. Assigning two owners ensures that you do not lose the function when one owner is unavailable.

If a user tries to access a site to which he or she does not have access, the user is prompted for authentication three times. After this, a site access request form is shown, which the user can send to the site owner. Site collection owners also receive any quota or autodeletion notices, and they have site collection administrator privileges.

> **Note**   Making a user a site owner also adds the user to the list of site collection administrators. Removing users from the list of site owners also removes them from the list of site collection administrators, but it doesn't change any other group membership or rights granted to them.

Windows SharePoint Services Sites Archiving and Autodeletion

Sites are usually created for the collaboration of project workgroups or project meetings. In most cases, team sites won't be used after projects are completed. You should plan a policy for archiving and removing such team sites to reclaim the storage consumed by them. The Windows SharePoint Services administration interface provides such a capability. Set it to notify owners of site collections if sites are not used for a period of time. (The default setting is 90 days.) Based on the policy for retaining data in your organization, you can set up the autodeletion feature to delete unused sites. As a best practice, you should archive these SharePoint sites before they are removed because the deletion is permanent and the content will not be retrievable. You can use smigrate.exe to archive the sites and then allow the autodeletion feature to delete the sites.

Planning and Managing Properties

SharePoint Portal Server 2003 displays the properties (or metadata) of items crawled by the content index server. The properties are on the Manage Properties Of Crawled Content page. Based on your business needs, you can manage which properties you want to be shown in the advanced search and trigger alerts when specific properties change. However, having too many properties takes longer and uses more resources when content is crawled.

You can customize the properties of a document based on your needs. For example, you can add a property such as **confidential** to your documents, to distinguish the confidential documents or allow users to search and quickly locate these types of documents. To add the property, add a column to your Document Library view.

When the documents are crawled, the new property is discovered and added to the list of properties that can be viewed through the Manage Properties tool. In this case, confidential is shown under:

```
"urn:schemas-microsoft-com:office:office" namespace.
```

You can configure the confidential property to be included in Advanced Search. You can also use this property to trigger an alert if the object has changed.

Summary

In this chapter, we have discussed some of the planning questions and best practices that should be considered before your SharePoint Products and Technologies implementation. We have discussed how to plan for search and indexing, keywords, Best Bets, user profiles, audiences, personal sites, and Windows SharePoint Services sites.

You absolutely should not skimp on the planning portion of your overall deployment. Furthermore, the quality of your planning will directly affect the quality of your deployment and the ability of the user to have a positive portal site experience.

Chapter 9

Capacity Planning

Capacity planning is one of the most important aspects of enterprise software deployment. Microsoft Office SharePoint Portal Server 2003 is no exception. Without careful planning and architecture design, it is likely your deployment will fail. This chapter will guide you through the steps involved in capacity planning and provide you with information on how to size your expected capacity and plan your topology. It will also cover testing your built topology to ensure it can handle the required traffic.

Topology Planning

This section will cover various topologies supported by SharePoint Portal Server. It will provide hardware requirements, software requirements, and infrastructure requirements for successfully deploying a SharePoint Portal Server solution. Many of the configurations in this chapter were tested using entry-level Dell servers. The medium and large farms were also tested using Hewlett-Packard (HP) ProLiant servers and disk arrays. The performance test results published in this chapter correspond to one of these reference configurations described below.

Common Infrastructure Requirements

SharePoint Portal Server requires several common infrastructure components. Not all of these are required for every topology, but they are covered here because they are common among multiple topologies.

Network Interfaces

In all topologies except single-server ones, ideally each front-end Web server should be equipped with at least two network interface cards (NIC). One will connect the servers to the external network, and one is for communications between the other server farm computers.

The Ethernet switches should be, at minimum, 100-megabit, full-duplex switches. If you anticipate growth beyond a five-server, high-availability medium server farm configuration, you should use gigabit (1000base-T) switches and NICs.

DNS

Each front-end Web server should have access to the corporate **domain name server** (DNS). During the construction and configuration of the servers, you should have the ability to create unique names for the corporate portal site, as well as for each divisional portal site and site collection. Make sure to reserve meaningful names for these portal sites.

Active Directory

A Microsoft Windows 2000 Server or Windows Server 2003 Active Directory domain or Microsoft Windows NT 4 domain is required for a SharePoint Portal Server 2003 deployment. For more information about Active Directory, please refer to the Windows 2003 Resource Kit.

Microsoft SQL Server, SharePoint Portal Server 2003, and Microsoft Windows SharePoint Services require both local and domain accounts for proper operations. For a listing of the required accounts, please see Chapter 12, "Deploying a Medium and Large Server Farm."

Software Licensing

There are three typical SharePoint Portal Server deployments: small, medium, and large farms.

Windows SharePoint Services requires Windows Server 2003 licenses. Windows Server is licensed on a Client Access License (CAL) and Server basis. All employees or employee devices that access a Windows Server 2003 server must have a CAL, and all servers that provide any Windows Server 2003 functionality must have a Server license.

The Windows Server External Connector license enables an unlimited number of nonemployees to access Windows SharePoint Services without any technical limitations or restrictions. (A *nonemployee* is a person who is not an employee, or similar personnel of the company or its affiliates, and is not someone to whom you provide hosted services using the server software.) This license must be obtained for every server that provides services to nonemployees. Partners and customers can be licensed by the External Connector whether or not they are members of the Active Directory.

SharePoint Portal Server 2003 is also licensed on a Client Access (CAL)/Server basis. All employees or employee devices that access a server running SharePoint Portal Server 2003 must have a SharePoint Portal Server 2003 CAL, and all servers that provide any SharePoint Portal Server 2003 functionality must have a SharePoint Portal Server 2003 server license.

The External Connector license enables an unlimited number of nonemployees to access SharePoint Portal Server 2003 without any technical limitations or restrictions. An External Connector license must be obtained for every server that provides services to nonemployees. Partners and customers can be licensed by the External Connector whether or not they are members of the Active Directory.

Because SharePoint Portal Server is built on Windows SharePoint Services, all SharePoint Portal Server users must also have the appropriate Windows Server 2003 licenses. (See the second paragraph in this section.)

SharePoint Portal Server ships with a version of Microsoft SQL Server 2000 Desktop Engine (MSDE). Customers who want to optimize performance and scalability can choose to deploy Microsoft SQL Server 2003 with Service Pack 3 (SP3) or later.

SQL Server is licensed on both a CAL/Server and per-processor basis. CALs are not required for per-processor licenses.

Customers can purchase CALs for all server products on either a per-device or per-user basis. Customers with shared kiosks can choose to license per device. Customers with multiple devices per employee can choose to license per user. Customers can license a combination of per-user and per-device CALs.

The Core CAL provides an efficient, cost-effective way for customers to license their SharePoint and Information Worker server solutions across all desktops with SharePoint Portal Server, Windows Server, Microsoft Exchange Server, and SMS CALs. The Core CAL includes Software Assurance (SA) so that your organization is always licensed for the most current technologies. Core CAL customers can also receive incentive pricing on Microsoft Office Live Communications Server.

SharePoint Products and Technologies Licensing Guidelines

The following licenses are required for an *internal* Windows SharePoint Services deployment:

■ Windows Server 2003 CALs for all employees or employee devices that access the server.

■ Windows Server 2003 Server licenses for each server providing SharePoint Services functionality.

■ Optional: SQL Server 2000 CAL and Server licenses *or* SQL 2000 processor licenses. (See the "SQL Server Licensing Guidelines" section that follows.)

The following licenses are required for an *external* Windows SharePoint Services deployment (extranet, Internet, or both):

■ Windows Server 2003 CALs for all employees or employee devices that access the server.

■ Windows Server 2003 Server licenses for each server providing Windows SharePoint Services functionality.

■ Windows Server 2003 External Connector License for each server that provides Windows SharePoint Services functionality to partners, customers, or both.

■ Optional: SQL Server 2000 processor licenses. SQL Server must be licensed per processor for external use. (See the "SQL Server Licensing Guidelines" section that follows.)

The following licenses are required for an internal SharePoint Portal Server 2003 deployment (intranet only):

■ Windows Server 2003 CALs for all employees or employee devices.

■ Windows Server 2003 Server licenses for each server providing either SharePoint Portal Server or Windows SharePoint Services functionality.

■ SharePoint Portal Server 2003 CALs for all employees or employee devices.

■ SharePoint Portal Server 2003 Server licenses for each server providing SharePoint Portal Server functionality.

■ Optional: SQL Server 2000 CAL and Server licenses *or* SQL 2000 processor licenses. (See the "SQL Server Licensing Guidelines" section that follows.)

The following licenses are required for an external SharePoint Portal Server 2003 deployment (extranet, Internet, or both):

- Windows Server 2003 CALs for all employees or employee devices.

- Windows Server 2003 Server licenses for each server providing either Share-Point Portal Server or Windows SharePoint Services functionality.

- Windows Server 2003 External Connector License for each server that provides either Windows SharePoint Services or SharePoint Portal Server functionality to partners, customers, or both.

- SharePoint Portal Server 2003 CALs for all employees or employee devices.

- SharePoint Portal Server 2003 Server Licenses for each server providing Share-Point Portal Server functionality.

- SharePoint Portal Server External Connector License for each server that provides Windows SharePoint Services functionality to partners, customers, or both.

- Optional: SQL Server 2000 processor licenses. SQL Server must be licensed per processor for external use. (See the "SQL Server Licensing Guidelines" section that follows.)

SQL Server Licensing Guidelines

The correct SQL Server licensing option depends on the type of SharePoint Products and Technologies deployment and current SQL Server license availability, as outlined in the following list:

- SQL Server 2000 is not required. Windows SharePoint Services ships with Microsoft SQL Server 2000 Desktop Engine (Windows) (WMSDE), which does not have the 2-gigabyte (GB) storage limit of MSDE. SharePoint Portal Server ships with MSDE. Customers can choose to deploy SQL Server 2000 for optimal performance and scalability.

- If your customer already owns SQL Server 2000 CALs and plans an internal SharePoint Products and Technologies deployment only, it might be more cost-effective to purchase only the required number of additional SQL Server 2000 Server licenses than to purchase per-processor licenses.

- If your customer does *not* already own SQL Server CALs and plans an *internal* SharePoint Products and Technologies deployment, they should then calculate and compare the cost of CAL/Server vs. per-processor licensing for their specific deployment.

- If your customer plans an *external* SharePoint Products and Technologies deployment, they must license SQL Server on a per-processor basis, regardless of whether or not their employees or employee devices are licensed with SQL Server CALs. Because SQL Server has dual licensing, it does not have an External Connector license for nonemployees.

Deploying a Single Server with MSDE

A single-server deployment with MSDE is the smallest and least scalable option for a SharePoint Portal Server solution because it is limited to five concurrent jobs and has a 2-GB storage limitation. This deployment type is recommended for testing and development as well as for small organizations that anticipate light usage of their corporate intranet. This is the least costly deployment option.

Hardware Recommendations

The reference configuration for a single server with MSDE deployment used throughout the chapter is:

- 1 x 2.4-gigahertz (GHz) Pentium-4 processor
- 1-GB main memory expandable to 4 GB
- Embedded ATA-100 IDE controller
- 2 x 40-GB IDE ATA-100 disks
- Embedded 10/100/1000-GB Ethernet interface card (NIC)

Deploying a Single Server Using SQL

A single-server deployment with SQL Server is a step above a single server with MSDE. Running SQL Server 2000 rather than MSDE provides additional scalability because MSDE can support only five concurrent jobs and a 2-GB database limit, while SQL Server does not have this restriction. This deployment type is recommended for small organizations with moderate usage of their corporate intranet or organizations and medium-sized organizations (less than 10,000 employees) with light usage of the corporate intranet.

Hardware Recommendations

The reference configuration for a single server with SQL deployment used throughout this chapter is:

- 1 x 2.4-GHz Pentium-4 processor
- 1-GB main memory expandable to 4 GB
- Embedded ATA-100 IDE controller
- 2 x 40-GB IDE ATA-100 disks
- Embedded 10/100/1000-GB Ethernet interface card (NIC)

Small Server Farm

A small server farm is a step above a single server with SQL Server. In this scenario, there are two servers in the farm—one runs the SharePoint Portal Server components, and the other runs SQL Server 2000. Having SQL Server on a separate system frees up some resources from the server running SharePoint Portal Server, allowing it to support more users. Also, it is often used in organizations where there is an existing SQL Server database or where administrative boundaries require certain administrators to manage SQL Server systems and other administrators to manage the intranet. Figure 9-1 depicts a small server farm topology infrastructure.

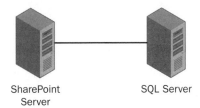

SharePoint   SQL Server
Server

Figure 9-1   Small server farm topology infrastructure

Hardware Recommendations

The reference configuration for a small server farm deployment used throughout the chapter are given in the following paragraphs.

For a server running SharePoint Portal Server, the following configuration was used:

- 1 x 2.4-GHz Pentium-4 processor

- 1-GB main memory expandable to 4 GB

- Embedded ATA-100 IDE controller

- 2 x 40-GB IDE ATA-100 disks

- Embedded 10/100/1000-GB Ethernet interface card (NIC)

    For SQL Server, the following configuration was used:

- 1 x 2.4-GHz Pentium-4 processor

- 1-GB main memory expandable to 4 GB

- Embedded ATA-100 IDE controller

- 2 x 40-GB IDE ATA-100 disks

- Embedded 10/100/1000-GB Ethernet interface card (NIC)

Load-Balanced Medium Server Farm

A load-balanced medium server farm is the first topology where SharePoint Portal Server really starts to scale out. In this scenario, there are four servers: two load-balanced front-end servers running the Web and search components, a dedicated indexing server, and a server running SQL Server. This topology performs well and can support many more users than a small server farm, but there is still no high-availability. This scenario would be used by small organizations with very heavy usage of their portal site or organizations with up to 50,000 users who have light to moderate usage of their intranet. Figure 9-2 depicts a load-balanced medium server farm topology infrastructure.

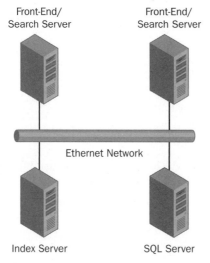

Front-End/   Front-End/
Search Server   Search Server

Ethernet Network

Index Server   SQL Server

Figure 9-2   Load-balanced medium server farm topology infrastructure

Hardware Recommendations

The reference configuration for a load-balanced medium server farm deployment used throughout the chapter are given in the following paragraphs.

For a combination of a front-end Web server with a search server (2 Servers), the following configuration was used:

- 1 x 2.4-GHz Pentium-4 processor
- 1-GB main memory expandable to 4 GB
- Embedded ATA-100 IDE controller
- 2 x 40-GB IDE ATA-100 disks
- Embedded 10/100/1000-GB Ethernet interface card (NIC)

For SQL Server, the following configuration was used:

- 1 x 2.4-GHz Pentium-4 processor
- 1-GB main memory expandable to 4 GB

- Embedded ATA-100 IDE controller

- 2 x 40-GB IDE ATA-100 disks

- Embedded 10/100/1000-GB Ethernet interface card (NIC)

For a server used as an index management and job server (1 server), the following configuration was used:

- 1 x 2.4-GHz Pentium-4 processor

- 1-GB main memory expandable to 4 GB

- Embedded ATA-100 IDE controller

- 2 x 40-GB IDE ATA-100 disks

- Embedded 10/100/1000-GB Ethernet interface card (NIC)

Highly Available Medium Server Farm with SQL Cluster

A highly available medium server farm is just like a load-balanced medium server farm, except that with a highly available medium server farm there is a SQL Cluster. The SQL Cluster adds the high availability because any server in this topology can fail and users will still be able to use their portal sites. In this scenario, there are five servers: two load-balanced front-end servers running the Web and search components, a dedicated indexing server, and two servers running SQL Server in an active/passive cluster. The index server is susceptible to failure, but even if it goes down, the farm will still be able to serve pages. Users just will not be able to get notifications and content indexes will not get updated until the server comes back online. Figure 9-3 depicts a load-balanced medium server farm topology infrastructure.

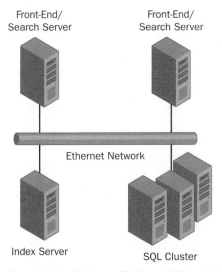

Figure 9-3 Highly available medium server farm topology infrastructure

Hardware Recommendations

The reference configurations for front-end Web and search servers in the server farm are given in the following paragraphs.

For a combination of a front-end Web server with a search server (2 servers), you following configuration was used:

- 2 x 2.8-GHz Xeon processors with 512-kilobyte (KB) Cache
- ServerWorks GC-LE chipset, supporting a 400-megahertz (MHz) FSB
- 2-GB main memory expandable to 6 GB
- Embedded Wide Ultra3 Smart Array 5i RAID controller
- 4 x 18.2-GB Ultra3 SCSI disks
- 2x embedded BCM5703 10/100/1000-GB Ethernet network interface card (NIC) ports
- Redundant power supply and fan

For a server used as an index management and job server (1 server), the following configuration was used:

- 2 x 2.8-GHz Xeon processors with 512-KB CacheServerWorks GC-LE chipset, supporting a 400-MHz FSB
- 2-GB main memory expandable to 6 GB
- Embedded Wide Ultra3 Smart Array 5i RAID controller
- 6 x 36.4-GB Ultra320 SCSI disks
- 2x embedded BCM5703 10/100/1000-GB Ethernet NIC ports
- Redundant power supply and fan

For a SQL Server–based database server (active/passive; 2 servers), the following configuration was used:

- 4 x 2.8-GHz Xeon processors with 512-KB CacheServerWorks GC-LE chipset, supporting a 400-MHz FSB
- 2-GB main memory expandable to 6 GB
- Embedded Wide Ultra3 Smart Array 5i RAID controller
- Smart Array 5300 controller
- 4 x 18.2-GB Ultra3 SCSI disks
- 14 x 72.8-GB Ultra320 SCSI disks with a SCSI-connected clustered storage subsystem (which supports up to 14 disks with HP Smart Array cluster storage)
- 2x NC3163 Fast Ethernet ports
- Redundant power supply and fan

Minimum Large Server Farm with a SQL Cluster

The minimum large server farm with a SQL cluster is the step above a highly available medium server farm. A minimum large server farm does not actually need a SQL cluster to be supported, but in practice, almost every large server farm will have a SQL cluster for high availability. This scenario has seven servers: two load-balanced front-end Web servers, two dedicated search servers, one dedicated indexing server, and two systems running SQL servers acting as an active/passive cluster. A minimum large server farm is mainly used by large organizations or medium-sized organizations with heavy portal site usage. The minimum large server farm configuration is really useful over the high availability medium server farm when there is a lot of searching in the portal site. Figure 9-4 depicts a minimum large server farm with a SQL cluster topology infrastructure.

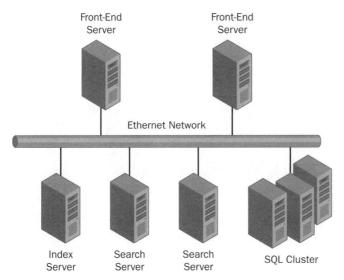

Figure 9-4   Minimum large server farm with SQL cluster topology infrastructure

Hardware Recommendations

The reference configurations for front-end and search servers in the minimum large server farm with SQL Cluster are:

For dedicated front-end Web servers (2 servers), the following configuration was used:

- 2 x 2.8-GHz Xeon processors with 512-KB CacheServerWorks GC-LE chipset, supporting a 400-MHz FSB

- 2-GB main memory expandable to 6 GB

- Embedded Wide Ultra3 Smart Array 5i RAID controller

- 4 x 18.2-GB Ultra3 SCSI disks

- 2x embedded BCM5703 10/100/1000-GB Ethernet NIC ports

- Redundant power supply and fan

For a server used as an index management and job server (1 server), the following configuration was used:

- 2 x 2.8-GHz Xeon processors with 512-KB CacheServerWorks GC-LE chipset, supporting a 400-MHz FSB

- 2-GB main memory expandable to 6 GB

- Embedded Wide Ultra3 Smart Array 5i controller

- 6 x 36.4-GB Ultra320 SCSI disks

- 2x embedded BCM5703 10/100/1000-GB Ethernet NIC ports

- Redundant power supply and fan

For dedicated search servers (2 servers), the following configuration was used:

- 2 x 2.8-GHz Xeon processors with 512-KB CacheServerWorks GC-LE chipset, supporting a 400-MHz FSB

- 2-GB main memory expandable to 6 GB

- Embedded Wide Ultra3 Smart Array 5i controller

- 6 x 36.4-GB Ultra320 SCSI disks

- 2x embedded BCM5703 10/100/1000-GB Ethernet NIC ports

- Redundant power supply and fan

For SQL Server–based database servers (active/passive; 2 servers), following configuration was used:

- 4 x 2.0-GHz XEON

- 2-GB main memory expandable to 32-GB Advanced ECC

- Embedded Wide Ultra3 Smart Array 5i Plus controller

- KGPSA-xx, PCI Fibre Channel HBA

- 4 x 18.2-GB Ultra3 SCSI disks

- HP StorageWorks modular SAN array (msa1000) with 2-GB Fibre Channel storage

- 28 x 72.8-GB Ultra3 SCSI disks (which supports up to 42 disks)

- 1x embedded NC7770 10/100/1000-GB Ethernet NIC ports

- Redundant power supply and fan

Windows SharePoint Services Server Farm (Optional)

For front-end Web servers (2 servers), the following configuration was used:

- 2 x 2.8-GHz Xeon processors with 512-KB CacheServerWorks GC-LE chipset, supporting a 400-MHz FSB

- 2-GB main memory expandable to 6 GB

- Embedded Wide Ultra3 Smart Array 5i RAID controller

- 4 x 18.2-GB Ultra3 SCSI disks

- 2x embedded BCM5703 10/100/1000-GB Ethernet NIC ports

- Redundant power supply and fan

Maximum Large Server Farm with a SQL Cluster

Large server farms scale out well. The maximum large server farm with SQL cluster is the largest single farm deployment you can have. You can scale a large farm to any configuration between the minimum large server farm and the maximum larger server farm, but because of space constraints, only the minimum and maximum configurations are presented in this. For more information on large farm scaling, please see Chapter 11.

The maximum supported large server farm with a SQL cluster consists of eighteen servers: eight load-balanced front-end Web servers, four search servers, four indexing management servers, and two systems running SQL servers acting as an active/passive cluster. Additionally, a nineteenth server running the optional document management components can be used. The maximum large server farm with SQL cluster is a highly available SharePoint Portal Server solution supporting large organizations with moderate to heavy usage. It provides protection from multiple points of failure. If you need to scale out beyond the maximum large server farm environment, you will need to use multiple farms and use inter-farm shared services to connect the farms. Inter-farm shared services is described in Chapter 14, "Shared Services."

This type of farm environment was not tested for this chapter, so no specific hardware recommendations are provided. If you are building a maximum large server environment, you should contact your hardware vendor, Microsoft representative, or both to discuss hardware recommendations.

Logical Deployment Considerations

The following are considerations for deploying SharePoint Portal Server 2003 in an organization:

- **A corporate portal site for all employees.** This is a required component of all SharePoint Portal Server 2003 installations. This portal site will usually use Windows Shared Services if multiple portal sites are present but not required. See Chapter 14 for more information on Shared Services.

- **Divisional portal sites for each division or project.** Additional portal sites can be created for divisions or important projects within the organization. Additional portal sites are not required, but medium and large deployments will usually have many portal sites.

- **Team site collection.** The team site collection will encompass teams and topics that are too small to warrant their own portal site. Team site collections can be hosted in the corporate portal site or its respective divisional portal site. A cross-corporate site collection can also be created to facilitate team sites that do not easily fall into a specific divisional portal site. The cross-corporate site collection is almost always stored in the corporate portal site.

- **A My Site for each employee.** My Sites are personal sites for each user. My Sites are optional in a portal site deployment. Each My Site is a SharePoint site with a special template applied. The user who owns the My Site will have full control of the site and can customize it as she wants. Architecturally, each My Site is considered a single Site collection.

- **Security.** Security considerations must be discussed and determined. By default, authenticated users will have reader access to everything in the portal site. All domain users will be authenticated users, therefore all users will have reader access to everything until the permissions are changed. Security should be planned before deploying SharePoint Portal Server 2003. Please refer to Chapter 24, "Information Security Policies for SharePoint Products and Technologies," for additional information on security practices.

Planning Services and User Accounts

There are two groups of accounts to plan for:

- Services accounts, which are used to run services such as SQL Server and SharePoint Portal Server

- User accounts, such as search, indexing, application pools, and administrative accounts

Planning Services Accounts

Services accounts are access accounts for SQL Server and SharePoint Portal Server services. The credentials for these services should not be used as user credentials. The following topics provide detailed information about the purpose of these accounts and the credentials that are assigned to them.

SQL Server Services Accounts

If you are using the default instance of a SQL Server 2000 installation, there are two services that need an account:

- MSSQLSERVER
- SQLSERVERAGENT

These should be created as domain accounts called *domain\spssql* with the SQL System Administrator database role. This account can be any domain user account, but it is not required to have special domain permissions.

If you are not using the default instance, these services will be shown as:

- MSSQL$InstanceName
- SQLAgent$InstanceName

Be sure to make that account a member of the local administrator group of each server on which SQL Server is installed.

SharePoint Portal Server Services Accounts

The SharePoint Portal Server services are as follows:

- **Microsoft SharePointPS Search (SharePointPSSearch).** Provides indexing and searching over the portal site and external content
- **Microsoft SharePoint Portal Administration (SPSAdmin).** Enables the server to administer SharePoint Portal Server services
- **Microsoft SharePoint Portal Alert (SPSAlert).** Schedules and sends alerts and alert results to users on one or more servers running SharePoint Portal Server
- **Microsoft SharePoint Timer (SPTimer).** Sends notifications and performs scheduled tasks for Windows SharePoint Services
- **Microsoft Single Sign-On (SSOSrv).** Provides single sign-on services for line-of-business applications. This service is not used in this solution

Use a single domain account—named *domain\spssql*—for these SharePoint Portal Server services. It is easier from an administrative standpoint to use the same account for these SharePoint Portal Server services and the SQL Server services. However, you can choose to use a different account for SharePoint Portal Server services and SQL Server services if you have different groups administering SQL Server and SharePoint Portal Server farms. Be sure to make that account a member of the local administrator group of each computer running SharePoint Portal Server. You must also add this domain account to the SharePoint Portal Server administrators group.

Planning User Accounts

You need two user accounts:

- Configuration database administration account
- Default content access account

The following topics describe these accounts.

Configuration Database Administration Account

The configuration database administration account is the user name and password that SharePoint Portal Server uses when connecting to the configuration database or when propagating full-text indexes from index management servers to search servers. This account must have administrator rights on both the index management server and the search server.

Default Content Access Account

This account is used as the default account for crawling content sources defined for a content index. For internal content, such as portal sites and site directories, you can use specific access accounts through exclude and include rules. This account should be a member of the SharePoint Portal Server administrators group so that it can access and crawl all content sources and their properties. In this case, the account uses Windows Integrated Authentication for accessing content by default. If this method of authentication fails, it uses Basic Authentication unless you have explicitly disabled Basic Authentication access.

Planning the Corporate Portal Site

The corporate portal site is the entry point from which all employees can get the latest corporate-wide information. Usually the corporate portal site is a parent portal site providing shared services, but this is not always the case. Sometimes a SharePoint Portal Server deployment includes only one portal site, which is the corporate portal site. In other cases, there are multiple portal sites, but they don't share services with the corporate portal site. However, the majority of SharePoint Portal Server deployments will have a corporate portal site providing shared servers to the divisional portal sites. A corporate portal site is required for a SharePoint Portal Server deployment.

When planning the corporate portal site, the following aspects need to be considered:

- Shared services, including search, user profiles, audiences, and alerts
- Personal sites
- Site groups/roles, permissions/rights
- Areas (topics)
- News, events, and announcements
- Keywords and Best Bets
- SharePoint sites

Each of these is covered briefly later in this chapter and will be covered in full detail in later chapters.

Planning Additional Portals

Additional portal site content is focused on the employees involved with a specific topic, usually a division or project. For example, employees in a human resources (HR) department will access their divisional portal site to find out about news, events, announcements, and documents related to HR. In organizations with many large ongoing projects, additional portal sites can be provisioned for these projects rather than for divisions. For example, a company that manufacturers airplanes can have a portal site for each different type of plane it manufacturers in addition to or instead of divisional portal sites. Typically, employees will access their divisional or project portal site more often than the corporate portal site. This arrangement saves time and keeps each employee more focused on the type of information they need instead of requiring them to search it out on the corporate portal site. In that scenario, each divisional or project portal site should share the search services of the corporate portal site, allowing users to search the enterprise from their divisional portal site.

Determining whether to use Shared Services is also important when planning divisional portal sites. Not using shared services can have a significant impact on farm resources, especially memory.

When planning a divisional or project portal site, consider the following areas:

- Team sites
- Associated divisional team sites to divisional portal sites
- Site groups/roles, permissions/rights

- Search scopes

- Areas (topics)

- News, events, and announcements

- Document libraries

- Keywords and Best Bets

Each of these is covered briefly later in this chapter and will be covered in full detail in later chapters.

Knowing when to create a new portal site versus creating a new site collection can be difficult. Here are some guidelines to help you make your decision:

- Create new site collections when collaboration is your primary need and you can use existing portal sites to meet your taxonomy needs.

- Create new areas in existing portal sites if you need to present static information and you don't need to create a new taxonomy.

- Create new portal sites if you need to implement a new taxonomy or present such a volume of static information that one or a few areas in existing portal sites will not be sufficient.

- Create a new portal site with new associated site collections if you need to implement the previous three bullet points in concert with each other.

Planning Roles, Groups, and Rights

Creating security groups in Active Directory instead of adding individual users allows you to manage user rights just by adding or removing users from groups, rather than assigning the same rights to many users individually. Based on your business need, you can use default site groups, which provide rights based on the type of actions each group can do. The default site groups include the following:

- **Reader.**   Has read-only access to the website

- **Contributor.**   Can add content to existing document libraries and lists

- **Web Designer.**   Can create lists and document libraries and customize pages in the website

- **Administrator.**   Has full control of the website

- **Content Manager.**   Can create and manage areas, lists, libraries, and sites

- **Member.**   Can view and personalize portal site content and create sites

> **More Info** You can also define your own custom roles and site groups with different rights. For more information, it is strongly recommended that you read Chapter 24 to thoroughly understand security before deploying Share-Point Portal Server.

You should plan for the following roles and groups:

- **Central administrator group (*domain\CentralAdminGroup*).** Responsible for administration of the entire server farm, server farm topology, and virtual websites. This group must be a member of the SharePoint Portal Server administrators group and of the SQL Server system administrators group.

> **Note** You can register only one domain group as the SharePoint Portal Server administrators group. Therefore, if you want to include other members, you must add them using the user and group management tools for your domain.

- **Corporate administrator group (*domain\CorpAdminGroup*).** Responsible for managing site groups, managing list permissions, creating sites, creating portal sites, and viewing usage analysis data. The corporate administrator group cannot be customized or deleted, and there must always be at least one member of this group. Members of this group always have access to, or can grant themselves access to, any item in the website. This group needs to be a member of Domain Admins to import user profiles from Active Directory.

- **Managing and updating news group.** Based on your company business rules and security policies, you might need to create a group that only manages and updates the company news. In this case, be sure to remove inheritance permissions by selecting unique permissions. This will remove site-level permissions and provide news update rights only to the assigned group. For this accelerator, you need to create groups for the corporate portal site news area and also for each divisional news area.

- **Managing and updating topics content group.** Based on your company business rules and security policies, you might need to create a group for each topic area and assign separate groups for managing each topic or subtopic area in the corporate and divisional portal sites. In this case, you need to create groups that can update and upload documents to each topic area.

Planning Search

This section describes the components of the SharePoint Portal Server search functionality. It provides guidelines on planning a customized version of each search component for your solution.

Overview of Search Functionality

There are four components that contribute to the SharePoint Portal Server search functionality:

- Content sources
- Content indexes
- Source groups
- Search scopes

For an in-depth discussion of each of these components, please refer to Chapter 21, "The Architecture of the Gatherer," and Chapter 22, "Managing External Content in Microsoft Office SharePoint Portal Server 2003." This chapter will discuss the planning requirements for content indexes only.

Planning Content Indexes

SharePoint Portal Server 2003 comes with two content indexes—Portal_Content and Non_Portal_Content. You can create additional content indexes as well; however, keep in mind that each search query has to be run on each index and the results must be aggregated before they are returned to the user. The result is that the more indexes you have, the longer search results take to generate.

> **Note**   Advanced search administration mode should be enabled so that you can create and manage additional indexes. In addition, when you create content sources, you can specify the index in which the content source will appear, and you can specify the source group.

When planning content indexes, consider the following factors:

- **Number of documents.**   If the number of documents is very large, you should consider breaking the content sources into many content sources with smaller scopes to make the size of the indexes more manageable. This is important because the index catalogs are copied across the network. Copying smaller files at different times can ease the network load, but it is recommended that you have a maximum of four content indexes. Searching will perform about the same with many smaller files as with one very large file.

- **Security.** Default content access is used as credentials for crawling all content sources. For content sources outside of your organization, consider using an account that has read-only access, such as the anonymous account. (See SharePoint Portal Server 2003 product documentation for information on using site and path rules.) The account should have appropriate access for other internal resources—such as site directories, portal site contents, and shared folders—that are part of the personal site. For shared folders, you should use an access account that is a member of the SharePoint Portal Server administrators group. This level of access allows for crawling all types of content and their properties in portals and site directories. To provide different accounts for crawling content, you must use include and exclude rules. You should add rules and include paths that you want to be crawled with different access accounts. These rules are applied to all content sources bound to a content index that creates additional crawling. To avoid duplicate or additional crawling, you should assign rules only to specific content sources. For details on how to build content indexes and content sources, see Chapter 21.

- **Scheduling.** Creating separate content indexes allows more flexible scheduling based on the nature of contents in each content source. Some content sources change quickly and need more updates, while other content sources are less volatile and require fewer updates.

- **Propagation.** Having smaller content indexes provides faster propagation of content indexes to search servers. However, there is a drawback: When a user initiates a search, the search engine has to run that query against each index and then aggregate the results. The more indexes that you have, the longer it takes.

- **Backup and restore.** Smaller content indexes also provide more flexibility when backing up and restoring. For more information about backing up and restoring content indexes, see Chapter 28, "Disaster Recovery in SharePoint Products and Technologies."

You should create content indexes for the corporate portal site, each divisional portal site, and any set of content sources that have a significant number of documents. For example, when crawling a large Internet site such as *www.microsoft.com*, it would be wise to have a separate content index for management purposes.

> **Note** SharePoint Portal Server does not allow spaces in content index names. Spaces are supported in source group names. Also, note that Non_Portal_Content and Portal_Content exist by default.

Updating Content Indexes

The four methods for updating content indexes are as follows:

- Full

- Incremental

- Incremental (inclusive)

- Adaptive

The method used to update the index can have a significant effect on performance. These update methods are discussed in Chapter 21.

Propagating Content Indexes

Propagation happens automatically at the end of every successful update (or crawl). The following should be taken into consideration when planning content indexes:

- The destination search server must be on a trusted domain.

- For every index to be propagated, there must be twice the size of the index in free space on the destination search server.

> **Note** Team sites under a SharePoint Portal Server portal site are crawled normally; however, these sites can be searched only from the portal site itself, not at the team-site level. To search from a team site, SQL Full Text indexing must be enabled. For information on how to enable SQL Full Text indexing, please refer to the SQL Server documentation.

Planning Alerts

Alerts provide notification when information of interest is added or updated on the portal site and associated content sources. You can define areas of interest and identify how and when you want to be notified. You can add an alert to track new matches to a search query, changes to content in an area, or a new site added to the Site Directory.

When configuring alerts, keep in mind that alerts for SharePoint Portal Server 2003 and Windows SharePoint Services are managed separately. The three key differences between SharePoint Portal Server alerts and Windows SharePoint Services alerts are as follows:

- SharePoint Portal Server alerts are managed by the user on the My Alerts page, which lives on the user's My Site. Windows SharePoint Services alerts are managed through the Manage My Alerts link on the Site Settings page of each team site.

- SharePoint Portal Server alert notifications can be delivered to the user's e-mail inbox, to the user's My Alerts Summary Web Part on the My Site, or to both. Windows SharePoint Services alert notifications can be delivered only through e-mail.

- SharePoint Portal Server users can set alerts on more items than Windows SharePoint Services users can.

- Search alerts consume 2 KB and the other types consume .5 KB of memory on the search process.

SharePoint Portal Server can track alerts for the following items:

- Search queries
- Documents and listings
- Areas
- News listings
- Sites added to the site directory
- SharePoint lists and libraries
- List items
- Portal site users

Windows SharePoint Services can track alerts on the following items within a site:

- Lists
- List items
- Document libraries
- Documents

When shared services are enabled at the corporate level, management of alert settings is possible only through the Corporate Portal Site Settings interface. Through this interface, you can set quotas for alerts per user and for all portal sites. You can define and adjust the default numbers based on the following items:

- The number of users
- How many alerts each user can have
- How many alert results you want to be returned per alert

You can adjust the defaults based on the number of users and the alerts-per-user setting to determine the maximum settings for alerts at the site level. For example, if your company has 20,000 users and you are setting a limit of ten search alerts per user and 20 other alerts per user, your maximum number of alerts for *all portal sites* is as follows:

20,000 x 10 = 200,000 is the maximum number of search alerts for all sites

20,000 x 20 = 400,000 is the maximum number of other alerts for all sites

Because all divisional portal sites consume shared services provided by the corporate portal site, these are maximum numbers allowed for all divisional portal sites and the corporate portal site combined. They are not per site.

> **Note**   Alerts on portal sites and Windows SharePoint Services team sites are not consolidated.

Planning User Profiles

User profiles have several uses, including the following ones:

- Searching for and connecting with people within your organization
- Generating a My Site in the portal site for individual users
- Providing better search results
- Targeting content to audiences

Importing User Profiles

You can import user profile information directly from Active Directory or enter it manually. You can also customize the properties of the user profile to meet the needs of your organization or to map it to Active Directory properties.

If you have already invested in an infrastructure based on Active Directory or any Lightweight Directory Access Protocol (LDAP)–compliant directory, you can import user information stored in the directories. With Active Directory, use Import Profile to import the user information to SharePoint Portal Server. Importing user profiles requires a domain account. To use the incremental import feature from Active Directory on a Windows Server 2000–based computer, a domain administrator account is required.

You can import user profiles from the same domain that SharePoint Portal Server is installed on or from any trusted domain (although this is not tested in this chapter). You can also configure and customize your connection to Active Directory to import users based on specific criteria as a script in an LDAP query—for example, all users who belong to a specific **organizational unit** (OU) or only users whose e-mail address property is not empty.

If you are using other platforms, you can add users manually. You can add more properties to the user profile if you need to extend the information that you want to be displayed about a user. However, any such updates will not be propagated, nor will they update Active Directory.

Updating User Profiles

After the first import from the directory, you can schedule incremental updates based on the frequency of users being added to Active Directory. In most cases, scheduling incremental updates daily and full updates weekly is sufficient.

> **Note** Removing a user from Active Directory and fully updating the user profile does not remove a user profile from the profile database. Nevertheless, a user who is removed from Active Directory is not able to access the SharePoint Portal Server because users are authenticated through Internet Information Services (IIS), which authenticates users through Active Directory.

Planning Audiences

Audiences allow organizations to target content to users based on their job or task, as defined by their membership in a Windows Server 2003 security group, distribution list, organizational reporting structure, or the public properties in their user profiles.

Audience Rules

Audiences are created based on a set of rules that you define. Definitions are based on the following items:

- Windows security group, distribution list, or organizational hierarchy
- User profile public property
- Organizational hierarchy
- Distribution lists

A rule is a simple query based on properties of user profiles or membership of users in security groups and distribution groups. If you have already created security groups or distribution groups in Active Directory, you can create audiences based on those groups. For example, you can define a rule for an audience group that reports to or under a specific manager (*domain\managerUserName*). You can also create an audience that belongs to a specific department if you have assigned a value to the Department field of user profiles.

Compiling Audiences

After you create or make changes to an audience, you must compile it for use. Compiling an audience group is simply a matter of executing queries to find users who meet the criteria defined in rules.

Audiences can be compiled at will, or they can be compiled by using a schedule that you create. Any changes to security or distribution group membership, security or distribution member properties, or user profile public properties will not be reflected in the audience until it has been recompiled.

Compiling audiences can be expensive in terms of processor time as well as disk I/O, especially if the audience membership query is complex. You should schedule audiences to be compiled at a time when the server farm and Active Directory are least busy, probably at night. Because audiences are built based on User Profiles, you should also schedule User Imports to occur before audience compilation. For large groups of audience compilation and complex audience memberships, there will be a hit on both the processor of the farm servers as well as Domain Controllers because SharePoint Portal Server might query the Active Directory to compile the audiences.

Planning for Growth

This section provides information to help design a deployment that meets your needs. The chapter describes performance considerations and testing, sizing guidelines, and strategies for scaling the design.

This section discusses the following items:

- How to estimate system requirements

- Choosing the appropriate farm solution for your scenario

- How and when to scale the solution

- Performance considerations

- Configuration of test systems

- Sizing recommendations

Estimating System Requirements

This section helps you to estimate your system requirements so that you can choose the appropriate hardware and farm deployment. SharePoint Portal Server 2003 can be configured in a number of ways and can scale to suit specific needs, such as general-purpose intranet, heavy search usage, or heavy team usage and collaboration. To choose the appropriate design, the following needs must be considered:

- Understand the users' work patterns and the specific tasks they perform.

- Obtain or estimate the size of the entire collection of documents that both SharePoint Portal Server 2003 and Windows SharePoint Services will store, including document versions, categories, and folders.

- Estimate the internal and external site content to be crawled and indexed.

Historical access information from Web logs and third-party monitoring tools can be used to determine current throughput rates and specific usage patterns if there is a current intranet. However, if no intranet exists, you must make an estimate based on a prediction as to what is required to support the overall business need.

End users see a portal site, viewing it either through a Web browser interface or, in some cases, the Microsoft Office System client. It is inappropriate to size the design based solely on the number of users. Base the system size and configuration on the type of transactions (or portal site functions) and on the frequency of transactions. The "transaction arrival rate" is called the *throughput rate*.

In this section, you will estimate the following factors:

- Peak throughput for each projected key portal and site type

- Current and future storage needs

Estimating Peak Throughput

When users browse intranets or the Internet, search for files, check out documents, or select from a list of choices, this usually causes the display of a new page of information. The more complex functions, such as document management, are especially resource-intensive and can initiate the display of multiple pages of information. In general, one user function is approximately equivalent to the display of one new HTTP page on the user's desktop. Therefore, throughput measurement is based on the premise that the number of HTTP pages per second roughly equates to the number of calculated operations per second.

To calculate the peak throughput rates your SharePoint Portal Server farm must support, you must obtain specific business-related sizing metrics. These sizing metrics differ depending on the type of portal site. For example, the typical user will access the corporate portal site much less frequently than he will access his divisional portal site or Windows SharePoint Services sites.

The following list provides key sizing metrics, along with typical values as a guideline:

- **Number of users.**   The number of potential users with access to the portal site.

- **Percent of active users per day.**   The percentage of the users who might access the portal site during the day. This is typically between 10 percent and 50 percent. This is an important number and one that is usually a point of contention. Most customers like to think that each user hits the corporate or divisional portal site each day, but your experience might prove otherwise.

- **Operations per user per day.**   Accesses to the portal site Home page, searches, category browses, document retrievals, media viewing, and so on. Depending on the user's role (whether it is reader, author, reviewer, or contributor), this number will usually range between 1 and 10 operations per day.

- **Hours per day.**   Hours in the business day. Portal site access can cross time zones, so 10 hours per day might be a typical number for a company spanning the United States.

- **Peak factor.**   A ratio of how much the peak usage exceeds the average usage. You should size the systems for peak usage so that performance does not degrade during busy periods. A typical ratio is 5 to 1.

Note   Peak factor is an approximate number that estimates the ratio of the peak portal site throughput to its average throughput. This number typically ranges from 1 to 5.

Next, using the following formula and the quantitative metrics of each portal site's usage characteristics, you will estimate the required portal peak throughput, in operations per second.

$$\frac{\text{Number of users} \times \text{Percent of active users per day} \times \text{Number of operations per active user per day} \times \text{Peak factor}}{360{,}000 \times \text{Number of hours per day}}$$

The constant 360,000 is derived from the following equation:

100 (percent conversion) × 60 (minutes per hour) × 60 (seconds per minute)

Break down the operations per active user per day by the type of site and related functions, such as the following ones:

- Corporate portal site access

- Divisional portal site access

- Windows SharePoint Services site usage

- My Site usage

The following example illustrates how to estimate required throughput for a divisional portal site component of the total workload. Table 9-1 shows sample characteristics representing a divisional portal site supporting approximately 10,000 users. This is a reasonably diverse workforce group, using a mix of common portal site functions and a small percentage of complex functions. Most users typically access the site through simple activities such as locating information by browsing categories, searching for documents that match their needs, or reading divisional news or announcements on the Home page.

Note Document collaboration functions (including document check-in and document upload) are weighted differently than other functions. These more complex activities take several steps to accomplish. Therefore, they should be rated as three times as intense as other functions.

Table 9-1   Characteristics Representing a Divisional Portal Site

Characteristic	Value
Number of potential users	10,000
Percent of active users per day	80
Number of common operations per active user per day	$32 \times$ (weight = 1.0) = 32
Number of complex operations per active user per day	$+ 8 \times$ (weight = 3.0) = 24
Number of operations per active user per day	56
Number of hours per day	12
Peak factor	4

$$\frac{10000 \text{ users} \times 80\% \text{ usage} \times 56 \text{ operations} \times 4 \text{ peak}}{360000 \times 12 \text{ hours per day}} = 41.48 \text{ ops/sec}$$

As shown, these characteristics yield a predicted peak throughput requirement of about 42 operations per second. To run just this portal site, a medium server farm with two load-balanced front-end Web servers, an indexing server, and a server running the SQL component would be needed. A rough estimate for performance is each 1 GHz of processing power in the front-end servers can support 9 to 10 operations per second. Therefore, each server in the farm should be approximately a 2 x 2-GHz Pentium 4 Server with 2 GB of RAM. This is a close estimate of the hardware requirements needed for the example. If more portal sites are being hosted on the same farm, higher hardware requirements are necessary.

Rough hardware estimates are based significantly on the type of farm being used. Because each farm type has resources broken down in different ways, they have different operations-per-second estimates. A single server farm with MSDE cannot exceed five concurrent database jobs, and therefore, cannot realistically exceed five operations per second. For cached operations, a slightly higher operations-per-second rate might be achieved, but on average, it will remain about five operations per second. A single server farm with SQL Server will be able to support around 6 to 7 operations per second for each 1 GHz of processing speed. If the server is constantly doing a lot of indexing, this number will be lower, as the server will be using processing resources on indexing.

A small server farm environment will be able to support approximately 7 to 8 operations per second per 1 GHz of processing speed. Again, if there is a lot of indexing, the number will be lower. You should restrict indexing activities to periods of light usage, such as late at night, in single-server and small server farm environments.

Medium server farm environment can handle more requests, not only because resource-intensive operations such as indexing are offloaded, but because a medium server farm can support more than one front-end server. It is the front-end Web servers and search servers that mainly affect the number of operations per second for users. A medium server farm can support approximately 9 to 10 operations per second per 1 GHz of processing speed on the front-end Web servers.

Large server farms can handle more requests still because the search and Web components are running on different servers. It's difficult to estimate the capacity of large server farms without knowing the breakdown of search requests versus normal requests. A rough estimate is that a large server farm can support 11 to 12 operations per second for each 1 GHz of processing power on the front-end Web servers, but this is a general approximation.

The numbers provided in this section are general guidelines and approximations, as actual results will vary based on the exact hardware you are running. It is important to run capacity planning tests on your servers to ensure they will be able to perform adequately. This testing is especially important in a large server farm environment, where it is harder to gauge the actual hardware requirements without knowing the exact environment specifications. For example, if there will be a lot of searching going on in a large server farm, it is important to have many search servers and to test the whole farm using a script that simulates many searches. Full coverage of testing servers for capacity will be provided in the "Testing for Capacity" section later in this chapter.

Estimating Current and Future Storage Needs

Estimate the size of the required content by analyzing the quantity and size of existing documents in shared folders and other existing systems. To determine your current and future storage needs, try to identify current access frequencies and patterns.

Once you have determined the total size of all documents you plan to store in your SharePoint Portal Server farm, including all team sites, you can start to plan disk space requirements. You must consider the number of versions for all documents you plan to store. Multiply the number of versions you expect by the total size of all documents to get the total storage size for documents.

The SQL Server component will be the place the documents are actually stored. It needs disk space equal to twice the total size of all documents, including versions, you want to store in all your portal sites. This free disk space is required on the drive where the SQL Server databases reside. Also, the storage requirement does not include any operating system or supporting system software. If you plan on storing large quantities of files, you should store the SQL Server databases that SharePoint Portal Server uses on a storage area network (SAN). You should refer to SQL Server documentation for information on what SAN products are compatible with SQL Server.

Note   SQL Server does not support storing database files on **Network-Attached Storage** (NAS), so the free storage requirement must be met on a local physical disk on the SQL Server or on a SAN.

Once you have determined total document storage for SQL Server, you must determine the total size of documents being indexed. Take the total size of each content source—file shares, exchange public folders, and websites—that you want to index, and add that sum to the total size of all files stored in the server farm. This number is the total size of all documents to be crawled. Take this number and divide it by two. That is the total storage required on each indexing server in your farm. Then divide the number by two again. That is the total space required on each search server in your farm.

In a single-server environment, all components run on the same system. This means you need all the storage space on a single system. A single-server environment needs free space equal to 2.75 times the total size of all documents stored if there are no external content sources. A small server farm separates the SQL Server storage component from the other components. In a small server farm, the SQL Server component needs twice the total size of documents to store in free space and the server that runs the SharePoint Portal Server components needs to have .75 times the total size of all documents being indexed in free space. Medium and large server farms follow the breakdown previously described.

Choosing the Farm Design

A well-planned deployment can scale cost-effectively to accommodate increasing usage or changing workloads while maintaining the required performance. This section covers the following topics:

- Single-server deployment

- Small server farm

- Medium server farm

- Large server farm

- Capacity planning

- Scaling

- Growth path from a medium server farm to a large server farm

Knowing the usage profile helps you to choose the appropriate architecture. For example, if your usage profile indicates heavy indexing and searching, you should deploy the large server farm design. Large server farms contain at least two dedicated search servers and provide a growth path that enables you to deploy additional dedicated search servers, in addition to index and job servers. If your usage profile suggests that a majority of the workload will come from heavy team collaboration and significant usage of Windows SharePoint Services sites, consider deploying a dedicated Windows SharePoint Services farm for hosting the Windows SharePoint Services sites.

Single-Server Design and Performance

The single-server topology is designed to support between 1 and 10,000 users, but the actual number of users it can support is dependent on the usage profiles and workload patterns. The preceding example shows there will be only 10,000 users accessing the portal, but because of the workload mix, a single-server solution would not be able to adequately handle the required 42 operations per second. A single server running MSDE as the back-end datastore is designed to support only 5000 users because of the concurrent job restriction MSDE has.

A single-server deployment has all SharePoint Portal Server components and the SQL Server component running on the same physical computer. This topology does not scale well. To add capacity, you must move to the next type of farm, and to do so, you must migrate your current back-end datastore to another server. Unless you have fewer than 5000 users or very light portal usage, you should not consider a single-server design for production.

A single-server solution is very good, however, for testing and development. If you want to stage custom-developed Web Parts or other types of portal modifications that could easily affect performance or stability of your main portal, you should use a single-server platform. Often developers run a single-server topology for their development workstations for fast development, debugging, and testing.

Small Server Farm Design and Performance

A small server is designed to support between 5000 and 15,000 users, but the number of users supported ultimately depends on usage profiles and workload patterns. Again, the preceding example has 10,000 users, but the given workload mix is still too heavy for this topology. Only a very powerful small server farm would be able to support 42 operations per second, and it would be more economically feasible to run a medium server on lower-end hardware than two high-end, expensive servers.

Small server farms scale better than a single-server topology. You still have to move to a medium farm if you want to scale your capacity to more users or more operations per second, but it is far easier to scale a small server farm than a single server. This is because a small server farm already has the back-end SQL Server component installed on a separate physical machine, making the process of adding a server as simple as changing some check boxes in SharePoint Central Administration and rebuilding content indexes.

Medium Server Farm Design and Performance

The medium server farm supports between 15,000 and 50,000 users, but the number of users supported is entirely dependent on the usage profiles and workload patterns. The example in the previous section shows that 10,000 users executing a given workload mix required a solution capacity of about 42 operations per second. As results in later sections show, a medium server farm can support about three times that capacity—or 30,000 users running the sample workload. Note that the example represents every active user accessing the portal in some manner about every 20 minutes, and is therefore a reasonably harsh workload. Less intense user activity will obviously translate to more supported users.

A medium server configuration consists of a three to five server farms, designed to allow high availability and scalability. The most common medium farm design consists of two front-end Web servers that also provide the search components for the farm, a dedicated index and job server, and a SQL Server component, which can be a two-node cluster. The remainder of this section will discuss the highly available medium server farm with a SQL cluster reference configuration. The other medium server configurations are similar, but they are not as scalable or highly available.

In the common medium server farm, each function is implemented on redundant servers, with the exception of the indexing and job server functions. (There can be only one index and job server per farm.) Even the failure of the index and job server does not immediately affect availability because the search services are still available to end users. However, no indexing of new content is possible until the index and job server becomes available.

In the medium server farm solution, the front-end Web servers also host the search components for the farm. Consequently, the performance of the front-end Web servers is predicated on their ability to respond to end-users' requests to serve pages and to respond to search queries.

You can scale a base-line medium server farm by using one of the following two methods:

■ Adding a front-end Web and search server to the Network Load Balancing cluster, thereby increasing the capacity and availability

> **Note**   In a medium server farm, you cannot add dedicated search servers, nor can you add index and job servers. To add such servers, you must deploy the large server farm. However, you can scale from a medium server farm to a large server farm after initial deployment.

■ Deploying the medium server farm with a separate dedicated Windows Share-Point Services farm to host SharePoint Portal Services sites

The five-server medium-server farm configuration was tested by applying a typical usage workload. This workload contains a mix of typical user functions as might be used on each of the four main types of portal sites or websites: Corporate, Divisional, Team Sites, and My Sites. This workload and the results obtained with it are considered to be representative of a majority of users and business usage. If a specific customer's workload differs substantially from the workload used, results and supported throughput for the various functions will vary from those presented here. Testing will give information for how to take such workload differences into consideration and how to estimate expected performance.

The tested highly available medium server farm with a SQL cluster (the configuration for which was stated previously in this chapter) provided a sustained throughput rate of 110 operations per second, where an operation corresponds to a portal function—for example browse, search, or open document—at an average CPU consumption of 80 percent on each of the 2 Network Load Balancing (NLB) Web front-end servers. The average CPU consumption of the active computer running SQL Server was approximately 35 percent (2 × 2.8 GHz CPUs). This indicates a 4 to 1 ratio between front-end Web server processors and SQL Server processors. A medium server farm, however, supports only two servers, so this solution cannot be scaled out by adding additional front-end Web servers. The observed network traffic rate between the front-end Web servers and the simulated client systems was approximately 5300 KB per second. The search service on the front-end Web servers was supporting approximately 8 search operations per second. User-perceived performance, as evidenced by the response times reported by the Segue Silk Performer reports and analysis, was typically sub-second for the simple functions such as navigating to the Home page, browsing, or reading news. Search operations responded in 1.5 to 2.0 seconds, depending on the query complexity, the number of indexes that were referenced, and related factors. Document management operations such as check-out/check-in completed within 2.0 to 2.5 seconds. Opening documents took no longer than 3 to 5 seconds on average, depending on document type and document size—larger documents obviously require more time to transfer to the client desktops.

Large Server Farm Design and Performance

The large server farm solution is targeted at large organizations, and particularly at customers whose usage profiles suggest heavy indexing and searching. The estimated number of seats the design can support will vary based on your customer's particular usage profile and workload patterns.

The large server farm solution provides a scalable architecture, consisting initially of at least six servers: two dedicated front-end Web servers, two dedicated search servers, a dedicated index and job server, and a SQL 2000 Server component, which can run in an active/passive cluster.

The large server farm solution is highly available and can be scaled in a number of ways, including:

- Adding dedicated front-end Web servers to the NLB cluster to increase both capacity and the availability of the solution

- Adding dedicated search servers and index servers, which is ideal for customers with heavy search and indexing requirements

- Deploying the large server farm solution with a separate dedicated Windows SharePoint Services farm to host the SharePoint Portal Services team sites

The tested minimum large server farm with a SQL cluster configuration provided a sustained throughput rate of 125 operations per second, where an operation corresponds to a portal site function (such as browse, search, open document, and so on), at an average CPU consumption of 80 percent on each of the two NLB front-end Web servers. The average CPU consumption of the active computer running SQL Server was approximately 25 percent (4 × 2.0 GHz CPUs). This indicates that a total of six front-end Web servers could be supported by a large server farm with a single active quad-CPU computer running SQL Server, providing a total capacity of about 375 operations per second.

The observed network traffic rate between the front-end Web servers and the emulated client systems was approximately 5600 KB per second. The search service on the two dedicated search servers was supporting approximately eight search operations per second total (per the workload definition), consuming only about 4.5 percent CPU on each of the search servers. User-perceived performance was similar to that of the medium server farm, with typically sub-second performance for the simple functions (access Home page, browse, read news, and so on). Search operations responded in 1.5 to 2.0 seconds, depending on the query complexity, number of indexes, references, and so on. Document management operations (such as check-out/-in) completed within 2.0 to 2.5 seconds. Opening documents took no longer than 3 to 5 seconds on average, depending on the file type (Microsoft Office Word, Microsoft Office Excel, Microsoft Office PowerPoint, and so on) and file size—larger files obviously requiring more time to transfer to the client desktop computers.

Adding Capacity

Monitoring servers frequently to determine when additional capacity is needed is an important factor in capacity planning. Information on how to monitor servers is not included in this chapter. You should refer to Chapter 10,"Performance Monitoring in Microsoft Office SharePoint Portal Server 2003," for detailed information on monitoring servers. For single servers and small farms, the only way to increase capacity is to move to the next farm level up when CPU and memory have hit their limits. To add capacity to a medium or large server farm, see Chapter 11.

Performance Considerations

Although much effort has been spent by Microsoft and its partners to design and use a workload that is representative of typical user type mixes and portal site functions use, the results obtained are clearly related to that workload definition and the portal site's corpus content. Everyone should test their servers for capacity before going live, but doing so is highly recommended and almost imperative if your workload differs significantly from the workload used during testing for this chapter.

The following is a summary of key performance results from the testing done for this chapter:

■ A single server with MSDE cannot handle more than five operations per second because of the five-job limit MSDE imposes. In this scenario, MSDE is the limiting factor.

- The single server with SQL Server configuration supported a sustained throughput of 15 operations per second at 80 percent average CPU consumption. The CPU was the limiting factor here. To scale this server to support more users would require going to a small server farm.

- The small server farm supported a sustained throughput of 18 operations per second at 80 percent average CPU consumption on the server running SharePoint Portal Server. The server running SharePoint Portal Server was the limiting resource in this scenario. The server running SQL Server was 32 percent busy on average. The best way to scale from this environment is to move to a load-balanced or highly available medium server farm.

- The load-balanced farm supported a sustained throughput of 39 operations per second, with the limiting resource being the two NLB front-end servers running at 80 percent average CPU. The server running SQL Server was 50 percent busy on average.

- The highly available medium server farm with SQL cluster configuration supported a sustained throughput of 110 operations per second, with the limiting resource being the two NLB front-end servers running at 80 percent average CPU consumption. SQL Server (2 × 2.8 GHz) was 35 percent busy on average. The SQL Server used could support a maximum of four front-end servers, providing a total of over 200 operations per second. However, a medium server farm topology does not support more than two front-end servers, so to scale from this configuration, you must increase the number of processors in your front-end servers or move to a large server farm configuration.

- The minimum large farm configuration with a SQL cluster supported a throughput of about 125 operations per second, with the limiting resource being the two NLB front-end Web servers running at 80 percent busy on average. SQL Server (4 × 2.0 GHz) was 25 percent busy. Adding a front-end Web server would add about 60 operations per second to the total capacity. The server running SQL Server (4 CPUs) could support a total of six front-end servers, yielding a total of over 375 operations per second.

- The search service, running on either the front-end Web servers or on dedicated servers, was not used heavily with the test workload, which employed between 10 percent and 25 percent search function activity, or 8 to 10 searches per second. However, search-specific testing showed that a single dedicated search server can support over 210 search operations per second. The second search server in the prescribed large server farm configuration is to ensure availability of the search service if the other server were to fail.

- The indexing server is easily able to handle real-time indexing of documents that are checked in. It also performs incremental-type re-indexing in a period of time suitable for frequent periodic indexing, and it can perform an index-inclusive operation suitable for overnight scheduling. Full re-indexing of large indexes containing significant content should be achievable over a weekend.

- Network traffic between the clients and front-end servers, and traffic between the front-end servers and other configuration systems (search servers, indexing server, and SQL Server) is not excessive and should be supportable using 100 megabit network segments. For the larger farm configurations, which have high operation rates, the prescribed network design of two virtual LANs was used. This design is used to segment differing network traffic (for instance, HTTP client/front-end traffic and other server intercommunication traffic) onto two separate LANs so that they do not saturate a network segment and user response times are not affected by nonclient traffic.

- Performing database and disk maintenance is strongly recommended. Periodic execution of an SQL Server query to adjust table statistics and re-index data-base tables will result in optimal SQL Server database performance. Periodic examination of logical disk volume fragmentation levels and appropriate reme-dial action will ensure that the I/O subsystem does not impede performance.

Testing for Capacity

Testing for capacity is one of the most important parts of capacity planning. It will determine whether your planned topology will actually support the number of users and operations per second you expect. Testing will be employed after you have planned your infrastructure using the information presented in the preceding sections. Once the topology is built, before putting it into production, it should be stressed with both the normal workload mix you expect and the peak workload mix you expect to ensure that it can easily support the load. There isn't much that's worse for a deployment than spending a lot of time and money planning and building a solution only to put it into production and have it fail because the system could not handle the load.

This section will discuss tools you can use to stress test your portal sites as well as how to use those tools. It will also provide some basic performance monitoring information, but more in-depth performance monitoring information can be found in Chapter 10. Before proceeding, you should know the most general workload pattern. Typical portal site activity for a general business solution is 20 percent corporate portal site, 15 percent divisional portal sites, 40 percent team sites, and 25 percent My Sites. Your custom workload pattern will probably be different, and you should apply the information presented to your custom pattern. The examples in this section will discuss the workload pattern for the general business solution.

Selecting the Stress Test Tool

Several tools on the market allow users to perform load simulation. In this book, the Microsoft Application Center Test (ACT) tool will be used to generate the tests, as it is available as part of Microsoft Visual Studio .NET and it allows you to generate load tests and create reports. If you would like to perform more advanced load simulation work, you will have to purchase third-party solutions such as LoadRunner, as these solutions have been designed to meet more advanced requirements.

Web Application Stress Tool

The Microsoft Web Application Stress tool is not recommended for testing the performance of SharePoint Portal Server 2003 portal sites, as it cannot handle many ASP.NET-related features, such as handling view states. This is why it will not be used for the load simulation of SharePoint Portal Server 2003 portal sites, although it still can be a useful tool for testing traditional ASP Web applications.

Application Center Test

ACT is designed to stress test Web servers and to analyze performance and scalability problems with Web applications. ACT can simulate a large group of users by opening multiple connections to the server and rapidly sending HTTP requests. ACT ships with the Enterprise Edition of Visual Studio .NET. Unfortunately, ACT does not have some advanced features that the Web Application Stress tool has, such as the ability to string multiple computers together to perform one large stress test. Each computer running ACT must perform its own test, and if you want to produce a large test, you must run ACT individually on many computers and manually aggregate the results. Figure 9-5 shows what the user interface of ACT looks like.

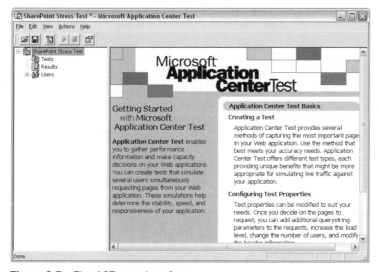

Figure 9-5 The ACT user interface

ACT allows you to create or record scripts (captured by Microsoft Internet Explorer) and run them at a later stage. Unfortunately, recording a script does not support authentication, so you must either record a script against a portal site with anonymous access enabled or write your own script. Creating a new test will provide you with the most basic test you can run. It contains just one line:

```
Test.SendRequest("http://localhost")
```

This script will send a request to the local server and ask for a response. The HTTP response code will be recorded. Scripts can then be customized and run several times. It is possible to configure scripts by right-clicking on them and selecting the properties, as shown in Figure 9-6.

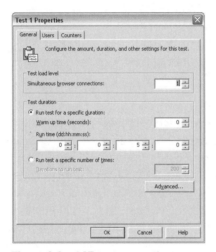

Figure 9-6 ACT test properties

ACT allows the user to configure several settings. One of them is the load level. A user can specify how many simultaneous browser connections (concurrent users) should hit the portal site. The other option is to also specify how long the scripts should run. Remember that the Visual Studio .NET edition of ACT does not allow you to connect multiple clients as the Web Application Stress tool did. Therefore, to perform large load tests, you have to run the stress scripts manually on each client and then merge the results to one report.

To simulate the load tests with multiple users, you have to configure a user group with the ACT tool. You can do that either manually or by importing a CSV file. Enabling user groups with multiple users allows the ACT tool to hit the portal site with unique users instead of using the same user multiple times. Make sure that the users within the ACT tool also have access rights to the portal site. Otherwise, there will be access problems.

Make sure that if you are using domain accounts the username field also includes the domain prefix, as shown in Figure 9-7. Also, to make your life easier, try to create user names that have an integer at the end that increments by 1 and use the same password for all of them. That way, you can have the ACT tool generate the users for you.

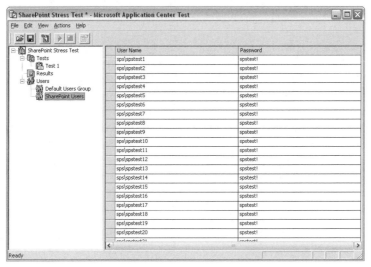

Figure 9-7   Users in ACT

Tools Used When Performing Load Simulations

There are a couple of tools that can help you understand the behavior and performance of your portal site. One of them is Network Load Balancing Manager, and the other one is the performance counter.

Network Load Balancing Manager

If you have any form of load-balanced server farm (medium or large farm), you should use Network Load Balancing (NLB) Manager during stress testing. NLB Manager allows you to create, configure, and manage all hosts of a Network Load Balancing cluster from a single computer. You can then use NLB manager to bring down nodes in the cluster to see the effect on performance. For more information on using NLB Manager, please see the Network Load Balancing section of Chapter 11.

Performance Monitor

Microsoft ships the performance monitor together with the operating system. It is extremely important to monitor the performance of CPU, Memory Usage, and Network Utilization on each of the servers running SharePoint Portal Server during stress testing. It is also imperative that you monitor SQL Server performance counters on the SQL Server component during testing. Before you start your performance measuring, you will have to select from a huge list of performance counters that might be of interest to you during the load simulation. You can monitor counters on remote servers, but this is not recommended during stress testing, as the resources required to send the performance data to the monitoring client might affect the test results. For more information on performance monitoring and exactly what to monitor with respect to SharePoint Portal Server, please refer to Chapter 10.

Scenarios for Load Stress Testing

One of the most important tasks before performing any stress tests is to understand what the different scenarios can be. These scenarios could be written down and then ordered by weight. It makes sense to test these scenarios, as they represent most common tasks the users will perform and therefore should result in the fastest response time possible. There are some tasks for which users simply expect a fast response time, while there are others where they can accept slower response times—for example, administrative tasks.

Performance scripts can be created to mimic anticipated load on the portal site. The scenarios that follow represent the most commonly occurring scenarios, but if your scenario differs, feel free to adjust according to your customized usage profile.

The Portal Home

SharePoint Portal Server allows you to create several portal sites. These are basically the main places for information in an enterprise implementation and will be one of the most requested locations in the intranet. It is important that at least the Home page opens up in a very fast manner. Normally, the corporate portal site will receive 20 percent of the total farm traffic, and the Home page of the corporate portal site will receive a significant amount of that traffic.

My Site

Personalization was one of the biggest demands of the users of the previous version of SharePoint Portal Server. In SharePoint Portal Server 2003, every user can go to his personal site by clicking My Site in the upper right corner. There is a personal and shared view for each user. The user can decide between the shared and personal view of the site and do some modifications. As most of the time people will access mainly their own sites, we will focus on the Personal View page and not on the Shared View.

The Shared View should be tested if you plan on using the corporate portal site as a corporate directory. Because the Shared View of the My Site, combined with user profiles, provides a very nice corporate directory, some organizations will make use of this feature. In this instance, you should make public My Site views a low percentage of testing because the public.aspx is one of the most expensive pages to render. If you do not plan on using Shared Views as a corporate directory, it is not necessary to include the Shared Views in your stress-testing plans.

Topics

Topics allow the users to browse the portal site's content by using a logical representation of grouping. Browsing topics is an easier way for users to find information and is also usually generates many hits on the server. It is important to test the latency of the topic structure because users are likely to use topics to find information. Users might find it unacceptable if the topic structure takes too long to load.

Team Sites

Windows SharePoint Services allows users to create team sites that are more project or department specific than the corporate or departmental portal sites. These sites can be used by teams to upload documents and collaborate and therefore will be requested many times as well. Microsoft's research shows that 40 percent of all farm traffic will be to team sites.

Custom Pages and Web Parts

Adding custom Web Parts to pages is what makes SharePoint Portal Server a flexible solution. These Web Parts can also have a huge impact on the overall performance of the system. Custom Web Parts that are not properly developed or that connect to external resources can dramatically slow down the performance of the system. For example, if you normally serve 24 pages a second, each page is served in about 40 milliseconds. All Web Parts on that page are rendered in that time. Therefore, it is important to test each of these Web Parts before importing them into a production portal site. This procedure would allow the administrator to identify whether the Web Part could be the bottleneck of the portal site.

Search

One of the most important features of a knowledge management solution is a powerful search engine that not only allows the user to find accurate information throughout the enterprise but also performs quickly. Therefore, the search performance is also another scenario that has to be tested. Research shows that 25 percent of the corporate portal site usage is for searches. If your organization plans to use searches extensively, it is even more important to thoroughly stress test the search function.

Mixed Scenario

A mixed scenario uses a combination of multiple scenarios to verify how the system performs when multiple parts of the portal site are being used at the same time. The mixed scenario represents actually the most realistic and therefore interesting scenario. A mixed scenario is the most important one to test, but doing so requires using customized ACT scripts.

What Does Not Need to Be Tested

This section focuses on the most widely used workload scenarios. Other scenarios—such as administrative tasks, document uploads, adding Web Parts to a portal site, and so on—do not occur as often as the scenarios just mentioned. If your organization has other scenarios, such as document uploads, that are more prevalent than the general case, you should modify your test plan accordingly.

Testing Methodology

Before running any tests, you should create a table in which you enter the number of concurrent users that would hit the portal site. You should start with one user and increment slowly with each subsequent test to see the impact on the portal site. You do not want to start with a high number of concurrent users and flood your portal site. That will not give you accurate test results, and you will most likely get frustrated trying to interpret the error-ridden results you get. You can increase the number of the concurrent user threads in the ACT tool in the properties of a test script as shown in Figure 9-8.

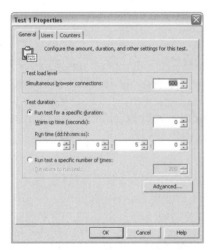

Figure 9-8   Setting the load level

The test load level indicates the number of simultaneous browser connections that the client will generate while performing the tests against the portal site. It is important to note that you will need to have enough users in the users profile to be able to concurrently hit the page. The load level should never be more than the number of users. If it is, the test will fail. The more user connections you have, the more load you will put on the server. You will also generate additional load on the client running the test as you. Generating too much load on the client will result in incorrect numbers, as the clients will not be able generate the expected load.

The ideal approach is to generate as much load as possible without affecting the clients while still maximizing load on the SharePoint Portal Server front-end Web servers. The client should have no more than 50 percent processor utilization during stress testing, and the average server load should average from 80 percent to 90 percent. A perfect testing methodology should enable the tester to eventually find the bottleneck that might be in the system. Although the next chapter will mention several important counters for the performance analysis, the most important ones are the following ones:

- ASP.NET Requests/Sec

- Processor utilization

- Disk Queue

- Pages/Sec

Looking at these counters should already give some valuable information about the portal site's bottleneck. This information will help determine in the decision-making process what might need to be upgraded to further enhance the portal site's performance if that is required.

By performing the incremental increase of the concurrent connections, you will find out that the more load you generate the smaller the increase for the requests per second (RPS) will be. The ACT tool shows RPS, but these are the same as the operations per second discussed previously. Eventually, you will get to the point where you no longer get a higher RPS when you add users. This is the maximum throughput for the current server. Table 9-2 shows the results of a simple ACT test that just loads the corporate portal site Home page with 1, 2, 5, 10, and 20 concurrent connections on a single server within a SQL Server environment.

Table 9-2   Results of a Simple ACT Test

Concurrent Connections	Test Results
1	Average requests per second: 12.83
	Average time to last byte (msec): 48.75
2	Average requests per second: 17.85
	Average time to last byte (msec): 56.09
5	Average requests per second: 20.97
	Average time to last byte (msec): 90.11
10	Average requests per second: 21.89
	Average time to last byte (msec): 137.15
20	Average requests per second: 22.06
	Average time to last byte (msec): 233.50

You can see that the RPS of the portal site stops growing at around 22 RPS. The other thing that is important to notice is that the latency increases as more load is generated.

Generating Load and Interpretation of the Results

The purpose of stress testing is to determine how a portal site will perform and to identify bottlenecks under load. Running scripts for the different scenarios that accurately simulate the expected production traffic will generate load on the servers. The purpose of a performance test should be to find out the maximum throughput under load. To better understand what might be acting as the bottleneck of the portal site, it makes sense to check for several counters on the different servers.

The most interesting point to find out is the throughput capabilities of the portal site. Throughput is the amount of work that the portal site can do in a given time period. In this case, that would mean finding out how many requests per second the portal site can handle. Splitting the performance counters into three groups makes sense. First of all, we have to make sure that the clients are not suffering too much under the load they are generating. Second, using different counters for the SQL server and the front-end servers will show us where the bottleneck lies (that is, at the front end or back end).

All the different scripts can be run with the ACT test tool, and there will be two kinds of results that can be analyzed. One type is the Web server responses that tell you whether there were any HTTP errors, how many pages have been processed, how long it took to open up the page, and so on. The other results are the performance counters that also indicate server hardware-related results.

Types of Scripts

As defined earlier, the most basic script contains just one line:

```
Test.SendRequest("http://sps")
```

What this script does is send a request to the server *http://sps* and requests the default page for the site. Because this is a corporate portal site, the default page is Default.aspx. The Web server processes the Default.aspx page and returns the result to the client computer. ACT times this whole transaction and uses that information to generate RPS data. Running this script will generate performance data for your server or server farm, but it is not particularly useful unless the only thing your users do is go to the Home page of the corporate portal site.

Using a mixed-scenario script is much more useful for testing the portal site. The following script performs the general workload mix on a specified corporate portal site. This script can be modified for divisional portal sites or to include other sites. It can also be modified for specific workload mix requirements of your organization. The code for the mixed scenario script is as follows:

```
RANDOMIZE
Test.SetGlobalVariable "g_SERVER", "http://<put your server name here>"
SERVER = Test.GetGlobalVariable("g_SERVER")
'*************************************************************************
' Mixed Scenario Script
'*************************************************************************
    Select Case int(2*RND)
        '50% GetHomePage
        Case 0
            Call GetHomepage
        Case 1
            Select Case int(10*RND)
                '20% GetMyPage
                Case 0, 1, 2, 3
                    Call GetSearch
                '15% GetSearch
                Case 4, 5, 6
                    Call GetSearch
                    '5% GetSiteReg
                    '5% GetCategories
                Case 7, 8, 9
                    Select Case int(3*RND)
                        Case 0
                            Call GetTeamSite
                        Case 1
                            Call GetSiteReg
                        Case 2
                            Call GetCategories
                    End Select
            End Select
    End Select


'*************************************************************************
' TM_GetHomepage
' Purpose: Gets the default homepage
'*************************************************************************
Function GetHomepage
    GetUrl SERVER & "/default.aspx", "Homepage"
End Function


'*************************************************************************
' TM_GetMyPage
' Purpose: Gets my page
'Note: In order to have this work you will have to import the users from the AD
' on the SharePoint Portal Server portal site and give them the necessary rights
'to have their own My Sites
'You will have to also use the PortalCramIt tool to generate the
'sites so that you will really hit existing My Sites
'*************************************************************************
Function GetMyPage
    GetUrlMyPri SERVER & "/MySite/default.aspx", "MyPage"
End Function


'*************************************************************************
' TM_GetSearch
```

```
' Purpose: Gets the default search page
'Note: We are searching here for the word home, you could of course
'change that
'*************************************************************************
Function GetSearch
    GetUrl SERVER & "/Search.aspx?k=Home", "GetSearch"
End Function


'*************************************************************************
' TM_GetCategories
' Purpose: Gets the main categories page
'*************************************************************************
Function GetCategories
    GetUrl SERVER & "/Topics/default.aspx", "GetCategories"
End Function


'*************************************************************************
' TM_GetTeamSite
' Purpose: Gets a Team Site Homepage
'Note: In order for this script to work you will have to create
'a team site and enter its name into the URL below
'*************************************************************************
'Get Team Site gets it own Object because can not access with Reader.
Function GetTeamSite
    GetUrl SERVER & "/sites/<name of an existing team site>/default.aspx", "GetTeam-
Site"
End Function


'*************************************************************************
' TM_GetSiteRegistry
' Purpose: Gets the site registry page
'*************************************************************************
Function GetSiteReg
    GetUrl SERVER & "/SiteDirectory/Lists/Sites/Summary.aspx", "GetSiteRegistry"
End Function


'*************************************************************************
' GetUrl
' Purpose: Gets the passed in URL.  Send the pagename to be logged
'Note: the number 200 can be replaced by any number you wish as long as these
'users have been generated in the AD
'*************************************************************************
Sub GetUrl(strURL, strPage)
RANDOMIZE
F = INT(200 * RND)
    Test.GetCurrentUser
    tStart = Timer()
        Set oResponse  = Test.SendRequest(strURL)
    tFinish = Timer()
    Test.GetNextUser
End Sub




Sub GetUrlMyPri(strURL, strPage)
```

```
RANDOMIZE
F = INT(200 * RND)
    Test.GetCurrentUser
    Set oUser = Test.GetCurrentUser
    oUser.Name = "domain\user" & F
    oUser.Password = "password"

    tStart = Timer()
        Set oResponse  = Test.SendRequest(strURL)
    tFinish = Timer()
    Test.GetNextUser
    Set oUser = Nothing
End Sub
```

After running the script, it is very important to see what the results of the test have been. ACT automatically generates for each test run a report file that can be analyzed as shown in Figure 9-9.

Average requests per second:	8.90
Average time to first byte (msecs):	100.91
Average time to last byte (msecs):	106.28
Average time to last byte per iteration (msecs):	106.28
Number of unique requests made in test:	5
Number of unique response codes:	1
Error Counts	
HTTP: 0	
DNS: 0	
Socket:	0
Additional Network Statistics	
Average bandwidth (bytes/sec):	710,950.39
Number of bytes sent (bytes):	4,567,107
Number of bytes received (bytes):	208,704,511
Average rate of sent bytes (bytes/sec):	15,223.69
Average rate of received bytes (bytes/sec):	695,681.70
Number of connection errors:	0
Number of send errors:	0
Number of receive errors:	0
Number of timeout errors:	0
Response Codes	
Response Code: 200 - The request completed successfully.	
Count:	2,669
Percent (%):	100.00

Figure 9-9   ACT test results

The most important information for the stress tester to determine is the average RPS that were achieved while running the test script. This number is equivalent to the number of operations per second the server can support. It is important to compare the numbers produced in testing with the numbers that were determined when planning. The RPS number achieved through ACT should be greater than or equal to the operations per second determined in planning the portal site. If it is not, your portal site will not be able to handle the load you planned for.

It is also important to note the average time to last byte. This is the amount of time a user would have to wait for a requested page. The number is in milliseconds, so a number greater than 1000 indicates that under the simulated load conditions an end user would have to wait more than 1 second for the requested page. This number is especially important to pay attention to if your users will not tolerate wait times.

While the scripts just shown actually already do generate good stress on the servers, there is one thing that was not taken into consideration so far: the caching of site components such as style sheets, .gif, .jpg, and so on. If you are testing for environments over slow links, this is very important. The following script opens the default Home page, default.aspx, and checks the modified date of the site's cascading style sheets (CSS) file against the local file if one exists. If the file had not been downloaded, the script will not download another copy. The code is as follows:

```
RANDOMIZE
Test.SetGlobalVariable "g_SERVER", "http://<serverURL>"
servername = "<servername or IP>"
SERVER = Test.GetGlobalVariable("g_SERVER")
Call GetHomepage

Function GetHomepage
    GetUrl SERVER & "/default.aspx", "Homepage"
    'in this script we have added only one file. You can add more of
    'these files if you want. (path of these ' '
    ' can be found out by looking at the page's source)
    GetLastModifiedUrl "/styles/sps.css"
End Function

Sub GetUrl(strURL, strPage)
RANDOMIZE
'usernumber can be changed to your preference
F = INT(200 * RND)
    Test.GetCurrentUser
    tStart = Timer()
        Set oResponse = Test.SendRequest(strURL)
    tFinish = Timer()
    Test.GetNextUser
End Sub

Sub GetLastModifiedUrl(strURL)
'Open a new connection to the Web server
    dim oConnection
Set oConnection = Test.CreateConnection(SERVERNAME, 80, False)
If (oConnection Is Nothing) Then
    Test.Trace("Error: Unable to create connection."&Servername)
    Else
        'Create a new Request
        Set oRequest = Test.CreateRequest
        Set oUser = Test.GetCurrentUser
```

```
    ' Set Request properties
    oRequest.Verb = "GET"
  oRequest.Path = strURL
  ' you can modify the date to your preference
    Call oRequest.Headers.Add("If-Modified-Since", "Wed, 2 Apr 2003 02:39:00 GMT")
    'Send the request
    Set oResponse = oConnection.Send(oRequest)
end if
End Sub
```

Summary

This chapter has provided you with the information necessary to plan, purchase, and test a SharePoint Portal Server installation in your organization. In the following chapters, you will learn how to build, customize, and manage your SharePoint Portal Server solution. Remember to always plan realistically based on your users' needs and test your installation for capacity before deploying it into production. Take the operations-per-second number you developed during planning by using the algorithm provided and compare this to the RPS number you achieved during testing. Make sure that the RPS number is higher than the required operations-per-second number. This will help ensure a successful deployment.

Chapter 10

Performance Monitoring in Microsoft Office SharePoint Portal Server 2003

After your intranet is up and running, changing conditions might require you to scale out the server farm. This chapter provides guidance on when and how to scale out. It provides information about how to monitor critical performance counters and analyze log data to determine the best scale-out strategy based on server farm behavior. It provides information about adding Web servers, search servers, and index servers. It also addresses strategies for splitting search indexes to improve search performance and for adding a dedicated Microsoft Windows SharePoint Services–based server farm.

Monitoring Server Farm Performance

This section describes the most important performance counters for gauging server farm performance and deciding how to scale out your server farm. However, it does not address scale-out issues related to custom Web Parts or applications. A scenario that employs custom code might require additional monitoring or change the interpretation of performance counters.

By monitoring a server's performance on a regular basis, you can recognize trends as they develop and prevent performance problems. Monitoring also helps you decide when to upgrade hardware and whether upgrades are actually improving the server's performance.

Use Microsoft Windows Server 2003 System Monitor and Performance Logs and Alerts to monitor the counters described in this chapter. For more information about performance monitoring, including counters, logs, alerts, and Windows Server 2003 System Monitor best practices, see "Monitoring Performance" in Windows Server 2003 Help.

General Counters

Table 10-1 lists the general performance counters that should be monitored for all SharePoint Portal Server–based servers as part of your normal monitoring strategy. Regular monitoring of these counters helps you understand the general health of the servers. Some of these counters are also key indicators that can help determine how and when to scale out the server farm.

Table 10-1   General Server Performance Counters

Object	Counter	Threshold	Description
Processor	Percent processor time_total	80 to 85 percent averaged over three intervals.	The total percentage of processor usage for a server.
Network interface	Bytes total per second_network interface	50 percent of the available network interface bandwidth—for example, a 100-MB network interface running at 50,000 KB per second.	The rate at which bytes are sent and received over each network adapter.
Logical disk	Percent idle time_ (drives C:, D:, and so on)	20 percent over idle time_.	Reports the percentage of time during the sample interval that the disk was idle. If this value is very low, the logical disk is very busy.
Paging file	Percent usage	Above 70 percent.	Review this value in conjunction with memory—available megabytes and page faults per second—to understand paging activity on the server.
Memory	Available MBs	128 MB—assuming 2 GB of RAM as prescribed on servers.	The amount of physical memory, in MBs, immediately available for allocation to a process or for system use on the server.
Memory	Page faults per second	20.	A high rate of page faults indicates a lack of physical memory.
System	Processor queue length	The number of CPUs + 1.	Exceeding the threshold indicates that the processors are not fast enough to process requests as they occur and that you are running out of processor power.
ASP.NET applications	Requests per second_total	Through ongoing monitoring, trends begin to emerge that equate requests per second with CPU consumption.	The number of requests executed per second; this roughly equates to the number of HTTP pages per second.

SharePoint Portal Server Counters

Each type of server—index, search, and front-end Web—has performance counters specific to its function in the server farm. This section lists the counters that should be analyzed for each server type to determine how and when to scale the server farm.

Front-End Web Servers—Large Server Farm

Analyze the counters in Table 10-2 to determine when to add a new dedicated front-end Web server to a large server farm. When the counters continuously approach or exceed any of the thresholds in Table 10-2, you should consider adding another dedicated front-end Web server to the server farm. However, you should also check the general counters in Table 10-1 to better understand the server's performance.

Table 10-2   Performance Counters for Dedicated Front-End Web Servers

Object	Counter	Threshold	Description
Processor	Percent processor time_total	80 to 85 percent averaged over three intervals.	The total percentage of processor usage for a server.
ASP.NET applications	Requests per second_total	Through ongoing monitoring, trends begin to emerge that equate requests per second with CPU consumption.	The number of requests executed per second; this roughly equates to the number of HTTP pages per second.
Web service	Get requests per second_total, individual portal, or IIS Virtual root	Through ongoing monitoring, trends begin to emerge that equate get requests per second with CPU consumption.	Generally speaking, this is the rate at which clients are requesting information from the front-end Web servers.

Leading Indicators for Front-End Web Servers

The counter **percent processor time** is the leading indicator of front-end Web server performance. You should sample percent processor time every 15 minutes; if it exceeds the indicated threshold on average, consider adding an additional front-end Web server. If your customer has very high performance expectations, you might need to establish a lower average threshold.

The value that requests per second reaches while percent processor time is at the threshold indicates the approximate maximum throughput for the server. Adding a front-end Web server should add this amount of capacity to the server farm.

Impact of Windows SharePoint Services Sites

Be sure to take into consideration the impact of extensive front-end traffic to Microsoft Windows SharePoint Services sites. If some of your Windows SharePoint Services sites are generating significant front-end traffic, you might want to scale out one or more of those sites to a separate server farm, as discussed in the "Dedicated Windows SharePoint Services Server Farm" section later in this chapter.

Front-End Web/Search Servers—Medium Server Farm

Table 10-3 lists the most important counters for evaluating the performance of a front-end Web server with the search component in a medium server farm.

Table 10-3   Performance Counters for Front-End Web/Search Servers

Object	Counter	Threshold	Description
Processor	Percent processor time_total	80 to 85 percent averaged over three intervals.	The total percentage of processor usage for a server.
Search	Query rate	10 per second.	The number of queries posted to the server per second; keep in mind that in the medium server farm configuration, the front-end servers are doing much more than searching.
Search	Succeeded queries	This counter should be used mostly for troubleshooting search problems.	The number of queries that produce successful searches. Monitor this counter along with the failed queries counter if you need to troubleshoot search problems.
Search catalogs	Number of documents	Microsoft has tested up to 5 million documents per content index.	The total number of documents in the catalog.
Search catalogs	Queries rate_ (index names or all instances)	Indicates which catalogs are searched most often by users.	The number of queries posted to indexes per second; in conjunction with other performance data, this can help determine if your index configuration can be optimized.
Web service	Get requests per second_total, individual portal, or IIS virtual root	Through ongoing monitoring, trends begin to emerge that equate get requests per second with CPU consumption.	Generally speaking, this is the rate at which clients are requesting information from the front-end Web servers.
ASP.NET applications	Requests per second_total	Through ongoing monitoring, trends begin to emerge that equate requests per second with CPU consumption.	The number of requests executed per second, which roughly equates to the number of HTTP pages per second.

Leading Indicators for Front-End Web/Search Servers

If the search catalog size exceeds 5 million documents, you must add an additional front-end Web/search server or move the indexing service to one or more dedicated Index servers. As the number of documents approaches 5 million, propagation and crawling times become unacceptably long.

The value that *requests per second* reaches while percent processor time is at the threshold indicates the approximate maximum throughput for the server. Adding a front-end Web server should add this amount of capacity to the server farm.

Separating the Effects of Searching from Other Front-End Traffic   When deciding to scale out front-end Web/search servers, you must determine how much of the CPU load is the result of search operations. As a rule of thumb, when the **query rate** counter exceeds the indicated threshold and search operations are consuming about 40 to 50 percent of the overall server capacity, you should consider scaling out to a large server farm. If the query rate is below the threshold but percent processor time is exceeding the threshold, front-end Web traffic is bringing the server to capacity and you should consider adding an additional front-end Web/search server to the medium server farm.

Be sure to take into consideration the impact of extensive front-end traffic to Windows SharePoint Services sites. If some of your Windows SharePoint Services sites are generating significant front-end traffic, you might want to scale out one or more of those sites to a separate server farm, as discussed in the "Dedicated Windows SharePoint Services Server Farm" section later in this chapter.

Other Factors That Influence Search Performance   Keep in mind that other factors can cause heavy search loads—for example, a large content index (which can slow down search performance) or heavy search query executions against a single portal in a shared services farm. Make sure that user expectations for search performance are realistic for your environment. Your customer's requirements for search response times, including commitments to service-level objectives that define specific response times for searches, can necessitate adding a server before the thresholds have been exceeded.

Dedicated Search Servers—Large Server Farm

Table 10-4 lists the most important counters for evaluating the performance of a dedicated search server in a large server farm.

Table 10-4   Performance Counters for Dedicated Search Servers—Large Server Farm

Object	Counter	Threshold	Description
Processor	Percent processor time_total	80 to 85 percent averaged over three intervals.	The total percentage of processor usage for a server.
Search	Query rate	20 per second.	The number of queries posted to the server per second. Keep in mind this counter should be watched on the dedicated search servers.
Search	Succeeded queries	This counter should be used mostly for troubleshooting search problems.	The number of queries that produce successful searches; monitor this counter along with the failed queries counter if you need to troubleshoot search problems.

Table 10-4   Performance Counters for Dedicated Search Servers—Large Server Farm *(continued)*

Object	Counter	Threshold	Description
Search catalogs	Number of documents	Microsoft has tested up to 5 million documents.	This counter identifies the total number of documents in the catalog.
Search catalogs	Queries rate_ (index names or all instances)	Indicates which indexes are most searched by users.	The number of queries posted to indexes per second. In conjunction with other performance data, this counter can help determine if your index configuration can be optimized.
Web service	Get requests per second_total, individual portal, or Windows SharePoint Portal Services site	With ongoing monitoring, trends emerge that equate requests per second with CPU consumption.	Generally speaking, this is the rate that clients are requesting information from the front-end Web servers.

Leading Indicators for Search Servers

When the percent processor time or query rate counters approach the indicated thresholds, consider adding a search server to the server farm. In addition, if the search catalog size exceeds 5 million documents, you must add a search server. As the number of documents approaches 5 million, propagation and crawling times become unacceptably long.

Evaluating search performance involves more than simply monitoring the counters in Table 10-4. For more information, see the "Other Factors That Influence Search Performance" section earlier in this chapter.

Scale-Out Limitations for Search Servers   You can have no more than four search servers per server farm.

Index Servers

Table 10-5 lists the most important counters for evaluating the performance of an index server in a large server farm.

Table 10-5   Performance Counters for Index Servers—Large Server Farm

Object	Counter	Threshold	Description
Processor	Percent processor time_total	80 to 85 percent averaged over three intervals.	The total percentage of processor usage for a server.
Search indexer catalogs	Number of documents	Microsoft has tested up to 5 million documents.	The number of documents in the catalog.
Search indexer catalogs	Index size MB	20 GB.	The current size of index data in megabytes.

Leading Indicators for Index Servers

The key performance thresholds for index servers are 80 to 85 percent processor time and 85 percent memory availability. However, the decision to add an index server is more a function of indexing and propagation time than of monitoring performance counters. When indexing and propagation cannot proceed fast enough to keep content indexes as up to date as your customer's business requirements demand, you should add another index server. For example, if it takes two hours for an incremental crawl and propagation when you need half-hour updates, consider adding an index server.

Factors Influencing Index Server Performance

Depending on business requirements, it might be acceptable to have as many as 5 million documents in one content index, but if the rate of change is high and alerts are popular, you might need two or three index servers for that data. Performance of an index server also depends on the location of the crawled content and the processing power of the index server. Crawl times depend on many factors, including the following ones:

- **Content location and network performance.** Content location and network performance are related. For example, when crawling content outside of your corporate LAN, performance might slow down. Crawling sites within your intranet with adequate bandwidth is generally faster.

- **Type of documents in the index.** You might be crawling sites that contain a variety of document types, such as Microsoft Word, Excel, or Visio, in addition to HTML files. Some file types are more resource intensive than others.

- **Frequency and type of content index updates.** The update schedule can be as frequent as a weekly full update with an incremental crawl every 15 minutes or something much less aggressive. You might be able to improve indexing performance by adjusting your crawling schedule to crawl less frequently if this can be done without affecting your ability to meet the business requirements.

Scale-Out Limitations for Index Servers

If your existing architecture is a medium server farm, adding an index server requires that you scale to a large server farm. This also requires the implementation of two dedicated search servers, which is the minimum supported configuration for a large server farm.

Microsoft recommends no more than four index servers per large server farm.

Advantages of Adding an Index Server   Adding an index server provides the following advantages:

- It gives you the ability to crawl more content more quickly.

- It enables you to separate your content indexes onto separate index servers based on your customer's specific indexing requirements. For example, you can separate internal content indexes from external content indexes.

- It enables you to use a separate index server for crawling specific content sources that require much more frequent indexing than other content sources.

Dedicated Windows SharePoint Services Server Farm

Monitor the Internet Information Services (IIS) logs to determine the amount of traffic going to the Windows SharePoint Services sites in the server farm. If you discover a large amount of traffic going to one or more Windows SharePoint Services sites, consider moving the busy sites to a dedicated Windows SharePoint Services server farm. If you see trends from ongoing monitoring that indicate your Windows SharePoint Services site traffic is increasing and will continue to increase, a separate dedicated Windows SharePoint Services site might be the best scaling option. You can elect to move one or more—or all—of the busiest Windows SharePoint Services site collections to a separate, dedicated Windows SharePoint Services server farm.

Separating one or more Windows SharePoint Services site collections to a dedicated server farm frees up resources on the front-end Web servers that are dedicated to supporting the corporate and divisional portals. It also enables you to independently scale out the dedicated Windows SharePoint Services server farm.

Microsoft SQL Server

The percent processor time counter is the leading indicator for Microsoft SQL Server performance. Examine percent processor time in conjunction with overall memory capacity, network traffic, and input/output (I/O) subsystem capacity.

Logs

Monitoring system performance in conjunction with IIS logs and SharePoint Portal Server Usage Analysis logs provides more in-depth information about how your sites are being used. Windows Server 2003 System Monitor helps you to understand resource consumption on a per-server basis. The logs provide in-depth Web traffic analysis data, such as which sites are most heavily used and by whom, how many visitors use the sites, and peak periods of activity.

Internet Information Services (IIS) Logs

IIS logs include detailed information, such as who has visited sites and what was viewed, in terms of total visits, average visits, page views, and trends over time. Careful analysis of the IIS logging data helps you to discover how much traffic is going to portal sites, how much is going to Windows SharePoint Services sites, and how much is going to search operations.

You can use IIS log data to help identify bottlenecks and performance issues. More importantly, you can use this data to identify the SharePoint Portal Server and Windows SharePoint Services sites that are used most often. This information helps you to understand the impact of Windows SharePoint Services sites on your front-end Web server traffic and to decide when to move one or more site collections to a dedicated Windows SharePoint Services server farm.

Setting Up Log Files

Set the logs to be created on a daily basis, which creates a new log file each day for each virtual server.

Set up SharePoint Portal Server to place the log files on a hard drive separate from the one that contains the operating system (drive C). Ensure that the local Administrators group and the IIS_WPG group have the appropriate permissions to access the log files directory.

Within the Logfiles directory, IIS creates a separate directory for each IIS virtual server log, with naming based on the virtual server instance number.

To view the directory and log file name for each virtual server through IIS Manager, follow these steps:

1. Right-click a virtual server, click **Properties**, and then select the **Properties** button next to **Active log format**.

2. The **Log File** name is displayed at the bottom of the screen.

Reading the Log File Data

The IIS logs are ASCII files that can be read using a text editor, but third-party utilities are typically used to analyze IIS logs and generate meaningful, formatted reports and graphical representations of usage data. How the IIS logging information is presented and accessed depends on the third-party tool used to present the IIS log data. You can also use Microsoft Commerce Server Web Analytics to gain this information.

IIS log files can also be logged in a database that complies with Open Database Connectivity (ODBC), such as a Microsoft SQL Server database, and SQL Server Query Analyzer can be used to generate reports. For more information about configuring IIS logs to an ODBC database, see "Log File Formats" at *http://www.microsoft.com /technet/prodtechnol/windowsserver2003/proddocs/standard/log_aboutlogging.asp*.

Configuring the Log Files

IIS logging is enabled by default for each virtual server. The recommended log file format is W3C, which is the default. This enables you to specify which fields are included in the log file. By limiting logging to the W3C fields that are most important to your customer, you can limit the log file size and simplify the analysis. Depending on the amount of traffic to your sites, the size of your log files can begin to consume valuable memory resources and CPU cycles. You need to balance the gathering of detailed data against the need to limit IIS log files to a manageable size and number.

The following W3C log file fields are the most important for analyzing Web traffic for scale-out decisions:

- **User name.**   The name of the user who accessed the server.
- **Server IP address.**   The IP address of the server on which the log entry was generated.
- **Server port.**   The port number to which the client is connected.
- **Method.**   The action the client was trying to perform—for example, a GET request.
- **URI stem.**   The resource accessed, such as an HTML page, a Common Gateway Interface (CGI) program, or a script (the most relevant resource for a scaling decision).
- **URI query.**   The query, if any, the client was trying to perform. One or more search strings that the client was seeking to match are recorded.
- **Protocol status.**   The status of the action, in HTTP terms.
- **Protocol substatus.**   Records additional status of the action, in HTTP terms.
- **Win32 status.**   The status of the action, in Windows operating system terms.

More Info   For a complete list of W3C log file fields, visit *http://www .microsoft.com/technet/prodtechnol/windowsserver2003/proddocs/standard /log_customw3c.asp*.

Usage Analysis Processing

Usage analysis processing provides usage reports on Windows SharePoint Services sites. This information can help you to determine which Windows SharePoint Services sites and subsites receive the most visitors.

Usage analysis data is taken from the IIS logs on the front-end Web servers and gathered into temporary files. When usage analysis processing takes place, the logs are merged into the content databases on the computer running SQL Server. For more information, see "Configuring Usage Analysis" in the online *SharePoint Portal Server 2003 Administrator's Guide*.

Usage analysis processing is disabled by default.

To enable usage analysis processing for all virtual servers in the server farm, follow these steps:

1. Click **Site Settings**.

2. Click **Go to Central Administration**.

3. Under **Component Configuration**, click **Configure usage analysis processing**.

4. Select **Enable logging**.

5. Specify a location for the usage analysis log files. The default location is *systemroot*\\system32\\logfiles\\STS. Within this directory, Usage Analysis Processing creates a folder for every virtual server, named according to the IIS virtual server instance number. Within each virtual server folder, Usage Analysis Processing creates a folder for each day.

6. Enter the number of log files to create, from 1 to 30. It is recommended that you set this number to be equal to the number of virtual servers on the front-end Web servers in the server farm. Splitting usage data into many smaller files rather than placing it into one big file reduces the amount of memory required to process all the usage data log entries.

7. Creating and updating the logs is processor intensive, so set processing to take place when site usage is low—for example, between 1:00 A.M. and 4:00 A.M.

Note Give the STS_WPG group read, write, and update permissions to the directory. Without these permissions, IIS cannot create or update the logs.

Usage Analysis Processing Reports

Even though the data is logged and stored for an entire site collection, when you view the data in HTML Administration pages, you can see the usage analysis data for a particular Windows SharePoint Services site or subsite but not for the entire site collection. A summary of the entire site collection usage is available from the top-level website for each site collection. Although you can see the total number of hits for an entire site collection, to see detailed information you must use the **Site Usage Report** page for the individual site or subsite.

Site usage reports are useful for identifying which content on your Windows SharePoint Services sites is being heavily used or used very little. This helps you to understand which sites are candidates for archiving and which sites should be kept online. In addition, the site collection usage reports help you track how much storage space your sites are using. This information is gathered as part of the quota tracking for Windows SharePoint Services sites.

For more information about viewing and analyzing usage analysis data, see "Analyzing Web Site Usage" in the online *SharePoint Portal Server 2003 Administrator's Guide*.

To view site usage data for a single site, follow these steps:

1. Navigate to the Windows SharePoint Services site and then click **Site Settings**.

2. Click **Go to Site Administration**.

3. Under **Management and Statistics**, click **View site usage data**. The **Site Usage Reports** page provides a report that contains the following information:

   - The pages that have been accessed on that site, including document libraries

   - The users that have accessed the site

   - The operating system of the user accessing the site

   - The browser type

   - The referrer URL

   - Data that can be displayed by monthly summary or daily summary

   - A site-usage summary for an entire site collection

4. Navigate to the top-level website, and select **Site Settings**.

5. Select **Go to Site Administration**.

6. Under **Site Collection Administration**, select **View Site Collection Usage Summary**. This provides a summary of the entire site collection usage.

To better understand what might be the bottleneck of the portal, it makes sense to check for several counters on the different servers. We can divide the counters in three different groups, as shown in Table 10-6.

Table 10-6   Counters by Platform

Platform	Counters
Client-Side Counters	Processor(_Total)\\% Processor Time
	Memory\Pages/sec
Windows 2003 and IIS Counters	File Cache Flushes/Hits
	ASP.net Application Restarts
	ASP.net Requests/Second
	ASP.net Requests Queued
	ASP.net Requests Rejected
	ASP.net Request Wait Time
	Processor(_Total)\\% Processor Time
	Memory\Pages/sec
	System\Context Switches/sec
	Process(inetinfo)\\% Processor Time
	Process(inetinfo)\Working Set
	Process(w3wp)\\% Processor Time
	Process(w3wp)\Working Set
	Process(LSASS)\\% Processor Time

Table 10-6   Counters by Platform   *(continued)*

Platform	Counters
SQL Counters	Memory\Pages/sec
	System\Context Switches/sec
	Process(sqlservr)\% Processor Time
	Process(sqlservr)\Working Set
	SQLServer:General Statistics\User Connections
	SQLServer:Databases\Transactions/sec
	SQLServer:Locks\Number of Deadlocks/sec
	SQLServer:Locks\Lock Waits/sec
	SQLServer:Locks\Lock Wait Time (ms)
	SQLServer:SQL Statistics\Batch Requests/sec

Operation Management

Hardware redundancy is an important element for high availability, but ongoing health monitoring is required to guarantee that this redundancy remains intact. For example, if one of the front-end Web servers fails and this failure remains undetected, it jeopardizes the high availability of the Web servers. Ongoing health monitoring and failure detection are vital to meeting the high availability goals of the infrastructure.

This part of this chapter focuses on the incident and performance aspects of managing the healthy operation of the architecture. These aspects include the following items:

- **Incident, or fault, management.**   Fault detection, fault registration, fault assignment, and fault resolution.

- **Performance management.**   Network and server capacity planning, availability, response time, throughput, and utilization. Statistics collection tools, traffic modeling techniques, and service probes are required to ensure that service level agreements are fulfilled.

Architectural Components

SharePoint Portal Server is a distributed application framework that uses multitier architecture. These components can be grouped as follows:

- Hardware

- Network infrastructure

- Operating system

- SharePoint Portal Server components

Healthy operation requires that you monitor each component and alert system administrators of problems. Most large enterprises already have policies in place for managing hardware, networks, and operating systems. The SharePoint Portal Server architecture does not introduce any new considerations with regard to those items.

Monitoring and Alerting Requirements

The more distributed an environment is, the more it requires monitoring. Failure to monitor the status of the architecture results in a reactive administrative model in which action is taken only after the problem has become serious enough for users to report it. The monitoring solution for this architecture provides a proactive administrative model in which problems are automatically detected before they escalate to a level that affects the system. To meet this aim, you should be aware of general monitoring principals and critical elements that need to be monitored.

It is imperative that alerts be used to bring any failure to the immediate attention of the system administrator so that it can be rectified. If this is not done, the infrastructure can slowly decay until it affects the performance of the website.

The monitoring and alerting infrastructure can also benefit scalability. Defining alerts based on system usage makes it possible to be proactive and start scaling the environment before users are affected. For example, an alert can be triggered when processor utilization on the Web servers is consistently above a preset limit. This can provide an indication that more servers or upgraded server hardware are required.

The following topics discuss several fundamental monitoring principles.

Monitoring Unobtrusively

A poorly designed or poorly implemented monitoring strategy can adversely affect system performance or operation. In general, the monitoring solution should have as minimal an impact as possible on the system it is monitoring, while providing all relevant information.

For example, when using a probe, it is sufficient to retrieve a single entry, which indicates that the server is functional, instead of retrieving multiple entries. The system should be probed only as often as absolutely necessary to provide adequate responsiveness. This limits the additional burden on the servers and applications. Probing a system too soon and too often returns failure data sooner, but it can place an obtrusive burden on the services.

Avoiding Cascading Failures

If a failure occurs, it can trigger other alerts in the monitoring solution. For example, if one set of servers running Internet Information Services (IIS) fails, this might place an additional load on the remaining servers, in turn generating alerts from those servers. If this happens, you should disable noncritical services or applications to reduce the load on the remaining servers. You should also evaluate system capabilities to proactively provide extra system capacity in case the problem recurs.

Maintaining a Problem History

You should design the monitoring solution to provide an accurate history of events and problems. For example, if the network management and monitoring system logs events in a standard format, the IIS-related entries can be periodically extracted, compiled, and archived in a central location for periodic review later. These extracted logs provide critical trend data that can be used to perform the following tasks:

- Identify recurring problems.

- Support capacity planning.

- Provide summary information about reliability and availability.

You should consider maintaining an issue log to track problems and solutions for future reference. If a problem recurs, future users can see how it was previously resolved.

Maintaining a Written Plan

You need a written plan that provides timely, accurate, consistent, and reusable responses for every failure, event, or problem. Executing a consistent plan for addressing recurring events helps avoid wasting time, resources, and money.

Using Effective Notification Techniques

Actively capturing real-time event information is useful only if the responsible parties are notified to implement the action plan. Event notification accomplishes the following four important goals:

- It notifies the parties responsible for fixing the problem.

- It notifies the parties responsible for administration of the system.

- It notifies the parties affected by the event. Users do not need to know the details of the problem, but they need to know if there is an interruption, or anticipated interruption, and when the problem will be resolved.

- It notifies each party to take appropriate action.

After you have captured an event and have notified the responsible people, you should do the following:

- Minimize the impact of the problem.

- Perform a root-cause analysis to determine the exact nature of the problem.

- Correct the problem.

- Create a plan for providing a long-term solution and a reusable action plan should the event recur.

Monitoring Performance Counters

Most large enterprises have some tools in place for monitoring hardware, software, and applications. Many of these products provide a central interface for monitoring and sending alerts to system administrators to notify them of hardware component failures and loads exceeding thresholds.

Microsoft products such as Microsoft SQL Server 2000, IIS 6.0, and SharePoint Portal Server 2003 include SNMP Management Information Bases (MIBs), which make this monitoring possible. An MIB is a set of objects that represent information about a device. The MIBs store the performance counter results, which are readable through Windows Server 2003 System Monitor (known as Performance Monitor in Microsoft Windows 2000).

Certain critical performance counters provide early indicators of loads approaching thresholds or irregular load behavior. This chapter provides an extensive list of available performance counters.

> **More Info**   For more information about how you can log performance counters, see Windows Server 2003 Help and Support Center and search for "monitoring server performance." You can access the Windows Server 2003 Help and Support Center by pressing the **F1** key.

Microsoft Operations Manager

Microsoft Operations Manager delivers enterprise-class operations management by providing comprehensive event management, proactive monitoring and alerting, reporting, and trend analysis. The Application Management Pack, which is the product support knowledge base included in Microsoft Operations Manager, helps you reduce the day-to-day support costs associated with running applications and services in a Windows-based environment.

The Microsoft Office SharePoint Portal Server 2003 management pack module monitors events placed in the Application event log. The module highlights events that indicate possible service outages or configuration problems so that you can quickly take corrective or preventative actions. For example, the management pack module alerts you of the following critical conditions:

- Data backup or restore failures
- Core services, such as search, alert notifications, and administration, failures
- Content source update failures
- Search propagation of one or more content indexes failures
- Audience compilation or profile import failures

Hardware Monitoring

To maintain server uptime, systems must operate within closely controlled environmental conditions. Otherwise, system components fail at a greater rate than they would under normal operating conditions. Therefore, it is important to monitor the following elements:

- **System temperature.**   The status of the thermal environment, which might move out of an acceptable range because of a failed system fan, opened computer hood, or high temperature in the external environment.

- **System fan status.**   The system and CPU fan, which affects the system temperature.

- **UPS battery condition.**   The battery low status of the uninterruptible power supply (UPS).

- **System reboot status.**   The server's condition and reboot counts.

- **Disk and array status.**   The status of system drives and arrays, such as hard and recovered read errors, seek errors, and data request timeouts.

- **SCSI status.**   The status of Small Computer System Interface (SCSI) systems, such as SCSI seek errors, timeouts, and read errors; Array Controller prefailure events; and tape rewrites, rereads, and noncorrectable tape errors.

- **NIC status.**   Packets received and transmitted with errors and packets discarded.

Some hardware vendors provide hardware management agents with defect detection and alerting features. Depending on the specific vendor implementation, you can tightly integrate the hardware management agents into Microsoft Operations Manager (MOM) or other third-party monitoring products that support standard SNMP MIBs. The ability to tightly integrate the various hardware-specific management agents into monitoring and alerting products is a major strength of operation management. When selecting the server hardware, evaluate the management facilities offered by the server vendor and determine how well they can be integrated into your overall solution.

The accelerator architecture has been tested on Hewlett-Packard ProLiant servers that are equipped with the Insight Manager tool. Insight Manager provides in-depth fault and performance management of ProLiant servers. Prefailure alerts provide notification of potential failures before they result in unplanned downtime. Remote Insight Lights-Out Edition speeds up problem diagnosis and resolution.

More Info   For more information about Insight Manager, see the Hewlett-Packard Web page at *http://www.compaq.com/manage*.

Network Infrastructure

The following topics summarize the dependencies between SharePoint Portal Server 2003 and these network infrastructure components:

- DNS server
- Proxy servers
- Network traffic
- Network Load Balancing
- Windows Server 2003
- SharePoint Portal Server counters
- Front-end Web servers
- System performance counters
- Application performance counters
- Search servers
- SQL Server–based servers

DNS Server

Each portal requires a host entry in DNS. This can be a server name or a host header name for virtual websites. These entries in DNS define the URLs that allow end users to access the portal. The performance counters for the DNS server are the same as those for the Windows operating system. (See Table 10-1 for details.)

Proxy Servers

If you specify content sources that require crawling other websites, make sure that the proxy settings are defined correctly in the Content Source configuration.

Network Traffic

The logical grouping of services to a virtual local area network (VLAN) enables a service group to make intensive use of a network segment. The services assigned to a VLAN are contained to just the allowed segments, based on access control lists (ACLs). Using ACLs ensures that one group does not affect the work of other groups. The VLAN configuration improves general network performance by not slowing down other groups that share the network.

Monitor the network traffic in the server farm subnet. If the subnet is too congested, you might consider hosting the front-end Web servers in a subnet different than that for back-end servers, such as SQL Server–based servers, index servers, and search servers.

In addition, consider adding a separate subnet for online backup and restore and monitoring by adding additional NICs to each server to reduce the network traffic on the VLAN that carries the end-user access traffic.

You can measure the traffic in the network by checking the SNMP MIBs of interface devices, calculated as total bytes per second.

Network Load Balancing

Event log records provide crucial information that can help you analyze and solve problems. Use the nlb.exe display command to display the most recent event log records produced by Network Load Balancing. For more information, see Chapter 4, "Windows SharePoint Services Architecture."

Windows Server 2003

Windows Server 2003 comes with tools for monitoring various services, including the Active Directory directory service. This information assists you in determining when the directory service is experiencing a problem as a result of the operating system. Windows Server 2003 probes are used across all servers to provide information about the status of the operating system.

Table 10-7 shows the most important operating system performance counters. You can observe these counters by using Windows Server 2003 System Monitor.

Table 10-7 Performance Counters and Thresholds for Windows Server 2003

Object	Counter	Interval/ minutes	Threshold	Description
Logical disk	Free mega- bytes	15	Less than 10 percent of logical disk size.	Shows unallocated disk space. If this threshold is met, the system is running out of available disk space.
Logical disk	% free space	15	15 percent.	Shows unallocated disk space. If this threshold is met, the system is running out of available disk space.
Logical disk	% disk time	15	90 percent.	% disk time is the percentage of elapsed time that the selected disk drive was busy servicing read or write requests.
Physical disk	Disk reads/sec, Disk writes/sec	15	Depends on manufacturer's specifications.	Checks the specified disk transfer rate to verify that this rate does not exceed the specifications. In general, Ultra Wide SCSI disks can handle 50 to 70 I/O operations per second.
Physical disk	Current disk queue length	1	Number of spindles plus 2.	This is an instantaneous counter. Observe the value over several intervals. For an average over time, use physical disk\average disk queue length.

Table 10-7 Performance Counters and Thresholds for Windows Server 2003 *(continued)*

Object	Counter	Interval/ minutes	Threshold	Description
Memory	Available MB	15	4 MB.	If this threshold is met, the system has run out of available memory. Imminent service failure is likely.
Memory	Page faults/sec	5	20 faults/sec.	A high rate of page faults indicates a lack of physical memory.
Network segment	% net utilization	15	Depends on type of network.	Determine the threshold based on the type of network. For Ethernet, 30 percent is the recommended threshold.
Paging file	Paging file % usage	15	Above 70 percent.	Review this value in conjunction with available bytes and pages/sec to understand paging activity.
Processor	% DPC time total	15	10 percent of all processor work deferred.	Indicates work that was deferred because the server was too busy. Possible processor congestion.
Processor	% processor time	1	85 percent averaged over three intervals.	Identifies processes that are using a high percentage of processor time. Upgrade to a faster processor, or install an additional processor.
Processor	Interrupts/sec	5	Depends on processor. For current CPUs, use a threshold of 1500 interrupts per second.	A dramatic increase in this counter value without a corresponding increase in system activity indicates a hardware problem. Identify the network adapter or disk controller card causing the interrupts. It might be necessary to install an additional adapter or controller card.
Server	Bytes total/sec	5	Dependent on network topology.	If the sum of bytes total/sec for all servers is roughly equal to the maximum transfer rates of the network, it might be necessary to segment the network.
Server	Work item shortages	1	3 shortages.	If the value reaches this threshold, consider tuning the InitWorkItems or MaxWorkItems entries in the registry. For more information about this topic, search the Microsoft Knowledge Base using the keyword "MaxWorkItems." See the Caution following this table regarding editing the registry.
Server	Queue length	5	4.	If the value reaches this threshold, there might be a processor bottleneck. This is an instantaneous counter. Observe the value over several intervals.

Table 10-7 **Performance Counters and Thresholds for Windows Server 2003** *(continued)*

Object	Counter	Interval/ minutes	Threshold	Description
System	Context switches/sec	15	70,000 switches/sec.	Indicates excessive transitions. There might be too many applications or services running, or their load on the system might be too high. Consider offloading this demand.
System	Processor queue length	1	6 averaged over 5 intervals.	The CPU is not fast enough to process requests as they occur. For domain controllers, if the replication topology is correct and the condition is not caused by failover from another domain controller, consider upgrading the CPU.

Caution Do not use a registry editor to edit the registry directly unless there is no alternative. The registry editors bypass the standard safeguards provided by administrative tools. These safeguards prevent entry of conflicting settings or settings that are likely to degrade performance or damage a system. Editing the registry directly can have serious, unexpected consequences that can prevent the system from starting and require that the Windows Server 2003 operating system be reinstalled. To configure or customize the Windows Server 2003 operating system, use the programs in Control Panel or Microsoft Management Console (MMC) whenever possible.

More Info For more information about operating system monitoring features, refer to the Windows Server 2003 Help and Support Center. You can access the Windows Server 2003 Help and Support Center by pressing the **F1** key.

SharePoint Portal Server Components

The following three critical SNMP MIBs must be monitored for each server in the SharePoint Portal Server architecture:

- Disk
- Processor
- Memory

These three general performance counters provide a quick indicator of server health. These indicators should be used only when required for further investigation of system behavior or troubleshooting purposes. Table 10-8 provides details about monitoring these performance counters.

Table 10-8   Performance Counters and Thresholds for All SharePoint Portal Servers

Object	Counter	Interval/ minutes	Threshold	Description
Logical disk	Free megabytes	15	<10 percent of logical disk size.	Shows unallocated disk space. If this threshold is met, the system is running out of available disk space.
Memory	Available MB	15	4 MB.	If this threshold is met, the system has run out of available memory; imminent service failure is likely.
Memory	Page faults/sec	5	700 faults/sec.	A high rate of page faults indicates a lack of physical memory.
Processor	% DPC time_total	15	10 percent of processor work deferred.	Indicates work that was deferred because the domain controller was too busy; possible processor congestion.
Processor	% processor time_total	1	85 percent busy averaged over 3 intervals.	Indicates the CPU is overloaded. To determine if CPU load is being used by a process, examine the "% processor time – process name" counter. Other processes have their respective counters as well.
System	Context switches/sec	15	70,000 switches/sec.	Indicates excessive transitions. There might be too many applications or services running, or their load on the system is too high. Consider offloading this demand.
System	Processor queue length	1	6 averaged over 5 intervals.	The CPU is not fast enough to process requests as they occur. If the replication topology is correct and the condition is not caused by failover from another domain controller, consider upgrading the CPU.
System	System uptime	5		Essential counter for measuring portal server reliability.

Front-End Web Servers

SharePoint Portal Server 2003 is a Web-based .NET application that runs on an IIS 6.0 Web server. Windows Server 2003 System Monitor is shipped with SNMP MIBs—for .NET applications, Web Services, and IIS—that monitor system behavior.

IIS 6.0 Application Pools

When you create a new portal and extend it to the other front-end Web servers in the server farm, you have the option to create a new application pool or use an existing application pool. The decision that you make has the following impacts:

- Creating a new application pool uses more memory, but it helps the stability of the portal.

- If you share one application pool among many portals, you have saved memory space at the cost of cascading failure to other portals if the application pool doesn't function properly.

It is essential that you properly configure the application pool to ensure the health and reliability of an Active Server Pages (ASP) .NET application. All the relevant settings are found on the application pool property sheet.

IIS 6.0 distinguishes between proactive and reactive recycling. IIS performs proactive recycling for known conditions and reactive recycling for unknown or dynamic conditions. For proactive recycling, IIS 6.0 checks the elapsed time, the number of requests completed, the scheduled time, and the amount of memory used. By default, events are only logged in the application event log if the recycling occurs based on the memory limit trigger.

Table 10-9 describes the available IIS 6.0 application pool settings, which are accessible through the IIS MMC snap-in.

Table 10-9   Application Pool Settings for IIS 6.0

Setting	Description
Idle timeout	Controls whether IIS shuts down idle worker processes. Worker processes serving the application pool are shut down after being idle for the specified amount of time.
Request queue limit	Controls the size of the request queue. This setting prevents large numbers of requests from queuing up and overloading the Web server.
CPU monitoring	Specifies what action is to be taken if a CPU usage threshold is reached.
Web garden	Controls the number of worker processes for the application pool.
Enable pinging	Specifies how often the Web Administration Service (WAS) pings each worker process in the application pool to detect its status.
Enable rapid fail protection	Configures IIS to remove the application pool from service if a specified number of crashes occur within the specified time period. If a worker process is removed from service, HTTP.sys responds to any incoming request with a "503 Service Unavailable" message.
Startup time limit	Specifies the amount of time a process is allowed for startup before IIS assumes that it has not started correctly and terminates it. Terminated processes are logged in the system event log.
Shutdown time limit	Tells the WAS how to cope with worker processes that hang during shutdown. If a worker process has not shut down during the specified time limit, it is terminated by the WAS.

ASP.NET supports two groups of performance counters: system and application. System performance counters are exposed in Windows Server 2003 System Monitor in the ASP.NET System performance counter object, and application performance counters are exposed in the ASP.NET Applications performance object.

> **Note**   There is a significant difference between the State Server Sessions counters found in the ASP.NET System performance object and the Sessions counters found in the ASP.NET Applications performance object. The former apply only to the server computer upon which the state server is running. The latter apply only to user sessions that occur in process.

System Performance Counters

ASP.NET supports the system performance counters detailed in Table 10-10. These aggregate information for all ASP.NET applications on a Web server computer, or they apply generally to a system of ASP.NET servers running the same applications. These can include Web server farms and Web gardens.

Table 10-10   System Performance Counters

Counter	Description
Application restarts	The number of times that an application has been restarted during the Web server's lifetime. Application restarts are incremented with each Application_OnEnd event. This value is reset every time the IIS host is restarted.
Applications running	The number of applications running on the server.
Requests disconnected	The number of requests disconnected due to a communications failure.
Requests queued	The number of requests waiting for service from the queue.
Requests rejected	The total number of requests not executed because of insufficient server resources to process them. This counter represents the number of requests that return a 503 HTTP status code, indicating that the server is too busy.
Request wait time	The number of milliseconds that the most recent request waited for processing in the queue.
Worker process restarts	The number of times a worker process has been restarted on the server computer.
Worker process running	The number of worker processes running on the server computer.

Application Performance Counters

ASP.NET supports the application performance counters detailed in Table 10-11, which you can use to monitor the performance of a single instance of an ASP.NET application. A unique instance appears for these counters, named __Total__, which aggregates counters for all applications on a Web server (similar to the global counters in Table 10-10). The __Total__ instance is always available. The counters will display zero when no applications are present on the server.

Table 10-11   Application Performance Counters

Counter	Description
Errors total	The total number of errors that occur during the execution of HTTP requests. Includes any parser, compilation, or run-time errors. This counter is the sum of the Errors During Compilation, Preprocessing, and Request Execution counters.
Errors total/sec	The number of errors per second that occur during the execution of HTTP requests; includes any parser, compilation, or run-time errors.
Requests failed	The total number of failed requests, including requests that timed out, requests that were not authorized (status code 401), or requests not found (status code 404 or status code 414). Note that the equivalent ASP counter also increments on requests rejected, which cannot be done (because the rejection is done by IIS and not the process model).
Requests not found	The number of requests that failed because resources were not found (status code 404 or 414).
Requests not authorized	The number of requests that failed due to no authorization (status code 401).
Requests succeeded	The number of requests that executed successfully (status code 200).
Requests timed out	The number of requests that timed out.
Requests total	The total number of requests since the service was started.
Requests/sec	The number of requests executed per second.
Transactions aborted	The number of transactions aborted.
Transactions committed	The number of transactions committed.
Transactions pending	The number of transactions in progress.
Transactions total	The total number of transactions since the service was started.
Transactions/sec	The number of transactions started per second.

Search Servers

This section describes performance counters available for the following search services:

■ SharePoint Portal Server Search service

■ SharePoint Portal Server Search Catalog content indexes

■ Index server

SharePoint Portal Server Search

Table 10-12 lists the most important search server performance counters available through Windows Server 2003 System Monitor.

Table 10-12   Search Performance Counters

Counter	Description
Current connections	The number of currently established connections between the Search service and all clients.
Queries	Cumulative number of queries posted to the server.
Failed queries	The number of queries that have failed.
Results	The cumulative number of results returned to clients.

SharePoint Portal Server Search Catalogs

Table 10-13 lists the most important content index performance counters available for each search catalog instance through Windows Server 2003 System Monitor.

Table 10-13   Content Index Performance Counters

Counter	Description
Current connections	The number of currently established connections between the Search service and all clients.
Queries	Cumulative number of queries posted to the server.
Failed queries	The number of queries that have failed.
Results	The cumulative number of results returned to clients.
Number of documents	The total number of documents in the catalog.
Index size (MB)	Size of catalog data in megabytes.

Index Server

Table 10-14 lists the performance counters available for each search index.

Table 10-14   Search Index Performance Counters

Counter	Description
Number of documents	The total number of documents in the catalog.
Index size (MB)	Size of catalog data in megabytes.

SQL Server

In addition to the general performance counters and alert settings detailed previously for each server, you can capture additional counters that are SQL Server–related, including the following:

- SQLServer:Databases Application Database: Log Growths

- SQLServer:Databases Application Database: Percent Log Used

- SQLServer:Databases Application Database: Transactions/sec

- SQLServer:General Statistics: User Connections

- SQLServer:Locks: Lock Waits/sec

- SQLServer:Locks: Number of Deadlocks/sec

- SQLServer:Memory Manager: Memory Grants Pending

Monitoring these elements helps to ensure that the SQL Server databases running within the portal architecture perform optimally and that any issues are dealt with promptly. It also allows for capacity planning and performance tuning of the environment, which enables you to provide continuous effective service.

Re-indexing Site Databases

It is critical that you re-index the site database tables after doing lots of updates, such as updating statistics or bulk loading of profiles, documents, or lists. By re-indexing the tables in the site database using a simple SQL script, you can improve database performance by 5 to 25 percent.

To re-index, run the following scripts against the site databases:

- UPDATE STATISTICS Personalization

- UPDATE STATISTICS UserInfo

- UPDATE STATISTICS WebMembers

- UPDATE STATISTICS Sites

- UPDATE STATISTICS Webs

- UPDATE STATISTICS Lists

- UPDATE STATISTICS WebParts

- UPDATE STATISTICS Docs

- DBCC DBREINDEX (Personalization, ", 0)

- DBCC DBREINDEX (UserInfo, ", 0)

- DBCC DBREINDEX (WebMembers, ", 0)

- DBCC DBREINDEX (Sites, ", 0)

- DBCC DBREINDEX (Webs, ", 0)

- DBCC DBREINDEX (Lists, ", 0)

- DBCC DBREINDEX (WebParts, ", 0)

- DBCC DBREINDEX (Docs, ", 0)

Establishing a Performance Baseline

Monitoring the health of the architecture requires a baseline. It also requires a clear understanding of load factors introduced by each component of SharePoint Portal Server 2003, such as:

- What is the impact of the load introduced by indexing content on resources in each server?

- What is the impact of the load on computers running SQL Server? How do computers running SQL Server behave under different load factors? Which parameters are more critical?

- How does IIS 6.0 behave under specific loads, and what can be observed on front-end Web servers?

- What should be expected when end users work with the portal through an office client?

- What is the difference between load generated by using different SharePoint Portal Server functions, such as browsing home pages, team site creation, My Site navigation, or uploading documents?

The IIS log and SharePoint Portal Server Usage Analysis Processing logs can provide a realistic picture of how a portal is used in each company. Analysis of IIS logs over time gives important information about the usage patterns of the portal. It also provides information about what specific portal functions are used more frequently, the number of users accessing the portal, and peak-time usage of the portal during the day. Tying this information to records collected from performance measurements of the server running SQL Server, the Index server, the Search server, and the Web server provides a full picture of architecture behavior. With this information, you can establish a server performance baseline.

You should revise the baseline as the load on your portal changes. For example, you might define a baseline for an out-of-the-box portal installation, and as you add more indexes or more users, define a new baseline. Compare the two to understand the impact of the load on different counters that you are monitoring. The baseline is a useful reference for capacity planning, for distribution of SharePoint Portal services and components to the other servers, and for adding new servers to the architecture.

Analyzing Logs

System log files can be scanned for events that indicate an error and for indications of performance problems. Log file analysis enables you to perform proactive monitoring, in which problematic conditions and indications of impending problems are identified before they affect customers. The following sections discuss the logs that are available for monitoring the health of the portal architecture.

Windows Server 2003 Event Logs

You can configure the level of information and types of events to be logged in Windows Server 2003 event logs. Check these event logs regularly to verify that the required operating system, SharePoint Portal Server, and IIS are running.

> **More Info**   The .NET Framework SDK provides customizable components for managing logs programmatically. For more information about managing event logs using these components, see the .NET documentation about event logs at *http://msdn.microsoft.com/vstudio/using/understand/perf /default.aspx?pull=/library/en-us/dnbda/html/exceptdotnet.asp.*

SQL Server 2000 Logs

SQL Server 2000 provides logs to monitor server processes, databases, and user activities. Checking SQL Server logs is the first step in analyzing database-related problems. After checking logs, you can trace problems by using other tools such as SQL Server Profiler for detailed analysis and resolution of problems.

When you create a new portal, SharePoint Portal Server creates three new databases, in addition to a configuration database that can be shared among different portals. When these databases are created, SharePoint Portal Server allocates default sizes for data files and transaction logs. To avoid the additional overhead added by the auto-grow feature of SQL Server, you can increase the initial size of data and transaction files based on your usage prediction. Continually using the auto-grow feature of data file and transaction logs can slow down database-related activities.

IIS 6.0 and SharePoint Portal Server Usage Analysis Processing Logs

The IIS and SharePoint Portal Server Usage Analysis Processing logs provide extensive information in log files that can detect how end users access and use SharePoint Portal Server with possible errors. These log files also can be used for peak-usage analysis and to determine which pages are most frequently used. Peak-usage analysis in conjunction with records obtained from performance monitoring logs can be used for capacity planning. Based on this information, you can decide if you need an additional server in the front-end Web server farm.

SharePoint Portal Server Diagnostic Tools

You can configure diagnostic tools through the SharePoint Portal Server Central Administration interface to detect errors and help with troubleshooting. You can configure these logs to record SharePoint Portal Server–related messages at the following levels:

- Do not run logging on this server

- Log critical events only

- Log informational events and critical events

- Log all tracing information

You can choose one of these options for each computer running SharePoint Portal Server. You can also configure a separate log that keeps track of information for a specific service. The SharePoint Portal Server services that provide logging capabilities are as follows:

- WWW Worker Process (w3wp.exe)

- Administration Service (spsadmin.exe)

- Search Service (spssearch.exe)

- Backup and Restore (spsbackup.exe)

- Notification Service (spsNotificationService.exe)

- Single Sign-On Service (ssosrv.exe)

Monitoring Custom Web Parts

Most customers customize the accelerator portal by developing new Web Parts, integrating with other applications, or using third-party Web Parts. Before adding a Web Part to the production portal, you should evaluate the impact of the load generated by new Web Parts.

Most companies have a separate development environment for this purpose, and some have staging environments that closely mimic the production portal configuration, which provides a more realistic picture of the impact of adding new Web Parts. In any case, you should thoroughly debug and test any custom Web Part and have a good understanding of the possible load that a new Web Part will generate in your accelerator portal.

Table 10-15 details the information you can use to compare the performance baseline of your portal with custom Web Parts against the results of your portal when it did not include the Web Parts. You can then determine the additional load and possible impact on other performance counters. These counters are available through Windows Server 2003 System Monitor.

Table 10-15   **Performance Monitoring of Custom Web Parts**

Type	Information	Sampling Frequency
General system information	Average CPU usage	Every two minutes
	Average virtual bytes	Every two minutes
	Average private bytes	Every two minutes
	Average pool paged bytes	Every two minutes
	Average pool nonpaged bytes	Every two minutes
	Average working set	Every two minutes
	Average context switches/sec	Every two minutes
	Average pages/sec	Every two minutes
	Average interrupts/sec	Every two minutes
	Physical disk—average current queue length	Every two minutes
	ISAPI requests processed	Total over a two-hour period
	ASP requests processed	Total over a two-hour period
	Total requests processed	Total over a two-hour period
	Web service—service uptime	Every two hours
ASP.NET	Average requests queued	Every two minutes
	Average request execution time	Every two minutes
	Average request wait time	Every two minutes
ASP.NET applications	Average requests executing	Every two minutes
	Requests total	Total over a two-hour period
	Output cache hits	Total over a two-hour period
	Output cache misses	Total over a two-hour period
	Average output cache entries	Every two minutes
Web service cache	File cache hits	Total over a two-hour period
	File cache misses	Total over a two-hour period
	File cache flushes	Total over a two-hour period
	Average current file cache memory usage	Every two minutes
	Average current files cached	Every two minutes
	Kernel: URI cache hits	Total over a two-hour period
	Kernel: URI cache misses	Total over a two-hour period

Table 10-15   Performance Monitoring of Custom Web Parts   *(continued)*

Type	Information	Sampling Frequency
Inetinfo process information	Average CPU usage	Every two minutes
	Average virtual bytes	Every two minutes
	Average private bytes	Every two minutes
	Average pool paged bytes	Every two minutes
	Average pool nonpaged bytes	Every two minutes
	Average working set	Every two minutes
	Average thread count	Every two minutes
Inetinfo process information	Average handle count	Every two minutes
	Average virtual bytes	Every two minutes
	Average private bytes	Every two minutes
	Average pool paged bytes	Every two minutes
	Average pool nonpaged bytes	Every two minutes
	Average working set	Every two minutes
	Average thread count	Every two minutes
	Average handle count	Every two minutes
	Average number deployed	Every two minutes
Web Administration Service (WAS) process information	Average CPU usage	Every two minutes
	Average virtual bytes	Every two minutes
	Average private bytes	Every two minutes
	Average pool paged bytes	Every two minutes
	Average pool nonpaged bytes	Every two minutes
	Average working set	Every two minutes
	Average thread count	Every two minutes
	Average handle count	Every two minutes
W3WP (worker process) process information	Average aggregate CPU usage	Every two minutes
	Average virtual bytes	Every two minutes
	Average private bytes	Every two minutes
	Average pool paged bytes	Every two minutes
	Average pool nonpaged bytes	Every two minutes
	Average working set	Every two minutes
	Average thread count	Every two minutes
	Average handle count	Every two minutes
	Average number deployed	Every two minutes

Table 10-15   Performance Monitoring of Custom Web Parts   *(continued)*

Type	Information	Sampling Frequency
All system processes	CPU usage	Every two hours
	Virtual bytes	Every two hours
	Private bytes	Every two hours
	Pool paged bytes	Every two hours
	Pool nonpaged bytes	Every two hours
	Working set	Every two hours
	Thread count	Every two hours

> **Note**   For an explanation of specific performance counters, refer to the Windows Server 2003 Help and Support Center. You can access the Windows Server 2003 Help and Support Center by pressing the **F1** key.

Indirect Monitoring

Monitoring the applications that directly use or access your portal provides an end-user view of the responsiveness and reliability of the system. Indirect monitoring provides a better picture of system response time to client requests, especially in environments that are geographically disparate. Indirect monitoring provides an accurate view of application performance and effectiveness.

There are third-party solutions that run scripts to simulate client sample loads from different locations at specific intervals. You can also use free tools and utilities, such as HTTPPing, to achieve the same goal. For more information about HTTPPing, visit the MSDN website at *http://msdn.microsoft.com*, and search for "HTTPPing."

Summary

In this chapter, we have outlined some methods and counters you'll need to use to effectively monitor SharePoint Portal Server 2003. In the next chapter, we'll outline how to use Microsoft Operations Manager to streamline performance monitoring of your servers.

Part IV

Deployment Scenarios

Chapter 11

Deploying a Single Server and a Small Server Farm

This chapter discusses how to deploy a single server or a small server farm. A *single-server* deployment has the database installed on the same server as Microsoft Share-Point Products and Technologies, whereas a *small farm* has SharePoint Portal Server 2003 or Windows SharePoint Services installed on one machine and the database installed on a separate server. In this chapter, we will cover the effect of these configurations on Microsoft Windows SharePoint Services and Microsoft Office Share-Point Portal Server 2003 deployments.

This chapter does not cover detailed step-by-step instructions on how to install Windows SharePoint Services and SharePoint Portal Server 2003. For that type of information, please refer to Chapter 2, "Installing Windows SharePoint Services," and Chapter 3, "Installing Microsoft Office SharePoint Portal Server 2003."

Single Server

The single server must be running Microsoft Windows Server 2003 (Standard, Enterprise, or Datacenter). You must configure the server as a Web server, running Internet Information Services (IIS) in IIS 6.0 worker process isolation mode, and you must be running ASP.NET. The computer must be using the NTFS file system. You can deploy a single-server configuration either as a stand-alone single server using Microsoft SQL Server 2000 Desktop Engine (Windows) (WMSDE) or as a single server with Microsoft SQL Server 2000 Service Pack 3a or higher.

> **Note**   The WMSDE is a build of MSDE specifically designed for Windows Components. MSDE has a 2-GB limit to the size of its database, and it limits the number of concurrent connections to 10. With WMSDE, both these limitations have been removed, but checks have been put in place so that only Windows Components can modify the structure of the database.

This section will now cover these two options when deploying Windows SharePoint Services and SharePoint Portal Server 2003.

Windows SharePoint Services

The quickest way to get started with Windows SharePoint Services is to install it on a single-server computer. This allows you to set up a small-scale installation to host several websites without performing many steps. Multiple sites and subsites are grouped in **site collections** on each **virtual server** in IIS that is extended with Windows SharePoint Services. An Internet Server Applications Program Interface (**ISAPI**) filter maps incoming URLs to specific sites on that virtual server. Scaling is achieved by adding site collections to an existing virtual server or by adding subsites to an existing site collection. Each virtual server has its own set of content databases in WMSDE or SQL Server. The configuration database directs each virtual server to the appropriate content database for a given website. The content for the top-level website and any subsites within a site collection is stored in the same content database.

When you install Windows SharePoint Services on a single server, you can choose between WMSDE and SQL Server as follows:

- **WMSDE.**   By using the default options during setup, WMSDE is automatically installed and used to create the database for your websites. You do not have to perform any other configuration steps to create the database. This installation scenario offers you the ability to host several websites without a great deal of overhead. You should consider using SQL Server instead of WMSDE if you anticipate supporting more than 1000 websites, if there are more than 10 active and large websites, or if you need a clustered database for high availability. Search features are available only for Windows SharePoint Services with Microsoft SQL Server 2000. If you are running WMSDE for your database, no search features are available. If you want to allow full-text searching on your websites, you must upgrade to SQL Server 2000.

- **SQL Server.**   Extract the Windows SharePoint Services installation files, and when the installation process starts, click Cancel. Run setup from the command line, and use the remotesql=yes property. This property allows you to install Windows SharePoint Services to work with an existing installation of SQL

Server 2000—that is, SQL Server must be installed prior to you starting the Windows SharePoint Services setup process. This installation scenario allows you to support a larger set of websites. When you use this method, you must perform additional steps to configure SQL Server and Windows SharePoint Services to work together. This is also true if you want to use SQL Server with SharePoint Portal Server. Refer to Chapters 2 and 3 for more information. Such additional steps could include the creation of additional accounts to use with SQL Server, configuring the SQL Server database to use Windows authentication, and connecting your extended virtual server to the SQL server where the configuration and content databases will be created.

For either option, the database size required for Windows SharePoint Services depends on the number and size of the websites your server supports. You should not consider using WMSDE if you will need to store more than 2 to 4 GB of data, if you want the database placed on a different server than Windows SharePoint Services, or if you want to use Windows SharePoint Services search capability. (Although there is no upper limit to the size of databases when you use WMSDE, you might find that when databases get to a certain size it will be easier to manage them by using SQL Server.) For more information on capacity planning, please refer to Chapter 9, "Capacity Planning."

For more information on Windows SharePoint Services installation and configuration considerations, please refer to Chapter 2.

Caution   During setup, in a default installation, Windows SharePoint Services extends the default virtual server (the default website in IIS) with Windows SharePoint Services. If you have a website running on the default website in IIS, Windows SharePoint Services will take over that website during installation. Also, before installing Windows SharePoint Services, verify that Microsoft FrontPage Server Extensions 2002 are not running on the virtual server on port 80. If FrontPage Server Extensions are running on the default virtual server, Windows SharePoint Services will not extend the virtual server during installation. (If you upgraded from Microsoft Windows 2000 to Windows Server 2003, FrontPage Server Extensions were installed by default to port 80.)

SharePoint Portal Server 2003

For SharePoint Portal Server 2003, the single server runs the Web component, index component, search component, and the job server; and it optionally runs the components for backward compatibility with Microsoft SharePoint Portal Server 2001 document libraries. SharePoint Portal Server 2003 is supported only on servers that are members of a Microsoft Windows NT 4.0, Windows 2000, or Windows Server 2003 domain. When you install SharePoint Portal Server 2003, setup automatically installs Windows SharePoint Services if it is not already installed. The single-server database options would be as follows:

- **WMSDE.**   In SharePoint Portal Server 2003 setup, choose to install SharePoint Portal Server with the database engine on the server. This installs the MSDE to store the databases. WMSDE has the same limited throughput ability and capacity with SharePoint Portal Server as it has with Windows SharePoint Services, as discussed in the previous section. It supports databases with a maximum size of 4 gigabytes (GB). If your deployment requires significant scalability or must store more than 2 to 4 GB of documents, you should use SQL Server in your deployment.

- **SQL Server.**   This server has SQL Server installed prior to the start of the SharePoint Portal Server installation process, and then in the installation process you choose the option to install SharePoint Portal Server without the database engine on the server.

For more information on SharePoint Portal Server 2003 installation and configuration considerations, please refer to Chapter 3.

Database Automation and Maintenance

Once you have installed Windows SharePoint Services or SharePoint Portal Server on a single server, the deployment is not complete until you have set up maintenance tasks and operational procedures. This is another differentiating aspect that you should take into consideration when you choose between WMSDE and SQL Server.

You can complete many of the tasks needed to maintain and back up Windows SharePoint Services and SharePoint Portal Server 2003 by using the administration Web pages. (See Chapter 10, "Performance Monitoring in Microsoft Office SharePoint Portal Server 2003," Chapter 28, "Disaster Recovery in SharePoint Products and Technologies," and Chapter 29, "Usage Analysis Tools in SharePoint Products and Technologies.") However, there are other SQL Server administrative tasks that you might want to complete, especially if the website is heavily used, business critical, or has a high profile. Using the SharePoint Portal Server Central Administration pages, such database-specific tasks that are not available include backing up the system databases, monitoring processes, checking for database errors, and the ability to alert someone when database-related events occur.

The automation and maintenance of database administration tasks is easier with SQL Server than with WMSDE. You can manage SQL Server 2000 installations by using the SQL Server Enterprise Manager, which allows for local and remote management of SQL Servers. It also includes administration wizards that are designed to make database administration easier. To manage WMSDE databases, you will have to use the osql command-line tool. Database administration is outside the scope of this book. More information on database administrative tasks, the SQL Server Enterprise Manager, and the osql utility can be found in SQL Server Books Online, the January 2004 update of which can be found at *http://www.microsoft.com/downloads/details.aspx?FamilyID=A6F79CB1-A420-445F-8A4B-BD77A7DA194B&displaylang=en*.

Migrating from WMSDE to SQL Server 2000

After you have used Windows SharePoint Services or SharePoint Portal Server 2003 with WMSDE for some time, you might run into performance or storage problems and need to move to a more scaled-out solution. If you find yourself in this situation, you can switch to using Microsoft SQL Server 2000 as your database instead of WMSDE.

You can upgrade WMSDE in-place to SQL Server, although it is not recommended. The Windows SharePoint Services instructions to upgrade are inherently difficult. Instead, you should back up your data, reinstall the operating system, install SQL, and then install SharePoint Portal Server 2003 and restore your data. This scenario has been tested and has proved to be much easier than upgrading.

If you are moving to a larger environment, with one or many front-end Web servers and one or many back-end database servers, the process is more complicated. For more information on migrating WMSDE to SQL Server on the same server or to a separate server, see the "Migrating from WMSDE to a Remote SQL Server or Server Farm" section in Chapter 2 and the "Migrating from WMSDE to SQL Server" section in Chapter 3.

Small Farm

A small server farm has the following two servers:

- One front-end Web server, running SharePoint Products and Technologies. This server could have installed Windows SharePoint Portal Services or SharePoint Portal Server 2003 running the Web component, index, search, and job services. This server can optionally run the components for backward compatibility with SharePoint Portal Server 2001 document libraries, or this can be installed on a separate server.

- One server running SQL Server 2000 with Service Pack 3a or higher. You cannot use WMSDE in a small server farm configuration, as WMSDE cannot be connected to remotely. You can use WMSDE only in a single-server configuration.

> **Note**   More than one SQL server could be installed—that is, the SQL Server component can be either a single server or a clustered server. As long as you are running any supported SQL Server configuration, SharePoint Products and Technologies will view it as a single-server installation. This chapter assumes that the SQL component is installed on one server.

Additional servers can be added to this topology to enable higher availability, higher capacity, or both. These configurations are classified as medium or large server farms and are discussed in Chapter 12, "Deploying Medium and Large Server Farms."

The reasons for having the database on a different server to server, which has SharePoint Products and Technologies, include:

■ Performance and availability. The number of users a SharePoint deployment can support increases when the database is on a separate server.

■ Administration or policy boundaries.

■ Security, as in an Internet or extranet deployment scenario, where the Web server can be separated from the SQL server with a firewall.

■ SQL Server 2000 is already present on a server running other databases.

> **More Info**   For more information on the type of farm you should deploy and planning considerations, please refer to Chapter 9, "Capacity Planning," and the chapters in Part 8, "Securing SharePoint Products and Technologies."

The front-end Web server must have Windows Server 2003 installed and be running IIS in IIS 6.0 worker process isolation mode with ASP.NET allowed. The computer must be using the NTFS file system.

This section will now cover the deployment aspects specific to Windows SharePoint Services and SharePoint Portal Server 2003.

Windows SharePoint Services

The process for installing Windows SharePoint Services with a separate SQL server, also known as a remote SQL server, is the same as installing Windows SharePoint Services on the same machine as SQL server as described earlier, except you will have to specify the name of the remote SQL Server server in the configuration options.

SharePoint Portal Server 2003

For SharePoint Portal Server, you must set up and configure a small server farm according to specific instructions that are detailed in Chapter 12. Briefly, the installation process consists of the following tasks:

- Domain Account creation

    - Create a domain account, which for the purposes of this chapter will be called *domain\spsadmin*.

    - Add **domain\spsadmin** to the local **Power Users** group on the **Share-Point Portal Server**.

    - Add the **domain/spsadmin** to the local **Administrators** group on any server that hosts the components for backward-compatible document libraries.

- Server Two: SQL Server

    - Configure the **MSSQLSERVER** and **SQLSERVERAGENT** services to start automatically using domain account names, and then confirm that the service starts successfully at startup.

    - Configure the **domain/spsadmin** to have the Security Administrators and Database Creators server roles on this SQL Server instance.

- Server One: SharePoint Portal Server 2003

    - As with a single-server installation, ensure that the FrontPage Server Extensions are not installed.

    - Install SharePoint Portal Server 2003 as detailed in Chapter 3, choosing the option **without database engine**.

    - In the **Account** name box, type **domain/spsadmin**. This will be used for administrative operations that create, modify, or grant access to the configuration or portal site databases.

> **Warning**   The following user rights are granted automatically to this account (the configuration database administration account) on the local server: Replace A Process Level Token, Adjust Memory Quotas For A Process, and Log On As A Service. If you change this account by using the Configure Server Farm Account Settings page, the rights are not revoked automatically for the previous account. However, you can remove these rights by using **Local Security Settings**. To open Local Security Settings, click **Start**, point to **Administrative Tools**, and then click **Local Security Policy**.

■ On the Component Assignment page, only one server should be present, the row of check boxes—**Web**, **Search**, and **Index** roles—should be assigned to this server, and this server should also be selected in the **Job server** list in the **Job Server Component** section.

■ Create a portal site. At the end of a successful portal site creation, the Operation Successful page appears. You can then further configure the portal site.

■ Optional: Install and configure the components for backward-compatible document libraries.

■ Check that the installation is configured correctly and can be accessed as planned. Such a check should include ensuring that the proxy server settings for Internet access are specified correctly and that you can access and create information objects such as areas, topics, document libraries, and lists as planned.

Summary

This chapter discussed the deployment of Windows SharePoint Services and SharePoint Portal Server 2003 in a single-server and small farm configuration. It described the reasons why you might want to install SharePoint Products and Technologies using WMSDE and why you might need to migrate to SQL Server, either on the same machine as a SharePoint Portal Server installation or on a separate server.

Chapter 12

Deploying Medium and Large Server Farms

This chapter discusses how to deploy a medium or large server farm. The majority of the chapter consists of step-by-step instructions that can be used as a guide for deploying a farm. This chapter does not cover how to determine which type of farm to use in given situations. For that type of information, please refer to Chapter 9, "Capacity Planning."

This chapter should be viewed as a getting-started guide for building a medium or large server farm. It will cover everything necessary for building both a medium server farm and a larger server farm. It will also contain instructions for how to migrate from a medium farm to a large farm.

Topologies

Many permutations of topologies can be built using Microsoft Office SharePoint Portal Server 2003, but only a small number of these topologies are supported by Microsoft. The simplest topologies are the single-server and small-server-farm topologies, which have been covered in previous chapters.

Medium and large server-farm topologies can get much more complex. A *medium* server topology requires at a minimum one front-end Web server running the search application, one index/job server running SharePoint Portal Server 2003, and one database server running Microsoft SQL Server 2000 with Service Pack 3a or later. Additional servers can be added to this topology to enable higher availability, higher capacity, or both, but you cannot have a medium farm with fewer than four servers.

Several topologies are not supported by Microsoft. When you install one of these topologies, it will appear to function—that is, you can create the topology on the

Components Selection page, but it will not be eligible for support and you will not be able to create a new portal site in it. In addition, unsupported topologies cannot be backed up or restored. When you open SPSBackup.exe, it will show an error "Topology not supported" and exit. It is strongly recommended that you stay away from these unsupported topologies. Installing the database component on one of the servers running SharePoint Portal Server is an unsupported topology for a farm. Installing two or more servers with all (Web/search/index) components is also not supported.

Here are the supported topologies:

- **Small Server Farm.**   One server running SQL Server 2000 and one server running SharePoint Portal Server 2003 assigned the Web, Search, Job, and Index services.

- **Medium Server Farm.**   One or two servers running SharePoint Portal Server 2003 assigned the Web service (more commonly known as front-end Web servers) and running SharePoint Portal Server 2003 assigned the Search, Job, and Index services; and one server running SQL Server 2000.

- **Large Server Farm.**   Two to eight servers running SharePoint Portal Server 2003 assigned the Web service (more commonly known as front-end Web servers), two to four servers running SharePoint Portal Server 2003 assigned the Search service, one to four servers running SharePoint Portal Server 2003 assigned the Index service (one of which *must* be assigned the Job Server role), and any number of servers running SQL Server 2000.

In all supported topologies, you can use a single additional server running SharePoint Portal Server 2003 for the purpose of running the backward-compatible document library.

Two factors differentiate a medium farm from a large farm. The first factor is the server component matrix—you will need more servers to run a minimum large farm. The second difference is that the Web and search components run on all front-end Web servers in a medium farm, while on a large farm these components must each run on separate servers. Medium server farms become large server farms by adding Web/search front-end servers, using Network Load Balancing (NLB) to distribute the load, and by adding search and indexing servers to the server component matrix. As long as you stay within the boundaries of a prescribed server farm, any combination of these can be employed. Only four index servers can exist in a large server farm because each search server can only consume four separate catalogs. For more information about how each of these components affects performance, please see Chapter 9. The most common medium-farm topology consists of two front-end Web servers running search and indexing/job servers, and one SQL component, for a total of four servers. The SQL component can be either a single server or a clustered server, but because the cluster acts like one system, it will be discussed here as one component. SharePoint Portal Server does not really care what the SQL Server topology is because this is abstracted from the server farm deployment.

Therefore, you can be running any supported SQL topology and SharePoint Portal Server views it as a single-server installation for topology purposes. This is the topology that will be covered when discussing medium server farms in this chapter. Because this topology employs NLB as well as all other components required by a medium farm, the instructions provided can be used to easily add servers to the topology.

As mentioned previously, a large server farm is very similar to a medium server farm, except that the search and Web components run on separate systems and large server farms can support more servers than a medium farm. The minimum topology for a large server farm is two front-end Web servers running SharePoint Portal Server 2003, two search servers running SharePoint Portal Server 2003, one index management server running SharePoint Portal Server 2003, and one database component running Microsoft SQL Server 2000 Service Pack (SP) 3a. The SQL component can be either a single server or a clustered server, but because the cluster acts like one system, it will be discussed here as one component. The large server farm can be scaled out by adding front-end Web servers, search servers, or index management servers. You cannot have more than four search servers or four index management servers in any farm. Because only four catalogs can be consumed by the search servers, having more than four index management servers will cause search to function improperly, as some content sources will not be searched.

Both medium and large server farms support running one server with the backward-compatible document libraries. There can only be one server in the farm that has these components. In addition, each medium and large server farm requires one job server. The job server role must be assigned to an index management server, in part, because the job server is responsible for indexing all portal site content and people. Here is a complete list of all the job server activities:

- Managing the indexing of all portal content

- Indexing people from the profile database

- Hosting the Single Sign-On administration pages

- Performing Audience calculations

- Running the Alert service for the server farm

- Importing profiles from Active Directory

The job server is an important role, but one that can be assigned only to an individual server in the server farm. This is an example of a *shared service*—a service that runs on a single server in the server farm but is consumed by all servers in the farm. Shared services is discussed more fully in Chapter 14, "Shared Services."

The way that the servers know which role they have been assigned in the farm is handled by the Admin service. When you make a component change between servers in a server farm on the Component Selections page, this information is written to the Configuration database. The Admin service, which runs on each server running

SharePoint Portal Server 2003, checks this configuration database for component assignment changes every 30 seconds. If it detects a change, the service turns on or off those portions of the SharePoint Portal Server code to run only the assigned services. For example, let's assume you have a server in a large server farm that has been assigned the index and job server roles. Now, let's assume that you decide to move the job server role to another index server in the farm. On both of these servers, *all* the SharePoint Portal Server code is installed, but when you make the service assignment change, the Admin service on the first server will "turn off" the job server role services and the Admin service on the second server will "turn on" the job server role services and assume these responsibilities. In this manner, each server in the farm will know its role in the farm, the services it is to run to "complete" the farm, and when to change its role to meet new role assignments you select on the Components Selection page.

Preparing for Deploying a Farm

Before building a server farm, you need to collect some information and create prerequisite accounts. Table 12-1 shows the information needed to create a portal site and includes the values for each item used for a medium farm in this chapter. The numbers and DNS entries filled in are examples. You should fill in your own IP Address Range and DNS entries based on your environment.

Table 12-1   Roles, IP Addresses, and Names in a Medium Farm

Physical Server	DNS Name	IP Address	Subnet Mask	Description	Notes
n/a	cluster.sps.test.local	172.16.12.200	255.255.0.0	Corporate portal virtual host	Used for NLB
SPS-01	SPS-01.sps.test.local	172.16.12.10	255.255.0.0	Host address for front-end Web/search server SPS-01	If only one NIC in server, bind this address and cluster address (below). If multiple NICs, choose the NIC connected to the internal network for this address.
SPS-01		172.16.12.200	255.255.0.0	Cluster address for front-end Web/search server SPS-01	If only one NIC in server, bind this address and host address (above). If multiple NICs, choose the NIC connected to the external network for this address.

Table 12-1 Roles, IP Addresses, and Names in a Medium Farm *(continued)*

Physical Server	DNS Name	IP Address	Subnet Mask	Description	Notes
SPS-02	SPS-02.sps.test.local	172.16.12.11	255.255.0.0	Host address for front-end Web server SPS-02	If only one NIC in server, bind this address and cluster address (below). If multiple NICs, choose the NIC connected to the internal network for this address.
SPS-02		172.16.12.200	255.255.0.0	Cluster address for front-end Web server SPS-02	If only one NIC in server, bind this address and host address (above). If multiple NICs, choose the NIC connected to the external network for this address.
SPS-03	SPS-03.sps.test.local	172.16.12.12	255.255.0.0	Index management server	
SQL-01	SQL-01.sps.test.local	172.16.12.9	255.255.0.0	Address of SQL Server (or active server if cluster)	If clustered, this information should be used for the SQL cluster's active node.
DocLib	DocLib.sps.test.local	172.16.12.15	255.255.0.0	Optional server for backward-compatible document libraries	

For a large server farm, the information in Table 12-2 will be used.

Table 12-2 IP Addresses and Names in a Large Farm

Physical Server	DNS Name	IP Address	Subnet Mask	Description	Notes
n/a	cluster.sps.test.local	172.16.12.200	255.255.0.0	Corporate portal virtual host	Used for NLB
SPS-01	SPS-01.sps.test.local	172.16.12.10	255.255.0.0	Host address for front-end Web server SPS-01	If only one NIC in server, bind this address and cluster address (below). If multiple NICs, choose the NIC connected to the internal network for this address.

Table 12-2   IP Addresses and Names in a Large Farm   *(continued)*

Physical Server	DNS Name	IP Address	Subnet Mask	Description	Notes
SPS-01		172.16.12.200	255.255.0.0	Cluster address for front-end Web server SPS-01	If only one NIC in server, bind this address and host address (above). If multiple NICs, choose the NIC connected to the external network for this address.
SPS-02	SPS-02.sps.test.local	172.16.12.11	255.255.0.0	Host address for front-end Web server SPS-02	If only one NIC in server, bind this address and cluster address (below). If multiple NICs, choose the NIC connected to the internal network for this address.
SPS-02		172.16.12.200	255.255.0.0	Cluster address for front-end Web server SPS-02	If only one NIC in server, bind this address and host address (above). If multiple NICs, choose the NIC connected to the external network for this address.
SPS-03	SPS-03.sps.test.local	172.16.12.12	255.255.0.0	Index management server	
SPS-04	SPS-04.sps.test.local	172.16.12.13	255.255.0.0	Search server	
SPS-05	SPS-05.sps.test.local	172.16.12.14	255.255.0.0	Search server	
SQL-01	SQL-01.sps.test.local	172.16.12.9	255.255.0.0	Address of SQL Server (or active server if cluster)	If clustered, this information should be used for the SQL cluster's active node.
DocLib	DocLib.sps.test.local	172.16.12.15	255.255.0.0	Optional server for backward-compatible document libraries	

SharePoint Portal Server farms use many different service accounts. These service account settings can all use the same account, or they can use different accounts if corporate policies dictate. For the purposes of this chapter, all service account settings will use the same account. Table 12-3 shows the different service accounts.

Table 12-3   Service Accounts

Server	Service Name	Access Account	Role
SQL Server	MSSQLSERVER	*domain\spssql*	Database system administrator
SQL Server	SQLSERVERAGENT	*domain\spssql*	Database system administrator
Web front-end(s), search, and index	SharePointPS search	*domain\spssql*	SharePoint Portal Server administrator
Web front-end(s), search, and index	SharePoint administration	*domain\spssql*	SharePoint Portal Server administrator
Web front-end(s), search, and index	SharePoint portal alert	*domain\spssql*	SharePoint Portal Server administrator
Web front-end(s), search, and index	SharePoint timer service	*domain\spssql*	SharePoint Portal Server administrator
Web front-end(s), search, and index	Configuration database	*domain\spssql*	Administrator right on search and index servers
Web front-ends	Default content access account	*domain\spssql*	Used for crawling content on the Internet. This should have elevated privileges to access content throughout the intranet. Keep in mind that even though this account can access all data, users will see only results for content that they have access to.

The SharePoint Portal Server administrator must have at least local Power User rights on each server running SharePoint Portal Server. To grant the account Power User permissions, follow these steps:

1. Open **Administrative Tools**, click **Computer Management**.

2. Expand **Local Users and Groups** and click the **Groups** folder.

3. Double-click the **Power Users** group.

4. Click the **Add** button.

5. Enter the name of the service account (**SPS\SPSSQL**) and click **OK**. Click **OK** again to finalize the group membership addition.

Configuring Network Load Balancing

Network Load Balancing (NLB) is a clustering technology that allows multiple servers that are configured the same to service clients. It distributes the incoming connections between all the servers in the cluster. In a SharePoint Portal Server farm environment, NLB is used to distribute load between all the front-end Web servers in the farm. This gives the farm redundancy and the ability to scale out.

> **Note**   Windows Network Load Balancing distributes load and provides failover for the Web servers only. Although the search services for the medium server farm operate on the Web server computers, search services use their own load-balancing mechanisms, and therefore Windows NLB does not affect them.

SharePoint Portal Server does not depend on NLB, so any load-balancing technology can be used. NLB is discussed here because it comes with all Windows Server 2003 editions. If your corporate environment uses a different load-balancing mechanism, feel free to use that instead.

NLB works by setting the same physical (MAC) address on all nodes of the cluster. In essence, this makes all the machines' network cards act like a single network card. The MAC address used for NLB cannot be manually configured. It is set by Windows based on the IP address chosen for the cluster. The following sections detail configuring and testing NLB for use in a SharePoint Portal Server farm.

To configure the first front-end NIC (SPS-01)

1. In **Control Panel**, click **Network Connections**.

2. Right-click **Local Area Network Connection** and then click **Properties**.

3. Under **This connection uses the following items**, click **Internet Protocol (TCP/IP)**.

4. Click **Properties**.

5. Click **Use the following IP address**, and type in the IP address with your assigned front-end static IP address. (This is the IP address for the machine, not the cluster.)

6. Type in the subnet mask associated with this IP address.

7. Type in the default gateway with your assigned front-end gateway.

8. Click **Advanced**.

9. Under **IP address**, click **Add**.

10. In the **IP Address** box, type the cluster IP address, as illustrated in Figure 12-1.

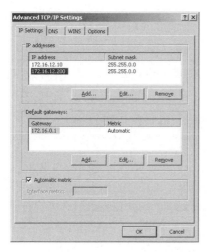

Figure 12-1   Setting the cluster IP address on SPS-01

11.   Type in the subnet mask associated with the cluster IP.

12.   On the **DNS** tab, remove all DNS entries.

13.   Deselect the **Register this connections addresses in DNS** check box.

14.   On the **WINS** tab, remove all WINS entries.

15.   On the LAN Connection Properties page, under **This connection uses the following items**, click **Network Load Balancing**.

16.   Click **Network Load Balancing** again, and then click **Properties**.

17.   On the **Cluster Parameters** tab, perform the following steps, as illustrated in Figure 12-2:

   a.   In the **IP Address** box, type the cluster IP (**172.16.12.200**).

   b.   Type the subnet mask associated with the cluster IP.

   c.   In the **Full Internet Name** box, type the DNS name.

   d.   Change the **Cluster operation** to the **Unicast** setting.

> **Note**   The Unicast setting can be used only when your server has multiple Network Interface Cards (NIC), while Multicast will be used when there is only one NIC. For a further explanation, please see the Windows Server 2003 Resource Kit or the "Network Load Balancing: Configuration Best Practices for Windows 2000 and Windows Server 2003" white paper.

   e.   Leave the **Allow remote control** check box unselected.

Figure 12-2   Configuring NLB cluster properties on SPS-01

18. On the **Host Parameters** tab, perform the following steps, as illustrated by Figure 12-3:

   a. Because this is the first Web/search server, enter **Priority 1**.

   b. In the **Dedicated IP Configuration** section, enter the address and subnet mask that you assigned to this machine in step 5.

   c. Do not change the initial host state settings.

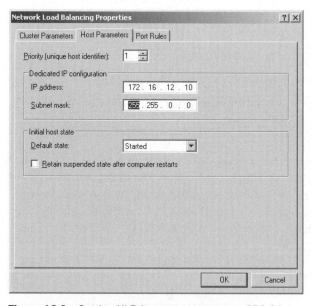

Figure 12-3   Setting NLB host parameters on SPS-01

19. On the **Port Rules** tab, in the **Filtering mode** section, verify that **multiple host** is enabled and that Portal Server is set to **None**, as shown in Figure 12-4.

Figure 12-4   Set NLB Port Rules on SPS-01

To configure additional front-end NICs (SPS-02)

1. In Windows Control Panel, click **Network Connections**.

2. Right-click **Local Area Connection** and then click **Properties**.

3. Under **This connection uses the following items**, click **Internet Protocol (TCP/IP)**.

4. Click **Properties**.

5. Click **Use the following IP address**, and type in the IP address with your assigned front-end static IP address. (This is the IP address for the machine, not the cluster.)

6. Type in the subnet mask associated with this IP address.

7. Type in the default gateway with your assigned front-end gateway.

8. Click **Advanced**.

9. Under **IP address**, click **Add**.

10. In the **IP Address** box, type the cluster IP address as shown in Figure 12-5.

11. Type in the subnet mask associated with the cluster IP.

12. On the **DNS** tab, remove all DNS entries.

13. Deselect the **Register this connections addresses in DNS** box.

14. On the **WINS** tab, remove all WINS entries.

15. On the LAN Connection Properties page, under **This connection uses the following items**, click **Network Load Balancing**.

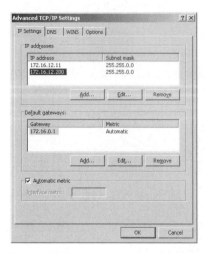

Figure 12-5 Setting the cluster IP address (SPS-02)

16. Click **Network Load Balancing** again, and then click **Properties**.

17. On the **Cluster Parameters** tab, perform the following steps, as shown in Figure 12-6:

   a. In the **IP Address** box, type the cluster IP (number 1 on the worksheet).

   b. Type the subnet mask associated with the cluster IP.

   c. In the **Full Internet Name** box, type the DNS name.

   d. Change the **Cluster operation** to the **Unicast** setting.

> **Note** The Unicast setting can be used only when your server has multiple Network Interface Cards (NIC), while Multicast will be used when there is only one NIC. For a further explanation, please see the Windows Server 2003 Resource Kit or the "Network Load Balancing: Configuration Best Practices for Windows 2000 and Windows Server 2003" white paper.

   e. Leave **Allow remote control** check box unselected.

18. On the **Host Parameters** tab, perform the following steps, as illustrated in Figure 12-7:

   a. Because this is your second Web/search server, select **Priority 2**. (For additional servers, choose numbers in ascending order—3 and then 4, and so on.)

   b. In the **Dedicated IP Configuration** section, enter the address and subnet mask that you assigned to this machine in step 5.

Figure 12-6   Configuring NLB cluster properties on SPS-02

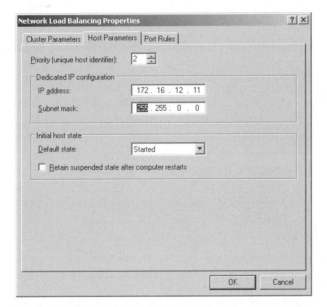

Figure 12-7   Configuring NLB host properties on SPS-02

19. On the **Port Rules** tab, in the **Filtering mode** section, verify that **Multiple host** is enabled and that **Affinity** is set to **None** as illustrated in Figure 12-8.

20. For large server farms: repeat these steps as necessary for each additional front-end Web server.

Figure 12-8 Configuring port rules on SPS-02

Verify the Cluster's Status

After configuring Network Load Balancing, it is absolutely paramount to test it and make sure it is working properly. Using Ping.exe and the Network Load Balancing Manager, you can quickly verify that your cluster is functioning properly.

1. In **Administrative Tools**, double-click **Network Load Balancing Manager**.

> **Note** If you run Network Load Balancing Manager from a node in the cluster, you might be presented with a warning that you need to use Multicast mode for successfully monitoring the cluster. If you did not select Multicast as the operating mode, you must run the Network Load Balancing Manager from a machine that is not in the cluster.

2. Right-click **Network Load Balancing Cluster**, and select **Connect to Existing**, as shown in Figure 12-9.

3. Enter the DNS of the cluster, and click **Connect**.

   Network Load Balancing Manager might take a minute or two to make all the connections. You should see all your servers in the cluster listed, and they should all be showing green, as shown in Figure 12-10.

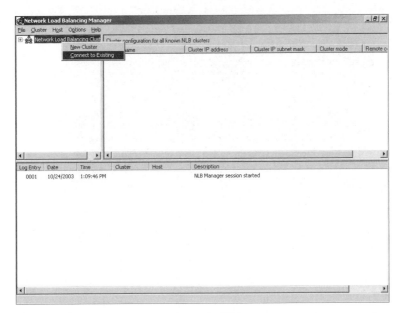

Figure 12-9   Connecting to a cluster in NLB manager

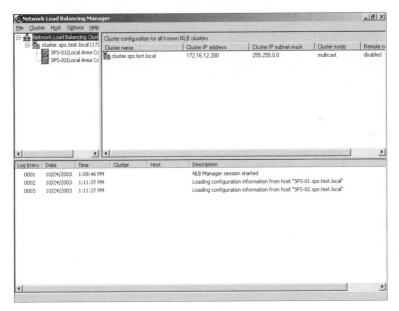

Figure 12-10   NLB Manager listing of all servers in a cluster

4. From a computer not in the cluster, run `ping -t <DNS name of cluster>`, as shown in Figure 12-11.

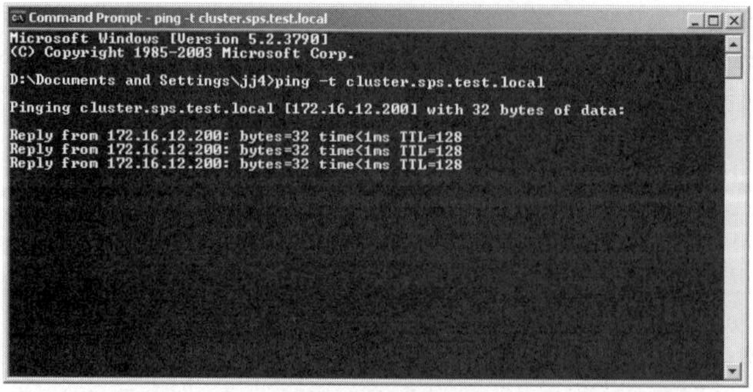

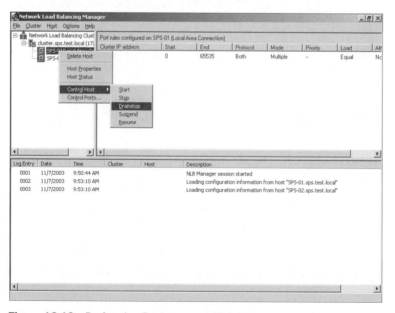

Figure 12-11 Starting the ping test for a cluster

This will test to make sure the cluster is operational by continuously pinging the cluster. To test the failover of the cluster, each machine in the cluster needs to be drainstopped. Drainstopping is used to tell the server to continue processing new requests but not accept any new requests, thus gracefully taking the server down. The ping should not stop even though one of the cluster nodes is down. To test failover, do the following:

1. Return to **Network Load Balancing Manager**.

2. Right-click the first server in the cluster (SPS-01), click **Control Host**, and then click **Drainstop**, as illustrated in Figure 12-12.

Figure 12-12 Performing Drainstop on SPS-01

3. You will see the server icon turn yellow and its state set to Converging. Wait about 10 seconds, right-click the cluster name, and choose Refresh. The icon

for the first node in the cluster (SPS-01) should be red now, which signals that it is stopped, as illustrated in Figure 12-13.

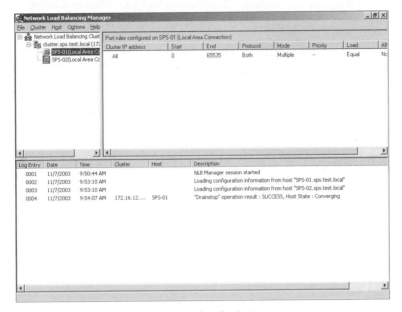

Figure 12-13   SPS-01 converging after Drainstop

4. Look at the computer running the ping command and make sure it is still getting a response from the cluster, as shown in Figure 12-14.

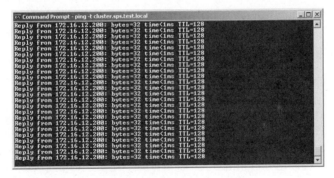

Figure 12-14   Ping test is still getting responses

5. Return to Network Load Balancing Manager.

6. Right-click the first server in the cluster (SPS-01), click **Control Host**, and then click **Start**, as shown in Figure 12-15.

7. You will see the server icon turn yellow and its state set to Converging. Wait about 10 seconds, right-click the cluster name, and choose Refresh. The icon for the first node in the cluster (SPS-01) should be green now, which signals that it is started.

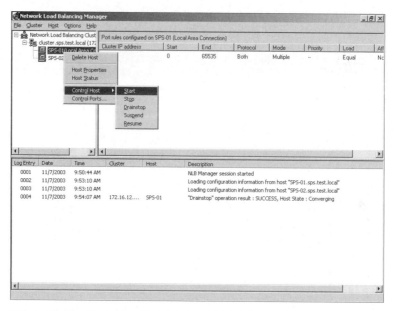

Figure 12-15   Restarting Network Load Balancing on SPS-01

8. Repeat steps 2 through 7 for each additional node in the cluster.

As long as the ping test passes for each node in the cluster, Network Load Balancing is configured properly. If one or more of the nodes fail the ping test, go back and reconfigure Network Load Balancing on each failed server as specified in the previous section.

Installing and Configuring SQL Server

SQL Server is required for a server farm installation or any installation that will have an extranet or Internet connectivity to the portal site. Running SQL Server on a separate machine from all other SharePoint Portal Server components is required, and it is recommended that you install SQL Server cluster if you want high availability. When installing on Windows Server 2003 Enterprise Edition, ensure that you are installing SQL Server 2000 and SQL Server Service Pack 3a. To verify that you have SQL Server 2000, on the CD, browse to **\X86\binn\ssnetlib.dll**. The version number should read 2000.80.311.0.

More Info   For detailed instructions on how to install SQL Server 2000, please refer to the SQL Server 2000 Resource Kit.

You must properly configure SQL Server services before installing SharePoint Portal Server 2003. To configure SQL Server services:

1. Configure the MSSQLSERVER service and the SQLSERVERAGENT service to start automatically, and confirm that both services start successfully at startup.

2. Configure the service accounts for the MSSQLSERVER service and the SQL-SERVERAGENT service to run as ***domain\spssql*** on the services corresponding to the instance of SQL Server you want to use.

3. For clusters, repeat this on each computer that is running SQL Server.

Installing Internet Information Services and SharePoint Portal Server

The SharePoint Portal Server client and administration functionalities depend on a specific Internet Information Services (IIS) configuration. Install IIS on all front-end search and index servers (SPS-01, SPS-02, SPS-03—and SPS-04 and SPS-05 for large server farms) as indicated in the following procedure.

To install Internet Information Services

1. Click **Start**, and then click **Manage Your Server**.

2. Click **Add or remove a role**.

3. Click **Next** to start the wizard. The Configure Your Server Wizard will gather information about your system, as shown in Figure 12-16.

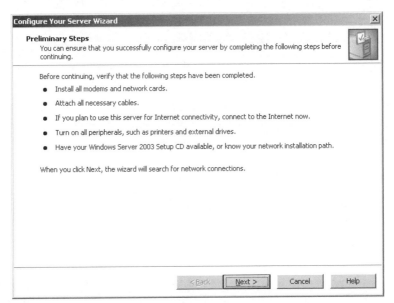

Figure 12-16 Starting the Configure Your Server Wizard

4. Click **Application server (IIS, ASP.NET)** from the list of choices, and click **Next** as illustrated in Figure 12-17.

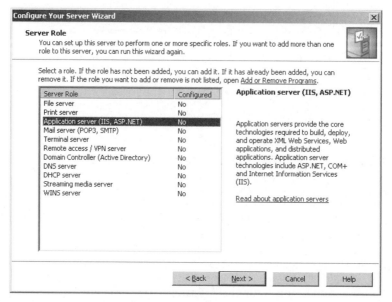

Figure 12-17   Selecting Application Server

5. Select the **Enable ASP.NET** check box.

6. Ensure that the **FrontPage Server Extensions** box is cleared. Click **Next** as shown in Figure 12-18.

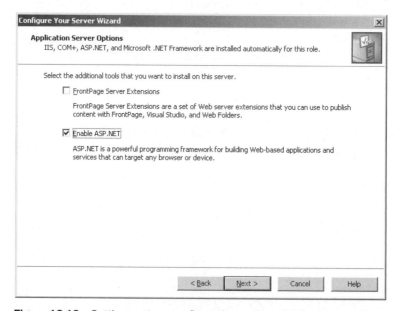

Figure 12-18   Setting custom configuration options for Application Server

7. Verify the install summary, and click **Next** to start configuration, as illustrated in Figure 12-19.

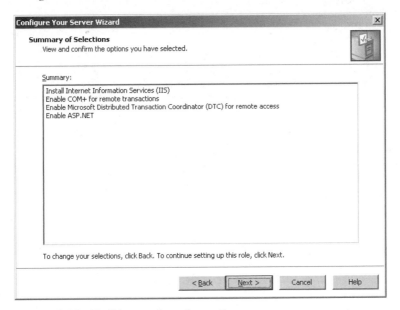

Figure 12-19   Verifying configuration options

8. Repeat these steps for additional servers (SPS-02, SPS-03).

Installing SharePoint Portal Server 2003

Install SharePoint Portal Server 2003 on all Web, search, and index servers (SPS-01, SPS-02, SPS-03—and SPS-04 and SPS-05 for large portal farms). Please refer to Chapter 3 for detailed instructions on installing SharePoint Portal Server 2003.

Configuring the SharePoint Portal Server System Architecture

When you complete the SharePoint Portal Server 2003 installation, the SharePoint Portal Server Central Administration page displays. Table 12-4 shows which configuration tasks are prescribed for medium and large server farms. These tasks are described in subsequent sections. You should complete the appropriate configuration tasks based on the type of server and server farm you are configuring. When you finish configuring the server farm accounts and connecting to the configuration database, you should add the servers to the server farm topology.

Table 12-4 Tasks Prescribed for Medium and Large Server Farms

	Medium Server Farm			Large Server Farm			
Configuration Task	First Front-end Web and Search Server	Second Front-end Web and Search Server	Index and Job Server	First Front-end Web Server	Second Front-end Web Server	Search Servers	Index and Job Server
Configure the server farm accounts	✓	✓	✓	✓	✓	✓	✓
Specify the configuration database	✓			✓			
Connect to existing configuration database		✓	✓		✓	✓	✓

Configuring the Server Farm Accounts

Perform the steps listed in the following procedure and shown in Figure 12-20 on all the SharePoint Portal Server–based servers.

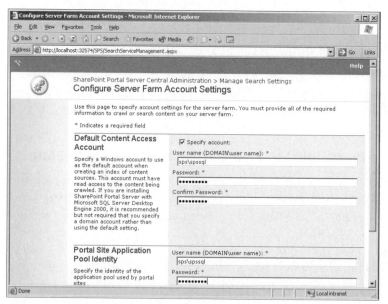

Figure 12-20 Configuring server farm accounts

To configure the server farm accounts

1. On the Configure Server Farm Account Settings page, in the **Default Content Access Account** section, click **Specify Account**.

> **Note** The Default Content Access Account can be any account, but to work properly, this account must have Read access to all content you plan on crawling.

2. In the **Portal Site Application Pool Identity** section, enter the domain and user name for the SharePoint Portal Server service account (*domain\sqlsps*).

3. Enter and confirm the account password.

4. Repeat these steps on each additional server.

Specifying the Configuration Database

SharePoint Portal Server uses a configuration database to store all information about the configuration and settings of a farm. This database needs to be created by the first server in your farm and used by each additional server you want to participate in the same farm.

To create the configuration database (SPS-01)

1. On the Specify Configuration Database Settings For SPS-01 page, perform the following steps, as illustrated in Figure 12-21:

    a. In the **Database Connections** section, click **Create configuration database**.

    b. In the **Configuration Database Server** section, in the **Database server** box, enter the name of the server (or virtual server if a cluster) running SQL Server 2000 (SQL-01).

    c. In the **Configuration Database Name** section, leave the default settings.

    d. Click **OK**. The Configure Server Farm Account Settings page appears.

e. In the **Contact E-mail Address** section, enter the e-mail address of a system administrator.

f. In the **Proxy Server Settings** section, set the appropriate proxy settings for accessing the Internet.

g. Click **OK**.

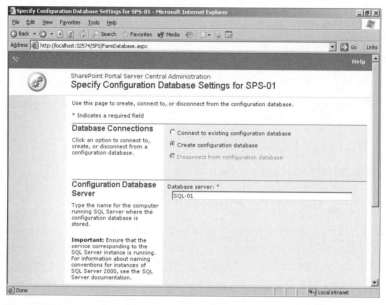

Figure 12-21 Creating the Configuration Database

Note Typically, you should use the default database name. If you have a special circumstance—such as needing to name the configuration database according to a naming scheme your company set up—you can specify your own name for the configuration database. Just make sure to write it down, as it will be needed when installing each additional farm server.

To specify the configuration database (SPS-02, SPS-03 and SPS-04, SPS-05 on large farms)

1. On the Specify Configuration Database Settings For *server_name* page, do the following:

a. In the **Database Connections** section, click **Connect to existing configuration database**.

  b. In the **Configuration Database Server** section, in the **Database server** box, enter the name of the server (or virtual server if cluster) running SQL Server 2000 (SQL-01).

  c. In the **Configuration Database Name** section, leave the default settings. (If a custom database name was specified, enter that here instead.)

  d. Click **OK**. The Configure Server Farm Account Settings page appears.

  e. In the **Contact E-mail Address** section, enter the e-mail address of a system administrator.

  f. In the **Proxy Server Settings** section, set the appropriate proxy settings for accessing the Internet.

  g. Click **OK**.

2. Repeat these steps for each additional server in the farm.

Adding Servers to the Topology

Now that all of the servers are added to the configuration database, you need to add them to the server topology.

To add servers to the server farm

1. On the Configure Server Topology page, click **Change Components**. Depending on the type of server farm you are adding, perform one of the following steps:

   For Medium Server Farms. On the Change Component Assignments page, in the **Component Assignment** section, there is a row of check boxes for each server and there are columns of check boxes to assign Web, search, and index roles. For each front-end Web server (SPS-01, SPS-02), select **Web** and **Search**. For the index server (SPS-03), select **Index** as illustrated in Figure 12-22.

   For Large Server Farms. On the Change Component Assignments page, in the **Component Assignment** section, there is a row of check boxes for each server and there are columns of check boxes to assign Web, search, and index roles. For each front-end Web server (SPS-01, SPS-02), select **Web**. For each search server (SPS-04, SPS-05), select **Search**. For the index server (SPS-03), select **Index** as illustrated in Figure 12-23.

2. In the **Job Server Component** section, select an index server from the **Job server** list.

3. In the **Document Library Server Component (Optional)** section, make sure the **Document library server** box is left empty.

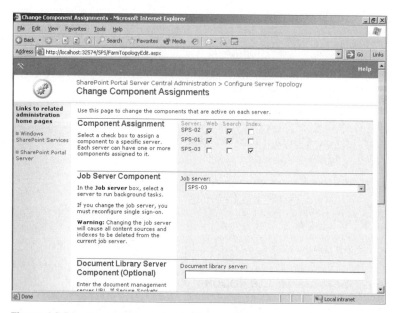

Figure 12-22 Assigning servers to the medium farm topology

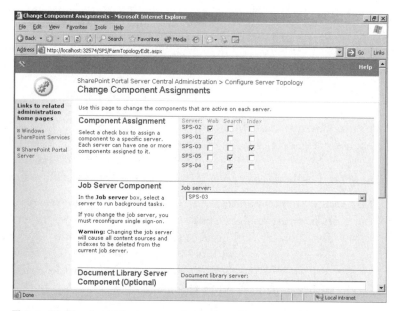

Figure 12-23 Assigning servers to the large farm topology

Specifying the Global E-mail Server

If you want portal sites in your farm to send e-mail alerts and e-mail invitations to other sites on those portal sites, you need to specify a global e-mail server for the farm, as outlined in the following procedure and illustrated in Figure 12-24.

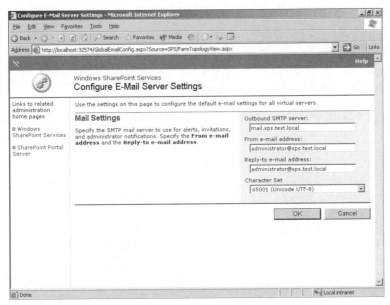

Figure 12-24   Configuring Global E-mail Server settings

To specify a global e-mail server

1. On the Configure Server Topology page, click the name of the current global e-mail server (should currently be "unknown").

2. Enter the Fully Qualified Domain Name (FQDN) of your e-mail server, an e-mail address to send from, and a reply-to e-mail address.

Note   The e-mail address you specify to have the e-mail sent from must have anonymous SMTP access. If your server requires authentication for the specified user, the portal site will be unable to send e-mail alerts.

Creating Portal Sites

Each portal site you want to have must be created separately on its own virtual server, and each will need to have its own URL. The following sections detail all the steps involved with creating new portal sites.

Creating Virtual Servers

Working in a load-balanced environment, the following IIS virtual server parameters must be configured the same on each front-end Web server:

■ Virtual Web name

- Virtual Web IP address

- Application pool

- Virtual Web-file system directory name and location

To create the virtual servers for a new portal site

1. Open **Administrative Tools** and then click **Internet Information Services**.

2. Right-click the **Web Sites** container, point to **New**, and then click **Web site**.

3. Follow the directions to start the wizard. On the Web Site Description page, enter a description (such as "SharePoint Cluster," which is used in Figure 12-25), and then click **Next**.

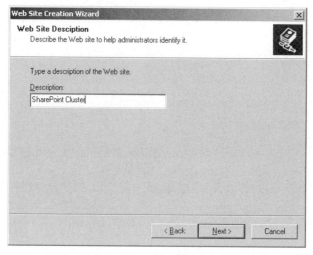

Figure 12-25   Entering a description for the virtual server

4. On the IP Address And Port Settings page, select the IP address of the cluster in the **Enter the IP address to use for this Web site** box. Leave the default TCP port of 80 in the **TCP port this Web site should use (Default 80)** box, as illustrated in Figure 12-26.

5. On the Web Site Home Directory page, enter the path to the folders that contain the Web site for the virtual server, as illustrated in Figure 12-27. (This can be any physical file folder except Inetpub\wwwbin, because that folder is already used by the default virtual server.) Deselect the **Allow anonymous access** check box, and then click **Next**.

6. On the Web Site Access Permission page, verify that only **Read** and **Run** scripts (such as Active Server Pages [ASP]) are selected, and then click **Next**. Finish the wizard.

7. Repeat the preceding steps on each front-end Web server.

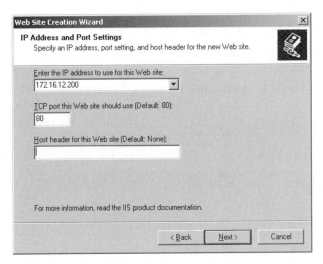

Figure 12-26 Configuring IP and Port Settings

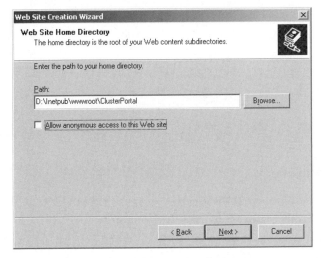

Figure 12-27 Configuring the home directory

> **More Info** For more information, see "Extending Virtual Servers" in the SharePoint Portal Server 2003 Administrator's Guide, which is accessible from the Start menu.

Creating a Portal Site

Once IIS is installed and configured on each server running SharePoint Portal Server and the farm topology is set up properly, it is time to create portal sites on the farm. Each portal site has its own content and settings. Each portal site hosted on the farm can be considered to be a separate entity. If you use shared services, which are covered in Chapter 23, "Personalization Services in SharePoint Products and Technologies" you can share indexing, My Sites, and user profiles between portal sites to conserve resources. This section will describe how to create the first portal site in the farm, but the same procedure can be applied for each additional portal site to be created. (See Figure 12-28.) A portal site farm must contain at least one portal site.

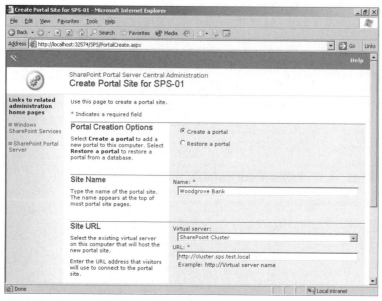

Figure 12-28   Creating a portal site

To create a portal site

1. Click **Start**, point to **All Programs**, point to **SharePoint Portal Server**, and then click **SharePoint Central Administration**.

2. In the **Portal Site and Virtual Server Configuration** section, click **Create a Portal Site**.

3. On the Create a Portal Site page, verify that **Create a portal** is selected.

4. Fill in the Site Name of the Portal (in this example, **Woodgrove Bank**), select the virtual server created previously (**SharePoint Cluster**), and enter the account and e-mail address of the portal site owner. (See Figure 12-28.)

5. Click **OK** to continue. Click **OK** to confirm portal creation. A progress bar will display the status of the creation.

Note   If portal site creation fails, check the log file to determine the cause of failure. Correct the problem and try again. Often a creation failure is related to accounts not having proper permissions.

After you have created the portal site on the first load-balanced server, you must extend it to subsequent virtual servers.

To extend the portal site to the virtual servers

1. On the Operation Successful page, in the **Server Extension Links** section, click **Link to a Virtual Server Extension Page for** *server-name* (*SPS-02*), as illustrated in Figure 12-29.

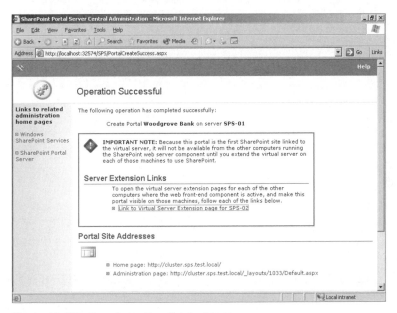

Figure 12-29   Portal creation finished page

2. The Virtual Server List administration page for that front-end Web server opens. Click the name of the virtual server to which you want to extend the portal site (SharePoint Cluster) as illustrated in Figure 12-30.

3. This opens the Extend Virtual Server administration page. Click **Extend and map to another virtual server**.

4. On the Windows SharePoint Services Extend And Map To Another Virtual Server page, in the **Server Mapping** section, click the name of the virtual server the portal site was created on in the list.

5. In the **Application Pool** section, click **Use an existing application pool**, select the portal site application pool that was created previously in this chapter, and then set the application pool. Click **OK**.

6. SharePoint Portal Server will now contact each front-end server to update its configuration. You might be prompted for local administrator credentials for all the other SharePoint Portal Server–based servers joined to the topology. On the Refresh Config Cache On Other Web Servers page, click **OK** as illustrated in

Figure 12-31. (You will see SPS-04, SPS-05 listed as well if you are performing a large farm installation.)

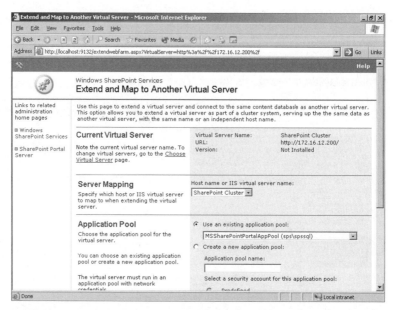

Figure 12-30   Extending the portal site to other virtual servers

7. Repeat as necessary for each front-end server.

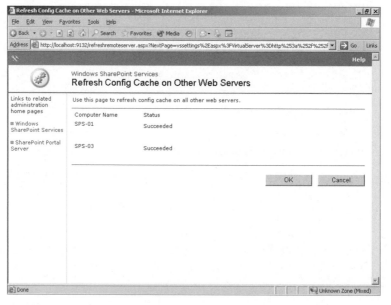

Figure 12-31   Extending the virtual server completed successfully

> **Note** If the server has Internet Explorer Enhanced Security Configuration enabled, you must add each server's administration website to Internet Explorer's Trusted Sites list.

Now that the portal site is created, it should be verified to ensure it is functioning properly.

Open Internet Explorer. In the address bar, type the address of the portal site you created (for example, **http://cluster.sps.test.local**). It should look similar to Figure 12-32.

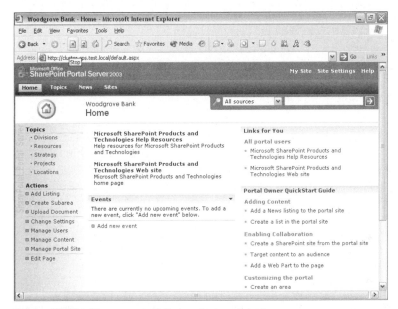

Figure 12-32 The successfully created portal site

Configuring Alternate URLs

The portal site has been created but is accessible only by the URL *http://cluster.sps .test.local*. This URL is the default portal URL and is used for crawling portal site content, but a different URL can be configured to allow easier access by end users. An alias record should be created in DNS for the URL end users will access, and that address should be specified in Alternate Access Mappings (shown in Figure 12-33) in SharePoint Central Administration.

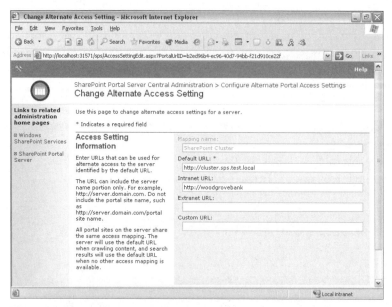

Figure 12-33 Setting alternate access URLs

Note If you do not know how to set up an alias record in DNS or do not have permissions to do so, you should contact your DNS administrator to get this set up.

More Info Extranets and Alternate Access Mappings will be covered in further detail in Chapter 13, "Installing and Configuring Windows SharePoint Services in an Extranet."

To configure Alternate Access Mappings

1. Click **Start**, point to **All Programs**, point to **SharePoint Portal Server**, and then click **SharePoint Central Administration**.

2. In the **Portal Sites and Virtual Server Configuration** section, click **Configure alternate portal site for intranet, extranet, and custom access**.

3. Click the arrow next to the mapping name to configure, and then click **Edit** on the menu.

4. In the **Intranet URL** box, enter the address of the alias that was set up in DNS (*http://woodgrovebank*).

5. Click **OK**.

Summary

In this chapter, you learned about medium and large server farms. You should be able to plan a farm and successfully build that farm. The chapter also covered configuring and testing Network Load Balancing. You are now ready to implement additional portal sites and customize your main portal site.

Chapter 13

Installing and Configuring Windows SharePoint Services in an Extranet

Note At the time we had to go to press with this chapter, the information on how to use Microsoft Office SharePoint Portal Server 2003 extranets was in the beta stages of being written. Therefore, this chapter will focus entirely on Microsoft Windows SharePoint Services. For more information on how to use SharePoint Portal Server extranets, please visit *http://office.microsoft.com/home /office.aspx?assetid=FX010909721033&CTT=6&Origin=ES790020011033*.

—Bill English

Business-to-business collaboration and resource sharing allows a company and its partners to work more effectively towards reaching business goals. A connection to the Internet facilitates the flexibility and convenience of accessing data at any time or place. Although an extranet portal might be convenient for your employees, your extranet is typically a mission-critical necessity for both partners and internal business units that work with them. Therefore, partners and business units are very sensitive to the timeliness of the extranet service. Business functions often depend on the data that is exchanged, so delays can be very costly. The extranet needs to be reliable, and the partners and business units need to be able to contact someone who can quickly resolve issues when they arise.

Although the title of this chapter and the preceding paragraph focus heavily on the concept of setting up an extranet for business partners, you will find information in this chapter about how to deploy a Windows SharePoint Services intranet as well. Because, after all, our internal customers are just as important as those who use the extranet!

If you are running an extranet that does not require advanced security, setting up access to the portal site is as easy as passing out the URL to the portal site and ensuring that each user has been added to the portal site with at least Read permission. Situations in which you might want to run an extranet without advanced security include using the portal site to offer public information for anonymous users and working in an enterprise where each division has its own portal site and security settings but you need to allow users from other divisions access to your portal site content. In either situation, advanced security such as SSL and client certificates might be in order, but it is plausible that using the built-in security in the portal site might be appropriate, too. It really depends on the sensitivity of the information being passed back and forth between the client and the server and how trusted the communication path is between these two parties.

Setting Up an Intranet and Extranet Deployment

This section describes the steps you need to take to configure the servers in your server farm to serve the same content for both an intranet and extranet.

You can install and configure Windows SharePoint Services to allow your server farm to provide the same content to both an intranet and an extranet site. There are two ways to make this happen:

- Use two virtual servers on separate server computers, configured differently, or

- Use two virtual servers on one machine. One virtual server running on port 80 exposed via the firewall and the second virtual server running on a different port that can be accessed via the internal network.

Following is the procedure to use two virtual servers on separate computers:

- One virtual server is configured with Integrated Windows authentication and an internal address so that internal users can be authenticated automatically and view the content from inside the intranet. For example, *http://My_Server*.

- The other virtual server is configured with another authentication type (for example, Basic authentication with Secure Sockets Layer [SSL]) and an external address so that external users can log in and view the content across the Internet (for example, *https://My_Server.extranet.example.com*).

Both of these virtual servers point to the same content: changes made to a site on the extranet are reflected on the intranet, and vice versa. The only differences are the URL used to access the content and the authentication method used to log in. It is recommended that both environments use Windows domain accounts to authenticate users, whether you choose Integrated Windows authentication, Basic authentication, or some other authentication method.

Caution Be aware that you can configure your virtual servers to use both Basic authentication and Integrated Windows authentication at the same time. When the client connects to the server, it will attempt authentication via the most secure method. If that method fails, it will attempt to authenticate the user via the next most secure method. The virtual server will continue this process for as many authentication methods as are configured until it succeeds or all methods fail.

You might consider this technique if you do not want to actually create two virtual servers. You can create only one virtual server and configure it to allow both authentication methods.

Preparing the Servers

Before you can install and configure Windows SharePoint Services for both an intranet and an extranet, you must be sure you meet the hardware and software requirements. The following sections help you review the requirements.

Hardware and Software Requirements

To be able to set up Windows SharePoint Services in an intranet and extranet configuration, you must meet the following criteria:

■ The front-end Web servers must be running Microsoft Windows Server 2003 (Standard or Enterprise Edition). Notice that the hardware requirements for Windows SharePoint Services are the same as the Windows Server 2003 installation requirements.

Note If you are installing Windows SharePoint Services on Windows Server 2003 Web Edition, you must be running the SQL database on a different server. They cannot coexist on this platform. Therefore, you must use the **remotesql=yes** parameter to install Windows SharePoint Services on a computer running Windows Server 2003 Web Edition. In addition, the Web Edition of Windows 2003 will not support running either the Index or Search applications for SharePoint Portal Server, which means that when running a server farm, you can use the Web Edition only if your Web front-end servers are not also configured to be Search, Index, or Job Servers.

- The front-end Web servers must be configured as Web servers (running Internet Information Services in IIS 6.0 worker process isolation mode) and must be running ASP.NET. For more information about installing and configuring IIS and ASP.NET, see the Windows Server 2003 Family documentation.

- The front-end Web servers must be using the NTFS file system. Microsoft Windows includes a conversion utility (Convert.exe) that you can use to convert an existing file allocation table (FAT) volume to NTFS—without losing data.

- The back-end servers must be running Microsoft SQL Server 2000 Service Pack 3 or later.

> **Note**   It is not required to have a dedicated SQL server in smaller deployments. Smaller organizations might choose to run a number of services on one machine, including Windows SharePoint Services and SQL. On the other hand, for large deployments you might want to have multiple SQL servers to balance the load across servers.

- The client computers must be running Microsoft Internet Explorer 5 or later (with the best results coming from Microsoft Internet Explorer 5.5 or later) or Netscape Navigator 6.2 or later to use Windows SharePoint Services website features.

Planning for Scale

You can use the same front-end Web server to host both your intranet and extranet virtual servers, or you can split them across two separate servers. If you anticipate a heavy load on either your intranet or extranet, you should use separate front-end Web servers for each environment so that heavy use of your extranet server does not affect the availability of your intranet server and vice versa. This section describes the steps you need to take to use separate front-end Web servers for each environment. You can also use multiple front-end Web servers to host both virtual servers, as in a standard server farm, to reduce potential downtime.

An important performance feature of Windows SharePoint Services is the ability to load balance across Web front-end servers, which will make the most of a server farm environment. Windows SharePoint Services works with most standard load-balancing methods available. Each method has its own set of pros and cons relative to cost, processing power, and scale. You can use any of the following methods with Windows SharePoint Services:

- **Software solutions, such as Network Load Balancing.**   Software, such as Network Load Balancing (NLB) services in Windows Server 2003. This method is inexpensive but offers only limited scalability. NLB runs on the Web front-end servers and uses the TCP/IP networking protocol to route requests. Because NLB (and other software load-balancing solutions) run on the Web front-end servers, it uses the Web front-end system resources, trimming the resources you can use for serving Web pages. However, the impact on system resources is not great, and a software solution can handle up to 32 Web front-end servers.

- **Software configuration solutions, such as using the domain name system to route requests.**   You can configure your domain name system (DNS) to create a primitive load-balancing system. For more information about DNS, see your Windows Server 2003 documentation.

- **Hardware load balancing.**   This method uses hardware such as a router or switch box. Load-balancing hardware uses your network to direct website traffic between your Web front-end servers. Load-balancing hardware is more expensive to set up than software but does not use up any of your Web front-end server resources to run and is the most scalable method. Windows Share-Point Services can be used with any load-balancing hardware. In addition, hardware load balancing provides the best use of your Web front-end server resources.

You do not need to perform any configuration steps to make Windows Share-Point Services work with any of these load-balancing methods. Simply set up the load-balancing method in your server farm, and either install or continue using Windows SharePoint Services.

Preparing the Database Back-End Servers

To set up your database back-end servers, you must perform the following steps:

- **Install SQL Server 2000, Service Pack 3.**   You can use SQL Server 2000 Standard or Enterprise Edition with Windows SharePoint Services. For more information about installing SQL Server, see the SQL Server 2000 documentation.

- **Set a strong password for your SQL Server administration account.**   You must know both the administrator user account and password to be able to connect between Windows SharePoint Services on the front-end Web servers and SQL Server on the back-end servers. You should set a strong password for the administration account. If you are using Windows Authentication (recommended), you should use a domain account with permissions to create databases in SQL Server. If you are using SQL Server authentication, the "sa" account should have a strong password. For more information about setting the administrator user name and password, see the SQL Server 2000 documentation.

- **Configure the authentication method for connections between the Web servers and SQL Server.**   For better security in your server farm, you should use Microsoft Windows NT authentication, rather than SQL Server authentication, for connections between your front-end Web servers and the database back-end servers. Windows NT authentication uses a domain user account to control access to SQL Server, rather than storing credentials in the registry and passing them across the network as in SQL Server authentication.

You configure the authentication method for SQL Server by using the SQL Server Enterprise Manager.

To configure authentication for SQL Server

1.   On the database back-end servers, click **Start**, point to **All Programs**, point to **Microsoft SQL Server**, and then click **Enterprise Manager**.

2.   Click the plus sign (+) next to **Microsoft SQL Servers**.

3.   Click the plus sign (+) next to **SQL Server Group**.

4.   Right-click the SQL server name, and click **Properties**.

5.   In the **Properties** dialog box, click the **Security** tab.

6.   Under **Authentication**, click **Windows only** and then click **OK**.

Configuring the Intranet Front-End Server

To configure your intranet front-end Web server, you must perform the following steps:

- **Configure the intranet server as a Web server.**   You must be running Internet Information Services (IIS) 6.0 on your Web server, and you must set it to run in IIS 6.0 worker process isolation mode instead of IIS 5.0 isolation mode. To communicate with SQL Server 2000 on the back-end servers, you must also configure the front-end Web server to use the TCP/IP protocol rather than Named Pipes (the default).

- **Create the intranet virtual server and configure the authentication method.**   If you are not using the default virtual server in IIS, you must create a new virtual server and map it to the host name of the server that will provide the content. The simplest way to set up an extranet is to use the default virtual server in IIS. Whichever method you choose, you must specify the authentication method (Integrated Windows authentication in this case) to use for the virtual server.

- **Install Windows SharePoint Services in the server farm configuration, and create the administration virtual server and configuration database.**   You must install Windows SharePoint Services on each front-end Web server. Using the remote SQL Server option allows you to install Windows SharePoint Services without also installing Microsoft Data Engine (MSDE). You must also create the administration virtual server and configuration database. You need to create the configuration database only when you configure the first front-end Web server;

for subsequent front-end servers (including the extranet server), you can simply connect to the Windows SharePoint Services configuration database.

■ **Extend the intranet virtual server.**   Before you can create sites, you must extend the intranet virtual server. The intranet virtual server is connected to the same content databases as the extranet virtual server so that they provide the same site content.

To perform these steps for a server farm, you should use the command-line administration tool, Stsadm.exe.

Configuring the Intranet Server as a Web Server

IIS is not enabled by default in Windows Server 2003. To make your front-end server into a Web server, you must enable IIS.

To enable IIS and configure it to use IIS 6.0 worker process isolation mode

1. Click **Start**, and then click **Manage Your Server**.

2. On the Manage Your Server page, click **Add or remove a role**.

3. On the Preliminary Steps page, click **Next**.

4. On the Server Role page, click **Application server (IIS, ASP.NET)** and then click **Next**.

5. On the Web Application Server Options page, accept the default of **ASP.NET** and then click **Next**.

6. On the Summary Of Selections page, click **Next**.

7. Click **Finish**.

8. Click **Start**, point to **Administrative Tools**, and then click **Internet Information Services (IIS)**.

9. In **Internet Information Services** manager, click the plus sign (+) next to the server name, right-click the **Web Sites** folder, and select **Properties**.

10. In the **Properties** dialog box, click the **Service** tab.

11. In the **Isolation mode** section, clear the **Run WWW service in IIS 5.0 isolation mode** check box and then click **OK**.

Note   The **Run WWW service in IIS 5.0 isolation mode** check box is selected only if you have upgraded to IIS 6.0 on Windows Server 2003 from IIS 5.0 on Windows 2000. New installations of IIS 6.0 default to IIS 6.0 worker process isolation mode.

Creating the Intranet Virtual Server and Configuring Authentication

When IIS is configured and ready to work with SQL Server, you can create the virtual server you need to host the intranet sites.

To create a virtual server

1. Click **Start**, point to **Programs**, point to **Administrative Tools**, and then click **Internet Information Services**.

2. Click the plus sign (+) next to the server name you want to add a virtual server to.

3. Right-click the **Web Sites** folder, click **New**, and then click **Web site**.

4. Click **Next**.

5. In the **Description** box, type the description of your virtual server and then click **Next**.

6. In the **Enter the IP address to use for this Web site** box, select the IP address you want to use, if appropriate, or use the default (All Unassigned) if that fits your deployment.

7. In the **TCP port this Web site should use (Default: 80)** box, type the port number to assign to the virtual server.

   You do not need to assign a host header, because the hosting is being handled through Windows SharePoint Services.

8. Click **Next**.

9. In the **Path** box, type or browse to the path on your hard disk where the site content will go.

10. If you do not want to allow anonymous access to your virtual server, clear the **Allow anonymous access to this Web site** check box.

11. Click **Next**.

12. On the **Web Site Access Permissions** page, select the permissions to use and then click **Next**. The default permissions, Read and Run Scripts (such as ASP), are recommended. The Execute (such as ISAPI applications or CGI) permission will be added automatically to the appropriate folders by Windows SharePoint Services.

13. Click **Finish**.

    Now you can configure the authentication method to use for the intranet virtual server.

To configure the authentication method for the intranet virtual server

1. On the intranet front-end Web server, in **Internet Information Services**, right-click the virtual server that will be used for the intranet site, and then click **Properties**.

2. On the **Directory Security** tab, under **Authentication and access control**, click **Edit**.

3. Select the **Integrated Windows authentication** check box, and clear all other authentication method check boxes.

4. Click **OK** to close the **Authentication Methods** dialog box.

5. Click **OK** again to close the **Properties** dialog box.

Installing and Configuring Windows SharePoint Services on the Intranet Front-End Web Server

You must install Windows SharePoint Services in the server farm configuration. To do so, you use the setupsts.exe command with the remotesql property on the command line.

To install Windows SharePoint Services with the Remote SQL Server option

1. Insert the Windows SharePoint Services compact disc into your CD drive.

2. Open a command prompt window, and navigate to the root folder on the CD drive.

3. Run the following command:

```
setupsts.exe remotesql=yes
```

4. Follow the prompts to install Windows SharePoint Services.

After setup, you can create the administration virtual server and configuration database. If you want to set up a server farm environment, you can use the command-line administration tool to create the configuration database and include the -hh parameter.

Table 13-1 displays the Stsadm.exe command-line utility that will create the configuration database or specify the connection to an existing configuration database. Setting the configuration database is required before a virtual server can be extended.

Table 13-1   Stsadm.exe Command-Line Utility

Required Parameters	Optional Parameters
-databaseserver (ds)	-connect
	-databaseuser (du)
	-databasepassword (dp)
	-databasename (dn)
	-hh
	-adcreation
	-addomain
	-adou

A sample syntax is as follows:

```
stsadm.exe -o setconfigdb [-connect] -ds <database server> [-du <database user>]
    [-dp <database user password>] [-dn <database name>] [-hh] [-adcreation]
    [-addomain <AD domain> [-adou <AD OU>]
```

To create the administration virtual server from the command line

1. Open a command prompt window, and navigate to the \Program Files \Common Files\Microsoft Shared\Web Server Extensions\60\bin folder.

2. Run the following command to create the administration virtual server:

```
stsadm.exe -o setadminport -port <port> -admapcreatenew -admapidname <id for
    application pool> -admapidtype <configurableid/NetworkService/LocalService
    /LocalSystem> -admapidlogin <user account for the application pool>
    -admapidpwd <password>
```

An example of this is as follows:

```
stsadm.exe -o setadminport -port 1035 -admapcreatenew -admapidname DefaultAppPool
    -admapidtype configurableid -admapidlogin DOMAIN\user1 -admapidpwd P@ssw0rd
```

In the preceding Stsadm.exe example, Setadminport sets the port number for the administration virtual server for Windows SharePoint Services. The ssl parameter is used to specify a Secure Sockets Layer (SSL) connection to the port. The admap... parameters are used to specify the IIS application pool to use or to create a new IIS application pool for the administration virtual server. See Table 13-2 for a listing of the required and optional stsadm.exe parameters relative to creating a virtual server from the command line.

Table 13-2   Stsadm.exe Parameters

Required Parameters	Optional Parameters
-port	-admapcreatenew
	-admapidloginname
	-admapidnametype
	-admapidpwdlogin
	-admapidtypepwd
	-ssl

Parameter	Definition
admapcreatenew	Specifies that a new application pool is created in Internet Information Services (IIS).
admapidlogin	The user name to use for running processes in the administrative application pool. This value must be a Windows NT user account name and must be qualified with a domain name—for example, DOMAIN\name.

Table 13-2   Stsadm.exe Parameters   *(continued)*

Parameter	Definition
admapidname	The administrative application pool ID.
admapidpwd	The password that corresponds to the admapidlogin.
admapidtype	The identity type to use for the administrative application pool. For example, you can use an account you have created in the directory (configurableid) or one of three predefined accounts (NetworkService/LocalService/LocalSystem).

Note   You can use any unused port between 1023 and 32767. The application pool account must have database owner (DBO) rights to the SQL Server computer to be able to create the configuration database. You should use a dedicated domain account for this account rather than a user's login account. Also, you should use the same account for each application pool that hosts the same content.

If you have used a domain account that does not already have database creation rights in SQL Server, you can give the account this access in SQL Server Enterprise Manager. This is a one-time only change. Once you have granted database creation permissions to the account used by the Windows SharePoint Services administration virtual server, this account can create any subsequent databases. You do not need database creation rights to connect to a configuration database, which you will do when you set up the front-end Web server for the extranet.

To grant database creation rights in SQL Server

1. On your SQL Server computer, click **Start**, point to **Programs**, point to **Microsoft SQL Server**, and then click **Enterprise Manager**.

2. In **Enterprise Manager**, click the plus sign (+) next to **Microsoft SQL Servers**, click the plus sign (+) next to **SQL Server Group**, and then click the plus sign (+) next to your SQL Server.

3. Click the plus sign (+) next to **Security**, right-click **Logins**, and then click **New Login**.

4. In the **Name** box, type the account in the form DOMAIN\name.

Note   If Windows SharePoint Services is running under the NT Authority \NetworkService account, the login ID should be "Domain\Machinename$".

5. Click the **Server Roles** tab.

6. In the **Server Role** list, select the **Security Administrators** and **Database Creators** check boxes, and then click **OK**.

After you configure the administrative virtual server (and grant SQL Server rights to the new application pool account, if necessary), you must restart IIS by typing **iisreset** on the command line. After IIS is reset, you can continue configuring Windows SharePoint Services to work with your remote SQL Server.

To create the configuration database from the command line

Run the following command to create the configuration database:

```
stsadm.exe -o setconfigdb -databaseserver <database server name>
  -databasename sts_config
```

The syntax shown is for Windows authentication. If you are using SQL Server authentication, you must also specify the -du and -dp parameters with the database username and password. To connect to the configuration database from subsequent front-end Web servers, use the following syntax:

```
stsadm.exe -o setconfigdb -databaseserver <database server name> [-databaseuser
  <database user> -databasepassword <password>] -databasename sts_config
```

Following is an example of what a command might look like:

```
stsadm.exe -o setconfigdb -My_server -databaseuser DOMAIN\user1 -databasepassword
  P@ssw0rd -databasename My_co_database
```

To create the administration application pool and configuration database using HTML Administration pages

1. When setup finishes, you are taken to the Configure Admin Virtual Server page.

2. In the **Application Pool** section, select **Create a new application pool**.

3. Under **Select a security account for this application pool**, select **Configurable**.

4. In the **User name** box, type the domain account to use for the application pool.

   This account must have DBO rights to the SQL Server computer to be able to create the configuration database. You should use a dedicated account for this account rather than a user's login account. Also, you should use the same account for each application pool that hosts the same content.

5. In the **Password** box, type the password for the account, confirm it, and then click **OK**.

   The application pool is created, and you are taken to a confirmation page. You must restart IIS to accept the change.

6. After restarting IIS, click the link to continue, and on the Create Configuration Database page, in the **Configuration Database** section, enter the server name and database name to use.

7. Select **Use Integrated Windows authentication (more secure, recommended)**.

8. In the **Active Directory Account Creation** section, select **Users already have domain accounts** if you are using a Windows domain, or **Automatically create active directory accounts for users of this site** if you are using Active Directory outside of a Windows domain.

9. If you selected **Automatically create active directory accounts** for users of this site, you must fill in the **Active Directory Domain** and **Organization Unit** information.

10. Click **Submit**.

11. On the SharePoint Central Administration page, in the **Server Configuration** section, click **Set default content database server**.

12. On the Content Database Server page, in the **Content Database Server** section, enter the server name, administrator account username, and password.

13. Click **Submit**.

Extending the Intranet Virtual Server

With the administration virtual server and configuration database in place, you can extend the virtual server to host the intranet sites. You can use either the command line or HTML Administration pages to extend the virtual server.

To extend the virtual server using the command line

1. Open a command prompt window, and navigate to the \Program Files \Common Files\Microsoft Shared\Web Server Extensions\60\bin folder.

2. Run the following command to extend the intranet virtual server:

```
stsadm.exe -o extendvs -url http://servername -ownerlogin <DOMAIN\username>
    -owneremail <e-mail address> [-ownername <display name> [-databaseuser
    <database user> -databaseserver <database server> -databasename
    <database name> -databasepassword <database password> -lcid <locale
    ID> -sitetemplate <template name> -apcreatenew -apidname
    <application pool name> -apidtype <configurableid/NetworkService/
    LocalService/LocalSystem> -apidlogin <DOMAIN\username> -apidpwd <password>]
```

Example:

```
stsadm.exe -o extendvs -url http://My_Server -ownerlogin DOMAIN\user1
    -owneremail someone@somewhere.com -ownername user1@domain.com -databaseuser
    user1@domain.com -databaseserver SQL_Server -databasename My_Co_Database
    -databasepassword P@ssw0rd -lcid 1033 -sitetemplate Sales_Template
    -apcreatenew -apidname NewAppPool -apidtype configurableid -admapidlogin
    DOMAIN\user1 -apidpwd P@ssw0rd
```

Note that while the apid… parameters are optional, it is recommended that you create a new application pool for the virtual server. Use a dedicated application pool account, not a user login account. The application pool account for a virtual server does not need database owner rights on the SQL Server computer. Note that the -du and -dp parameters are not needed if you are using Windows authentication to connect to SQL Server.

To extend the virtual server using HTML Administration pages

1. On the Central Administration page, in the **Virtual Server Configuration** section, click **Extend or upgrade virtual server**.

2. On the Virtual Server List page, click the name of the virtual server to extend.

3. On the Extend Virtual Server page, in the **Provisioning Options** section, click **Extend and create a content database**.

4. In the **Application Pool** section, select **Create a new application pool**.

5. Under **Select a security account for this application pool**, click **Configurable**.

6. In the **User name** box, type the domain account to use for the application pool.

    You should use a dedicated account for this account rather than a user's login account. Also, you should use the same account for each application pool that hosts the same content.

7. In the **Password** box, type the password for the account and then confirm it.

8. In the **Site Owner** section, in the **User name** box, type the user name for the site owner (in the format DOMAIN\username if the username is part of a Windows domain group).

9. In the **E-mail** box, type the e-mail address that corresponds to the account.

10. In the **Database Information** section, enter the following database connection information:

    ■ In the **Database server** box, type the server name for your SQL Server.

    ■ In the **Database name** box, type the name to use for your content database.

11. If you want to specify a path for the URL, in the **Custom URL path** box, type the path to use.

12. If you are using quotas, select a template in the **Select a quota template** box of the **Quota Template** section.

13. In the **Site Language** section, select the language to use.

14. Click **OK**.

> **Note**   For a basic test scenario where you are hosting the same content from two virtual servers, you can create a second virtual server on the intranet front-end server and extend it using the **Extend and connect to an existing content database**. On the Extend And Connect To An Existing Content Database page, select the first virtual server you extended. When you click OK, the content will be hosted from both virtual servers.

Configuring the Extranet Front-End Server

To configure your extranet front-end Web server, you must perform the following steps:

- **Configure the server as a Web server.**   You must be running IIS 6.0 on your Web server, and you must set it to run in IIS 6.0 worker process isolation mode instead of IIS 5.0 isolation mode.

- **Switch to using the TCP/IP protocol for the connections between the Web servers and SQL Server.**   To communicate with SQL Server 2000 on the back-end servers, you must configure the front-end Web servers to use the TCP/IP protocol rather than Named Pipes (the default).

- **Create a virtual server and configure the authentication method.**   Before you can create sites for your extranet, you must create the virtual server to contain them in IIS and specify the authentication method to use (Basic authentication with Secure Sockets Layer in this case).

- **Install Windows SharePoint Services in the server farm configuration.**   You must install Windows SharePoint Services on each Web front-end server. Using the remote SQL Server option allows you to install Windows SharePoint Services without also installing Microsoft Data Engine (MSDE). You must also create an application pool for the extranet sites and connect to the configuration database after installation.

- **Extend the virtual server.**   Before you can create sites, you must extend the extranet virtual server. The extranet virtual server is connected to the same content databases as the intranet virtual server so that they provide the same site content.

To perform these steps for a server farm, you should use the command-line administration tool, Stsadm.exe.

IIS is not enabled by default in Windows Server 2003. To make your front-end servers into Web servers, you must enable IIS.

To enable IIS and configure it to use IIS 6.0 worker process isolation mode

1.   Click **Start**, and then click **Manage Your Server**.

2.   On the Manage Your Server page, click **Add or remove a role**.

3. On the Preliminary Steps page, click **Next**.

4. On the Server Role page, click **Application server (IIS, ASP.NET)** and then click **Next**.

5. On the Web Application Server Options page, accept the default of **ASP.NET** and then click **Next**.

6. On the Summary Of Selections page, click **Next**.

7. Click **Finish**.

8. Click **Start**, point to **Administrative Tools**, and then click **Internet Information Services (IIS)**.

9. In Internet Information Services manager, click the plus sign (+) next to the server name, and then right-click the **Web Sites** folder and select **Properties**.

10. In the **Properties** dialog box, click the **Service** tab.

11. In the **Isolation mode** section, clear the **Run WWW service in IIS 5.0 isolation mode** check box, and then click **OK**.

When IIS is configured and ready to work with SQL Server, you can create the virtual server you need to host the extranet sites.

To create a virtual server

1. Click **Start**, point to **Programs**, point to **Administrative Tools**, and then click **Internet Information Services**.

2. Click the plus sign (+) next to the server name you want to add a virtual server to.

3. Right-click the **Web Sites** folder, click **New**, and then click **Web site**.

4. Click **Next**.

5. In the **Description** box, type the description of your virtual server and then click **Next**.

6. In the **Enter the IP address to use for this Web site** box, select the IP address you want to use.

7. In the **TCP port this Web site should use (Default: 80)** box, type the port number to assign to the virtual server.

8. In the **Host Header for this site (Default: None)** box, type the header you want to use and then click **Next**.

9. In the **Path** box, type or browse to the path on your hard disk where the site content will go.

10. Clear the **Allow anonymous access to this Web site** check box, and then click **Next**.

11. On the Web Site Access Permissions page, select the permissions to use and then click **Next**.

    If other users are allowed to contribute to the site, you must select at least the **Read**, **Write**, and **Browse** check boxes. If your virtual server allows scripts to be run, you must also select the **Run scripts (such as ASP)** check box. If you want to allow ISAPI applications or CGI scripts to be used on your virtual server, you must also select the **Execute (such as ISAPI applications or CGI)** check box.

12. Click **Finish**.

    Now you can configure the authentication method to use for the extranet virtual server.

To configure the authentication method for the extranet virtual server

1. On the extranet front-end Web server, in **Internet Information Services**, right-click the virtual server that will be used for the extranet site, and then click **Properties**.

2. On the **Directory Security** tab, under **Authentication and access control**, click **Edit**.

3. Select the **Basic authentication** check box, and clear all other authentication method check boxes.

4. Click **OK** to close the **Authentication Methods** dialog box.

5. On the **Directory Security** tab, under **Secure communications**, click **Edit**.

6. In the **Secure Communications** dialog box, select the **Require secure channel (SSL)** check box and then click **OK**.

7. Click **OK** again to close the **Properties** dialog box.

> **Note**   You must have a certificate before you can enable SSL. For more information about SSL certificates, see the topics "About Certificates" and "Setting Up SSL on Your Server" in IIS 6.0 online Help. For more information about IIS authentication methods, see the topic "About authentication" in IIS 6.0 online Help.

After you have configured the authentication method, you can install Windows SharePoint Services.

Installing and Configuring Windows SharePoint Services on the Extranet Front-End Web Server

You must install Windows SharePoint Services in the server farm configuration. To do so, you use the setupsts.exe command with the remotesql property on the command line. Follow the procedure detailed earlier in this chapter, "To install Windows SharePoint Services with the Remote SQL Server option."

To set the application pool for the administration virtual server and connect to the configuration database from the command line

1. Open a command prompt window, and navigate to the \Program Files \Common Files\Microsoft Shared\Web Server Extensions\60\bin folder.

2. Run the following command to create the administration virtual server:

    ```
    stsadm.exe -o setadminport -port <port> -admapcreatenew -admapidname
        <id for application pool> -admapidtype configurableid -admapidlogin
        <DOMAIN\username> -admapidpwd <password>
    ```

    Example:

    ```
    stsadm.exe -o setadminport -port 1035 -admapcreatenew
        -admapidname NewAppPool -admapidtype configurableid
        -admapidlong DOMAIN\user1 -admapidpws P@ssw0rd
    ```

> **Note**   You can use any unused port between 1023 and 32767. You should use a dedicated account for the application pool account rather than a user's login account. Also, you should use the same account for each application pool that hosts the same content.

3. Restart IIS by running **iisreset** on the command line.

4. Run the following command to connect to the configuration database:

    ```
    stsadm.exe -o setconfigdb -ds <database server name> [-du <database user>
        -dp <password>] -dn sts_config
    ```

    The syntax shown is for Windows authentication. If you are using SQL Server authentication, you must also specify the -du and -dp parameters with the database username and password.

To set the application pool for the administration virtual server and connect to the configuration database using HTML Administration pages

1. When setup finishes, you are taken to the Security And Configuration Database page.

2.   In the **Application Pool** section, select **Define a new application pool**.

3.   Under **Select a security account for this application pool**, select **Configurable**.

4.   In the **User name** box, type the domain account to use for the application pool.

   This account must have DBO rights to the SQL Server computer to be able to create the configuration database. You should use a dedicated account for this account rather than a user's login account. Also, you should use the same account for each application pool that hosts the same content.

5.   In the **Password** box, type the password for the account, confirm it, and then click **OK**.

6.   The application pool is created, and you are taken to a confirmation page. You must restart IIS to accept the change. To restart IIS, type **iisreset** on the command line.

7.   After restarting IIS, click the link to continue, and on the Create Configuration Database page, in the **Configuration Database** section, enter the server name and database name for the existing configuration database.

8.   Select **Use Integrated Windows authentication (more secure, recommended)**.

9.   Select the **Connect to existing database** check box.

10.   In the **Active Directory Account Creation** section, select **Users already have domain accounts** if you are using a Windows domain, or **Automatically create active directory accounts for users of this site** if you are using Active Directory outside of a Windows domain.

11.   If you selected **Automatically create active directory accounts for users of this site**, you must fill in the **Active Directory Domain** and **Organization Unit** information.

12.   Click **Submit**.

13.   On the Central Administration page, under **Server Configuration**, click **Set default content database server**.

14.   On the Set Default Content Database Server page, in the **Content Database Server** section, enter the server name, administrator account username, and password.

15.   Click **Submit**.

Extending the Extranet Virtual Server

With the administration virtual server and configuration database in place, you can extend the virtual server to host the extranet sites. You can use either the command line or HTML Administration pages to extend the virtual server.

To extend the extranet virtual server

1. Open a command prompt window, and navigate to the \Program Files \Common Files\Microsoft Shared\Web Server Extensions\60\bin folder.

2. Run the following command to extend the extranet virtual server.

   ```
   stsadm.exe -o extendvsinwebfarm -url https://www.servername.extranet.com
       -vsname <virtual server name> [-apcreatenew -adpidname <application pool
       name> -apidtype configurableid -apidlogin <DOMAIN\name> -apidpwd <password>]
   ```

   The -vsname parameter is the IIS name of the internal virtual server you extended earlier. For example, if you are using a site named "mysite" in IIS, the -vsname value would be mysite. It is recommended that you create a new application pool for the virtual server. Use a dedicated application pool account, not a user login account. The application pool account for a virtual server does not need database owner rights on the SQL Server computer. Note that the -du and -dp parameters are not needed if you are using Windows authentication to connect to SQL Server.

To extend the virtual server using HTML Administration pages

1. Click **Start**, point to **Programs**, point to **Administrative Tools**, and then click **SharePoint Central Administration**.

2. In the **Virtual Server Configuration** section, click **Extend or upgrade virtual server**.

3. On the Virtual Server List page, click the virtual server you want to extend.

4. On the Extend Virtual Server page, click **Extend and map to another virtual server**.

5. On the Extend And Map To Database Another Virtual Server page, in the **Server Mapping** section, in the **Host name or IIS virtual server name** list, select the name of the host or virtual server that you want to use.

6. In the **Application Pool** section, click **Create a new application pool**.

7. Under **Select a security account for this application pool**, click **Configurable**.

8. In the **User name** box, type the domain account to use for the application pool.

   You should use a dedicated account for this account rather than a user's login account. Also, you should use the same account for each application pool that hosts the same content.

9. In the **Password** box, type the password for the account and then confirm it.

10. Click **Submit**.

11. To set up the SMTP parameters after extending the virtual server, click **Start**, point to **Programs**, point to **Administrative Tools**, and then click **Share-Point Central Administration**.

12. Under **Virtual Server Configuration**, click **Configure virtual server settings**.

13. On the Virtual Server List page, click the virtual server you want to configure.

14. Under **Virtual Server Management**, click **Virtual server e-mail settings**.

15. Under **Mail Settings**, configure the **Outbound SMTP** server, the **From** address, and the **Reply-to** address.

16. Click **OK**.

Creating Sites

After following the steps just shown, you are ready to create sites for your users. This is the last step in the process for setting up your intranet/extranet server farm. After this step, you can start adding users and managing the sites.

To create a site

1. Open a command prompt window, and navigate to the \Program Files \Common Files\Microsoft Shared\Web Server Extensions\60\bin folder.

2. Run the following command to create a site:

```
stsadm.exe -o createsite -url <url>  -ownerlogin <DOMAIN\username>
    -owneremail <email address> [-ownername <display name> -lcid <lcid>
    -sitetemplate <site template> -title <title> -description <site description>]
```

Repeat this step for every site you want to create. Note that because both your intranet and extranet virtual servers connect to the same content database, the same sites are available in each environment.

Next Steps

Your server farm is now set up for serving the same content on both an intranet and extranet. You can start adding users and managing sites, or you can perform the following optional, but recommended, steps:

- You should help protect your administration virtual server either by using a firewall to block access or by using Secure Sockets Layer (SSL) for the port.

- As your sites increase in number and size, you will want to be able to add content databases or change connections to the content databases.

Summary

This chapter has described the setup process for configuration of Windows Share-Point Services to provide both an intranet and extranet deployment to serve the same content to both sets of clients.

We have addressed the crucial issues from preparing your servers to configuring SQL Server and IIS. As indicated in this chapter, a topic of prime importance is planning for and securing the extranet. Therefore, you need to pay special attention to the sections that deal with setting up authentication methods.

Chapter 14

Shared Services

This chapter discusses the shared services functionality of Microsoft Office Share-Point Portal Server 2003. Shared services provide common storage and management capabilities for alerts, audiences, user profiles, My Sites, and search between multiple portal sites on the same farm or between farms. This chapter will discuss when and why shared services should be used and how to enable shared services.

Multiple Portal Sites

There are many reasons an organization would choose to run multiple portal sites on the same server farm. For example, there could be a corporate news portal site that has information about what is going on in the company and then portal sites for each division, such as Legal, Human Resources (HR), or Marketing. That is a perfectly fine structure, but you could also choose to have a corporate portal site with divisional topics in that portal site, and then have portal sites for each major team. For example, a software company might have portal sites for each product. It is really up to each individual organization to determine the structure of the server farm.

There are several things to consider when determining how many portal sites to use, however. The first consideration is resources. Full portal sites consume a significant amount of RAM. They can also use a lot of processing power, depending on the number of users. In a single-server environment or small server farm, it is expensive to host many non–shared services portal sites. Each non–shared services portal site will have its own search applications—catalogs, content sources, search scopes, and crawling schedules—as well as its own My Site directories and audiences.

The benefit of multiple non–shared services portal sites is that each portal site is a completely separate entity. This scenario might be useful for partner extranets, where you want no connection to your corporate portal site. In such a scenario, you would want partners to have access to controlled information about your company. For example, giving partners access to the corporate portal site would give them access to see public My Sites of any user of the portal site. If you just want to give partners access to contact information for specific users of your company, you would need to have a completely separate portal site for partners (or even separate portal sites for each partner) or get very deep into changing permissions on public My Sites on the corporate portal site.

The major disadvantage of multiple non–shared services portal sites is that additional administrative effort and administrative costs are incurred. It is difficult to manage multiple discrete portal sites, as each additional site takes more time to set up, configure, and maintain. Each portal site has different settings, and keeping track of what settings each site has can be daunting and time consuming for the SharePoint Portal Server administrator. Depending on the number of non–shared services portal sites, you might need to share the burden of administration among multiple server administrators. This will add cost as well. Also, having multiple non–shared services portal sites can be confusing for users who have accounts on each of those portal sites—for example, a salesperson who has an account on the corporate portal site as well as on the partner portal site. That user will have a different My Site on each portal site and will get different search results on each portal site. These factors should be taken into consideration.

The other increased cost of running multiple non–shared services portal sites is resources. A single-server environment with 4 GB of RAM can host up to 10 non–shared services portal sites without incurring a performance penalty. The amount of content in the portal site and the site's peak usage will ultimately determine how many non–shared services portal sites can be hosted on a single server. If usage is light, up to 10 non–shared services portal sites can be hosted, but if usage of all the portal sites is heavy, you should not run more than 4 or 5 non–shared services portal sites. To increase the capacity of the farm, additional machines must be purchased and the farm must be reconfigured. Both are costly ventures, requiring skillful planning to ensure minimal downtime. In addition, much data will be stored multiple times. Audience compilation and user profiles will be stored in a separate database for each portal site, so any information that is present in multiple portal sites will be stored multiple times. Search catalogs will be built on a per–portal site basis, meaning that if any content source, such as company press releases, is present in more than one portal site, it is indexed in both the corporate portal site and the partner portal site. That same content will be crawled twice, taking up processor time, and it will be stored in two different catalogs, taking up twice the space.

Use Intra-Farm Shared Services

Intra-farm shared services can be the answer to the problem with multiple portal sites we just discussed. It will not help in a situation where multiple non–shared services portal sites are needed to separate the entities, but it will help alleviate the resource and management difficulties. Additional portal sites in a farm running shared services will take up far fewer resources, except for the corporate portal site. The corporate portal site is the top-level, or parent, portal site of the farm. This portal site will host all the shared services—search applications, audiences, user profiles, and My Sites. It will consume roughly the same amount of memory as a non–shared services portal site. With shared services enabled, you will be able to host up to 100 portal sites on a single server without incurring a performance penalty. Again, as with non–shared services portal sites, the total number of portal sites per server that can be hosted ultimately depends on site content and usage.

> **Note** You do not want to enable shared services on a server farm where there is only one portal site. Because shared services add additional databases for the shared services data, running shared services with only one server will actually give you slightly lower performance. You can always enable shared services later when a second portal site needs to be created.

Administration is easier with shared services also. Because there is only one location to configure search, audiences, user profiles, and My Sites for the entire farm, these components are much simpler and faster to manage. Troubleshooting can be easier as well. Search can be a problematic component of SharePoint Portal Server to fix when it breaks. Because there is only one search application for the entire server farm with shared services, there will be only one instance to monitor and fix, rather than several.

Each portal site will still have its own Site Settings configuration, which will be the responsibility of the portal site owner to manage, but resource-intensive operations, such as audience compilation and crawling, will be reserved for farm administrators. The link for each of these will still show up on the Site Settings page, but you will get a notice that shared services is enabled and that you will need to contact the administrator of the corporate portal site, as shown in Figure 14-1.

The end-user experience will be improved with shared services as well. If a user performs an "All Content Source" search on any portal site in the farm, that user will get the same search results as if he searched directly from the parent portal site. When the user visits his My Site, it will be the same no matter what portal site he is using. This is because the My Site link actually redirects the user to the My Site on the corporate portal site no matter what portal site he is using, unless you manually designate a separate personal site portal. You might consider using a separate personal site portal if you have a huge number of personal sites and you want to segregate all those sites on a different server to increase performance. As you can see in Figure 14-2, the URL for My Site (as seen in the status bar in the lower left corner) points to portal.woodgrovebank.com even though the user is on the Partners portal site. All public My Sites will be the same for all portal sites in the farm as well. All this leads to a more seamless end-user experience while still implementing multiple portal sites.

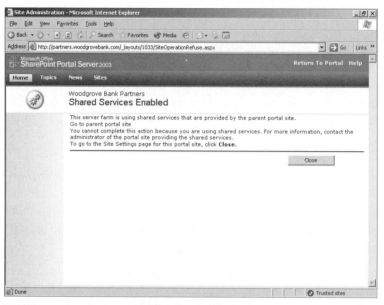

Figure 14-1 Shared services enabled warning

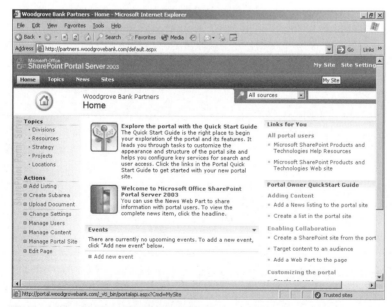

Figure 14-2 My Site URL redirection

> **Note** The only time the user experience is not seamless is when the user clicks to go to his My Site from a child portal site and then wants to navigate back. Usually in the upper-right corner of the portal site, there is a link to go up to the level above where he is. For a user's My Site, this link will always be the root of the corporate, or parent, portal site. If the user comes from a different portal site and wants to use the link, it might be somewhat awkward. In this instance, the user should use the browser's Back button to return to the site he was on.

Configuring Shared Services

To use shared services, you first must enable shared services on the server farm. Shared services provide common storage and management capabilities for alerts, audiences, user profiles, My Sites, and search. If you run a multiple portal site environment on your server farm without activating shared services, you are required to manage each of the preceding issues separately on each portal site.

Shared services can be enabled from any server in the farm from which you can access SharePoint Central Administration. Usually, it is configured from a front-end Web server.

> **Note** After you enable shared services, you cannot easily change the selections that you are making in the following steps. Be sure to make appropriate decisions for your organization before continuing.

To enable shared services

1. Click **Start**, point to **All Programs**, point to **SharePoint Portal Server**, and then click **SharePoint Central Administration**.

2. On the SharePoint Portal Server Central Administration page, in the **Component Configuration** section, click **Manage shared services for the server farm**.

3. On the Managed Shared Services page, in the **Shared Services Provider** section, click **Provide shared services**.

4. In the **Portal site that provides shared services** list, click the name of the corporate portal site as shown in Figure 14-3.

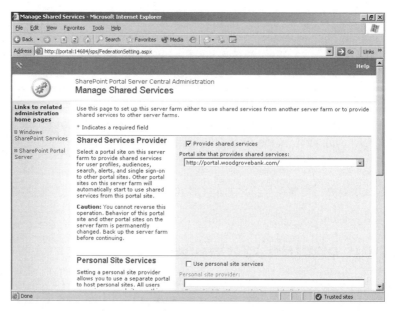

Figure 14-3   Selecting the corporate portal site to enable shared services

5. If you want to share My Sites by using a separate personal sites portal, select the **Use personal site services** check box and enter the URL of the portal site hosting the My Sites (the corporate portal site) as shown in Figure 14-4.

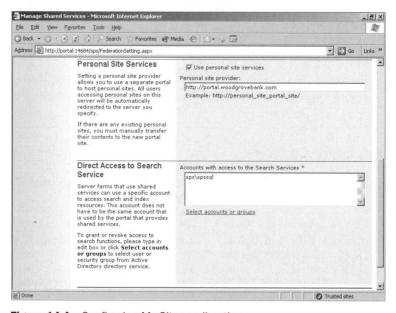

Figure 14-4   Configuring My Sites redirection

6. In the **Direct Access to Search Service** section, enter the domain account used for managing search and content services (DOMAIN\spssql).

> **Note**   Server farms that use shared services can use a specific account to access search and index resources. This account does not have to be the same account that is used by the portal site that provides shared services.

Adding Portal Sites

Using shared services is pointless unless you have multiple portal sites. Using the steps that follow will create an additional portal site. These are the same steps for creating both a non–shared services portal site (when shared services is not enabled) and a child portal site (when shared services is enabled). In our example, our main portal site is at *partners.woodgrovebank.com*. The portal site to be created in our example will be accessible at *partners.woodgrovebank.com*.

To create an additional portal site, first create a new virtual server in Internet Information Services (IIS) by following these steps:

1. On a front-end Web server, open **Internet Information Services Manager**.

2. Expand the server.

3. Right-click the **Web Sites** folder, point to **New**, and then click **Web Site**.

4. Click **Next** to start the wizard. Enter a description for the website as shown in Figure 14-5. Click **Next** to continue.

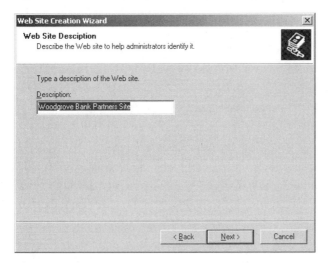

Figure 14-5   Creating a new virtual server

5. Enter an IP address to bind to if you have multiple network interface cards (NIC); otherwise, enter a host header as shown in Figure 14-6. Click **Next** to continue.

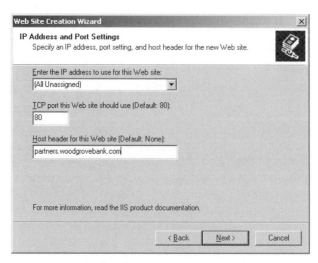

Figure 14-6   Configuring a host header

6. Enter a path for the website. This path cannot be the same as one used by another website. You should create a new folder under your default home directory for IIS sites (located by default at C:\Inetpub\wwwroot). Clear the **Allow anonymous access to this Web site** check box. Click **Next** to continue.

7. Leave **Web Site Access Permissions** at their default (Read, Run scripts). Click **Next** to continue. Click **Finish** to complete the wizard.

8. Repeat steps 1 through 7 on each front-end Web server.

9. Go to **SharePoint Portal Server Central Administration**.

10. In the **Portal Site and Virtual Server Configuration** section, click **Create a portal site**.

11. Enter a name for the portal site, and select the virtual server you just created as shown in Figure 14-7. Enter an owner account and e-mail address. Click **OK**. Click **OK** again to confirm portal site creation.

12. For additional front-end servers, on the SharePoint Portal Server Central Administration page, in the **Portal Site and Virtual Server Configuration** section, click **Extend an existing virtual server from the Virtual Server List page**.

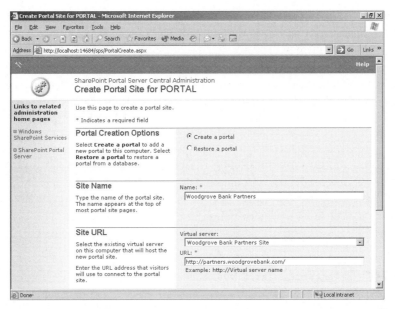

Figure 14-7 Creating a new portal site

13. This opens the Extend Virtual Server Administration page. Click **Extend and map to another virtual server**.

14. On the Windows SharePoint Services Extend And Map To Another Virtual Server page, in the **Server Mapping** section, click the name of the virtual server the portal site was created on in the list.

15. In the **Application Pool** section, click **Use an existing application pool**, select the portal site application pool that was created previously in this chapter, and then set the application pool. Click **OK**.

16. Repeat steps 12 through 15 for each additional front-end server.

Recovery Considerations

You can restore portal sites by using the SharePoint Portal Server Data Backup and Restore utility, which is covered in detail in Chapter 30, "Default Tools to Customize Windows SharePoint Services." However, the following rules apply when restoring portal sites to farms that use shared services:

■ Within a shared services server farm, the corporate (parent) portal site provides all shared services for the divisional (child) portal sites in the server farm. If the corporate portal site is disabled or deleted, all divisional portal sites become unavailable until the corporate portal site is restored.

■ When the corporate (parent) portal site no longer exists on the server farm, the divisional (child) portal sites continue to operate as if they were still members of an intra-farm shared services configuration. However, you cannot connect to a divisional portal site while the corporate portal site is down or disabled. If the corporate portal site cannot be restored, an independent portal site can be restored to the server farm, and it will automatically become the master portal site. This makes it possible to repair the server farm after the corporate portal site is lost.

The Backup and Restore utility is sensitive to the type of portal site being restored. If the corporate (parent) portal site is available, any portal site being restored automatically becomes a divisional (child) portal site and consumes shared services from the corporate portal site. You cannot restore a divisional portal site into a server farm that is missing the corporate portal site. The corporate portal site must be restored before a divisional portal site can be restored.

Inter-Farm Shared Services

Inter-farm shared services are much like regular shared services, except that a different farm hosts the shared applications—search, audiences, profiles, and My Sites. This model allows additional scalability because large farms that are at capacity can have their services shared with an additional farm. It can also work well for smaller farms that want more portal sites but don't want to make the jump to a larger farm topology. By adding a single server or small server farm, more portal sites can be supported in the organization.

> **Note**   To use inter-farm shared services, all server farms must be in the same domain and all SharePoint database access accounts must have permission to access the configuration and content databases of the corporate (parent) portal site.

Only SharePoint Portal Server farms that use SQL Server are supported in an inter-farm scenario. Servers using MSDE cannot participate in inter-farm shared services.

To configure inter-farm shared services

1. Open **SharePoint Portal Server Central Administration** on one of the front-end Web servers. In the **Component Configuration** section, click **Manage shared services for the server farm**.

2. In the **Shared Services Consumer** section, select the **Use shared services** check box.

3. Enter the name of the configuration database server and configuration database for the farm you would like to share services from, as shown in Figure 14-8.

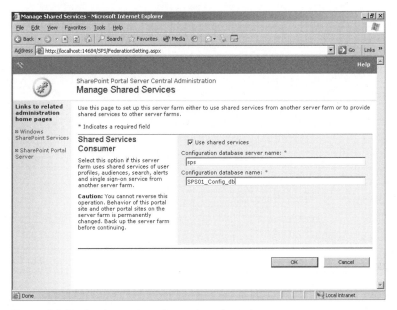

Figure 14-8   Setting up inter-farm shared services

Summary

In this chapter, you learned about shared services and works. Shared services is incredibly useful when hosting multiple portal sites on the same farm, by sharing search, My Sites, profiles, and audience information between farms. This lowers the resource cost of hosting portal sites and allows more than 15 portal sites to be hosted on a single farm. Finally, this chapter detailed how to set up and configure both inter-farm and intra-farm shared services.

Part V

Administration of Windows SharePoint Services

Chapter 15

Configuring Windows SharePoint Services

It is important to plan the Microsoft Windows SharePoint Services configuration prior to actually doing the install so that you make the best use of your administrative time. For instance, if you think through who needs access to data in the site collections, you can capitalize on security inheritance and minimize the number of times you need to set up security. However, most of the configuration options we will discuss in this chapter can be changed once the site collection is created.

Configuration of a Windows SharePoint Services site is accomplished using the Windows SharePoint Services Central Administration Web page. Site and Site Collection Administration is accomplished using the Site Settings Administration Web pages that are accessed directly from the Windows SharePoint Services site.

The Management User Interface for Windows SharePoint Services

Because the focus of this chapter is on the administration of the Windows SharePoint Services installation as a whole and not on specific sites, we'll be using the Windows SharePoint Services Central Administration HTML pages.

One way you can gain access to SharePoint Central Administration (shown in Figure 15-1) is to go to Start, Programs, Administrative Tools, and then SharePoint Central Administration. This will take you to the Windows SharePoint Services Central Administration page. If the title at the top of the screen references SharePoint Portal Server, make sure you click the Windows SharePoint Services link in the left-most column of the screen.

Figure 15-1 Windows SharePoint Services Central Administration settings

Using the SharePoint Central Administration Pages

Each of the four main menu selections has submenu items that have several options. As you work with these menus and submenus, remember that you can always return to the Windows SharePoint Services Central Administration page by using the Back button on your Web browser or by clicking the Windows SharePoint Services link in the left-most column of the Central Administration page.

Configuring Virtual Servers

You can configure settings for the virtual server by clicking the Configure Virtual Server Settings link (which was also shown in Figure 15-1). After clicking the link, you might have a number of virtual servers listed, as shown in Figure 15-2. Select the one you want to configure.

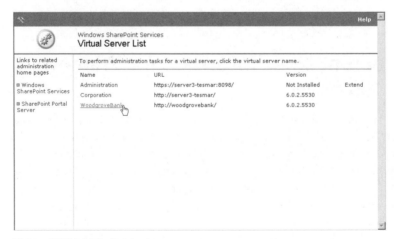

Figure 15-2 List of virtual servers

The following option can be set at the virtual server level and will affect all sites on that virtual server:

The **Self-Service Site Creation** setting can be set at the virtual server level and will affect all sights on a virual server. This setting, shown in Figure 15-3, allows you to either enable or disable Self-Service Site Creation. Microsoft Windows SharePoint Services allows members of the Administrator site group to create subsites off of their websites by default. These subsites can by fully functioning SharePoint sites— complete with a home page, document libraries, and so on—and they can even have their own unique permissions. If administrators decide this is a capability they would like to extend to users, they can enable the Self-Service Site Creation feature. The user does not need administrator permissions on the server or virtual server, only permissions on the website where Self-Service Site Creation is hosted. The user simply enters some basic information and the new top-level website is created with the user as the owner and administrator. When you enable Self-Service Site Creation, you free yourself from having to create top-level websites on demand for your users—they can do it themselves.

> **Note** This feature allows users to create top-level sites, not just subsites in another collection. Users with this capability can create entirely new site collections.

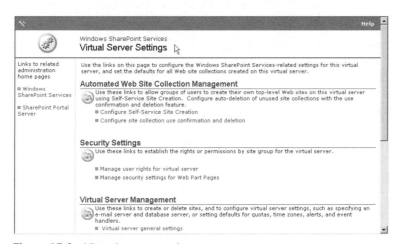

Figure 15-3   Virtual server settings

Command-Line Administration

On occasion, you might want command-line tools to accomplish some tasks either because it is not convenient to use the HTML administration pages or because you want to automate a procedure. In such cases, you can use a command-line utility.

Windows SharePoint Services includes Stsadm.exe for command-line administration of Windows SharePoint Services servers and sites. The Stsadm.exe tool provides a method for performing the Windows SharePoint Services administration tasks to run once, to be used in batch files, or to be used within a script. The command-line tool has a more streamlined interface than HTML Administration pages, yet it allows you to perform many of the same tasks.

> **Note** You must be an administrator of the server computer to be able to use the Stsadm.exe tool, and the command must be run from the server running Windows SharePoint Services.

Configuring Self-Service Site Creation from the Command Line

Use the enablessc operation to turn on and configure Self-Service Site Creation from the command line. The enablessc operation requires the URL parameter, and optionally takes the requiresecondarycontact parameter. For example, to turn on Self-Service Site Creation for a server called *My_Server* and require two contact names for each site, you would use the following syntax:

```
stsadm -o enablessc -url http://My_Server -requiresecondarycontact
```

To disable Self-Service Site Creation, use the disablessc operation. The disablessc operation takes only the URL parameter. To turn off Self-Service Site Creation for My_Server, use the following syntax:

```
stsadm -o disablessc -url http://My_Server
```

Configure Site Collection Using Confirmation and Deletion

Websites based on Microsoft Windows SharePoint Services can become inactive for many reasons. Perhaps a site was set up for documents relating to a project that is finished, or perhaps a user was trying out Windows SharePoint Services and created a site that he or she no longer needs. Because inactive sites take up space on the servers, it's important to check with site owners to see whether their sites are still needed or have become inactive. In Windows SharePoint Services, new administrative options allow you to automatically send notices to site owners requiring them to confirm that their sites are in use. You can also delete unconfirmed sites automatically. These features give you a way to control the number of unused websites on your server.

After a specified time defined by the administrator, the site owners are sent an e-mail notification asking the owners to either reactivate or delete their unused websites. The notification e-mail text contains links to confirm that a site is active or to delete a site. After the notification is sent, there are three possible outcomes:

- If a site is in use, the site owner will click a link to confirm that the site is active and preserve the site. When the owner clicks the confirmation link, the timer is restarted, and the owner will be notified again after the same time period.

- If a site is not in use, the site owner can delete the site by following instructions in the notification e-mail or do nothing. The site owner continues to receive periodic e-mail notifications (the period is defined by the administrator) until use is confirmed or the site is deleted.

- If a site is not in use, you have turned on the automatic deletion feature, the site owner is queried a specific number of times (a number configured by the administrator), and use is not confirmed, the site is automatically deleted.

Automatic deletion is an advanced administrative feature that can delete unneeded sites without any administrative intervention and without any backup mechanism. To prevent a site from being deleted without any notification, you must turn on site use confirmation before you can turn on automatic deletion. Also, the site owner must always be sent at least two confirmation notices before a site can be deleted.

By default, site use confirmation is turned off. To require confirmation of use, you can specify the interval to wait before sending the first notification and how frequently to continue sending notifications if site use is not confirmed. Notices are sent to the e-mail address specified in the site for the site collection owner and the secondary owner (if a secondary contact has been identified).

Warning Be sure to back up websites regularly so that you can restore a recent copy if a site is unintentionally deleted.

As an example, if you specify 60 days in the Start Sending Notifications box, when a user creates a site, the first notification will be sent after 60 days. If the user confirms that the site is in use at that time, another 60 days will pass before the user gets another notification.

Note The exact time of the physical deletion will depend on when you have scheduled the background process called Checking For And Automatically Deleting Unused Web Sites. This process can be set to run daily, weekly, or monthly and is set at the virtual server level, so it will potentially affect all sites on that virtual server.

The Start Sending Notifications Days field must be a value between 30 and 365. (The initial notification value controls when the first confirmation notice is sent to a new site or to a site that has been confirmed as in use. This value does not control the frequency of notifications, only the number of days to wait before the initial notification.)

Regardless of the value you place in the Start Sending Notifications field, if you choose daily notification, the value must be between 28 and 168 days. As you look at the options, it will be obvious that the relationship between the values in the fields must make sense. For instance, you can't set the Start Sending Notifications field for 15 days, and the Check For Unused Site Collections setting to monthly notification, because that makes no sense. It would be impossible to start sending notifications 15 days after the site was last used if the system is only checking on a monthly basis. However, when you set incompatible values, the user interface will give you a warning, as it always does, at the top of the window in red lettering. See Figure 15-4.

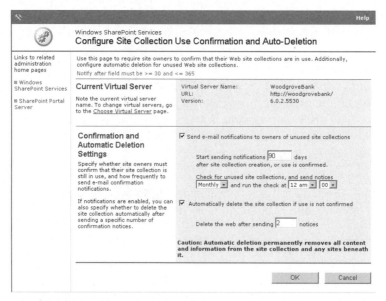

Figure 15-4   Error for Automatic Deletion settings

Manage User Rights for Virtual Server Settings

As an administrator, if you want to allow or limit certain actions your users perform, you can disable or enable the associated right on the virtual server. For example, if you do not want users to be able to add pages to a website, you can disable the Add And Customize Pages right. When you disable a right on a virtual server, it cannot be assigned to any site group and, as a result, cannot be granted to any user of a site on the virtual server.

> **Note**   If a user already has a right, and you disable that right, the right is also disabled for that user.

Manage Security Settings for Web Part Pages

This setting is used for administration of the Web Parts and Web Part Pages you use on this virtual server. Specify whether users can create connections between Web Parts in a website and whether the Online Web Part Gallery is available. (See Figure 15-5.)

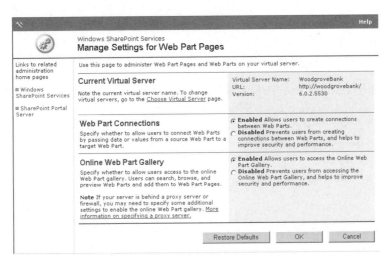

Figure 15-5   Web Part connections

Web Part Connections and Online Web Part Gallery Settings

Use these settings to control whether users can connect Web Parts within a site and whether they have access to the online Web Part gallery. The online Web Part gallery contains many Web Parts that users can use on their sites. Adding Web Parts or making connections to Web Parts might affect your server security and performance. For example, if you allow Web Part connections and a user connects a complex Web Part to a large data set, the Web Part Page that contains those Web Parts could load very slowly when a user goes to it. Also, if a user connects to a Web Part that contains a scripting error or malicious code, that Web Part could open a security hole in the user's site or, potentially, on your server. However, in most scenarios, the default settings that allow Web Part connections and an Online gallery will be the preferred setting because the feature of connecting Web Parts presents powerful collaboration solutions.

You can change these configuration options at the virtual server level. By default, both security options are enabled at the server level. You need to change these options only if you do not want to allow either Web Part connections or access to the online Web Part gallery.

When making virtual server setting changes in a farm environment, if a change is made on one virtual server, SharePoint will display a page asking if you want to synchronize the other servers in the farm.

You must be an administrator of the local server computer or a member of the SharePoint administrators group to configure security and performance options for Web Parts and Web Part Pages.

Virtual Server General Settings

The Virtual Server General Settings page contains several options that apply throughout the virtual server. When you configure a setting for a virtual server, it takes priority over settings applied on specific sites of that virtual server. For example, if you disable alerts for a virtual server, no site or subsite can use alerts. For more information about how each setting is treated at different levels, see the specific topic for that setting.

The settings you can configure on the Virtual Server General Settings page are detailed in the following sections.

Time Zone to Use for the Virtual Server

Select a time zone to use for all sites created on this virtual server as shown in Figure 15-6. The time zone setting can also be changed for a top-level or subsite. To change the time zone for a site, click Site Settings, and then under the heading Administration, click Go To Site Administration. Now from the Top-Level Site Administration menu, click Change Regional Settings under the heading Management And Statistics.

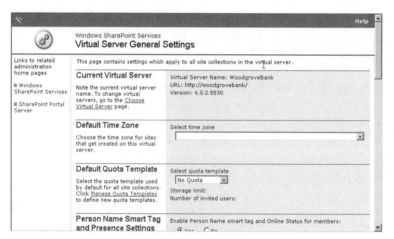

Figure 15-6   Time Zone and Quota Template settings

Configuring Time Zone from the Command Line

If you prefer to change the time zone setting from the command line, use the Stsadm.exe command with the following parameters:

Stsadm.exe –o setproperty –pn defaulttimezone

You will need to know the numerical value for the time zone you want to use. Replace the defaulttimezone parameter with this numerical value.

Default Quota Template for Sites Created Under the Virtual Server

You can specify the default quota template to use. (See Figure 15-6.)

Microsoft Windows SharePoint Services allows you to specify quotas for sites so that you can manage site and server resources. You can create multiple sets of quotas, called *quota templates,* and use them in different Site Collections of the server farm or to suit different users. You can use locks to stop sites from exceeding your storage quota limits and to block all users from accessing a site if necessary.

When you create a top-level website, you can create it using the default template or a different template. Quota templates and the settings specified in them are stored in the configuration database for your server or server farm. Quota values apply to top-level websites and are applied when you create such sites. You can specify a default template to use for all top-level websites created on a virtual server, for example, or you can specify the template to use when you create the top-level website. The values listed in the quota template are copied into the database for the top-level website and are referenced from there.

Note   If you change the values for a quota template, those changes apply only to new top-level websites created using that template, not to existing ones. If you want to apply the template changes to existing sites, you can use the SharePoint Central Administration User Interface and re-apply the quota template to existing sites. Alternatively, you can use the Windows SharePoint Services object model or make the change with a SQL Server query. Likewise, when you delete a quota template, the template is removed from the configuration database, but any top-level websites created using that template will retain the quota values. If you want to remove quotas from all sites using a particular quota template, you must use the object model or perform a SQL Server query.

If there are no templates, you can create a template by using the Manage Quota Templates page. Note that when you specify a default template for the virtual server, you can still select a different template when you create a site.

Applying Quota Template Changes from the Command Line

If you prefer to apply the quota template from the command line, use the Stsadm.exe command with the following parameters:

Stsadm –o setproperty –pn defaultquotatemplate –pv <property value>

Replace <`property value`> with the actual name of the template.

Name Smart Tag and Presence Settings

Use this setting to enable or disable presence information for site members. Online presence allows users of your site to see whether other users are online and to send instant messages to them. To use online presence, your users must have Microsoft

Office 2003 installed, must be running Microsoft Windows Messenger version 4.6 or later or MSN Messenger version 4.6 or later on their client computers, and must have valid accounts with the .NET Messenger or Exchange Instant Messaging service. Note that the e-mail address for the instant messaging account must be the same as the e-mail address for the user account in Windows SharePoint Services. See Figure 15-7.

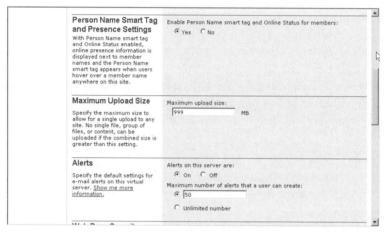

Figure 15-7   Smart Tag, Upload Size, and Alert settings

Maximum Upload Size

This is the place to specify the maximum file size to allow when files are uploaded to a website on this virtual server. See Figure 15-7.

Setting the Maximum File Upload Size from the Command Line

If you prefer to change the maximum file upload size setting from the command line, use the Stsadm.exe command with the following parameters:

Stsadm –o setproperty –pn max-file-post-size –pv <property value>

Replace <property value> with a numerical value, in megabytes (MB).

> **Note**   Even though you can increase the Maximum Upload Size to a much larger number, Microsoft's recommendation is not to exceed 50 MB for best performance. Note that this applies to the Upload Multiple Files feature in Office 2003. We have successfully tested uploading much larger file sets using the Web Folder client with the drag-and-drop method.

Alert Settings

This setting allows you to enable or disable alerts for all sites under the virtual server, and it allows you to configure default settings for alerts. See Figure 15-7.

Because websites based on Microsoft Windows SharePoint Services are meant to help groups of users work together, they tend to grow quickly and change often. Keeping up with these changes can be difficult for users, especially if they aren't checking on the site every day. To help users stay in touch with changes on a site, Windows SharePoint Services includes a feature called *Alerts*, an e-mail notification service. (They will also appear in the My Alerts when this Web Part is present on site pages.) When documents, lists, or items in a list on a server running Windows SharePoint Services are created, modified, or deleted, users who sign up for alerts receive messages informing them that changes have been made.

> **Note**   Before alerts can work for a particular site, the e-mail server settings must be configured at the server or virtual server level. In SharePoint Team Services v1.0 from Microsoft, alerts were called *Web subscriptions*.

Users can create alerts to track items within a site, such as:

- **Lists.**   Users are notified of changes to the list, such as when an item is added, deleted, or changed in a list.

- **List items.**   Users are notified of changes to a particular item in a list.

- **Document libraries.**   Users are notified of changes to the document library, such as when a document in a document library is added, deleted, or changed, or when Web discussions are added, changed, deleted, closed, or activated for a document.

- **Documents.**   Users are notified of changes in a particular document or when Web discussions are added, changed, deleted, closed, or activated for a document.

When a user creates an alert for one of these items, she can specify what types of events will trigger an alert. Alerts can be generated whenever a document or list item is added, updated, or deleted in a document library or list, or when a Web discussion on a document or list changes. A user can specify one of these events or select all of them to be notified whenever anything changes on the list, list item, document, or document library they want to track.

Users also have the ability to decide how often they want to receive alerts: immediately, daily, or weekly. Immediate alerts are sent as individual e-mail messages, and daily or weekly alerts are combined into summary messages for the entire website.

Users can change their alerts by using the My Alerts On This Site link on the Site Settings page of their website.

Configuring Alerts from the Command Line

You can manage alerts from the command line by using the GetProperty and SetProperty operations with Stsadm.exe. You can set the properties shown in Table 15-1 to configure how alerts work.

Table 15-1   Managing Alerts from the Command Line

Property	Description
alerts-enabled	Turn alerts on or off.
alerts-limited	Specify whether users are limited to a specific number of alerts.
alerts-maximum	Specify the maximum number of alerts users can create.
job-immediate-notification	Specify how often to check for immediate alerts (in minutes).
job-daily-notification	Specify the time of day (using a 24-hour clock) to send out daily alerts.
job-weekly-notification	Specify the day of the week and time of day (using a 24-hour clock) to send out weekly alerts.

The following example shows the syntax to use to turn off alerts:

```
stsadm.exe -o setproperty -p <port> -pn alerts-enabled -pv false
```

Note   A user must have the View Items right (included in the Contributor site group by default) to sign up for alerts.

Web Page Security Validation

Use this setting to enable or disable security validation for website pages. This setting specifies how long to wait before the security validation expires for a given page.

Web Page Security Validation enhances security by imposing a time limit on pages when the user is submitting information to the server. This feature ensures that the connection between the browser and the server is more secure and that data is not altered on a user's behalf without his knowledge. When users take too long before submitting changes to the server, they receive a message informing them that they must go back to the previous page and retry the operation.

In most installations, a setting of 30 minutes is usually appropriate. If site users experience frequent time-outs because of long data transfer times, consider increasing the interval. However, you should not turn off Web Page Security Validation, as it helps to maintain the security of your server.

Select Never to keep the validations from expiring. However, this is not recommended, as you would obviously be creating a security vulnerability. See Figure 15-8.

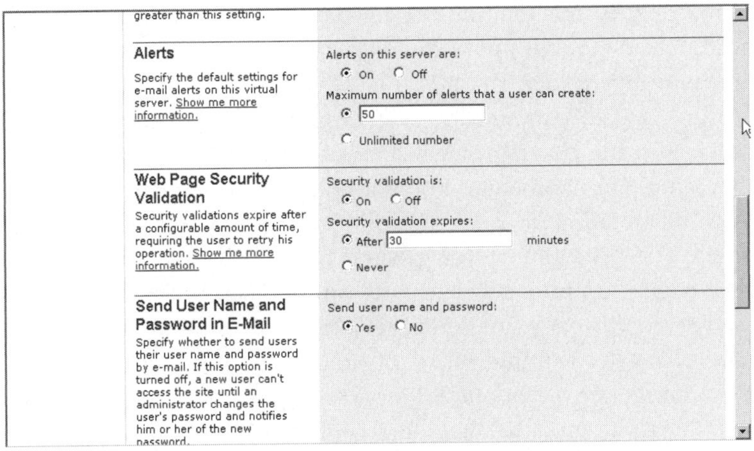

Figure 15-8   Security Validation and User Name/Password settings

Sending User Names and Passwords in E-mail

Use this setting to specify whether user names and passwords are sent in e-mail messages to new users. This setting is used for Active Directory user account mode only. See Figure 15-8.

E-mail Inserts

Use this setting to enable or disable e-mail-enabled document libraries and to specify the public folder path for e-mail attachments and how frequently to check for new attachments. See Figure 15-9.

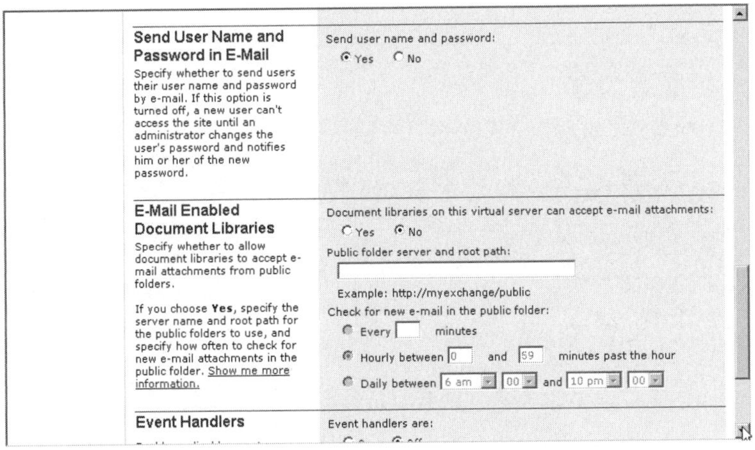

Figure 15-9   E-Mail-enabled Document Library settings

Windows SharePoint Services includes the ability to link a document library with a public folder based on Microsoft Exchange 2000 or later. Any documents attached to messages in the public folder can be automatically inserted into the document library, and the document library displays the document as well as the from address, subject line, and date and time that the attachment was inserted into the document library. Note that the body text of the e-mail message is not preserved. It remains in the public folder, but it is not transferred to the document library.

Therefore, a user can simply send e-mail with an attached document to the public folder, and the document will be automatically added to the correct document library on a SharePoint site. For example, if you are using an XML template to store invoice information, a user could fill out the XML invoice and e-mail it to the public folder. The XML file then is posted to the document library and would be available for rolling up into larger reports on invoices or for easy retrieval.

To configure this page, in the Public Folder Server And Root Path box, type the name of the computer running Microsoft Exchange Server and the path to the root folder for Exchange Server public folders on that server. See Figure 15-9.

If you choose to allow e-mail attachments, specify the frequency and times to check for e-mail attachments in the public folder.

Event Handlers

Use this setting to enable or disable event handlers.

Windows SharePoint Services allow you to bind an event handler to a document library. With this feature, you can use document library events to start other processes, such as workflow processes. You can develop managed code that leverages document library events and create an application based on Windows SharePoint Services to perform whatever actions you need. When you combine document libraries, your own event-handling managed code, and possibly XML forms, you can create even complex workflow processes that are easy for users to work with. See Figure 15-10.

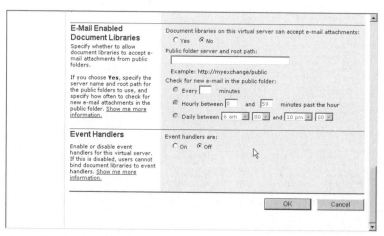

Figure 15-10   Event Handler settings

For example, in the healthcare industry, when a new patient is admitted to a hospital, a lot of paperwork needs to be generated and it needs to be done in a specific order. You can write an application that interacts with XML forms in a document library to accomplish the following tasks:

- Track when a new admissions form is added to the document library

- Extract the insurance information, and forward it to the billing application

- Notify the staff in the appropriate section of the hospital to pull the patient's chart

Table 15-2 shows events that can be tracked for document libraries.

Table 15-2 Events Tracked for Document Libraries

Event	Description
Insert	A new document is added to the document library
Update	An existing document is edited
Delete	An existing document is deleted
Move	A document is moved or renamed
Copy	A document or folder is copied
Check In	A document is checked in
Check Out	A document is checked out
Cancel Check-Out	Changes made to a checked-out document are undone

If you are following along on your own server's Central Administration Pages, we have now explored all the options under Virtual Server General settings. Now click the Back button in your Internet Explorer and resume with the second menu item under the main heading Virtual Server Management. See Figure 15-11.

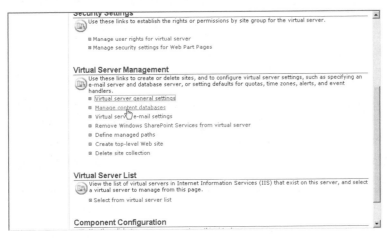

Figure 15-11 Virtual server management

Manage Content Databases

You can create or delete content databases, or change the capacity settings for a particular content database. You can create multiple content databases for each virtual server.

Microsoft Windows SharePoint Services uses a database to store and manage site content. Just as each virtual server can host multiple top-level websites, each virtual server can rely on multiple content databases to store site content. If you are running Windows SharePoint Services on a single server, hosting just a few sites, you can probably use the same content database for all your sites. If you want to add capacity in a server farm, you will most likely need several content databases to store site data for each virtual server.

To make it easier to manage site content for large server farms, you can also set limits on how many top-level websites can store content in a single content database. You can specify a warning limit and a maximum limit for the number of sites. When a warning limit or maximum limit is reached, an event is logged in the server's Windows NT Event Log so that you can take action. When a maximum limit is reached, no more sites can be created using that content database.

When you create a new site, the databases are queried and the new site's content is added to the database that has the most available space. For example, suppose your virtual server has three content databases, all are set to warn you when they reach 2000 sites, and all have a maximum of 2025 sites. When the first content database reaches 2000 sites, an event is logged. When it reaches 2025 sites, no more sites can be created in that database. When you are close to the limit on two of the three content databases and you know that you'll need to host more than 2000 additional sites, it is time to create another content database.

You can specify any number of sites for the warning and maximum number of sites. To determine an appropriate number for your situation, divide the amount of available disk space on the database server by the estimated size for each site (plus a buffer). If you are using quotas, divide the disk space by the disk space quota (plus a buffer).

A buffer allows the number of sites to grow beyond the warning level but not exceed your disk space. The size of the buffer is up to you, but make sure to provide enough space for growth so that you don't exceed the maximum number before you can react to a warning event. When the maximum number is reached, no more sites can be created in that content database. Be sure to create a buffer large enough so that your users can continue to create sites as required, without having to constantly create new content databases.

Content databases are created and managed at the virtual server level. When you create a new content database (or when you extend a virtual server), you specify the database connection settings for the content database. You can update these settings if, for example, the database server name changes.

You can create or delete content databases, and specify settings such as the database server to use for the content and how many top-level websites to allow per content database in a server farm setting, by using pages in HTML Administration. In

HTML Administration, you can view the full list of content databases for your virtual server and see at a glance the current warning and maximum level of sites for the content database.

Managing Content Databases by Using HTML Administration

You can specify a default server to store content databases for all your virtual servers. This allows you to create a new content database when you extend a virtual server, without having to specify a location or supply the user name and password.

To specify a default content database server

1. Click **Start**, point to **All Programs**, point to **Administrative Tools**, and then click **SharePoint Central Administration**.

2. On the Central Administration page, under **Server Configuration**, click **Set default content database server**.

3. In the **Database section**, type in the database server name.

   If you are using Microsoft SQL Server authentication, you must also supply the administrator account user name and password.

4. Click **OK**.

You can create multiple content databases for each virtual server. There are two situations in which you create a new content database: when you extend a new virtual server, and when your other content databases are getting full. You use a different method to create the content databases in each of these cases.

In most cases, you create a content database when you extend a virtual server. When you extend a virtual server, the warning level is set to 9000 sites and the maximum is set to 15,000 sites. To change this after the virtual server is extended, you use the Manage Content Databases page. You can also create additional content databases by using this page.

To create a new content database for a virtual server

1. Click **Start**, point to **All Programs**, point to **Administrative Tools**, and then click **SharePoint Central Administration**.

2. On the Central Administration page, under **Virtual Server Configuration**, click **Configure virtual server settings**.

3. On the Virtual Server List page, click the virtual server you want to configure.

4. On the Virtual Server Settings page, under **Virtual Server Management**, click **Manage content databases**.

5. On the Manage Content Databases page, under **Content Databases**, click **Add a content database**.

6. In the **Database** section, select either **Use default content database server** or **Specify database server settings**.

    If you select **Specify database server settings**, type in the database server name and database name. If you are using SQL Server authentication, you must also supply the administrator account user name and password.

7. In the **Database Capacity Settings** section, type a number in the **Number of sites before a warning event is generated** box.

8. Type a number in the **Maximum number of sites that can be created in this database** box.

9. Click **OK**.

You can also change database connection settings, warning levels, and maximum site levels for a content database.

To change settings for a content database

1. Click **Start**, point to **All Programs**, point to **Administrative Tools**, and then click **SharePoint Central Administration**.

2. On the Central Administration page, under **Virtual Server Configuration**, click **Configure virtual server settings**.

3. On the Virtual Server List page, select the virtual server you want to configure.

4. On the Virtual Server Settings page, under **Virtual Server Management**, click **Manage content databases**.

5. On the Manage Content Databases page, under **Content Databases**, click the name of the database you want to change.

6. To change database status, in the **Database Status** box, select **Ready** or **Offline**.

7. To change the number of sites allowed for a content database, in the **Database Capacity Settings** section, enter a new warning and maximum number.

8. Click **OK**.

If you want to remove a content database, you do so from the Manage Content Databases page as well. Note that when you remove a content database, the site data stored in that database is not deleted. You can reconnect to the content database later to restore the sites.

To remove a content database

1. Click **Start**, point to **All Programs**, point to **Administrative Tools**, and then click **SharePoint Central Administration**.

2. On the Central Administration page, under **Virtual Server Configuration**, click **Configure virtual server settings**.

3. On the Virtual Server List page, select the virtual server you want to configure.

4. On the Virtual Server Settings page, under **Virtual Server Management**, click **Manage content databases**.

5. On the Manage Content Databases page, under **Content Databases**, select the database you want to change.

6. On the Manage Content Database Settings page, in the **Remove Content Database** section, select the **Remove content database** check box.

7. Click **OK**.

You can reconnect to a content database that you have removed by adding it again. To reconnect to an existing content database, you need to use the same database server and database name. There are additional steps if you are reconnecting to a content database after restoring the database to a new server farm. For more information, refer to Chapter 28, "Disaster Recovery in SharePoint Products and Technologies."

When you remove a content database, the site data stored in that database is not deleted. You can reconnect to the content database later to restore the sites.

Removing a Content Database from the Command Line

The Unextendvs property can be used with the Stsadm command line to remove Windows SharePoint Services from a particular virtual server. And if you use the deletecontent parameter, you can delete the content databases for the virtual server at the same time. A sample syntax is as follows:

```
stsadm.exe -o unextendvs -url <url> [-deletecontent] E-mail settings -
```

Specify the outbound e-mail server to use and the e-mail addresses to use when sending e-mail from the server. E-mail settings can also be configured at the server level and used as the default settings.

Microsoft Windows SharePoint Services sends alerts and other administrator messages by using an SMTP server. This feature is also required for end-users to request access to a site or list. You can specify which SMTP server to use and set the e-mail address to use for sending alerts and receiving replies for all sites. See Figure 15-12.

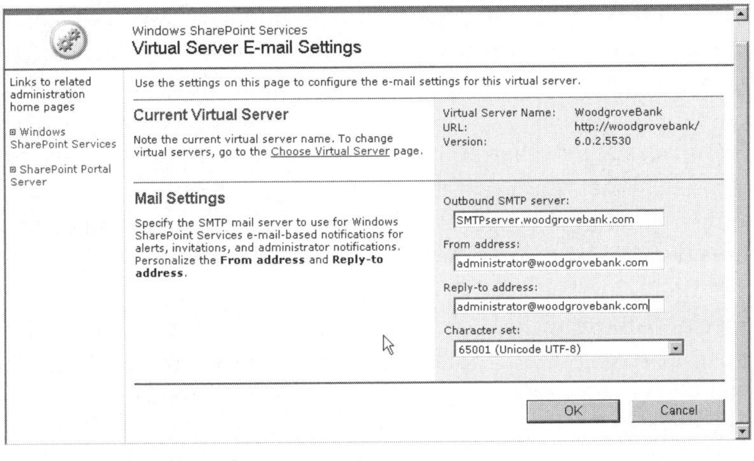

Figure 15-12   Mail settings

Remove Windows SharePoint Services from a Virtual Server

You can remove Windows SharePoint Services either permanently or temporarily by using HTML Administration or the command-line administration tool. Both of these tools allow you to either preserve or delete content when you remove Windows SharePoint Services.

You can use the unextendvs operation with the stsadm.exe command-line utility to remove Windows SharePoint Services from a virtual server. For example, to remove Windows SharePoint Services from a virtual server but preserve the content databases, use the unextendvs operation with syntax such as the following:

```
Stsadm -o unextendvs -url http://My_Server
```

To remove Windows SharePoint Services from a virtual server and remove the content databases permanently, use the unextendvs operation with syntax such as the following:

```
Stsadm -o unextendvs -url http://My_Server -deletecontent
```

If you want to remove Windows SharePoint Services from a server computer entirely, you can uninstall it by using Add Or Remove Programs in Control Panel. Uninstalling Windows SharePoint Services does not remove any related products, such as the Microsoft SQL Server 2000 Desktop Engine (WMSDE), that were installed. You must uninstall these programs separately.

Define Managed Paths

Using this setting, you can add or remove included and excluded paths to control which areas of the URL namespace are managed by Windows SharePoint Services.

Many organizations installing Microsoft Windows SharePoint Services already have a Web server or server farm in use and must be able to identify areas of the existing URL namespace that should not be managed by Windows SharePoint Services. For example, if you have a Web application on your Web server already and you install Windows SharePoint Services, you need a way to specify that Windows SharePoint Services will not attempt to control content in or settings for that path.

In addition, the Define Managed Paths setting allows you to specify the paths to use for Self-Service Site Creation. You can restrict Self-Service Site Creation users to specific paths when they create sites. By default, the /sites path is created and added as a path for Self-Service Site Creation users when you enable Self-Service Site Creation. You can create other paths for Self-Service Site Creation users, or you can remove the /sites path when you manage paths.

Note that you can also specify inclusions and create new paths when you use Create A Top-Level Web Site from Windows SharePoint Services Central Administration. If you select the Define Managed Paths item under Web Site Address, you will find that you can specify paths to include or exclude, and you can even add new paths.

You can manage two categories of paths: included and excluded. An *included path* indicates that Windows SharePoint Services manages that path. An *excluded path* indicates that a different application manages the path and that Windows

SharePoint Services should leave it alone. Included paths can be further categorized into the following two types:

- **Explicit inclusions.**   Includes only the specific path that you set. Use explicit inclusions, for example, if you want Windows SharePoint Services to manage a specific path (such as /portal) but not any possible sites below it (such as /portal/webapp).

- **Wildcard inclusions.**   Includes any sites below the path that you set so that you don't have to add them individually. This is the type of inclusion to use for Self-Service Site Creation, when you want users to be able to create top-level websites underneath a specific path, such as /sites.

> **Note**   Web server performance declines linearly with the number of inclusions and exclusions. You can minimize the performance impact by using wildcard inclusions rather than many explicit inclusions, and by putting as many excluded applications under the same excluded path as possible.

Included and excluded paths are used only for directories, not pages in a website, and they are recursive. (For example, if you exclude /mango, Windows Share-Point Services ignores any URL beginning with /mango/ or equal to /mango.) Exclusions take precedence over inclusions, so if you accidentally set a particular path to be both included and excluded, the path is excluded. Inclusions are evaluated by length; longer URLs are checked before shorter URLs, so an inclusion for *http://My_Server/sites/teams* is evaluated before an inclusion for *http://My_Server /teams*.

You can manage paths by using HTML Administration or the command-line administration tool. You can use the addpath and deletepath operations to manage paths on the command line. Both operations take the -url and -type parameters. The -type parameter has three values: exclusion, explicitinclusion, and wildcardinclusion. For example, to add a new wildcard inclusion to manage all sites at the top level of *http://My_Server*, you would use syntax such as the following:

```
Stsadm -o addpath -url http://My_Server/ -type wildcardinclusion
```

You can also remove an included or excluded path by using the command line. For example, to remove an exclusion for the site at *http://server1/hrweb/webapp*, you would use syntax such as the following:

```
Stsadm -o deletepath -url http://My_Server/hrweb/webapp
```

Create or Delete a Top-Level Website

You can create a new top-level website or delete an existing top-level website. If you are an administrator of the server computer, you can also create sites and subsites by using the Stsadm.exe command-line tool. To create a top-level website, use the createsite operation. To create a subsite, use the createweb operation.

> **Note** You can also use the createsiteinnewdb operation to create a top-level website and a new content database at the same time.

The createsite operation takes the following required parameters: url, ownerlogin, owneremail, and the following optional parameters: ownername, lcid, sitetemplate, title, description, and quota. For example, to create a top-level website called site1 on *http://server_name/sites*, you would use syntax similar to the following:

```
Stsadm.exe -o createsite -url http://My_Server/sites/site1 -ownerlogin
    <DOMAIN\user> -ownermail someone@example.com -ownername <display name>
```

Select from Virtual Server List

Note that this item simply loops you back to the virtual server list so that you can choose a different virtual server if you are done configuring the last one you selected.

Configure Data Retrieval Service Settings

A data retrieval service implements a new data-binding technology that enables data consumers and data sources to communicate with each other through SOAP and XML. Data retrieval services are XML Web services that return XML data from different data sources. A data retrieval service is installed and runs on a server extended with Microsoft Windows SharePoint Services. Windows SharePoint Services comes with a default set of data retrieval services for working with data in SharePoint lists, OLEDB, and XML data sources. Client applications and data-bound Web Parts, such as the Spreadsheet Web Part, can use a data retrieval service to query the data source supported by the particular data source.

Configuring Data Retrieval Services from the Command Line If you are using a third-party data retrieval service, you can register a service by using the command line. Register these services by using Stsadm.exe with the binddrservice and removedrservice operations. The binddrservice and removedrservice operations register individual data retrieval services for specific settings. When you register a service, it appears on the HTML Administration pages under the appropriate setting. For each operation, you specify the following required parameters: servicename and setting. The setting parameter takes any of the following values: enabled, responsesize, timeout, or update.

For example, to register a data retrieval service called *Service1* to the list of services that an administrator can enable or disable, you would use the following syntax:

```
Stsadm.exe -o binddrservice -servicename Service1 -setting enabled
```

And to remove Service1 from the list of services that can allow data updates, you would use the following syntax:

```
Stsadm.exe -o removedrservice -servicename Service1 -setting update
```

The binddrservice operation registers a data retrieval service for the list of data retrieval services that pertain to a specific setting on the Data Retrieval Services Settings page. Specify the service name and then the setting. Settings include enabled, responsesize, timeout, and update.

The required parameters for the Binddrservice operation are –servicename and –setting. There are no optional parameters for this operation.

Following is sample syntax for the Stsadm.exe command when using the binddrservice operation to register a data retrival service:

```
Stsadm.exe -o binddrservice -servicename <service name> -setting <enabled/response-
    size/timeout/update>
```

Use the properties listed in Table 15-3 to configure data retrieval services for your virtual server, server, or server farm. Specify whether data retrieval services are enabled, whether the virtual server should inherit the server farm settings, the time an adapter will wait for a response from the back-end data source, the maximum size for data returned from the back-end source, and whether adapters can execute requests that contain updatable queries.

Table 15-3   Properties to Configure Data Retrieval Services

Property Name	Values
data-retrieval-services-enabled	true/false
data-retrieval-services-inherit	true/false
data-retrieval-services-response-size	An integer value in kilobytes (KB) between 1 and 100,000
data-retrieval-services-timeout	An integer value in seconds between 1 and 100,000
data-retrieval-services-update	true/false

Authentication

Securing your corporate computers and the information on them is a vast topic. It will range from protecting corporate assets from viruses and unauthorized access to protecting them from acts of nature. However, we will limit our discussion here to the concept of *authentication*. Authentication is the process by which the user's identity will be verified as one that is allowed to log in. It is different than authorization, which is verifying that the identity has authority to access specific resources. None of the work we have done so far will do us much good if we have not carefully thought through and configured the appropriate access for the sites we've created, so let's explore authentication methods supported by Windows SharePoint Services.

Authentication Methods

You configure authentication for websites based on Microsoft Windows SharePoint Services by configuring authentication methods in Internet Information Services (IIS). Windows SharePoint Services uses the authentication method you specify for a virtual server in IIS to control authentication for all top-level websites and subsites of that virtual server. Windows SharePoint Services works with the following authentication methods in IIS:

- **Anonymous authentication.** Anonymous authentication provides access to users who do not have Microsoft Windows NT server accounts on the server computer (for example, website visitors). IIS creates the anonymous account for Web services, which is often named IUSR_*computername*. When IIS receives an anonymous request, it impersonates the anonymous account.

  You can enable or disable anonymous access in IIS for a particular virtual server, and enable or disable anonymous access for a site on that virtual server, by using HTML administration pages for IIS Administration pages. Anonymous access must be enabled in IIS before you can enable it for a website on that virtual server.

  Once you have enabled anonymous access for the virtual server with the HTML administration pages for IIS, you will need to actually enable this same level of access for each individual website. To do so, from the website page itself (a feature that is not available from Central Administration), click Site Settings, click Go To Site Administration under the heading Administration, and then click Manage Anonymous Access under the heading Users And Permissions. Note that by default, anonymous users can access nothing and you will need to choose either Entire Web Site or Lists And Libraries.

- **Basic authentication.** Basic authentication is an authentication protocol supported by most Web servers and browsers. Although Basic authentication transmits user names and passwords in easily decoded clear text, it has some advantages over more secure authentication methods in that it works through a proxy server firewall and ensures that a website is accessible by almost any Web browser. If you use Basic authentication in combination with Secure Sockets Layer (SSL) security, you can help protect the user names and passwords, making your user information more secure.

Note It is strongly recommended that you use SSL any time you use Basic authentication to ensure a secure deployment.

- **Integrated Windows authentication.** Integrated Windows authentication (also known as Windows NT Challenge Response) encrypts user names and passwords in a multiple-transaction interaction between client and server, thus making this method more secure than Basic authentication. Disadvantages are that this method cannot be performed through a proxy server firewall, and some Web browsers (most notably, Netscape Navigator) do not support it. You can, however, enable both this method and Basic authentication at the same time, and most Web browsers will select the most secure option. (For example, if both Basic and Integrated Windows authentication are enabled, Microsoft Internet Explorer will try Integrated Windows authentication first.)

- **Certificates authentication.** Certificates authentication provides communications privacy, authentication, and message integrity for a TCP/IP connection. By using the SSL protocol, clients and servers can communicate in a way that prevents eavesdropping, tampering, or message forgery. With Windows Share-Point Services, SSL helps secure authoring across firewalls and allows more secure remote administration of Windows SharePoint Services. You can also specify that SSL be used when opening any website based on Windows Share-Point Services.

You can change authentication methods for virtual servers hosting websites based on Windows SharePoint Services, and you can change the authentication method used for the SharePoint Central Administration site. You can also enable Secure Sockets Layer (SSL) security in IIS to help protect your sites or the administration port for your server.

> **Caution**   It should be strongly noted that enabling SSL after establishing the Windows SharePoint Services site is very difficult. The reason is that Windows SharePoint Services in some cases uses the https:// protocol behind the scenes when interfacing with the database. This then makes changing the URL after the fact a difficult task.

Changing Authentication Methods

Each virtual server can use a different authentication method in Internet Information Services (IIS). You can even enable multiple authentication methods if you are using the same website content in more than one environment. For example, if you have a website that is primarily for internal use within your organization, you would most likely choose Integrated Windows authentication. (It should be noted here that Internet Explorer must be your organization's standard browser.) If, however, your use of the site changes and you must allow your organization's members to access the site externally through a firewall, you might also want to enable Basic authentication.

> **Note** Basic authentication is less secure than Integrated Windows authentication. It is recommended that you use Basic authentication with SSL to help make your environment more secure.

When you change authentication methods in IIS, you do not need to change any settings in Windows SharePoint Services. For example, if you decide to use Integrated Windows authentication instead of Basic authentication, you make the change only in IIS.

To change authentication methods

1. Click **Start**, point to **All Programs**, point to **Administrative Tools**, and then click **Internet Information Services (IIS) Manager**.

2. Click the plus sign (+) next to the server name that contains the virtual server you want to change.

3. Click the plus sign (+) next to **Web sites**.

4. Right-click the virtual server, and then click **Properties**. (See Figure 15-13.)

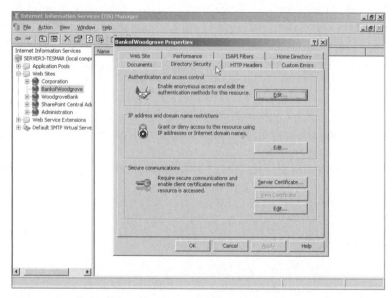

Figure 15-13 Properties of the virtual server

5. On the **Directory Security** tab, under **Authentication and access control**, click **Edit**.

6. Select the check boxes for the authentication methods you want to enable, and clear the check boxes for the authentication methods you want to disable. (See Figure 15-14.)

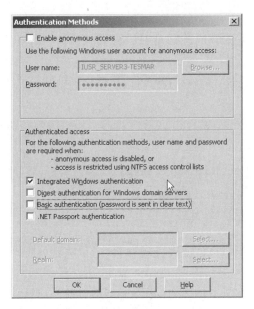

Figure 15-14   Authentication methods

7.   Click **OK** to close the **Authentication Methods** dialog box.

8.   Click **OK** again to close the **Properties** dialog box.

Server Farm Configuration

Certain settings that must be made at the server or server-farm level will have a significant impact on your Windows SharePoint Services sites. You can configure these settings from the SharePoint Central Administration page for your server. This page controls settings for a particular server in a server farm, and it also contains links to other servers in the server farm so that you can configure settings for those servers as well. Most of these settings can also be controlled from the command line, using the Stsadm.exe tool. The following actions can be taken from the SharePoint Central Administration page:

Setting the Administrative Group for Windows SharePoint Services

To install Windows SharePoint Services, you must be a member of the local administrators group on the server computer. This group also gives users the permissions needed to control settings on the Central Administration pages and to run the command-line tool Stsadm.exe. You can also allow a specific domain group, in addition to the local administrators group, to have administrative access to Windows SharePoint Services. You can add users to this group rather than to the local administrators group to separate administrative access to Windows SharePoint Services from administrative access to the local server computer.

Members of the SharePoint administrators group do not have access to the IIS metabase, so they cannot perform the following actions for Windows SharePoint Services:

■ Extend virtual servers (They can, however, create top-level websites or change settings for a virtual server.)

■ Manage paths

■ Change the SharePoint administrators group

■ Change the configuration database settings

■ Use the Stsadm.exe command-line tool

Members of the SharePoint administrators group can perform any other administrative action using the HTML Administration pages for Windows SharePoint Services.

Members of both the SharePoint administrators group and the local administrators group have rights to view and manage all sites created on their servers. This means that a server administrator can read documents or list items, change survey settings, delete a site, or perform any action on a site that the site administrator can perform.

Configuring Default E-mail Settings

Windows SharePoint Services sends alerts and other administrator messages by using an SMTP server. You can specify which SMTP server to use and set the e-mail address to use for sending alerts and receiving replies for all sites by using the SharePoint Central Administration e-mail settings. You can also specify different settings for a specific virtual server. At either level, you can specify the following settings: outbound SMTP server, from address, reply-to address, and character set to use.

Using HTML Administration to Configure E-mail Settings

You use the Configure E-Mail Server Settings page to specify e-mail settings for your server.

To specify e-mail settings for a server or server farm

1. On the SharePoint Central Administration page, under **Server Configuration**, click **Configure e-mail server settings**.

2. In the **Outbound SMTP server** box, type the name of the SMTP mail server to use for sending messages.

3. In the **From address** box, type the e-mail address to send e-mail messages from.

This address appears in the **From** box of any e-mail messages from the server. No e-mail messages are sent to this address, so you can use an unmonitored e-mail address if you want.

4. In the **Reply-to address** box, type the e-mail address that users can reply to.
    If a user replies to an e-mail message from the server, it will be sent to this address. You should use an address that is monitored for the reply-to address.

5. In the **Character set** box, select the character set to use.

6. Click **OK**.

You can also specify e-mail settings for a particular virtual server. The virtual server settings override the settings specified on the SharePoint Central Administration pages. Use these steps when you want a virtual server to use a different SMTP server for alerts than the one specified in the server settings.

To specify mail settings for a virtual server

1. On the SharePoint Central Administration page, under **Virtual Server Configuration**, click Configure virtual server settings.

2. On the Virtual Server List page, click the name of the virtual server you want to configure.

3. Under **Virtual Server Management**, click **SharePoint e-mail configuration**.

4. In the **Mail Settings** section, in the **Outbound SMTP server** box, type the name of the SMTP mail server to use for sending messages.

5. In the **From address** box, type the e-mail address to send e-mail messages from.
    This address appears in the **From** box of any e-mail messages from the server. No e-mail messages are sent to this address, so you can use an unmonitored e-mail address if you want.

6. In the **Reply-to address** box, type the e-mail address that users can reply to.
    If a user replies to an e-mail message from the server, it will be sent to this address. You should use an address that is monitored for the reply-to address.

7. In the **Character set** box, select the character set to use.

8. Click **OK**.

Using the Command Line to Configure E-mail Settings

You can also configure e-mail settings from the command line by using the e-mail operation with Stsadm.exe. The e-mail operation takes the following required parameters: outsmtpserver (the outgoing SMTP server), fromaddress (the e-mail address to send messages from, which can be an unmonitored address), replytoaddress (the e-mail address to send replies to, which must be a monitored address), and code-page (the codepage to use). In addition, you can use the optional url parameter to specify settings for a particular virtual server.

The e-mail operation uses the following syntax:

```
stsadm.exe -o email -outsmtpserver <smtp server> -fromaddress <from address>
  -replytoaddress <reply-to address> -codepage <codepage> [-url <url>]
```

For example, to configure the e-mail settings to use the server \\SMTPServer and to use someone@example.com as both the from and reply-to address, you would use syntax similar to the following:

```
stsadm.exe -o email -outsmtpserver SMTPServer -fromaddress someone@example.com
  -replytoaddress someone@example.com
```

To set the http://myserver virtual server to use a different codepage, you would use syntax similar to the following:

```
stsadm.exe -o email -outsmtpserver SMTPServer -fromaddress someone@example.com
  -replytoaddress someone@example.com -codepage <codepage> -url http://myserver
```

Manage Site Owners and Users

Using HTML Administration Pages to Manage Users and Cross-Site Groups

To manage users and cross-site groups, you follow the Manage Users link on the Site Settings page to the Manage Users page. By using this page, you can view a list of users and cross-site groups, check which site group a user or cross-site group is assigned to, add new users and cross-site groups, delete users and cross-site groups, or assign users and cross-site groups to site groups. When you add new users or cross-site groups, you also have the option to send an e-mail message to them, inviting them to use the site. You can even include a custom message in the invitation e-mail message. For example, you can describe your site and what it should be used for, or you can add a personal message to the default e-mail invitation.

> **Note** If you do not see the Manage Users option on your Site Settings page, you are probably in a subsite that uses the permission settings of a higher-level website of the server or virtual server. To work with user accounts and permissions, either go to the parent-level website or change to using unique permissions for the subsite.

If you want to view which site groups a user is a member of, you use the Manage Users page.

To view site group membership for a user or cross-site group

1. On the website you want to manage, click **Site Settings**.

2. On the Site Settings page, under **Administration**, click **Manage Users**.

    The users and cross-site groups added to the website and the site groups they are a member of are displayed on the Manage Users page.

3. From the Manage Users page, you can change which site group a user or cross-site group is a member of.

To change site group membership for a user or cross-site group

1. On the Manage Users page, select the check box next to the user or cross-site group name you want to change.

2. Click **Edit Site Group of Selected Users and Groups**.

3. In the **Site Group Membership** area, select the site group you want the user or cross-site group to be a member of.

4. Click **OK**.

You can also add new users and cross-site groups to your site from the Manage Users page.

To add a new user or cross-site group

1. On the Manage Users page, click **Add Users**.

2. In the **Step 1: Choose Users** section, in the text box, type the user's e-mail address or the cross-site group's name.

3. In the **Step 2: Choose Permissions** section, select the site group that the user will belong to and then click **Next**.

4. In the **Step 3: Confirm Users** section, verify the e-mail address, user name, and display name information.

5. In the **Step 4: Send E-mail** section, if you want to send an invitation, select **Send the following e-mail to let these users know they've been added**, and type the subject and body text information to send in the e-mail message.

6. Click **Finish**.

You can delete users or cross-site groups from all site groups by using the Manage Users page. Note that this does not delete the user or cross-site group account, but it does remove all rights to the website.

To delete a user or cross-site group from all site groups

1. On the Manage Users page, select the check box next to the user or cross-site group you want to delete.

  2. Click **Remove Selected Users**.

  3. On the confirmation message that appears, click **OK** to remove the users.

Managing Users in a Site Collection

Every website with unique permissions has a Manage Users page that the site's administrator can use to add, modify, or delete users. In addition to this page, the top-level website in a website collection also includes a page that server administrators or the site collection administrator can use to view and delete users. This page lists all users for the site collection, including the users of the top-level website and users of any subsites in the site collection. When you remove a user from this list, the user is removed from all sites and subsites in the site collection.

To remove a user from a top-level website

  1. On the top-level website, click **Site Settings**.

  2. Under **Administration**, click **Go to Site Administration**.

  3. On the Top-Level Site Administration page, under **Site Collection Administration**, click **View site collection user information**.

  4. Select the check box next to the user you want to remove, and then click **Remove Selected Users**.

Managing Users from SharePoint Central Administration

If you are an administrator on the server computer or a member of the SharePoint administrators group, you might have administrative rights to change settings on the Site Settings page for any individual site on your server. What happens when a top-level website owner leaves your organization or a user must be added to or removed from a site that you do not have administrative rights for? The SharePoint Central Administration page includes a link for managing users for sites even if the administrator does not have rights to the site. You can add users or cross-site groups, remove users or cross-site groups, change site-group membership, and change owners without having to be an administrator on a specific site. You do, however, need to know the URL for the site and the specific user name that you want to change.

To change the owner of a site collection

  1. Click **Start**, point to **All Programs**, point to **Administrative Tools**, and then click **SharePoint Central Administration**.

  2. On the SharePoint Central Administration page, under **Security Configuration**, click **Manage site collection owners**.

  3. On the Manage Site Collection Owners page, in the website URL box, type the URL to the site, and then click **View**.

  4. The information for the current site owner and secondary owner is automatically filled in on the page when you click **View**.

5. In the **Site Owner** section, in the **User name** box, type the account name for the new owner.

6. If you have a new secondary contact name, type the account name in the **Secondary Owner** section.

7. Click **OK**.

If you are an administrator on the server computer and need to change the owner of a site that you do not have administrative access to, you can make the change from the SharePoint Central Administration page.

To add a new site user

1. Click **Start**, point to **All Programs**, point to **Administrative Tools**, and then click **SharePoint Central Administration**.

2. On the SharePoint Central Administration page, under **Security Configuration**, click **Manage Web site users**.

3. On the Manage Web Site Users page, in the **Site URL** box, type the URL to the site, and then click **View**.

4. In the **Add a User** section, in the **Account name** box, type the account name for the new user.

5. In the **Display name** box, type the full name for the new owner.

6. In the **E-mail address** box, type the e-mail address for the new user.

7. In the **Site group** box, select a site group to add the user to, and then click **Update**.

You can also delete a user or change a user's site-group membership from this page.

To delete a site user or change site-group membership

1. Click **Start**, point to **All Programs**, point to **Administrative Tools**, and then click **SharePoint Central Administration**.

2. On the SharePoint Central Administration page, under **Security**, click **Manage Web site users**.

3. On the Manage Web Site Users page, in the **Site URL** box, type the URL to the site, and then click **View**.

4. In the **Enter Site User** section, in the **Account name** box, type the user account you want to change or delete, and then click **View**.

5. To change site-group membership, select the check box for the site group you want the user to be a member of and then click **Update**.

6. To remove the user from all site groups, select the **Delete this user account** check box and then click **Update**.

Using the Command Line to Manage Users

You can add a user account to your site by using the adduser operation. The adduser operation takes the url (of the site where you want to add the user), userlogin, useremail, username, and role parameters, plus the optional parameter siteadmin. You use the siteadmin parameter to specify that the user is the site collection administrator or owner of the site collection. Note that if you are using Active Directory account creation mode, you do not need to specify the userlogin parameter; you would use the useremail parameter to identify the user instead. (For more information about Active Directory Account creation mode, see Chapter 2, "Installing Windows SharePoint Services.")

For example, to add User1 as an administrator for http://My_Server/site1 in domain account mode, you would type

```
stsadm.exe -o adduser -url http://My_Server/site1 -userlogin DOMAIN1\User1
 -useremail user1@domain.com -username "User 1" -role administrator
```

You use the deleteuser operation to remove users from a site. The deleteuser operation takes the url and userlogin parameters. To remove User1 from http://server1/site1, you would type

```
stsadm.exe -o deleteuser -url http://My_Server/site1
-userlogin DOMAIN1\User1
```

You can assign a user to a site group from the command line by using the userrole operation. The userrole operation takes the url, userlogin, role, and add or delete parameters. For example, to add the user User1 to the Contributor site group for site http://server1/site1, you would type

```
stsadm.exe -o userrole -url http://My_Server/site1 -userlogin DOMAIN1\User1
-role contributor -add
```

Note that this does not remove the user from any site groups she was previously a member of.

Configuring Antivirus Protection

Windows SharePoint Services now allows you to help protect your users from uploading or downloading files that contain viruses. When you have installed an antivirus scanner that is compatible with Windows SharePoint Services, you can enable the antivirus protection feature for your server. When you enable the antivirus protection feature, files are checked for viruses when a user adds a document to a document library or list, or when a user views a document in a document library or list. If a virus is found, the scanner attempts to clean the file; if the file cannot be cleaned, the scanner blocks the file from being added or viewed.

Consult your antivirus software vendor to find out whether they offer a virus scanner for use with Windows SharePoint Services and for information about installing the virus scanner. Or, for a list of antivirus software vendors that support antivirus protection for Windows SharePoint Services, see the Windows SharePoint Services Partners website.

> **Note** If a file is uploaded and is later identified as containing a virus, the user will not be able to open the file. In this situation, however, the user might still be able to save the file locally and open it from his computer.

You enable and configure antivirus protection at the server level. When enabled, antivirus protection is available for all document libraries on all sites and subsites on your server or for all servers in your Web farm. You can use HTML Administration pages or the command-line tool to configure antivirus protection.

You must install Windows SharePoint Services–compatible antivirus software on any server computer running Windows SharePoint Services before you can enable antivirus protection in Windows SharePoint Services. If you are in a server-farm configuration, antivirus software must be installed on every Web front-end server in the server farm. Consult your antivirus software vendor to find out whether they offer a virus scanner for use with Windows SharePoint Services and for information about installing the virus scanner.

> **Note** McAfee Security is providing a virus scanner for customers using Windows SharePoint Services. For information about their virus scanner, go to the McAfee website (http://www.McAfee.Com). Or, for a list of antivirus software vendors that support antivirus protection for Windows SharePoint Services, see the Windows SharePoint Services Partners website.

Using HTML Administration Pages to Configure Antivirus Protection

You use the Configure Antivirus Protection page in the SharePoint Central Administration pages to enable and configure antivirus protection.

To enable antivirus protection for your server or Web farm

1. Click **Start**, point to **Programs**, point to **Administrative Tools**, and then click **SharePoint Central Administration**.

2. On the SharePoint Central Administration page, under **Security Configuration**, click **Configure antivirus protection**.

3. Select the **Scan documents on download** check box.

4. Select the **Scan documents on upload** check box.

5. If desired, select the **Attempt to clean infected documents** check box.

6. In the **Time out scanning after ___ seconds** box, type the number of seconds to allow before timing out the scanning process.

   The default time is 300 seconds, or 5 minutes. This should be enough time to allow the antivirus processes to finish without affecting performance. The default time is recommended, but you can adjust this time if you are experiencing performance issues.

7. In the **Allow scanner to use up to ___ threads** box, type the number of threads to allow the scanning process to take up.

   By default, the number of threads is set to 5, which should be sufficient for even a large number of sites. The default number of threads is recommended, but you can reduce the number of threads if you are experiencing performance slowdown.

8. Click **OK**.

Using the Command Line to Configure Antivirus Protection

You can also configure antivirus protection by setting properties on the command line. To set a property, you use the Stsadm.exe tool with the setproperty operation. The properties listed in Table 15-4 are available for use in configuring antivirus protection.

Table 15-4   Properties Available for Use in Configuring Antivirus Protection

Property Name	Description	Values
avcleaningenabled	Specifies whether antivirus cleaning is enabled or disabled	yes/no
avdownloadscanenabled	Specifies whether documents are scanned on download	yes/no
avnumberofthreads	Specifies the number of threads to use for antivirus processes	A numerical value, the number of threads to use
avtimeout	Specifies how long to wait before timing out an antivirus process	A numerical value, in seconds
avuploadscanenabled	Specifies whether documents are scanned on upload	yes/no

The following example shows the syntax to use when setting an antivirus property:

```
stsadm.exe -o setproperty -pn <property name> -pv <property value>
```

For example, to set the avtimeout property to 200, you would use the following syntax:

```
stsadm.exe -o setproperty -pn avtimeout -pv 200
```

Configuring Site Quotas and Locks

If you are using Windows SharePoint Services in a large environment, such as at an Internet Service Provider (ISP) or in a large intranet, you need to be able to maintain control over your server resources and carefully monitor areas such as storage space and site security. You must be able to ensure that one user's site cannot use so many resources that other sites can no longer function. Windows SharePoint Services allows you to specify quotas for sites so that you can manage your site and server resources. You can set quota limits for the following item:

- **Storage.**   When you set a quota limit for storage, you can set two values: a warning value and a maximum value. When a site passes the warning limit, an e-mail message is sent to the site administrator and owner notifying them that their site is nearing their storage quota. When a site meets the maximum limit, another e-mail message is sent to the owner and administrator, and no new content can be added to the site.

> **Note**   The size of the data reported by quotas does not necessarily match the size of the storage in SQL Server. This is because the quota feature estimates storage figures for empty sites (sites that contain no user content) and includes those figures in the quota, as well as the actual storage from the database. The estimated size of an empty site includes the real size of the template pages for Windows SharePoint Services, such as the forms pages and pages in the _layouts directory, which are not normally counted because there is only one copy of these pages for all sites. Although each site has a unique URL to the pages, the site does not have a unique instance of the page.

You can create multiple sets of quotas, called quota templates, and use them in different areas of your Web farm or to suit different users. For example, in an ISP setting, you could have the following quota templates:

- **Free.**   Applied to free or demonstration sites, it restricts users to 10 MB of storage and 5 users.

- **Standard.**   Applied to monthly-fee sites, it allows site owners up to 25 MB of storage and 50 registered users.

- **Premium.**   Applied to extranet sites for large corporate customers, it allows organizations up to 10 GB of storage and unlimited user accounts.

You must be an administrator of the local server computer or a member of the SharePoint administrators group to be able to manage quotas and quota templates.

Enabling Quotas

The quota feature is disabled by default in Windows SharePoint Services—there are no default quota values or templates. To enable quotas, you use the following methods:

- To use quotas for your server or Web farm, you create a quota template.

- To use quotas for a particular virtual server, you assign a default quota template to that virtual server.

- To use quotas for a particular top-level website, you assign a quota template to the top-level website when you create the site.

- To use a set of quota values for a single site only, you can apply specific quota limits to the site itself, independent of any quota template.

You can reverse your decision to use quotas at any point in the hierarchy. For example, applying a default quota template to a virtual server does not mean that all top-level websites under that virtual server must use the quota limits—it only means that they can. Settings that you apply to a single site can be cleared if you no longer want to use quotas.

About Quota Templates

Quota templates and the settings specified in them are stored in the configuration database for your server or server farm. Quota values apply to top-level websites and are applied when you create a top-level website. You can specify a default template to use for all top-level websites created on a virtual server, for example, or you can specify the template to use when you create the top-level website. The values listed in the quota template are copied into the database for the top-level website and are referenced from there.

Note   If you change the values for a quota template, those changes apply only to new top-level websites created using that template, not to existing top-level websites. If you want to apply the template changes to existing sites, you must use the Windows SharePoint Services object model to make the change with a SQL Server query. Likewise, when you delete a quota template, the template is removed from the configuration database, but any top-level websites created using that template will retain the quota values. If you want to remove quotas from all sites using a particular quota template, you must use the object model and perform a SQL Server query.

Managing Quota Templates

You manage quota templates from the SharePoint Central Administration pages for your server or Web farm. You can create or delete templates or change the values in the templates.

To create a quota template

1. Click **Start**, point to **All Programs**, point to **Administrative Tools**, and then click **SharePoint Central Administration**.

2. On the Central Administration page, under **Component Configuration**, click **Administer quotas and locks**.

3. On the Administer Quotas And Locks page, click **Manage Quota Templates**.

4. On the Manage Quota Templates page, in the **Template name** area, click **Create a new quota template**.

5. In the **Template to start from:** box, select a template to base your new template on.

6. In the **New template name** box, type the name to use for your new quota template.

7. Select the **Limit site storage to a maximum of: ___ MB** check box, and then type the amount of storage to allow at a maximum.

8. In the **Storage Limit Values** section, select the **Send warning e-mail when site storage reaches ___ MB** check box, and then type the amount of storage to allow before sending a warning e-mail.

9. In the **Invited User Limits** section, select the **Limit invited users to a maximum of: ___ users**, and then type the number of users to allow.

    The user limit option is availablenly in Active Directory account mode.

10. Click **OK**.

    When you click **OK**, the new template is added to the list of available templates and the page is refreshed.

You can delete a quota template if you change your quota structures. However, remember that deleting a quota template will not delete quota values from sites that were created using the quota template. If you want to remove quotas from all sites using a particular quota template, you must use the object model and perform a SQL Server query.

To delete a quota template

1. Click **Start**, point to **All Programs**, point to **Administrative Tools**, and then click **SharePoint Central Administration**.

2. On the Central Administration page, under **Component Configuration**, click **Administer quotas and locks**.

3. On the Administer Quotas And Locks page, click **Manage Quota Templates**.

4. On the Manage Quota Templates page, in the **Template name** area, click **Edit an existing template**.

5. In the **Template to modify:** box, select the quota template you want to delete.

6. Click **Delete**.

7. When you click **OK**, the template is removed from the list of available templates and the page is refreshed.

You can change individual quota values in a template. The new values apply only to new top-level websites created using the quota template. The changed values are not applied to existing sites unless you use the object model to update the values in the database.

To change an existing quota template

1. Click **Start**, point to **All Programs**, point to **Administrative Tools**, and then click **SharePoint Central Administration**.

2. On the Central Administration page, under **Component Configuration**, click **Administer quotas and locks**.

3. On the Administer Quotas And Locks page, click **Manage Quota Templates**.

4. On the Manage Quota Templates page, in the **Template name** area, click **Edit an existing template**.

5. In the **Template to modify:** box, select the quota template you want to change.

6. Update the options you want to change, and then click **OK**.

7. When you click **OK**, the template is updated and the page is refreshed.

Specifying a Quota Template for a Virtual Server

When you extend a new virtual server, you can specify a quota template to use as the default quota template for that virtual server on the Extend And Create Content Database page. Any new top-level websites that you create under the virtual server will automatically use the values in the default quota template. You can change the default quota template for a virtual server from the Virtual Server Settings page. Keep in mind that changing the default quota template does not change quota values for existing top-level websites. Only newly created top-level websites will use the new quota template.

To change the default quota template for a virtual server

1. Click **Start**, point to **All Programs**, point to **Administrative Tools**, and then click **SharePoint Central Administration**.

2. On the Central Administration page, under **Virtual Server Configuration**, click **Configure virtual server settings**.

3. On the Virtual Server List page, select the name of the virtual server you want to change.

4. Under **Virtual Server Management**, click **Virtual server general settings**.

5. In the **Default Quota Template** section, select the quota template to use as the default template when new top-level websites are created.

6. Click **OK**.

Specifying Quota Values for a Specific Site

If you want to specify a different set of limits for a particular site, you can do so. Specifying quota values for a single site is an easy way to turn on quotas on a site-by-site basis. Similarly, if you need to make an exception to a quota template for a particular site, you can change the quota value for just that site. Keep in mind, however, that it is possible to lock a site simply by changing the quota value. If you already have quotas set for a particular site and want to update the value, be sure to check the site's current quota levels before making the change. For example, suppose the current quota level for site storage is 25 MB and a site has 21 MB. If you change the value to 20 MB, the site will be locked as soon as you save the change. To prevent locking a site accidentally, be sure to check the current storage or invited user count for the site before making a change to the quota values.

If you do not know what the existing quota values are for a site, you can use the SharePoint Central Administration page to view the current values and the current data (storage used and number of users) for the site.

To view current quota values and data for a site

1. Click **Start**, point to **All Programs**, point to **Administrative Tools**, and then click **SharePoint Central Administration**.

2. On the Central Administration page, under **Component Configuration**, click **Administer quotas and locks**.

3. On the Administer Quotas And Locks page, click **Site Quota Settings and Locks**.

4. In the **Select a top-level Web site** section, type the URL in the **Enter the top level Web site URL** box, and then click **View Data**.

5. In the **Site Quota Information** section, view the settings listed to see the quota settings and current values.

To view the current data for a site, you can also use the Site Collection Usage Statistics Summary page for the top-level website.

To view quota data for a site

1. On the site you want to view data for, click **Site Settings**.

2. Under **Administration**, click **Go to Site Administration**.

3. Under **Site Collection Administration**, click **View site collection usage summary**.

After you have checked the site quota data, you can change the quota values for a site. Note that this action does not change the quota template, and the change does not affect any site except the site you specify.

To change quota values for a site

1. Click **Start**, point to **All Programs**, point to **Administrative Tools**, and then click **SharePoint Central Administration**.

2. On the Central Administration page, under **Component Configuration**, click **Administer quotas and locks**.

3. On the Administer Quotas And Locks page, click **Site Quota Settings and Locks**.

4. In the **Select a top-level Web site** section, type the URL in the **Enter the top-level Web site URL** box, and then click **View Data**.

5. In the **Site Quota Information** section, change the **Limit storage to a maximum of __ MB** amount, **Send warning e-mail when site storage reaches __MB** amount, or **Maximum users allowed:** amount setting.

6. Click **OK**.

> **Note**   The user limit option is available only in Active Directory account mode.

Managing Locks

You can use locks to stop sites from exceeding your storage quota limits and to block all users from accessing a site if necessary. Sites are locked automatically when they exceed the maximum storage quota. You can also lock a site manually, if, for example, it is in violation of your site use policies. Depending on the type of lock, the result of a locked site is different. The differences are as follows:

■ When a site is locked for exceeding a storage quota limit, users who attempt to upload new content see a disk full error.

■ When a site is locked manually, users who attempt to view the site will see an access denied message.

Sites can be unlocked by different methods, depending on the reason for the lock. Site administrators can unlock sites by themselves if the sites are locked for exceeding quota limits. Only a server administrator can clear a manual lock. Table 15-5 lists the lock reasons and methods for unlocking sites.

Table 15-5   Lock Reasons and Methods for Unlocking Sites

Lock Reason	Server Administrator Action to Unlock	Site Administrator Action to Unlock
Storage limit exceeded	Change the quota value, or clear the Adding Content Prevented lock	Delete excess site content or documents
Manual lock by server administrator	Clear the All Access Prevented lock	None

If you need to lock a site and deny all users access to it, either temporarily or permanently, you do so by using the Site Quota Settings And Locks page.

To lock a site manually

1. Click **Start**, point to **All Programs**, point to **Administrative Tools**, and then click **SharePoint Central Administration**.

2. On the Central Administration page, under **Component Configuration**, click **Administer quotas and locks**.

3. On the Administer Quotas And Locks page, click **Site Quota Settings and Locks**.

4. In the **Select a top-level Web site** section, type the URL in the **Enter the top-level Web site URL** box, and then click **View Data**.

5. In the **Site Lock Information** section, select **Adding content prevented** or **No access**.

6. If you want to further document the reason for the lock, type an explanation in the **Additional lock reason information:** box.

7. Click **OK**.

When a site has been locked manually, you can unlock it by using the Site Quota Settings And Locks page.

To unlock a site

1. Click **Start**, point to **All Programs**, point to **Administrative Tools**, and then click **SharePoint Central Administration**.

2. On the Central Administration page, under **Component Configuration**, click **Administer quotas and locks**.

3. On the Administer Quotas And Locks page, click **Site Quota Settings and Locks**.

4. In the **Select a top-level Web site** section, type the URL in the **Enter the top-level Web site URL** box, and then click **View Data**.

5. In the **Site Lock Information** section, select **Not locked**, and then click **OK**.

Configuring Usage Analysis

If you want to know what kind of impact your website has, you need to track how many users visit your site, the type and number of hits your site receives, and other site-usage information. Microsoft Windows SharePoint Services includes features that analyze the usage of your site. Summary and detailed usage reports supply information such as:

- Number of page hits for each individual page
- Number of unique users
- Browser and operating system information
- Referring domains and URLs

Tracking usage information can be useful for identifying which content on your site is being heavily used (and therefore should be kept) and which content is not being heavily used (and might be a candidate for archival). In addition to site usage statistics, you can also keep track of how much storage space your site is taking up and the level of activity your site is generating. This information is gathered as part of the quota tracking for sites. For more information about quotas, see the "Configuring Site Quotas and Locks" section earlier in this chapter.

The usage reports rely on usage log data gathered from the websites and stored in the content database for each virtual server. The log data is a summary record of transactions on your website. When you view a usage report in Windows SharePoint Services, the data is arranged into a list format. You must be a member of the administrator role (or have the View Usage Data right) for a site to view the site usage statistics.

You configure the settings for processing the usage log by using commands in HTML Administration pages. From the SharePoint Central Administration page, you can control the following items:

- **Whether or not to log usage data.**   Usage analysis is not enabled by default. If you want to use the usage analysis features for your server, you must enable the usage analysis logging process. Log files are created daily to track usage information. When the log file is processed, a flag is added to indicate that is has been processed. If you do not want to track usage analysis data and you want to conserve disk space, you can turn off data logging for usage analysis.

- **Where the log files are stored and how many log files to create.** By default, the log files are in c:\Windows\system32\LogFiles\STS. Inside this folder is a folder for every virtual server, and under those folders are folders for each day. You can specify any other location you prefer. You can specify that up to 30 log files are created.

> **Note** If you choose a different log file location, you must be sure to give the STS_WPG user group Read, Write, and Update permissions to the directory. Without these permissions, the usage log files cannot be created or updated by IIS. For more information about setting permissions for a directory, see the Microsoft Windows Help system.

- **Whether or not to process the usage logs and when to do so.** By default, the log files are set to be processed every day at 1:00 A.M. You can schedule the usage log to be processed at a more convenient downtime for your websites. You can also specify the end time for the usage log processing. If your websites are primarily used by internal employees, for example, you might schedule the log to be processed at night, when demand on the sites is lower than during working hours. If you have multiple servers, you can stagger the processing. For example, you can configure the processing to start at midnight and stagger it by 15 minutes so that server1 starts at 12:00, server2 starts at 12:15, server3 at 12:30, and so on.

In Microsoft Windows SharePoint Services, usage analysis data is gathered from the front-end Web servers and collected into temporary files. When the daily log processing takes place, the data is merged into the content databases on the back-end servers. Usage data is collected for an entire site collection on one server at a time. Even though the data is logged and stored for an entire site collection, when you view the data in HTML Administration pages, you can see only the data for a particular website or subsite, not for the entire site collection.

> **Note** Although you can see the total number of hits for a site collection on the Site Collection Usage Summary page, for detailed information you must use the Site Usage Report page for the individual site or subsite.

Usage data is kept for up to three months in the database for historical purposes. Daily information is stored for 31 days, and monthly information is stored for

24 months. Note that usage analysis processes rely on the Microsoft SharePoint Timer service to manage the timing of log processing.

> **Note**   Because usage analysis processing runs only once a day, when you enable usage analysis processing, you will not see any data until the next day. Log processing is done only for a single day's worth of data. If you turn off the log processing for a week but leave the data logging turned on, the next time you turn on processing, it will process only one day's worth of log files. The log files for all of the days before that will remain unprocessed.

You control settings for usage analysis processing from the SharePoint Central Administration page. You must be an administrator of the local server computer or a member of the SharePoint administrators group to configure usage analysis settings.

> **Note**   When you configure usage analysis processing for a server, it takes effect for any existing virtual servers. If you later add a virtual server, you must configure usage analysis processing again to enable usage analysis for the new virtual server.

To configure usage analysis processing for a server

1. Click **Start**, point to **All Programs**, point to **Administrative Tools**, and then click **SharePoint Central Administration**.

2. Under **Component Configuration**, click **Configure usage analysis processing**.

3. In the **Logging Settings** section, select the **Enable logging** check box.

4. In the **Log file location** box, type the location to store the log file.
   The default location for the log file is c:\Windows\system32\Log-Files\STS.

5. In the **Number of log files to create** box, type a number from 1 to 30.
   In general, you should use a number that is one to three times the number of database servers in your server farm, with a maximum number of 30 log files.

6. In the **Processing Settings** section, select the **Enable usage analysis processing** check box.

7. Under **Run processing between these times daily**, specify the range of times to start the usage analysis log processing. In the **Start** box, select the earliest time of day to begin running log processing. In the **End** box, select the latest time to begin running log processing.

8. Click **OK**.

Managing HTML Viewers

Included with Windows SharePoint Services is the ability to connect to an HTML viewing server. The HTML viewing server provides support for users who want to view the content of files on the Windows SharePoint Services website but do not have Microsoft Word, Excel, or PowerPoint from Office 97 (or a newer release of Microsoft Office) installed on their local computer. Even users who have only a Web browser (Microsoft Internet Explorer or Netscape Navigator) can view content by having the native Office file format converted to HTML at the time the user opens the file. Although there is a slight delay while the transformation takes place, the converted file is extremely close to the WYSIWIG formatting of the original. In addition to transforming files on the fly for end users, administrators can use a batch process mode of HTML Transformations to convert the contents of entire folders to HTML.

> **Note** By default, the HTML viewing service supports only the following document types: .doc, .xls, .ppt, and .pps.

Transformation of a supported document can take from 1 to 30 seconds, depending on the complexity and size of the document as well as the speed and available resources of the dedicated computer. To provide for this ability and assure a fast response time, you should dedicate a separate computer to this service as the process is very CPU intensive.

After the server is set up, it can be administered through the Configure HTML Viewer page in SharePoint Central Administration pages. For more information about setting up an HTML Transformation Server, see the "HTML Transformations Service for Windows SharePoint Services" white paper on the Office 11 Resource Kit (Beta) website.

To configure Windows SharePoint Services to use HTML Transformations

1. Click **Start**, point to **Administrative Tools**, and then click **SharePoint Central Administration**.

2. Under **Server Configuration**, click **Configure HTML Viewer**.

3. Select the **Turn on HTML Viewer** check box.

4. In the **Path to HTML Viewer Server** box, type the full URL to the transformation server.

5. In the **Maximum Cache Size** box, type the maximum size to allow for the HTML viewing cache.

6. In the **Maximum File Size** box, type the maximum file size to view.

7. In the **Timeout Length** box, type the length of time to wait before ending an HTML viewer process.

8. Click **OK**.

Managing and Customizing Search

Microsoft Windows SharePoint Services enables users to search all website content on a particular virtual server. Because all site information (including documents) is stored in a database, the search model will allow searching of all site content.

The type of search you use for Windows SharePoint Services depends on the other software you are running in your server system, as outlined here:

- If you have Microsoft SharePoint Portal Server "v2.0" installed, you can use the search features included with SharePoint Portal Server "v2.0" to search your websites from a portal site.

- If you are running Microsoft SQL Server 2000, Windows SharePoint Services uses the SQL Server 2000 full-text searching features to search for website content.

Search features are available only for Windows SharePoint Services with SQL Server 2000 or with SharePoint Portal Server "v2.0". If you are running Microsoft SQL Server Desktop Engine 2000 (MSDE) for your database and do not have SharePoint Portal Server "v2.0" , no search features are available. If you want search, you must either upgrade to SQL Server 2000 or use SharePoint Portal Server "v2.0" to search your website.

Understanding Search in Windows SharePoint Services

Search is available per virtual server. This means that search is either turned on or off for all top-level websites and subsites on a particular virtual server. Subsites inherit the search settings from parent sites. If search has not been enabled for a virtual server, the search links will not appear in the websites that reside on that virtual server.

Search can query most lists and all document libraries on your site. Search cannot query lists of lists (such as the Quick Launch bar) or surveys. Users can search the entire site or a single list page within the site (for example, for a particular contact in the Contacts list).

Searching with SQL Server 2000

If you are using SQL Server 2000, you can enable full-text searching for your websites. SQL Server 2000 full-text searching is a good solution for searching Windows SharePoint Services websites in small or medium organizations; however, SQL Server 2000 full-text search does not scale well to large server farms. Search catalogs can use up to 40 percent of the hard disk space that data uses. There is a hard limit of 256 search catalogs per server; plus you will encounter performance issues when you reach 1 million rows in the search catalog table. If you are running a large server farm, it is not advisable to offer search features for all of them. Consider adding search for premium customers if you are an ISP or Application service provider (ASP), or for only a limited number of sites if you are hosting websites based on Windows SharePoint Services inside a large organization.

SQL Server 2000 full-text search supports only one language for each database. If you are supporting Windows SharePoint Services websites in several languages and want to enable full-text search in those languages, consider hosting each language on a separate virtual server with a separate database for each language.

SQL Server 2000 performs linguistic analysis on full-text search catalogs. The following list includes the languages for which linguistic analysis packages are available:

- Neutral
- Dutch
- English (UK)
- English (US)
- French
- German
- Italian
- Japanese
- Korean
- Simplified Chinese
- Spanish (Modern)
- Swedish
- Traditional Chinese
- Thai

The neutral linguistic analysis package is provided for use with languages not on this list. For more information about SQL Server, full-text search, and languages, see the SQL Server 2000 documentation. You can download the documentation from the following site: *http://www.microsoft.com/sql/techinfo/productdoc/2000/books.asp.*

When you enable full-text search in Windows SharePoint Services, a new, empty catalog is created by default and named ix_*databasename*. Content is added to this catalog as it is added to your new website. Aside from enabling and disabling full-text search, any search management or monitoring must be done from within SQL Server 2000 with the SQL Server administration tools. For more information about managing full-text search in SQL Server 2000, see "Administering Full-Text Features Using SQL Enterprise Manager" in the SQL Server Books Online system at *http://www.microsoft.com/sql/techinfo/productdoc/2000/books.asp*.

Enabling Search for SQL Server 2000

To use search with Windows SharePoint Services and SQL Server 2000, you must have full-text searching installed on your SQL Server computer. Full-text searching is usually installed by default, but if it is not installed on your server, you can install it easily with the SQL Server Setup tools.

To install full-text indexing with SQL Server 2000

1. On your SQL Server computer, run the SQL Server 2000 Setup program.

2. On the setup screen, click **SQL Server 2000 Components**, and then click **Install Database Server**.
   The Microsoft SQL Server 2000 Installation Wizard opens.

3. On the **Welcome** screen, click **Next**.

4. On the **Computer Name** screen, select the computer type, and then click **Next**.

5. On the **Installation Selection** panel, select **Upgrade, remove, or add components to an existing instance of SQL Server**, and then click **Next**.

6. On the **Instance Name** panel, clear the **Default** check box, and then in the **Instance Name** box, select your SQL Server instance for Windows SharePoint Services and click **Next**.

7. Select **Add components to your existing installation**, and then click **Next**.

8. On the **Select Components** panel, in the **Sub-Components** list, select **Full-Text Search**, and then click **Next**.

9. Click **Next** again to begin the installation.

10. Click **Finish**.

After you have configured SQL Server 2000 to support full-text searching, you're ready to enable search for Windows SharePoint Services.

To enable search for Windows SharePoint Services

1. On your server computer running Windows SharePoint Services, click **Start**, point to **All Programs**, point to **Administrative Tools**, and then click **Share-Point Central Administration**.

2. Under **Component Configuration**, click **Configure full-text search**.

3. In the **Search Settings** section, select the **Enable full-text search and indexing** check box.

4. Click **OK**.

> **Note** Full-text searching does not include any file types other than .doc, .xls, .ppt, .txt, and .htm in the search results
>
> If you are using the full-text searching for Microsoft SQL Server 2000, the following filters are installed by default: .doc, .xls, .ppt, .txt, and .htm. You can install custom filters to allow you to search other file types. For more information about adding filters to SQL Server full-text searching, see the SQL Server 2000 documentation as stated above along with the site URL.

Configuring Blocked File Extensions

Microsoft Windows SharePoint Services provides the ability to restrict certain kinds of files from being uploaded or retrieved, based on the file extension. For example, a file with the .exe file extension could potentially contain code that runs on client computers when it is downloaded. Because it has the .exe file extension, the file can be run on demand when it is downloaded. If files with the .exe file extension are blocked, users can neither upload nor download a file with the .exe extension, and potentially dangerous content in the .exe file cannot be downloaded. This feature does not prevent all exploits based on file types, nor is it designed to do so.

Summary

In this chapter, we have addressed the process for configuring Windows SharePoint Services sites.

The first crucial step is, of course, the planning. You will achieve a much better site for your users if you carefully plan what data you will share and exactly who should have access to that data. If your users have a good experience the first time they access the site, they will be much more likely to return and use this very powerful tool for managing corporate information assets.

We have addressed how to use the management user interface both through SharePoint Central Administration as well as through Site Settings on the Web page itself. Often times you can configure a particular setting by going through either Central Administration or Site Settings. At first this might seem confusing, but as you become more familiar with the interface, you will find it is a great advantage.

Chapter 16

Windows SharePoint Services Site Administration

This chapter will focus on skills and topics you will need to effectively administer Microsoft Windows SharePoint Services sites for your enterprise. You will learn how to create sites and then how to apply templates, lists, documents, and other workspaces to your sites so that you can maximize Windows SharePoint Services. In addition, you will find information about how to configure security for the sites and subsites in your collections.

Your users can contribute to sites by using nothing more than a Web browser. However, if you use a Windows SharePoint Services–compatible client program, such as Microsoft Office 2003, you can work seamlessly with the site, saving files to libraries, editing documents in the client program, and moving or linking that information to your site.

You can add information to the SharePoint site, such as events, names, and phone numbers of people with whom your team communicates, and to-do items. You can also do the following:

- Post documents to share with other team members

- Hold newsgroup-style discussions

- Take a poll of the team to make a decision

As team members add or delete documents, lists, discussions, and surveys, Windows SharePoint Services automatically updates links to the content so that it's always easy to find. You can also create alerts so that you are notified of changes to the site.

Pages in the site will display lists of information, allowing team members to organize the information any way they want, such as by subject, due date, or author. For example, you can do the following:

- Restrict the display to see only the set of information that applies to you

- Hide information that doesn't interest you

- Change the order in which the information is listed

- Set up customized views to make it easy for your team members to focus quickly on pertinent information

To use the features described, you will want to acquaint yourself with the management interface where most of these features will be available to create and configure. From the site's Web page, select Site Settings from the top of the window. (See Figure 16-1.) This will take you to the page for site administration. Throughout this chapter, we will be exploring administration tasks that you will access through this menu structure.

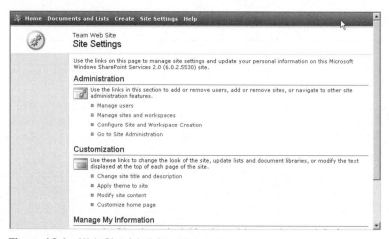

Figure 16-1   Web Site Administration main menu

Using Templates

When creating sites to serve business needs, one of the first things you will need to decide is what you want your site to look like. For instance, do you want to include sections for announcements, members, and events? Will you want a separate part of the page to display news items or links to other pages? Fortunately, you don't have to build this view of information each time you create a new site because Windows

SharePoint Services includes predefined views called *site templates*. Alternatively, you will be able to customize a site and then save a site template based on that new design for use on other sites. A site template includes all the pages, information, and styles needed to create a site, including any list templates used in the site. Another kind of template, called a *list template*, includes all the pages, information, and styles needed to create a single list.

The first time you access the newly created site, you will have the opportunity to select a template from a page that shows all templates available on the server and site collection. This set is filtered based on the site language and the site definition ID that your site is based upon. As mentioned earlier, these templates can be customized for the site. (See Figure 16-2.)

Note Each template maintains its identify via site definition ID. For example, a site based on the Meeting Workspace template has a different site definition ID than a site based on the Team Site template. As an example, if you create a Meeting Announcements custom list template from the Announcements list in a site based on a Meeting Workspace template, that template is not available from within a site based on the Team Site template.

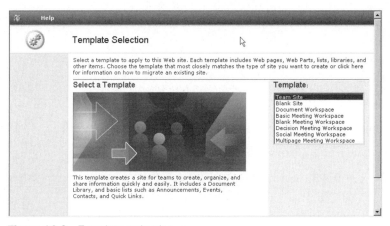

Figure 16-2 Template selection

Templates are also known as *site definitions*. Later we will explore how you can create your own customized templates or site definitions. For now, we'll focus on the site definitions that are available on the server by default.

Team Site Template

Figure 16-3 shows what the default Team Site template looks like.

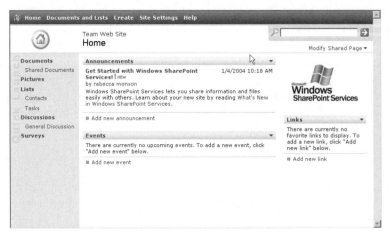

Figure 16-3   Team website

From here, you can customize the team's website. However, note the number of features that are available by default for your use on this page. You can easily add announcements, events, and links by simply clicking the Add button in each of the Web Parts. Direct your attention to the lefthand column of the screen, where you will see other features that are included by default in the Team Site template. (Refer to Figure 16-3.)

The items provided include:

- A shared document library, where users of the site can easily create and upload documents

- A link to make it easy for users to create a picture library

- Two predefined lists already created:

  - A contacts list, where you can add information about people your team works with

  - A task list, to keep track of work that you or your team needs to complete

- A general discussion board, which is a place to hold newsgroup-style discussions on topics relevant to your team.

- A link to make it easy to create a survey to quickly poll team members about a particular concept or topic. If the survey is set up so that respondents' names are visible, the All Responses view enables you to see how each team member responded.

Blank Site Template

The Blank Site template is shown in Figure 16-4.

Figure 16-4   A website using the Blank Site template

This page can be customized exactly as you want through the Modify Shared Page drop-down menu in the upper-right corner of the screen. (Refer to Figure 16-4.) Unlike the Team Site template, the Blank Site template will not automatically set up any document or picture libraries for you, nor will it set up lists or discussion forums.

Document Workspace

A Document Workspace site is a Microsoft Windows SharePoint Services site that is centered on one or more documents. Colleagues can easily work together on a document—either by working directly on the Document Workspace site copy or by working on their own copy, which they can update periodically with changes that have been saved to the Document Workspace site copy.

Creating a Generic Document Workspace Site

You might need to contact an administrator to grant you permission to create Document Workspace sites. Once you have the required permission, you can use the following steps to create a generic document workspace site:

1. Go to a Microsoft Windows SharePoint Services website where you have permission to create Document Workspace sites.

2. On the top link bar, click **Create**.

3. On the Create page, under **Web Pages**, click **Sites and Workspaces**.

4. Enter a title, description, and URL, and click a permission setting. Then click **Create**.

5. On the Template Selection page, click **Document Workspace** in the **Template** box, and then click **OK**.

You have just created a generic Document Workspace site, and by clicking on **Add new document**, you can upload any document on which you plan to collaborate. (See Figure 16-5.)

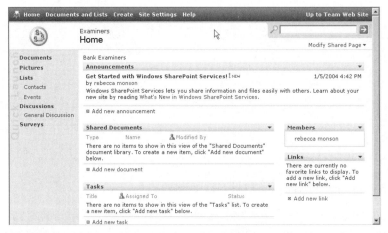

Figure 16-5 Generic Document Workspace site

A Document Workspace site includes many of the same Web Parts included with sites based on the Team Site template, such as:

- Announcements
- Contacts
- Events
- General Discussion
- Links
- Members
- Shared Documents
- Tasks

Creating a Private Document Workspace Site

An alternate method is to create a private Document Workspace site for a document already published in a document library. (See Figure 16-6.) To do this, follow these steps:

1. In a Web browser, go to the document library where the document is stored.

2. Point to the name of the document, and click the **Edit** arrow that appears.

3. Click **Create Document Workspace**.

Figure 16-6   Creating a Document Workspace site

When you create a Document Workspace site that is based on a document in a document library, the Document Workspace site carries the same name as the document on which it is based. (See Figure 16-7.) The document is then stored in a separate document library in the new Document Workspace site. This document can be published back to its source location, in the original document library, from the Document Workspace site. To publish your document back to the source, all you need to do is click the drop-down arrow to the right of the document and select the Publish To Source Location menu item. The Source Location is the originating document (and document library) from which the document workspace was created.

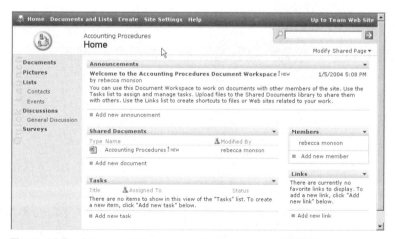

Figure 16-7   Document Workspace site based on a single document

> **Note**   The ability to publish a document back to its original location is available only in a Document Workspace site created from a document that is already stored in a document library. This feature is not available in Document Workspace sites created by using the Create page on a Windows SharePoint Services site. This is because when a workspace is created and then a document is added to the workspace, there is no source location to which to publish the document.

Meeting Workspace Sites

When you create your websites, you can base them on one of the following five Meeting Workspace site templates:

- Basic Meeting Workspace
- Blank Meeting Workspace
- Decision Meeting Workspace
- Social Meeting Workspace
- Multipage Meeting Workspace

These templates are designed to optimize planning, posting, and working together on meeting materials, as well as following up after a meeting or series of meetings.

Basic Meeting Workspace

This template includes all the basics to plan, organize, and track your meeting. The template contains the following lists and their associated Web Parts: Objectives, Attendees, and Agenda. (See Figure 16-8.)

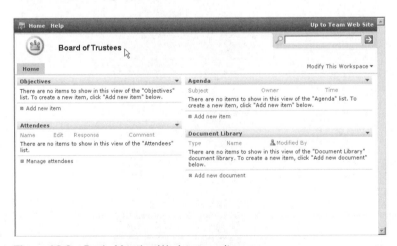

Figure 16-8   Basic Meeting Workspace site

Blank Meeting Workspace

This template creates a blank Meeting Workspace site for you to customize based on your requirements. (See Figure 16-9.)

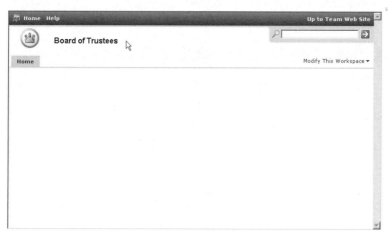

Figure 16-9   Blank Meeting Workspace site

Decision Meeting Workspace

This template includes features for reviewing documents and recording decisions reached at the meeting. The template contains the following lists, library, and their associated Web Parts: Objectives, Attendees, Agenda, Document Library, Tasks, and Decisions. (See Figure 16-10.)

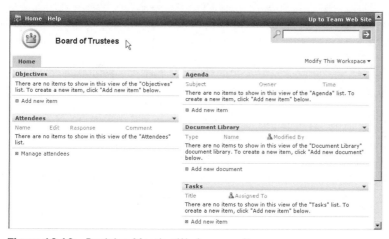

Figure 16-10   Decision Meeting Workspace site

Social Meeting Workspace

This template helps you plan social occasions. It features a discussion board and a picture library to post pictures of the event. The template contains the following lists, library, and their associated Web Parts: Attendees, Directions, Image/Logo, Things To Bring, Discussions, and Picture Library. (See Figure 16-11.)

Figure 16-11   Social Meeting Workspace site

Multipage Meeting Workspace

The Multipage Meeting Workspace site template includes all the basics to plan, organize, and track your meeting with multiple pages. This Meeting Workspace site contains the following lists and their associated Web Parts: Objectives, Attendees, and Agenda. It also contains two blank pages for you to customize based on your requirements. (See Figure 16-12.)

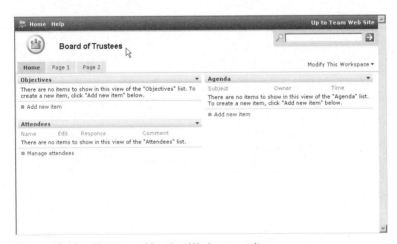

Figure 16-12   Multipage Meeting Workspace site

Customizing, Saving, and Using Templates

Although you cannot open any of the templates and edit them, you can change the workspace that is created from one of these templates. Basic customization can be done from within the browser by using links from the Home, Create, and Site Settings pages of the website. From the browser, you can perform basic customizations such as the following:

- Add a list.

- Change the layout of the home page.

- Change the picture on the home page.

- Add a Web Part to a Web Part Page.

- Change a site's display name (not the URL).

- Apply a theme.

The Windows SharePoint Services Help files contain more information about customizing websites from within the browser.

Once you have customized the workspace site, you can save it as a site template so that other users in the site collection can create similar sites later. Saving a site template you have customized to your specifications qualifies as a best practice that makes it easy to have a consistent look and feel across your sites.

To create a site template based on a website, you must be a member of the Administrators site group for the current website. To add the new site template to the Site Collection gallery, you must have the Add Item right for the Site Template gallery, which is included by default in the Web Designer and Administrator site groups for the top-level website in a site collection. Administrators of a site collection can also import a site template created by another user or software vendor, and they can add the new template to the available site templates in the site collection. You must go to the Site Administration page for the top-level website in a site collection to manage the Site Template gallery.

When a user creates a site template, it is automatically added to the Site Template gallery for the site collection.

To add a template to the Site Template gallery

1. On the top-level website, click **Site Settings**.

2. Under **Administration**, click **Go to Site Administration**.

3. Under **Site Collection Galleries**, click **Manage site template gallery**.

4. On the Site Template Gallery page, click **Upload Template**.

5. In the **Name** box, type the path to the template, or click **Browse**.

   You can upload multiple templates by clicking **Upload Multiple Files**.

6. Click **Save and Close**.

To delete a template in the Site Template gallery

1. On the top-level website, click **Site Settings**.

2. Under **Administration**, click **Go to Site Administration**.

3. Under **Site Collection Galleries**, click **Manage site template gallery**.

4. On the Site Template Gallery page, click the **Edit** icon next to the template name.

5. On the Site Template Gallery: <*Name*> page, click **Delete**.

   Site templates do not include the following items:

   ■ Security settings, such as a list of users or groups with permissions to the site from which the template was created

   ■ Personalizations to Web Part Pages

   ■ Web discussions from the original site

   ■ Alerts from the original site

   ■ Web Part assemblies that were added to the original site

To create a site template

1. On the site, click **Site Settings**.

2. Under **Administration**, click **Go to Site Administration**.

3. Under **Management and Statistics**, click **Save site as template**.

4. In the **File name** box, type the file name to use for the site template file.

5. In the **Template title** box, type the title you want to use for the template in the Site Template gallery.

6. In the Template **description** box, type a description for the site template.

7. If you want to include the existing site content, select the **Include content** check box.

8. Click **OK**. (See Figure 16-13 and Figure 16-14.)

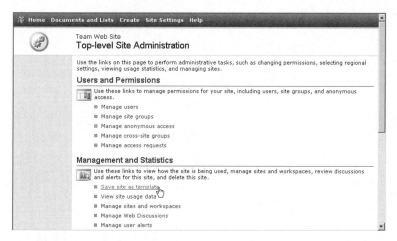

Figure 16-13   Creating a new site template

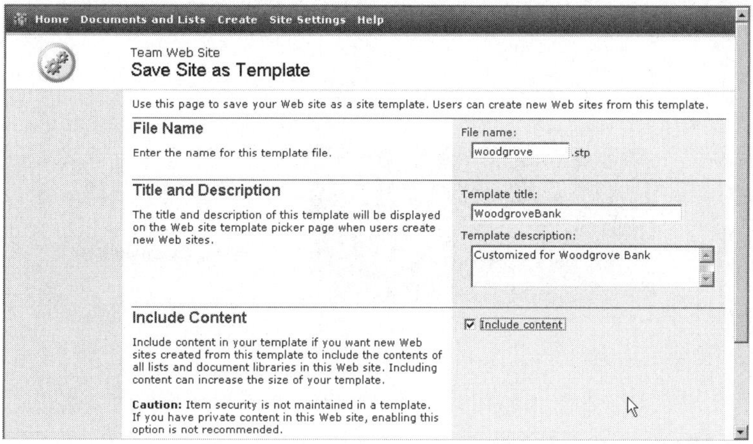

Figure 16-14   Saving a site as a template

Once you have saved the template, it automatically will be a part of the Site Template gallery and available to the site collection. (See Figure 16-15.)

The next time you create a site that is part of the collection under the site where you saved the template, this new template will be an available option. (See Figure 16-16.)

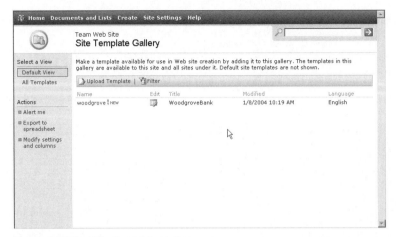

Figure 16-15   Site Template gallery

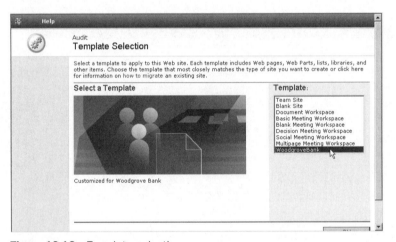

Figure 16-16   Template selection

Selecting a Customized Template from the Command Line

Administrators can also create sites based on the site templates available in the Server Template gallery from the command line by using stsadm.exe. To create a site based on a template in the Central Template gallery, the administrator must use the createsite (to create a top-level website) or createweb (to create a subsite) operations on the command line, and specify the template name as _GLOBAL_#*number*, where *number* refers to the template ID. For example, if you have a site template in the Central Template gallery with the ID 2, you could use the following syntax to create a site based on that template:

```
Stsadm.exe -o createsite -url <url> -ownerlogin <DOMAIN\username> -owneremail
    <someone@example.com> -sitetemplate _GLOBAL_#2
```

> **Note** To find the template ID for a global template, you can use the enumtemplates operation. The enumtemplates operation with the Stsadm.exe command lists the templates currently in the Central Template gallery.

Site Creation Process

Depending on the amount of customization and control you want to allow your users, you can let them create either top-level websites or subsites. The Self-Service Site Creation feature gives users the ability to create top-level websites on their own. For more information on the Self-Service Site Creation feature of SharePoint Portal Server 2003, see Chapter 15, "Configuring Windows SharePoint Services."

Users can also create subsites of any site for which they have the Create Sites And Workspaces right. The Create Sites And Workspaces right is included in the Administrator site group by default, so any member of the Administrator site group for a site can create a subsite of that site. You can assign this right to other site groups by using the Manage Site And Workspace Creation page.

If you want to control top-level website creation yourself, you can disable Self-Service Site Creation and create top-level websites (site collections) on your users' behalf from SharePoint Central Administration. To create a top-level website outside of Self-Service Site Creation, you must be an administrator of the local machine on which the site will reside or a member of the SharePoint administrators group.

> **Note** When you are running a server farm with multiple host names or are in Active Directory account mode, you cannot create a top-level website from SharePoint Central Administration. To perform this action in Active Directory account mode, you must use the command line or object model.

To create a top-level website from SharePoint Central Administration

1. Click **Start**, point to **All Programs**, point to **Administrative Tools**, and then click **SharePoint Central Administration**.

2. Under **Virtual Server Configuration**, click **Create a top-level Web site**.

3. On the Virtual Server List page, click the virtual server under which you want to create the top-level website.

4. To create a site under a predefined URL path for the virtual server, on the Create Top-Level Web Site page, select **Create site under this URL**; in the **Site name** box, type the name for the top-level website; and then in the **URL path** box, select the path to use.

   The name and URL path are combined with the server name to create the full URL to the site. For example, on *http://servername*, if you create a top-level website at the /sites URL path and use Site001 as the name, the full path to the new top-level website is *http://servername/sites/site001*.

5. To create a site at a predefined URL path, select **Create site at this URL**, and then in the **URL path** box, select the URL to use for the top-level website. The site is created at the top level of the URL path you select. For example, on *http://servername*, if you select /portal as the path, the site is created at *http://servername/portal*.

6. In the **Site Collection Owner** section, type the account name (in the form DOMAIN\username) and e-mail address (in the form someone@example.com) for the user who will be the site owner and administrator.

7. If you want to identify a user as the secondary owner of the new top-level website (recommended), in the **Secondary Owner** section, type the account name and e-mail address for a secondary owner and administrator of the new site.

8. If you are using quotas, in the **Quota Template** section, select a quota template to use.

9. In the **Site Language** section, select the language to use for the top-level website.

10. Click **OK**.

The site owner can select a template for the site when first browsing to the URL, or you can browse to the URL on the confirmation page and select one yourself. You must alert the site owner and secondary owner when you have created the site with the URL. They are not notified automatically when you create a site.

Creating Subsites

You can create a subsite of a current site by using the Manage Sites And Workspaces page.

1. On a site, click **Site Settings**.

2. Under **Administration**, click **Manage sites and workspaces**.

3. On the Manage Sites And Workspaces page, click **Create**.

4. On the New SharePoint Site page, in the **Title and Description** section, type the title and description for the new subsite.

5. In the **URL name** box, type the URL for your subsite.

6. In the **User Permissions** section, select either **Use same permissions as parent site** or **Use unique permissions**.

   Select **Use same permissions as parent site** if you want to share users with the parent site, or select **Use unique permissions** if you want to maintain a separate list of users for your subsite.

7. In the **Language** section, select the language to use.

8. Click **Create**.

9. On the Template Selection page, select a template to use, and then click **OK**.

Creating Sites and Subsites from the Command Line

If you are an administrator of the server computer, you can also create sites and subsites by using the Stsadm.exe command-line tool. To create a top-level website, use the createsite operation. To create a subsite, use the createweb operation.

 Tip You can also use the createsiteinnewdb operation to create a top-level website and a new content database at the same time.

The createsite operation takes the following required parameters: url, ownerlogin, and owneremail. It also takes the following optional parameters: ownername, lcid, sitetemplate, title, description, and quota. For example, to create a top-level website called site1 on *http://server_name/sites*, you would use syntax similar to the following:

```
Stsadm.exe -o createsite -url http://server_name/sites/site1 -ownerlogin
    <DOMAIN\user> -owneremail <someone@example.com> -ownername <display name>
```

The createweb operation requires the url parameter and takes the following optional parameters: lcid, sitetemplate, title, description, convert (used to convert an existing folder to a website), and unique (used to specify unique permissions for the subsite). To create a subsite called subsite1 under the site you just created, you would use syntax similar to the following:

```
Stsadm.exe -o createweb -url http://server_name/sites/site1/subsite1
```

Allowing Access to Websites

One of an administrator's main concerns will be granting the appropriate access to the appropriate users for each site and site collection. This topic explains the rights and site groups you can assign to users by using operations in Stsadm.exe and by using HTML Administration. We will discuss the concepts and then the tools provided by Microsoft to ease the burden of this administrative task.

Microsoft Windows SharePoint Services provides the ability to control site access by all the following means:

- **Site groups.** Site groups let you specify which of your users can perform specific actions in your site. For example, a user who is a member of the Contributor site group can add content to Windows SharePoint Services lists, such as the tasks list, or a document library.

- **Anonymous access control.** You can enable anonymous access to allow users to contribute anonymously to lists and surveys or to view pages anonymously. Most Internet websites allow anonymous viewing of the site but ask for authentication when someone wants to edit the site or buy an item on a shopping site.

> **Note** You can also grant access to "all authenticated users" to allow all members of your domain as well as trusted domains to access a website, without having to enable anonymous access.

- **Per-list permissions.** You can manage permissions more finely by setting unique permissions on a per-list basis. For example, if you have a document library containing sensitive financial data for the next fiscal year, you can restrict access to that list so that only the appropriate users can view it. Per-list permissions override site-wide permissions for the lists.

- **Subsite permissions.** Subsites can either use the same permissions as the parent website (inheriting both the site groups and users available on the parent website) or use unique permissions different from those of the parent site (so that you can create your own user accounts and add them to site groups).

User Rights Available for Windows SharePoint Services

Windows SharePoint Services includes 21 rights. One of those 21 rights, Self-Service Site Creation, is available only on a top-level website and is not available for use on subsites. The 21 rights are used to create the five default user site groups. You can change which rights are included in a particular site group (except for the Guest and Administrator site groups) or create a new site group to contain a specific list of rights. Table 16-1 is a list of rights and the groups those rights are granted to by default.

Table 16-1   User Rights for Sites

Right Name	Rights Granted	Default Groups
Add and Customize Pages	Grants permission to create ASP.NET, ASP, and HTML pages for a website	Web Designer, Administrator
Add Items	Grants permission to add items to lists or documents to document libraries	Contributor, Web Designer, Administrator
Add/Remove Personal Web Parts	Grants permission to add and remove Web Parts to personalize Web Part Pages	Contributor, Web Designer, Administrator
Apply Style Sheets	Grants permission to apply a style sheet to the entire website	Web Designer, Administrator
Apply Themes and Borders	Grants permission to apply a theme or border to an entire website	Web Designer, Administrator
Browse Directories	Grants permission to browse the directory structure of a website	Contributor, Web Designer, Administrator
Cancel Check-out	Grants permission to cancel the check-out action performed by another user	Web Designer, Administrator
Create Cross-Site Groups	Grants permission to create or delete cross-site groups, or to change membership of a cross-site group	Contributor, Web Designer, Administrator
Create Sites and Workspaces	Grants permission to create a new subsite or workspace, such as a Document Workspace or Meeting Workspace	Reader, Contributor, Web Designer, Administrator
Delete Items	Grants permission to delete list items and documents from the website	Contributor, Web Designer, Administrator
Edit Items	Grants permission to edit existing list items and documents in the website	Contributor, Web Designer, Administrator
Manage Lists	Grants permission to create, edit, or delete lists and change their settings	Web Designer, Administrator
Manage List Permissions	Grants permission to change permissions for a list or document library	Administrator
Manage Personal Views	Grants permission to create, edit, or delete personal views on lists	Contributor, Web Designer, Administrator Contributor, Web Designer, Administrator
Manage Site Groups	Grants permission to create, delete, and edit site groups, both by changing the rights assigned to the site group and by changing which users are members of the site group	Administrator

Table 16-1 User Rights for Sites *(continued)*

Right Name	Rights Granted	Default Groups
Manage Web Site	Grants permission to perform administration tasks for a particular site or subsite	Administrator
Update Personal Web Parts	Grants permission to update Web Parts to display personalized information	Contributor, Web Designer, Administrator
Use Self-Service Site Creation	Grants permission to use the Self-Service Site Creation tool to create a top-level website	Reader, Contributor, Web Designer, Administrator
View Items	Grants permission to view items in lists, documents in document libraries, and Web discussion comments	Reader, Contributor, Web Designer, Administrator
View Pages	Grants permission to browse pages in the website	Reader, Contributor, Web Designer, Administrator
View Usage Data	Grants permission to view reports on website usage	Administrator

Defining Site Groups

Windows SharePoint Services uses site groups to manage site-wide security. Each user is a member of at least one site group. Each site group possesses corresponding rights. Rights are actions that users can perform, such as Manage Lists. With Windows SharePoint Services, you can use the following default site groups: Guest, Reader, Contributor, Web Designer, and Administrator. In addition, Windows SharePoint Services allows you to edit the rights assigned to a site group, create a new site group, or delete an unused site group. You manage site groups in Windows SharePoint Services with either HTML Administration pages or the command-line administration tool. You cannot change the rights assigned to the Guest and Administrator site groups, and you cannot assign users directly to the Guest site group.

> **Note** You can add user accounts to a website without assigning them to a site group. For example, if you are creating new user accounts for the website, you can create the user accounts and then assign the users to site groups later. You can also remove a member from all site groups. However, a user who is not assigned to a site group has no access to the website.

Windows SharePoint Services includes the following site groups by default:

■ **Guest.** The Guest group has limited rights to view pages and specific page elements. This site group is used for giving users access to a particular page or list without granting them rights to view the entire site. Users cannot be explicitly added to the Guest site group; rather, users who are given access to lists or document libraries by way of per-list permissions are automatically added to the Guest site group. The Guest site group cannot be customized or deleted.

- **Reader.**   The Reader group has rights to view items, view pages, and create a top-level website using Self-Service Site Creation. Readers can only read a site; they cannot add content. Note that when a reader creates a site using Self-Service Site Creation, she becomes the site owner and a member of the Administrator site group for the new site. This does not affect the user's site group membership for any other site.

- **Contributor.**   The Contributor group has Reader rights, plus rights to add, edit, and delete items; browse directories; manage personal views; add, remove, or update personal Web Parts; and create cross-site groups. Contributors cannot create new lists or document libraries, but they can add content to existing lists and document libraries.

- **Web Designer.**   The Web Designer group has Contributor rights, plus rights to cancel check-out, manage lists, add and customize pages, define and apply themes and borders, and apply style sheets. Web Designers can modify the structure of the site and create new lists or document libraries.

- **Administrator.**   The Administrator group has all rights from other site groups, plus rights to manage site groups, manage list permissions, create sites and workspaces, and view usage analysis data. The Administrator site group cannot be customized or deleted, and there must always be at least one member of the Administrator site group. Members of the Administrator site group always have access to, or can grant themselves access to, any item in the website.

> **Note**   The owner and secondary owner of a site collection are members of the Administrator site group for their site, but they are also identified separately in the configuration database as site collection owners. This owner flag can be changed only by using the Manage Site Collection Owners page in Central Administration or by using the site owner operation with Stsadm.exe. If you remove an owner from the Administrator site group for the site, the owner retains the owner flag in the database and can still perform website administrative tasks.

These site groups are defined per website. Users assigned to the Administrator site group are administrators only for a particular website. To perform any administrative tasks that affect settings for all websites and virtual servers on the server computer, a user must be an administrator for the server computer (also known as a local machine administrator) or a member of the SharePoint administrators group, rather than a member of a site's Administrator site group.

Customizing Rights for Site Groups

You can create a new site group or customize an existing site group (except for the Guest and Administrator site groups, which cannot be customized) to include only the rights you want. For example, if you want only the Web Designers to be able to edit lists on the site, you can remove the Edit Items right from the Contributor site group.

Some rights depend on other rights. You must be able to view items before you can edit items. If a right is removed from a site group, any rights dependent on that right are also deleted. For example, when the View Items right is deleted, the Add Items, Edit Items, and Delete Items rights are also deleted. In the same way, if you add a right that requires another right, the required right is also added. So, if you grant the Edit Items right to a user, the View Items right is granted automatically.

Using HTML Administration Pages to Manage Site Groups

You can manage site groups from the Site Administration page for your Web site. To manage site groups, follow the Manage Site Groups link on the Site Administration page to the Manage Site Groups page. (See Figure 16-17.) On this page, you can view a list of site groups, change which rights are included in a site group, add a new site group, or delete a site group.

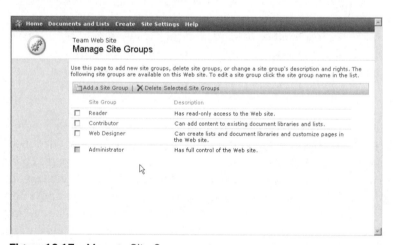

Figure 16-17   Manage Site Groups page

To view a list of site groups

1. On the Site Settings page for your website, under **Administration**, click **Go to Site Administration**.

2. On the Site Administration page, under **Users and Permissions**, click **Manage site groups**.

3. The site groups available for the website are displayed on the **Manage Site Groups** page. (See Figure 16-17.)

To add a new site group

1. On the Manage Site Groups page, click **Add a Site Group**.

2. In the **Site Group Name and Description** area, type the name and description for your new site group.

   In the **Rights** area, select the rights you want to include in the new site group.

3. Click **Create Site Group**.

   Figure 16-18 illustrates this process.

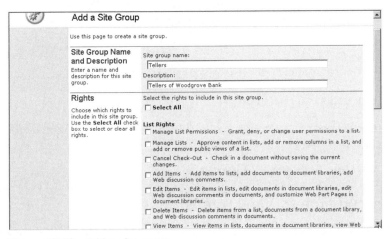

Figure 16-18   Add a site group

You can create a new site group based on an existing site group, and even copy the members of the existing site group into your new site group.

To copy an existing site group

1. On the Manage Site Groups page, click the site group you want to copy.

2. On the Members Of *"Site Group Name"* page, click **Edit Site Group Permissions**.

3. On the Edit Site Group *"Site Group Name"* page, click **Copy Site Group**.

4. On the Copy The Site Group *"Site Group Name"* page, in the **Site Group Name and Description** area, type the name and description for your new site group.

5. If you want to copy the users from the existing site group into your new site group, select the **Copy users from** *"Site Group Name"* check box.

6. In the **Rights** area, select any additional rights that you want the site group to contain, and clear any rights that you do not want the site group to contain.

7. Click **Create Site Group**.

You can also edit an existing site group to change the rights assigned to that site group.

To edit an existing site group

1. On the Manage Site Groups page, click the site group you want to change.

2. On the Members Of "*Site Group Name*" page, click **Edit Site Group Permissions**.

3. On the Edit Site Group "*Site Group Name*" page, select the rights you want to include and clear any rights that you do not want.

4. Click **OK**.

If you find that a site group is not used, you can delete the site group.

To delete an existing site group

1. On the Manage Site Groups page, select the check box next to the site group you want to delete.

2. Click **Delete Selected Site groups**.

Using the Command Line to View Site Groups

You can view the list of site groups from the command line in Windows SharePoint Services by using the enumroles operation. This operation takes the -url parameter, and then simply lists the names of the site groups for that URL, so you can use the correct site group name when assigning permissions to users. For example, to view the list of site groups for a site at *http://myserver/site1*, you would type the following command:

```
Stsadm -o enumroles -url http://myserver/site1
```

Assigning Per-List Permissions

Windows SharePoint Services provides the ability to control permissions on a per-list basis. If you have sensitive information stored in a list and you do not want to expose the information to all members of your site, you can set permissions for just that list to control which users can view, edit, or add items to that list. You can grant permissions to a list or document library to individual users, to groups of users, or to a site group. Per-list permissions work for any list or document library in a web-site based on Windows SharePoint Services (for example, Announcements, Tasks, Shared Documents, and so on).

List permissions can be changed by any user who has the Manage List Permissions right (by default, included in the Administrator site group) or Full Control permissions for that list. By default, all members of a website (all users assigned to a site group, except for the Guest site group) have access to all lists and document libraries on that website. Each site group has a predefined level of permissions for all lists and document libraries. The default list permissions are as follows:

- View items (given to the Reader site group by default)
- View, insert, edit, delete items (given to the Contributor site group by default)
- View, insert, edit, delete items; change list settings (given to the Web Designer site group by default)
- View, insert, edit, delete items; change list settings; change list security

In addition, you can set advanced permissions, which allow you to grant any of the following rights for a user or site group:

- Manage Lists (given to the Web Designer site group by default)
- Manage List Permissions
- Manage Personal Views (given to the Contributor site group by default)
- Cancel Check-Out (applies only to document libraries; given to the Web Designer site group by default)
- Add List Items, Edit List Items, and Delete List Items (given to the Contributor site group by default)
- View List Items (given to the Reader site group by default)

> **Note**   Members of the Administrator site group always have the highest level of permissions for all lists and document libraries. You cannot change list or document library permissions for the Administrator site group. Also, any site group that has the View Lists Item right (such as Reader) can continue to see the list name, description, number of items, and time when the list was last modified, even though they cannot view the list contents directly.

To control permissions for a list, go to the list itself or to the Customize *"Listname"* page for the list.

View Permissions for a List

Navigate to the list, and then in the left pane, click **Modify Settings And Columns**. (See Figure 16-19.)

Figure 16-19   Viewing permissions for a list

On the Customize "*Listname*" page, in the General Settings section, click **Change Permissions For This <list/document library>**. (See Figure 16-20.)

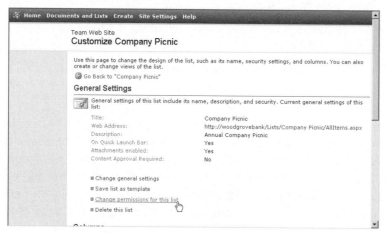

Figure 16-20   Changing permissions on a list

The Change Permissions: "*Listname*" page displays the users and any groups that have access to the list, and it shows the permissions level each user or group is assigned. You can change the list permissions for all members of a particular site group by modifying that site group's permissions.

To change list permissions for a particular site group

1. Navigate to the list, and then in the left pane, click **Modify settings and columns**.

2. On the Customize "*Listname*" page, in the **General Settings** section, click **Change permissions for this <list/document library>**.

3. Select the check box next to the site group you want to change. (See Figure 16-21.)

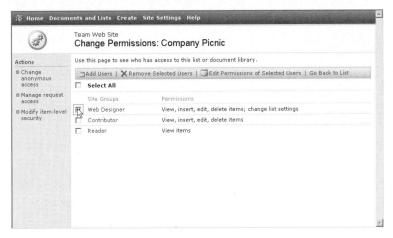

Figure 16-21   Changing permissions given to a site group

For example, click the check box next to **Web Designer** to change the permissions for all members of the Web Designer site group.

4. Click **Edit Permissions of Selected Users**.

5. In the **Choose Permissions** section, select the level of permissions to allow and click **OK**.

You can also grant permissions to individual users or to user groups instead of to all members of a site group. Remember that when you grant a user or group permissions to a specific list in your site, they are added to the Guest site group if they are not already members of the site. Note that a member of the Guest site group cannot navigate to a page within the site unless you give them the exact page URL.

To assign list permissions to a specific user or group

1. Navigate to the list, and then in the left pane, click **Modify settings and columns**.

2. On the Customize "*Listname*" page, in the **General Settings** section, click **Change permissions for this <list/document library>**.

3. On the list toolbar, click **Add Users**.

4. In the **Step 1: Choose Users** section, in the **Users** area, in the text box, type the network domain name or e-mail address for the user or group you want to assign permissions.

5. In the **Step 2: Choose Permissions** section, under **Permissions**, select the level of permissions for the user or group, and then click **Next**.

6. In the **Step 3: Confirm Users** section, verify that the e-mail address, user name, and display name for the user or group are correct.

7. If you want to notify the user or group of their permissions with an e-mail message, in the **Step 4: Send E-Mail** section, select the **Send the following e-mail to let these users know they've been added** check box, and fill in the text you want to send.

8. Click **Finish**.

If you want to restrict your list to a specific set of users, you must both grant access to the individual users and remove access from other site members.

To remove list permissions for a user, group, or site group

1. Navigate to the list, and then in the left pane, click **Modify settings and columns**.

2. On the Customize "*Listname*" page, in the **General Settings** section, click **Change permissions for this <list/document library>**.

3. Select the check box next to the site group, user, or group you want to remove permissions for, and then click **Remove Selected Users**.

If you no longer want to use unique permissions for a particular list, you can reset the permissions to use the website's general permissions.

To reset permissions to the default state

1. Navigate to the list, and then in the left pane, click **Modify settings and columns**.

2. On the Customize "*Listname*" page, in the **General Settings** section, click **Change permissions for this <list/document library>**.

3. Click **Inherit permissions from the parent Web site**.

4. Click **OK** to change to inherited permissions.

Note The Inherit Permissions link does not appear unless the list permissions have already been customized.

Controlling Access for All Authenticated Users

If you want all authenticated users of your intranet to be able to access your website, rather than adding each user individually or in groups, you can configure your site to allow all users on your network rights to use the site. You can also specify which site group (either Reader or Contributor) to assign to all authenticated users.

To allow all authenticated users rights to a top-level website

1. On your site, click **Site Settings**.

2. Under **Administration**, click **Go to Site Administration**.

3. On the Site Administration page, under **Users and Permissions**, click **Manage anonymous access**.

4. In the **All Authenticated Users** section, under **Allow all authenticated users to access site**, select **Yes**.

5. Under **Assign these users to the following site group**, select a site group.

6. Click **OK**.

Controlling Anonymous Access to a Website

If you want users to be able to contribute to your site anonymously, you can configure your site to allow anonymous access. Anonymous access is used to allow users to browse sites without authenticating (a standard Internet scenario), respond anonymously to surveys, or even contribute to a list or document library anonymously.

Anonymous access relies on the anonymous user account on your Web server. This account is created and maintained by your Web server (Internet Information Services [IIS]), not by Windows SharePoint Services. On IIS, the anonymous user account is usually IUSR_*ComputerName*. When you enable anonymous access in Windows SharePoint Services, you are enabling that user account for your website.

Enabling Anonymous Access

Anonymous access is disabled by default and is controlled at the site level. If you want to allow anonymous access (such as for an Internet site, where you want visitors to be able to browse without authenticating), you must enable anonymous access by assigning rights to the anonymous user. To enable anonymous access, you must first be sure that IIS is configured to allow anonymous access, and then on the Site Settings pages for your website, you can enable anonymous access.

To allow anonymous access for a virtual server in Internet Information Services

1. Click **Start**, point to **All Programs**, point to **Administrative Tools**, and then click **Internet Information Services (IIS) Manager**.

2. Right-click the virtual server you want to enable anonymous access for, and then click **Properties**.

3. Click the **Directory Security** tab.

4. In the **Authentication and access control** section, click **Edit**.

   The Authentication Methods dialog box appears.

5. Select the **Enable anonymous access** check box. (See Figure 16-22.)

6. Click **OK** to close the **Authentication Methods** dialog box.

7. Click **OK** to close the **Properties** dialog box.

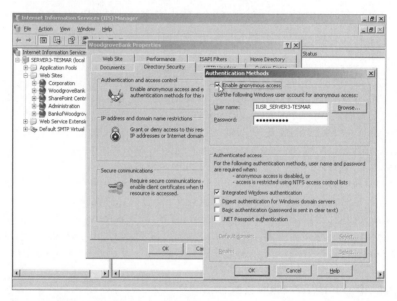

Figure 16-22   Enabling anonymous access

You might need to restart IIS for this change to take effect. After anonymous access has been turned on for the virtual server in IIS, you can enable anonymous access for a specific top-level website.

To enable anonymous access for a top-level website

1. On your site, click **Site Settings**.

2. Under **Administration**, click **Go to Site Administration**.

3. On the Site Administration page, under **Users and Permissions**, click **Manage anonymous access**.

4. In the **Anonymous Access** section (shown in Figure 16-23), select a level of access to allow:

   ■ **Entire Web site**

   ■ **Lists and libraries**

   ■ **Nothing**

5. Click **OK**.

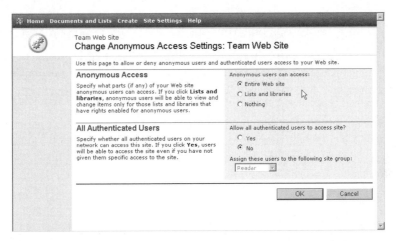

Figure 16-23   Changing anonymous access settings: team website

Per-List Permissions and Anonymous Access

You can control anonymous access for your entire site by using the Manage Anonymous Access page, or you can control anonymous access for specific lists by using the per-list permissions feature. If anonymous access is disabled for your site, it cannot be enabled for a particular list in the site.

To enable anonymous access for a list

Verify that anonymous access is enabled for your site by performing the following steps:

1. Navigate to the list, and then in the left pane, click **Modify settings and columns**.

2. In the **General Settings** section, click **Change permissions for this <list/ document library>**.

3. On the left of the screen under **Actions**, click on **Change anonymous access**.

4. Select the level of permissions to give anonymous users, and then click **OK**.

Creating Unique Permissions for a Subsite

When you create a subsite, you can choose whether to inherit the permissions from the parent website or to create unique permissions for your subsite. (See Figure 16-24.) Depending on your choice, you get one of the following results:

- If you choose unique permissions, the default site groups are created (Guest, Reader, Contributor, Web Designer) but are not populated. The Administrator site group is also created, and the subsite creator is assigned to this site group. You can add users to the subsite and assign them to site groups, and they will have permissions only on your subsite, not on the parent website.

- If you choose to inherit permissions, all the security from the parent website is used for the subsite, with the exception of per-list permissions. If you add a user to a list, the user is added to the parent website.

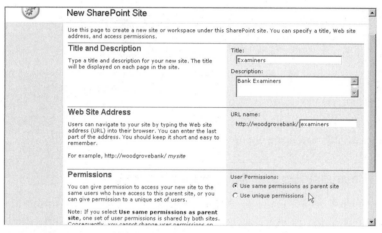

Figure 16-24   Subsite permissions

Switching to a Different Permissions Model

If you set up your subsite with unique permissions but find that you need to share permissions with your parent website instead, you can switch to inherited permissions. There are some drawbacks to making this switch, however, such as:

- Switching from unique to inherited permissions is not reversible. The users and site groups from your subsite are deleted when you switch to inherited, and your subsite reverts to the permissions set for the parent website.

- Items that have per-list permissions set lose those permissions. All lists revert to the site-wide permissions.

You can also switch from using inherited permissions to using unique permissions. In this case, the transition is simpler. The current permissions are duplicated when you switch, and the link to the parent website's permissions structure is broken.

From that point on, any changes you make to the permissions affect only the sub-site. When you switch from inherited to unique permissions, per-list permission settings remain intact.

> **Note**   Switching between permissions models can create some strange scenarios. For example, any user who has the Create Subsites right can create a subsite. By default, this right is included only in the Administrator site group, but if you assign it to another site group, members of that group can create subsites with unique permissions and become administrators of the new subsites. If such a user then chooses to switch to using the parent website's permissions, the user will no longer be an administrator of the subsite.

You use the Site Settings page for your subsite to switch to a different permissions model.

To set unique permissions by using HTML Administration pages

1. On the subsite, click **Site Settings**.

2. Under **Administration**, click **Go to Site Administration**.

3. On the Site Administration page, under **Users and Permissions**, click **Manage permission inheritance**.

4. In the **Permissions** section, select **Use unique permissions**.

5. Click **OK**.

If you want to return to using the same permissions as the parent website, you can also change back by using HTML Administration pages.

Managing Site Creation Rights

By default, when Self-Service Site Creation is enabled, all members of the Reader, Contributor, Web Designer, and Administrator site groups have the Use Self-Service Site Creation right. They can use this right to create a top-level website on a virtual server from the Create Web Site page. Another right, the Create Subsites right, is available to members of the Administrator site group by default. This right allows the user to create a subsite or a workspace site from the Create page or the Manage Sites And Workspaces page.

You control which users have the Use Self-Service Site Creation right by changing the rights in a site group. You can control which users have the ability to create sites and workspace sites by changing which site groups have the Create Subsites right, or by using the Enable Site And Workspace Creation page in Site Settings. You must be a member of the Administrator site group for a site to control these rights.

For detailed instructions on how to implement Self-Service Site Creation, see Chapter 15, "Configuring Windows SharePoint Services."

Security and User Rights

User rights grant users the ability to perform certain actions on a website and restrict other users from performing those actions. Some rights do not completely restrict certain actions. The Apply Themes And Borders and Apply Style Sheets rights allow users to make changes to an entire website. Any user with the Add And Customize Pages right, however, can perform the same changes on a page-by-page basis in the actual HTML code. Be aware that if you give a user the Add And Customize Pages right (by assigning them to a site group that contains the right), you are also giving them the ability to change the theme, border, and style sheets for individual pages in your website.

When you assign rights to site groups, be sure to assign the appropriate rights, and do not unintentionally allow members of the site group to perform more actions than you want on your website. Conversely, be sure that members of the site group are not unintentionally restricted from performing the actions they need to perform.

Statistics

If you want to know what kind of impact your website has, you need to track how many users visit your site, the type and number of hits your site receives, and other site-usage information. Microsoft Windows SharePoint Services includes features that analyze the usage of your site. Summary and detailed usage reports supply information such as the following:

- Number of page hits for each individual page
- Number of unique users
- Browser and operating system information
- Referring domains and URLs

Analyzing Website Usage

Tracking usage information can be useful for identifying which content on your site is heavily used (and therefore should be kept) and which content is not being heavily used (and might be a candidate for archiving). In addition, it shows the sort of information your visitors are most interested in so that you know where to invest your future efforts. You can also keep track of how much storage space your site is taking up and the level of activity your site is generating. This information is gathered as part of the quota tracking for sites.

The usage reports rely on usage log data gathered from the websites and stored in the content databases for each virtual server. The log data is a summary record of transactions on your website. When you view a usage report in Windows SharePoint Services, the data is arranged into a list format. You must be a member of the administrator role (or have the View Usage Data right) for a site to view the site usage statistics.

To configure usage analysis processing for a server

1. Click **Start**, point to **All Programs**, point to **Administrative Tools**, and then click **SharePoint Central Administration**.

2. Under **Component Configuration**, click **Configure usage analysis processing**.

3. In the **Logging Settings** section, select the **Enable logging** check box.

4. In the **Log file location** box, type the location to store the log file.

    The default location for the log file is %Windir%\system32\LogFiles\STS.

5. In the **Number of log files to create** box, type a number from **1** to **30**.

    In general, you should use a number that is one to three times the number of database servers in your server farm, with a maximum number of 30 log files. However, note that more log files will increase the traffic load on the servers, thereby potentially degrading performance. It is actually the traffic on the server and sites that will dictate the size of the log files, so this is the main factor to consider when deciding how many log files to create.

6. In the **Processing Settings** section, select the **Enable usage analysis processing** check box.

7. Under **Run processing between these times daily**, specify the range of times to start the usage analysis log processing. In the **Start** box, select the earliest time of day to begin running log processing. In the **End** box, select the latest time to begin running log processing.

8. Click **OK**. (See Figure 16-25.)

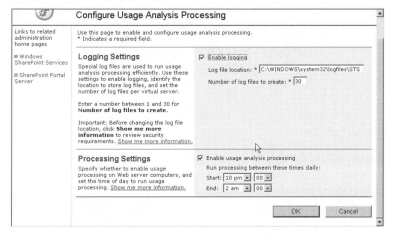

Figure 16-25   Configuring usage analysis processing

You can view a Site Usage Report about a site from the Site Administration page. (See Figure 16-26.)

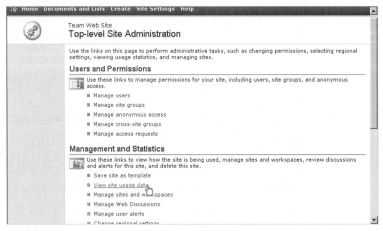

Figure 16-26   Viewing site usage data

To view site usage report data

1. On the site you want to view data for, click **Site Settings**.

2. Under **Administration**, click **Go to Site Administration**.

3. Under **Management and Statistics**, click **View site usage data**.

You can view the quota settings for an entire site collection. Note that this feature is not available at the subsite level.

To view quota settings for a site collection

1. From the portal, click **Site Settings**.

2. Click **Go to SharePoint Portal Server central administration**.

3. Click **Windows SharePoint Services** in the left window pane.

4. Under **Component Configuration**, click on **Manage quotas and locks**.

5. Click **Manage site collection quotas and locks**.

6. Type the URL of the top-level website, and click **View Data**.

   Two new fields will be revealed to you: Site Lock Information and Site Quota Information.

To view usage data and quota information for a site collection

1. On the top-level website of the site collection, click **Site Settings**.

2. Under **Administration**, click **Go to Site Administration**.

3. Under **Site Collection Administration**, click **View site collection usage summary**.

This page will also show you the amount of disk space used by the content in the site collection as well as the total number of users who have been added to the site collection.

Managing Alerts

Because websites based on Microsoft Windows SharePoint Services are meant to help groups of users work together, they tend to grow quickly and change often. Keeping up with these changes can be difficult for users, especially if they aren't checking on the site every day. To help users stay in touch with changes on a site, Windows SharePoint Services includes a feature called alerts, an e-mail notification service. When documents, lists, or items in a list on a server running Windows SharePoint Services are created, modified, or deleted, users who sign up for alerts receive messages informing them that changes have been made.

> **Note** Before alerts can work for a particular site, the e-mail server settings must be configured at the server or virtual-server level. In SharePoint Team Services from Microsoft, alerts were called *Web subscriptions*, but the functionality has not changed significantly.

Users can create alerts to track items within a site, such as:

- **Lists.** Users are notified of changes to the list, such as when an item is added, deleted, or changed in a list.

- **List items.** Users are notified of changes to a particular item in a list.

- **Document libraries.** Users are notified of changes to the document library, such as when a document is added, deleted, or changed in a document library or when Web discussions are added, changed, deleted, or closed.

- **Documents.** Users are notified of changes in a particular document or when Web discussions are added, changed, deleted, or closed.

When a user creates an alert for one of these items, he can specify what types of events will trigger an alert. Alerts can be generated whenever a document or list item is added, updated, or deleted in a document library or list, or when a Web discussion on a document or list changes. Users can specify one of these events or select all of them to be notified whenever anything changes on the list, list item, document, or document library they want to track.

Users also have the ability to decide how often they want to receive alerts: immediately, daily, or weekly. Immediate alerts are sent as individual e-mail messages, and daily or weekly alerts are combined into summary messages for the entire website.

Users can change their alerts by using the My Alerts On This Site link on the Site Settings page of their website. (See Figure 16-27.)

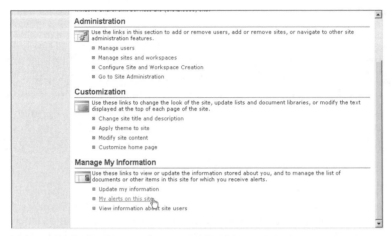

Administration

Use the links in this section to add or remove users, add or remove sites, or navigate to other site administration features.

⊠ Manage users

⊠ Manage sites and workspaces

⊠ Configure Site and Workspace Creation

⊠ Go to Site Administration

Customization

Use these links to change the look of the site, update lists and document libraries, or modify the text displayed at the top of each page of the site.

⊠ Change site title and description

⊠ Apply theme to site

⊠ Modify site content

⊠ Customize home page

Manage My Information

Use these links to view or update the information stored about you, and to manage the list of documents or other items in this site for which you receive alerts.

⊠ Update my information

⊠ My alerts on this site

⊠ View information about site users

Figure 16-27   Setting up alerts with HTML Administration pages

Note   A user must have the View Items right (included in the Contributor and Reader site groups by default) to sign up for alerts.

To configure alerts at the virtual-server level

1. From the portal page, click **Site Settings**.

2. Under **General Settings**, click **Go to SharePoint Portal Server central administration**.

3. Under **Portal Site and Virtual Server Configuration**, click **Configure virtual server settings from the Virtual Server List page**.

4. On the next screen, which is the Virtual Server List page, click the name of the virtual server you want to configure.

5. Under **Virtual Server Management**, click **Virtual server general settings**.

6. Under **Alerts**, turn on the alerts for this virtual server and specify either unlimited or the maximum number of alerts that a user can create.

To configure e-mail settings at the virtual-server level

1. From the Portal site, click **Site Settings**.

2. Under **General Settings**, click **Go to SharePoint Portal Server central administration**.

3. In the left window pane, click **Windows SharePoint Services**.

4. Under **Server Configuration**, click **Configure default e-mail server settings**.

5. Specify the **Outbound SMTP server, From e-mail address**, and **Reply-to-e-mail address** settings.

6. Click **OK**.

Customizing the Message Text for Alerts

For Windows SharePoint Services, you can customize the contents of the alert messages. Keep in mind that while you can alter the contents of the message, there is still no mechanism for identifying and extracting exact text changes within a document or list item. You can, however, customize the text in the message and re-order, add, and remove fields from the message.

> **Note**   You must be an administrator on the local server computer to edit the XML templates for Windows SharePoint Services.

The message text for immediate, daily, and weekly alerts is based on content in a series of XML templates on the server computer. To customize the message text, you must edit the XML templates that contain the message text. The templates are stored on the front-end Web server at \\Program Files\Common Files\Microsoft Shared\Web Server Extensions\60\Template*LCID*\XML, where *LCID* is the locale ID. (See Figure 16-28.)

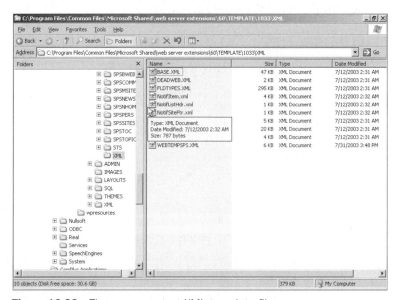

Figure 16-28   The message text XML template files

Table 16-2 shows the parts of an e-mail alert for immediate notification of changes to a list item and which part each XML file constructs.

Table 16-2   Immediate E-mail Notifications Constructed by XML Files

XML File	Displayed Content
NotifSiteHdr.xml	Alert result http://*Server_Name*/sites/*Site_Name* - *Site_Display_Name*
NotifListHdr.xml	*List_Display_Name* Summary
NotifItem.xml	*File_Name* was modified by *User_Name* at 10/12/2003 8:01 P.M.
NotifSiteFtr.xml	Go to My Alerts to edit, delete, or view your alerts.

To create a custom message for an alert, make customizations to the appropriate XML file as indicated in Table 16-2.

> **Caution**   Editing any of the XML templates for Windows SharePoint Services can break the templates and, consequently, break the mechanism for sending alerts. Be sure to edit only the message text in the template and keep a backup copy of the original templates in case you need to revert to the originals. For more information about customizing XML templates, see the Windows SharePoint Services Software Development Kit.

You can edit the XML templates to include any of the tags shown in Table 16-3.

Table 16-3   Tags for Use in XML Message Text Files

Tag	Description
AlertFrequency	The time interval for sending an alert. Possible values include 0 (immediate), 1 (daily), or 2 (weekly).
EventType	The type of event. Possible values include 1 (item added), 2 (item modified), 4 (item deleted), 16 (discussion added), 32 (discussion modified), 64 (discussion deleted), 128 (discussion closed), and 256 (discussion activated).
ItemName	The title of the item.
ItemUrl	The absolute URL for the item.
ListName	The name of the list.
ListUrl	The absolute URL for the list.
ModifiedBy	The display name of the user who modified the item.
MySubsUrl	The absolute URL for the My Alerts On This Site page in Site Settings.

Table 16-3   Tags for Use in XML Message Text Files   *(continued)*

Tag	Description
SiteLanguage	The locale identifier (LCID) for the language used on the site. For example, 1033 is the LCID for U.S. English.
SiteName	The title of the site.
SiteUrl	The absolute URL for the site.
TimeLastModified	The time at which the item was last modified.

You can use any XML editing tool, such as Notepad, to edit the templates. Keep in mind that any changes you make to this message text are used for all alert messages sent to all users of your server. If you are in a server farm environment, you must edit the templates on each server in the server farm or copy the edited templates to each server in the server farm. You must be an administrator of the local server computer to edit the XML templates for Windows SharePoint Services.

Note   In the XML templates, you use numerical values instead of text to specify frequency and event types. So, if you want to set the AlertFrequency to weekly, you would use the value 2 in the template rather than typing "weekly". See the description column in Table 16-3 for the tag named AlertFrequency.

Configuring and Managing Alerts

You can view alerts for a website or subsite and delete alerts that are no longer needed. If you are a server administrator or a member of the SharePoint administrators group, you can use SharePoint Central Administration pages to configure settings for alerts, such as the following:

- View alert settings.
- Turn alerts on or off.
- Specify how many alerts users can create.

You can also use the Stsadm.exe command-line tool to configure alert settings if you are a server administrator. Using the command line, you can do the following:

- Turn alerts on or off.
- Specify how many alerts users can create.

Alerts use the Windows SharePoint Services e-mail settings to send alert items. When you configure alert settings, be sure that you also double-check the e-mail settings for your virtual server. For step-by-step instructions, see the "To configure alerts at the virtual-server level" section earlier in the chapter.

Managing Alerts with HTML Administration

You can use HTML Administration pages to view and delete alerts on your site. To manage alerts, you use the Manage User Alerts page in the Site Administration pages.

1. On the Site Settings page for the website, under Administration, click **Go to Site Administration**.

2. Under **Management and Statistics**, click **Manage user alerts**.

3. On the Manage User Alerts page, select a user name in the **Display alerts for __ box**, and then click **Update**.

4. To delete an alert, select the check box next to the alert, and then click **Delete Selected Alerts**.

Configuring Alerts for a Virtual Server

You can also change alert settings for a virtual server. Changes you make on the virtual server affect all websites under that virtual server. To change settings for a virtual server, you use commands on the Virtual Server Settings page. You must be a member of the SharePoint administrators group or an administrator of the local computer to change virtual server settings.

1. On the server that contains the virtual server, click **Start**, point to **All Programs**, point to **Administrative Tools**, and then click **SharePoint Central Administration**.

2. On the Central Administration page, under **Virtual Server Configuration**, click **Configure virtual server settings**.

3. On the Virtual Server List page, click the virtual server you want to configure.

4. On the Virtual Server Settings page, under **Virtual Server Management**, click **Virtual server general settings**.

5. In the **Alerts** section, next to **Alerts on this server are**, click **On** or **Off**.

6. Under **Maximum Number of alerts that a user can create**, specify a number of alerts. If you want users to be able to create as many alerts as they want, select **Unlimited number**.

7. Click **OK**.

Using the Command Line to Configure Alerts

You can manage alerts from the command line by using the GetProperty and SetProperty operations with Stsadm.exe. You can set the properties shown in Table 16-4 to configure how alerts work.

Table 16-4   Properties for the Stsadm.exe Command-Line Utility

Property	Description
alerts-enabled	Turn alerts on or off.
alerts-limited	Specify whether users are limited to a specific number of alerts.
alerts-maximum	Specify the maximum number of alerts users can create.
job-immediate-notification	Specify how often to check for immediate alerts (in minutes).
job-daily-notification	Specify the time of day (using a 24-hour clock) to send out daily alerts.
job-weekly-notification	Specify the day of the week and time of day (using a 24-hour clock) to send out weekly alerts.

The following example shows the syntax to use to turn off alerts:

```
Stsadm.exe -o setproperty -p <port> -pn alerts-enabled -pv false
```

Summary

In this chapter, we have covered a number ways you can administer and manage your websites. You have learned how to create sites and subsites. We have addressed the various templates you can use as you create new sites and the features each will provide by default. You should have a good understanding of the default site groups and the 20 rights that you can assign to those groups. We have talked about various access methods, including setting up anonymous access for sites that will be used by the public at large. We covered setting up alerts so that you or others can be notified when content on a website or in a specific document library changes. Finally, we briefly addressed how to set up website usage analysis so that you can identify which content on your sites is heavily used to aid in your planning for performance.

As we have discussed each item, we've identified how to do the task from the HTML Administration pages and, in most cases, have indicated how to complete the same task with the command-line utility, stsadm.exe.

This chapter is by no means exhaustive of all that you will eventually want to know about administering your websites, but it should be a great springboard to launch most of your administrative tasks.

Part VI

Administration of Microsoft Office SharePoint Portal Server 2003

Chapter 17

Configuring SharePoint Portal Server 2003

As a classic example of a multitiered distributed architecture, Microsoft Office Share-Point Portal Server 2003 presents some unique administration requirements. While the administration tools provided with Microsoft Windows SharePoint Services discussed in the previous two chapters serve to configure and manage each server individually, they do not suffice when faced with the multitude of servers that are usually involved in using SharePoint Portal Server 2003. If multiple database servers, Web servers, and other component servers are present in this environment, each will require a single place to go that allows for configuration and management of the individual servers and of the farm as a whole.

The Web-based tool provided with SharePoint Portal Server 2003 is called Share-Point Central Administration. By maintaining a list of all portal sites in the farm, this tool allows the administrator to configure the many services provided by each portal site on a per-portal-site basis. Furthermore, by using the list of all servers in the farm, the administrator is able to quickly navigate to those servers to perform server-level management of the servers' portal site services. It also allows the administrator to perform ongoing management tasks such as portal site management, which includes site content and security administration, user profile and personal site management, audience creation and management, as well as search and index management.

This chapter will concentrate on showing the portal site configuration tasks an administrator will have to perform both after installation and on an ongoing basis as new servers are added or removed from the farm. This will include the configuration of virtual servers and the subsequent creation of portal sites on those virtual servers.

A Quick System Overview

To properly set the stage for what the administrator does in configuring SharePoint Portal Server 2003, let us review the many component services that provide the product with its functionality. A total of four types of servers are part of a server farm for which configuration tasks must be performed:

- **Web.**   This type of server receives HTTP requests from the client community and serves the portal site content in the form of Web Pages.

- **Index.**   These servers crawl all portal site content, as well as chosen external content, and created index files used when users utilize the search feature of the portal site.

- **Search.**   This type of server receives queries from users' search requests, handles the queries by using the index files created by the index servers, and returns the matching results.

- **Job.**   This server coordinates scheduled jobs, such as content crawls by the index server or profile imports from Active Directory.

Additionally, there are three more server types that provide support services to the farm:

- **Database Server.**   All portal site configuration information, site security settings, and content is stored in multiple databases in one or more required database servers.

- **E-Mail Server.**   These optional servers will relay alert messages from the portal site to administrators and users.

- **HTML Viewer Server.**   This optional type of server installed from the Office 2003 Resource Kit can be set up to convert standard Microsoft Office documents to HTML on behalf of users who do not have Microsoft Office or the Office Viewers installed.

To qualify as a potential Web, index, search, or job server in the farm, each of these types of servers will need to have SharePoint Portal Server 2003 installed on them. Not only must each server be assigned its role in the farm, but each service that the server will provide must also be configured and tailored to the specific environment to achieve the desired effect.

SharePoint Central Administration

After installing SharePoint Portal Server 2003, you might notice that you do not yet have a working portal site. You will have to designate all the server types just mentioned and configure their services before you can create a portal site.

The install does create an administration website on the server. This is the site from which the SharePoint Portal Server Central Administration Web pages are served via Internet Information Services (IIS). During installation, a random port is generated for this administration website as a simple form of security and to avoid using port 80, which will be needed for the actual portal site users will access. Therefore, to administer a portal site through a server named *woodgrove* on which the administration website was installed on port 9999, the administrator would use the following URL in his browser to navigate to the main portal site administration page: *http://woodgrove:9999/sps/*. Figure 17-1 depicts the SharePoint Portal Server Central Administration Web page displayed in the browser for this scenario.

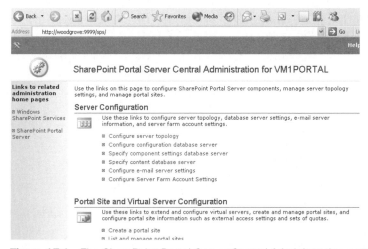

Figure 17-1   The SharePoint Portal Server Central Administration page

There are two considerations with this random port assignment: first, this means that each server for the portal site has a different administration port; second, you might need to secure this port. Even though only user accounts armed with the knowledge of the random portal site and with appropriate administrator privileges can modify settings, all traffic is still unencrypted between the administrator's workstation and the server being managed. This can be an issue in your environment because some configuration pages require assigning service accounts and their passwords.

To resolve the first problem, we want to simplify remote administration by changing the port number so that it is consistent on all servers on the server farm. This allows the administrator to type the URL for the central administration pages without going through the Site Settings page for each server. You will need to be logged on as a member of the local administrator's group to perform these tasks.

Standardize the port number for the Central Administration pages

1. Open a command prompt.

2. Navigate to **%Program Files%\Common Files\Microsoft Shared\web server extensions\60\BIN**.

3. Type **stsadm.exe -o setadminport -port** *port_number*, and then press **Enter**.

   For example, to specify 8088 as the common port, type
   stsadm.exe -o setadminport -port 8088

4. Close the command prompt.

5. Update the shortcut for SharePoint Central Administration on the **All Programs** menu for other servers. Do this by using the following steps:

   a. On the taskbar, click **Start**, point to **All Programs**, point to **SharePoint Portal Server**, and then point to **SharePoint Central Administration**.

   b. Right-click **SharePoint Central Administration**, and then click **Properties**.

   c. On the **Web Document** tab, in the **URL** box, replace the existing port number with the updated port number.

   For example, if the updated port number is 8088 and the existing URL is *http://localhost:10505/sps/Default.aspx*, change 10505 to **8088** so that the URL is *http://localhost:8088/sps/Default.aspx*.

   d. Click **OK**.

Keep in mind that this affects the port for the Windows SharePoint Services Central Administration pages as well because they are served out of the same virtual server.

To resolve the security issue, encryption is required and available by configuring IIS with a security certificate and then configuring the administration website to require a secure channel with Secure Sockets Layer (SSL). Refer to the SharePoint Portal Server 2003 documentation on Office Online at *http://office.microsoft.com/home/default.aspx* for details on how to set this up. Assuming that the SSL certificate is already installed on the servers, the following command will set all servers for the portal site to require SSL when accessing the administration pages:

```
stsadm.exe -o -setadminport -ssl
```

Granting Administrative Access to the Portal Server Farm

One of the first configurations relating to a portal server that you need to understand and set is administrative access control. There are two high-level administrator types for a portal site.

Users who are members of the local Administrators group on a portal server have full administrative access to the server's configuration and potentially all the portal site's content. If the user has Administrators group membership on a portal server that is playing the Web front-end server role, that user will be able to access all content and perform all site administration tasks. On non-front-end Web servers, such members are able to determine settings for the entire farm of servers with respect to their farm service roles simply by navigating to the SharePoint Portal Central Administration page on that server.

Another way to grant portal site administrator privilege to a user is to assign user accounts (or group accounts) to what is called the SharePoint administrators group account. The account is defined by navigating to the Set SharePoint Administrative Group Account link found in the Security Configuration section of the SharePoint Portal Server Central Administration page. Even though the location implies a user account, in actuality, any Active Directory account can be assigned here, including group accounts.

> **Tip** It is considered a best practice to assign an Active Directory Global Group account as the SharePoint administrators group account to avoid accidentally losing administrative access should the user account be deleted.

There are a few tasks that a user associated to the SharePoint administrators group account cannot perform. Following is a list of tasks that only the local administrator can perform:

- Extend or unextend a virtual server
- Change the SharePoint administrators group
- Manage paths (inclusions and exclusions)
- Change the configuration database

The SharePoint Portal Server Central Administration Page

The main SharePoint Portal Server Central Administration page has four categories of links leading to appropriate configuration subpages. These categories and links allow for configuration of each of the components' servers, services, and features that relate to the functionality of the farm. The four categories are Server Configuration, Portal Site and Virtual Server Configuration, Security Configuration, and Component Configuration. The remainder of this chapter will be organized by these categories. The Portal Site and Virtual Server Configuration links will be covered last as part of an overall discussion on virtual servers as they relate to portal site creation.

Server Configuration

The Server Configuration category of links is used to configure server topology such as Web, index, search, and job server assignments; database server settings; e-mail server information; and server farm account settings. This area, depicted in Figure 17-2, is the first area to go to every time a new server is added to the server farm.

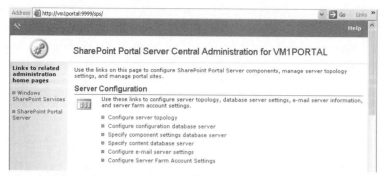

Figure 17-2 The Server Configuration links on the SharePoint Portal Server Central Administration page

Configure Server Topology

This link is to a page that is used to view and assign the components of SharePoint Portal Server for each server in the farm and to remove servers from the farm. This page also allows administrators to change the components that servers in the farm will service. In effect, the four server types discussed earlier are defined by assigning respective servers one or more components to service. For example, a Job Server is defined by assigning to it the Job service component.

There are three main sections to the Configure Server Topology page: Database Server Settings, Component Assignments, and Problems With This Configuration. Figure 17-3 shows the first two sections of the page.

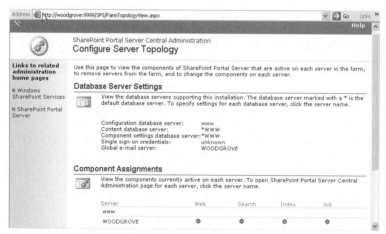

Figure 17-3 The Configure Server Topology page, which is used for component assignment

Database Server Settings

Because everything, including configuration, is stored in a database, it makes sense to have to configure database settings first. There are four databases that are used in the portal site, but only the first three are configurable with respect to which SQL Server will host that database. Following is an explanation of those three databases and a few other items appearing in this section of the Configure Server Topology page:

- **Configuration Database Server.** The configuration database maintains connections between servers and content databases, stores server settings, and identifies which content is to be provided by which virtual servers. There is one configuration database per stand-alone server or per server farm. Each server in the farm must be associated with the configuration database by connecting it to that database. The default name of the database is *SPS_01_Config*.

  Typically, the page will already display the server assigned during the product's post-installation Portal Configuration Wizard. Therefore, clicking the listed server will show a page displaying the name of the existing configuration database (as well as the database server name). Also, the option of disconnecting the managed server from that database will be displayed. This is the preferred method for removing a server running SharePoint Portal Server from the server farm.

- **Content Database Server.** The content database is where all portal site content will be placed. By default, the server hosting the portal site content database is the same as the configuration database. This can be changed here to distribute the database load. Also, because the portal site will have many sites—and potentially thousands—more than one database on more than one server can be manually defined. However, only one server is designated as the default database server on whose databases new sites will be created. When you create a new site, the databases on the designated default database server are queried and the new site's content is added to the database that has the most available space. The default database name for the first portal site content database is composed of the first eight characters of the first portal site's name, followed by a number, and followed by _SITE. For example, if the portal site is named Woodgrove, the content database would be *Woodgrov1_SITE*. Keep in mind that even though this is the default database used for both portal and team sites, a separate database can be defined and used to contain team sites.

- **Component Settings Database Server.** This database stores service information for each portal site in a deployment. For example, each time SharePoint Portal Server 2003 updates an index, it creates a gatherer log entry in a table in the component settings database for the portal site. The default database name will start the same way as the content database but end with _SERV. Using the same example as in the previous paragraph, the database would be named *Woodgrov1_SERV*.

- **Profile Database Server.** The profile database is used to store the content for the My Site feature, which gives each portal site user a personal site. It will always default to the same server as the configuration database server and cannot be changed here. This database name will end with _PROF. Using the same example as before, the database would be named *Woodgrov1_PROF*.

- **Global E-Mail Server.** Even though this is not a database server, it appears in this section and should be configured for the farm. The farm can operate without having an e-mail server defined; however, the alert feature will not function. The alert feature allows users to subscribe to lists and documents and be alerted via e-mail when those lists or documents change. The configuration page allows you to set the SMTP e-mail server name or IP address (which can be Microsoft Exchange, the IIS SMTP service, or any third-party SMTP server that accepts Anonymous connections) that the alerts should show the change notification as coming from and to whom replies will be sent, as well as the character set used for the e-mails. Keep in mind that this is a global setting for the farm. If a certain server needs to be pointed to a different e-mail server (such as for a portal server residing outside of a firewall), that server can have its e-mail server setting changed on its Windows SharePoint Services Central Administration page.

- **Single Sign-On Credentials.** If you are wondering about Single Sign-On credentials, they too do not have anything to do with databases and are configured with an optional setting used in highly customized portal site implementations. Single Sign-On allows you to store and map an application's account credentials to user account credentials. This prevents users from having to sign on again when portal-based applications retrieve information from business applications, such as third-party enterprise resource planning and customer relations management (CRM) systems.

By using Single Sign-On, you can centralize information from multiple back-end applications through a single portal site that uses application definitions. By using application definitions, you can minimize and automate the sign-on process to these applications in a more secure environment. In addition, SharePoint Portal Server 2003 provides an easy interface for developers to create and extend this feature.

Component Assignments

The Component Assignments area lists all servers that have been assigned some role in the server farm. Servers that are assigned as database servers or e-mail servers will not have a hyperlink, while servers that play one of the following key component roles will have a hyperlink: Web, Search, Index, and Job. This makes sense because the hyperlink leads to the SharePoint Central Administration pages as serviced by the virtual server on that server, which of course requires SharePoint Portal Server 2003 to be installed on that server.

To assign or change the component roles that the listed servers will play, click the Change Components button at the bottom of the page. This can be useful if, for example, you add servers to your server farm. You add a server to the farm by first installing SharePoint Portal Server 2003 on the server. You will then be able to see it as a server to which you can assign one of the four component roles (Web, Search, Index, or Job).

You will need to have at least one Web server to service the client HTTP requests and serve out the portal site content. Because a portal site needs to offer search capability, you will have to assign at least one index server to create indexes from the content it crawls and one search server to handle the client requests using these indexes. Finally, you will need to assign one job server to handle scheduling of the index crawls among other services. All four roles must be assigned to a server before a portal site can be created.

To change component assignments for the server farm

1. On the SharePoint Portal Server Central Administration For *server_name* page, in the **Server Configuration** section, click **Configure server topology**.

2. On the Configure Server Topology page, click **Change Components**.

3. On the Change Component Assignments page, in the **Component Assignment** section, do one of the following:

    - Select a check box to assign a component to a server.

    - You can assign more than one component to each server.

    - Clear a check box to remove the assignment of a component to a server.

4. In the **Job Server Component** section, in the **Job server** list, select a job server.

5. If you have installed the server component for backward-compatible document libraries, in the **Document Library Server Component (Optional)** section, in the **Document library server** box, type the URL of the server to run the document library server component.

6. If you are not using SSL, the URL should be of the form http://*server_name* or *server_name*.

7. If SSL is enabled or enforced on the document library server, the URL must be an https address (for example, https://*server_name*).

8. Click **OK**.

In a single-server scenario, one server plays all roles. However, in larger environments you will want to distribute the services for availability and performance reasons. Refer to Chapter 9, "Capacity Planning," to determine how many servers of each server type you will need. Also refer to Chapter 12, "Deploying Medium and Large Server Farms," for additional details on recommended server role configuration scenarios.

Problems With This Configuration

Found at the bottom of the Configure Server Topology page, the Problems With This Configuration section simply provides reminders of any missing server-role component configurations. If all required components have been configured, you will see the following message:

"There are no issues at this time. Your farm is fine."

Otherwise, you will see messages reminding you of configuration tasks you should perform.

One last item to cover on this page is the Remove Server button. Click this button to remove servers from the farm only in the following situations:

■ The server does not have SharePoint Portal Server installed on it.

■ The server running SharePoint Portal Server is unresponsive or offline.

■ The server is running the optional component for backward-compatible document libraries only.

Before you remove a server from the server farm, you must remove all dependencies from the server, unless it is the last computer remaining in the server farm.

Configure Server Farm Account Settings

This is a very important page, as it relates to the user accounts used by the various services to perform their tasks as well as to some connectivity settings the services might need. If you are wondering why we've skipped the four links following the Configure Server Topology link in the Server Configuration section of the SharePoint Portal Server Central Administration page, it is because navigating to them will show that they point to the same configurations discussed on the Configure Server Topology page.

You can configure the following settings on the Configure Server Farm Account Settings page:

Contact E-mail Address

As part of the HTTP header in the requests it makes to crawl content, SharePoint Portal Server 2003 provides an e-mail address to each website it crawls when creating an index. If a problem occurs while crawling (for example, the crawler is hitting the site too much), the administrator of the website can contact this address. All portal sites on the server provide this e-mail address to the crawled site while creating indices. For this reason, the e-mail address for the server farm administrator is typically specified.

Configuration Database Administration Account

The configuration database administration account is the user name and password that SharePoint Portal Server uses when connecting to the configuration database or when propagating full-text indexes from index management servers to search servers.

At a minimum, this account must be a member of the Power Users local group on all the front-end Web servers, index management servers, and search servers. This account must also be a member of the local Administrators group on the document library server. In addition, this account must be a member of the Security Administrators and Database Creators server roles on Microsoft SQL Server.

Default Content Access Account

The default content access account is the user name and password used by the index component servers to crawl content outside the portal site. There are many aspects to consider when choosing this account, including the following ones:

- When SharePoint Portal Server connects to external servers to create content indexes of sites hosted on the external Internet server, it connects to those servers by first providing the default content access account to establish a connection. If this account has not been configured, SharePoint Portal Server provides the anonymous account. The account used must have Read permissions for the websites and servers being crawled.

- If there is a proxy server to pass through to get out to the Internet to crawl external content, the account mentioned above must have proxy permissions on the proxy server to browse externally to be able to crawl the sites and create a content index of these Internet sites. Without permissions, the index servers can crawl only content on the local intranet.

- The access account should be a member of the SharePoint administrators group. If the access account is not a member of the SharePoint administrators group, the server will crawl the site but the content index will not be secure because all users will be able to access the documents. In the case of intranet crawls, it means that some data might not be included in the content index because the account might not be able to access all the sites under a Windows SharePoint Services site.

Portal Site Application Pool Identity

This account is used by the default application pool (MSSharePointPortalAppPool) created by SharePoint Portal Server to contain all portal sites. It is the account used by the application pool to do the initial lookup to determine which content database stores the user-requested URL's data. It is also used to access the indices on search servers, and it plays a role in importing data from Active Directory if the Profile Import feature is enabled.

The following is a list of security considerations for this account:

- In a multiserver portal site, the account must be a domain account and must have the db_owner role on the Configuration Database.

- This account must be a member of the local Administrators group on document library servers.

Proxy Server Settings

With this link, you can set SharePoint Portal Server 2003 index servers to use a proxy server when they create crawls of external websites so that they can create full-text indexes of those sites. Proxy servers are generally used to enhance the security of intranets by working along with a firewall to prevent unauthorized access in from or out to the Internet. Proxy servers can also enhance performance by caching recently accessed Web pages, which minimizes download time.

By default, SharePoint Portal Server uses the proxy server setting defined for the default content access account. The default content access account derives its proxy server setting from the current proxy server settings in the Microsoft Internet Explorer application on the crawling server.

Changes to the proxy settings for the SharePoint Portal Server computer do not affect other applications on the server. For example, configuring the server to use a proxy server that is different from the proxy server used by Internet Explorer does not affect Internet Explorer.

Changing the proxy settings on the Search Server Settings page affects servers running the index component only. For other servers, you can change the proxy settings from the Configure Server Farm Account Settings page.

Security Configuration

The Security Configuration section is used to view or configure security settings for Microsoft SharePoint Products and Technologies for servers in the server farm, including blocked file types and antivirus configuration if third-party antivirus software has been installed. Figure 17-4 displays the Security Configuration section, which is the next area on the SharePoint Portal Server Central Administration page that you might want to configure before creating your first portal site.

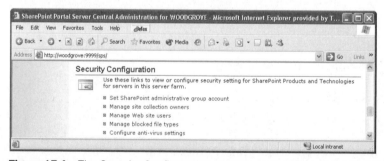

Figure 17-4 The Security Configuration section on the SharePoint Portal Server Central Administration page

Set SharePoint Administrators Group Account

As mentioned previously, the SharePoint administrators group account is where you assign a domain user or group as the administrator of the farm.

Manage Site Collection Owners and Manage Website Users

The purpose of these two links relate to managing access to sites and will be discussed in Chapter 18, "Managing SharePoint Portal Server 2003."

Manage Blocked File Types

Windows SharePoint Services provides the ability to restrict certain kinds of files from being uploaded or retrieved, based on the file extension. By default, several standard file extensions are blocked, including any file extensions that are treated as executable files by Microsoft Windows Explorer. Files with curly braces, { or }, are also blocked automatically. Because the list of blocked file types is maintained by file extension, all files that use a file extension on the list cannot be uploaded or downloaded, regardless of the file's intended use.

The list of file extensions is controlled for the entire server or server farm and is recorded in the configuration database. Additional file extensions can be blocked (up to 1024 file types) by adding them to the list.

One thing to keep in mind is that when the list of file extensions is changed, the change affects both new files being added to a website and files already posted to a website. Users will be able to rename or delete a file with a blocked file extension but will not be able to perform any other actions.

Even though this option appears in the Security Configuration section, it is important to realize that technically this is just a file-extension checking mechanism. For example, if the .mp3 file type is blocked and the user renames the file as *.mpz*, the portal site will not block the uploaded file.

Configure Antivirus Settings

When you install an antivirus scanner that is compatible with SharePoint Portal Server 2003, you can enable the antivirus protection feature for all servers for the portal site on the Configure Antivirus Settings page. In a server farm deployment, you will have to install antivirus software on every front-end Web server in the server farm.

Remember that having such antivirus software installed on your front-end servers will affect their performance and scalability. You will have to configure your servers with additional processing power to compensate for the additional overhead.

Component Configuration

The Component Configuration links are used to manage search settings, configure Single Sign-On, manage shared services, and to configure usage analysis, HTML viewer settings, and diagnostic settings. If you have installed the optional backward-compatible document library component (for compatibility with SharePoint Portal Server 2001), you can also configure document libraries (Web Storage System–based) from here. All the links in this section found on the SharePoint Portal Server Central Administration page are shown in Figure 17-5.

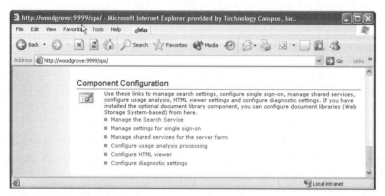

Figure 17-5   The Component Configuration section on the SharePoint Portal Server Central Administration page

Manage the Search Service

This link leads to a page that allows the administrator to manage how and when the index servers crawl content, to specify where the index servers store temporary files, and to specify other Search Service–related settings. Refer to Chapter 21, "The Architecture of the Gatherer," and Chapter 22, "Managing External Content in Microsoft Office SharePoint Portal Server 2003," for details about the index and search services. Chapter 18 will also cover these links in the context of ongoing management tasks relating to the search services.

Manage Settings for Single Sign-On

As stated earlier, Single Sign-On is a feature relating to integration with enterprise-level third-party applications. For more information see Chapter 26, "Single Sign-On in SharePoint Portal Server 2003."

Configure HTML Viewer

Included with Windows SharePoint Services is the ability to connect to an HTML Viewer server. An HTML Viewer server provides support for users who want to view the content of files on the Windows SharePoint Services website but do not have Microsoft Office Word, Excel, or PowerPoint from Microsoft Office 97 (or a later release of Office) installed on their local computers. Even users who have only a Web browser (Microsoft Internet Explorer or Netscape Navigator) can view content by having the native Office file format converted to HTML on the fly. Although a slight delay occurs while the transformation takes place, the converted file is extremely close to the WYSIWYG formatting of the original. In addition to the process of transforming files on the fly for end users, administrators can use a batch process mode to convert the contents of entire folders to HTML ahead of time and give users better response when requesting those documents.

By default, the HTML Viewer server supports only the following document types: .doc, .xls, .ppt, and .pps.

Transformation of a supported document can take from 1 to 30 seconds, depending on the complexity and size of the document as well as the speed and available resources of the dedicated computer. To provide for this ability and assure a fast response time, you should dedicate a separate computer to this service.

To install the service, find the htmlview.exe file in the Microsoft Office 2003 Resource Kit and extract it on a server that will handle the conversion process. Using the required instructions found with the HTML Viewer files, you will have to install Microsoft Office 2003 along with the HTML Viewer on the chosen server.

Installing Office for the HTML Viewer

To create an Office HTML Viewer server, you must install a customized version of Office 2003 to the dedicated Office HTML Viewer server. Before creating this installation, find the ENG11PROBYPASS.MST and HTMLTRBACKEND.MSI files from the package that included this document. Copy these two files (ENG11PROBYPASS.MST and HTMLTRBACKEND.MSI) to the local computer and folder where the setup.exe for Office 2003 will be run.

Office 2003 must be installed in order to create an Office HTML Viewer server. From the command prompt of the workstation, enter the following command line from the folder where the ENG11PROBYPASS.MST file is stored:

```
setup TRANSFORMS=ENG11PROBYPASS.MST
```

Or you can add the path to the file using the TRANSFORMS property, as shown in the following example:

```
setup TRANSFORMS="<path>\ENG11PROBYPASS.MST"
```

You can also add further customizations, but they are not needed and, in fact, might conflict with settings in the ENG11PROBYPASS.MST file.

You should accept the default install location for Office (C:\Program Files\ Microsoft Office\).

Tip You should not use Office 2003 from the console on the Office HTML Viewer server. It is only for use by the HTML Viewer server. The customizations to Office on the server provide for a specialized installation. Use of Office from the console could slow down the server. Also, if an HTML viewing action takes place while Office is in use for other purposes, it would dramatically affect the responsiveness of all other applications or services on the server.

Note The specialized installation of Office on the Office HTML Viewer server is provided to help mitigate any possible security threats by reducing the exposure of Office access points to external users. The configuration of Office used for the Office HTML Viewer sets macro security to High. Setting macro security to High turns off macro support for executables. Macros embedded in documents or files will not run during the file conversion process. Any documents or files that retrieve data on the fly from remote servers or custom applications will not function. Content within the document or file must be static to be converted. However, VBA projects (source code) in any documents or files will make a roundtrip through the HTML viewing process.

Running the Office HTML Viewer Windows Installer Package

After the Microsoft Office 2003 install process completes, run the Microsoft Office HTML Viewer install package on the Office HTML Viewer server by using the following command line:

HTMLTRBACKEND.MSI

This file is a Windows Installer file that places necessary Office HTML Viewer executables and Office customizations on the computer.

You can also run this file by double-clicking it from within Windows Explorer or referencing it in the Run utility (Start menu, Run option). When it starts, a setup dialog box requesting you to specify where to install files appears. You should accept the default install location. If the HTMLTRBACKEND.MSI file does not start, it is likely that MSIEXEC.EXE is not installed on the computer or it is not the most recent version. The latest version of MSIEXEC.EXE is available from the *www.microsoft.com* website.

When the HTMLTRBACKEND.MSI file finishes, the installation and customization process of Office 2003 is also complete. It is now necessary to instruct Windows SharePoint Services where to find the Office HTML Viewer server.

After installing the HTML Viewer service on a host, the administrator can configure the portal site to use the viewer by navigating to its configuration page from the SharePoint Portal Central Administration page depicted on Figure 17-6.

Keep in mind that the resource requirements for this service are very high and can severely affect the performance of any server not dedicated to this task. It is therefore recommended to dedicate a server to host this service. The steps and parameter settings are explained next.

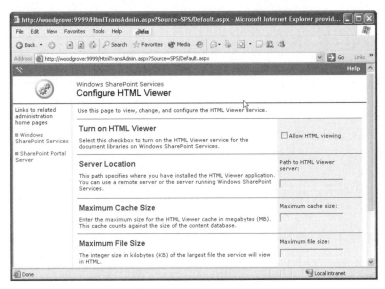

Figure 17-6   The HTML Viewer Configuration page

To configure Windows SharePoint Services

1. In the **Path to HTML Viewer Server** box, type the full URL to the server hosting HTML viewing.

2. In the **Maximum Cache Size** box, type the maximum size to allow for the HTML viewing cache.

3. In the **Maximum File Size** box, type the maximum file size to view.

4. In the **Timeout Length** box, type the length of time to wait before ending an HTML Viewer process.

5. Click **OK**.

Configure Diagnostic Settings

This link leads to a page that allows the administrator to change logging settings for the various services and processes, view and manage her diagnostic logs, and configure automatic reporting settings for certain types of events.

Logging Settings

The Logging Settings section on the Configure Diagnostic Settings page shows a list of components that run on the various portal servers, allowing each to have its logging settings modified. The components that allow their logging levels to be modified are as follows:

■ WWW Worker Process

■ Notification Service

- Single Sign-On Service

- Administrative Service

- Search Service

- Search Filter Process

- Backup – Restore

- Audience Job

- Third Party Applications

  For each component, you can edit the logging level as follows:

- Do not log event for this component

- Log critical events only

- Log informational events and critical events

- Log tracing information

> **Note**   You should select Log Tracing Information only for troubleshooting purposes. Logging tracing information might affect performance and disk use.

You can also choose to save a copy of the log automatically after a specified number of days, and you can choose to delete logs automatically after a specified number of days to save disk space.

View Diagnostic Logs

This section allows for viewing and deleting the log files created by the components defined in the Logging Settings section just described.

To view and delete diagnostic logs

1. On the SharePoint Portal Server Central Administration For *server_name* page, in the **Component Configuration** section, click **Configure diagnostic settings**.

2. On the Configure Diagnostic Settings For *server_name* page, in the **View Diagnostic Logs** section, in the **Diagnostic logs** list, select a diagnostic log, and then do one of the following:

   a. To view the selected log, click **View Log**.

   b. To delete the selected log, click **Delete**. You cannot delete a log file that is in use.

   c. To delete unused log files, click **Delete Unused Log Files**.

Automatic Error Reporting

SharePoint Portal Server 2003 can be configured to automatically send reports to Microsoft of errors that cause it to crash. Automatic error reporting uses a connection that uses the HTTP over SSL (https) protocol, which is more secure than an ordinary Internet connection. The data that Microsoft collects is used strictly for the purpose of tracking down and solving problems that users are experiencing. The information is stored in a secure database with limited access.

You can view the Microsoft Error Reporting Data Collection Policy from a link in the Automatic Error Reporting section. There is a link to this page on the SharePoint Portal Server Central Administration For Server *server_name* page.

The procedure to configure automatic error reporting for this server involves configuring the Error Reporting settings from Local Computer Policy in Microsoft Management Console. You must be logged on to the computer as a member of the local Administrators group to complete this procedure.

To configure automatic error reporting

1. On the taskbar, click **Start**, and then click **Run**.

2. Type **gpedit.msc** and then click **OK**.

3. In Group Policy Object Editor, under the **Local Computer Policy** node, expand the **Computer Configuration** node.

4. Right-click **Administrative Templates**, and then click **Add/Remove Templates**.

5. In the **Add/Remove Templates** dialog box, click **Add**.

6. Select **AER_LanguageID.ADM**, and then click **Open**. For example, for English, you would select **AER_1033.ADM**. For more information about language IDs, see "Regional and Language Settings" in the SharePoint Portal Administrator's Guide.

7. Click **Close** to close the **Add/Remove Templates** dialog box.

8. Under the **Computer Configuration** node, expand the **Administrative Templates** node.

9. Expand the **Application Error Reporting** node.

10. Click the **Queued Reporting** node.

11. In the details pane, right-click **Bypass queue and send all reports**, and then click **Properties**.

12. On the Properties page, on the **Setting** tab, click **Enabled**.

13. Click **OK**.

14. Close Group Policy Object Editor.

Portal Site and Virtual Server Configuration

At this point, we have configured almost all the core service features for the portal servers in the farm. We are now ready to discuss the configuration options and procedures relating to the creation of portal sites. The links in the Portal Site And Virtual Server Configuration section are used to extend and configure virtual servers required to host portal sites and team sites, create and manage portal sites, and configure portal site information such as external access settings and quota configurations.

Because all websites including portal sites need to be serviced through a virtual server preconfigured in IIS, we will begin our discussion there and end with the actual portal site creation procedure. Figure 17-7 depicts the links of the Portal Site And Virtual Server Configuration section we will be discussing.

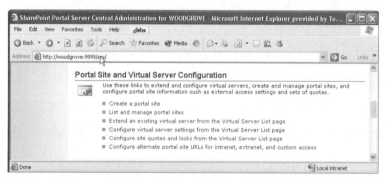

Figure 17-7   The Portal Site And Virtual Server Configuration section on the SharePoint Portal Server Central Administration page

Extending Portal Virtual Servers

As with Windows SharePoint Services, for a virtual server to provide front-end Web services for sites, it must be extended. Extending a virtual server associates the appropriate application pool, installs the Windows SharePoint ISAPI filter to the virtual server, and creates the appropriate files in the virtual server's folder.

However, in the portal site scenario, you do not have to extend the virtual server before creating your portal sites. This is different from Windows SharePoint Services, which requires that this step be performed before any sites can be created. The portal site creation process auto-extends the virtual server as part of the process. That said, you might be wondering why the Extend An Existing Virtual Server From The Virtual Server List Page option even exists on the SharePoint Portal Server Central Administration page. It is there to configure front-end Web servers that are added to the farm after the portal site has been created. Read the "Creating Portal Sites" section at the end of this chapter for details on how to extend virtual servers in a multiportal farm.

Once you have extended a virtual server, it will appear on the Virtual Server List page that appears when you click Configure Virtual Server Settings from the

Virtual Server List page. Selecting a virtual server on that page brings you to the Virtual Server Settings page depicted in Figure 17-8, which will allow you to configure that server. We now will examine the various configuration options the Virtual Server Settings page provides. Keep in mind that any settings that contradict similar settings that you have defined at the portal site level will be superseded by the virtual server's settings.

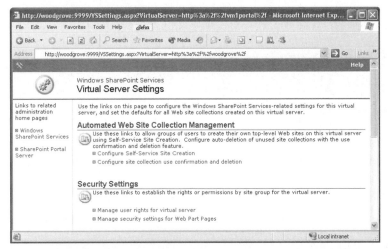

Figure 17-8   The Windows SharePoint Services Virtual Server Settings page

Configure Self-Service Site Creation

You might want to give your user community the ability to create new sites for themselves on the fly by enabling Self-Service Site Creation. If this feature is enabled, any user can create new top-level websites without an approval process.

Careful consideration must be given before turning this feature on, as you are potentially relinquishing control over the propagation of sites and site content in your organization. If you turn it on and don't check its usage, you might find yourself with a portal site filled with unused sites created at the user community's whim. To address this issue, a "dead-web cleanup" feature is provided that is described in the next section.

Configure Site Collection Use Confirmation and Deletion

To help mitigate the loss of disk and database space as a result of unused site collections, this option allows the administrator to set time limits that define how long to wait to delete unused site collections. There are also parameters that allow the administrator to define how many times to e-mail the owners of these unused sites to warn them of the deletion. If activity on the site is detected or if the owner of the site responds to the e-mailed warning, the site will not be deleted. Keep in mind that this feature will work only if the usage analysis processing is turned on at the portal site level.

Security Settings

This area of the SharePoint Portal Central Administration page, depicted previously in Figure 17-8, is used to configure the list of available rights for any sites hosted by a particular server, as well as how to handle Web Part Pages. Details follow for each of the two links.

Manage User Rights for the Virtual Server

This link is also referred to as the Virtual Rights Mask. It is used if you want to make sure that certain rights are not available to anyone using any of the site collections hosted by the virtual server, regardless of site group membership. You can disable those rights by deselecting the rights you want to block.

A situation in which you'd use this setting is when you want to ensure that users cannot change the themes to their sites. You can disable the Apply Themes right at the virtual server level so that users must use the default theme of the site template when any site or workspace is created.

Manage Security Settings for Web Part Pages

Web Parts are the main programming mechanism through which the portal site Web pages provide their functionality. A Web Part has server-side code, client-side code, or both that eventually translates to user-viewable rendered HTML. The code behind these Web Parts can pass parameter values and other data to other Web Parts that have been written by the programmer to receive that data. Web Parts that have been written with this kind of functionality are called "Connected" Web Parts because they use the Web Part Connections programming feature.

Connected Web Parts pass data to each other, and therefore might expose that data and violate existing security policy constraints. Also, these kinds of Web Parts tend to have more code running either at the client or server to support the connections. As an administrator, you can turn off Web Part Connection support at the virtual server level to improve security or to improve the performance of the server.

The other configuration you might want to set on this page pertains to whether or not you want to have your user community see Web Parts that have been published on the Microsoft website. The feature is turned on by default, but if it's disabled, it will cause the site pages to show only the default Web Parts created at install time as well as those posted by the administrator.

Virtual Server Management

Because Microsoft SharePoint Portal 2003 is based on Windows SharePoint Services, which in turn handles all Web requests through an ISAPI filter in IIS, it follows that some virtual server configuration tasks are required. The settings for these tasks are available via the Virtual Server Management section of the Virtual Server Settings page depicted in Figure 17-9. Refer to Chapter 15, "Configuring Windows SharePoint Services," for details about most of the settings found here. The most important link in this section is the Define Managed Paths link, which will be described next.

Figure 17-9   The Virtual Server Management section on the Virtual Server Settings page

Define Managed Paths

When client URL requests come in to the server on the listening port (usually port 80) defined on any virtual server that has been extended with Windows SharePoint Services, the Windows SharePoint Services ISAPI filter first looks at the URL to determine whether the path requested is to be serviced by Windows SharePoint Services. The filter makes that determination by comparing the requested path to the Managed Path list. By default, all paths under the virtual server's home folder are implicitly included.

However, an administrator might want the same virtual server that serves the portal site to also serve other subwebs that are not part of Windows SharePoint Services. For example, the administrator might want the path /tsweb, which represents a Web interface to terminal services, to be excluded from any portal Windows SharePoint Services processing. This is accomplished on this page by explicitly excluding the path.

On this page, it is also possible to append additional managed paths. For example, the default path intended for team site hosting, created at install time, is the /sites URL. If another path is preferred, such as /dept or /team, simply add the paths using the Add A New Path section of the page. Then, when a team site is created, the administrator will be able to select these additional paths as alternate creation paths for the new team site.

Create Top-Level Website

The virtual server hosting a portal site can also host team sites. This is accomplished by creating site collections, also known as top-level websites. When creating a site collection, the administrator will need to provide the desired URL path, a Site Collection Owner, Secondary Owner, Quota Template, and a Site Language.

The /sites URL is the default URL path created at installation of the portal site intended for team sites. If additional paths were added on the Define Managed Paths page, the administrator will see them in the URL Path drop-down combo box.

Delete Site Collection

When you specify the URL for the top-level website that the administrator wants to delete and click OK, that site and all subsites along with their content will be deleted.

Configure Data Retrieval Settings

Windows SharePoint Services makes use of data retrieval services for working with data in SharePoint lists, OLEDB, and XML data sources. For example, client applications and data-bound Web Parts, such as the Spreadsheet Web Part, use data retrieval and provider services to query the data source supported by the particular data source. Keep in mind that while the Web Parts provided with Windows SharePoint Services have predefined retrieval services, developers can create Web Parts that define their own custom database connections.

Each extended virtual server has such a set of data retrieval services installed and configured to handle client requests. This page allows the administrator to temporarily disable the service in troubleshooting scenarios, limit the KB size of data returned to clients so as to limit server and network loads, and set the time-out if the data source does not respond within the specified duration.

Configure Site Quotas and Locks

The only way to control the use of space in your content databases is to assign quota limits to the team sites that will be using that space. This is accomplished by clicking Configure Site Quotas And Locks from the Virtual Server List page in the Portal Site And Virtual Server Configuration section on the SharePoint Portal Server Central Administration page, defining quota templates, and then assigning quota templates as defaults for all site collections defined on the virtual server.

Any number of templates can be defined, each with its own storable limit values. There are two sets of values, one is the maximum space allowed for the site to occupy, and the second is the amount of space at which the owner of the site will be notified via e-mail that the limit is being approached.

Configure Alternate Portal Site URLs

Administrators often deploy portal sites that users can access by using different URLs. In these scenarios, it is 4important that functionality, such as search results for portal site and document library (Web Storage System–based) content, be appropriate for the URL that was used to access the portal site. External URLs must be provided to the user in a form that is appropriate for how the user is currently accessing the portal site. For example, let us assume that internal users are given *http://woodgrove/* as the base URL for accessing the portal site and its subsites. Let's also assume that the portal is also accessible to external users who use *http://www.woodgrove.com* as the base URL. When users utilize the search feature, they expect links in the result set to work. The only way for this to happen is to tell the portal site to provide the appropriate alternate URL based on where the request came from.

Without alternate access settings, search results might be displayed in a way that would make them inaccessible to users. Users might receive search results that they cannot access whenever they access the portal site by using a URL that is different from the original URL used for crawling the content.

To define URL alternate access settings, the administrator will need to navigate to the Configure Alternate Portal Access Settings page available via Configure Alternate Portal Site URLs For Intranet, Extranet, And Custom Access on the Central Portal Administration page. Figure 17-10 shows this page with one entry for the Woodgrove portal site that has an External Extranet URL of *http://www.woodgrove.com* and a Custom URL of *http://portal*. This means that intranet users can use either the current default *http://woodgrove* URL or the custom *http://portal URL*, while external users will have to use *http://www.woodgrove.com*.

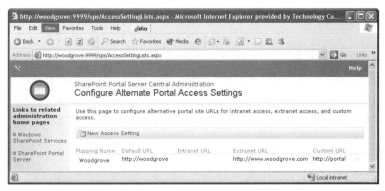

Figure 17-10   Alternate access URLs for a portal

Note   Remember that there must be name resolution, such as DNS, that will return the IP address of the portal site to requesting users.

Caution   This feature does not require the definition of custom http headers in IIS. However, if custom http headers are defined in IIS, you must remember to match them up to the alternate access URLs. Otherwise, those alternate URLs will not be serviced by IIS.

The Microsoft SharePoint Portal Server Search (SharePointPSSearch) service consults the alternate access setting entries when crawling a document. If the URL of the document matches one of the mapping entry URLs, the URL is replaced with the mapping ID for the entry. When the search result is displayed, the mapping ID is replaced by the appropriate URL if the user is requesting the document from an access point listed in the alternate access setting entries. If there is no appropriate alternate mapping, the search results display the default URL. Figures 17-11 and 17-12 show the same search results for a query. Note the status bar at the bottom of each, which shows that the appropriate alternate address URL has been placed for the link.

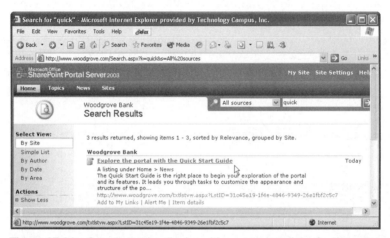

Figure 17-11   Search results display with appropriate links for the extranet users

Figure 17-12   Search results display with appropriate links for the intranet users using the custom URL

When defining alternate access, every entry must have a default URL. Each entry can have additional alternate access methods for either intranet, extranet, or custom access. Each URL must be different from all other URLs. These mappings are stored in the configuration database. SharePoint Portal Server 2003 uses the default URL for any requested URL that is not found in the mapping table. Also, you cannot delete entries for virtual servers that currently host portal sites or document libraries.

Caution   If an entry has been deleted but URLs for that mapping ID still exist in the index, those results will be displayed with a message stating that the content is not currently accessible. The server farm administrator will have to update the content index in order to update the URLs.

Creating Additional Application Pools

Windows SharePoint Services allows you to create application pools and associate them with separate virtual servers. By creating new application pools and assigning websites and applications to them, you can isolate portal sites and help enhance security between them while maintaining the availability of your other applications. Figure 17-13 shows how an additional application pool is created from within the IIS administration tool.

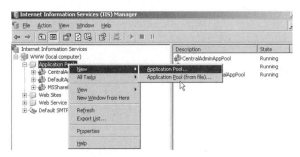

Figure 17-13   Creating an additional application pool

An application pool is a configuration in IIS that links one or more applications to a set of one or more worker processes. Because worker process boundaries separate applications in an application pool from other applications, problems caused by applications in one application pool do not affect applications in another application pool. For example:

- If one application pool identity is compromised and SharePoint Portal Server 2003 uses only one application pool, the administrator must disable all portal sites on the server. However, if the server farm administrator creates an application pool for each portal site and uses different application pool identities, the compromise of one application pool identity affects only one portal site, not all portal sites. Companies that provide SharePoint Portal Server services to other parties might want to create additional application pools, with separate application pool identities, to help enhance security and service continuity.

Note   When you create separate application pools, you can no longer manage the credentials by using the Configure Server Farm Account Settings page. Specifying the application pool identity of the portal site on this page applies only to MSSharePointPortalAppPool. You must use IIS Manager to manage any new application pools.

■ IIS shuts down an application pool if its processes falter several times. If all portal sites share an application pool and IIS shuts down that application pool, none of the sites will be operational. Therefore, using multiple application pools helps improve and ensure reliability. The server farm administrator might want to create one application pool for the parent portal site and another application pool for all the child portal sites to enhance reliability of the sites. Both application pools could use the same application pool identity.

■ If the server farm hosts more than 50 portal sites, it is required that additional application pools be created so that no single application pool has more than 50 portal sites sharing it. All application pools could use the same application pool identity. The limit is because, by default, IIS will recycle an application pool that grows beyond a certain memory limit. Splitting the application pools allows IIS to be more efficient about memory usage.

Note   Having multiple application pools increases memory usage. Each portal site with its own application pool uses approximately 150 megabytes (MB) of memory. When portal sites share an application pool, the first portal site uses approximately 150 MB, and each additional portal site uses 15 MB to 30 MB.

By default, SharePoint Portal Server 2003 creates a single application pool, named MSSharePointPortalAppPool, that hosts all virtual servers on which portal sites are created. Although this default setting is sufficient for many customers, others might want to move the virtual servers into separate application pools. For example, moving the virtual servers into separate application pools could be a requirement for customers who provide hosting services to different clients by using the same SharePoint Portal Server 2003 server farm. You can separate portal sites into different security contexts by specifying unique identities for each application pool.

> **Note**   Each portal site still has the db_owner database role on the configuration database and can affect other portal sites in the server farm by writing to the configuration database.

Remember and be careful to switch *all* components of the Web server to the new application pool, including the virtual directories (for example, _vti_bin, _layouts, and so on). If this is not done, the portal site will become inaccessible. Also, do not forget to assign the appropriate user account to the application pool. Figure 17-14 shows the Identity tab of the properties page for an application pool where this is done.

Figure 17-14   Creating an additional application pool

Creating Portal Sites

It is important to realize that more than one portal site can be hosted by a Microsoft SharePoint Portal 2003 server. This section will describe the overall steps required to create additional portal sites beyond the first one in a multi-front-end server farm.

From what we've learned so far, we know that for each portal site we need an additional virtual server to be created in IIS. We also know that even though we do not extend portal virtual servers directly, the portal site creation process, displayed in Figure 17-15, extends them for us. Extending a virtual server involves associating the Windows SharePoint Services ISAPI filter to it, as well as entering folder references for Managed path exclusions or inclusions.

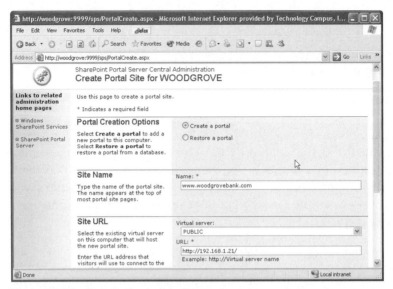

Figure 17-15 Creating a portal site

So you might be wondering why the Extend A Virtual Server link exists in the first place. Its purpose is to give administrators something to use on additional front-end servers once the portal sites have been created. The idea is to go to each front-end Web server's Central Administration page and extend the virtual server that will host a given portal site. On the Extend Virtual Server page, instead of creating a content database for it, you will map the virtual server to the original virtual server on which the portal site was created.

Summary

This chapter has shown that Microsoft SharePoint Portal Server 2003 provides a complete set of configuration tools that allow the administrator to define all the operational settings for the myriad servers and services that play various roles in the portal site. We also saw that some configuration tasks need to be performed from a command line by using the stsadmin.exe tool. Furthermore, the Web-based SharePoint Portal Central Administration page provides a single place for the administrator to do these configuration tasks from any browser-capable workstation. From there, the administrator can configure all servers at once or configure each server on a case-by-case basis.

The next chapter will continue our discussion of Microsoft SharePoint Portal Server 2003 from the perspective of ongoing administration of the portal sites themselves.

Chapter 18

Managing SharePoint Portal Server 2003

If one thinks of Microsoft Windows SharePoint Services as providing a collaboration engine targeted to helping members of individual teams and small workgroups collaborate and share data, one can look at Microsoft Office SharePoint Portal Server 2003 as the product that brings those teams and workgroups together, allowing them to find each other and to leverage each other's work. In fact, part of the intent of the portal product is to provide a central place for all workers in an organization to quickly and easily find information in workspaces that they might not be members of.

When looking at and using Microsoft Windows SharePoint Services, users had no way to easily find all the team sites that were created and it was left to the administrator to create a Web page of links that pointed to those team sites. Also, searching for data is always limited to the team site from which you do the search request.

Essentially, Microsoft SharePoint Portal Server 2003 takes all the Windows SharePoint Services sites and makes them navigable, as well as searchable from the central portal site. Furthermore, a new kind of site is introduced, called portal areas, which can be created as part of the portal site. Using special area templates, these portal area sites include additional enterprise-level features such as support for alerts based on users' subscriptions to lists and list content, as well as support for content displayed based on users' audience membership. Another kind of site is also introduced, called personal sites, wherein each user is given his own site to use for private storage of data with the capability of making that data available to other users of the portal.

In this chapter, we first will learn how a portal system administrator can make use of and manage these additional features. Starting on the Site Settings page of the portal site, we will look at some differences between portal-level security and team site security and the special considerations that should be made when managing portal-level security. We will also cover the management tasks related to the alert feature. This topic will show how an administrator can help individual users manage their alerts. We will then look at how to change the default look of the portal site to a customized one by assigning custom logos and custom cascading style sheet files. From there, we will see how to manage portal site content with respect to area pages, the Topic Assistant, and audience targeted links. Finally, we will look at how to manage audience recalculation and show how administrators can manage users' personal sites. For a discussion on searching and indexing, please refer to Chapter 21, "The Architecture of the Gatherer," and Chapter 22, "Managing External Content in Microsoft Office SharePoint Portal Server 2003."

Administering Portal Site Settings

To administer a portal site, use the Site Settings link found at the top right-hand corner of any portal area page. Only users with portal administrator and area administrator type permissions will see this link. The ensuing Site Settings page is divided into four sections called General Settings, Portal Site Content, Search Settings, and Indexed Content. These sections are followed by sections named User Profile, Audiences, and Personal Sites. Each section will be discussed in detail next.

General Settings

The General Settings section contains links to manage which users are explicitly allowed to access the portal site, as well as a link allowing the administrator to control how anonymous access is handled by the portal site. The ability to manage the alert feature of a portal site is provided here as well. Figure 18-1 shows the General Settings section of the portal site's Site Settings page.

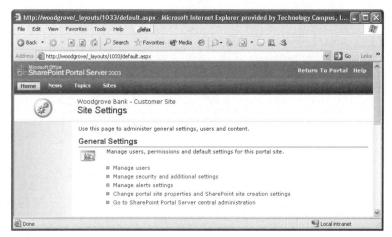

Figure 18-1 The General Settings section of a portal site's Site Settings page

Manage Users

As a portal administrator, you will want to control who can access the portal site and what level of privilege they have with respect to accessing and modifying content. Just as with Windows SharePoint Services, administrators can add users and groups from Microsoft Windows NT or Active Directory domains as users of the portal site. Permissions are assigned in the same way as in Windows SharePoint Services sites by associating users and groups to Site Groups. Please refer to Chapter 16, "Windows SharePoint Services Site Administration," for a discussion on how to add users using this interface.

Manage Security And Additional Settings

This link takes the portal administrator to the Manage Security And Additional Settings page, which contains many links useful for day-to-day management of the portal. This page is also divided into five grouped sections of links. Figure 18-2 displays the Manage Security And Additional Settings page and shows two of the five grouped sections of links found there.

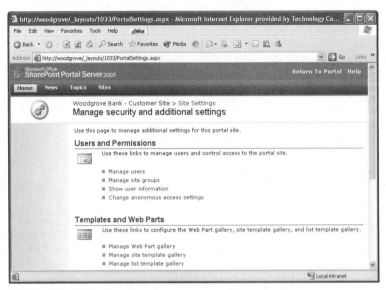

Figure 18-2   The Manage Security And Additional Settings page

The full list of grouped sections and their main purposes are as follows:

- **Users And Permissions.**   Used to manage who can access the portal and with what privilege

- **Templates And Web Parts.**   Used to manage a site's or area's Web Parts as well as Web Parts installed for the whole portal site

- **Discussion Settings.**   Used to view and delete document discussions

- **Storage Space.**   Used to identify where the most storage-intensive content is found, and offers the ability to delete it as well

- **Regional Settings.**   Used to set locale, default search result sort order, and time zone of the portal server

Users And Permissions

Controlling who can access the portal site and what level of access they will have to its content is performed through the Manage Users and Manage Site Groups links, which work exactly as they do in Windows SharePoint Services team sites. Please refer to Chapter 16 for more detail on managing users and site groups.

> **Caution**   Despite the security similarities between Windows SharePoint Services and SharePoint Portal Server, it is important keep in mind that while the former has the concept of Sites and Site Collections, the latter does not. A *portal* is a site collection and an *area* is a sub-web.

The Show User Information link, which does not exist with Windows SharePoint Services, takes the administrator to a page summarizing all users that have a Microsoft SharePoint Portal 2003 profile. A profile is created either when an authenticated user successfully accesses the portal site for the first time or automatically by the profile import process (which creates a profile for users based on Active Directory) if it has been enabled by the portal administrator. By following the link for a listed user, the administrator can edit the user information by adding notes about the user and can even designate the user as a Site Collection Administrator.

> **More Info**   You might notice that user accounts that have been granted access to portal areas and team sites continue to show in site groups and permission lists in the portal site even after they have been deleted from the domain. The only two ways to get rid of them are to delete each entry in every site and site group or to delete them from the Manage Site Collection Users page, which will effectively remove them from all sites and site groups in that collection.

One of the few differences in portal security from Windows SharePoint Services security is the existence of the additional Content Manager site group. By default, members of the Content Manager site group can approve or reject content posting requests and manage area settings. In addition, Content Managers can target areas for viewing by one or more audiences, which will be discussed later.

Another security-related difference relates to the permission set that can be granted to a portal's site group. For example, users can be granted or denied the Use Personal Features permission, which allows administrators to control which users or groups can use the portal site's alert feature and the portal site's personal site feature. Other permissions that do not exist for team sites relate to portal site feature management. Table 18-1 lists the differences in the two sets of permissions.

Table 18-1 Rights Differences Between Windows SharePoint Services and SharePoint Portal Server 2003

Windows SharePoint Services Rights	Description
Manage List Permissions	Grant, deny, or change user permissions to a list
Manage Lists	Approve content in lists, add or remove columns in a list, and add or remove public views of a list
Cancel Check-Out	Check in a document without saving the current changes
Add Items	Add items to lists, add documents to document libraries, add Web discussion comments
Edit Items	Edit items in lists, edit documents in document libraries, edit Web discussion comments in documents, and customize Web Part Pages in document libraries
Delete Items	Delete items from a list, documents from a document library, and Web discussion comments in documents
View Items	View items in lists, view documents in document libraries, view Web discussion comments, and set up e-mail alerts for lists
Manage Site Groups	Create, change, and delete site groups, including adding users to the site groups and specifying which rights are assigned to a site group
View Usage Data	View reports on website usage
Create Subsites	Create subsites such as team sites, Meeting Workspace sites, and Document Workspace sites
Manage Web Site	Grants the ability to perform all administration tasks for the website as well as manage content and permissions
Add and Customize Pages	Add, change, or delete HTML pages or Web Part Pages, and edit the website using a Windows SharePoint Services–compatible editor
Apply Themes and Borders	Apply a theme or borders to the entire website
Apply Style Sheets	Apply a style sheet (.css file) to the website
Browse Directories	Browse directories in a website
Use Self-Service Site Creation	Create a website using Self-Service Site Creation
View Pages	View pages in a website
Manage Personal Views	Create, change, and delete personal views of lists
Add/Remove Private Web Parts	Add or remove private Web Parts on a Web Part Page
Update Personal Web Parts	Update Web Parts to display personalized information
Create Cross-Site Groups	Create a group of users that can be granted access to any site within the site collection

Table 18-1 **Rights Differences Between Windows SharePoint Services and SharePoint Portal Server 2003** *(continued)*

SharePoint Portal Server Rights	Description
View Area	View an area and its contents
View Pages	View pages in an area
Add Items	Add items to lists, add documents to SharePoint document libraries, add Web discussion comments
Edit Items	Edit items in lists, edit documents in SharePoint document libraries, and customize Web Part Pages in SharePoint document libraries
Delete Items	Delete items from a list, documents from a document library, and Web discussion comments in documents
Manage Personal Views	Create, change, and delete personal views of lists
Add/Remove Personal Web Parts	Add or remove Web Parts on a personalized Web Part Page
Update Personal Web Parts	Update Web Parts to display personalized information
Cancel Check-Out	Check in a document without saving the current changes
Add and Customize Pages	Add, change, or delete HTML pages or Web Part Pages, and edit the portal site by using a Windows SharePoint Services–compatible editor
Create Area	Create an area on the portal site
Manage Area	Delete or edit the properties for an area on the portal site
Manage Area Permissions	Add, remove, or change user rights for an area
Apply Style Sheets	Apply a style sheet (.css file) to an area or the portal site
Browse Directories	Browse directories in an area
Create Personal Site	Create a personal SharePoint site
Create Sites	Create SharePoint sites by using Self-Service Site Creation
Use Personal Features	Use alerts and personal sites
Manage Alerts	Change alert settings for the portal site, and manage alerts for users
Manage User Profiles	Add, change, or delete user profile information and properties
Manage Audiences	Add, change, or delete audiences
Manage Portal Site	Specify portal site properties and manage site settings
Manage Search	Add, change, or delete index and search settings in the portal site
Search	Search the portal site and all related content

As you read through this chapter and learn about all the management responsibilities you will have as an administrator of a portal site, you will undoubtedly want to delegate some of those responsibilities. You can achieve this delegation of responsibilities by creating custom site groups that have one or more of the five additional rights that pertain to portal area management permissions:

■ **Manage Alerts.**   Privilege to change alert settings for the portal site and manage alerts for users

■ **Manage User Profiles.**   Right to add, change, or delete user profile information and properties

■ **Manage Audiences.**   Permission to add, change, or delete audiences

■ **Manage Portal Site.**   Right to specify portal site properties and manage site settings

■ **Manage Search.**   Privilege to add, change, or delete index and search settings in the portal site

The **Change anonymous access setting** link is required if the portal site administrator wants to enable anonymous access for the portal site. The Anonymous Access setting is set to Nothing by default, meaning that even if the virtual server hosting the portal site allows anonymous HTTP requests, the portal site will not honor the request. The requesting user would experience this kind of scenario by being prompted to log on to the portal site.

> **Tip**   Remember to turn on anonymous access both at the IIS virtual server as well as on the portal site's Anonymous Access Settings page if you want users to access the portal site anonymously, such as in a public Internet portal scenario. You'll also need to give the Anonymous user account Reader (or higher) permissions in the portal site. Also, note that anonymous, basic, and NTLM/integrated authentication on the virtual server with SPS is not supported by Microsoft.

Figure 18-3 shows that one of the following three levels of anonymous access can be chosen:

1. **Areas And Content.**   Selecting this option allows all anonymous users to see all content, but it does not allow them to use the search feature. In this mode, the search Web Part does not show on the portal area pages for anonymous users.

2. **Areas, Content And Search.**   This mode will allow anonymous users to see all content and will show the user the search Web Part at the top right of each portal area page.

3. **Nothing.**   This is the default setting, which prevents anonymous users from entering the portal home page or any other portal area page.

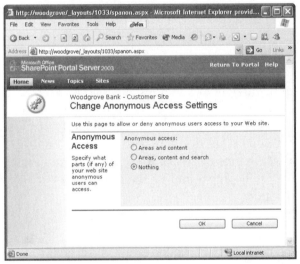

Figure 18-3   Changing the level of access to content for anonymous users of the portal site

Keep in mind that granting user access to the portal site does not necessarily grant access to the team sites or portal area pages listed by that portal site. While each team site is still administered as discussed in Chapter 16, the procedure to manage portal area security is slightly different. Figure 18-4 shows the News portal area page as seen by an administrator of that portal area along with the Manage Security link. By selecting the Manage Security link in the Action bar on the left side of the page, the administrator will be led to the area's Manage Security Settings page, where he will be able to assign users, assign site groups, or allow inheritance of security from the parent area.

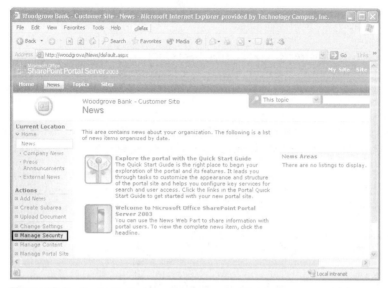

Figure 18-4   Controlling who can access portal areas

Each area page can be thought of as, and is, analogous to a team site. Just like team sites, portal areas can inherit permissions from their parent area or can have inheritance canceled by administrators. However, the method to cancel inheritance for portal area pages is very different from the way it is done on team sites. All the administrator needs to do is change the list of users and site groups that appears on the area page by adding or removing a user or site group, which effectively cancels inheritance for that portal area.

Tip   Always read the description at the top of the portal area page to determine whether inheritance is in effect or has been blocked. Figure 18-5 shows the News area page with inheritance turned on. If the administrator turns inheritance off by changing the list of users and site groups, the description will state "these permissions are not inherited" and will also offer a link. Keep in mind that if you re-enable inheritance by selecting the link labeled "Inherit permissions from the parent area", you will lose any changes you've made to the list of allowed users and site groups.

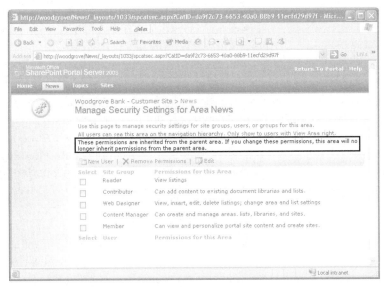

Figure 18-5 Manage Security Settings for the Area page with inheritance turned on

Templates And Web Parts

This section of the Manage Security And Additional Settings page is analogous to the Site Collection Galleries discussed in Chapter 16. The difference is that this section pertains to Web Parts and templates installed and available from the portal level down instead of only a SharePoint Services site's Web Parts and templates, which have a per-virtual-server focus. The administrator can add and remove Web Parts and upload and manage site templates to the portal site. The advantage of uploading Web Parts and templates to the portal site is that they become available to all portal site users regardless of which server they are hosted on.

> **Note** One thing to remember, however, is that the administrator will still be responsible for installing Web Parts (and setting the Web Part security) on each front-end server. There is no "replication" of Web Parts that occurs.

Discussion Settings

Websites based on Microsoft Windows SharePoint Services include Web discussions, which are threaded discussions that allow users to collaborate on HTML documents or on any document that can be opened with a browser (such as .htm, .xls, .doc, and .ppt files) on a server running Windows SharePoint Services. Anyone with discussion permissions can attach comments to a Web page or any document that can be opened with a browser. Users place comments in the document or have them appear in the discussion pane at the bottom of the Web browser window.

> **Note**   Web discussions are not the same as Discussion Boards and should not be confused with them. Discussion Boards are a feature of Windows SharePoint Services sites that provide a forum for conversing about any topics that interest your team and are created on the same Create Page location used to create lists and libraries. Web discussions are also supported by Windows SharePoint Services, but they relate to documents and Web pages only.

Anyone reviewing a Web page can use the Web Discussions toolbar in Internet Explorer to view and reply to any discussion. The Web Discussions toolbar is available in Microsoft Internet Explorer 4.0 or later to users of a Windows SharePoint Services–compatible client program, such as a Microsoft Office 2003 program.

> **Note**   When you add discussion comments to a Web page, your text is stored in a database on a discussion server. The Web page you are discussing must be located on the same computer as the discussion server where your comments are stored.

The Manage Web Discussions page allows the portal administrator to list, access, and delete any document discussions pertaining to files stored in Document Libraries. The following tasks are possible:

- To see all discussion threads associated with your site, click **All Web discussions**, and then click **Update**.

- To see discussion threads filtered by a particular URL, type a path in the Web discussions in folder http://*server_name*/ box, and then click **Update**.

- To view a particular discussion thread, click the URL for the thread.

- To delete a particular discussion thread, select the check box next to the thread, and then click **Delete**.

- To delete all discussion threads on your site, click **Delete all discussions**.

These tasks are particularly useful if you want to observe which documents have had discussions added to them or if you want to delete them to free up space.

Storage Space

One of the administrator's day-to-day portal management tasks will involve monitoring and freeing up space used by the various content types, especially document and image libraries. The storage section facilitates this task by offering the Manage Storage Space Allocation link. Navigating to it leads to a similarly named page that allows the portal administrator to view portal site lists, all document libraries, and their documents along with the amount of space that each uses. (See Figure 18-6.)

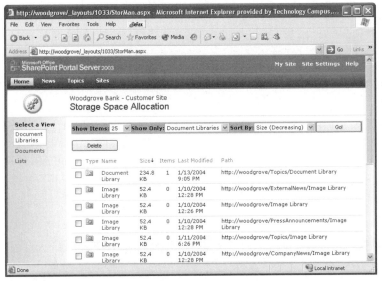

Figure 18-6   Document Library view on the Storage Space Allocation page

Figure 18-6 shows the Document Library view that helps the administrator quickly identify which document libraries in which areas are responsible for the greatest use of space. The vertical task bar on the left shows the ability to view the list by individual document, which will show an ordered list of all documents across all libraries of the portal areas. There is also the ability to view non-library lists such as Task, Events, and Contact lists in terms of their storage space usage. From there, the administrator can navigate to or delete the listed libraries, documents, or list items to free up space. It will be up to the administrator to ensure that libraries have been backed up before deleting them, as there is no such indication in the provided interface. This could be accomplished by sending an e-mail to the owner of the library as listed in the library's property pages.

This feature works only at the portal level, meaning that you won't see Windows SharePoint Services site-based document libraries or lists in this page.

Regional Setting

This last section of the Manage Security And Additional Settings page allows the portal administrator to set the locale, time zone, and time format for the portal site. The reason it is important to set the time zone is that you want the creation or modification timestamp for content to be accurately recorded in the content database. In scenarios where the Web front-end servers reside in a different time zone than the user as well as the content databases, this is crucial. The configuration of the default sort order used when displaying lists chosen as a function of the locale is also important. For example, if the locale is French, the sort order would typically be French as well, which takes into account additional sorting rules related to that language's additional characters and character modifiers.

Manage Alerts Settings

When users want to be notified via e-mail that a document has changed or that search results for a particular query have changed, they create a SharePoint Portal alert. Because this feature is used at the users' discretion, administrators might need to manage them to keep users' alerts under control. The Manage Alerts Settings page exists to help administrators with this task. Figure 18-7 shows this page, which the administrator can access by clicking the like-named link on the General Settings section of the Site Settings page.

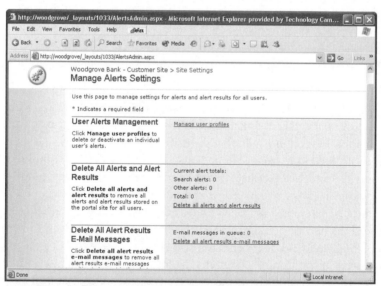

Figure 18-7   Alerts management options on the Manage Alerts Settings page

The following list describes each of the settings found on the Manage Alerts Settings page and their usage:

- **User Alerts Management.**   If a user decides one day that she has created too many alerts and does not want to track down where each was created to cancel each alert, the administrator can delete all the user's alerts for her by following the Manage User Profiles link. The resulting page will list all users who have subscribed to alerts. By hovering the cursor over a user name in the list and clicking on the drop-down arrow that appears, the administrator can choose to deactivate the user's alerts temporarily or delete all of them.

> **Note**   If a user has her Create Alerts right revoked, she will retain her current alerts and receive alert messages for them. If appropriate, use the link described next to eliminate them after revoking permissions.

- **Delete All Alerts And Alert Results.**   The administrator can follow the Delete All Alerts And Alert Results link, which will ask for confirmation of the action before executing it. This is typically done in environments where it is decided, after deployment, that a given portal site should no longer support alerts. After disabling the feature, deleting all alerts and alert results would prevent any previously created alerts from contributing to the e-mail message queue. See the following note on how to disable the feature.

- **Delete All Alert Results E-Mail Messages.**   This link is used to clear the portal site's e-mail queue of any alerts. It comes in handy when the queue has accumulated too many alerts—for example, in situations where the e-mail server to which they were sent has been down for a long time. Clearing the queue would avoid bombarding the users' mailboxes with all the queued-up alerts. Of course, careful consideration must be given before clearing the queue, as users would not get notified for changes listed in the queue at the time of deletion.

- **Alert Quotas.**   This group of settings allow the portal administrator to limit the total number of alerts both at the portal level as well as for the users.

- **Default E-Mail Address For Alerts.**   The portal administrator can use this setting to specify to the alert system which e-mail property in the users' profiles to use when users create their alerts. Only fields that have been defined as e-mail fields will show in the drop-down selection. You should select the Always Use User Profile Field check box to prevent users from entering another e-mail address.

- **SMTP Server For E-Mail Alerts.**   The change default e-mail settings link is used if the administrator wants a particular server to use different mail server settings than those defined as default on the Central Portal Administration pages. The settings are defined for a particular virtual server chosen by the administrator and will override the portal-defined default. This is useful in scenarios where a particular server does not have access to the default portal e-mail server based on its location.

Change Portal Site Properties And SharePoint Site Creation Settings

The purpose of following this link is for the portal administrator to change how the portal area pages are displayed to the requesting browsers. There are four customizations that the linked page provides:

- **Portal Site Name and Description.**   The Name property will affect what is displayed at the top of each area page in the portal site. The Description property is not displayed and is for the administrator's own use.

- **Custom Portal Site Logo.**   This setting allows the administrator to designate a different logo file than the default set at install time. Any path relative to the local server is acceptable, but the administrator will have to ensure the logo file has been copied to all Web front-end servers for this to work. To avoid having to do this, a single accessible URL can be defined instead. Keep in mind that this URL can be served in a load-balanced scenario, assuming the logo file is copied to all load-balanced Web servers.

- **Location For Creating SharePoint Sites.**   If this setting is left blank or if its default value of /_layouts/language/scsignup.aspx is used, any sites created from within the portal site will be created in the default content database. If portal administrators want newly created sites to default to using an alternate content database, they will have to change this property to a URL that points to a Web server running Windows SharePoint Services with Self-Service Site Creation enabled (keeping in mind that the server needs to have a content database defined for it to use on its administration pages). A few additional rules to remember include:

  - The URL must end with /_layouts/language/scsignup.aspx.

  - The URL for creating sites from the Sites Directory is limited to 2048 ASCII characters. In addition, no component of the URL, such as the virtual directory or virtual server, can exceed 128 characters.

  - Leaving the URL blank reverts the value back to /_layouts/language/scsignup.aspx.

- **Custom Cascading Style Sheet.**   By default, the portal site uses a file called sps.css, which is found in the /_layouts/*language code number*/styles folder. A Web designer can design an alternate cascading style sheet file to customize the look of the portal pages. To have the portal site use this new .css file, the administrator needs only to place it in a centrally accessible location and specify the URL in this property.

> **Tip**   Avoid editing the sps.css file directly, as it can be overwritten when upgrading or installing a fix or running a repair on the installation from the Add/Remove Programs Control Panel applet. Placing a custom .css file in a centrally accessible URL ensures that it will be available regardless of what happens with the portal server's installation.

Portal Site Content

The Portal Site Content section of the portal site's Site Settings page, shown in Figure 18-8, allows the administrator to define additional area pages, change the portal site's navigational structure, configure the automated association of content links to pertinent area pages with the Topic Assistant, manage the content of portal area targeted links, as well as import data from Microsoft SharePoint Portal Server 2001. Each of these options shows up as a separate link, each of which we will examine next.

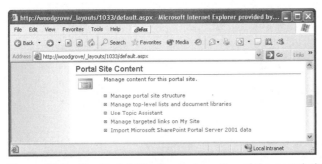

Figure 18-8   The Portal Site Content section of the portal site's Site Settings page

Manage Portal Site Structure

Before embarking on a discussion of how to manage the portal site structure, let's look at what the portal site is composed of in terms of Web pages and content. The first thing to realize is that each portal site has a home page. This home page can be edited and customized, but it can never be deleted. All other pages in the portal site are referred to as areas or area pages. In SharePoint Portal Server 2003, areas serve two purposes. First, they provide a navigational structure or map of the portal site and related content. By adding, moving, or deleting areas, administrators can change the view of the portal site for users. Second, they provide a centralized structure for storing and organizing content into content-specific areas, which results in giving users a structure for information browsing. Areas direct readers to the information they seek through an organized hierarchy of topics. Areas are intended to provide a flexible way to both describe and find documents as well. By default, the installation creates three top-level areas called News, Topics, and Sites. These can be deleted or modified at will, and additional ones can be created as well. You can think of an area as both a category as well as a team site that will contain content pertinent to that category. In any deployment of SharePoint Portal 2003, the true challenge lies in deciding how to categorize content and organize the navigational structure of the portal site.

One of the main features a portal area page has that a regular team site page does not is its association with the Portal Site Map, which defines the portal site's navigation structure. Figure 18-9 shows that on the News area page, and on every other area page, there is a horizontal navigation bar of links running along the top of the page as well as a vertical navigation bar along the left side called Current Location. As just mentioned, these navigation bars are automatically updated to reflect the structure defined on the Portal Site Map.

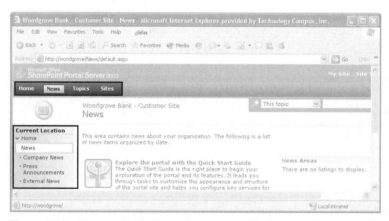

Figure 18-9   The portal site News area page with focus on the navigation bars

When administrators follow the Manage Portal Site Structure link found on the task bar below the Current Location navigation bar, they are taken to the Portal Site Map page, which shows a tree-like view of the area page hierarchy. The top level is, of course, the home page. Any portal areas that fall one level indented below the home page will show up as links on the top navigation bar. Any area pages that are placed at levels below the area in focus will show up on the left-hand vertical navigation bar (assuming that the area has not been excluded from portal site navigation on the Display tab of the Site Settings page for the area). This page allows the administrator to create new portal area pages, manage existing ones, and alter the navigation bars of these pages simply by dragging and dropping the areas to different locations in the tree structure. The Portal Site Map can be seen in Figure 18-10, with the News area node expanded. Notice the relationship between the structure shown on the map and the display of that area page in Figure 18-9.

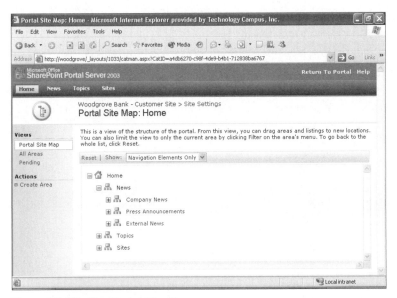

Figure 18-10   The Portal Site Map

Beyond creating, deleting, and moving area pages to alter the navigational structure of the portal site, the Portal Site Map allows the administrator to edit each area's properties. This is achieved by hovering the cursor over the area in the Portal Site Map, clicking on the drop-down menu, and selecting Edit. Alternately, as each portal area is viewed, the administrator can click the Change Settings link in the Action menu on the left-hand column to edit the area's properties as well. This leads to the area's Change Settings page shown in Figure 18-11. The Change Settings page is composed of the following five categorized tabs of properties:

- **General.**   This tab allows the administrator to change the title that appears on the area page, its relative URL path name, area description, contact e-mail that will appear on the area page if defined, location in the site structure, as well as creation and modification dates.

- **Publishing.**   This tab is useful if the administrator wants an area page to appear only as of a certain date and to be automatically removed from the navigation links after the expiration date. Keep in mind that not only are the links unavailable but the page itself (as well as its content) is also no longer available to users.

- **Page.**   Just as team sites are created from Windows SharePoint Services templates, portal area pages are created from area templates. This tab has two sections. The Subarea Templates section specifies which template should be used for subsequent creations of subareas below the currently selected one. The Area Templates section allows the administrator to change the template of the currently selected area.

- **Display.**   This tab is used to control whether or not to exclude the area page from the navigation bars, to determine the order in which to place the link on the navigation bars, and to associate a custom image to show on the area page.

- **Search.**   This tab allows the administrator to set content created in this area to be excluded from search results, as well as to configure whether the Topic Assistant should suggest content links to be published for this area.

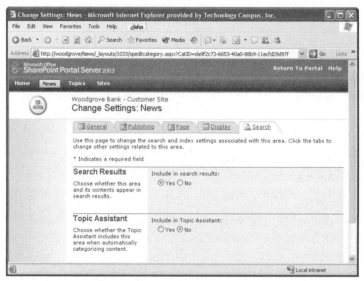

Figure 18-11   The Search tab of the Change Settings page of an area

Manage Top-Level Lists and Document Libraries

Following this link takes administrators to the portal site's Documents And Lists page for the Home area, which allows them to create and view content lists just as any Windows SharePoint Services site. Also, keep in mind that each area that is created has its own set of content lists, as though it was its own team site that could be managed by following the Manage Content link on the left-hand navigation bar under Actions. See Chapter 16 for more details on list and content types.

Manage Targeted Links on My Site

Portal administrators can target content to the personal sites of portal users. Users who click My Site on the navigation bar to view their personal site will see all the content that is targeted to them for the audiences to which they belong through Web Parts, such as the News For You or Links For You Web Parts.

Audiences are defined as users who meet certain criteria. Users are said to be members of an audience if they meet that audience's membership criteria. Criteria examples defined when an audience is created include a user account's group membership or a user account's property, such as Title or Department as stored in the portal profile of the account.

Content is targeted to personal sites by adding listings to the Targeted links on the My Site area or News area, and then editing the display properties of the listings to target specific audiences. Users then see the content that is targeted to them in the Links For You and News For You Web Parts on their personal sites. Content added to the Targeted links on the My Site area is displayed in the Links For You Web Part. Content added to the News area is displayed in the News For You Web Part.

> **Note**   Portal content administrators can target portal listings such as people, links to portal site or Windows SharePoint Services site content, news, and custom text. To view and manage which listings are targeted, the adminis- trator can select the Portal Listings link on the area's Documents And List- ings page, which is available from the Manage Content link of any area.

Import Microsoft SharePoint Portal Server 2001 Data

This link is used as part of the upgrade procedure when upgrading from Microsoft SharePoint Portal Server 2001. In such a scenario, before installing Microsoft Share- Point Portal 2003, the administrator would first run the upgrade tool provided on the product CD. This tool would create a file called V1Export.XML containing all the data of the original portal. After installing the newer version, the administrator would then navigate to this page and import the data from this file by specifying its path.

Here are some additional notes related to upgrading and importing data from Microsoft SharePoint Portal 2001:

- Some data from SharePoint Portal Server 2001 is imported during upgrade, but it cannot be used in SharePoint Portal Server 2003. This includes portal custom- ization and most SharePoint Portal Server 2001 custom Web Parts.

- To use the document management capabilities of SharePoint Portal Server 2001, you must install the optional components for backward-compatible document libraries.

- Security roles are exported from SharePoint Portal Server 2001 but are not imported to SharePoint Portal Server 2003. You can keep this information as a record to use when deciding how to assign users to site groups.

- After completing an upgrade to SharePoint Portal Server, you will not be able to back up and restore the client components for backward-compatible docu- ment libraries.

- The portal content and dashboard folders are not deleted during upgrade and appear in the Documents area of the portal site. After you have migrated all the content from these folders, it is recommended that you delete the folders.

Search Settings And Indexed Content

One of the most powerful features of SharePoint Portal Server 2003 is its search capability. This section of the Site Settings page has six links that allow the administrator to configure all aspects of how search indexes are created, how external content is crawled, and how results are skewed for queries received from users. For details concerning the configuration and management of the search and indexing feature of Microsoft SharePoint Portal 2003, please refer to Chapter 22.

User Profile, Audiences, And Personal Sites

This section of the portal's Site Settings page, shown in Figure 18-12, allows the portal administrator to configure automatic importing of profiles from Active Directory domains, manage the audience membership recalculation schedule, and manage users' personal sites for them when the need arises.

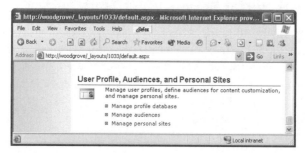

Figure 18-12   The User Profile, Audiences, And Personal Sites section of the portal Site Settings page

Manage Profile Database

Each user of the portal site needs to have a profile. A profile consists of a list of properties such as telephone number, address, e-mail, department, and so on. A profile is created for each user the first time the user visits the portal site and successfully authenticates to it, a profile can be precreated manually by the administrator, or it can be automatically created from data imported from Active Directory. Keep in mind that if users edit properties, their edits will be overwritten with the information that is in Active Directory the next time an import is scheduled. The exception to this rule applies to custom fields for which no Active Directory association has been made. Another feature allows the administrator to select which data from a user's profile properties should appear in the My Site area of that user and, then, can also be modified by that user. To add a profile property, click the Add Profile Property link in this section of the page.

The advantage of populating data into these profiles is that it can be used by the search service to help users find other users. For example, in a large organization, a portal user in one country might need to find the department manager of a division in another country. If the portal profiles have been filled in with meaningful data, the search service will be able to find the person. Clicking on the Manage Profile Database leads to a like-named page with the following links:

- **Add User Profile.** This link is used to precreate a profile for a user who has yet to visit the portal site.

- **View User Profiles.** This link is used to see a list of existing profiles from which the administrator can view and modify a user's profile properties.

- **Configure Profile Import.** This link is used to define which domain or forest to import the user account data from and automatically create profiles for the user even before he visits the portal site. Part of this configuration requires specifying a service account with read privileges to the domain/forest to be used for gathering the data. Also, a schedule can be defined that dictates how often to check for new users to create their profiles and import their data. There are two types of schedules, full and incremental. Full will re-read and re-import data for users already possessing a profile (effectively overwriting any data that might have been modified by the user or administrator). Incremental will create profiles and import data only for new users discovered since the last full import. Keep in mind that the Profile Import Account needs to have the domain administrator privilege assigned to it for this feature to work.

- **View Import Log.** This link is used by the administrator to troubleshoot problems with profile import configuration. Information such as when the last import was attempted and any error details is available here.

At the bottom of the Manage Profile Database page is the User Profile Properties section, which allows the administrator to define additional properties and to edit behaviors of properties. Behaviors include the ability for users to include them in their My Site, edit them, and map them to Active Directory.

Manage Audiences

Audiences allow organizations to target content to users based on their job or task, as defined by their membership in a Windows 2003 security group, distribution list, organizational reporting structure, or the public properties in their user profiles. Audiences are managed centrally across one or more server farms hosting Share-Point Portal Server 2003. They apply across one or more portal sites in a deployment, not to individual areas, sites, or items. Following the Manage Audiences link from the Site Settings page of a portal site takes you to the Manage Audiences page, which is shown in Figure 18-13.

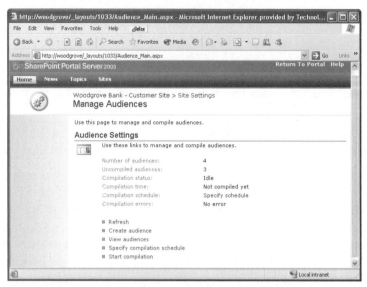

Figure 18-13 Manage Audiences administration page

You must have the Add, Change, or Delete Audiences right to manage audiences. As an audience manager, you can view all members of a specific audience and find the audiences to which a specific user belongs, as well as manage the rules defining audiences and compile audiences as the rules and members of an audience change.

The process for targeting content requires that you first create an audience (unless one already exists that you can use). Then you target an item, such as a document or news listing, to one or more audiences. You can do this at the time you create an item or at a later time. If you didn't originally create the item in a specific area and if you didn't specify an audience, you can follow the steps that appear at the end of the chapter to target an item and to store it in an area that uses the Targeted Content Web Part, called Links For You. Finally, audience membership must be compiled either manually or at scheduled intervals.

> **Note** Audiences are not used to assign rights and permissions. SharePoint Portal Server uses site groups to assign rights and permissions to users within the portal site. Audiences are used to manage how content is distributed and displayed, not to enforce security. They push information to a user; they do not restrict or permit access to information.

The Create Audience link on the Manage Audiences page allows the administrator to create an audience and define the rules of membership. Rules of membership are always dependent on the property values of a user's profile matching the criteria defined by the rule. More than one rule can be associated with an audience, along with a definition as to whether all rules must be met or whether only one rule must be met to satisfy audience membership.

Audience membership must be recompiled on a regular schedule to ensure that all new users are added and any users who no longer meet audience rules are removed. This compilation should be scheduled to occur after the profile import schedule has run if it is enabled.

Manage Personal Sites

Each user has a personal site called My Site that she can edit and use for her own purposes. From the bottom of the Site Settings page, the Manage Personal Sites link allows the administrator to specify the location that will store the user's personal sites and define a default naming convention for the user's personal site folders that will be created for her by the portal site. This link also allows the administrator to specify which Active Directory or local groups will be made members of the Site Reader group for each personal site as it is created.

By default, the Personal Site Location property is set to *personal*, meaning that all users' personal My Sites will be created under the /personal URL of the portal site. The available drop-down box will list managed paths that have been defined for the portal site. It is up to the administrator to decide whether to select a different managed path (which he would have created already) for the storage and servicing of My Sites.

> **More Info** Managed paths are created on the Define Managed Paths page, which is available from the Virtual Server Settings page of a virtual server. An included managed path is a path for which matching URL requests will be handled by Windows SharePoint Services. An excluded path will be handled by IIS in the traditional manner and not be passed to the Windows SharePoint Services.

The next parameter that needs defining is how to name the folders that will be created for each user's personal site. There are three conventions to choose from:

- **User name (do not resolve conflicts).** Example: http://portal_site /location/username/

- **User name (resolve conflicts by using domain_username).** Example: http://portal_site/location/username/ or http://portal_site/location/domain_ username/

- **Domain and user name (will not have conflicts).** Example: http: //portal_site/location/domain_username/

There is no right or wrong method, but the most consistent method in terms of predictability is the third option. Having a predictable name is useful because then you can "guess" the URL to someone's personal site simply by knowing his name.

The last setting to define for personal sites relates to which users or groups will be automatically assigned the Site Reader site group for each personal site. This will grant them the ability to see the public portion of any user's personal site. When users add content to their personal sites, they can decide whether that content should be private or public, meaning that anyone in the Site Reader site group can access it. Any local or Active Directory user or group can be assigned.

Another point regarding personal site management is that many administrators also want to know how to get into other users' personal sites to manage them. Remember that local administrators and SharePoint administrative group members have administrator access to all content, so all that is needed is the URL to the user's personal site. Having this URL can be useful for allowing the administrator to delete a user's content to free up space when she uses too much space in her personal sites or to delete the accounts of users who no longer need their personal site.

The preceding information regarding the usefulness of an administrator having users' URLs is true even for users whose accounts have been deleted. As long as you know the URL to the personal site, you can navigate to it and manage it if you are an administrator.

Caution   Be careful not to delete user accounts until you have cleaned up their personal sites. Despite the fact that you can get into their sites and delete public content, you will not be able to get into their private content. This is because anything marked as private, even private views of portal and team pages, is tied to the security identifier (SID) of the user account. Therefore, only that user account can access private items. If the account is deleted, there is no easy way to get to the content.

So how can an administrator access private items? Simply by running a browser session in the context of the user account in question. Use the Run As option to start a browser session and provide the credential information for the user you want to impersonate within the browser (assuming you can get it or reset the user's password). Even though you might be logged in at the console as yourself, the browser will act as though the user had logged in as it sends requests to the portal site.

Changing Owners of Portal Sites

What happens when a portal site owner leaves your organization or when you must add a user to or remove a user from a site for which you do not have administrative rights? If you are an administrator on the server and need to change the owner of a portal site to which you do not have administrative access, you can make the change from the Microsoft Office SharePoint Portal Server Central Administration page or from the command line by using the siteowner operation with Stsadm.exe.

> **Note**   Local server administrators and members of the SharePoint administrators group can perform any task that a portal site administrator can perform for a site collection.

When you create a portal site, you are automatically listed as the site owner. Depending on your configuration, you might also be required to specify a secondary owner for the portal site. Confirmation notifications are automatically sent to the site owner and to the secondary owner, if one exists.

The owner and secondary owner of a portal site are members of the Administrator site group. They are also identified separately in the configuration database as site owners. One can change this owner flag either by using the Manage Site Collection Owners page in SharePoint Portal Server Central Administration or by using the siteowner operation with Stsadm.exe.

> **Note**   If you remove an owner from the Administrator site group for the site, the owner retains the owner flag in the database and can still perform website administrative tasks.

The SharePoint Portal Server Central Administration page includes a link for managing users for sites. Administrators on the server computer and members of the SharePoint administrators group can use this link to change portal site owners, add users or cross-site groups, remove users or cross-site groups, and change site group membership, all without having to be an administrator on a specific site. Administrators do, however, need to know the URL for the portal site.

To change the owner of a portal site, follow these steps

1. From the home page of the portal site, click **Site Settings**.

2. On the Site Settings page, in the General Settings section, click **Go to SharePoint Portal Server central administration**.

3. On the SharePoint Portal Server Central Administration page, in the Security Configuration section, click **Manage site collection owners**.

4. On the Manage Site Collection Owners page, in the Site URL section, type the URL of the portal site, and then click **View**. The information for the current site owner and secondary owner appears on the page.

5. In the Site Collection Owner section, type the user name (in the form *DOMAIN\username*) for the user who will be the site owner and administrator.

6. If you have a new secondary contact name, type the user name in the Secondary Owner section.

7. Click **OK**.

To change the owner of a portal site by using Stsadm.exe, you must know the URL for the portal site and the specific user name that you want to change. You can use the siteowner operation to change the owner or secondary owner of a portal site. The syntax for changing the owner of a portal area is:

```
stsadm.exe -o siteowner -url <url>   [-ownerlogin <DOMAIN\username> | -
secondownerlogin <DOMAIN\username>]
```

Summary

In this chapter, we saw that the portal administrator has many responsibilities and management tasks relating to maintaining a portal site. Each feature the portal site adds to Windows SharePoint Services results in its own management requirements, for which there are administration tools available through the Web-delivered Site Settings page. First, the management of who can access the portal site, the level of access to the portal site, and whether or not anonymous access is allowed can be controlled. Next, management of alerts gives the administrator the ability to control alert usage and helps users clear out alerts when they get out of hand. With the addition of areas and content categorization features, management tools in the form of the Portal Site Map and the Topic Assistant are provided. To help manage the ability to target content to users that meet preset criteria, the administrator can use the audience management links. Finally there are management tools to manage personal sites as well.

Part VII

Information Management in SharePoint Products and Technologies

Chapter 19

Working with Documents in SharePoint Products and Technologies

One of the reasons customers are compelled to use Microsoft SharePoint Products and Technologies is because of its strong document collaboration features. In this chapter, we'll take a look at these features and illustrate how to administer document collaboration in SharePoint Products and Technologies.

But first, we'll outline why you'll want to move from storing your documents in a file server to storing them in a Microsoft SQL Server database. Storing files in SharePoint document libraries provides the following advantages over storing files in simple network file shares:

- The ability to centrally store custom properties associated with documents and groups of documents so that you more effectively store, organize, and retrieve large groups of documents.

- The use of shared or personal views to sort and filter documents that are of interest.

- The use of content approval so that users with the Manage Lists right can approve or reject which documents get added to a document library.

This chapter is primarily concerned with document collaboration in SharePoint Products and Technologies document libraries. A **document library** is a location where a collection of files is stored. Document libraries can be created within a Microsoft Office SharePoint Portal Server 2003 **portal site** and a Windows SharePoint Services **site**.

> **Note** This chapter will cover document collaboration approval routing within a **backward-compatible document library**, but no other features of the backward-compatible document library will be described. The backward-compatible document library component can be installed independently of SharePoint Portal Server 2003. The backward-compatible document library component enables you to store documents using the SharePoint Portal Server 2001 formatting and authorization process. For more information on the backward-compatible document library, refer to the *Microsoft Office SharePoint Portal Server 2001 Administrator's Guide*.

There is no single interface for SharePoint Products and Technologies; instead, you can access document libraries using the following familiar interfaces:

- Browser
- My Network Places\Web folder
- Compatible programs such as Microsoft Office applications

This flexibility allows you to work efficiently no matter where you are, but some functions are easier to achieve in one interface than in others. At the end of this chapter, in addition to understanding what information and document collaboration features are available, you should also be able to manage documents using the different methods and understand when you should use the different methods.

Understanding the Document Storage Options

SharePoint Products and Technologies support two types of content stores. The primary store is the SQL Server content store. Based on Microsoft SQL Server technology, the SQL Server content store provides a single, consistent data storage solution for document content, list content, and metadata. You can use common Microsoft Windows and SQL Server management tools and development tools to easily manage, tune, and back up SQL Server content stores.

When you install SharePoint Portal Server 2003, you have the option of installing the backward-compatible document store. The backward-compatible document store is an updated version of the **Web Storage System**–based document store used in SharePoint Portal Server 2001. The backward-compatible document store is provided for users who require features from SharePoint Portal Server 2001, such as document routing and approval, folder-level security, minor-level version numbers, and multiple **document profiles** for each folder.

The primary interfaces for the document collaboration features in SharePoint Products and Technologies are SharePoint libraries, which you can add to any SharePoint portal site or Windows SharePoint Services website. A library consists of the virtual folder where the files are stored, the files themselves, and the user-definable descriptive information (metadata) associated with each item in the library.

Libraries allow you to share files with site users. The kind of library you use depends upon the kind of files that you are sharing. If you need to store a group of XML-based business forms, use a **form library**. To share a collection of digital pictures or graphics, use a **picture library**. For most other file types, including documents and spreadsheets, use a document library.

Form Libraries

Form libraries provide a simple way for you to share and track XML-based forms (.xml files) that are used to gather the same type of information. For example, you can create a form library for your team's status report forms to provide a single location for team members to quickly fill out, save, and view their forms.

A form template is associated with each form library. This form template defines the structure and appearance of all forms created from the form library, as well as the appropriate application with which to open the form.

Although any file type can be stored in a form library, there are several advantages to storing only .xml files, which require a Windows SharePoint Services–compatible XML editor, such as Microsoft Office InfoPath 2003. These advantages include the ability to use form library columns (which can be designed to display specific information stored within each form in the library) and the ability to merge data from multiple forms into a single form.

Note   For more information on the use of SharePoint Products and Technologies and InfoPath, refer to Chapter 40, "Microsoft Outlook 2003 Integration with SharePoint Products and Technologies."

Picture Libraries

Picture libraries provide a simple way to share and organize digital pictures in a corporate server environment. For example, an organization could create a picture library for marketing graphics—providing a single location for team members to view, share, edit, and download corporate logos or other marketing material.

Although pictures can be stored in other types of lists and libraries, there are many advantages to using picture libraries. These advantages include viewing pictures with one of three unique display styles (detailed list, thumbnails, or a filmstrip); sharing pictures by using slide shows or by sending pictures directly to compatible programs; downloading pictures directly to a computer; and editing pictures with Windows SharePoint Services–compatible image editors, such as Microsoft Office Picture Manager. If you don't have Microsoft Office Picture Manager installed on the computer that you are using to locate a picture library or your Web browser is not configured to support ActiveX controls, you'll receive an error if you try to edit a picture held in a picture library, as illustrated in Figure 19-1.

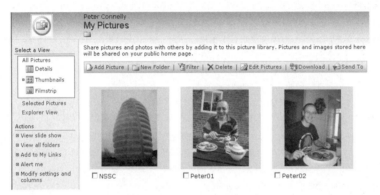

Figure 19-1 My Pictures, a picture library created by default when a user creates a personal website

Tip The Thumbnail style is best for browsing through a large set of pictures. Thumbnail images of the following extensions can be created: .gif, .jpeg, .jpg, .jpe, .jfif, .xbm, .bmp, .dib, .png, .wmf, .emf, .tif, and .tiff.

The Filmstrip style displays a strip of smaller pictures and a larger picture of the selected picture. This allows you to review many pictures and at the same time view in detail one of the pictures. Use the Selected Pictures view if you need to filter the items listed in My Pictures. The default display style for this view is Thumbnail.

As you can with other document libraries, you can add, create, delete, and edit items listed, as well as subscribe to e-mail notifications. If a Windows SharePoint Services–compatible program (such as a Microsoft Office 2003 program) is installed, you can upload multiple files.

Performance Considerations

Whether a document library is created in a portal site or a Windows SharePoint Services site, to maintain optimum server performance and ease navigation of the document libraries and folder structures, use the following guidelines as the upper limits for organizing files:

- 1000 files in a folder
- 1000 folders per document library
- 1000 document libraries per site
- 50 megabytes (MB) per file

When a site is maintained within these parameters, throughput is as follows:

- 10 saves per second per content database
- 300 reads per second per content database

When organizing content, you need to make a decision on the number of portal sites, site collections, sites, and document libraries.

All sites within a site collection use the same **content database**. If the expected traffic for the combined sites in a site collection exceeds the available throughput, separate the sites into multiple site collections. The site with heavy traffic can then be moved to a separate content database. If throughput is not an issue, you don't have to use more than one site collection for related files. Managing related files within one site collection allows easier navigation and control of security.

> **Note**   You must be a member of the Administrators group on the local server or a member of the SharePoint administrators group to create a site collection. Alternatively, if Self-Service Site Creation is enabled, end users can create their own site collections.

For more guidelines about running SharePoint Products and Technologies, see Chapter 8, "Planning Your Information Structure Using Microsoft Office SharePoint Portal Server 2003."

Content-Related Considerations

In general, create sites within a site collection so that you can place documents and lists that are related in the same site. This approach makes navigation more convenient and ensures that all related documents will be included in search results. It also ensures that if you need to create a lookup column in a list or document library that is based on metadata of a document library, you can do so. The use of the lookup feature to share information already stored in a site ensures data integrity. However, if a site contains more than 1000 document libraries and lists, performance begins to degrade.

> **Note**   If Self-Service Site Creation is enabled for a virtual server, you must belong to a site group that has the Use Self-Service Site Creation right to create a site collection. That right is turned on in all default site groups. If Self-Service Site Creation is not turned on, you must belong to a site group that has the Create Subsite right to create a site. The Create Subsite right is included by default in the Administrator site group.

Document Libraries

Document libraries can contain custom properties that store metadata about the files in the libraries. Document libraries also provide fine-grained security for granting access to files. Any files that can use the same set of properties and security settings can be stored in the same document library. (You can use views and filters to allow users to display any set of properties that they want to.) However, if a set of files requires a unique set of properties, it will need a separate document library. Similarly, if a set of files requires unique user permissions, that set will also require a different document library. Other settings that are per document library include file versioning, content approval, the default document template, and any event code written for the document library.

> **Note**   You must be a member of a site group with the Manage Lists right to create and change document libraries. The Manage Lists right is included by default in the Web Designer and Administrator site groups.

Document libraries can contain folders and files, which can be organized in the same familiar way as they are on your computer's C: drive or a file share, as directories and files. Users who contribute content to document libraries will become very familiar with the hierarchy and structure of the document libraries. However, for a visitor to your sites who has only reader rights or even for the occasional contributor, other features of SharePoint Products and Technologies will be needed to allow them to find information.

Document libraries can be viewed through the browser or through a **Web folder** view using My Network Places. The browser view of a document library contains a navigation area, which identifies your current location, the views you can choose, and any actions that are available to you.

When a document library is created, two views are available:

- **All Documents view.**   This is the default view and lists the documents in a similar way as a spreadsheet. This view enables you to have some information about the document without the need to open each document or rely on users to make the file name meaningful. Some columns display user-definable descriptive information, known as *document properties* or *metadata*, as illustrated in Figure 19-2. These document properties are displayed in columns next to the document name.

There can be multiple columns, and the information can be presented as Yes or No check boxes, drop-down menus, date and time, currency, a link, free text, or other choices. Document metadata can be promoted and demoted between Office-compatible files and the SQL Server content database. (See Chapter 20, "Working with Information Components in SharePoint Products and Technologies.") To view the metadata that has been read from the document, create columns that match the property names used in the document. Whether you create a column to display a document's metadata or not, the metadata will still be read and stored in the content database. The important point here is that when you create a column in the document library with a matching name to the property in the file, Windows SharePoint Services automatically demotes this property from the column in the document library and moves it into the property of the file.

Tip   If some columns do not appear in the view, property information can be found by clicking View Properties from the drop-down list associated with the file.

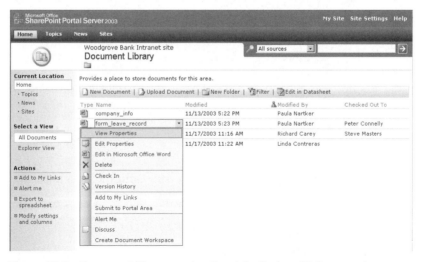

Figure 19-2   Document library—using the default view, All Documents, you can view the properties of a file

■ **Explorer view.** This view enables you to work with files and folders in a similar way that you work with files and folders in Microsoft Windows Explorer. Any user with the Reader permission will see the Forms folder, but you must have the Manage Lists right to access the contents of this folder. This folder is present in every document library or list and contains the Web pages used internally by Windows SharePoint Services to display the contents of the document library within a browser and the template document, which the document library uses. For example, in the Forms folder, you will see Upload.aspx, which is the upload document Web page that is displayed when you upload a document into the document library, and AllItems.aspx, which is the Web page that implements the All Documents view. Because the Forms folder is an internal structure folder, you should not store documents within it. You can use the Explorer view to copy and paste files and folders to and from the desktop, as well as to select multiple files and folders to copy.

When you try to view documents in a document library in Explorer view, you might experience problems, such as not being prompted for your credentials; the Web page not being displayed correctly; Microsoft Internet Explorer displaying a blank, white Web page; or the Web page displaying the words "Action Cancelled." These issues occur if both the following conditions are true:

1. You use Windows SharePoint Services in an Internet service provider (ISP)–hosted configuration with Basic authentication and Anonymous authentication enabled;

2. The WebClient service is disabled on the client computer.

By default, the WebClient service is disabled on Windows 2003 and set as automatic on Windows XP, but local site configurations might have altered these default settings. To work around this issue, enable the WebClient service on the client computer. To do so, follow these steps:

Note Because there are several versions of Microsoft Windows, the following steps might be different on your computer. If they are, see your product documentation to complete these steps.

1. Click **Start**, right-click **My Computer**, and then click **Manage**.

2. Expand **Services and Applications**, and then click **Services**.

3. In the right pane, double-click **WebClient**.

4. Click the **General** tab.

5. Do one of the following:

    a. To configure the WebClient service to start automatically when the computer starts, click **Automatic**.

    b. To configure the WebClient service so that you start the service manually, click **Manual**, click **Apply**, and then click **Start**. However, note that when you configure a service to use a manual startup type, the service does not start automatically when the computer starts.

6. Click **OK**.

By default, your portal site and most Windows SharePoint Services websites come with built-in libraries. The name of the document library will vary depending on the site template used to create the site. This is detailed in the following section.

More Info Site templates were covered in Chapter 16, "Administering Microsoft Windows SharePoint Services." Area templates will be covered in Chapter 20, "Working with Information Components in SharePoint Products and Technologies."

Portal Site Document Libraries

In a default installation of SharePoint Portal Server 2003, each **area** or **topic** within a portal site contains two libraries—except for the Sites area, which contains none. The two libraries created in each area or topic are as follows:

- **Document Library.** This library is of type Document Library, with versioning and content approval disabled. It defaults to using a Microsoft Word document template for all new documents created using the browser interface. The **document templates** are copied from <*driveletter*>:\Program Files\Common Files\Microsoft Shared\web server extensions\60\TEMPLATE\LCID, where *LCID* is the Locale ID. A subfolder structure exists for each area and topic. For example, the subdirectory SPSHOME is the template directory for the home page, SPSNEWS is the template directory for the News area of the portal, and SPSTOPIC is the template directory for the Topics area. The subdirectory STS contains the template subdirectories for the Windows SharePoint Services websites. The document libraries created for these sites are detailed in the next section.

- **Image Library.** This library is of type Picture Library.

Documents can therefore be physically located as content within a specific area or topic as well as associated with other areas or topics.

> **Tip** A user, who has only reader rights on the portal site, cannot directly navigate to the area and topic document libraries. The only method the user has of getting to a particular document library is via the results of a search query. It is therefore important that users who contribute content make their information easy to find by using features such as audiences, listings, keywords, Best Bets, and document properties (metadata).
>
> As a member of the Contributor, Content Manager, Web Designer, or Administrator site group, you can navigate to the portal document libraries by clicking the Manage Content link under the Actions section in the navigation area on the left.

Websites Document and Picture Libraries

When a website is created, the default site template creates various document and picture libraries. The templates and libraries they create are as follows:

- The Team Site, Document Workspace, and Multipage Meeting Workspace site templates create a document library named Shared Documents.

- The Blank Meeting Workspace and Blank site templates create no document libraries.

- The Basic Meeting Workspace and Decision Meeting Workspace site templates create a document library named Document Library.

- The Social Meeting Workspace site template creates a picture library named Picture Library.

My Site

Portal site users who are assigned to at least the Member site group can create a personal website—My Site. See Chapter 23, "Personalization Services in SharePoint Products and Technologies."

> **Note** A person with the Create Sites and Create Personal Site rights can also create a personal site.

The default personal site template creates three document libraries—My Pages, Private Documents, and Shared Documents; it also contains one picture library—My Pictures. The document library Private Documents is private to the user, whereas My Pages, Shared Documents, and My Pictures are shared on a user's public home page. Private Documents should be used in a similar way to My Documents. The My Lists section within the quick launch area allows the user to quickly gain access to their document libraries, as illustrated in Figure 19-3.

Figure 19-3 My Site quick launch area—My Lists section

Document Templates

You can store any kind of file in a document library. However, there are some advantages to using document libraries in conjunction with client programs compatible with Windows SharePoint Services, such as Microsoft Office 2003:

- You can set up a template that automatically starts the appropriate program and formats documents consistently when team members create new documents in the document library.

- You can open and modify your documents from within Windows SharePoint Services–compatible client programs as though the documents resided on any other network place or on your hard disk.

All the default document libraries, except for the My Pages document library within My Site, do not have versioning and approval enabled but do have a word template associated with them. Microsoft Office Word will run when a user clicks New Document on any of the default document library pages. The My Pages document library uses a Web Part Page document template, which, when the user clicks New Document on the My Pages document library page, results in the display of the My Pages: New Web Part Page.

Later, if you have a file in your site that you want to use as a template for new documents, you can modify the document library to use that file as the template.

The default document templates are:

- Microsoft Office Word document
- Microsoft Office FrontPage Web page
- Microsoft Office Excel spreadsheet
- Microsoft Office PowerPoint presentation
- Basic Page
- Web Part Page

More Info   When a SharePoint site is created, a number of XML files are used to create the document libraries just described. For example, each Windows SharePoint Services site definition on a front-end Web server has one ONET.XML file located in the Local_Drive\Program Files\Common Files\Microsoft Shared\Web Server Extensions\60\TEMPLATE\LCID\ Site_Definition_Name\XML folder. ONET.XML specifies the document templates that are available for creating document library lists on the New Document Library page and specifies the files used in the document templates. The default document templates for Windows SharePoint Services website document libraries are held within *<driveletter>*\Program Files\Common Files\Microsoft Shared\Web Server Extensions\60\TEMPLATE\LCID\Sts\. For example, the default Word document template is held in doctemp\word\wdtmpl.doc. When a document library for a Windows SharePoint Services website is created that uses this document template, wdtmpl.doc is copied to the document library's Form directory and renamed as template.doc. Similar ONET.XML files and document templates exist for My Site and areas within portal sites. These are stored in associated XML and DOCTEMP subdirectories, located in area-specific and My Site–specific subdirectories in the *<driveletter>*\Program Files\Common Files\Microsoft Shared\Web Server Extensions\60\TEMPLATE\LCID folder. See Chapter 20 for more information on area templates and Part VIII, "Securing SharePoint Products and Technologies" for more information on how to customize document templates. Making changes to an originally installed ONET.XML file on a server running Windows SharePoint Services is not supported and can break existing sites.

To create a customized document template or to create a document template based on an existing document template, navigate to the document library, click Modify Settings And Columns, and then in the General Settings area to the right of the DocumentTemplate and the path to the template, click (Edit Template). Edit the template and then save it. The template for your document library must be stored in the Forms folder of the document library that uses it. If you customize the template after documents have been added to the document library, changes to the template will not be reflected in the existing documents. If you save the template with a different name, the path to the template should be changed by clicking Change General Settings in the General Settings section of the Modify Settings And Columns page. On the Document Library Settings "document library" page, in the Document Template section, specify the path to the file that you want to use as a template. The path is relative to the current website.

Templates for document libraries can be in any file format that a client program compatible with Windows SharePoint Services can open (.doc, .xls, and so on). However, there are advantages to using a Web-based file format (.htm or .mht) for a template:

- Team members don't need to have the appropriate client program installed to read a document that's based on a Web page (.htm) or Web archive (.mht).

- Using the Web Discussions feature, you can attach threaded discussions within a document that's based on a Web page or Web archive.

Caution   Template files include personal information such as server URLs and user account names. Share template files only with trusted users and groups.

Naming Conventions

Some basic naming conventions include the following:

- The following characters are not allowed in file or folder names, although they can be used in property names and values: / \ : * ? " < > | # <TAB> { } % ~ &

- A file name or folder name cannot end in a period or contain two or more consecutive periods.

- File and folder names cannot be longer than 128 characters. Also note that the complete URL for the file or folder cannot be longer than 260 characters.

Creating Document Libraries

If you require additional document libraries, they can be created. The method to use depends on whether the document library is to reside within a portal site area or topic or in a specific type of website.

The following procedures apply to portal areas and Topics.

To use the Manage Content link

1. Navigate to the area or Topic where the document library resides.

2. Click **Manage Content** in the navigation area in the **Actions** section.

3. On the top link bar, click **Create**.

4. On the Create Page page, click **Document Library**.

5. In the **Name** box, type a name for the list. This is a required field.

6. In the **Description** box, type a description of the purpose of the library.

7. In the **Navigation** section, click **Yes** if you want a link to this list to appear on the Quick Launch bar. This is only meaningful on websites that have a quick launch area. Portal areas and Topics do not have a Quick Launch area.

8. In the **Document Versions** section, click **Yes** if you want a backup copy of a file to be created each time a file is checked into the library.

9. In the **Document Template** section, specify the type of file used as a template for new files in this document library.

10. Click **Create**.

The following procedures apply to Team sites, Blank sites, Document Workspace sites, and Multipage Meeting Workspace websites.

To use the Create link on the Navigation area

1. On the top link bar, click **Create**.

2. On the Create Page page, click **Document Library** and follow the procedure just shown.

You can open the new document library by clicking Documents and Lists on the top link bar and then clicking the document library name in the Document Libraries section. If you chose to add the document library to the Quick Launch bar, you can also click the document library name there to open it.

To use the Create link on the Document and Lists page

1. On the top link bar, click **Documents and Lists**.

2. On the Documents And Lists page, click **Create**.

3. On the Create Page page, click **Document Library** and follow the procedure just shown.

My Site has the Documents And Lists link on the top navigation bar. It also has the following additional way of creating document libraries:

1. Click the **Create List** link under the **Actions** section.

2. On the Create Page page, click **Document Library** and follow the procedure just shown.

The following procedures apply to Meeting Workspace sites, Blank Meeting sites, Decision Meeting sites, and Social Meeting sites:

1. From the **Modify This Workspace** menu, click **Site and Settings**.

2. Click **Modify site content** under the Customization section.

3. On the Modify Site Content page, click **Create new content**.

4. On the Create Page page, click **Document Library** and follow the procedure just shown.

Once you've created your document library, consider creating extra columns to match the metadata you want to capture for the documents that will be located here, and then assign defaults. Also create the folder structure that you have planned for this document library.

If you're going to do a bulk transfer of documents, batch together documents with the same metadata values. Set the defaults of the columns to those values of the first batch of documents and then use the Upload Multiple Files feature on the first batch of documents. Change the default values of the columns to the metadata of the second batch of documents and upload them. Continue this process until you have uploaded all the documents. The Upload Multiple Files feature is detailed later in this chapter.

Nesting Folders within a Document Library

The folder structure of a document library is usually similar to the folder structure of a typical file store. For optimal performance, each folder should contain fewer than 1000 files. Performance and ease of navigation will degrade as the number of files in a folder increases. The depth of the folder structure might also be limited by the number of characters in the file and folder name. There can be no more than 260 total characters in the URL for a file in a document library. The maximum file or folder name length is 128 characters, including the extension.

Security can't be configured at the folder level. All folders within a document library inherit the security settings of the document library in which they reside.

If a folder structure has few files but lots of subfolders, consider adding properties to the document library. Users do not have to remember where to place documents. While navigating through the subfolder hierarchy, they just need to enter property values. Views can then be added to the document library instead of adding subfolders to display the subset of documents that contain the appropriate property value. For example, create a property named "Team member" for a Team Documents folder instead of a subfolder for each team member. Then create a view that displays only those documents belonging to a particular team member.

You must be a member of a site group with the Add Items right to add files to a document library. The Add Items right is included by default in every built-in site group except the Reader site group.

Security of Document Libraries

Security is essential to both document collaboration tasks and the search function. In document collaboration, you need to restrict the viewing of a document to those who edit or approve it, until it's ready for a larger audience. This can be achieved by using content approval features within SharePoint Products and Technologies. Security is also important to prevent users from finding documents to which they should have no access when they perform searches. For this, SharePoint Products and Technologies provide user authentication, and groups and permissions rights.

Managing security on information is difficult because it's relative—that is, it means different things to different people. Information can be sensitive. It can also be dynamic and change as the business changes or as the processes or people within a business change. Often the decision on who sees what will be delegated to a user who owns the information, a business owner. However, the user will need to understand the technical implementation of security on document libraries within a portal site and how they can differ from security features provided in a Windows SharePoint Services site. The following section provides this detail.

Portal Site Document Libraries

Portal area and topic document libraries take their security from the portal site. Submitting documents to a portal site area—that is, creating a link on portal site pages—in conjunction with audience targeting would enable you to filter documents for the users to your sites.

Windows SharePoint Services Document Libraries

Websites have security set at the document library and list level as well as at the site level. If you have sensitive information stored in a document library and you don't want to expose the information to all members of a site, you can set permissions for just that document library to control which users can view, edit, or add items to that list. You can grant permissions to a list or document library to individual users, to groups of users, or to a site group. Per-list permissions work for any list or document library in a website based on Windows SharePoint Services. Per-list permissions aren't available for lists that are part of portal areas. Portal area lists inherit their security from the area itself.

List permissions can be changed by any user who has the Manage List Permissions right (by default, included in the Administrator site group) or users who have all permissions selected for that list. By default, all members of a website (all users assigned to a site group, except for the Guest site group) have access to all lists and document libraries on that website. Each site group has a predefined level of permissions for all lists and document libraries. The default list permissions are as follows:

- View items (given to the Reader site group by default)
- View, insert, edit, and delete items (given to the Contributor site group by default)
- View, insert, edit, and delete items; change list settings (given to the Web Designer site group by default)
- View, insert, edit, and delete items; change list settings; change list security (No group is assigned these permissions by default. A Web Site Administrator will have full control of the website.)

In addition, you can set advanced permissions, which allows you to grant any of the following rights for a user or site group:

- Manage Lists (given to the Web Designer site group by default)
- Manage List Permissions
- Manage Personal Views (given to the Contributor site group by default)
- Cancel Check-Out (applies only to document libraries; given to the Web Designer site group by default)
- Add List Items, Edit List Items, and Delete List Items (given to the Contributor site group by default)
- View List Items (given to the Reader site group by default)

> **Note**   Members of the Administrator site group always have the highest level of permissions for all lists and document libraries. You cannot change list or document library permissions for the Administrator site group. Also, any site group that has the View List Items right (such as Reader) can continue to see the list name, description, number of items, and time when the list was last modified, even though they cannot view the list contents directly.

To view, change, or remove permissions on a website document library, complete the following steps:

1. Using a browser, navigate to the document library and then in the left pane, click **Modify settings and columns**.

2. On the Customize Document Library page, in the **General Settings** section, click **Change permissions for this document library**. The Change Permissions: Document Library page is displayed, as illustrated in Figure 19-4.

Depending on the task needed, perform either of the following steps:

1. View the details, and then click **Go Back to Document Library**.

2. Click the box next to the group or user you want to change and perform either of the following steps:

   a. Click **Edit Permissions of Selected Users**. In the **Choose Permissions** section, select the level of permissions to allow, and then click **OK**.

   b. Click **Remove Selected Users**.

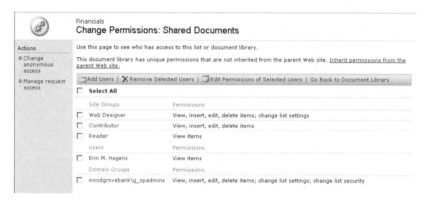

Figure 19-4   Change Permissions: Document Library

To assign document library permissions to a specific user or group

1. Navigate to the list, and then in the left pane, click **Modify settings and columns**.

2. On the Customize Document Library page, in the **General Settings** section, click **Change permissions for this document library**.

3. On the list toolbar, click **Add Users**.

4. In the **Step 1: Choose Users** section, in the **Users** area, in the text box, type the network domain name or e-mail address for the user or group you want to assign permissions.

5. In the **Step 2: Choose Permissions** section, under **Permissions**, select the level of permissions for the user or group, and then click **Next**.

6. In the **Step 3: Confirm Users** section, verify that the e-mail address, user name, and display name for the user or group are correct.

7. If you want to notify the user or group of their permissions with an e-mail message, in the **Step 4: Send E-Mail** section, select the **Send the following e-mail to let these users know they've been added** check box, and fill in the text you want to send, as illustrated in Figure 19-5.

8. Click **Finish**.

   If you want to restrict your list to a specific set of users, you must both grant access to the individual users and remove access from other site members.

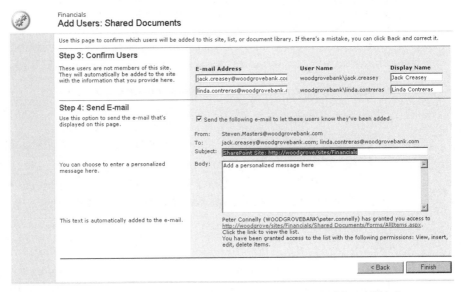

Figure 19-5   Document library permissions: Confirm Users and Send E-Mail

Caution   Remember that when you grant a user or group permissions to a specific document library in your site, they are added to the Guest site group if they are not already members of the site. Note that members of the Guest site group cannot navigate to a page within the site unless you give them the exact page URL.

To reset permissions of the document library to the default state

1. Navigate to the list, and then in the left pane, click **Modify settings and columns**.

2. On the Customize *Document Library* page, in the **General Settings** section, click **Change permissions for this document library**.

3. Click **Inherit permissions from the parent Web site**. The **Inherit permissions from the parent Web site** link does not appear unless the list permissions have already been customized.

4. Click **OK** to change to inherited permissions.

Per-List Permissions and Anonymous Access

You can control anonymous access for your entire site by using the Manage Anonymous Access page, or you can control anonymous access for specific document libraries by using the per-list permissions feature. If anonymous access is disabled for your site or if Internet Information Services (IIS) is not configured to allow anonymous access, it cannot be enabled for a particular document library in the site. In such circumstances, the check boxes are unavailable (grayed out).

To enable anonymous access for a document library

1. Verify that anonymous access is enabled for your site.

2. Navigate to the document library, and then in the left pane, click **Modify settings and columns**.

3. On the Customize *Document Library* page in the **General Settings** section, click **Change permissions for this document library**.

4. In the **Action** pane, click **Change anonymous access**.

5. On the Change Anonymous Access Settings page, click the check box for the level of permissions that you want to grant to anonymous users.

6. Click **OK**.

Note that you'll also need to add the Anonymous User account to your site as at least a Reader before enabling Anonymous access, and you'll need to configure the virtual server for Anonymous access too. If you don't, the options will remain grayed out, as illustrated in Figure 19-6.

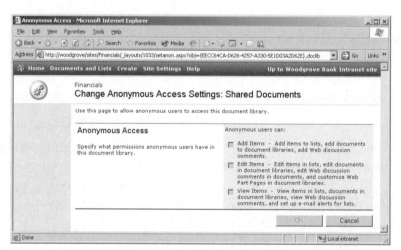

Figure 19-6   Change Anonymous Access Settings: Document Library

Access Denied

Although users who have List access to document libraries will be able to view the contents of a document library, many options visible to the user will not be available to them. In such cases, when the user comes to complete a task, a Windows security dialog box will prompt a user for a name and password. Failure to provide a user name that has the necessary rights will result in either an access denied message being displayed or, if the Request For Access feature is enabled, a Web page being displayed that the user can complete and send to the owner of the website. The Request For Access Web page and the resultant e-mail is illustrated in Figure 19-7.

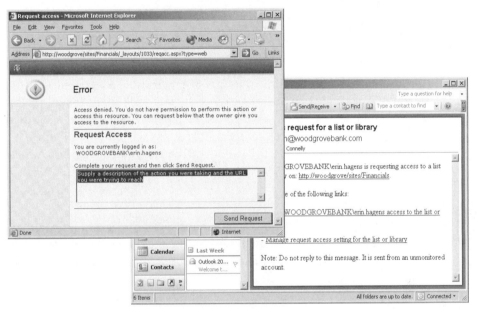

Figure 19-7   Error: Request For Access and Owner E-mail

At first glance, the text of the e-mail to the owner does not specify the list or the library for which the user is having access difficulties. However, this information is contained in the hyperlinks. To give the user the required access, click the grant link. This will redirect you to the list or document library where the user had the access problem. This e-mail is sent to you only if the user can't access the document library or list. If the user has some access right but doesn't have the necessary access rights to complete a task, the more general Access request for a site e-mail is sent. An example of such a scenario would be if a user had list rights to a document library and tried to check out a document. In this case, the e-mail the user receives might lead him to believe that there is a website access problem when it is a document library access issue. To prevent misdiagnoses and to enable you to decide whether this user should have access, you should train end users to include in the e-mail a description of the task they were trying to complete and the name of the document library or list.

By default the Request Access feature is enabled at the website level and on document libraries. There is no such equivalent feature for portal document libraries.

To enable Request Access at the document level

1. Navigate to the document library, and then in the left pane, click **Modify settings and columns**.

2. On the Customize *Document Library* page, in the **General Settings** section, click **Change permissions for this document library**.

3. In the **Action** pane, click **Manage Request Access**.

4. On the Manage Request Access: *Document Library* page, clear or select the check box for **Allow Requests for Access**.

5. Click **OK**.

This method of enabling Request Access doesn't permit you to change the recipient of e-mail—that is, you cannot specify a different e-mail recipient for each document library or list. To change the Request For Access e-mail address, you need to edit Allow Request Access at the site level, as illustrated in Figure 19-8. If Request For Access is disallowed at the site level, the Allow Requests For Access at the document library is unavailable.

Warning   Even with the Allow Request For Access feature enabled, under certain circumstances users will be redirected to the Access Denied Web page—for example, if a user has only reader rights on the portal and she then clicks on a website Add To My Links. The reason for this particular access denied message is that the My Links feature is part of a user's personal website. To have a personal website, the user must be at least assigned Member rights on the portal site. Occasionally, when using SharePoint Products and Technologies, the Access Denied message or the Windows Security dialog box will appear. These are obtuse methods of stating that the user is trying to attempt an activity for which she currently doesn't have permission. Such messages can also occur because of browser and proxy server configuration settings. In most cases, the message isn't generated because of a misconfiguration or a bug within SharePoint Products and Technologies. End users and support staff should be warned of the possibilities of and reasons for the Access Denied and Windows Security dialog box appearing so that access permission problems can be resolved efficiently.

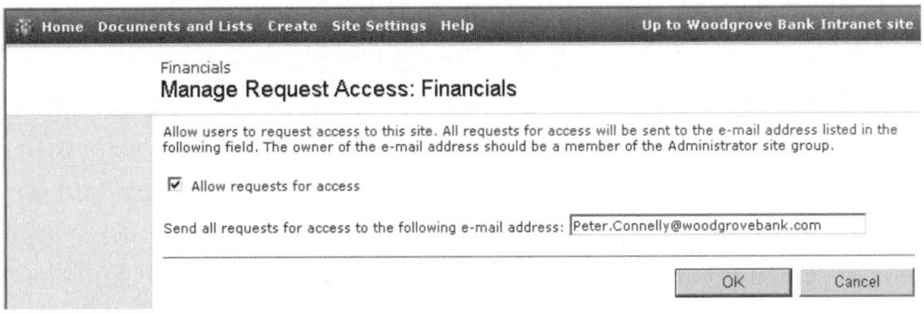

Figure 19-8   Manage Request For Access: Document Library

For more information on security settings and configuration, see Chapter 6, "Security Architecture for SharePoint Products and Technology."

Uploading Documents into a Document Library

There are several ways of storing documents within a document library, some of which are detailed in this section. The main tools you'll use to upload documents are the browser and Microsoft Office applications.

Outside an Office Application

To upload a document using a browser, navigate to the wanted document library; click the Upload Document button in either the All Documents or Explorer view. On the portal area and Topic Web pages, there is also an Upload Document link under the Actions section in the navigation area on the left.

Uploading Files Using the All Document View

The Document Library: Upload Document Web page will be displayed when you upload a document. This Web page is different than the document profile page because that page contains a set of properties that will be applied to the document during a check-in process. Portal site area and Topic document libraries are created with four columns. Therefore, on the Upload Document form, four properties (Name, Title, Owner, and Status) are presented on the form, as well as an extra check box, the Add A Listing For This Document check box. (See Figure 19-9.) The Name field is the filename, a link to where the document is located within the SQL Server database, but the other fields are created and mapped to the four columns created in the document library. Website document libraries are created with only one column, Title. Therefore, the Upload Document form will look different. The Add A Listing For This Document check box will enable you to create a link item for this document in a Portal Listings list. See Chapter 20 for more information on listings.

The Title property is not visible from the default All Document view, but it's visible if you view the properties of a document. You can rename the Title property, but you cannot delete it. This is the only property that cannot be deleted. You can choose to make the Title property visible by clicking the Modify Settings And Columns link and then clicking the All Document link under the Views section. You'll notice on the Document Library: Edit View page that you have a number of built-in properties you can choose from as well as any custom properties that you have added. Columns, and therefore fields, on the Upload Document form can be deleted or modified and new ones can be created. The order in which the fields appear on the form can be changed. A red asterisk by the side of the field denotes a mandatory field, thereby ensuring consistency within a document library. By placing fields in the Upload Document form, you can increase the amount of information (metadata) that can be stored in the SQL content database and used to assist users in finding this document and in determining whether the document contains the information they are searching for. For more information on the search process, see Chapter 21.

Note   Users who belong to the Reader or Contributor site group on a site cannot add or modify column settings.

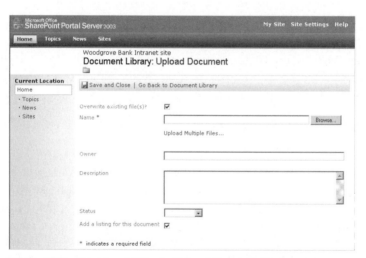

Figure 19-9   Document Library: Upload Document form

In the Name field, enter the location from where the file can be uploaded. In most cases, using the Browse button prevents typing errors. It is recommended that you enter appropriate information in the other default fields. When you click the Save And Close link, the "Form Validation Error" Web page is displayed (as illustrated in Figure 19-10) if any of the following conditions exist:

- If the file is empty
- If the file doesn't exist

- If the file exceeds the maximum file size

- If the file has a filename that includes braces—for example, a filename.(doc)

- If the file is a blocked file type

The default maximum upload file size limit is 50 MB and applies to the combined size if you are using the Multiple Upload file feature.

Figure 19-10   Form Validation Error

A similar Upload Document form, now labeled Web File Properties, will also be displayed if, for example, Microsoft Office 2003 or Office XP is used to save a file to a document library. These properties can be viewed and edited by using either the browser or Microsoft Office applications.

Uploading Files by Using Explorer View

Although the Upload Document link is available in the Explorer view, the simplest method for moving files to the new site is to drag and drop files or folders into the Explorer view of a document library.

To drag and drop files by using the Explorer view

1. On the top link bar, click **Documents and Lists**.

2. Click the document library to which you want to add files.

3. In the **Select a View** list, click **Explorer View**.

4. Open a Windows Explorer window, and find the folder with the files that you want to copy to the document library.

5. Select the desired files, and then drag them into the document library in the browser window.

Add Files by Using Upload Multiple Files

If Microsoft Office 2003 is installed, the Upload Document form will contain an Upload Multiple Files link. Once clicked, an Explorer-like view consisting of two panes will be displayed, as illustrated in Figure 19-11. The left pane is the navigation pane, which starts with a desktop view of your computer. The right pane lists the files found in the selected folder, with a check box next to each file. By selecting the check boxes, you can choose the files you want to upload. The Overwrite Existing File(s) check box is available. If selected, this setting will be used for all files—that is, if a file of the same name exists in the document library, it will be replaced.

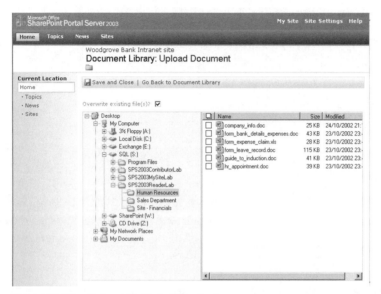

Figure 19-11   Upload Multiple Files feature

If you use this feature on portal document libraries, you cannot upload a document and add a listing for the documents—that is, using the bulk upload method, the Add A Listing For This Document option is not available. If you want a link to be added to the Portal Listings list for an area or topic for any documents you are uploading, you'll need to use the Submit To Portal Area or Add A Listing features. See Chapter 20 for more information on this topic. Also, if you have defined extra columns in your document library and have assigned default values to those columns, during the bulk upload method the default values will be taken for the fields for each document.

To upload files into a document library by using My Network Places

1. Click the **Start** menu, click **All Programs**, point to **Accessories**, and then click **Windows Explorer**.

2. In the **Folders** list, click **My Network Places**.

3. In the right pane, double-click **Add Network Place**.

4. Follow the instructions in the **Add Network Place Wizard** to add a shortcut to the server running Windows SharePoint Services.

5. After you've created the new network place, open a Windows Explorer window and find the folder with the files that you want to copy to the document library.

6. Select the desired files, and then drag them into the document library in the network place.

To add files by using a mapped network drive

Another method of uploading documents into a document library is to use a *mapped network drive*. Note that this functionality doesn't work if you have the client components installed for the backward-compatible document library. Using a mapped network drive to upload documents into a document library can be achieved by completing the following steps:

1. Click **Start**, and then click **My Computer**.

2. On the **Tools** menu, click **Map Network Drive**.

3. In **Drive**, select a drive letter.

4. In **Folder**, type the name of the Web server and document library in the form **Server_Name\Document_Library**\.

   The mapped network drive opens in Windows Explorer to show the contents of the document library.

5. Open a Windows Explorer window, and then find the folder with the files that you want to copy to the document library.

6. Select the desired files, and then drag them into the document library in the mapped network drive.

Within an Office Application

To upload a file, applications compatible with Windows SharePoint Services allow you to save files to document libraries by using the file management tools in those applications. For example, using Microsoft Word, you can use the Save or Save As actions from the File menu and then click My Network Places to choose the Web Folder view of the document library. If a network place does not exist for the document library, you might need to create one. See Chapter 39, "Using Microsoft Office InfoPath with SharePoint Products and Technologies."

Warning   If you copy and paste the document library's URL from the address area of the browser, you might find that the URL now contains the following characters: %20. You have to replace the "%20" characters with spaces before the document library is displayed in a Web Folder view.

Blocked File Types

Microsoft Windows SharePoint Services provides the ability to restrict certain kinds of files from being uploaded or retrieved, based on the file extension. For example, a file with the .exe file extension could contain code that runs on client computers when it is downloaded. Because it has the .exe file extension, the file can be run on demand when it is downloaded. If files with the .exe file extension are blocked, users can neither upload nor download a file with the .exe extension, and potentially dangerous content in the .exe file cannot be downloaded. This feature does not prevent all exploits based on file types, nor is it designed to do so.

By default, several standard file extensions are blocked, including any file extensions that are treated as executable files by Windows Explorer. Files with curly braces, { or }, are also blocked automatically.

The list of file extensions is controlled for the entire server or **server farm** and is recorded in the **configuration database**. Because the list of blocked file types is maintained by file extension, all files that use a file extension on the list cannot be uploaded or downloaded, irrespective of the file's intended use. If .asp is on the list of extensions to block, the feature blocks all .asp files on the server, even if they're used to support website features on another server in the server farm. If a file ends in a period (.), the preceding characters are checked against the list of blocked file extensions as well. For example, if .exe is on the list of blocked file extensions, a file named "filename.exe." is also blocked. The following list shows different ways of representing the same file, all of which are blocked if the .hta extension is on the list of blocked file extensions:

- filename.hta
- filename.hta.
- filename.hta.{3050F4D8-98B5-11CF-BB82-00AA00BDCE0B}
- filename.hta::$DATA

You can determine which files are blocked for websites on your servers by modifying the list of blocked file extensions. You can block additional file extensions (up to 1024 file types) by adding them to the list in the SharePoint Central Administration pages, or you can remove a block by deleting the file extension from the list. When you change the list of file extensions, the change affects both new files being added to a website and files already posted to a website. For example, if a document library contains a .doc file and you add the .doc file extension to the list of blocked file extensions, users will no longer be able to open the .doc file in the document library. Users will be able to rename or delete a file with a blocked file extension but will not be able to perform any other actions.

To configure blocked file types, click Manage blocked file types, under Security configuration on the SharePoint Central Administration page. On the Manage Block File Type page, you can add or delete a file type.

For more information on configuring blocked file types, see Chapter 28, "Disaster Recovery in SharePoint Products and Technologies."

Modifying Columns

When you have a number of documents in a document library, you'll find it useful to have some information about them available—information that will allow you to find the document you need without having to open each document or rely on people to make filenames meaningful. Document libraries and lists can be easily customized to display custom properties about the documents. You only need to navigate to the document library or list, click on Modify Settings And Columns, and choose to add a new column. The default is that any new column is added to the default view. Additionally you can mark any column as "required" information and you can provide a default value for the column, which can be a static text value or a calculated value. If a column is marked as required and the user does not enter a value for that column, the default value will be used. If you have not provided a default value for a required column, the user will need to enter a value for that column.

The Name property of the column is a custom property that will be associated with a document when it is stored. A number of information, or column, types are available, such as text, user choices, numbers, currency, and dates. You also have the ability by means of lookup references to reference other information that is already stored in a list or document library in the current website, thus ensuring data integrity. You can create the following numbers of each column type for each document library or list:

- Single line of text and single choice—that is, where a user is provided with a drop-down menu or radio buttons—columns: 64

- Multiple lines of text and multiple choice—where a user is provided with check boxes—columns: 31

- Number and Currency columns: 32

- Hyperlink or Picture columns: 32

- Date and Time columns: 16

- Lookup columns: 16

- Yes/No columns: 16

- Calculated columns: 8

In the preceding list, where more than one column type is mentioned, the number given is the total for all columns of those types. For example, you could have 14 Number and 18 Currency columns, but not 32 of each column type.

> **More Info**   See the *SharePoint Portal Server 2003 Administrator's Guide* for information types and options. You can also create your own custom field types. To find out how to do this, see the *Microsoft Windows SharePoint Services Software Development Kit.*

If the name of the column matches the custom property of the document, the property is propagated into the document content. When a document is saved into a document library, the property form is generated in HTML and, depending on the method used to save a document, will be labeled as either the Upload Document form or Web File Properties. All documents within a document library share the same property form. This form was discussed earlier in the chapter and might also be known as a document's profile.

If you're a frequent contributor to a document library, you'll become very familiar with the property form and its ease of use. Only add properties that you are sure will be useful. Before you add new properties, check the built-in properties. You might find that an existing property meets your needs. Place important properties so that they appear at the top of the property form by using the Change The Order Of Fields feature. Remember that properties are also used during the search process; therefore, ensure that users understand the importance of including a title and description and that data is stored in the property. Data stored in a property name is not searchable; therefore, keep the number of properties that use, for example, the Yes/No check box option to a minimum. Only data that is stored in the property is searchable.

Document libraries and lists can be filtered or sorted on any of the custom or built-in properties. Custom views can be created for frequently used filters and sorts, thereby ensuring ease of use for users of the document library.

When you create a custom view of a document library and you group the view by a column that stores date and time information, you might find that some list items are incorrectly grouped in the view. To achieve the desired results, create a new column that uses the following formula: =TRUNC([OriginalDateTimeColumnName]. Then group the list items in the new column. When you use this formula, although the data type that is returned for items in the column uses Date and Time format, the formula truncates the data type so that items in the column use the Date Only format. See Microsoft Knowledge Base Article 823509, "List Items in a Column That Stores Date and Time Information Are Grouped Incorrectly in a View."

Check-In/Check-Out Processes

Microsoft Windows SharePoint Services gives users the ability to keep versions of documents and to check documents in and out.

About Document Versioning

Document versioning allows you to keep multiple versions of a document. This functionality is not enabled by default. By enabling document versioning, if a change needs to be reversed, you can restore the previous version and continue working. A Version History command is included on the drop-down list users see when they click the arrow next to a document name and on the toolbar in the Edit Properties or View Properties page for the document. The Version History command is also available in client applications compatible with Windows SharePoint Services, such as Microsoft Office Word 2003, Microsoft Office Excel 2003, and Microsoft Office PowerPoint 2003. When the user clicks Version History, a list of the previous versions of the document appears. The user can open an old version, restore a version (replacing the current version), or delete an old version.

Important When a file is deleted from a library, all previous versions are deleted as well.

Versions can be created for all file types except HTML files that contain images or embedded objects. If you want to create versions as HTML, you must use the archive, or thicket, MHTML format (often saved as .mht) when saving to this website. This restriction applies to other compound documents. Although you can save several versions of a compound document—say, a Microsoft Word document with a link to a Microsoft Excel spreadsheet held within a document library—the link within the Microsoft Word document will always point to the most recent version of the Excel spreadsheet and not to the version of the spreadsheet that matched the version of the Word document at time of creation. If you want to match information from several sources at a particular instance, you need to include the content within one document and not link to it. In SharePoint Server 2001, compound documents were supported only in **standard folders**.

By default, picture and document versioning is turned off for the document libraries that are created for each portal site area, Topic, and SharePoint site. You can enable and disable versioning once a document library is created. When you create a new library, you have the option of turning on versioning. This means that you can turn on versioning for libraries that store important information and turn off this feature for libraries that don't need versioning.

When versioning is enabled, versions are automatically created whenever a user updates a document in a document library. Version control in SharePoint Products and Technologies is different than the versioning in the backward-compatible document libraries, where version numbers have a major and minor number. See the *SharePoint Portal Server 2003 Administrator's Guide* for more information on version history in the backward-compatible document library. In SharePoint Products and Technologies, versioning has only a major number, which is incremented by one as versions are created, starting with an initial major version number of one. Versions are created in the following situations:

- When a user checks out a file, makes changes, and checks the file back in
- When a user opens a file, makes changes, and then saves the file for the first time

Note If the user saves the file again, without closing the file, a new version is not created. If the user closes the application she is using to edit the file and then opens it and saves the file again, another version is created.

- When a user restores an old version of a file (and does not check it out)
- When a user uploads a file that already exists, in which case the current file becomes an old version

Members of the Administrator, Content Manager, and Web Designer site groups can determine whether document versioning is enabled for a particular document library.

Tip If the information stored in a document library is valuable, you should turn on versioning. However, when turned on, versioning requires much more storage space on the Web server. If Web server disk space is low or the files stored in the library are not critical or are backed up by using another means, you should not enable versioning.

To enable versioning for a document library

By default, versioning is not enabled on document libraries. To enable versioning, complete the following steps:

1. Navigate to the document library, and on the left link bar, click **Modify settings and columns**.

2. On the Customize Document Library page, click **Change general settings**.

3. On the Document Library Settings page, in the **Document Versions** section, under **Create a version each time you edit a file in this document library?**, click **Yes**.

4. Click **OK**.

Tip To find whether versioning is enabled for a document library, use the procedure just shown to check the settings.

To view the contents of previous versions of a file

1. Using your browser, navigate to the document library. In the row where the name of the file appears, point to the file, click the triangle on the bar that appears, and then click **Version History** on the menu that appears.

2. In the **Modified** column, click the version of the file that you want to view, as illustrated in Figure 19-12.

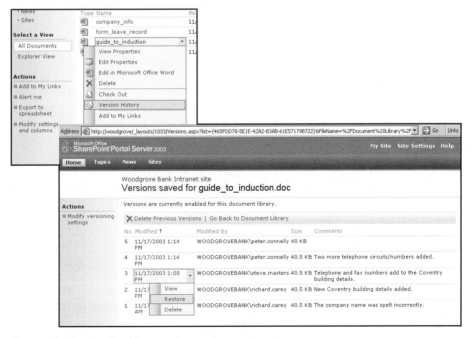

Figure 19-12 Version History, view and restore

> **Note**   The Version History command is also available in client applications that are compatible with SharePoint Products and Technologies, such as Microsoft Office Word 2003, Excel 2003, and PowerPoint 2003.

To restore a file to a previous version

Once you have ascertained that you want a previous document to become the most recent version, perhaps by viewing the version as just shown, you can restore a file by completing the following steps:

1. On the page that displays the library, in the row where the name of the file appears, point to the file, click the triangle on the bar that appears, and then click **Version History** on the menu that appears.

2. In the **Modified** column, point to the version of the file that you want to restore, click the triangle on the bar that appears, and then click **Restore** on the menu that appears.

3. When prompted to confirm that you want to replace the current version of the file with the previous version, click **OK**.

To delete previous versions of a file

Storing multiple versions of a document will affect the storage and your quota. Therefore, it's a good practice to manage your documents on a regular basis. To delete a previous version of a file, you can do either of the following:

- Delete one previous version of a file by completing the following steps:

    1. On the page that displays the library, in the row where the name of the file appears, point to the file that you want to delete, click the triangle on the bar that appears, and then click **Version History** on the menu that appears.

    2. In the **Modified** column, point to the version of the file that you want to delete, click the triangle on the bar that appears, and then click **Delete** on the menu that appears.

    3. When prompted to confirm that you want to delete the previous version of the file, click **OK**.

- Delete all previous versions of a file by completing the following steps:

    1. On the page that displays the library, in the row where the name of the file appears, point to the file that you want to delete, click the triangle on the bar that appears, and then click **Version History** on the menu that appears.

2. Click **Delete Previous Versions**.

3. When prompted to confirm that you want to delete all previous versions of the file, click **OK**.

About Checking Documents In and Out

Checking documents in and out allows users to obtain exclusive write access to a document, eliminating the need to merge changes from multiple authors. When a user checks a document out, he is the only user who can save changes to the document. The document is flagged as if it's in a long-term check-out status. This is also known as an explicit check-out or file lock. Other users can read the document, but they cannot make changes. The user who has the document checked out can update the document and see the latest version of the document, but other users will not see the updates until the document has been checked back in. When the document is checked in, you can provide comments on the amendments to or purpose for this version of the document. Members of the Administrator, Content Managers, and Web Designer site groups (or members of any site group with the Cancel Check-out right) for a site can override a document check-out if necessary and force the document to be checked in with the previous version.

To force a document to be checked in, you use the same command as the user would use to check in a document normally.

To cancel a check-out and return to the previous version

If you check out a document but then decide you don't want to check in the changes you made, you can undo the check-out as follows:

1. Navigate to the document, click the down arrow next to the document's title, and then click **Check In**.

2. On the Check In page, select **Discard changes and undo check out** and then click **OK**.

3. On the confirmation message that appears, click **OK** to check in the document.

Editing Documents in the Document Library

To edit a document, you do not have to explicitly *check out* the document. Navigate to the document library, and click on the name of the file. If the file extension is bound to an application, such as Microsoft Word, the file will open in read-only mode. This will also be the case if the document is checked out to you. If you look at the Office application title bar, you'll see (read-only) after the filename. The File drop-down menu will not have the options to check the document in or out. However, when Microsoft Word 2003 opens the document, it automatically sets a short-term lock on the file to prevent other users from editing the open file. This is also known as an implicit check-out, but if you have not previously explicitly checked out the document, your user name will not be placed in the checked-out column on the website. When you close the file in Microsoft Word 2003, it releases the short-term lock and the document is then available for other users to edit.

When you save the document back to the document library (assuming you have the permissions to do so) and you're using a Microsoft Office 2003 application, the Web Files Properties box will be displayed with the same fields as on the Document Library: Upload Document page. Once the document is saved, the explicit Check Out and Check In options will be available from the drop-down File menu or on the Shared Workspace pane, as illustrated in Figure 19-13, but you can continue editing the document and saving it without checking the document in or out. Applications that are compatible with Windows SharePoint Services will use short-term file locking when opening a document stored in a document library.

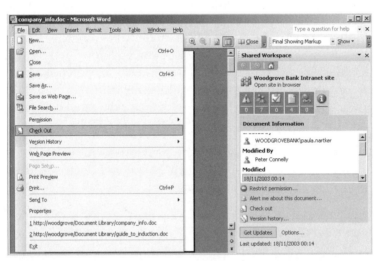

Figure 19-13   Microsoft Word 2003 File menu and Shared Workspace pane

Check in and **Check out** states are not dependent on the Save, Save As, Copy, or Move action. If versioning is enabled, the version number increments as described in the previous section whether the document is checked out or checked in. Nor are Check In and Check Out dependent on versioning being enabled. You should check out a document if you want to edit it; this will prevent a second user from opening the same document, making changes to that document, and then finding (because whoever opened it first has a short-term lock on the file) that she is unable to save her changes to the document. Because the second person has no visible evidence when she views the document library that anyone else is accessing the file, she might think there is a problem with the website.

> **Warning** As a contributor to a document library, you should always check the status of a document before attempting to edit it. It is advisable that you check it out first and therefore place a long-term lock on the document prior to editing the file.
>
> The most visually obvious method of finding out whether a document is checked in or checked out is by using, within a browser, the All Documents view of the document library where the document is located. The Checked Out To column displays the name of the person the document is checked out to. If the column is blank, the document is not checked out.
>
> If you're using the Explorer view of a document library within a browser or you use My Network Places to view a document, there's no icon associated with the file to indicate whether the file is checked in or out.
>
> If you have opened a file in a Microsoft Office 2003 application, you can use the Shared Workspace pane to see which of the Check Out or Check In options are available.

Content Approval

Content approval allows you to create a list or library in which any items or documents submitted by users are not immediately visible to all site users—that is, pending or rejected documents will not be visible in the All Document view of a document library. You can view a list of the items you submitted and check their approval status using the My Submissions view. And if you know the URL (or can guess it), you'll be able to see documents that were submitted by other users that are in a pending or rejected state, even if you don't have Manage List rights. This is because Content Approval is not a security feature.

Members of the Administrator site group and users with the Manage Lists right use the Approve/Reject Items view of the list or library to set an item or file as approved, rejected, or pending. They can also enter comments regarding their decisions. For example, you can create a document library where all documents must be approved before all site users can view them.

Submissions by members of the Administrator site group or users with the Manage Lists right are automatically approved. However, other members of the Administrator site group or users with the Manage Lists right can still reject the items.

Note   Rejecting an item or file does not delete it or prevent users from viewing it. Such a document will retain all its versions if versioning is enabled on the document library. You'll be able to edit, save, check out, and check in your document while in a pending or rejected state. This enables you to prepare a document, and only when you have collaborated with other people, perhaps using Web discussion threads, would you ask your content manager or administrator to approve the document. However, a member of the Content Manager or Administrator site group cannot change the status of a document while it is in a checked-out status.

To help prevent users from viewing rejected or pending items, the submitter or a user who is a member of the Administrator site group or a site group with the Manage Lists right must manually delete the items.

When approval is set on a list or a document library, the Upload Document form (Upload.aspx) will display extra text, warning you that this document requires content approval. The equivalent form for new list items is NewForm.aspx, which also contains the warning text, as does the form, EditForm.aspx, which appears when you edit the properties of a document or a list item.

To enable content approval for a document library

1. Navigate to the document library, and on the left link bar, click **Modify settings and columns**.

2. On the Customize *Document Library* page, click **Change general settings**.

3. On the Document Library Settings page, in the **Content Approval** section, under **Require content approval for submitted items?**, click **Yes**.

4. Click **OK**.

To find whether content approval is enabled for a document library, use the procedure just shown to check the settings. Also, when a document library has content approval enabled, two new views will be listed in the Select A View section, under Approve/Reject Items, as illustrated in Figure 19-14, and My Submissions. In these two views, the columns Approval Status and Approver Comments are visible, but the Checked Out To column that is present in the All Documents view is not visible.

Figure 19-14   Content Approval: Approve/RejectItems view

To approve or reject a document

To complete the following steps, you must be a member of the Administrator site group or a member of a site group with the Manage Lists right:

1. On the page displaying the list or library for which you want to approve or reject items, click **Approve/reject Items**.

2. Point to the item you want to approve or reject, click the down arrow on the menu that appears, and then click **Approve/reject**.

3. Click either **Approve**, **Rejected**, or **Pending**.

4. Type a comment (optional) explaining why you approved the item, rejected the item, or left the item pending.

5. Click **OK**.

Folders created in a document library, where content approval is enabled, will not be visible to all users until the folders are approved. Folders act, as far as content approval is concerned, in a similar fashion to documents that are added to a document library. For example, rejecting a folder does not delete it or prevent users from viewing it.

Approval Routing in a Backward-Compatible Document Library

In backward-compatible document libraries, you can use an approval process as a method of reviewing and approving documents in enhanced folders before publishing them on the portal site. After you approve a document, a public version is automatically created. Users who are assigned as readers on the folder containing the document can then search for and view the document on the portal site. The main points concerning the approval process are as follows:

- When you create a subfolder, an approval process is inherited from the parent folder along with role assignments. However, any subsequent changes to the approval process on the parent folder are not inherited. You must manage the approval process for each folder individually.

- Alternatively, you can establish different approval process configurations for individual folders and subfolders by clicking the Approval tab on the Properties page of the specific folder.

> **Note**   You can make changes to an approval process, but these changes affect only documents submitted for approval after the changes have been made. Changes to the approval process for a folder do not affect documents already pending approval.

- If you choose not to configure an approval process, Microsoft Office SharePoint Portal Server 2003 will publish documents automatically upon submission, without review or approval.

To configure an approval process

1. Choose the appropriate document approvers.

2. Supply e-mail addresses for approvers to allow SharePoint Portal Server to alert them when a document is ready for review. This is not required, but it is recommended. If you do not provide e-mail addresses, users see only alert requests for approvals on the portal site and do not receive the alert results in an e-mail message.

3. Create an e-mail message to send to approvers when a document is submitted for their approval.

4. Choose an approval route.

Using the backward-compatible document library, SharePoint Portal Server has two approval routing options, serial and parallel, which are illustrated in Figure 19-15. These approval routing options are not available if you store documents in document libraries in the SQL content database.

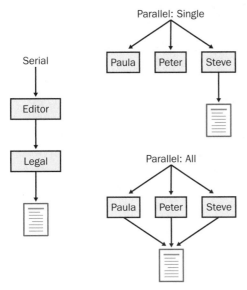

Figure 19-15   Approval routing in a backward-compatible document library

- **Serial approval (one after another).**   When the author submits the document by using the Publish command, the first member of the Approvers list receives a request for approval by e-mail. After the first person on the list approves the document, the next person on the list is asked to approve it, and so on. SharePoint Portal Server publishes the document only after all approvers on the list have approved the document. If any person on the list rejects the document, SharePoint Portal Server cancels the approval process and returns the document to the document library in a checked-in state.

- **Parallel approval (all at once).**   This approval model is based on the number of approvals required to publish the document. The coordinator can choose one of two strategies: one approval publishes the document, or all approvers must approve the document for publication to take place. When the author submits the document by using the Publish command, SharePoint Portal Server sends a request for approval to all approvers. The approval e-mail informs approvers of the location of the document. If the required number of approvers approves the document, SharePoint Portal Server publishes it. If the document does not receive the required number of approvals, SharePoint Portal Server cancels the approval process and returns the document to the document library in a checked-in state.

As a coordinator, you have the ability to stop an approval process, either by using the Bypass Approval command or the Cancel Publish command. This capability is useful if a document is under approval and one or more of the approvers are not available. The Bypass Approval command skips all remaining approvers and publishes the document to the portal site. The Cancel Publish command cancels the approval process and returns the document to a checked-in, unpublished state in the document library.

> **Warning**   If you are both a coordinator on a folder and an approver for that folder, when you receive an approval request, the Approve, Bypass Approval, Reject, and Cancel Publish options are all available to you on the same menu. Ensure that you do not accidentally choose Bypass Approval or Cancel Publish when you want to approve or reject a document.

Summary

This chapter discussed the document library and the different methods of managing documents within a document library. Document libraries can contain documents and folders. Folders are static and are the traditional way of organizing and capturing metadata, but now with SharePoint Products and Technologies there are other methods, such as columns, views, and filters. This chapter also discussed versioning, check-in procedures, check-out procedures, and content approval.

Many techniques used with document libraries can be generalized for use with lists. Uploading documents or adding items to lists are not the only methods of collaborating, nor is navigating through document libraries and folders the best way of finding information. You must make sure that others can find information held in document libraries and lists, and this is the subject of Chapter 20.

Working with Information Components in SharePoint Products and Technologies

For the purposes of this chapter, information components include any Microsoft SharePoint component that contains information, such as documents, list items, libraries, lists, areas, topics, and keywords. In the previous chapter, we used documents and document libraries to store and find information. Document libraries are just a list of documents along with the profile information you choose to associate with them. In this chapter, we'll expand on the ideas of a list and discuss how to make information easy to find.

Lists, sites, and workspace sites are other locations where information can be stored. Sites and workspace sites were discussed in Chapter 16, "Administering Windows SharePoint Services." **Lists** will be discussed in this chapter as will **Topics**, **areas**, **listings**, **keywords**, keyword **Best Bets**, and document **metadata**. Lists, like document libraries, hold information, whereas Topics, areas, listings, keywords, keyword Best Bets, and document metadata help users find information.

Lists

A list can be created in several places. First, a user can create a list on a portal site, where the collection of information is shared throughout the organization. A user can also create a list on a Windows SharePoint Services site for collaboration within a team, or a user can create a list on her personal website to share or host information.

Sites include a set of built-in lists and document libraries. Except for the Announcements list, these lists are empty when you create the site. You can immediately fill them with items pertinent to your needs. The Announcements list contains a sample announcement to help you get started.

Each list appears on a page that includes commands for adding items, sorting and filtering items, switching to a different view of the list, and changing the design of the list. You can copy the list to a Windows SharePoint Services–compatible spreadsheet, such as Microsoft Excel 2003, and you can create an alert to be notified of changes to the list from this page.

List Management

You can use the lists that come with your site as is, you can modify or delete lists that you don't use, and you can create your own custom lists. The lists featured on your sites will vary, depending on the site template your site uses. SharePoint Products and Technologies uses two types of templates:

- **Site definitions.** Site definitions include the set of basic pages and schema from which all SharePoint sites and lists are derived. Site definitions contain all the configuration data for the site and are stored on the file system of each front-end Web server as Web pages and XML files. A site definition can actually contain multiple configurations, but all the configuration data in a site definition uses the same set of lists that a user can create. For example, the Social Meeting, Multipage Meeting, and Decision Meeting templates that are listed on the Template Selection page are based on the Meetings site definition. There is currently no user interface to customize these definitions or to add new ones. To do this, the XML files need to be edited manually. To change the XML files see the white paper "Build Custom SharePoint Sites and Portal Areas with Templates and Site Definitions," by Dino Dato-on, September 2003.

- **Custom templates.**   You can save an existing site as a custom template (.stp file). An .stp file contains only the information about what is customized in the site and doesn't contain the definition of the entire site. Custom templates are a way of packaging a set of changes to an existing site definition and making those available for new sites and lists. Every custom template is based on a site definition. Custom templates are stored in the database and made available through the central template gallery or through site collection template galleries. When you save an existing site as a custom template, the .stp file is added to the site template document library in the root of the site collection and can be used by all subsites. Custom templates can be created using the browser or the stsadm.exe command line, as described later in this section.

Each site definition is specified in the ONET.XML file. This file also contains list definitions for each type of list defined for your deployment. You can customize both the site and list definitions, allowing new portal sites, areas, Topics, and Windows SharePoint Services sites to take on your organization's corporate identity, ensure information integrity, and reduce the effort needed for the creation of each list. You should not modify an originally installed site definition; instead, you should copy an existing definition and edit that. (See "Creating a Site Definition from an Existing Site Definition," in the Microsoft Windows SharePoint Services Software Development Kit.) Making changes to the originally installed ONET.XML file can have the following effects:

- Use of repairs and service packs could result in the loss of your modifications.

- Custom templates based on the original site definitions might not work.

- Site definitions with references to original list definitions might not work.

Customizing site definition files has certain disadvantages, including the following:

- Customization of a site definition requires more effort than creating custom templates. The person who edits the XML files needs in-depth knowledge of the XML schema, whereas a business user can save and create a custom template.

- It is difficult to edit a site definition after it has been deployed.

- Doing anything other than adding code can break existing sites.

- Users cannot apply a SharePoint theme through a site definition.

- Users cannot create two lists of the same type with different default content.

- Customizing site definitions requires access to the file system of the front-end Web server.

Each list type only needs to be defined once, but each different site or area definition can use or re-use each individual list type as many times as you want. Once a list type is defined you can create lists using the browser by navigating to the Create page as illustrated in Figure 20-1.

Figure 20-1   Create page

How you navigate to the Create page is dependent on whether you want to create a list on a portal site or a Windows SharePoint Services site. In a portal site, under the Actions section, click Manage Content and then click Create. In Windows SharePoint Services sites, on the top-link bar, click Create. Once on the Create page, you can choose the list you want to create. By default, the list types are as follows:

- **Links.**   You can use link lists to post hyperlinks, either intranet or Internet addresses, to Web pages of interest to your team. By default, creating a site creates a link list, the contents of which are displayed in a Web Part on the home page of an area, Topic, or site. In an area or Topic—that is, in SharePoint Portal Server 2003—this list is called *Portal Listings*; on a Windows SharePoint Services site, it is called *Links*. To see all the links in this default list, click either Manage Content in the Actions list or the Links title on the website home page. You can also create additional link lists to organize your links.

> **Note** Portal site listings are the most important links in SharePoint Portal Server. Portal site listing lists are specialized link lists where you post your hyperlinks. Using the browser, you cannot customize or delete lists of portal site listings. For example, when you choose to add a listing to a portal area, this creates an item within a SharePoint list called Portal Listings that contains a pointer. Similarly, when you upload a document to a portal site document library and you select the Add listing for this document check box, or when you choose to submit an item to a portal area, you are creating a portal site listing that contains the URL of the document or item. Each link within the portal site listing list has a number of attributes or properties, and it is through these properties that a portal site listing is associated with an audience. Therefore, portal site listings are tightly integrated with areas, Topics, and audiences that allow users to find information. Listings are discussed in greater detail later in this chapter.

- **Announcements.** A place to post information for the team.

- **Contacts.** Information such as name, telephone number, e-mail address, and street address for people who work with your team.

- **Events.** A list of important dates.

- **Tasks.** A to-do list for team members.

- **Issues.** A list you can use to manage a set of issues or problems. You can assign, prioritize, and follow the progress of issues from start to finish.

- **Custom list.** A list with a customized set of defined columns. When you want to create a list that is unlike any of the built-in lists, create a custom list. You can base them on the designs used for the built-in lists, or you can create custom lists from scratch. To create a custom list, navigate to the Create page, as described earlier in this chapter, and then click Custom List. Complete the field properties Name (required), and in the Description box, type a description of the purpose of the list. The content, or *metadata*, of these two fields is important for search purposes. In the Navigation section, if you want a hyperlink to this list to appear on the Quick Launch bar, click Yes, and then click Create. Add columns to your list as described in Chapter 19, "Working with Documents in SharePoint Products and Technologies."

- **Custom list in datasheet view.** Use a custom list in datasheet view when you want to specify your own custom columns and you want to use a spreadsheet-like environment. This is convenient for data entry, editing, and formatting. Datasheet views require that you have a Microsoft Windows SharePoint Services–compatible datasheet program installed, such as Microsoft Office 2003 and the Microsoft Office List Datasheet Component, which is installed by default when you install Office 2003. Datasheet programs allow you to quickly add, delete, and update list entries just as you would in a spreadsheet program, such as Microsoft Excel, without having to switch to a separate program.

■ **Data imported from a spreadsheet.**   If you want to start with a list of information in a spreadsheet, you can define a range of cells to use as a list in your site. Windows SharePoint Services imports the data from the spreadsheet and displays it the same way it displays the built-in lists—that is either in Standard or Datasheet view. As you have imported the data into a list from a spreadsheet, you might find the Datasheet view more useful. The Datasheet view is a very powerful feature; you can apply themes to a Datasheet view and make the Datasheet view the default view. For more information on the Datasheet view, navigate to any list on a site, click Edit In Datasheet, and then at the bottom of the list, click the Help link as illustrated in Figure 20-2.

Figure 20-2   Assistance with Datasheet view

There are other ways of displaying help for the Datasheet view—for example, right-click any cell inside the Datasheet view, and click Help from the drop-down menu list, or if the Datasheet view is in focus, press F1. If the Datasheet view is not in focus, pressing F1 will display Internet Explorer Help.

When you create a list by importing data from a spreadsheet, there is no inherent relationship between the original spreadsheet and the list on the site. If you change the spreadsheet, the list on the site is not updated. Likewise, changes to the list on the website are not reflected in the original spreadsheet. If you want to synchronize the list to Microsoft Access or Microsoft Excel, you need to create a link between the Datasheet view and Access or the Excel worksheet. Once a link is created, data changes in one can be synchronized in the other. See the Datasheet view help for more information.

> **Caution** If you want to use a Microsoft Office Excel spreadsheet that has been saved as a Web page, the sheet must not use interactivity—that is, the Add Interactivity option must be cleared in the Save As dialog box in Excel.

Other important list-related features you can configure are assigning per-list permissions, attaching files to a list item, copying the contents of a list to a spreadsheet, changing the name of the list or document library, and deleting a list. These are detailed in the following sections.

Specify List Permissions

Area and Topic lists take their security from the portal site. Lists created in Windows SharePoint Services sites have security set at the list level. Lists (excluding document libraries) can be set to require content approval, but not versioning. However, lists do have item-level permissions, and this is available on all lists, wherever they are located in SharePoint Products and Technologies. The item-level permissions allow you to specify whether users can read and edit only their own items or their own plus the items of others. This setting is found at the list level. To modify the setting, navigate to the list, click Modify Settings and Columns, and then in the General Settings section, click Change General Settings. You can then modify the setting by means of the option buttons in the Item-Level Permissions section, as illustrated in Figure 20-3.

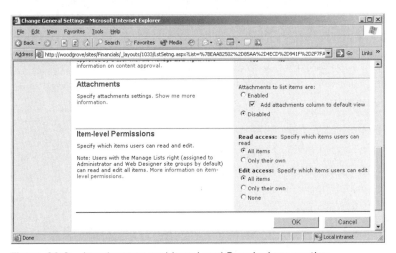

Figure 20-3 Attachments and Item-Level Permissions section

Attach a File to a List Item

At the list level, you attach a file to any one of the following types of lists: announcements, events, discussions, contacts, and custom lists. Navigate to the list, and click Modify Settings and Columns. In the General Settings section, click Change General Settings and modify the option buttons and check boxes in the Attachment section (also shown in Figure 20-3). If you change the Attachment setting from enabled to disabled, all attachments will be deleted. When you click the OK button, a dialog box will be displayed warning you of this. At that time, you can cancel your action.

Once the Attachment setting is enabled, navigate to the list in which you want to attach a file, and then do either of the following procedures:

- To attach an existing list item, point to the item, click the down arrow that appears, and then click **Edit Item**, click **Attach File**, and then click **Browse** to locate the file you want to attach to the list item. Then click **Open**. Click **OK**, and then click **Save and Close**.

    or

- To add a new list item, click **New Item**. In the fields provided, type the title of the list item and any other information that is required. Click **Attach File**, and then click **Browse** to locate the file you want to attach to the list item. Then click **Open**. Click **OK**, and click **Save and Close**.

To copy the contents of a list to a spreadsheet

You can copy the contents of lists, except for the Portal Listings list, into a Windows SharePoint Services–compatible spreadsheet program, such as Microsoft Excel 2003. For example, if you export a list to Microsoft Excel 2003, you can create PivotTables and charts to analyze the information or apply text formatting. In Excel, the exported list is a Web Query that stays updated with changes to the original list in your SharePoint site. You can also export the results of a survey to a spreadsheet program. Here are the steps to do this:

1. Go to the page that displays the list or survey you want to export.

2. Choose the view that contains the columns you want to export. You might have to create a new view if none of the existing views meets your needs, or you might choose to select one of the views and delete the unwanted data once it has been copied to your spreadsheet.

3. In the **Actions** section or on the top of the survey, click **Export to spreadsheet**. If the **File Download** and **Opening Query** dialog boxes are displayed, warning you of the harm and the confidentiality risk some files can cause your computer, click **Open**.

To change the name or description of a list or library

Just as the name and description of a document or list item are important metadata, so are the name and description for lists and document libraries. Therefore, you need to maintain these items so that they reflect the information they contain. To update information, follow these steps:

1. Navigate to the list, document library, survey, or discussion board in which you want to change the name or description.

2. Click **Modify settings and columns**. If the page displays a survey, click **Modify survey and questions**.

3. Under **General Settings**, click **Change general settings**.

4. In the **Name** and **Description** boxes, type the new information you want.

5. At the bottom of the page, click **OK**.

To delete a list or library

Once information in a list is no longer needed, the list can be deleted. To delete a list, perform the following steps:

1. On the page that displays the list or library, click **Modify settings and columns**.

2. Under **General Settings**, click **Delete this list**, **Delete this document library**, **Delete this picture library**, **Delete this form library**, or **Delete this discussion board**.

List Templates

Creating a list is similar to creating a document library; use the Manage Content link on areas or the Create link on the Document And Lists page. The Create page is then displayed. When you choose a list to create, you are selecting a list template to use in the creation of the list. SharePoint Products and Technologies include many list templates by default, and users can customize an existing list and save the customized list as a new list template. Similarly, you can customize a library and save the customized library as a new library template. Ensure that when you create a template you give the template a meaningful name so that both you and your users know the purpose of the template. List templates and library templates created by other users or software vendors can also be imported to the site collection list template gallery.

A template can be created using the browser, in which case they are known as *custom* templates and are stored in the SQL database. Otherwise, you can create a template as a list definition that is stored in the file system of each front-end Web server. List definitions have their own subfolder at *Local_Drive*\Program Files\Common Files\Microsoft Shared\Web Server Extensions\60\TEMPLATE*LCID* *Site_Definition_Name*\LISTS*List_Definition_Name* that includes a SCHEMA.XML file. In this location name, LCID is the *Locale I*; *Site_Definition_Name* represents the area, Topic, or site; and *List_Definition_Name* is the list type. For example, STS is the *Site_Definition_Name* for Windows SharePoint Services sites, SPSCOMU is the *Site_Definiton_Name* for the Community Area template, and ANNOUNCE is the *List_Definition_Name* for the Announcements list. Figure 20-4 shows the Explorer view of the list definition folder.

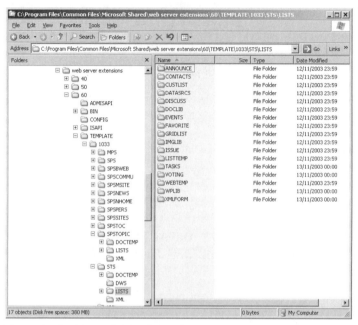

Figure 20-4   List definition folder for the Windows SharePoint Services sites

Each list definition folder includes a number of Web pages that are used to display the list's content and the SCHEMA.XML file, which defines the views, forms, toolbar, and special fields for new lists that are created through the list definition. The following kinds of tasks can be performed in a SCHEMA.XML file to customize a list definition:

■ Add custom fields based on field types defined in FLDTYPES.XML. Each front-end Web server in a deployment of Microsoft Windows SharePoint Services has one FLDTYPES.XML file located in the *Local_Drive*\Program Files\Common Files\Microsoft Shared\Web Server Extensions\60\TEMPLATE\LCID\XML folder that is used during site or list creation to define how field types are rendered in the different modes for viewing list data. Changes to this file should be made with extreme caution because the changes are global to a Windows SharePoint Services deployment and affect all site definitions on the front-end Web server. Field types are described in Chapter 19.

- Create a custom view for lists created through the list definition.

- Create custom forms for working with list items.

- Specify the default description that is displayed for the list in the user interface.

- Define the Actions area that is displayed in the side navigational area of list views.

Warning   Making changes to an originally installed SCHEMA.XML file on a server running Microsoft Windows SharePoint Services is unsupported and can break existing sites. Whenever possible, create a new site or list template as opposed to modifying original schema files.

However, you don't have to physically edit these files—you can create your own list templates using a browser. These are known as the custom list templates. Custom templates remain tied to a particular site definition (for example, the one for a SharePoint site or a Meeting Workspace site) so that if the site definition is not present or is changed, the custom template will not work. Each list template, whether it's a list definition template or a custom list template, appears as an option on the Create page for any site or subsite of a particular Windows SharePoint Services site collection if the template is stored in the top-level site's list template gallery.

On a portal site, there is only one list template gallery—that is, there isn't a separate list template gallery per area, subarea, or Topic. When you navigate to an area or Topic and create a custom list template, it's stored in the portal's list template gallery with an association as to which area or Topic you created this list template from. On a portal site, the Create page for the area or Topic displays only custom templates you created there. They don't appear on the Create page of any other area, subarea, or Topic. So, for a portal site, the Create page behaves as if there is a separate list template gallery for each area, subarea, or Topic. The portal's list template gallery doesn't make visible this association of the custom list template to the area, subarea, or Topic. Therefore, to assist in the use of custom list templates and to prevent unnecessary troubleshooting exercises, you should include in the list template description the area under which a particular list template was created.

You must have the Manage Lists right to create a list template. The Manage Lists right is included in the Web Designer and Administrator site groups by default. To add or import a list template to the site collection gallery, you must have the Add Item right for the list template gallery, which is included by default in the Web Designer and Administrator site groups for the top-level website in a site collection.

A custom list template is a file that includes all the design information about the list, such as:

- The columns and fields in the list
- Any views created for the list
- List content (optional)

Custom list templates do not include the following items:

- Security settings, such as a list of users or groups with permissions to the list from which the template was created.
- Lookup field links. Although lists can contain lookup fields that reference data in another list, that other list (and its data) is not included when you save a list template.

Caution   Template files include personal information such as server URLs and user account names. You should share template files only with trusted users and groups.

Custom list templates are stored as files with the .stp extension. To create a list template, complete the following steps:

1. Navigate to the list you want to save as a template.
2. Under **Actions**, click **Modify settings and columns**.
3. On the Customize *<List Name>* page, under **General Settings**, click **Save list as template**.
4. In the **File name** box, type the filename to use for the template file.
5. In the **Template title** box, type the title you want to use for the template in the list template gallery.
6. In the **Template description** box, type a description for the template.
7. If you want to include the existing content, select the **Include content** check box.
8. The Operation Completed Successfully Web page should be displayed. From this page, you can go to the list template gallery.
9. Click **OK** to return to the Customize *<List Name>* page.

Custom templates hold the following advantages over customization of site definitions:

- Custom templates are easy to create.

- Almost anything that can be done in the user interface can be preserved in the template.

- Custom templates can be modified without affecting existing sites that have been created from the templates.

- Custom templates are easy to deploy.

  Custom template disadvantages include the following:

- Custom templates should first be created in a development environment, and once they're tested, placed in production environment. However, because they can be easily created, the tendency is for this not to occur. List definitions, because they require file access rights on the front-end Web servers, are more tightly controlled, and best-practice deployment strategies will usually prevail.

- They are less efficient in large-scale environments.

- If the site definition, on which the custom template is based, doesn't exist on the front-end server or servers, the custom template will not work.

Managing the List Template Gallery

List templates are managed at the site collection level in a *List Template gallery*. Other galleries created at the site level are the *Web Part gallery* and the *Site Template gallery*. You must be a member of the Administrator site group in the top-level website in a site collection to manage the List Template gallery.

When a user creates a list template, it is automatically added to the List Template gallery for the site collection. If you want to import a list template from a .stp file, you can do so from the List Template Gallery page.

To add a template to the List Template gallery, complete the following steps:

1. On the top-level website, click **Site Settings**.

2. On a portal site, under **General Settings**, click **Manage security and additional settings**. On a Windows SharePoint Services website, under **Administration**, click **Go to Site Administration**.

3. Under **Templates and Web Parts** on a portal site or under **Site Collection Galleries** for a Windows SharePoint Services website, click **Manage list template gallery**.

4. On the List Template Gallery page, click **Upload Template**.

5. In the **Name** box, type the path to the template, or click **Browse**.

6. You can upload multiple templates by clicking **Upload Multiple Files**.

7. Click **Save and Close**.

To delete or edit a template in the list template gallery, navigate to the List Template gallery as stated previously and click the Edit icon next to the template name. The properties page for the chosen template is displayed. You can modify the metadata associated with the template or delete the template by clicking Delete.

A List Template gallery is a document library, and therefore, all the features discussed in Chapter 18, "Managing SharePoint Portal Server 2003," are available to you, including versioning and content approval.

Sharing Templates

You can share list and site templates with users outside of your site collection by giving them a copy of the .stp template file, which is actually a .cab file that can be renamed with the .cab file extension and opened in Microsoft Windows Explorer. You can give them a copy of the template file, just like any other file, by sending it in an e-mail message, posting it to a network share or website, or making a copy on a disk.

The advantage of this is that lists and libraries created in one site collection can be used across the enterprise by simply creating a central repository of all list templates. Then, when a new site collection is created, the list templates can be immediately imported (this is a manual process) into the List Template gallery to make these customized lists available to the users in the new site collection. Better still, these customized lists can be imported into a List Template gallery for a top-level site, and then the site itself can be templated, including the List template content and the new site template used to create new site collections that automatically include the desired List templates.

To create a copy of a template, you must perform the following steps:

1. Create the template.

2. Navigate to the template gallery (whether site or list), right-click the file, and then click **Save As** to save the file to a network share or your local computer.

Managing the Central Template Gallery

The *Central Template gallery* allows you to save site custom templates, which then become available for top-level site creation and subsite creations. It is meaningless to store list custom templates in the Central Template gallery, and they can cause an Invalid Site Template error message if stored and then selected from the site Template Selection page. If you want your list custom templates to be centrally stored and available in newly created sites, save a top-level site template with content. This will incorporate any List templates that are in the List Template gallery into the site collection.

> **Note** The maximum size for the template content is 10 megabytes (MB).

To manage the Central Template gallery, you need to use the stsadm.exe executable, which can be found (by default) under the %ProgramFiles%\Common Files\Microsoft Shared\Web server extensions\60\bin directory. To add, delete, or list templates in the Central Template gallery, use the following options with the stsadm.exe program, remembering to execute stsadm.exe from the directory where it is located:

- The **addtemplate** operation takes the required filename and title parameters and the optional description parameter. Create a template, save the file to a network share or your local computer, and then add the template to the Central Template gallery using the following syntax:

```
stsadm.exe -o addtemplate -filename <filename> -title <template title> -
description <description of the template>
```

- The **deletetemplate** operation takes the required title parameter and the optional lcid parameter. To delete a template from the Central Template gallery, you would use the following syntax:

```
stsadm.exe -o deletetemplate -title <template title> -lcid <language>
```

Note After you add or delete a template from the Central Template gallery, you need to restart the Web service in Internet Information Services (IIS). You can restart all of IIS at once by running **iisreset/restart** on the command line, or just restart the specific websites in Internet Information Services (IIS) Manager. If you're in a server farm environment, you must restart the Web services for each front-end Web server in your server farm.

- The **enumtemplates** operation takes the optional lcid parameter. To list all templates in the Central Template gallery, you would use the following syntax:

```
stsadm.exe -o enumtemplates
```

To list only templates for a specific language, you would use the following syntax:

```
stsadm.exe -o enumtemplates -lcid <language>
```

Topics

The Topics area is also a good place for subject matter developers to use when they want to organize and publish information about a particular subject. Readers in the portal can also use the Topics feature to browse for published information. Topics can contain lists, discussion boards, document libraries, and other collaboration tools that enable people to work together. You must be a member of the Administrator, Web Designer, or Content Manager site group to add, edit, or delete a Topic. It is usual to assign a person who will manage a Topic area, both from the content perspective and the user access perspective.

From a technical perspective, Topics are created from area templates that host specific Web Parts, such as *Area Details* and *Area Contents* Web Parts. Additional Web Parts can be added once a Topic area is created. See Chapter 31, "Working with Web Parts," for more information on the purpose and use of each built-in Web Part. Topics behave like other areas and are managed in the same way. (For more information on area management, see the next section in this chapter.) However, Topics usually contain highlights of other areas or frequently used content that are related For greater discoverability, you can add listings to more than one Topic.

Listings

As detailed earlier, whenever an area, subarea, or Topic is created, a specialized link list, called Portal Listings, is created. This is combined with a Web Part on most area or Topic Web pages to display a subset of link items that is dependent on the user and the targeting of those links, through the **audience** feature. For more information on audiences see Chapter 23, "Personalization Services in SharePoint Products and Technologies."

Throughout the browser interface, many methods are provided that allow you to add link items to the Portal Listings lists. Such methods are labeled as Add Listing, Add Person, Submit To Portal Area, Select A Portal Area For This List, Select A Portal Area For This Document Library, and Add A Listing For This Document. This section of this chapter is about listings—that is, the ability to add a listing to an area, subarea, or Topic. For greater discoverability, you can add listings to more than one area or Topic.

The names of the methods used to add a link item to a Portal Listings list can be obtuse—for example, when you create a site, the areas section asks you to click on the location link if you want to select one or more areas for this site. The word *location* used in this context can be misleading, as it is also used to specify where in the area and Topic hierarchy of a portal site you want an area or Topic to reside. For a site, the location link, if selected, allows you to add a link item to the Portal Listings list. That is, a pointer to this newly created site is added as a link to each location selected. The default location is set to none—that is, no link item is added to any Portal Listings list.

An example of an obvious label for adding a listing is when you upload a document in a portal document library and you select the Add Listing check box. This is illustrated in Figure 20-5.

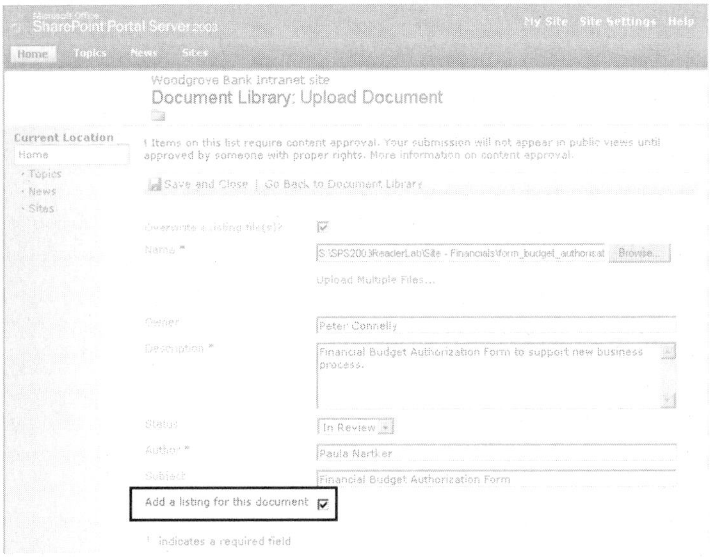

Figure 20-5   Add Listing check box

When you click Save And Close, the Add Listing Web page is displayed, as illustrated in Figure 20-6.

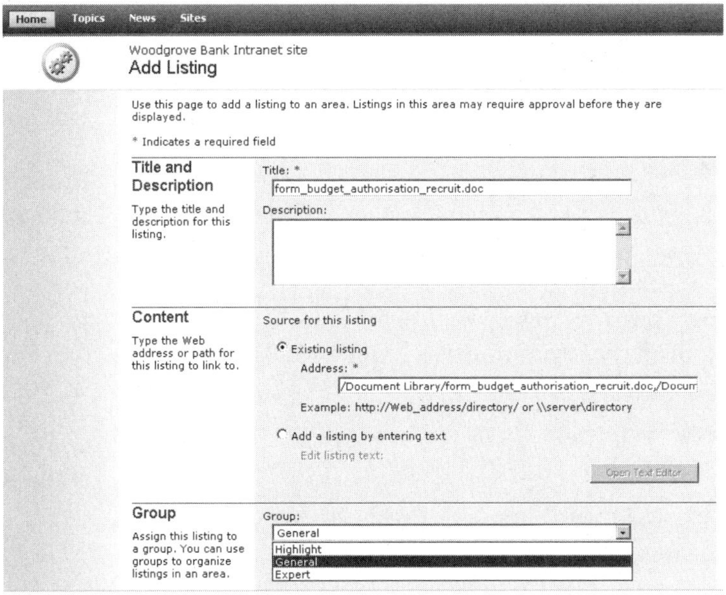

Figure 20-6   Add Listing Web page

In the Group section, select a group from the list. By default, three groups are created: *Highlight*, *General*, and *Expert*. Listings, when they're displayed on the area or Topic Web page, will be grouped by these names. In the Image section, enter the address for a graphics file you want to display with this listing and select the target audience you want to see this listing. For more information on Audiences, see Chapter 23.

In the Location section, click Change location to display the Choose Location page, as illustrated in Figure 20-7. Click the appropriate check boxes to list the listing in a different portal area or to select additional areas.

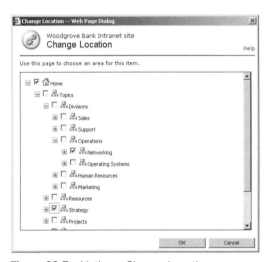

Figure 20-7   Listings: Change Location

The Add Listing Web page displays attributes of the link item and can be thought of as equivalent to a property page for the listing. There are more attributes for a listing than those displayed on the Add Listing Web page. To modify all the attributes of a listing, you'll need to navigate to an area's Portal Listings list and select Edit from the listings item's drop-down menu. A Change Settings *<Listing Name>* Web page is displayed with four tabs: General, Publishing, Display, and Search, as illustrated in Figure 20-8.

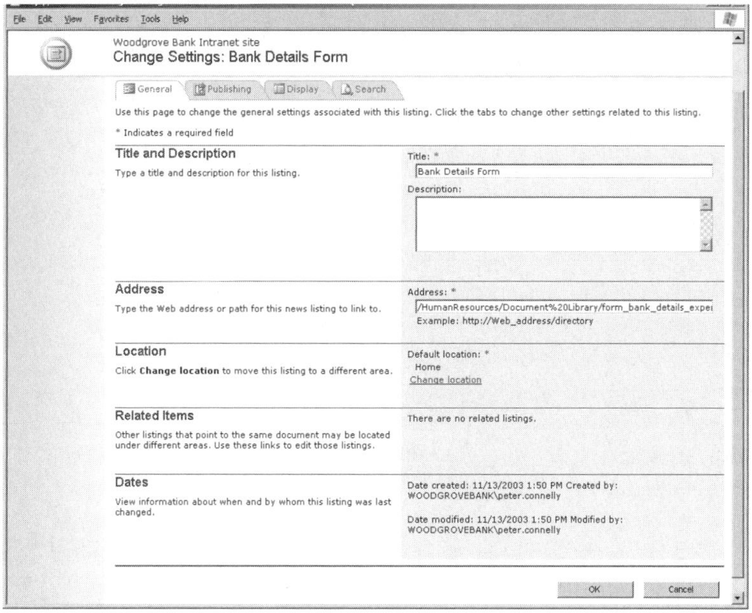

Figure 20-8   Change Settings for a Listing

Additional properties include: Start and Expiration dates for the listing and approval status on the Publishing tab; and whether you want to include the listing in search results on the Search tab. Because the whole purpose of a listing is to allow users to find information, the text you type on this page is important if you are to meet your goal.

The methods used to add a link item to a Portal Listings list mentioned earlier in this section include navigating to a document library, clicking the document's drop-down menu, and selecting Submit To Portal Area. Doing this will display the Add Listing page.

A second method is to navigate to an area's Portal Listings list by clicking Manage Content on the area's Web page and selecting Portal Listings on the Document And Lists page. The Portal Listings list is displayed in the All Listings view. An alternative method of getting to the same page that doesn't work for all areas is to navigate to the area, click Edit Page, and then click Manage Grouping And Ordering. The Portal Listings list is now displayed using the Grouping And Ordering view, as illustrated in Figure 20-9.

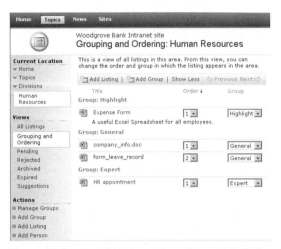

Figure 20-9   Portal Listings: Grouping and Ordering view

Because Portal Listings is a specialized list, you'll be presented with a number of views. From any of these views except the Suggestions view, you can then click Add Listing. The disadvantage of adding a listing using this method is that you must know the exact address of the information component you want to add. However, by using this method, you can create a listing that has no information component, and you can enter the text for the listing using the Open Text Editor button.

When you add a listing, you are not storing the information component in a Portal Listing list; you are only adding a link that points to where the information component is physically located. If you relocate, rename, or delete the information component, the link item in the Portal Listings list will no longer be valid and you will have a broken link. The Portal Listings list is a link list, and hence the same scenario can occur for any link list you create. However, because the Portal Listings lists play such an important role in allowing users to find information, broken links in these link lists will cause greater user frustration. There is no inherent check for broken links in link lists. Therefore, you will need to train users who submit listings to take responsibility for the listing as well as the information component it points to. The most common cause of broken lists in Portal Listings is the renaming of documents in document libraries.

To manage listings, navigate to the Portal Listings list. Here, you can complete many listings management tasks, such as viewing the approval status of the listing; approve, reject, and delete listings; and edit the settings for a listing. You can also add a person as a listing, manage groups, change the order of listings within groups, and add a group.

To enable content approval on a Portal Listings list, navigate to the area or Topic, click Change Settings, and on the Publishing tab, select the Yes option button for Require Approval To Publish New Listings.

Warning Although all areas contain a Portal Listings list, not all areas contain a Web Part that displays the link items contained in the Portal Listings list. Areas based on the Topic Area, News Area, News Home Area, and Community Area templates will display listings by default. When you create an area based on the Contents Area template, the listings are not automatically shown. To do so, you will need to enable the Show Listings property of the Browse Topics By Web Part. See Chapter 31 for information on how to customize Web Parts. For areas based on the Site Directory Area template a Grouped Listings Web Part can be added to display the listings. See Part VIII for more information on customizing Web Part Pages and Web Parts. The default areas (Topics and Sites) that are created from the Content Area and Site Directory Area template when a portal site is created will also not show listings by default. The browser logic allows you to choose any area as a location for a listing. Because there is always a Portal Listing list, it will always succeed, but as stated earlier it might not be visible through a Web Part when users visit that area. You can either use the Grouped Listings Web Part to display listings or tell users where they can add listings. Also, as an administrator of a portal area, you should check the Portal Listings that don't have an associated Web Part to be sure that users have not created listings in those lists, and perhaps relocate them in other, more suitable areas.

Areas

To make it easy for users to navigate, browse, and find what they need, you can divide portal site content into areas. Areas let you organize content—from documents to people to sites—into sets of related information, even though the content can be stored in different sources and formats. To control all the content in an area, the portal site administrator can assign a subject matter expert for the area. The manager can then control what content appears in the area and who has access to it. Areas provide three types of functionality in a portal site:

- They provide a navigational structure or map of the portal and related content. By adding, moving, or deleting areas, you can change the view of the portal for users.

■ They provide a centralized structure for information browsing. Areas direct readers to the information they seek through an organized hierarchy of Topics.

■ Areas provide a flexible way to both describe and find documents. Area managers can approve or reject content requests, manage area settings, and assign users to roles for this area. You can target areas for viewing by one or more audiences.

To find all areas in a portal site, use the Portal Site Map page, which you can navigate to by clicking Manage Portal Site in the Actions list. Only members of the Administrator site group of the portal site can use this feature. You can also find all areas in a portal site by entering the following URL query: *http://PortalSiteName /Search.aspx?tp=category*. This is the same as executing an advanced search and selecting Search By Type: Areas. The search results page for this query does not display areas and Topics in their hierarchical structure. For more examples of encoding your query in a URL, see Microsoft SharePoint Products and Technologies 2003 Software Development Kit: Using GET on Search Page.

Create, Modify, or Delete an Area

To create a subarea, navigate to the area under which you want the subarea to appear. Although this approach is not required, it will ensure that you don't accidentally create a subarea at the wrong location. You can move subareas once they are created. Subareas under Home are displayed on the primary navigation area; therefore, the subareas Topics, News, and Sites are technically subareas of the Home area.

In the Actions list, click Create Subarea. Then in the Title And Description section, type a title and description for the area. In the Publishing Dates section, you can specify start and end dates. The start date is the date you want the area to appear on, and the default is the current date. If you leave the expiration date blank, the area will be displayed indefinitely. If you didn't navigate to the required area before you started the subarea creation process, the current area is represented as the default location in the Location section. To display the area in a different location, click Change Location, and on the Change Location page, select a location in which to display this area. Then click OK.

When you create a subarea, only a small proportion of the area's settings are available to you. To customize an area or to change the settings you entered when the subarea was created, navigate to the subarea and click Change Settings in the Actions list. You'll be presented with a Change Settings: *subarea* Web page with five tabs: General, Publishing, Page, Display, and Search, as illustrated in Figure 20-10.

Figure 20-10   Area change settings

You can use the Area Change Settings page to do the following:

■ Specify contact information.

■ Change the location of the area. This is equivalent to a move.

■ Alter the publication dates.

■ Change the default listing approval settings. The default is No Approval Is Required. If approval is required, new listings must be approved by a user with Manage Area rights. The site groups Content Manager and Administrator have this right. You can also specify whether to automatically approve all listings added by a user with the Manage Area right.

■ Restrict the site template that any subareas created beneath the area can use.

■ Change the area template of the area. The default area templates include: Content, Topic, News, News Home, Site Directory, and Community.

■ Specify whether to hide the area—that is, whether to place a link to this area in the portal site navigation facilities. For example, if you choose to exclude an area from portal site navigation, a link to the area will not appear in the top navigation bar, in the Location section, or on the Topics Web page. This does not prevent users from seeing this area, but they will need to know the URL for the area if they are to navigate to it. Hidden areas can still be included in the portal search features if required. By default, two hidden areas are created under the Home area when a portal site is created: Search and Targeted Links On My Site. These two areas facilitate the SharePoint Portal Server search feature and the targeted links feature on My Site. You can see these two areas by navigating to the Manage Portal Site from the portal Home page and using the All Areas view. These two areas cannot be deleted, as they are intrinsic to the workings of the search and personal links features. Although you can create subareas beneath these two areas, it is meaningless to do so.

- State how you want listings in the area to be sorted—manually or alphabetically.

- Enter an address for the graphic files that you want to associate with the area.

- Choose whether to include the area and its contents in search results.

- Choose whether the Topics Assistant includes the area when automatically categorizing content—that is, you can choose whether the Topics Assistant should suggest item links to be added to the area's Portal Listings list.

The Area Change Settings page doesn't allow you to delete the area, manage the security for the area, or add an area to a listing. To achieve these functions, click Manage Portal Site in the Actions list on any area page of the portal site. On the Portal Site Map page, rest the pointer on the area you want to complete the task and click the arrow that appears. A drop-down menu appears, as illustrated in Figure 20-11. Click an appropriate option—for example, Delete. For this option, a confirmation window appears. Click OK if you want to delete the area. To view your changes, click Return To Portal on the title bar of the page.

Figure 20-11   Area Portal Site Map

You should not delete the top-level areas—such as Home, Topics, News, or Sites—because the built-in logic of some components depends on these areas existing. If you don't want these areas to appear on the top navigation bar, navigate to the area and click Change Settings. On the Display tab, check the Exclude From Portal Site Navigation check box.

> **Tip**   You might experience an operation time-out problem if you try to delete a large number of portal areas—for example, if you try to delete 500 or more portal areas at the same time. You're more likely to experience this issue on a server that uses a slower processor. If you experience this problem, delete a smaller number of portal areas at any one time.

You can also use the Portal Site Map page to alter the location of an area by using drag and drop. If you needed to reorganize the location of several areas, it would be quicker to use the Portal Site Map page, rather than the Change Settings option, for each area involved. You can also limit the view of areas displayed on the Portal Map by selecting a different view, using the drop-down box next to the Show button, or choosing the Filter option on the area's drop-down menu.

Area Architecture

Each area is created as a subsite off the root of the portal site in a set of subdirectories. The subsite Web directory hierarchy is completely independent of the portal area hierarchy that is visible through the browser and the Portal Site Map page discussed earlier in this chapter. Using a product such as Microsoft FrontPage 2003, you can see the out-of-box portal area subsites (such as News, SiteDirectory, Topics, and ExternalNews) and the first level of Web directories (C1, C2, and C3), as illustrated in Figure 20-12.

Figure 20-12 Area Web directory hierarchy as shown in Microsoft FrontPage 2003

The reason for two hierarchies is that the Web directory hierarchy lacks the ability to represent the key features that portal areas have, such as the ability for dynamically moving an area from one parent area to another. Therefore, the designers of SharePoint Portal Server 2003 had to create a separate Web directory hierarchy that also had to take into account the need to limit the number of websites under the same parent for scalability reasons.

Each Web directory (such as C1, C2, and so on) is known as a Web *bucket*. Every bucket including the portal root directory can include only 20 regular websites plus 20 buckets. The first 20 areas of a portal site will appear under the portal root. If you create a document workspace from a document held in a document library under the portal's Home area and the number of subsites in the root has not reached 20, the document workspace site will also appear under the root.

Once the root has 20 Webs, any new Web will be created in a Web bucket. Buckets are filled in a round-robin fashion so that once the portal root has 20 Webs, the next Web will be created under the C1 directory and the next under the C2 directory. You can see where in the Web hierarchy an area is created by looking at the URL of the area. Once all the first-level buckets (C1 through C20) have their full complement of 20 websites each, a second level of directories is created. The second level of directories would be C1/C1, C1/C2, C1/C3, through C1/C20; C2/C1, C2/C2, through C2/C20; and C20/C1 through C20/C20. Therefore, the portal root accommodates 20 Webs, the first bucket level contains a maximum of 400 Webs and the second bucket level contains a maximum of 8000 Webs. Once the second level is full a third level would be created, and so on. Only when a bucket is needed will it be created, as illustrated in Figure 20-12, where the highest first-level bucket is C11. Once an area is deleted the Web slot in the bucket hierarchy is available for reuse when you create a new area.

Area Security

You can specify security at the area level, and then all subareas, document libraries, or lists within that area will inherit from the area. To set security permissions, navigate to the Portal Site Map page and choose Manage Security from the area's drop-down menu.

Keywords and Keyword Best Bets

Keywords are used to mark specific items as more relevant for a particular word included in search. Doing this will cause certain items to show up more prominently in search results—specifically, with a yellow star. The primary purpose of keywords is to help readers search for and find information based on keywords or a synonym of a keyword.

Administrators and subject matter experts create keywords for common searches, and then add keyword Best Bets for each keyword that marks items most relevant to that search. You can filter the IIS log to get a better understanding of what users are looking for. For example, you can filter to learn the 10 most frequently searched keywords in each portal and assign keyword Best Bets based on this analysis. If you intend to filter the IIS logs on a regular basis, you should obtain software to analyze the log, as manually reviewing log entries is a very time-consuming exercise.

Keywords are created in a hierarchical structure that enables you to manage the keywords and keyword Best Bets, as can be seen in Figure 20-13. You can create additional keywords under existing keywords based on subject matter. Instead of creating a flat structure that presents thousands of keywords at a time, you can create a structure that enables you to quickly navigate through the hierarchy to the keyword you want to manage. This capability is useful for organizing keywords, but the hierarchical structure doesn't identify any relationship between the keywords as far as searching is concerned. The keyword Best Bets for lower-level keywords don't appear in search results for the higher-level keywords. For example, create a keyword named *Residential* with a subkeyword *Bungalow* and then associate a specific document as a Best Bet for the keyword *Bungalow*. When you enter the word *Residential* in the Search box and click the execute search green arrow button, the specific document will not appear in the search result set as a Best Bet. But when you search for the word *Bungalow*, the specified document will be returned as a Best Bet. The keyword hierarchy is there to assist in finding keywords and keyword Best Bets on the Keywords Web page.

To create keywords, you must have the Create Area right. To edit and delete keywords, you must have the Manage Area right. To add, edit, and delete keyword Best Bets, you must have the Add Items, Edit Items, and Delete Items rights.

Creating and Managing Keywords

To manage keywords, click Site Settings on the portal site, and in the Search Settings and Indexed Content section, click Manage Keywords. From the Keywords Web page, you can view the keyword hierarchical structure and documents that are registered as keyword Best Bets. You can also create keywords and add keyword Best Bets from the Actions section of the action pane or from a keywords drop-down menu, as illustrated in Figure 20-13. You can also add, edit, and delete keywords and keyword Best Bets by clicking existing keywords or keyword Best Bets, and then clicking the appropriate action.

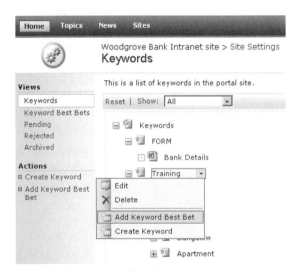

Figure 20-13   Manage Keywords and keyword Best Bets

Views of Keywords and Keyword Best Bets

On the Keywords page there are five views available to you:

- **Keywords.**   This view shows all keywords that are created for this server. By default, the items that are selected as keyword Best Bets are shown under the appropriate keywords. Keyword Best Bets are marked with icons to show their status. You can choose to show only the keywords by clicking Keywords Only in the Filter By list on the toolbar.

- **Keyword Best Bets.** This view shows a flat list of all keyword Best Bets. Each keyword Best Bet in the list shows the keyword with which it is associated, the user who created it, and its status. You can organize the list into groups by using any of these properties. To organize by groups, click the property in the Group By list. You can filter the view to show only items with a particular status by clicking Filter on the toolbar, and then clicking a status in the Status list that appears on the page. You can also choose whether to include the description for each keyword Best Bet by clicking Show More or Show Less on the toolbar. From this view, to add a keyword Best Bet, click Add Keyword Best Bet on the toolbar. To edit or delete keyword Best Bets or to change the status of a keyword Best Bet, click the item and then click the appropriate action.

- **Pending.** This view is similar to the Keyword Best Bets view, but it shows only keyword Best Bets that are marked as pending approval.

- **Rejected.** This view is similar to the Keyword Best Bets view, but it shows only keyword Best Bets that are rejected.

- **Archived.** This view is similar to the Keyword Best Bets view, but it shows only keyword Best Bets that are marked for archiving.

As with many other information components, when you create a new keyword or keyword Best Bet, only a subset of the properties is available to you. For example, you are unable to view or set the Start and Expiration dates during which you want an item to be displayed as a keyword Best Bet. To set or to modify the settings, click on the item and choose Edit from the drop-down menu. Doing this also displays contact information for the person who created the keyword.

The main drawback of creating a keyword Best Bet from the Keywords page is that you need to know the correct address of the information component and cut and paste it or correctly type it. There is no method of associating, say, a document with a keyword when you upload or save it. However, if you find an information component as a result of a search, you can associate it with a keyword Best Bet by completing the following steps:

1. Identify the item that you want to make a keyword Best Bet, and click the **Item Details** link.

2. Click the **Make Best Bet** link in the **Actions** section.

3. In the **Keyword** section, click the **Change Parent Keyword** link.

4. In the **Keyword Chooser** dialog box, click the check box associated with the appropriate keyword for the item. You can associate an item with multiple keywords.

Approval and Publishing

Keyword Best Bets must be approved before they can be used in a search. Keyword managers can choose to approve new keyword Best Bets automatically or require an approval process. By default, approval is required. To alter this setting, click Edit on any keywords drop-down menu and then modify the settings within the Keyword Approval section on the Publishing tab.

Keyword Best Bets can be in several different states depending on their approval status and publishing dates. The manner in which the status of keyword Best Bets is shown depends on how you are viewing keywords and keyword Best Bets.

Document Metadata

Another information component is *metadata*. A document's metadata is also known as the document custom properties. It's the user-definable descriptive information that is associated with each item in a document library. Lists also have metadata also known as fields. Metadata is stored in the Microsoft SQL Server content store for documents in the Docs table, and it can be displayed in the columns of a document library or list. This aspect of metadata was detailed in Chapter 19, "Working with Documents in SharePoint Products and Technologies." However, there are restrictions as to which metadata is displayable in a column. It is limited to custom properties. For example, the document property Subject is crawled and placed in the SQL Server database and used for searching, but it will not be displayed if a column is named Subject, whereas the custom property owner is crawled for search capabilities and would be viewable in a column labeled Owner.

Metadata is used during the crawl of a document, and you can select which properties to exclude during the search process by completing the following steps:

1. Click **Site Settings**, and in the **Search Settings and Indexed Content** section, click **Manage properties from crawled documents**.

2. On the Manage Properties of Crawled Content page, on the toolbar, select or clear **Hide excluded properties** to hide or show excluded properties in the list.

By default, excluded properties are hidden and do not appear on the Manage Properties of Crawled Content page. SharePoint Portal Server formats the name of excluded properties as strikethrough text. When you click a property, not only can you change the settings of a property, but you can select and view up to five crawled documents or pages that contain the property, as illustrated in Figure 20-14.

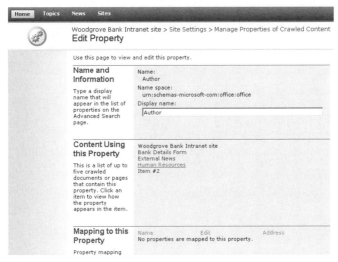

Figure 20-14   Manage Properties of Crawled Content: Edit Property Web page

For more information on search techniques and indexing, please see Chapter 22, "Managing External Content in Microsoft Office SharePoint Portal Server 2003."

Summary

This chapter discussed how to use information components other than documents and document libraries. The information components detailed in this chapter included lists, Topics, listings, areas, keywords, keyword Best Bets, and metadata.

Although lists, like document libraries, enable you to store information and are organized to facilitate collaboration, they might not suit the casual user of a site, as such a user might not know the physical location of the lists and document libraries. Many of the information components can be used to represent the business-oriented view of the content and are a reader-oriented approach to organizing information. This is one of the strengths of SharePoint Products and Technologies—it allows you to organize information into multiple views that assist in sharing and finding information.

Chapter 21

The Architecture of the Gatherer

The gatherer is the crawling component of the Search service. The purpose of the gatherer is to crawl content sources, extract the source's data, and break that data down so that it can be placed in an **index** and searched. The gatherer also processes client queries so that they are optimized and can return a larger set of hits to the user. To accomplish these tasks, this service contains several components. Some components are used in both the indexing and searching processes.

Default Indexes

When you create a portal site, Microsoft Office SharePoint Portal Server 2003 automatically creates two index files, which are the Portal_Content index and the Non_Portal_Content index. The Portal_Content index is created so that the information contained on the portal site can be crawled and indexed. By default, this index contains a content source for the portal site and a content source for People. If you have installed the backward-compatible document library component, a content source for each document library is also created. The Non_Portal_Content index file holds content not held on the portal site. By default, this index contains only a site's directory content source.

An administrator can add content indexes as needed. To create more indexes, an administrator must use advanced search administration mode. When additional content sources are created, an administrator can specify which content index should hold the content source's index. For information on creating indexes, see Chapter 22, "Managing External Content in Microsoft Office SharePoint Portal Server 2003."

Role of the Gatherer

The gatherer, which runs as part of the SharePointPS Search service, is responsible for crawling and extracting information from documents held in a content source. Once the content has been extracted, the responsibilities of chunking, word breaking, and noise word removal are all handled by the gatherer component of the Search service.

For the gatherer to function properly, it must have an IFilter (Index filter) and a protocol handler available before it can connect to a content source and extract data. In the following sections, we'll discuss the process of how the gatherer works and how you can use the gatherer error messages to diagnose problems that you might encounter when crawling a content source.

The Indexing Process

The entire indexing process starts with a set of source documents called a *content source*. A content source is a starting point for crawling a file system, database, or website for text and property information to include in an index. The end result of the indexing process produces an index file and a property store that together are called a *catalog*. The purpose of this multistep process is to extract the data from the original set of disparate documents and place that data into a single index file that is formatted so that it can efficiently respond to search queries.

The SharePoint Portal Server search engine, called SharePointPS Search (MSSearch.exe), is responsible for the process of crawling the documents and calling components that are needed to break down the information. These components include protocol handlers that access the documents, filters that convert the format, word breakers for each supported language, and noise word files used to remove unnecessary words. The whole process results in a catalog that is about 40 percent of the size of the original set of documents. Figure 21-1 shows the different components involved in the indexing process.

The indexing process begins when the content source is triggered to start crawling the target content. The first step in crawling the content is performed when the gatherer reads the URL of the target content and then loads the appropriate protocol handler and IFilter.

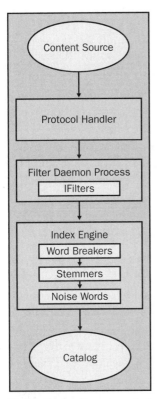

Figure 21-1 Components involved in the indexing process, including protocol handlers, filters, word breakers, stemmers, and noise word files

Protocol Handlers

Protocol handlers are needed to make the initial connection to a content source. Protocol handlers tell the gatherer how to connect to the target content. SharePoint Portal Server includes protocol handlers for the following document types:

- File shares
- Web pages
- Web pages using Secure Sockets Layer (SSL)
- Microsoft Exchange Server public folders
- Lotus Notes databases

Other protocol handlers can be installed, such as an FTP protocol handler, that will enable the Search service to connect to a File Transfer Protocol (FTP) site as a content source. In addition, you can write your own protocol handlers to connect to a content source by using any transport protocol you want. Please reference the SharePoint Software Development Kit (SDK) for more information.

Filters

When a file is created, it is formatted in the proprietary format of the application in which it was created. In other words, a document created in Microsoft Excel is in a different format than a document created in Notepad. SharePoint Portal Server must convert the contents of each document to a generic format before it can place the content into an index. The process of changing the format of the document is called *filtering*.

The purpose of a filter is to remove the proprietary formatting while extracting the text of the document as well as the document's properties. When a document is run through a filter, it is converted into an unbroken string of Unicode characters. Filtering is run by the filter daemon process (Mssdmn.exe).

IFilters

The actual component that is responsible for knowing how to interpret the format of files is called an IFilter (or Index filter). The gatherer uses IFilters for scanning documents for text and properties and for extracting the text and metadata from these documents. It also filters out embedded formatting while keeping information about the position of the text within the document.

SharePoint Portal Server includes IFilters for the following: Microsoft Office files, HTML files, Tagged Image File Format (TIFF) files, and text files. However, the IFilter for Microsoft Publisher is included in SharePoint Portal Server Service Pack1. SharePoint Portal Server accepts filters for other applications also. IFilters for popular file types such as PDF can be obtained from the vendor. If the gatherer component has no IFilter for a particular file type, it will attempt to extract the text of a document using a generic filter called the Null IFilter.

If an IFilter is not available for a document type that you would like to include in an index, another option is to contact the vendor of the application used to create the document or to create a customized IFilter component by using the SharePoint Portal Server SDK. An IFilter must be registered with the operating system and associated with a file type before SharePoint Portal Server can use it in the indexing process. If you obtain an IFilter from a vendor, these instructions should be included by the vendor. The IFilter must be registered on the computer running SharePoint Portal Server that is crawling that file type. File types are indicated by file extension, such as .doc for a Microsoft Word document. Once an IFilter is registered and a file type has an IFilter associated with it, documents of that file type can be crawled and included in the index. If no filter is registered for a file type, only the file properties are included in the index.

Filtering Limitations

SharePoint Portal Server has a limit to the amount of text data that it can filter from a single document. This limit applies only to the text in the document. It does not apply to graphics or any other type of content. By default, the limit is 64 KB of text in a single document. If a document has more text than the limit, SharePoint Portal Server stops the indexing process, considers the document indexed, and moves on to the next document.

SharePoint Portal Server has a registry value that limits the maximum file size that it will crawl. The registry value is called Max Download Size and is located in the HKLM/Software/Microsoft/SPS Search/Gathering Manager key. By default, the entry for this registry value is set at 16 MB. SharePoint Portal Server also has a registry entry that defines how many times larger the file can be than the text. This registry value is contained in the HKLM/Software/Microsoft/SPS Search/Gathering Manager/Max Grow Factor key. By default, this value is set at four. This means that the text in a file can be only up to four times larger than the file size.

Plug-Ins

After the protocol handler and IFilter have been loaded, the gatherer then connects to the content source and begins streaming data out of the content source, obeying the rules you've created for the content source. (Please refer to Chapter 22 and the discussion on creating and managing content sources to learn about the Site Hit Frequency, Site Path, and other rules that can be created as part of the content source.)

The gatherer first streams out the metadata and then streams out the content of the document. The metadata includes the document's properties and its permissions. Permissions gathered from the document are referenced when the result set is built, and any documents the user does not have access to are clipped from the result set before it is presented back to the user.

The data streams are sent through a series of plug-ins, which are components that perform certain functions on the data stream. By default, four plug-ins— Schema, Indexer, PQS, and AutoCat—ship with SharePoint Portal Server 2003 and are used to perform different functions.

Schema Plug-In

The Schema plug-in is a new feature in this version of Search for SharePoint Portal Server. This plug-in is responsible for adding new objects to the schema used by SharePoint Products and Technologies as they are discovered during the crawling process. When needed, this plug-in is also responsible for alias name resolution to Active Directory account names. This is useful for the profile database.

Indexer Plug-In

The Indexer is responsible for several functions, including word breaking, stemming, and noise word removal. Each of these is discussed in the following sections.

Word Breakers

The data stream from the content source is an unbroken string of Unicode characters. Word breakers are needed to determine where the word boundaries are so that the string can be broken back into individual words. SharePoint Portal Server uses word breakers provided by Windows 2000 Server Indexing Service and also provides word breakers of its own. The word breakers provided by the Microsoft Windows 2000 Server Indexing Service are for documents that are in Dutch, Italian, Swedish, and German. SharePoint Portal Server provides word breakers for English, French, Spanish, Japanese, Thai, Korean, Chinese-Traditional, and Chinese-Simplified.

If multiple languages are used in a single document, SharePoint Portal Server recognizes that multiple word breakers are needed. If no word breaker is available for a particular language, the neutral word breaker is used. In this case, words are broken at neutral characters such as spaces and punctuation marks.

Stemmers

Many words in a language have several inflections that can be used. In English, even a simple word such as "get" can also take the form of "getting," "got," or "gotten." Because of this, a component is needed to convert different variations of a word. Components that convert all the variations of a word are called *stemmers*. Stemmers also affect the formats of numbers, dates, and times so that they are handled consistently. Stemmers are used only in processing queries and are not used in the indexing process.

Noise Word Removal

Some words in a language are not useful for performing searches. Put another way, these words provide no search value when executed in a search query. For example, in the English language, words such as "the" and "a" are not useful in a search because they provide no real search value: nearly every document will have these words, making them indiscriminate in a search query. Words like these are considered to be *noise words*. Noise words are different in each language, so, as with word breakers, SharePoint Portal Server uses several different files to contain noise words. Each file is a list of words that are removed during the indexing process.

Noise Word File Management

By default, SharePoint Portal Server stores noise word files in the \Program Files\SharePoint Portal Server\DATA\Config directory of the server. The location of the DATA directory can be changed during the server installation process.

Another set of the same noise word files is copied to the to local_drive\Program Files\SharePoint Portal Server\Data\Applications\Application UID\Config directory. These files can be used to specify noise word files that apply at the application level instead of at the server or server-farm level. For example, if SharePoint Portal Server and Microsoft SQL Server are installed on the same server, each can have different noise word lists. Table 21-1 lists each language supported and the corresponding noise word file included by default in SharePoint Portal Server 2003.

Table 21-1   Noise Word Files Available in SharePoint Portal Server 2003

Language	Corresponding Noise Word File
Chinese-Simplified	noisechs.txt
Chinese-Traditional	noisecht.txt
Czech	noisecsv.txt
Dutch	noisenld.txt
English-International	noiseeng.txt
English-US	noiseenu.txt
Finnish	noisefin.txt
French	noisefra.txt
German	noisedeu.txt
Hungarian	noisehun.txt
Italian	noiseita.txt
Japanese	noisejpn.txt
Korean	noisekor.txt
Neutral	noiseneu
Polish	noiseplk.txt
Portuguese (Brazil)	noiseptb.txt
Russian	noiserus.txt
Spanish	noiseesn.txt
Swedish	noisesve.txt
Thai	noisetha.txt
Turkish	noisetrk.txt

> **Note   The neutral noise word file** (noiseneu.txt) is used if a document contains text from a language that does not have a noise word list.

Changes to Noise Word Files   Noise word files can be edited with any text editor. Before doing this, an administrator should be clear on how changes to noise word files affect the content index integrity. Adding words, removing words, or deleting noise word files affects query behavior as well as the contents of an index. Also, for changes in the noise wordfile to be reflected in the index, you will need to run full index jobs on all your content sources.

Removing Words from a Noise Word File   A two-step process is needed to allow a successful search on a word that is listed in a noise word file. First the word must be removed from the noise word file. Next, the index must be reset and a full update must be run. In the indexing process, noise words are removed from text before the text is included in an index. Even after a word is removed from the noise word file, that word must be integrated into the index. Resetting the index and re-indexing all content is the only way to accomplish this.

Adding Words to a Noise Word File   Adding noise words to a noise word file will cause those words to be removed from the index. This decreases the size of the index, which helps performance. It can also decrease the accuracy of the searches on the index if the added noise word is needed by users.

What kind of words should be added to a noise word file? This will be different for each environment, but the general rule is that if the word presents no search value to your users, it can be (and in some cases *should be*) placed in the noise word file.

For example, your company's name likely has no real search value because a search query on your company's name against all your indexed data will return such a large result set that the list will be meaningless. Other types of words that can be placed in the noise word file to ensure that those words do not appear in the index could include the following types of words:

- Politically, culturally, or sexually inappropriate or insensitive words

- Names of high-profile employees, such as the names of CEOs or company presidents

- Commonly used product names or generic terms that are specific to your company or industry

- Any other words that present no search value in your organization, such as slang words

Placing a word in the noise word file results in that word not appearing in the index. In turn, this means that a query against that word will return an empty result set.

Deleting Noise Word Files   A noise word file should never be deleted. If you delete the file, the neutral noise file will be used and all single characters will be removed as noise words. If you want to include all words in the content index, even noise words, you should delete all entries from the noise word file for the language you are using. Leave the empty file in the directory.

PQS Plug-In

The Persistent Query Service (PQS) plug-in is responsible for matching the data stream from the content source with the alert subscriptions that have been created by your users. Alerts are really little more than SQL Select Statements that reside in the SQL databases. The information is filtered through these statements, and when there is a match, a notification is generated.

Your users will need to be educated about this process because it can be a bit confusing. For example, let's assume one of your users creates a search query to look for the word "SharePoint" on the MSDN (Microsoft Solutions Developer Network) library site. After executing the search, your user selects the Alert Me feature and then selects To Be Notified Immediately.

Now, your user believes that he will be notified as soon as there is a change in content in the online MSDN library concerning the word "SharePoint." But this is not the case. The gatherer does not place hooks in the content source so that the user is automatically notified on the fly. Instead, the user's configuration really results in the user being notified within 5 minutes *after* the PQS plug-in becomes aware that there has been a change in the MSDN Library that matches the user's alert rule.

If you are crawling this site on a nightly basis, the user will not be notified until after the next crawl.

Now, refer to the "Frequency of Updates" section later in this chapter. You'll notice that an incremental crawl is executed on all portal content every 10 minutes by default. So, every 10 minutes, new or modified portal content is sent through the PQS plug-in, thereby delivering faster notifications to your users than content that is crawled only once per day. Therefore, if you crawl content incrementally on a once-per-day schedule, which is quite common for many content sources, the effect is that the user is really notified on a daily basis, not an immediate basis, as the user interface (UI) would indicate.

Therefore, a best practice is as follows:

- If you need fast notifications on content in the portal site, do nothing, as this is accomplished by default.

- If you need fast notifications on content outside the portal site, you'll need to match your crawling schedule with the notification schedule.

- Determine the crawling schedule for your content sources by first determining the frequency at which users need to be notified of new content in that content source.

AutoCat Plug-In

The Auto Categorization (AutoCat) plug-in is the component that makes the Topic Assistant feature possible. This feature is used to automatically categorize content external to the portal site and assign it to the Topic area in accordance with how you have trained the Assistant.

Building the Catalogs

Once the data stream has passed through the plug-ins, the data is then placed in one of two areas. First, the metadata for the documents, including the exact URLs to each document, are placed in the SPS.EDB file. The actual content of the documents is first written to word lists in RAM, very quickly written to shadow indexes on disk, and then merged into a Master Index on a nightly basis.

Therefore, crawled information is held in two places—the SPS.EDB ESE (Extensible Storage Engine) database and the index files or catalogs on the NTFS file system.

If you encounter errors in the gatherer crawling process, these errors will be recorded in the gatherer logs, which will be discussed later in this chapter.

Adding File Types to the Indexing Process

The extension, or file type, of a file indicates to SharePoint Portal Server which filter it should use to convert the text in the file to a Unicode character string. File types determine which IFilter will convert the document in the indexing process. Administrators can also add new file types so that they can be included in the indexing process. If the file's extension does not appear in the File Type list, those files will not be crawled by the gatherer. The file type can be associated with an existing IFilter; however, IFilters are designed to filter documents in only one format. If the new file extension is from an application that does not have an IFilter, it cannot be properly indexed. SharePoint Portal Server also accepts third-party IFilters for custom file types.

When a file type is added it applies only to content that is stored outside the portal site and included in the content index through content sources. Therefore, as long as you have a protocol handler to connect to an external content source, an IFilter to extract the data from the documents in that content source, and the file type added to the portal site, then those documents should be available for crawling, indexing, and searching.

You can add file types to be included in the content index. All files with a file extension in the list will be included in the index. When you add a file type to SharePoint Portal Server 2003 and register its IFilter, the file type is readable/searchable by the portal site. After adding a new file type, it appears on the Include File Types page.

If you delete a file type, the file format is no longer compatible with or searchable from SharePoint Portal Server 2003. Changes in file types will not take effect in the index until you have run a full index on all your content sources. So plan your file types carefully and give yourself time for new file types to be included in the index as you execute new Full Updates on your content sources.

Note   You must register the IFilter for new file types. If you add a new file type but no IFilter is registered, only the file properties are included in the index.

To add a file type

1. On the Site Settings page, in the **Search Settings and indexed content** section, click **Configure search and indexing**.

2. On the Configure Search And Indexing page, in **General Content Settings and Indexing Status**, click **Include File Types**.

3. On the Include File Types page, click **Add File Type**.

4. On the Add File Type page, in the **File Extension** box, type the file name extension for the file type that you want to add to the list of file types for the content index.

5. Click **OK**.

The Architecture of Index Updates

Once the content of a site and the content sources are indexed, the index needs to be updated to maintain accuracy. When you add documents to the portal site or modify existing documents, SharePoint Portal Server modifies the index to include the changes. When an index is updated, it follows the same process of breaking down the information in documents that it does when the index is first created. However, the changes are not immediately merged into the master index.

The process of merging changes into the master index is highly resource intensive. To make this process more efficient. SharePoint Portal Server merges only a group of changes into the master index. Until there are enough changes to merge into the master index, they are saved in separate lists and indexes. Figure 21-2 shows the different lists and indexes involved in the update process.

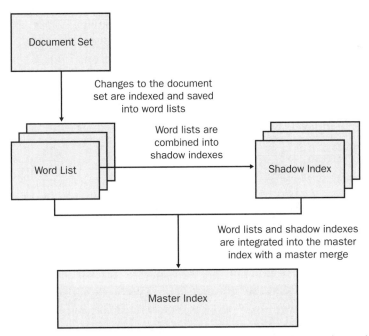

Figure 21-2   The creation of word lists and shadow indexes prior to doing a master merge in the SharePoint Portal Server Search service

Word Lists

When a document is indexed, the index information goes first to a *word list*. A word list is a small, temporary index that contains index information for only a few documents. Creation of a word list is very quick and does not require updating of any stored data in the master index. This saves changes so that a merge with the master index can take place less often.

Word lists are stored in memory and are not updated. When another set of documents is indexed, another word list is created.

Shadow Indexes

When the number of word lists exceeds the maximum allowable number, the SharePointPS Search service performs a shadow merge, which transforms word lists into a *shadow index*. Shadow indexes are highly compressed and are saved to a disk, which frees up memory that was occupied by word lists. The number of word lists that accumulate before triggering a shadow merge can vary based on settings in SharePoint Portal Server. See the "Balancing Resources" section of this chapter for more information.

Master Merge

The master index is persistent, disk-resident, highly compressed, and optimized for querying. Word lists and shadow indexes are part of the entire catalog that makes up the content index, so queries from search requests are performed against all word lists and shadow indexes as well as the master index. Having a large amount of the catalog in the form of word lists uses a large amount of memory. Also, because queries are performed against the master index as well as all shadow indexes and word lists, a large amount of either or both of these can slow down search queries. By default, the SharePointPS Search service performs a master merge whenever a full crawl or propagation is completed or a threshold of a maximum number of word lists and shadow indexes is reached. A master merge combines shadow indexes with the master index.

Balancing Resources

A master merge is triggered when the number of word lists and shadow indexes reaches a maximum threshold. The use of word lists uses memory resources while saving on processor resources that would otherwise be used performing master merges. However, because each word list must be searched during a query, too many word lists can affect search performance. Similarly, shadow indexes can merge word lists and avoid the resource-intensive process of master merges, but again too many can slow search performance. The Balancing Resources setting in the Central Administration site allows an administrator to balance the use of word lists and shadow indexes with resources used by master merges and the performance of search queries.

By default, the setting called Resource Usage is set to three, which balances memory and processor usage with index and query performance. Setting this to a lower number sets a lower threshold for the maximum number of word lists and shadow indexes that are allowed. This means that more frequent master merges occur when the Resource Usage setting is lowered to a two or a one. Lower this setting if your server does not have enough resources to give to word lists and shadow indexes. Setting Resource Usage to a higher number indicates that the server can use more resources for crawling and indexing. This allocates more cache and memory for word lists as well as more threads within the crawling, indexing, and search processes.

Index Builds

Update types describe the different way content is re-crawled for changes. Although all updates to content indexes follow the same procedure, settings in SharePoint Portal Server determine when and how the updated documents are checked. Indexes can be updated manually from the Manage Content Indexes page, or Share-Point Portal Server can schedule updates to occur automatically.

SharePoint Portal Server offers four types of updates to suit the demands of different portal sites. More than one type of update can be used on a single index to accommodate changing demand throughout a day. Table 21-2 lists each update type supported in SharePoint Portal Server 2003 and a description of what the update does. Each update type is explained in detail in this section of the chapter.

Table 21-2 Update Types in SharePoint Portal Server 2003

Update Type	Description
Full update	Crawls all content. Adds new content to and removes deleted content from the content index.
Incremental update	Crawls new and changed content. Adds new content to and removes deleted content from the content index.
Incremental (inclusive) update	Crawls new and changed content, including Web Part Pages and pages included in the SharePoint Portal Server application. Adds new content to and removes deleted content from the content index.
Adaptive update	Crawls content that is likely to have changed, based on site history. Adds new content to and removes deleted content from the content index.

Full Update

During a full update, SharePoint Portal Server crawls and updates all content in the content source or content index without regard to whether the content has been indexed before. A full update adds new content, modifies changed content, and removes deleted content from a content index.

Because all content is crawled during a full update, it is the most time-consuming and resource-intensive of the update types. During a full update, the processor time is at 100 percent. Full updates should be used less often than other types of updates; however, there are some circumstances when a full update is needed. Table 21-3 lists when a full update is needed and why.

Table 21-3   Update Types in SharePoint Portal Server 2003

Circumstance	Reason Update Is Needed
Update rules for content sources are changed	Update rules control what content is included in the content index. If a new rule is created that affects only one content source, a full update is needed only on that one content source.
A noise word file is changed	A noise word file contains words that are excluded from an index. If a word is added to the noise file the index must be updated to remove the word. If a word is removed from the noise file the word must be added to the index.
A content index is reset	Resetting an index removes all information from it. The index then needs to be completely rebuilt with a full update.
The search server has a power failure	A power failure can cause disruptions in the crawling process. If documents seem to be missing from the index, a full update is needed.
When a file type is added or removed	The only method to update the index is to perform a full index update on the affected content sources.
If files are renamed in the content source	An incremental or adaptive update does not reflect file name changes in the index. Only a full index update will accomplish this task.

Incremental Update

An incremental update of a content source crawls and updates only modified and new content. In an incremental update, SharePoint Portal Server does not index unchanged content. For this reason, performing an incremental update is faster than performing a full update.

A periodic incremental update captures changes to the content source. Perform incremental updates to keep pace with content changes without using the resources needed for a full update. In general, incremental updates should be used unless there is a reason for performing a full update, such as reducing the amount of content that is crawled.

Reducing Index Size by Excluding Links

If you change settings to reduce the amount of content that is crawled (for example, you exclude links to content that was previously crawled or you reduce the crawling depth for the content source), the changes will not be reflected with an incremental update. Instead, three full updates are needed before any previously crawled pages are actually excluded from the content index. This behavior is by design. SharePoint Portal Server must perform three crawls before removing any content to safeguard against removing content from sites that are only temporarily unavailable.

The purpose of this behavior is to avoid unneccesary alerts to users. Let's say a user places an alert on a document and that document is linked to a content source. If the link to the document is unavailable during a crawl, SharePoint Portal Server notes that the link was temporarily unavailable but does not delete the content from the index. If it actually deleted the content from the index, the user would be alerted to this. Then when the link to the document later became available, the user would be alerted again to the change. SharePoint Portal Server checks three times before deleting any content to avoid removing content that is only unavailable because of a broken link.

Reducing Index Size by Excluding Document Types

Content that is excluded by methods other than excluding links can be removed with an incremental update. For example, suppose a content source is initially configured to index only the document types .doc, .htm, and .ppt. Later the index is modifed so that it includes only .doc and .htm document types, which excludes content with a document type of .ppt. An incremental update can incorporate this change into the content index. A full update is not needed for the content to be removed from the index.

Optimizing Resources with an Incremental Update

The best way to optimize resources in SharePoint Portal Server is to configure an incremental update to run daily. With this schedule, a full update is needed only weekly. This creates a balance between resources and updates, and it allows for daily updates of changed content and periodic full updates of all content.

> **Note**   If an incremental update is the first update you create—that is, you have not previously performed a full update—that incremental update is actually a full update. Subsequent incremental updates will be true incremental updates.

You should plan to run incremental updates when you need new and modified content to be indexed quickly but you don't need rule changes, file type or noise word changes, or changes in deleted content to be immediately reflected in your index.

Incremental (Inclusive) Update

SharePoint Portal Server 2003 changed the incremental update to make it more efficient and less resource intensive. To allow for changes that the incremental update does not check for, SharePoint Portal Server 2003 included a new type of update called the *incremental (inclusive) update*. This update is similar to the incremental update except that the incremental (inclusive) update removes deleted content from the index. Otherwise, this update is similar to the incremental update in SharePoint Portal Server 2001. The incremental (inclusive) update is more resource intensive than the regular incremental update and should therefore be run less often. The incremental update is the least resource-intensive update.

Adaptive Update

An adaptive update builds a statistical model for the content source and crawls only the content that, statistically speaking, is more likely to have changed since the last update. Unlike the incremental update, the adaptive update increases its efficiency by "learning" which content changes and at what frequency, and then it molds its crawling schedule accordingly.

How Adaptive Updates Work

To decide which documents to crawl, adaptive updates gather change information each time an update is performed on a content source. This information is used to determine which documents are most likely to change. Because of this, the efficiency of adaptive updates increases over time and over multiple updates. As more updates are performed, more statistical samples are available to the algorithm. After a week of daily adaptive updates, the system settles into a steady state. A steady state is a state in which the system has acquired enough information for the adaptive update to function at optimal efficiency.

Improving Performance with Adaptive Updates

The algorithm used by adaptive updates computes statistical information regardless of the type of update SharePoint Portal Server performs. If incremental updates are run first and then later adaptive updates are used, performance improves immediately because the system is already in a steady state. This is because SharePoint Portal Server has already accumulated sufficient statistical information to apply the algorithm.

Performance improvement between an adaptive update and an incremental update depends on the number of documents and the frequency of changes to the documents. The higher the percentage of documents that change infrequently, the better the performance is. Adaptive updates show the most significant performance improvement in collections of more than 2500 documents.

If no other updates have been performed, the first time an adaptive update is performed is equal to performing a full update. The second time an adaptive update is performed is equal to performing an incremental update. Because of this, performance improvements are not seen until the third time an adaptive update is performed.

Safeguards for Adaptive Updates

An adaptive update is faster than an incremental or full update, but there is a chance that an adaptive update could miss some updated content. Adaptive updates check only content that is likely to have changed, so if a document does not change often it might be overlooked by adaptive updates. To account for this, SharePoint Portal Server places a two-week maximum between crawls on documents. This is a safeguard to ensure that all changes get included in the index.

You should not use adaptive updates if having a fully accurate index is important in your environment. This recommendation is given because adaptive updates are never 100 percent accurate in crawling all the modified content. Instead, adaptive updates only crawl that content that the algorithm predicts is most likely to have changed. A document that is seldom modified might not have its changes appear for up to two weeks in the index. You must consider the advantages of using the adaptive update performance features against the potential delay of getting updated information into the index.

Frequency of Updates

By default, when SharePoint Portal Server is installed, four updates are scheduled to run. These updates are as follows:

- An incremental update of portal site content that occurs every 10 minutes

- An incremental update of the people content source that occurs every hour

- An incremental (inclusive) update of portal site content that occurs once a night

- An incremental update of nonportal site content that occurs once a night

In general, an update schedule should be based on how quickly new content needs to be available for searches or alerts. This need must be balanced against the resources and time required to crawl content.

Starting an Update

An update can be started only if the update status is Idle. The update status for a content index is in the Update Status column on the Configure Search And Indexing page on the SharePoint Portal Server Central Administration page. For the content source, the update status can be viewed in the Update Status column on the Manage Content Sources page.

Before beginning an update, the content index is in the "initializing" state. If there are a large number of alerts or people profiles, the content index can stay in the "initializing" state for a period of time.

> **Note**   If power to the server is interrupted during an update, the update continues after power is restored. For a full update, the crawl restores the previous checkpoint and then resumes. For an incremental update, the crawl restores the previous checkpoint and then redoes all work that occurred after the previous checkpoint. The content index is still available for queries during this time.

Updates and Permissions

All updates pick up permission changes. Access control lists are indexed as part of a document's properties. However, only the full update picks up changes to membership in local groups. Because of this, you should not use local groups to secure content that SharePoint Portal Server crawls.

The Gatherer Log

Each time SharePoint Portal Server 2003 creates or updates a content index, it also creates a gatherer log. The gatherer log is located in a table in the component settings database for the portal site and can be viewed by selecting links on the Site Settings—Configure Search And Indexing page of a portal. This log contains data about URLs accessed by SharePoint Portal Server while it is creating an index. An administrator can also configure the log to record successful accesses, indexing warnings, access errors, and accesses disallowed by rules, which it does not log by default.

Viewing Gatherer Logs

The latest gatherer log can be viewed on the SharePoint Portal Server Central Administration page, but only if the administrator has enabled advanced search administration mode. This view of the gatherer log includes summary or detailed information as well as customized views of the log.

By default, the gatherer log shows only the information from the last crawl. When a new crawl begins, the log entries from the new crawl can overwrite previously recorded entries. However, the gatherer log does not overwrite entries that are less than five days old. Log entries over five days old are considered to be obsolete. If no crawl is performed for more than five days, the log remains unchanged until a new crawl begins. Then all entries are deleted.

Saving Gatherer Logs

Administrators can save old versions of the gatherer log for statistical purposes such as trend analysis or even to to debug problems with index restrictions. By changing property settings of a gatherer log on the SharePoint Portal Server Central Administration page, an administrator can view log entries from previous crawls. The other alternative is to pull the logs directly from SQL Server using active data objects (ADO). The logs are named gathererlog_ID#, where ID# is a number between one and four according to the action that was logged. Table 21-4 shows the ID# that corresponds to the action that was logged.

Table 21-4   Log Numbers and Corresponding Action

Number	Action Logged
1	Portal content
2	Nonportal content
3	Auto Categorization training
4	Profile import

Index Propagation

SharePoint Portal Server 2003 allows the indexing process and the process of querying indexes to be performed on physically separate servers. A server dedicated to performing the indexing process is called the *index management server*, while a server dedicated to processing client search queries is called the *search server*. This allows SharePoint Portal Server to create extensive indexes without affecting the performance of the search server. Once the index management server completes the indexing process, the index is propagated to the search server so that queries can be processed locally.

Preparing for Propagation of an Index

By default, propagation occurs automatically after an index management server creates or updates a content index by using any type of update. Propagation occurs only if your Index Server and Search Server roles are assigned to different servers in the farm. If both roles are assigned to the same server in the farm, there is no index propagation. If needed, propagation can also be forced on the SharePoint Portal Server Central Administration page.

A manual propagation is needed if indexing is paused or propagation fails for some reason, such as network problems or lack of disk space on the search server. Another reason to force a manual propagation is when a new search server is added to the server farm.

A single search server can accept up to four propagated indexes from index management servers. Before forcing propagation from an index management server to a search server, make sure the following actions are performed:

- Configure a search service account for the server farm. This account must have local administrator permissions on the search server.

- Verify that the search server belongs to the same domain as the index management server or to the same trusted domain.

- Check the available disk space on the destination server. SharePoint Portal Server needs more than double the size of the propagated index to complete propagation.

Once propagation begins, the contents of a new index are not accessible on the search server. If propagation has a failure and does not complete, the index remains inaccessible, even if a previous propagation was successful. The index will remain inaccessible until a propagation completes successfully.

Security During Propagation

When propagating indexes from an index management server to a search server, the transmission does not, by default, have safeguards that protect it from unauthorized access. If the propagation is over a network that is not secure, the use of Internet Protocol Security (IPSec) is recommended. IPSec is an industry-defined set of standards that verifies, authenticates, and optionally encrypts data at the IP packet level.

Propagating a SharePoint Portal Server 2003 Content Index

Perform the following steps to propagate a SharePoint Portal Server 2003 content index:

1. On the SharePoint Portal Server Central Administration For Server *server_name* page, click **Configure search and indexing**.

2. On the Manage The Search Service For SharePoint Portal Server page, in the **Indexes** section, click **Manage propagation**.

3. On the Search Propagation page, rest the pointer on the index name and then click the arrow that appears.

4. On the menu that appears, click **Force Propagation**.

Stopping the Propagation of a Content Index

You might stop propagating a content index if, for example, you lose your network connection or if the propagation is taking an exceedingly long time. Propagation of indexes containing a large number of documents takes longer than propagation of indexes containing fewer documents. The time for propagation also depends on the network connection to the search servers.

Indexes are propagated to all search servers. If you stop propagation of an index, you will not be able to see it on any search server unless you stopped the propagation after it was successful on some servers but not on others. When this occurs, the propagation page will show that the propagation was successful, but with errors on specific servers.

Perform the following steps to stop content index propagation:

1. On the SharePoint Portal Server Central Administration For Server *server_name* page, click **Configure search and indexing**.

2. On the Manage The Search Service For SharePoint Portal Server page, in the **Indexes** section, click **Manage propagation**.

3. On the Search Propagation page, rest the pointer on the index name and then click the arrow that appears.

4. On the menu that appears, click **Stop Propagation**.

> **Note**   There is no concept of pause or resume in propagation. If the propagation does not complete for any reason it must be started again from the beginning.

Summary

A portal site can contain a disparate set of documents that number in the hundreds of thousands. One of the overriding advantages of using portal sites is the ability to make documents in different formats and locations available for searching. The process of indexing these documents can take a significant amount of time and resources. Processor and disk resources are heavily used while an index is being created. Indexes also need to be updated constantly, while still remaining available for client searches.

SharePoint Portal Server contains several components that optimize both the indexing and searching processes. These components work together to break down the text and property information to create efficient indexes. Many of these same components also process client queries so that a client can receive a thorough result set without needing to submit multiple queries.

Chapter 22

Managing External Content in Microsoft Office SharePoint Portal Server 2003

One requirement for building a robust information management system is to pull together information that is located in disparate data islands. Microsoft Office SharePoint Portal Server 2003 does an outstanding job of helping you pull that information into the portal site without having to actually *move* it to the portal site's database.

SharePoint Portal Server accomplishes this through the crawling and indexing features—features that enable us to extract data from external sources of content (called **content sources**) and then place that extracted data in text files (that cannot be edited) that can be searched with the results displayed in a result set. Therefore, by simply crawling and indexing information, you can greatly expand the usefulness of the portal site in assisting users when they need to find information quickly and easily.

The tools that we'll discuss in this chapter focus on both administrative and user-oriented subjects. For administrators, we'll focus on the creation and management of content sources, search scopes, source groups, and index files. We'll also discuss ways to craft the result set for your end users, including the use of the thesaurus, the noise word file, keywords, and Best Bets.

From an end-user's perspective, we'll focus on how queries are executed in the Search Web Part and outline some considerations when training your end users for this activity in the portal site. First, let's start by differentiating between Basic Search Administration Mode and Advanced Search Administration Mode in the Search Administration pages.

Advanced Search Administration Mode

By default, when SharePoint Portal Server 2003 installs, the Basic Search Administration Mode is installed with it. This mode (shown in Figure 22-1) does not include an interface for working with the index files or the source groups. In addition, you'll need this mode turned on to view the gatherer logs. When you enable Advanced Search Administration Mode, you will receive the ability to create and manage index files, work with source groups, and view the gatherer logs.

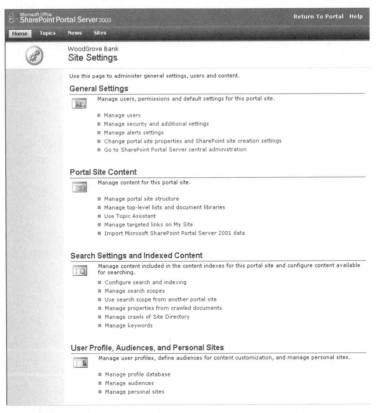

Figure 22-1 Basic Search Administration Mode user interface

To enable Advanced Search Administration Mode, click Enable Advanced Search Administration Mode on the Configure Search And Indexing page (also shown in Figure 22-1). Remember that this is a one-way, one-time change that is user-specific and cannot be reversed.

Creating and Managing Content Sources

SharePoint Portal Server 2003 content aggregation can extend past its physical server farm and actual portal site through the use of content sources. A *content source* is really a set of rules that informs the gatherer service about where to connect to crawl content that is hosted on servers outside the portal. The content can be located in a multitude of places that are outlined in Table 22-1. SharePoint Portal Server 2003 can crawl the following content types in content sources:

Table 22-1   SharePoint Portal Server 2003 Content Sources

Content Source	Description
Microsoft Exchange Server public folders	SharePoint Portal Server 2003 can crawl Exchange Server folders, including messages, discussions, and collaborative content. Including Exchange Server folder content in a SharePoint Portal Server can open Exchange-based discussions and collaborative content.
File share	File shares are still in wide use in many organizations. SharePoint Portal Server 2003 can use file shares as content sources. For example, the WoodGrove Bank Share-Point Portal Server 2003 implementation can use the following file shares as content sources: \\WoodGroveBank\shareddocs\ file://WoodGroveBank/shareddocs/
Web content	SharePoint Portal Server 2003 can crawl a variety of Web content as content sources, including singe static Web pages, entire websites, SharePoint Portal Server sites, and Microsoft Windows SharePoint Services sites content, including HTML content, documents, and lists.
Windows SharePoint Services–based sites and SharePoint Team Services–based sites	SharePoint Portal Server 2003 can index content hosted in these two site platforms. This indexing feature in the site itself is a SQL-based full-text indexing engine, which is different than the MSSearch.exe indexing engine that we are discussing in this chapter.
Lotus Notes database	Content stored in Lotus Notes databases is not off limits to SharePoint Portal Server 2003 as a content source. Using a Lotus Notes database as a content source requires the Lotus Notes administrator to make some configuration changes to the Lotus Notes Index Management Server, and then to make configuration changes to the Lotus Notes protocol handler.

You can create as many content sources as you need, but once you get above a few hundred content sources, the user interface will become unworkable. However, you can still manage this many and more by using the command-line parameters. The SharePoint Portal Server object model is the recommended method of working with content sources in large server farms with hundreds or thousands of content sources.

In smaller installations, the more content sources you have, the more scheduling you'll need to manage because you won't want all your content sources firing at the same time to index their respective data. While it is not unusual for organizations to have hundreds of locations from which they could *potentially* crawl content, it is also conceivable that creating several hundred or even thousands of content sources would present significant resource needs and (perhaps) administrative difficulties.

Therefore, you'll need to balance several competing needs as you work with SharePoint Portal Server. First, you'll need to ensure that you crawl only data that you really need in your index. For example, if you need to crawl 100 documents that are located in a file share hosting 3,000 documents, crawling all 3,000 documents to get the data from the 100 documents into your index would be foolish. Your index would be filled with data that your users wouldn't want appearing in their result sets. Indexing needless information only clutters your index and the result sets, leading to a less positive end-user experience when they use the portal site's search functionality.

So, what would you do? A best practice is to move these 100 documents into their own file share and crawl that file share individually. Remember the old adage: garbage in, garbage out. If you fill your index with needless information, the result sets will not be tight and pinpointed toward what the user is really after. Keeping your indexes clean and trim will help lead to a positive end-user experience when they input a search query. Remember that the goal of creating content sources is to enable your users to find information quickly and easily. A cluttered index leads to a result set that forces your end users to hunt through the list to find the information they are after. Such hunting is neither quick nor easy, and it's likely to "turn off" your end users from wanting to use the search features in the portal site. This is why, later in this chapter, we'll spend time looking at ways to craft the result set for your end users.

Second, you'll need to ensure that content sources are not created on a whim or at every request from a user. It is conceivable employees from your sales department will decide that they'd like to have a host of sale-oriented articles on a website indexed for their own use. While SharePoint Portal Server can certainly handle this task, it might not be wise to set up content sources at the request of each user because you could end up creating many additional content sources that are really unnecessary. A best practice to guard against this is to create a SharePoint Portal Server planning team that lives in perpetuity and that approves the creation of new content sources.

Third, you'll need to ensure that you create enough content sources to pull in the information your users need to perform their jobs and collaborate effectively, but not so many that you can't manage them. Content source management can become a real issue in information-intensive environments. Hardware resources can be unnecessarily taxed, and without proper planning you can actually degrade the performance of your indexing server when you try to crawl a content source.

For example, one procedure that occurs every night on nearly every server in most environments is the backup procedure. There are others, such as antivirus scanning and disk defragmenting. But for purposes of our conversation here, we'll focus on the backup procedure in our example. Because the crawling function is highly processor- and RAM-intensive on both the crawling server and the content source server, a best practice is to schedule your crawl schedules around the other servers' activities.

So, if you have 30 content sources that you want to crawl, a best practice is to ascertain (as best you can) the regular routines that are run on that server and when they are run, and then schedule the index update builds during times when that server is not taxed by routines or client demand. Doing this can be a tall order, but if those servers are in different time zones, having this information might widen the crawling window for you. Therefore, you'll need to think through what content really needs to be crawled and indexed versus how many content sources you'll have, when the sources can be crawled, and how you'll do this without creating bottlenecks on either server during peak crawling periods.

Default Content Sources

SharePoint Portal Server 2003 installs with several default content sources, as follows:

- **Portal Site Content (This Portal).**   An incremental update of portal site content is conducted every 10 minutes in the background, and an incremental (inclusive) update is performed each night. Portal site content includes content hosted in areas plus linked content via portal listings.

- **People Content (People).**   An incremental update of people content occurs every 60 minutes in the background. This content source crawls people profiles and personal sites and includes both public and private documents. However, remember that permissions are applied to result sets before they are presented to the user so that the user will see only documents for which the user has permissions.

- **Non–Portal Site Content (Site Directory).**   An incremental update of non–portal site content is conducted every night to ensure that all non–portal site content is included in the index. Non–portal site content includes all site collections created in the Sites Directory, but it can include other content sources as configured by the portal administrator or administrators.

The SharePoint Timer service works in conjunction with the Scheduled Tasks on the local server to run these (and other) scheduled events. You can learn about the default times by opening Control Panel and then Scheduled Tasks. In that location, you'll see the various scheduled tasks for crawling portal site and non–portal site content. If you have set up other schedules, such as audience compilations or user profile imports, those will appear here too. You can change the timing of such scheduled events by using the Schedule tab in the properties of the scheduled event.

Creating a New Content Source

Whether you're creating or managing a content source, you'll do this in the same location: the Manage Content Sources page. You'll navigate to this page by clicking Site Settings, clicking Configure Search And Indexing, and then clicking Manage Content Sources in the Other Content Sources section.

The Site Settings page governs search settings and indexed content integral to searching and indexing across a SharePoint Portal Server 2003 implementation. Table 22-2 shows the page sections for SharePoint Portal Server site settings.

Table 22-2   SharePoint Portal Server 2003 Site Settings Page Sections

Section	Description
Configure search and indexing	Governs the configuration of search and indexing on the local SharePoint Server.
Use search scope from another portal site	Enables you to use the search scope from an existing SharePoint Portal Server 2003 implementation. This feature is useful if you are deploying multiple SharePoint Portal Server 2003 implementations across an organization and you want to standardize the search scope matrix in each portal site.
Manage properties from crawled documents	Enables you to manage properties from documents you crawl with SharePoint Portal Server 2003.
Manage crawls of the Site Directory	Enables you to manage the crawls of all the sites to be included in your search results.
Manage keywords	Enables the management of keywords throughout your portal site.

To create a new content source, click Add Content Source on the Manage Content Sources page (shown in Figure 22-2).

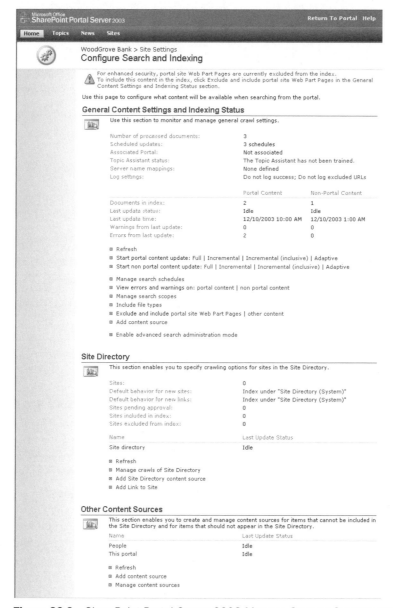

Figure 22-2   SharePoint Portal Server 2003 Manage Content Sources page

At this stage, you'll need to specify what type of content source you want to create:

- **Exchange Server content.** Using Exchange Server content as a content source enables you to tie SharePoint Portal Server into Exchange Server content such as public folders, public e-mail list folders, and other collaborative content.

- File share enabling you to tie SharePoint Portal Server 2003 into your existing shared network drives.

- Web content Web pages, websites, Windows SharePoint Services team sites, other SharePoint Portal Server 2003 portal sites, and sites residing on previous versions of SharePoint Portal Server and SharePoint Team Services.

- Site Directory

- Lotus Notes databases

Crawling Web Content Sources

When you create a new content source (and even after you've created it), you can specify how "deep" the content source should crawl the content. When it comes to websites, you can configure several different options:

1. Click **This site**—follow links to all pages on this site.

2. Click **This page only**.

3. Click **Custom - specify page depth and site hops**. If you click the custom option, you can limit the page depth and the site hops. To do this, select the **Limit page depth** and **Limit site hops** check boxes, and then specify the limits.

The *page depth* is the number of links followed within sites. A *site hop* occurs when a link from one website leads to another website. If you specify that the number of site hops on a website content source be unlimited, SharePoint Portal Server 2003 can access an unlimited number of sites through the initial site. If you choose to reduce the page depth, three full updates must occur before any previously crawled pages are excluded. Three full updates are hard-coded into the product to ensure that temporarily unavailable content is not prematurely removed from the index while generating false positive and unnecessary alerts.

You can also select the Participate In Adaptive Updates check box to include this content source in adaptive updates. Note that if you select the Participate In Adaptive Updates check box, changes will show up more quickly in search results, but updates will tax more server resources. Adaptive updates are described in Chapter 21, "The Architecture of the Gatherer." Thereafter, some of the other duties you'll need to accomplish when setting up a new content source will be performed in these steps:

1. Select a source group if you have enabled Advanced Search Administration Mode. In the **Source Group** section, perform one of the following options:

   - Type a description of the source group for this content source if you want to create a new source group for this content source in the **Source group** box.

   - Select one of the existing source groups if you want to use an existing source group for this content source.

2. Perform one of the following steps to confirm or specify updates and rules for Web content as a content source:

   ▪ Click **OK**.

   ▪ Click **Advanced**. Specify rules to include or exclude content, specify scheduled updates, or start an update on the *content_source_type* content source page.

Managing Rules for Including or Excluding Content

You can create rules that include or exclude content from the content index. These rules are called site restrictions and site path rules. A *site restriction rule* is the main rule for a site. You can show or hide the other rules for a site by clicking the plus sign (+) or minus sign (-) next to the site restriction. The other rules for a site are called *site path rules*. The site restriction defines the overall rules for a site, and the site path rules are rules for specific parts of the site. The Site Path rules are nested inside the Site Restrictions rule.

Site Path Rules are evaluated in the order they appear in the list. If there is a site rule match, all the path rules are evaluated and applied in the order they appear.

You can use site restrictions and site path rules to accomplish the following tasks:

▪ Override the settings for the default content access account when crawling a specific site or path

▪ Specify the granularity for crawling lists

▪ Allow crawling of sites where addresses pass parameters—for example, the address includes a question mark (?)

▪ Allow sites to be traversed for links without content being added to the index

▪ Exclude an area from the index completely

Including or excluding content is a best practice for tuning SharePoint Portal Server search capabilities, and it's a good tool to offer the best possible search results that meet your business requirements.

Rules can use general expressions and wild cards, as shown in the following examples:

▪ "http://woodgrovebank/folder*" applies to all Web resources that have a URL that starts with "http://woodgrovebank/folder"

▪ "http://server?web*" applies to resources such as "http://serveraweb2/file.htm" and "http://serverbweb3/file.htm"

▪ "*/*.doc" applies to every Microsoft Office Word document encountered

Document shortcuts are subject to the same site and path restrictions as other documents and content sources in the portal site. If a user adds a document shortcut to the portal site, SharePoint Portal Server 2003 updates that shortcut in the same way as other content sources. If site or file type restrictions prohibit the inclusion of a shortcut in the index, SharePoint Portal Server does not include content from that document shortcut in the index.

The settings described by these rules will become effective only after a new crawl occurs. If you change rules during a crawl, any content that has not been crawled yet and that is described by the rule will be affected by the changes.

You can add a rule to include specific paths in the content index, to exclude specific paths from the index, to specify how SharePoint lists are handled, or to provide a specific account to access a specific path.

Add a rule that includes or excludes content

Perform the following steps to add a rule that includes or excludes content from your SharePoint Portal Server 2003 searches:

1. On the Configure Search And Indexing page, in the **General Content Settings and Indexing Status** section, click **Exclude and Include Content**.

2. On the Exclude And Include Content page, click **Add Rule**.

3. On the Add Rule page, in the **Path** box, type a path for the content affected by this rule. You can use general expressions and wildcard characters to define which resources are subject to this update rule.

4. In the **Crawl Configuration** section, perform one of the following four options:

   ■ To exclude all documents in this URL space, click **Exclude all items in this path**. If you select this option, when the search component encounters a resource within this space, it will neither crawl the resource nor follow links contained within the resource.

   ■ To include all documents in this URL space, click **Include all items in this path**. If you select this option, you can also do the following:

      ■ To suppress the inclusion of a page of links but still crawl the content that the page links to, select the **Include linked content, but do not include source** check box.

      ■ To follow complex links (URLs that include question marks (?) followed by parameters), select the **Follow complex links** check box.

   ■ To allow alerts on individual SharePoint list items, click **Allow alerts on individual SharePoint list items**. This option will allow alerts to be generated when individual list items in Web Parts are changed, added, or deleted. By default, SharePoint lists are crawled as one item. If you do not click **Allow alerts** on individual SharePoint list items, alerts for the list will be sent if any item in the list is changed.

■ To crawl each SharePoint list item individually, click **Index SharePoint list items individually**.

5. In the **Specify Authentication** section, do one of the following:

■ To use the default content access account, click **Use default crawling account to log in**. If the default crawling account cannot access this path, enter a user name and password combination that can crawl the content source.

■ To prevent Basic authentication from being used, select the **Prohibit the server from passing plain text passwords** check box. The server will attempt to use NTLM authentication.

6. Finally, to use a client certificate for authentication, click **Specify client certificate**, and then select a certificate from the list.

Working with Content Indexes

A content index is a full-text index of content stored on a SharePoint Portal Server 2003 portal site. These content indexes do not include the indexes from the Microsoft SQL Server Full Text Index engine that can be used in each Windows SharePoint Services site. The content indexes are populated by the Indexing Service as it receives crawled content from the Gatherer Service.

Content indexes do not have a hard-coded limit. Successful testing has reached 5 million documents indexed to a single index file.

Creating a Content Index

The reasons for creating additional index files are a bit complex. You'll need to bear in mind a couple of competing issues when you decide to create a new index file.

First, bear in mind that if a user's search spans multiple index files, this will increase the load on your server when the query is executed and it will also take more time to search each index file and then compile a single result set.

Second, ranking is performed within each index file but is not performed again in the aggregate result set. So, if a search query pulls records from multiple index files, there will be no overall ranking of the result set. Therefore, the best practice here is to try, if you can, to limit the number of index files that you create. However, if you find yourself creating a plethora of index files, group the content sources together in such a manner so as to limit the number of times most search queries will need to traverse multiple index files.

Third, if an index file should become corrupt (which can occur if your server suddenly loses power or if there is a read/write failure in your hardware), bear in mind that if you reset the index, you'll be starting simultaneous, full-index updates on each content source that writes to that index file. If you have a high number of content sources writing to that index file, it is possible to overload your server with the execution of multiple full-update builds to rebuild the content in that index file.

Fourth, if you're running in a server farm environment where the indexes are created on an Index server and then propagated to a Search server, bear in mind that the larger the index file, the longer the copy operation will last between the Index server and the Search server. When the Index server is crawling a content source, that information is being written to the local copy of the index on the Index server. Only after the crawling operations are completed will the index file be copied from the Index server to the Search server. Because this is a normal file copy operation, the larger the file, the more time that will be required to copy this file from the Index server to the Search server. Depending on available bandwidth between servers, this could end up being an hour or more of copy time between servers for extremely large index files. For the portal site content incremental update that occurs every 10 minutes, this could mean that your copy operations do not finish before the next incremental crawl commences. A best practice is to perform a test copy of the largest index file to discern the amount of time required to copy a file from the Index server to the Search server and then verify that the copy time is within acceptable limits.

If you need to create a new index file, perform these steps:

1. On the Configure Search And Indexing page, in the **Content Indexes** section, click **Manage content indexes**.

2. On the Manage Content Indexes page, click **New Content Index**.

3. On the Create Content Index page, in the **Name and Information** section, perform the following: type a unique name for this index in the **Name** box. The name must be unique for this portal site. The description is not required to be filled in and is there for your purposes.

4. In the **Source Group** box, type the source group name. This name should be thought out in advance of creating the index file because source groups play a pivotal role in the creation of search scopes.

5. In the **Server** list, select the server on which the index will reside.

6. Click **OK**.

Tip   Universal Naming Convention (UNC) names are not accepted here. The address must be a valid file system path for the server on which the index is being created.

Editing the Properties of a Content Index

Editing the properties of a content index takes place when you need to modify index-specific information such as description, source group, status, and logging options. Such options might have to be changed, depending on the particular requirements of your organization. The logging information available as part of content-index properties is also useful in troubleshooting any content-index issues you might encounter.

In the properties of a content index, you can learn the following information:

- **Name and description of the content index.** The name is not configurable, but the description is.

- **Source group.** You can see to which source group the index file is assigned and assign the file to a new source group if needed. To assign the file to a new source group, simply type in the name of the new source group and then click **OK** at the bottom of the screen.

- **Status information.** The status information includes the file size, the number of documents in the index, the last update, warnings and error message counters, and a link to the gatherer log for this index file.

- **Logging options.** These two check boxes will allow you to specify additional information that should be placed in the gatherer logs. If documents that you think should appear in the index are not appearing, enable these two selections, rerun a full index, and then view the gatherer log for additional troubleshooting information.

- **Excluded and included paths.** You can view the number of included and excluded paths and then click on a link that will allow you to further modify these rules.

Because this information is held in the properties of the index files, you'll want to enable Advanced Search Administration Mode to quickly open the properties of these index files.

Managing Content Indexes

Managing content indexes is an important element of SharePoint Portal Server 2003 site maintenance because resetting and updating content indexes keeps the index up to date and ensures a successful search experience based on the latest portal site content. The management tasks include:

- Resetting a content index and thus stopping index updates and emptying the selected content index entirely. This is an option best used if you suspect file corruption or other issues with the selected content indexes. Resetting the content index file will automatically start a full update for all content sources assigned to that file.

- Starting, stopping, or pausing index build jobs.

- Deleting a content index. You'll delete a content index file only when the file is no longer needed and there are no content sources assigned to that index file.

Content index management is performed from the **Manage Search Settings And Indexed Content** section of the Site Settings page in SharePoint Portal Server 2003.

Resetting a Content Index

Resetting a content index is the best way to empty an index file and force a full-update index to run for all the content sources that are using that index file. You'll want to do this if the index file becomes corrupted or if you want to quickly start a manual full update of all assigned content sources.

Perform the following steps to reset a content index:

1. On the Manage Content Indexes page, rest the pointer on the index name and then click the arrow that appears.

2. On the menu that appears, click **Reset Content Index**.

3. On the message box that appears, click **OK**.

Resetting the index stops any updates that are in progress and empties the index completely. In a server farm configuration, the old index exists on the search servers until index propagation has occurred.

Deleting a Content Index

Deleting a content index is performed from the **Manage Search Settings And Indexed Content** section on the Site Settings page. You'll delete a content index only when you've either moved the content sources to another index file or if you no longer need the content in the index to appear in the search results for your users.

> **Note**   You can delete a content index only if you have enabled Advanced Search Administration Mode. You cannot delete the Portal_Content or Non_Portal_Content indexes.

Perform the following steps to delete a content index:

1. On the Manage Content Indexes page, point to the content index name and then click the arrow that appears.

2. On the menu that appears, click **Delete**.

3. In the confirmation message box that appears, click **OK**.

Deleting a content index also deletes the indexes on the search servers in a server farm configuration.

Managing and Editing Search Scopes and Source Groups

Search scopes give users the opportunity to search a portion of the overall index, thereby placing less demand on the server and returning a sharper, more focused result set. Search scopes can be defined by topics and areas, by source groups, or by both.

Source groups are a new feature of SharePoint Portal Server 2003. (They are not supported in Windows SharePoint Services.) Source groups enable an administrator to group together unique combinations of content sources and index files so that they can be used in one or more search scopes. The advantage of using source groups lies in their granularity: by creating a 1-to-1 relationship between content sources and source groups, you can build search scopes that allow users to search multiple layers of granularity in their result sets.

For example, let's suppose that you have three Windows SharePoint Services sites in the research department: Data Modeling, Chemicals, and Team Discussions. Each site has a distinct purpose, and you need to index the information in these sites so that your users can search it. Now, let's further suppose that your users sometimes need to search just the Chemicals documents and at other times they need to search across all three teams in the research department. Through the smart use of source groups and content sources, you can accommodate both types of searches.

What you would do is create a content source to each site—one for Data Modeling, another for Chemicals, and a third for Team Discussions. In the properties of the content source (keeping in mind that you must have Advanced Search Administration Mode enabled), you would type in a unique source group name for each content source, such as Research Data Modeling Source Group, Research Chemicals Source Group, and Research Team Discussions Source Group.

Then you would create three search scopes—each one based on a source group. Therefore, you would create a Research Data Modeling Search Scope, a Research Chemicals Search Scope, and a Research Team Discussions Search Scope. Finally, you would create a search scope that encompasses all three source groups, named (perhaps) Research Department Search Scope.

In this scenario, if a user wanted to find documents related to plastics in the Chemicals site, the user could select the Research Chemicals Search Scope and execute her query against that individual index from the Chemicals Content Source. However, if the user wanted to search across all three sites for documents related to plastics, she would select the Research Department Search Scope and her search would be executed against the portion of the overall index that was built from all three of those content sources.

Implementing a robust search scope hierarchy is no easy task, and it is really more art than science. One suggestion to capture and build a hierarchy that your users will love is to capture the search terms they executed in the Internet Information Server (IIS) logs and use that to inform your scope hierarchy creation.

In addition, the tighter and more robust your search scopes are, the leaner and more accurate the result set will be when users execute a search query (assuming that they use the search scopes you developed). Accurate results coupled with a faster response time (because the query is not being executed against the entire index) will result in a better end-user experience and increase the positive reaction to your SharePoint Portal Server deployment.

It is important to include discussions about the best use of search scopes, source groups, index files, and content sources in your predeployment planning meetings. Even though they're complex, such discussions can lead to a better deployment and a better end-user experience during the initial stages of a new SharePoint Portal Server 2003 deployment.

Adding a Search Scope

Perform the following steps to add a search scope:

1. On the Manage Search Scopes page, on the toolbar, click **New Search Scope**.

2. On the Add Search Scope page, type a name for this search scope.

3. Decide whether you want to limit the scope by topics or other portal areas. In the **Topics and Areas** section, click **Include all contents** if this search scope is not limited by topic or area. To limit this search scope by topic or area, click **Limit the search scope to items in the following topics or areas**, and then click **Change areas**.

4. On the Change Location page, select areas to use for this search scope. You can select one or more areas, but each selected area includes all of its subareas. Only items in the selected areas show up in search results when using this search scope. When you are finished selecting areas, click **OK**.

5. In the **Content Source Groups** section, click **Include all content sources** if this search scope is not limited to certain groups of content sources. Click **Exclude all content sources** to limit the search scope to only the default content source for this portal site. To limit the search scope to particular content source groups, click **Limit the search scope to the following groups of content sources**, and then select the content source groups that apply.

6. Click **OK**.

Using Search Scopes from Other Portal Sites

In a shared services environment, you might find that you'll want all your users to use the same set of search scopes regardless of which portal site they are executing searches in. This will enable you to also set up a single list of search scopes and make them available across multiple portal sites.

To configure searches in this way, you'll need to use the **Use Search Scope from Another Portal Site** link in the Site Settings of your portal site. Click the **Associate This Portal To Another Portal** option button, and then enter the URL for the associated portal site.

Windows SharePoint Services Search and MSSearch

The search engine that runs in a Windows SharePoint Services site is the SQL Server full-text search engine. The search engine that runs the SharePoint Portal Server search functionality is MSSearch.exe. These are two different, distinct engines that produce two different indexes. These indexes cannot be merged or shared, nor is there any support for attempting to merge these two engines to gain a common index for the portal site and all sites associated with the portal site.

The Topic Assistant

The Topic Assistant provides a way for you to automatically have items in the portal site categorized into areas based on the existing items in those areas. In other words, when properly trained, the Topic Assistant could take a document about flat-panel monitors stored in an area dedicated to content about monitors and include it in an area dedicated to LCD technology. This reduces the time and effort it takes to manage areas, allowing items on the portal site to appear in search results and the portal site map according to the areas to which they belong.

As you add items to lists and document libraries in a particular area, the Topic Assistant can learn (by looking at the index) from your manually added content in that area and other areas and then suggest items to list under alternate areas that it deems are appropriate for that content to appear in. The content manager of that area then can approve or reject these suggestions. As areas are added to the portal site and as items are added to areas, the Topic Assistant continues to learn and suggest items for each area.

The effectiveness of the Topic Assistant is highly dependent on the size of the training set, the appropriateness of the content in each area, and the level of precision set when configuring the feature. There must be a minimum of two areas configured to be included by the Topic Assistant with at least ten documents each to begin the training process. Every time the content index is crawled, the Topic Assistant makes its suggestions. The content index is crawled by selecting the Train Now link on the Topic Assistant page. A best practice is to well exceed the minimum requirements to train the Topic Assistant so that more accurate portal listings are created.

Manage Crawls of Site Directory

Whenever you create a new site collection in the Site Directory, that site collection's URL is placed in the Manage Crawls Of Site Directory list. By default, the listing is approved and crawling of that URL is enabled.

There might be times when you'll want to temporarily stop indexing a site collection—perhaps when the site's administrator contacts you to ask for a temporary hold on indexing while she uploads additional information that she wants included in the next indexing process.

The default behavior is to Crawl This Site. However, you can also select to either Require Approval For Crawling or Do Not Crawl This Site from the list that is associated with the portal site listing. When you select the Require Approval For Crawling option, what you're really doing is moving those sites out of the Approved Sites list and into the Requested Sites list. Doing so does not delete the listing itself, but rather places it in a holding pattern that requires an administrator to manually approve the listing before the content source can be crawled.

Note that site collections are not automatically crawled unless they are created through the Sites Directory in the portal. You'll need to create a content source for the site collection and then ensure that the collection's portal site listing is enabled in this area before you'll enjoy a successful crawl of the site collection.

If you select the Do Not Crawl This Site option, you're moving the listing to the Rejected Sites list. Of course, the listing can be manually re-enabled by selecting the Crawl This Site option and the effect of moving a listing to either the Rejected Sites list or the Requested Sites list is the same: a crawl will not occur on any site listed in either list. To permanently remove a listing from being crawled, click Delete.

Site collections built through the Site Directory are not included in the crawling of the default portal content source. However, they are included in the Site Directory content source, and their information is placed in the nonportal content index file.

Manage Keywords and Best Bets

Keywords are an excellent way to capture a summary of a document in a single word or phrase. SharePoint Portal Server 2003 supports the nesting of keyword lists and the association of any URL-accessed– or Universal Naming Convention (UNC)–based resource. In addition, you can create Best Bets, which is a method of specifying that a particular document or resource will be displayed in the Best Bets Web Part above the regular result set for configured search queries.

For example, let's assume you have the keyword *human resources* in your keyword list. Let's further assume that you have associated the Human Resource Policy Manual with this keyword as a Best Bet. What will happen is this: when a user enters the phrase *human resource* in the Search Web Part, the Human Resource Policy Manual will appear in the Best Bet Web Part above the result set. You'll use Best Bets to manually configure certain documents or resources to appear ahead of any other resource in the result set. This feature allows you to specify certain documents and resources to appear when the user enters a keyword. This is an excellent way to craft the result set for the end user by specifying obvious documents and resources for a given search query.

End-User Experience

MSSearch uses free-text queries in the Search Web Part in SharePoint Portal Server 2003. With free-text queries, you can enter a group of words or a complete sentence. The indexing service finds pages that best match the words and phrases in the free-text query. It does this by finding pages that match the meaning, rather than the exact wording, of the query. The indexing service ignores Boolean, proximity, and wildcard operators.

You can use free-text queries to search both contents and property values. If you submit only the query text without specifying the type of query or the property, the indexing service uses the free-text query and the Contents property by default.

For example, if you enter "blue shoes" (without the quotation marks) in the Search Web Part, you will get back documents that contain the word "blue", the word "shoes", and both "blue" and "shoes". In other words, search will find documents that contain either or both words.

To search for an exact phrase, enclose the phrase in quotation marks, such as "blue shoes". When such a phrase is entered, search will return only documents that contain the exact phrase "blue shoes".

Crafting the Result Set Using the Thesaurus

Another way to expand the set of documents that is received from a catalog is to use thesaurus files. Thesaurus files allow the user to type a phrase in a search query and receive results that are altered by the administrator. The thesaurus also enables the server farm administrator to affect search ranking by assigning weights to words. Table 22-3 lists the thesaurus files available in SharePoint Portal Server 2003.

Table 22-3   SharePoint Portal Server 2003 Thesaurus Files

Language	Thesaurus File
Chinese-Simplified	tschs.xml
Chinese-Traditional	tscht.xml
Czech	tscsv.xml
Dutch	tsnld.xml
English-International	tseng.xml
English-US	tsenu.xml
Finnish	tsfin.xml
French	tsfra.xml
German	tsdeu.xml
Hungarian	tshun.xml
Italian	tsita.xml
Japanese	tsjpn.xml

Table 22-3   SharePoint Portal Server 2003 Thesaurus Files   *(continued)*

Language	Thesaurus File
Korean	tskor.xml
Neutral	tsneu.xml
Polish	tsplk.xml
Portuguese (Brazil)	tsptb.xml
Russian	tsrus.xml
Spanish	tsesn.xml
Swedish	tssve.xml
Thai	tstha.xml
Turkish	tstrk.xml

The neutral thesaurus file is always applied to queries, in addition to the thesaurus file associated with the query language. If a query is in a language that does not have its own thesaurus file, only the neutral thesaurus file is applied.

Editing Thesaurus Files

Thesaurus files are XML files that can be edited in a text editor. When editing thesaurus files, use only well-formed XML (that is, matching opening and closing tags around each entry) or the file will not load properly. If the XML is malformed, SharePoint Portal Server logs an error in the Microsoft Windows Server 2003 event log referencing the file and line.

By default, SharePoint Portal Server stores thesaurus files in the Program Files\SharePoint Portal Server\DATA\Config directory of the server. The location of the DATA directory can be changed during the installation of SharePoint Portal Server. This directory contains one additional file called Tsschema.xml. Do not modify this file.

There are four ways to craft the result set for your end users via the thesaurus. The first way is to enter expansion sets, which essentially means that if a user searches on the word "boots", we're going to automatically expand that query to include the words "shoes" and "sandals" (for example). Expansion-set terms are equal, so if you place the three words "boots", "shoes", and "sandals" in the same expansion set, a search on any one of these three terms will expand the query to include the other two.

Common instances of when you'll want to use expansion sets includes expanding acronyms to include their spelled-out form, finding commonly misspelled forms of the searched words, and finding common synonyms for names and terms that might exist in your industry. For example, if you have a difficult-to-spell term—such as "pyrotechnic"—in your index, you might want to create common misspellings of this word in an expansion set so that even if users misspell the word, they will still receive a result set of the documents that they are looking for.

A second method of using the thesaurus is to create the opposite of an expansion set, which is called a *replacement set*. In this scenario, you specify a term or set of terms that you *don't* want users searching on, and instead, you replace it with terms that you *do* want users searching on. For example, let's suppose that you don't want users searching on the term "pyrotechnic", but you do want them searching on the term "explosive". In this scenario, you'll create a replacement set that replaces the term "pyrotechnic" with the term "explosive".

Common instances of when you'd want to do this include when replacing culturally insensitive words or words that would violate your human-resources policies. We know of one administrator that listed all the offensive words in a replacement set and replaced it with the title to the human resource (HR) policy manual. In this instance, when a user searched on an offensive term, the result set came back with a link to the HR manual. That's a pretty good use of the thesaurus!

Believe it or not, another common use for replacement sets is for misspelled words. You can handle commonly misspelled words either through expansion or replacement sets, whichever method seems to best fit your needs and environment.

The third method of crafting the result set using the thesaurus is to use the weighting schemes. Weighting (or ranking) determines which documents will appear ahead of other documents in the result set. Terms are assigned a weight between 0.1 and 1.0, and these differences are absolute, not proportional. Therefore, 0.8 is not twice as "heavy" as 0.4, and 0.5 is just as much higher as 0.8 when compared to 0.4. So, select the terms that you want to weight, place them in the same expansion set, and then add weighting as illustrated in the default thesaurus file.

Finally, you can employ *stemming*, which means placing a term in an expansion set and then following that term with two stars, as in "run**". What this will do is force a search in the index on all terms that begin with the three letters "r-u-n". A best practice here is to use this method with caution, because you can get unintended effects in the result set from doing this. We suggest that you use a dictionary to start with the root word you want to stem and then follow that word down the dictionary list of words to see all the possible words that will be included in the search to ensure that the result set will be what the user really expects.

In our example the result set would include documents that contain the word "run", but also the word "runaway", "runabout", "running", and "runt". Such a dissimilar set of words might not be desirable as part of an overall search query, so be sure to think this through before using it.

As you might have gathered by now, the use of the thesaurus is really more art than science, and more skill than technology. Because the default thesaurus is really a blank slate, you'll need to use it over time to figure out how it can best serve your needs. A best practice here is to use a software product to capture the search queries entered into the Search Web Part, and then use that list to help you build an intelligent and useful thesaurus for your environment.

Using Multiple Thesaurus Files

During installation of the thesaurus files, a copy of the thesaurus files is saved to the *<local_drive>*\Program Files\SharePoint Portal Server\Data\Applications\Application UID\Config directory. These files can be used to specify thesaurus files that apply at the application level instead of at the server or server-farm level. For example, if SharePoint Portal Server and another application that is included in the portal site are installed on the same server, each can use different thesaurus files.

Attribute Mapping for Advanced Search

SharePoint Portal Server 2003 allows you to specify which attributes should appear in the Advanced Search Web Part by allowing you to configure a custom list in the drop-down list.

To configure Attribute Mapping for Advanced Search, click Manage Properties Of Crawled Documents and then drill down into the property you want to enable for advanced searching. On the Edit Property page, in the Search Options section, select the Include This Property In Advanced Search Options check box.

Note that when you select this check box, the Include This Property In The Content Index and Allow Property To Be Displayed check boxes are automatically selected and then dimmed so that you can't clear them. In a sense, this saves us from ourselves because there would be no reason to select a property to appear in Advance Search and then not index the property or allow the property to be displayed.

Optionally, you can also have the property appear in item details in the result set by selecting the Display This Property In Item Details In Search Results check box. Doing this will ensure that this specific property is displayed in the search results.

Finally, you can tie alerts to modifications in the property. What this means is that even if the content of the document does not change, but only the values in this property do, alerts can be generated.

Summary

This chapter covered how you can manage external content via SharePoint Portal Server 2003 through the use of content sources that tie into SharePoint Portal Server 2003 content indexes. This chapter also covered managing and editing search scopes and discussed their significance in SharePoint Portal Server 2003 searches.

Chapter 23

Personalization Services in SharePoint Products and Technologies

As the body of corporate knowledge on a portal site increases, it becomes increasingly difficult for individuals to find relevant information, and to have it presented in an intuitive way. Content presented on home pages for corporate and divisional portal sites is typically general in focus and forces workers to access multiple pages to view role-specific and user-specific content.

Microsoft Office SharePoint Portal Server 2003 creates a portal site that knows who you are and what information you care about and work with, thus providing a personal context for users. Based on Web Part Pages technology, SharePoint Portal Server delivers customization and personalization that is flexible, secure, and reliable. SharePoint Portal Server provides a rich set of features focused on ensuring that users have easy access to relevant information from a variety of entry points.

- **Web Part Pages and Web Parts.** SharePoint Portal Server provides site managers with a flexible policy for personalization and customization. Site managers can customize the portal site to users based on specific criteria. Portal site users can personalize the site to facilitate collaboration or to provide custom views of their projects, including by using websites based on Microsoft Windows

SharePoint Services to facilitate team collaboration. This topic is discussed in detail in Chapter 30, "Default Tools to Customize SharePoint Services."

- **User profiles.**   User profiles allow you to search for and connect with people within your organization based on information people publish about themselves.

- **Audiences.**   SharePoint Portal Server allows you to target content to people according to their membership in a particular audience.

- **My Site.**   My Site is a personal Windows SharePoint Services site that provides personalized and customized information for you.

- **Alerts.**   SharePoint Portal Server can alert you about new or updated information on topics that match your interests.

If a corporation has divisions or customers in different countries or multilingual regions, the need arises to provide information and content in multiple languages. This chapter discusses how personalization services can be used to implement multilingual scenarios.

Personalization services can be provided by a corporate portal site and consumed by different divisional portal sites through SharePoint shared services. This chapter discusses the personalization services of SharePoint Portal Server 2003.

User Profiles

User profiles enable you to search for and connect with people within your organization. User profile information is also used to generate a personal site in the portal site for individual users. Users can personalize their view of this site, called *My Site*. In addition, user profile information is used by index and search services to provide better search results, and it is used in targeting content to audiences. You can import user profile information directly from Active Directory directory service or enter it manually. You can also customize the properties of the user profile according to the needs of your organization or to map to Active Directory properties, such as Territory or Geography.

As a portal site user, you can view and change your own user profile from My Site, a default area in the portal site that provides personalized information for you. You can change only profile properties that are marked as editable by profile administrators. You can view your own profile by using either the private view or the public view. You can edit your profile from either view, but the actual profile details are only displayed on the public view by default. The private view contains private information that is viewable only by you. Portal site users with the Manage Profiles right can manage profiles and quick links only. Other private information, such as your Private Documents Library, is only viewable to you and global administrators.

The public view of the user profile is visible to all other portal site users when they click your name in the portal site. For example, when viewing search results, you can click the author name to view the public user profile for the author.

Adding User Profiles

After clicking My Site a user profile is automatically created for you. During profile creation SharePoint Portal Server attempts to retrieve data from the Active Directory directory service which is configured as an import source. Users who do not have user profiles available by using Active Directory directory service as an import source must enter their user profile properties manually. Once user profiles are added or imported, you can update information by editing each user profile. Editing a user profile does not change the set of properties displayed in that user profile. You can add, edit, or delete the individual profile properties on the Manage Profile Database page in the User Profile Properties section.

Add a user profile manually

You can add user profiles manually if you do not want to or cannot import user profile information automatically from an Active Directory directory service. For any properties that you do not specify manually SharePoint Portal Server will attempt to import values from the Active Directory directory service specified in the configuration settings.

1. Use one of the following methods:

    ■ On the Manage Profile Database page in the **Profile and Import Settings** section, click **Add user profile**.

    ■ On the View User Profiles page, click **New Profile** on the toolbar.

2. Type values for the required properties and for any other properties you want to include for this user.

3. On the toolbar, click **Save and Close**.

4. To leave this page without adding a user profile, click **Cancel and Go Back** on the toolbar.

It is also possible to edit and delete user profiles using the View User Profiles page, which is shown in Figure 23-1. If you delete a user profile, you also delete the properties and values for that user. Personalized links and alerts for that user are also deleted. The personal site for that user is not deleted. Before deleting the user, you should use the Manage Personal Sites option in the User Profile, Audiences, and Personal Sites section on the Site Settings Administration page to delete the personal site and copy items from the personal site for archiving purposes. Although you can import any properties mapped to Active Directory directory service during the next scheduled import, you permanently lose any custom properties that you added. You also lose any values for properties mapped to Active Directory that have changed since the last import.

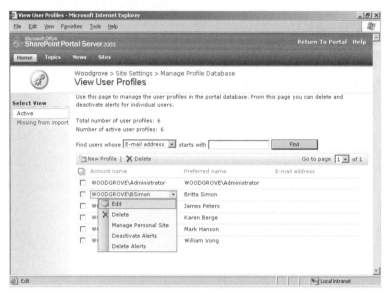

Figure 23-1   Add, edit, or delete user profiles on the View User Profiles page

> **Note**   If you delete a user profile for a user that remains in Active Directory directory service, that user profile is automatically recreated the next time user profiles are imported. If a user account is deleted in Active Directory, it will not be deleted automatically from the profile database during the next import. Instead, the SharePoint profile will be marked as deleted. Then you can use the selector on the Manage User Profiles page to manually delete the user profile. Remember that this action deletes only the user profile— you'll still need to delete permission assignments and the user's My Site manually.

Importing User Profiles

You can import user profile information from Active Directory. This saves time in entering user information for every user in your organization, because otherwise all user profiles will have to be added manually. However, the user information might not include all the properties you want to show for each user. Also, if you do not import user profiles from Active Directory, you will lose some audience features and the ability to create audiences based on SharePoint-specific criteria. We do not reconnect back to Active Directory to dynamically pull the user profiles for Share-

Point Portal Server because by copying and holding the user profiles in SharePoint Services, you are free to create new SharePoint-specific profile objects without extending the Active Directory schema. In addition, there is no performance decrease on your domain controllers by not servicing user profile requests from SharePoint Portal Server 2003. Finally, by not writing back to the Active Directory, we do not turn SharePoint into a meta-directory service that would create additional management and security issues.

A user profile based on Active Directory information can contain values in profile properties that are mapped to Active Directory or are unique to SharePoint Portal Server. Active Directory is used to uniquely identify users and resources on the network. By importing user profile information from Active Directory, you keep a single central repository for storing SharePoint-specific user information within your organization.

To import user profile information, you must first configure the import settings. You set up an import account for a specific server running Active Directory directory service in your organization. Then you enable full or incremental imports and schedule when those imports should regularly occur.

After you have configured the import settings, you can import user profile information from the list of actions in the Profile and Import Settings section on the Manage Profile Database page, which is shown in Figure 23-2. You can also stop any import currently in progress and view a log of past imports.

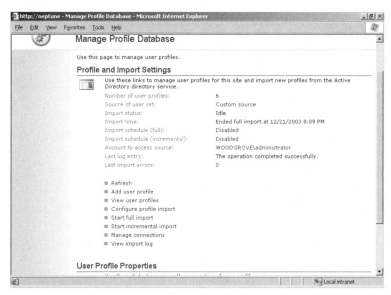

Figure 23-2   Manage user profiles on the Manage Profile Database page

This page has two views. The **Active** view includes all active user profiles that were imported during the last full import. The **Missing from import** view includes the user profiles that were imported in the past but were not imported in the previous three full imports because the user profile information was not available from

Active Directory. This usually means that the person has been deleted from the Active Directory, which might happen when someone leaves the company. The user profile is not deleted automatically. Instead, you should decide how you want to delete or preserve their personal site. Then delete their profiles on a case-by-case basis. If you just want to delete all of them, you can use the Check All check box to quickly delete them.

To configure import settings

To import user profile information from Active Directory, you must configure import settings first.

1. On the title bar of the portal site, click **Site Settings**.

2. In the **User Profile, Audiences, and Personal Sites** section, click **Manage profile database**.

3. On the Manage Profile Database page, click **Configure profile import**.

4. In the **Source** section, select the server running Active Directory from which to import user profiles. This can be from the **Current domain**, the **Entire forest**, or a set of **Custom source** domains that include the current domain. If you select **Custom source**, the Manage Connections page appears when you click **OK** on this page.

5. In the **Access Account** section, type the account name and password for an account that has rights to Active Directory.

6. In the **Full Import Schedule** section, select **Schedule full import**.

7. In the **Incremental Import** section, click **Schedule incremental import** to show this option on the Manage User Profiles page.

8. For each type of import you have enabled, select a start time from the **Start at** drop-down list. To schedule imports at this time every day, select **Every day**. To schedule imports on certain days of the week, select **Every week on** and then select the days on which you want to import user profiles. To schedule imports once a month, select **Every month on this date** and then select the day of the month on which to import user profiles.

9. Click **OK**.

To start full import

After configuring the import settings, you can start importing user profile information.

1. On the Manage Profile Database page, in the **Profile and Import Settings** section, ensure that **Source of user set** lists the correct set of users.

2. To select a different set of users, click **Configure profile import**.

3. After verifying the set of users, click **Start full import**.

During a *full import*, values of Active Directory properties overwrite the values of user profile properties mapped to Active Directory. If the value for an Active Directory property is empty, any customizations in the value of the user profile property mapped to Active Directory will be retained. Deleted Active Directory accounts will not be deleted from the profile database during a full import.

Another type of import exists: the *incremental import*. During an incremental import, profile information about users whose Active Directory records have changed or have been added since the last import is overwritten. Incremental imports will significantly shorten the time it takes to complete the import. To perform incremental imports, the account must have the Replicate Changes permission for Active Directory directory services provided by Windows 2000 Server. The permission is not required for Windows 2003 Active Directory.

Incremental imports can be started from the Manage Profile Database page. If a full or incremental import takes too much time or if server performance drops to an unacceptably low level, you can stop the import, which can also be done using the Manage Profile Database page.

To view an import log

You can view a log of past imports, which can be used for troubleshooting purposes. You can do this by going to the Manage Profile Database page, in the **Profile and Import Settings**, and clicking **View import log**.

To view active and missing user profiles

The View User Profiles page has two views. The **Active** view includes all active user profiles that were imported during the last full import. The **Missing from Import** view includes the user profiles that were imported in the past but were not imported in the previous three full imports because the user profile information was not available from Active Directory.

1. On the Manage Profile Database page, in the **Profile and Import Settings** section, click **View user profiles**.

2. On the View User Profiles page, in the **Action** pane, click the view that you want to see.

    ■ To view active user profiles, click **Active**.

    ■ To view missing user profiles, click **Missing from import**.

Managing Active Directory Connections

When you configure import settings for user profiles, you can choose to import user profile information from servers running Active Directory for your current domain, from servers running Active Directory for your entire forest, or from servers running Active Directory on one or multiple custom domains. You can import user profile information only from Active Directory, environments running Microsoft Windows NT 4.0 domain controllers will not be able to benefit from this.

To add an Active Directory server

If you decide to import user profile information from one or multiple domains, on the Configure Profile Import page, select the **Custom source** option in the **Source** section. Next add the servers to the set of servers available to import user profile information.

1. On the Manage Connections page, click **New Connection**.

2. In the **Connection Settings** section on the Add Connection page, type a domain name in the **Domain name** box.

> **Note** By default, a domain controller is automatically detected for you. To select a controller, click **Select a domain controller** and type a domain controller name in the **Domain controller name** text box for the Active Directory server that you want to add.

3. To access this server by using a secured socket layer (SSL) secure connection, select the **Use SSL-secured connection** check box.

4. To limit the amount of time spent attempting to access a server that is not responding, type a value in the **Time out** box.

5. In the **Search Settings** section, type a name in the **Search base** text box. If you do not enter anything in the **Search base** text box, SharePoint Portal Server enters the appropriate information.

6. In the **User filter** section, you can add query clauses to further filter the user profile data that you are importing.

7. The default value in the **User filter** text box is a specific Lightweight Directory Access Protocol (LDAP) query. Specifying an LDAP query enables you to granularly define the data that will be imported into the profile database.

8. In the **Scope** section, select how deeply in the Active Directory server to search for user profiles to import. You can limit the scope by selecting **One level** or search more deeply by clicking **Subtree**.

9. Type a value in the **Page size** box to limit the amount of data imported in each user profile.

10. Type a value in the **Page time out** box to limit the amount of time spent attempting to access a page that is not responding.

You can also edit the settings for existing servers or delete servers from the set used when importing user profile information from the Manage Connections page.

Deleting a server from the list of connections removes the connection to that server so that user profiles found only on that Active Directory server are not imported.

LDAP Search Filters

Active Directory connections provide the possibility to specify an LDAP query that granularly defines the data that is imported into the profile database. An LDAP query consists of the following four parts:

- **Base distinguished name.**   For example: DC=Woodgrove, DC=COM.

- **LDAP search filters.**   Search filters enable you to define search criteria.

- **The LDAP display name of the attributes to retrieve.**   This is managed by specifying user profile properties, which will be described in the next section.

- **The scope of the search.**   Valid values are "onelevel" or "subtree".

The following table gives examples of LDAP search filters.

Table 23-1   Examples LDAP Search Filters

Search Filter	Description
(objectClass=*)	All objects
(&(objectCategory=person) (objectClass=user) (!cn=amy))	All user objects but "amy"
(sn=sa*)	All objects with a surname that starts with "sa"
(&(objectCategory=person)(object-Class=contact)(|(sn=Purcell)(sn=Bezio)))	All contacts with a surname equal to "Purcell" or "Bezio"
(&(objectCategory=person) (objectClass=user) (!(userAccount-Control:1.2.840.113556.1.4.803:=2)))	Imports user profile information of only user accounts that are enabled

Additional Notes for Better Import Setting

The following list provides information on importing user profiles.

- If possible, search on indexed attributes only. Try to use index attributes that you expect will generate the fewest number of hits, therefore higher performance.

> **Note**   A comprehensive list of indexed attributes for Windows 2000 and Windows .NET can be found in the Active Directory Schema section of the Active Directory guide.

- Search on objectCategory instead of objectClass since objectClass is not an indexed property.

- Stay away from searching for text in the middle and at the end of a string. For example, "cn=*hille*" or "cn=*larouse*".

- Properly scope your searches by specifying innermost search base and minimum search scope so as to not retrieve more than is necessary.

Managing User Profile Properties

The set of properties that are included in the user profile might not contain all the information about users in your organization that you want to include on the site. You can add new properties to enhance those included in the user profile. You can also edit existing properties to change how those properties are displayed in the user profile. You can also map properties to properties in Active Directory directory services. When you add or edit a property mapping, you must run a full import before the changes take effect.

To add a profile property

If the default user profile page does not include all the properties that you want to show for each user, you can add additional properties.

1. In the **User Profile Properties** section on the Manage Profile Database page, click **Add profile property**.
   -or-
   On the View Profile Properties page, click **New Property**.

2. On the Add User Profile Property page, type a name for the property in the **Name** box. This name is not displayed on the user profile, but instead is used programmatically whenever the property is accessed by SharePoint Portal Server 2003.

3. Type a display name for the property in the **Display name** text box. The display name is the name for the property that is shown on the personal and public views of the user profile.

4. Select a property type in the **Type** list and if applicable, type the length in the **Length** text box. These define the acceptable values for this property and cannot be changed once the property is created.

5. To display this property to the user and administrator on the personal and edit views of the user profile, select **Private – Only the user and users with the Manage Profile right can view the settings for this property.** To display this property to all users in the public view of the user profile, select **Public – All users of the site can view the settings for this property.**

6. To allow users without the Manage Profile right to change the value of this property, select **Allow users to edit this property.** Otherwise, select **Do not allow users to edit this property.**

7. In the **Display Settings** section, you can choose whether or not the property is displayed in the **Details** section of the user profile in the public view. You can also choose whether the property is displayed on the Edit My Profile page.

8. To map this property to a property in Active Directory directory service, select a property from the **Active Directory property to map** drop-down list.

9. Click **OK**.

On the View Profile Properties page shown in Figure 23-3, the properties available for user profiles are listed and organized by sections. You can add, delete, and edit properties from this page. You can also add, edit, and delete sections and move properties within and between sections.

> **Note**   Sections are only used for display in the Details section of the user's public view of My Site. It is not used when editing a user profile.

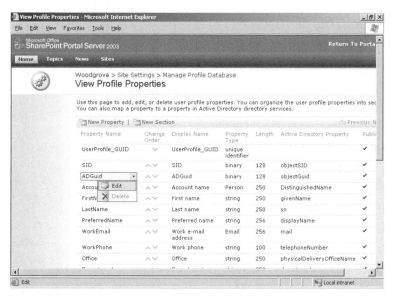

Figure 23-3   The View Profile Properties page can be used to add, edit, and delete profile properties and sections

Audiences

The audience feature is supported only in SharePoint Portal Server 2003. Audiences allow organizations to target content to users based on their job or task, as defined by their membership in a Windows 2003 security group, a distribution list, an organizational reporting structure, or the public properties in their user profiles. Only users imported into the Profile Database populate audiences.

There are three components to using audiences effectively. First, you must add an audience. Second, you target an item such as a document or news item to one or more audiences. Third, you put the targeted item in one of the areas that uses the Links for You Web Part to show targeted items to portal site users. You can also target Web Parts to audiences. In this case, the targeted Web Part will only be displayed when the audience matches the current user. This is discussed in Chapter 30.

By default, SharePoint Portal Server includes an audience named *All portal site users*. In addition to this audience, you can create other audiences, such as by department or by security group. These audiences can span one or more portal sites in a deployment.

Managing Audiences

Audiences are managed centrally across one or more server farms hosting SharePoint Portal Server 2003. They apply across one or more portal sites in a deployment, not to individual areas, sites, or items. You must have the Add, Change, or Delete Audiences right to manage audiences. As an audience manager, you can create, edit, or delete audiences, view all members of a specific audience, and find the audiences to which a specific user belongs, as well as manage the rules defining audiences and compile audiences as the rules and members of an audience change.

> **Note**   Audiences are not used to assign rights and permissions. SharePoint Portal Server uses site groups to assign rights and permissions to users within the portal site. Audiences are used to manage how content is distributed, not to enforce security. They push information to a user, instead of restricting or permitting access to information.

To create an audience

You can create an audience and define audience rules to define audience membership.

1. On the Managing Audiences page, click **Create audience**.

2. Alternatively, on the View Audiences page, click **New Audience** on the toolbar.

3. On the Create Audience page, type a name and description for the audience.

4. Click **Satisfy all of the rules** or **Satisfy any of the rules**. Complex rules, for example rules that combine OR and AND operators, can be created only through the Object Model.

5. Click **OK**.

6. The Add Audience Rule page appears. See the "To add audience rule" procedure for more information.

> **Tip**   You must add rules to an audience and then compile the audience before content can be targeted to the audience.

You can add, edit, or delete audiences from the View Audiences page, which is shown in Figure 23-4. Deleting an audience does not delete content; rather, content is no longer targeted to members of that audience. If that content is only targeted to that audience, it is no longer seen on the site.

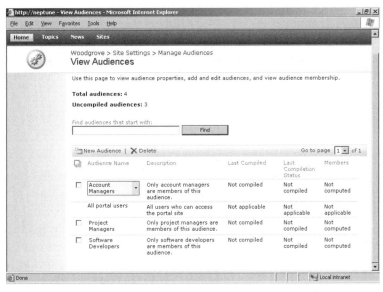

Figure 23-4   Add, edit, or delete audiences on the View Audiences page

Compiling Audiences

Changes made to audiences and audience rules are not reflected in audience membership until the audience is compiled. During compilation, all existing audiences will be compiled. You should start audience compilation after creating a new audience or after important changes in user profile information have taken place. You can schedule audience compilation during offline hours. If you're using scheduled profile imports, you should schedule audience compilation after profile imports have taken place. You can also start a compilation manually at any other time if you must update an audience before the next scheduled compilation.

When you compile an audience, the property values in user profile and membership in distribution lists, security groups, and reporting structure are checked to see if they match the audience rules you have created. Users that match the audience rules for an audience are included in that audience and receive content targeted to that audience.

From the Manage Audiences page, you can start a compilation. You can also view the compilation status and most recent compilation time and see the number of uncompiled audiences.

To specify compilation schedule

You can set compilation schedule from the Manage Audiences page.

1. On the Manage Audiences page, click **Specify compilation schedule**.

2. On the Specify Compilation Schedule page, click **Enable scheduling** to turn on audience scheduling.

3. Select a start time from the **Start at** drop-down list. To schedule compilations at this time every day, select **Every day**. To schedule compilations on certain days of the week, select **Every week on** and then select the days you want to compile audiences. To schedule compilations once a month, select **Every month on this date** and then select the day of the month on which to compile audiences.

4. Click **OK**.

Viewing Audience Membership

You can check the membership of an audience to see if the audience is targeting the right users. This is particularly helpful after adding or editing an audience, after adding or editing audience rules, or after changing the property or organizational structure used by an audience rule. The audience membership summary shows the last time the audience was compiled and the number of members in the audience at that time.

To view audience members

You can determine the members of an audience.

■ On the View Audiences page, click the audience whose membership you want to view and then click **View Membership**.

    -or-

    On the View Audience Properties page for an audience, in the **Audience Member** section, click **View membership**.

■ To view a different page of multiple page audience membership, click the page number in the **Go to page** drop-down list.

Managing Audience Rules

Audience rules determine who is or is not a member of an audience. An audience includes all the members who match the audience rules when the audience is compiled. Changes to audience rules do not change the membership of the audience until the next time the audience is compiled.

To ensure that an audience is current, you must compile the audience after adding, editing, or deleting an audience rule. Audiences also must be compiled if the values of public properties used by the audience rule change or new users are added, even if the audience rules itself is not changed.

You can define audience rules based on profile properties, organizational hierarchy, distribution lists, or Windows NT security groups. Using audience rules, you can specify audience membership using complex expressions. Audience rules use simple queries to include or exclude users from membership in an audience. Each rule includes an operand, an operator, and a value.

The *operand* is the user or the property you want to include in the query for this rule. The *operator* indicates how users compared to the value should be queried to include or exclude them from the audience. The *value* is the point of comparison used by the query.

For example, using the following audience rule you could build an audience based on distribution list membership in combination with the value of a profile property:

```
MEMBER OF "IT Staff" (DL)
AND
Office CONTAINS "Tokyo"
```

To add audience rule

Define audience membership based on rules.

1. On the View Audience Properties page, in the **Audience Rules** section, click **Add rule**.

2. On the Add Audience Rule page, click **User** to add a rule based on distribution list membership, security group, or reporting structure, or click **Property** to create a rule based on a user property.

3. If you clicked **Property**, click the relevant property in the drop-down list.

4. In the **Operator** drop-down list, click an operator to indicate how you want to compare the user or property with a given value.

5. In the **Value** text box, type a value to which to compare the user or property selected for this rule.

6. Click **OK**.

You can edit audience rules on the View Audience Properties page. You can delete an audience rule on the Edit Audience Rule page. Deleting an audience rule changes how the membership of an audience is determined when the audience is compiled. The audience is compiled using the remaining audience rules. If the deleted audience rule was the only remaining audience rule, the audience membership is empty and content targeted to only that audience is not seen.

Show Targeted Items to Portal Site Users

You can display targeted items in the following three ways:

- Any items can be displayed in the Links for You Web Part on My Site.

- News items can be displayed in the News for You Web Part on My Site.

- Any items can be displayed on the default home page of the portal site or on any area which has a Links for You Web Part or a Grouped Listings Web Part, which is grouped by audience.

Whether individual users see items targeted to these locations depends on whether the users are members of the audience to which the items are targeted.

To add an item targeted to the Links for You Web Part on My Site

You can display any item on the Links for You Web Part.

1. Click **Site Settings**, and in the **Portal Site Content** section, click **Manage targeted links on My Site**.

2. On the Targeted links on My Site page, click **Add Listing** to target a link to the **Links for You** Web Part on **My Site**.

3. On the Add Listing page, in the **Title and Description** section, type a title and a description for the listing.

4. In the **Content** section, for existing items, click **Existing listing** and type the address for the location of the item.
   If you are adding a completely new item, click **Add a listing by entering text** and then click **Open Text Editor**. Type and format the text for the item, and then click **OK**.

5. In the **Group** section, you can click the group to which you want to assign this listing. By default, listings are in the **General** group.

6. In the **Image** section, you can decide to type an address for an image to represent this listing when it appears in the portal site.

7. In the **Audience** section, select the audience that you want to target from the **Available audiences** list and then click **Add**. If the list of available audiences is long, you can type part of the audience name into the **Find audiences that start with** text box to go directly to the audience in the list. You can select more than one audience.

8. On the Add Listing page, click **OK**.

> **Note** You can also add a person to the Links for You Web Part by clicking **Add Person** from the Quick Launch bar. This is a useful way to provide information to a team about a manager or new employee.

You can edit or delete an item targeted to the Links for You Web Part on My Site on the targeted links on My Site page. If this is a news item that you would prefer to target to the News for You Web Part, click Move. On the Move Listing page click Change location and then select the News area or one of its subareas. If you want to target this item to the home page of the portal site, you can change the area to Home or one of its subareas. If you change this to any other area, this item is not targeted to any users on the home page or in My Site.

To show the item in the News for You Web Part on My Site

You can target items to the News for You Web Part.

1. On the title bar of the portal site, click **Site Settings**.

2. In the **Portal Site Content** section, click **Manage portal site structure**.

3. In the **Show** list, click **All**.

4. Select the item that you have targeted to an audience.

5. Drag the icon of the targeted item to the **News** area or one of its subareas.

> **Note** After you have dragged the item, the page will refresh. Dragging an item to a new area moves the item. To add a link to the item in the new location without removing the item from its old location, click the new area and then click **Add Listing**.

To show the item on the default portal site page

You can show items on the default portal site page to provide relevant information to your end users. By doing this you're basically telling your end users that certain information is probably of interest to them. This is an entirely different tool with an entirely different purpose than setting security permission on areas, which makes sure your end users are not allowed to see certain information.

1. On the title bar of the portal site, click **Site Settings**.

2. In the **Portal Site Content** section, click **Manage portal site structure**.

3. In the **Show** list, click **All**.

4. Select the item that you have targeted to an audience.

5. Drag the icon of the targeted item to the **Home** area.

You can show items using this procedure in locations other than the default portal site page. You can show targeted items to portal site users in one of the areas that use the Links for You Web Part.

To target an item to an audience

To target an item to an audience, you must edit the display properties of the item in the portal site map to select the audience or audiences to which to target the item.

1. On the navigation bar of the portal site, click **Site Settings**.

2. In the **Portal Site Content** section, click **Manage portal site structure**.

3. On the Portal Site Map page, click the arrow next to **Show** on the toolbar and then click **All** to change the default view to show all items.

4. Select an item to target. You must select a specific item, such as a document or a news item. Selecting an area does not work because content is targeted by item and not by area.

5. Click the arrow next to an item to select it. In the drop-down menu that appears, click **Edit**.

6. Click the **Display** tab to select an audience.

7. On the Display Properties page, in the **Audience** section, click the audience you want from the available audiences list and then click **Add**.

8. Click **OK**.

> **Note**   Another way to target an item to an audience is by going to the page where the item is located and selecting **Edit Page**. Use the item's drop-down menu, and select **Modify Shared Web Part**. Expand the **Advanced** section, and click the **Target Audiences Select** button.

Personal Sites

A personal site, named *My Site* in the SharePoint Portal Server 2003 user interface, is your personal starting point for accessing and contributing to your organization's intranet through the portal site. A portal site has two natural entry points: the portal site home page and your personal site. The portal site home page shows information based on the viewpoint of your organization. Your personal site is about you: it contains information directed by you to reflect your information interests. It also contains information about you to help other users to find out more about you.

Every personal site has a private storage area for personal content and work in progress, which provides personalized and customized information for you. On a Windows operating system, the My Documents folder fulfills a similar role, providing a private directory. The private storage area of My Site should be seen as a replacement for the My Documents folder.

The personal site also contains a public storage area for easily sharing the projects and documents you are working on. The public storage area should be seen as a replacement for a personal file share. The public storage area enables you to customize the information you use or present to other people in your organization. Because the personal site includes some profile information from the Active Directory directory service, it also provides information to others about the role you play within a team or organization.

Just as you share information with other people in your organization through the public view of your personal site, you can also find and connect with other people through the public views of their personal sites.

When a user name appears in the portal site, you can click the name to view the public view of that person's personal site. Everything that a person chooses to share is available for you to see. You can see a person's shared links to sites, people, and documents that might help you to get your work done. You can also see what workspaces you have in common. The *business card* shows contact information, like a user's cell phone. The About Me section contains a message written by a person. Also, by default, the personal site contains information about the organizational hierarchy related to that person.

To create your personal site

When you first click My Site on the navigation bar of the portal site, SharePoint Portal Server 2003 creates your personal site for you. Once your personal site is created, it appears every time you click My Site on the navigation bar of the portal site.

Personal Site Views

Your personal site consists of two views: a private view for personal information that only you can see, and a public view seen by everyone else. The private view is shown by default when you view your own personal site.

To change the view of your personal site

You can switch between the private and public view of your personal site.

■ To switch to the private view from the public view, click **Private** in the **Select View** section of the action pane.

■ To switch to the public view from the private view, click **Public** in the **Select View** section of the action pane.

Personal Site Navigation

As with most other SharePoint sites, your personal site has a top link bar with the following links:

■ **Home.**   This link returns you to the home page of a personal site. If that page is your personal site, you see the private view. If it is another person's personal site, you see the public view.

■ **Documents and Lists.**   This link shows all the lists for your personal site and the number of documents in each list. You can also create lists of various types from this page.

■ **Site Settings.**   This link provides administration, customization, and information management pages for your personal site.

■ **Help.**   This link shows help for the current page.

■ **Up To.**   This link will get you back to the home page of the portal site.

Private View

The private view of your personal site provides a personalized view of the portal site and the documents, sites, and people found in the portal site. This view contains content targeted to you based on your membership in a particular audience. For example, if you are a new employee, you might find links to key training resources.

The private view of the home page for your personal site includes several Web Parts for organizing information specific to you. The private view Web Part layout can be customized by changing to **Shared View**. In **Shared View**, any changes made to Web Part properties or layout will be reflected to all users' personal sites. By default, these Web Parts include the following:

■ **My Calendar.**   Meetings and appointments scheduled in Microsoft Exchange Server 2003. You must provide the address of a Microsoft Outlook Web Access server to use My Calendar.

■ **My Links Summary.**   A summary of links that you have created on your personal site for regular use. To add a link, click **Add new link**. Links in this list that you share also appear on the public view of your personal site.

■ **Links for You.**   Links to items targeted by audience managers in your organization to certain audiences. Links for the audiences to which you belong appear in this Web Part.

■ **My Alerts Summary.**   All the alerts you receive are listed here. To view the item that sent the alert, click the alert in the list. To change the properties of a specific alert, click the arrow next to the alert in the list. To manage all your alerts, click **Manage Alerts** in the **Select Action** section of the action pane.

■ **News for You.**   News items are targeted by the audience managers in your organization to certain audiences. The news items for the audiences to which you belong appear in this Web Part.

You can add, remove, or modify Web Parts for the home page of your personal site just like you do for any other Web Part page. The private view of the home page for your personal site is shown in Figure 23-5.

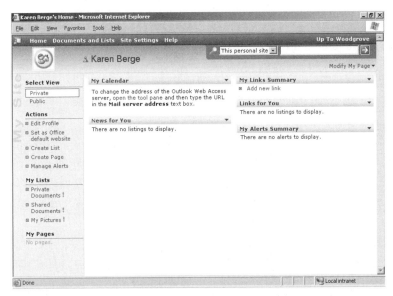

Figure 23-5   Private view of a personal site

When using Microsoft Office, you can set your personal site as the Office default website. You can expand your personal site by creating lists of various types and new Web Part pages. You can choose whether to share lists or pages with other people in your organization. You can also manage alerts. The My Lists link in the action pane provides links to all the lists on your personal site that are not hidden. To view hidden lists, click Documents and Lists on the top link bar of your personal site. The My Pages link in the action pane provides links to the pages on your personal site that are in the My Pages document library.

To edit your profile

You can provide information about you by editing your profile.

1. In the action pane, in the **Actions** section, click **Edit Profile**.

2. On the Edit Profile page, type information for the properties that you want to display to other people in your organization. Some of these properties, such as the **About me** property, have formatting menus to change the appearance of your user profile. The site administrator decides what properties are available for you to edit.

3. To save these changes, click **Save and Close** on the toolbar. To leave your user profile without making changes, click **Cancel and Go Back**.

Public View

The public view of your personal site is a convenient way for you to manage the way that other people in your organization find you and your work. The design, layout, and Web Parts on the public view cannot be personalized. They are designed to look consistent across the organization. Other people in your organization can see your public view even if you have never created a personal site. The public view can be customized through Microsoft FrontPage.

The public view shows the following information:

- **Your public profile.** Depending upon your organization, your profile can include such things as your picture, information about you, and contact details. Your profile allows other people in your organization to learn information about you and to contact you.

- **Organization.** Organizational information, such as your manager and reporting structure.

- **Recent Documents.** Your five most recently modified documents on the intranet, listed in order starting with the most recent and highlighted so that other people in the organization can find them. All your recent documents that are crawled by the portal are listed here, and not just documents stored in your personal site. You can click the **Recent Documents** link to display all documents by this author.

- **Shared Links.** These are links that you specifically decide to share with other people on your personal site.

- **Shared Workspace Sites.** SharePoint sites, Document Workspace sites, and Meeting Workspace sites that you share with other people in your organization. For other people to see these workspace sites in the public view of your personal site, you must first invite them to join the workspace sites. Only workspaces created under you personal site will show up here, not all workspaces across the portal.

- **Shared Lists and Shared Pages.** Action pane links to your shared lists and shared pages. People can see only the lists and pages to which they have access.

The public view is shown in Figure 23-6.

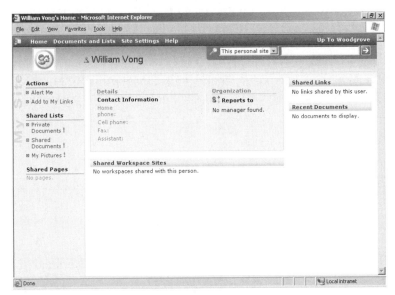

Figure 23-6   Public view of a personal site

Your personal site also includes all the functionality of Windows SharePoint Services sites. You can create document and picture libraries, calendars, surveys, tasks, and other SharePoint lists. You can create other pages on your personal site. Any of the documents you create in your personal site can be shared with other users by adding them to public document libraries.

Managing Personal Sites

Site administrators control the location and site naming format for the personal sites on the portal site from the Manage Personal Sites page. If you are using shared services, you can create and store personal sites for any portal site on a different portal site in the server farm. Site administrators can also select the users and security groups that are part of the default Reader site group. You can view and manage site settings for individual personal sites from the View User Profiles page.

To select the personal site location

The personal site location is the name of the directory where you want to create and store personal site directories for users. This directory is created immediately under the root directory. For example, if you click **personal**, all the personal site directories are created under http://*servername*/personal. You can change this location at any time without affecting the location of existing personal sites.

1. Click **Site Settings**, and then in the **User Profile, Audiences, and Personal Sites** section, click **Manage personal sites**.

2. On the Manage Personal Sites page, in the **Personal Site Location** section, in the **Location** list, select the location where you want to create and store all personal sites.

3. Click **OK**.

To select the site naming format for personal sites

The site naming format describes the naming convention to use when creating directories for the personal sites for specific users, and how to resolve conflicts with existing directories. This is important because user names can potentially conflict with one another across multiple domains.

1. Click **Site Settings**, and then in the **User Profile, Audiences, and Personal Sites** section, click **Manage personal sites**.

2. On the Manage Personal Sites page, in the **Site Naming Format** section, select the naming format to use when creating and storing information for personal sites. For example, you can specify that a new personal site is created in a directory with the format *domain_username*.

3. Click **OK**.

To add accounts and groups to the Reader site group for personal sites

Personal sites are important when organizations want to share information about their employees, at least within the company itself. In most cases, you should consider giving all your employees reader access to all personal sites. You can decide which users can view personal sites by adding accounts and groups to the Reader site group.

1. Click **Site Settings**, and then in **the User Profile, Audiences, and Personal Sites** section, click **Manage personal sites**.

2. On the Manage Personal Sites page, in the **Default Reader Site Group** section, type the accounts or groups that you want to add to the Reader site group in the text box, separating accounts and groups by using commas.

3. You can also select accounts or the groups to add to the Reader site group by clicking **Edit**. The Default Reader Site Group page appears.

4. On the Default Reader Site Group page, in the **Find by** list, click the option for the name or alias of the user or security group for which you are searching.

5. Type the text for the name or alias for which you are searching, and click **Find**. All names or aliases starting with that text are returned in search results.

6. In the **Results** box, click the users or aliases that you want to add and then click **Add**.

7. Search for and add as many users as you want, and then click **OK**. The Default Reader Site Group page is closed.

8. Click **OK**.

Portal Site Alerts

Alerts notify you when information that interests you is added or updated on the portal site and associated content sources, thus providing you with the ability to search in the future. You can define your areas of interest and identify how and when you want to be told about something new or updated that you might want to investigate.

Alerts are important tools for portal site users. As information from diverse sources is pulled together, sifting through so much content can be a time-consuming task. Alerts provide a proactive solution to staying informed. Alerts in SharePoint Portal Server 2003 build on the concept of subscriptions in SharePoint Portal Server 2001, extending and refining the feature to make it even more powerful.

An alert can be added to track the following types of items:

- Search queries

- Documents and listings

- Areas

- News listings

- Sites added to the Site Directory

- SharePoint lists and libraries

- List items

- Portal site users

- Backward-compatible document library folders

For example, you can add an alert for an area in the portal site, such as a topic area, as shown in Figure 23-7. An *area page* is any area of the portal site other than the home page.

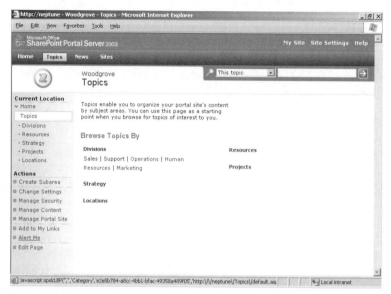

Figure 23-7   Add area alert

The portal site sends alert results whenever changes are made to the content that you added an alert for. You can view alert results on the portal site or receive them in e-mail messages. You can specify how frequently you want to receive alert results by e-mail and receive them immediately, as a daily summary, or as a weekly summary. When you no longer need to follow changes for the item, you can delete your alerts at any time.

You can manage your alerts and alert results from My Alerts, a page available from My Site. This does require "User personal features" rights. In addition, by using Microsoft Office Outlook 2003, you can view all alerts and alert results from all alert providers, including alerts from Windows SharePoint Services.

To edit an alert

After adding alerts you can manage them on your personal site.

1. On the title bar of the portal site, click **My Site**.

2. In the **Actions** list, click **Manage Alerts**.

3. In the list of alerts, click the alert you want to edit.

4. In the **Actions** list, click **Edit Alert**.

5. Change the settings.

6. Click **OK**.

To activate or deactivate an alert

If you deactivate an alert, you will not receive alert results until you reactivate it.

1. On the title bar of the portal site, click **My Site**.

2. In the **Actions** list, click **Manage Alerts**.

3. In the list of alerts, click the alert that you want to activate or deactivate.

4. In the **Actions** list, click **Activate Alert** or **Deactivate Alert**.

5. Click **OK**.

> **Note** If your alert generates an excessive number of results, the portal site might automatically deactivate it to conserve resources. Activate the alert to begin receiving results again. If you activate this alert and then your alert is automatically deactivated again, edit the alert to reduce the number of alert results you receive. For example, under Alert Results on the Edit Alert page, you can narrow the scope of your alert results by specifying that the results contain a specific word or phrase.

To delete an alert result

This deletes alert results but does not delete an alert. You will continue to receive alert results.

1. On the title bar of the portal site, click **My Site**.

2. In the **Actions** list, click **Manage Alerts**.

3. In the list of alerts, click the alert whose results you want to delete.

4. Under the result you want to delete, click **Delete alert result**.

5. Click **OK**.

> **Note** If you receive alert results in e-mail messages, you can click **Delete These Results from My Alerts** in the message to automatically delete the results listed in the message.

The Manage Alerts page also offers the possibility to delete all alert results in one single action.

Manage Portal Site Alerts Settings

Administrators have the possibility to manage alerts on a portal site level via the Manage Alert Settings page. From this administration page you can accomplish the following tasks:

- Managing individual user alerts

- Deleting all alerts and alert results

- Deleting all alert results e-mail messages in the alerts queue

- Setting alert quotas, setting and/or locking the user's default alert e-mail address

- Setting the Simple Mail Transfer Protocol (SMTP) server used for sending e-mail alert notifications

To enable portal site alerts

Alerts are an important feature within SharePoint Portal Server. You must enable this feature before users can benefit from alerts.

1. On the title bar of the portal site, click **Site Settings**.

2. In the **General Settings** section, click **Go to SharePoint Portal Server central administration**.

3. In the **Portal Site and Virtual Server Configuration** section, click **Configure virtual server settings** from the Virtual Server List page.

4. Click the name of your Virtual Server.

5. In the **Virtual Server Management** section, click **Virtual server general settings**.

6. In the **Alerts** section, you can enable alerts on the virtual server and specify the maximum number of alerts per user.

To manage portal site alerts

Administrators can manage alerts for all users.

1. On the title bar of the portal site, click **Site Settings**.

2. In the **General Settings** section, click **Manage alerts settings**.

3. In the **User Alerts Management** section, click **Manage user profiles** to go to a page where you can delete or deactivate an individual user's alerts.

4. In the **Delete All Alerts and Alert Results** section, click **Delete all alerts and alert results** to remove every alert and alert result stored on the portal site for all users. Click **OK** to confirm that you want to delete all alerts and alert results for all users. This action cannot be undone.

5. In the **Delete All Alert Results E-mail Messages** section, click **Delete all alert results e-mail messages** to remove all alert results e-mail messages waiting to be sent in the alerts notification queue. Click **OK** to confirm that you want to delete all unsent alert results in the queue. This action cannot be undone.

6. In the **Alert Quotas** section, specify limits for the number of alerts per user, the number of alerts per site, and the number of alert results per site.

7. In the **Default E-Mail Address for Alert** section, you can specify a User Profile field to use as the source of the default e-mail address when a user adds an alert. Select **Always use user profile field** to prevent users from changing the default e-mail address supplied by the User Profile.

8. In the **SMTP Server for E-Mail Alerts** section, click **Change default e-mail settings** to configure SMTP server settings. If an SMTP server is already configured, the name and status are displayed.

You can configure SharePoint Portal Server 2003 alert notifications to use any SMTP server. Only a member of the SharePoint administrators group can configure an SMTP server.

Using the Command Line to Configure Alerts

You can manage alerts from the command line by using the **GetProperty** and **SetProperty** operations with Stsadm.exe. You can set the properties shown in the following table to configure how alerts work.

Table 23-2   Command Line Properties to Configure Alerts

Property	Description
alerts-enabled	Turns alerts on or off
alerts-limited	Specifies whether users are limited to a specific number of alerts
alerts-maximum	Specifies the maximum number of alerts users can create
job-immediate-notification	Specifies how often to check for immediate alerts (in minutes)
job-daily-notification	Specifies the time of day (using a 24-hour clock) to send out daily alerts
job-weekly-notification	Specifies the day of the week and time of day (using a 24-hour clock) to send out weekly alerts

The following example shows the syntax to use to turn off alerts:

```
stsadm.exe -o setproperty -p <port> -pn alerts-enabled
-pv false
```

Using the Command Line to Configure E-Mail Settings for Windows SharePoint Services

You can also configure e-mail settings from the command line by using the e-mail operation with Stsadm.exe. The e-mail operation takes the following required parameters: *outsmtpserver* (the out-going SMTP server), *fromaddress* (the e-mail address to send messages from; can be an unmonitored address), *replytoaddress* (the e-mail address to send replies to; must be a monitored address), and *codepage* (the codepage to use). In addition, you can use the optional *url* parameter to specify settings for a particular virtual server.

> **Note** The valid codepages are listed on the Configure Default E-mail Server Settings page in SharePoint Central Administration, in the Character set box. To specify a codepage on the command line, use the number for the character set, rather than the full name. For example, use the number **65001** to specify the codepage for 65001 (Unicode UTF-8).

The e-mail operation uses the following syntax:

```
stsadm.exe -o e-mail -outsmtpserver <smtp server>
  -fromaddress <from address> -replytoaddress <reply-to address>
  -codepage <codepage> [-url <url>]
```

For example, to configure the e-mail settings to use the server \\SMTPServer, and to use someone@example.com as both the *from* and the *reply-to* address, you would use syntax similar to the following:

```
stsadm.exe -o e-mail -outsmtpserver SMTPServer
  -fromaddress someone@example.com
  -replytoaddress someone@example.com
  -codepage 65001
```

To set the http://myserver virtual server to use codepage 65001, you would use syntax similar to the following:

```
stsadm.exe -o e-mail -outsmtpserver SMTPServer
  -fromaddress someone@example.com -replytoaddress someone@example.com
  -codepage 65001 -url http://server_name
```

SharePoint Site Alerts

SharePoint sites include an alerts feature comparable to the portal site alert mechanism. The SharePoint site alerts feature is an e-mail notification service. When users who have signed up for alerts create, modify, or delete documents, lists, or items on a server running Windows SharePoint Services, they receive messages informing them of these changes. Users can create alerts to track lists, list items, document libraries, and documents within a site. Users manage these alerts via the My Alerts on this Site page, which is shown in Figure 23-8.

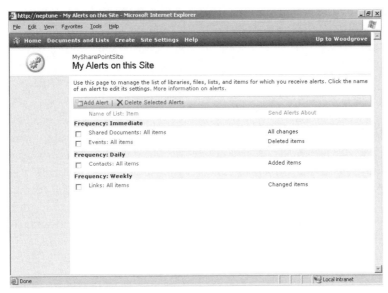

Figure 23-8 Manage alerts on the My Alerts on this Site page

Troubleshooting Alerts

If you cannot create alerts to be notified of changes to Web content, take the following actions:

- The server administrator must check whether the alerts feature is turned off. This feature must be turned on before you can use it.

- The Windows SharePoint Services timer service is responsible for coordinating the processing of alerts. The server administrator must turn on this feature for alerts to function.

- Check whether the site group to which you belong has permission to create alerts.

If alerts are sent to the wrong e-mail address, do the following:

- Check whether the correct e-mail address was specified when you were invited to the site. You might need to update your account information.

- Check whether the alerts are being sent to the mail account that you use for instant messaging. When you enable instant messenger integration, the e-mail address that you specify is also used for alerts.

If a user who is removed from a site still receives alerts from it, do the following:

■ After removing a user from a website, site group, or cross-site group you should manually remove any alerts created by the user. This is also true for any lists or libraries for which you change security settings to limit access. If a user has set up alerts for the list or library, the user will continue to receive them after you change the security settings.

Summary

This chapter shows the personalization services that are available in SharePoint Products and Technologies. First it covers how profiles are used to store user information and how this information can be imported from Active Directory. Based on user profiles, you can create audiences that are used to target content to certain groups of users within your organization. The chapter also discusses the role of personal sites within SharePoint Portal Server and what you can do with them. Finally, the chapter explains what alerts are, how you can manage them, and how to solve problems with alerts.

Chapter 24

Information Security Policies for SharePoint Products and Technologies

In today's world, you cannot really secure a network without having information security policies in place. Such policies are really business rules—rules that define acceptable and sometimes required behavior regarding your company's information. Information security policies continue to become more complex because the technologies that host an organization's mission-critical information are also becoming more complex every year, if not every month. From cell phones to laptops, from PDAs to servers, the access vectors and potential security holes are increasing as the technology complexity increases. Information security policies are one method of plugging many security holes by prescribing acceptable behavior as information is developed and stored.

The more an organization follows information security policies, the more dependent an organization becomes on these rules in a host of situations, such as guiding a manager on acceptable behavior about how information is accessed, informing a legal team as to whether a manager has performed due diligence, or acting as reference documents for internal security audits.

Some will say that the problem with information security policies is that the rules are only as effective as the people who obey them. But the presence of information security policies in an organization is fast becoming a legal assumption: those companies that operate *without* information security policies (hereafter referred to simply as *policies*) might be subject to the charge that reasonable care for an organization's information was not executed. Regardless of an organization's size, purpose, or location, effective information security is vital, so we are covering it in this resource kit.

The purpose of this chapter is to outline those types of policies that should be considered when implementing either Microsoft Windows SharePoint Services or Microsoft Office SharePoint Portal Server 2003. Our purpose is not to write the policies for you or even to give you a sample set of policies from which to work, but rather to highlight the types of policies that will be affected when implementing SharePoint Products and Technologies.

Password Policies

Because SharePoint Products and Technologies require domain services for authentication, it is wise to have password policies in place for your network. In all likelihood, if you have any policies in place in your organization, chances are good that you already have policies that address the issues listed in this section. However, the implementation of SharePoint Products and Technologies is an appropriate time to review those policies because most of the information held in SharePoint Products and Technologies can be compromised by obtaining a SharePoint-pervasive username and password combination.

Like most policy domain areas, there are sub-areas that should be addressed as the policies are written. Password policies are no exception. The following are some of the issues to be considered when developing your password policies:

- Minimum password length

- Password complexity and strength

- Prohibition of reusing old passwords

- Prohibition of written storage of passwords

- Prohibition against printing or displaying passwords

- Periodic forced change in passwords

- Method to manage expired passwords

- Authorized means to transmit new passwords to remote users

- Limits on consecutive attempts to enter a password

- Acceptance or prohibition of single sign-on services

- Prohibition of passwords sent through e-mail

- Requirement for encrypted storage of passwords

- Reliance on domain services for authentication

- Requirement for non-anonymous authentication before access to information is allowed

- Use of duress passwords (Duress passwords trigger scripts during a duress situation—that is, if a gun is pointed at your head and you are asked to log on to the server, a duress password would log you on, but because of the password entered, a script would be triggered to delete all predetermined sensitive data.)

- Requirement to change all administrative passwords if any have been compromised

- Password sharing prohibition

- User responsibility for all actions taken with his username and password combination

- Security notice in logon system banner

- Prohibition against leaving systems without logging off or locking the system

- Use of biometric devices required for logon to portal

- Use of smartcard devices required for logon to portal system

Note   Throughout this chapter, we will introduce issues that should be considered when writing your policies. Each issue introduced might or might not apply to your environment. For example, some organizations might have a strong password complexity policy while another environment might not due to culture, industry, or other factors. We are not recommending that each issue be implemented as presented here, only that each issue should be *considered* as the policies are written.

Most of these issues relating to password policies should be covered in your network policy, but one that directly affects SharePoint Products and Technologies is the single sign-on policy. If your organization prohibits single sign-on capabilities, meaning that users must log on to each application that requires unique authentication, you will be unable to use the single sign-on feature in SharePoint Portal Server 2003.

Also, the Active Directory Mode feature of Windows SharePoint Services needs to be considered in a Windows SharePoint Services–only installation. Given that this feature allows site administrators the ability to create new user accounts in Active Directory, if you are going to use this feature, you should have policies surrounding who can be a site administrator and under what circumstances a new user account can be created in Active Directory from a Windows SharePoint Services site.

In addition, if you are going to use SharePoint Products and Technologies in an extranet environment—especially for its customer relationship features—in which users outside your company will be authenticating in your domain to access their portion of the portal site, implementation of a policy specifying how you will securely transmit passwords to those users and whether or not e-mail may be used will have paramount importance.

Moreover, in situations in which you will be sharing sensitive information with other companies (maybe even competitors), you will probably want a robust set of password policies to be required by all parties to the agreement, necessitating the development of such policies before the project can begin.

As we mentioned previously, much of the information in SharePoint Products and Technologies is secured *only* through username and password combinations. The compromise of passwords in your environment could lead to sensitive information being exposed to the wrong people and this, in most cases, would be disastrous.

Personal Use of Sites

We would like to think there is no need to mention this, but it is possible that users will create their own websites, give only themselves permission to the site, and then use that site for private purposes. The authors of this resource kit know of multiple times when a company's servers were used to set up Internet-based businesses without the knowledge of or the consent of the company's owners.

Creating policies that prohibit personal use of company systems will help prevent this problem. Few things irritate system administrators more than the misuse of company systems for personal gain at the expense of system performance, storage space, and additional administrative effort.

Because it will be very easy—especially for the SharePoint Products and Technologies administrators—to set up personal websites (we are not referring to the My Site feature here, but rather to rogue Windows SharePoint Services sites) for personal gain (if you have enabled Self-Service Site creation or if the user is already a member of the Administrator site group in a site), a strict prohibition should be approved by your managers and then communicated to your users as part of their SharePoint Products and Technologies training.

The following issues should be addressed in this domain:

- Use of SharePoint Products and Technologies sites for personal use is strictly prohibited.

- Personal use of computers is prohibited.

- Incidental personal use of business systems is permissible. (Consider this issue only if your users are allowed to use company systems for personal use.)

- Storage of personal data is prohibited on company systems.

You might have noticed that the third bullet point contradicts the others. We include this point to emphasize that in certain situations, *some* personal use of computers and SharePoint Products and Technologies will be permissible. We can think of nonprofits who allow their employees to host in-kind websites to the organization's mission after gaining approval. Again, this list is not meant to dictate what should and should not be in your policies, but rather to alert you to the issues that should be considered when writing these policies.

Information Storage Policies

Because more and more mobile devices, such as laptops, PDAs, and Tablet PCs (along with older technologies, such as floppy disks), will be connecting to your SharePoint sites, it is important to define what types of devices can permanently hold your mission-critical information. The last thing you want is a member of the Compensation Committee Site downloading sensitive information to an unsecured PDA and then leaving that device in an airport or hotel. It would be an understatement to say that this is an undesirable scenario for any organization.

Therefore, you should consider the following issues when it comes to how your mission-critical, private, secret, or sensitive information is stored:

- Acceptable use of mobile devices.

- No sensitive information on mobile devices.

- Definition of what a mobile device is.

- Mobile devices must store all information in encrypted form.

- Mobile devices must be password-protected.

- Default permissions for all files on the network.

- No write-down permissions for company information.

- Information ownership must be assigned.

- Prohibition of taking ownership of information without authorization.

Administrative Policies

In many organizations, we often find that there is poor communication between the human resources department and the system administration people. Reasons for this vary from company to company, but it is common for the system administrators to be some of the last people to learn that a person has changed departments or has left the company.

In SharePoint Portal Server 2003, when a user account is deleted in Active Directory, that deletion is not implemented in the user profile database in SharePoint Portal Server 2003. Even though the account is marked for deletion in the user profile database, those accounts must still be deleted manually by a SharePoint administrator.

If you need to remove a user's profile from the user profile database before it is removed through a full import, you will need to propagate policies to this effect. In this domain area, here are some issues to consider:

- Worker status changes are sent to System Administrators in a timely fashion.

- Users must inform System Administrators about changes in status.

- Transfer of ownership of information after user leaves company.

- Schedule of file deletion after user leaves company.

- User notifications need to be cleaned up by the SharePoint Administrator.

Logging Events

One of the ways to troubleshoot any system is to have a robust logging system in place that can help you troubleshoot problems should they arise. One area to log for SharePoint Products and Technologies is the Internet Information Services (IIS) platform. Because all of the client calls will come through IIS to the Windows SharePoint Services filter, you can capture who is connecting, when they are connecting, and which pages they are requesting. In addition, you can purchase third-party software that will give you more vigorous reporting capabilities.

Logging is also a security concern because you can track attack vectors that hackers might use to compromise your system. A robust logging system is essential for good security, and those logging policies to be considered that relate to SharePoint Products and Technologies include the following:

- Logs are required for all application systems that host sensitive information.

- Logs must support auditing requirements.

- Logs must provide accountability and traceability during an audit.

- Content of SharePoint Products and Technologies logs must include specified information.

- Required retention period for logs.

- Information to capture when a compromise is suspected.

- Logging required before a system can be placed in the production domain.

- Clock synchronization on all SharePoint Products and Technologies servers with a master clock of all servers in production domain.

- Persons authorized to view logs.

- Logs must be reviewed on a regular basis by authorized personnel.

Authorized Web Parts and Applications

Because SharePoint Products and Technologies is designed with a distributed administrative architecture, it is important to remember that authorized users will be able to install Web Parts on a site. It would be very easy for authorized users to download Web Parts that have been created on the Internet and then install those parts on their sites. Remember that site and portal administrators delegate the right to add Web Parts to a Web Parts page, and there are protections in place for the administrator to control how much a Web Part can do. Liberal delegation of this right might lead to compromised security in your SharePoint implementation. Unsuspecting users could download an infected or a compromised Web Part, install it, and expose your critical information to hackers on the outside.

Because of this potential vulnerability, you should seriously consider restricting which software can and cannot be installed in SharePoint Products and Technologies. Points to consider when creating policies in this area include the following:

- Prohibition against downloading third-party software to your corporate systems.

- Requirement to scan downloaded Web Parts before use in a production system.

- Testing for viruses must be performed on a non-cabled, stand-alone server.

- Multiple virus screenings must be performed on all downloaded software from the Internet to corporate systems.

- Virus scanning software must be employed on all SharePoint Products and Technologies systems.

- Requirement to run all third-party Web Parts in a test environment prior to deployment in a production environment.

Change Control

Because SharePoint Products and Technologies will be hosting some of your most mission-critical and sensitive information, it is best to ensure that you have a strong change control program in place for your servers. By controlling who can make administrative modifications to your system, you can maintain stability in your production environment and ensure that only authorized changes are made to your systems.

Pay attention to the Site Collection Use And Confirmation feature that allows SharePoint Products and Technologies to automatically delete a site collection if site use is not confirmed by the site owners after a specified number of days. In many environments, automatic deletion of entire site collections will be unacceptable. You will want to factor into your policies the exact settings you wish to have for this feature because an undesired configuration could result in the loss of a site collection.

This area actually touches a number of security policy areas, including backup and restore, information retention times, and change control. The topic is introduced here because the deletion of a site collection is significant, and the fact that this deletion can be automated makes this a more important consideration when you create your policies.

Considerations that will have particular interest to your SharePoint administrators include the following:

- Formal change control procedure is required for all administrative changes.

- System changes must be consistent with overall security architecture.

- Training is required before authorization will be given to administrate a site, portal, or server.

- Changes on supporting systems must be tested before introduction into production systems.

- Automatic deletion of content is prohibited.

- Automatic deletion of content is allowed only after content is backed up.

Information Privacy

While it might seem obvious, you should spell out in your policies who actually owns content that is developed in your SharePoint Products and Technologies systems and who owns the intellectual rights to that information.

In most organizations, this has already been explained in a policy. But best practice would say to include the SharePoint Products and Technologies systems in that policy. If you have not done so, here are some topics to consider for inclusion in information privacy policies:

- Right of management to examine data on SharePoint Products and Technologies systems.

- Company ownership of all content developed on company-owned systems.

- Right of company, without notification, to add system administrators to sites as administrators.

- Permissible information to collect on employees when creating a contacts list.

- Permissible information to disclose on self in the My Site area.

- Expressions of personal views in My Site.

- Information about children of employees may not be collected.

- Requirement of disclaimer when collecting information.

- Existence of personnel records in SharePoint Products and Technologies prohibited without proper security.

- Disclosure of worker change of status notification.

- Marketing or promotion of employee-owned businesses prohibited on company systems.

Data Classification Schemes

Different firms have different levels of confidentiality, but it is certainly worth assigning a security level to every document in your organization so that workers know how to handle the data. As the document is developed in SharePoint Products and Technologies, the security level of the document can become a defining (and indexable) piece of metadata. Most classification schemes use one or more of the following document categories: *public*, *confidential*, *secret*, and *private*. Each organization will have its own scheme, and our point is not that you should copy what we have written here, but instead that you implement a classification scheme and then use that scheme as new information is developed. Because most content that is developed is automatically considered confidential, it might be important in your organization to spell that out to those content developers. Doing so will ensure that they do not disseminate confidential information.

Items to consider when developing this policy include the following:

- Data classification scheme is required for all company data.

- Labeling requirements for all company data.

- Information is treated as confidential whenever the classification is unknown.

- Departments may create additional classifications if authorized.

- Content developers are responsible to assign data classification to all documents during development.

- Owner of content must meet classification requirements.

- Declassification of content must follow prescribed procedures.

- Co-presenting of different classified content prohibited.

- Classified content must be hosted in SharePoint Products and Technologies sites with required permissions.

Extranet Considerations

When users connect over the Internet, a whole new set of security issues is introduced. If you already have external connection security policies in place, chances are good that they will apply to SharePoint Products and Technologies and will cover a user's connection to the portal site. Port 80 is the most often attacked port, and even with the use of Secure Sockets Layer (SSL), external connections offer an obvious attack vector to a would-be hacker. Creating policies that detail acceptable behavior for your users when they connect to the portal site will help ensure that their connection is done securely.

If you do not already have such policies in place, consider the following:

- All Internet Web servers must be firewall protected.

- SharePoint Products and Technologies servers must be in the perimeter network.

- Internet portal servers must be placed on a separate subnet.

- Connection to intranet portal servers from the Internet requires encryption and certificates.

- Employee-owned computers must meet minimum software requirements.

- Vendor connectivity to intranet from the Internet is prohibited.

- Customer connectivity to customer sites from the Internet requires encryption and certificates.

Summary

In this chapter, we have discussed information security policy considerations as they relate to SharePoint Products and Technologies. It is important to remember that there is a host of other policies that should be written if you want to create an effective set of policies for your company. The introduction of SharePoint Products and Technologies into any environment presents some unique security challenges that should be considered before you deploy SharePoint Products and Technologies in your production environment.

Part VIII

Securing SharePoint Products and Technologies

Chapter 25

Firewall Considerations for SharePoint Portal Server Deployments

When a Microsoft Office SharePoint Portal Server deployment provides services across an extranet or is accessible from the Internet by the general public, the threat of compromise to those services is significantly increased in comparison with an intranet deployment. To assure a high level of protection, external access to the SharePoint Portal Server deployment must occur through a *firewall* (shown in Figure 25-1). The firewall inspects all incoming and outgoing traffic, and then allows or disallows the traffic based on the preconfigured policies. Configuration of the firewall is an important part of your overall solution that requires careful consideration.

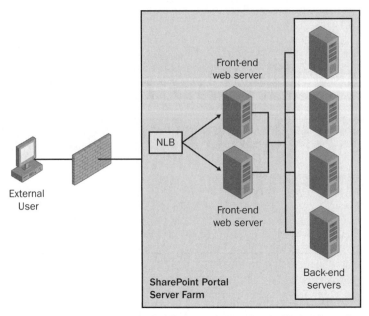

Figure 25-1   SharePoint Portal Server deployment behind a firewall

On a simple level, firewalls perform packet filtering: when traffic comes to the firewall, it compares the data in the Internet Protocol (IP) header with the preconfigured rules to determine whether to allow or deny access. However, to protect SharePoint Portal Server deployments from external attacks, it is also necessary to check and verify the payload inside the HTTP header. A Microsoft Internet Security and Acceleration (ISA) Server 2000 firewall is an application-layer firewall that, in addition to packet filtering, provides the ability to examine the content contained in the application-level protocols such as HTTP. Using ISA Server provides the ability to publish portal sites to the Internet without compromising the security of your internal network. In this chapter, we will look into issues you need to consider when you configure ISA Server 2000 to protect the SharePoint Portal Server deployments from unauthorized access.

ISA Server 2000 Web Publishing

When you set up the external ISA Server 2000 firewall, you first need to consider how to use ISA Server 2000 Web publishing rules for making the internal SharePoint site available for external users.

When a client on the Internet requests an object from a front-end Web server, the request is actually sent to an IP address on the ISA Server computer. Web publishing rules that are configured on the ISA Server computer forward the request, as applicable, to the server running SharePoint Portal Server located behind the firewall. The servers running SharePoint Portal Server require no special IP configuration.

This is because the servers benefit from the ISA Server network address translation (NAT) architecture. Web publishing rules determine how ISA Server should intercept incoming HTTP requests for a server located behind the ISA Server computer, and how ISA Server should respond on behalf of this server. Requests are forwarded downstream to the server (or a server farm) running SharePoint Portal Server. If possible, requests are serviced from the ISA Server cache. Essentially, Web publishing rules map incoming requests to the appropriate server behind the ISA Server computer.

> **Note**   Web publishing uses the ISA proxy service as well as the firewall service. Therefore, ISA Server 2000 has to be installed in integrated mode.

When Web publishing is used, Secure Sockets Layer (SSL) connections to the SharePoint site are terminated at the ISA Server 2000 firewall so that the traffic can be decrypted and the HTTP payload examined. For a Web publishing rule, you can configure how HTTPS (HTTP over SSL) requests should be redirected from ISA Server to the internal SharePoint site—as HTTP requests or as HTTPS requests. This is known as *SSL bridging*.

You can further enhance your solution by configuring link translation. Link translation provides the ability to replace text strings in an HTTP response based on a dictionary that is set up at the ISA Server. This functionality allows you to address the problem of broken links that might result from using internal computer names when responding to external clients. We will discuss setting up link translation later in this chapter.

An additional layer of protection can be provided by enabling basic credentials delegation on the ISA Server. In this scenario, the external users are authenticated at the ISA Server. If the authentication at the ISA Server is successful, the user credentials are then forwarded to the internal SharePoint site for authentication. The SharePoint authentication is transparent to the users; the users submit their credentials only once.

> **Note**   Link translation and basic credentials authentication are available in ISA Server 2000 Feature Pack 1. Feature Pack 1 can be downloaded from *http://www.microsoft.com/isaserver/featurepack1/howtogetfp1.asp*.

We will start with setting up a Web publishing rule for a SharePoint Portal Server deployment. We will then look into configuring SSL bridging, link translation, and basic authentication delegation.

Note You can also publish a SharePoint site using the server publishing rules on ISA Server 2000. However, Web publishing has many advantages over server publishing. Server publishing bypasses the proxy service and therefore cannot use advanced publishing filters such as SSL bridging, link translation, and basic authentication delegation. We will look into limited scenarios where you might need to consider using server publishing later in this chapter.

Assumptions

There are several assumptions that we will make before looking into the ISA server configuration. We assume you have successfully completed several steps that need to be performed when you deploy a portal site across the extranet or as an Internet site.

The steps to be completed are as follows:

■ Extend the portal site into a new website. An additional optional step is to use a separate application pool to isolate worker processes. You can then either create a new portal site in the new site or map an existing portal site to the new site.

■ On the server running SharePoint Portal Server, configure the new site to use the Basic Authentication method in IIS, and remove Integrated Windows Authentication. This is necessary because if an external user authenticates to a SharePoint site using Basic authentication, and the site is configured to use both Basic and Integrated Windows authentication, the user will not be able to view search results when he uses a search query on the site. However, if the site is configured to use only Basic authentication, the user will be able to view the results of a search.

■ You might need to configure split DNS so that different fully qualified domain names (FQDNs) are used for accessing the portal externally and internally.

Assuming that these steps have already been performed, the sample settings for the portal site that are used for examples in this chapter are summarized in Table 25-1.

Table 25-1 Sample Settings for the Portal Site

Parameter	Value
External fully qualified domain name (FQDN)	external.contoso.com
External IP address	207.46.245.214

Table 25-1 Sample Settings for the Portal Site   *(continued)*

Parameter	Value
Internal name	Internal
Internal IP address	192.168.1.1

Setting Up a Web Publishing Rule

A default installation of ISA Server 2000 blocks both inbound and outbound access. When you install ISA Server, it configures a default Web publishing rule. The default rule is configured so that all requests are discarded. To make the portal site available for external users, you need to set up at least one Web publishing rule.

To publish a website using a Web publishing rule, you need to create and configure the following items on the ISA Server machine:

1. Destination set

2. Web publishing rule

3. Listener for incoming Web requests

Creating a Destination Set

A *destination set* is made up of one or more FQDNs or IP addresses and a set of one or more path statements. Path statements can be used to direct requests to specific folders under the root of the Web server.

Destination sets are used to control both inbound and outbound access. The Web publishing rule matches a request for a particular FQDN in the HTTP header with an entry in a destination set to determine where to redirect the incoming traffic.

To create a destination set for a Web publishing rule for a portal site, perform the following steps on ISA Server 2000:

1. Open the ISA Management MMC snap-in (by clicking **Start**, pointing to **Programs**, pointing to **Microsoft ISA Server**, and then clicking **ISA Management**).

2. In the console tree of ISA Management, click **Policy Elements**, right-click **Destination Sets**, select **New**, and then click **Set**.

3. In the **New Destination Set** dialog box, in the **Name** box, type a name for the destination set. Optionally, in the **Description** box, type a description for this destination set. Click **Add**.

4. In the **Add/Edit Destination** dialog box, make sure that the **Destination** option button is selected. In the **Name** box, type the FQDN that external clients will use to connect to the SharePoint site—for example, **external.contoso.com**.

5. Click **OK** to create the destination set.

> **Note** References throughout this chapter pertain to the advanced view of the ISA Management console. To display this view, in the **View** menu click **Advanced**.

Creating a Web Publishing Rule

After creating the destination set, the next step is to create a Web publishing rule to redirect the request from an external client to the portal site on the internal network. To create a Web publishing rule, do the following:

1. In the ISA Management MMC console, click **Publishing**, right-click **Web Publishing Rules**, select **New**, and then click **Rule**.

2. In the **Welcome to the New Web Publishing Rule Wizard** dialog box, type a name for the Web publishing rule. Click **Next**.

3. In the **Destination Sets** dialog box, from the **Apply this rule to** list, select **Specified destination set**. Then, in the **Name** list, select the destination set that you have just created. Click **Next**.

4. In the **Client Type** dialog box, select **Any request**, and then click **Next**.

5. In the **Rule Action** dialog box, do the following:

   a. Click **Redirect the request to this internal Web server** (name or IP address).

   b. Type the IP address of the portal site. In our example, the address is **192.168.1.1**. Instead of the IP address, you can use an unqualified or a fully qualified domain name for the portal site, which in our example is **internal**. However, you need to make sure that this name is resolved to a correct internal IP address by the ISA Server. The name can be resolved either using a hosts file entry or a DNS server.

   c. Click **Send the original host header to the publishing server** instead of the actual one (specified earlier). This setting preserves the FQDN specified in the external HTTP request header.

   d. Click **Next**.

6. In the **Completing the New Web Publishing Rule Wizard** dialog box, click **Finish**.

Configuring the Listener for Incoming Web Requests

By default, when you install ISA Server, incoming Web request properties are configured so that no IP address listens for requests, which means that external clients cannot connect to the published portal site. When you configure incoming Web request properties to listen for requests on an external interface, you set ISA Server to allow Web publishing.

To configure a listener for the published portal site, perform the following steps:

1. Open the ISA Management MMC console, right-click your server node, and select **Properties**.

2. In the **Properties** dialog box, click the **Incoming Web Requests** tab.

3. On the **Incoming Web Requests** tab, select one of the following:

   ■ **Use the same listener configuration for all IP addresses**

   ■ **Configure listeners individually per IP address**

   You can use the same listener configuration for all IP addresses bound to the external interface, or you can use different listener configurations for each of the IP addresses. In our example, we will configure listeners individually.

4. If you selected **Configure listeners individually per IP address**, click the **Add** button.

5. In the **Add/Edit Listeners** box, do the following:

   a. In the **Server** list, select your ISA Server name.

   b. In the **IP Address** list, select the external IP address that resolves to the external FQDN of the published portal site. In our example, it is **207.46.245.214**.

6. Click **OK**. A warning appears that the changes will be applied only after the restart of the Web proxy service. You can select either the **Save the changes, but don't restart the service(s)** option and then manually restart the Web proxy service or the **Save the changes and restart the service(s)** option.

You now need to test the Web publishing rule from an external client. Before starting your test, make sure that the Web proxy service has restarted on the ISA Server computer. To test the Web publishing rule, on a computer that is not connected to your corporate network, start Microsoft Internet Explorer and open http://*<external FQDN>*. The external FQDN must be the same name that you used in the destination set. This FQDN must resolve to the IP address that you configured in the incoming Web requests listener. In our example, we would open *http://external.contoso.com*. Because the portal site is set up to support Basic authentication, you should see the credentials dialog box. After authenticating yourself, you should be able to browse the site.

SSL Bridging

When a Web publishing rule is used to publish a portal site, SSL connections to the site are terminated at the ISA Server 2000 firewall. You can then specify how HTTPS (HTTP over SSL) requests should be redirected to the internal portal site—as HTTP requests or as HTTPS requests. If requests are redirected as HTTPS requests, ISA Server re-encrypts the packets before passing them on to the portal server. This process is referred to as *SSL bridging*. With SSL bridging, because the SSL traffic is decrypted at the ISA Server 2000, it can be inspected before it is forwarded to the internal network.

For SharePoint Portal Server deployments that use SSL to secure communications with external clients, SSL bridging can be used in the following ways:

- HTTPS requests are forwarded as HTTPS requests from ISA Server to the portal site (shown in Figure 25-2). In this scenario, when a client sends a request over SSL, ISA Server decrypts the request, and then encrypts it again and forwards it to the server. When the server returns the encrypted response to ISA Server, ISA Server decrypts the response, and then encrypts it again and sends it to the client. In this case, to forward traffic to the portal site, ISA Server negotiates a new SSL session with the portal site.

- HTTPS requests are forwarded as HTTP requests from ISA Server to the portal site (shown in Figure 25-3). In this scenario, when a client sends a request over SSL, ISA Server decrypts the request and forwards it to the server. When the server returns the HTTP response to ISA Server, ISA Server encrypts the response and sends it to the client. In this case, the portal site does not have the encryption overhead because all encryption is handled by the firewall.

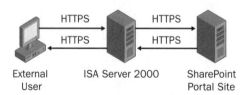

Figure 25-2   SSL bridging: HTTPS to HTTPS

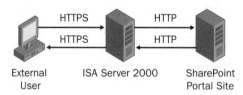

Figure 25-3   SSL bridging: HTTPS to HTTP

Setting up SSL bridging on ISA Server 2000 firewall consists of several steps, as follows:

1. Export an X.509 certificate from the portal site.

2. Import the certificate into the ISA Server 2000 machine certificate store.

3. Configure the incoming Web requests listener to listen for SSL requests.

4. Make sure the Web publishing rule is configured to forward either HTTPS or HTTP traffic, as required, to the internal portal site.

5. If using HTTPS-to-HTTP bridging, disable SSL on the portal site. You might need to refer to Chapter 27, "Securing an Extranet Using SSL and Certificates," for a detailed discussion of enabling and disabling SSL on the SharePoint sites.

We will now look into how to perform steps 1 through 4.

Exporting Certificate from SharePoint Portal Site

ISA Server 2000 uses the same digital certificate as the portal site for SSL bridging. Therefore, the first step for enabling SSL bridging on the ISA Server is to export the certificate from the portal site.

> **More Info**   For detailed information on how to install certificates and configure SSL on SharePoint sites, refer to Chapter 27.

1. On the computer running SharePoint Portal Server, open **Internet Information Services (IIS) Manager**.

2. In the console tree, click the computer name; then click the **Web Sites** node, right-click the site you are exporting the certificate from, and select **Properties**.

3. Click the **Directory Security** tab. In the **Secure Communications** section, click **Server Certificate**.

4. In the **Welcome to the Web Server Certificate Wizard** dialog box, click **Next**.

5. In the **Modify the Current Certificate Assignment** dialog box, click **Export the current certificate to a .pfx file** and then click **Next**.

6. In the **Export Certificate** dialog box, type the full file name (including path and extension) of the file where you would like the certificate to be saved and then click **Next**.

7. In the **Certificate Password** dialog box, type a password in the **Password** and **Confirm Password** boxes. You will need this password at a later stage. Click **Next**.

8. In the **Export Certificate Summary** dialog box, verify that the FQDN used in the certificate is the external FQDN; in our example, it is **external.contoso.com**. Check other certificate details, and then click **Next**.

9. In the **Completing the Web Server Certificate Wizard** dialog box, click **Finish**.

Importing the Certificate into ISA Server 2000

The next step is to import the certificate file into the ISA Server 2000 machine certificate store. Before starting to import the certificate to the ISA Server 2000, verify the following:

- The Certificate .pfx file can be accessed from ISA Server machine.
- The Certificates MMC console is available on ISA Server.

If the Certificates MMC snap-in is not available, you need to add the Certificates snap-in to the existing MMC console. To add the Certificates snap-in, do the following:

1. Open the console where you would like the snap-in to be added. To open a blank console, click **Start**, click **Run**, and then type **mmc** in the **Open** box. Click **OK**.

2. In the MMC console window, select **File**, and then **Add/Remove Snap-in**.

3. In the **Add/Remove Standalone Snap-in** dialog box, click **Add**.

4. In the **Add/Remove Standalone Snap-in** dialog box, select **Certificates** from the list of available snap-ins, and then click **Add**.

5. In the **Certificates** snap-in dialog box, select the **Computer account** option, and click **Next**.

6. In the **Select Computer** dialog box, select **Local computer: (the computer this console is running on)**. Click **Finish**.

7. Click **Close** in the **Add/Remove Standalone Snap-in** dialog box, and then click **OK** in the **Add/Remove Snap-in** dialog box.

To import the certificate file using the Certificates MMC console, perform the following steps:

1. In the Certificates MMC console, expand the **Certificates (local computer)**, right-click the **Personal** certificate store, and select **All Tasks - Import**.

2. In the **Welcome to the Certificate Import Wizard** dialog box, click **Next**.

3. Type the file name of the certificate .pfx file in the **File name** box, or use the **Browse** button to navigate to the file. Click **Next**.

4. In the **Password** box, type the password you created when you exported the certificate from the portal site, and click **Next**.

5. Verify that **Certificate store** text box points to the **Personal** store, and that **Place all certificates in the following store** is selected.

6. In **Completing the Certificate Import Wizard** dialog box, click **Finish**.

7. Click **OK** to confirm the successful import of the certificate.

Configuring the Listener for Incoming Web Requests to Use a Certificate

The next steps are to enable the listener for incoming Web requests to listen for requests on TCP Port 443 (the default SSL port), and then to associate the listener with the certificate you imported in the previous step.

To enable the listener for incoming Web requests to use the certificate, do the following:

1. Open the ISA Management MMC console, right-click your server, and select **Properties**.

2. In the **Properties** dialog box, click the **Incoming Web Requests** tab.

3. In the **Identification** section, select **Enable SSL listeners**. This is a global setting for all listeners and cannot be configured on a per-listener basis.

4. After you've selected the check box, a message appears. It says that SSL requests will be accepted only if each listener is configured with an appropriate certificate. Click **OK**.

5. In the **Identification** section, highlight the listener you would like to configure and click **Edit**.

6. In the **Add/Edit Listeners** dialog box, select the **Use a server certificate to authenticate to web clients** check box, and then click **Select**.

7. In the **Select Certificate** dialog box, select the certificate you imported in the previous section, and click **OK**.

8. In the **Add/Edit Listeners** dialog box, verify that the external FQDN of the portal site is listed as the certificate common name in **Use a server certificate to authenticate web clients**. In our example, it is **external.contoso.com**. Click **OK**.

    A warning appears that says that the changes will be applied only after the restart of the Web proxy service. You can select either the **Save the changes, but don't restart the service(s)** option and then manually restart the Web proxy service or the **Save the changes and restart the service(s)** option. If you do not see the certificate in the **Select Certificates** dialog box, check the steps undertaken in the previous sections to make sure that the certificate has been exported correctly and that it has been added to the correct certificate store.

Configuring SSL Bridging on the Web Publishing Rule

The default configuration for SSL bridging is to forward external HTTPS requests as HTTPS requests to the internal website. This configuration provides an end-to-end secure connection between the external client and the portal site. If this is the configuration that you require, you do not need to perform any additional configuration steps.

However, it is possible to configure the Web publishing rule to bridge incoming HTTPS connections to the ISA Server as HTTP connections from ISA Server to the internal portal site. In this case, the internal portal site should not be configured to request SSL connections. If this is your preferred configuration, do the following:

1. Open the ISA Management console, click **Servers and Arrays**, click your server name, and then click **Publishing**. Click **Web Publishing Rules**, right-click the rule you would like to configure, and select **Properties**.

2. In the **Properties** dialog box, click **Bridging** tab.

3. On the **Bridging** tab, select **Redirect SSL requests as: HTTP requests (terminate the secure channel at the proxy)**.

4. Click **Require secure channel (SSL) for the published site**. Depending on your company security policy, you might need to select **Require 128-bit encryption**.

5. Click **Apply**, and then click **OK**.

When you configure the SSL-to-HTTP bridging for a SharePoint Portal Server extranet site, you might encounter two issues with accessing the search results links from an external client, as follows:

■ Because the portal site is not SSL-enabled, the links' URLs in the search results page are generated with HTTP protocol, not HTTPS protocol. Therefore, when a user clicks any of them, the HTTP request will be sent back to the portal site. However, the Web publishing rule as configured requires an HTTPS connection for the portal site, so the HTTP connection request will fail.

■ The links' URLs in search results use the internal name of the portal site, which cannot be resolved to an IP address by the external client. In addition, the destination set in the Web publishing rule uses an external FQDN, which is different from the internal name.

Both of these issues can be addressed by configuring the link translation on the ISA Server. The second issue—broken links because of using internal names—can also be addressed by configuring alternate portal site access settings on the portal site. We will look into configuring link translation in the next section. Configuring alternate portal access settings is discussed in detail in Chapter 13, "Installing and Configuring Windows SharePoint Services in an Extranet."

Testing SSL Bridging Configuration

Before you go any further, you need to test your SSL bridging configuration. On an external computer that is not connected to your network, start Internet Explorer and type in **https://<*external FQDN*>**. In our example, we would open **https://external.contoso.com**. A security alert might appear because the certificate of the root CA that issued the portal site certificate is not installed on the external client's machine. If the security alert appears, click Yes to proceed. Because the SharePoint site is set up to support Basic authentication, you should see the credentials dialog box. Enter your credentials, and you should be able to see the portal site's home page.

If an error message—specifically, "500 Internal Server Error"—is returned to the browser, you might need to reconfigure the Web publishing rule. The reason this error might occur is the difference between the common name in the certificate and the name of the server in the Web publishing rule where the requests are redirected. The common name in the certificate is the external FQDN, whereas the name of the server in the Web publishing rule is the server internal name. In our example, the common name is *external.contoso.com* and the internal name is *internal*. The workaround is to use the external FQDN for the name of the server the requests are redirected to.

To change the name, go to the Web publishing rule Properties, click the Action tab, and in the Redirect The Request To This Internal Web Server (Name Or IP Address) box, type **external FQDN**. However, for this configuration to work, ISA Server must be able to resolve the external FQDN to the internal IP address of the SharePoint site—in our example, 192.168.1.1. To enable this name resolution, you can create a hosts file entry that maps the FQDN to an internal IP address. The solution is either to set up a split DNS or to add an entry to the hosts file on the ISA Server computer. For instructions on how to set up a split DNS, refer to Chapter13. If you want to use the hosts file, add a line to it with an external FQDN and an internal IP address—for example: **192.168.1.1 external.contoso.com**

Note   The hosts file is located in the %SystemRoot%\System32\Drivers\Etc folder on the ISA Server computer.

Configuring Link Translation

Using link translation on an ISA Server addresses several problems that external users might encounter when connecting to an internal SharePoint site through a firewall. Link translation is implemented as a Web application filter that is installed in Feature Pack 1 for ISA Server 2000. By default, this filter is disabled.

Link translation provides an ability to address these problems by replacing text strings in the URIs that are returned from the portal to text strings that are contained in a link translation dictionary used by the Web publishing rule on an ISA Server. The link translation filter can be used for both SSL-protected portal sites as well as the sites without SSL protection. In the previous section, we discussed the access problem that occurs with the use of the SSL listener when HTTP links are returned to external clients. However, for the SharePoint sites without SSL protection, the problem with using an internal server name in the responses to the external users is the same as for sites with SSL-to-HTTP bridging enabled on the firewall. This issue can be addressed either by using link translation on the ISA Server or by configuring the alternate access settings on the portal site. Refer to Chapter 13 for a detailed discussion of the alternate portal access settings.

To enable link translation for different types of content, do the following:

1. Open the ISA Management console, click **Servers and Arrays**, and then click your server. Click **Extensions**, and then click **Web Filters**.

2. Right-click the **Link Translator Filter** in the right pane of the console, and select **Enable**.

3. A warning appears that says that the changes will be applied only after the restart of the Web proxy service. You can select either the **Save the changes, but don't restart the service(s)** option and then manually restart the Web proxy service, or the **Save the changes and restart the service(s)** option.

4. By default, the link translator filter works only with the HTML documents, as identified by the content-type HTTP header. To enable link translation on other content groups, right-click the **Link Translator Filter**, select **Properties**, click the **Content Groups** tab, and then choose the content groups, as required. The available content groups are as follows:

    - Application

    - Application data files

    - Audio

    - Compressed files

    - Documents

    - HTML documents (selected by default)

    - Images

    - Macro documents

    - Text

- Video

- VRML

To configure link translation for the Web publishing rule, do the following:

1. In the ISA Management MMC console, click **Servers and Arrays**, click your server name, and then click **Publishing**. Click **Web Publishing Rules**, right-click the rule you would like to configure, and select **Properties**.

2. In the **Properties** dialog box, click the **Link Translation** tab.

3. On the **Link Translation** tab, click **Perform link translation** and **Prevent caching of responses on external proxy servers**. Click **OK**.

When you configure link translation for a Web publishing rule, a default link translation dictionary is created. This dictionary might be sufficient for your portal site. However, depending on your individual site, you might need to add some custom entries to the dictionary. To add a custom entry to the link translation dictionary, do the following:

1. In the **Properties of the Web** publishing rule, click the **Link Translation** tab. Click **Add**.

2. In the **Add/Edit Dictionary Item** dialog box, type the text string to be replaced and the replacement text string. Click **OK**.

> **More Info**   For additional information on the ISA Server 2000 link translation, refer to the Feature Pack 1 product documentation.

Delegation of Basic Authentication

Delegation of Basic authentication provides the ability for an ISA Server 2000 firewall to authenticate an external user at the ISA Server, and then, provided the authentication is successful, to forward this user's credentials to the internal SharePoint site for authentication. When ISA Server forwards user credentials to the SharePoint site, the SharePoint site authenticates the users without requesting credentials for a second time.

> **Note**   Basic authentication credentials are transmitted unencrypted. Therefore, Basic authentication should always be done over HTTPS; otherwise, it is not secure. This includes credentials passed between the ISA Server and the SharePoint site.

When Basic authentication delegation is enabled, the ISA Server firewall drops requests that have not been authenticated before sending the traffic associated with these requests to the internal SharePoint site. Therefore, authenticating users at the ISA Server provides additional protection to the internal SharePoint site, and it decreases unsuccessful authentication overhead on the computer running Share-Point Portal Server.

ISA Server performs pre-authentication of users, identifies them, and logs their activity on the ISA Server machine, thus providing administrators with a single location for information on an external client IP address, as well as the user name.

To set up the delegation of Basic authentication from the SharePoint site to the ISA Server, you need to perform two steps at the ISA Server:

1. Configure the listener for incoming Web requests for Basic authentication.

2. Enable the delegation of Basic authentication credentials on the Web publishing rule for the SharePoint site.

To configure the listener for incoming Web requests to support Basic authentication, do the following:

1. Open the ISA Management console, click **Servers and Arrays**, right-click your server name, and select **Properties**.

2. In the **Properties** dialog box, click the **Incoming Web Requests** tab.

3. In the **Connections** section, click **Ask unauthenticated users for identification**. This is a global setting and applies to all incoming listeners.

4. In the **Identification** section, select the listener you would like to configure and click **Edit**.

5. In the **Add/Edit Listeners** dialog box, in the **Authentication** part, select **Basic with this domain** and clear all other authentication mechanisms.

    If your company security policy requires two-level authentication—by certificate as well as by user name and password—you might need to select **Client certificate (secure channel only)** in addition to Basic authentication.

6. If the domain for user credentials validation is different from the ISA Server computer's domain, you can specify a default domain for the users. This setting is optional because the users can specify the domain themselves by typing their user name in the *<domain name>\<user name>* format. To set up the default domain, click the **Select domain** for the Basic authentication setting, type the domain name, and click **OK**.

To configure the Web publishing rule to use delegation of Basic authentication credentials, do the following:

1. In the ISA Management console, click **Servers and Arrays**, click your server name, click **Publishing**, and then click **Web Publishing Rules**.

2. Right-click the Web publishing rule you would like to configure, select **Properties**, and then click the **Action** tab.

3. On the **Action** tab, select the **Allow delegation of basic authentication credentials** check box. This check box is available only with Feature Pack 1. Click **OK**.

> **More Info**   For additional information on the ISA Server 2000 Basic authentication credentials delegation, refer to the Feature Pack 1 product documentation.

ISA Server 2000 Server Publishing

In general, it is not recommended to use ISA Server 2000 Server publishing for HTTP servers. Server publishing is used for other protocols such as File Transfer Protocol (FTP), and other servers such as SQL Server. When Server publishing rules are used instead of Web publishing rules, the ISA Server firewall does not examine HTTP traffic before forwarding it to the internal SharePoint Portal Server. To examine the HTTP traffic, ISA Server uses Web application filters that require the Web proxy service. However, the Web proxy service is bypassed by ISA Server 2000 Server publishing. With Server publishing, SSL-encrypted HTTP traffic is forwarded to the internal server without being inspected first by the firewall. Server publishing does not support link translation and Basic credentials authentication. With Server publishing, the requests are never serviced from the ISA Server cache. Basically, Server publishing provides packet filtering and secure NAT.

There are a limited number of scenarios in which you might need to consider using Server publishing to make a portal site available externally. Sometimes, administrators use Server publishing instead of Web publishing to be able see the actual source IP address in the IIS logs on the computer running SharePoint Portal Server. When you publish a Web server using a Web publishing rule, the source IP address that appears in your Web server log files is the internal address of the computer running ISA Server. When you use a Server publishing rule, the actual source IP address of the request is shown in the IIS logs.

In other scenarios, Server publishing is used in combination with Web publishing. For example, consider a scenario in which you have a single ISA Server 2000 server that is used to provide access to two portal sites, as shown in Figure 25-4. One site is an extranet site where Basic authentication is required. This site is protected by SSL, and Basic authentication delegation is configured on the ISA server.

Another site is an Internet site that does not require authentication and is open to the general public.

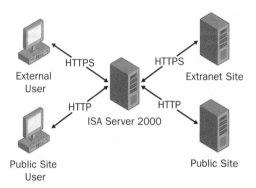

Figure 25-4   Combining Web publishing and Server publishing for SharePoint sites

Because the first site delegates authentication to ISA Server, all incoming requests listeners require authentication. (The Ask Unauthenticated Users For Identification setting is a global one and affects all incoming listeners.) To allow anonymous access to the second site for the general public, we can configure a Server publishing rule to make the second site available for external access.

However, to make this configuration work, we also need to make sure there are two external IP addresses that can be used for the first site and the second site, respectively. Server publishing rules do not provide the ability to publish a service more than once on the same external interface. In our example, because we have two different portal sites to publish, we need to have two external IP addresses that can be bound to the same external interface. We will then use one IP address for the Web publishing rule to publish the first site, and another IP address for the Server publishing rule to publish the second site. It is important to note that the incoming requests listener for the first site must be configured for only one IP address using the option to configure listeners individually per IP address.

When you use Server publishing to publish a SharePoint site, to make sure that the links on the external clients are not broken, verify that the internal SharePoint Portal Server is configured to use alternate portal site access settings for external clients. Refer to Chapter 13 for detailed instructions.

Setting Up a Server Publishing Rule

To configure the Server publishing rule for a SharePoint site, perform the following steps on ISA Server:

1. Verify that the listeners for incoming Web requests is not configured to listen on an IP address that will be used to publish SharePoint sites using a Server publishing rule. The Server publishing rule must not conflict with the incoming Web requests listener configuration.

2. Create a protocol definition that allows incoming HTTP requests. (This step is not required for HTTPS traffic.)

3. Create a Server publishing rule by using the protocol definition created in the previous step.

More Info For additional information on the ISA Server 2000 Server publishing rules, refer to the ISA Server 2000 product documentation.

Summary

In this chapter, we considered various configuration options for an ISA Server 2000 firewall that you can use to provide Internet access to and protection of SharePoint Portal Server deployments. An ISA Server 2000 firewall is an application-layer firewall that, in addition to packet filtering, provides the ability to examine the HTTP payload. ISA Server 2000 with Feature Pack 1 installed is a flexible and feature-rich firewall that enables administrators to secure access to the SharePoint Portal Server deployments without compromising the security of the internal network. Using Web publishing features such as SSL bridging, link translation, and Basic authentication delegation provides additional protection layers while at the same time ensuring that the external users' connections to portal sites from outside the firewall are efficient and transparent.

Chapter 26

Single Sign-On in SharePoint Portal Server 2003

Single sign-on is a new feature in Microsoft Office SharePoint Portal Server 2003 that provides storage and mapping of credentials such as account names and passwords so that the portal site–based applications can retrieve information from the third-party applications and back-end systems, for example, Enterprise Resource Planning (ERP) and Customer Relations Management (CRM) systems. The single sign-on functionality is implemented by the Microsoft Single Sign-On (SSOSrv) service. SSOSrv is a credential storage service that allows the saving and retrieval of credentials. The use of single sign-on functionality stops users from having to authenticate themselves more than once when the portal site–based applications need to obtain information from other business applications and systems.

In a single sign-on environment, these back-end applications and systems are referred to as **enterprise applications**. To enable customers to interact with an enterprise application directly from the portal site, SharePoint Portal Server 2003 stores and maps assigned credentials within an **enterprise application definition**. By using application definitions, you can automate, and secure the sign-on process to the corresponding enterprise applications from a portal site–based application.

The single sign-on functionality enables scenarios where multiple Web Parts access different enterprise applications, which each use a different type of authentication. Each Web Part can automatically sign on to its enterprise application without prompting the user to provide credentials each time. There are endless uses of single sign-on functionality within an enterprise environment. For example, let's consider two different scenarios—a human resources intranet site and a business intelligence site, as follows:

■ A standard human resources (HR) portal site or page might include several Web Parts that display employee information from a back-end employee management system. This employee data is stored in a dedicated HR database system, frequently based on SAP or PeopleSoft. These HR databases do not support Microsoft Windows IDs, might not run on Windows-based operating systems and, in fact, might include proprietary logon protocols. The Web Parts on the portal site should retrieve the individual employee data without prompting for a separate logon. In this example, the individual employee does not have a separate logon to the HR system, but uses a group account that provides generic read access to the database. In other words, the employee does not know the user name and password required to log on to the system he or she is accessing.

■ An executive might use a portal site to provide a dynamic, aggregated view of relevant business information. This data is stored in two places: Siebel stores the customer relationship information, and SAP tracks accounts and payments. To see an integrated view, the portal must log on to and access both back-end systems. Prompting the user for additional passwords is an unacceptable user experience. In this example, the executive does not need to know the user names and the passwords required for logon to the back-end systems. In addition, multiple Web Parts are used to ensure this integration. By default, each Web Part separately authenticates the user to the appropriate back-end system.

As these examples show, by using single sign-on you can centralize information from multiple back-end applications through a single portal that uses application definitions. In addition, SharePoint Portal Server 2003 provides a programming interface for developers to use and extend this feature.

Single Sign-On Architecture

For each enterprise application that SharePoint Portal Server connects to, there is a corresponding enterprise application definition configured by an administrator. This application definition is used by a Web Part to integrate with the enterprise application within a portal site. The application definition controls how credentials for a particular business application are stored and mapped. The code within the Web Part uses the application definition to retrieve credentials that are then used to integrate with an enterprise application. This process is transparent to the portal site users.

There are two primary types of enterprise application definitions used with the SSOSrv service, as follows:

- **Individual enterprise application definitions.**   In this scenario, individual users know and can manage their own credentials stored within the enterprise application definition.

- **Group enterprise application definitions.**   In this scenario, the individual user does not know his or her credentials stored within the enterprise application definition, but is associated with a managed group account.

The single sign-on administrator, rather than the individual user, chooses the account type when configuring the enterprise application definition.

The SSOSrv service stores encrypted credentials in a Microsoft SQL Server database. When you set up the single sign-on on the job server, you specify two settings for the single sign-on database: the name of the computer running SQL Server where the credentials store will be located, and the name of the database that will become the credentials store for your Web farm. These settings are stored in the SharePoint Portal Server configuration database.

All credentials in the credentials store are encrypted using the single sign-on encryption key. When you configure single sign-on for the first time, the encryption key is created automatically. You can regenerate the key if required and re-encrypt the credentials store; for example, you might have a policy to change the key after a certain amount of time.

How Single Sign-On Works

When individual enterprise definition is used, on the first access to the Web Part that integrates with the enterprise application, if a user's credentials have not been stored in the single sign-on database, the user is redirected to the logon form that prompts the user for appropriate credentials for the enterprise application. The number, the order, and the names of the fields in the logon form are configured by the administrator within the application definition; the logon form is generated automatically based on these configuration settings. The developer needs to write the code within the Web Part to check whether the credentials exist in the database, and to redirect the user to the logon form if necessary. The user-supplied credentials are then stored in the credentials store and mapped to the Windows account that is this user's account for SharePoint Portal Server. Then, the user is redirected back to the original Web Part. The code in the Web Part then submits the credentials from the credentials store to the application in the way that is relevant to this application, and retrieves the necessary information that is then presented to the user within the Web Part. This process is shown in Figure 26-1. The steps are as follows:

1. A user accesses the Web Part that integrates with the enterprise application for the first time. The Web Part code checks whether the user credentials for the required application are stored in the single sign-on database. If they are stored, the process continues from step 6 in this list.

2. If there are no credentials stored for this user for the required application, the user's browser is redirected to the logon form for this application.

3. The user supplies credentials for the application.

4. The supplied credentials are mapped to the user's Windows account and stored in the single sign-on database.

5. User is redirected to the original Web Part.

6. The Web Part retrieves the credentials from the single sign-on database.

7. The Web Part submits the credentials to the enterprise application and retrieves the necessary information.

8. The Web Part is displayed to the user.

On subsequent access, when the user requests the Web Part, to get the necessary data from the enterprise application the credentials are retrieved from the single sign-on database. The process is transparent to the user. (See Figure 26-1.)

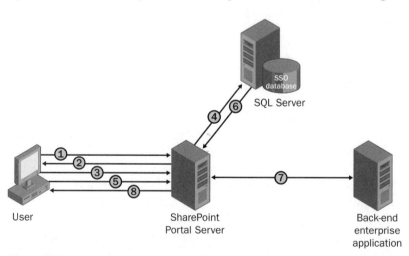

Figure 26-1   Accessing an enterprise application using single sign-on

When group enterprise definition is used, the account mapping is configured by the administrator. The administrator specifies the credentials for accessing the enterprise applications that are valid for all members of a Windows group. If the user who accesses the Web Part belongs to the mapped Windows group, the access credentials are already stored in the single sign-on credentials store. The code in the Web Part retrieves the credentials, submits them to the enterprise application, and retrieves the necessary information. The Web Part is then displayed to the requesting user. In this scenario, the whole process is transparent to the user. The user is not aware of any authentication information required for the enterprise application; it is only known to the administrator.

Security Recommendations Regarding the Topology of the Server Farm

When using the single sign-on service, you can help enhance security by distributing your resources in the server farm. Specifically, the configuration of the front-end Web server, the job server, and the computer storing the single sign-on database can affect security.

- **Less secure configuration.** Everything is deployed on one server. This configuration is less secure because the front-end Web server, the single sign-on database stored in SQL Server, and the encryption key are on the same computer. This configuration is not recommended.

- **More secure configuration.** Two-computer configuration where one computer is the front-end Web server. The second computer is the job server containing the single sign-on database stored in SQL Server and the encryption key.

- **Recommended configuration for better security.** Configuration of three or more computers in which the front-end Web server, the job server containing the encryption key, and the server containing the single sign-on database stored in SQL Server are different computers.

If you are using single sign-on in a shared services scenario, the user credentials stored in the parent server farm are available to the administrators of all child server farms. It is recommended that you run applications using single sign-on on the parent portal site only and use an iFrame in the application for child portal sites. You should disable the single sign-on service on child server farms. We will discuss how to disable the SSOSrv service later in this chapter.

Configuring Single Sign-On

To configure single sign-on for the first time, you must complete the following tasks:

1. Determine and set up necessary Windows accounts.

2. Enable the single sign-on service on the job server.

3. Configure the single sign-on settings.

4. Create a new application definition.

5. Provide account information for the application definition.

6. Enable the single sign-on service on the front-end servers.

Step 1: Set Up Single Sign-On Accounts

The SSOSrv service uses the following four types of accounts:

■ Configuration account for single sign-on

■ Single sign-on administrator account

■ Single sign-on service account

■ Enterprise application manager account

Before configuring single sign-on, you must determine and, where necessary, create and set up these accounts.

Configuration Account for Single Sign-On

Configuration Account for single sign-on is the Windows account that will be used to configure the SSO. When setting up single sign-on, you use this account to log on to the job server. This account must meet the following requirements:

■ Be a member of the local Administrators group on the job server.

■ Be a member of the local Administrators group on the computer running SQL Server that stores the single sign-on database.

■ Be either the same as the single sign-on administrator account, or be a member of the group account that is the single sign-on administrator account. (The single sign-on administrator account is discussed in the next section.)

Single Sign-On Administrator Account

The single sign-on administrator account can be either the Windows Global group or the individual user account, and it will be used to set up and manage the single sign-on service. This account cannot be a local domain group account or a distribution list.

Make sure that the following requirements are met for the single sign-on administrator account:

■ The single sign-on service account must be this user or a member of this group.

■ The configuration account for single sign-on must be this user or a member of this group.

We will specify this account as the single sign-on administrator account in step 3, "Configure the Single Sign-On Settings on the Job Server." After it has been configured, this user account or members of this group account will have full access to the single sign-on administration pages and will be able to make configuration and application definition changes.

Single Sign-On Service Account

The single sign-on service account is the user account that will run as the single sign-on service. Make sure the following requirements are met:

■ The single sign-on service account must be the same as the single sign-on administrator account or a member of the group account that is the single sign-on administrator account.

■ The single sign-on service account must be a member of the local group STS_WPG on all servers running SharePoint Portal Server 2003 in the server farm.

To make the user a member of STS_WPG, do the following:

1. On the taskbar, click **Start**, point to **Administrative Tools**, and then click **Computer Management**.

2. In the console tree, under the **System Tools** node, expand the **Local Users and Groups** node.

3. Click **Groups**.

4. Double-click **STS_WPG**.

5. In the **STS_WPG Properties** dialog box, click **Add**.

6. Add the user.

The single sign-on service account must be a member of the local group SPS_WPG on all servers running SharePoint Portal Server in the server farm.
To make the user a member of SPS_WPG, do the following:

1. On the taskbar, click **Start**, point to **Administrative Tools**, and then click **Computer Management**.

2. In the console tree, under the **System Tools** node, expand the **Local Users and Groups** node.

3. Click **Groups**.

4. Double-click **SPS_WPG**.

5. In the **SPS_WPG Properties** dialog box, click **Add**.

6. Add the user.

The single sign-on service account must be a member of the public database role on the SharePoint Portal Server configuration database.

> **Note**   On a single server deployment, if the single sign-on service runs under an account that is a member of the local Administrators group, you do not need to ensure that the user has the public right on the configuration database. However, for security reasons it is recommended that you do not run the service under an account that is a member of the local Administrators group.

To assign rights on the configuration database, do the following:

1. On the SQL Server computer, open **SQL Server Enterprise Manager**.

2. Expand the **Microsoft SQL Servers** node.

3. Expand the **SQL Server Group** node.

4. Expand the **(local) (Windows NT)** node.

5. Expand the **Security** node.

6. Click **Logins**, and then do one of the following:

   - If the logon name does not exist, right-click **Logins**, click **New Login**, and then in the **Name** box, type the account for the user in the format *DOMAIN\user_name*.

   - If the logon name already exists, right-click the logon name, and then click **Properties**.

7. Click the **Database Access** tab.

8. In the **Specify which databases can be accessed by this login** section, select the check box for the configuration database.

9. In the **Database roles for *database_name*** section, select the **public** check box.

10. Click **OK**.

11. Close **SQL Server Enterprise Manager**.

The single sign-on service account must be a member of the Server Administrators server role on the SQL Server instance where the single sign-on database is located.

> **Note**   On a single server deployment, if the single sign-on service runs under an account that is a member of the local Administrators group, you do not need to ensure that the user is a member of Server Administrators server role on the SQL Server instance where the single sign-on database is located. However, for security reasons, it is recommended that you do not run the service under an account that is a member of the local Administrators group.

To make the user a member of the Server Administrator role

1. On the SQL Server computer, open **SQL Server Enterprise Manager**.

2. Expand the **Microsoft SQL Servers** node.

3. Expand the **SQL Server Group** node.

4. Expand the **(local) (Windows NT)** node.

5. Expand the **Security** node.

6. Click **Logins**, and then do one of the following:

   ■ If the logon name does not exist, right-click **Logins**, click **New Login**, and then in the **Name** box, type the account for the user in the format *DOMAIN\user_name*.

   ■ If the logon name already exists, right-click the logon name, and then click **Properties**.

7. Click the **Server Roles** tab.

8. Select the **Server Administrators** check box.

9. Click **OK**.

10. Close **SQL Server Enterprise Manager**.

Enterprise Application Manager Account

The enterprise application manager account can be the Windows Global group account, or individual user account, that will be used to set up and manage application definitions. This account cannot be a local domain group or a distribution list.

You do not need to perform any configuration steps now; we will configure this account to become the enterprise application manager account in step 3,

"Configure the Single Sign-On Settings on the Job Server." However, it is useful to notice the rights that this account will have after it has been specified as the enterprise application manager account, as follows:

- This account or members of this group have rights to create, modify, or delete application definitions from the single sign-on administration pages.

- This account or members of this group do not have rights to configure single sign-on. Only members of the single sign-on administrator account can configure single sign-on.

- Rights that this user or members of this group have are automatically contained in the single sign-on administrator account.

Step 2: Enable the Single Sign-On Service on the Job Server

To enable the SSOSrv service, do the following on the job server:

1. On the taskbar, click **Start**, point to **Administrative Tools**, and then click **Services**.

2. On the **Services** management console, double-click **Microsoft Single Sign-on Service**.

3. Click the **Logon** tab.

4. Under **Log on as**, click **This account**.

5. In the **This account** box, type an account name that you determined as a single sign-on service account in the previous step.

6. In the **Password** and **Confirm password** boxes, type the password.

7. Click **Apply**.

8. Click the **General** tab.

9. In the **Startup type** list, click **Automatic**.

10. In the **Service status** section, if the service status does not display **Started**, click **Start**.

11. Click **OK**.

Step 3: Configure the Single Sign-On Settings on the Job Server

To configure the single sign-on settings, you must be logged on as the configuration account on the job server. As we discussed earlier in step 1, "Set Up Single Sign-On Accounts," this account must be a member of the local Administrators group on the job server, and must also be a member of the group account that you specify as the single sign-on administrator account.

You cannot configure single sign-on remotely. To configure single sign-on, go to the computer running as the job server, log on as the configuration account, and then do the following:

1. On the SharePoint Portal Server Central Administration for *server_name* page, in the **Component Configuration** section, click **Manage settings for single sign-on**.

   Alternatively, click **Start**, point to **All Programs**, point to **SharePoint Portal Server**, and then click **SharePoint Portal Server Single Sign-On Administration**.

2. On the Manage Settings for Single Sign-On for *server_name* page, in the **Server Settings** section, click **Manage server settings**.

3. On the Manage Server Settings for Single Sign-On page, in the **Single Sign-On Settings** section, in the **Account name** box, type the name of the single sign-on administrator account that you determined in step 1, "Set Up Single Sign-On Accounts." The format of the account is *DOMAIN\group_name* or *DOMAIN\user_name*.

4. In the **Enterprise Application Definition Settings** section, in the **Account name** box, type the name of the enterprise application manager account that you determined in step 1, "Set Up Single Sign-On Accounts." The format of the account is *DOMAIN\group_name* or *DOMAIN\user_name*.

5. In the **Database Settings** section, do the following:

   a. In the **Server name** box, type the name of the database server on which you want to store the settings and account information for single sign-on.

   b. In the **Database name** box, type the name of the single sign-on database. If the database does not exist, it is created.

6. In the **Time Out Settings** section, do the following:

   a. In the **Ticket time out (in minutes)** box, type the number of minutes to wait before allowing a ticket, or access token, to time out.

   b. In the **Delete audit log records older than (in days)** box, type the number of days to hold records in the audit log before deleting.

7. Click **OK**.

8. If a message box appears stating that you have reconfigured single sign-on, click **OK**.

> **Note**   The audit log is overwritten after the number of days you specify. Because the log contains a record of any illicit operations or logon attempts, it is recommended that you maintain backup copies of the logs. The logs reside in the single sign-on database in the SSO_Audit table. This table is automatically backed up when you back up the database.

Step 4: Create an Application Definition

To create an application definition, you need to be logged on as a member of single sign-on administrator account or as an enterprise application definition manager account. To create an application definition, do the following:

1. On the SharePoint Portal Server Central Administration for *server_name* page, in the **Component Configuration** section, click **Manage settings for single sign-on**.

    Alternatively, click **Start**, point to **All Programs**, point to **SharePoint Portal Server**, and then click **SharePoint Portal Server Single Sign-On Administration**.

2. On the Manage Settings for Single Sign-On for *server_name* page, in the **Enterprise Application Definition Settings** section, click **Manage settings for enterprise application definitions**.

3. On the Manage Enterprise Application Definitions page, click **New Item**.

4. On the Create Enterprise Application Definition page, in the **Application and Contact Information** section, do the following:

    a. In the **Display name** box, type a display name for this application definition.

    When administrator changes the settings for the application definition at a later stage, the application definition is listed using its display name.

    The display name is what the user sees on the logon form when entering credentials on the first access.

> **Tip**   If you enter a long name with no spaces in it for the display name, the entire name might not be displayed.

    b. In the **Application name** box, type an application name for the application definition. The application name is used by developers.

> **Tip**   If you enter a long name with no spaces in it for the application definition name, the entire name might not be displayed.

    c. In the **Contact e-mail address** box, type an e-mail address for users to contact for this application.

5. In the **Account Type** section, do one of the following:

- If you want all users to log on by using a single account, select **Group**. Users do not need to enter any credentials with this option.

- If you want users to log on by using their own account information, select **Individual**.
  Each user will have to provide credentials when accessing the Web Part for the first time.

> **Tip**   If you specify a group account as the account type, so that all users log on by using a single account, ensure that you have the appropriate number of client licenses for the application that you are accessing.

6. In the **Logon Account Information** section, select one or more fields to map to the required logon information in the necessary order for this enterprise application. The number and the order of the fields are defined by the enterprise application logon requirements. For each field, do the following:

    a. Type a display name for each field as a reminder of the required information. For an individual user application definition, the display name is what the users see on the logon form when entering their credentials for the enterprise application. For a group application definition, the display name of the field is what the administrator sees when entering the mapped group account credentials for the enterprise application.

    b. If the field contains sensitive information, such as a password, click **Yes** for **Mask** so that the information is not displayed within this field when it is being filled in or viewed.
  For example, for access to Oracle, you might enter the following:
  Field 1 = Oracle user name
  Field 2 = Oracle user password (select Yes for the Mask option)
  Field 3 = Oracle database name

If you need to access the SAP application, for SAP credentials you might enter the following:

Field 1 = SAP user name

Field 2 = SAP password (select Yes for the Mask option)

Field 3 = SAP system number

Field 4 = SAP client number

Field 5 = language

7. Click **OK**.

Step 5: Provide Account Information for an Application Definition

After you have created the application definition, for group application definition you have to specify the logon account credentials. For individual application definitions, you can specify credentials for the users or, alternatively, the users may enter their credentials in the logon form on the first access.

To specify the logon account information for the application definition, do the following:

1. On the SharePoint Portal Server Central Administration for *server_name* page, in the **Component Configuration** section, click **Manage settings for single sign-on**.

   Alternatively, click **Start**, point to **All Programs**, point to **SharePoint Portal Server**, and then click **SharePoint Portal Server Single Sign-On Administration**.

2. On the Manage Settings for Single Sign-On for *server_name* page, in the **Enterprise Application Definition Settings** section, click **Manage account information for enterprise application definitions**.

3. On the Manage Account Information for an Enterprise Application Definition page, in the **Account Information** section, do the following:

   a. In the **Enterprise Application Definition** list, select the name of the application definition. If you created the application definition to use an individual account, the **user account name** box is displayed on the page. If you created the application definition to use a group account, the **group account name** box is displayed.

   b. In the **User account name** or **Group account name** box, type the account name that will be mapped to the application credentials.

   c. Click **OK**.

4. On the Provide *application_definition_display_name* Account Information page, in the **Logon Information** section, enter the credentials to be used for the logon to the enterprise application. The number, the order and the names of the fields displayed follow configuration in the Logon Account Information section of the application definition.

Step 6: Enable the Single Sign-On Service on the Front-End Web Servers

After you have configured the single sign-on settings on the job server, you need to enable the single sign-on service of the front-end Web servers. To enable the single sign-on service on each front-end Web server, follow the instructions given earlier in step 2, "Enable the Single Sign-On Service on the Job Server."

Managing Single Sign-On

After you have configured the single sign-on for the first time, you are likely to need to perform administration tasks at a later stage, including the following:

- Creating and deleting the application definitions

- Managing account credentials mapped within the application definitions

- Regenerating, backing up, and restoring the encryption key

- Enabling auditing of the encryption key

- Disabling the SSOSrv service

In this section, we will discuss the single sign-on administration tasks. If you need to change your single sign-on configuration, make sure you consider the following:

- The single sign-on configuration and encryption key management tasks cannot be done remotely. To configure single sign-on or manage the encryption key, go to the computer running as the job server and specify the settings locally.

- If you change the job server to another server, you must reconfigure single sign-on. After changing the job server, you must delete the entire registry key HKEY_LOCAL_MACHINE\SOFTWARE\Microsoft\ssosrv\Config on the old job server.

- If you reconfigure single sign-on and you want to change the account that you specified for managing the single sign-on service (the single sign-on administrator account), the user who reconfigures the single sign-on and the single sign-on service account must be a member of both the current single sign-on administrator account that manages the service and the new account that you want to specify.

Editing an Application Definition

You can edit the display name, the e-mail contact, and the logon fields for an enterprise application definition. You cannot edit the application definition name or change the account type.

To edit an application definition, do the following:

1. On the SharePoint Portal Server Central Administration for *server_name* page, in the **Component Configuration** section, click **Configure the Single Sign-on component and manage enterprise application definitions for portals**.

   Alternatively, click **Start**, point to **All Programs**, point to **SharePoint Portal Server**, and then click **SharePoint Portal Server Single Sign-On Administration**.

2. On the Manage Settings for Single Sign-On for *server_name* page, in the **Application Settings** section, click **Manage settings for enterprise application definitions**.

3. On the Manage Enterprise Application Definitions page, rest the pointer on the display name for the application definition, and then click the arrow that appears.

4. On the menu that appears, click **Edit**.

5. On the Edit Enterprise Application Definition page, in the **Application and Contact Information** section, you can edit the display name and the e-mail contact.

6. In the **Display Name** box, type a display name for this application definition. The display name is what the user sees.

7. In the **E-mail Contact** box, type an e-mail address for users to contact for this application.

8. In the **Account Information** section, select one or more fields to map to the required logon information for this application definition.

9. Type a display name for each field as a reminder of the required information. The display names for the fields will appear on the logon page for the application.

10. To ensure that sensitive information, such as a password, is not displayed when viewing account information, click **Yes** for **Mask?**

11. Click **OK**.

Deleting an Application Definition

When you delete an application definition, it is removed from the single sign-on database. In addition, all credentials associated with the application definition are removed. To delete an application definition, do the following:

1. On the SharePoint Portal Server Central Administration for *server_name* page, in the **Component Configuration** section, click **Configure the Single Sign-on component and manage enterprise application definitions for portals**.

Alternatively, click **Start**, point to **All Programs**, point to **SharePoint Portal Server**, and then click **SharePoint Portal Server Single Sign-On Administration**.

2. On the Manage Settings for Single Sign-On for *server_name* page, in the **Application Settings** section, click **Manage settings for enterprise application definitions**.

3. On the Manage Enterprise Application Definitions page, rest the pointer on the display name for the application definition, and then click the arrow that appears.

4. On the menu that appears, click **Delete**.

5. On the confirmation message box, click **OK**.

Managing Account Information for an Application Definition

You can update or delete individual account information for a single application definition, or you can remove an account from all application definitions.

For group application definitions, you can update the account information, but you cannot remove the Windows account from a group application definition because there is a one-to-one correspondence between a group application definition and the account. If necessary, you can delete the group application definition.

To manage account information for an application definition, do the following:

1. On the SharePoint Portal Server Central Administration for *server_name* page, in the **Component Configuration** section, click **Manage settings for single sign-on**.

Alternatively, click **Start**, point to **All Programs**, point to **SharePoint Portal Server**, and then click **SharePoint Portal Server Single Sign-On Administration**.

2. On the Manage Settings for Single Sign-On for *server_name* page, in the **Enterprise Application Definition Settings** section, click **Manage account information for enterprise application definitions**.

3. On the Manage Account Information for an Enterprise Application Definition page, in the **Account Information** section, do the following:

    a. In the Enterprise Application Definition list, select the name of the application definition.

    b. If you created the application definition to use an individual account, the User account name box appears. If you created the application definition to use a group account, the Group account name box appears. In the User account name or Group account name box, type the account name to modify.

4. In the **Enterprise Application Definition** section, you can perform one of the three operations: update the account information for the application corresponding to this application definition, delete the stored credentials for this account for this application, and delete the stored credentials for this account from all application definitions.

> **Note**   For individual application definitions, all three options are available. For group application definitions only the update option is available; both delete options are grayed out.

To update the account information for this application, do the following:

1. Click **Update account information**.

2. Click **OK**.

3. On the Provide *application_definition_display_name* Account Information page, in the **Logon Information** section, enter the credentials to be used for the logon to the enterprise application. The number, the order, and the names of the fields displayed follow configuration in the Logon Account Information section of the application definition.

4. Click **OK**.

To delete the stored credentials for this user account from this application definition, do the following:

1. Click **Delete stored credentials for this account from this enterprise application definition**.

2. Click **OK**.

3. To delete the user credentials, click **OK** on the confirmation message box.

To remove this user account credentials from all application definitions, do the following:

1. Click **Delete stored credentials for this account from all enterprise application definitions**.

2. Click **OK**.

3. To delete the user credentials from all application definitions, click **OK** on the confirmation message box.

Creating the Encryption Key

The encryption key is used as part of the encryption process for credentials used with single sign-on. The key helps to decrypt encrypted credentials stored in the single sign-on database. The first time you configure single sign-on and enterprise application definitions on the Manage Server Settings for Single Sign-On page, the encryption key is created automatically. You can regenerate the key if the previous credentials are compromised or if you have a policy to change the key after a certain number of days.

When you create an encryption key, you can choose to re-encrypt the existing credentials with the new key. When you re-encrypt the SSOSrv service credential store, events are logged in the Microsoft Windows Server 2003 application event log. Once re-encryption is initiated, you can monitor the application event log to verify that the credential store has been re-encrypted. Event ID 1032 is recorded in the application event log when re-encryption is started. Event ID 1033 is recorded in the application event log when re-encryption has ended. If there are any failures during re-encryption, an event is recorded in the log.

If the job server is restarted or SSOSrv is stopped on the job server during the re-encryption process, you should look in the event log for errors. If the event log reports an error, you must restart the re-encryption process from the Manage Encryption Key page.

Note   If the re-encryption process is preempted in any way, it will have to be re-run. If the re-encryption process is preempted, it reverts back to its original state

The re-encryption process is a long-running operation. It is recommended that you change or restore the encryption key during non-peak periods.

During the re-encryption process, Write operations such as updating credentials and changing application definitions are not allowed. Read operations such as retrieving credentials continue to work as normal.

Note   To re-encrypt the existing credentials, the single sign-on service account must be a member of the Server Administrators server role on the SQL Server instance where the single sign-on database is located. For other requirements for single sign-on service account, refer to the section "Single Sign-On Service Account" earlier in this chapter.

You cannot create the encryption key remotely. To re-generate the encryption key, go to the computer running as the job server, log on as the single sign-on administrator account, and do the following:

1. On the SharePoint Portal Server Central Administration for *server_name* page, in the **Component Configuration** section, click **Manage settings for single sign-on**.

   Alternatively, click **Start**, point to **All Programs**, point to **SharePoint Portal Server**, and then click **SharePoint Portal Server Single Sign-On Administration**.

2. On the Manage Settings for Single Sign-On for *server_name* page, in the **Server Settings** section, click **Manage encryption key**.

3. On the Manage Encryption Key page, in the **Encryption Key Creation** section, click **Create Encryption Key**.

4. On the Create Encryption Key page, to re-encrypt the credentials for the single sign-on database, select the **Re-encrypt all credentials by using the new encryption key** check box, and then click **OK**.

> **Note**   If you do not re-encrypt the existing credentials with the new encryption key, users must retype their credentials for individual application definitions, and administrators for group application definitions must retype group credentials.

Backing Up the Encryption Key

After creating the encryption key, you should back it up. You must back up the key to a 3.5-inch floppy disk. You should lock up the backup disk for the encryption key in a safe place.

> **Note**   Because the encryption key is the key that decrypts the encrypted credentials stored in the single sign-on database, the backup copy of the key should not be stored with the backup copy of the database. If a user obtains a copy of both the database and the key, the credentials stored in the database could be compromised.

You cannot back up the encryption key remotely. To back up the encryption key, go to the computer running as the job server, log on as the single sign-on administrator account, and do the following:

1. On the SharePoint Portal Server Central Administration for *server_name* page, in the **Component Configuration** section, click **Manage settings for single sign-on**.

    Alternatively, click **Start**, point to **All Programs**, point to **SharePoint Portal Server**, and then click **SharePoint Portal Server Single Sign-On Administration**.

2. On the Manage Settings for Single Sign-On for *server_name* page, in the **Server Settings** section, click **Manage encryption key**.

3. Insert a 3.5-inch disk into a disk drive on the computer running as the job server.

4. On the Manage Encryption Key page, in the **Encryption Key Backup** section, in the **Drive** list, click the letter of the disk drive, and then click **Back Up** to back up the encryption key.

5. In the completion message box that appears, click **OK**.

6. Remove the 3.5-inch disk from the disk drive.

Restoring the Encryption Key

You cannot restore the encryption key remotely. To restore the encryption key, go to the computer running as the job server, log on as the single sign-on administrator account, and do the following:

1. On the SharePoint Portal Server Central Administration for Server *server_name* page, in the **Component Configuration** section, click **Manage settings for single sign-on**.

    Alternatively, click **Start**, point to **All Programs**, point to **SharePoint Portal Server**, and then click **SharePoint Portal Server Single Sign-On Administration**.

2. On the Manage Settings for Single Sign-On for Server *server_name* page, in the **Server Settings** section, click **Manage encryption key**.

3. Insert a 3.5-inch disk into a disk drive on the computer running as the job server.

4. On the Manage Encryption Key page, in the **Encryption Key Restore** section, in the **Drive** list, click the letter of the disk drive, and then click **Restore** to restore the encryption key.

5. Click **OK**.

    When the restore completes, the Manage Settings for Single Sign-On for Server *server_name* page appears.

6. Remove the 3.5-inch disk from the disk drive.

> **Note**   Restoring the encryption key and re-encrypting the single sign-on credentials store with the restored key is a long-running process. It is recommended that you restore the encryption key during non-peak periods.

Enabling Auditing for the Encryption Key

You should enable auditing for the encryption key. Then, if the key is read or written to, there will be an audit trail in the security log in Microsoft Windows Server 2003 Event Viewer.

To enable auditing for the encryption key, you need to modify the registry using regedit and then enable auditing using Group Policy Object Editor.

1. To modify the registry, do the following:

   a. On the taskbar, click **Start**, and then click **Run**.

   b. Type **regedit** and then click **OK**.

   c. In **Registry Editor**, navigate to HKEY_LOCAL_MACHINE\SOFTWARE \Microsoft\ssosrv\Config.

   d. Right-click **Config**, and then click **Permissions**.

   e. In the **Permissions for Config** dialog box, click **Advanced**.

   f. In the **Advanced Security Settings for Config** dialog box, click the **Auditing** tab, and then click **Add**.

   g. In the **Select User, Computer, or Group** dialog box, in the **Enter the object name to select** box, type **everyone**.

   h. Click **OK**.

   i. In the **Auditing Entry for Config** dialog box, in the **Failed** column, select the **Full Control** check box, and then click **OK**.

   j. Click **OK**, and then click **OK** again to close all dialog boxes.

   k. Close **Registry Editor**.

   To enable auditing, do the following:

1. On the taskbar, click **Start**, and then click **Run**.

2. Type **mmc** and then click **OK**.

3. In the console, on the **File** menu, click **Add/Remove Snap-in**.

4. In the **Add/Remove Snap-in** dialog box, on the **Standalone** tab, click **Add**.

5. In the **Add Standalone Snap-in** dialog box, in the **Available Standalone Snap-ins** list, click **Group Policy Object Editor**, and then click **Add**.

6. In the **Select Group Policy Object** dialog box, ensure that **Local Computer** appears in the **Group Policy Object** box, and then click **Finish**.

7. In the **Add Standalone Snap-in** dialog box, click **Close**.

8. In the **Add/Remove Snap-in** dialog box, click **OK**.

9. Expand the following nodes:

   - **Local Computer Policy**

   - **Computer Configuration**

   - **Windows Settings**

   - **Security Settings**

   - **Local Policies**

   - **Audit Policy**

10. In the details pane, double-click **Audit object access**.

11. In the **Audit object access Properties** dialog box, select the **Failure** check box, and then click **OK**.

    You can verify that auditing is working by doing the following:

    a. Log off.

    b. Log on as a user who should not have access to the registry key.

    c. Try to read the registry key.

    d. Look in the security log in Windows Server 2003 Event Viewer for audit entries.

Disabling the Single Sign-On Service

To disable the single sign-on service on the server farm, you must disable it on each front-end Web server, on the job server, and on any server running the single sign-on service.

If you want to delete all credentials associated with application definitions, you must delete each enterprise application definition.

To disable the single sign-on service, do the following on each front-end Web server, job server, and any server running the single sign-on service:

1. On the taskbar, click **Start**, point to **Administrative Tools**, and then click **Services**.

2. On the **Services** management console, double-click **Microsoft Single Sign-on Service**.

3. On the **General** tab, in the **Startup type** list, click **Manual**.

4. In the **Service status** section, click **Stop**.

5. Click **OK**.

Creating a Web Part That Uses Single Sign-On

After you have configured the single sign-on and created the application definitions, you need to develop a Web Part that implements the single sign-on functionality and retrieves information from the corresponding back-end application programmatically.

SharePoint Portal Server 2003 provides a programming interface for developers to use and extend the single sign-on feature. There are two namespaces provided solely for interaction with the single sign-on functionality, as well as one class in a more generic Microsoft.SharePoint.Portal namespace, as follows:

- The Microsoft.SharePoint.Portal.SingleSignOn namespace contains core classes that allow you to work with account credentials and application definitions in the single sign-on credentials store. These core classes and their functionality are listed in Table 26-1. The required assembly is Microsoft.SharePoint.Portal.SingleSignon, located in Microsoft.SharePoint.Portal.SingleSignon.dll.

- The Microsoft.SharePoint.Portal.SingleSignOn.Security namespace contains two classes that control the ability to access Single Sign-On resources programmatically from the code. These two classes and their functionality are listed in Table 26-2. The required assembly is Microsoft.SharePoint.Portal.SingleSignOn.Security, located in Microsoft.SharePoint.Portal.SingleSignOn.Security.dll.

- The SingleSignonLocator class in the Microsoft.SharePoint.Portal namespace allows you to locate a URL for the logon form for the SSOSrv service. It has the GetCredentialEntryUrl(strAppName, [port]) method that returns the URL for the logon form for a given application definition. The method takes two parameters: strAppName, which is a name of an application that is configured in the corresponding application definition, and the optional port number for SSL. If you do not specify the port number, and SSL is not enabled on the server, the port number will default to port 80 (that is, the port value will be omitted from the URL). If the second parameter is absent and SSL is enabled on the server, the port number is assumed to be the standard SSL port 443. However, if you require the URL returned to be formatted for SSL on a particular port, you need to specify it. For example, you would pass the specified port when the system cannot detect which SSL port to use, such as when multiple SSL port mappings exist. The required assembly for this class is Microsoft.SharePoint.Portal, located in Microsoft.SharePoint.Portal.dll.

Table 26-1   Microsoft.SharePoint.Portal.SingleSignOn Namespace Core Classes

Class	Description
Application	Exposes functionality to add, get, and delete enterprise application definitions
Credentials	Exposes functionality to manage user and group credentials and access tokens
SSOReturnCodes	Contains all the return codes for SSOSrv service that the SingleSignonException class will throw
SingleSignonException	Instantiates an exception from the SSOSrv service with a specific error code

Table 26-2   Microsoft.SharePoint.Portal.SingleSignOn Security Namespace Classes

Class	Description
SingleSignOnPermission	Allows security actions for SingleSignOnPermission to be applied to code using declarative security.
SingleSignOnPermissionAttribute	Represents a custom permission that controls the ability to access Microsoft SharePoint Products and Technologies resources to manage user and group credentials and access tokens.

For example, let's look into a code in the Web Part that retrieves the account credentials for a back-end enterprise application from the single sign-on credentials database. The corresponding application definition is configured to use individual accounts. The code checks whether a requesting user's credentials have already been stored in the single sign-on credential database. If not, the user is redirected to the Single Sign-On logon form to enter the required credentials for accessing the back-end application.

The code should implement the following sequence:

1. Call the GetCredentials method of the Credentials class. Specify the application name for which the credentials need to be retrieved from the single sign-on database.

2. If the SSOSrv service cannot find credentials for the user for the enterprise application specified, the GetCredentials method throws a SingleSignonException. If the LastErrorCode property of the SingleSignonException is SSO_E_CREDS_NOT_FOUND, call the GetCredentialEntryUrl(String) method—or the Get-CredentialEntryUrl(String, Int) method—of the SingleSignonLocator class to build the URL to the single sign-on logon form.

3. After the URL for the logon form has been retrieved, redirect the browser to this URL. The logon form is created by the SSOSrv service. It prompts the user to enter credentials for the enterprise application in a number of fields. The order, the number and the display names for these fields are configured within the application definition under Logon Account Information. For example, if the enterprise application uses user name and password for authentication, two fields will be present in the logon form. For SAP, you may need five fields. After the SSOSrv service saves the credentials, the form redirects control back to the original Web Part.

The code in your Web Part will be similar to the following example that shows how to redirect the user to the logon form to save credentials for an enterprise application called SampleApp:

```
protected override void RenderWebPart(HtmlTextWriter writer) //RenderWebPart
{
    string[] rgGetCredentialData = null;
    try
    {
    //Try to get the credentials for this application.
    //Before running this code, make sure that an individual
    //application definition for application called "SampleApp"
    //has been added.
        Credentials.GetCredentials(1,"SampleAPP", ref rgGetCredentialData);
    }
    catch (SingleSignonException ssoe)
    {
    //This exception will be thrown if this user does not have
    //credentials for the "SampleApp" application.
        if(SSOReturnCodes.SSO_E_CREDS_NOT_FOUND == ssoe.LastErrorCode)
        {
        //Send the user to the single sign-on logon form.
        //The logon form will:
        //- Prompt the user for credentials for this application
        //- Save credentials for this user for this application
        //- Then redirect the user back to this Web Part
            string strSSOLogonFormUrl = SingleSignonLocator.GetCredentialEntryUrl
                ("MyIndividualApplicationID");
            writer.Write("<a href=" + strSSOLogonFormUrl +">Click here to save your
                credentials for the Enterprise Application.</a>");
            writer.WriteLine();
        }
    }
}
```

After the user credentials for the enterprise application have been stored in the single sign-on database, the custom code in the Web Part should retrieve the credentials using GetCredentials method, then submit them to the enterprise application in a manner that is relevant to this application, then retrieve the necessary data from this application, and then finally render the data in the Web Part. Referring back to Figure 26-1 that shows eight steps described in the section "How Single Sign-On

Works," the preceding code corresponds to steps 1 through 5. In addition to this code, you have to implement steps 6 through 8.

Your code for interacting with the enterprise application such as submitting credentials and retrieving information will be different depending on the type of application you are accessing. You need to consider that in an enterprise environment, where a user interacts with many systems and applications, it is likely that the environment does not maintain the user context through multiple processes, products, and computers. This user context is crucial to provide single sign-on capabilities because it is necessary to verify who initiated the original request. To overcome this problem, SharePoint Portal Server provides ability to use a Single Sign-On (SSO) ticket (not a Kerberos ticket). An SSO ticket is an encrypted access token that can be used to get the credentials that correspond to the user who made the original request. Also, in the enterprise environment you might consider using Microsoft Biz-Talk Server as a transformation engine for the authentication requests, as well as requests for data, between your Web Part and a format that is understood by the enterprise application.

An example of such enterprise application integration (EAI) infrastructure is shown in Figure 26-2. In this scenario, a Web Part gets the information from a line of business (LOB) back-end application using BizTalk Server 2004. The LOB application requires authentication. In this example, we will assume that the enterprise application definition for the LOB application has already been created, and the user credentials have been stored in the SSO database.

The authentication process shown in Figure 26-2 consists of several steps, as follows:

1. The Web Part calls Microsoft.SharePoint.Portal.SingleSignon.Credentials .ReserveCredentialTicket() with the user. This method reserves a credential ticket for the user and then returns an encrypted access token (SSO ticket) to the calling Web Part.

2. The Web Part passes the SSO ticket to the BizTalk Server 2004 native SOAP adapter by calling a Web service that runs on BizTalk Server. The SSO ticket is passed within the header of the SOAP request. When the SOAP adapter receives a request containing an SSO ticket, the ticket is stored as the SSO Ticket property in the context property of the BizTalk message. For details on configuring BizTalk 2004 SOAP adapter for integration with SharePoint Portal Server single sign-on, refer to *http://msdn.microsoft.com/library/default.asp?url=/library/en-us /operations/htm/ebiz_ops_adapt_file_eixk.asp*.

3. BizTalk passes the SSO ticket to the adapter for the LOB application that has the ability to call into SSO to redeem user's credentials using an SSO ticket. The LOB adapter calls Microsoft.SharePoint.Portal.SingleSignon.Credentials .GetCredentialsUsingTicket().method with the encrypted SSO ticket along with the enterprise application definition name to retrieve the security credentials

for the given application from the SSO credentials database. Alternatively, to redeem the ticket and obtain the user credentials from the SSO credentials database, you can use BizTalk Enterprise SSO object model and call Microsoft.BizTalk.SSOClient.Interop.ISSOTicket.RedeemTicket() method with the encrypted SSO ticket and with the enterprise application definition name.

4. The LOB adapter performs the necessary authentication and accesses the LOB application.

> **Note**   Only members of the SSO administrators group can call the Microsoft.SharePoint.Portal.SingleSignon.Credentials.GetCredentials-UsingTicket() method to get credentials for another user using an SSO ticket.
> For details on necessary permissions to call Microsoft.BizTalk .SSOClient.Interop.ISSOTicket.RedeemTicket() method, refer to *http://msdn .microsoft.com/library/default.asp?url=/library/en-us/sdk/htm /frlrfmicrosoftbiztalkssolookupinteropissoticketclassredeemtickettopic.asp.*

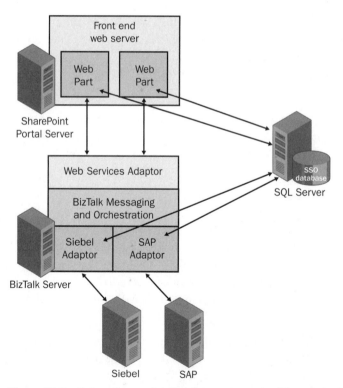

Figure 26-2   Enterprise application integration using SharePoint Portal Server single sign-on

If the Web Part that uses single sign-on is partially trusted (installed in the \bin directory of a virtual server), you must assign a custom Code Access Security Permission (SingleSignOnPermission) to it. To add the SingleSignOnPermission, make the following changes to one of the WSS policy files—either WSS_MediumTrust.config or WSS_MinimalTrust.config, depending on which one is in use:

1. To the <SecurityClasses> section, add:

```
<SecurityClass Name="SingleSignonPermission"
   Description="Microsoft.SharePoint.Portal.SingleSignon.Security
   .SingleSignonPermission, Microsoft.SharePoint.Portal.SingleSignon.Security,
   Version=11.0.0.0, Culture=neutral, PublicKeyToken= 71e9bce111e9429c"/> .
```

2. To the <Permission Set> section, and specifically to the PermissionSet where Name is "ASP.Net", add:

```
<IPermission class="SingleSignonPermission" version="1" Access="Minimal" />
```

The Access modifier in the above permission may be set to Minimal, Credentials, or Administer, as follows:

- **Minimal.** Allows a user to reserve a ticket

- **Credentials.** Allows a user to redeem credential tickets

- **Administer.** Allows a user to configure the SSOSrv service and maintain applications and credentials

> **Note** These instructions grant a specific level of SingleSignonPermission to all assemblies in the \bin directory of a virtual server. For more information about how to restrict the permission grant to just a single assembly and not all the assemblies in the \bin directory, see the "Code Access Security For Developers" section in the Microsoft SharePoint Products and Technologies SDK at *http://msdn.microsoft.com/library/default.asp?url= /library/en-us/spptsdk/html/smpscCodeAccessSecurityDevs.asp.*

Summary

SharePoint Portal Server 2003 provides single sign-on functionality implemented by Microsoft Single Sign-On service. The SSOSrv service provides storage and mapping of credentials such as account names and passwords so that portal site–based applications can retrieve information from third-party enterprise applications such as ERP and CRM systems. The credentials are encrypted and stored in the SQL Server database. For each enterprise application, you need to configure the corresponding single sign-on application definition. SharePoint Portal Server 2003 provides a programming interface to use the single sign-on feature. After you have configured the application definition, you need to create a Web Part that programmatically implements the single sign-on functionality using classes provided by SharePoint Portal Server, and then retrieves the data from the corresponding back-end application. There are numerous uses for single sign-on functionality in the enterprise environment.

Chapter 27

Securing an Extranet Using SSL and Certificates

When extranet users from outside the firewall connect to your Microsoft Office Share-Point Portal Server for deployment, it is highly recommended to secure the communication by using Secure Sockets Layer (SSL) protocol. SSL is a public key–based security protocol implemented by the Secure Channel (Schannel) security provider, and it provides a secure way of establishing an encrypted communication link with users.

Certificates are digital identification documents that allow both servers and clients to authenticate each other. If you want the server and client browser to set up an SSL connection over which encrypted information can be sent, certificates are required. Certificates include keys that are used to establish an SSL-encrypted connection. A public key and a private key form an SSL key pair. This key pair is used by a Web server to negotiate an encrypted connection with the client browser.

SSL confirms the authenticity of your website and, optionally, the identity of users who access your SSL-protected SharePoint site. To activate the SSL security features for SharePoint Portal Server, you must obtain and install a valid server certificate. A server certificate enables users to authenticate your server, check the validity of Web content, and establish a secure connection. The server certificate also contains a public key, which is used in creating a secure connection between the client and the server.

This chapter describes how to enable and configure SSL for a SharePoint Portal Server 2003 deployment.

Enabling SSL for a SharePoint Portal Server 2003

In this section, we will discuss how to create, install, and validate a digital server certificate. We will also cover how to install the certificate across your network load-balanced front-end Web servers. We will then define how to require SSL for communication between the clients and the front-end Web servers and will also look into additional optional steps that you might require to further protect access to your SharePoint Portal Server 2003 deployment, such as requiring client certificates and enabling a certificate trust list.

There are several assumptions that we will make before configuring SSL. The steps in this chapter assume the following:

- You have installed SharePoint Portal Server and created a portal site.

- The portal site is functioning correctly.

- If you are using network balancing, it is functioning correctly.

- Updates and search are functioning correctly.

- You are using Microsoft Certificate Services. The default certificate templates or types of certificates are available, depending on whether you have Microsoft Certificate Services installed on a computer running Microsoft Windows 2000 Server or Microsoft Windows Server 2003, respectively. Specifically, the client authentication certificate and the server authentication certificate are available. If they are not available, contact your certificate server administrator for the type of certificate to use for client or server authentication certificates.

- You are enabling SSL on the Default Web Site.

> **Note**   If you are enabling SSL on another virtual server, substitute the name of that virtual server for Default Web Site in the instructions in this chapter.

The process for obtaining and installing a server certificate and then enabling SSL on a SharePoint Portal Server consists of multiple steps, as follows:

1. Ensure that you can access the home page of the portal site.

2. Create a server certificate request by using the certificate wizard.

3. Submit the certificate request, and obtain the server certificate from the certificate server.

4. Install the server certificate on your primary front-end Web server.

5. Verify that the certificate is valid.

6. Test that the home page of the portal site is accessible over HTTP and HTTPS.

7. Require SSL on the portal site.

8. Test that the home page of the portal site is accessible over HTTPS.

9. Export the server certificate from the primary front-end Web server.

10. Install the server certificate on the remaining network load-balanced front-end Web servers.

11. Test that home page of the portal site is accessible over HTTPS.

12. Test SSL from the index management server.

13. Modify settings to update search.

14. Configure import settings for user profiles to use SSL via secure Lightweight Directory Access Protocol (LDAP). This step is optional.

15. Request client certificates. This step is optional.

16. Create a Certificate Trust List. This step is optional.

> **Note**   If you are not using a server farm, steps 9 through 13 are not required.

In this section, we will look at each step of this process. In addition, later in this chapter we will discuss troubleshooting, including information to assist you in diagnosing configuration problems.

To ensure that you can access the home page of the portal site

Before you enable SSL, ensure that you can access the home page of the portal site by using the HTTP protocol. You can do this in one of two ways:

- If you know the URL for your portal site, open a browser window and type the URL for the portal site.

- If you do not know the URL for your portal site, go to the SharePoint Portal Server Central Administration for *server_name* page, and then do the following:

  1. In the **Portal Site and Virtual Server Configuration** section, click **List and manage portal sites**.

  2. On the Manage Portal Sites page, click the URL for the portal site on which you are enabling SSL.

To create a server certificate request by using the Certificate Wizard

A server certificate must be created on your primary front-end Web server. To create a server certificate for your SharePoint Portal Server deployment, do the following on the primary front-end Web server:

1. Open Internet Information Services (IIS) Manager. In the console tree, expand the computer name node, and then expand the **Web Sites** node. Right-click **Default Web Site**, and select **Properties**.

> **Note**   In this chapter, we are enabling SSL on the Default Web Site. If you are enabling SSL on another virtual server, in the instructions in this section substitute the name of that virtual server for Default Web Site. Your virtual server name will also appear in the Mapping Name column on the Configure Alternate Portal Access Settings page.

2. On the **Directory Security** tab, in the **Secure communications** section, click **Server Certificate**.

3. On the Welcome to the Web Server Certificate Wizard page, click **Next**.

4. On the Server Certificate page, click **Create a new certificate**, and then click **Next**.

5. On the Delayed or Immediate Request page, click **Prepare the request now, but send it later**, and then click **Next**.

6. On the Name and Security Settings page, do the following:

    a. In the **Name** box, type a name for your certificate. It is recommended that you use the same name as the website that you are configuring, such as *Default Web Site*.

    b. In the Bit length list, select a bit length to indicate the strength of the encryption key or accept the default of 1024. Click **Next**.

7. On the Organization Information page, do the following:

    a. In the **Organization** box, type or select the name of your organization.

    b. In the **Organizational unit** box, type or select your team or division name. Click **Next**.

8. On the Your Site's Common Name page, in the **Common name** box, type the name that you will use to access the website, and then click **Next**.

The name can be a computer name, a fully qualified domain name (FQDN), or—if you are using network load-balanced or multiple front-end Web servers—the name of the entire server farm.

> **Note**   If you are implementing crawling over SSL, the common name must equal the base URL of the website. The base URL is the URL that was entered on the Create Portal Site for *server_name* page when the portal site was created. You can determine the base URL by going to the Configure Alternate Portal Access Settings page and looking at the Default URL column for Default Web Site (under Mapping Name). If you created a virtual server other than Default Web Site and you created the first portal site on that new virtual server, for the base URL, look at the Default URL column for your virtual server name listed in the Mapping Name column. If the base URL (Default URL) is not equal to the common name that you want to use, you can edit the mapping name and change the default URL on the Change Alternate Access Setting page.

9. On the Geographical Information page, do the following:

   a. In the **Country/Region** list, click the name of your country or region.

   b. In the **State/Province** list, type or select the name of your state or province.

   c. In the **City/Locality** list, type or select the name of your city or locality.

   d. Click **Next**.

10. We will now create a folder where we will save the certificate request. Leave the IIS Certificate Wizard open. Open Windows Explorer, and create the following folder hierarchy on your operating system drive:

    <system_drive>:\Certificates*<common_name>*

    where *common_name* is the common name you entered in step 8 of this procedure.

11. Return to the IIS Certificate Wizard. On the Certificate Request File Name page, do the following:

    ■ Click **Browse**, and navigate to the folder that you created in step 10 of this procedure. Click **Save**, then click **Next**.

12. On the Request File Summary page, click **Next**.

13. On the Completing the Web Server Certificate Wizard page, click **Finish**. Click **OK** to close the **Default Web Site Properties** dialog box.

To submit the certificate request, and obtain the server certificate from the Certificate Server

If you use Microsoft Certificate Services, use the following steps to request a server certificate from the certificate server.

> **Note**   The following procedure is based on Microsoft Certificate Services installed on Windows Server 2003. The user interface will be slightly different if you are using Microsoft Certificate Services installed on Windows 2000 Server.
>
> If you use another certificate authority (CA), use the steps supplied by the CA provider.

1. In your Web browser, type the URL of the CA server. Next, on the Welcome page, click **Request a Certificate**.

2. On the Request a Certificate page, click **Advanced certificate request**. On the Advanced Certificate Request page, click **Submit a certificate request by using a base-64-encoded CMC or PKCS #10 file**, or **submit a renewal request by using a base-64-encoded PKCS #7 file**.

3. Leave the Web browser open on the Submit a Certificate Request or Renewal Request page, and do the following:

    a. In a text editor such as Notepad, open file **certreq.txt** in the directory *<system_drive>*:\Certificates*<common_name>*. This is the directory that you created in the previous section.

    b. Select and copy the contents of the file, and then close the text editor.

4. Return to the Submit a Certificate Request or Renewal Request page. Paste the copied text into the **Saved Request** box, and then click **Submit**.

5. On the Certificate Issued page, do the following:

    a. Leave the **DER encoded** option selected.

    b. Click **Download certificate**.

    c. In the **File Download** dialog box, click **Save**.

    d. In the **Save As** dialog box, navigate to *<system_drive>*:\Certificates *<common_name>*.

    e. Click **Save**.

    f. Click **Close** to close the **Download Complete** dialog box.

    g. Click **Download certificate chain**.

    h. In the **File Download** dialog box, click **Save**.

    i. In the **Save As** dialog box, navigate to *<system_drive>*:\Certificates *<common_name>*.

    j. Click **Save**.

    k. Click **Close** to close the **Download Complete** dialog box.

> **Note** If you are using Microsoft Certificate Services, make sure the file you saved is the .p7b file.

    l. Close the Web browser.

To install the server certificate on your primary front-end Web server

After the server certificate has been issued by the CA, it must be installed on the primary front-end Web server. To install the certificate, do the following on the primary front-end Web server:

1. Open Internet Information Services (IIS) Manager. In the console tree, expand the computer name node, and then expand the **Web Sites** node. Right-click **Default Web Site**, and then click **Properties**.

2. On the **Directory Security** tab, in the **Secure communications** section, click **Server Certificate**.

3. On the Welcome to the Web Server Certificate Wizard page, click **Next**.

4. On the Pending Certificate Request page, select **Process the pending request and install the certificate**, and then click **Next**.

5. On the Process a Pending Request page, do the following:

    a. Click **Browse**, and navigate to *<system_drive>*:\Certificates *<common_name>*.

    b. In the **File name** box, type ***.p7b**, and then press **Enter**.

    c. Select the file with the .p7b extension (usually named **certnew.p7b**), and then click **Open**.

    d. Click **Next**.

> **Note**   If you received the certificate from a provider other than Microsoft Certificate Services, select the file with the extension defined in the certificate provider's instructions.

6. On the SSL Port page, in the **SSL port this web site should use** box, type **443**, and then click **Next**.

> **Note**   443 is the default port for SSL. You can select a different port than 443 if required.

7. On the Certificate Summary page, click **Next**. On the Completing the Web Server Certificate Wizard page, click **Finish**.

8. Click **OK** to close the **Default Web Site Properties** dialog box.

To verify that the certificate is valid

You should verify that IIS recognizes that the server certificate is valid. If this is not the case, you can try reinstalling the certificate or installing missing certificate chains.

1. Open Internet Information Services (IIS) Manager. In the console tree, expand the computer name node, and then expand the **Web Sites** node. Right-click **Default Web Site**, and then click **Properties**.

2. On the **Directory Security** tab, in the **Secure communications** section, click **View Certificate**.

3. Verify the following in the **Certificate** dialog box:

   ■ On the **General** tab, confirm that the certificate is valid.

   ■ On the **Certification Path** tab, verify that the **Certificate status** box contains the statement "This certificate is OK."

   If the certificate status is not OK, you will see a red X or a yellow warning icon. If this happens, try reinstalling the certificate or the certificate authority root. For more information, see the "Troubleshooting" section at the end of this chapter.

4. Click **OK** to close the **Certificate properties** dialog box, and then click **OK** to close the **Default Web Site Properties** dialog box.

To test that the home page of the portal site is accessible over HTTP and HTTPS

You should ensure that you can access the home page of the portal site by using HTTP and HTTPS with the NetBIOS name of the computer. To do this, open a browser and type the URL for the portal site, using the NetBIOS name of the server.

> **Note** If you installed the portal site on a port different than 80, or if you configured SSL on a port other than 443, you must include the port number in the URL.

When you access the portal site using HTTPS, you might receive several warnings that at this stage can safely be ignored, as follows:

- "Revocation information for the security certificate for this site is not available." This warning signifies that your server is unable to connect to the certificate server to verify that the certificate you have just obtained has not been revoked. To continue, click **Yes**.

- "The name on the security certificate is invalid or does not match the name of the site." The reason for this alert is the difference between the common name in the certificate and the NetBIOS name in the URL. To continue, click **Yes**.

You should be able to see the home page of your portal site.

To require SSL on the portal site

At this point in the process, SSL is enabled. However, you can still use Hypertext Transfer Protocol (HTTP) to access your site. To protect the extranet deployment, you must require SSL so that the external clients have to connect to the portal site using HTTPS.

> **Note** SSL must be required on all front-end Web servers.

To require SSL, do the following:

1. Open Internet Information Services (IIS) Manager. In the console tree, expand the computer name node, and then expand the **Web Sites** node. Right-click **Default Web Site**, and then click **Properties**.

2. On the **Directory Security** tab, in the **Secure communications** section, click **Edit**.

3. In the **Secure Communications** dialog box, select the **Require secure channel (SSL)** check box, and then click **OK**.

4. Click **OK** to close the **Default Web Site Properties** dialog box.

5. This step is critical. In the **Inheritance Overrides** dialog box, click **Select All**, and then click **OK**.

> **Note**   If you do not accept the inheritance overrides, you must remove the certificate, remove the requirement for SSL, and then start from the first procedure in this chapter, "To ensure that you can access the home page of the portal site." See the "Troubleshooting" section at the end of this chapter for the steps to remove the certificate and remove the requirement for SSL.

To test that the home page of the portal site is accessible over HTTPS

You should ensure that you can access the home page of the portal site by using HTTPS with the NetBIOS name of the computer. Refer to the procedure "To test that the home page of the portal site is accessible over HTTP and HTTPS" earlier in this chapter for details of the warnings that might be displayed when you access the site over HTTPS. As before, you can safely ignore them.

When you attempt to access the portal site by using HTTP, you should see a page that states "The page must be viewed over a secure channel."

If the home page of the portal site does not display when you access it using HTTPS, see the "Troubleshooting" section at the end of this chapter.

To export the server certificate from the primary front-end Web server

We will now export the server certificate from the primary front-end Web server so that we can install and use it on the remaining front-end Web servers. To export the certificate, you must do the following on the primary front-end Web server:

1. Open Internet Information Services (IIS) Manager. In the console tree, expand the computer name node, and then expand the **Web Sites** node. Right-click **Default Web Site**, and then click **Properties**.

2. On the **Directory Security** tab, in the **Secure communications** section, click **Server Certificate**.

3. On the Welcome to the Web Server Certificate Wizard page, click **Next**.

4. On the Modify the Current Certificate Assignment page, click **Export the current certificate to a .pfx file**, and then click **Next**.

5. On the Export Certificate page, save it, for example, in the folder that we have been using for certificate files, *<system_drive>*:\Certificates*<common_name>*. Browse to the folder, click **Save**, and then click **Next**.

> **Note** You should copy the file to a network share because you will need to access the file from the remaining front-end Web servers when you install the certificate on them.

6. On the Certificate Password page, in the **Password** box, type a password. You will be prompted for this password when you install the certificate on another front-end Web server. Then, in the **Confirm password** box, type the password again, and click **Next**.

7. On the Export Certificate Summary page, click **Next**.

8. On the Completing the Web Server Certificate Wizard page, click **Finish**.

9. Click **OK** to close the **Default Web Site Properties** dialog box.

> **Note** If you use a different methodology from the one outlined in this chapter to export the server certificate from the primary front-end Web server and import it to the remaining front-end Web servers, on subsequent front-end Web servers you might encounter issues such as warnings in the event log that the private key is missing or invalid. For more information, see the "Troubleshooting" section at the end of this chapter.

To install the server certificate on the remaining network load-balanced front-end Web servers

You now need to install the certificate on the remaining front-end Web servers. On each remaining network load-balanced front-end Web server, you must do the following:

1. Open Internet Information Services (IIS) Manager. In the console tree, expand the computer name node, and then expand the **Web Sites** node. Right-click **Default Web Site**, and then click **Properties**.

2. On the **Directory Security** tab, in the **Secure communications** section, click **Server Certificate**.

3. On the Welcome to the Web Server Certificate Wizard page, click **Next**.

4. On the Server Certificate page, click **Import a certificate from a .pfx file**, and then click **Next**.

5. On the Import Certificate page, click **Browse**, and navigate to the location of the .pfx file that you exported in the previous section. Click **Open**, and then click **Next**.

6. On the Import Certificate Password page, in the **Password** box, type the password that you used when you exported the certificate on the primary front-end Web server, and then click **Next**.

7. On the SSL Port page, in the **SSL port this web site should use** box, type **443** or the custom port if you are using one, and then click **Next**.

> **Note**   If you have chosen an alternate custom port number for SSL on the primary front-end Web server, use that same number on the other front-end servers.

8. On the Imported Certificate Summary page, click **Next**.

9. On the Completing the Web Server Certificate Wizard page, click **Finish**.

10. Click **OK** to close the **Default Web Site Properties** dialog box.

11. Verify that the certificate is valid, and then test that you can access the home page of the portal site (referring to instructions in procedures "To verify that the certificate is valid" and "Test that the home page of the portal site is accessible over HTTP and HTTPS" earlier in this chapter). If you required SSL on the primary front-end Web server, you need to do the same on the remaining front-end Web servers (referring to the procedure "To require SSL on the portal site" earlier in this chapter if necessary), and then you need to test the access once again.

> **Note**   You might need to install the certificate authority root. If you receive a certificate warning that states, "The security certificate was issued by a company you have chosen not to trust," you must install the Trust Root Authority, as described in "Obtaining and Installing the Certificate Authority Root," in the "Troubleshooting" section later in this chapter.

To test the home page of the portal site

After testing the NetBIOS server name for each of the front-end Web servers in your server farm, you must test the common name of your server farm.

You should test that you can access the home page of the portal site from the browser by using HTTPS with the common name of your server farm. This time, you should not receive a security alert stating that the certificate name is invalid or does not match the name of the site when you access the portal site with HTTPS.

To test SSL from the index management server

Before you perform the following steps, verify that the index management server has access to the front-end Web servers over the port that you have specified for SSL, such as the default port 443. This is especially important for perimeter network (also known as *DMZ, demilitarized zone*, and *screened subnet*) deployments or segmented-network deployments.

To view your portal site from the index management server, open a new browser window, and type the HTTPS URL for the portal site that is on the primary front-end Web server or the computer that hosts the parent portal site for shared services.

As before, you can ignore the warning "Revocation information for the security certificate for this site is not available." It signifies that your server is unable to connect to the certificate server to verify that the certificate you just obtained has not been revoked. To continue, click **Yes**.

If an authentication prompt appears, type your user name and password, and then click **OK**. The home page of the portal site should be displayed.

If you receive a certificate warning that states, "The security certificate was issued by a company you have chosen not to trust," you must install the Trust Root Authority, as described in "Obtaining and Installing the Certificate Authority Root" in the "Troubleshooting" section at the end of this chapter. If you receive any other warning, review the steps you used to create and install the certificate, and try again.

To modify settings to update search

We will now modify SharePoint Portal Server settings so that the content from the SSL-protected portal site is included in the index.

As before, Default Web Site in IIS is our portal site. To include content from the SSL-protected portal site in the index, first you modify the alternate portal site access settings to use HTTPS, as follows:

1. On the SharePoint Portal Server Central Administration for *server_name* page, in the **Portal Site and Virtual Server Configuration** section, click **Configure alternate portal site URLs for intranet, extranet, and custom access**.

2. On the Configure Alternate Portal Access Settings page, rest the pointer on **Default Web Site**, click the arrow that appears, and then click **Edit** on the menu that appears.

3. On the Change Alternate Access Setting page, in the **Default URL** box, change **http** to **https**, and then click **OK**.

If you previously specified an account for the site restriction rule for a site and do not want to use the default content access account (default crawling account), specify the account again after applying alternate portal site access settings, as follows:

1. On the Site Settings page, in the **Search Settings and Indexed Content** section, click **Configure search and indexing**.

2. On the Configure Search and Indexing page, in the **Other Content Sources** section, click **Manage content sources**.

3. On the Manage Content Sources page, rest the pointer on **This portal**, click the arrow that appears, and then click **View Gatherer Log** on the menu that appears.

4. On the Gatherer log details page, in the **Actions** list, click **Exclude and Include Content**.

5. On the Exclude and Include Content for Portal_Content page, rest the pointer on the name of the site restriction for the site (for example, *server_name*), click the arrow that appears, and then click **Edit** on the menu that appears.

6. On the Edit Rule page, in the **Specify Authentication** section, click **Specify crawling account**. In the **Account** box, type the user name or ID that can access the resources in this URL space. Examples are *user_name*, *user_name@org*, or *DOMAIN\user_name*. In the **Password** box, type the password for this user name. This password is protected and can be used only to access the needed resources for the purpose of crawling content. In the **Confirm password** box, type the password for this user name again, and click **OK**.

7. Click **Configure Search and Indexing** at the top of the Exclude and Include Content for Portal_Content page.

8. On the Configure Search and Indexing page, in the **Other Content Sources** section, click **Manage content sources**. On the Manage Content Sources page, rest the pointer on **Site directory**, click the arrow that appears, and then click **View Gatherer Log** on the menu that appears.

9. On the Gatherer log details page, in the **Actions** list, click **Exclude and Include Content**. On the Exclude and Include Content for Non_Portal_Content page, rest the pointer on the name of the site restriction for the site (for example, *server_name*), click the arrow that appears, and then click **Edit** on the menu that appears.

10. On the Edit Rule page, in the **Specify Authentication** section, click **Specify crawling account**. In the **Account** box, type the user name or ID that can access the resources in this URL space. In the **Password** box, type the password for this user name. In the **Confirm password** box, type the password for this user name again, and then click **OK**.

If the proxy server settings for the index management server differ from the default proxy server settings, reset the proxy server settings for the index management server after applying alternate portal access settings.

> **Note**   The default proxy settings are those specified on the Configure Server Farm Account Settings page. The settings for the index management server are those specified on the Search Server Settings page. When you apply alternate portal site access settings, the proxy server settings specified on the Search Server Settings page are overwritten by the settings on the Configure Server Farm Account Settings page.

To reset proxy settings, do the following:

1. On the SharePoint Portal Server Central Administration for *server_name* page, in the **Component Configuration** section, click **Manage the Search Service**.

2. On the Manage Search Settings page, in the **Servers and Topology** section, click the name of the index management server.

3. On the Search Server Settings page, in the **Proxy Server Settings** section, specify the proxy server information for the index management server, and then click **OK**.

You will now need to perform a full update on the **People**, **Site directory**, and **This portal** content sources, as follows:

1. On the Site Settings page, in the **Search Settings and Indexed Content** section, click **Configure search and indexing**.

2. On the Configure Search and Indexing page, in the **Other Content Sources** section, click **Manage content sources**.

3. On the Manage Content Sources page, rest the pointer on **People**, click the arrow that appears, and then click **Start Full Update** on the menu that appears. Rest the pointer on Site directory, click the arrow that appears, and then click **Start Full Update** on the menu that appears.

4. Rest the pointer on **This portal**, click the arrow that appears, and then click **Start Full Update** on the menu that appears.

The updates can take a while. After the updates for the **People**, **Site directory**, and **This portal** content sources have completed, check the gatherer log for errors such as "access denied" and for certificate warnings, as follows:

1. On the Manage Content Sources page, rest the pointer on **People**, click the arrow that appears, and then click **View Gatherer Log** on the menu that appears.

2. Rest the pointer on **Site directory**, click the arrow that appears, and then click **View Gatherer Log** on the menu that appears.

3. Rest the pointer on **This portal**, click the arrow that appears, and then click **View Gatherer Log** on the menu that appears.

On the index management server, if you have the proxy settings in Microsoft Internet Explorer specified as the same as those on the Search Server Settings page, you might receive a security alert when you access the portal site. This alert could include the following information:

- Whether the certificate was issued by a company you trust

- Whether the certificate date is valid

- Whether the name of the certificate is valid

If a warning icon (a yellow triangle with an exclamation point in it) accompanies either or both of the first two items, you must fix the issue. If you see a warning icon next to the third item, you can bypass the certificate name check by doing the following:

1. On the SharePoint Portal Server Central Administration for *server_name* page, in the **Component Configuration** section, click **Manage the Search Service**. On the Manage Search Settings page, in the **Servers and Topology** section, click the name of the index management server.

2. On the Search Server Settings page, in the **SSL Certificate Warning Configuration** section, select the **Ignore SSL Certificate name warnings** check box, and then click **OK**.

> **Note**   If you choose to ignore certificate name warnings, it is recommended that you do not use the index management server to crawl sites on the Internet.

To configure import settings for user profiles to use SSL via secure LDAP (optional)

This is an optional step. If you configured use of Active Directory for user profiles by following the steps in the *Microsoft Office SharePoint Portal Server 2003 Administrator's Guide*, you need to ensure that you select the **Use SSL-secured connection** check box on the Add Connection page, as follows:

1. On the Site Settings page, in the **User Profile, Audiences, and Personal Sites** section, click **Manage profile database**.

2. On the Manage Profile Database page, in the **Profile and Import Settings** section, click the link next to **Source of user set**.

3. On the Configure Profile Import page, in the **Source** section, click **Custom source**, and then click **OK**.

4. On the Manage Connections page, rest the pointer on the name of your connection, click the arrow that appears, and then click **Edit** on the menu that appears.

5. On the Edit Connection page, in the **Connection Settings** section, ensure that the **Use SSL-secured connection** check box is selected.

6. Click **OK**.

> **Note**   You must have secure LDAP enabled on your domain. For instructions on configuring secure LDAP, refer to *http://go.microsoft.com/fwlink /?LinkId=20732* and *http://go.microsoft.com/fwlink/?LinkId=20735*.

To require client certificates (optional)

This step is optional. You might require client certificates to provide additional security for accessing your portal site from outside the firewall. When you request certificates from the clients, it means that clients that do not have certificates installed will not be able to access the portal site. For example, you might require client certificates if you need a stronger two-level authentication, in which clients are required to provide something they have (a certificate) and users are asked to provide something they know (authentication credentials).

To require client certificates, do the following on each front-end Web server:

1. Open Internet Information Services (IIS) Manager. In the Internet Information Services management console, expand the tree view, and then expand **Web Sites**. Right-click **Default Web Site**, and then click **Properties**.

2. Click the **Directory Security** tab.

3. In the **Secure communications** section, click **Edit**.

4. In the **Secure Communications** dialog box, make sure the **Require secure channel (SSL)** check box is selected, and in the **Client certificates** section, click **Require client certificates**.

5. Click **OK** to close the **Secure Communications** dialog box, and then click **OK** to close the Default Web Site Properties page.

6. If one or more **Inheritance Overrides** dialog boxes appear, click **Select All**, and then click **OK** for each dialog box.

> **Note** You can map client certificates to Windows security accounts and then use client certificates for authentication. This process is called an *account mapping*. You enable account mapping by selecting **Enable client certificate mapping** check box from the **Secure Communications** dialog. For more information and detailed instructions, refer to the white paper "Enabling Client Certificates and Using Client Certificates When Crawling Content with SharePoint Portal Server 2003," located at *http://www.microsoft.com/technet/prodtechnol/office/sps2003/maintain/clicerts.asp?frame=true*.

To create a certificate trust list (optional)

This step is optional. After you have required client certificates, you can further tighten the access security by specifying the list of certificate authorities (CAs) that your portal site trusts. A client with a certificate issued by a CA that is a member of this list will be allowed access, whereas clients with certificates issued by other CAs will be denied access to your portal site.

Before you can add the certificate authorities to a certificate trust list, the certificate authorities must be installed on the server. The steps for installing the certificate authorities on the server are found in "Obtaining and Installing the Certificate Authority Root" in the "Troubleshooting" section at the end of this chapter.

Both the CA that issued the client certificate and the CA that issued the server certificate must be considered trusted certification authorities. If the server certificates and client certificates are issued by the same certification authority and you successfully performed certification validation in the procedure "To verify that the certificate is valid" earlier in this chapter, the CA is installed on the server.

To check if the CA is installed on the server, you may do the following:

1. Obtain the client certificate without a private key (.cer file). The client certificate without the private key can be exported from the computer where the certificate is installed.

2. Right-click the **.cer** file, point to **Open With**, and then click **Crypto Shell Extensions**.

3. In the **Certificate** dialog box, click the **Certification Path** tab. The certification path should show no errors in the chain. If errors are shown, you must download and install the certificate authority root on each front-end Web server following the steps in "Obtaining and Installing the Certificate Authority Root" in the "Troubleshooting" section at the end of this chapter.

4. Click **OK** to close the **Certificate** dialog box.

We will now create a certificate trust list (CTL). You must create a certificate trust list on each front-end Web server.

> **Note**   After you create a certificate trust list, put all of your certificate authorities for client and server certificates in this list. Do not create a new certificate trust list for each certificate authority that you add.

To create a CTL, do the following on each front-end Web server:

1. Open Internet Information Services (IIS) Manager. In the Internet Information Services management console, expand the tree view, and then expand **Web Sites**. Right-click **Default Web Site**, and then click **Properties**.

2. Click the **Directory Security** tab.

3. In the **Secure communications** section, click **Edit**.

4. In the **Secure Communications** dialog box, select the **Enable certificate trust list** check box, and then click **New**.

5. In the **Certificate Trust List Wizard**, do the following:

    a. On the Welcome to the Certificate Trust List Wizard page, click **Next**.

    b. On the Certificates in the CTL page, click **Add from Store**.

    c. In the **Select Certificate** dialog box, select one or more certificates that you want to use, and then click **OK**.

    d. On the Certificates in the CTL page, click **Next**.

    e. On the Name and Description page, type a name in the **Friendly name** box, and then click **Next**. For example, you can use a friendly name such as *All CAs* as a reminder to place all additional certificate authorities in this one list.

    f. On the Completing the Certificate Trust List Wizard page, click **Finish**.

6. Click **OK** In the message box that appears, click **OK** to close the **Secure Communications** dialog box, and then click **OK** to close the **Default Web Site Properties** dialog box.

7. Close Internet Information Services (IIS) Manager.

Note   If you have required client certificates and you would like to add the content of your SSL-protected site to the index, you must install the client certificate on the index management server. For more information and detailed instructions, refer to the white paper "Enabling Client Certificates and Using Client Certificates When Crawling Content with SharePoint Portal Server 2003," located at *http://www.microsoft.com/technet/prodtechnol /office/sps2003/maintain/clicerts.asp?frame=true*.

Troubleshooting

In this section, we will concentrate on the common problems that you might come across, and how to resolve them. We will start with how to obtain and install the CA root, and then address what to do if the common name does not resolve. After that, we will look into the problems of certificates not being trusted and inheritance overrides not being accepted. In addition, we will discuss the course of action in case the home page of the portal site does not appear on one or more front-end Web servers.

Obtaining and Installing the Certificate Authority Root

If any of your SSL tests failed, and you use Microsoft Certificate Services, you might need to install the certificate authority root on your servers by using the following procedure.

Note   If you use another certificate authority, use the steps supplied by the certificate authority provider.

1. In your Web browser, type the URL of the CA server.

2. On the Welcome page, click **Download a CA certificate, certificate chain, or CRL**.

3. On the Download a CA Certificate, Certificate Chain, or CRL page, do the following:

    a. In the **CA certificate** list, select the certificate that begins with "Current."

    b. In the **Encoding method** section, ensure that **DER** is selected.

    c. Click **Download CA certificate chain**.

    d. In the **File Download** dialog box, click **Save**.

    e. In the **Save As** dialog box, specify a location for the file, and then click **Save**.

    f. Click **Close** to close the **Download Complete** dialog box.

Note   The file type that you downloaded should be a .p7b file.

4. Close your Web browser.

5. Open the **Certificates** MMC console, as follows:

    a. On the taskbar, click **Start**, and then click **Run**. In the **Open** box, type **mmc** and then click **OK**.

    b. On the console **File** menu, click **Add/Remove Snap-in**.

    c. In the **Add/Remove Snap-in** dialog box, on the **Standalone** tab, click **Add**.

    d. In the **Add Standalone Snap-in** dialog box, in the **Available Standalone Snap-ins** list, click **Certificates**, and then click **Add**.

    e. In the **Certificates snap-in** dialog box, click **Computer account**, and then click **Next**.

    f. In the **Select Computer** dialog box, click **Local computer: (the computer this console is running on)**, and then click **Finish**.

    g. Click **Close** to close the **Add Standalone Snap-in** dialog box.

    h. Click **OK** to close the **Add/Remove Snap-in** dialog box.

6. In the **Certificates** console, expand the **Certificates (Local Computer)** node.

7. Expand the **Trusted Root Certification Authorities** node.

8. Right-click **Certificates**, point to **All Tasks**, and then click **Import**.

9. On the Welcome to the Certificate Import Wizard page, click **Next**.

10.   On the File to Import page, do the following:

   a.   Click **Browse**, and navigate to the location of the certificate file that you saved.

   b.   In the **File name** box, type ***.p7b**, and then press **Enter**.

   c.   Select the file with the **.p7b** extension, and then click **Open**.

   d.   Click **Next**.

11.   On the Certificate Store page, do the following:

   a.   Click **Place all certificates in the following store**.

   b.   In the **Certificate store** box, specify **Trusted Root Certification Authorities**.

   c.   Click **Next**.

12.   On the Completing the Certificate Import Wizard page, click **Finish**.

13.   Click **OK** to close the successful import message box.

Common Name Does Not Resolve

If the common name does not resolve, restart the front-end Web servers and the index management servers. If restarting the servers does not fix the problem, ping the common name. If the ping does not resolve to an IP address and states that the host cannot be found, contact your network administrator.

Certificate Is Not Trusted

This error appears if you installed the .cer or .pfx file. If you receive this error, you must add the certificate authority root. See the preceding section in this chapter, "Obtaining and Installing the Certificate Authority Root."

Inheritance Overrides Not Accepted

If you did not accept the inheritance overrides described in the procedure "To require SSL on the portal site," you must remove the certificate, remove the requirement for SSL, and then start again. To do this:

1.   Open Internet Information Services (IIS) Manager. In the console tree, expand the computer name node, and then expand the **Web Sites** node. Right-click **Default Web Site**, and then click **Properties**.

2.   On the **Web Site** tab, in the **Web site identification** section, click **Advanced**.

3.   In the **Advanced Web Site Identification** dialog box, in the **Multiple SSL identities for this Web site** section, click each IP address and click **Remove** until no IP addresses are listed.

4. Click **OK** to close the **Advanced Web Site Identification** dialog box.

5. On the **Directory Security** tab, in the **Secure communications** section, click **Server Certificate**.

6. On the Welcome to the Web Server Certificate Wizard page, click **Next**.

7. On the Modify the Current Certificate Assignment page, click **Remove the current certificate**, and then click **Next**.

8. On the Remove a Certificate page, click **Next**.

9. On the Completing the Web Server Certificate Wizard page, click **Finish**.

10. On the **Directory Security** tab, in the **Secure communications** section, click **Edit**.

11. In the **Secure Communications** dialog box, clear the **Require secure channel (SSL)** check box, and click **OK**, and then click **OK** to close the **Default Web Site Properties** dialog box.

12. Go to the first procedure in this chapter, "To ensure that you can access the home page of the portal site," and start again.

If following this procedure does not resolve the problem, refer to your IIS documentation. Solutions may include deleting the virtual server and re-extending the portal site to the new virtual server.

Home Page of the Portal Site Does Not Appear

If the home page of the portal site does not appear, you should test that SSL is enabled correctly on the primary front-end Web server and on each network load-balanced front-end Web server. To test SSL, create a virtual directory that points to the root folder of your website, and test whether you can reach this directory over SSL.

> **Note** If you are using shared services, run this test on the computer that hosts the parent portal site for shared services.

To perform the test, on the primary front-end Web server and on each remaining network load-balanced front-end Web server, do the following:

1. Create a file called default.htm with some text that indicates the front-end Web server. For example, your file might contain the following:

```
<h1>Test SSL on front-end Web server server_number</h1>
```

The server number will change for each server. For example, if you have three front-end Web servers in addition to the primary front-end Web server, your file for the first server would contain the following:

```
<h1>Test SSL on front-end Web server 1.</h1>
```

Your file for the second server would contain the following:

```
<h1>Test SSL on front-end Web server 2.</h1>
```

2. Move this file to the root folder of your site. By default, the root folder for the Default Web Site is *<system drive>*:\Inetpub\wwwroot.

3. Open Internet Information Services (IIS) Manager. In the console tree, expand the computer name node, and then expand the **Web Sites** node.

4. Right-click **Default Web Site**, point to **New**, and then click **Virtual Directory**.

5. On the Welcome to the Virtual Directory Creation Wizard page, click **Next**.

6. On the Virtual Directory Alias page, in the **Alias** box, type the name for the virtual directory, for example, **test**, and then click **Next**.

7. On the Web Site Content Directory page, in the **Path** box, specify the path to the website root directory, such as *<system drive>*:\Inetpub\wwwroot, and then click **Next**.

8. On the Virtual Directory Access Permissions page, click **Next**. Do not change the default values that are selected.

9. On the You have successfully completed the Virtual Directory Creation Wizard page, click **Finish**.

10. On the SharePoint Portal Server Central Administration for *server_name* page, under **Links to related administration home pages**, click **Windows SharePoint Services**.

11. On the Windows SharePoint Services Central Administration page, in the **Virtual Server Configuration** section, click **Configure virtual server settings**.

12. On the Virtual Server List page, click **Default Web Site**.

13. On the Virtual Server Settings page, in the **Virtual Server Management** section, click **Define managed paths**.

14. On the Define Managed Paths page, in the **Add a New Path** section, do the following:

   a. In the **Path** box, type **/test**.

   b. In **Type**, click **Excluded path**.

   c. Click **OK**.

15. Open a new browser window, and type **https://*server_name*/test/default.htm**.

As before, you can ignore the warning "Revocation information for the security certificate for this site is not available." To continue, click **Yes**.

If an authentication prompt appears, type your user name and password, and then click **OK**. If the test page appears, it means that SSL is correctly enabled on the server that you are testing. If it doesn't appear, go to the next section.

Portal Site or Test Page Fails to Display on One or More Front-End Web Servers

If the home page of the portal site or test page does not appear, check the event log for an error with an Event Source of Schannel, an Event ID of 36869, and a description stating that "The SSL server credential's certificate does not have a private key information property attached to it." This most often occurs when a certificate is backed up incorrectly and then later restored. This message can also indicate a certificate enrollment failure.

If this event ID exists, perform the steps from the section "Inheritance Overrides Not Accepted" earlier in this chapter. Then follow the instructions in this chapter starting with the procedure "To export the server certificate from the primary front-end Web server." The error was most likely due to the use of an alternate method for exporting the server certificate, and the private key was not included.

If this event ID does not exist, check your network connections and network connectivity, or restart your server.

Summary

In this chapter, we looked into how to protect the SharePoint Portal Server deployment by enabling and configuring SSL on the front-end Web servers. This process consists of multiple steps, including obtaining a server certificate and installing it on all front-end Web servers, validating the certificate, requiring SSL, and modifying search settings to include the content of a SSL-protected site in the index. You might also need to configure import settings for user profiles via secure LDAP. Depending on your requirements, you might require client certificates to provide two-level authentication and create a Certificate Trust List to make sure that only the clients with certificates from the trusted CAs are allowed to connect to your site.

Part IX

Maintaining a Server in Windows SharePoint Services

Chapter 28

Disaster Recovery in SharePoint Products and Technologies

What do you do when things go wrong? Really, really wrong. You should not wait to ask yourself this question when you are in need of an immediate answer. The most important thing in solving critical problems is to think ahead and record your problem-resolving strategy in a disaster recovery plan. Before you can do that, you must be aware of the problem-solving tools available. This chapter covers operational tasks common in disaster recovery scenarios using the native tools provided by Microsoft Office SharePoint Portal Server 2003 and Microsoft Windows Share-Point Services. In addition, this chapter discusses how to leverage SQL Server backup and restore processes to safeguard your data in SharePoint Products and Technologies solutions.

Backup and Restore Utilities

Windows SharePoint Services is shipped with its own backup and restore tool, Stsadm.exe. Stsadm.exe is also widely used in SharePoint Portal Server deployments. The SharePoint Migration Tool is another tool that ships with Windows SharePoint Services; it is used to migrate sites. In addition to these Windows SharePoint Services tools, SharePoint Portal Server is shipped with another tool: the SharePoint Portal Server Data Backup and Restore utility. Finally, the Resource Kit CD will also contain a backup tool named SPBackup.exe, which can be used to back up site collections that have recently been changed. The rest of the section provides you with a detailed overview of the use and purpose of these tools.

General Overview

Table 28-1 provides a general overview of the available backup and restore utilities.

Table 28-1   Overview of Backup and Restore Utilities

Tool	Purpose
Stsadm.exe	Makes a full-fidelity backup of site collections.
SharePoint Migration tool (Smigrate.exe)	Backs up and restores sites and subsites. Does not make a full-fidelity backup; you might lose some customizations or settings during the process.
SharePoint Portal Server Data Backup and Restore utility (Spsbackup.exe)	Backs up and restores all databases, except the configuration database. Restores content indexes and content sources.
SPBackup.exe	Determines which site collections have changed and generates a batch file that backs up changed site collections using the Stsadm.exe tool.

The Stsadm.exe Utility

Windows SharePoint Services includes Stsadm.exe for command-line administration of Windows SharePoint Services servers and sites. Within SharePoint Portal Server, Stsadm.exe can be used to make a full-fidelity, complete backup of site collections. Please remember that Stsadm.exe cannot be used to back up or restore the portal site. Microsoft SQL Server 2000 is not required when you want to use the Stsadm.exe tool. You must be a member of the Administrators group on the server computer to be able to use the Stsadm.exe tool. The Stsadm.exe tool provides a method for performing the Windows SharePoint Services administration tasks to run once, to be used in batch files, or to be used within a script. The command-line tool has a more streamlined interface than the site administration pages, yet it allows you to perform many of the same tasks. Stsadm.exe can be used to back up the following:

- Site collections
- Subsites

- Pages in the sites
- Files in document libraries or lists
- Security and permission settings
- Feature settings

> **Caution**   Using Stsadm.exe to back up or restore team or personal sites on a machine running SharePoint Portal Server 2003 is not supported by Microsoft. You are advised to use the Spsbackup.exe utility for disaster recovery or portal-specific needs and Smigrate.exe to export, import, or migrate personal or team sites.

You can back up an entire site collection and all the sites and content beneath it, but not an individual subsite (or any other finer level of granularity, for that matter). However, you can restore content and subsites within a site collection by restoring the site collection to a different site and manually copying the lost data to the original location.

You can use Stsadm.exe from the command line or from batch files. Stsadm.exe must be run on the Web front-end server itself. To create a backup of the site at the specified URL, use the following syntax (using the overwrite parameter to replace an existing kbackup file): `stsadm.exe -o backup -url <url> -filename <filename> [-overwrite]`.

The SharePoint Migration Tool

The SharePoint Migration Tool (Smigrate.exe) that ships with Windows SharePoint Services is used to migrate sites. The SharePoint Migration Tool is available in the Program Files\Common Files\Microsoft Shared\Web Server Extensions\60\Bin folder on your server computer. Alternatively, you can get a copy of this file by going to *http://central .workplace.corasworks.net/support/smigrate/smigrate.zip*. The SharePoint Migration tool does not make a full-fidelity backup because you might lose some customizations or settings in the process. To use the SharePoint Migration Tool, you must be a site administrator for both the site or the site collection being backed up and the destination site.

> **Note**   Using the Smigrate.exe tool to back up, restore, or migrate personal sites is supported with the following exceptions:
>
> 1. Web Parts added to personal sites after creation time must be re-added.
> 2. Links added to the MyLinks Web Part must be re-added.
> 3. Before restoring each personal site, a new site must be created on the target virtual server with the same name as the old site but without a template being applied.

You can use the SharePoint Migration Tool from the command line or from batch files. To back up a site, you use the SharePoint Migration Tool with the following parameters:

```
smigrate.exe -w <Web site URL> -f <backup filename> [-e -y -u <username> -pw
   <password>]
```

All backup files end with the .fwp extension. If you do not specify the .fwp extension, it will be added automatically. The optional –e paramater excludes subsites during backup. The optional –y parameter overwrites an existing backup file. The optional –u parameter specifies the user name of the website administrator. The optional –pw parameter specifies the password for the website administrator. Use an asterisk (*) to be prompted to type a password.

> **Note**   You can also use Microsoft FrontPage 2003 to create a backup file by opening a site via File\Open Site, specifying the URL of the site, and choosing Tools\Server\Backup Web Site. You can restore a site via FrontPage 2003. First you should open the nontemplated site to which you want to restore the backup. You can do this by choosing File\Open Site, specifying the URL of the site, and then choosing Tools\Server\Restore Web site.

During a backup, the SharePoint Migration Tool produces a cabinet file (.cab) with an .fwp extension to back up the site and then uses this .fwp file to restore the site or site collection. Developers can modify the backed-up site template before the site is restored by changing the file extension of the .fwp file to .cab and extracting the manifest.xml file. After changes are made to the manifest.xml file, the .fwp file can be repackaged and the site can be restored by using the SharePoint Migration Tool.

You can only use the SharePoint Migration Tool or FrontPage to restore a backup to a site if the site exists but no template has been applied to the site yet. You can create a nontemplated site in the following ways:

- Using the Windows SharePoint Services pages, you can create a new site on the New SharePoint Site page. After creating the site, you should stop the creation process on the Template Selection page before choosing and applying a template.

- Using the Stsadm.exe tool, use the CreateWeb operation without using the –sitetemplate parameter—for example: `stsadm.exe -o createweb -url http://woodgrove/MySubSite`

- Using FrontPage, select File\New\Subsite, and then select any template except for SharePoint Team Site. This will apply a FrontPage site template to the site;

it will not apply a Windows SharePoint Services site template to the site, and the site can be used to restore sites that were backed up.

- Using the Windows SharePoint Services Object Model.

At this point, the SharePoint Migration Tool can be used to restore a site or site collection. To restore a site or site collection, you use the SharePoint Migration Tool with the following parameters:

```
smigrate.exe -r -w <Web site URL> -f <backup filename> -u <username> -pw <password>]
```

The –r parameter restores a site to a new location.

SharePoint Portal Server Data Backup and Restore Utility

The SharePoint Portal Server Data Backup and Restore utility is installed by default when SharePoint Portal Server is installed. You must run the SharePoint Portal Server Data Backup and Restore utility from the server itself in a single server scenario or from any of the front-end Web servers in a server farm scenario. SQL Server 2000 Client Tools must also be installed on the server from which backups and restores are performed. The SharePoint Portal Server Data Backup and Restore utility performs the following functions:

- Backs up and restores all databases within the server farm or all databases of a single portal site. That is, all databases except the configuration database.

- Restores content indexes and content sources on the corporate portal site.

- Backs up Windows SharePoint Services site databases.

- Supports moving a portal site from one farm to another.

- Restores an index server.

Note   The configuration database is not included in the backup because it would be impossible to guarantee a successful restore of it. The configuration database that is to be restored would need to match the existing topology exactly. Furthermore, existing team sites stored across *all* the content databases would have to match exactly the sites in the configuration database being restored. Because there is no way to guarantee this, it is useless to back up the configuration database. The correct restore procedure indicates that you must rebuild your farm—which will rebuild the configuration database and ensures a new configuration database is created that is guaranteed to work.

The SharePoint Portal Server Data Backup and Restore utility creates an XML-based manifest file that lists all the individual backup files for SharePoint Portal Server and Windows SharePoint Services databases. To use the SharePoint Portal Server Data Backup and Restore utility successfully, the following accounts must have access to the directory containing the backup files:

■ The account for the Microsoft Windows NT service corresponding to the SQL Server instance must have write access to the directory if you want to create a backup; the account needs read access if you want to restore a backup.

■ The search service and the account that the Microsoft SharePoint Portal Server Search service runs under must have write access to the directory.

■ The current user must have write access to the directory.

The current user must also have the following rights:

■ The user is a member of the Local Administrators group on the (optional) backward-compatible document library server.

■ The user is a member of the Backup Operators group on the content index servers.

■ The user is a member of the SQL Server 2000 System Administrator's role if you want to restore a backup. For a backup, it is required that the user account has write access to the configuration database and backup permission on the particular databases that are being backed up.

Note After making a backup, you must click the Reset button before performing any other actions.

You can run the SharePoint Portal Server 2003 Data Backup and Restore utility from the Start menu or by typing **Spsbackup** from the command line in the \bin directory of the server running SharePoint Portal Server. This tool provides a graphic user interface that is easy to use, as shown in Figure 28-1.

You can also run the SharePoint Portal Server 2003 Data Backup and Restore utility by using the Spsbackup.exe command-line utility, which enables you to write a script that backs up the SharePoint Portal Server databases on a schedule. Run Spsbackup.exe with the following command-line parameters:

```
spsbackup { /all | /teamdbs | /ssodb | /doclib |
{ /portal site portal siteUrl [ /service { sitedbs | index } ] } } /file
    backupfilepath\fileprefix [/overwrite]
```

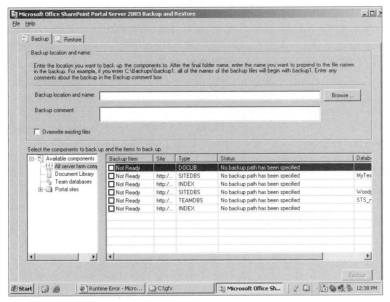

Figure 28-1 Using the SharePoint Portal Server 2003 Data Backup and Restore utility

You must choose one of the following parameters for the type of data to back up:

- **/all.** Backs up all data from all portal sites and team databases.

- **/teamdbs.** Backs up all team databases.

- **/ssodb.** Backs up all data from single sign-on databases.

- **/doclib.** Backs up all data from backward-compatible document libraries.

- **/portal site *portal siteUrl*.** Backs up the portal site with the specified portal site URL.

You might also add the following optional parameter to the /portal site portal siteUrl parameter:

- **/service.** Backs up a specific service, either sitedbs or index.

The following parameters are added next:

- **/file backupfilepath\fileprefix.** This required parameter specifies the files that contain the backup image. backupfilepath is the directory to the location of backup files, and fileprefix is the first few characters in the file names of the backup files.

- **/overwrite.** This optional parameter overwrites any previous backup image.

- **/DMLocalPath.** During a backup of the backward-compatible document library, the backup of the Web Storage System is stored to a local drive. This location will only hold the document library backup temporarily because the SharePoint Portal Server Data Backup and Restore utility pulls the backup file out of there and copies it to the backup file path specified using the /file parameter. If there is not enough disk space in the default location on the local drive, you can specify a different local path on the server.

The SPBackup.exe Utility

The SPBackup.exe tool determines which site collections have changed and generates a batch file that, when run on a server running Windows SharePoint Services, backs up changed site collections using the Stsadm.exe tool. The batch file created by SPBackup.exe will not back up SharePoint Portal Server 2003 portal sites. However, when run on a server running SharePoint Portal Server, SPBackup.exe will generate a batch file that backs up team sites, personal sites, and workspace sites on the server. You must install SPBackup.exe to the same folder as Stsadm.exe.

> **On the Resource Kit CD**   The SPBackup.exe tool can be found on the Resource Kit CD.

The SPBackup.exe tool uses the following syntax: Spbackup {-a | -d | -w} [-f filename]. You can use the –a parameter to generate a file that backs up all modified site collections. The –d parameter generates a file that backs up all site collections that have changed in the past day. The –w parameter generates a file that backs up all site collections that have changed in the past week, and the –f filename parameter specifies the name of the batch file to create. If this argument is omitted, the batch file will be named SPBakOut.bat.

SAN Snapshoting

Taking a snapshot of the databases hosted on a SAN (storage area network) will be supported if all the databases are backed simultaneously. This includes the configuration database. This is the only scenario where the backing up of a configuration database is supported. You must restore a snapshot image to the same machine on which the backup was taken.

> **Note**   Except in SAN Snapshoting, backing up the configuration database is not recommended because the configuration database is not restored during a restore operation. Instead, it is rebuilt on the fly during the restore operation.

Recovering SharePoint Sites and Personal Sites

Windows SharePoint Services site collections cannot be restored individually from a complete database backup. If you restore a database, all content is overwritten, including site collections, subsites, documents, lists, and content within those sites. Restoring an entire database simply to recover a single site collection, personal site, document, or list is not recommended, because all users of that site are affected when the database is restored. This is particularly annoying in situations where one or several sites are damaged. In such scenarios, you want to get the server back up and running in the shortest time possible. Instead, use the Stsadm.exe utility for backing up and restoring the individual personal sites and site collections. Use the SharePoint Migration Tool to back up and restore individual sites.

Backing Up Site Collections

The –o backup parameter of the Stsadm.exe tool backs up only the specified site collection; it does not back up an entire virtual server. If you specify the virtual server root URL, only one site collection belonging to that virtual server is backed up, which is the site collection that lives at the root of the virtual server. Other site collections are not backed up. The following example shows how to use the Stsadm.exe backup parameter to back up a site collection on a portal site. The over-write parameter overwrites the existing backup file name.

```
stsadm -o backup -url http://www.woodgrove.com/sites/myexamplesitecollection
-filename myexamplesitecollectionbackup.bak -overwrite
```

If you add additional site collections to your server farms, you can use the Stsadm.exe enumsites parameter to list all the site collections that have been created within a SharePoint virtual server. The enumsubwebs parameter lists all subsites within a site collection. Use the enumsites parameter in your script to parse the list of sites. Then, using the Stsadm.exe backup parameter, walk through the list to create a backup of each site collection. The following examples show how to use the enumsites and enumsubwebs parameters to enumerate the site collections in a Windows SharePoint Services virtual server and to enumerate all subsites in a site collection.

```
stsadm -o enumsites -url http://www.woodgrove.com/
```

```
stsadm -o enumsubwebs -url
http://www.woodgrove.com/sites/myexamplesitecollection
```

The following example shows how to use the SharePoint Migration tool to back up a site collection.

```
smigrate -w http://www.woodgrove.com/sites/ myexamplesitecollection -f
    c:\backup\mybackup.fwp
```

The amount of disk space required to back up each site collection depends on the amount of content within the site collection and how long the backups are kept on the disk before being moved to a tape drive. You can estimate the maximum amount of hard disk space required for site collection backups by using the following formula:

The number of site collections × Disk quota = Maximum disk space required

For example, if you have 10 site collections with the quotas set for 100 MB, you need 1000 MB of disk space for backing up site collections. This also means that the Windows SharePoint Services databases containing the site collections are affected by 1000 MB.

Restoring Site Collections

To restore individual site collections, use the Stsadm.exe tool with the Restore option. There are three options for restoring sites with the Stsadm.exe backup:

- **Restore a site collection over an existing site.**   When you overwrite an existing site, all existing site data—including subsites and content—are completely overwritten.

- **Restore a site collection to a new site on the same server.**   This is the recommended option for recovering data without overwriting the entire site collection. When you restore a site collection to a new site on the same server, you can copy the data from the restored site collection or subsite back to its original site.

- **Restore a site to a separate server.**   The separate server must have a separate installation of SharePoint Products and Technologies. This option is more complex and requires additional hardware to purchase and manage. Also, the following settings and configurations of the backup server must match those of the restore server:

    - The type of installation configuration.

    - The schema or XML files on the file system defining fields or global customizations.

    - Managed paths.

    - Domain. The user's domain should be the same. For example, suppose a server is in domain A and you would try to restore on a server in domain B. If domain B and domain A are not connected, the user might not be able to access the site.

    - Solution package. For example, if the Office value pack is installed on the source server but not on the target server, a restored site might not work.

    - Any user-added front-end templates, Web Parts, and changes to layouts.

    - Any changes made by the user to the IIS metabase.

To restore a site from a backup file, either to a new site or a separate server, use the Stsadm.exe restore parameter. Use the overwrite parameter to replace any existing site at the new location. Before running this command, ensure that a content database exists for the restored site collection. To create a new content database, go to the Manage Content Databases page from the Virtual Server Settings page, as shown in Figure 28-2. On this page, select Add A Content Database.

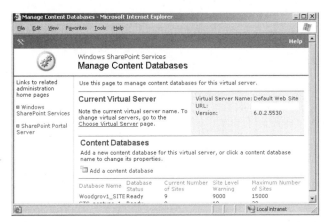

Figure 28-2   Creating a new content database on the Manage Content Databases page

The following example restores a site collection to the original site or to a new site:

```
stsadm -o restore -url http://www.woodgrove.com/sites/myexamplesitecollection
 -filename myexamplesitecollectionbackup.bak -overwrite
```

The following example restores a site collection by using the SharePoint Migration Tool:

```
smigrate -r -w http://www.woodgrove.com/mysitecollection -f c:\backup\mybackup.fwp
```

Backing Up and Restoring Personal Sites

Like site collections, personal sites—which are discussed in Chapter 23, "Personalization Services in SharePoint Products and Technologies,"—can be backed up using the Stsadm.exe utility. By default, personal sites content is contained in the site database of the portal site. You could use the SharePoint Portal Server Data Backup and Restore utility to back up the personal sites content, but then you would not be able to restore individual personal sites. Instead, you would have to restore the entire site database. Stsadm.exe can back up and restore individual users' personal sites, including all subsites, files in document libraries or lists, security and permission settings, and feature settings.

The Stsadm.exe enumsites parameter lists all personal sites that have been created on the portal site. The enumsubwebs parameter lists all subsites within a site collection. Use the enumsites parameter to parse the list of personal sites, and then back up each personal site to a file. The following example shows how to enumerate personal sites on the portal site:

```
stsadm -o enumsites -url http://www.woodgrove.com/
```

The following example shows how to use the Stsadm.exe backup parameter to back up an individual personal site:

```
stsadm.exe -o backup -url http://www.woodgrove.com/personal/woodgrove_kberge
 -filename "MySite.bak"
```

To restore a personal site from an Stsadm.exe backup file, use the **Stsadm.exe** command with the restore parameter. The following example shows how to use the restore parameter to restore a personal site to its original site or another site:

```
stsadm.exe -o restore -url
http://www.woodgrove.com/personal/woodgrove_kberge
 -filename "MySite.bak" -overwrite
```

The amount of disk space to back up personal sites depends on the following factors:

- The number of personal sites

- The amount of content in each personal site

- The amount of time that personal site backups are kept on disk before they are moved to a tape drive

You can estimate the maximum amount of disk space required for backing up the individual personal sites by using the following calculation:

The number of My Sites × Disk quota = Maximum disk space required

For example, if you have 2000 users, each with a personal site and 100-MB storage limit set on each personal site, the maximum amount of disk space required for the personal sites backup is approximately 200 GB. This also means that the portal site database, which contains the personal sites data, is equally affected by the extra 200 GB of data. Keep in mind that most personal sites will not use disk space in amounts approaching the quota. Therefore, the average disk space required for personal sites will be much lower than the quota. Set the quota high enough to accommodate the occasional large personal site. Setting the quota too low could result in support calls from users needing more space.

Recovering Individual SharePoint Sites

Although strictly speaking the SharePoint Migration Tool is used for site migration, it provides much value in disaster-recovery scenarios. The SharePoint Migration Tool can be used to back up and restore or migrate individual sites. The following example shows how to use the SharePoint Migration Tool to back up an individual site; the –e parameter is used to exclude subsites during backup:

```
smigrate -w http://www.woodgrove.com/mysitecollection -f c:\temp\myback.fwp -e
```

> **Note**   If you are migrating to a large number of sites, you should manually back up each site separately and restore each site after backup to prevent possible memory usage errors.

The Stsadm.exe tool and the SharePoint Migration Tool offer similar capabilities. However, you should bear in mind the following important differences. The Stsadm.exe tool can be used to back up an entire site collection. It is also only capable of restoring the entire site collection. To perform a backup or restore with the Stsadm.exe tool, you must be an administrator on the Windows SharePoint Services machine and run the command locally. The SharePoint Migration Tool can be used to back up and restore one individual site or subsite as long as you are an administrator of that site. You can run the SharePoint Migration tool from a machine that does not have Windows SharePoint Services installed. Another very important difference is between the Stsadm.exe tool and the SharePoint Migration Tool is the data that actually gets backed up and restored. The backups and restores made with Stsadm.exe are full-fidelity operations, which means that all data and customizations are preserved. The SharePoint Migration tool is not full-fidelity, so security, personalization, and global administration settings will be lost on the restored site.

Recovering Portal Sites

You can restore portal sites using the SharePoint Portal Server Data Backup and Restore utility or the SharePoint Portal Server Central Administration page.

The SharePoint Portal Server Data Backup and Restore utility is sensitive to the type of portal site being restored. If a corporate portal site is available, any portal site being restored automatically becomes a divisional portal site and consumes shared services from the corporate portal site. You cannot restore a divisional portal site into a server farm that is missing the corporate portal site. The corporate portal site must be restored before a divisional portal site can be restored. The SharePoint Portal Server Data Backup and Restore utility restores all databases. After that, the portal site is created, the team databases are added to the virtual server, and all content indexes on the appropriate servers are restored. This is the best way available to recover a portal site as completely as possible.

> **Note**   Some information for the portal site is not restored and must be configured after restore has completed. This includes proxy settings, custom Web Parts, customized templates, e-mail settings, and various registry settings described in the documentation.

To restore a portal site from the SharePoint Portal Server Data Backup and Restore utility

To restore the portal site from SharePoint Portal Server, perform the following steps:

1. On the front-end Web server where SharePoint Portal Server is installed, start the SharePoint Portal Server Data Backup and Restore utility.

2. Click the **Restore** tab, and then click **Browse** to browse to the latest backup manifest file.

3. On the left side of the window, under **Available Components**, click **All Server farm components** under **Select the component to restore and the items to restore**.

4. On the right side of the window, all other portal sites have the restore status of **Cannot be selected**; the portal site that you need to restore has a restore status of **Parameters needed**.

5. Select the portal site labeled **Parameters needed**, and then click **Edit**.

6. By default, the original values of the portal site to be restored are displayed, including the portal site name, portal site URL, database file names, and information. Ensure that all these parameters are correct, and then click **OK**.

> **Note**   If a portal site must be restored and the databases for the portal site still exist in SQL Server, you must enter new database names for the portal site's database because the SharePoint Portal Server Data Backup and Restore utility cannot restore over an existing database.

7. The portal site's status is set to **Ready**. Select the **Ready** check box, and then click **Restore**.

8. After the portal site has been restored, click **Extend** to extend the restored portal site to the second front-end Web server.

> **Note**   You must unextend the virtual server for the portal site before restoring the portal site on the first front-end Web server with the SharePoint Portal Server Data Backup and Restore utility. Once you have done this, you only have to extend the virtual server on the other front-end Web servers.

To restore a portal site from SharePoint Portal Server Central Administration
The SharePoint Portal Server Central Administration page also offers the option to restore a portal site. This option can be used to restore a portal site to an empty virtual server on a different server farm. This option restores the portal site without restoring the search configuration and content indexes. The information in the existing site, services, and user profile databases are restored, but the default search configuration for new portal sites is used. To fully restore a portal site, you should use the SharePoint Portal Server Data Backup and Restore utility.

1. On the SharePoint Portal Server Central Administration page, in the Portal Site and Virtual Server Configuration section, click **Create a portal site**.

2. On the Create Portal Site page, in the Portal site Creation Options section, click **Restore a portal site**.

3. In the Restore Portal site From Database section, perform the following steps:

   a. In the **Site database server** list, select the content database server.

   b. In the **Site database name** box, type the name of the content database from which you want to restore the portal site.

   c. In the **User profile database server** list, select the database server that hosts the user profile database.

   d. In the **User profile database name** box, type the name of the user profile database from which you will restore user profile information for the portal site.

   e. In the **Services database server** list, select the database server that hosts the services database.

   f. In the **Services database name** box, type the name of the services database from which you will restore services for the portal site.

4. In the Site URL section, perform the following steps:

   a. In the **Virtual Server** list, click the existing virtual server on the server that hosts the portal site.

   b. In the **URL** box, type the URL that users use to connect to the portal site.

   By default, this URL is **http://server_name/**.

5. Click **OK**. On the Create Portal site Confirmation page, click **OK** to begin to restore the portal site.

Restoring the Backward-Compatible Document Library

The backward-compatible document library is an optional component based on the Web Storage System, which can be used in organizations that are migrating from SharePoint Portal Server 2001 to SharePoint Portal Server 2003.

To restore data to a backward-compatible document library

The backward-compatible document library can be backed up using the SharePoint Portal Server Data Backup and Restore utility. You can restore data to a backward-compatible document library on the same server or a new server.

1. Delete all document libraries by using the SharePoint Portal Server Central Administration page on the Change Document Library Settings page.

> **Tip** Because you have lost your Document Management server, you are not actually deleting the document libraries. What you are doing is deleting the entries for them in the configuration database. When you still have a working Document Management server, deleting the document library this way deletes both the entry in the configuration database and the physical document library.

> **Note** For SharePoint Portal Server, delete any document libraries associated with portal sites by using the Site Settings page for each portal site. Delete any document libraries not associated with portal sites by using the following URL: *http://ServerName:PortNumber/sps/DmWorkspaceDelete .aspx?WorkspaceName=NameOfWorkspace*.

2. Remove the document management server from the server farm topology by removing it from the component assignments.

3. Remove the document management server from the server farm.

4. Install the document management component of SharePoint Portal Server on the newly built server.

5. Add the document management server to the server farm.

6. Add the document management server to the server farm topology by adding it to the component assignments. If you want to restore the data to a server with a new name, you should reconnect to the document libraries using the same names that you used on the previous server.

7. Restore the document management components to the server using the Share-Point Portal Server Data Backup and Restore utility. If necessary, you can use the Change Document Library Settings page to connect to the document library and associate it with a portal site.

Recovering Different Types of Servers

In SharePoint Products and Technologies solutions, different servers can play different roles: the role of front-end Web server, search server, index management and job server, or database server. In a single-server scenario, all roles are fulfilled by the same server. In small, medium, or large server farm scenarios, several servers work together performing different roles to provide portal site services. At this point, you've seen how to use Stsadm.exe, the SharePoint Portal Server Data Backup and Restore utility, and the SharePoint Portal Server Central Administration page to back up and restore information. This section contains additional information about recovering each type of server.

Backing Up and Restoring Front-End Web Servers

Front-end Web servers are distinct from other servers in a SharePoint Portal Server server farm because they can store application customizations (such as custom WPWeb Parts) on the local file system that cannot be recovered using the SharePoint Portal Server Data Backup and Restore utility. It is recommended that you back up these servers by using the Automated System Recovery Wizard in the Backup Utility of Windows Server 2003. The front-end Web servers also provide the Internet Information Services (IIS) 6.0 virtual servers, application pools, and customized data for all the portal sites and Windows SharePoint Services sites. Each of the front-end Web servers contains IIS metadata, which contains configuration data for the virtual servers and application pools for the sites and for customized components including templates, assemblies, and Web Part packages.

Maintain the data for each individual front-end Web server in a central location, such as a shared network folder, so that these components can easily be copied and reinstalled when a server must be recovered. For example, create a shared network folder with a subdirectory for each front-end Web server in the server farm, and use a regularly scheduled script to do the backup. You should also copy the data on the shared network folder to a tape and include it in your normal tape backup and rotation strategy. Schedule your backup script to run on a regular basis, taking into account how often data is changed on the front-end Web servers.

If a front-end Web server fails, you can quickly re-image it using your standard image. Then you can copy, restore, and reinstall the necessary components on the recovered server. The following data should be copied or backed up to the shared library for each front-end Web Server:

- IIS metabase
- Root directories of Windows SharePoint Services–extended virtual servers
- Custom Web Part assemblies
- Custom templates
- Add-in software

The following sections discuss these components in detail.

IIS Metabase

IIS automatically backs up the metabase on each front-end Web server to the %WinDir%System32\inetsrv\MetaBack directory. Back up the entire MetaBack directory for each individual front-end Web server to its own server subdirectory on the shared network location.

> **Note**   You cannot just copy the metadata from one front-end Web server to another because the metadata is unique to each implementation of IIS 6.0.

You can also use the **iisback.vbs** command-line utility to schedule and perform regular backups of the metabase on each front-end Web server remotely, beyond the normal automatic backup schedule. You should also manually create IIS 6.0 metabase backups before and after making any changes to virtual servers or application pools so that the configuration can be quickly restored if necessary.

Root Directories

The root directory of a Windows SharePoint Services–extended virtual server contains the Web.config files, which are text files that contain custom XML elements or options for Web Parts and Web Part pages for each virtual server on the front-end Web Servers. You should back up the complete root directory for each front-end Web server to the shared library on a regular basis. The tree must be restored to the same path from which it was copied, and it must correspond to the paths identified within the IIS 6.0 metadata.

Custom Web Part Assemblies

Custom Web Part assemblies should be kept in the shared directory and reinstalled on the front-end Web servers when new servers are added to the server farm or restored after a failure. Custom Web Part assemblies are located by default in either the bin folder under the virtual server root directory of the computer running SharePoint Portal Server or the Global Assembly Cache (GAC) folder %WinDir%assembly, depending on your software development best practices and standards.

Assemblies are unique, and each one can have different installation instructions. Some assemblies require that you edit the registry. Keep the directions for installing each assembly along with each assembly in the shared directory.

Custom Templates

If you have customized any site templates, these should be included in your regular script or backup process for each front-end Web server and copied to the network shared library. Copy the following directories:

- systemroot\Program Files\Common Files\Microsoft Shared\Web Server Extensions \60\config\

- systemroot\Program Files\Common Files\Microsoft Shared\Web Server Extensions \60\template\

Add-in Software

Add-in software includes the following:

- Language template packs for Windows SharePoint Services

- Web Part page solutions (third-party-developed aspx pages that include Web Parts)

- Templates that work with Microsoft Office

- Microsoft Office Web Parts and Components, which is a collection of Web Parts

If you are using any add-in software packages, they must be reinstalled after restoring a front-end Web server. The backups should be located in the shared directory so that they can be reinstalled after a front-end Web server has been restored or when a new front-end Web server is added to the server farm.

Optional Backups

There is other data that is not intended to be restored to the front-end Web server but that is interesting enough to archive for analysis and long-term off-line reference. You might consider backing up the following log files:

- **Internet Information Services (IIS) logs.**   %WinDir%System32\Logfiles \W3svc<IIS-instance-number>*.log.

- **Usage analysis log.**   %WinDir%System32\LogFiles\STS\ (available only if usage analysis is enabled).

- **Other Windows SharePoint Services logs.**   STSAdm.log and OWSTimer.log from the %PersonalFolder%Local Settings\Temp directory. For STSAdm.exe, %PersonalFolder% is the personal folder of the person who installed Windows SharePoint Services on the front-end Web server. The STSAdm.log contains information related to operations performed using the Stsadm.exe tool. By default, the server log level is set to 0, which causes only errors to be logged. For OWSTimer.log, %PersonalFolder% is the personal folder of the account that the Owstimer.exe service process is running as, which is the same as the administrative application pool identity. The OWSTimer.log contains error information reported by the SPTimer service.

Front-End Web Server Backup Size

The size of a front-end Web server backup depends on your customer and how much customization is done on the front-end Web servers. A reasonable estimate based on a medium server farm solution consisting of two front-end Web servers is approximately 50 MB for each server. You can estimate the maximum amount of hard disk space required for front-end Web server backups by using the following formula:

The number of front-end Web servers × 50 MB = Estimated disk space required

You must also plan adequate space for backing up the IIS log files. You can estimate the space required by using the following formula:

The number of days of logging × Daily log file size = Estimated disk space required

For example, if you want to preserve 30 days of logs with an average daily log file size of 1 GB, you need 30 GB.

To recover a front-end Web server

To restore a front-end Web server, perform the following steps:

1. Install your standard image by using your standard imaging tools and best practices.

2. Configure Microsoft Network Load Balancing or your third-party load-balancing solution, and test it to ensure that load balancing is functioning properly with the new server.

3. Copy the Inetpub and IIS metabase data for the front-end Web server from its shared backup directory, and then restore the IIS metabase and reinstall any custom assemblies, templates, and add-in software components. If you did not use a standard port number for SharePoint Central Administration, you must change the port number to use Central Administration on that server.

4. Connect the server to the existing configuration database for the server farm.

5. Add the front-end Web server to the server topology as a Web server. If this server is a front-end Web server in a medium server farm, enable the search component and force propagation of the content indexes to ensure that the search server has current information.

Backing Up and Restoring Search Servers

Search servers typically do not need the same level of protection as database servers or front-end Web servers because searching can be set up to be redundant within medium and large server farms. In a medium server farm, the front-end Web servers also provide search services for the server farm; in a large server farm, two dedicated search servers provide search services. In either solution, if one of the search servers becomes unavailable, the redundant search server continues to provide search services until the failed server is recovered. If a search index contains corrupted data, forcing propagation of the content indexes usually overwrites the corrupted data.

To recover a search server

If you want to recover a failed search server:

1. Remove the failed server from the server farm topology.

> **Warning**   Removing a search server using the topology manager causes all content indexes to be deleted from the search server.

2. Restore the server by using your standard image, or install SharePoint Portal Server on a newly built server.

3. After the server is recovered, connect it to the existing configuration database for the server farm and add it to the server farm topology and component assignments as a search server.

4. In a medium server farm, configure the search server as a front-end Web server.

5. Force propagation of the content indexes to the restored search server to immediately update the indexes.

Backing Up and Restoring Index Management Servers

The SharePoint Portal Server Data Backup and Restore utility can be used to back up and restore content indexes on the index management servers. In the case of index management servers, redundancy is less relevant compared to other types of servers. In the event of a failure, this type of server has little immediate impact on the availability of the solution. However, the server does require attention because new content is not indexed or searchable until the index management server has been recovered. Searching continues to be available, but the search indexes become out of date as new content is added.

If a content index contains corrupted data, you can force a full index rebuild to overwrite the corrupted index. Rebuilding a content index is accomplished by indexing the locations specified by the content sources and storing the results in the content index on the index server. You can also reset a damaged content index from the SharePoint portal site Configure Search and Indexing page in the Administration console if Advanced Search Administration mode is enabled. You can enable Advanced Search Administration mode in the Administration console, although it is recommended that you enable it during installation.

When you reset a content index, you are emptying the index and you must perform a full update of that index to rebuild it. This can be a time-consuming and resource-intensive process in an environment in which there is a great deal of content. In addition, during a full content index reset, any user who has search alerts set will receive all the alerts. If an index becomes corrupted beyond recovery or if an index management server fails, you can restore the indexes from the latest backup.

To recover an index management server

With the loss of an index management server, the content indexes for the server farm, in addition to all content sources for the portal sites, are lost unless the content indexes have been backed up using the SharePoint Portal Server Data Backup and Restore utility. To recover an index management server, perform the following steps:

1. Remove the failed server from the server farm topology before restoring it.

2. Restore the server by using your standard image, or install SharePoint Portal Server on a newly built server.

3. Connect to the configuration database for the server farm, and add the server to the topology as an index and job server.

4. Restore the content indexes from the latest SharePoint Portal Server Data Backup and Restore Utility backup set. If a backup of the indexes does not exist, manually re-create any indexes and divisional content sources.

Backing Up Databases by Using SQL Server Backup Tools

SQL Server 2000 is the data store for SharePoint Products and Technologies. This means you can leverage all the knowledge you have about backing up SQL Server databases. You can use the SQL Server backup tools in addition to the native SharePoint Products and Technologies backup tools Stsadm.exe and the SharePoint Portal Server 2003 Data Backup and Restore utility. In some ways, these backup tools overlap each other, but they also complement each other. You should use Stsadm.exe if you need the finest granularity possible. Using Stsadm.exe, you can restore site collections and personal sites without having to restore the entire site database.

The SharePoint Portal Server 2003 Data Backup and Restore utility offers the most complete solution: it backs up all relevant databases as well as content sources and indexes. This is very important in deployments where it takes a long time to build indexes for all content sources. If you understand the types of databases used in SharePoint Products and Technologies, the SQL Server backup tools provide an important advantage compared to the SharePoint Portal Server 2003 Data Backup and Restore utility.

With the SQL Server backup tools, you can get a full-fidelity, complete backup of the databases used by SharePoint Products and Technologies. You can restore any or all of these databases. In a scenario where portal databases are backed up using the SQL Server backup tools, you need to remember that the index is not restored. You can restore the portal site via the SharePoint Portal Server Central Administration page after you have restored the portal databases by using the SQL Server backup tools. For this scenario to work, the spsadmin service account must either be a member of the Administrator's group on the Web front-end server or be a Windows SharePoint Services administrator. According to recommended security practices, you should not grant the spsadmin account administrator rights; on the server, the spsadmin account should be granted as few privileges as possible. By default, the content access account is granted Windows SharePoint Services administrator rights. You should create a new Windows security group, and add both the content access account and the spsadmin service account to this group. Then, using the Windows SharePoint Services administration Web pages, you should change the Windows SharePoint Services administrator account to be this Windows security group. From Windows SharePoint Services Central Administration, locate the Security Configuration section and click Set SharePoint administration group. You must have installed the SQL Server 2000 client tools to be able to use the SQL Server backup tools or use the OSQL command-line tools that are installed with the Windows Microsoft Data Engine. Both kinds of tools provide you with the possibility to perform differential backups of the relevant databases.

A *differential backup* backs up the parts of the database that have changed since the last full database backup. It also backs up any activity that took place during the differential backup, as well as any uncommitted transactions in the transaction log. Performing a differential backup minimizes the time that is necessary for backing up a frequently modified database.

> **Note** Perform a differential backup only if you have performed a full database backup. Remember that you don't back up the configuration database.

Windows SharePoint Services uses two types of databases: content databases and configuration databases. Data in the lists and libraries on SharePoint sites go into the content database. The virtual server settings, such as the mapping of a site URL to the physical storage location, go into the configuration database. SharePoint Portal Server uses two additional types of databases: the profile database and the services database. User profiles are stored in the profile database. Services information, such as gatherer logs and subscription schedules, goes into the services database.

> **Tip**   You should always restore all SharePoint Portal Server databases together. Restoring just one of the databases is not supported by Microsoft. Restoring a single Windows SharePoint Services content database is supported, though. For more information, see the SQL Server documentation.

> **Note**   This section does not discuss how to back up data located in the Windows Microsoft Data Engine (WMSDE). You will need to use the OSQL command-line tools to do this. For more information, again, see the SQL Server documentation.

Recovering Different Server Topologies

Having discussed each type of server in a SharePoint Products and Technologies solution, it is now time to see how you can recover different server topologies in case of total server failure. It is possible to back up the configuration database before backing up the content databases and, in the intervening time, have new sites created that would not be available after the restore operation was completed. Besides, the configuration database must be rebuilt during the restore operation to ensure that it exactly matches the farm and site configurations in the restored databases.

To restore data, SQL Server Enterprise Manager allows administrators to schedule backups for each database in the system. For example, you could schedule full backups of the content, profile, and services databases every Sunday at 1:00 A.M. and schedule differential backups every other day at 1:00 A.M. SQL Server also provides command-line options that administrators can use to back up and restore data to servers. For more information, see the SQL Server documentation.

> **Note**   This section does not discuss how to back up data located in the Microsoft SQL Server Database Engine (MSDE or WMSDE). You'll need to use the OSQL command-line tools to do this. For more information, again, see the SQL Server documentation.

Hot Server Farm Swapping via SQL Log Shipping

If you want to use the SQL Log Shipping feature as a disaster recovery method for your SharePoint Portal Server or Windows SharePoint Services deployment, you'll be interested to learn that this is a supported method of disaster recovery. But, before you can use this method, you'll first need to prepare your environment to take advantage of this ability to hot-swap a server farm from one group of servers to another. Configuring log shipping between a live server farm and a mirror server farm in a different domain is supported. When failing over to the mirror farm in this scenario, the Domain Controller of the live farm's domain must be available in order to authenticate users by mapping their Security Identifiers (SID).

First, you'll need to build a mirror server farm in a remote location, using the same IIS settings on each WFE server as what presently exists on the live server farm. You'll also need to ensure you're using the same operating system (and service pack) and SharePoint language as the live server farm. You do not need to have the same number of servers in the mirror server farm, and the server roles do not need to be identically distributed. In addition, you do not need to have the same server names, hardware, or network load-balancing settings as the live server farm.

To enable SQL Log Shipping, all databases need to have a recovery mode of Full or Bulk-logged. The default configuration of our databases is as follows:

- _SITE – full recovery mode
- _PROF – simple recovery mode
- _SERV – simple recovery mode

Check the mode of each database and ensure that each is set to either Full or Bulk-logged. If necessary, change the mode by using either Enterprise Manager or Transact-SQL.

After you have prepared your mirror farm environment, you'll then need to perform a full backup of your live farm by using the SharePoint Portal Server backup/restore tool. In a Windows SharePoint Services–only server farm, you will need to back up all content databases and restore them to the mirror server farm. The mirror farm in this case would have its own configuration database and the content databases would be added to the mirror farm's virtual servers by using the Windows SharePoint Services Manage Content Databases administration pages.

Next, restore the full backup to the mirror farm by using the SPS Backup/Restore tool. If you did not change the recovery mode of the databases before making the backup, you have to change the recovery mode of the _PROF and _SERV databases to a compatible mode (as outlined in the preceding paragraphs) after restoring the databases, by using either Enterprise Manager or Transact-SQL.

Then apply the same customizations to the mirror farm as existed in the live farm, such as customized pages, custom code, or custom-built Web Parts.

After you have applied the customizations to the mirror farm, you'll then enable SQL Server log shipping between _SITE, _PROF, and _SERV databases for each portal site. Do *not* ship logs between config DBs. Also, enable log shipping for content databases hosting team or personal sites. (These sites can be hosted on different virtual servers from the portal sites or on the same virtual server.) Configure update frequency according to your Service Level Agreements and network traffic requirements.

To enable SQL Log Shipping, the databases on the secondary server need to be in Standby or No Recovery mode. This configuration can be accomplished only by manually restoring all databases a second time, using either Enterprise Manager or Transact-SQL:

- If no customizations have been applied to the mirror farm, the same database backups created by the SPS Backup/Restore tool can be used to perform the second restore to put the databases in standby or no recovery mode.

- If some customizations have been applied to the mirror farm, use either Enterprise Manager or Transact-SQL to back up and restore the databases on the secondary SQL server to put the databases in Standby or No Recovery mode.

Note   In Enterprise Manager, you specify standby mode by selecting the Leave Database Read-Only And Able To Restore Additional Transaction Logs option from the Recovery Completion State section in the Options tab in the Restore Database dialog box. No Recovery mode can be specified by selecting the Leave Database Nonoperational But Able To Restore Additional Transaction Logs option. In Transact-SQL, you use the RESTORE DATABASE command with the WITH STANDBY or WITH NORECOVERY options to reach the corresponding mode. When specifying standby mode, also select the Terminate Users In Database check box. Doing this is important because the mirror farm databases are read-only and could have some connections that would cause transaction logs to fail to be applied.

In the SQL Log Shipping wizard, when presented with the Add Destination Database dialog box, choose the Use Existing Database option and select the corresponding database. In this dialog box, you can also select the Allow Database To Assume Primary Role option, which lets the destination database become a new log shipping source database and thus permits a possible role reversal between primary and secondary servers.

Perform weekly full backups of the live farm and restores to the mirror farm to ensure the configuration DB is kept up to date with any server farm configuration or search configuration changes.

What if your live server farm fails? What then? Well, here are the steps to restore a downed farm to a mirror farm:

1. Change the role of the secondary SQL server to a primary server to bring the portal databases online.

   a. Before running any stored procedures to change roles, ensure that there are no open connections to the databases participating in SQL Log Shipping. The stored procedures will fail if SQL Server cannot obtain exclusive access to the databases.

      In every machine that you installed SharePoint Portal Server 2003, stop the **Sharepoint Portal Administration** (spsadmin) service.

      Close all other connections made through Enterprise Manager, Query Analyzer, or any other utilities.

   b. During the initial log shipping configuration, you could have selected the **Allow database to assume primary role** option. If you want the secondary server to be the primary server and start log shipping from that server, you need this option. Regardless of your choice, you can follow the same procedure to upgrade your secondary server to a primary server. This option affects only whether you can use the new primary server as a log shipping source or not.

2. Delete existing portal sites, and detach (rather than delete) databases.

3. Restore portal sites (and team sites living on the same vserver) by performing the following steps:

   a. On mirror farm, navigate to the **http://<servername:port>/sps /portalcreate.aspx** page.

   b. Select the **Restore a portal** option.

   c. Provide database names for the mirror _SITE, _PROF, and _SERV databases.

   d. Specify the same portal site URL and virtual server name as for the live site.

4. Restore team sites (those living on vservers that do not contain portal sites) by completing the following steps:

   a. In Windows SharePoint Services Central Administration, click **Configure virtual server settings**, click on the virtual server name, and click **Manage Content Databases**.

   b. Click to select the database name, select the **Remove content database** check box, and click **OK**.

   c. On the Manage Content Databases page, select the **Add a content database and specify the name of the restored content database for this virtual server** option.

   d. Repeat these steps for each content database.

5. Apply any site-specific customizations not enabled by step 4 of Environment Preparation (adding custom Web Parts, for example).

6. Change VIP from live farm to point to mirror farm.

7. Start full crawl for each content index.

Here are some considerations to make when performing these tasks. First, we recommend a periodic execution of "delete portals and detach databases; reconnect them to mirror farm config DB" steps to ensure there are no hidden surprises when actual fail-over occurs. Running these steps in a test environment will ensure that any custom code you've written will be transferred to the new farm environment, and doing so will keep your skills up on how to do this in the event you encounter a real disaster-recovery scenario.

Second, avoid using static URLs embedded in content because this could be problematic on the mirror farm.

Third, users should consider the mirror farm to be read-only when the live farm fails. Users will have access to data and can make changes to that data, but these changes will be lost when the live farm is brought back online.

Fourth, log shipping is not a substitute for periodic full backups using Share-Point Portal Server backup and restore! Ensure that you are performing regular back-ups of your data. This is always a best practice.

Remember, while the mirror farm is actively engaged in log shipping, all portal databases are in read-only standby mode and remain in this state until there's a role change. Essentially, this means that performing weekly SharePoint Portal Server backups and restores to the mirror farm requires disabling SQL Log Shipping.

> **More Info**   For more information, see the white paper "INF: Microsoft SQL Server 2000: How to Set Up Log Shipping" at *http://support.microsoft.com /default.aspx?scid=kb%3Ben-us%3BQ323135*, the Microsoft Knowledge Base article 314515 at *http://support.microsoft.com/default.aspx?scid=kb; en-us;314515*, and the article "Log Shipping in SQL Server 2000" at *http: //www.microsoft.com/technet/prodtechnol/sql/2000/maintain/logship1.mspx*.

Troubleshooting a Single-Server Restore

If you use the Backup And Restore tool to back up a single-server deployment of SharePoint Portal Server 2003 that uses the Microsoft SQL Server 2000 Desktop Engine (MSDE) and restore the data to another server in a different domain or to a different server farm deployment, you might experience problems with receiving alerts when content on the portal site changes. You might also find that content is missing from the search results when you search the portal site.

To restore data to a single server

You can either build a server with the same name or with a new name by following these steps:

1. Install SharePoint Portal Server.

2. Create the configuration database.

3. Restore everything except for the configuration database. This can be done using the SharePoint Portal Server Data Backup and Restore utility. Click the **Edit** button on the **Restore** tab of this utility to specify the settings for each component, and select a new name for the server if you are restoring to a server with a different name.

   These issues might occur if the user account that is used to restore the Share-Point Portal Server data is different from the account that created the portal site. The account that is used when restoring data should already be a member of the Administrators site group.

To assign group membership

Administrator site group membership can be assigned to a user on the Edit Site Group Membership page.

1. Connect to your portal site, and then click **Site Settings**.

2. On the Site Settings page, under **General Settings**, click **Manage users**.

3. On the Manage Users page, select the check box next to the user account that you want to assign to the Administrators site group, and then click **Edit Site Groups of Selected Users**.

4. On the Edit Site Group Membership page, in the **Site Group Membership** area, select the **Administrator - Has full control of the Web site** check box, and then click **OK**.

Recovering a Server Farm

If an entire server farm is lost beyond recovery, you have little choice but to rebuild it. Remember that the type of a portal site (corporate, divisional) being restored is embedded in the backup image so that the portal site retains the same or a compatible type after it is restored. Table 28-2 shows what types of portal sites can be restored to different kinds of destination deployments.

Table 28-2   Federation Matrix. Shared Services Matrix

Backup\Dest	Independent portal site	Intra-federatedShared Services child	Inter-federated Shared Services child	Master
Independent portal site	YES	YES	YES	YES
Child	NO	YES	YES	NO
Master	YES	YES	YES	YES*

* Should automatically set itself to a master

The first column of headers lists backup types. The first row of headers lists the restore destination deployment. "No" means that you are not allowed to restore the backup to the destination. Intra-federated portal sites are part of the same server farm as the master portal site, the shared service provider. Inter-federated portal sites are part of a different server as the master portal site. Both inter-federated and intra-federated portal sites are known as shared services consumer portal sites.

To recover a server farm

1. Install and configure SQL Server 2000.

2. Load your standard image for each of the servers in the server farm by using your standard imaging tools and processes.

3. Set up the front-end Web servers:

   a. Configure Network Load Balancing on the front-end Web servers.

   b. Copy the Inetpub and IIS metabase data for each front-end Web server from the shared backup directory. Then restore the IIS metabase and reinstall any custom assemblies, templates, and add-on software components.

   c. Use SharePoint Portal Server Central Administration on the first front-end Web server to create a new configuration database, and add the server to the topology as a Web server. If this is a medium server farm with the search components located on the front-end Web server, add the server to the topology as a search server.

   d. Add the second front-end Web server to the topology, and connect it to the new configuration database. If this is a medium server farm with the search components located on the front-end Web server, add the server to the topology as a search server.

   e. Add the index management server and the search server to the topology, connecting to the new configuration database.

   f. Install SQL Server 2000 Server Client Tools and the latest SQL Server 2000 Service Pack on the first front-end Web server in the server farm.

4. Restore the portal sites:

    a. Start the SharePoint Portal Server Data Backup and Restore utility on the first front-end Web server in the server farm.

    b. Click the **Restore** tab, and then click the most recent backup manifest file to restore. Any changes made since the last backup are lost.

    c. Restore the corporate portal site from the most recent backup. This automatically demotes it to an independent portal site with shared services disabled when it is restored. The content indexes for the corporate portal site are also restored when the corporate portal site is restored.

    d. Select the corporate portal site from the list of available portal sites.

    e. Click **Edit**, ensure that all the default restore parameters are correct, and then click **Restore**.

    f. After the portal site has been restored, use SharePoint Portal Server Central Administration to enable shared services on the restored corporate portal site.

    g. Restore each of the divisional portal sites and Windows SharePoint Services site collections from the SharePoint Portal Server Data Backup and Restore utility manifest file, and extend them to the other front-end Web servers in the server farm.

Repairing SharePoint Portal Server

If SharePoint Portal Server itself or Windows SharePoint Services is damaged, you can repair the installation of SharePoint Portal Server or Windows SharePoint Services using the SharePoint Portal Server 2003 CD-ROM. You can also repair the optional backward-compatible document library using the same CD-ROM. If you do so, the client components are repaired as well. You can repair the client components separately for the backward-compatible document library by using Add Or Remove Programs in Control Panel.

To repair client components using the command line

You can also use the command line to repair client components by following these steps:

1. On the taskbar, click **Start**, point to **All Programs**, point to **Accessories**, and then click **Command Prompt**.

2. Type **"path\setup" /f "path\SPSClient.msi"**, where *path* is the path to the setup.exe and SPSClient.msi files. Include the switch /f to repair the client components. For example, to repair the client components, where Setup.exe and SPSClient.msi are in E:\Client Files, you would type **E:\Client Files\setup" /f "E:\Client Files\SPSClient.msi**.

> **Note**   If you have removed one or more of the installation prerequisites, you cannot repair the client components unless you disable the prerequisite check. You can disable the prerequisite check by adding **DISABLEPREREQ=1** to the command line. To disable the prerequisite check in the preceding example, you would type **E:\Client Files\setup" /f "E:\Client Files\SPSClient.msi" DISABLEPREREQ=1**.

Uninstalling SharePoint Portal Server

If everything fails and SharePoint Portal Server is damaged beyond recovery, you can always remove SharePoint Portal Server. To fully remove SharePoint Portal Server, you must remove the following, in this order:

1. SharePoint Portal Server

2. Windows SharePoint Services

3. SQL Server Desktop Engine (if installed)

4. Backward-compatible document library (if installed)

5. Internet Information Server (IIS)

> **Warning**   Most files and subfolders located in installation folders will be removed. All Microsoft SQL Server databases will be detached, but not removed, from the database server. When you remove SharePoint Portal Server, all user data is left in the database files. These files are also left behind if you remove SQL Server Desktop Engine or Microsoft SQL Server.

Writing a Disaster Recovery Plan

You should write a disaster recovery plan that provides timely, accurate, consistent, and reusable solutions for emergency situations. Executing a consistent recovery plan in case of emergencies helps avoid wasting time, resources, and money, not to mention preventing a lot of stress. A disaster recovery plan should reflect a well-planned data protection strategy based on your customer's specific data protection requirements. The primary objective of disaster recovery is to minimize downtime by providing the most reliable recovery plan to restore data in the event of a server crash, database corruption, or any other form of data loss. A well-planned and thoroughly tested database recovery strategy and reliable database protection software are essential to maintain the availability of SharePoint Products and Technologies solutions.

The first step in building a disaster recovery plan is to create a strategy to monitor server health. You can rely on performance counters (which are discussed in detail in Chapter 10, "Performance Monitoring in Microsoft Office SharePoint Portal Server 2003") and diagnostic logging to provide this information. Actively capturing real-time event information is useful only if the responsible parties are proactively monitoring server health and ready to act upon this information when necessary. If problems arise, you should perform the following tasks:

- Minimize the impact of the problem.

- Perform a root-cause analysis to determine the exact nature of the problem.

- Correct the problem.

- Create a plan for providing a long-term solution and a reusable action plan should the problem reoccur.

Best Practices

This section contains best practices that should be considered during the creation of a disaster recovery plan.

Backup and Restore Strategy

To provide the most flexibility when restoring your customer's data, use the SharePoint Portal Server Data Backup and Restore utility in combination with using the Stsadm.exe utility to back up the Windows SharePoint Services site collections and My Sites. The backups should be made directly to a shared disk location and then backed up to tape following your best practices.

Back Up Regularly Using Scripts

Create scripts using Stsadm.exe and Spsbackup.exe to back up all the databases and indexes on a schedule. It is highly recommended that you perform backups when server usage is low. Because most large companies have defined requirements on mission-critical backups and restores, your schedule of backups will depend on your customer's requirements. You might need to back up more or less frequently if your customer needs to meet a Service Level Agreement or has more stringent data recovery standards in place.

The following code example uses the SharePoint Back And Restore tool to back up a portal site. The code can be copied into a batch file.

```
"C:\Program Files\SharePoint Portal Server\BIN\spsbackup" /portal site
    "http://woodgrove /file C:\\backup\MyPortal siteBackup.bak /overwrite
```

The following code example uses the Stsadm.exe tool to back up all site collections within a portal site. The code can be copied into a VBScript file (.vbs).

```
Option Explicit
Const STSADM_PATH =
    "C:\Program Files\Common Files\Microsoft Shared\web server extensions\60\BIN\stsadm"
Dim objFso, objFolder, objFiles, objFile, objShell, objExec, strResult, objXml, objSc,
    objUrl, strUrl, strFileName, strCmd
Set objFso = CreateObject("Scripting.FileSystemObject")
Set objFolder = objFso.GetFolder("C:\backup\")
Set objFiles = objFolder.Files
WScript.Echo "Begin backup"

' Delete all backup files currently present in the backup folder.
For Each objFile in objFiles
    objFile.Delete(True)
Next

' Retrieves all site collections in XML format.
Set objShell = CreateObject("WScript.Shell")
Set objExec = objShell.Exec(STSADM_PATH & " -o enumsites -url http://woodgrove/")
strResult = objExec.StdOut.ReadAll
WScript.Echo strResult

' Load XML in DOM document so it can be processed.
Set objXml = CreateObject("MSXML2.DOMDocument")
objXml.LoadXML(strResult)

' Loop through each site collection and call stsadm.exe to make a backup.
For Each objSc in objXml.DocumentElement.ChildNodes
    strUrl = objSc.Attributes.GetNamedItem("Url").Text
    strFileName = "C:\backup\" & Replace(Replace(strUrl, "http://", ""), "/", "_") &
        ".bak"
    strCmd = STSADM_PATH & " -o backup -url """ + strUrl + """ -filename """
        + strFileName + """"
    WScript.Echo "Backing up site collection " & strUrl & " to file
        " & strFileName & " using the following command " & strCmd
    objShell.Exec(strCmd)
Next

WScript.Echo "Backup of portal site collections successful"
```

The following code example shows how to call the previous VBScript file. The code can be copied into a batch file.

```
cscript [path to backup script]mybackupscript.vbs
```

Back Up to Disk or to Tape

When backing up a database, back up to a shared disk on a remote server. Consider using a clustered disk share and RAID 1 or RAID 5 protection to provide additional levels of fault tolerance for the shared backup disk. Backing up a database to a file on the same physical disk as the database is not recommended. If the disk containing the database fails, there is no way to recover it because the backup is located on the same failed disk.

After you back up the databases to a shared disk, copy them to a second location or back them up to a second medium such as tape. Archive the second copy in a secure offsite location. Keeping a week's worth of backups on disk allows recent backups to be restored more easily, because they do not have to be recovered from tape. Recovering from tape takes much longer than recovering from disk. However, it does consume a significant amount of disk space to maintain a week's worth of backups on disk.

Use your company's standard software tools and processes for backing up the data to tape and follow your best practices for tape media management and offsite storage.

Backup Schedule

It is recommended that you schedule regular backups of your SharePoint Portal Server deployment, and that you validate the integrity of those backup files by periodically restoring backups. You should verify that all the SharePoint Portal Server features perform as expected and that all data is present. Make sure you include a backup schedule in your disaster recovery plan. Table 28-3 shows an example of a backup schedule.

Table 28-3   Backup Schedule Example

Type of Backup	Day 0	Day 1	Days 2–365
SQL Server database	Nightly backup to disk; no same-day recovery	Restore from disk. Nightly copy of day 0 backup data to tape.	Restore from tape
Site collection	Nightly backup to disk; no same-day recovery	Restore from disk. Nightly copy of day 0 backup data to tape.	Restore from tape
Shadow copy	7 P.M. snapshot copy to disk; same-day restore after backup completes	Restore from disk until 7 P.M.	Not available

Single Item Recovery

Documents cannot be recovered unless they are present during the latest backup; document libraries include versioning so that a copy of each published version is saved. Team sites are usually restored to a temporary site from which users can retrieve the files they need. Portal sites are restored over the existing portal site; no individual document or list restore is available for portal sites, unless you restore a portal site to another server. You can expect a growing number of third-party vendors to provide document-level backup solutions. For an up-to-date list of third-party backup solutions, visit the Backup And Storage Management page in the Products And Utilities section of the MSD2D.com website (*http://www.msd2d.com*).

Summary

This chapter provides a thorough overview of what to do when you need to recover from a disaster. It discusses the native tools in SharePoint Products and Technologies that are used to back up and restore data. It also shows how to restore SharePoint sites, personal sites, portal sites, and backward-compatible document libraries. The recovery of different kinds of servers as well as different kinds of server topologies is discussed. The chapter provides information about repairing and uninstalling SharePoint Products and Technologies if all else fails. The chapter concludes with a discussion about what a disaster recovery plan should cover and what best practices should be kept in mind in disaster recovery scenarios.

Chapter 29

Usage Analysis Tools in SharePoint Products and Technologies

Usage analysis allows you to track how websites on your server are being used. The Internet Information Services (IIS) log and usage analysis logs from Microsoft Windows SharePoint Services and Microsoft SharePoint Portal Server can provide a realistic picture of how a portal site is used in each company. The viewing and managing of these logging mechanisms will be discussed in this chapter.

Tying this information to records collected from performance measurements of the server running SQL Server, the index server, the search server, and the Web server provides a full picture of architecture behavior. Peak usage analysis in conjunction with records obtained from performance monitoring logs can be used for capacity planning. Based on this information, you can decide if you need an additional server in the front-end Web server farm. Diagnostic logging provides another related logging mechanism, but this is not discussed in this chapter.

Managing Usage Analysis

If you want to view usage data, you can use the site administration pages or Microsoft Office FrontPage 2003. Before you're able to perform this usage analysis, you need to configure usage analysis processing. You control settings for usage analysis processing from SharePoint Central Administration. You must be an administrator of the local server computer or a member of the SharePoint administrators group to configure usage analysis settings.

From SharePoint Central Administration, you can control the following:

- **Whether or not to log usage data.**   Usage analysis is not enabled by default. If you want to use the usage analysis features for your server, you must enable the usage analysis logging process. Windows SharePoint Services log files are created daily to track usage information. When the log files are processed, a flag is added to indicate that the log file has been processed. You can check whether the log file has been processed by opening the file using Notepad or any other text editor. If you see an ampersand (&) after the top-level site Uniform Resource Locator (URL), the log file has been processed. Log files are not automatically deleted. They are preserved in the following path: %WinDir%system32 \LogFiles\STS. This is the default path, but it can be customized. If you do not want to track usage analysis data and you want to conserve disk space, you can turn off data logging for usage analysis.

  Usage analysis data is generated by Windows SharePoint Services and gathered into the Windows SharePoint Services log files, which are stored on the front-end Web servers. The name of the default log files folder is called STS. When usage analysis processing takes place, the Windows SharePoint Services logs are merged into the content databases on the computer running SQL Server or the Microsoft SQL Server Desktop Engine (Windows) (WMSDE). The log data is a summary record of transactions on your website. The IIS logs contain a complete overview of Web traffic, including calls to Web services, requests for images, and so on; the summary record contains only the information necessary to provide a usage overview.

  Usage data is kept for a limited time in the content database for historical purposes. Daily information is stored for 31 days and monthly information for 31 months. All usage data is stored as a binary image in the Webs table. Daily information is stored in the DailyUsageData column, and monthly information is stored in the MonthlyUsageData column.

- **Where the log files are stored and how many log files to create.**   By default, the log files are in %WinDir%system32\LogFiles\STS. You can specify any other location you prefer for this root log folder.

> **Note**   If you choose a different log file location, you must be sure to give the STS_WPG user group **Read**, **Write**, and **Update** permissions to the directory. Without these permissions, the usage log files cannot be created or updated by Windows SharePoint Services.

Inside this folder is a folder for every virtual server named using the Windows SharePoint Services virtual server globally unique identifier (GUID), and under those folders, a different folder for each day will be generated. The path of these folders cannot be modified.

You can configure the limit of logs to be created on a daily basis, with a maximum number of 30 log files. If you set a maximum number of n log files, this applies to each virtual server. This means that the log folders of each of the virtual servers will contain at most n log files. In other words, if this number is set to 1 there will be 1 log file for each virtual server. Having many virtual servers and having many log files might reduce performance during logging. You should consider increasing the number of log files if a front-end Web server (standalone or member of a Web farm) has log files with more than a million entries.

The front-end Web server might not have enough memory to memory-map a really large log file, which leads to a situation in which the log file might not get processed. Each hit that a front-end Web server receives uses approximately 200 bytes (B) in a log file. As a result, approximately 200 megabytes (MB) of RAM are used to memory-map a log file that contains a million hits. Memory mapping occurs only for several minutes during usage processing. Because log files are processed serially, when you have several log files, a smaller memory footprint results when a log file is processed.

> **Note**   Windows SharePoint Services logs HTTP 2.x information to the log files and does not log HTTP 3.x or HTTP 4.x information to the log file. When you use multiple log files, the log files are created at the same time, and all hits from one website are contained in the same log file. Usage data for a website is updated one time each day.

The number of requests that are sent to the back-end server during usage processing is proportional to the number of websites on the server. However, the memory footprint on the back-end server is not affected by the number of websites. The additional load that usage processing generates does not significantly affect the performance of the back-end servers on the server farm.

■ **Whether or not to process the usage logs and when to do so.**   The tracking of usage data takes up a lot of disk space on the Web front-end server and the server where the content database is located. If you want to conserve disk space, you can stick to the default option and leave usage analysis processing disabled. In this scenario, you could use third-party tools to analyze the IIS logs. However, if you want to use the site administration pages to view usage data, you need to enable the processing of the usage logs.

By default, the log files are set to be processed every day at 1:00 A.M. During this process, the content of the Windows SharePoint Services logs is aggregated, summarized, and written to the content database. You can schedule the usage log to be processed at a more convenient downtime for your websites or for your SQL Backup schedule. You can specify an interval, by specifying the start time and end time of the interval, during which the usage processing job starts. The job is guaranteed to start at some time within the interval, but you cannot control when the job ends.

If your websites are primarily used by internal employees, for example, you might schedule the log to be processed at night, when demand on the sites is lower than during working hours.

Because usage analysis processing runs only once a day, when you enable usage analysis processing, you will not see any data until the next day. Log processing is done only for a single day's worth of data. If you turn off the log processing for a week but leave the data logging turned on, the next time you turn on processing, it will process only the previous day's log files. The log files for all the days before that will remain unprocessed.

When you configure usage analysis processing for a server, it takes effect for any existing virtual servers. If you later add a virtual server, you must configure usage analysis processing again to enable usage analysis for the new virtual server.

To configure usage analysis processing for a server

To configure usage analysis processing (shown in Figure 29-1), perform the following steps:

1. Click **Start**, point to **All Programs**, point to **Administrative Tools**, and then click **SharePoint Central Administration** or **Windows SharePoint Services Central Administration**. The configuration takes effect for any existing virtual server, so it does not matter which of these pages you use.

2. Under **Component Configuration**, click **Configure usage analysis processing**.

3. In the **Logging Settings** section, select the **Enable logging** check box.

4. In the **Log file location** box, type the location to store the log file.

5. In the **Number** of log files to create box, type a number between 1 and 30.

6. In the **Processing Settings** section, select the **Enable usage analysis processing** check box.

7. Under **Run processing** between these times daily, specify the range of times to start the usage analysis log processing. In the **Start** box, select the earliest time of day to begin running log processing. In the **End** box, select the latest time to end running log processing.

8. Click **OK**.

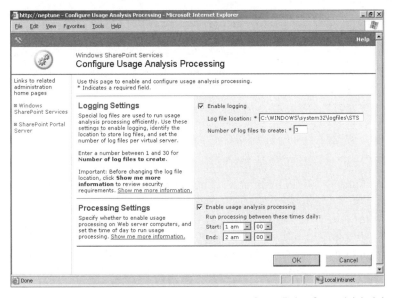

Figure 29-1   Configuring usage analysis using SharePoint Central Administration

You can also configure usage analysis processing at the command prompt by using the Stsadm.exe tool. This tool can be used to schedule the timed job responsible for starting the processing of log files.

You use the **getproperty** operation with Stsadm.exe to retrieve information about timed jobs. The **getproperty** operation takes the propertyname parameter as well as the -url parameter.

If you want to retrieve the usage analysis job settings, type the following command at the command prompt:

stsadm -o getproperty -pn job-usage-analysis -url http://<virtual server URL>

You use the **setproperty** operation with Stsadm.exe to schedule timed jobs. The **setproperty** operation takes the propertyname and propertyvalue parameters as well as the -url parameter. For a timed job, the propertyvalue parameter is the frequency and time when you want the job to be performed. If you want to schedule the usage analysis job, you can type the following command at the command prompt:

stsadm -o setproperty -pn job-usage-analysis -pv "daily between hh:mm:ss and hh:mm:ss" -url http://<servername>

For example, to schedule a job to be processed daily between midnight and 1:00 A.M., you would specify the propertyvalue parameter as

stsadm -o setproperty -pn job-usage-analysis -pv "daily between 0:00:00 and 01:00:00" -url http://woodgrove

> **Note**   You can set the start and end time of the interval to be the same in order to process the log files at a precise time. Remember to set this time at least a few minutes in the future to allow the timer job to schedule the process.

> **Warning**   When configuring usage analysis processing via SharePoint Central Administration, any changes in the processing schedule can be retrieved via the getproperty operation of stsadm.exe. Because of a bug, changes in the scheduling of the usage analysis job via the setproperty operation of stsadm.exe will not be visible in the SharePoint Central Administration pages. The changes are valid nonetheless.

Analyzing Website Usage

Usage analysis processing provides usage reports on Windows SharePoint Services sites. Site usage reports are useful for identifying which content on your Windows SharePoint Services sites is being heavily used or is used very little. This helps you to understand which sites are candidates for archiving and which sites should be kept online.

When you view a usage report in Windows SharePoint Services, the data is arranged into a tabular report. You must be a member of the administrator role (or have the **View Usage Data** right) for a site to view the site usage statistics. Summary and detailed usage reports supply information such as the following:

- Number of page hits for each individual page

- Number of unique users

- Browser and operating system information

- Referring domains and URLs

To view single site usage data

To view a site usage report (as shown in Figure 29-2), perform the following steps:

1. Navigate to the Windows SharePoint Services site, and then click **Site Settings**.

2. Click **Go to Site Administration**.

3. Under **Management and Statistics**, click **View site usage data**. Data can be displayed by monthly summary or daily summary.

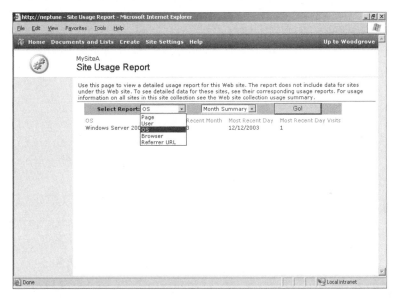

Figure 29-2   Viewing single site usage data in the site administration pages

Usage data is processed for an entire site collection on one server at a time. The usage data is collected and stored per site, which is why it can be viewed only per site, not per site collection. Even though the data is logged and stored for an entire site collection, when you view the data in the site administration pages, you can see only the data for a particular website or subsite, not for the entire site collection. You can use the Site Collection Usage Summary page to see the total number of hits for a site collection; for detailed information, you must use the Site Usage Report page for the individual site or subsite. The site collection usage reports also help you track how much storage space your sites are using. This information is gathered as part of the quota tracking for Windows SharePoint Services sites.

To view a site collection usage summary

This report provides a summary of the entire site collection usage. You can view the usage data and storage information for an entire site collection at the same time. (See Figure 29-3.)

1. Navigate to the top-level website, and select **Site Settings**.

2. Select **Go to Site Administration**.

3. Under **Site Collection Administration**, select **View Site Collection Usage Summary**.

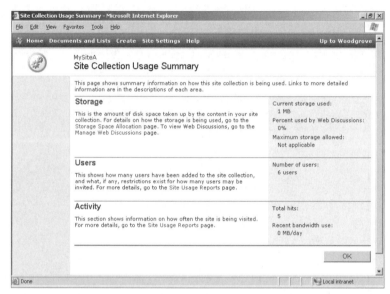

Figure 29-3   Viewing the site collection usage summary in the site administration pages

Internet Information Services (IIS) Logs

IIS logs include detailed information—such as who has visited sites and what was viewed—in terms of total visits, average visits, page views, and trends over time. The SharePoint Products and Technologies log files contain a subset of the data available in the IIS logs. This subset contains the information that is most relevant to the SharePoint Products and Technologies administrator. The IIS logs, however, contain valuable information as well. Careful analysis of the IIS logging data helps you to discover how much traffic is going to portal sites, how much is going to Windows SharePoint Services sites, and how much is going to search operations. The IIS logs also contain hits to pages that are excluded in the Windows SharePoint Services logs, specifically pages in the _layouts folders. These folders contain Windows SharePoint Services application pages, which are not important to users trying to track the use of the content in their site.

Configuring the Log Files

IIS logging is enabled by default for each virtual server. The recommended log file format is W3C, which is the default. This enables you to specify which fields are included in the log file. By limiting logging to the W3C fields that are most important to your customer, you can limit the log file size and simplify the analysis. Depending on the amount of traffic to your sites, the size of your log files can begin to consume valuable memory resources and CPU cycles. You need to balance the gathering of detailed data against the need to limit IIS log files to a manageable size and number.

Setting Up Logging

Set the logs to be created on a daily basis, which creates a new log file each day for each virtual server. Ensure that the local Administrators group and the IIS_WPG group have the appropriate permissions to access to the log files directory. Within the Logfiles directory, IIS creates a separate directory for each IIS virtual server log with naming based on the virtual server instance ID.

To view the directory and log file for each virtual server through IIS Manager

1. Right-click a virtual server, click **Properties**, and then select the **Properties** check box next to **Active log format**.

2. The **Log File** name is displayed at the bottom of the screen.

Reading the Log File Data

The IIS logs are ASCII files that can be read using a text editor, but third-party utilities or FrontPage are typically used to analyze IIS and generate meaningful, formatted reports and graphical representations of usage data. How the IIS logging information is presented and accessed depends on the tool used to present the IIS log data. IIS log files can also be logged in a database that complies with Open Database Connectivity (ODBC), such as a Microsoft SQL Server database, and SQL Server Query Analyzer can be used to generate reports.

Viewing Website Reports Using FrontPage

In a previous section, you've seen how to view usage data using the site administration pages. Various website reports, including a report about usage data, is available using the Reports view from FrontPage 2003. The Reports view allows you to display a variety of reports that provide detailed information on the files, shared content, problems, and workflow status of your website, in addition to statistics on site usage. All reports except the usage reports are always available in FrontPage and will not be discussed in this chapter. The usage reports are available only if SharePoint Team Services, FrontPage Server Extensions, or Windows SharePoint Services is installed on a server. If FrontPage is used to view usage reports about Windows SharePoint Services sites, FrontPage retrieves the usage data from the content database.

To display a particular report, activate Reports View by clicking the Web Site tab at the top of the working area of the FrontPage window and then clicking the Reports View button at the bottom of the tab. Then select the particular report you want to see from the drop-down menu at the left end of the Reports toolbar. (The menu button is labeled with the name of the currently displayed report, such as Site Summary.)

Alternatively, in any FrontPage view you can choose the particular report you want to see from the View, Reports submenu. (See Figure 29-4.) This will activate Reports View and show the selected report.

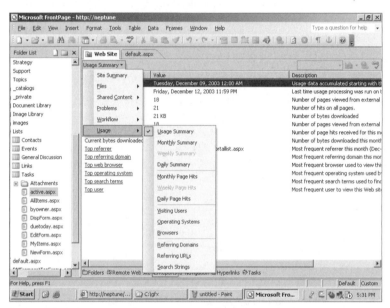

Figure 29-4   Viewing website reports in FrontPage 2003

The usage reports displays activity statistics collected by the Web server. The following table discusses all the reports that are part of the Usage view.

Table 29-1   Usage Reports

Report	Description
Usage Summary	Displays overall statistics for your site collected since inception. The inception date is one of the reported statistics.
Monthly and Daily Summaries	Displays total visits, total page hits, total hits of all kinds, and percentage of hits.

Table 29-1 Usage Reports *(continued)*

Report	Description
Monthly and Daily Page Hits	Displays, by period, the number of times that Web visitors requested each page in your site.
Visiting Users	Displays the identities of site visitors to your site. However, unless you require Web visitors to identify themselves by user name and password, this report will be blank. In intranet or extranet environments, this report provides valuable information.
Operating Systems	Reports how many visits came from computers running Windows 95, Windows 98, Windows NT, Windows 2000, Windows 2003, Macintosh, various forms of UNIX, and so forth.
Browsers	Reports how many visits came from various browsers, such as Microsoft Internet Explorer 5.0 and later, and various versions of Netscape.
Referring Domains	Reports the names of all websites—anywhere—that contain hyperlinks that Web visitors followed to your site.
Referring URLs	Reports the locations of all Web pages that contain hyperlinks that Web visitors followed to your site.
Search Strings	Reports a history of keywords that Web visitors entered on Search forms on one of the large search engines such as Yahoo! or AltaVista. This tells you how people are finding your site and what topics interest them. In intranet or extranet environments, this report will probably remain empty.

Note Because weekly usage data is not stored in the content database, the Weekly Summaries and Weekly Page Hits reports are not available when FrontPage reports are used to analyze usage data on a server where Windows SharePoint Services is installed.

When you generate reports in FrontPage, you can save or copy the data to HTML or into other Microsoft applications, such as Microsoft Office Excel. This is useful for archiving report data or for sharing it with others. You can save report data from the following types of reports: Files, Shared Content, Problems, Workflow, and Usage. You do this by clicking **Save As** on the **File** menu. You cannot save the Site Summary and Usage Summary reports. You can copy website report data to another Office program, such as Excel or a Web page in your website, by right-clicking anywhere in the aforementioned reports and clicking **Copy Report**.

Troubleshooting

If you see a "no data" message when you try to view the Site Usage Report page, you should first check whether logging and usage processing is turned on. This is turned off by default. You should also check whether the site is new. If the site is new (created today) or has not been used before today, no data will appear until the usage log processing has been done (usually within 24 hours). After that, make sure there has been activity on your site within the last 31 days. Daily usage data is kept only for the past 31 days, so if there has not been activity you will see the "no data" message.

If you find you're having trouble processing usage analysis data, you should check whether the SharePoint Timer Service is enabled or needs to be restarted. If you need to enable or restart the SharePoint Timer service on a Web server computer, you can do so by using the **Services** control panel.

> **Note**   To enable or restart the SharePoint Timer service, you need to be a member of the local computer's Administrators group or you need to have been granted permissions to manage services on the local computer.

Summary

This chapter shows how to manage usage analysis. The chapter also discusses how to analyze website usage using the site administration pages and website reports in FrontPage. In addition, it shows how to configure IIS log files to paint a complete picture of portal site usage. It also assists you in troubleshooting usage analysis and scheduling the timed jobs responsible for processing the Windows SharePoint Services log files.

Chapter 30

Default Tools to Customize Windows SharePoint Services

Websites based on Microsoft Windows SharePoint Services are designed to be flexible and highly customizable. This allows you to make the sites as effective as they can be. You can tailor a site to fit your users' needs by adding or removing pages, changing the appearance of pages, changing the site navigation, adding or removing Web Parts, and making other customizations. Here are the three main tools for implementing customizations:

- **The Browser.** Basic customization can be done from within the browser, using links from the Home, Create, and Site Settings pages of the website.

- **Customizing websites by Using Web Page Editing Tools.** Additional customization can be done by using a Windows SharePoint Services–compatible Web page editor, such as Microsoft Office FrontPage 2003. With a Web page editor, you can perform customizations such as adding borders to pages, inserting graphics, and adding components to the home page. You can also customize text files—such as .css, xml, and .aspx pages that are stored on the file system—by using applications other than FrontPage.

- **Customizing websites Programmatically.** You can perform advanced Web development customizations by using the programming model behind

Windows SharePoint Services. You can use the programming model to make website customizations such as adding, editing, deleting, and retrieving data from SharePoint lists; creating new lists and setting list metadata (such as the fields in a list); working with documents in document libraries; and performing administrative tasks such as creating websites, adding users, and creating roles.

In any deployment, all three tools will likely be used to customize your sites. Whatever method you use to customize websites, you must have the following rights, all of which are included in the Web Designer and Administrator site groups by default:

- Manage Lists
- Add and Customize Pages
- Apply Themes and Borders
- Apply Style Sheets

Other users of your site cannot gain access to the pages required to perform these tasks unless you specifically assign them to a site group that contains these rights.

This chapter and the following chapter will introduce you to basic concepts that will allow you to complete customization tasks by using default tools such as the browser and the Stsadm command-line tool, and by replacing files on the file system.

Customizing Web Part Pages

Before we can talk about customizing any of the portal sites, we must cover certain basic concepts. The majority of sites created using Microsoft SharePoint Products and Technologies consist of Web Part Pages, which are special Web pages that contain one or more Web Parts. Web Parts are reusable components that can contain any kind of Web-based information, including analytical, collaborative, and database information. See Chapter 31, "Working with Web Parts," for more information.

There are two kind of Web Part Pages: **ghosted** and **unghosted**. Ghosted pages are pages stored on the file system that do not come from the child virtual directories _layouts and _vti_bin. Unghosted pages are stored in the database. Applications such as FrontPage 2003 can customize ghosted and unghosted Web Part Pages. A ghosted page becomes unghosted once the page or one of its properties has been modified—for example, by using FrontPage 2003. The main reasons for SharePoint Products and Technologies to store some templates in the file system (ghosted) and some in the database (unghosted) have to do with security and scalability. For more information on ghosted and unghosted Web Part Pages, see Chapter 37, "Using Visual Studio .NET to Create Web Parts."

Shared View vs. Personal View

A Web Part Page can have two views:

- **Shared view.**   This is the view of the Web Part Page that every user with the appropriate rights on a site can see. Any changes to a shared view Web Part Page will appear to all users.

- **Personal view.**   This view of a Web Part Page is available only to a particular user. Changes made to the personal view of a Web Part Page are visible only to the user who altered his or her personal view of the Web Part Page.

By default, changes to Web Part Pages are made only to your personal view. As an administrator, you will be shown Web Part Pages in shared view until you personalize them, and then the personal view becomes your default view of that Web Part Page. For the My Site Web Part Page, the personal view is the default view even for administrators. As the administrator for a page, you can decide to change the shared view of a Web Part Page or your own personal view. An administrator cannot change the personal views of specific users. As an administrator, when you first display a Web Part Page, the page is in shared view and the Modify Shared Page link is shown in the upper-right corner, beneath the Search box. For a Web page that forms part of a portal site, you will need to click Edit Page in the Actions list for the Modify Shared Page link to appear. For a Web Part Page that is displayed as a personal view, the link is Modify My Page. To switch between these two views, click either Modify Shared Page or Modify My Page, and then click either Personal View or Shared View, as shown in Figure 30-1. When you switch from the shared view to the personal view, notice that the URL now has *PageView=Personal* appended to it.

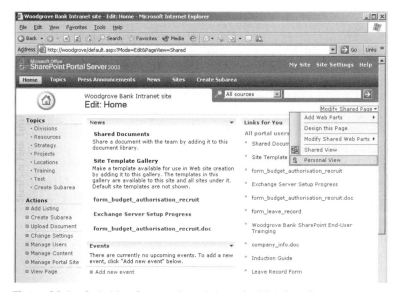

Figure 30-1   Switching from a shared view of a Web Part Page to a personal view

The personal view is detailed in Chapter 23, "Personalization Services in SharePoint Products and Technologies"; this chapter will concentrate on the shared view.

Web Part Page Zones

Web Part Pages include a number of zones, and each zone can contain a number of Web Parts. Although you can customize the basic layout of these Web Part Pages using FrontPage 2003, the browser is a much more efficient way to add and remove Web Parts from these zones because it offers easy drag-and-drop functionality of Web Parts within zones and between zones. Web Parts can reside outside the zones; these are called *static* Web Parts and cannot be customized using the browser.

To change the layout, the Web page must be in design view. Click Modify Shared Page, and then click Design This Page. The page is redisplayed, and the zones are now clearly visible. On a portal site, the word *Edit* will be placed before the page name, as shown in Figure 30-2.

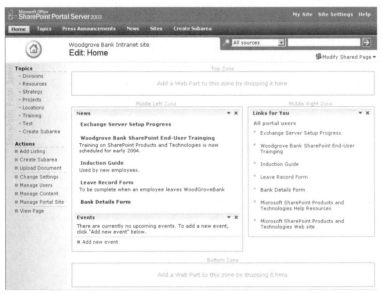

Figure 30-2   Changing the layout of a portal site home page: four zones and two navigation bars

To perform a drag-and-drop operation, click the Web Part title bar so that a cross with arrows appears, and then drag the Web Part to the desired location.

Each Web Part Page, zone, and Web Part has a number of attributes or properties associated with it. Some Web Part properties can be customized using the browser, and this is detailed in Chapter 31. Web Part Page and zone properties cannot be edited using the browser, but their settings can affect what you can and cannot do using the browser. For example, each zone has a property named AllowPersonalization. If this property is set to False, Web Parts that are located in that zone cannot be modified by individual users, and when all zones have this setting, there is only the shared view for the page. However, to an administrator, it might look as if there is a shared and personal view of the page, so you might find that you can switch between shared view and personal view, but you cannot design the personal view. Other zone properties can stop you from adding, moving, deleting, connecting, and customizing Web Parts within a zone.

To complete your changes, click Modify Shared Page, and then click Design This Page. This will remove the tick symbol by the side of this option, the page will be redisplayed, and the zones will no longer be visible.

Most Web pages that are created for you, as a result of you choosing a particular area or site template, have a number of zones and navigation bars. For example, the portal site home page has top, middle left, middle right, and bottom zones and has two navigation bars. (Refer back to Figure 30-2.) The two navigation bars are as follows:

- The horizontal navigation bar at the top of the page shows all top-level areas in a portal site (top-level areas are areas under the Home area), regardless of where the user is. If you looked at the code in the default.aspx file for the portal site home page, it would look something like this:

```
<SPSWC:CategoryNavigationWebPart runat="server" id="HorizontalNavBar"
```

- The vertical navigation bar on the left side of the page shows two controls: the subareas (if any), which is dependent on the user's location, plus an Actions list. The code within the default.aspx file for this would look like:

```
<SPSWC:CategoryNavigationWebPart runat="server" id="VerticalNavBar" Display-
Style="VerticalOneLayer"/>
<SPSWC:ToolBar runat="server" id="ActionBar" RenderIfEmpty="false" Orientation=
"Vertical"
```

All but the Sites area or areas based on the Site Directory area template follow this format, where all zones are configured so that users cannot personalize them. Administrators can change the zone property AllowPersonalization to True to allow users to personalize the Web Parts within the zone. Administrators can also create new zones. When you navigate to the Sites area or areas based on the Site Directory Area template page, you get redirected to a view of a list. Web Part Pages that display the contents of lists and libraries are described later in this chapter.

Note On Windows SharePoint Services sites, the same principle of zones and navigation bars exist, except that the code specifics are different.

Most Web Part Pages on Windows SharePoint Services sites contain only two or three zones, and some include more than one Web Part Page. For example, if you create a website based on the Social Meeting site template, you will see Home, Discussion, and Photos Web Part Pages, each of which consist of three zones—left, center, and right. You can create Web Part Pages that can contain many zones; however, using a browser you cannot add or delete zones on a Web Part Page. You will need to use a tool, such as FrontPage 2003. See Chapter 32, "Using Microsoft Office FrontPage 2003 to Customize Windows SharePoint Services Sites," for details on how to do this.

Web Part Page Creation

The browser is the best tool for adding new Web Part Pages. Web Part Pages can be added to form part of a site's navigation design, added as an item to a document library, or created when you create a list or a library or you add a view to that list or library.

Adding Navigation Web Pages

On a portal site, when you add an area, subarea, or topic, you are adding a Web Part Page to the site. As stated earlier, all area Web Part Pages that have been created for you when you create a portal site or areas that you created using the default area templates cannot be personalized by users. The other zone properties set by default allow users to add, remove, resize, and move Web Parts and allow users to change Web Part settings for all users if the user has the necessary rights, unless the settings on the individual Web Parts override these. Zone properties can be altered by using a tool such as FrontPage 2003.

For Windows SharePoint Services sites based on the default workspace site templates, Social Meeting, Decision Meeting, Blank Meeting, and Basic Meeting, click Modify This Workspace in the upper-right corner, and then click Add Pages. Type the page name, and then click Add. This will add a three-zone page to your website. To manage or delete these Web Pages, click Modify This Workspace, and then click Manage Pages. A tool pane will be displayed, and the Web Part Page is displayed in design mode. Click the down arrow to reorder, add further pages, and delete or alter the settings, such as the page name of the site's Web page. Remember that you cannot alter the page name of the home page for these sites through the browser. Click OK, Cancel, or the Close button in the upper-right corner of the tool pane to close it. These sites do not have a personalized view.

Using the browser, you cannot add or customize the navigation Web Part Pages for the websites created from the other default site templates—that is, Team Site, Document Workspace, Multipage Meeting, and the Blank Site templates. Using the browser, you can customize only zones and Web Parts on the Home Web Part Page for these sites. The navigation Web Part Pages for these sites are: spsviewlsts.aspx on portal sites and viewlsts.aspx on the website for the Documents And Lists page; spscreate.aspx on portal sites and create.aspx on websites for the Create page; and default.aspx or settings.aspx for the Site Settings page. These Web Part Pages are stored in the virtual directory, as follows:

- For portal sites: *http://<servername>/_layouts/LCID*

- For a Windows SharePoint Services website: *http://<servername>/sites/<sitename> /_ layouts/LCID*

In all situations, these virtual directory URLs map to *Local_Drive*\Program Files\Common Files\Microsoft Shared\Web Server Extensions\60\TEMPLATE \LAYOUTS*LCID* where **LCID** is the **locale ID**. Whenever you **extend** a virtual server, a virtual directory _layouts is created and by default is mapped to the system file directory mentioned earlier. All _layouts virtual directories created for any sites under these virtual servers also have their _layout virtual directories mapped to this system file directory. Therefore, if you change the files or place new custom files in this directory, you will be customizing all extended virtual servers and the **site collections** that are hosted on the server. If you want to customize your deployment on a virtual server by virtual server basis, copy the system file directory to another location, and then, using the Microsoft Internet Information Services (IIS) Manager, remap the _layouts virtual directory to the new file structure by expanding the website, right-clicking the virtual directory _layouts, and clicking Properties. On the Virtual Directory tab, as shown in Figure 30-3, click the Browse button next to the Local Path box, navigate to the file structure, and then click OK twice.

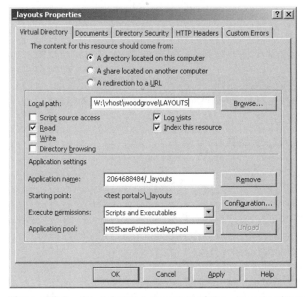

Figure 30-3   Changing the mapping of the _layouts virtual directory

There are other virtual directories—such as _vti_bin, _wpresources, and _layouts/images—that map, by default, to the same file directory for all virtual servers on a front-end Web server. The process detailed earlier can be used for these virtual directories; if you want to customize your deployment on a virtual server by virtual server basis, however, ensure that the process is carefully documented, and if you have a Web **server farm** deployment, ensure that it is completed on all servers.

Caution   Any service packs or hotfixes will not know that you have remapped these virtual directories. You will manually have to copy to the new directories any files that the service packs or hotfixes replace. This requirement should be reflected in your change management and testing procedures. You might also find that Microsoft will not support such a configuration.

Adding Web Pages to Document Libraries

Navigate to the Create page for area, subareas, topics, and the Windows SharePoint Service websites based on the default site templates: Team Site, Document Workspace, Multipage Meeting, and Blank Site. The Create page can be found by clicking Manage Content on area pages or Create on websites. Then, in the Web Pages section, click Web Part Page. The New Web Part Page page is displayed as in Figure 30-4, and on that page you can choose the layout and number of zones you require. These Web Part Pages are stored in document libraries, which can be viewed, managed, or deleted like any other item within a document library, as detailed in Chapter 19, "Working with Documents in SharePoint Products and Technologies."

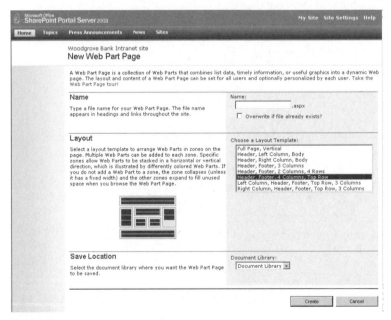

Figure 30-4   New Web Part Page

You cannot add templates to the Web Part Page creation form, and you cannot embed Web Parts in any of the predefined templates. The white paper "Microsoft SharePoint Products and Technologies: Creating Custom Web Part Page Templates" by David Long, Lana Fly, and Scott Ruble, July 2003, describes how to create a new, customized creation form that contains an unlimited number of custom page templates that can contain embedded Web Parts. Sample Web Part Page templates that accompany this article are available for download. You can modify these sample templates to fit your needs. The information in this white paper also applies to SharePoint Portal Server.

For Windows SharePoint Services sites based on the default workspace site templates, Social Meeting, Decision Meeting, Blank Meeting, and Basic Meeting, you need to create a Web Part Page elsewhere and then upload it to a document library. Remember that not all websites contain document libraries; you might first need to create one by clicking Site Settings on the Modify This Workspace drop-down list, clicking Modify Site Content, and then clicking Create New Content.

List and Library Web Part Pages

When lists or libraries are created, a number of Web Part Pages are created for you. You cannot edit these Web Part Pages, and therefore you cannot see the zones or Web Parts that are an integral part of these Web Part Pages using the browser.

Lists and libraries come with a set of **views**, such as All Documents, Explorer View, Approve/Reject Items, and My Submissions for document libraries; All Contacts for a contacts list; Threaded and Flat for discussions; All Events, Calendar, and Current Events for an events lists; and Overview, Graphical Summary, and All Responses for a survey. The All Responses survey view displays a list of every response, but you have to click each response separately to see each respondent's response. The All Responses option is designed so that you can view a list of all the respondents and the date they responded. You can use the Graphical Summary view when you want to determine the frequency of each response or the percentage of responses per item.

Views make it quick and easy to see information in a variety of ways. Each view is a Web Part Page linked to the Quick Launch bar on the page that displays the list or library. Through the browser, you can add new views and modify or delete existing ones by clicking Modify Settings And Columns in the Actions list; by doing this you are adding, modifying, or deleting Web Part Pages.

Security for Web Parts and Web Part Pages

Security for Web Part Pages and Web Parts is integrated with security for SharePoint Products and Technologies, as detailed in Chapter 6, "Security Architecture for SharePoint Products and Technologies." A subset of rights affects Web Part Pages and Web Parts, dependent on whether the Web page has been created and stored in a document library or on a site. Also, there are rights unique to Web Part Pages and Web Parts. This is detailed in the tables in this section. You can control who can do what to a Web Part Page and the Web Parts on it by allowing, for example, the following actions:

- A site reader to view, but not to personalize, a Web Part Page

- A site contributor to browse and personalize a Web Part Page on a site, but not to make changes to a Web Part Page or its Web Parts for all users in shared view

- A Web designer to browse, create, customize, and make changes to a Web Part Page and its Web Parts on a site or in a document library for all users in shared view

If at one time any user has had View Pages or View Items rights but they have been removed, the user can still delete personalizations made to Web Part Pages. The Web Part will revert to its shared property values.

> **Note**   Although Web Parts are detailed in Chapter 31, it is easier to describe the security implications for Web Part Pages and Web Parts together in this section.

Once a user has personalized a Web Part Page, there is no automatic way to replace these personalized changes by a system administrator or a user with appropriate permission. However, a system administrator or a user with appropriate permission can go to the Web Part Maintenance page as discussed in Chapter 31 and delete all personalized changes there. Any personalized changes made by any user will revert to the shared property values.

Table 30-1 summarizes how the different rights affect a user's experience when working with Web Part Pages and Web Parts on a site and in a document library.

Table 30-1 **Rights that Affect a User's Experience**

This right	Allows you to	And applies to
Add and Customize Pages	Create and delete a Web Part Page.	A Web Part Page on a site, but not in a document library
	Edit a Web Part Page by using a Windows SharePoint Services–compatible HTML editor, such as FrontPage 2003.	
	Make changes to a Web Part Page that applies to all users in shared view.	
	Make changes to a Web Part Page that apply to all users in shared view by adding Web Parts to and removing Web Parts from a Web Part Page.	
View Pages	Browse a Web Part Page.	
View Items	View a Web Part on a Web Part Page.	A Web Part Page in a document library
	Open a Web Part Page in a document library.	
Add Items	Create a new Web Part Page in a document library.	
Edit Items	Edit a Web Part Page.	
	Edit a Web Part Page by using a Windows SharePoint Services–compatible HTML editor.	
	Make changes to a Web Part Page that apply to all users in shared view.	
	Make changes to a Web Part Page that apply to all users in shared view by adding Web Parts to and removing Web Parts from a Web Part Page.	
Delete Items	Delete a Web Part Page in a document library.	
Add/Remove Private Web Parts	Add a Web Part to and remove a Web Part from a Web Part Page.	A Web Part Page on a site and in a document library
	This right is dependent on and automatically granted with the Update Personal Web Parts right by default.	
Update Personal Web Parts	Make changes to a Web Part Page that apply only to the current user in personal view. This right is dependent on and must be granted with the Add/Remove Private Web Parts right.	

Table 30-2 summarizes the Web Part Page and Web Part rights granted by default to each site group.

Table 30-2   Summary of Rights Granted by Default

Right	Reader	Contributor	Web Designer	Administrator
View Pages	Granted	Granted	Granted	Granted
View Items	Granted	Granted	Granted	Granted
Add/Remove Private Web Parts	Denied	Granted	Granted	Granted
Update Personal Web Parts	Denied	Granted	Granted	Granted
Add Items	Denied	Granted	Granted	Granted
Edit Items	Denied	Granted	Granted	Granted
Delete Items	Denied	Granted	Granted	Granted
Add and Customize Pages	Denied	Denied	Granted	Granted

As Table 30-3 shows, default site groups provide different abilities depending on whether the Web Part Page is located on a site or in a document library.

Table 30-3   Various Abilities Provided by Default Site Groups

Site Group	Abilities on a Team Website	Abilities in a Document Library
Administrator Web Designer	Create, browse and delete a Web Part Page.	
	Edit a Web Part Page by using a Windows SharePoint Services–compatible HTML editor, such as FrontPage 2003.	
	Make changes to a Web Part Page that applies to all users in shared view.	
	Personalize a Web Part.	
	Add a private Web Part to a Web Part Page or delete a private Web Part from a Web Part Page.	
Contributor	Browse a Web Part Page and its Web Parts.	Browse a Web Part Page and its Web Parts.
	Personalize a Web Part.	Personalize a Web Part.
	Add a private Web Part to a Web Part Page or delete a private Web Part from a Web Part Page.	Add a private Web Part to a Web Part Page or delete a private Web Part from a Web Part Page.
		Create and delete a Web Part Page.
		Edit a Web Part Page by using a Windows SharePoint Services–compatible HTML editor.
		Make changes to a Web Part Page that apply to all users in shared view
Reader	Browse a Web Part Page and its Web Parts	

Other Customizations

The default installation of SharePoint Portal Server 2003 or any of the websites based on Windows SharePoint Services have a distinctive look that might not fit in with your organization's standards or corporate identity. This section will introduce you to some common customizations that you might want to complete on **SharePoint sites** that you have created or on sites that are created for you when you install SharePoint Products and Technologies.

Serverwide Configurations

There are a number of virtual directories that map to file directories for all virtual servers on a **front-end Web server**. Table 30-4 details these mappings.

Table 30-4   Virtual Directories Mapping to File Directories

Virtual Directory	Physical Directory in the File System
_layouts,	C:\Program Files\Common Files\Microsoft Shared\Web Server Extensions\60\template\layouts
_layouts/images.	C:\Program Files\Common Files\Microsoft Shared\Web Server Extensions\60\template\images
_wpresources	C:\Program Files\Common Files\Microsoft Shared\Web Server Extensions\wpresources
_vti_bin,	C:\Program Files\Common Files\Microsoft Shared\Web Server Extensions\60\isapi

These virtual directories do contain files that you might want to customize, for example:

■ The images virtual directory contains many .gif files that are used as logos on many different Web Part Pages. See the following procedure. This directory also contains thumbnail and preview image files for your custom themes.

■ The classes for cascading style sheets that determine the styles and formatting applied to pages in Windows SharePoint Services are defined in OWS.CSS, which is located in the virtual directory _layouts*LCID*\STYLES. For example, see Knowledge Base article 824495, "How to Change the Color of the Horizontal Top Bar," for more information.

■ Third-party developers can add a custom reportrich.aspx file to the _layouts*LCID* folder to provide rich charts for issues lists. The functionality of a custom reportrich.aspx file will be called automatically when users select a report type on the Report page.

■ One copy of the Help files is installed per server into the virtual directory_vti_bin \HELP*LCID*\STS\\ so that users from all sites hosted by the server see the same Help files.

Any changes to files in these directories will affect all site collections hosted on the server and will be at risk of being lost during the application of service packs and hotfixes. By changing files once, you can have your corporate identity set on all sites. If you want to have a different identity per virtual server, you could create a copy of these directories and alter the mapping using the IIS Manager, as described earlier in this chapter.

To change the picture on the home page

If you wanted a different logo for a portal site home pages, do the following:

1. Open the *Local_Drive*\Program Files\Common Files\Microsoft Shared\Web Server Extensions\60\template\images directory. This assumes the default mapping of the virtual directory is http://<*virtualserver*>/_layouts/images.

2. Copy the images that you want to appear on the home pages of your websites to this directory.

3. Rename the image files **home.gif** and **homepage.gif** to **home.org.gif** and **homepage.org.gif,** respectively. These files contain the logos used on the left and right sides of the home page, respectively.

4. Rename the new image files **home.gif** and **homepage.gif**.

All sites with the appropriate virtual directory mapping now display new logos on their home pages. Portal sites use the spshome.gif by default. The name of this file can be changed on a portal site by portal site basis using the browser, as described later in this chapter. To find the name of the .gif file you want to customize, navigate to a page that displays the logo, right-click the image, and then click Properties. Notice the file name at the end of the URL, as illustrated in Figure 30-5.

> **Caution**   If you change any of the default files, you might lose your customization on an upgrade or on the application of a hotfix or a service pack. To prevent this loss, use FrontPage 2003 to change the URL of the image file to one you have stored in a document library or place an image file in the same physical directory as spshome.gif, but use a unique file name.

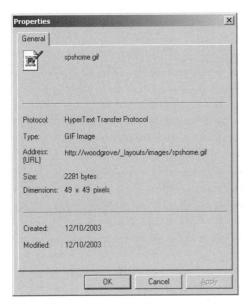

Figure 30-5   How to find the filename of a logo

Site-Level Customization

Many of the previous chapters have detailed customization of sites; for example, Chapter 16, "Administering Windows SharePoint Services," discussed the different site definition files and custom templates, and Chapter 20, "Working with Information Components in SharePoint Products and Technologies," covered list definitions, custom templates, and customization by adding columns and views, as well as areas. As mentioned in this chapter, if you do create a custom list you must ensure when you deploy it to other template galleries on other sites that the site definition with the same site definition ID as the original site is available on the new site; otherwise, it will not appear on the Create page of that site. Site definition IDs might not match up with the same site definitions on all sites. This might occur if any one of the following conditions is true:

- You create a list template on a Windows SharePoint Portal Services site, and then you import the list template to a portal site.

- You create a list template on a portal site, and then you import the list template to a Windows SharePoint Portal Services site.

- You create a list template on a Windows SharePoint Services site, and then you import the list template to another Windows SharePoint Services site that uses a different site definition ID.

When you create a list, you can select a list template from the set of list templates on the server and on the site collection. This set of list templates is filtered according to the site language and the site definition ID that your Windows SharePoint Services site is based on. For example, a site that is based on the Basic Meeting Workspace template has a site definition ID that is different from a site that is based on the Team Site template. If you create a Meeting Announcements custom list template from the Announcements list on a site that is based on a Basic Meeting Workspace template, the Meeting Announcements list template that you create is not available on a site that is based on the Team Site template. To work around this issue, create the list template on the Windows SharePoint Services site or on the portal site where the list template will be used. For example, if Windows SharePoint Services sites that are based on the Team Site template require a survey template, create the survey template on a site that is based on the Team Site template.

The rest of this section will mention customizations not mentioned elsewhere in this resource kit, such as the following:

- The portal site name and description.

- A custom portal site logo. You must type a URL address for the location of the graphics file.

- The location for creating SharePoint sites.

- The URL address of the cascading style sheet file you want to use for this portal site.

These changes can be achieved by clicking Site Settings on a portal site and then, in the General Settings section, clicking Change Portal Site Properties And SharePoint Site Creation Settings. For both the portal site logo and the cascading style sheet file, if the file location is a local relative path (for example, /_layouts /*LCID*/blue.css), you must copy the cascading style sheet file to that location on each front-end Web server. For better performance, it is recommended that you copy the files to the _layouts folder on each front-end Web server.

You could store all your logos within a picture library and your cascading style sheets within a document library, enabling you to use the versioning and approval features. You would then type the URL of the picture library or the document library in the text boxes. Ensure that the rights on these libraries allow all users to view the files; otherwise, the user will be prompted for a set of user credentials that do have rights to view the files. Although the user can select the Cancel option on the Security dialog box, it can be very annoying. In such cases, you might want to create a central location where you place all contact pictures and logos, with reader rights for all the users to your sites.

On a Windows SharePoint Services website, the Site Settings page provides you with other options: Change Site Title And Description, Apply Theme To Site,

Modify Site Content, and Customize Home Page, which allows you to edit the home page with the tool pane displayed.

You can customize Windows SharePoint Services websites created from a portal site by clicking Manage Sites in the Actions list on an area page. This displays a list of sites created. Rest the pointer on the site you want to edit, click the arrow that appears, and then click Edit Item on the menu that appears. You are presented with a page similar to the one you used when you created the site, which allows you to amend the Title, URL, Description, Owner, Division, Region, and Spotlight properties. You can change all but the URL property. If you change the URL property, unless you have created a site at the new URL, users will receive the error message "The Web site that is referenced here is not in the configuration database." These properties are visible only on the portal site; therefore, if you want the website to have the same title as the title property on the portal site, you must navigate to the website, click Site Settings, and then click Change Site Title And Description.

List and Library Configurations

The names and descriptions of lists and libraries can be modified by navigating to the list or library. Under the Actions section, click Modify Settings And Columns, and in the General Settings section, click Change General Settings. You can also choose to customize views with different styles and groupings, as well as limit the amount of data that is returned to the user.

When you create a view, in the Audience section you can choose to create a shared view that all site users can share or a personal view. However, if a website has many users and each creates a shared view, the list of shared views can get very long. Personal views enable each user of a SharePoint site to create her own views, which are not visible to other users. Having both types of views allows site administrators to ensure that only views that are useful for most users appear in the list of shared views, while still allowing users to create personal views that help them view list information in the most convenient way for them.

Note The types of views you can create might vary based on the template your site uses. Also remember that only shared views can be specified as the default view.

Remove !New Tag from New Items

When you add a new entry to announcements, events, or links on a website, the new entry always includes a tag that is made up of the exclamation point character (!) and the word *New* (!New). To prevent the !New tag from appearing next to new entries on your website, use the Stsadm.exe tool to change the Days To Show New

Icon property to zero by typing the following commands in a command-prompt window:

```
CD \Program Files\Common Files\Microsoft Shared\web server extensions\60\BIN
stsadm.exe -o setproperty -pn days-to-show-new-icon -pv 0 -
url Your_Virtual_Server_URL
```

Themes

A theme is a unified set of design elements that influence the fonts and color schemes when you apply it to a website. Applying a theme is a quick and easy way to ensure your site is visually consistent and appealing.

Each Windows SharePoint Services site and subsite has its own theme setting that can be configured using the browser. You can also add your own custom themes, as detailed in the following procedure. When you apply a theme, it will not affect the layout of your site. In addition, applying a theme will not change any individual Web pages that you have applied themes to by using a Web page editor compatible with Windows SharePoint Services, such as FrontPage 2003. When you create pages, the default theme is applied automatically. If you change or remove the default theme, the change is applied to the entire site.

To apply or remove a theme on your site, you must have the Apply Themes And Borders right for that site. The Apply Themes And Borders right is included by default in the Web Designer site group.

To add a custom theme to the list of available themes

By default, you are provided with 20 themes to choose from on the Apply Theme To Web Site page. If you want to add a custom theme, complete the following procedure:

1. On the navigation bar, click **Site Settings**, and then, in the **Customization** section, click **Apply theme to site**.

2. In the **Address** bar on the browser, replace the file name **themeweb.aspx** with **spthemes.xml**.

    For example, if the **Address** bar showed http://*server_name*/_layouts/1033/themeweb.aspx, you would change the path to http://*server_name*/_layouts/1033/spthemes.xml.

3. Edit the XML file, and add a new section for your custom theme, similar to the following code:

    ```
    - <Templates>
    <TemplateID>newtemplateid</TemplateID>
    <DisplayName>NewTemplateDisplayName</DisplayName>
    <Description>Description</Description>
    <Thumbnail>../images/image.png</Thumbnail>
    <Preview>../images/image.gif</Preview>
    </Templates>
    ```

Areas

By default, all area templates have a generic look and feel, and although we have detailed in this chapter some methods of applying a corporate identity, you cannot apply themes to an area by using the browser. You will need to use a tool, such as FrontPage 2003, to achieve this. If you want to change the contents for all new areas, change ONET.XML as specified in Chapter 20, "Working with Information Components in SharePoint Products and Technologies," and in the webcast "Building Custom Microsoft SharePoint Sites with Templates and Site Definitions" at *http://www.microsoft.com/seminar/shared/asp/view.asp?url=/Seminar/en/20031101SharePoint_T407/manifest.xml&rate=1.*

Summary

This chapter detailed the basic customization that can be done from within the default tools, such as the Stsadm command-line tool and the browser, using links from the Home, Create, and Site Settings pages of the website. Some of the basic customizations covered include the following:

- Changing the layout of the home page and other Web Part Pages
- Changing the picture on the home page
- Changing a site's display name (not the URL)
- Adding views to list and libraries
- Applying a theme

The SharePoint Portal Server 2003 and Windows SharePoint Services Help files contain more information about customizing websites from within the browser. The next chapter completes the coverage of browser-based customization by looking specifically at Web Parts.

Chapter 31

Working with Web Parts

Websites based on Microsoft SharePoint Products and Technologies allow users to add **Web Parts** to **Web Part Pages**. This chapter will introduce you to basic concepts, which allow you to customize Web Parts and which complete the review of using default tools—such as the browser and the **Stsadm.exe** command-line tool—and using a text-based editor to set configuration parameters in files on the file system.

A Web Part is a modular unit of information that has a single purpose. For example, the list of built-in Web Parts available in SharePoint Products and Technologies includes the following:

- SharePoint Portal Server 2003–specific Web Parts; for example:

    - Area Contents: Used to display the content of areas and topics.

    - Grouped Listings: Used to display listings in an area—that is, the link items stored in an area's Portal Listings list.

- Microsoft Windows SharePoint Services–specific Web Parts; for example:

    - Members: Used to display a list of site members and their online status.

- List View Web Parts. Web Parts that display a view of a list or library, available on portal and Windows SharePoint Portal Services websites; for example:

    - Contacts: Allows you to display the Contacts list on a Web Part Page.

- Web Parts that can be used on portal and Windows SharePoint Services web-sites; for example:

    - Content Editor Web Part: Displays unstructured Web content, such as text or images.

    - Form Web Part: Allows you to add an HTML form.

    - Image Web Part: Displays a picture.

These and other built-in Web Parts will be explained later in this chapter.

SharePoint Products and Technologies are built on top of the Microsoft .NET Framework 1.1, and Web Parts are therefore Microsoft ASP.NET Web Form custom server controls. Web Part Pages include a number of zones, where each zone can contain a number of Web Parts. Web Part Page Zones are detailed in Chapter 30, "Default Tools to Customize Windows SharePoint Services." Web Parts can also be placed directly on a Web Part Page—that is, outside a Web Part Page Zone—by Page Authors at design time, and therefore the layout and properties of these Web Parts are fixed by the designer of the Web Part. They cannot be minimized or closed, nor can their properties be modified in the browser. Such Web Parts are called **static Web Parts**. A static Web Part and its properties are stored in the Web Part Page (the .aspx file), not in the SQL **content database** for the site.

Dynamic Web Parts are Web Parts that are contained in a **Web Part Page Zone** and can be customized by using the browser. Users with the right to Add/Remove Private Web Parts or to Add And Customize Pages can, using the browser, add a dynamic Web Part into any zone on most Web Part Pages, on any site that is a SharePoint Portal Server site, or on any site that is based on Windows SharePoint Services. Even if a Web Part Page contains Web Part Page Zones, this does not imply that a Web Part can always be added to the Web Part Page. One example of a Web Part Page to which you cannot add a Web Part by using the browser is any Web Part Page that is based on the Site Directory area template. This, together with zones and security rights for Web Parts, was discussed in Chapter 30. You can add dynamic Web Parts to pages by dragging and dropping them in a browser, as described in Chapter 23, "Personalization Services in SharePoint Products and Technologies," and in Chapter 30.

Basic Customization of Dynamic Web Parts

A dynamic Web Part is stored in the content database rather than in the Web Part Page (the .aspx file); therefore, changes do not affect the underlying .aspx page. Once a Web Part is added to a Web Part Page, you can customize it by setting properties. When you set Web Part properties in the browser, the scope of the modification depends on whether the page is in **Personal view** or **Shared view**. Changes made in Personal View apply only to the current user and take precedence over changes made in Shared View. A member of the Administrator site group can use Shared View to set default values for all users of that page.

Even if a Web Part is displayed on a Personal View, it does not follow that you can personalize the properties of that Web Part. When a Web Part is created, the properties of the Web Part are defined by the developer and are stored, based on the setting of the WebPartStorage attribute in the property definition, as follows:

- **Shared.**   This setting means that the property is stored with the same value for all users. An example of this is a Web Part that displays weather information and has a URL to a weather site as one of its properties.

- **Personal.**   This setting means that the property is stored per user. In a Web Part that displays weather information, for example, if you want to allow a user to choose the geographic area for which to find the weather, you could define a property that contains a ZIP code, which would be stored on a per-user basis.

- **None.**   This setting means that the property is not stored in the database, and the value is assigned programmatically by the developer. The value stored in the .aspx file is ignored. Static Web Parts can have only this type of property.

Using a browser to change a shared or personal property for a Web Part, click the downward arrow on the right side of the Web Part title bar, and then click Modify My Web Part (in Personal View) or Modify Shared Web Part (in Shared View). On a Windows SharePoint Service Web Site, the page automatically changes to Design View with an outline around each Web Part Page Zone and a tool pane (also known as a *task pane*) for setting properties appears; for a Web Part Page that forms part of a portal site, you will need to click Edit Page in the Actions list for the downward arrow to appear, as illustrated in Figure 31-1.

Note   For the downward arrow to appear on the News Web Part on a portal site home page, you will have to switch the page into design mode.

Once you are in design mode on a portal site, an extra link will be added to the horizontal navigation bar from which you can add subareas.

Figure 31-1 Modifying Web Part settings

When a Web Part is first added to a Web Part Page Zone on a Web Part Page, the Web Part is instantiated by using a combination of all the Shared and Personal properties defined for the Web Part. Once a user personalizes a Web Part (for example, when the user moves the Web Part to a different zone), a copy of the user's personal properties is stored in the database. The next time that Web Part is instantiated on a user's personal view, the Shared and new Personal properties are again combined, reflecting the changes.

A Web Part added to your personal view is called a *Private Web Part*. Private Web Parts are available only to the user who added or imported the Web Part. No other users can see your private Web Parts.

The process of setting personal property values is known as *personalization*, and the process of setting properties for all users is known as *customization*. Personalization and customization affect storage in the content database.

All Web Parts can have a set of common properties that you can use to control a Web Part's appearance and behavior, such as its height and width. Each Web Part can also have a set of custom properties that are created by the developer. The default tool pane displays the shared, personal, common, and custom Web Part properties. A tool pane consists of tool parts, which can be likened to how Web Part Page Zones hold Web Parts. When you modify a Web Part, the default properties pane has two tool parts: WebPartToolPart and CustomPropertiesToolPart. These tool parts contain logic that is used to decide how to display the Web Part properties. Web Part properties have certain attributes that the tool parts use; for example, if the *browsable* attribute for the Web Part property is set to False, the property will not show up in the CustomPropertiesToolpart. The default property tool pane can be customized by the developer, who can add custom **tool parts** that can be used to manipulate custom properties beyond the default capabilities of the default property pane.

When you use the tool pane to edit the settings of a Web Part's properties, each property's attribute is checked; for example, if you are using your personal view of a Web Part Page, only Web Part properties whose storage attribute is set to Personal will be shown. If you display a Web Part Page in Shared View, Web Part properties with the storage attribute of either Personal or Shared will show up. Using the setting of the browsable attribute, the common and custom properties are displayed in groups, depending on the Web Part. The grouping of a Web Part's property is defined by the developer of the Web Part, who sets the category attribute for the property. The WebPartToolpart tool part will display properties that have their categories' attributes set to Appearance, Layout, or Advanced. The categories Appearance, Layout, and Advanced are used for the common, also known as *base*, Web Part properties. The CustomPropertyToolPart will display all custom properties. If a custom property does not specify a category attribute, the CustomPropertyToolPart logic will assign a default category name of *Miscellaneous*. If the custom property specifies a category attribute, the CustomPropertyToolPart logic will create a new group heading for it.

> **Note**   If a developer tries to specify a category attribute of Appearance, Layout, or Advanced, the custom property will *not* appear under the group heading in the tool pane that was specified. The custom property will be displayed under the Miscellaneous group heading instead.

When you modify a Web Part on a default portal site or a website based on the default site templates using a browser, the group headings that might be visible in the tool pane are Appearance, Layout, Advanced, Custom Properties, and Miscellaneous. The tool pane category groups and the properties that can be displayed within each group are described in the following sections.

Appearance Properties

The Appearance properties, as specified in the following list, can be customized, personalized, or both if the zone in which the Web Part is placed allows this.

- **Title.** Specifies the title of the Web Part as it appears in the browser. The value of this property is used when you search for Web Parts by using the Search command on the Find Web Parts menu of the tool pane.

- **Height.** Allows you to choose whether the Web Part should have a fixed height specified in various units (centimeters, inches, millimeters, points, picas, or pixels) or whether the Web Part should be sized to fit the zone, where the height of the Web Part is automatically adjusted to fit the zone. If this property is not set or if it is set programmatically to Empty, the Web Part is allowed to grow to be as big as its content within the limits of the zone that contains it.

- **Width.** Allows you to make the same choices for width as for height.

- **Frame State.** When this property is set to Minimize, only the title of the Web Part is displayed. Otherwise the title and contents are displayed. Users can choose to "Restore" a minimized Web Part within the browser.

- **Frame Style.** Also known as the FrameType property, it allows you to specify one of the following with regard to the title bar and border of the Web Part:

  - To use the specified value of the Web Part Page Zone FrameType property, select **Default**. This is the default.

  - To display the content, but not the title bar and frame, select **None**.

  - To display the title bar, content, and frame, select **Title Bar and Border**.

  - To display the title bar and content, but no frame, select **Title Bar Only**.

Layout Properties

The Layout section allows you to specify how the Web Part is placed or viewed on the page. These properties, listed here, can be personalized if the zone in which the Web Part is placed allows this.

- **Include on Page.** This property specifies whether the Web Part is actually present on the page. If this property is not checked, the Web Part, along with any customizations, is present in the Web Part Page gallery for this page, and users can add it later should they want to. Galleries are detailed later in this chapter. Using the browser, the same effect can be achieved by clicking the arrow on the right side of the Web Part title bar and clicking Close. This property is called *IsIncluded* by the underlying **Common Language Runtime (CLR)** class for a Web Part.

- **Visible on Page.** Specifies whether the Web Part is displayed on the page. A Web Part whose *Visible on Page* property is not checked (False) will be visible only when the Web page is in design mode. Sometimes it is desirable to have a "behind the scenes" Web Part that feeds data to other Web Parts via Web Part connections. A similar concept exists with ASP.NET custom controls, where a control can be present on a page but not be displayed.

- **Direction.** Specifies the direction of the reading order of the text in the Web Part: left to right, right to left, or default. When set to default, the text direction is determined by the language settings.

- **Zone.** Specifies the zone to which this Web Part belongs.

- **Part Order.** Specifies the location of the Web Part within the zone. The value for this property is an integer greater than zero. For example, a value of two means that the Web Part is second from the top if the orientation of the Web Parts within a zone is laid out top to bottom.

Because static Web Parts are not placed within zones, the Visible on Page, Zone, and Part Order properties are ignored. Also, static Web Parts do not have the ID property, which is set by the Web Part infrastructure when you include a dynamic Web Part on your Web Part. This allows for the retrieval of the Web Part from the content database.

Advanced Properties

The Advanced Properties section contains the following shared properties, and therefore the Advanced Properties section is visible only in Shared View. These properties can be customized if the zone in which the Web Part is placed allows this.

- **Allow Minimize.** Specifies whether a Web Part can be minimized by the user at run time within the browser. If the check box next to this property is not set (False), the Minimize option will not be available on the Web Part's drop-down menu and the Frame State property option buttons will be disabled or not visible, depending on whether you are in Shared View or Personal View.

- **Allow Close.** Specifies whether a Web Part can be closed—that is, removed from the page and moved into the Web Part Page gallery by the user at run time within the browser. When this property is set to False, the Close option will not appear on the Web Part's drop-down menu. Galleries will be discussed later in this chapter.

- **Allow Zone Change.** Specifies whether the Web Part can be moved to a different zone by the user at run time within the browser. When this property is set to False, you cannot drag the Web Part to another zone, but you are still able to close the Web Part. When you add the Web Part back to the page from the Web Part Page gallery, you can only place it in the zone from which it originated.

> **Note**   Properties values are used while viewing Web Parts in the browser. They do not affect how the Web Part behaves when you use an HTML-compatible editor such as FrontPage 2003. For example, even when Allow Zone Change is not selected, it is possible in FrontPage 2003 to move the Web Part from one zone to another. To prevent a user from minimizing, removing, or moving the Web Part by using the browser, you set the Allow Minimize, Allow Remove, and Allow Zone Change properties to False.

- **Allow Export Sensitive Properties.**   Applies only in the personal view and controls whether a user can export sensitive data by selecting Export from the Web Part menu to a **Web Part description (.dwp) file**, which is an XML document. The .dwp file captures a snapshot of the property settings for a Web Part and a reference to the assembly (.DLL) and the .NET class used to create it. An assembly is the .NET term for the smallest unit of deployment, and deployment will be described later in this chapter. If the Allow Export Sensitive Properties check box is not set (False), not all Web Part properties will be exported; only properties not flagged by the developer as controlled properties will be exported. The developer can use the ControlledProperties property to prevent the viewing and distribution of one or more property values that might contain sensitive information. This property also controls whether a Web Part property can be accessed by the **Web Part Services Component (WPSC)** that runs on the client computer or whether it can be used in the default Web service. For more information, see the Client-side Communication topic in the SharePoint Products and Technologies 2003 *SDK*.

- **Detail Link.**   Specifies the URL of an HTML file containing additional information about the Web Part. When you click the Web Part title, the file is displayed in the same window that hosted the Web Part Page. To return to the Web Part Page, click the browser's Back button. The detail link is disabled when viewing the Web Part in design mode. If this were not the case, you would not be able to move the Web Part by using a drag-and-drop operation because any attempt would be redirected to the HTML file.

- **Description.**   Specifies the screen tip that appears when you rest the mouse pointer on the Web Part title or the Web Part icon. When you search for Web Parts by using the Search command on the Find Web Parts menu of the tool pane, the value of this property is used.

- **Help Link.**   Specifies the location of an HTML-formatted file containing Help information that will help the end user interact with the Web Part. The Help information is displayed in a separate browser window when you click the Help command on the Web Part menu.

- **Icon File (Large).**   Also known as the PartImageLarge property; specifies the location of a file containing a large Web Part icon. This icon is used when the Web Part is listed in a gallery. The image size must be 16 by 16 pixels.

- **IconFile (Small).**   Known as the PartImageSmall property; is not currently used by the Web Part infrastructure and is reserved for future use, so this property is irrelevant in Windows SharePoint Service 2.0 and SharePoint Portal Server 2003.

- **Missing Assembly Error.**   Specifies a message that appears when you import a Web Part for which the assembly file is missing or incorrect. An assembly can contain one or more Web Parts. If this property is not set, a system default message will be displayed.

- **Target Audiences.**   By clicking the Select button, the Select Audiences – Web Page dialog box is displayed. This allows you to target a Web Part to a specific audience. Add selected audiences from the available audiences list, and click OK. If no audiences are targeted, the Web Part is viewed by all portal users. To view the audiences that the Web Part targets, display the Select Audiences – Web Page dialog box. This property is valid only on portal site Web Part Pages.

Custom Properties

Custom Properties are displayed under group headings in the Web Part tool page as specified by their category attribute in the tool part CustomPropertiesToolPart, as described earlier in this chapter. Any property that is not displayed under the Advanced, Layout, or Appearance group headings is a custom property. The custom properties displayed in the Web Part tool pane are dependent on the Web Part that you modify.

A group heading that is often visible when you are editing a Web Part is Miscellaneous. If a developer does not specify a category attribute, or if Default or Miscellaneous is specified, all the Web Part's custom properties are displayed under the Miscellaneous heading of the tool pane. For example, the Grouped Listings Web Part and Web Parts based on the Grouped Listings Web Part have the Cache Timeout and Cache Per User properties listed under this Miscellaneous section.

On a portal site where you are using the default area templates, the developers have specified a category attribute of *Custom Properties* for some Web Part custom properties. You will therefore see a group heading of Custom Properties on the tool pane for these Web Parts.

Other section names might appear, depending on the value of the category attribute. You might also see properties at the top of the tool pane under no category section. For example, Group Listings Web Parts have a Change Location link, and if you add a list to a Web Part Page you will see the properties *Selected View* and *Toolbar Type*. These custom properties will be discussed later in this chapter when the built-in Web Parts are described.

Adding New Web Parts

You can add new Web Parts on a Web Part Page by using the browse, search, or import methods. Also, when you use a drag-and-drop operation to place a list or a library into a Web Part Page Zone, a Web Part is automatically created that displays a view of the list or library. To add a new Web Part to a Web Part Page by using the browser, on the Modify Shared Page menu (Shared View) or the Modify My Page menu (Personal View), point to Add Web Parts, and then click Browse, Search, or Import.

Browse and Search

If you click Browse, you are presented with four galleries: the Web Part Page gallery, <Site Name> gallery, Virtual Server gallery, and Online gallery. If you click Search, you can limit your selection to Web Parts with names that contain your search text. Both the Browse command and the Search command, once you have searched for a Web Part, will display a list of the four available galleries, with a number in brackets next to each gallery that shows how many Web Parts are available in that gallery. When you select a gallery, a list of the Web Parts is displayed. In the case of the <Site Name> gallery, also known as the *team site gallery*, the number of Web Parts displayed in the tool pane will include Web Parts from the Web Part Gallery list, together with the name of the lists or libraries that are created for the area or site in which the Web Part Page resides. The Web Part Gallery list can be viewed by navigating to the Manage Web Part Gallery link by clicking Site Settings and then, when you are on a portal site, by clicking Manage Security And Additional Settings, or when you are on a Windows SharePoint Services site, by navigating to the Top-Level Site Administration page. An example of a portal site's team site gallery in a tool pane is illustrated in Figure 31-2, where there are 21 built-in Web Parts and four lists or libraries contained within the portal's Home area. The lists or libraries visible on the task pane are Document Library and Image Library. For a Windows SharePoint Services site, the team site gallery would contain only six built-in Web Parts, plus any lists or libraries contained within the site.

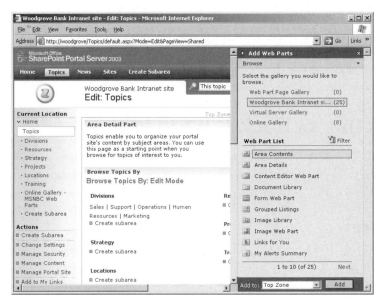

Figure 31-2   Add Web Parts - Browse

Drag the Web Part or a Web Part that displays a list or library that you want to add to the page from the task pane into a Web Part Page Zone on the Web Part Page. You can then close the task pane or select more Web Parts. The drag-and-drop operations for adding Web Parts to a page are available in browsers that support rich user interaction. You do not need to use the drag-and-drop method of adding a Web Part to a page; the task pane includes a drop-down list for choosing a Web Part Page Zone on the page and an Add button for adding the selected Web Part to the selected zone. (Refer back to Figure 31-2.) Additionally, these alternative controls together with the keyboard shortcuts make Web Parts accessible to users who do not use a mouse. For more information on keyboard shortcuts, refer to either the *SharePoint Portal Server 2003 Administrator's Guide* or the *Windows SharePoint Services Administrator's Guide*.

Import

The third method of adding a new Web Part to a Web Part Page is to Import the Web Part. You can import a Web Part to a page even if the Web Part is not yet included in a gallery, as long as you can locate the .dwp file for the Web Part; the assembly for the Web Part is available in the **Global Assembly Cache (GAC)** or in the bin directory for the virtual server, and the Web Part is added to the safe control list. The GAC is a machine-wide code cache, where you place assemblies (.DLL files) that are shared among several applications.

To add a Web Part by referencing a .dwp file, on the Web Part Page, click Modify Shared Page (Shared View) or Modify My Page (Personal View), point to Add

Web Parts, and then click Import. In the task pane, type the path to the .dwp file, or click the Browse button and then browse to the location of the .dwp file. The selected Web Part appears in the task pane. Drag the Web Part to a Web Part Page Zone on the page, or use the Add To menu to select a Web Part Page Zone and then click Add.

Purpose and Use of Each Built-In Web Part

When you first install a SharePoint site, built-in Web Parts will be visible from the Add Web Parts tool pane in the <Site Name> gallery and the Online gallery. This section will describe the built-in Web Parts visible within these two galleries.

<Site Name> Gallery

The <Site Name> gallery contains Web Parts that are available to a particular site. The number of built-in Web Parts installed in this galley depends on whether the site is a portal site or a Windows SharePoint Services site and on the number of lists or libraries created in an area or site. The built-in Web Parts are described in the following sections.

Area-Specific Web Parts

These Web Parts are available on portal sites and My Site. They enable you to display area-specific information. By default, the area information that these Web Parts will display is specific to the area Web Page on which they are placed. So, for example, if you place the Grouped Listings Web Part on the portal's home page, you will see the targeted links held within the Home Portal Listings list. You can, however, use the Location link in the Current Area Override section of the Properties tool pane to configure the Grouped Listings Web Part to use the Topic or any other area's Portal Listings list.

All these Web Parts have the Appearance, Layout, and Advanced properties mentioned earlier, plus the Change Location property and the following Web Part–specific custom properties:

- **Area Contents.**   Used to display the contents of subareas; by default, it is placed on the Topics Web Part Page, where it is labeled *Browse Topics By*. The custom properties for this Web Part allow you to specify the number of top-level columns, the number of areas shown by default, the number of listings shown by default, the use of vertical layout for areas and listings and the alignment of areas horizontally. These properties show top-level area listings, the subtitle, Listings, area icons, listing icons, and descriptions, and they specify the description trim size.

- **Area Details.** Used to display area details such as description and contact details. By default, this property is placed on many of the area Web Pages and has custom properties to show the subtitle. It allows you to fix the image width and height in pixels, and you can decide whether you want the picture of the area's contact to be displayed.

- **Grouped Listings.** Used to display listings—that is, target items held within a Portal Listings list. This Web Part is included in most area templates. This might not be immediately obvious because the title for the Web Part when it is included on area pages would be different or have no title at all. The custom properties include Maximum Number Of Listings, Fixed Image Width And Height In Pixels, Ignore Listings In Anchor Area, Subarea Layers, Display Template, Group By, Sort Listings By, Sort Direction, Display Column, Highlights Visibility, More Info Link Text Label, More Info Link URL, Description Trim Size, and Show Subtitle. This Web Part also has two custom properties— Cache Timeout and Cache Per User—which appear under the Miscellaneous group heading. A Web Part can be designed to store frequently used data in **cache** on a shared (all users) basis or on a per-user basis to expedite data retrieval. If the data is to be stored in cache, you can also specify the timeout value, which specifies the length of time during which the Web server should retrieve the data from cache. If the time has expired, the Web server should reference the data source, which could be the original .aspx file or the content database. The data will then be copied into the cache and would be valid for the timeout value specified. The Web Part cache can be configured to be either held in memory or in an SQL database, on a Virtual Server basis, by configuring the Web.config file; however, static Web Parts can use cache only if it is memory. A decision on Web Parts and caching should be part of the design process and involve both developers and administrators. For more information, see the *"Web Parts and Caching"* topic in the *SharePoint Portal Server 2003* or *Windows SharePoint Services SDK*. Other Web Parts that are based on the Group Listings Web Part and described in this chapter are News, News Area, Links For You, and News For You.

- **News.** This Web Part is placed by default on a portal site's home page and the News Web Part Page. It is based on the Grouped Listings Web Part—that is, it will display links contained in the Portal Listing List and has the same custom properties as stated earlier. The maximum number of Listings is set to five. This Web Part uses the expanded display template and sorts listings by creation date. If you place this Web Part on a different area page, it would not show the items listed in the News Portal Listing list. To configure this Web Part to display the News links, you would need to change the location *Home > News* by using the link in the Current Area Override section, which is how this Web Part is configured on a portal site's home page.

- **News Area.** This Web Part is placed by default on the News Web Part Page. It is based on the Grouped Listing Web Part, with the maximum number of listings set to 3. It ignores listings in the anchor area, uses a minimum display template, groups the listings by area, and sorts listings by creation date in descending order. The subarea layers property is set to one. Therefore, the Web Part will display the links in the Portal Listings list for the subareas beneath the current area Web Part; for example, if you placed this Web Part on the Topics page, it would display any links that were stored in the Portal Listings list for the subareas Divisions, Resources, Strategy, Projects, and Locations. If you placed this Web Part on the portal site's home page, any links that were stored in the Portal Listings list for Topics, News, and Sites would be displayed.

- **Topic Assistant Suggestion.** Used to display topic assistant suggestions for this area. The information that you view in this Web Part is a subset of the information you could view if you displayed an area's Portal Listings list and chose the Suggestions view. The custom properties allow you to specify the maximum number of items to display, (the default is 50), fix the width of the Web Part to the first table row, specify the widths of columns, and customize the display text if the Topic Assistant has suggested no items for this area.

> **Tip**   A Web Part that is not in any of the galleries but is very useful is the Web Part named *Portal Owner QuickStart Guide* that is displayed on a portal site's home page. In the Miscellaneous category section, the property HTML for Links' text box contains code. This code displays links that, when clicked, open a separate window displaying Help files. This Web Part can be exported and then imported on any other Web page and amended to suit your requirements.

Generic Web Parts

By default, these Web Parts are available in the <Site Name> gallery on all SharePoint sites; however, a person with administrative permissions could remove the Web Part from the gallery or make the Web Part unsafe to use. All these Web Parts are accompanied by a Help file that can be accessed by clicking the arrow on the right side of the Web Part title bar and clicking Help. This is available in Web Part Page design or view mode. The Generic Web Parts include the following:

- **Content Editor Web Part.** Used to format text, tables, and images. The Content Editor Web Part is intended for adding HTML content to a Web Part Page; it is not designed to link to a website. You can add content to this Web Part by using the Rich Text Editor or HTML source editor or by providing a link to a text file. These options are provided under the Content Editor section of the Properties tool pane. If you need to link to a website, consider using the Page Viewer Web Part. The HTML <FORM> element is not allowed in the Content Editor Web Part. If you need to add a Web Part that uses the <FORM> element, consider using the Page Viewer Web Part or the Form Web Part. Use this Web Part for the following requirements:

- You want to permit users to quickly enter richly formatted text.

- You want to display content that is editable by users with the appropriate permissions.

- You want to use Microsoft JScript or Microsoft Visual Basic Scripting Edition (VBScript) to develop the functionality of the Web Part.

- You want to incorporate existing JScript or VBScript files into a Web Part.

- You do not need to use the built-in Web Part connection interfaces to connect your Web Part.

- Client-side script is not a security concern.

- **Form Web Part.**   Used to connect simple form controls to other Web Parts. Both Web Parts must run on the same site server. To use this Web Part, you must connect with another Web Part by using a **Web Part Connection**. This allows the contents of one Web Part to change depending on an item selected in another Web Part. In this case, the text you type in the text box, once you click the Go control, will filter the contents of the Web Part to which you have connected. To form the connection between the Form Web Part and the other Web Parts, click the arrow on the right side of the Form Web Part title bar and choose Connections. Then click Prove Form Value To, and select the Web Part you want the Form Web Part to connect to. You can connect the Form Web Part to one or more Web Parts on a Web Part Page. You can also modify the Form Web Part to display option buttons, check boxes, and other controls by using either the Source Editor custom property or by using FrontPage 2003. More information can be found in this Web Part's Help file.

- **Image Web Part.**   Used to display pictures and photos. This Web Part is included in many of the Windows SharePoint Service site templates to display a logo on the site's home Web Part Page. You can control the vertical alignment, horizontal alignment, and background color of the image inside the Image Web Part by modifying its custom properties. In this way, you can match the image with other Web Parts on the page. This is another Web Part that is often used with Web Part connections so that, instead of entering a file path or a hyperlink to the image file in the Image Link custom property, you would connect the Web Part to this Image Web Part. When a user selects an item in that Web Part, it provides a file path or a hyperlink to the Image Web Part so that the image can be dynamically changed based on the user's selection.

■ **Page Viewer Web Part.**   Used to display linked content, such as files, folders, or Web pages. The linked content is isolated from other content on the Web Part Page and therefore can be used only in a browser that supports the HTML <IFRAME> element. If you use this Web Part to display a file or folder, Microsoft Internet Explorer is required. This Web Part displays the content asynchronously from the rest of the page. This means that you can view and use other Web Parts on the page if the link happens to take a long time to return the content. Use this Web Part for the following requirements:

■ You want to incorporate existing content (such as a website or document) into a Web Part.

■ You want to display existing content with no additional functionality.

■ You want to display an entire Web page within a Web Part.

■ You want to isolate a Web Part from the rest of the Web Part Page.

■ You want to use nested forms. Web Part Pages are .aspx pages that use ASP.NET server controls. Nested forms are not permitted inside an ASP.NET server control unless they are isolated with an <IFRAME> element. Because the Page Viewer renders content within an <IFRAME> element, you can use it to display pages that contain a <form> tag.

■ You want to retrieve data from a server that requires authentication. In this case, the Page Viewer Web Part forwards authentication credentials from the client.

■ **XML Web Part.**   Used for Extensible Markup Language (XML) and to apply Extensible Stylesheet Language (XSL) to define how the XML is displayed. In the Properties tool pane, you can add XML by using the XML Editor or entering a URL to an XML file. Similarly, the XSL can be entered using the XSL editor, or you can link to an XSL file. The content displayed in the XML Web Part cannot contain an HTML <FORM> element. If you need to use the <FORM> element, consider using the Page Viewer Web Part or the Form Web Part. You might use the XML Web Part to display the following:

■ Structured data from database tables or queries

■ XML-based documents

■ XML forms that combine structured and unstructured data, such as weekly status reports or travel expense reports

Personal or Targeted Web Parts

Many of these targeted or personal Web Parts are either on the portal's home page or on My Site.

- **Links for You.**   Used to display links targeted to you. This is one of the default Web Parts placed on your Private View of the My Site Web Part Page and a portal site's home page. This is based on the Grouped Listings Web Part. Only a subset of the properties is available to you to personalize on your personal website, My Site.

- **My Alerts Summary.**   Used to display your alerts and alert results. This is one of the default Web Parts placed on your Private View of the My Site Web Part Page.

- **My Calendar.**   Used to display your calendar. This is one of the default Web Parts placed on your private view of the My Site Web Part Page. To configure this Web Part, click open the tool pane. You need to set three properties: *Exchange folder name* (by default, this is Calendar), the *Mail server address* (for example, *http://mail.woodgrovebank.com/exchange*), and your *mailbox* ID.

- **My Inbox.**   Used to display your inbox. This Web Part interfaces with Microsoft Exchange 2000 and 2003 and is very similar to the My Calendar Web Part in that you have to configure the same three properties. However, the default for the Exchange folder name for this Web Part is *inbox*.

- **My Links.**   One of the default Web Parts placed on your Private View of the My Site Web Part Page.

- **My Mail Folder.**   Used to display the mail folder you specify. It works with Microsoft Exchange 2003. This defaults to your inbox, but it can be changed by amending the Exchange folder name custom property that is displayed in the Mail Configuration category section on the Properties tool pane.

- **My Tasks.**   Used to display your tasks as stored in Exchange.

- **My Workspace Sites.**   Used to display your workspace sites.

- **News for You.**   One of the default Web Parts placed on your Private View of the My Site Web Part Page.

- **Your Recent Documents.**   One of the default Web Parts placed on your Shared View of My Site Web Part Page that displays documents you recently opened.

Windows SharePoint Services–Specific Web Parts

There is only one Web Part specific to Windows SharePoint Services:

- **Members.**   Use this Web Part to see a list of the site members and their online status. This Web Part is available by default on a Windows SharePoint Services website but not on a portal site.

List and Library Web Parts

When you create lists or libraries, you will find them listed in the Browse or Search tool pane under the <Site Name> gallery. You can then use a drag-and-drop operation to move them onto the Web Part Page. The default view will be used to display items stored in a list or a library. These Web Parts are often called *List View Web Parts* or *data lists*. You can change the view, edit the current view, and change the toolbar type by using the List View section in the Properties tool pane, as illustrated in Figure 31-3.

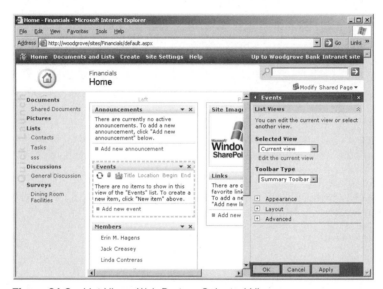

Figure 31-3   List Views Web Parts – Selected View

Be careful when switching to a different view from the current view. You might remove changes you have made to the current view and might disable Web Part connections that depend on columns in the current view. You are prompted for confirmation if you switch views.

The title property for the List View Web Part is set to the name of the list, with the detailed link set to the Web Part Page that displays the list and the Help list set to the List View Part Summary topic in the User's Guide. These Web Parts are often used in combination with a Form Web Part. They also cannot be exported to a .dwp file.

Online Gallery

The default Web Parts displayed in the Online gallery are based on the Content Editor Web Part and reference Web services over the Internet. The URL for this Web service is specified in the OnlineLibrary element of the Web.config file for a site. This gallery provides a way for the IT administrator to deploy Web Parts so that many servers can share access to a common, centrally maintained gallery of Web Parts. The built-in Web Parts are listed here and are illustrated in Figure 31-4.

- MSNBC Business Needs

- MSNBC Stock Quotes

- MSNBC Entertainment News

- MSNBC Sports News

- MSNBC Stock News

- MSNBC Weather

- MSNBC Technology News

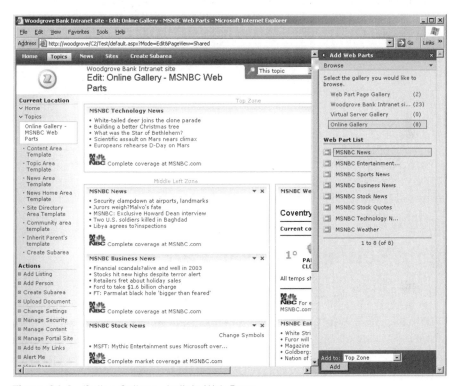

Figure 31-4   Online Gallery – built-in Web Parts

Connecting Web Parts

Web Parts can connect to other Web Parts using standard interfaces. For example, if you connect an Image Web Part to a List View Web Part, which has a column containing hyperlink data type, you can make the image in the Image Web Part change depending on the row that is selected in the List View Web Part.

Perhaps the most interesting and innovative new feature for Web Parts is an infrastructure in which Web Parts can use standard interfaces to communicate with each other. Users can use simple menu selections to connect Web Parts that are able to exchange data, and the Web Parts can be developed completely independently of each other. For example, a graphing Web Part from one vendor could be connected to a datasheet view Web Part from another, or a stock quote Web Part could show the current share price for the company selected in another Web Part that lists suppliers.

The Web Part infrastructure provides rich support for communication between Web Parts. Developers can use standard interfaces to create Web Parts that can exchange information with each other. Users can connect Web Parts to each other by using simple menu commands in the browser.

Additionally, the Web Part infrastructure provides transformers that allow Web Parts to communicate with each other even if their interfaces are not exactly complementary. The Web Part infrastructure automatically detects an interface mismatch and displays a dialog box that allows the user to map values from one interface to the other.

Note   You can create connections only when the page is in Design View.

Connections can have a performance impact. For example, if you allow Web Part connections and a user connects a complex Web Part to a large data set, the Web Part Page that contains those Web Parts could take a long time to load when a user browses to it. You can control whether users can connect Web Parts to each other within a site on a Virtual Server basis.

Managing Settings for Web Part Pages

Web Part Page security settings are set at the virtual server level and affect all sites on that virtual server. You can specify whether users can create connections between Web Parts in a site and whether the Online Web Part gallery is available. By default, both security options are enabled at the server level. You need to change these options only if you do not want to allow either Web Part connections or access to the Online Web Part gallery. If you have multiple servers in a server farm environment and you want to change these settings for all virtual servers, you must configure these options for each virtual server on each server in that server farm. You must be an administrator of the local server computer or a member of the SharePoint Administrators group to configure security and performance options for Web Parts and Web Part Pages. Navigate to these configure options for Web Parts and Web Part Pages by clicking SharePoint Central Administration from the Administrative Tools menu. On the SharePoint Central Administration page, click Configure Virtual Server Settings From The Virtual Server List Page and then click the virtual server that you want to configure. On the Virtual Server Settings page, click Manage Security Settings For Web Part Pages and select the options you want to enable or disable, as illustrated in Figure 31-5, and then click OK.

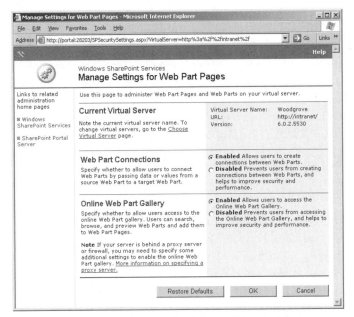

Figure 31-5   Manage Security Settings for Web Part Pages

You can also return to using the default server settings of enabling users to both connect Web Parts and use the Online gallery by clicking Restore Defaults.

Working with Web Part Galleries

Windows SharePoint Services provides the following four types of galleries that can contain Web Parts:

- Web Part Page gallery
- <Site Name> gallery
- Virtual Server gallery
- Online gallery

Web Part Page Gallery

A Web Part Page gallery contains Web Parts that are already added to the current page. This might seem paradoxical at first. Why would you need to add a Web Part that is already added to the page? This is useful because you can add a Web Part to a page and then close the Web Part. To close a Web Part, click the arrow on the right side of the Web Part title bar and then click Close. A closed Web Part is no longer visible on the page, but it is still a member of the Web Part Page gallery for that page. The Web Part is still associated with the page by an entry in the content database of the server, which also stores any shared or personalized property settings for the Web Part. Each Web Part Page has its own Web Part Page gallery.

You can add a Web Part to a page, personalize it extensively, close it, and then later add it back to the page with the personalization intact. To bring back a closed Web Part, select it from the Web Part Page gallery and drag it to the designated position.

When you first create a Web Part Page, there are no Web Parts within this gallery.

To truly delete a Web Part from a page, you must click the Modify My Page menu (or the Modify Shared Page menu in Shared View) and then click Design This Page to add the Delete command to the drop-down menu of the Web Part. To delete a Web Part from the Web Part Page gallery, perform either of the following steps:

- Add the Web Part back on to the page, click the arrow on the right side of the Web Part title bar, and then click **Delete**.

    Or

- Browse to the Web Part Maintenance page, select the check box to the right of the Web Part, and click **Delete**. Make sure you are in the view you want, either Personal View or Shared View. A note at the bottom of the page displays whether you are in Personal View or Shared View. If the Web Part Page is stored in a document library, rest your mouse pointer on the title, click **Edit Properties** on the **Edit** menu, and then click **Open Web Part Page in maintenance view**. If you are viewing the Web Part Page, you can navigate to the Web Part Maintenance page by appending *?Contents=1* to the Web Part Page's URL—for example, *http://woodgrove/sites/Financials/default.aspx?contents=1*. You can alternatively specify the view from the query as well, by adding Page-View=Shared or PageView=Personal when used with contents=1. This will take you to the correct view—for example, *http://woodgrove/default.aspx?Contents=1&PageView=Personal*.

> **Tip**   The Web Part Maintenance page is an extremely useful page if you are having persistent problems with a Web Part or a Web Part connection. Also, if the Web Part that the user closes initially is bad and does not allow the page to render, the only way to delete the offending Web Part by using the browser is to use the Web Part Maintenance page.

\<Site Name\> Gallery

This Web Part Page gallery is typically managed by a site collection administrator, who decides which Web Parts are displayed in the gallery and thereby determines which Web Parts are visible in the team site gallery for sites in the site collection. There is only one \<Site Name\> gallery for each site collection. Site collection administrators can use the Web Part Gallery page to add or remove Web Parts from the list of Web Parts available for use or to upload new Web Parts.

> **Caution**   When you add a Web Part to a site gallery, the .dwp file is copied into the content database for that site. If you make a change to the .dwp file, you must import it again or the change is ignored.

You can also have Windows SharePoint Services automatically create a default .dwp file for a Web Part assembly when you install the Web Part, if the assembly for the Web Part is already installed on the server and has been added to the safe controls list. The generated default .dwp is added to the Web Part Page gallery and will appear by default in the team site gallery.

To do display Web Parts in the <Site Name> gallery, follow these steps:

1. On the home page, click **Site Settings**.

2. On the Site Settings page, if it is a portal site, click **Manage security and additional settings**; on a Windows SharePoint Services website in the Administration area, click **Go to Site Administration.**

3. Click **Manage Web Part Page gallery**, which is under the Templates And Web Parts section on a portal site, and on a Windows SharePoint Services site in the Site Collection Galleries area. The Web Part Page Gallery page is displayed and lists the Web Parts currently added to the <Site Name> gallery, as illustrated in Figure 31-6. If you click the Web Parts .dwp file name, you will see a preview of the Web Part.

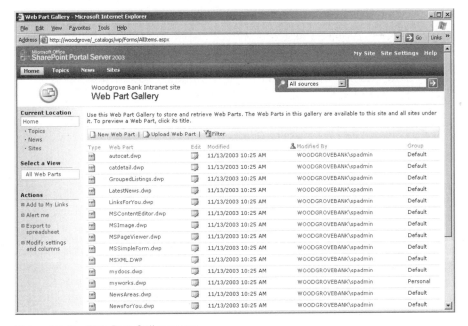

Figure 31-6   Web Part Gallery page

4. Click **New Web Part**.

5. On the Web Part Gallery: New Web Part Page, as illustrated in Figure 31-7, select the check box for any Web Part that you want to add to the site gallery. These are all the Web Parts that are identified as safe in the SafeControls section of an applicable Web.config file.

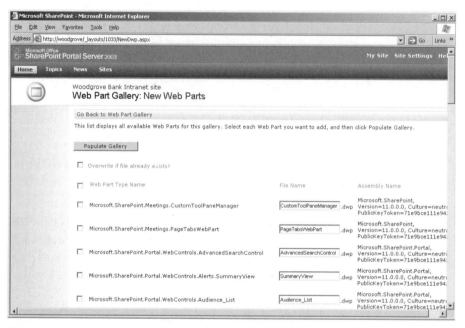

Figure 31-7 Web Part Gallery: New Web Parts

6. Optionally, type a name for the .dwp file for each Web Part that you selected. A default file name is entered automatically, based on the class name.

7. Click **Populate Gallery**. A minimal .dwp file is created automatically and added to a gallery named <Site Name> Gallery.

Web Parts that are added to a <Site Name> gallery become available to that site and to all sites under it.

If you have installed a Web Part Package and you need to add the Web Parts to the gallery, you can use the Upload Web Part button to add the new Web Parts to the gallery.

Web Parts can be organized into groups for easy filtering in the gallery. You can specify which group a Web Part belongs to when you add a Web Part to the Web Part Page gallery. Groups are optional—you can add a Web Part without specifying a group.

You can remove a Web Part from the gallery by clicking the Edit icon next to the .dwp file name on the Web Part Gallery page and then clicking Delete. You can also export the Web Part or view the XML. Deleting the Web Part makes it unavailable to users through the <Site Name> gallery. If a user has already used a Web Part in the site and you delete the Web Part from the site gallery, the Web Part will remain on the Web Part Page and will still work because all you did was remove the Web Part from showing up in the gallery by removing the .dwp. However, if an administrator on the server computer removes the Web Part assembly that contains the Web Part from the server or marks the assembly as unsafe in the Web.config file for the server, the Web Part will no longer run and the user will see an error message.

Virtual Server Gallery

This is the gallery where the Web Parts are installed when you use the Stsadm.exe tool. There are no built-in Web Parts in this gallery when you first install a Share-Point site. To add Web Parts to the Virtual Server gallery, add them to the <local drive>\inetpub\wwwroot\wpcatalog directory—that is, to the root directory for each of your virtual servers. You can use the Stsadm.exe command-line tool to do this, as explained in the "Web Part Assembly Deployment" section later in this chapter. The biggest benefit of adding your Web Parts to the Virtual Server gallery is that you can deploy localized Web Parts. Then, depending on the language you have chosen to create your site from, you will see Web Parts only in that language. For example, if you have German Web Parts, they will be displayed only when the language used to create the site is German. If you have a subsite that is English, English Web Parts will be displayed. So, in a site collection you can have sites displaying specific languages on the Web pages and the matching language in the Virtual Server gallery. This is done by creating culture subdirectories under the wpcatalog folder—for example, *wpcatalog\neutral\WebPart1.dwp* and *wpcatalog\de-DE\GermanWebPart1.dwp*. You will need to install language packs to be able to create sites based on site templates that use specific languages. These are available from the Microsoft Windows SharePoint Services website. The Virtual Server Gallery lists Web Parts that are available to all sites on that virtual server.

Online Gallery

The Online gallery is an additional set of Web Parts that is available from Microsoft. When you connect to an Online gallery, Windows SharePoint Services makes an HTTP request to the remote server that hosts the Web Part Page gallery. When the remote server receives the HTTP request, it uses the criteria contained in the request to perform a search operation and sends back a response. Windows SharePoint Services then displays the search results in the Add Web Parts tool pane. When you add a Web Part to a page, you might be prompted to agree to an End User Licensing Agreement (EULA). After you accept the EULA, Windows SharePoint Services retrieves the .dwp file that describes the Web Part from the remote server and adds the Web Part to the page. The Online gallery is enabled by default, but you can disable it as detailed earlier in this chapter. If the Online gallery is not listed under Add Web Parts, one or both of the following conditions are true:

- Access to the online Web Part Page gallery is disabled on the virtual server.

- Your server is behind a proxy server or firewall; the proxy server settings are not specified in the Web.config file for the virtual server.

To resolve this issue, enable access to the online Web Part Page gallery on the virtual server. If your server is behind a proxy server or firewall, you must also edit the Web.config file to include the proxy server settings for the virtual server where you want to enable the online Web Part Page gallery. In a server farm environment, you must edit the Web.config file for each virtual server in every front-end Web server in the server farm.

To configure the Web.config file, follow these steps:

1. Start a text editor, such as Notepad.

2. Locate and open the Web.config file for the virtual server where you want to enable access to the online Web Part Page gallery. The default location of the Web.config is in the following folder: <local drive>:\Inetpub\wwwroot. Check that this is the correct location by using the Internet Information Server (IIS) Manager, and under the **Web Sites** section, right-click the appropriate virtual server, select Properties, and then click the **Home Directory** tab where you can take note of the local path name.

3. Locate the </system.web> entry near the end of the Web.config file.

4. Copy and paste the following lines to the Web.config file, immediately after the *</system.web>* entry, where *<ProxyServer>* is the name of your proxy server and *<Port>* is the port that you are using:

```
<system.net>
  <defaultProxy>
  <proxy proxyaddress="http://<ProxyServer>:<port>" bypassonlocal = "true"/
>
</defaultProxy>
</system.net>
```

5. Save the Web.config file, and then close the text editor.

Repeat steps 1 through 5 for each virtual server where you want to enable access to the online Web Part Page gallery.

If your organization runs Windows SharePoint Services on multiple servers, you might want to create an online Web Part Page gallery as a central location for deploying Web Parts to all your SharePoint sites.

More Info The white paper "Technologies: Building an Online Web Part Gallery," by Nilly Banerjee (Microsoft Corporation, July 2003), details how to create an Online Web Part Page gallery as a central location for deploying Web Parts to multiple servers.

Web Part Assembly Deployment

You create Web Parts in C# or Visual Basic .NET by using the Web Part Library Template in Microsoft Visual Studio .NET as described in Chapter 37. This will be necessary if the built-in Web Parts do not meet your needs. These Web Parts are then compiled into assemblies; however, Web Parts are more than just the assemblies. A Web Part might have class resources such as images, JScript files, or Help files. These files might also be localized and deployed in locations that are different from the location of the Web Part. Additionally, the Web Part must be added to the SafeControl list for the specific virtual server before users can take advantage of its functionality.

A Web Part package is a cabinet (.cab) file that contains the following items:

- Manifest.xml (mandatory)
- Web Part assemblies (optional)
- Class resource files (optional)
- .dwp files (optional)

Developers can use either of the following methods to create a .cab file:

- Use Visual Studio .NET to create a CAB Project.
- Use MakeCAB.exe, a command-line tool included with Windows 2000 and later.

Visual Studio does not support creating .cab files with internal directories. However, localized Web Parts might require a .cab file with internal directories. Because of this, you must use a tool such as MakeCAB.exe or another third-party CAB utility to deploy localized Web Parts.

Server Administrators can use the Stsadm.exe tool to deploy .cab files created by developers. Stsadm.exe is a command-line tool that you can use to manage a Windows SharePoint Services computer. The following three Stsadm.exe options apply to Web Part package deployment:

- AddWPPack
- DeleteWPPack
- EnumWPPacks

To use the Stsadm.exe command to deploy a Web Part package on a server computer, open a command prompt and then type the following command:

```
CD \Program Files\Common Files\Microsoft Shared\web server extensions\60\BIN
stsadm.exe -o addwppack -filename PathtoWebPartPackname [-lcid language] [-url URL] [-globalinstall] [-force]
```

If you want to deploy a Web Part to a particular virtual server, use the –url parameter. The –force parameter forces a reinstall, and if you specify the LCID for the Web Part, you must also use the –globalinstall parameter. The –filename parameter points to a physical location where the Web Part resides, for example:

```
stsadm.exe -o addwppack -filename c:\SPS2003Labs\northwindcab.cab
```

If you have already installed a Web Part on a server and want to distribute it to other servers, on the server where the Web Part is already installed, use the –name parameter, as in the following command:

```
stsadm.exe -o addwppack -name WebPartPack_name [-url URL] [-globalinstall] [-force]
```

For example:

```
stsadm.exe -o addwppack -name northwindcab.cab
```

To delete a Web Part package from specified virtual servers, type the following command:

```
stsadm.exe -o deletewppack -name WebPartPackname [-lcid language] [-url URL]
```

To list all the Web Part packages installed on a computer, type the following command:

```
stsadm.exe -o enumwppacks [-name WebPartPackname][/language] [-url URL] [-farm]
```

To decide whether to install a Web Part package in the GAC or in the Bin directory, ask the following questions:

- Do you want to make this package available to all applications on your computer?

- Do you trust the assemblies and resources of the package completely?

If you answer yes to both of these questions, it might be appropriate to install the Web Part package into the GAC by using Stsadm.exe with the –globalinstall option. By default, assemblies in the GAC are fully trusted and are available to all virtual servers. Assemblies placed in the GAC can have a constraining policy applied to them as well. For more information, read "Microsoft Windows SharePoint Services and Code Access Security," which is available at *http://msdn.microsoft.com/library/default.asp?url=/library/en-us/odc_sp2003_ta/html/sharepoint_wsscodeaccesssecurity.asp.*

Note You can still install a Web Part package into the GAC and enable the Web Part only for a specific virtual server, using the safe controls list; however, this does not prevent nonextended virtual servers from using the assembly.

See Table 31-1 for a list of the differences between installing assemblies to the GAC and installing them in the Bin directory.

Table 31-1 Installation Differences Between the GAC and the BIN Directory

Item	GAC	Bin directory
Assembly location	local_drive:\Windows \Assembly	local_drive:\virtual_server_file system_location\bin
Class resources	<local drive>:\Program Files\Common Files \Microsoft Shared\Web Server Extensions\wpresources URL: *http://virtual_server /_wpresources*	<local_drive>:\ virtual_server_file system_location\wpresources URL: *http://virtual_server /wpresources*
Default Security Trust Level	Full	Partial (WSS_Minimal)
Accessible by all Virtual Servers	Yes (The assemblies and types must be enabled in the Safe-Controls list for each virtual server.)	No (The Web Part package is accessible only from the virtual server on which the assembly is installed.)
Prerequisites for using Stsadm.exe	The assembly must be a strong-named assembly.	
Requires using the -globalinstall switch	Yes	No

Note If you install the assembly to the Bin directory and the assembly requires code access security permissions that exceed the default policy for the Bin directory, you can assign these permissions after the deployment is complete. For information about code access security, see Chapter 37, "Using Visual Studio .NET to Create Web Parts" and the white paper "Microsoft Windows SharePoint Services and Code Access Security," which is available at *http://msdn.microsoft.com/library/default.asp?url=/library/en-us /odc_sp2003_ta/html/sharepoint_wsscodeaccesssecurity.asp*.

You can use Wppackager to package and create an MSI for a Web Part solution. In addition, while packaging the Web Part, you can specify additional permissions to set for the Web Part during installation. This automates the installation of Web Parts, ensuring components are deployed and code access security permissions are applied to Web Part assemblies consistently and in a repeatable manner. Administrators can install Web Part assemblies directly to the GAC or to the Bin directory for the specified virtual servers according to the specified deployment plan. Administrators can also easily remove the Web Part solution by using Add Or Remove Programs on the front-end Web server.

 More Info   See the white paper *"Using Wppackager to Package and Deploy Web Parts for Microsoft SharePoint Products and Technologies,"* by Parikshit Pol, Andrew Birck, and Emilio Concepcion (Microsoft Corporation, September 2003).

Summary

This chapter completes the review of the basic concepts for Web Part Pages and Web Parts and the customization of the default Web Part Pages and built-in Web Parts by using default tools such as the browser and the command-line tool Stsadm.exe. You can use Stsadm.exe to deploy Web Part packages to the GAC or to the Bin directory for specified virtual servers. This allows you to deploy Web Part packages across an entire organization or to only a limited set of sites, according to your requirements.

Chapter 32

Using Microsoft Office FrontPage 2003 to Customize SharePoint Products and Technologies Sites

Customizing your SharePoint site using Microsoft Office FrontPage 2003 can be done without coding, a degree in Web design, experience with XML or XSLT, or an understanding of database technologies. The WYSIWYG authoring environment combined with dynamic Web templates, auto-updating data views, prebuilt Web Parts, and Web connectors and built-in conditional formatting capabilities streamline the Web design and development process. With FrontPage 2003, site administrators and even end users themselves can rapidly extend and customize their SharePoint sites in hours—rather than days or weeks.

The combination of design and coding tools in FrontPage 2003 provides more control and greater flexibility over the layout of text, tables, navigation elements, graphics, Flash content, and other design elements on a Web page. Plus, you can apply fully customized themes and templates to design the SharePoint site you want.

SharePoint Products and Technologies Fundamentals

There are some fundamental SharePoint Products and Technologies concepts that serve as the building blocks for customizing websites.

Web Parts

Web Parts are a major asset of SharePoint Products and Technologies. Web Parts are modular units of information that can be inserted into pages. Third parties or corporate developers can develop Web Parts for SharePoint Lists, and document libraries can be inserted into pages as Web Parts from within FrontPage 2003, or even from the browser. Web Parts used in the website—such as Announcements, Contacts, and Shared Documents—can be accessed from the Web Parts task pane, as can Web Parts located on the server and online in the Online Gallery of Web Parts.

Lists

Because Microsoft SharePoint Portal Server 2003 is built on Microsoft Windows SharePoint Services, you can add both predesigned and custom lists to sites created with SharePoint Products and Technologies. For example, you can create a picture library to share a collection of digital pictures or create an issue tracking list to maintain a history on a specific issue. You can also use calendar views for any SharePoint list that has a date and time column. In addition, you can add attachments to list items, including HTML pages, documents, and images.

SharePoint lists are collections of information you can share with visitors to your website. Lists can contain a variety of data types, including text, numbers, hyperlinks, pictures, and more. Default lists on Windows SharePoint Services sites include Contacts, Events, Links, and Announcements. You can easily create new lists from various ready-made list templates or even custom lists by using the FrontPage 2003 List Wizard. Lists you create are made available to others on your site and also in the Web Parts task pane. The primary reason for putting information in Windows SharePoint Services lists is that the lists are updatable by authorized users from their browsers, making it easy for content owners to keep information on the site current.

Libraries

SharePoint libraries are central repositories for files, including Word documents, Excel spreadsheets, PowerPoint presentations, pictures, forms, and more. You can think of libraries as file shares that are exposed within Web pages. Users can upload files to SharePoint libraries from their browser, and hyperlinks are automatically created to the files contained in them—no more waiting for a Webmaster to create a link to a document you post to a file share.

Form libraries are new with Windows SharePoint Services. Form libraries are used to store XML-based business forms, such as expense reports or travel requests. Form libraries are very powerful when combined with an XML editor such as Microsoft Office InfoPath. With InfoPath, you can create a form and then associate that form with the form library so that InfoPath opens with the appropriate form when a user clicks Fill Out This Form. When the user is finished completing the form and then saves it, it is automatically stored in the form library. Even more importantly, you can designate which fields from the form to display in columns in the form library, thereby making the form data available to visitors to the site.

Areas

Default portal sites created with SharePoint Portal Server 2003 contain a top-level site and a number of subordinate sites. Areas are new in SharePoint Portal Server 2003 and are a great way to organize information on a portal site. The portal site is a hierarchy of rich subordinate sites that enable content managers to add lists, images, and documents to one or more areas. Content managers can approve or reject items that are submitted to the area. In addition, security can be managed at the area level, allowing only specific users to make contributions or changes to the area.

Personal Sites

SharePoint Products and Technologies make it easy for users to store, find, and retrieve information and documents. My Site is a personal Windows SharePoint Services site that provides personalized and customized information for each user for quick access to links to documents, people, or websites, as well as alerts to track changes to content within the portal site and the organization. From My Site, you can also update your user profile and share links with other portal site users.

Views

Views are rules for how to present the data in a Web Part. By default, each list or library has a default view, and that view can be changed from the browser. The default view as defined in the browser is also the default view inserted into a page with FrontPage 2003. Views can be used to present data that is sorted by one or two fields, or even filtered according to a series of criteria that you set.

The true power to customize a site with FrontPage 2003 can be exploited by inserting views of data into pages where needed. For example, while you might have a complete staff list that includes address, title, areas of specialty, and more on an e-mail list page, you can reuse that staff list by presenting a view that includes only the name and e-mail address. Additionally, on a regional e-mail address page you could present a view of that same data that includes only the name and phone number for team members in a specific region. The ability to reuse data across your website saves time and reduces errors because you no longer have to duplicate information to use it in different places.

Browser-Based Customization

SharePoint Products and Technologies make updating sites and their content from the browser easier than ever. As you learn to customize SharePoint sites, you will become accustomed to editing some things from the browser and others from within FrontPage 2003. Here is a brief list of the items you will probably continue to edit from the browser even after you become proficient at customizing sites with FrontPage 2003:

- **Creation of lists, document libraries, discussions, and surveys.**   Creation of content Web Parts is most commonly done via the browser. You can create content Web Parts from your site at *http://<myserver>/_layouts/1033/create.aspx*.

- **List or document library contents.**   Adding and editing content contained inside of Web Parts on the site is done via the browser. You can even edit content in a datasheet view (such as a spreadsheet) to speed the editing of existing content and the addition of new content.

- **Changing fields in lists, document libraries, discussions, and surveys.**   If you want to add, reorder, remove, or add fields to lists or document libraries, you can certainly do these things via the browser.

- **Personal views.**   SharePoint Products and Technologies users can alter the shared view of a page that everyone sees to create views of a Web page that only they can see. These personal views can include different or rearranged Web Parts, and they do not have to include the Web Parts that everyone else sees in the shared view. These personal views are created and managed in the browser by each user.

How to Edit Sites in FrontPage 2003

Everything that can be done with SharePoint Products and Technologies from a browser can also be done from within FrontPage 2003 and much more. There are very strong capabilities in FrontPage 2003 that help the user avoid going back and forth between the browser and FrontPage 2003 to customize a site. But, first we need to get the site open in FrontPage 2003.

Opening a Site

Opening a site in FrontPage 2003 is easy. All you need is the Web address or URL of the site you plan to edit, as well as a user name and password (if necessary) and sufficient permissions to edit the site. Contact your server administrator if you have questions about the website address or permissions to edit the site.

To open a SharePoint site in FrontPage 2003

1. With FrontPage 2003 open, click **Open Site** (shown in Figure 32-1) on the **File** menu.

Figure 32-1   Open Site menu

The **Open Site** dialog box (shown in Figure 32-2) is displayed.

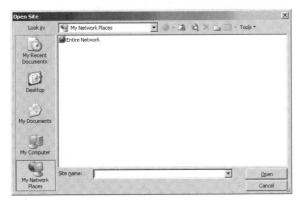

Figure 32-2   Open Site dialog box

2. In the **Site name** box, type the website address (the URL) of your website. Examples include *http://localhost*, *http://servername*, or *http://www.example.com*. Then click the **Open** button. If prompted, provide the user name and password for opening the website in FrontPage 2003.

> **Tip**   You can also open a site in FrontPage 2003 by browsing to it in Internet Explorer, and then choosing Edit With Microsoft Office FrontPage from the File menu or clicking the Edit button on the Standard Buttons toolbar. FrontPage 2003 will open not only the current page but the entire SharePoint Products and Technologies portal site that contains the current page.

Becoming Familiar with FrontPage 2003

The FrontPage 2003 user interface gives you easy access to the tools you need. The left part of the screen allows you to view your website by folder list or by navigation pane (shown in Figure 32-3).

Figure 32-3   Internet Explorer Edit With Microsoft Office FrontPage 2003 toolbar button

The Folder List displays all the folders and files in your site. You can move or rename files or folders, and FrontPage 2003 will prompt you to automatically fix all the hyperlinks. When you view your site in the navigation pane, you can see the navigational structure and link bars in your site.

The Folder List also holds some significant SharePoint Products and Technologies capabilities. Right-click on any document library or on any list (found in the Lists directory). A dialog box that contains five tabs—General, Settings, Fields, Security, and Supporting Files—is displayed. Using these tabs is a very efficient way to make changes to these properties.

The middle of the screen shows the page that is currently being edited, with page tabs (shown in Figure 32-4) available to make it easy to switch to other opened pages in your site.

Figure 32-4   Page tabs

The Web Site tab at the top of the editing pane is used to give you options for managing your website, such as viewing the remote website, reports, navigation, hyperlinks, and tasks.

The bottom of the screen allows you to switch between Design, Split, Code, and Preview page views. (See Figure 32-5.)

Figure 32-5   Design, Split, Code, and Preview page views

- **Design View.**   Design view is the WYSIWYG editing mode. This view is the one used most often by FrontPage 2003 users, even those who are experts at coding HTML. The reason is simple: the buttons and menu options allow you to create Web pages faster. For example, creating a table in a text editor requires a lot of typing. Creating a table in the FrontPage 2003 Design view by clicking the Table button takes only a few seconds.

■ **Split View.**   Split view allows you to see the HTML code in one part of the window and the WYSIWYG view in another part. When you make a change in the WYSIWYG window, the HTML code is automatically updated, and vice versa. The Split view is a great tool for users who know HTML and want to have the best of both worlds—that is, fast coding in WYSIWYG mode with precision control of the HTML code at the same time.

■ **Code View.**   Code view allows you to see and edit the HTML code for a page. You can continue to use most menu options, but you must be familiar with HTML coding to be productive in this view.

■ **Preview View.**   Preview view allows you to see what your Web page will look like in the browser before saving your page. This view is particularly handy when you have made a change that you are not sure you want to keep.

> **Tip**   New tools in FrontPage 2003 make creating code in Code view faster than ever. The new Code View menu in the Edit menu and shortcut keys in FrontPage 2003 make creating and editing code fast and easy. You can use the Code View menu and the corresponding keyboard shortcuts to quickly increase or decrease indents, select a tag or block, find a matching tag or block, insert a tag or comment, and more. In addition, new Intellisense technology makes code completion automatic if desired, and Code Snippets make it easy to reuse commonly used code among website editors.

Instant Updates

Many Web developers are accustomed to publishing files or sending them to a server via an FTP program when they are finished making their updates. When FrontPage 2003 users open a website created with SharePoint Products and Technologies, the changes they make are updated on the server immediately after they save the page they are working on. Therefore, FrontPage 2003 users simply need to save their pages when they are finished editing them. Saving pages is accomplished by clicking the Save option in the File menu.

Caveats to Editing SharePoint Portal Server Sites in FrontPage 2003

There are some differences in how websites created with Windows SharePoint Services and how portal sites created with SharePoint Portal Server 2003 are edited with FrontPage 2003. This section outlines some of the more important differences.

Web Part Display

Web Parts in Windows SharePoint Services sites are displayed in FrontPage 2003 with live data. However, some Web Parts in portal sites created with SharePoint Portal Server 2003 might be displayed with static previews that do not include live data.

Moving or Backing Up Websites

Portal sites created with SharePoint Portal Server 2003 should be moved or backed up by using SharePoint Portal Server 2003 backup tools instead of using FrontPage 2003 Backup, Restore, or Web Package options. Therefore, these features are disabled by default in FrontPage 2003 when editing sites created with SharePoint Portal Server 2003.

Working with Areas and Sub-Areas

SharePoint Portal Server 2003 sites can include Areas and Sub-Areas, which can be nested many levels underneath the root web. When opened in FrontPage 2003, all areas and subareas are represented as subordinate sites, and all are displayed underneath the root of the site. For example, if Area1 is below the root-level site and Area11 is below Area1, Area11 is simply a subsite of the root-level site and not a subsite of the Area1 site.

FrontPage 2003 users are not able to delete an Area or Sub-Area in a site created with SharePoint Portal Server 2003. When the root site of a site created with SharePoint Portal Server 2003 is open in FrontPage 2003, it is possible to create subordinate sites under that root. Subsequently, subordinate sites under those newly created subordinate sites are also possible, thus nesting them multiple levels deep. Yet Areas and Sub-Areas of the portal, represented as subordinate sites in FrontPage 2003, cannot have nested subordinate sites. When an Area or Sub-Area is open in FrontPage 2003, the Subordinate Site option seen when you right-click on a folder in the Folder List and then click New is unavailable. Visually, in the FrontPage 2003 user interface, you cannot differentiate between a subordinate site and an Area; both are represented with the same folder icon.

Editing Personal Sites

One of the biggest advantages to My Sites in SharePoint Portal Server 2003 is that each user browses to the same URL but each sees his or her own unique content. SharePoint Portal Server 2003 does this by assigning a unique GUID to each user and storing customization and content options for each GUID. The My Site template is shared by all users, so if a FrontPage 2003 user edits the default.aspx page in the My Site website, the change would affect all users with My Sites. The easiest way to open the My Site default.aspx page in FrontPage 2003 is by browsing to it in Internet Explorer, and then choosing Edit With Microsoft Office FrontPage from the File menu or clicking the Edit button on the Standard Buttons toolbar.

For example, if a Web designer opens the My Site Web in FrontPage 2003 and then replaces the logo in the upper left corner of default.aspx with her own image, all users on the portal site will see that new image when they browse to My Site. This has the benefit of allowing portal site administrators to use FrontPage 2003 to easily make changes to the My Site template that affect all existing and new users' My Sites.

Changing Styles

The look and feel of a portal site created with SharePoint Portal Server 2003 is determined by the Cascading Style Sheet (CSS) files that define the selectors or styles to apply to elements in the portal site. The style sheets used by SharePoint Portal Server 2003 sites are located by default on the server in the C:\Program Files\Common Files \Microsoft Shared\Web Server Extensions\60\Template\Layouts\1033\Styles folder. The two style sheets used by default are the sps.css and ows.css files. (Note that 1033 represents the language ID for U.S. English; replace this number with the appropriate language ID if you aren't using U.S. English versions of SharePoint Portal Server 2003.) These files are not publicly accessible and require administrative access to modify them.

Because you might not have administrative access to modify style sheets on the server, you can instead create a new style sheet and then associate the pages on the site you are authorized to edit with that new style sheet. If the new style sheet includes definitions for formatting choices for the same selectors that are in the server's style sheets, the new style sheet formats will be used. This is because if multiple style sheets are applied to a site or page, the selectors in the one that is applied last are used.

The easiest way to create a new style sheet is to start with one of the existing style sheets and then make edits to it. You can open a copy of the server-based style sheets in FrontPage 2003 by clicking Open on the File menu, typing the URL for the style sheet in the File Name box, and then clicking Open.

> **Tip**   The default URL for sps.css is *http://<myserver>/_layouts/1033/styles /sps.css*, and the URL for ows.css is *http://<myserver>/_layouts/1033/styles /ows.css*.

The style sheet opens in FrontPage 2003. Save the style sheet with a new name in the portal site opened in FrontPage 2003 by clicking Save As on the File menu. Make edits to the style sheet as desired, and then save the new style sheet. Next, browse to your website created with SharePoint Portal Server 2003 and then click the Site Settings link. To apply the new style sheet to other SharePoint Portal Server 2003 areas and subordinate sites, you should open the site in FrontPage 2003 and use the Style Sheet Links dialog box, which can be selected from the Format menu.

> **Tip** If you have a custom Theme you want to apply to a site created with SharePoint Portal Server 2003, you can browse to the style sheet it uses (at the default location of *http://<myserver>/_layouts/1033/styles/ows.css*), save it with a new name, and then apply it to the SharePoint Portal Server 2003 site by using the technique just described.

Identifying the selectors that correspond to the elements to change in the site is made easier with a CSS Selector tool that allows you to hover your mouse over an area on a page and then see a ToolTip that displays the name of the selector used in that area. Each page you want to use the CSS Selector tool in should have the following modifications:

1. Replace the body tag with the following code:

    ```
    <body marginwidth="0" marginheight="0" scroll="yes" onmouseover="classInfo();">
    ```

2. Add the following code to the <body> section of your page:

    ```
    <script language="vbscript">
    sub classInfo()
      if window.event.srcelement.classname <> "" then
        stsclass.innertext =
          window.event.srcelement.classname
      else
        stsclass.innertext=""
      end if
    end sub
    </script>
    <div>
      <a id="stsclasstitle" width="25">
      <font face="Arial">Classname</font></a>
      <a id="STSclass" width="275">
      <font face="Arial Black"> </font></a>
    </div>
    ```

3. Preview the page in the browser. Move your cursor over the style you want to identify. The Selector will be displayed at the top of the page.

FrontPage 2003 Features Disabled when Editing a SharePoint Portal Server 2003 Site

Some features in FrontPage 2003 are disabled by default when you open a portal site created with SharePoint Portal Server 2003. These features are disabled so that they do not conflict with the way that portal sites are implemented.

Publishing

FrontPage 2003 users are accustomed to using the Publish feature to move pages or websites from one location to another. However, SharePoint Portal Server 2003 pages and sites should be moved using the SharePoint Portal Server 2003 backup command-line utility instead of the FrontPage 2003 Publish functionality. (For more information, see Chapter 18, "Managing SharePoint Portal Server 2003.")

> **Tip**   The commands affected are Publish Site (on the File menu), Import File From Site (on the File menu), Remote Web Site (on the View menu), and Publish Selected Files (when you right-click a file or files in the Folder List).

Navigation

Portal sites created with SharePoint Portal Server 2003 have their own navigational structure and are edited using SharePoint Portal Server 2003 tools. Therefore, you cannot insert FrontPage 2003 link bars or navigation bars into sites created with SharePoint Portal Server 2003 and maintain the integrity of the existing SharePoint Portal Server 2003 navigation.

> **Tip**   The commands affected are Navigation (on the Insert menu) and Link Bars (when you click Web Component on the Insert menu).

Navigation View

Navigation view is managed by Windows SharePoint Services, and because Share-Point Portal Server 2003 uses its own navigational scheme, this view is not used when editing portal sites created with SharePoint Portal Server 2003.

> **Tip**   The commands affected are Navigation (on the View menu), the Navigation button (when you click the Web Site tab), and the Navigation button at the bottom of the Folder List.

Themes

FrontPage 2003 cannot be used to apply Themes to portal sites created with Share-Point Portal Server 2003, nor can themes be applied to individual pages in those portal sites. Themes should instead be applied to portal sites created with SharePoint Portal Server 2003 by clicking Change Portal Site Properties And SharePoint Site Creation Settings on the Site Settings page of the SharePoint Portal Server 2003 site and entering the Custom Cascading Style Sheet location.

> **Tip** The commands affected are Apply As Default or Apply To Selected Page(s) (when you click Theme on the Format menu).

FrontPage 2003 Features to Understand when Editing a SharePoint Portal Server 2003 Site

With some features in FrontPage 2003, you can experience unanticipated results when editing portal sites created with SharePoint Portal Server 2003, so it is recommended that you understand these features.

Optimize HTML

FrontPage 2003 Optimize HTML is a tool that allows you to clean up HTML code by removing comments, white space, unused content, and HTML generated from Word HTML and other tools. Using Optimize HTML on pages in a portal site created with SharePoint Portal Server 2003 will not harm the pages; however, FrontPage 2003 might have difficulty displaying some pages after Optimize HTML has been used on them. Instead, optimize your HTML by hand.

> **Tip** The command affected is Optimize HTML (on the Tools menu).

Dynamic Web Templates (DWT)

FrontPage 2003 allows you to create dynamic page templates that define regions that are editable by users. These templates are called Dynamic Web Templates (DWT), and they stay attached to pages even after they are created to make updating many pages at one time fast and easy. Most commonly, DWTs use Themes or attach to an external style sheet to define formatting for the pages attached to them. Because SharePoint Portal Server 2003 sites include links to style sheets used across the portal site, applying a DWT to a portal site very likely would replace the links to the SharePoint Portal Server 2003 style sheet, which could cause formatting problems on the pages attached to the DWT. DWTs can be used without problems on new pages in a portal site. However, because Themes and style sheets are commonly used in conjunction with DWTs, you should fully understand the effect of DWTs on portal sites created with SharePoint Portal Server 2003.

> **Tip** The command affected is Dynamic Web Template (on the Format menu).

Additional FrontPage 2003 Features that Can Be Disabled when Editing a SharePoint Portal Server 2003 Site

FrontPage 2003 and SharePoint Portal Server 2003 make it possible for you to specify features to disable in FrontPage 2003 when portal sites created with SharePoint Portal Server 2003 are opened in FrontPage 2003.

Template Locations

Disabling features is done by flagging an attribute in an XML file called onet.xml that is associated with each SharePoint Portal Server 2003 template used in a portal site. The attribute in the onet.xml file tells FrontPage 2003 (and other authoring tools) to disable specific features.

To change the list of features and functionality to disable in FrontPage 2003 when SharePoint Portal Server 2003 sites are opened, you will need to edit the onet.xml file that corresponds with each template used on the site. Table 32-1 shows the list of templates used in SharePoint Portal Server 2003 sites, with their locations on the server:

Table 32-1   Default Site Template Locations

Site	Default Template Location on the Server
Root Site	C:\Program Files\Common Files\Microsoft Shared\Web Server Extensions\60\Template\1033\SPS\XML\
MySite (personal sites)	C:\Program Files\Common Files\Microsoft Shared\Web Server Extensions\60\Template\1033\SPSMSITE\XML
CompanyNews, ExternalNews, PressAnnouncements, and all areas under the News area	C:\Program Files\Common Files\Microsoft Shared\Web Server Extensions\60\Template\1033\SPSNEWS\XML
News	C:\Program Files\Common Files\Microsoft Shared\Web Server Extensions\60\Template\1033\SPSNHOME\XML
SiteDirectory	C:\Program Files\Common Files\Microsoft Shared\Web Server Extensions\60\Template\1033\SPSSITES\XML
Topics	C:\Program Files\Common Files\Microsoft Shared\Web Server Extensions\60\Template\1033\SPSTOC\XML
Divisions, HumanResources, Locations, Marketing, Operations, Projects, Resources, Sales, Strategy & Support, and all areas under the Topics area	C:\Program Files\Common Files\Microsoft Shared\Web Server Extensions\60\Template\1033\SPSTOPIC\XML
Community Template	C:\Program Files\Common Files\Microsoft Shared\Web Server Extensions\60\Template\1033\SPSCOMMU\XML

DisableWebDesignFeatures Example

The attribute that flags FrontPage 2003 to disable features is named DisableWeb-DesignFeatures, and the list of features to disable follows it in the XML file. Here is a sample onet.xml file:

```
<Project Title="Team Web Site" ListDir="Lists"
xmlns:ows="Microsoft SharePoint"
AlternateHeader="PortalHeader.aspx"
DisableWebDesignFeatures="wdfbackup;
wdfrestore;
wdfpackageimport;
wdfpackageexport;
wdfthemeweb;
wdfthemepage;
wdfnavigationbars;
wdfnavigationview;
wdfpublishview;
wdfpublishselectedfile;
wdfopensite">
```

The example shows that features are being disabled (as shown by the inclusion of the DisableWebDesignFeatures attribute), and the list of features disabled follows. Table 32-2 shows the list of features you can disable:

Table 32-2   DisableWebDesignFeatures List

Feature to Disable	Value in onet.xml	Command Blocked in FrontPage 2003	Command Type	Result
Backup site	wdfbackup	Backup (when you click Server on the Tools menu)	Menu command	Command disabled
Restore site	wdfrestore	Restore (when you click Server on the Tools menu)	Menu command	Command disabled
Web Package import	wdfpackageimport	Import (when you click Packages on the Tools menu)	Menu command	Command disabled
Web Package export	wdfpackageexport	Export (when you click Packages on the Tools menu)	Menu command	Command disabled
Theme site	wdfthemeweb	Apply As Default (when you click Theme on the Format menu)	Task pane, context menu	Command disabled
Theme page	wdfthemepage	Apply To Selected Page(s) (when you click Theme on the Format menu)	Task pane, context menu	Command disabled

Table 32-2   DisableWebDesignFeatures List   *(continued)*

Feature to Disable	Value in onet.xml	Command Blocked in FrontPage 2003	Command Type	Result
Insert Navigation	wdfnavigationbars	Navigation (on the Insert menu) and Link Bars (when you click Web Component on the Insert menu)	Menu command	Command disabled
Show Navigation View	wdfnavigationview	Navigation (on the View menu)	Menu command	Command disabled
Show Navigation View	wdfpublishview	Navigation button (when you click the Web Site tab)	View selector button	Show alert
Show Navigation View	wdfpublishview	Navigation button at the bottom of the Folder List.	View selector button	Show alert
Show remote site view	wdfpublishview	Publish Site (on the File menu)	Menu command	Command disabled
Show remote site view	wdfpublishview	From Site (when you click Import on the File menu)	Dialog box button	Button disabled
Show remote site view	wdfpublishview	Remote Web Site (on the View menu)	View selector button	Show alert
Publish selected file	wdfpublishselectedfile	Publish Selected Files (when you right-click a file in the Folder List)	Folder pane, context menu	Command disabled
Open Site	wdfopensite	Open Site (on the File menu)	Menu command	Show alert
New subordinate site	wdfnewsubordinate site	Subordinate Site (when you right-click a folder in the Folder List and then click New)	Folder pane, context menu	Command disabled

Tip   At times, you might want a site created with SharePoint Portal Server 2003 to be locked down completely so that it cannot be edited in FrontPage 2003. For example, if you have processes and procedures for staging content on a different server and then publishing it when approved, you can restrict the site from even being opened in FrontPage 2003. Do this by including the wdfopensite value in the onet.xml file.

Most Common Changes Made in FrontPage 2003

This section includes instructions on how to make the most commonly needed changes in Microsoft Office FrontPage 2003.

Web Page Changes

FrontPage 2003 aids us in customizing our Web pages. The next several sections describe only some of these changes.

Adding Text

Adding text to pages in a SharePoint site is as simple as clicking on a region of the page outside of any Web Part Zone and then typing and formatting the text as desired.

Tip Some pages are formatted by using tables, and you might have to insert a new table row or column to create an area that is editable. You can insert a table row or column by clicking on the Table menu.

Adding Images

Adding images to your site is also straightforward.

To open a SharePoint site in FrontPage 2003

1. First you should make sure that the images are in your website. You can add images to your website by clicking the **Import** option on the **File** menu.

2. Once the files are in your website, make sure that the page you want the image on is open in **Design View**, and then you can simply move the image from the **Folder List** onto your page by performing a click-and-drag operation.

   Deleting images is as easy as clicking on the image you want to delete and then pressing the DELETE key.

Tip If you plan to insert another image after you delete a logo, press the ENTER key after you press the DELETE key. That will insert a space you can move your new image into by performing a click-and-drag operation.

Changing Images

After you add a new image to your site, you might want to make some changes to the image, such as cropping or resizing (and then resampling to reduce the size of the file) or rotating images. The Pictures toolbar is the key to making these changes.

Click on an image to open the Pictures toolbar. (See Figure 32-6.) If you do not see it, click Toolbars on the View menu and then click Pictures.

Figure 32-6   Pictures toolbar

The Pictures toolbar includes the functions listed in Table 32-3.

Table 32-3   Pictures Toolbar Functions

Image	Description
	Click to insert a picture from a file.
A	Click to add text. You can insert text on top of a picture except when adding text to a .gif file. The text can be added, but it doesn't display in Internet Explorer.
	Click to automatically create a thumbnail image to place on the page. When the user clicks the image, she is sent to the large version of the image.
	Click to position the image in a specific spot on the page.
	Bring the image forward.
	Send the image backward.
	Flip the image.
	Change the contrast on the image.
	Change the brightness of the image.
	Crop the image.
	Make a color in the image transparent. Use this when you want the background color or image to show through.
	Click to change the color of the image.
	Click to add a bevel border around the image.
	Click to select an image or a portion of an image.

Table 32-3 Pictures Toolbar Functions *(continued)*

Image	Description
□ ○ ⊄	Click to add hotspots to image. The image and the hotspots make up an image map. When a visitor clicks on that region of the image, he is sent to a different page or place on the page.
⬚	Click to make hotspots visible on the image.
⬚	Click to restore an image to where it was before you started changing it.

You can use these functions to crop, rotate, or colorize images, or even turn them into image maps.

Adding Pages

You will create a new Web page for any number of reasons, such as for consolidating multiple Web Parts for easy viewing or hosting common Web Part content in a different format.

To add a new page to an existing SharePoint site

1. With a SharePoint site open in FrontPage 2003, click the **Page** option (shown in Figure 32-7) of the **Create a new normal page** button on the Standard FrontPage 2003 toolbar.

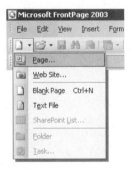

Figure 32-7 Page option

Tip Alternatively, you can click the New option from the File menu and then click the More Page Templates link.

The Page Templates dialog box (shown in Figure 32-8) is displayed.

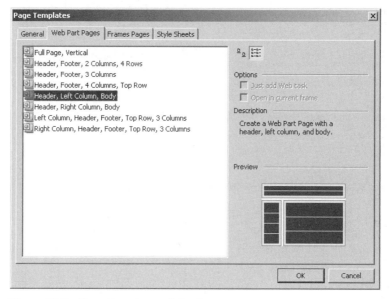

Figure 32-8   Page Templates dialog box

2. Choose a template from one of the four tabs, and click the **OK** button.

Tip   As you click on each template, notice the Description on the center right of the dialog box below Options and above Preview. It can be very helpful in choosing the correct template. Below that there is a preview of how the page will look.

If a Web Part Page template was chosen, a new page is created using the chosen template, and a new tab labeled new_page_1.aspx is added to the top of the editing pane. The file extension will vary if another type of template is chosen.

Lists and Document Library Views

One of the most commonly asked questions is how to change the way lists are viewed, such as changing the fields displayed and the sort order of list items, when you insert a List View Web Part (LVWP) into a page. The granularity within FrontPage 2003 is finer than can be achieved in a browser. Additionally, many users want to be able to insert these LVWPs in other pages in their site or insert additional lists or library views on their home page. This section describes how to make these changes.

Changing Fields Displayed in Lists

When you insert an LVWP into a page, it automatically displays data from specific fields in the list. For example, inserting the Announcements LVWP into a page by using the browser displays the announcement title, submittal date and time, submitter display name, and first few lines of the body for all recent announcements (shown in Figure 32-9) by default.

Figure 32-9 Sample Announcements List View Web Part

Incidentally, inserting the same Announcement LVWP into the page by using FrontPage 2003 will result in a slightly different default view that includes only the Title and Modified fields and a Full Toolbar. No difference in functionality results, just a different default.

The default fields might be fine for some applications. But SharePoint Products and Technologies let you change the columns displayed by the LVWP to any List View Page previously defined for the list. In fact, choosing the Edit The Current View link when modifying an LVWP in the browser, using the Data View Details task pane for the LVWP in FrontPage 2003, or choosing the Properties option from a list or library folder in the Folder List in FrontPage 2003 provides the ability to choose any of the fields on the list we would like to see displayed. None of these methods requires the creation of a separate List View Page.

To change the fields displayed in an LVWP by using FrontPage 2003 using the Data View Details task pane

1. From the page that contains the LVWP in FrontPage 2003, right-click the **LVWP**, and choose **List View Properties** from the menu to open the **Data View Details** task pane. (See Figure 32-10.) By default, it opens docked to the right side of FrontPage 2003.

Figure 32-10 Data View Details task pane

2. Click the **Fields** link to open the **Displayed Fields** dialog box. (See Figure 32-11.)

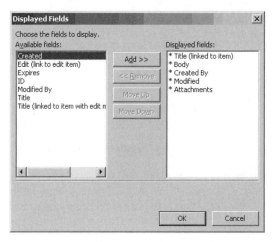

Figure 32-11   Displayed Fields dialog box for the Announcements list

3. To add fields to the LVWP, click on the ones you want in the **Available fields** box and then click the **Add** button.

Tip   You can use CTRL+click to select multiple items, and then click the Add or Remove button.

4. To remove fields from display, click on the ones you want to remove in the **Displayed fields** box and then click the **Remove** button. You will notice that some fields cannot be removed from some views. These fields are marked with an asterisk (*).

Tip   Try changing to a different list style if there are fields you want to remove from the view on your page that are not removable. Changing list styles is covered next.

5. You can also change the order of the fields displayed by clicking the field in the **Displayed fields** box and then clicking the **Move Up** or **Move Down** button. When the fields are displayed as you want them, click the **OK** button. Save your Web page by clicking the **Save** option on the **File** menu. The fields displayed are changed.

Changing List Styles

In FrontPage 2003, there are ready-made templates called styles for LVWPs that rearrange the presentation of the list data. You can take advantage of these styles by changing the list style of the LVWP.

To change the list style of an LVWP

1. Right-click on the **LVWP**, and then click **List View Properties** to open the **Data View Details** task pane (shown earlier in Figure 32-11).

2. Click the **Style** link to open the **View Styles** dialog box. (See Figure 32-12.)

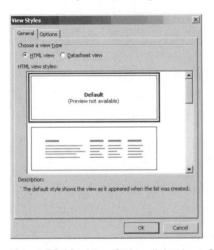

Figure 32-12   View Styles dialog box, General tab

3. Click the style you would like to use in the **HTML view styles** scroll box, and then click **OK**. Save your Web page by clicking the **Save** option on the **File** menu. The style for the LVWP is changed.

Changing the Title Bar Displayed

By default, a list view Web Part is displayed with a title bar that contains the name of the list, such as Announcements, Events, or Lists. The title bar also includes a clickable down arrow, located on the far right side, that allows the user to access the Web Part menu.

You can change the display of the title bar of any list. First, right-click on the LVWP in FrontPage 2003, and then click Web Part Properties or double-click anywhere on the LVWP to open the Web Part Properties dialog box. You can then select from one of the following Frame Style values:

■ **Default.**   This setting displays the default title bar display for the list. For Announcements, it includes the title bar and the border.

■ **None.**   This setting removes the title bar and the border that surrounded the list. (See Figure 32-13.) If you choose this option, you might want to add some static text above the list so that the user knows what she is looking at.

Figure 32-13   Announcements list with no title bar

■ **Title Bar And Border.**   This setting displays the title bar and the border.

■ **Title Bar Only.**   This setting displays just the title bar, with no border. (See Figure 32-14.)

Figure 32-14   Announcements list with no border

Changing Toolbars Displayed

By default, an LVWP that is added by using the browser is displayed with the option to add new items at the bottom of the list.

To change the toolbar options for an LVWP

1.   Right-click on the **LVWP**, and then click **List View Properties** to open the **Data View Details** task pane.

2.   Click the **Style** link to open the **View Styles** dialog box. (See Figure 32-15.) Click the **Options** tab.

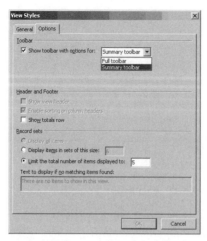

Figure 32-15   View Styles dialog box, Options tab

You can select from one of the following toolbar options:

- **No Toolbars.**   If you deselect the check box to the left of Show Toolbar With Options For, all options for adding or filtering items will be removed. (See Figure 32-16.)

Figure 32-16   Announcements list with No Toolbars

- **Summary Toolbars.**   Be sure that the check box to the left of Show Toolbar With Options For is selected, and choose Summary Toolbar from the drop-down list. This is the default when the LVWP is added by using the browser. The link option for adding items will be displayed at the bottom of the list.

- **Full Toolbars.**   Be sure that the check box to the left of Show Toolbar With Options For is checked, and choose Full Toolbar from the drop-down list. A toolbar just under the Title Bar will be displayed with the option to add an item to the list or filter the items in the list. (See Figure 32-17.)

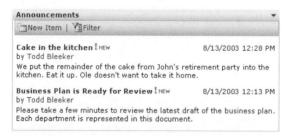

Figure 32-17   Announcements list with Full Toolbars

Changing the LVWP Filter

You can choose to display only a subset of the data in a List or document library by using a filter. For example, the Announcements list might contain postings from many different people. However, if we wanted to display the list with only the announcements that the authenticated user created, we can insert the LVWP into a page and then choose to filter it to display only those records.

To change the toolbar options for an LVWP

1. Right-click on the **LVWP**, and then click **List View Properties** to open the **Data View Details** task pane.

2. Click the **Filter** link to open the **Filter Criteria** dialog box. (See Figure 32-18.) By default, the **Announcements LVWP** added by using the browser already has two filter criteria. The date each announcement Expires cannot be Null and must be Great Than Or Equal To The [*Current Date*].

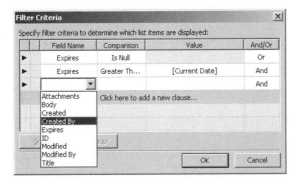

Figure 32-18   Announcement list Filter Criteria dialog box

3. Click on the **Click here to add a new clause** gray bar, and select the field you would like to filter on by clicking the **Field Name** drop-down box. To limit the list to only the viewing user's announcements, select **Created By**.

4. Click the **Comparison** drop-down box and then select the comparison option you want to use (such as Equals, Greater Than, or Less Than). **Equals** is chosen for us by default.

5. Click the **Value** drop-down list and then choose or type the value you want to compare against. For our example, we want to choose **[Current User]** from the drop-down list.

6. By default, **And** has been selected for how our new criteria will filter with the other criteria items. We could change the value to **Or**, as was done in the criteria set by default in the **Announcements** list, but we want it to remain as **And**.

7. When you are finished, click the **OK** button. Save your Web page by clicking the **Save** option on the **File** menu. The LVWP is now displayed with only the data that meets the criteria set.

Changing the LVWP Sort Order

To change the sort order of fields displayed in a LVWP for a list or document library, follow these steps:

1. Right-click on the list, and then click **List View Properties** to open the **Data View Details** task pane (shown earlier in Figure 32-11).

2. Click the **Sort & group** link to open the **Sort and Group** dialog box. (See Figure 32-19.)

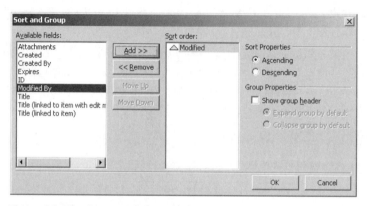

Figure 32-19 Sort And Group dialog box

3. If there are fields in the **Available Fields** box that you want to sort against, click them and then click the **Add** button.

4. If the fields you want to sort against are already in the **Sort order** box, you can click them and then click the **Move Up** or **Move Down** button to change their priority.

5. If there are fields in the **Sort order** box that you do not want to sort against, click the fields and then click the **Remove** button. By default, the **Announcements LVWP** added by using the browser is sorted by the date that the announcement was Modified in Descending order.

6. Make sure that the **Ascending** option button is selected for each field you want to sort against if you want the sort to go from lowest to highest, or that the **Descending** option button is selected if you want the sort to go from highest to lowest.

7. Click **OK** when you are finished. Save your Web page by clicking the **Save** option on the **File** menu. The LVWP is now displayed with the sort order you specified.

Changing List Grouping and Sorting to Make a Collapsible LVWP

Grouping list content is a great way to make a long list of data easier to navigate. For example, if we had lots of announcements, we might want to group them by the person who created the announcement. The LVWP could be displayed with each group collapsed, and when we wanted to see the announcements that were created by a certain person we would click on the plus sign (+), and the list of announcements for that creator would expand. Similarly, we would click on the minus sign (–), and the list of announcements for that creator would collapse.

To change the sort order of fields displayed in a list or document library

1. Right-click on the **LVWP**, and then click **List View Properties** to open the **Data View Details** task pane.

2. Click the **Sort & group** link to open the **Sort and Group** dialog box. (See Figure 32-19, shown earlier in the chapter.)

3. Click fields you want to sort on first, and then click the **Add** button to add them to the **Sort order** box. For our example, we want to add **Created By** to the **Sort order** box.

4. Make sure that the **Ascending** option button is selected for each field you want to sort against if you want the sort to go from lowest to highest, or that the **Descending** option button is selected if you want the sort to go from highest to lowest. The default value of Ascending will work for our example.

5. Because Group properties apply to all items in the Sort Order box, we need to make sure that the fields are in the correct sequence. We don't want to group them by Modified Date and then group them by the Created By value. We could reverse the order, but we really just want to remove Modified from the Sort Order box. If we did want both fields, we could move the Created By field to the first position in the Sort Order box by selecting Created By and clicking the Move Up button. For our example, we just remove **Modified** by selecting it from the **Sort order** box and clicking the **Remove** button.

6. Make sure that the **Show group header** check box is selected. It is not selected by default, so we must select the **Show group header** check box.

7. Choose the default way to show each group's content, expanded or collapsed. By default, each group will be expanded and its contents will be visible. For our example and for most applications of this option, you will want to select the **Collapse group by default** option button.

8. Click **OK** when you are finished. Save your Web page by clicking the **Save** option on the **File** menu. View the modified page in the browser. The LVWP is grouped and sorted as you indicated. (See Figure 32-20 and Figure 32-21.) The number in parenthesis (*2* in this example) is the number of announcements that are grouped inside that item.

Figure 32-20   Announcements list grouped by Created By—Collapsed

Figure 32-21   Announcements list grouped by Created By—Expanded

Notice that when each group of announcements is expanded, the sort order is no longer the Modified date in descending order. But if we had left the Modified date as grouped in the **Sort Order** box, each date would have been grouped, requiring the user to click a second time to open each group of announcements modified on a given date. That would have been tedious for the user.

Inserting List or Library Views

Inserting list or document library views into pages is a great way to bring the information needed to the place where it is needed. For example, if you have a page that discusses a project you are working on, you can easily include a view of a team member list or a document library right in the page that discusses the project instead of linking the user to another page and then hoping they come back when they are finished. Now that you have learned how to filter, sort, and group LVWPs, you know that you can include only a subset of a list on a page as well.

To insert an LVWP for a list or document library into a page

1. Open or create the page you want to insert the view into by using Front-Page 2003.

2. Click the location you want the view to go, and then click the **Insert Web Part** option on the **Data** menu to open the **Web Parts** task pane. (See Figure 32-22.)

Figure 32-22   Web Parts task pane

3. Choose the gallery of Web Parts you will use. Use the *<Site Name>* **Gallery** to look for Web Parts in the active site. Use **Virtual Server Gallery** to find a Web Part that is part of your virtual server. Use the **Online Gallery** to find a Web Part in the online library. FrontPage 2003 defaults to the list of Web Parts on the Team Web Site Gallery.

4. Click the name of the Web Part that you want to insert into the page from the Web Part List. If you can't find a Web Part that you think should be listed, look to see if there is more than one page of Web Parts. If there is, the **Next** link should be present. Try clicking on that.

5. Click the **Insert Selected Web Part** button at the bottom of the task pane. The Web Part is inserted into your page.

6. If you are on a part of the page that doesn't have a Web Part Zone, the **New Web Part Zone** button on the bottom of the task pane will be enabled. Clicking this button will create a new Web Part Zone that you and your browser users can add Web Parts to. If you don't place your Web Parts in a Web Part Zone, you will end up with static Web Parts that the users will not be able to change in the browser.

7. Save your Web page by clicking the **Save** option on the **File** menu. FrontPage 2003 will ensure that the page is saved as an .aspx page, as is required. The list is now displayed on your page.

Inserting Interactive Buttons

You might want to insert a button into a page independent of the overall navigational structure of your site. You can create Interactive Buttons from within FrontPage 2003 without leaving FrontPage 2003 to use a graphics program to create separate graphics files for each button you want to use. Even more importantly, FrontPage 2003 automatically creates separate buttons for normal, hovered, and pressed states and automatically includes the Microsoft JScript code necessary to give the buttons their interactivity. Nice.

To insert an Interactive Button into a page

1. Open or create the page you want to insert an Interactive Button into using FrontPage 2003.

2. Click the location you want the Interactive Button to go, and then click the **Interactive Button** option on the **Insert** menu to open the **Interactive Buttons** dialog box. (See Figure 32-23.)

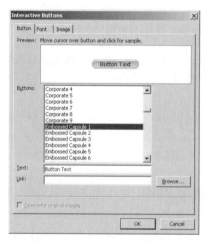

Figure 32-23   Interactive Button dialog box

3. Click the button style you want to use in the **Buttons** scroll box.

4. Type the text you would like to appear on your button in the **Text** box.

5. Type the URL for the page you want the button to link to in the **Link** box.

6. Click the **Font** tab if you want to change the font used on the button, and click the **Image** tab if you want to change the button size or give it a transparent background around the edges.

7. Click the **OK** button when you are finished, and then you will see the button on your page. When you save your page, you will be prompted to save three images for every button. One represents the *normal* state, one represents the *hovered* state, and one represents the *pressed* state. When you view your page

in the browser, the button will be included. When you hover the cursor over the button, the button changes; and when you press the button, it changes until the next page is loaded.

Advanced Customization

Once you are familiar with using FrontPage 2003 to customize websites created with SharePoint Products and Technologies, you will find that these sites have the potential to be unique and highly effective. This section outlines how you can use features in FrontPage 2003 to make creating and managing your site easier and give your site enhanced functionality.

Repeating the Same Content on Multiple Pages

Most websites start small and then grow larger as content is added to the site. As sites grow in size, they can become more difficult to manage because when content that appears on more than one page in your site changes, you have to spend time opening and editing multiple pages, which can be a tedious task that is prone to errors. FrontPage 2003 can help manage content that appears on multiple pages in some key ways.

Dynamic Web Templates (DWT)

Most website designs include a common header on all pages, common navigation on the side, and a common footer on all pages that contains copyright information, contact information, or terms of use. Perhaps the content for the page even has a separate designated area for the page title. (See Figure 32-24.)

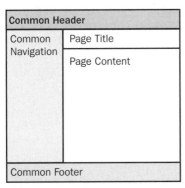

Figure 32-24   Simple page design

In a corporate setting, the website is often designed and created by one person or team, and then updated and maintained by another person or team, such as the content owners. A new feature with FrontPage 2003 is that Web developers can create Web pages that contain editable regions, in which users can create and edit content, and leave the rest of the page uneditable. For example, a Web developer can create pages that have a header, navigational area, footer, and page title in them that the users cannot edit, but also open a large portion of the page for editing. This gives the Web developer control over the formatting on the page and prevents the user from accidentally removing or changing the page header, footer, or navigation, yet it gives the content owner freedom to create and edit his own content on the page.

Control of editable portions of Web pages is determined by the use of a Dynamic Web Template (DWT). DWTs can be thought of as page templates with definitions for editable regions that stay attached to pages even after they are created.

For example, you could create a DWT that is attached to 30 pages on your site, and if you wanted to change a section of the footer on all those pages, you would change it one time on the DWT and it would automatically update the footer on all 30 pages. Because you can have more than one DWT in a site, you could have some pages attached to one DWT, some pages attached to another DWT, and some pages unattached and therefore freely editable.

To create a DWT

1. Using FrontPage 2003, create the DWT. DWT pages are simply Web pages, so start with whatever page design you like. If you want to apply the home page look and navigation to other pages on your site, you can start with the default.aspx page and then remove the content you do not want on every page.

2. Name the page with a .dwt file extension. If the left-hand navigation is included on the DWT, each page will include the link bars that are on the home page. Any time one of the link bars changes, the link bars will automatically be updated on all the pages that use them.

3. Specify which region of the page you would like to be editable by authorized FrontPage 2003 users. You do this by selecting the area you want to designate as editable, clicking **Dynamic Web Template** on the **Format** menu, and then clicking **Manage Editable Regions**, which opens the **Editable Regions** dialog box. (See Figure 32-25.)

Figure 32-25   Editable Regions dialog box

4. Type a name for the region in the **Region name** box, such as "content", click the **Add** button, and then click the **Close** button. The editable region in the DWT has now been defined. Save the DWT by clicking **Save** on the **File** menu.

5. Attach the pages you want to use the DWT design. If you want to attach more than one page to a DWT at one time, the easiest way is to multiple-select them in the folder list by using CTRL+click (for selective choices) or SHIFT+Click (for consecutive choices).

Tip If a DWT includes Web Parts or other ASP.NET controls or code, the attached pages must have the .aspx file extension. You will be prompted to save pages with the .aspx file extension when this condition occurs.

6. Once the page or pages are selected, click **Dynamic Web Template** from the **Format** menu, and then click **Attach Dynamic Web Template** to open the **Attach Dynamic Web Template** dialog box. Click the name of the DWT you want to attach to these pages, and then click **Open** to attach the DWT to each of the pages.

7. Open a page attached to the DWT and then edit the regions marked as editable. In this example, the editable region would be marked on the page with an orange border and the name given to the editable region would be "content."

Tip Users are unable to edit regions that are controlled by the DWT.

Advanced Find and Replace

You can use the enhanced find and replace features in FrontPage 2003 to make updates to Web pages or directly to the HTML code. For example, you could replace all the links to a particular graphic file or change an e-mail address that appears throughout your site by using the find and replace feature in FrontPage 2003. To access this feature, click Find on the Edit menu. Or you can use the keyboard shortcuts CTRL+F for Find and CTRL+H for Replace. This opens the Find And Replace dialog box. (See Figure 32-26.)

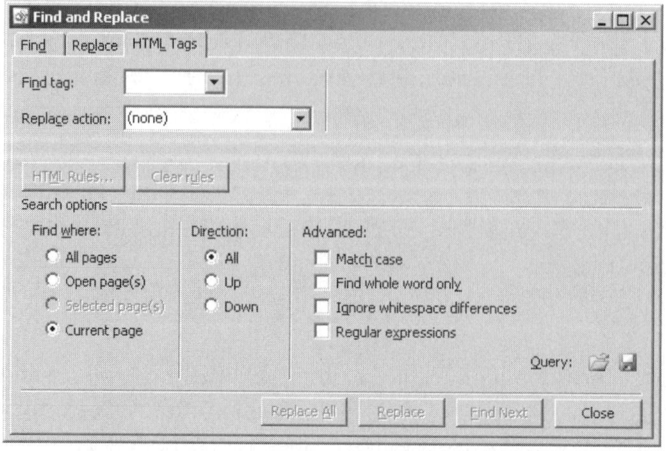

Figure 32-26   Find And Replace dialog box—HTML Tags tab

A powerful aspect of the find and replace feature in FrontPage 2003 is the ability to set a series of criteria (including the use of regular expressions) for searches, including a specific set of actions to take once content is found that meets the search criteria. For example, you could use Find And Replace not only to find specific tags, but to replace only the contents in the tag. Find And Replace is a slick tool you can use to make updating and managing your website easier.

Themes

Themes are great ways to change fonts, formatting, and graphical elements on one page or throughout an entire website.

Cascading Style Sheets (CSS)

FrontPage 2003 Themes use industry-standard Cascading Style Sheets (CSS) to define formatting rules. However, the FrontPage 2003 user interface shields you from the technical intricacies so that you can create a custom Theme without ever opening a CSS file. In fact, although the themes use CSS, the CSS files cannot be successfully edited directly; they must be altered by using the Customize Theme user interface.

Find a Theme to Copy

If you want to create a custom Theme with your own colors, fonts, formatting, buttons, and more, you might want to customize an existing Theme rather than create a new one. There are hundreds of formatting options, and it is often easier to find an existing Theme that resembles the look you want and then customize it rather than start from a blank Theme and then make each formatting choice yourself.

For example, Themes allow you to specify formatting choices for such detailed items as the colors behind calendar entries or the font color used on the date-picker pop-up window. If you start with a Theme that already uses colors similar to the ones you want to use, you will not have to change the formatting for such detailed items because they will already be acceptable. Instead, you can concentrate on changing the formatting for the items that are important to you, such as body text formatting, hyperlink formatting, and more.

To customize an existing Theme, you should first look through the existing Themes in FrontPage 2003 to see what existing Themes contain fonts and formatting that are the most similar to those you want to use. Scroll through the list of available Themes that are installed on your computer using the Theme task pane. Click on the Theme option from the Format menu to open the Theme task pane. (See Figure 32-27.)

Figure 32-27   Theme task pane

Saving Your Custom Theme

To find a Theme that most closely matches the look of your finished site (discussed in previous section), and then save a copy of it as your own Custom Theme, follow these steps:

1. Using FrontPage 2003, click **Theme** on the **Format** menu to open the **Theme** task pane. (See Figure 32-27 shown earlier.)

2. Hover the cursor over the Theme you want to start with, click the down arrow on the right, which results in a pop-up menu being presented, and then

click the **Customize** option to open the **Customize Theme** dialog box. (See Figure 32-28.)

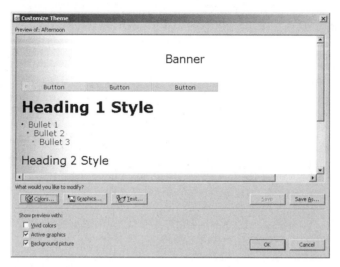

Figure 32-28 Customize Theme dialog box

3. Click the **Save As** button to open the **Save Theme** dialog box. (See Figure 32-29.)

Figure 32-29 Save Theme dialog box

4. Type a new name for your Theme in the **Enter new theme** title box, click **OK**, and then click **OK** again. This process has saved your new Theme, but it has not applied it to your site yet.

Tip You can create a custom Theme from scratch if you do not want to start with one of the existing Themes and then customize it from there. Instead of choosing an existing them and then clicking Customize, simply click the Create New Theme option at the bottom of the Theme task pane. Click the Save As button, name your Theme, and then click the OK button two times. You new custom Theme is then saved.

Applying Your Custom Theme to Your Site

To apply your custom Theme to your site, find the Theme you just created in the Themes task pane, select a theme scroll box, hover the cursor over it, click the down arrow on the right (which results in a popup menu), and click Apply As Default Theme. If changes are made to your Theme from this point forward, FrontPage will prompt you to apply the new changes to your website. Responding affirmatively to the prompt will propagate your changes to all your pages. New pages will automatically use the custom theme.

Changing Colors, Graphics, and Fonts

Once your Custom Theme is applied to your site, change colors, graphics, and fonts in your site by using the Customize Theme dialog box (shown earlier in Figure 32-29) by following these steps:

■ Click the **Colors** button, and then click the **Custom** tab to change the colors of headings, the page background, hyperlinks, and more.

■ Changing graphics such as buttons, bullets, page banners, and background images is done by clicking the **Graphics** button. You can also change the font style on buttons here as well.

■ Changing body text formats and heading formats is done by clicking the **Text** button. Additional styles can be added by clicking **More Text Styles** and then clicking **New**.

■ When you are finished changing colors, graphics, and fonts, you click **OK** twice, and when prompted whether or not to save your changes, click **Yes**.

Advanced Theme Customization

There are over 300 styles you can change in each Theme. This collection of styles can change even the smallest elements in a website created with SharePoint. The vast majority of custom Themes that are created do not make changes to more than a fraction of the styles available. If the element you want to change is not exposed in the color, graphics, or fonts areas, you will need to find out what CSS style needs to be changed to affect that element.

> **More Info**   For more information on how to determine which CSS needs to change, you can read an article in the FrontPage 2003 Developer's Toolkit titled "Customizing Themes for Sites Created with Windows SharePoint Services." It includes details about how to hover your cursor over a screenshot of a default page of a site created with SharePoint and see a ToolTip that shows the corresponding style to change. The FrontPage 2003 Developer's Toolkit is available at *http://www.frontpagedevkit.com/wss/articles/themes-custom.htm*.

Once you know what style you want to change, you can change it by clicking the Text button on the Customize Theme dialog box (shown previously in Figure 32-29), and subsequently clicking the More Text Styles button, which opens the Style dialog box. (See Figure 32-30.)

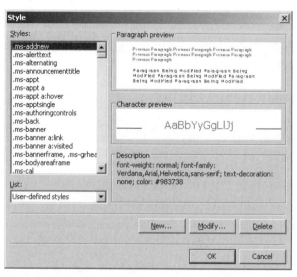

Figure 32-30   Style dialog box

The Styles scroll box displays all the styles currently in use in the Theme. Click the style you want to change, and then click the Modify button to open the Modify Style dialog box. (See Figure 32-31.)

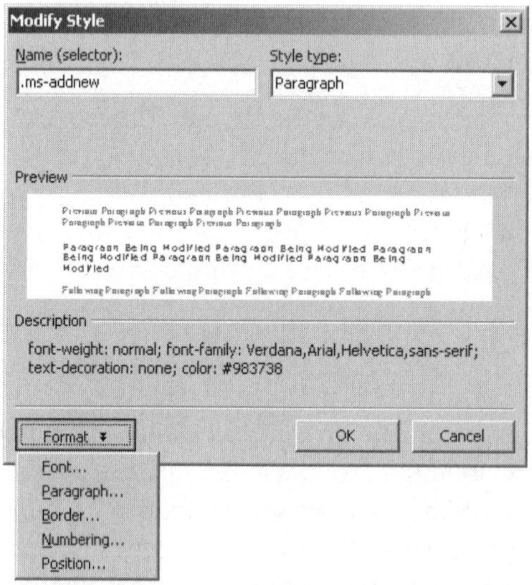

Figure 32-31   Modify Style dialog box

Click the Format button, and then click the option that represents the change you want to make—Font, Paragraph, Border, Numbering, or Positioning. Each of these options give you full control over the formatting possibilities. For example, you could choose to change font color, increase the amount of space before or after the text, add a border only to the top of the text, or position the text to wrap to the right. The options are virtually unlimited.

When you are finished making your updates, click the OK button until you are asked whether you want to save the Theme, and then click Yes. You might need to repeat these steps for each style you want to change until your custom Theme is just the way you want it.

Image Tracing

You do not have to use default sites provisioned by SharePoint Products and Technologies. In fact, you can create a brand new page that doesn't contain any Share-Point Products and Technologies functionality at all and then add list or document library views back into your site as needed. Because Windows SharePoint Services elements can be formatted to suit professional designs, some sites created with Windows SharePoint Services do not look like default sites and therefore are not recognizable as sites created with Windows SharePoint Services.

One new tool in FrontPage 2003, called image tracing, makes converting a professional design, which is usually delivered in the form of a large graphics image of what the site will look like when it is completed, into a fully functional website. Image tracing allows you to place your site design into the background of a page you are working on in Design view and then create your page on top of it. When your page is complete, you can remove the tracing image. The tracing image is used only for the purposes of editing and therefore will not be visible when you view your page in the browser.

To use image tracing

1. From within FrontPage 2003, import the design graphic into your site by clicking **Import** on the **File** menu.

2. Open an existing page or create a new page, and then highlight the **Tracing Image** option on the **View** menu. Click the **Configure** option under the **Tracing Image** option to open the **Tracing Image** dialog box. (See Figure 32-32.)

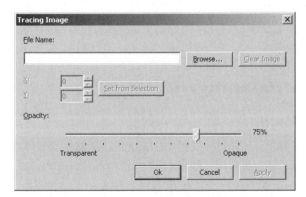

Figure 32-32   Image Tracing dialog box

3. Click the **Browse** button, click on your design graphic, and then click **Open**. Use the **Opacity** slider bar to adjust the opacity or transparency of the tracing image. You will see a lightened version of the design graphic in the background of your page. You can use all the familiar tools to create your Web page, but you will be creating it on top of the tracing image. This ability to see your design while working on your page greatly simplifies the process of creating a page to exacting specifications from a designer.

4. When you are finished designing your page and no longer need the tracing image, open the **Tracing Image** dialog box again, delete the path to the tracing file, and then click **OK**.

Adding Effects to Your Pages with Behaviors

FrontPage 2003 makes adding JScript effects to your Web pages easier than ever. You can insert a graphic into a page, and then use Behaviors to change the status bar when clicked, launch a pop-up window, play a sound, open a separate browser window, and more. You can also use Behaviors to call JScript that you create when you click on text or hover over it. Click Behaviors on the Format menu to provide access to the many options in the Behaviors task pane. (See Figure 32-33.)

Figure 32-33 Behaviors task pane with Insert options showing

Layers (Absolute Positioning)

Some website designs call for design elements that overlap. For example, your design might dictate placing an image on a page and then placing text on top of that image that overlaps multiple table cells. FrontPage 2003 Layers Support gives you the ability to position multiple design elements in the same area on a page. Click Layers on the Format menu, and then click the Insert Layer button for each layer you would like to insert. This opens a blue box where you can place content of nearly any kind.

> **Tip**   Combine Layers with Behaviors (discussed earlier in this chapter) to add interactivity. For example, you could set one layer to trigger display of another layer by adding a behavior to the first layer.

Working with the Data Source Catalog

The Data Source Catalog acts as the central repository of all your data sources. It is the single location from which all your data sources can be accessed and managed. It doesn't matter whether the data source exists on your server or on an external server. If you have access rights to the data source, you can interact with it by using the Data Source Catalog.

Adding a Data Source

FrontPage 2003 uses the Data Retrieval Services in Windows SharePoint Services to provide data access. These services retrieve data from many sources and present it in an XML format for consumption. Great Plains and SQL Server also have separate non–FrontPage 2003 data-retrieval services that can be added on to Windows Share-Point Services. Table 32-4 lists the many data source types that can be accessed using FrontPage 2003:

Table 32-4   Data Source Types

Data Source Type
Windows SharePoint Services lists
Windows SharePoint Services document libraries
OLEDB databases
XML files
Server-side scripts
XML Web Services

To add a data source to the Data Source Catalog

1. From within FrontPage 2003, click **Insert Data View** on the **Data** menu to open the **Data Source Catalog** task pane. (See Figure 32-34.)

Figure 32-34 Data Source Catalog task pane

2. Determine what type of data source to add. Recently used data sources are listed at the top of the **Data Source Catalog** task pane under **Recent**.

3. Expand the folder for the type of data source chosen by clicking the plus sign (+) to expose the existing data sources. Clicking the minus sign (–) would collapse the list, making it easier to see the other folders.

4. Follow the steps under one of the following sections for the specific data source type you want to add.

Adding a SharePoint Products and Technologies Data Source

By default, you cannot specify the columns, sorting, filtering, or grouping on the SharePoint Products and Technologies List data source created by FrontPage 2003. You just get a default query. However, if you select the data source and then choose Copy And Modify, you will create a new data source that will have the ability to specify the columns, sort, filter, and group. The Copy And Modify feature works with all data source types but is most useful with lists and document libraries.

To add a SharePoint list

1. Under the **SharePoint Lists** folder, click the **Create new SharePoint list** link to open the **SharePoint List** dialog box to the **Lists** tab.

2. By default, FrontPage 2003 shows the **Lists** tab, and you simply select the type of SharePoint list you want to add from the list.

Tip On the top right side of the SharePoint List dialog box, there are two toggle buttons. The default Large Icons button on the left is one that presents the SharePoint lists by using difficult-to-read large icons. Click the **List** button on the right to see the SharePoint lists presented in a readable list.

3. Try the New List Wizard if you are unsure what type you want to add. Otherwise, type a name for the new list in the **Specify the name for the new list** box under the **Option** section on the right side of the dialog box.

4. To add a SharePoint library instead, you have two options. You can click the **Document Libraries** tab of the already open **SharePoint List** dialog box, or you can choose to **Cancel** the dialog box, **Expand** the SharePoint Libraries folder, and click the **Create New Document Library** link to reopen the **SharePoint List** dialog box to the same **Document Libraries** tab.

5. On the **Document Libraries** tab in the **SharePoint List** dialog box, select the type of document library you want.

6. Again, for additional help, you can double-click the **New Document Library Wizard** option. Otherwise, type a name for the new document library in the Specify The Name For The New Document Library box under the **Option** section.

7. There isn't a separate folder in the Data Source Catalog task pane for SharePoint surveys, so choose either of the two previously mentioned methods to open the SharePoint List dialog box and then click the **Surveys** tab.

8. Double-click the **New Survey Wizard** option, or type a name for the new survey in the **Specify the name for the new survey** box under the **Option** section.

9. New surveys will be added to the **SharePoint Lists** folder in the **Data Source Catalog** task pane.

Adding a Database Connection Data Source

This example creates a database connection to the Customers table in the Northwind sample database for Microsoft SQL Server.

To create a new database connection

1. In the **Data Source Catalog** task pane, expand the **Database Connections** folder and click the **Add to catalog** link. This opens the **Database Data Source Properties** dialog box. (See Figure 32-35.)

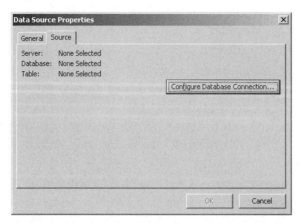

Figure 32-35   Initial Database Data Source Properties dialog box

2. Accept the defaults for fields on the **General** tab. On the default **Source** tab, click the **Configure Database Connection** button to bring up the Configure Database Connection Wizard, Page 1. (See Figure 32-36.)

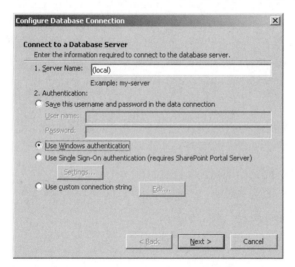

Figure 32-36   Configure Database Connection Wizard, Page 1

3. Enter the name of the server—in this example, our database is on the (local) server.

4. Choose the authentication type; the following choices are available:

  ■ **Save this username and password in the data connection**. This option allows you to type in a specific database user name and password that identifies you to the data source.

  ■ **Use Windows Authentication**. This option uses integrated security—your Windows credentials are used for authentication at the data source. If you choose this option, make sure that integrated security is supported by the data source (for example, Microsoft SQL Server) and that it is configured to accept Windows sign-on credentials. If your SQL Server is on a physical machine other than the Windows SharePoint Services machine, you will need to use one of the other authentication types.

- **Use Single Sign-On authentication (requires SharePoint Portal Server)**. This option can be used when this site is part of a portal site created by using SharePoint Portal Server 2003 and the administrator has enabled and configured Single Sign-On.

- **Use Custom connection string**. This option lets you specify an OLEDB connection string used to connect to the database. This option can be used for fine-grained control of the connection.

In this example, we use the Use Windows Authentication option. This assumes that the SQL Server and Windows SharePoint Services exist on the same machine. If connecting to an external database is required (common), you must use another authentication type because Windows Authentication allows only "one hop" of the credentials. So, you cannot authenticate against an external SQL server using the Windows credentials captured by the Windows SharePoint Services server.

To use the Use Windows Authentication option to create a new database connection

1. Click **Next** to navigate to the Configure Database Connection Wizard, Page 2. (See Figure 32-37.)

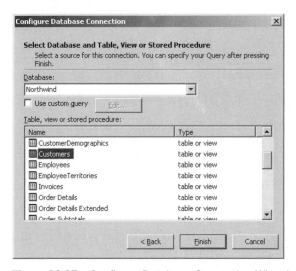

Figure 32-37   Configure Database Connection Wizard, Page 2

2. Select the table, view, or stored procedure that you want to use as the source of data for this connection. Note that stored procedures will be available only if the Enable Update Query Support setting has been turned on in the Data Retrieval Services settings on the Windows SharePoint Services server. In this example, we choose the Northwind database in the drop-down list of databases.

3. Select **Customers** from the Table, View, or Stored Procedure list.

> **Tip** If you select the Use Custom Query check box, you can specify any SQL query you want.

4. Click **Finish** to complete this wizard and you are returned to the **Data Source Properties** dialog box. (See Figure 32-38.)

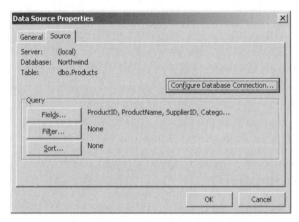

Figure 32-38   Database Data Source Properties dialog box

5. Click the **Fields** button on the **Data Source Properties** dialog box to open the **Displayed Fields** dialog box. (See Figure 32-39.)

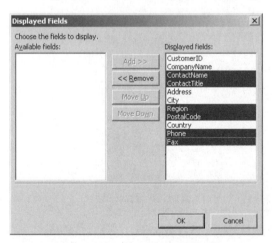

Figure 32-39   Displayed Fields dialog box

6. Using the CTRL key, highlight all the fields in the **Displayed fields** box on the right except the CustomerID, CompanyName, Address, City, and Country fields

and click the **Remove** button. Click the **OK** button to remove the fields from the data source.

7. Click the **Filter** button on the **Data Source Properties** dialog box to open the **Filter Criteria** dialog box. (See Figure 32-40.)

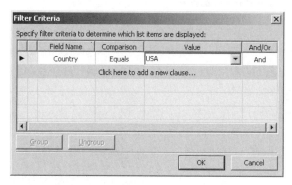

Figure 32-40   Filter Criteria dialog box

8. Click the **Click here to add a new clause** gray bar, choose **Country** from the **Field Name** drop-down list, leave the Comparison value as the default Equals, and type the text **USA** into the **Value** text box. (This text box looks like a drop-down list, but it is initially empty.) Click the **OK** button to apply the filter.

9. Click the **Sort** button on the **Data Source Properties** dialog box to open the **Sort** dialog box. (See Figure 32-41.)

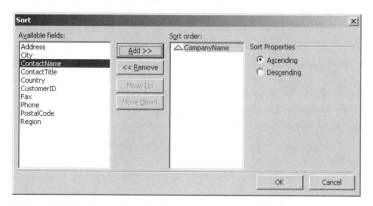

Figure 32-41   Sort dialog box

10. Click the **CompanyName** in the **Available fields** box, leave the default Sort Properties option of Ascending, and then click the **Add** button. **CompanyName** will be added to the **Sort order** box. Click the **OK** button to apply the sort.

11. Click **OK** on the **Data Source Properties** dialog box to complete database connection setup.

The new data source, named "Customers on Northwind" in our example, is listed in the **Database Connections** folder in the **Data Source Catalog** task pane.

Adding an XML FileData Source

FrontPage will automatically create a data source in the catalog for any XML file in the site. This works the same as SharePoint lists and document libraries.

To add a new XML File data source

1. First you must have an XML file. You have the following options for obtaining an XML file:

   - Create a new XML file. (In FrontPage 2003, create a new Text file and then save it as XML.)

   - Search your hard drive for an XML file installed with some other sample. (This is the option we took.)

   - Use an XML file you find on the Internet.

     For this example, we will use an XML file available on the Internet called *cust-ord.xml.*

> **More Info**   Download the actual XML file used in this example, and save it on your local machine as cust-ord.xml. The File is available at *http://www.sharepointcustomization.com/resources/whitepapers/webpartdocs/cust-ord.xml.*

A fragment from this XML file follows:

```
<?xml version="1.0" encoding="utf-8" ?>
<CustomerOrders>
  <Customer>
    <CompanyName>Ernst Handel</CompanyName>
    <Orders>
      <OrderID>10258</OrderID>
      <OrderDate>1996-07-17T00:00:00</OrderDate>
      <Products>
        <ProductName>A Widget</ProductName>
        <Quantity>65</Quantity>
        <UnitPrice>17.0000</UnitPrice>
        <total>1105.0000</total>
      </Products>
    </Orders>
  </Customer>
  <Customer>
    <CompanyName>Frankenversand</CompanyName>
    <Orders>
      <OrderID>10267</OrderID>
```

```
      <OrderDate>1996-07-29T00:00:00</OrderDate>
      <Products>
        <ProductName>B Widget</ProductName>
        <Quantity>70</Quantity>
        <UnitPrice>44.0000</UnitPrice>
        <total>3080.0000</total>
      </Products>
    </Orders>
  </Customer>
</CustomerOrders>
```

2. In the **Data Source Catalog** task pane, expand the XML Files folder and click
    the **Add to catalog** link. This opens the XML Data Source Properties dialog
    box. (See Figure 32-42.)

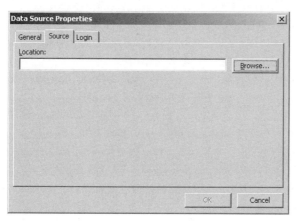

Figure 32-42   XML Data Source Properties dialog box

3. Accept the defaults for fields on the **General** and **Login** tabs. On the default
    Source tab, click the **Browse** button to bring up the traditional **File Open** dia-
    log box.

4. Navigate to the XML file you want to use. Select it and click the **Open** button.
    Then click **OK** on the **XML Data Source Properties** dialog box.

5. If the XML file isn't already located within your website, you will be prompted
    to import it. Click **OK** on the Alert Message box. (See Figure 32-43.)

> **More Info**   If the XML file is located at an HTTP URL, it does not need to be
> imported to the local site. For example, you can use an external XML file
> such as an RSS feed without importing it. This is why the proxy settings can
> be important for these data sources.

Figure 32-43   Import Alert Message box

6. Subsequently, an **Import** dialog box (shown in Figure 32-44) will prompt you to place the imported file somewhere on your site. For now, save the XML file to the default location, the website root, by clicking the **OK** button.

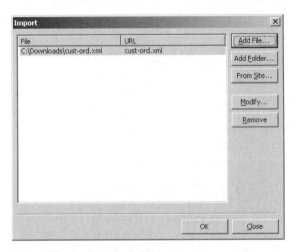

Figure 32-44   Import dialog box

An XML data source corresponding to the imported XML file should now exist in the XML files folder of the Data Source Catalog task pane.

Adding a Server-Side Script Data Source

A server-side script begins to run when a browser requests any kind of script file (such as an .asp file) from the Web server. The Web server then calls the script, which processes the requested file from top to bottom, executes its commands, and sends back a block of data as XML. Because scripts run on the server instead of on the client browser, the Web server does all the work that is involved in generating the XML that is returned to FrontPage.

To add a new server-side script data source

1. Expand the Server-Side Scripts folder in the **Data Source Catalog** task pane, and click the **Add to Catalog** link to open the **Script Data Source Properties** dialog box. (See Figure 32-45.)

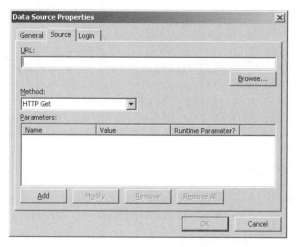

Figure 32-45   Script Data Source Properties dialog box

2. Type the path to the script in the URL box, and then select from the **Method** drop-down list whether to run the script using an **HTTP Get** (default) or an **HTTP Post**.

3. To add the parameters to use when running the script from a Web page, click the **Add** button.

> **Tip** If there is a proxy server involved, note that the Data Retrieval Services do not look for the proxy settings in the default web.config file. To make data requests through a proxy, the administrator must enable the proxy server by changing the web.config located by default in the C:\program files \common files\microsoft shared\web server extensions\60\config\ folder on the WSS server.

Adding an XML Web Service Data Source

To add a new XML Web service, follow these steps:

1. Expand the XML Web Services folder in the **Data Source Catalog** task pane, and click the **Add to Catalog** link to open the XML Web Services Data Source Properties dialog box. (See Figure 32-46.)

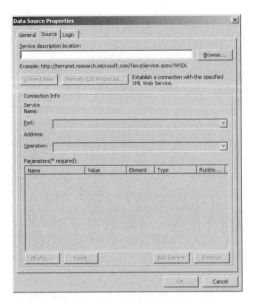

Figure 32-46 XML Web Services Data Source Properties dialog box

2. In the **Service description location** box in the **Data Source Properties** dialog box, type the URL for the Web service.

3. Click **Connect Now** to read the Web Service Description Language (WSDL) associated with the Web Service. FrontPage 2003 will create an XML Web Service data source based on that definition.

> **Tip** As discussed in the previous section, Data Retrieval Services do not look for the proxy settings in the default web.config file. See the previous tip.

Referencing External Catalogs

Each Windows SharePoint Services site has a collection of data sources that consists of at least the lists and document libraries on that site; in addition, it can have other data sources that the site administrator or users have added.

The Data Sources Catalog from any Windows SharePoint Services site can be made available at your site. This is a powerful feature that allows the user to share data sources instead of having to re-create them.

To reference a catalog from a different site

1. Click the **Manage Catalog** link near the bottom of the **Data Source Catalog** task pane to open the **Manage Catalog** dialog box. Click the **Add** button to open the **Collection Properties** dialog box. (See Figure 32-47.)

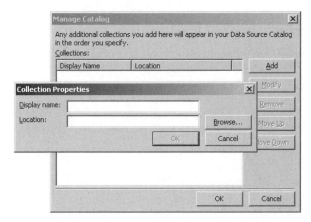

Figure 32-47   Collection Properties dialog box

2. In the **Collection Properties** dialog box, type the display name and location for the collection you want to add.

Searching for Data Sources

As a site changes and users create or reference multiple data sources, it is often difficult to keep track of the sources that you are interested in. This is when the search feature of the catalog becomes useful.

To search for a data source

1. Click the **Find a Data Source** link near the bottom of the **Data Source Catalog** task pane to open the **Find a Data Source** task pane. (See Figure 32-48.)

Figure 32-48   Find a Data Source task pane

2. In the **Search** box, enter the location you want to search.

3. In the **For** box, type the search term.

4. Click **Search Now**.

Note that the search occurs on the name of the data source. The search process simply looks for the presence of the search string within the data source name without worrying about word boundaries.

Deleting Data Sources

Deleting a data source is as simple as right-clicking it and selecting Remove. FrontPage 2003 creates a data source for each SharePoint list or document library in your site. So, these data sources can be removed only by removing the SharePoint list or document library.

Working with Data

FrontPage 2003 makes working with data easier than ever by allowing you to modify and present live data from a variety of data sources (as shown earlier in Table 32-4) to create sophisticated data-driven websites that lower maintenance costs and allow users to post data to your website by using only their browser.

Data-driven websites in FrontPage 2003 are enabled by the Windows Share-Point Services Data Retrieval Service and support a complete set of WYSIWYG tools for creating and modifying XSLT. They are industry-standard Web Parts for sorting, grouping, filtering, and conditionally formatting data. You can use these Web Parts to create high quality, dynamic Web pages for presenting live data.

You can also use a Windows SharePoint Services–based XML editor such as Microsoft Office InfoPath to create XML forms that are saved to a form library. (For more information, see Chapter 39, "Using Microsoft Office InfoPath with SharePoint Products and Technologies.") The XML data is not just stored to the form library, but fields in the form data can be presented to site visitors as lists. These lists can be sorted, filtered, and even connected to other Web Parts to extend the data even further.

Data Views

Data View Web Parts, also known as Data Views, are the primary component used for data presentation when building data-driven websites using FrontPage 2003 and Windows SharePoint Services. Data Views never store static data. Instead, Data Views always point back to the original data source for the data found in the Data Source Catalog. The display is managed using the formalism of an Extensible Stylesheet Language Transformation (XSLT), which is a powerful, industry-standard language used for formatting the presentation of XML data. A Data View retrieves data from the data source in the form of XML and applies the XSLT to it. This gives the developer a powerful and standards-based way to display formatted data.

XSLT is an XML-based language that enables you to transform one class of XML document to another. XSLT offers great flexibility for presenting and exchanging data between disparate devices and business systems. For example, with XSLT style sheets, you can dynamically transform an XML purchase order from one schema to another before sending the order to a supplier. In addition, with XSLT you can dynamically transform an XML document so that it can be rendered on a variety of Internet-enabled devices.

From within FrontPage 2003, you can format the data within a Data View by directly applying formatting from Design view. FrontPage 2003 applies formatting to all data points at the same level in the XML by modifying the XSLT style sheet attached to the page. You can change the XSLT style sheet without having to know anything about XSLT. FrontPage 2003 even generates the XPATH query for you. This new feature in FrontPage 2003 is the first-of-its-kind WYSIWYG XSLT editor on the market today.

Data-Driven Web Sites

FrontPage 2003 has many features for building live, data-driven webs. Central to any data-driven Web page is the ability to collect and present live customer data on the fly on a page—that is, you are effectively building a page based on data (hence the term *data-driven*). These features fall into the following two categories:

- **Sites based on ASP or ASP.NET.**   This method uses the Database Results Wizard and the Database Interface Wizard. You can create Web pages that display interactive views of data by using ASP code or ASP.NET controls.

- **Sites based on Windows SharePoint Services.**   This method uses the Data Source Catalog and Data View task panes. With it, you can access a wide range of data sources. (See Table 32-4 earlier in the chapter).

In the following sections, we focus on the second category.

Windows SharePoint Services Data Retrieval Service

The key technology enabling this versatile data access is the Data Retrieval Service, which is a new data-binding mechanism in Windows SharePoint Services. The Data Retrieval Service enables data consumers and data sources to communicate with each other through Simple Object Access Protocol (SOAP) and XML. In essence, it is an XML Web service that returns XML data from different data sources or manipulates data against those data sources. The Data Retrieval Service is installed and runs on any server running Windows SharePoint Services.

The Data View is a special Web Part that acts as a client to the Windows SharePoint Services Data Retrieval Service, as it can retrieve and manipulate data from any data source registered in the Data Source Catalog. As we mentioned before, the Data Retrieval Service is a Web service; thus, it returns data in the form of XML and the Data View uses XSLT to format the data. (See Figure 32-49.)

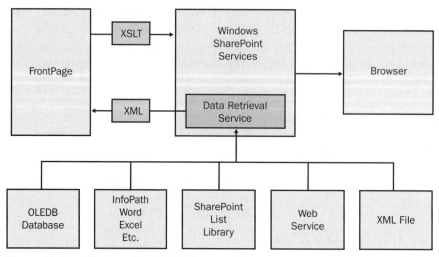

Figure 32-49 Windows SharePoint Services Data Retrieval Service

A key feature of the Data View is that it provides WYSIWYG authoring of XSLT to produce formatted views of data. The visual editor produces XSLT code that is inserted directly into the HTML of your page. Once inserted on your page, you can use any WYSIWYG formatting tools from within the Data View in FrontPage 2003, such as adding table columns with certain font formatting, and FrontPage 2003 will generate the new XSLT on the fly. You can also change or add to the XSLT in the Code view of the FrontPage 2003 editor.

Because of the Data Retrieval Services Web service architecture, live data is available at authoring time. Furthermore, data is available as XML regardless of how it is stored at the data source.

Data Views can be connected to build rich pages that combine data from multiple sources, provide rich views on top of hierarchical data (such as master-detail), or both.

Adding a Data View

Add a new page to the root directory of the FrontPage 2003 Folder List, and name it DataView.aspx. We will use this empty page in the next several sections.

We start interacting with a Data View on a Web page by selecting the desired data source from the Data Source Catalog task pane. The Data Source Catalog is described in detail in a previous section of this chapter.

Inserting Data View into the Page

To add a Data View to your Web page, follow these steps:

1. From within FrontPage 2003, open the empty page DataView.aspx in Design mode. Click **Insert Web Part Zone** from the **Data** menu to create Zone 1 at the top of the empty page.

> **Tip**   Like any other Web Part, a Data View can reside either within or out-side a Web Part Zone. A Web Part that is not in a Web Part Zone is called a Static Web Part and is subject to certain limitations in its ability to be cus-tomizable at run-time. It is common practice to put Web Parts inside a Web Part Zone, and we have followed that convention here.

2. Click **Insert Data View** on the **Data** menu to open the **Data Source Catalog** task pane. (See Figure 32-48.) As described in the previous section, there are many data sources that you can use. (See Table 32-4 earlier in the chapter.) Notice that FrontPage 2003 has automatically created data sources for the lists and document libraries that exist in your Windows SharePoint Services site.

3. Expand the **Database Connections** folder by clicking the plus sign (+), which exposes the Customers on the Northwind data source that we created earlier in the section about the Data Source Catalog task pane.

4. Position the cursor on the **Customers on Northwind** data source, and click the right arrow at the end of the name.

5. Click the **Insert Data View** option at the top of the context menu.

6. Save the new page and then view it in your browser. (See Figure 32-50.)

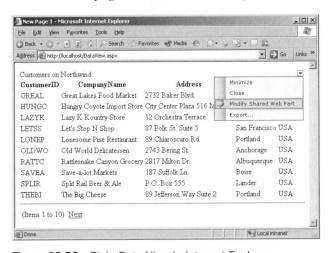

Figure 32-50   Plain Data View in Internet Explorer

As you can see, with a few simple drag-and-drop actions, your Web page can easily be extended with data from the source of your choice. The display comes complete with pagination. Because the Data View is essentially a Web Part, all the advantages of the Web Part Infrastructure—such as runtime customization, applying themes, shared and personal views, and so on—are available to the user from the browser or to the developer from within FrontPage 2003. If we hadn't placed the Data View into the Web Zone, the drop-down menu in the top right corner would not have been available.

Formatting the Data View

What we have seen so far are just the basics. Data Views have many rich and powerful capabilities built into them, such as grouping, filtering, sorting, toolbars, layout and formatting capabilities, the ability to work with hierarchical data, and more. In the next few sections, we will explore formatting the Data View in more detail.

One of the most powerful features of the Data View is that it allows XSL-based WYSIWYG formatting of data, thus providing multiple presentation options with just a few mouse clicks. The power of WYSIWYG lies in the fact that you can work entirely in the Design View. The powerful design tools in FrontPage 2003—such as formatting toolbars and so on—are readily available to format the output any way you want right in Design View.

Applying Styles

FrontPage 2003 provides several built-in styles to format the data in the Data View. Application of these styles is done using the Style link in the Data View Details task pane. Similar to the way we formatted the SharePoint Announcements list earlier in this chapter, we will continue formatting the Data View we added to the DataView.aspx page in the previous section.

To apply a style to the Data View

1. Ensure that the **Data View Details** task pane is displayed for the Data View. If it is not, you can display it by right-clicking anywhere in the **Data View** and choosing **Data View Properties** in the pop-up menu.

2. In the **Manage view settings** section at the top of the **Data View Details** task pane, click the **Style** link. This opens the **View Styles** dialog box.

3. In the list of available HTML styles, change the selection from the Basic Table to the Two Column Repeating form with border style (which is the fifth choice in the list). The style name shows as a ToolTip when you hover the cursor over the style.

4. Click the **Options** tab and in the Record Sets section at the bottom of the dialog box, change the value in the text box to the right of **Display items in sets of this size** from 10 to 4. Click the **OK** button to apply the changes.

5. You might be warned that changing the view style will remove any custom formatting and asked if you want to continue. Click the **Yes** button.

6. Save the DataView.aspx page and then view it in your browser. (See Figure 32-51.)

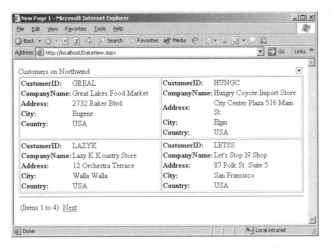

Figure 32-51   Data View with new style in Internet Explorer

As mentioned before, Data Views provide WYSIWYG formatting using XSL Transformations. The mouse clicks and other actions performed in the previous steps generated XSLT code and put this code inline within the HTML of your page.

To see this, ensure that DataView.aspx is open in Design view in FrontPage 2003, and click anywhere on the Data View. Now switch to Split view by clicking on Split in the View Selection bar at the bottom left of the page. This displays both the code and the design surface simultaneously. The code corresponding to the Data View is automatically highlighted in the code pane. Notice that XSLTs appear as CDATA with the <dvwp:XSL> tag. FrontPage 2003 generated these stylesheet transformations because of your actions in the WYSIWYG user interface.

Manually Editing XSLT

The auto-generated XSLTs can also be manually edited to allow a high degree of flexibility to the author of the page. We will look at a simple illustration of this. Suppose that you wanted to change the string CompanyName in the Data View so that it is italicized instead of boldfaced. Again, we will continue formatting the Data View we added to the DataView.aspx page in the previous section.

To manually edit the XSLT

1. Position the cursor anywhere on the **Data** View on the DataView.aspx page and switch to the **Split** view. By positioning the cursor first, FrontPage 2003 will position the Code pane at the location of the cursor on the page, making it easier to find the code associated with the element on the page.

2. In the code pane, locate the set of lines in the highlighted text that set the format for CompanyName.

It should look like the following fragment. (If you have followed the steps exactly the way they were shown in the previous sections, it should start at or close to line 180.)

```
<tr>
 <td width="25%" class="ms-vb">
    <b>CompanyName:</b>
 </td>
   <td width="75%" class="ms-vb">
    <xsl:value-of select="@CompanyName"/>
   </td>
</tr>
```

3. Change the third line to the following:

```
<i>CompanyName:</i>
```

4. Save the DataView.aspx page and then view it in your browser or choose the **Design View** tab at the bottom of the FrontPage user interface. (See Figure 32-52.) Return the page to the FrontPage 2003 Design view.

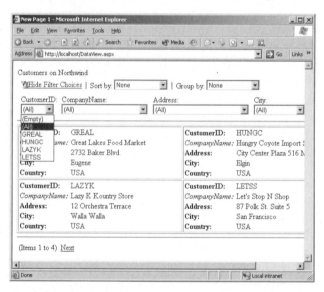

Figure 32-52　Data View with custom XSLT in Internet Explorer

This example is admittedly rather simple. The same effect could have been achieved within the Design view by simply selecting the desired text and clicking Format/Font. But without teaching you XSL, the example highlights the ability to edit FrontPage 2003–generated XSLT transformations directly within the Code pane of FrontPage 2003. XSLT editing can be used to accomplish things that are not available in the Design view.

Working with Data View Toolbars

The Data View is more that just a great way to present data; it also allows the user to interact dynamically with the data by grouping, filtering, and sorting. These actions are enabled using the Data View toolbar.

> **Note**   Grouping, filtering, and sorting can also be done at design time. When done at design time, these operations determine the shape, contents, and order rows in the Data View itself; at run time, these operations affect what data is presented to the user, not the actual contents of the Data View.

By default, when a Data View is inserted into a page, it does not come with a toolbar. However, the page author can choose to add one to the view. The following steps build on the DataView.aspx from the previous section.

To add a toolbar to the Data View

1. Ensure that the **Data View Details** task pane is displayed for the Data View.

2. In the **Manage view settings** section at the top of the **Data View Details** task pane, click the **Style** link. This opens the **View Styles** dialog box.

3. Click the **Options** tab and in the Toolbar section at the top of the dialog box, select the check box to the left of Show Toolbar With Options For.

4. Filter, Sort, and Group are all selected by default. Click the **OK** button to apply the changes.

The toolbar has a button to specify the filter and two drop-down lists to specify the sorting and grouping. When you click the Filter button in the browser, the Filter Choices pane is displayed. This allows you to specify a filter on the desired column. Note the following:

- Any Data View column can be used for filtering.

- The user interface (UI) for choosing the filter is a drop-down list. The only possible filter is of the form column=value, where *value* is one of the known-to-exist values for that column (and therefore is presented as an entry in the drop-down list).

- Filter choices are limited to the values on the immediate page.

Sorting is accomplished by choosing a column to sort on from the drop-down list. A directional arrow appears next to the drop-down list, showing the sort order—ascending or descending. Clicking the arrow changes the sort order from one to the other.

Grouping is accomplished by choosing a column to group by from the drop-down list. Groups can be expanded and collapsed. The Data View toolbar is enabled only at the top level of the Data View; subviews cannot have toolbars of their own.

Setting Data View Record Options

The Data View allows the author to control the number of records displayed. This is done under the Options tab of the View Styles dialog box, within the Record Sets category. The following three options are available, which appear as option buttons:

- **Display all items.**   This option displays all records in the view on a single page.

- **Display items in sets of size.**   This option displays records in sets of the specified size. Navigation buttons are provided at the bottom of the Data View, which allow the user to move to the next set of records (next), the previous set of records (previous), or the first set of records (reset).

- **Limit the total number of items displayed to.**   This option is the same as the one just listed, except the number of records displayed is limited by the specified size. These are design-time settings; the end user cannot modify this in the browser.

Conditional Formatting

Data Views offer another powerful feature: the formatting applied to the various fields in the view can be driven by conditions on the data. For instance, this feature will allow us to underline the CompanyName for companies in a specific city. Data Views also allow conditional display; whether a field is displayed or not can be controlled by predicates on other data within the view. The following steps build on the DataView.aspx from the previous section.

To add a conditional formatting to the Data View

1. Ensure that the **Data View Details** task pane is displayed for the Data View.

2. Select a **Data View** field value for the field we want to format on a given condition. In our example, the value for a CompanyName should be selected (such as "Great Lakes Food Market").

3. In the **Manage view settings** section at the top of the **Data View Details** task pane, the **Conditional Formatting** link will now be enabled. Click it to open the **Conditional Formatting** task pane. (See Figure 32-53.)

Figure 32-53   Conditional Formatting task pane

4.   Choose **Apply Formatting** from the **Create** menu to open the **Condition Criteria** dialog box. (See Figure 32-54.)

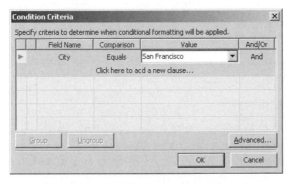

Figure 32-54   Condition Criteria dialog box

5.   Click the **Click here to add a new clause** gray bar, choose **City** from the **Field Name** drop-down list, leave the Comparison value as the default Equals, and type the text **San Francisco** into the **Value** text box. Click the **OK** button to apply the criteria.

6.   This will open the **Modify Style** dialog box. (See Figure 32-55.)

Figure 32-55   Modify Style dialog box

In the previous steps, we specified the conditions that trigger the application of special formatting. This dialog box allows you to spell out what this formatting is.

7. Note the many options available for formatting. For our example, choose **Font** from the **Format** menu to open the **Font** dialog box. (See Figure 32-56.)

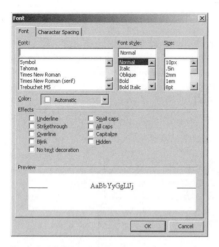

Figure 32-56 Font dialog box

8. In the **Effects** section of the **Font** dialog box, simply check **Underline**. Then click the **OK** button twice to save the changes and close the dialog boxes. The new formatting condition is added to the Existing Conditions section of the Conditional Formatting task pane. (See Figure 32-57.) Note that the context menu on the condition allows us to edit the condition, modify the style, or do both.

Figure 32-57 Existing Conditions in Conditional Formatting task pane

9. Save the DataView.aspx page and then view it in your browser. (See Figure 32-58.)

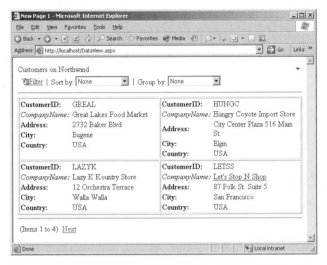

Figure 32-58 Data View with Conditional Formatting in Internet Explorer

Conditional formatting can also be used to control visibility. For instance, in our previous example we could have chosen to not display the name of the company if the City was San Francisco. The steps in accomplishing this are almost exactly the same as the steps previously outlined except instead of choosing Apply Formatting from the Create menu, we would choose Hide Content from the Create menu.

Conditional formatting can apply to only one field at a time; thus, it is not possible to create a single criterion that will modify the style/visibility of two fields. To accomplish this, you have to create two criteria. You can, however, compose a single criterion of multiple predicates on different columns (such as underline the Company-Name when the City=San Francisco OR City=Walla Walla AND Country=USA).

Data Views as Web Parts

At its heart, the Data View is a Web Part. This means that in addition to all the formatting, grouping, sorting, filtering, and so on, it automatically leverages all the features of the Web Part Infrastructure available in Windows SharePoint Services. Specifically, this means the following:

- Data Views support personal and shared views (when inside a Web Part Zone), just like every other Web Part. This means that a user can make personalizations that are visible only to him; the user can also customize the shared view of the same Data View.

- Data Views support run-time customization by using a browser-based interface when inside a Web Part Zone.

- Data Views have the standard set of customizable properties shared by all Web Parts, such as Title, Height, Width, Frame State, and so on.

- Data Views support Web Part connection authoring, but they require FrontPage 2003 to create the connection string.

> **More Info**   For more information about working with Web Parts in SharePoint Products and Technologies, see Chapter 31, "Working with Web Parts." For more information about using Visual Studio .NET to create Web Parts, see Chapter 37, "Using Visual Studio .NET to Create Web Parts."

Grouping, Filtering, and Sorting

In the previous section, we examined how the Data View toolbar can be used to group, filter, and sort the data displayed. This was performed at run time in the browser by the end user. The author might want to perform similar operations at design time.

Conceptually, when a filter condition is applied to a Data View at run time using the Data View toolbar, it affects only the presentation of the data; the Data View itself contains the entire set of records. When a Data View is filtered at design time, however, the filter is actually limiting what records are available in the Data View. Similar comments apply to design time vs. run time sorting and grouping.

In this section, we examine how Data Views can be filtered, sorted, and grouped at design time. These operations can be performed under the Manage View Settings category of the Data View Details task pane.

We want the Data View to contain records for companies whose names start with an "L". These records should be sorted by the Company Name field, and they should also be grouped by the same field. The following steps build on the DataView.aspx from the previous section.

To group, filter, and sort the data displayed at design time

1. Open DataView.aspx in FrontPage 2003 Design view.

2. Ensure the Data View Details task pane is displayed. If it is not, you can display it by right-clicking anywhere in the **Data View** and choosing **Data View Properties** in the pop-up menu.

3. Select a **Data View** field value for the field we want to format on a given condition. In our example, the value for a CompanyName should be selected (such as "Great Lakes Food Market").

4. In the **Data View Details** task pane, click **Filter** under the **Manage view settings** category to open the **Filter Criteria** dialog box. (See Figure 32-44 earlier in the chapter.) Note that the Data View filter defaults to the filter originally created for the Customers on the Northwind data source.

5. Click the **Click here to add a new clause** gray bar, choose CompanyName from the Field Name drop-down list, change the Comparison value to **Begins With**, and type the text **L** into the **Value** text box. Click the **OK** button to apply the criteria.

6. Save the DataView.aspx page and then view it in your browser. (See Figure 32-59.) Only companies that begin with the letter "L" will be displayed.

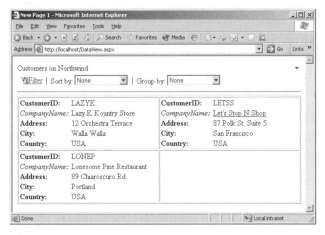

Figure 32-59   Data View with additional filtering in Internet Explorer

The filter criteria are XPath expressions. If it's available, the Filter Criteria dialog box is simply a visual editor that translates the UI into XPath. However, like all visual editors that sit on top of a language formalism, there are things that cannot be expressed visually but can be achieved by directly editing the XPath. The XPath behind a filter can be edited by clicking the Advanced button in the Filter Criteria dialog box, and it can also be edited from the conditional clause composition dialog box for conditional formatting.

Sorting and grouping are related operations, and they go hand in hand. If you are sorting by a field, the effect is that all records that have the same value for this field are displayed one after the other. This is an elementary form of grouping. Thus, you can group only fields for which you have specified sorting.

1. In the **Data View Details** task pane, click **Sort and Group** under the **Manage view** settings category to open the **Sort and Group** dialog box. (See Figure 32-60.) Note that Data View Sort and Group defaults to the values originally created for the Customers on the Northwind data source.

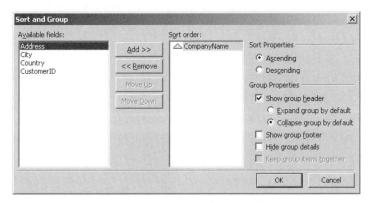

Figure 32-60   Sort and Group dialog box

2. The Data View is already sorted on the CompanyName field; you can optionally add group headers or group footers to each group. A group is defined as a set of records that have the same value for the grouping field. When you add a group header, the records in the group will be bunched together under a header; the header displays the value of the grouping field. You can also expand or collapse a group of records. In the **Group Properties** section of the **Sort and Group** dialog box, select the **Show group header** check box and the **Collapse group by default** option button.

3. Save the DataView.aspx page and then view it in your browser. (See Figure 32-61.)

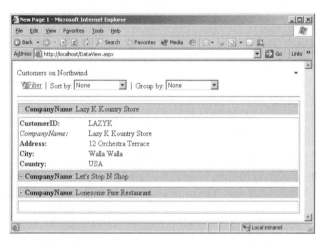

Figure 32-61   Data View with grouping in Internet Explorer

You can click the plus sign (+) to expand the group and subsequently click the minus sign (–) to collapse the group.

In addition to or instead of displaying a header, you can choose to display a footer. This causes records in a group to be bunched with a footer containing the title of the group. However, you cannot expand and collapse a group unless you display the header.

You might also want to show all records belonging to a group in a single screen regardless of how many records you have chosen to display at one time. FrontPage 2003 allows you to specify that the group size should override the set size in a Data View—this is accomplished by selecting the Keep Group Items Together check box in the Sort And Group dialog box.

If you check the Hide Group Details check box, only the group captions are displayed and the individual fields are hidden.

Working with Hierarchies

The Data View works with data in XML format. The XML formalism can be used naturally to describe hierarchical data. Consequently, the Data View has built into it the intelligence to deal with data hierarchies. In this section, we will examine these features.

Sample XML Source

In this section we will use the cust-ord.xml file we imported in that section.

Our sample XML file contains the data we need throughout the rest of this section. The cust-ord.xml contains a list of customers. For each customer, there is the list of orders and for each order, there is a list of the products that comprise that order. Shown in Figure 32-62 is an illustration of the XML's hierarchical structure.

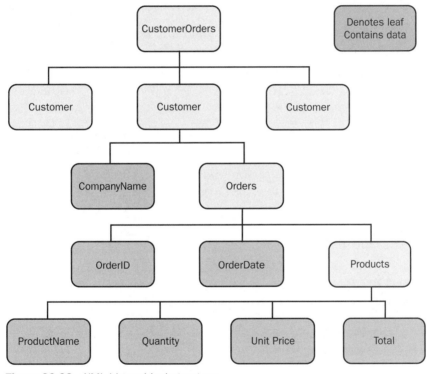

Figure 32-62   XML hierarchical structure

Our sample file contains 63 Customer records. Each of them has zero or more Orders, and each Order has zero or more Products.

Add Data View

The cust-ord.xml file contains data that is hierarchically organized. We will now select data from various places in the hierarchy and create a Data View that presents the data in the desired way. Specifically, we want to display the name of each company and the names, quantity, unit price, and total price of the products they have ordered.

In doing so, we want to preserve the hierarchy—that is, we want the product information for a given company to appear under that company name. Add a new page to the root directory of the FrontPage 2003 project, and name it Hierarchy.aspx.

To add an initial Data View of the XML to your Web page

1. From within FrontPage 2003, open the empty page Hierarchy.aspx in Design mode. Click **Insert Web Part Zone** from the **Data** menu to create Zone 1 at the top of the empty page.

2. Click **Insert Data View** on the **Data** menu to open the **Data Source Catalog** task pane.

3. Expand the XML Files folder by clicking the plus sign (+), exposing the cust-ord.xml data source that we created earlier in the section about the Data Source Catalog task pane.

4. Position the cursor on the data source, and click the right arrow at the end of the name.

5. Click the **Show Data** option on the resulting context menu to open the **Data View Details** task pane. (See Figure 32-63.)

Figure 32-63   Data View Details task pane showing XML data

6. Under the **Work With Data** section, you see the actual data in this file displayed. Note the following:

   ■ The hierarchy inherent in the structure is preserved.

   ■ You can use the left and right arrow buttons to navigate among the records in the file.

7. Click **CompanyName** and select **Insert Data View**. Doing this inserts only the name of the company in the view. Notice that because FrontPage 2003 detected that you have selected only one field from your data to insert as a view, it picked the most appropriate style, which is the bulleted list.

8. In the **Manage View Settings** section of the task pane, click the **Style** link to open the **View Styles** dialog box. (See Figure 32-13 shown earlier in the chapter.)

9. In the list of available HTML styles, change the selection to the **Repeating Form** style (which is the second choice in the list). The style name shows as a ToolTip when you hover the cursor over the style.

10. Click the **Options** tab and in the **Record sets** section at the bottom of the dialog box, change the value in the text box to the right of **Display items in sets of this size** to **2**. Click the **OK** button to apply the changes.

11. Add details to the product data for each customer by using a **Subview**. Position the cursor below the line under the first record just above the second record in the **Data View** (in this case, just above Frankenversand).

12. Click the **Products** node in the **Work with data** section of the **Data View Details** task pane, and then click the **Insert Subview** link in the same section.

13. Click anywhere in the subview just added, and then click the **Style** link to open the **View Styles** dialog box.

14. This time, change the selection to the **Two-column repeating form with border** style (which is the fifth choice in the list). Click the **OK** button to apply the change.

15. Save the Hierarchy.aspx page and then view it in your browser. (See Figure 32-64.)

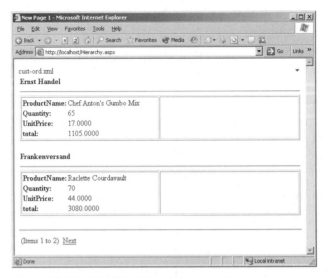

Figure 32-64 XML Data View in Internet Explorer

Windows SharePoint Services-Based Lists as Data Views

Data is stored in Windows SharePoint Services in the form of lists. SharePoint lists can act as a data source to a Data View. Windows SharePoint Services also ships with several Web Parts, each of which is tailored to access data in a particular Share-Point list. FrontPage 2003 allows the conversion of these Web Parts into Data Views. The advantage of converting them to Data Views is that the rich formatting, filtering, sorting, grouping, and other features can be used on this data.

> **Tip** The List View Web Part itself allows operations such as filter, sort, group, and so on. However, when these operations are compared with Data Views on a feature-by-feature basis, the Data View is more comprehensive in its ability to work with and enable presentation of data.

We will be converting a List View Web Part (LVWP) to a Data View Web Part (DVWP). In the process, FrontPage 2003 will generate the XSLT necessary to (almost) exactly match the Collaborative Application Markup Language (CAML) that was used to render the LVWP. To mimic the interaction that we expect in an LVWP, FrontPage 2003 generates several events. Whenever an LVWP is converted to a DVWP, you will see some extra functionality because this is what makes conversion valuable.

If you don't care about trying to mimic the LVWP, create the DVWP from scratch by choosing Show Data on the context menu of a SharePoint list in the Data Source Catalog. Select the specific fields that you want to insert, and click Insert Data View. Doing this will cause less XSLT to be generated, and then you can build your links and formatting using the table and other formatting tools in FrontPage 2003.

In the following example, we will actually convert the Links LVWP into a DVWP and leverage Data View–specific features to create a customized presentation. To follow along with this example, we suggest that you add a few links to the default Links Web Part.

Again, we will add a new page to the root directory of the FrontPage 2003 project. This time we'll name it Links.aspx.

To convert the Links LVWP into a DVWP

1. From within FrontPage 2003, open the empty page Links.aspx in Design mode. Hover the cursor over the **Insert** option on the **Table** menu. On the resulting flyout menu, click the **Table** option. Accept all the defaults, and click the **OK** button to insert the table.

2. Position the cursor in the first cell. Click **Insert Web Part Zone** from the **Data** menu to create Zone 1. This will contain the "before" view.

3. Position the cursor in the first cell of the second row. Click **Insert Web Part Zone** from the **Data** menu to create Zone 2. This will contain the "after" view.

4. Click the **Click to insert a Web Part** link in Zone 1 to open the **Web Parts** task pane. (See Figure 32-65.)

Figure 32-65   Web Parts task pane

5. Select **Links** in the **Web Part List** section of the **Web Parts** task pane, and click the **Insert Selected Web Part** button at the bottom of the task pane. You will briefly see a message stating that FrontPage 2003 is "Fetching information about the Web Part from the web server...".

6. Click the **Click to insert a Web Part** link in Zone 2.

7. Select **Links** in the **Web Part List** section of the **Web Parts** task pane, and click the **Insert Selected Web Part** button at the bottom of the task pane.

8. Right-click anywhere on the Web Part in Zone 2, and choose **Convert to XSLT Data View** in the resulting pop-up menu.

   As soon as the Web Part is converted to a Data View, FrontPage 2003 automatically displays the Data View Details task pane. You can see all the fields that are available in this SharePoint list under the Work With Data category.

9. Click the **Style** link for the Data View, and change the HTML view from Basic table to the **Repeating form (centered)** style (which is the third choice in the list). This style is not an available choice on the Web Part in Zone 1.

10. Click the **Options** tab, and in the Toolbar section deselect the **Show toolbar with options for** option. Click the **OK** button to apply the changes.

11. In the **Data View**, select and delete any one of the rows that contain a field that begins with "URL:". Press the DELETE key to remove the field from the Data View.

12. Select any one of the remaining rows with a link, and set the data to be left-aligned using the toolbar.

13. Save the Links.aspx page and then view it in your browser. (See Figure 32-66.)

Figure 32-66 Converted view in Internet Explorer

As you can see, you can use Data Views to format and display SharePoint lists data, thereby enabling powerful authoring capabilities that seamlessly integrate the authoring platform provided by FrontPage 2003 with the data-driven infrastructure of Windows SharePoint Services.

Using Reports to Measure Site Use and Performance

FrontPage 2003 includes powerful tools to help track site use and performance, and identify potential problems so that you can take action to fix them. These tools are available to use on sites created with Windows SharePoint Services and SharePoint Portal Server 2003, and usage analysis reports are available as long as the server administrator has turned reporting on. Site usage analysis reports are run on a regular basis, with the frequency and time determined by the server administrator.

To access reports from within FrontPage 2003, open your website, and select Reports from the View menu. You can choose from a variety of reports, including Site Summary, Files, Shared Content, Problems, Workflow, and Usage. (See Figure 32-67.)

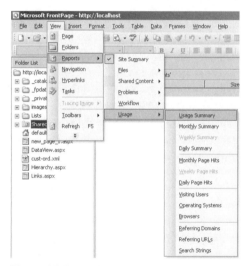

Figure 32-67   Reports in FrontPage 2003

The Site Summary report presents key information about your site, including the number of hits and downloads, number of files and pictures in your site, the number of files that aren't linked to and therefore might not be necessary, slow pages, older files, links to reports displaying lists of all of the pages, and more. You can use this report to find many common problems with your site and then fix them.

You can also use the usage analysis reports to find out which pages in your site are being accessed most frequently and which pages might not be necessary or might need to be updated on your site because they are not accessed frequently.

The usage summary report also gives you a snapshot of your site's usage at a glance, including number of visits, page hits, bytes downloaded, top referrers, top referring domains, and more.

Summary

Microsoft Office FrontPage 2003 and SharePoint Products and Technologies really deliver a powerful set of tools. After we covered some basic SharePoint Products and Technologies fundamentals such as Web Parts, Lists, Libraries, Areas, Personal Sites, and Views, we touched on browser-based customization of SharePoint Products and Technologies and took a high-level tour of FrontPage 2003 itself.

We learned that there are some caveats to editing SharePoint Portal Server 2003 sites in FrontPage 2003. But Microsoft has provided a high level of granularity in our ability to disable some functions.

Then we turned to the most common changes people make using FrontPage 2003 when editing a SharePoint site. We covered adding text, images, and pages and changing almost everything about how a list can be displayed. In the section about Advanced Customization, we discussed using Dynamic Web Templates, Themes, and other new features in FrontPage 2003.

We boned up on using the Data Source Catalog and the huge variety of data sources available through FrontPage 2003. Then we turned our attention to getting the most out of Data View Web Parts. These display workhorses capitalize on the power of XSLT and the Data Retrieval Service in Windows SharePoint Services. We covered displaying, filtering, sorting, grouping, and more. This was followed by a brief example of an XML hierarchy.

We demonstrated how SharePoint lists can be converted to Data Views for additional capabilities for formatting the output. And finally we discussed the various prepackaged reporting functionalities available from within FrontPage 2003.

The next two chapters go a layer deeper and discuss the object models underlying SharePoint Products and Technologies in detail.

Chapter 33

The Windows SharePoint Services Object Model

There are 18 namespaces in nine assemblies in the Microsoft Windows SharePoint Services object model. These namespaces are used within SharePoint sites on the server that is running Windows SharePoint Services. This chapter will give a structured overview of the Microsoft .NET–managed namespaces that can be used to customize a Windows SharePoint Services deployment.

The types and members of the following three namespaces are not intended to be used directly from your code: Microsoft.SharePoint.ApplicationPages, Microsoft .SharePoint.ApplicationRuntime, and Microsoft.SharePoint.Library. Therefore, they will not be described in this chapter. The Microsoft.SharePoint.WebPartPages and Microsoft .SharePoint.WebPartPages.Communication namespaces are specific to building Web Parts. The Microsoft.SharePoint.WebPartPages namespace will be discussed in Chapter 37, "Using Visual Studio .NET to Create Web Parts."

Microsoft.SharePoint Namespace

The Microsoft.SharePoint namespace provides types and members that can be used for working with a SharePoint site and its subsites or lists. This namespace can be found in the Windows SharePoint Services assembly (in Microsoft.SharePoint.dll) and has three major top-level classes that are shown in Table 33-1.

Table 33-1 Major Top-Level Classes of the Microsoft.SharePoint Namespace

Name	Description
SPList	Represents a list and opens access to its fields, views, and other properties
SPSite	Represents a site collection (a top-level site and its subsites) and is used for managing existing sites and for accessing site and list data
SPWeb	Represents an individual SharePoint site and provides access to all its lists, files, folders, Web Parts, and other objects

The SPSite Class

The code example will show you how to use the SPSite class and the SPWeb class. Each SPSite object, or site collection, is represented within a SPSiteCollection object that consists of the collection of all site collections on the virtual server. The SPWeb method represents a SharePoint site.

```
SPGlobalAdmin myGlobalAdmin = new SPGlobalAdmin();
SPSiteCollection mySiteColl = myGlobalAdmin.VirtualServers[0].Sites;
foreach ( SPSite mySite in mySiteColl)
{
  foreach ( SPWeb mySubSite in mySite.AllWebs )
  {
    output.Write("\r" + mySubSite.Url);
  }
}
```

Microsoft.SharePoint.Administration Namespace

The Microsoft.SharePoint.Administration namespace is used for managing the server or server farm in a deployment of Windows SharePoint Services. This namespace can be found in the Windows SharePoint Services assembly (in Microsoft.SharePoint.dll).

Table 33-2 shows the major top-level classes of the Microsoft.SharePoint .Administration namespace.

Table 33-2 Major Top-level Classes of the Microsoft.SharePoint.Administration Namespace

Name	Description
SPGlobalAdmin	Represents the top-level object that provides access to all servers and usage settings in the Windows SharePoint Services deployment
SPVirtualServer	Represents a virtual server and provides access to server-wide settings

This section contains a couple of code examples that show how to use some of the classes within the Microsoft.SharePoint.Administration namespace.

The AddWPPack Method

The first code example shows how to install and enable a Web Part package and add it to the virtual server Web Part gallery. This action can also be performed using the Stsadm.exe tool. The code example shows how to do this programmatically.

The SPGlobalAdmin represents the top-level object for administration and as such takes an important place in the code examples in this section. You can install and enable a Web Part package by using the AddWPPack method of the SPGlobal-Admin class. The signature of the AddWPPack method looks like this:

```
public void AddWPPack(
    string strPathname,
    string strBaseName,
    uint nLang,
    string strURL,
    bool bGlobalInstall,
    bool bForce,
    System.IO.TextWriter logWriter
);
```

The strPathname parameter contains the full file system path for the Web Part package .cab file to install. You can create a Web Part package .cab file using Microsoft Visual Studio .NET. Open the Web Part library project for which you want to create a .cab file, and choose File\New\Project. On the New Project dialog that appears, choose Setup and Deployment Projects\Cab Project. Make sure the Add to Solution option button is selected. Right-click the Cab project in the Solution Explorer, and choose Add\Project Output. On the Add Project Output Group screen, choose what you want to include in the .cab file. A .cab file will be generated the next time you compile the solution.

The strBaseName parameter contains the file name of the installed Web Part package that needs to be enabled. You should either specify strPathname or strBaseName.

The nLang parameter contains an unsigned 32-bit integer that specifies the locale ID for the Web Part package. This parameter can be 0 or any valid LCID (1033 for English).

The strURL parameter contains the URL for the virtual server. The strURL parameter is used in conjunction with the strBaseName or strPathname parameter. If strURL is set to null, the Web Part package specified by the strName parameter is enabled for all virtual servers on the front-end Web server, or the Web Part package specified by the strPathname parameter is installed on all virtual servers on the front-end Web server.

The bGlobalInstall parameter can be set to true to install the Web Part package to each front-end Web server in a server farm.

The bForce parameter can be set to true to overwrite an existing Web Part package with a new version.

Finally, the logWriter parameter contains a System.IO.TextWriter object that is used to write an error log to the text stream.

Before you can call the AddWPPack method, you should create an instance of the SPGlobalAdmin class. The following code example can be copied into a Web Part. Because this is just an example, the AllowUnsafeUpdates property of the SPGlobalAdmin class is set to true so that updates are allowed to the database as a result of a GET request. If you do not set this property, the AddWPPack method will fail after an HTTP GET request. This opens a security risk. In real world situations you would probably call the AddWPPack method in a non-HTTP context, from either a command-line executable or a Windows application. If you want to call the AddWPPack method in an HTTP context, you should send an HTTP POST request and add the AdminFormDigest control to the form body, which is discussed later in the "Microsoft.SharePoint.WebControls Namespace" section.

```
SPGlobalAdmin myGlobalAdmin = new SPGlobalAdmin();
myGlobalAdmin.AllowUnsafeUpdates = true;
myGlobalAdmin.AddWPPack(@"C:\projects\ResKitCab\Debug\ResKitCab.cab", null, 1033,
    null, true, true, null);
```

The EnumWPPack Method

The following code example shows how to return a string containing all the Web Part packages installed on the virtual server. You can do this by using the EnumWPPack method of the SPGlobalAdmin class. The signature of the EnumWPPack method looks like this:

```
public string EnumWPPacks(
    string strName,
    string strURL,
    bool bEntireFarm
);
```

The strName parameter contains the name of a Web Part package or null. The strURL parameter contains the URL for the virtual server or null. The bEntireFarm parameter has the value true when you want to list the Web Part packages currently installed on a server farm; otherwise, it contains false or null. The return value contains information about Web Part packages that are installed. The format of this string depends on which parameters are used.

Before you can call the EnumWPPacks method, you should create an instance of the SPGlobalAdmin class. The code example shown here can be copied into a Web Part. This code example will return the host name, the name of the .cab file and the locale, and the virtual server name.

```
SPGlobalAdmin myGlobalAdmin = new SPGlobalAdmin();
strReturn = myGlobalAdmin.EnumWPPacks(null, "http://woodgrove/", true);
```

The Log Method

This code example will show how to create a log with the Log method of the SPGlobalAdmin class that indicates the severity of a problem in the Windows SharePoint Services environment and provides details. The signature of the Log method looks like this:

```
public void Log(
   int iSeverity,
   string strMessage
);
```

The iSeverity parameter specifies the level of severity to report in the log. Table 33-3 shows the possible values that the iSeverity parameter can contain.

Table 33-3   Values of the iSeverity Parameter

Value	Description
0	Error
1	Warning about a problem
2	Ignorable but a potential problem
3	Infrequent and happens once per thread, but only information, not a problem
4	Uncommon and happens several times per thread, but only information, not a problem
5	Common and happens numerous times per thread, but only information, not a problem
6	Frequent and happens many times per thread, but only information, not a problem
7	Verbose log that provides all information
8	TestingProgram only used by test application

The strMessage parameter contains a description that will be used in the log for the specified error. The Log method will log the message and severity to a file in %temp%\<*applicationname*>.log.

```
SPGlobalAdmin myGlobalAdmin = new SPGlobalAdmin();
myGlobalAdmin.Log(8, "a test message");
```

Microsoft.SharePoint.Dsp Namespace

The Microsoft.SharePoint.Dsp namespace provides the base class for the data retrieval service adapters used in Microsoft Windows SharePoint Services. This namespace can be found in the Microsoft.SharePoint.Dsp assembly (in Microsoft.SharePoint.Dsp.dll). The adapters define a protocol for data consumers to query heterogeneous data sources and for the data sources to return query results back to the consumers, integrating different types of data into a unified format so that they can be related, analyzed, and manipulated easily.

Each data retrieval service provides a data-binding scheme that enables data consumers and data servers to communicate with each other through Simple Object

Access Protocol (SOAP) or the object model of Windows SharePoint Services. The client side of the data retrieval services consists of data consumers, such as applications, data-driven Web Parts, or data-bound server controls. The server side of the data retrieval services is a group of adapters, which are Web services that return XML data from different data sources or that perform data-manipulation operations in those data sources. The following adapters are used in Windows SharePoint Services:

- **Microsoft.SharePoint.Dsp.OleDb.** Provides the data retrieval service adapter for performing queries against OLE DB data sources. This namespace can be found in the Microsoft.SharePoint.Dsp.OleDb assembly (in Microsoft .SharePoint.Dsp.OleDb.dll).

- **Microsoft.SharePoint.Dsp.SoapPT.** Provides the data retrieval service adapter for performing pass-through queries against arbitrary Web services. This namespace can be found in the Microsoft.SharePoint.Dsp.SoapPT assembly (in Microsoft.SharePoint.Dsp.SoapPT.dll).

- **Microsoft.SharePoint.Dsp.Sts.** Provides the data retrieval service adapter for performing queries against sites and lists in Windows SharePoint Services. This namespace can be found in the Microsoft.SharePoint.Dsp.Sts assembly (in Microsoft.SharePoint.Dsp.Sts.dll).

- **Microsoft.SharePoint.Dsp.XmlUrl.** Provides the data retrieval service adapter for performing queries against arbitrary XML data sources. This namespace can be found in the Microsoft.SharePoint.Dsp.XmlUrl assembly (in Microsoft.SharePoint.Dsp.XmlUrl.dll).

The Microsoft.SharePoint.Dsp.Sts namespace has both an object model and a SOAP interface, whereas the other three namespaces have only an object model.

The adapters provide an object model that can be used by other Microsoft .NET–managed assemblies. Server components can load the assembly of a service directly, eliminating the overhead of calling the service through SOAP. All adapters implement the IDspAdapter interface of the Microsoft.SharePoint.Dsp namespace, and by dynamically loading the data retrieval service assemblies, the same client code can be written to talk to any of the adapters.

Microsoft.SharePoint.Meetings Namespace

The Microsoft.SharePoint.Meetings namespace provides types and members that can be used to customize Meeting Workspace sites. This namespace can be found in the Windows SharePoint Services assembly (in Microsoft.SharePoint.dll). A Meeting Workspace site is a SharePoint site for centralizing all the information and materials for one or more meetings.

Table 33-4 shows the classes of the Microsoft.SharePoint.Meetings namespace.

Table 33-4   Classes of the Microsoft.SharePoint.Meetings Namespace

Name	Description
CustomToolPaneManager	Represents a custom ToolPane Manager Web Part. This Web Part-enables you to implement tool panes using the extensible tool-pane framework.
PageTabsWebPart	Represents the PageTabs Web Part and is responsible for rendering the page tabs on the Meeting Workspace site.
PropertyBag	Represents a property bag and is responsible for rendering the Modify This Workspace link on the Meeting Workspace site. It also returns some global variables on the site that are needed for scripting.
SPMeeting	Provides methods and properties to work with Meeting Workspace sites.

The SPMeeting Class

Methods and properties for working with Meeting Workspace sites can be found in the SPMeeting class. The IsMeetingWorkspaceWeb method of the SPMeeting class determines whether the specified SharePoint site was created by using a Meeting Workspace site template. The signature of this method looks like this:

```
public static bool IsMeetingWorkspaceWeb(
   Microsoft.SharePoint.SPWeb web
);
```

The web parameter contains the SharePoint site for which you want to determine whether a Meeting Workspace site template was used. The method will return a boolean that will give the value False if no Meeting Workspace site template was used. In this code example, we will make use of the IsMeetingWorkspaceWeb method and check which SharePoint sites are Meeting Workspace sites.

```
SPSite siteCollection = new SPSite("http://server_name");
SPWeb site = siteCollection.RootWeb;
SPWebCollection subSites = site.Webs;

foreach (SPWeb subSite in subSites)
{
Boolean blnTest = SPMeeting.IsMeetingWorkspaceWeb(subSite);
output.Write(blnTest + "--" + subSite.Url + "<br>" );
}
```

Microsoft.SharePoint.Security Namespace

The Microsoft.SharePoint.Security namespace provides a set of code access permission and attribute classes designed to protect a specific set of resources and operations, such as access to the Windows SharePoint Services object model, the ability to do unsafe saving on HTTP Gets, and enabling Web Part to Web Part connections. Saving is considered unsafe when security validation is not included in a Web form. This can be done by adding a FormDigest or AdminFormDigest control to the Web page. The Microsoft.SharePoint.Security namespace can be found in the Windows SharePoint Services Security assembly (in Microsoft.SharePoint.Security.dll). The purpose of the attribute classes, as described in Table 33-5, is to provide support for declarative security so that developers can specify the custom permission when using declarative syntax for security actions such as requests, demands, or assertions.

Table 33-5   Classes of the Microsoft.SharePoint.Security Namespace

Name	Description
SharePointPermission	Controls the ability to access SharePoint Products and Technologies resources
SharePointPermissionAttribute	Allows you to declaratively specify SharePoint Products and Technologies resources your class can use
WebPartPermission	Controls the ability to access Web Part resources
WebPartPermissionAttribute	Allows you to declaratively specify Web Part resources your class can use

The Microsoft.SharePoint.Security namespace maps onto a unique assembly that matches the namespace and is installed into the global assembly cache (GAC) only. This is also true for the Microsoft.HtmlTrans.Interface and Microsoft.SharePoint .DSP namespaces. So before the Microsoft.SharePoint.Security namespace can be used in your project, you have to add a reference to the right assembly, Microsoft .SharePoint.Security.dll. Unfortunately, Visual Studio.NET does not allow you to reference assemblies directly in the GAC, so you will have to copy the assembly out of the GAC manually and add the reference yourself.

The GAC is located under *<DriveLetter>*:\windows\assembly. To copy files out of the GAC, you will have to open a command prompt and go to the following folder: *<DriveLetter>*:\WINDOWS\assembly\GAC\Microsoft.SharePoint.Security \11.0.0.0__71e9bce111e94.

> **Note**   You will not see this folder when using Windows Explorer. You will have to use the command prompt.

After that, you should copy the DLL to another location, like this:

```
copy microsoft.sharepoint.security.dll [DriveLetter]:\microsoft.sharepoint
    .security.dll
```

Now you are ready to add a reference to the Microsoft.SharePoint.Security assembly.

The SharePointPermission Class

This code example uses the SharePointPermission class, which represents a custom permission that controls the ability to access Microsoft SharePoint Products and Technologies resources. The SharePointPermission class cannot be inherited.

The constructor of the SharePointPermission class expects, like all code-access permission objects, a System.Security.Permissions.PermissionState enumeration value. This value represents a value specifying whether an entity, at creation, should have full or no access to resources. This value can be set to None to indicate that a new instance is fully restricted or Unrestricted. Next the code example accesses the UnsafeSaveOnGet property of the SharePointPermission class to get a value indicating whether saving to the SharePoint Products and Technologies database is allowed during an HTTP-GET request. Because this code example uses the PermissionState.Unrestricted value, it will return True.

```
SharePointPermission myPermission = new SharePointPermission(PermissionState
    .Unrestricted);
output.Write(myPermission.UnsafeSaveOnGet);
```

> **Note** You can copy this code into the RenderWebPart method of a Web Part. Remember to import the Microsoft.SharePoint.Security namespace.

Microsoft.SharePoint.SoapServer Namespace

The Microsoft.SharePoint.SoapServer namespace contains classes that implement the Windows SharePoint Services Web Service on the server. This namespace can be found in the Windows SharePoint Services assembly (in Microsoft.SharePoint.dll). The numerous methods provided by the Windows SharePoint Services Web service are designed for accessing content on a site, including methods for working with lists or site data, as well as methods for customizing meetings, imaging, Document Workspace sites, or search. In most cases, the members of these classes are not designed to be called from the server and are not tested in this configuration. The methods provided by a Web service are designed to be called remotely from client applications. An excellent example of client applications that use the Web services provided by the Microsoft.SharePoint.SoapServer namespace is Office 2003 itself.

The Simple Object Access Protocol (SOAP) interfaces used in these services provide .NET developers with object models for creating solutions that work with Windows SharePoint Services remotely from a client or custom application. The interfaces are integrated with the server-side object models of the Windows SharePoint Services assembly, and their design has been optimized to reduce the number of roundtrips transacted between client computer and server.

Web services provide their functionality through the _vti_bin virtual directory, which maps to the *<DriveLetter>*:\Program Files\Common Files\Microsoft Shared\Web Server Extensions\60\ISAPI directory in the server.

The Alerts Service

The Alerts service provides methods for working with alerts for list items in a SharePoint site. This code example will show you how to create a simple Windows form that uses the GetAlerts method of the Alerts Web service to retrieve information about alerts within a SharePoint site.

First we have to create a new Window Application project and add a reference to the Alerts Web service, that is http://*servername*/_vti_bin/alerts.asmx. We will drag a label and a button onto the form and add the following code in the button click event handler. This code will first declare and initialize a variable for the Alerts Web service, that we have called in our example *WebAlerts*. Next we have to authenticate the current user by passing the default credentials to the Alerts Web service from the system credential cache. Then we can use the GetAlerts method to get all the alerts on this SharePoint site. The following information will be displayed in the label control: the name of the server, the URL of the server, the title of the SharePoint site, and the number of alerts that are made on the SharePoint site.

```
WebAlerts.Alerts alertService = new WebAlerts.Alerts();
alertService.Credentials = System.Net.CredentialCache.DefaultCredentials;

WebAlerts.AlertInfo allAlerts = alertService.GetAlerts();

label1.Text = "Server: " + allAlerts.AlertServerName +
"\nURL: " + allAlerts.AlertServerUrl +
"\nWeb Title: " + allAlerts.AlertWebTitle +
"\nNumber: " + allAlerts.Alerts.Length.ToString();
```

Microsoft.SharePoint.Utilities Namespace

The Microsoft.SharePoint.Utilities namespace is used for various utilities purposes, including encoding of strings and processing of user information. This namespace can be found in the Windows SharePoint Services assembly (in Microsoft.SharePoint.dll). Table 33-6 shows the classes of the Microsoft.SharePoint.Utilities namespace.

Table 33-6   Classes in the Microsoft.SharePoint.Utilities Namespace

Name	Description
SPEncode	Provides methods for encoding strings
SPPropertyBag	Stores arbitrary key-and-value pairs that contain custom property settings
SPUtility	Provides tools for converting date and time formats, for getting information from user names, for securing access to sites, and for various other tasks in managing a deployment of Windows SharePoint Services

The SPProperty Bag Class

The SPPropertyBag class of the Microsoft.SharePoint.Utilities namespace stores arbitrary key-and-value pairs that contain custom property settings. First you have to make an instance of the SPGlobalAdmin class in the Microsoft.SharePoint.Administration namespace. Next the Config property of the SPGlobalAdmin class gets a global configuration object, SPGlobalConfig. The Properties property of the SPGlobalConfig class will contain global configuration settings that are used in the Windows SharePoint Services deployment. In the following code example, we will add a key-and-value pair to our property bag by using the Add method. Modifications to the property bag will not be saved until we call the Update method of the SPPropertyBag class.

```
string strReturn = "";
SPGlobalAdmin myGlobalAdmin = new SPGlobalAdmin();
myGlobalAdmin.AllowUnsafeUpdates = true;
SPGlobalConfig myGlobalConfig = myGlobalAdmin.Config;
SPPropertyBag myBag = myGlobalConfig.Properties;
int myValue;

try
{
  myValue = Int32.Parse(myBag["mykey"]);
  myValue++;
  myBag["mykey"] = myValue.ToString();
}
catch (Exception err)
{
  myValue = 1;
  myBag.Add("mykey", myValue.ToString());
  strReturn += err.Message;
}
myBag.Update();
strReturn = myValue.ToString();
output.Write(strReturn);
```

The SPEncode Class

The SPEncode class from the Microsoft.SharePoint.Utilities namespace provide static methods so you do not need to instantiate the class before using them. You may use the methods of the SPEncode class to help prevent malicious script blocks from being able to execute in applications that execute across sites. In code that calls members within the Windows SharePoint Services assembly, the encoding methods of the SPEncode class are more effective than methods of the System.Web.HttpUtility and System.Web.HttpServerUtility classes. The SPEncode methods for encoding URLs and HTML can be used to encode a larger set of characters than the methods of the HttpUtility and HttpServerUtility classes.

The following code example makes use of the ScriptEncode method to escape characters that would otherwise conflict with the script. For example, a quotation mark (") is replaced with \".

```
strReturn =  SPEncode.ScriptEncode("alert(\"hi\")");
```

Microsoft.SharePoint.WebControls Namespace

The Microsoft.SharePoint.WebControls namespace contains Microsoft ASP.NET server controls that are used on site and list pages in a SharePoint site. This namespace can be found in the Windows SharePoint Services assembly (in Microsoft.SharePoint.dll). The major class, SPControl, provides methods for getting or setting the context of requests and serves as the base class from which other controls in this namespace derive.

In general, although the set of Web controls within the Microsoft.SharePoint .WebControls namespace are used extensively in SharePoint Products and Technologies, they are of very limited usefulness to a third-party developer. In this section, the most interesting controls will be shown. If you want to find out more about the other controls, the best approach would be to see how the controls are used in the layouts .aspx files and experiment.

The SPControl Class

The SPControl class provides methods for getting or setting the context of the request and serves as the base server control from which other controls in the Microsoft.SharePoint.WebControls namespace derive. As such, SPControl is very important when programming the Windows SharePoint Services object model.

The SPControl class can be used in a Web Part, in a custom Web service (in _vti _bin), or in an ASPX page or a Web Application (in _layouts). The following code uses the GetContextSite method to return the site collection that serves as the context for the current HTTP request. It also uses the GetContextWeb method to return the website that serves as the context for the current HTTP request. Finally, it shows how to retrieve the top-level website from the current site collection.

```
SPSite siteCollection = SPControl.GetContextSite(Context);
SPWeb site = SPControl.GetContextWeb(Context);
SPWeb topLevelSite = SPControl.GetContextSite(Context).RootWeb;
```

The FormDigest Control Class

The FormDigest class inserts a security validation within the form of an .aspx page. To make posts from a Web application that modifies the contents of the database, you must include the FormDigest control in the form making the post. The FormDigest control generates a security validation, or message digest, to help prevent the type of attack whereby a user is tricked into posting data to the server without knowing it. The security validation is specific to a user, a site, and a time period, and it expires after a configurable amount of time. When the user requests a page, the server returns the page with security validation inserted. When the user then submits the form, the server verifies that the security validation has not changed. If you want to do website or lower-level operations in your page, you need to use the FormDigestol.

> **Note** When performing global administration operations, you will need a different control for performing security validation: the AdminFormDigest control.

To add a FormDigest Control to a Web Application

This procedure shows how to add a FormDigest control to the Visual Studio .NET toolbox and add it to a Web form.

1. Open your Web application in Visual Studio.NET.

2. Go to the design view of a Web form, right-click the toolbox, and select Add/Remove Items.

3. In the Customize Toolbox dialog, click Browse.

4. Browse to the Microsoft.SharePoint.dll, which is located by default in *<DriveLetter>*:\Program Files\Common Files\Microsoft Shared\Web Server Extensions\60\ISAPI\Microsoft.SharePoint.dll. Click Open.

5. Under the .NET Framework Components tab, locate FormDigest, select the check box, and click OK.

6. Now you will find the FormDigest control added to the toolbox. Drag the FormDigest control on the Web form.

If you switch to HTML view, you will notice a new page directive which registers the FormDigest control to the page.

```
<%@ Register Tagprefix="SharePoint" Namespace="Microsoft.SharePoint.WebControls"
    Assembly="Microsoft.SharePoint, Version=11.0.0.0, Culture=neutral, PublicKeyToken=
    71e9bce111e9429c" %>
```

You will also notice a FormDigest control which is included in the form.

```
<sharepoint:FormDigest id="FormDigest1" runat="server"></sharepoint:FormDigest>
```

Now you are ready to make posts from the Web application to modify the contents of the content database.

Adding a FormDigest Control Programmatically

You can also add a FormDigest control programmatically. This example shows how to add a FormDigest control to a Web Part. The first step is to create a new instance of the FormDigest control. Next you should call the Render method of the FormDigest control to send the content of the control to an HtmlTextWriter object, which is responsible for writing the content that is rendered on the client. The following code can be copied into the RenderWebPart method of your Web Part:

```
FormDigest myDigest = new FormDigest();
myDigest.RenderControl(output);
```

Adding an AdminFormDigest Control

As discussed previously, the FormDigest control can be used if you want to perform website or lower-level operations in your page. However, you should add an AdminFormDigest control if you want to perform global operations. The Admin-FormDigest control is not a part of the Microsoft.SharePoint.WebControls namespace, but because it is closely related to the FormDigest control it is discussed in this section. The following code shows how to add the AdminFormDigest control programmatically.

```
SPGlobalAdmin globalAdmin = new SPGlobalAdmin();
Page.RegisterHiddenField("__REQUESTDIGEST", globalAdmin.AdminFormDigest);
```

The Theme Control

The Theme class of the Microsoft.SharePoint.WebControls namespace can be helpful in making your Web Part page adopt the right theme. The Theme class outputs a .css link and will be very useful if you are using the correct class IDs. To use this class, you will have to make a new instance of the Theme control. After that, you will have to call the Render method of the Theme control to send the content of the control to an HtmlTextWriter object. The HtmlTextWriter object is responsible for writing the content that is rendered on the client. The following code example can be copied into the RenderWebPart method of your Web Part:

```
Theme myTheme = new Theme();
myTheme.RenderControl(output);
```

Microsoft.HtmlTrans.Interface Namespace

The Microsoft.HtmlTrans.Interface namespace allows you to write custom applications that can create an HTML version of documents that are stored on a server running Windows SharePoint Services. Users who do not have the required client application or viewer installed on their computers will get an HTML version of the requested document. This namespace can be found in the Microsoft HtmlTrans Interface assembly (in Microsoft.HtmlTrans.Interface.dll). To use this functionality, make sure that the HTML Viewer feature is enabled in the SharePoint Administration pages.

The Microsoft.HtmlTrans.Interface namespace consists of two interfaces: IHtmlTrLoadBalancer and IHtmlTrLauncher. An implementation of these interfaces also relies on an XML configuration file, named Htmltransinfo.xml, which resides on the server running Windows SharePoint Services.

- **IhtmlTrLoadBalancer.**   The IHtmlTrLoadBalancer interface helps to select the server on which to run the custom converter application.

- **IhtmlTrLauncher.**   The IHtmlTrLauncher interface launches the custom converter application and returns the HTML results to Windows SharePoint Services.

The Htmltransinfo.xml file, that is located in *<DriveLetter>*:\Program Files\Common Files\Microsoft Shared\web server extensions\60\TEMPLATE\XML, redirects the document request to a handler page, which calls the load balancer and launcher components. The <HtmlTrInfo> element contains mapping instructions for directing a request to the URL for handling a request when the client computer does not have Microsoft Office 2003 installed. An entry in the Htmltransinfo.xml configuration file uses the following format:

```
<HtmlTrInfo>
<Mapping Extension="ext" AcceptHeader="application/vnd.my-app"
   HandlerUrl="myapphandler.aspx" ProgId=""/>
</HtmlTrInfo>
```

Using the Microsoft.HtmlTrans.Interface Namespace

The following sequence of events occurs when a user requests a document from a server running Windows SharePoint Services:

1. Windows SharePoint Services looks in the Htmltransinfo.xml file at the <Mapping> element that is nested in the <HtmlTrInfo> element to identify the file extension of the document. If found, Windows SharePoint Services retrieves the matching AcceptHeader attribute of the <Mapping> element. If the file extension is not found, Windows SharePoint Services prompts the user to download the document.

2. Windows SharePoint Services checks the AcceptHeader attribute value of the <Mapping> element against the Accept-Header HTTP header of the request to see whether the client computer recognizes the requested document type. If so, Windows SharePoint Services delivers the document in its native format.

3. Windows SharePoint Services also retrieves the ProgId attribute of the <Mapping> element from the Htmltransinfo.xml file and attempts to open the file on the client computer by using the component designated by the ProgId. If this attempt fails, Windows SharePoint Services continues with the HTML conversion process.

4. If the client computer does not recognize the requested document type, Windows SharePoint Services prompts the user: "Do you want to convert the document for viewing in the browser?" If the user chooses not to convert the document, Windows SharePoint Services prompts the user to download the document instead.

5. If the user chooses to convert the document, Windows SharePoint Services forwards the request to the handler page specified by the HandlerUrl attribute in the Htmltransinfo.xml file. The handler page manages the conversion process and delivers the converted file to the user for viewing in the browser.

Implementing Custom Document Conversion

To implement custom document conversion on the Windows SharePoint Services platform you must create the following:

- An entry in the Htmltransinfo.xml file for the document type.

- A handler page that launches the document conversion process and returns the HTML output to the user.

- A set of custom conversion components.

You must choose among three methods to build the set of custom conversion components:

- Build custom implementations of the IHtmlTrLoadBalancer and IHtmlTr-Launcher interfaces to launch a custom converter application and return its results to Windows SharePoint Services.

- Build a set of custom conversion components that do not use the Microsoft .HtmlTrans interfaces at all.

- Call the custom implementations of the IHtmlTrLoadBalancer and IHtmlTr-Launcher interfaces provided as part of the Microsoft Office 2003 Resource Kit and provide a custom converter application for the IHtmlTrLauncher implementation to call.

Summary

This chapter provides an overview of all namespaces available in Windows Share-Point Services and the major classes within them. Code examples illustrate how to use the Windows SharePoint Services object model.

Chapter 34

The SharePoint Portal
Server Object Model

Introduction

The Microsoft Office SharePoint Portal Server object model encompasses a number of namespaces—about 50 in total—that provide a way to manipulate SharePoint Portal Server configuration and information. Because the object model is so large, it cannot possibly be fully covered here; however, this chapter will discuss the most important and frequently used namespaces, classes, and methods. It will provide an overview of these components and provide samples useful for administrators.

Out of the approximately 50 namespaces provided in the SharePoint Portal Server object model, only 16 of them are supported. The remaining namespaces are reserved for Microsoft's internal use. If you were to go through some of the .aspx pages provided with SharePoint Portal Server, you might notice that the reserved namespaces are frequently used.

This chapter will focus on the SharePoint Portal Server object model from the administrative perspective. It will cover the basics of the object model and provide some code samples that would be of use to administrators. Other general background information would be useful for administrators to know about, should they run into a problem with a Web Part or add-on, but the chapter does not provide in-depth developer information. Developers will get a general understanding of the object model from reading this chapter but should refer to the SharePoint Products and Technologies SDK for an in-depth reference.

The Microsoft.SharePoint.Portal Namespace

All code and references in the SharePoint Portal Server object model stem from the Microsoft.SharePoint.Portal namespace. The definition for this namespace is found in Microsoft.SharePoint.Portal.dll. When creating projects, you will need to reference this file. If you are developing on a computer running SharePoint Portal Server, the file will be registered for you during installation; it can be found in Program Files\Common Files\Microsoft Shared\web server extensions\60\ISAPI. Otherwise, you will need to copy the file to your development machine and explicitly add a reference to it from your project. The Microsoft.SharePoint.Portal.dll file contains the code for most namespaces under Microsoft.SharePoint.Portal. The following namespaces are not included in this assembly:

- Microsoft.SharePoint.Portal.Admin.Search

- Microsoft.SharePoint.Portal.SingleSignOn

- Microsoft.SharePoint.Portal.SingleSignOn.Security

Included in the Microsoft.SharePoint.Portal namespace are two very important classes—PortalApplication and PortalContext. These two classes are the basis for any code written against the SharePoint Portal Server object model. The PortalContext object is extremely important because it is the entry point for using almost every other object in the SharePoint Portal Server object model. The PortalApplication class provides functions that can get a PortalContext object. The following code shows how to get a PortalContext object from an HTTP Context object:

```
C#
PortalContext context = PortalApplication.GetContext(Context);
VB.NET
Dim Context As PortalContext = PortalApplication.GetContext(Context)
```

This example shows how the PortalContext will be derived in almost every Web Part that uses the SPS object model. To get a PortalContext object from a console application or Windows Forms application, the Microsoft.SharePoint.Portal.Topology namespace must be used.

Microsoft.SharePoint.Portal.Topology

The Microsoft.SharePoint.Portal.Topology namespace provides functions for interacting with a SharePoint Portal server farm. Using this namespace, you can add servers to a farm, change the configuration database, get a listing of servers in the farm, and in fact build a farm completely through the functions in this namespace. You can also use objects in this namespace to get Microsoft Windows SharePoint Services objects in the Microsoft.SharePoint.Administration namespace. For example, you can get a collection of VirtualServer objects that the farm uses and then perform Windows SharePoint Services operations on those VirtualServer objects to add a Web Part to all virtual servers in the farm.

Another crucial function that the Microsoft.SharePoint.Portal.Topology namespace provides is allowing you to get a PortalContext object from a Console application or a Windows Forms application. For this, you would use the Topology-Manager object to get a specific PortalSite object for the portal site you want to connect to. The following code snippet demonstrates how to get a PortalContext object from a console or Windows Forms application:

```
C#
TopologyManager topology = new TopologyManager();
PortalSite portal = topology.PortalSites[new Uri("http://test-server")];
PortalContext context = PortalApplication.GetContext(portal);
```

```
VB.NET
TopologyManager()
Private Portal As PortalSite = topology.PortalSites("http://test-server")
Private context As PortalContext = PortalApplication.GetContext(portal)
```

It is important to remember that the URI you pass as an indexer in the preceding sample must be the default portal site URL. For example, if you have a portal site available at *http://test-server* and the URL *http://192.168.0.1* also points to that site, you can only use *http://test-server* in the code example. Otherwise, the code will throw an exception since the object model gets the reference of the site from the database, and only the default URL is stored.

Microsoft.SharePoint.Portal.UserProfiles

The Microsoft.SharePoint.Portal.UserProfiles namespace is one of the most useful namespaces for Windows Forms and Console applications. It is often used to perform administrative functions. For example, if you do not have Active Directory to import user profiles from, you could use the namespace to import user profiles from any other directory service. You could also pre-create My Sites, otherwise known as Personal Sites, for all users with this namespace so that the server does not have a load spike in production when a user clicks to create a My Site. Creating My Sites are expensive in terms of processor time because they are the same as creating a new Site collection, so it can be beneficial to expend the processor time to create these before the servers go into production.

With this namespace, you can also work with a user's profile and My Site. You can add properties to the profile, add links to all users' My Sites, or create reports to see how many users are using their My Site. This namespace provides excellent functionality for administrative functions. Because this namespace provides administrative functions, several code samples will be provided in this section for administrators, whereas other sections might provide just a description of the namespaces.

The following code snippet demonstrates how to import user profiles from a text file. It assumes that each property is delimited by a colon (:) character. Although this is a simple example, it can easily be modified to provide user profile imports for any other type of directory service, be it a database, a Lightweight Directory Access Protocol (LDAP) service, or a corporate directory.

```csharp
C#
public static void Import (string filename)
{
TopologyManager topology = new TopologyManager();
    PortalSite portal = topology.PortalSites[new Uri("http://test-server")];
    PortalContext context = PortalApplication.GetContext(portal);
    //initialize user profile config manager object
    UserProfileManager profileManager = new UserProfileManager(context);
    //Open Text File containing user information
    System.IO.FileInfo file = new FileInfo(filename);
    System.IO.StreamReader fs = file.OpenText();
    string read;
    while ((read = fs.ReadLine()) != null)
    {
        //parse line
        string[] userInfo = read.Split(":".ToCharArray());
        //create user profile if it doesn't exist
        string userAccount = userInfo[0];
        if (!profileManager.UserExists(userAccount))
            profileManager.CreateUserProfile(userAccount);
        //Get the userprofile so it can be changed
        UserProfile userProfile = profileManager.GetUserProfile(userAccount);
        // Set users Preferred name to their first + last name.
        userProfile["PreferredName"] = userInfo[2] + " " + userInfo[1];
        userProfile["WorkEmail"] = userInfo[0] + "@domain.com";
        userProfile.Commit();
    }
fs.Close();
}


VB.NET
Public Shared Sub Import(filename As String)
        Dim topology As New TopologyManager()
        Dim portal As PortalSite = topology.PortalSites(New Uri("http://test-
            server"))
        Dim context As PortalContext = PortalApplication.GetContext(portal)

        'initialize user profile config manager object
        Dim profileManager As New UserProfileManager(context)

        'Open Text File containing user information
        Dim file = New FileInfo(filename)
        Dim fs As System.IO.StreamReader = file.OpenText()
        Dim read As String
        read = fs.ReadLine()
        While Not (read Is Nothing)
            'parse line
            Dim userInfo As String() = read.Split(":".ToCharArray())
```

```
'create user profile if it doesn't exist
Dim userAccount As String = userInfo(0)
If Not profileManager.UserExists(userAccount) Then
    profileManager.CreateUserProfile(userAccount)
End If 'Get the userprofile so it can be changed
Dim userProfile As UserProfile = profileManager.GetUserProfile(userAccount)
' Set users Preferred name to their first + last name.
userProfile("PreferredName") = userInfo(2) + " " + userInfo(1)
userProfile("WorkEmail") = userInfo(0) + "@domain.com"
userProfile.Commit()
read = fs.ReadLine()
End While
fs.Close()
End Sub
```

The next example demonstrates how to add the corporate Web site URL to every user's Links Web Part. This Web Part is shown on the users' My Site. You can use this code to add any links that you deem necessary for all users. The sample code is a function that adds the passed URL and title to the "Corporate" category. With modifications, you could also use the code to add certain links to specific sets of users.

C#
```csharp
public static void Add(string url, string title, bool IsPublic)
{
    TopologyManager topology = new TopologyManager();
    PortalSite portal = topology.PortalSites[new Uri("http://test-server")];
    PortalContext context = PortalApplication.GetContext(portal);
    //initialize user profile config manager object
    UserProfileManager profileManager = new UserProfileManager(context);
    foreach (UserProfile profile in profileManager)
    {
        profile.QuickLinks.Add(title, url, "Corporate", IsPublic);
    }
}
```

VB.NET
```vbnet
Public Shared Sub Add(url As String, title As String, IsPublic As Boolean)
        Dim topology As New TopologyManager()
        Dim portal As PortalSite = topology.PortalSites(New Uri("http://test-
            server"))
        Dim context As PortalContext = PortalApplication.GetContext(portal)

        'initialize user profile config manager object
        Dim profileManager As New UserProfileManager(context)

        Dim profile As UserProfile
        For Each profile In  profileManager
            profile.QuickLinks.Add(title, url, "Corporate", IsPublic)
        Next profile
    End Sub
```

The next example shows how to create My Sites for all users in the profile database in one shot. It is often useful to create sites for all users before the

SharePoint farm goes live to save the performance hit of creating the site during peak times.

```csharp
C#
public static void Create()
{
    //Connect to the portal and get the portal context.
    TopologyManager topology = new TopologyManager();
    PortalSite portal = topology.PortalSites[new Uri("http://test-server")];
    PortalContext context = PortalApplication.GetContext(portal);
    //initialize user profile config manager object
    UserProfileManager profileManager = new UserProfileManager(context);
    foreach (UserProfile profile in profileManager)
    {
Console.Write("Creating a Personal Site for " + profile["PreferredName"] + "..." );
        try
        {
                profile.CreatePersonalSite();
                Console.Write("Success!\n");
        }
        catch (PersonalSiteExistsException)
        {
                Console.Write("Site already exists!\n");
        }
        catch
        {
                // Write code to Log or Display Error
        }
    }
}
```

```vbnet
VB.NET
Public Class CreateProfiles
        Public Shared Sub Create()
                'Connect to the portal and get the portal context.
                Dim topology As New TopologyManager
                Dim portal As PortalSite = topology.PortalSites(New Uri("http://test-
                    server"))
                Dim context As PortalContext = PortalApplication.GetContext(portal)

                'initialize user profile config manager object
                Dim profileManager As New UserProfileManager(context)

                Dim profile As UserProfile
                For Each profile In profileManager
                    Console.Write(("Creating a Personal Site for "
                       + profile("PreferredName") + "..."))
                    Try
                        profile.CreatePersonalSite()
                        Console.Write("Success!" + ControlChars.Lf)
                    Catch
                        Console.Write("Site Already Exists!" + ControlChars.Lf)
                    End Try
                Next profile
        End Sub
```

This final example will create a report which displays all users in the profile database and the URL of their My Site. It will display "None" for the URL if the user does not have a My Site. It will also display the total number of users who have already created a My Site. This report could easily be modified to calculate the size of each user's My Site and the total size of all My Sites, among other useful information.

```csharp
C#
public static void Report()
{
    int usersWithProfiles = 0, usersWithoutProfiles = 0;
    //Connect to the portal and get the portal context.
    TopologyManager topology = new TopologyManager();
    PortalSite portal = topology.PortalSites[new Uri("http://test-server")];
    PortalContext context = PortalApplication.GetContext(portal);
    //initialize user profile config manager object
    UserProfileManager profileManager = new UserProfileManager(context);
    foreach (UserProfile profile in profileManager)
    {
        Microsoft.SharePoint.SPSite personalSite = profile.PersonalSite;
        if (personalSite == null)
        {
            Console.WriteLine(profile["PreferredName"] + " : " + "NONE");
            usersWithoutProfiles++;
        }
        else
        {
Console.WriteLine(profile["PreferredName"] + " : " + personalSite.Url);
            usersWithProfiles++;
        }
}
Console.WriteLine("Users with Personal Site: " + usersWithProfiles.ToString());
Console.WriteLine("Users without Personal Sites: " + usersWithoutProfiles.ToString());
}
```

```vbnet
VB.NET
Public Shared Sub Report()
    Dim usersWithProfiles As Integer = 0
    Dim usersWithoutProfiles As Integer = 0
    'Connect to the portal and get the portal context.
    Dim topology As New TopologyManager()
    Dim portal As PortalSite = topology.PortalSites(New Uri("http://test-server"))
    Dim context As PortalContext = PortalApplication.GetContext(portal)
    'initialize user profile config manager object
    Dim profileManager As New UserProfileManager(context)
    Dim profile As UserProfile
    For Each profile In  profileManager
        Dim personalSite As Microsoft.SharePoint.SPSite = profile.PersonalSite
        If personalSite Is Nothing Then
            Console.WriteLine((profile("PreferredName") + " : " + "NONE"))
            usersWithoutProfiles += 1
        Else
            Console.WriteLine((profile("PreferredName") + " : " + personalSite.Url))
            usersWithProfiles += 1
        End If
```

```
        Next profile
        Console.WriteLine(("Users with Personal Site: " + usersWithProfiles.ToString()))
        Console.WriteLine(("Users without Personal Sites: "
            + usersWithoutProfiles.ToString()))
    End Sub
```

Microsoft.SharePoint.Portal.WebControls

The Microsoft.SharePoint.Portal.WebControls namespace provides several base classes for Web Parts and for interacting exclusively with a portal site. You would not use this namespace from a Console or Windows Forms application because it can only be used from Microsoft ASP.NET. The classes in this namespace are incredibly useful because they take a significant amount of work out of developing repeatedly used functions such as a cacheable Web Part. Table 34-1 provides a description of each of the classes in this namespace.

Table 34-1 Description of Classes in the Microsoft.SharePoint.Portal.WebControls Namespace

Class Name	Description
AudiencePicker	This class provides the same graphical audience picker that is used when targeting content to particular audiences.
BaseAreaWebPart	This class is an inheritable base class that acts like an area. It creates a Web Part that is cacheable, increasing its performance. The Web Parts in the default areas inherit from this Web Part.
BreadCrumbTrail	This class provides a hierarchical view of where the user is in relation to other areas. It will show the parent area and subareas.
CategoryNavigationWebPart	This Web Part implements the top horizontal navigation bar for the portal site and the side navigation bar.
CacheableWebPart	This class provides a base class for a Web Part that implements output caching. Output caching is important to achieve high performance for Web Parts that do not change frequently.
CategoryPicker	This class provides a graphical category hierarchy. It is very similar to the Portal Site Map, provided with SharePoint Portal Server, allowing you to see a list of areas.
HtmlMenu	This class implements an HTML menu much like the drop-down menu SharePoint sites use in many lists.
HtmlMenuButton	This class implements the drop-down button that will display an HtmlMenu class when clicked on.
HtmlMenuItem	This class represents a particular item on an HtmlMenu class.
SearchBox	This class implements a text box and the search functionality behind that box. If you want to develop a more advanced search, this class would be the starting point.

Table 34-1   Description of Classes in the Microsoft.SharePoint.Portal.WebControls Namespace   *(continued)*

Class Name	Description
SearchResults	This class implements the SharePoint Portal Server Search Results Web Part. If you want to develop a more advanced search results part, this class would be the starting point.
TextEditor	This class implements the rich text editor control used throughout SharePoint sites.

Other Namespaces

The SharePoint Portal Server object model provides several other namespaces. These namespaces are much less frequently used than the previously discussed namespaces. A short discussion of these namespaces will be provided in this section. For more information on these Namespaces, please refer to the "Reference" section of the SharePoint Products and Technologies SDK.

- **Microsoft.SharePoint.Portal.Admin.Search.**   This namespace provides functions for interacting with the search catalogs. You can manage the catalogs by adding or removing content sources, forcing propagation of the catalogs, and forcing a type of crawl (Full, Incremental, and so on) on a specific search catalog. This namespace, however, does not let you work with individual content sources, only full search catalogs, so you cannot crawl a particular content source directly using the functions, only a particular catalog, such as Portal_Content.

- **Microsoft.SharePoint.Portal.Search.**   The Microsoft.SharePoint.Portal.Search namespace provides only one single class—QueryProvider. With this class, you can call the search service. Although this class does provide the search ability, it is better to use the Search Web service. The Search Web service is more robust and easier to use, plus the code that calls the QueryProvider class can only be run on the local server running SharePoint Portal Server.

- **Microsoft.SharePoint.Portal.Search.ObjectModel.**   This namespace provides classes and functions for manipulating search scopes. With the namespace, you can add, remove, move, update, and list the search scopes on a particular portal site.

- **Microsoft.SharePoint.Portal.Search.WebQueryService.**   This namespace implements the Search Web service, the SPSQueryService class. Using the Search Web service explicitly instead of going through this class is generally easier and allows your code to be run from remote machines.

- **Microsoft.SharePoint.Portal.SingleSignOn.**   This namespace contains classes and functions required for accessing the Single Sign-On service provided with SharePoint Portal Server. You can add different applications, set up the credentials systems, and request credentials from this namespace.

- **Microsoft.SharePoint.Portal.SingleSignOn.Security.**   This namespace contains classes for managing access to the Single Sign-On credentials.

- **Microsoft.SharePoint.Portal.Security.**   This namespace contains functions for working with security in the portal sites. It contains the classes for users, roles, and permissions. If you want to use code to create roles or add users to roles, you would use this namespace.

- **Microsoft.SharePoint.Portal.Audiences.**   This namespace contains functions for working with SharePoint Portal Server audiences. You can get users in particular audiences, create audiences, and rebuild audiences with this namespace. You can use the functions in this namespace to build a Web Part that tailors its information based on audience membership, giving you more flexibility than just targeting a Web Part.

- **Microsoft.SharePoint.Portal.Alerts.**   The Microsoft.SharePoint.Portal.Alerts namespace and its subnamespaces, Microsoft.SharePoint.Portal.Alerts.Types and Microsoft.SharePoint.Portal.Alerts.NotificationTypes, allow you to work with alerts. You can change alerts, remove alerts, add alerts, and enable/disable alerts programmatically.

- **Microsoft.SharePoint.Portal.SiteData.**   The Microsoft.SharePoint.Portal .SiteData namespace provides functions for working with areas. It contains the code for creating areas, removing areas, applying certain area templates, and associating keywords with areas. With this namespace, you can also associate audiences with areas and work with area listings. If you want to manipulate areas through code, you would work with this namespace. For most administrators, it is faster and easier to perform the functions exposed here through the SharePoint Portal Server user interface or Microsoft Office FrontPage 2003.

Summary

This chapter provided a general overview of the SharePoint Portal Server object model. It also provided sample code snippets that would be useful to administrators for performing administrative functions. If you want to do more development work, it is strongly recommended that you download the SharePoint Products and Technologies SDK from the Microsoft Developer Network (MSDN) website. The SDK provides much more in-depth information into SharePoint Portal Server development.

Chapter 35

Building Applications Using Windows SharePoint Services Data

Microsoft Windows SharePoint Services, released shortly after Microsoft Windows Server 2003, has taken team services to a whole new level. With the built-in ability to create websites by using document libraries, lists, and so on, Windows SharePoint Services has become nearly as easy to use as Microsoft Office Word or Excel.

Windows SharePoint Services is also based on Microsoft .NET, thus extending the functionality of Windows SharePoint Services components and enabling development of Windows SharePoint Services sites by using Microsoft Visual Studio, Microsoft FrontPage, or even Notepad. The built-in functionality is exceptional—users can create and manage most of the common content themselves. This functionality is nearly the same as in Microsoft Office SharePoint Portal Server 2003, although security in Windows SharePoint Services provides limited control over individual Web Parts. Unlike SharePoint Portal Server 2003 sites, Windows SharePoint Services sites are intended to be team sites—that is, they are completely independent of any other site. Even though two or more sites can share the same database (and user authorization), the sites themselves are distinct—even navigation between them is a manual process.

Using Windows SharePoint Services Components

Because Windows SharePoint Services (and SharePoint Portal Server) are built on .NET, the entire object classes are made available to any ASP.NET application by adding a reference to the assemblies. This means that you can add a Windows

SharePoint Services document library to your application outside of the Windows SharePoint Services environment. This functionality cannot be underestimated: the ability to access internal components enables you to create external functionality on a grand scale. Rather than moving data from point A to point B, writing display pages, and so forth, we can use the same Windows SharePoint Services component, including its user interface in both sites, and still maintain security.

> **Note** Not all Windows SharePoint Services component objects can be used in an ASP.NET application. Some require parts of the framework that prevent use outside of a Windows SharePoint Services site. Although all lists and document libraries are supported, additional ones are being added.

Sharing Windows SharePoint Services Component Data

Although we can instantiate a Windows SharePoint Services component within our application, the focus of our example in this chapter is to access the data (or content) within a component within a Windows SharePoint Services site. In other words, we're going to set up a standard Windows SharePoint Services site, set up a component there, and then get (and display) the data it holds in an ASP.NET application.

Why would we do this? Simple: we can use a Windows SharePoint Services component to do all the work (add, update, delete, and so on) within a secured environment (even our intranet) but make this data available (view-only, in our example) on an ASP.NET application in a completely different environment. This is a great way to use your intranet content on your external sites *and* maintain security! In the next section, we will demonstrate how to share Windows SharePoint Services component data with ASP.NET.

Sharing Windows SharePoint Services Component Data with ASP.NET

To demonstrate how to share Windows SharePoint Services component data with ASP.NET, we'll use a hypothetical company named Contoso, Inc. This section requires some familiarity with Windows SharePoint Services Administration and basic knowledge in objects, Visual Studio, and Visual Basic .NET.

The Business Requirements

Contoso, Inc. has a special application named How Cool that it sells and supports. Presently, its corporate site is built on ASP.NET, and with only 25 people on staff, they've decided to use Windows SharePoint Services for internal department sites, document management, and knowledge management. The Support Group has its own site called the "How Cool Support Area," where it hosts running discussions, posts follow-up alerts on support calls, and performs other such functions.

The Support Group has just released How Cool Version 2, and after receiving many repeat calls regarding some minor upgrade issues, it set up a Problem/Solutions Knowledge Base List Web Part to enable various support people to post common problems and their solutions. Since doing this, support people were able to cut their research time in half. After a review, the Support Group found that many clients had already been to the company website seeking support before they called in, so it decided that offering this same list to outside customers would be an ideal way to reduce outside calls to the Support Group. The Support Group wanted to offer the list to customers with some differences, including making the information read only, making the information searchable, and doing this in a way that required minimum effort for the Support Group to maintain.

The Technical Requirements

Your mission as a developer is to expose the content held in the Windows SharePoint Services site component using a page in an external-facing ASP.NET application.

The Sample Setup Process

The setup process we will use for this sample project consists of presetup steps and setup steps, as detailed in the following list:

- Presetup Steps

    - Set up a user account, and grant it the permissions necessary to create the sites.

    - Add the new user account to Microsoft SQL Server.

    - Create new Internet Information Services (IIS) virtual directories to hold the sites.

    - Create a new Windows SharePoint Services site as the Support Site.

    - Choose the Windows SharePoint Services template.

    - Create a new ASP.NET application to simulate the External Site.

    - Create an ASP.NET Home Page in the External Site.

- Setup Steps

    - Verify the Windows SharePoint Services content database for the site.

    - Use Windows SharePoint Services Site Administration to add a Web Part.

    - Add some data to the Web Part.

    - Locate the Web Part GUID.

- Use Visual Studio to create a new ASP.NET page.

- Code the DataList.

- Test the new page.

- Try it out: verifying the new entries.

Presetup Steps

First we need to set up a user account and grant it the permissions necessary to create the sites. For the setup we'll use in our example, Windows SharePoint Services must already be installed. Verify this by clicking Start, choosing All Programs, pointing to Administrative Tools, and selecting SharePoint Central Administration. (If necessary, consult the Windows SharePoint Services Administrator's Guide for installation instructions and requirements.) You must also have permissions to create a Windows account if one is not available and an account that has privileges to administer Microsoft Internet Information Services (IIS). A Windows SharePoint Services Share-Point Administrators group member account is not automatically permitted access to IIS Administration, only Windows SharePoint Services and SharePoint Portal Server.

Creating a New Windows SharePoint Services Administrator Account

Windows SharePoint Services security requires that an account be used to administer Windows SharePoint Services sites and that it belong to the SharePoint Administrator's group. A base account is usually set up when Windows SharePoint Services is installed, and in many environments—including development environments—only one account is used. However, it is best practice to designate a specific account to manage particular sites to better control the hierarchy of security. (IIS and access control lists [ACL] are used to prevent Administrators from accessing sites they do not own.) For this example, any SharePoint Administrator account can be used, but we will follow best practices and create a new account named WSSASPTester.

To create a new Windows user account

1. If you are using NTLM (basic Windows Accounts), click **Start**, point to **All Programs**, point to **Administrative Tools**, and select **Computer Management**.

2. Click the plus sign (+) next to **Local Users And Groups** to expand it, and then click the **Users** folder. The list of users should appear on the right side of the screen.

3. Right-click the **Users** folder, and from the menu, select **New User**. This opens the New User screen.

4. Enter the user information for the new account, WSSASPTester, as follows:

   - User name: **WSSASPTester**

   - Full Name: **WSSASPTester Tester**

■ Description: **WSSASPTester Tester Account**

■ Password/Confirm Password: *<enter desired password>*

5. Change the check-box options. First deselect the **User must change password at next logon** option, and then select the **User Cannot Change Password** and **Password Never Expires** options. The Account Is Disabled box should be clear.

6. Click **Create** to create the account.

7. In the right pane of the window, right-click the new **WSSASPTester** account, and from the menu, select **Properties**.

8. On the Properties window, click the **Member Of** tab. By default, you should see the Users group.

9. At the bottom of the window, click the **Add** button to open the **Select Groups** window. From the **Select Groups** window, click **Advanced**.

10. In the lower left corner, open the **Select Groups Advanced** window and then click the **Find Now** button. This should display a list of groups and users for the server.

11. Scroll the bottom window until you locate the group with the name *STS_WPG*. (The instance number is the IIS instance number specific to your systems installation.) Click the group name in the lower box to select it.

12. Without deselecting the **OWS group**, scroll down until you find the **VS Developers Group**. Hold down the control key and click to select the **VS Developers Group** as well. With both selected, click **OK** to close the advanced window, and click **OK** again on the **Select Groups** window. This returns you to the Account Properties page.

13. Click **Apply** to save the account settings, and then click **OK** to close.

To create a new Active Directory directory service user account

1. If you are using Active Directory, click **Start**, point to **All Programs**, point to **Administrative Tools**, and select **Active Directory Users and Computers**.

2. Click the plus sign (+) next to the *<server>.local name* to expand it (if it isn't already), and click the **Users** folder. The list of users should appear on the right side of the screen.

3. Right-click the **Users** folder, and from the menu, choose **New**, and select **User**. This opens the **New Object - User** screen.

4. Enter the user information for the new account, WSSASPTester, as follows:

■ First name: **WSSASPTester**

■ Initials: (leave blank)

- ■ Last name: **Tester**

- ■ User logon: **WSSASPTester**

- ■ (Leave the @domain setting as is.)

5. When finished, click **Next**.

6. Enter the password for the account that meets the Active Directory directory service security requirements. Depending on the system settings, the default requires you to use a password of at least 8 characters, containing numbers and both uppercase and lowercase letters.

7. Next, change the check-box options. First deselect the **User must change password at next logon** option, and then deselect the **User Cannot Change Password** and **Password Never Expires** options. The Account Is Disabled box should be clear.

8. Click **Next**, and then click **Next** again to create the account.

9. In the right pane of the window, right-click the new WSSASPTester account, and from the menu, select **Properties**.

10. On the Properties window, click the **Member Of** tab. By default, you should see the Domain Users group for the Active Directory instance.

11. At the bottom of the window, click the **Add** button to display the Select Groups window.

12. From the Select Groups window, click **Advanced** in the lower left corner to open the Select Groups Advanced window.

13. Under Common Queries, find the **Name:** line. Leave the drop-down menu selection as **Starts With**, and in the box next to it, enter **OWS** and then click the **Find Now** button.

> **Note**   Active Directory can contain a large number of users and groups; it is highly recommended that you use the keyword search function.

This should display a group with the name *STS_WPG*. (The instance number is the IIS instance number specific to your systems installation.) This group has the following description: Microsoft SharePoint role 'admin' for web 'http://<your web>'. (Double-check that the site shown *is* the server you are working with.)

14. Click the group name in the lower box to select it, click **OK** to close the Advanced window, and click **OK** again in the Select Groups window.

This account will also need rights to work as a Visual Studio developer.

15. Click the **Add** button again to open Select Groups, and click **Advanced** to open the Select Groups Advanced window.

16. Just like in the earlier steps, in the **Name:, Starts With** query, enter **VS** and click **Find Now**. This should display the VS Developers Group.

17. Click the group name in the lower box to select it, click **OK** to close the Advanced window, and click **OK** again in the Select Groups window. The Account Groups screen is displayed.

18. In the Account Properties window, click **Apply** and then click **OK** to close the window.

To add the new account to SQL Server

This section assumes you are using SQL 2000 Standard or Enterprise. If you are using the MSDE Database installed by SharePoint Portal Server out of the box, this does *not* apply—to add a user to MSDE, you must use the MSDE ISQL Tool and the sp_adduser stored procedure. In either case, the user privileges described here are the same.

An account to be used to access data in the Contoso, Inc. Support Group must also be able to create a database in SQL Server to hold content for the site. To enable this, the user must have SQL Server Administration privileges either through the Administrator account or the internal 'sa' account.

1. Log in as an SQL Administrator.

2. Click **Start**, point to **All Programs**, point to **Microsoft SQL Server**, and select **Enterprise Manager** to open the SQL Server Enterprise Manager console.

3. Under Microsoft SQL Servers, locate the **Windows SharePoint Services** database instance. If the instance is not shown—that is, only (local) is shown—you need to register the server as follows:

   a. Right-click **SQL Server Group**, and select **New SQL Server Registration**.

   b. Click **Next** on the opening page of the wizard.

   c. In the box just below Available Servers, enter the instance name for Windows SharePoint Services as *<server>***SHAREPOINT**. (If your server name is S2003E, this would be S2003E\SHAREPOINT.)

   d. Click the **Add** button. The name you entered should appear under Added Servers.

   e. Click the name to select (highlight) it, and click the **Next** button.

   f. On the Authentication Mode screen, select **Windows Authentication** and click **Next**. When you are successfully connected, click **Close**.

   g. Click the plus sign (+) to expand the **SQL Server** group, and then click the *<server>***SHAREPOINT** database instance.

h. Click the plus sign (+) next to the **Security** folder to expand it.

i. Click the **Logins** icon to display the users in the right window pane.

To add WSSASPTester as a login name for SQL Server

1. Right-click the **Login** icon, and from the menu, select **New Login**.

2. On the SQL Server Login Properties page, find the ellipsis (…) button beside **Name** to open the user list.

> **Note** Make sure the domain name listed under List Names From is correct. If this is a local system account, do not assign a domain-level account.

3. Scroll the list until you find *WSSASPTester*. Double-click the name, and it should appear in the Add Name box. When it does, click **OK**.

4. Back on the SQL Sever Login Properties page, click the **Server Roles** tab. Scroll down the list until you locate **Database Creators**, and click the check box to select it.

5. Click the **Database Access** tab, and be sure that the **master**, **model**, **tempdb**, and **msdb** check boxes are selected.

6. Click **OK** to finish adding the account.

Creating Virtual Sites and New IIS Virtual Directories to Hold Them

For this example, we'll need two sites to work with: a Windows SharePoint Services site and an empty ASP.NET site. You can start with either a subsite or a top-level site. For this example, we're going to assume we're starting from scratch, including the virtual site. Follow these steps:

1. Create file system directories to hold the virtual sites. These can be located anywhere, but for our example, we are putting them at the top of the E drive.

2. Create a new directory named **e:\OurNewSharePointSite**. (This will hold the Windows SharePoint Services site.)

3. Create another new directory named **e:\OurNewASPNetSite**.

4. Open the IIS administration console.

5. Click the plus sign (+) next to the server name to expand the tree.

6. Click the plus sign (+) next to the **Web Sites** folder to expand the tree.

7. Right-click the **Web Sites** folder, and select **New** and then **Web Site**. (This opens the Web Site Creation Wizard.)

8. In the opening window of the wizard, click Next.

9. Enter the description of the website as **OurNewSharePointSite**.

10. Leave the IP default setting, and enter the **TCP Port Number** as any number *other than* port 80 or 8080 (or any administration site port). For our example, **OurNewSharePointSite** will be on port **382**. When you have entered the port number, click **Next**.

11. On the Web Site Home Directory window, click **Browse** and navigate to the directory for the SharePoint site (**e:\OurNewSharePointSite**).

12. Click **e:\OurNewSharePointSite** to select it, and then click **OK**. The path shown should be the directory you selected. Click **Next** to continue.

13. On the Web Site Access Permissions page, leave the default settings (which are **Read** and **Run**) selected and click **Next** to complete the wizard.

14. Click **Finish** to close. The new site should appear in the list of websites.

15. Repeat steps 5 and 6 for **OurNewASPNetSite** using a different port number (not 80 or 8080). In our example, we will use port **383**.

As a best practice, we need to set the Application Pool settings for the Windows SharePoint Services site, OurNewSharePointSite, so that it uses the common application pool for all SharePoint sites. If SharePoint Portal Server is installed, always use the application pool created by SharePoint Portal Server 2003, named MSSharePointPortal-AppPool, as the setting for any SharePoint Portal Server 2003 or Windows SharePoint Services sites. If SharePoint Portal Server 2003 is not installed, use MSSharePoint-AppPool. To set the application pool used by the site, follow these steps:

1. In the IIS Management console under the **Web Sites** folder, right-click the **OurNewSharePointSite** site, and then from the menu, select **Properties**.

2. On the Site Properties page, select the **Home Directory** tab.

3. On the bottom of the tab, find the **Application Pool** drop-down list.

4. Select either **MSSharePointPortalAppPool** or **MSSharePointAppPool** (depending on your installation), and click **OK**.

You might have noticed that we used OurNewSharePointSite as the name of our Windows SharePoint Services site in IIS. This name has no connection to the SharePoint site name; it is simply the virtual directory that will hold the site.

> **Tip**   Leave the default privileges on the site. By default, a newly created virtual server in Windows SharePoint Services inherits the settings from defaults set on the Central Administration pages. You can change these default settings once the virtual server is created.

When you have completed this, you should see both sites in the IIS Management console.

Creating the Windows SharePoint Services Site as the Support Site

Creating a Windows SharePoint Services site is done through the Windows SharePoint Administration console known as SharePoint Central Administration. To open the console, click Start, point to All Programs, point to Administration Tools, and click SharePoint Central Administration. This opens the Windows SharePoint Services Central Administration page.

Note that if SharePoint Portal Server is also installed on your system, there are actually two consoles: one for Windows SharePoint Services and one for SharePoint Portal Server. The title of the page indicates which one you are on, showing either "Windows SharePoint Services/Central Administration" or "SharePoint Portal Server Central Administration." (The colors are also slightly different.) Make sure you are using the correct one, as they are very similar. You alternate between the two consoles by using the links on the left side of the page under Links To Related Administration Home Pages.

Like the FrontPage extensions they replace, new websites created in IIS are not extended with Windows SharePoint Services. For us to use the site we just created (OurNewSharePointSite), the virtual directory needs to be extended to include the Windows SharePoint Services extensions.

On the Windows SharePoint Services Administration page, find the Virtual Server Configuration section and click Extend Or Upgrade Virtual Server. This opens the Virtual Server List page, which displays the list of sites found that do not have Windows SharePoint Services extensions installed. The site you've just created should appear with the following information:

Name	URL	Version	
OurNewSharePointSite	http://\<server>:\<port>/	Not Installed	Extend

The *\<server>* is the name of your server or Localhost, depending on your installation. The port number is the one you selected when creating the site in the IIS Management console.

> **Note**   You can show all sites via the Go To Complete List link at the top of the page.

Notice that both sites created are listed. However, we want to extend only OurNewSharePointSite. In the list, the name of the site is a link that will extend the site and add the Windows SharePoint Services extensions. Click the name to launch the Windows SharePoint Services Extend Virtual Server page. This page shows the current virtual server to be extended. Under the Provisioning Options section, you will see the following two options:

- **Extend and create a content database.**   This option allows you to create a new database for this site that can be used to host new sites.

- **Extend and map to another virtual server.**   This option allows you to extend a virtual server and connect to the same database as another virtual server. This option is primarily for clustering or large installations and is beyond the scope of our example.

To extend this site, click Extend and create a content database that opens the Extend And Create Content Database page.

There are seven subsections, with options under each on this page: Current Virtual Server, Application Pool, Site Owner, Database Information, Custom URL, Quota Template, and Site Language. Most of these settings are important in a real site installation. However, for this example we will use the default settings for all sections except as follows:

- For the Application Pool section, click the Use An Existing Application Pool option button. If SharePoint Portal Server is installed, select StsAppPool1. If only Windows SharePoint Services is installed, select StsAppPool.

> **Note**   When creating a new site, ALWAYS select Using An Existing Application Pool. If SharePoint Portal Server is installed, always use the Application Pool created by SharePoint Portal Server 2003 called MSSharePointPortal-AppPool as the setting for any SharePoint Portal Server 2003 or Windows SharePoint Services sites. If SharePoint Portal Server 2003 is not installed, use MSSharePointAppPool.

- For the Site Owner section, the account specified will default to the account you are currently using. It appears in the form of <domain - server>\<user account>. Leaving the domain or server name as is, change the account to the one we created named WSSASPTester (in our example, S2003E\WSSASPTester). Enter an e-mail address for the site owner as WSSASPTester@<*domain*>.

> **Note**   Do not worry if the e-mail address is not real. Windows SharePoint Services does not check this.

■ For the Database Information section, leaving the Use Default Content Database Server option selected is sufficient in most default installations. However, it is best, particularly in test scenarios, to set up your own database. To do this, simply deselect the Use Default option and enter a name that relates to the Windows SharePoint Services site. For our example, we'll use the name Contoso1.

> **Note**   If you do use the default content database server, a new database will be created as STS_<*server*>_<*IIS Instance number*>. Although you can find it easily enough by locating the site settings in the IIS MetaBase.xml file, it is much easier to specify a name to match the site.

Click OK to start the extension process. In most cases, you will have no difficulties in this process. However, a common error message you'll encounter is "Unable to create the database—extensions may not be complete" or something similar. If you are using a development system and have difficulties that appear to be related to accounts or privileges, you can default to using the Administrator account. However, you should do this only as a last resort and *never* on a QA, staging, or production system.

When the Windows SharePoint Services extension process has been completed, you will receive the Virtual Server Successfully Extended page. You'll notice that there is a link shown next to New Top-Level Web Site URL, as well as an OK button at the bottom of the page. This OK button is a little odd with regard to navigation, as it will return you to the Extend Virtual Servers page—apparently under the assumption that you would extend multiple virtual servers and then set them up later.

In our case, we want to quickly create the Contoso, Inc. Support Group site, so our interest is in the link. The link should look something like this: *http://<server>: <port>*. The server in our example is S2003E using port 382, so this appears as: *http://s2003e:382*.

> **Note**   This will also be the URL needed to navigate to the site from your browser.

Click this link to launch the Windows SharePoint Services site Template Selection page.

Troubleshooting Hint

Depending on how your installation was configured and whether both SharePoint Portal Server and Windows SharePoint Services are installed, you might get the following error when you click the link that simply says:

> Unable to connect to database. Check database connection information and make sure the database server is running.

> This error can be caused by one or more issues. The most common issue, which is explained in Microsoft Knowledge Base Article #833183, is that the MSSQL$SHAREPOINT SQL Service instance is not running. (The correction is to set the service, start it through the services in the Administrative Tools, and manually start it.)

> Another common problem is that Windows SharePoint Services is installed before SharePoint Portal Server, the configuration database, or both are installed on the SQL Server Default instance. This problem can usually can be corrected by removing the extensions from the site and running the extension process again. However, when selecting the Database options, select the SQL Default Instance (just the server name) instead of the *<server>*\SHAREPOINT instance.

Choosing the Windows SharePoint Services Template

When a Windows SharePoint Services site has been created but a base site has not yet been established, it immediately launches the Site Template Selection page.

As you can see, a wide range of prebuilt templates are available, from the standard Team Site template to the Great Plains Site template. Note that this is just a simple example of the flexibility in Windows SharePoint Services. As the number of available application-related packages increases, from CRM to ERP, more prebuilt site templates will be available. You can also create your own, but explaining how to do that is beyond the scope of this example.

We'll use the Decision Meeting Workspace Site template for the site in our example, as it is an appropriate selection to meet the needs of a typical support group. Preconfigured items include Document Management document library and Tasks, Decisions, and Agenda lists. After some minor customization, the Decision Meeting Workspace Site template could easily provide the resources needed by a substantial support organization.

To set the Template Style, click Decision Meeting Workspace and then click OK. After creating the Windows SharePoint Services site, you will be brought to the Home Page of the site.

Notice the title is automatically set to Team Web Site; don't confuse this with the Team Site template. All Windows SharePoint Services template sites have the same title. You can change this at any time via the Site Settings.

Create an ASP.NET Application

To create the non–Windows SharePoint Services site for this example (by definition, a site that does not have WSS extensions installed), we need to create a new ASP.NET application to use as our external site. When we created the virtual sites earlier in the chapter, the site OurNewASPNETSite was created at port 383. To create a new application, we need to open it by using Visual Studio and then create a home page.

> **Note** For the purposes of our examples, we will be using Visual Basic .NET. C# users should have no difficulty translating this example into a C# project.

First open Visual Studio, and then from the top menu, select File and New Project. From the left side of the New Project selection page, scroll down and click the Visual Basic Projects folder to open the VB Templates on the right site of the page. On the right side, locate the ASP.NET Web Application Template and click to select it.

In the Location section, enter the path of the virtual site we created, http://localhost:383 (where *localhost* is the local system or the name of the system you are working on), and click OK. Once the project has opened, Visual Studio might have automatically opened a page named WebForm1.aspx. If it has, close it because we will not be using it. (You can delete this file if you want.)

Right-click the References folder in the Solution Explorer, and select Add Reference. This opens the Add Reference window with three tabs: .NET, COM, and Projects. If you are not already on the .NET tab, click it to open it. Click the Component Name title bar in the window to sort the components by name in reverse order. Locate the Windows SharePoint Services component, and click it to select it.

Congratulations! You've just added Windows SharePoint Services functionality to your site. Well, sort of—this reference enables you to access the objects from within the code of your aspx pages. To actually use the Windows SharePoint Services objects, you'll need to include a reference to the library using the <% Register page directive of the HTML file, as shown here:

```
<%@ Register Tagprefix="WebPartPages" Namespace="Microsoft.SharePoint.WebPartPages"
    Assembly="Microsoft.SharePoint, Version=11.0.0.0, Culture=neutral,
    PublicKeyToken=71e9bce111e949c" %>
```

Once you've registered, you can create Windows SharePoint Services objects on the page, as in the following example:

```
<form runat="server" ID="form1">
    <WebPartPages:ListViewWebPart runat="server" ID="Listviewwebpart1"
     Description="Test List part!" Dir="default" IsIncluded="true"
     FrameState="Normal" FrameType="Standard">
    </WebPartPages:ListViewWebPart>
</form>
```

To complete this, let's quickly build a home page that displays a simple image for testing.

> **Note** Visual Studio does not default to showing all files, which can make it hard to find parts of the project. To save some time, at the very top of the Solution Explorer window, click the Show All Files icon (which is the third icon from the left).

To build a home page for testing

1. From the top menu, click **Project** and select **Add New Item**.

2. In the right pane, click **Web Form** to select it.

3. In the **Name** box on the bottom of the window, clear whatever is there, enter **Default.aspx**, and then click **Open**.

4. We need an image to put on the home page, so right-click **LocalHost (Or Server)** in the Solution Explorer window, select **Add**, and then click **Add Existing Item**.

5. At the bottom of the page, in the **Files of type** drop-down list, select **Image Files**.

6. Next, from the top of the page, use the **Look In** drop-down list to navigate to the **c:\Windows (or c:\Winnt)** folder. From there, click any bitmap (BMP) or JPG file.

7. Click the **Open** button to add it to the project. You should have the Default.aspx file open in the editor.

8. If you are in HTML mode, click **Design mode**. (The layout grid should be showing.)

9. In the Solution Explorer pane, click the new image you added, drag it to the Default.aspx page, and drop it near the top left corner of the page.

10. In the Solution Explorer pane, right-click **Default.aspx** and from the menu, select **Set As Start Page**. (This sets the Default.aspx page as the page to open if we are running the debugger.)

11. Now save your project by selecting **File** and then **Save All** from the top menu. (You can also press **Ctrl+Shift+S** to save everything.)

12. Then from the top menu again, select **Build** and then **Build Solution**. (You can also press **Ctrl+Shift+B**.) An Output window should appear and indicate that the build was successful.

Now we need to test the application to make sure it works. Open your browser, and navigate to the new site—in our example, the URL is *http://localhost:383* (or *http://<servername>:383*). You should see the new page with the image as we created it.

Setup Steps

At this point, you have two sites, *OurNewSharePointSite* and *OurNewASPNETSite*, up and running. For the first part of this example, we're going to do the following:

- Verify the content database for the site.

- Use Windows SharePoint Services Site Administration to add a Web Part.

- Add some data to the Web Part.

- Locate the Web Part GUID.

- Use Visual Studio to create a new ASP.NET page.

- Code the DataList.

- Test the new page.

- Try it out: verifying the new entries.

Verify the Content Database for the Site

When using Web Parts outside of the Windows SharePoint Services environment, it is helpful to be able to locate information about it (the GUID and so on) that is stored in the content database for the site. For our example, we will use this database to check out information about the Web Part, so we need to locate the one created for OurNewSharePointSite.

> **Note** Knowing how to locate the correct content database for a site is also useful for working with sites that others have created—not everyone follows a convention.

As mentioned previously in the creation of the OurNewSharePointSite site, the content database you selected should have a distinctive name. In our example, we named it Contoso1. If you opted instead to use the default content database (that is, you left the Use The Default Content Database option selected when you created the site), a new database would have been created using a default name of STS_<*servername*>_<IIS *Instance number*>.

Once you have located the IIS instance number, open the SQL Server Enterprise Manager. (You do this by clicking Start, pointing to All Programs, selecting Microsoft SQL Server, and clicking Enterprise Manager.) In SQL Server Enterprise Manager, click the plus sign (+) next to the SQL Servers Group and then click the plus sign (+) next to the Server Instance for Windows SharePoint Services, <*server*>\SHAREPOINT, to expand it. Click the Databases folder and find your database.

To verify the site, click the plus sign (+) next to the database name, and then click Tables. The database tables will appear in the window pane on the right. Right-click the table named Sites, and from the menu select Open Table and then click Return All Rows. This will display all the records from the table in a grid.

Notice that there is only one entry. This entry should match the site we created (*http://s2003e/382*). Also note the ID column—this is the GUID assigned to the site when it was created by Windows SharePoint Services. This GUID is internal to Windows SharePoint Services and SharePoint Portal Server 2003. (It does not correspond to a Registry Entry.)

> **Note**   Almost all objects "created" by Windows SharePoint Services (or SharePoint Products and Technologies) use GUIDs to keep them unique. This allows complete reuse because objects are instances instead of copies.

Adding a Web Part to OurNewSharePointSite

To complete the setup for our Windows SharePoint Services site, we are going to simply change the name and add a new Web Part to act as our Problem/Solutions Knowledge Base. To do this, we need to log in under the WSSASPTester account to author the site.

> **Tip**   You can use Administrator to do this, but it's better to be sure your security settings are correct for the site by using the Site Owner account.

In your browser, navigate to the new OurNewSharePointSite using the URL *http://<servername>:382* (or by using the port you used when you created it).

The next step is to add a Web Part to this page. On the top right of the page, find the Modify This Workspace link and click it to open the drop-down list menu. Select Add Pages to open the Add dialog box. Under Page Name, enter the new page name, SupportKBPage, and then click Add.

This opens the new page in the browser for editing.

In the menu on the right, you should see the Add Web Parts With Create Lists option. Locate the General Discussion Web Part at the bottom of the list. Click and drag it to the left column of the new Workspace page. The new Web Part should appear with the title General Discussion.

Note that we could have defined a completely new Web Part list and defined our own fields to be included, because much more data would generally be required for a support-related issue (such as the date of the call, who called in, and so on). A prebuilt Web Part and one you create both work the same.

We need to change some properties of the General Discussion Web Part so that it is easy to identify. In the title bar of General Discussion, click the drop-down arrow to show the menu and select Modify Shared Web Part. This should open the General Discussions properties window on the right side of the page. To show this as a true discussion, we'll make the following changes:

1. Change the Selected View to **Threaded**. (You will receive a message "Switching to a different view removes changes you made to this view, and may disable Web Part connections that depend on columns in this view." Click **OK** to close this message.)

2. Change the Toolbar Type to **Full Toolbar**.

3. Scroll down to find the **Appearance** submenu, and click the plus sign (+) next to it to open it. Change the title from General Discussion to **Problem/Solutions Knowledge Base**.

4. Scroll down a bit further and change Frame Style to **Title Bar and Border**.

5. Scroll down to the **Advanced** submenu, and click the plus sign (+) to expand it. Deselect the **Allow Minimize**, **Allow Close**, and **Allow Zone Change** options. (This forces the Web Part to appear on the page and specifies that it cannot be moved or closed by the user.)

6. Scroll to the bottom of the window, and click the **Apply** button.

7. Click **OK** to close the Web Part properties.

Add Data to the Web Part

The first thing we need to do is add some data to the Web Part so that we can see something from the ASP.NET application. On the Problem/Solutions Knowledge Base Web Part, click New Discussion. This opens the New Item page. For the subject, enter **How Cool Problem/Solutions**, and for the text, you can enter anything you want. The text you enter could be a description of the discussion, a list of team members, and so on. Right now we're just entering text to get the discussion started.

Click Save and then click Close from the menu to save this discussion thread. We need to add another item just for good measure. Click New Discussion in the title bar of the Problem/Solutions Knowledge Base Web Part to open the New Item page. Type some text. (What you enter is not important.) For the example, we've typed in text describing a problem with the solution, and as you'll notice, we've taken advantage of the built-in text formatting.

Click Save and then click Close from the menu at the top, which returns you to the new page. You should now see the two new discussion threads in your Web Part.

Using Text Formatting in the messages is particularly important. When the user clicks the plus sign (+) next to the discussion to expand it, she gets to see the nicely formatted information.

The formatting also supports the use of HTML links. (You can see this function simply by entering **http://**<*link info*>.) We must warn you, however, if you expose links to external users, you must consider security. If you do use links, they should be accessible to anonymous users.

Locate the Windows SharePoint Services Web Part GUID

As you probably know, Windows SharePoint Services and SharePoint Portal Server use system GUIDs to manage Web Parts and objects within the environment. In true object-oriented fashion, this arrangement allows one object to be reused by all users.

In our example, we selected a discussion list that is actually a List View Object. When we created it, Windows SharePoint Services created a GUID to identify the settings and data we gave it. When the Web Part is rendered on a page, the GUID is used to get the object and then add the settings and data to it when it is displayed. This process is how Windows SharePoint Services keeps track of almost every item created—from a list to a document library.

As in Windows SharePoint Services and SharePoint Portal Server, if we want to access a Web Part, Web Part data, or both, we also need the GUID because it is the only way to locate the item we want to access. Using the GUID, we can pursue the following options:

- Instantiate the same object on a different page.

- Use the GUID to instantiate the same object in a different Windows SharePoint Services site.

- Use Microsoft Office to move data between Windows SharePoint Services Web Parts and Access, Word, and Excel.

- Access the data directly in the content database (as in our example).

There are three ways to get the GUID for a specific Web Part: by using Notepad, by using FrontPage, or by querying the content database.

To use Notepad to locate a Web Part GUID

1. Open your Web browser, navigate to the site (in our example, *http://s2003e:382*).

2. Navigate to the new page we created to display the discussion Web Part.

3. Right-click the page, and select **View Source**. This opens the page's HTML code in Notepad.

4. In the **Edit** menu, click **Find** (or press **Ctrl+F**) to open the **Find** dialog box.

5. Search for the title of the Web Part by typing in its name, **Problem/Solutions Knowledge Base**.

    The first occurrence in the file will be the title assigned to the TD tag; the next occurrence should be the actual title between <span> tags.

6. Scroll down (and be careful because there is no formatting), and locate the **ctx.listName** setting. This is the actual GUID of the list, and it is enclosed in braces { }.

> **Note**   You will see the WebPartID, which also has a GUID. This is *not* the GUID for the Web Part; it is the Web Part Page GUID for the page, not for the part.

In the following code snippet, you can see the TD Title and <span> titles highlighted. Lower in the text, you can see the highlighted GUID on the ctx.listName line:

```
<tr class="ms-WPHeader">
<td accesskey="W" tabindex="0" title="Problem/Solutions Knowledge Base - Use
the General Discussion to hold newsgroup-style discussions on topics
relevant to your team." id="WebPartTitleWPQ5" style="width:100%;"><div
id="MSOFixedWidthTitle" fixedWidth="400px"
style="overflow:hidden;text-overflow:ellipsis;" class="ms-WPTitle"><a
href="http://s2003e:382/Lists/General%20Discussion/AllItems.aspx"><nobr>
<span>Problem/Solutions Knowledge Base</span><span id="WebPartCaptionWPQ5">
    </span></nobr></a></div></td><td align="right"
onkeydown="MSOMenu_KeyboardClick(WebPartWPQ5_MenuLink, 13, 40)"
style="width:10px;padding-right:2px"><a
onclick="MSOWebPartPage_OpenMenu(MSOMenu_WebPartMenu, this,
WebPartWPQ5,'False');" id="WebPartWPQ5_MenuLink" style="cursor:hand;"><img
src="/_layouts/images/Menu1.gif" tabindex="0" class="ms-HoverCellInActive"
onmouseout="this.className='ms-HoverCellInActive'"
onmouseover="this.className='ms-HoverCellActiveDark'" border="0"
align="absmiddle" title="Web Part Menu" alt="Web Part Menu" /></a></td>
</tr></table></td></tr><tr><td class="ms-WPBorder" valign="top"><div
WebPartID="3e75d5c4-15e2-4c5d-8286-50cfbbe80124" HasPers="false"
id="WebPartWPQ5" allowMinimize="false" allowRemove="false"
allowDelete="false" allowExport="false"
… …
… …
border=0><SCRIPT>
ctx = new ContextInfo();
ctx.listBaseType = 3;
ctx.listTemplate = 108;
ctx.listName = "{CD68E7BA-2DEA-4E40-AB44-46CE32A5E468}";
ctx.listUrlDir = "Lists/General Discussion";
```

Again note that the WebPartID is *not* the GUID for the Web Part.

To use FrontPage to locate a Web Part GUID

Using FrontPage is almost as easy as using Notepad to locate a Web Part GUID, although you do have to open the site to do it this way, as the following steps demonstrate:

1. Open Microsoft Office FrontPage 2003 and from the top menu, select **File** and then click **Open Site**.

2. Type in **http://s2003e:382**, which is the URL for OurNewSharePointSite.

3. When the site opens, the Site Folders list should appear on the left side of the screen. If it does not, you need to open it by going to the top menu and selecting **View**, and clicking **Folder List** (or by pressing **Alt+F1**).

4. Scroll through the folders until you find the Pages folder, and click the plus sign (+) next to the folder to expand it (that is, to open it).

5. Find the page named SupportKBPage.aspx (which is the page we created when we set up the Windows SharePoint Services site). Double-click this page to open it in the editor.

    Depending on your settings, the page will open in either Design, Split, or Code mode. We want to use Design mode to quickly locate our Web Part.

6. Select **Design** mode. In Design mode, notice that the page items appear as components. You can click any item and, as a block, it is selected.

7. Click the title bar of our Web Part, **Problem/Solutions Knowledge Base**, to select it. (Notice that the List View Options drop-down menu appears as a little page when you select it.) The Web Part selection should look something like this:

    <FPSELECTWEBPARTIMG>

8. With the Web Part selected, change from Design to **Code** mode. You'll notice that the code for the Web Part is already selected:

    <FPWEBPARTCODEIMG>

9. Scroll down through the selected code until you locate the following line:

    <ListName xmlns=http://schemas.microsoft.com

    The GUID appears between the <ListName...> and </ListName> tags and includes the curly braces ({ }).

To use SQL Server

In content databases, several key tables are used to create, manage, and store Web Part data. The most notable tables used are as follows:

- **Docs.** Stores a reference to every document library

- **Lists.** Stores a reference to every list

- **Links.** Stores a reference to every link

- **Sites.** Stores references for every site in this site tree

In addition, there is a table named UserData in which user-entered data is stored. In our example, we are using a List table (because discussions are a list type), which means the reference information is stored in the Lists table.

By default, Windows SharePoint Services databases use Windows Authentication for security reasons. Therefore, you should log in to the system as **WSSASPTester** to open the SQL Server database, although you can do this from any account that has access to the Windows SharePoint Services database we created (for example, Administrator, sa, and so on).

1. Open the SQL Server Query Analyzer by clicking **Start**, pointing to **All Programs**, selecting **Microsoft SQL Server**, and clicking **Query Analyzer**.

2. In the Connect To SQL Server dialog box, enter your server instance name. (By default, for Windows SharePoint Services this is *<server>*\SHAREPOINT.) In our example, our server is *S2003E*, so the server name would be entered as: **s2003e\SHAREPOINT**.

3. If you are using WSSASPTester or Administrator, select **Windows Authentication**. If you are using a SQL Server account, such as sa, you need to click **SQL Server authentication** and enter the Login name and password.

4. Click **OK** to log in to the database, and open **Query Analyzer**.

5. On the very top menu bar, there is a drop-down list that indicates the database you are currently accessing. If you logged in as WSSASPTester, this should already be pointing to Contoso1. If anything else is shown, such as "master," use the drop-down list to locate and select **Contoso1**. In the Query window, enter the following select statement:

   ```
   SELECT tp_ID FROM Lists WHERE tp_Title LIKE '%Problem/Solutions%'
   ```

   Entering this information should return a single row in the Query Results window. The GUID for the list is the column named tp_ID. (Note that the GUID does not have curly braces in the database.)

> **Note**   If you *do not* find the row using the query just shown, the list might have used the Default Title, General Discussions. If this is the case, substitute **General Discussions** for Problem/Solutions in the select statement and try again.

Use Visual Studio to Create a New ASP.NET Page

In our example, our goal is to display the same data from the Web Part in the Windows SharePoint Services site, OurNewSharePointSite, in the ASP.NET application site, OurNewASPNETSite, with as little difficulty and required maintenance as possible. Basically, we're going for a "set it and forget it" arrangement because we don't want to have to change code or make changes if the data changes.

To do this, we have several options that include using a custom object you create to instantiate a cloned Web Part within the ASP.NET site. However, these methods are complicated because of several factors, including security, access to style sheets, image objects, and so on. In addition, to use a Web Part within the confines of an ASP.NET site requires Windows SharePoint Services extensions to be installed on that site.

As is usually the case, and as it is with our example, our Windows SharePoint Services site and ASP.NET sites are completely isolated from one another. The general assumption is that to provide security, the ASP.NET site users should have zero access to the Windows SharePoint Services site or its objects. Although we have both sites on the same machine, using TCP/IP, these two sites could be in London and New York City.

To accomplish our goal of displaying the data from an internal Windows SharePoint Services site to an external ASP.NET site, we will use a direct connection to the Windows SharePoint Services database and use a DataList control in ASP.NET to display the data directly from the database table.

Getting to the data is the first requirement, and the key to this is accessing the GUID for the list, as we did in the previous section. This key enables us to pull the data from SQL Server to use it as we need to in the ASP.NET page.

Updating the Home Page   In our example, we left our ASP.NET site with a single page named Default.aspx and referred to it as the home page. We added a single image to it to test the site and make sure it was operational.

For the next steps and to keep the example simple, we are going to add our functionality to a new page named ProbSolutionKB.aspx. We'll add a link to it from the home page (Default.aspx) so that we can access it for testing. Open Visual Studio and open the project created for the ASP.NET site (in our example, port 383).

In the original setup, we set the Default.aspx page to be the start page of the project when we run the application. If you have not done this, you should do it now. In Visual Studio Solution Explorer, right-click Default.aspx and select Set As Start Page from the menu.

To start off, we want to make this example more realistic by making the home page look a little better. (This is not required.) We're going to modify the Default.aspx page (which is the home page for the site) by adding a heading to it using a table and adding a new image. We'll also add a link to the new page to be created.

In Visual Studio, first add the image for the How Cool Version 2 product, HowCoolV2sm.jpg (or any other image). (You can even keep the CoffeeBean.bmp we used in the setup if you prefer.) Regardless of how you choose to use Visual Studio—that is, whether you use the Design mode or code by hand—we want to accomplish the following tasks:

- Add a background color to the page.

- Create a main table that will surround the page objects.

- Create a table within the main table to handle our page layout.

- Add the image to the page as a heading logo.

- Add a link to the page to be created.

First we need to upload the HowCoolV2sm.jpg image to the project. Right-click the project name, select Add, and then click Add Existing Item, which brings up the Add Existing Item dialog window. Browse to the file location where the image is located, click to select it, and then click Open.

Note   If you navigate to the folder and do not see the file, check to see whether the Files Of Type drop-down list is set to Image Files or All Files. (There are several selections, and the default is usually set to be VB Code Files or C# Code Files.)

To open the file for editing, in the Solutions Explorer, double-click Default.aspx (unless it is already open). If the editor opens in the Design view, switch to the HTML view. Cut and paste (or type in) the new Default.aspx HTML code as shown in the following code sample. (*Omit* the <%@ Page directive from our example, and leave the line as it is in your project. It should be the same but it might not be!)

```
<%@ Page Language="vb" AutoEventWireup="false" Codebehind="Default.aspx.vb"
    Inherits="localhost._Default"%>
<!DOCTYPE HTML PUBLIC "-//W3C//DTD HTML 4.0 Transitional//EN">
<HTML>
<HEAD>
<title>Contoso - How Cool v2 Home Page</title>
<meta name="GENERATOR" content="Microsoft Visual Studio .NET 7.1">
<meta name="CODE_LANGUAGE" content="Visual Basic .NET 7.1">
<meta name="vs_defaultClientScript" content="JavaScript">
<meta name="vs_targetSchema"
    content="http://schemas.microsoft.com/intellisense/ie5">
</HEAD>
<body topmargin="0" bottommargin="0" leftmargin="0" rightmargin="0"
    title="Contoso (c)2004">
<form id="Form1" method="post" runat="server">
<table width="100%" align="center" cellpadding="0" cellspacing="0"
    bgcolor="#660000">
    <tr>
            <td height="5"></td>
    </tr>
    <tr>
        <td>
            <table width="90%" align="center" cellpadding="0" cellspacing="0"
                bgcolor="#660000" border="0">
                <tr bgcolor="#ffffff">
                    <td valign="middle" align="left" bgcolor="#ffffff">
<font style="FONT-WEIGHT: bold; COLOR: black; FONT-FAMILY: verdana,arial; FONT-VARIANT:
small-caps"> Contoso, Inc.<br>Welcome to the How Cool Home Page</font></td>
                    <td valign="middle" align="right" bgcolor="#ffffff">
```

```
<IMG SRC="http://localhost:383/How CoolV2sm.jpg"></td>
                         </tr>
                         <tr bgcolor="#ffffff">
                                 <td Colspan=2 align=center><hr color=#660000></td>
                         </tr>
                         <tr bgcolor="#ffffff">
                                 <td Colspan=2 align=center><br><font style="FONT-
SIZE: 9pt; FONT-WEIGHT: bold; COLOR: black; FONT-FAMILY: verdana,arial;">
<a href="ProbSolutionKB.aspx">How Cool v2 Support Problem/Solutions Knowledge Base
</a></font><br><br></td>
                         </tr>
                 </table>
         </td>
    </tr>
    <tr>
         <td height="5"></td>
    </tr>
</table>
</form>
</body>
</HTML>
```

Regardless of what you add for code here, be sure that you add the new link shown for ProbSolutionKB.aspx. (In the preceding example, this new link, `<a href= "ProbSolutionKB.aspx">How Cool v2 Support Problem/Solutions Knowledge Base</a>`, appears in boldface type.) Save your work either by pressing Ctrl+S or by selecting File from the top menu and then clicking Save Default.aspx. To build the project to ensure there are no errors, from the top menu, select Build and then click Build Project.

Assuming you have no build errors, next you need to test the new home page in your browser (not within Visual Studio). Do this by either opening Internet Explorer and navigating to the URL of the site (in our example, *http://s2003e:383*) or, in Visual Studio in the Solution Explorer pane, right-clicking the name (Default.aspx) and selecting Browse With from the menu. In the Browse With dialog box, select Microsoft Internet Explorer from the Browser List and then click Browse.

Note   You could also simply build and start the project by pressing the F5 key or, from the top menu, selecting Debug and then clicking Start. Because Default.aspx is already set as the start page, it will automatically open (if there are no build errors). If you do use this method, verify that the page works and then stop debugging so that we can add the new page in the next section.

If you click the link for the Knowledge Base page, you should get a message that says "The page cannot be found," but the link should be correct (*http://s2003e: 383/ProbSolutionKB.aspx*). Once you have tested the page, close the browser.

Build the New Page   Now that we've redone the home page, we can use the code to get started on our new page to give our new site a consistent look and feel. First, we need to open a new page. To do this, in Visual Studio, in the Solution Explorer pane, right-click the project name, select Add, and then click Add New Item. Then select WebForm under Templates, and in the lower part of the window under Name enter **ProbSolutionKB.aspx**. Click Open. If it is in Design mode, switch to HTML mode.

Because we've already redone the home page, we can use most of the HTML code to get our new page started. If the Default.aspx page is not open (keeping in mind that you can switch pages via the tabs at the top of the page), double-click the name in the Solution Explorer to open it. If it is in Design mode, switch to HTML mode.

In the HTML editor, select and copy the following code:

```
<body topmargin="0" bottommargin="0" leftmargin="0" rightmargin="0"
title="Contoso (c)2004">
<form id="Form1" method="post" runat="server">
<table width="100%" align="center" cellpadding="0" cellspacing="0"
bgcolor="#660000">
    <tr>
        <td height="5"></td>
    </tr>
    <tr>
        <td>
            <table width="90%" align="center" cellpadding="0" cellspacing="0"
                bgcolor="#660000" border="0">
                <tr bgcolor="#ffffff">
                    <td valign="middle" align="left"
bgcolor="#ffffff"><font style="FONT-WEIGHT: bold; COLOR: black;
    FONT-FAMILY: verdana,arial; FONT-VARIANT: small-caps">Contoso, Inc.
    <br>Welcome to the How Cool Home Page</font></td>
                    <td valign="middle" align="right"
bgcolor="#ffffff"><IMG SRC="http://localhost:383/HowCoolV2sm.jpg"></td>
                </tr>
                <tr bgcolor="#ffffff">
                    <td Colspan=2 align=center><hr color=#660000></td>
                </tr>
                <tr bgcolor="#ffffff">
                    <td Colspan=2 align=center><br><font style="FONT-
SIZE: 9pt; FONT-WEIGHT: bold; COLOR: black; FONT-FAMILY: verdana,arial;">
<a href="ProbSolutionKB.aspx">How Cool v2 Support Problem/Solutions Knowledge Base
</a></font><br><br></td>
                </tr>
            </table>
        </td>
    </tr>
    <tr>
        <td height="5"></td>
    </tr>
</table>
</form>
</body>
</HTML>
```

Switch to the new page, ProbSolution.aspx, and in the HTML editor, select from the <BODY start tag to the end of the code and delete it. Then copy the code from the preceding code sample and paste it in. We now need to change the heading and title so that we know which page we are using in the browser. First, change the <TITLE>ProbSolutionKB.aspx</TITLE> line to be **<TITLE>Problem/Solutions Knowledge Base</TITLE>**. Next we want to change the heading on the page itself from "Contoso, Inc." to "Contoso Support" and "Welcome to the How Cool Home Page" to the Support Group telephone number. Change the highlighted code in the page from this code

```
<tr bgcolor="#ffffff">
        <td valign="middle" align="left" bgcolor="#ffffff">
<font style="FONT-WEIGHT: bold; COLOR: black; FONT-FAMILY: verdana,arial;
   FONT-VARIANT: small-caps">Contoso, Inc.<br>
Welcome to the How Cool Home Page</font>
</td>
        <td valign="middle" align="right" bgcolor="#ffffff">
<IMG SRC="http://localhost:383/HowCoolV2sm.jpg"></td>
</tr>
```

to the following code

```
<tr bgcolor="#ffffff">
        <td valign="middle" align="left" bgcolor="#ffffff">
<font style="FONT-WEIGHT: bold; COLOR: black; FONT-FAMILY: verdana,arial;
   FONT-VARIANT: small-caps">OurSoftware Support</font><br>
<font style="FONT-WEIGHT: bold; FONT-SIZE: 8pt; COLOR: black; FONT-
   FAMILY: verdana,arial">Support main line: 898-392-3383</font>
        </td>
        <td valign="middle" align="right" bgcolor="#ffffff">
<IMG SRC="HowCoolV2sm.jpg"></td>
</tr>
```

Next, we need to change the link to allow us to get back to the home page and add a link to refresh this page by making it call itself (which is explained later). The code you've cut and pasted so far should now look like the following:

```
<tr bgcolor="#ffffff">
        <td Colspan=2 align=center><br>
<font style="FONT-SIZE: 9pt; FONT-WEIGHT: bold; COLOR: black;
   FONT-FAMILY: verdana,arial;">
<a href="ProbSolutionKB.aspx">How Cool v2 Support Problem/Solutions Knowledge Base
   </a></font><br><br>
        </td>
</tr>
```

Change the code in boldface type in the preceding code sample to the code shown in boldface type in the following code sample:

```
<tr bgcolor="#ffffff">
        <td Colspan=2 align=center><br>
<font style="FONT-SIZE: 9pt; FONT-WEIGHT: bold; COLOR: black;
   FONT-FAMILY: verdana,arial;">
```

```
<a href="ProbSolutionKB.aspx">Return To Home</a></font>    
<a href="ProbSolutionKB.aspx">Refresh Page</a></font><br><br>
        </td>
</tr>
```

Save your work by pressing **Ctrl+S** or selecting File and then clicking Save ProbSolutionKB.aspx. Then test the page by right-clicking the name in the Solution Explorer window pane, selecting Browse With, and then selecting Internet Explorer. Again, do not use the Visual Studio internal browser to test this page, as it will mask problems that the other browsers do not.

Add a DataList to the Page   In this next part of this example, we have to add a component (a DataList object) to the page and write some procedural code that will load data from the Windows SharePoint Services Web Part into our ASP.NET Page.

Adding a DataList to the ASP.NET page is done in the HTML editor in either Design mode by means of a drag-and-drop operation, or it's done by simply coding the object in by hand. (Most folks prefer to use both. They use a drag-and-drop operation to place the object on the page and then switch to the HTML editor to change the attributes.) For this example, we did both, as you will likely do on real projects.

If it is not open already, open the ProbSolutionKB.aspx page in the HTML editor and make sure it is in HTML mode. Then in the table we created in HTML, add a new Table Row and put a marker there as shown in the following code:

```
<tr bgcolor="#ffffff">
    <td Colspan=2 align=center valign=middle><font style="FONT-SIZE: 7pt;
COLOR: black; FONT-FAMILY: verdana,arial"><a href="Default.aspx">Return to Home
    </a></font>    <font style="FONT-SIZE: 7pt;
    COLOR: black; FONT-FAMILY: verdana,arial"><a href="ProbSolutionKB.aspx">
    Refresh Page</a></font></td>
</tr>
<tr>
    <td colspan="2" width="100%">PUTCONTROLHERE</td>
</tr>
```

Switch to Design mode and you'll see the marker "PUTCONTROLHERE" on the page. Click the Toolbox, and under the Web Forms click DataList and drag it until you see the cursor (|) appear in or next to the marker text. (If you do not see the toolbox, from the top menu, select View and then click Toolbox or press **Ctrl+Alt+X**.)

On the page, delete the text marker (PUTCONTROLHERE) so that only the control remains in the table row. Right-click the DataList, and then from the menu select Properties. This should open the Properties window for the DataList, which allows you to work with the majority of settings for determining how the DataList will appear.

For the example, right-click on the list and select Properties. From the Properties page, select AutoFormat and choose a style. (Doing this is not required, but for this example, the Colorful 1 style was selected.)

While we would ordinarily use a cascading style sheet (CSS) to assign CSS classes to each of the areas (such as Heading, Item, Selected, and so on), for this example, we have simply changed the font in each section to be Verdana, Arial (which are typical fonts for screen displays) instead of accepting the default font on the page (which is usually a Courier or Times font). As in the step just mentioned, doing this is not required, but it is usually done because the default settings are not exactly pretty.

Because the DataList has no bindings assigned, you can actually test the page at this point, although you will not see the DataList. (It must be populated with data to show.) The next step is to add the code required to populate the DataList when the page opens. If it is not already, make sure your browser is closed (and not debugging), and open the ProbSolutionKB.aspx page (in Design or HTML mode). Right-click the page in the Editor, and from the menu, select View Code to open the Visual Basic (or C#) Editor.

The first thing we need to be sure of is that our new DataList is listed as an object in our code. If you created the list by means of a drag-and-drop operation in Design mode, this entry is already made for you. If you did not create it that way, you must add it before you can use it in the code. In the Code editor, find the Region named Web Form Designer Generated Code and click the plus sign (+) next to it to expand it. Below the END SUB line for the InitializeComponent Sub, you should see a line that starts with "Protected WithEvents".

If you do not see this line (which is typical if you added the DataList by hand), you need to add it.

Verifying the Data   Before continuing with the code, we need to switch to SQL to understand the data we need to get in order to load the DataList on our page. To do this, we need the GUID of the Web Part we're going to use and query the database created for the Windows SharePoint Services site.

Open the SQL Server Query Analyzer (by clicking Start, pointing to All Programs, clicking Microsoft SQL Server, and clicking SQL Query Analyzer). If you are prompted for a login, enter **WSSASPTester** and select Windows Authentication. You can use any other login that has privilege, but *you must make sure* that you are pointing to the Windows SharePoint Services database (in our example, Contoso1).

There are a few queries you can run to see the data from the Query Analyzer. For our example, our Web Part was created with the GUID of

{CD68E7BA-2DEA-4E40-AB44-46CE32A5E468}

We will use this as our key to get information in the Windows SharePoint Services database. Note, however, that not all information found in these tables is needed. For example, in the Lists table, there is a considerable amount of information about the List, but we are interested only in the Title and Description.

In the UserData table—which is generic for all types of lists, documents, and so on—there are many fields used to accommodate the kinds of data that can be stored in Web Parts. For example, there are 64 "generic" nvarchar fields used to store data. If your Web Part uses two such fields, they will be assigned to [nvarchar1] and [nvarchar2]. However, where your data is located will depend on your list, and you will have to query the UserData table to determine where the data actually is.

The quickest way to determine this is to create a specific entry in your list (or Web Part) that uses every field added with a title such as "FIRSTTEST." You can then use this entry to query the UserData table, find the FIRSTTEST row, and check which fields are being used.

So while we can get lots of information about a particular list (or Web Part), we need to determine the exact data we want. In our example, we searched the User-Data table for our first entry and found that the fields "nvarchar1" and "ntext2" represent the title and the description, respectively. This allows us to set up the specific query we'll need in the ASP page, as you will see in the following example:

```
/* In these examples, the List GUID created is {CD68E7BA-2DEA-4E40-AB44-
   46CE32A5E468} */
/* This selects the entire row from Lists: */
SELECT * FROM [Contoso1].[dbo].[Lists]
WHERE [tp_ID] = '{CD68E7BA-2DEA-4E40-AB44-46CE32A5E468}'

/* To simply get the basic info, use this: */
SELECT [tp_Title], [tp_Description], [tp_ItemCount]
FROM [Contoso1].[dbo].[Lists]
WHERE [tp_ID] = '{CD68E7BA-2DEA-4E40-AB44-46CE32A5E468}'

/* This returns the all columns for ALL items for the given list: */
SELECT * FROM [Contoso1].[dbo].[UserData]
WHERE [tp_ListId] = '{CD68E7BA-2DEA-4E40-AB44-46CE32A5E468}'

/* After looking at the data, only two fields are required (we get the    */
/* ItemOrder and Unique ID just to show which fields can be used to  */
/* create special sorting options programmatically:                      */
SELECT [tp_ItemOrder], [uniqueidentifier1], [nvarchar1], [ntext2]
FROM [Contoso1].[dbo].[UserData]
WHERE [tp_ListId] = '{CD68E7BA-2DEA-4E40-AB44-46CE32A5E468}'
Order by tp_Ordering, uniqueidentifier1
```

Once you have the query as you need it (as we did for both the Lists and User-Data tables), save this to Notepad for the next step.

Coding the DataList

At this point, we have all we need to code the DataList. After adding the Web Part in Windows SharePoint Services, getting the GUID by using Notepad, and then figuring out the queries we need to get our data, all that remains is creating the code to execute the SQL code and populate the DataList on our page.

In Visual Studio, if it is not already open, you need to open the ProbSolutionKB .aspx file. In the Editor, right-click and from the menu, select View Code to open the Code Editor. If the Region "Web Form Generated Code" is expanded (visible), click the plus sign (+) next to it to minimize it and get it out of your way while you edit.

The next bit of code is all added:

- We add a local reference to the System.Data.SqlClient namespace so that we can access the database.

- We add a subroutine to handle populating the database.

- We add a call to the subroutine in the Page_Load subroutine to execute it when the page loads.

Using the following sample code, type in the code shown in boldface type. We've commented each section so that you can follow it:

```
GUIDGUIDGUIDGUID' ADDED for access to the SQL Database
Imports System.Data.SqlClient

Public Class ProbSolutionKB
    Inherits System.Web.UI.Page

+ #Region " Web Form Designer Generated Code "

    Private Sub Page_Load(ByVal sender As System.Object, ByVal e As System.EventArgs)
        Handles MyBase.Load
        'Put user code to initialize the page here
        '
        ' If this was only to load once, then you can uncomment
        ' the IF statement; without this, the page will reload
        ' each time (this means added items will be found on refresh):
        '
        Dim AGUIDInStringFormat As String = "{CD68E7BA-2DEA-4E40-AB44-46CE32A5E468}"
        '
        If IsPostBack Then   ' Use this to run ONLY ONCE when loaded
            '    LoadTheDataGrid(AGUIDInStringFormat)
        Else                 ' Use this to reload every time
            LoadTheDataGrid(AGUIDInStringFormat)
        End If
        '
    End Sub

    Private Sub LoadTheDataGrid(ByVal OurStringGUID As String)
        '
        Dim SQLConn As New SqlConnection
        Dim SQLDataAdapter As New SqlDataAdapter
        Dim SQLSelectString As String
        Dim SQLSelectListHeaderString As String
        Dim SQLSelectListDetailString As String
        Dim DiscussionData As DataSet
        Dim TotalItems As Integer
        '
        ' Open the database using a SQL Login:
        '
        SQLConn.ConnectionString = "Integrated Security=SSPI;Persist Security
            Info=False;Initial Catalog=Contoso1;Data Source=s2003e;"
        SQLConn.Open()
        '
```

```
' We know the GUID assigned to the SPECIFIC Windows SharePoint Services
    Object in three ways:
' Display the page and do a View Source (fastest)
' Open the page in FrontPage and change to the Source view
' Search the lists table in SQL for the Name of the list
'

' Once we have the GUID, we can use direct SQL to get the
' information we want from the List directly from SharePoint database:
'

' Setup the SQL Statement - this returns the Title and
' Description of the list:
'

SQLSelectListHeaderString = "SELECT [tp_Title],[tp_Description]
    FROM LISTS WHERE [tp_ID] = '" & OurStringGUID & "' "
'

' Setup the Detail SQL Statement - this returns all of the
' List Items from the UserData table.
' NOTE: YOU MUST ORDER the Query by the tp_Ordering column.
' In Discussion lists, this column is used to keep track of
' the threads. For the Main Topic, it assigns a unique 14 digit
' to the message; the first reply appends another 14 digits
' and the next appends again and so on:
' Main Topic 1: 12345678901234
' First Reply:  1234567890123412345678901234
' Second Reply: 123456789012341234567890123412345678901234
'

' Main Topic 2: 23948798746242
' First Reply:  2394879874624229871234987234712345678901234
' Second Reply: 2394879874624229871234987234712345678901234
'

' Order By this column ensures that discussion threads will be
' kept with the correct messages.
'

SQLSelectListDetailString = "SELECT [tp_ItemOrder],[uniqueidentifier1],
    [nvarchar1], [ntext2] FROM [Contoso1].[dbo].[UserData] WHERE [tp_ListId] =
    '" & OurStringGUID & "' AND tp_ModerationStatus = 0 AND tp_IsCurrent = 1
    Order by tp_Ordering, uniqueidentifier1 "
'

' Create a new data set to hold both Select Results:
'

DiscussionData = New DataSet
'

' LISTS (Information about the object from the LISTS table):
' Set the SQL Select command:
SQLDataAdapter.SelectCommand = & _
        New SqlCommand(SQLSelectListHeaderString, SQLConn)
' Add the table to the Data Set:
DiscussionData.Tables.Add("Lists")
' Get the Data:
SQLDataAdapter.Fill(DiscussionData.Tables("Lists"))
' Clear the Adapter:
SQLDataAdapter.Dispose()
'

' USERDATA
' (Detail Items contained in the List from the USERDATA table):
```

```
SQLDataAdapter.SelectCommand = & _
        New SqlCommand(SQLSelectListDetailString, SQLConn)
DiscussionData.Tables.Add("UserData")
SQLDataAdapter.Fill(DiscussionData.Tables("UserData"))
SQLDataAdapter.Dispose()
'
' Capture the total number of entries we found (NOTE: This
' number is also in the Lists Table as column tp_ItemCount,
' but better to use what is returned):
'
TotalItems = DiscussionData.Tables("UserData").Rows.Count
'
' We're done with the data connection so close it:
'
SQLConn.Close()
'
' Now we'll dynamically bind the data to the DataList...
'
' Create a new DataTable and create Columns for us to fill:
'
Dim OurDT As New DataTable
Dim OurDRs As Integer
Dim BuildDataRow As DataRow
Dim GetIndex As Integer
'
' Add two columns, Subject title and Message
'
OurDT.Columns.Add("Title", GetType(String))
OurDT.Columns.Add("DescText", GetType(String))
'
' Loop through the table and build the DataTable:
'
For GetIndex = 0 To (TotalItems - 1)
    BuildDataRow = OurDT.NewRow()
    BuildDataRow("Title") = & _
DiscussionData.Tables("UserData").Rows(GetIndex).Item("nvarchar1")
    BuildDataRow("DescText") = & _
DiscussionData.Tables("UserData").Rows(GetIndex).Item("ntext2")
    OurDT.Rows.Add(BuildDataRow)
Next
'
' Now establish a new DataView from the table just created:
'
Dim OurDataView As DataView = New DataView(OurDT)
'
' Bind it to the DataList control and we're done!
'
DataList1.DataSource = OurDataView
DataList1.DataBind()

    End Sub
End Class
```

When you are done editing, save your work by pressing **Ctrl+S** or by selecting File from the top menu and clicking Save ProbSolutionKB.aspx.

Now, before we finish, we have to add the Binding to our DataList on the HTML code side. This basically sets the fields we expect to use (in this case, Title and Desc-Text from the code) and sets how they will be formatted when they are displayed.

From the top tabs, select ProbSolutionKB.aspx or double-click the name in the Solution Explorer to open it in the editor. If you are in Design mode, switch to HTML mode. Look at the following code to see what changes need to be made to the base code:

```
<tr>
    <td colspan="2" width="100%">
    <asp:datalist id="DataList1" runat="server" BorderColor="#CC9966"
        BorderStyle="None" BackColor="White" CellPadding="4" GridLines="Both"
        BorderWidth="1px" CellSpacing="2" width=100%>
        <SelectedItemStyle Font-Size="X-Small" Font-Names="verdana,arial"
            Font-Bold="True" ForeColor="#663399" BackColor="#FFCC66">
            </SelectedItemStyle>
        <HeaderStyle Font-Size="Smaller" Font-Names="verdana,arial" Font-Bold="True"
            ForeColor="#FFFFCC" BackColor="#990000"></HeaderStyle>
        <HeaderTemplate>
            How Cool 2: Problem/Solutions Knowledge Base
        </HeaderTemplate>
        <EditItemStyle Font-Size="X-Small" Font-Names="Verdana,Arial">
            </EditItemStyle>
        <AlternatingItemStyle Font-Size="X-Small" Font-Names="verdana,arial">
            </AlternatingItemStyle>
        <ItemStyle Font-Size="X-Small" Font-Names="verdana,arial"
            ForeColor="#330099" BackColor="White"></ItemStyle>
        <ItemTemplate>
            <font style="FONT-WEIGHT: bold; FONT-SIZE: 8pt; COLOR: #000066;
                FONT-FAMILY: verdana,arial">Reported Issue:</font><br>
            <font style="FONT-WEIGHT: bold; FONT-SIZE: 10pt; COLOR: black;
                FONT-FAMILY: verdana,arial">
<%# DataBinder.Eval(Container.DataItem,"Title")%>
            </font>
            <hr color="#990000">
            <font style="FONT-SIZE: 10pt; COLOR: black; FONT-FAMILY: Verdana,arial">
<%# DataBinder.Eval(Container.DataItem,"DescText")%>
            </font>
            <br>
        </ItemTemplate>
        <FooterStyle Font-Size="XX-Small" Font-Names="verdana,arial" HorizontalAlign=
            "Right" ForeColor="#660099" BackColor="#FFFFCC"></FooterStyle>
        <FooterTemplate>OurSoftware How Cool 2 Support email: <a href=
            "mailto:HC2@OurSoftware.com">HC2@OurSoftware.com</a></FooterTemplate>
    </asp:datalist>
    </td>
</tr>
```

Notice the changes made to the DataList, including the following:

- Added "How Cool 2: Problem/Solutions Knowledge Base" as the heading
- Added the Item Template section
- Added two DataBinder statements for the two fields we will populate the list with
- Added a footer for the support group

Again, when you are done editing, save your work by pressing **Ctrl+S** or by selecting File from the top menu and clicking Save ProbSolutionKB.aspx.

Now check to make sure everything is OK by building the project. From the top menu, select Build and then click Build Solution. If you discover any errors, check them against the code listed previously. (Problems are usually limited to only typos.)

Testing the New Page

Because we've already added the link to the home page and have set Default.aspx to be the Project Startup page, we're ready to test the page. For a comparison, open your browser and navigate to the Windows SharePoint Services site (OurNewShare-PointSite), *http://s2003e:382*. Click the Page tab to open the SupportKBPage, and you should see the Problem/Solution Knowledge Base Discussion Web Part with the two entries we made when it was created.

> **Note**   You should have seen these entries when testing in SQL Server Query Analyzer.

Now from Visual Studio, press the F5 key (or from the top menu, select Debug and click Start). Doing this will build the project and then start the Start Page—in our case, Default.aspx. It also will help you if any problems occur because Debug mode will enable you to open the project and view the source code that might be causing a problem.

If all goes well, your default browser should open to the home page.

Click the link (as shown, "How Cool v2 Support Problem/Solutions Knowledge Base") and this should open the ProbSolutionKB.aspx page. If it opens successfully, you should see our final result.

> **Note**   A common problem here occurs if you do not have the correct account access to SQL Server. Make sure you have an account that has access to the Windows SharePoint Services database specifically.

> **Note**   We mentioned how important it was to format text when you entered it in the Windows SharePoint Services site Web Part. As you can see, the formatting you applied in there is carried over into the DataList.

Try It Out: Verifying New Entries

Now that we know we can display the contents of the Web Part, it's time to check out the dynamic nature of it. As you recall, one of our objectives is to cut down or eliminate maintenance. With what we've just built, we have satisfied that and then some. When entries are added to the Web Part, they are automatically available to our ASP.NET application through the database. This means that Add, Edit, Update, and Delete are not our concern—the Web Part handles all that. We look only for current data.

You might have noticed that in the example, we included a link on the ProbSolutionsKB.aspx page that links the page back to itself. We called this link Refresh Page, and it is there for a reason.

If it is not already open, open your browser and navigate to the ProbSolutionsKB.aspx page (via the Home Page link or by typing in the URL **http://s2003e:383/ProbSolutionsKB.aspx**). Click the Refresh Page link and the page should be reloaded. (You can also use the Reload button on your browser or press the F5 key.)

In another browser window, navigate to the OurNewSharePointSite site with the URL *http://s2003e:382*. From the home page, click the SolutionKBPage tab to display it and the Problem/Solutions Knowledge Base Web Part.

On the Web Part, click New Discussion and enter a new discussion. In this one, we will simply enter a new one for testing. However, in the Text area, we will enter a LINK as well. We don't have to explicitly indicate a link—Windows SharePoint Services already does this when you enter **http://<*server*>**.

Click Save and then click Close to save this item. You should now see it in the Problem/Solutions Knowledge Base discussion list. Switch back to the browser showing the ASP.NET page, ProbSolutionKB.aspx, and click Refresh Page (or press the F5 key). Your new entry should appear in the list. If you'd like, try the link as well; it should bring you to the Team Site home page.

Summary

This example is just one simple way in which to provide an external face to your SharePoint Portal Server or Windows SharePoint Services site. This example is intentionally simple because it offers a quick way to provide secured data to a public or nonsecured display, likely something most developers can grasp quickly. However, in a full production environment, there are many ways in which to access Windows SharePoint Services and SharePoint Portal Server data via the database, depending on your needs. I would encourage you to look into the SharePoint Products and Technologies Web Services layer, which provides extended access to all the services available.

Chapter 36

Building Applications for Microsoft Office SharePoint Portal Server 2003

Sometimes you will want to create a remote client application that interfaces with your portal site functionality and data outside of the Web interface provided by Microsoft. Perhaps you will want to tap into the search capabilities of Microsoft Office SharePoint Portal Server 2003, or you will want to create an alternative means of managing your portal site areas. In any case, SharePoint Portal Server Web services represent another major advantage to using Microsoft SharePoint Products and Technologies. These Web services allow remote clients to register with the portal site, retrieve and manipulate areas and subareas, retrieve user profile information, and search the SharePoint Portal Server index of resources. Third parties or corporate developers could develop remote client applications that provide SharePoint Portal Server functionality and data in venues other than the portal site.

SharePoint Portal Server Web Services

There are three Web services that SharePoint Portal Server 2003 exposes to the remote client developer: the Area Web service (AreaService), the User Profile Web service (UserProfileService), and the Query Web service (search). Each Web service is described in the following sections along with an example of how to use it. The next section describes how to create and configure a new Microsoft Windows–based application in C# that each example assumes as its starting point.

> **Note** Of course, the SharePoint Portal Server API for developers is more extensive than these three Web services. Windows SharePoint Services object model (and its numerous associated Web services) is covered in detail in Chapter 33, "The Windows SharePoint Services Object Model," and the SharePoint Portal Server 2003 object model is covered in detail in Chapter 34, "The SharePoint Portal Server Object Model Introduction."

Visual Studio .NET Setup

Use the following steps to create a remote client (a C# Windows-based application) in Microsoft Visual Studio .NET that will demonstrate the functionality that is available using the SharePoint Portal Server 2003 Web services.

1. Using Visual Studio .NET, create a new C# Windows-based application from the application templates.

2. Right-click the **References** folder, and then click **Add Web Reference**.

3. In the Start Browsing for Web services dialog, click the link for the Web services on the local machine. (For simplicity, this example assumes that you are using a pristine, local installation of SharePoint Portal Server 2003; if SharePoint Portal Server is installed on another server you will need to type in the fully qualified URL to the Web service on that server.)

4. In the Services column, click **AreaService**. If prompted, enter your credentials.

5. Once the methods are retrieved, type **AreaWebService** into the Web reference name text box, and then click **Add Reference**. This will close the dialog box and create a proxy to the Web service that you can use in code.

6. Follow steps 2 through 5 for both search and UserProfileService, naming them **SearchWebService** and **UserProfileWebService**, respectively. At the end of this step, there will be three items listed in the Web References folder (shown in Figure 36-1) of the project's Solution Explorer.

Figure 36-1 Web services in the Web Reference folder

7. From the **Toolbox**, drag a button, text box, tree view, and list box onto Form1 using the default name assigned to them by Visual Studio .NET: **button1**, **textBox1**, **treeView1**, and **listBox1**, respectively.

8. Double-click **button1** to get to the button1_Click function in the code-behind. You will be repeatedly replacing code in this function as you explore the SharePoint Portal Server 2003 Web services.

9. Double-click **treeView1** to get the treeView1_AfterSelect function in the code-behind. You will also place code in this function.

The following C# Windows-based application examples should run locally on your development PC using your default NTLM credentials accessing the local installation of SharePoint Portal Server 2003 from the MyComputer zone. Failing that approach, or to access a SharePoint Portal Server 2003 elsewhere, you will need to either implement Code Access Security (CAS) as described in Chapter 34, "The SharePoint Portal Server Object Model Introduction," Chapter 35, "Building Applications Using Windows SharePoint Services Data," and Chapter 37, "Using Visual Studio .NET to Create Web Parts," to establish trust for the C# Windows-based application or to set up anonymous access to your portal site (only recommended for exploring what can be done with these Web services). You are now ready to begin working with the SharePoint Portal Server 2003 Web services.

AreaService Web Service

You created a proxy to the SharePoint Portal Server 2003 AreaService Web service named *AreaWebService* in the Visual Studio .NET Setup section of this chapter. Let's begin our exploration of this Web service by retrieving the characteristics of the Home area and its subareas in a default installation of SharePoint Portal Server 2003. Clicking a node in the tree view will populate the list box with the characteristics of that area. Start by creating two private functions that perform activities that will be called from multiple places.

Create a getUserCredentials function to simplify the way you authenticate to the Web services. If SharePoint Portal Server 2003 is installed locally on your PC, you can use the URL that you use to access your portal (typically *http://localhost/*) for the URI as shown in the code; otherwise, use the same URL referenced by your Web services.

```
private System.Net.NetworkCredential getUserCredentials()
{
    //1. Return a network credential from the credential cache
    //   for the currently authenticated user.
    //   This assumes integrated security is in use and that the
    //   currently authenticated user has sufficient rights.
    return
        System.Net.CredentialCache.DefaultCredentials.GetCredential(
        new Uri("http://localhost/"), "NTLM");
}
```

Create a populateListbox function to simplify the way you authenticate to the Web services.

```
private void populateListBox(AreaWebService.AreaData area)
{
  //1. Empty the listbox
  listBox1.Items.Clear();

  //2. Put the Area name in the text box
  textBox1.Text = area.AreaName + " Area";

  //3. Add each characteristic of the area to the listbox
  listBox1.Items.Add("AppearanceDate:" + area.AppearanceDate);
  listBox1.Items.Add("AreaID:         " + area.AreaID);
  listBox1.Items.Add("Bool1:          " + area.Bool1);
  listBox1.Items.Add("Bool2:          " + area.Bool2);
  listBox1.Items.Add("Bool3:          " + area.Bool3);
  listBox1.Items.Add("CreationDate:   " + area.CreationDate);
  listBox1.Items.Add("Datetime1:      " + area.Datetime1);
  listBox1.Items.Add("Depth:          " + area.Depth);
  listBox1.Items.Add("Description:    " + area.Description);
  listBox1.Items.Add("ExpirationDate:" + area.ExpirationDate);
  listBox1.Items.Add("HonorOrder:     " + area.HonorOrder);
  listBox1.Items.Add("InheritUrl:     " + area.InheritUrl);
  listBox1.Items.Add("Int1:           " + area.Int1);
  listBox1.Items.Add("Int2:           " + area.Int2);
  listBox1.Items.Add("Int3:           " + area.Int3);
  listBox1.Items.Add("IsPublicNav:    " + area.IsPublicNav);
  listBox1.Items.Add("LargeIconUrl:   " + area.LargeIconUrl);
  listBox1.Items.Add("LastModified:   " + area.LastModified);
  listBox1.Items.Add("ListingCount:   " + area.ListingCount);
  listBox1.Items.Add("Navigation:     " + area.Navigation);
  listBox1.Items.Add("NText1:         " + area.NText1);
  listBox1.Items.Add("NVarChar1:      " + area.NVarChar1);
  listBox1.Items.Add("NVarChar2:      " + area.NVarChar2);
  listBox1.Items.Add("NVarChar3:      " + area.NVarChar3);
  listBox1.Items.Add("NVarChar4:      " + area.NVarChar4);
  listBox1.Items.Add("Order:          " + area.Order);
  listBox1.Items.Add("Owner:          " + area.Owner);
  listBox1.Items.Add("OwnerEmail:     " + area.OwnerEmail);
  listBox1.Items.Add("OwnerGuid:      " + area.OwnerGuid);
  listBox1.Items.Add("OwnerPicture:   " + area.OwnerPicture);
  listBox1.Items.Add("ParentID:       " + area.ParentID);
  listBox1.Items.Add("SmallIconUrl:   " + area.SmallIconUrl);
  listBox1.Items.Add("Synonyms:       " + area.Synonyms);
  listBox1.Items.Add("System:         " + area.System);
  listBox1.Items.Add("UrlNavigation:  " + area.UrlNavigation);
  listBox1.Items.Add("UrlOverride:    " + area.UrlOverride);
  listBox1.Items.Add("WebUrl:         " + area.WebUrl);
}
```

Place the following code in the button1_Click function:

```
private void button1_Click(object sender, System.EventArgs e)
{
  //1. Instantiate the proxy for the AreaService Web Service
```

```
AreaWebService.AreaService areaWS =
  new AreaWebService.AreaService();

//2. Set credentials for authentication to the Web service
areaWS.Credentials = getUserCredentials();

//3. Establish a variable for the home area data
AreaWebService.AreaData homeArea =
  areaWS.GetAreaData(areaWS.GetHomeAreaID());

//4. Add the home area and its sub areas to the treeview
TreeNode node = treeView1.Nodes.Add(homeArea.AreaName + " Area");
node.Tag = homeArea.AreaID;
foreach(Guid areaGuid in areaWS.GetSubAreas(homeArea.AreaID))
{
  //5. Establish a variable for each home sub area and
  //   add it to the treeview as a child of the home area
  AreaWebService.AreaData area = areaWS.GetAreaData(areaGuid);
  TreeNode childNode = node.Nodes.Add(area.AreaName + " Area");
  childNode.Tag = area.AreaID;
}

//6. Expand the treeview node
node.Toggle();

//7. Default listBox nodes to characteristics of the home area
populateListBox(homeArea);
}
```

Finally, place the following code in the treeView1_AfterSelect function:

```
private void treeView1_AfterSelect(object sender,
  System.Windows.Forms.TreeViewEventArgs e)
{
  //1. Instantiate the proxy for the AreaService Web Service
  AreaWebService.AreaService areaWS =
    new AreaWebService.AreaService();

  //2. Set credentials for authentication to the Web service
  areaWS.Credentials = getUserCredentials();

  //3. Establish a variable for the clicked node's area data
  AreaWebService.AreaData clickedArea =
    areaWS.GetAreaData(new Guid(e.Node.Tag.ToString()));

  //4. Populate the list box using the area data
  populateListBox(clickedArea);
}
```

Press F5 in Visual Studio .NET to compile and run the application. Click the button1 button in the resulting dialog box to populate the list box as shown in Figure 36-2.

The values in the list box represent the Home area and its subareas. Clicking a node in the list box will result in its characteristics filling the list box.

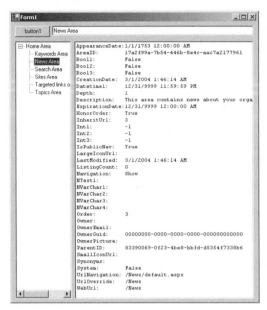

Figure 36-2 News area returned by the AreaService Web service

Most of the characteristics have their roots in the familiar tabbed Change Settings screens for an area in SharePoint Portal Server 2003. The fields might differ in name somewhat, for instance the Title field is called *AreaName* in the Web service and the Start Date is called *AppearanceDate* in the Web service. There are also a few fields that seem unfamiliar. For instance, Bool1, Bool2, Bool3, Datetime1, Int1, Int2, Int3, NText, NVarChar1, NVarChar2, NVarChar3, and NVarChar4 are all user-defined values that programmers can set and get that accept various evident datatypes.

If the ListingCount were greater than 0 for an area, you could use the GetArea-Listings method of the AreaService Web service to get a list of area listing GUIDs. Subsequently, you could use the GetAreaListingData method to get and set a subset of the area listing's characteristics.

Of course, you can use CreateArea and CreateAreaListing to generate new areas and area listings. Likewise, you can use DeleteArea (if not a system area like the Home page) and DeleteAreaListing to remove areas and area listings. There are examples of these functions in the SharePoint Products and Technologies Software Development Kit (SDK).

There are also many Web service methods that start with Begin and have associated methods that start with End. These methods can be used to complete that functionality asynchronously.

Search Web Service

You created a proxy to the SharePoint Portal Server 2003 search Web service named *SearchWebService* in the "Visual Studio .NET Setup" section earlier in this chapter. This Web service lets us query the SharePoint Portal Server 2003 search index for resources that match a pattern or query. A simple string of search terms can be used to query the search index. By default, results of this type of query are returned in order of relevance rank, descending from most relevant to least relevant. Booleans and wildcards are not currently supported out of the box with the default search constructor Web Part by SharePoint Portal Server 2003. The Microsoft SQL Syntax for Full-text Search (MSSQLFT) dialect can also be used to query the search index. Use an MSSQLFT query with the SQL SELECT response format to specify different sort orders.

You will use the same set of controls for this sample application as you did for the first one. However, they will all perform different functions. The text box will be the string that you want to search for, the button will initiate the search, the tree view will contain our search results including a hyperlink to the resource, and the list view will just be used for providing feedback to the user.

As with the AreaService Web service, you need to provide credentials to the search Web service. So, you will use the getUserCredentials function created earlier in this chapter to help with this functionality.

Place the following code in the button1_Click function:

```
private void button1_Click(object sender, System.EventArgs e)
{
  //1. Setup a variable containing the XML required for querying
  //   the Web service. Double quotes in the XML must be escaped
  //   with a backslash. The SEARCHSTRING will be replaced later with
  //   the actual string of keywords that the user wants
  //   to search for.
  string queryString =
    "<?xml version=\"1.0\" encoding=\"utf-8\" ?>" +
    "<QueryPacket xmlns=\"urn:Microsoft.Search.Query\" " +
        "Revision=\"1000\">" +
      "<Query domain=\"QDomain\">" +
        "<SupportedFormats>" +
          "<Format>" +
            "urn:Microsoft.Search.Response.Document.Document" +
          "</Format>" +
        "</SupportedFormats>" +
        "<Context>" +
          "<QueryText language=\"en-US\" type=\"STRING\">" +
            "SEARCHSTRING" +
          "</QueryText>" +
        "</Context>" +
        "<Range>" +
          "<StartAt>1</StartAt>" +
          "<Count>9</Count>" +
        "</Range>" +
      "</Query>" +
    "</QueryPacket>";

  //2. Instantiate the proxy to the SearchWebService Web Service
  SearchWebService.QueryService queryWS =
    new SearchWebService.QueryService();

  //3. Set credentials for authentication to the Web service
  queryWS.Credentials = getUserCredentials();
```

```
//4. Clear the list box and treeview from previous searches
treeView1.Nodes.Clear();
listBox1.Items.Clear();

//5. Verify that the search Web service status is ONLINE
if(queryWS.Status().Equals("ONLINE"))
{
  //6. Replace the search string in the XML with the string
  //   of keywords that the user wants to search for.
  string query = queryString.Replace(
    "SEARCHSTRING",
    textBox1.Text);

  //7. Submit the query returning a dataset
  DataSet ds = queryWS.QueryEx(query);

  //8. Process the results of the query, one row in the dataset
  //   for each resource found by the search
  foreach(DataRow row in ds.Tables["table"].Rows)
  {
    //9. We will use the link to the resource and its title
    string hrefLink =
      row["DAV%3ahref"].ToString();
    string displayTitle =
row["urn%3aschemas.microsoft.com%3afulltextqueryinfo%3adisplaytitle"].ToString();

    //10. The last modified date, content length, description,
    //    rank, sourceGroup, and sdid1 (search ID)
    //    are returned from the default search
    //    but are not used in this example
    string getLastModified =
      row["DAV%3agetlastmodified"].ToString();
    string getContentLength =
      row["DAV%3agetcontentlength"].ToString();
    string description =
row["urn%3aschemas.microsoft.com%3afulltextqueryinfo%3adescription"].ToString();
    string rank =
      row["urn%3aschemas.microsoft.com%3afulltextqueryinfo%3arank"].ToString();
    string sourceGroup =
row["urn%3aschemas.microsoft.com%3afulltextqueryinfo%3asourcegroup"].ToString();
    string sdid1 =
      row["urn%3aschemas.microsoft.com%3afulltextqueryinfo%3asdid1"].ToString();

    //11. Add each resource into the treeview
    TreeNode node = treeView1.Nodes.Add(displayTitle);

    //12. Save the URL with the node
    node.Tag = hrefLink;
  }

  //13. Determine if any resources were found by the search
  if (treeView1.Nodes.Count > 0)
  {
    //14. Message the user to click on any item to view it
    listBox1.Items.Add("Click on any item to view it.");
  }
```

```
    else
    {
      //15. Message the user that no resources were returned
      listBox1.Items.Add("No resources were returned.");
    }
  }
  else
  {
    //16. Message the user if search is not ONLINE
    //     Currently, the only other value is OFFLINE
    listBox1.Items.Add("Search is currently "
      + queryWS.Status());
  }
}
```

Notice that in line 1 of the code we set up a variable containing the XML required for querying the Web service. To do an MSSQLFT search instead of a STRING search, just change `type=\"STRING\"` to `type=\"MSSQLFT\"`. But if you do that, the text box needs to contain a query rather than just a string when the button is clicked.

In line 7 of the code, you submit the query XML using QueryEx to return a dataset. Using Query rather than QueryEx will return an xmlNode with basically the same data. The dataset is just a little easier to work with, even though the names of the fields are long. Speaking of the field names, notice that %3a is the escape sequence for a colon. Mentally substituting those three characters when looking at the preceding code will make the field names easier to understand.

Finally, place the following code in the treeView1_AfterSelect function:

```
private void treeView1_AfterSelect(object sender,
  System.Windows.Forms.TreeViewEventArgs e)
{
  //1. Setup a variable representing a latent process with
  //    IE (iexplore.exe) as the application and the URL
  //    in the clicked node's tag as the document to open
  System.Diagnostics.ProcessStartInfo iexploreStartInfo = new
    System.Diagnostics.ProcessStartInfo(
      "iexplore.exe", e.Node.Tag.ToString());

  //2. Starting the process opens IE to the URL
  System.Diagnostics.Process iexplore =
    System.Diagnostics.Process.Start(iexploreStartInfo);
}
```

Replace the text in the text box with the keywords you want to search for. In our example, you searched for the word "microsoft". Click the button. If searching a brand new portal site, there should be a number of resources found (typically five), as shown in Figure 36-3.

Click any resource listed in the tree view and your browser will open directly to that resource's URL.

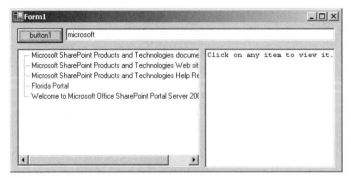

Figure 36-3   Resources returned using the search Web service

By default, all portal site sources are searched. To get a list of the sources that are available to be searched, you can use the GetPortalSearchInfo method of the search Web service.

Again, there are many Web service methods that start with Begin and have associated methods that start with End. These methods can be used to complete that functionality asynchronously.

UserProfileService Web Service

You created a proxy to the SharePoint Portal Server 2003 User Profile Web service named *UserProfileWebService* in the "Visual Studio .NET Setup" section of this chapter. Basically, this Web service lets you retrieve user profiles and their schema using a variety of different user IDs: GUID, index, and user account name. GUID and index will be useful when SharePoint Portal Server provides those tokens to us as the ID for a user.

Again, you will use the same set of controls for this sample application as you did for the both the AreaService Web Service and the search Web Service examples. For this example, allow the user to initially type an account name into the text box. When the user clicks the button, you will attempt to retrieve the account name specified in the text box from SharePoint Portal Server 2003. You will save all successful searches in the tree view and present all profile details in the list view. If the user's profile is not found, you will present a message in the list view indicating that status. If the user clicks on a previously successful account in the tree view, you will re-retrieve the profile using the GUID that you saved when the profile was initially retrieved.

As with the previous Web services, you need to provide credentials to the UserProfileService Web service. So, you will use the getUserCredentials function created earlier in this chapter to help with this functionality.

Place the following code in the button1_Click function:

```
private void button1_Click(object sender, System.EventArgs e)
{
  //1. Establish a proxy to the UserProfileService Web Service
  UserProfileWebService.UserProfileService userProfileWS =
    new UserProfileWebService.UserProfileService();
```

```
//2. Set credentials for authentication to the Web service
userProfileWS.Credentials = getUserCredentials();

//3. Clear the list box on each request
listBox1.Items.Clear();

try
{
  //4. Give names to the PropertyData array indexes
  int userProfile_GUID = 0;
  int accountName = 1;

  //5. Retrieve the PropertyData array for account name
  //   provided by the user in the text box
  UserProfileWebService.PropertyData[] userData =
    userProfileWS.GetUserProfileByName(textBox1.Text);

  //6. If successful, add account name to the treeview
  TreeNode node = treeView1.Nodes.Add(
    userData[accountName].Value);

  //7. Save the GUID with the node
  node.Tag = userData[userProfile_GUID].Value;

  //8. For every property in the profile
  foreach(UserProfileWebService.PropertyData userProperty
          in userData)
  {
    //9. Add the name and value to the listbox
    listBox1.Items.Add(userProperty.Name + ": "
      + userProperty.Value);
  }
}
catch
{
  //10. Message the user if the account name is not found
  listBox1.Items.Add("Account Name Not Found");
}
}
```

Finally, place the following code in the treeView1_AfterSelect function:

```
private void treeView1_AfterSelect(object sender,
  System.Windows.Forms.TreeViewEventArgs e)
{
  //1. Establish a proxy to the UserProfileService Web Service
  UserProfileWebService.UserProfileService userProfileWS =
    new UserProfileWebService.UserProfileService();

  //2. Set credentials for authentication to the Web service
  userProfileWS.Credentials = getUserCredentials();

  //3. Clear the list box on each request
  listBox1.Items.Clear();

  //4. Show the clicked accountName in the text box
  textBox1.Text = e.Node.Text;
```

```
try
{
  //5. Retrieve the PropertyData array for GUID saved when
  //    the user was first retrieved
  UserProfileWebService.PropertyData[] userData =
    userProfileWS.GetUserProfileByGuid(
    new Guid(e.Node.Tag.ToString()));

  //6. For every property in the profile
  foreach(UserProfileWebService.PropertyData userProperty
            in userData)
  {
    //7. Add the name and value to the listbox
    listBox1.Items.Add(userProperty.Name + ": "
      + userProperty.Value);
  }
}
catch
{
  //8. Message the user if the account name is not found
  listBox1.Items.Add("Account Name Not Found");
}
}
```

Type an account name into the text box in the format domain\username or just a username, and click the button. If the account is found, it will be added to the tree view of previous successful retrievals and its properties will be presented in the list box, shown in Figure 36-4.

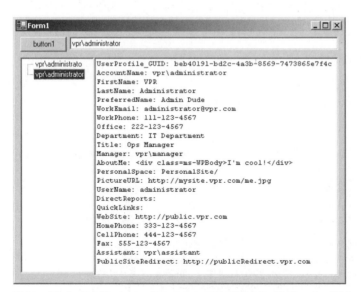

Figure 36-4   Profile properties returned by UserProfileService Web service

Clicking any previously retrieved profile in the tree view will re-retrieve that profile using the GUID stored in the tree view node's tag property.

Summary

The examples provided in this chapter are rudimentary and somewhat crude. However, they demonstrate the capabilities available to a remote client accessing SharePoint Portal Server 2003 Web services.

We covered all three Web services provided by SharePoint Portal Server 2003. The AreaService Web service allowed us to manage nearly every aspect of a SharePoint Portal Server 2003 area. The search Web service gave us a window into the resources indexed by SharePoint Portal Server 2003, and the UserProfileService Web service lets us retrieve profile information using various user IDs.

The next chapter describes how you can use Visual Studio .NET to create Web Parts.

Chapter 37

Using Visual Studio .NET to Create Web Parts

Microsoft SharePoint Products and Technologies offers a managed object model that can be used to create your own custom solutions in a developer-friendly way using Microsoft Visual Studio .NET. This chapter and Chapter 31, "Working with Web Parts," introduce you to the basic things you need to know to be successful in Web Part development.

Web Part Architecture

To understand how the Web Part architecture works, you need to look at the smallest piece within the architecture, the Web Part itself, and then zoom out gradually to less granular levels. This is the approach that is taken by this section.

Web Parts

Web Parts are the basic building blocks of a Web Part Page, each one of them providing its own specific set of features. For example, a news Web Part is responsible for showing news items. You are responsible for deciding how many and which Web Parts should be placed on a Web Part Page.

SharePoint Products and Technologies comes with several Web Parts that users can use right away, and many more are available in the online Web Part gallery. For more information about these Web Parts, see Chapter 31. Several other software vendors offer free or commercial Web Parts that you can use. In addition, you can create your own Web Parts using Visual Studio .NET, which is the topic of this chapter.

Every Web Part derives from the Microsoft.SharePoint.WebPartPages.WebPart class. Because the Web Part base class derives from System.Web.UI.Control, every Web Part is a Microsoft ASP.NET Web control. This means Web Parts, like all controls, participate in page rendering, property settings, post-back events, and state management.

Placing Web Parts

Web Parts can be placed on Web Part Zones. A Web Part Zone is a server control that derives from the Microsoft.SharePoint.WebPartPages.WebPartZone class. Web Part Zones are located on a Web Part Page, and every Web Part Zone can contain one or more Web Parts.

At this point, you might assume that every Web Part should be placed within a Web Part Zone, which is not the case. Placing a Web Part within a Web Part Zone has its advantages. By doing this, you tap into the power of the customization and personalization services offered by the SharePoint framework, discussed in Chapter 23, "Personalization Services in SharePoint Products and Technologies."

You can also place a Web Part on a Web Part Page outside of a Web Part Zone. The advantage of doing this is that you ensure the properties of such a Web Part are static. Because the Web Part properties cannot be customized or personalized, the Web Part will always have the same set of properties. The properties of a static Web Part are not stored in the database but rather in the page itself.

Finally, because a Web Part is an ASP.NET Web control, it can also be used outside a Web Part Page as a standard Web form control. A Web Part can be placed directly on any .aspx page in the same way as you would with any other custom control. Essentially, this is the very similar to placing a Web Part outside a Web Part Zone.

Web Part Pages

Every SharePoint site consists of Web Part Pages. A Web Part Page is a special type of Web page that can contain one or more Web Part Zones. Every Web Part Page derives from the Microsoft.SharePoint.WebPartPages.WebPartPage class, which in turn is derived from the System.Web.UI.Page class.

When working with Web Part Pages it's important to realize that a Web Part Page can be in one of two states: ghosted or unghosted. This concept can be confusing when you're new to SharePoint Products and Technologies, but basically, ghosted pages are Web Part Pages that are stored on the file system, and unghosted pages are stored in the SharePoint database.

Ghosted pages are all Web Part Pages that are rendered from the root virtual directory main application root and its subfolders, as well as Web Part Pages stored in SharePoint document libraries. Ghosted pages do not include pages that come from the child virtual directories _layouts and _vti_bin. Examples of ghosted pages are the default home page and the new Web Part Pages. A ghosted page becomes unghosted once the page or one of its properties has been modified, for example, using Microsoft FrontPage 2003 or Web folders. The state of a Web Part Page has significant consequences during Web Part Page rendering.

Web Part Page Rendering

In a SharePoint Products and Technologies environment, each page request that hits Microsoft Internet Information Services (IIS) is handed over to the ASP.NET HTTP pipeline. The HTTP pipeline is a chain of managed objects that sequentially processes the request and makes the transition from a URL to plain HTML text.

At installation time, the SharePointHandlerFactory registers itself as the IHttp-Handler for all .aspx requests. This association between types of resources and types of handlers is stored in the configuration file of the SharePoint site. More exactly, the default set of mappings is defined in the <httpHandlers> section of the Web.config file. The line below illustrates the code that defines the HTTP handler for .aspx resources once Windows SharePoint Services is installed.

```
<add verb="*" path="*.aspx"
  type="Microsoft.SharePoint.ApplicationRuntime.SharePointHandlerFactory"/>
```

The SharePointHandlerFactory IHttpHandler requires that all page requests are Web Part Pages, that is, that they derive from the Microsoft.SharePoint.WebPartPages. WebPartPage class. The line below shows the @Page directive that ensures that the Web page is a Web Part Page.

```
<%@ Page language="C#"
  Inherits="Microsoft.SharePoint.WebPartPages.WebPartPage" %>
```

If the @Page directive is missing, it defaults to a Web Part Page type and the request is passed to the Web Part infrastructure for rendering. Any requests whose @Page directives identify Web Part Page types are also passed to the Web Part infrastructure. If an @Page directive identifies a page that is not a Web Part Page, the following error is returned: "To run as a WebPartPage, this page must derive from a class which is derived from the Microsoft.SharePoint.WebPartPages.WebPartPage object."

Once the request is passed to the Web Part infrastructure, Windows SharePoint Services determines whether the page is ghosted or unghosted. For ghosted pages, the request is handed off to the ASP.NET infrastructure for rendering; otherwise, the page is rendered by the SafeMode parser that is part of the Web Part infrastructure. The following steps are taken during this page rendering process:

- Retrieves the page's collection of Web Parts, determines whether the page is in personal or shared view, and resolves personalization and customization considerations.

- Verifies that every part in a Web Part Zone is in the SafeControls list. If a page is parsed by the SafeMode parser all server controls, even those that are not a part of a Web Part Zone, are validated against the SafeControls list, which is located in the Web.config file.

After this, the infrastructure creates each Web Part until all the parts are rendered on the page and the page is returned to the requestor.

Web Part Rendering

Rendering a Web Part is handled by the standard ASP.NET rendering process. The Render method of the WebPart class is inherited from the System.Web.UI.Control class and is used by the Microsoft.SharePoint.WebPartPages.WebPart base class to add the frame around the content provided by the Web Part. The Render method also calls the RenderWebPart method so the Web Part can generate the HTML that is rendered inside the Web Part frame. Although the Render method on the base class is defined as overridable, it is not recommended that you do so. Instead, implement any rendering for the Web Part in the RenderWebPart method. The entire rendering process is shown in Figure 37-1.

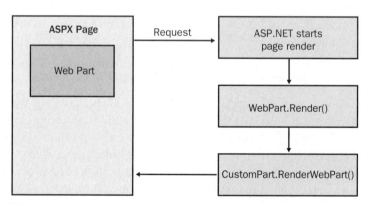

Figure 37-1   Rendering Web Part Pages and Web Parts

Page States Explained

We have seen that Web Part Pages can be in different states. The main reasons for SharePoint to store some templates in the file system (ghosted) and some in the database (unghosted) have to do with security and scalability.

When a client requests an unghosted page, the Web Part Page is rendered by the SafeMode parser. The SafeMode parser ensures unghosted pages are not allowed to run untrusted code. This security feature prevents a user from injecting code into Web Part Pages that might, maliciously or unintentionally, bring down a server or hijack data. Once a pages is transitioned from a ghosted to unghosted state, the SharePoint administrator knows that page cannot influence the behavior of the server in such ways. Remember, a ghosted page becomes unghosted once the page or one of its properties has been modified, for example, using FrontPage 2003 or Web folders. Pages that are created through the SharePoint user interface are ghosted, but pages that are newly uploaded will be unghosted. In other words, if you upload a new file to a SharePoint folder or document library, the page is automatically and permanently considered unghosted.

Additionally, without the SafeMode parser, all pages would have to be routed through ASP.NET, which would mean all pages would be compiled and their associated assemblies would be loaded into memory. On a site with thousands of operational pages, the memory requirement would be huge. In the current design, using the SafeMode parser, page compilation is limited to a very small number of pages relative to the actual number of pages within a SharePoint-extended virtual server.

Another benefit of unghosted pages becomes clear in Web farm scenarios. SharePoint Products and Technologies does not offer any features that replicate physical files or data from one front-end Web server to another. This means if you change a Web Part Page on front-end Web server A, you should make the same change on front-end Web server B. Unghosting a page allows only one copy of the page to exist for any given number of front-end Web servers.

Strong-Naming Assemblies

Every Web Part exists within an assembly. The Web Part assembly, a dynamic-link library (DLL) file, contains one assembly manifest that describes the assembly itself and contains several global attributes. Assemblies are referenced by using their names. An assembly name consists of a text name, which is usually the name of the assembly without the file extension. In addition to this name, the assembly name can consist of an assembly version number and a culture reference. The assembly name can be further qualified by using a public key token. The assembly name, version number, culture, and public key token of an assembly are called the assembly's full name, also known as the *strong name*.

The next XML fragment is taken from the Web.config file located in the Windows SharePoint Services extended virtual server root directory.

```
<SafeControl Assembly="ResKitLibrary, Version=1.0.0.0, Culture=neutral, PublicKey-
  Token=3fab337e00400dc5" Namespace="ResKitLibraryNamespace" TypeName="*" Safe="True" />
```

The Web.config file is used to specify the settings for the specific virtual server where Windows SharePoint Services or SharePoint Portal Server is installed. It clearly shows how the Web Part assembly name consists of several parts. The first part refers to the name of the assembly, followed by the assembly version number and the culture. It also includes a public key token related to the strong name of the assembly. The <SafeControl> element also contains a Namespace attribute referring to one of the namespaces used within the assembly and a TypeName attribute referring to the simple type name. For example, if a control is named *MyControl* and the namespace is *MyNamespace*, the TypeName attribute would contain *MyControl* and not *MyNamespace.MyControl*.

> **Note**   This differs from the type name described in Web Part description files (.dwp). Web Part description files require the full type name for the TypeName node. A SafeControl entry only requires the simple type name. Please refer to Chapter 31 for detailed information about Web Part description files.

If you specify a wildcard (*), every type name is selected. You can also explicitly specify the type name. Finally, the <SafeControl> element can contain a Safe attribute. If the Safe attribute is omitted, the SafeControl entry defaults to True. If a Web Part fails to meet the SafeControl validation, you will get an error message informing you that "A Web Part or Web Form Control on this Web Part Page cannot be displayed or imported because it is not registered on this site as safe."

The Safe attribute indicates whether a server control is considered to be safe to be executed. This attribute can be set to False if you temporarily want to disable a Web Part. This provides fine-grained control to the administrator of what is running on the server. Suppose you have installed an assembly from company A that contains a set of ten Web Parts. And suppose that one of the Web Parts contains a critical error that can bring down the server. By setting the Safe attribute to False, the administrator can prevent this Web Part from running on the server without having to remove the entire assembly. Therefore, business functionality involving all other Web Parts can remain intact.

If you want to import and place a Web Part on a Web Part Page, you should register the Web Part as a safe control. Failing to do so will prevent the Web Part import and rendering. You can register the Web Part as a safe control by adding a <SafeControl> element to the Web.config file

Web Part library assemblies can installed into one of two locations. First, you can place the DLL in the bin directory of the Windows SharePoint Services extended virtual server root directory. In this case, the Web Part is available only to the virtual server containing this directory. Second, you can place the DLL in the Global Assembly Cache (GAC). This makes the assembly accessible to all applications on the server. Assemblies installed in the GAC are granted Full Trust by the policy files used by either Windows SharePoint Services or ASP.NET. A Web Part library can only be placed in the GAC if it is signed. You can refer to the procedure "To create a strong name key pair file," later in this chapter, if you want to know more about this topic.

Code Access Security

The Microsoft .NET Framework provides a security mechanism called code access security (CAS). Code access security is a process that helps limit the access code has to protected resources. This could be code from a third party or code that you have written yourself. Although code access security is something that has been around for quite some time, SharePoint Products and Technologies is the first technology to really bring it to the forefront. SharePoint Products and Technologies uses .NET code access security to control access to protected resources. With code access security, you can assign to an assembly a configurable level of trust that corresponds to a predefined set of permissions.

> **Note** If you want to know more about code access security, you can also refer to the "Microsoft Windows SharePoint Services and Code Access Security" white paper, which can be found on MSDN, the Microsoft Developer Network.

To allow the administrator to easily switch levels of trust assigned to an application, Windows SharePoint Services includes code groups of its own, next to the default policies that are installed by ASP.NET. Windows SharePoint Services include two security policy files: WSS_Minimal and WSS_Medium. You can specify a level of trust that corresponds to a predefined set of permissions for ASP.NET applications, ranging from "Minimal" to "Full." SharePoint Products and Technologies defines two additional levels of trust of its own: "WSS_Minimal" and "WSS_Medium." The exact location of the security policy files can be found in the <securityPolicy> section in the Web.config file, as shown here:

```
<securityPolicy>
  <trustLevel name="WSS_Medium"
policyFile="C:\Program Files\Common Files\Microsoft Shared\Web Server Extensions\60\
config\wss_mediumtrust.config" />
  <trustLevel name="WSS_Minimal"
policyFile="C:\Program Files\Common Files\Microsoft Shared\Web Server Extensions\60\
config\wss_minimaltrust.config" />
</securityPolicy>
```

The default trust level is WSS_Minimal, but this can be changed using the level attribute of the <trust> element, as shown here:

```
<trust level="WSS_Minimal" originUrl="" />
```

The SharePoint Products and Technologies class libraries use code access security to protect certain resources and operations by specifying the permissions that they require to run. The members of the SharePoint class libraries demand SharePointPermission with the ObjectModel property set to true. You should take note of this and ensure that any assemblies you create that use the WSS object model have this permission.

> **Note** If you look at the .NET Framework Class Library information, which can be found on MSDN, you will notice a Requirements section that outlines the permissions required in order to execute a method.

If the default permission level does not suit your needs, there are several ways to make sure your code has the required permissions. One option is to consider installing the assembly in the Global Assembly Cache (GAC) because the code in it, by default, has Full trust. Installing assemblies in the Global Assembly Cache is not recommended; it's best to assign the assembly the lowest level of permissions possible. Another option is to consider raising the trust level for the virtual server extended with SharePoint. Yet another option is to create a custom security policy and assign the needed permissions to the specific assembly or set of assemblies.

> **Note** If you want to know more about raising the trust level for assemblies, you can refer to "Microsoft Windows SharePoint Services and Code Access Security" on MSDN.

If your code tries to write data to the WSS database on an HTTP Get, or if the code needs to enable Web Part to Web Part connections, your code might also need two other permissions specific to Microsoft SharePoint Products and Technologies: SharePointPermission.UnsafeSaveOnGet and WebPartPermission.Connections. If you want to use the classes and the members in the Microsoft.SharePoint.Portal.SingleSignOn namespace, your code will need an additional permission: SingleSignOnPermission.Access. Your code might also need one or more of the default .NET permissions if it tries to perform an action or access a resource that is protected by the common language runtime.

Changing trust levels for the virtual server is an easy approach to granting or revoking permissions. Changing the trust level is a global change affecting all assemblies. There might be situations in which an administrator might want to either grant more permissions or reduce the number of permissions granted to specific assemblies. To do this, you must create a custom code group and add this to the security policy file.

To create a custom security policy

To customize one of the built-in policy files, you should make a copy of one of the built-in policy files and make changes to the copy to ensure that you can reuse the original file if necessary. The following procedure describes how to give access to the Microsoft SharePoint object model to a specific assembly:

1. Copy the wss_minimaltrust.config file, which is located by default at <Local Drive>:\Program Files\Common Files\Microsoft Shared\Web Server Extensions\60\config\wss_minimaltrust.config.

2. Rename the file *new_file_name*.config.

3. Use a text editor to open *new_file_name*.config.

4. Under the <SecurityClasses> element, add a reference to the SharePointPermission class, as follows:

```
<SecurityClasses>
..
  <SecurityClass Name="SharePointPermission"
  Description="Microsoft.SharePoint.Security.SharePointPermission,
  Microsoft.SharePoint.Security,Version=11.0.0.0, Culture=neutral,
  PublicKeyToken=71e9bce111e9429c "/>
</SecurityClasses>
```

5. Search in your .config file for the <PermissionSet> element where the name attribute equals ASP.Net.

6. Copy this entire tag and all of its children, and paste a copy of it immediately following the one you copied.

```
<PermissionSet
  class="NamedPermissionSet"
  version="1"
  Name="new_permission_set_name">
</PermissionSet>
```

7. Add the following <IPermission> element to the <PermissionSet> element where the name attribute equals New_Permission_Set_Name:

```
<IPermission class="SharePointPermission" version="1" ObjectModel="True" />
```

8. Next you must create a code group to specify when the common language runtime should apply the permission set. By default, the AllCode code group is a FirstMatchCodeGroup in ASP.NET policy files. Therefore, the common language runtime stops assigning permissions to an assembly after the first match to a specific code group. To apply the custom permissions, you must declare the specific code group assigning the custom permissions to your assembly as the first code group within the AllCode group. This ensures that the common language runtime assigns your New_Permission_Set_Name permission set and stops without proceeding to the default $AppDirUrl$/* code group that is used to assign permissions based on whether the assembly is located in BIN directory. You can do this by adding the following <CodeGroup> element to your .config file. In the following example, the

membership condition for the new code group is based on strong-named member-ship. Therefore, the <IMembershipCondition> element contains a PublicKeyBlob attribute. The next step discusses how to obtain the public key blob.

```
<CodeGroup class="UnionCodeGroup" version="1" Permission-
  SetName="New_Permission_Set_Name">
  <IMembershipCondition class="StrongNameMembershipCondition"
    version="1" PublicKeyBlob=".. .." ="[see the next step]" Name="
      MyAssemblyName " /> </CodeGroup>
```

9. To retrieve the public key blob for an assembly, use the Secutil.exe tool as follows: `secutil.exe -hex -s MyAssemblyName.dll`

10. The Secutil tool extracts strong name information or the public key for an X.509 certificate from an assembly and converts this information into a format that can be incorporated into code. Please notice that the Secutil tool returns a string in the form of `""0X…"".…"`. You should not include the 0X notation marker when copying the public key blob to the policy file.

11. Save and close your .config file.

12. Open the Web.config file for your Windows SharePoint Services virtual server, and add the following <trustLevel> element:

```
<trustLevel name="MyCustomTrustLevel"
            policyFile="new_file_name.config" />
```

13. Go to the <trust> element in the Web.config file, and adjust it so that it refers to your custom trust level.

```
<trust level="MyCustomTrustLevel" originUrl="" />
```

14. Save and close the Web.config file, and run iisreset.

> **Caution**   Failing to run iisreset can result in the display of the following error message: "Assembly *AssemblyName* security permission grant set is incom-patible between app domains." In ASP.NET programs, strong-named assem-blies are loaded in a neutral domain. These assemblies are not unloaded until the process is stopped.
>
> Therefore, if the security policy for a strong-named assembly is altered, the common language runtime will cause an error message to appear when it detects that differing grant sets have been applied to the same assembly. This behavior typically occurs in scenarios where the trust level for a strong-named assembly has been changed.
>
> Another way to resolve this is to manually recycle the site's associated application pool in the Internet Services Manager for IIS. To do this, in IIS Manager, expand the local computer, expand Application Pools, right-click the application pool, and then click Recycle.

Creating a Web Part

In the "Web Part Architecture" section at the beginning of the chapter, you learned that a Web Part is a special kind of Web control that derives from the Microsoft.Share-Point.WebPartPages.WebPart class. If you first start developing Web Parts with Visual Studio.NET, you should download the Web Part template from the Microsoft Developer Network (MSDN). The installation of this template isn't mandatory, but it makes Web Part development a lot easier. The Web Part template provides support for both C# and Microsoft Visual Basic .NET development.

> **Note** If you want to know more about Web Part Templates you can also refer to the "SharePoint Products and Technologies Templates: Web Part Templates for Visual Studio .NET" white paper, which can be found on MSDN.

To create a new Web Part library project

After installing the Web Part template the creation of a Web Part is easy. You can use Visual Studio.NET to create a new Web Part library project. Web Part libraries contain Web Parts.

1. Start Visual Studio .NET.

2. On the **File** menu, point to **New** and then click **Project**.

3. In the **New Project** dialog box, click **Visual C# Projects** and then select the **Web Part Library** template.

> **Tip** If you want to create a Visual Basic .NET project, select the Web Part Library template from Visual Basic Projects instead.

Now a reference to the Microsoft.SharePoint DLL is added and a Web Part class and a.dwp file are created. The default name of the Web Part class is WebPart1.cs. This class does not need much work before it can be used; just locate the RenderWebPart method and replace SPEncode.HtmlEncode(Text) with SPEncode.HtmlEncode("Hello World!") then you will be ready to create your first Web Part. The RenderWebPart method is shown below (in C#).

```
/// <summary>
/// Render this Web Part to the output parameter specified.
/// </summary>
/// <param name="output"> The HTML writer to write out to </param>
```

```
protected override void RenderWebPart(HtmlTextWriter output)
{
  output.Write("SPEncode.HtmlEncode("Hello World!"));
}
```

> **Note**   In this example, the use of SPEncode.HtmlEncode is superfluous, but in general you should HTML encode your strings so that script injection bugs are avoided at all times.

Next you should create a name for the Web Part so that it can be identified uniquely. Strong naming the Web Part library assembly is a crucial step in accomplishing this.

To create a strong name key pair file

The first step you need to take if you want to strong name an assembly is generating a strong name key pair file, which can be done using the Strong Name tool (sn.exe), which is installed with the .NET Framework SDK.

1. Create a file containing the key pair. From a command prompt on the drive where you installed Visual Studio .NET, type the following: `cd \Program Files\Microsoft Visual Studio .NET\FrameworkSDK\Bin\` or `\Program Files\Microsoft Visual Studio.NET 2003 \SDK\v1.1\Bin` if you are using Visual Studio.NET 2003.

2. Type the following: `sn.exe -k c:\mykey.snk`

3. Next open the AssemblyInfo.cs file to set the version number of the assembly. Remember, the version number is also a part of the assembly name. The following code shows how to use the AssemblyVersion property to set the version number of the assembly to 1.0.0.0.

    `[assembly: AssemblyVersion("1.0.0.0")]`

It is best to set the version number to a known value instead of using a wildcard (*) for the minor parts. When a Web Part is added to the page, Windows SharePoint Services uses the assembly's full name to determine the Web Part type. As long as the version number does not change, Windows SharePoint Services will always be able to find Web Part X, version V, from assembly Y. This information is stored in the SharePoint database. If you are using a wildcard the version number is changed the next time you compile your assembly. At that point, you will have Web Part X, version Q, from assembly Y, which does not match to the record in the SharePoint database. This results in a mismatch stating that the Web Part is not safe.

Adjust the AssemblyKeyFile property so that it refers to the strong name key pair file to make sure the name of the assembly is unique after compilation.

`[assembly: AssemblyKeyFile(@"c:\mykey.snk")]`

There are two default locations where the .NET common language runtime will look for .NET assemblies when operating within the context of a WSS-extended server. One of them is the Global Assembly Cache, and the other one is the bin directory of your WSS extended virtual server root directory (for example, the c:\inetpub\wwwroot \bin folder).

To specify the build output path

During Web Part development, changing the build output path to the BIN folder of your SharePoint virtual server is recommended so that you don't have to copy the assembly file every time after compilation.

1. In the **Solution Explorer**, right-click your project name, and then click **Properties**.

2. Under **Configuration Properties\Build\Outputs**, set the **Output Path** to the Bin folder within the root folder of the Windows SharePoint Services extended virtual server, for example: c:\inetpub\wwwroot\bin.

Deploying a Web Part

Now you are ready to compile the Web Part. However, before you're able to use the Web Part, there are a couple of steps left that you need to take. The <SafeControls> section of the Web.config file specifies which Web Parts are trusted. So, you need to register your own Web Part as a safe control. The following code shows an example of the <SafeControls> section:

```
<SafeControls>
  ..
  <SafeControl Assembly="Microsoft.SharePoint.Solutions.GreatPlains, Version=11.0.0.0,
    Culture=neutral, PublicKeyToken=71e9bce111e9429c" Namespace="Microsoft.SharePoint
      .Solutions.GreatPlains" TypeName="*" Safe="True" />
  <SafeControl Assembly="Microsoft.SharePoint.WebParts.QuickQuote, Version=11.0.0.0,
    Culture=neutral, PublicKeyToken=71e9bce111e9429c" Namespace="Microsoft.SharePoint
      .WebParts.QuickQuote" TypeName="*" Safe="True" />
</SafeControls>
```

The Assembly attribute of the <SafeControl> element shows the assembly name of the Web Part assembly, and optionally a version number, a culture reference, and a public key token. Now you should determine the public key token of your Web Part library assembly so that you can create a safe control entry for your Web Part in the Web.config file. The easiest way to accomplish this is to copy the assembly DLL file into the Global Assembly Cache. Locate the DLL file, right-click the DLL, and copy the public key token. After this, don't forget to remove the assembly .DLL file from the Global Assembly Cache. You could also use the Strong Name tool (SN.exe) to obtain the public key token.

1. From a command prompt on the drive where you installed Visual Studio .NET, type the following: cd \Program Files\Microsoft Visual Studio .NET\FrameworkSDK\Bin\ or \Program Files\Microsoft Visual Studio.NET 2003\SDK\v1.1\Bin if you are using Visual Studio.NET 2003.

2. Type the following: `sn.exe -T [MyAssemblyPath\MyAssemblyName.dll]`

Note   The –T flag is case sensitive. Only the –T (in uppercase) will give you the correct public key token.

3. Next, create your own <SafeControl> element. The following example shows a Web Part library named *ResKitLibrary* in the ResKitLibrary namespace.

```
<SafeControl Assembly="ResKitLibrary, Version=1.0.0.0, Culture=neutral, Public-
    KeyToken=3fab337e00400dc5" Namespace="ResKitLibraryNamespace" TypeName="*"
    Safe="True" />
```

Before you can import your Web Part on a Web Part Page, you need to create a Web Part Definition (.dwp) file. The .dwp file is an XML file that contains property settings for a Web Part. The most important properties when installing a Web Part in the .dwp file are the <Assembly> and <TypeName> elements. The <Assembly> element contains the assembly name, simple or full, of the Web Part assembly; the <TypeName> element contains the full type name for the Web Part. The following code shows the content of an example .DWP file:

```
<?xml version="1.0" encoding="utf-8"?>
<WebPart xmlns="http://schemas.microsoft.com/WebPart/v2" >
  <Title>TestPart</Title>
  <Description>Our TestPart</Description>
  <Assembly>ResKitLibrary, Version=1.0.0.0, Culture=neutral,
    PublicKeyToken=3fab337e00400dc5</Assembly>
  <TypeName>ResKitLibrary.TestPart</TypeName>
</WebPart>
```

Now, for the final stage, you're ready to import the Web Part into a Web Part Page.

To import your Web Part into a Web Part Page

To import your Web Part into a Web Part Page, simply upload the .dwp file. After uploading the Web Part, you can display the Web Part by dragging it into one of the zones of the Web Part Page.

1. Open a Web Part Page on your server.

2. Click Modify My Page or Modify Shared Page (depending on whether you are in Personal View or Shared View) in the upper-right corner of the page, and click Add Web Parts from the menu.

3. Click Import.

4. Browse to the location of your .dwp file and click the Upload button. After uploading, the page will refresh and your Web Part should be displayed under Imported Web Part.

5. Drag the icon next to your Web Part to a zone on the Web Part Page.

The end result is shown in Figure 37-2.

Figure 37-2   The end result

> **More Info**   If you want to know more about Web Part Deployment, you can also refer to the "Using Wppackager to Package and Deploy Web Parts for Microsoft SharePoint Products and Technologies" white paper, which can be found on MSDN, and "Web Part Assembly Deployment."

Debugging Web Parts

The previous "Hello, World!" Web Part example was simple to create in terms of code. As soon as you start doing serious Web Part development, you will need the available Web Part debugging techniques.

When debugging Web Parts, there are two important questions to ask. The first question concerns how you wish to attach to the process that runs your Web Part: either manually or automatically. The other question depends on who is generating the symbol table (.pdb), to which the debugger must have access to debug the code: you or ASP.NET.

If you want to start the debugging process manually and you already have code-behind assemblies and a symbol table in place, you do not have to change any settings within Visual Studio .NET. In this scenario, you will not be able to debug inline code.

If you want to debug code within the .aspx page itself and you want ASP.NET to generate the symbol table, for any pages that it compiles you need to set the trust level in the Web.config file to at least WSS_Medium.

If you want Visual Studio .NET to automatically attach itself to the process that runs your Web Part, you need to set the debugging settings to true. You can do this by setting the debug attribute of the <compilation> element in the Web.config file to True, like this: `<compilation batch="false" debug="true" />`. You should also make sure that debugging is enabled for your Web Part library project. You can do this by right-clicking the project name in the Solution Explorer and choosing **Properties**. Then choose **Configuration Properties | \Debugging**, and set **Enable ASP.NET Debugging** to True.

The next step in the debugging process, regardless of the scenario that applies to you, is to set breakpoints in your code. For example, the RenderWebPart method would be a good place to set a breakpoint. You can set breakpoints by opening your Web Part assembly in Visual Studio.NET, going to the line of code where you want to enter a breakpoint, right-clicking the line, and then clicking **Insert Breakpoint**.

To manually attach to the process

You can manually attach to the W3wp.exe process to debug your Web Part. This method is less useful in situations where you are in the middle of a repeated development and debugging cycle. On the other hand, this method is extremely helpful in situations where you are attempting to debug code access security–related problems. In a scenario in which you are automatically attaching to a process, you might have to artificially raise the trust level (to at least WSS_Medium). This could possibly hide security exceptions that might be encountered only at lower trust levels.

1. Set up a Web Part Page with the Web Part you want to debug on your local SharePoint server.

2. Attach the debugger to the ASP.NET process: W3wp.exe.

   a. On the **Debug** menu, click **Processes**.

   b. Select the **Show system processes** and **Show processes in all sessions** check boxes.

   c. In the **Available Processes** list, select **W3wp.exe** and then click **Attach**.

   d. In the **Attach to Process** dialog box, select **Common Language Runtime** and then click **OK**.

   e. Click **Close**.

You are now ready to step through your code.

To use a start-up page and automatically attach to the process

You can automatically attach to the W3wp.exe process for debugging purposes. This method is probably the one you will use most often during Web Part development.

1. Right-click the project name in the Solution Explorer, and then click **Properties**.

2. Click **Configuration Properties**, and then click **Debugging**.

3. Under **Start Action**, set **Debug Mode** to **URL** and then set **Start URL** to the URL of the Web Part Page that uses your Web Part.

4. Click **OK**, and then save your project.

5. On the **Debug** menu, click **Start**. The debugger should launch the browser with your Web Part Page, attach to the process, and allow you to debug automatically.

After attaching to the W3wp.exe process, you are now ready to step through the code. Request the Web Part Page with the target Web Part in it. As the Web Part Page and the Web Part render, depending on where the breakpoint is set you will notice that the control switches to the Visual Studio debugger. Once the control is in the debugger, you can step through the code and identify the problem by using the debugger's available functionality.

Using the CallStack Attribute

Windows SharePoint Services overrides the CallStack attribute. This attribute is located in the Web.config file. The CallStack attribute controls whether a call stack and an exception message are displayed when a system-level exception occurs while ASP.NET processes a request to send a page to all local and remote clients. By default, Windows SharePoint Services disables the CallStack attribute and displays a limited set of exceptions to prevent information disclosure.

To enable the CallStack attribute

To receive a call stack and an exception message when an exception occurs, enable the CallStack attribute.

1. In Windows Explorer, browse to the root folder of the Windows SharePoint Services extended virtual server, for example: local_drive:\InetPub\wwwroot\bin\.

2. Double-click the **Web.config** file.

3. In the Web.config file, search for the <SharePoint> element.

4. In the <SharePoint> element, locate the <SafeMode MaxControls="50" CallStack="false"/> tag and change it to <SafeMode MaxControls="50" CallStack="true"/>.

5. Save and close the file.

When exceptions occur, you now receive ASP.NET exception messages with stack trace information.

> **Note**   The CallStack attribute enables this functionality for all local and remote clients.

Using Tracing in ASP.NET

You can use the tracing feature in ASP.NET to monitor the environment of the server on which you are programming. You can use tracing on a specific page or for an entire application.

To enable ASP.NET tracing on a local server

You can use tracing on a local server computer without enabling it for remote clients.

1. In Windows Explorer, browse to the root folder of the Windows SharePoint Services extended virtual server, for example: local_drive:\InetPub\wwwroot\bin\.

2. Double-click the Web.config file.

3. In the Web.config file, search for the <system.web> element.

4. In the <system.web> element, add the following line:

   ```
   <trace enabled="true" pageOutput="true"/>
   ```

5. Save and close the file.

The environment information now appears at the bottom of the test page that includes the Web Part.

Creating Child Controls on a Web Part

Now that you've seen how to create a simple Web Part and how to debug a Web Part you're ready for the next level: creating child controls on a Web Part. This provides you with the possibility to create more sophisticated Web Parts. This section describes how to add TextBox and Button controls to a Web Part.

The first thing you need to do is to declare two member variables at the top of the Web Part class named myTextBox and myButton, like this:

```
private TextBox myTextBox;
private Button myButton;
```

> **Tip**   Make sure you have added the System.Web.UI.WebControls namespace.

Next you need to override the CreateChildControls method, which is the place to instantiate child controls, initialize them, and add them to the control tree. The CreateChildControls method is called automatically by the framework. The following code example shows a CreateChildControls method that can be copied into a Web Part class. The method adds two controls to the control tree: a TextBox control and a Button control. The Click event of the button control is associated with an event handler named myButton_Click.

```
protected override void CreateChildControls ()
{
  myTextBox = new TextBox();
  myTextBox.Text = "hi!";
  Controls.Add(myTextBox);
  myButton = new Button();
  myButton.Text = "Push the button!";
  myButton.Click += new System.EventHandler(myButton_Click);
  Controls.Add (myButton);
}
```

The implementation of the event handler depends very much on your specific needs. The following example can be copied into a Web Part class and shows how to retrieve the value of the TextBox control:

```
private void myButton_Click(object sender, System.EventArgs e)
{
  string strValue = myTextBox.Text;
}
```

Remember that the Render method of the WebPart class is responsible for adding the frame around the content provided by the Web Part, so you should not override the Render method. Instead, you should override the RenderWebPart method, which is called by the Render method. The RenderWebPart method is called whenever the Web Part needs to be displayed, so it is called every time the Web Part Page that contains your Web Part is called.

If you are not sure about the control execution life cycle, you can call the Ensure-ChildControls method from any code that needs to access a child control. The Ensure-ChildControls method checks whether the child controls have been created. If the child controls have not been created, it invokes the CreateChildControls method.

> **More Info**   If you want to know more about the control execution life cycle, you can also refer to the "Control Execution Life Cycle" white paper, which can be found on MSDN.

The RenderWebPart is also the place to call the RenderChildren method, which renders the children of a Web Part control into an HtmlTextWriter object. The following code shows a basic RenderWebPart implementation that makes sure the TextBox and Button controls are rendered.

```
protected override void RenderWebPart(HtmlTextWriter output)
{
  EnsureChildControls();
  RenderChildren(output);
}
```

Figure 37-3   A Web Part with child controls

This concludes the section about creating child controls on a Web Part. A Web Part is a special kind of ASP.NET Web control, so if you need more information about this topic you can read more on developing ASP.NET Web controls on MSDN.

Web Part Caching

One of the factors that separate a great Web Part from an average Web Part is performance. You can enhance performance by caching data. You should not use the ASP.NET Session state in Web Parts because the current implementation of the Safe-Mode parser does not allow Session state to be defined at the page level as is possible with the ASP.NET parser. This means the administrator can enable Session state for all Web Part Pages or for none of them. Enabling Session state for all pages degrades server performance.

Instead you can use the Web Part cache to store data to enhance performance. The Web Part cache can be used in different modes: None, Database, and CacheObject. The None mode disables caching. In the Database mode, all data is stored in the SharePoint database. In this mode, Shared and Personal cache entries are limited to 2 MB. If this limit is exceeded, the cache entry will be lost, and no error will be displayed. Personal storage data will be charged against the user's quota. The final Web Part cache mode, the CacheObjectMode, uses the ASP.NET cache object to store data. This is also the default mode of the Web Part cache object. Only administrators—not developers—can set the cache type using the <WebPartCache> element in the <SharePoint> section of the Web.config file, like this:

```
<SharePoint>
  ..
  <WebPartCache Storage="CacheObject" />
</SharePoint>
```

You can use the CacheType property of the WebPart class to determine the type of caching used by the Web server. This property is read-only, so it cannot be used to change the type of caching. Developers can retrieve the cache type at run time using the following code:

```
if ( CacheType == CacheType.None )
{
  output.Write("Caching is disabled.");
}
else
{
  output.Write("Caching is enabled.");
}
```

The PartCacheWrite method of the WebPart class stores a value in the Web Part cache. You need to provide this method with a storage type (None, Personal, or Shared). You also need to provide a key-value pair and determine how long you want to keep a value stored in the Web Part cache. The following code example shows how to write data to the Web Part cache:

```
PartCacheWrite(Storage.Shared, "mykey", "myvalue", TimeSpan.FromMinutes(5));
```

The PartCacheRead method of the WebPart class can be used to retrieve values from the Web Part cache again. This is shown in the following code example:

```
String strValue = PartCacheRead(Storage.Shared, "mykey").ToString();
```

The PartCacheInvalidate method of the WebPart class can be used to outdate data in the Web Part cache. You can either outdate all contents of the Web Part cache, outdate contents of a specific storage type, or mark only a specified cache value of a specified storage type as outdated. The following code example shows how to outdate a specific cache value and storage type:

```
PartCacheInvalidate(Storage.Shared, "mykey");
```

Web Part Tools

Already several tools exist that can help you during Web Part development. MSDN and the Resource Kit CD-ROM contain valuable aids. The tools that are most relevant to this chapter are discussed briefly in this section.

- **GhostHunter.**   The GhostHunter Web Part identifies all ghosted pages on a site and optionally reverts unghosted pages back to their original form.

- **InstallAssemblies.**   This is an assembly installation tool for Windows SharePoint Services. It is designed for use within development environments. The tool can be used to deploy packages using the AddWPPack functionality of the Stsadm.exe tool, which is discussed in detail in Chapter 31. The tool can also install assemblies using traditional XCopy methods.

- **Plex.exe.**   This tool is useful when using the backward-compatible document library. Plex.exe can be used for Web Storage System–based document libraries to view document properties.

- **SharePoint Configuration Analyzer (sca.exe).**   SharePoint Configuration Analyzer is a diagnostic tool that verifies settings on your server that are critical to running Microsoft Windows SharePoint Services or Microsoft SharePoint Portal Server and to hosting Web Parts on your server. SharePoint Configuration Analyzer also reports on Web Part usage on your server and retrieves a set of log files, configuration files, and Web Part packages used by Windows SharePoint Services and Internet Information Services (IIS).

- **SharePoint Explorer (spex.exe).**   If you come from a SharePoint Portal Server 2001 background you will be familiar with this tool, which is known under different names: Platinum Explorer, plex.exe, WSS Explorer, or Exchange Explorer. SharePoint Explorer is the first cousin of this tool, and it can be used to view Web Part and Web Part Page properties.

- **UberConnector.**   The UberConnector Web Part offers a flexible way of exposing and hooking into various connection interfaces. This tool is valuable when creating connectable Web Parts.

- **WebPartDeployment tool.**   This tool can be used to import and delete Web Part Packages.

- **Wppackager.**   Use Wppackager to package and deploy Web Parts for use with SharePoint Products and Technologies. Wppackager can be downloaded from MSDN.

Summary

This chapter shows the basics you need to be aware of to be successful in Web Part development. It discusses the Web Part architecture. After that, the chapter explains what strong naming is and the role it plays in doing Web Part development. Next, the chapter details how to adjust the trust policy so that code identity–based security allows your Web Parts to do what they need to do—nothing more, nothing less. Then, the chapter shows how to build a basic "Hello, world!" Web Part and how to import this Web Part into a Web Part Page. It also shows how to create Web Parts that are more sophisticated by showing how to create Web Part child controls. The chapter concludes with an explanation of Web Part caching.

Part X

Microsoft Office 2003 Integration with SharePoint Products and Technologies

Chapter 38

Windows SharePoint Services with the Microsoft Office System

Microsoft Windows SharePoint Services provides the collaborative backbone to a Microsoft Office system. Sharing and managing documents and data are only part of what can be done with Windows SharePoint Services. You can create SharePoint sites from your Office applications as part of your regular work routine, so you can be more productive without needing extensive training or specialized technical knowledge.

You can use Web services included as part of Windows SharePoint Services to interact directly with Windows SharePoint Services, or use the Shared Workspace object model to build document-centric collaborative solutions.

As with Microsoft Office, Windows SharePoint Services delivers a solid core of functionality that you can extend with your own code. Such features as Document Workspace sites and Meeting Workspace sites enable users to share data seamlessly, cooperate on tasks, and exchange e-mail and instant messages without leaving their familiar Microsoft Office applications.

Windows SharePoint Services and Microsoft Office Integration Features

This chapter focuses on areas where you can begin to integrate Windows SharePoint Services with the Microsoft Office applications. Topics covered include:

- **Integration with Access.**   You can export tables from Microsoft Office Access 2003 to SharePoint lists, and you can import or link SharePoint lists to database tables in Access 2003.

- **Integration with Excel.**   You can use new integration features in Microsoft Office Excel 2003 to access, analyze, and manipulate data stored on SharePoint sites. Excel 2003 provides two-way synchronization between Excel spreadsheets and SharePoint lists, so you can work with lists when you are offline and then synchronize the changes when you reconnect. Additionally, you can export Excel data to a SharePoint site as a custom list.

- **Integration with Outlook.**   Users typically use e-mail to share much of their work, so Windows SharePoint Services provides extensive integration with Microsoft Office Outlook 2003. On a Contacts list or Events list SharePoint site, you can click Link To Outlook to create a read-only contact or calendar folder in Outlook 2003. This folder is synchronized with the online list whenever you use Outlook to connect to the SharePoint site. Additionally, when you receive a Windows SharePoint Services alert, the alert contains additional information that Outlook 2003 can use to run enhanced rules for sorting and filing your alerts.

- **Integration with FrontPage.**   You can use Microsoft Office FrontPage 2003 to modify and customize the look and feel of SharePoint sites. With FrontPage 2003, you can manage list views, edit pages, add Web Parts to pages, and design templates for SharePoint sites. FrontPage 2003 also includes reporting capabilities that you can use for tracking and reporting site page data and usage statistics.

Table 38-1 shows Windows SharePoint Services integration features for each program in Office 2003.

Table 38-1   Windows SharePoint Services Integration Features

Feature Overview	Microsoft Office Programs
Open and Save from File menu	Excel, FrontPage, InfoPath, Microsoft Project, OneNote, Outlook, PowerPoint, Publisher, Visio, Word
Shared Workspace task pane	Excel, Microsoft Project, OneNote, PowerPoint, Visio, Word
Create shared attachment	Outlook
Synchronize calendar and contact list sites	Outlook

Table 38-1   Windows SharePoint Services Integration Features   *(continued)*

Feature Overview	Microsoft Office Programs
Document updates for shared attachments	Excel, PowerPoint, Visio, Word
Automatically collect metadata	Excel, PowerPoint, Word
Check in and check out	Excel, PowerPoint, Word
Version tracking	Excel, PowerPoint, Word
Store inline discussions on the server	Excel, PowerPoint, Word
Import SharePoint list as data	Access, Excel
Export data as SharePoint list	Access, Excel

Microsoft Office Access 2003 Integration

Using the Microsoft Office System, you can interact with Windows SharePoint Services data programmatically. A good starting point is with support in Microsoft Office Access 2003 of SharePoint lists.

From within Access, you can treat a SharePoint list just like any other data source. You can import data from Windows SharePoint Services, export Access data to a SharePoint site, or link Windows SharePoint Services data to an Access database.

As with other data sources, Access uses the DoCmd.TransferDatabase method to interact with SharePoint lists. For example, to export a table to a Windows SharePoint Services database, you can use this syntax:

```
DoCmd.TransferDatabase acExport, "Windows SharePoint Services", _
 "http://server_name/sites/site_name", _
 acTable, "Customers", "Customers"
```

The previous example exports the Customers table from the current database to a SharePoint list, also named Customers, on the specified SharePoint site.

To import a SharePoint list to Access or to add a link to a SharePoint list from an Access database, you can also use the TransferDatabase method, but the syntax is somewhat more complex. Here's a Microsoft Visual Basic for Applications command to add a link to a SharePoint list named Parts:

```
DoCmd.TransferDatabase acLink, "Windows SharePoint Services", _
 "WSS;HDR=NO;IMEX=2;" & _
 "DATABASE=http://server_name/sites/site_name;" & _
 "LIST={800BE2B7-FA3C-4CFC-BBB3-8500C4EDCF22};" & _
 "VIEW=;RetrieveIds=Yes;TABLE=Parts", acTable, , _
 "Parts"
```

The difficulty in constructing this command is that Windows SharePoint Services uses globally unique identifiers (GUIDs) to identify lists. For example, that's how it stores ten different Contact lists in the same database. When you use Access to import or add link data in Windows SharePoint Services, it matches the names to the GUIDs.

When you interact with the Jet engine directly through VBA, you need to match them manually. The long string in the example that starts with `"Windows SharePoint Services"` and ends with `"TABLE=Parts"` identifies a particular SharePoint list.

To programmatically import or add links to data in Windows SharePoint Services, there are two ways to identify the correct GUID. The easy way is to add a link manually between the desired SharePoint list and the Access database, and then open the linked table in design view. The Description property of the linked table contains the necessary linking string. Obviously, this is less than useful when linking to arbitrary lists. You can also use the Windows SharePoint Services Web service interface to Windows SharePoint Services, which exposes a Lists.GetList method. This method gets the name of a list on a specified SharePoint site and returns detailed information, including the GUID that identifies the list. The Windows SharePoint Services Web service interface is discussed in more detail later in this document.

If you created a link between a SharePoint list and an Access database, you can work with it just like any other table. You can execute SQL statements to retrieve or change data, or open a Recordset and manipulate the list programmatically. Access treats the SharePoint list similar to another table and all the table-oriented code you already know works. An optimistic locking model coordinates concurrency issues, such as when two users work with the same data at the same time between Windows SharePoint Services and Access.

Microsoft Office Excel 2003 Integration

Microsoft Office Excel 2003 also integrates with SharePoint lists by implementing an extension to the Excel 2003 object model to make working with lists distinct from other activities. The Worksheet object in Excel is extended with a ListObjects collection that contains individual ListObject objects. The ListObject contains collections of ListColumns and ListRows, and the individual ListColumn and ListRow objects have properties that tie them to Excel Range objects.

By default, the ListObjects collection contains native Excel 2003 lists. But you can hook up one of these lists to a SharePoint site by calling the Publish method of the corresponding ListObject object.

To create a list from the rectangular area extending from A1 to C8, you could run the following VBA code:

```
Public Sub PublishList()
    ' Get the collection of lists for the active sheet
    Dim L As ListObjects
    Set L = ActiveSheet.ListObjects
    ' Add a new list
    Dim NewList As ListObject
    Set NewList = L.Add(xlSrcRange, Range("A1:C8"), , True)
    NewList.Name = "PartsList"
    ' Publish it to a SharePoint site
    NewList.Publish Array("http://server_name/sites/site_name", _
    "NewParts"), True
End Sub
```

When adding the list, the third parameter indicates that this particular list has headers. When the list is published, Windows SharePoint Services uses these headers as column names for the list. The second argument to the Publish method of the ListObject object indicates that this list is linked to the SharePoint list. This enables the use of the Refresh and UpdateChanges methods to keep the two versions of the list synchronized.

The Refresh method copies the current schema and data from the SharePoint list to the worksheet. For example:

```
Public Sub RefreshList()
    ActiveSheet.ListObjects("PartsList").Refresh
End Sub
```

Any unsaved changes you make to the data in the worksheet are overwritten when you call the Refresh method.

The UpdateChanges method is more complex. If a value in the worksheet changes, UpdateChanges copies it to the SharePoint list. If a value in the SharePoint list changes, the method copies the change to the worksheet. But what happens if both values change? The method detects the conflict and acts on it according to a parameter that you supply. For example, you can leave the decision to the user by calling the UpdateChanges method this way:

```
Public Sub UpdateList()
    ActiveSheet.ListObjects("PartsList").UpdateChanges (xlListConflictDialog)
End Sub
```

With the xlListConflictDialog constant supplied, Excel displays a dialog box if it detects any conflicts between the local version of the data and the version on the SharePoint list. The user decides how to resolve these conflicts.

You can control the behavior of the UpdateChanges method by specifying the following constants:

- **xlListConflictDiscardAllConflicts.**   Indicates to accept the version of the data stored on the SharePoint list

- **xlListConflictError.**   Indicates to raise an error if a conflict occurs

- **xlListConflictRetryAllConflicts.**   Indicates to overwrite the version of the data stored on the SharePoint list

Integration with Outlook

Microsoft Office Word 2003, Microsoft Office Excel 2003, Microsoft Office Power-Point 2003, and other applications are great for composing documents, one of the primary collaboration benefits that Windows SharePoint Services provides. But, true collaboration is really about communicating, a great portion of which is done in Microsoft Office Outlook 2003.

You can synchronize your data in Microsoft Office Outlook 2003 with data from Windows SharePoint Services, so you can keep a local copy of Outlook items from your SharePoint site. Calendar synchronization with Outlook 2003 works only in one direction—from Windows SharePoint Services to Outlook 2003. After you synchronize with the team calendar on a SharePoint site, you can work offline and view the synchronized data side by side with other personal calendars or shared calendars.

Windows SharePoint Services automatically updates the synchronized data in Outlook 2003. The synchronization occurs from Outlook—so at regularly timed intervals or when a refresh of the folder is forced, a refresh will occur by navigating to the folder in Outlook or by selecting Refresh after clicking on the folder in Outlook. Of course, for the synchronization to succeed, you will need to have access to the site.

This feature can help you be more productive, especially if you are a mobile user. You can quickly create a contact list in Windows SharePoint Services by importing contacts from the global address list in Outlook. You can quickly import contacts from the global address list in Outlook by selecting Import Contacts on a Windows SharePoint Services contacts list.

Integration with FrontPage

Microsoft Office FrontPage 2003 is a Web editor that is fully integrated with Windows SharePoint Services. FrontPage 2003 provides a variety of WYSIWYG tools you can use to customize and manage your SharePoint sites, including an improved table editing tool and a collection of dynamic templates for SharePoint sites. With FrontPage 2003, you can edit and control SharePoint site components (for example, team sites, Web Parts, or navigation) and customize the look and feel of a SharePoint site.

You can also use FrontPage 2003 to prepare usage analysis reports for SharePoint sites so that you can track who is using your site and how they are using it. To edit Web pages in a SharePoint site, you must be a member of a site group with the Add And Customize Pages right for that SharePoint site.

With FrontPage 2003, you can use Windows SharePoint Services and Web Parts to create data-driven websites. Web Parts are reusable, modular pieces of code that you can easily add to SharePoint sites. You can use FrontPage 2003 to create Web Parts that connect to live data from a variety of sources. For example, to add current company sales data to your SharePoint site, you can use FrontPage 2003 to create a Web Part that is linked to your company sales database.

FrontPage 2003 includes some powerful productivity tools for developing websites built on Windows SharePoint Services and ASP.NET database-driven Web applications.

FrontPage 2003 has the capacity to easily insert Web Part zones, which are regions in a page where Web Parts can reside and which can be controlled by the user. In addition, FrontPage 2003 has WYSIWYG tools for performing drag-and-drop operations with Web Parts and it has a gallery of ready-made Web Parts from which to select.

The Data View Web Part can display data from a variety of data sources, including traditional databases, XML data sources, and Web services. You can use FrontPage 2003 to create custom Data views and to link Data views together.

WYSIWYG XSLT Web Editor

Data View Web Parts use the power of XML and XSL to create Extensible Stylesheet Language Transformations (XSLT). XSLT is used to obtain the granular level of formatting.

Editing detailed XSLT can be a time-consuming and tedious task. Below is just a snippet of the XSLT code:

```
<xsl:template name="dvt_1.body">
    <xsl:param name="Rows"/>
    <xsl:param name="FirstRow"/>
    <xsl:param name="LastRow"/>
    <xsl:for-each select="$Rows">
        <xsl:variable name="KeepItemsTogether" select="false()"/>
        <xsl:variable name="HideGroupDetail" select="false()"/>
        <xsl:variable name="GroupStyle" select="'auto'"/>
        <xsl:if test="true()">
            <xsl:if test="not($HideGroupDetail)" ddwrt:cf_ignore="1">
                <tr>
                    <xsl:attribute name="style">display:auto;<xsl:if
                        test="position() mod 2">
background-color: #EEF0C6;</xsl:if></xsl:attribute>
                        <td class="ms-vb" style="font-family: Arial; font-
                        size: 10pt; color:#333399">
<xsl:value-of select="@ProductName"/></td>
                        <td class="ms-vb" style="font-family: Arial; font-
                        size: 10pt; color:#333399">
<xsl:value-of select="format-number(@Quantity, '#,##0.#;-#,##0.#')"/></td>
                        <td class="ms-vb" style="font-family: Arial; font-
                        size: 10pt; color:#333399">
<xsl:value-of select="ddwrt:FormatDate(string(/dsQueryResponse/Rows/Row/
    @OrderDate) ,1033 ,1)"/></td>
                </tr>
            </xsl:if>
        </xsl:if>
    </xsl:for-each>
</xsl:template>
```

With FrontPage 2003, you never have to look at the XSLT code if you don't want to (although you can if you want more control). Instead, you can work with an array of visual tools that enable you to apply styles in the same manner as you would apply formatting in previous versions of FrontPage and in other Microsoft Office programs.

In addition, special tools are included such as the ability to use conditional formatting, which allows you to apply styles according to conditions. For example, the alternating row colors could be achieved by applying a rule regarding whether the row number was even or odd.

Table 38-2   Integration Features Between Windows SharePoint Services and Each Version of Microsoft Office

Feature	Office 2000	Office Windows XP	Office 2003 Editions
Save and open files from SharePoint sites	Yes (Excel, FrontPage, PowerPoint, Project, Word)	Yes (Excel, FrontPage, PowerPoint, Project, Visio, Word)	Enhanced (Excel, FrontPage, InfoPath, OneNote, Outlook, PowerPoint, Project, Publisher, Visio, Word)
Create new documents in Web browser	No	Yes (Excel, FrontPage, PowerPoint, Word)	Yes (Excel, FrontPage, InfoPath, PowerPoint, Project, Publisher, Word)
Collect metadata automatically	No	No	Enhanced (Excel, PowerPoint, Word)
Promote and demote file properties and metadata automatically	Data stored, but not displayed (Excel, FrontPage, PowerPoint, Word)	Yes (Excel, FrontPage, PowerPoint, Word)	Enhanced (Excel, FrontPage, InfoPath, PowerPoint, Visio, Word)
Track document versions	No. Use Web browser to view and manage document versions.	No. Use Web browser to view and manage document versions.	Enhanced (Excel, PowerPoint, Visio, Word)
Check out and check in documents	No. Use Web browser to manually check out and check in documents.	No. Use Web browser to manually check out and check in documents.	Enhanced (Excel, PowerPoint, Visio, Word). Use Web browser to manually check out and check in other types of documents.
Manage Microsoft Project documents, risks, and issues	No	No	Yes
Upload multiple documents	No	No	Yes
Inline discussions	Yes	Yes	Yes
Microsoft Office Components for SharePoint Products and Technologies	No	No	Yes
Person Names Smart Tag	No	No	Yes
Integration with Microsoft Business Solutions	No	No	Yes

Table 38-2   **Integration Features Between Windows SharePoint Services and Each Version of Microsoft Office**   *(continued)*

Feature	Office 2000	Office Windows XP	Office 2003 Editions
Document Workspace Sites			
Shared attachments	No	No	Outlook attachments
Create Document Workspace sites automatically	No	No	Yes, with shared attachments
Shared Workspace task pane	No	No	Yes (Excel, OneNote, PowerPoint, Project, Visio, Word)
Document updates for shared attachments	No	No	Yes (Excel, PowerPoint, Visio, Word)
View and edit a shared attachment	Yes	Yes	Yes
Meeting Workspace Sites			
Create Meeting Workspace sites automatically	No	No	Yes (Outlook meeting, or from SharePoint events list)
Outlook Integration			
Synchronize calendar and contact list sites	No	No	Yes (Outlook)
Alerts	Yes	Yes	Yes, improved (alerts on lists, more alert information)
Alert integration with Outlook	No	No	Yes (Outlook)
Excel Integration			
Two-way synchronization with SharePoint lists	No	No	Yes
Export list data to Excel spreadsheet	No	Yes	Yes
Create custom list from Excel spreadsheet	No	No	Yes

Table 38-2 Integration Features Between Windows SharePoint Services and Each Version of Microsoft Office *(continued)*

Feature	Office 2000	Office Windows XP	Office 2003 Editions
Access Integration			
Link table to SharePoint list	No	No	Yes
Export list data to Access database table	No	No	Yes
Create custom list from Access database table	No	No	Yes
FrontPage Integration			
Edit and customize Windows SharePoint Services websites	No	No	Yes
Create and customize data-driven Web Part Pages	No	No	Yes
Solution packages	No	No	Yes
Browse and search Web Part galleries	No	No	Yes
Manage list views	No	No	Yes
Design templates	No	No	Yes
Web Part connections	No	No	Yes
Back up and restore site	No	No	Yes
InfoPath Integration			
Business Document Library	N/A	N/A	Yes
Edit documents in InfoPath	N/A	N/A	Yes
Aggregate business reports	N/A	N/A	Yes

Summary

Microsoft Office and Windows SharePoint Services are natural partners in a synergistic, context-rich sharing environment. Microsoft Office 2003 provides a full range of productivity tools that are easy to use. Windows SharePoint Services provides a shared work environment that includes libraries for storing documents, lists of relevant information, and easy-to-manage security. Using these products together, users can create team websites quickly and easily and greatly enhance productivity.

Chapter 39

Using Microsoft Office InfoPath with SharePoint Products and Technologies

Microsoft Office InfoPath 2003 is a new information gathering program that is part of the Microsoft Office System. It is a desktop application that enables teams and organizations to efficiently gather the information they need through rich, dynamic forms based on XML. An InfoPath form collects information from a user in a structured manner. After the form has been filled out, it is submitted to a fixed storage location. A submitted InfoPath form is an XML document. You can use these forms to create XML-based business solutions for a variety of tasks. InfoPath 2003 provides the ability to develop and deploy dynamic forms that enable the users to accurately and efficiently collect information using data standards defined by your company.

An example of an InfoPath form is shown in Figure 39-1. InfoPath natively uses XML standards for input and output and enables nontechnical end users to view and create XML documents belonging to a custom-defined XML schema. Flexible structural editing enables the users to expand the XML document by validly adding optional and repeating elements. InfoPath uses existing custom-defined XML schema to constrain and guide editing.

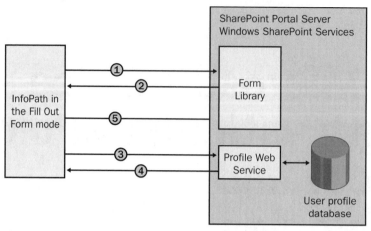

Figure 39-1   An InfoPath form

InfoPath uses and produces XML schemas and XSLT files, and it is integrated with XML Web services standards. Data can be submitted in XML format through Simple Object Access Protocol (SOAP) or through the HTTP POST method.

You can publish forms from a form editor compatible with Microsoft Windows SharePoint Services, such as InfoPath 2003, directly to a Windows SharePoint Services form library, which can enable team collaboration by providing a single location for InfoPath forms to be stored and shared. In addition, Windows SharePoint Services includes several integration features that you can use to take better advantage of form editors compatible with Windows SharePoint Services, such as InfoPath 2003. We will discuss these features later in this chapter.

InfoPath Form Templates

An InfoPath form template is a file or set of files that define the data structure, appearance, and behavior of an InfoPath form. The form template includes the XML Schema that determines the structure for the data when the form is filled in by a user. When a user fills in a form, the form references the form template it is based on, regardless of whether it is installed on the user's local computer or is stored on a networked location, such as a company's intranet or a server running Windows SharePoint Services.

InfoPath provides two distinct modes in which you can work:

■ *Fill out a form* mode is a familiar Microsoft Office–like environment where users can fill out forms while the XML file for the form is created behind the scenes. This allows users to work with forms without needing to know anything about XML. Figure 39-1 shows InfoPath in this mode, with the sample form open.

- *Design* mode is a WYSIWYG environment for developing form templates. Every form a user fills out is based on a form template, which is created in design mode. In design mode, you can view a form's underlying XML Schema, drag controls onto a form, set data validation and conditional formatting, and preview your forms to test their appearance and functionality. You can build a custom form from scratch or customize existing sample forms. Figure 39-2 shows InfoPath in the design mode, with an open form template for the sample form.

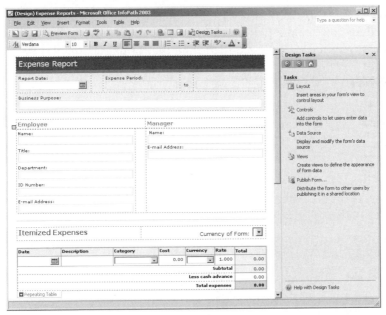

Figure 39-2   InfoPath in the design mode

To enable data capture that is optimized for end users, InfoPath provides flexible views of the abstract data structures of XML. This approach uses the XML paradigm of separating the data in a document from the formatting. These flexible views are based on Extensible Stylesheet Language Transformations (XSLTs), which enable the content of the editing views to be organized differently than the structure of the XML document. Views show the XML document as nested field groups containing text fields and other user interface (UI) controls. Within a form template, you can define multiple views for your form.

When designing a form template, developers define many elements, including the form's structure; the types of controls on a form; the form's data validation rules; the views that define the layout of data; the default content of the form; and what users can and cannot modify when filling it out.

In InfoPath, the collection of fields and groups that define and store the data for an InfoPath form is called a *data source*. Form fields contain data, and groups contain and organize the fields; the data source is made up of fields and groups. The controls on the form are bound to the fields and groups in the data source, and this binding allows data entered into a control to be saved. Information entered into a bound control is saved in the field it is associated with. InfoPath supports the following data sources: XML documents, Extensible Schema Definition (XSD) schemas, databases (Microsoft SQL Server or Microsoft Access), and XML Web services. When you design a form, InfoPath Data Source Setup Wizard prompts you to select the type of data source you want to use. Regardless of the type of data source you ultimately decide to use in your project, InfoPath reads the available metadata from the data source and displays it in the Data Source view, as shown in Figure 39-3. You can then drag data source fields onto the form as you are designing it, providing a binding between the data source fields and the form controls.

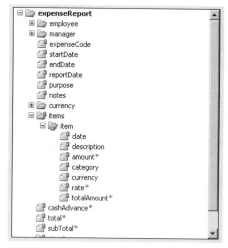

Figure 39-3   Form data source

The programming environment for InfoPath is Microsoft Script Editor (MSE). Microsoft JScript and Microsoft Visual Basic Scripting Edition (VBScript) are the programming languages used in MSE to design custom business logic for a form.

The InfoPath object model can be used to interact with the application, its forms, and data that the form contains. The object model also contains properties that can be used to return references to the XML Document Object Model (DOM). The DOM interacts with XML documents (or files) that are used in an InfoPath form, including the XML data that an InfoPath form produces.

All form templates are composed of several individual form files. These files ensure that when users fill out a form based on a form template, it opens, displays, and functions properly. InfoPath form templates include the following files: form definition file (XSF), XML Schemas, XML templates, and view, presentation, script, and custom business logic files. Table 39-1 describes these files and lists their extensions.

Table 39-1 InfoPath Form Template Files

Name	Extension	Description
Form definition	.xsf	An InfoPath-generated file that contains information about all of the other files and components used in a form. This file serves as the manifest for the form template. The XSF schema is available from *http://www.microsoft.com /downloads/details.aspx?FamilyID=fe118952-3547-420a-a412-00a2662442d9&displaylang=en*.
XML Schema	.xsd	The XML Schema files that are used to constrain and validate a form's underlying XML document files.
XML template	.xml	The .xml file that contains the default data that is displayed in a view when a new form is created.
View	.xsl	The presentation style sheet files that are used to present, view, and transform the data contained in a form's underlying XML document files.
Presentation	.htm, .gif, .bmp, and others	The files used to create custom user interface elements.
Business logic	.js, .vbs	The script files (JScript and VBScript) that contain programming code used to implement specific editing behavior, data validation, event handlers, control of data flow, and other custom business logic. If your form does not use any scripting, these files are not created.
Binary	.dll, .exe	The custom Component Object Model (COM) components that provide additional business logic. These files are external to the form template file and must be registered separately. These files are only required when your form uses COM components.
Form template	.xsn	The compressed file format (.cab) that packages all the form files into one file.

A form template can be stored as individual files within a normal folder. When designing a form, you can work with the form template's individual form files. However, for ease of deployment, InfoPath automatically packages these files into a single file, making it easy to transport the files as a set. This file is a *cabinet file* (.cab) that is renamed with an .xsn extension.

Note You can extract the form template files from an .xsn file to a temporary folder by clicking Extract Form Files on the InfoPath File menu.

When you receive and open an InfoPath form, InfoPath reads a processing instruction in the XML document to determine the location of the form template that the XML document is based on. If this is the first time you have accessed the form template, it is downloaded to the local cache for form templates. If there is a locally cached copy of the form template and it is older than the copy on the server, the cached copy is updated from the server.

Form Libraries

Form libraries provide the primary integration point between Windows SharePoint Services and InfoPath. Form libraries are located on Windows SharePoint Services sites and act as a file server, where users can fill out and store forms based on the same form template.

A *form library* is a special type of document library that can contain and promote any information from an XML file. All documents stored within it are based on a specified XML document. In InfoPath, all forms in the library are based on an InfoPath form template. In a nutshell, form libraries provide a simple way to use and share InfoPath 2003 forms. An example of a form library is shown in Figure 39-4.

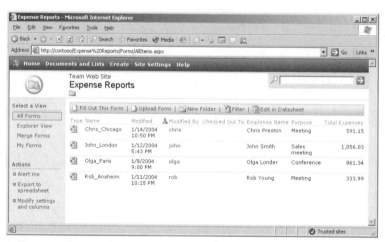

Figure 39-4   Form library that stores InfoPath forms, default view

Because only one form template is associated with each form library, every form created from the library has the same structure and appearance. For example, you could create a form library that provides a single location for your team members to quickly fill out, save, and view their expense report forms.

The form library is the main distribution point for a specified InfoPath form template; it allows the form to be maintained, deployed, and shared for use by the members of an organization. The template for a form library must be stored in the Forms folder of the library that is based on it. The default name for the form template for a library is *template.xml* (or *template.xsn* for packaged InfoPath templates).

A user can visit the form library to fill out new forms based on the form template. When the user completes the form, InfoPath automatically saves the resulting form directly to the form library. The user can later revisit the form library to edit existing forms.

Storing InfoPath forms in the form library provides the ability to use additional Windows SharePoint Services functionality, such as *form library columns* and *merging forms*. The form library also makes the exposed form information available for searching as part of the SharePoint site.

Form library columns are populated with data extracted from the specified fields in the forms stored in the form library. This allows users to view information without having to open and view each form (Figure 39-4). Form library columns also provide a way to sort and group forms according to their content. With these columns, the user can create custom views to organize the forms and their content within the form library. For example, if you stored your team's expense reports in a form library, the form library columns could display the employee's name, the business purpose, and the total expenses claimed. This would be displayed for each form in the form library, as shown in Figure 39-4. You could then sort the expense reports by any column, such as business purpose, or filter the reports by, for instance, employee name.

Merging forms provides the ability to aggregate forms data by merging several forms into a single form. For example, you can merge several individual expense reports into the summary report. A form designer can define how the data in various fields should be merged in the resulting document.

The following sections describe how to perform various tasks using form libraries as well as the InfoPath forms that these libraries store.

Creating a Form Library

You can create a form library from InfoPath or from a SharePoint site. In any case, to create form libraries, you must have permission to modify the site where the form library will be stored.

Creating a form library from InfoPath

InfoPath includes the Publishing Wizard that provides an ability to publish form templates to shared locations on your computer or company network, to a SharePoint 2003 site, or to a Web server. To create a form library from InfoPath, perform the following steps:

1.   Open the form template in InfoPath design mode.

2.   On the **File** menu, select **Publish**. Alternatively, click **Publish Form** in the **Design Tasks** pane. The InfoPath Publishing Wizard starts. On the Welcome page, click **Next**.

3. From the list of shared locations, select **To a SharePoint form library** (Figure 39-5).

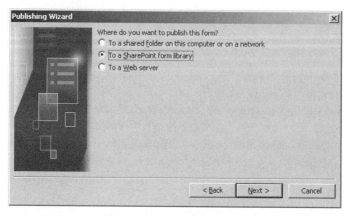

Figure 39-5 Publishing Wizard select location page

4. Select **Create new form library (recommended)**.

5. Specify the URL of the SharePoint site where you want to create the form library.

6. Type the name and description of the form library. The name and description will be displayed on the form library page on the SharePoint site. The name is mandatory; the description is optional.

7. On the next page, specify the names of the fields that you would like to promote (Figure 39-6). This process is called a *field*, or *properties*, *promotion*. It allows a designer to select fields from a form data source that will become form library columns in the SharePoint form library.

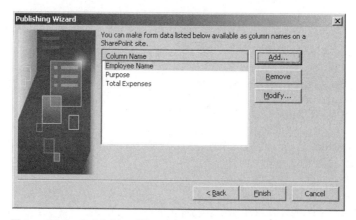

Figure 39-6 Publishing Wizard form library columns page

Form template designers define what form data will be displayed on the form library page. The form data is displayed in a table; the data in the columns comes from the fields promoted by the designer in the form template. By promoting the fields, the designer creates a table layout for the form library page that is displayed in the library's default view **All Forms**.

It is important to point out that the contents of promoted fields can be searched on a SharePoint site. Therefore, if you want to make a particular form data searchable, make sure the field that contains the data is promoted.

The Publishing Wizard allows the designer to add, delete, and modify the list of promoted columns. Figure 39-7 shows the **Select a Field or Group** dialog box that is displayed when you click either the **Add** or **Modify** button on the Form Library Columns page of the wizard. It allows you to select a field to be promoted, specify the name for the column for this field's data, and specify an operation to be performed if the field is a repeated field. Examples of available operations include first, last, sum, average, minimum, maximum, and so on. Operations available for a field depend on the type of data stored in this field. For example, numerical operations such as sum or average are not available for the text fields.

Note   Field promotions are applied to the form library during the publication process. They are identified in the file properties.xfp that is stored in the library Forms folder. The form library promotes form data whenever a user submits the form to the server.

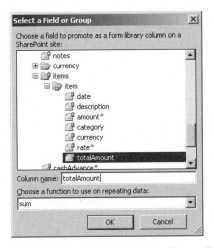

Figure 39-7   Select a Field or Group dialog box

8. On the wizard's last page, check the appropriate boxes if you want to send a notification e-mail and/or open the form library, and then click **Finish**.

Creating a form library from a SharePoint site

When you first create a form library from a SharePoint site, you need to specify a form template to base the library on. However, if you do not have a form template installed at the time of creating the library, choose the default blank form as the form template for your form library. This form template is a placeholder file. Before you can start filling out and adding forms to this library, you will need to create the form template that will serve as the basis for all forms created in the form library and change the blank template to the new template you have created. We will look into modifying the form template a library is based on, later in this chapter.

To create a form library from a SharePoint site, do the following:

1. Go to the SharePoint site where you would like the form library to be created. On the top link bar, click **Create**.

2. On the Create Page page, under **Document Libraries**, click **Form Library**. The New Form Library page is displayed (Figure 39-8).

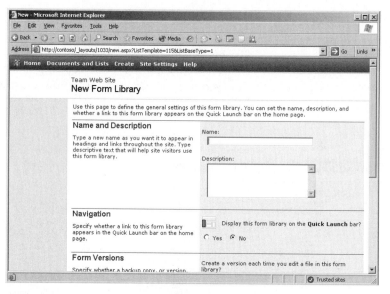

Figure 39-8   New Form Library page

3. In the **Name** box, type a name for the library. Supplying the name is mandatory.

4. In the **Description** box, type text that describes the purpose of the library. The description is optional.

5. In the **Navigation** section, choose whether you want to add a link to this library on the **Quick Launch** bar.

6. To create a backup copy of a form file each time it is checked into the library, in the **Document Versions** section, click **Yes**.

7. In the **Form Template** section, select the form template you want to specify as the basis for all forms in the library. If there is no custom form template installed, choose the default blank form.

8. At the bottom of the page, click **Create**.

Creating a new form library from a custom library template

Custom templates are a way of packaging up settings and, optionally, content for a form library and making those available for new form libraries. As we shall see later in this section, an existing form library can be saved as a custom template. New form libraries can be created from this custom template on the current site or another site. Custom library templates are stored in the database and made available through the central or site collection template galleries.

A form library template is a file that includes all of the design information about the form library, including the library columns and promoted fields; any views created for the library; and, optionally, content of the library. The form library template does not include security settings such as a list of users or groups with permissions to the form library from which the custom template was created. The form library template is stored as a file with the .stp extension.

Members of the Administrator group for a site can create templates based on that site. To create a custom template from the existing form library, perform the following steps:

1. Go to the form library and click **Modify settings and columns**.

2. Under **General Settings** section, click **Save form library as template**.

3. On the Save as Template page (Figure 39-9), specify the file name for the template .stp file; title and description for the library's template that will be displayed on the Create page when the template is used for creating a new form library; and whether the content of the form library should be included in the template.

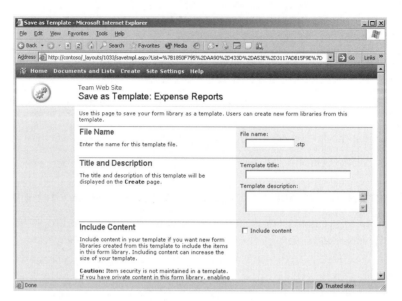

Figure 39-9   Save as Template page

4. Click **OK** to save all changes.

To export a form library template for use by other SharePoint sites, perform the following steps:

1. On the top-level site from which the form library template is to be exported, click **Site Settings**.

2. Under **Administration**, click **Go to Site Administration**.

3. Under **Site Collection Galleries**, click **Manage list template gallery**.

4. Right-click the list template you want to save, and select **Save Target As**.

5. Specify a location to which to save the template .stp file, and click **OK**.

To import a form library template to a SharePoint site, do the following:

1. On the top-level site for which you want to import a form library, click **Site Settings**.

2. Under **Administration**, click **Go to Site Administration**.

3. Under **Site Collection Galleries**, click **Manage list template gallery**.

4. On the List Template Gallery page, click **Upload Template**.

5. In the **Name** box, type the path to the template .stp file, or click **Browse**. You can upload multiple templates by clicking **Upload Multiple Files**.

6. Click **Save and Close** to add the form library template.

To create a form library from an existing form library template, do the following:

1. Go to the Documents and Lists page for the SharePoint site.

2. Click **Create**.

3. In the **Document Libraries** section, select the desired template from the list.

4. On the New Form Library page, in the **Name** box, type a name for the library; in the **Description** box, type text that describes the purpose of the library (optional); and in the **Navigation** section, choose whether you want to add a link to this library on the **Quick Launch** bar.

5. Click **Create** to save changes.

Modifying an Existing Form Library

Modifying an existing form library means changing the form template this library is based upon. This operation requires special consideration because changes made to a form template might result in data loss in the existing forms in the form library that are based on this form template. For example, if you remove a control in a form template that collected specific data, the control will no longer appear in the existing forms that are based on that form template, and the data will be lost. However, if you are making additive schema changes, and/or changes to the user interface, no data loss should occur. If in doubt, to prevent compatibility issues with existing forms, do not modify the existing library. Instead, publish the changed form template to a different location.

You can modify a form template in an existing form library from InfoPath or from this library page on the SharePoint site.

To modify an existing form library from InfoPath

1. Open the form template in InfoPath design Mode.

2. Make changes to the template.

3. On the **File** menu, select **Publish**. The InfoPath Publishing Wizard starts. On the Welcome page, click **Next**.

4. From the list of shared locations, select **To a SharePoint form library**.

5. Click **Modify existing form library**.

6. Specify the URL of the SharePoint site.

7. From the list of form libraries, choose the form library whose form you want to modify.

8. On the next page, click **Overwrite the existing form template**.

9. Specify the promoted column names. If required, you can add, delete, or modify the fields you would like to be used as column names in the library's default view.

10. On the wizard's last page, check the appropriate boxes if you want to send a notification e-mail message and/or open the form library, and then click **Finish**.

To modify an existing form library from a SharePoint site

1. On the SharePoint site, open the form library.

2. On the form library page, under **Actions**, click **Modify settings and columns**.

3. On the Customize page, in the **General Settings** section, to the right of the **Template** location, click **Edit Template**.

4. InfoPath opens the existing form template in the design mode. Make the changes to the template.

5. Save the changed form template.

If you have already uploaded the changed template to the SharePoint library you would like to modify, you can specify the location of this template as a template to base the form library on. To achieve that, do the following:

1. On the Customize page, under **General Settings**, click **Change general settings**.

2. On the Form Library Settings page, under **Form Template**, in the **Template URL** box, type the path and filename of the form template that has been uploaded to the form library.

Creating and Modifying a Form Library View

A view of a form library allows you to see a particular selection of items, or to see the items sorted in a particular order and/or filtered according to specific criteria. Views provide an ability to see the contents of specified form fields in a form library page in a predefined way without opening a form. The default view All Forms is created by the designer when the InfoPath template is published to the library.

The fields in the form template may be promoted for different reasons, including displaying form data in the library page, making the data searchable, and taking advantage of the ability to show summary information in the custom views of the form library. When your requirements change, it might be necessary to modify the field promotions for the library to enable creation of different data representation in the library's views.

To modify field promotions for a library

Field promotions are identified in the form template file named properties.xfp. You can modify the promoted fields in InfoPath design mode either at the time of template publishing using the Publishing Wizard, or at the template design time. To modify the field promotions at design time, perform the following steps:

1. Open the form template in InfoPath design mode.

2. On the **Tools** menu, select **Form Options**.

3. Click the **Form Library Columns** tab. Using the **Add**, **Remove**, and **Modify** buttons, define the form fields to be promoted to the library columns.

   Clicking either the Add or the Modify button displays a dialog shown on Figure 39-7. It is the same dialog as the one used by the Publishing Wizard. From this dialog, you can select the fields to be promoted. If you select a repeating field, you need to specify how to treat the repeating entries. For example, you could choose plain text, merge, sum, average, and so on.

4. Specify a column name to associate with the form field when it is displayed in the column in the form library, if you want the column name to be different from the name of the field.

To create a new view

Custom views allow a form library designer to create custom presentations of form data and their related content. With the aid of standard document properties and promoted fields, these views allow designers to provide focused views that sort and filter the data in a specific way. Custom views can be shared or personal. For example, in a library that stores expense reports, you can create a summary view that displays the summary of all expenses. To create a new view for a form library, perform the following steps:

1. On the form library page, under **Actions**, click **Modify settings and columns**.

2. In the **View** section, click **Create a new view**.

3. Specify the type of view you want to create: **Standard**, **Datasheet**, or **Calendar**.

4. On the Create View page (Figure 39-10), under **Name**, type a name for a new view.

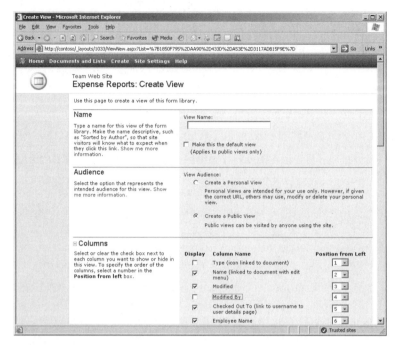

Figure 39-10 Create View page

5. Under **Audience**, specify whether the form is shared or personal.

6. Under **Columns**, select the columns you want to be displayed in your new view. The columns available for selection include the form's document properties, as well as promoted fields.

7. If you want to, change the order of the columns for your new view.

8. Configure other settings for the new view as applicable. Depending on the type of the view you are creating, the available settings will be different. Options for **Standard** and **Datasheet** views include the following: sort options; filter and group options; totals options that specify operations to perform for the selected columns, for example, count, sum, and average; and style options, folders options, and items limit.

> **Note** Totals option of Average for columns that store dates is available in the **Datasheet** views only.

9. Click **OK** at the bottom of the page to save all changes.

To modify an existing view

To modify the settings associated with the existing view, do the following:

1. On the form library page, under **Actions**, click **Modify settings and columns**.

2. On the Customize page, in the **View** section, click on the specific view that you want to modify.

3. On the Edit View page, modify the settings for the view, such as number and type of columns, sort options, filter and group options, and so on.

   For example, you can show or hide the columns by selecting the check box next to each column you want to display and clear the check box next to each column you want to hide.

4. Click **OK** at the bottom of the page to save all changes.

Working with Forms in the Form Library

After a form library has been created, the users can fill out, save, and upload new forms; edit existing forms; and merge forms to import or aggregate the data. It is sometimes necessary to relink the forms to their form library. It is also possible to deploy the fully trusted forms to the form library, and to submit the form data to the form library programmatically.

To fill out a new form

1. On the page that displays the form library, click **Fill Out This Form** (shown in Figure 39-13)

2. InfoPath opens a new form based on this form library template. Fill out the form.

To edit an existing form

1. On the page that displays the form library, click the form you would like to edit.

2. InfoPath opens the form in the Fill Out Form mode. Edit the form.

To save a form to the form library

1. In InfoPath, from the **File** menu, select **Save** or **Save As**. You need to use **Save As** if the form file has previously been saved on your file system, so that you can work with it offline.

2. If using **Save As**, specify the URL of the form library. If you have been working with this form library on this computer before, it will be listed as a Web folder under My Network Places, so you can just select it. Alternatively, type the URL in the file name box.

To upload a form to the form library

1. On the page that displays the form library, click **Upload Form**.

2. On the Upload Form page (Figure 39-11), click **Browse** to locate the form you want to upload, and then click **Open**. There is a check box that allows you to specify whether or not you want to overwrite the existing files.

    If you want to add multiple forms at once, on the Upload Form page, click **Upload Multiple Files**, specify the form files you want to upload, and then click **Save and Close**.

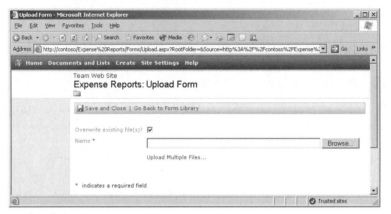

Figure 39-11   Upload Form page

Merging Forms in a Form Library

The Merge Forms feature of Windows SharePoint Services integrates with the Merge Forms feature of InfoPath to provide a mechanism for data aggregation and comparison across one or more files present in a specific form library. The form template specifies whether the Merge Forms feature is enabled for a given form, what the merged form's appearance will be, and which data is included or merged into the new form.

To merge forms in a form library, perform the following steps:

1. On the form library page, select **Merge Forms** view (Figure 39-12).

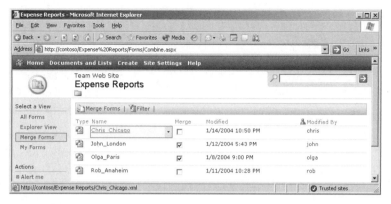

Figure 39-12 Merge Forms view

2. To merge one or more form files, select or clear the **Merge** box for these forms.

3. Click **Merge Forms**.

4. InfoPath creates a new form that merges the contents of all selected files and opens it in the Fill Out Form mode (Figure 39-13). The selected files remain unchanged.

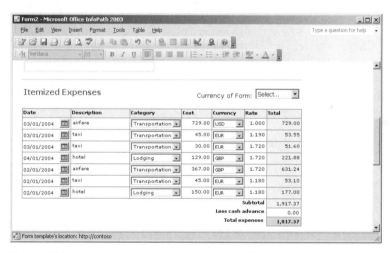

Figure 39-13 Aggregated data in the merged form

The Merge Forms feature in a form library provides the following functionality:

- **Importing form data.** If you select just one form for merging, the data from this form will be imported into the new merged form. For example, if your status reports are stored in a form library, you can use the Merge Forms view to import the contents of a previous status report into a new status report, effectively carrying forward the information from a previous reporting period.

- **Aggregating form data.** If you select two or more forms for merging, the information from these forms will be combined into the new merged form. Following the previous example, you can merge the status reports of all team members into a single status report.

The aggregation of data resulting from merging forms can include all of the data contained in the merged forms, or only a portion of the original data. When a form designer enables merging on the form, the data that is merged must be saved in a repeating field or in a field that is part of a repeating group; these repeating fields and groups are bound to list controls, repeating tables, or repeating sections. Data saved in a rich text box will be merged into one rich text box. The default operations are as follows:

- For repeating elements, data is inserted at a matching location in the resulting document.

- For nonrepeating elements, the attributes of the elements of the merged documents are added to the resulting document.

To enable form merging, perform the following steps:

1. Open the form template in InfoPath design mode.

2. Select **Form Options** from the **Tools** menu.

3. On the **General** tab in the **Form Options** dialog box, select the **Enable form merging** check box.

When the default merge capability is not sufficient, you can create customized merge behaviors that operate directly on the underlying XML of the aggregated files. This allows InfoPath to merge data from different form templates (for example, schemas), override the default merge operation for forms based on the same template, and execute custom merge operations on any type of group or element (for example, merge a nonrepeating field). For these scenarios, you can create an XSL

Transformation (XSLT), which contains aggregation instructions for the merge. These aggregation instructions are XML attributes (and their values) in the namespace *http://schemas.microsoft.com/office/InfoPath/2003/aggregation.*

> **More Info**   For more information on custom merge operations, refer to the InfoPath SDK. It is available for download from *http://msdn.microsoft.com /library/default.asp?url=/downloads/list/infopath.asp.*

Relinking a Form to Its Form Library

If you rename the form library's form template or change its location, the form template and the forms stored in the form library might become unsynchronized. This can result in problems when working with the forms, such as not being able to open and edit the forms. Because forms must point to the correct version and location of the form template to open and function properly, it might be necessary to relink the existing forms in the library to the form template. Forms that are not correctly synchronized with the form library's form template are displayed on the Relink page.

> **Note**   You only need to relink the forms (.xml files) that reference an old or incorrect form template. The Relink page might display other file types stored in the form library.

To relink the form files to the form library, do the following:

1. On the SharePoint site, open the form library.

2. On the form library page, under **Actions**, click **Modify settings and columns**.

3. On the Customize page, in the **General Settings** section, click **Relink forms to this form library**.

4. On the Relink page (Figure 39-14), select the **Relink** check box next to each form you want to relink, and then click **Relink Forms**.

> **Note**   The relink feature will not work for forms that were created with a different form template than that of the form library.

Figure 39-14   Relink Forms page

Deploying Fully Trusted Forms

By default, InfoPath forms published to SharePoint form libraries are restricted from accessing system resources and are not allowed to use any software components that are not marked as safe for scripting. Such forms (and their templates) are said to be *sandboxed*. A sandboxed form template is cached for offline use, is automatically updated, and has restricted access to system resources. When a user fills a sandboxed form out, the form is placed in a local cache and denied access to system resources. Up until now in this chapter, we have been discussing the sandboxed forms. This type of form is sometimes referred to as *standard forms*; they inherit their permissions from the domain in which it is opened.

You can avoid these limitations by creating a fully trusted form. Fully trusted forms have more permissions than sandboxed forms do. For example, they can contain code that uses external objects for accessing system resources; they can use software components or Microsoft ActiveX controls that are not marked as safe for scripting; and they can use custom business logic provided by COM components. In addition, some members of the InfoPath object model are set to security level 3, which means that they can only be used in a fully trusted form. For example, to access the Microsoft Office CommandBars object, you use the CommandBars property of the InfoPath object to set a reference to it. Because this property is set to security level 3, it cannot be used in a form that is not fully trusted.

Unlike sandboxed forms, fully trusted forms must be installed on the client computer. That is why they are sometimes referred to as *custom installed forms*. Deploying a fully trusted form involves deploying form files in two locations.

- The form's XML template file is deployed to a SharePoint form library.

- The form is deployed to the computers of users who will be using the form.

Once the appropriate files have been deployed, clicking the XML template file in the SharePoint form library will start an instance of the form on the client computer.

The following steps demonstrate how to convert an existing form to a fully trusted form and then make the form compatible with a newly created SharePoint form library.

Step 1: Create a Fully Trusted Form

You can convert a standard form to a fully trusted form manually. This process can be tedious and complicated.

> **More Info** For more information about fully trusted forms, including manual conversion of a standard form into a fully trusted form, see the article "Understanding Fully Trusted Forms" in InfoPath SDK documentation at *http://msdn.microsoft.com/library/default.asp?url=/downloads/list/infopath.asp*.

To simplify the conversion, InfoPath provides a form registration tool named RegForm. This tool is a command-line utility program with features that allow you to do the following:

- Automatically make a backup copy of the form template

- Make the necessary changes to the .xsf file and XML template file to make the form fully trusted

- Update the version number of the form template

- Package the files in the .xsn CAB file format

- Create a custom installation program for installing the fully trusted form

The RegForm tool is installed as a part of InfoPath SDK installation. It is located at the *<InfoPath SDK installation folder>*/Tools. To use RegForm, open Command Prompt, navigate to the folder that contains the RegForm tool, and then type the following at the command prompt:

```
RegForm /U urn:MyForm:MyCompany /T Yes C:\MyForms\MyTrustedForm.xsn
```

Replace the values for the /U option and the name of the form template file with your own requirements and file location. The /U option provides the Uniform Resource Name (URN); the /T option indicates that the form should be marked as a fully trusted form; and the last parameter is the file and path name of the form template that is to be converted.

The tool will create a .js file and a .bak file in the same folder that contains the form template that you are converting. The .bak file is a copy of the original form template file before the changes were made to it; the .js file is a script file that can be used to install the fully trusted form.

In addition to creating a .js file for installing a fully trusted form, the RegForm tool supports creating an .msi file if you have Microsoft Visual Studio .NET installed. To create a Microsoft Installer file (.msi), use the /MSI option, as shown in the following example:

```
RegForm /U urn:MyForm:MyCompany /T Yes /MSI C:\MyForms\MyTrustedForm.xsn
```

Replace the values for the /U option and the name of the form template file with your own requirements and file location.

The tool creates an .msi file in the same folder that contains the form template that you are converting. The RegForm tool also creates a Visual Studio .NET setup project in the %temp%\RegForm directory. You can use this project to modify the installation routine to fit your requirements.

> **Note**   If you use the /MSI option and you do not have Visual Studio .NET installed, the RegForm tool creates the default .js file for installing the fully trusted form.

Other options can be used with the RegForm tool to provide more control over the values that it uses, such as the form template name, company name, and version number. You can use the /? switch to view the RegForm tool command-line Help.

Step 2: Extract the Form's XML Template File

You must extract the form's XML template file so that it can be deployed to a form library. To do this, open your form in design mode, click Extract Form Files on the File menu, and then select a folder to which the form files will be extracted. By default, the XML template file is named template.xml.

Step 3: Create a SharePoint Form Library from the Share Point site

To perform this task, use instructions provided in the section "Creating a form library from a SharePoint site" earlier in this chapter

Step 4: Upload the Form's XML Template to the SharePoint Form Library and Set it as the Default Form

Upload the XML template file to the form library using instructions provided in the section "To upload a form to the form library" earlier in this chapter. Your form file should have the name *template.xml*. If the form is not named *template.xml*, follow these additional steps to set the template as the form library's default template: on the Customize page, under General Settings, click Change general settings; then on the Form Library Settings page, under Form Template, in the Template URL box, type the path and filename of the template that you uploaded to the form library in the previous steps.

Step 5: Deploy the Form to Client Computers

At this point, your form's XML template file has been copied to a new SharePoint form library and it has been set as the SharePoint form library's default template. The form will not work, however, unless it has been installed on the computer of each user. There are several approaches that you should take to accomplish this task:

- Place a link to the form's installation package (.msi) in the form library's Description field. To achieve this, type a link to your form's .msi file along with the appropriate instructions to the user in the Description box on the Form Library Settings page.

- Another possibility is to use an HTML editor, such as Microsoft FrontPage, to add instructions on how to install the form to the form library's main page. If you do this, make sure you make a backup copy of the page.

Note   For updates on this topic, refer to the InfoPath SDK.

Submitting a Form Programmatically

In InfoPath, you can set up a form template so that the users are able to submit the data in their form directly to an HTTP location, a database, or a Web service. If this feature is enabled, the Submit command is available on the File menu in the Fill Out Form mode. To programmatically specify the URL for submitting the InfoPath form to the SharePoint form library, add a script to the form's OnSubmitRequest event handler, as described in the following procedure.

1. In InfoPath design mode, open the form template.

2. On the **Tools** menu, select **Submitting Forms**.

3. Select **Enable submit**, select **Submit using a custom script** from the **Submit** drop-down list box, and then click **OK** to open the Microsoft Script Editor.

4. Add a script similar to the following to the **OnSubmitRequest** event handler for the form:

```
function XDocument::OnSubmitRequest(eventObj)
{
    // If the submit operation is successful, set
    // eventObj.ReturnStatus = true
    var blnSubmitSuccess = false;
    var fFileExists = false;
    // Specify the URL of the file you want to submit here.
    var strUrl = "http://MyServer/MyFormLibrary/MyForm.xml";
    try
    {
        // Create an XMLHTTP object to transport the file.
        var objXmlHttp = new ActiveXObject("MSXML2.XMLHTTP.5.0");
        // Attempt to open to a form using the specified URL to
        // check if a form with the same name already exists
        // in the form library.
        try{
        objXmlHttp.Open("HEAD", strUrl, false);
        objXmlHttp.Send();
        fFileExists = true;
            }catch(e)
            {
                XDocument.UI.Alert("Submit failed due to the following error
.\n\n" + ex.number + " - " + ex.description + "\n\nThe file already exist");
                fFileExists = false;
            }
        // If no form at the same URL has been found, proceed
        // to submit. If you need logic to replace the previous
        // file, you can call
        // objXmlHttp.Open("DELETE", strUrl, false) to delete
        // the form from the form library before proceeding.
        if (objXmlHttp.Status == 404 || !fFileExists)
        {
            // Submit the form to the form library.
            objXmlHttp.Open("PUT", strUrl, false);
            objXmlHttp.Send(XDocument.DOM.xml);
```

```
                        // 200 or 201 status code indicate the form has
                        // been submitted successfully.
                        if (objXmlHttp.Status == 200 || objXmlHttp.Status == 201)
                        {
                            blnSubmitSuccess = true;
                        }
                }
        }
        catch (ex)
        {
            XDocument.UI.Alert("Submit failed due to the following error.\n\n"
    + ex.number + " - " + ex.description);
        }
        if (blnSubmitSuccess)
        {
            XDocument.UI.Alert("The form was submitted successfully.");
            eventObj.ReturnStatus = true;
        }
        else
        {
            eventObj.ReturnStatus = false;
        }
}
```

In this script, the URL for the form is defined by strUrl string variable that is set to a static value of http://MyServer/MyFormLibrary/MyForm.xml. However, if you specify a static URL in the form template, when a user selects Submit from the File menu in the InfoPath, a form will always be submitted to the same location, overwriting the previous one. This is useful when submitting an .xml template for a fully trusted form.

However, for standard (sandboxed) forms that might not be the desired behavior; therefore, make sure that you customize the sample code to use a dynamic location. For example, you can add a field to the form specifically for the document title, make it a required field so that a user must fill it out with the text, and then in the code append ".xml" to this text to create a file name for the URL location of the form. Provided this field is named *Title*, your code will look similar to the following:

```
var strTitle = XDocument.DOM.selectSingleNode("//my:Title").text;
var strUrl = "http://MyServer/MyFormLibrary/"+ encodeURI(strTitle) + ".xml";
```

Tip   *My* is an InfoPath default name for a custom namespace for a form's XML schema.

Integrating InfoPath Forms with Web Services for SharePoint Portal Server

In certain scenarios, you might wish to prepopulate your forms with information that can be obtained from other systems in the enterprise so that users do not have to fill out repetitive data or data that is available elsewhere. You can prepopulate your forms using the Web services provided by SharePoint Portal Server 2003. InfoPath natively supports these Web services, so you can easily write a code to call a Web services method from an event handler within your form. If the data that is required to prepopulate an InfoPath form can be obtained from SharePoint Portal Web services, you can call the appropriate Web services in the form's OnLoad() event handler.

SharePoint Portal Server provides a suite of Web services that allow client computers to interact with the back-end database component. In addition, the Web server capabilities of SharePoint Portal Server allow the server to host custom Web services and applications that interact with the back-end database to provide targeted functionality to client applications. InfoPath can capitalize on these applications and Web services to provide an integrated experience for the user.

For example, when a user fills out an expense report form, you might want the form fields that contain directory-style user information to be obtained from the user profile database on the portal site. Examples of these types of fields include user full name, employee ID, department, e-mail, phone number, and other similar data. Such data is usually stored in a user's profile database on the SharePoint Portal Server. The expense report form can call a custom Web service on a SharePoint Portal Server to obtain information related to the person who is filling out the form. InfoPath then uses this information to prepopulate the fields of the form.

The sample custom Web service provides user profile information to the caller. This Web service obtains user profile information by using the Share Point Portal Server object model to query the user profile database. The user profile information is generally public, directory-style information that is related to a specific person. The sample Web service provides the GetMyProfile() method that detects the identity (that is, the user name) of the caller and returns the user profile associated with that identity.

```
[WebMethod]
public Profile GetMyProfile()
```

> **Note**   SharePoint Portal Server provides a User Profile Web service, but that service does not detect the identity of the caller; the caller must pass the account name to the service to obtain user profile information. Depending on your business logic, you can either write a custom Web service or use the one provided.

In the form template, an OnLoad() event handler checks whether the user is online, calls a GetMyProfile() method to obtain all information related to the user, and then programmatically prepopulates the appropriate form fields with this information.

The illustration of this process is shown on Figure 39-15, as follows:

1. A user starts InfoPath in the **Fill Out Form** mode and points to the form template in the form library on the SharePoint site. Alternatively, the user can click Fill Out Form on the form library's page.

2. The form is downloaded to the client computer and put in the local cache.

3. InfoPath opens the form and executes OnLoad() event handler that calls the GetMyProfile() method of the Profile Web Service on the SharePoint Portal site.

4. The required data is returned to InfoPath. The form fields are populated with the returned data, and the form is displayed to the user.

5. The user fills out the rest of the form and saves it back to the form library.

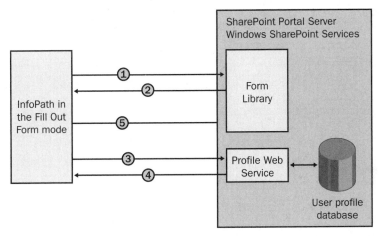

Figure 39-15   Prepopulating InfoPath form with data from user profile database

More Info   For a working code sample that shows prepopulating an InfoPath form with the data exposed by a custom Web service on portal site, plus a detailed explanation of this code, refer to the article "Integrating Microsoft SharePoint Products and Technologies and Microsoft Office InfoPath 2003," located at *http://msdn.microsoft.com/library/default.asp?url=/library /en-us/odc_sp2003_ta/html/sharepoint_integrating_sps_and_infopath.asp.*

Summary

Microsoft Office InfoPath 2003 is a new Microsoft Office desktop application that lets you design your own data collection forms that turn the user-entered data into XML documents. InfoPath forms are based on form templates that define the data structure, appearance, and behavior of a form. After a user fills out an InfoPath form, it is submitted to fixed storage locations, such as a company's intranet or a server running Windows SharePoint Services. Windows SharePoint Services includes several integration features that you can use to take better advantage of InfoPath 2003.

On Windows SharePoint Services sites, form libraries act as a file server where users can fill out and store forms based on the same form template. Using the form libraries columns, the data within specified form fields can be displayed and searched on the SharePoint site. In addition, a Merge Forms feature allows users to aggregate the data from multiple InfoPath forms into a single document. Form libraries provide the primary integration point between Windows SharePoint Services and InfoPath.

Chapter 40

Microsoft Outlook 2003 Integration with SharePoint Products and Technologies

Just as Microsoft SharePoint Products and Technologies has been evolving, so has its level of integration with compatible e-mail and calendar applications such as Microsoft Outlook. For Microsoft Outlook 2000 and Microsoft Outlook 2002, there were two main points of SharePoint integration. The first point of integration was the ability to display a SharePoint Team Services or SharePoint Portal Server site page when the user switched to a particular Outlook folder. The second point of integration was Outlook Web Access Web Parts that displayed data from a user's Microsoft Exchange mailbox. Microsoft Office Outlook 2003 provides much richer SharePoint integration, including the ability to display a local read-only copy of SharePoint events and contacts lists and the option to create Meeting and Document Workspace sites related to message file attachments and meeting requests.

This chapter discusses the many ways in which Outlook 2003 and SharePoint Products and Technologies work together.

Viewing SharePoint Products and Technologies Data in Outlook

Outlook users can export any single contact or event item from a SharePoint list to Outlook and view any page in a SharePoint site from within Outlook. In addition, Outlook 2003 allows you to link any SharePoint contacts or events list to Outlook. Outlook stores a copy of the data from the SharePoint list locally, and updates occur automatically at periodic intervals.

Folder Home Pages

A **folder home page** is a Web page that Outlook displays when the user switches to a particular Outlook folder. The most familiar example is the Outlook Today page that displays information about your Inbox, Calendar, and Tasks folders when you click the top-level folder of the hierarchy that contains your Inbox.

While you can customize the resource DLL file that contains the Outlook Today page, a more common approach for an organization using SharePoint Products and Technologies is to replace the built-in Outlook Today page with a home page of a departmental Microsoft Windows SharePoint Services site or a corporate SharePoint Portal Server 2003 portal site page. This technique works with any version of Outlook starting with Outlook 2000.

To replace the Outlook Today page with another HTML page

1. Right-click the folder at the top of the hierarchy that contains the main Inbox folder. (Depending on the Outlook version, it might or might not be labeled Outlook Today.) Then choose **Properties**.

2. On the Home Page tab of the Properties dialog (Figure 40-1), change the value for **Address** to the URL of the SharePoint page you want to display.

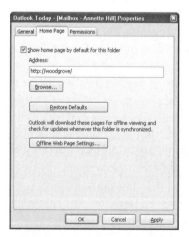

Figure 40-1   A SharePoint site page used as a custom home page for an Outlook folder

> **Tip** You can display a page in a SharePoint site as a folder home page for any Outlook folder by applying the procedure just shown to any folder. For example, if you work with multiple SharePoint sites, you might create a folder in Outlook named *My SharePoint Sites*, add a subfolder for each site, and then set the home page of each subfolder to display that site's home page.

Outlook 2003 stores the value for the custom Outlook Today page URL in the Windows registry, under the HKEY_CURRENT_USER\Software\Microsoft\Office \11.0\Outlook\Today key, in a string value named UserDefinedUrl. An administrator can set the default for that value to a SharePoint site page by using the Custom Installation Wizard or Custom Maintenance Wizard in the Office Resource Kit to deploy or update Outlook, or the administrator can enforce that value with a group policy by using the policy template described later in this chapter, in the "Managing Integration Features in Outlook" section. The Windows Server 2003 Deployment Kit: Designing a Managed Environment, available for download from Microsoft's website, provides the foundation you need to understand and deploy Group Policy within Microsoft Windows Server 2003.

Because SharePoint Products and Technologies provides support for the **vCard** and **iCalendar** standards for data interchange, Outlook users can add any single contact or event from a SharePoint list to their Outlook Contacts or Calendar folder.

To add a contact or event from a SharePoint list to Outlook

1. In a contact or events list, click the hyperlink for the item you want to add to Outlook.

2. Click the **Export Contact** or **Export Event** link.

3. When the **File Download** dialog appears, click **Open** to open the .vcf (vCard) or .ics (iCalendar) file that you created.

4. Click **Save and Close** to add the resulting contact or appointment to your Outlook folders.

You cannot export a recurring series of events using this technique. If you open a recurring event from the All Events view, you will not see an Export Event link. You can, however, export any individual occurrence from a recurring series by opening it from the Calendar view and then following the procedure just shown.

Linking Events and Contacts in Outlook 2003

In Microsoft Office Outlook 2003, you can view any contacts or events list from a Windows SharePoint Services site as a read-only Outlook folder. Outlook stores the data from the SharePoint list in a Personal Folders .pst file on the user's hard drive. Because the list information resides in a local file, these event and contact items are available in Outlook even when the user is not connected to the network. The user cannot, however, create new items in the SharePoint lists through Outlook. The user still must browse to the SharePoint site to create, delete, or modify items.

To link a contacts list or calendar to Outlook 2003

1.   View the SharePoint list that you want to link to Outlook.

2.   Click the **Link to Outlook** link. (Netscape Navigator users will see **Link to Contacts** or **Link to Calendar**.)

3.   Click **Yes** at the **Do you want to add the folder to Outlook?** prompt.

You can now see the linked folder in the Other Contacts or Other Calendars list in the Outlook navigation pane, as well as in the Folder List.

> **Tip**   As with any other Outlook contacts folder, the user can enable the local copy of a contacts list for display in the Outlook Address Book and use those contacts to resolve names in e-mail messages.

To remove a linked SharePoint list from Outlook

■   Right-click the name of the folder in the navigation pane, and select **Delete** *foldername*.

Removing a linked SharePoint list from Outlook does not delete the list from the SharePoint site.

By default, Outlook checks each linked SharePoint list for updates whenever the user switches to that folder in Outlook and every 20 minutes thereafter, and it copies new or updated items to the local .pst file. Users can perform a manual update of a linked SharePoint list at any time while they are displaying the folder.

To update the Outlook copy of a linked SharePoint list

■   Right-click the Outlook folder, and then click **Refresh**.

Outlook monitors the progress of the update in the Outlook Send/Receive Progress dialog and maintains information in the status bar (shown in Figure 40-2) on the number of items in the linked folder, the time of the last update, and the next scheduled update. (Note that if the user is displaying multiple calendar folders side by side, this information does not appear in the status bar.)

Figure 40-2   Status bar information for a linked SharePoint list

Administrators can change the automatic update interval or disable the linking feature completely with registry entries or group policies, as described in the "Managing Integration Features in Outlook" section later in this chapter. If the linking feature is disabled, a user who clicks the Link To Outlook link in a SharePoint list will receive the following message: "The folder cannot be added to Outlook because your system administrator does not allow Outlook folders to be linked to a Windows SharePoint Services Web site."

Using an Stssync Link

You can make Outlook 2003 users aware of a SharePoint events or contacts list by sending them an e-mail message containing a special link using the **stssync** protocol. When the user clicks on the link, she will get the same "Do you want to add the folder to Outlook?" prompt as she would get by clicking on the Link To Outlook link on the list's Web page.

An stssync link takes this format:

*stssync://sts/?ver=**version**&type=**folder-type**&cmd=**command-name**&base-url=**sts-url**&guid=**the-guid**&site-name=**site-friendly-name**&list-name=**list-friendly-name**&list-url=**list-url**&user-id=**uid***

Table 40-1 lists the different parameters for an stssync link that work with Outlook 2003.

Table 40-1   Stssync Protocol Parameters

Parameter	Description
ver	Required. Must be 1.0.
type	Required. Must be calendar or contacts, depending on the type of list (case-insensitive).
cmd	Required. Must be add-folder.
base-url	Required. The URL to the SharePoint list being added. Should not end in a / character.

Table 40-1   Stssync Protocol Parameters   *(continued)*

Parameter	Description
guid	Required. The GUID that, together with the base-url, uniquely identifies the list. Must be in the following format: "{"+ 8 hexadecimal characters + "-" + 4 hexadecimal characters + "-" + 4 hexadecimal characters + "-" + 12 hexadecimal characters + "}". To obtain the GUID, navigate to the site and click Modify Settings And Columns; the GUID will be the value for the List parameter in the URL for the listedit.aspx page.
site-name	Required. The friendly display name of the site that contains the list being added. Outlook uses this parameter together with the list-name to create the folder name in the SharePoint Folders hierarchy in Outlook.
list-name	Required. The display name of the list being added. Outlook uses this parameter together with the site-name to create the folder name in the SharePoint Folders hierarchy.
list-url	Required. A string that, when added to the sts-url parameter, creates the full URL for the list. Should start with a / character.
user-id	Optional. A number greater than zero, with fewer than eight digits. Uniquely represents a user on the SharePoint site.

The base-url, site-name, list-name, and list-url parameters can include spaces and special characters such as "\," and Unicode characters. Replace spaces with %20. For the characters "&", "\", "[", "]", or "|", precede the character with the "|" character. For example, if an events list is named Holidays & Events, the value of the corresponding list-name parameter would be Holidays%20|&%20Events. For each Unicode character, enclose the 4-digit hexadecimal representation of the character in square brackets "[ ]". For groups of consecutive Unicode characters, concatenate the groups and use one set of brackets to enclose all the characters. For example, if an events list is named Über Evénts, the value of the corresponding list-name parameter would be [00DC]ber%20Ev[00E900F1]ts.

The complete URL for an events list named Über Evénts on the Woodgrove Portal at *http://woodgrove/Lists/ber%20Evts/AllItems.aspx* with a GUID of {0C600187-1CC6-4AA0-A80E-5AD683397570} would be:

stssync://sts/?ver=1.0&type=calendar&cmd=add-folder&base-url=http://woodgrove/Lists/ber%20Evts&guid={0C600187-1CC6-4AA0-A80E-5AD683397570}&site-name=Woodgrove%20Portal&list-name=[00DC]ber%20Ev[00E900F1]ts&list-url=/AllItems.aspx

Understanding the SharePoint Folders.pst File

The first time you link a SharePoint list, Outlook creates a file named SharePoint Folders.pst in the user's profile folder under \Documents and Settings\\%username%\Local Settings\Application Data\Microsoft\Outlook\ and creates a folder in the item corresponding to the list, naming the folder after the site and the list (*site name - list name*). When you link additional SharePoint lists from the same site or even from different sites, Outlook creates additional folders in the same SharePoint Folders.pst file.

The SharePoint Folders.pst file uses the new Unicode format introduced in Outlook 2003. (Chapter 6 in the Office 2003 Resource Kit includes a section titled "Unicode Enhancements in Outlook 2003.") This means that the file cannot be opened in earlier versions of Outlook.

If the SharePoint Folders.pst file is moved to a new location (while Outlook is not running) or if it is closed or removed from the current Outlook profile, links to the SharePoint lists will be broken. The user can open the .pst file in Outlook again and see the SharePoint data that was previously copied. The file will function as a normal .pst file where users can create, modify, and delete items, but it will no longer receive updates from the SharePoint lists. The next time the user clicks the Link To Outlook link on a SharePoint list, Outlook will not reuse the original Share-Point Folders.pst file. Instead, it will create a new file named SharePoint Folders(2).pst to hold the linked folder.

Transferring Outlook Data to a SharePoint Site

There are at least five ways to transfer data from Outlook to a SharePoint site:

- Create a new list from Outlook data exported to a Microsoft Office Excel worksheet.

- Import contacts from the Outlook address book.

- Send a document via e-mail to a Microsoft Exchange public folder that has been linked to a SharePoint document library.

- Send a file as an attachment to a message, and accept the option to create a related Document Workspace site.

- Send a meeting request, and accept the option to create a related Meeting Workspace site.

Chapter 41, "Integrating Exchange Server 2003 with SharePoint Products and Technologies," describes how to enable e-mail for a SharePoint document library so that users can mail files to an Exchange public folder and have them transfer automatically to the document library. The creation of document and meeting workspaces in Outlook 2003 is covered in a separate section later in the chapter.

Note   An additional but less direct method would be to create a link to an Excel worksheet with a SharePoint list. You then copy and paste Outlook data into the worksheet and synchronize the worksheet with the server. You could copy Outlook data directly from selected items in an Outlook folder displaying a table view, or you could export from an Outlook folder to an Excel worksheet and copy from that sheet into the linked worksheet.

Creating a New List from Outlook Data

If you export data from an Outlook folder to an Excel worksheet .xls file, Windows SharePoint Services can use this file to create a new list with a column for each column in the worksheet.

To create a new SharePoint list from Outlook data

1. In Outlook, on the **File** menu, click **Import and Export** and use the wizard to export the desired data to an Excel .xls file.

2. Open the file in Excel, and select the cells to be imported, including the column headings.

3. On the **Insert** menu, click **Name**, click **Define**, and create a named range from the selected cells. Save the worksheet file.

4. On the SharePoint site, click **Create** and then click **Import Spreadsheet**.

5. Give the new list a name and description, and then click **Browse** to locate the worksheet file containing the data exported from Outlook.

6. Click **Import** to complete the import process.

   If the imported data includes date fields, you can display the SharePoint list in a calendar view. It will not, however, display a Link To Outlook link as a normal SharePoint events list would.

Importing Outlook Data from the Address Book

When the user clicks the Import Contacts button for a SharePoint contacts list, the browser runs a JScript script that launches the Outlook 2003 address book. (This technique works in Outlook 2002 as well.) The user then selects one or more names from the address lists. Names can be mixed and matched from personal contacts lists stored in Outlook, from enterprise contact information in the Exchange Server Global Address List (GAL), or from other address lists that might be present.

Tip The script that runs when the user clicks Import Contacts requires an Address Book Control component included with Outlook. By default, this component is not installed during Outlook setup but is configured as Installed On First Use. When you deploy Outlook, you might want to mark the Address Book Control component as Run From My Computer, as explained in Chapter 4 of the *Microsoft Office 2003 Editions Resource Kit* (Microsoft Press, 2003) under "Customizing Office Features and Short-cuts," so that it will already be installed locally when users want to import Outlook data into a SharePoint contacts list.

Table 40-2 lists the fields that Windows SharePoint Services can import from either personal or Exchange contacts and the matching column names in a Share-Point contacts lists. Any fields left blank in the Outlook contact or GAL entry are also left blank in the corresponding item in the SharePoint list.

Table 40-2 Import Mappings from Outlook Contacts and Exchange GAL to SharePoint

Outlook Contact Field	Exchange GAL Field	Column in SharePoint List
First Name	First Name	First Name
Last Name	Last Name	Last Name
E-mail	E-mail	E-mail Address
Company	Company	Company
Job Title	Title	Job Title
Business Phone	Telephone Number	Business Phone
Home Phone	Home Phone	Home Phone
Mobile	Mobile	Mobile Phone
Business Fax	Fax	Fax Number
Street Address	Street	Address
City	City	City
State	State/Province	State
Zip/Postal Code	Zip/Postal Code	Postal Code
Country/Region	Country/Region	Country
Web Page	n/a	Web Page
Notes	n/a	Notes

Unless you're working in a Microsoft Exchange Server environment where the administrator has modified the security settings for Outlook, after you choose the names to import, an Outlook security prompt will appear and you'll need to click Yes for Windows SharePoint Services to complete the import.

> **Note**   It is not possible to add new fields to the import list. Even though GAL entries include Web Page and Notes fields, Windows SharePoint Services does not import information from those GAL fields, even though it does import that information from Outlook contacts. Also, Windows SharePoint Services does not import the Full Name value from either Outlook contacts or GAL entries.

If you include a distribution list among the names to import, Windows SharePoint Services creates an item in its contacts list for each entry in the distribution list. If you want to import one or more Outlook contact records that do not have e-mail addresses, you'll need to add "dummy" addresses and save the contacts first, because the address book displays only contacts with e-mail addresses.

Document and Meeting Workspace Sites

When an Outlook 2003 user sends a file attachment or creates a meeting request, Outlook offers the opportunity to create a related Document Workspace or Meeting Workspace site on a server running Windows SharePoint Services. The site-creation process is transparent to the sender of the document or meeting request. Outlook names the site after the document or meeting, adds the sender to the Administrator site group, adds the recipients to the Contributor site group, and uploads the meeting details or the file attachments to the site.

Controlling Where a User Can Create Workspace Sites

To create a Meeting or Document Workspace site, the user must be a member of a site group with the Create Subsites right for the parent site. By default, SharePoint Products and Technologies grants this permission only to the Administrator site group. On SharePoint Portal Server, users are automatically in the Administrator site group on their personal (My Site) sites.

On the personal site on SharePoint Portal Server, if the user clicks the Set As Office Default Website link and responds Yes to the prompt that appears, My Site will then appear at the top of the list of available locations in the Meeting Workspace and Attachment Options task panes in Outlook. An administrator can use registry values or group policy to control which other sites are suggested in the site creation interface, as described in the "Managing Integration Features in Outlook" section later in this chapter.

If you want users to create Document and Meeting Workspace sites in a site other than their personal sites, you might want to set up a new top-level SharePoint site just to hold workspace sites. This will allow you to manage quotas and other settings for all workspace sites as part of a site collection. You'll need to grant the Create Subsites right to one or more site groups in that master workspace site.

Granting the Create Subsites Permission

There are at least three ways you can grant the Create Subsites right so that users can create Document or Meeting Workspace sites in a site where the user is not a member of the Administrator site group:

- Edit the settings for an existing site group to add the Create Subsites right.

- Create a new site group (perhaps named "Workspace Creator") with the Create Subsites right, and assign users to it.

- In the Site Settings page for the site, use the Configure Site And Workspace Creation link to select site groups and add the Create Subsites right to them.

Working with Meeting Workspace Sites from Outlook

When you create an Outlook 2003 meeting request, you can also create a Meeting Workspace site or link the meeting to an existing workspace site. Outlook creates the Meeting Workspace site by calling the Meeting Web Services on the SharePoint server using Simple Object Access Protocol (SOAP). The Meeting Workspace site can also track which Outlook 2003 meeting-request recipients have responded to the meeting request.

To create or link to a Meeting Workspace site

1. Create a new appointment, and click **Invite Attendees**. This converts the appointment into a meeting request.

2. On the Appointment page of the meeting request, click the **Meeting Workspace** button to display the **Meeting Workspace** task pane (shown in Figure 40-3).

3. To change the parent site and template, in the task pane click **Change Settings**. You will see the additional options shown in Figure 40-4. Otherwise, skip to step 8.

4. Select the site where you want to create the workspace site from the **Select a location** list, or choose **Other** and type in a new URL pointing to a SharePoint site.

5. To create a new workspace site, select the language and meeting template. Outlook uses the subject of the meeting request as the site name, subject to a 122-character limit.

   6. To link to an existing workspace site, select it from the list of those available in the site. If you are creating a recurring meeting, you can link it only to an empty meeting workspace, not to a single or multiple meeting workspace.

   7. Click **OK** to finish changing the settings.

   8. Click **Create** to create the workspace site, or click **Link** if you choose to link to an existing workspace site. Outlook will add a link to the workspace site to the body of the meeting request.

   9. Add attendees, and send the meeting request.

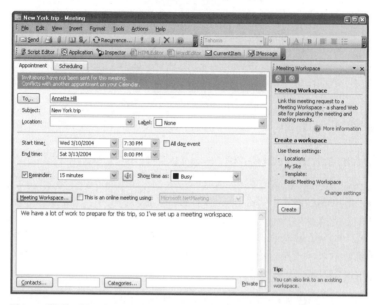

Figure 40-3   Meeting Workspace task pane in Outlook 2003

Figure 40-4   Meeting Workspace settings

> **Note**   You cannot create a new Meeting Workspace site under an existing Meeting Workspace site.

When you send the meeting request, Outlook attempts to add the attendees to the workspace site and include them in the Contributor site group. If the meeting-request recipients include a distribution list, either from the user's Contacts folder or the Exchange GAL, Outlook expands it automatically and adds each individual member of the list to the workspace site. If you receive a notification that Outlook was unable to add all attendees to the site, you'll need to manually add them as site users. You might receive such a notification if you invite someone who is not already a user in the Active Directory or if Outlook is working with an Exchange account offline and has the address book download set for "No Details."

> **Important**   Don't create the Meeting Workspace site until you have filled in the Subject for the meeting request. If you leave the Subject blank, Outlook will create a Meeting Workspace site with the name *UntitledXXX*, where *XXX* is a number calculated based on the number of existing "untitled" named sites.

Administrators can disable the Meeting Workspace button and control the available Meeting Workspace site locations using registry entries or group policies, as described in the "Managing Integration Features in Outlook" section later in this chapter.

After you send the meeting request, it will appear in the Outlook calendar (see Figure 40-5) with a special Meeting Workspace icon (F). Outlook provides several ways to view the Meeting Workspace site:

- Right-click the meeting in the Calendar folder, and then click **View Meeting Workspace**.

- Open the meeting, and click the link in the body of the item or the **Go to workspace** link in the task pane.

- When the reminder for the meeting fires and the **Reminders** dialog appears, select the meeting, click **Meeting Services**, and then click **View Meeting Workspace**.

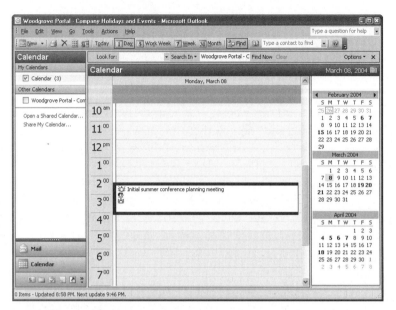

Figure 40-5   Outlook Appointment with Meeting Workspace

If the meeting request was for a recurring meeting or if you linked a new meeting to an existing workspace site, the home page of the Meeting Workspace site will list all the dates for the recurrences. Each date will have its own set of SharePoint lists and libraries in the Meeting Workspace site.

To remove the link from a meeting to a workspace site

■   Open the meeting from your Calendar folder, and then click the **Remove** button.

This removes the link between the meeting and the Meeting Workspace site, but doesn't delete the Meeting Workspace site.

Tracking Attendee Responses

If the sender of the meeting request and all the recipients are working in the same Microsoft Exchange organization, as people respond to the meeting request, their responses will be tallied on the Meeting Workspace site. You can also choose to tally meeting-request responses when some or all recipients work with a non-Exchange server, such as POP3 (Post Office Protocol) or IMAP4 (Internet Message Access Protocol), as long as the server supports Transport-Neutral Encapsulation Format (TNEF) and the meeting organizer sends the meeting request in Rich Text Format (RTF), not as an iCalendar item.

Users will need training in the specific techniques for sending a meeting request in Rich Text Format, which depend on whether the user is sending with an Exchange account or from a POP or IMAP account. In either case, the first step is to make sure that each Internet attendee's address is set for RTF.

To change an attendee's message format

1. Double-click the underlined attendee name or address in the meeting request.

2. If Outlook displays the attendee's contact record, double-click the attendee's e-mail address.

3. In the **E-mail Properties** dialog, under **Internet format**, choose **Send using Outlook Rich Text Format**.

If the sender is using a Microsoft Exchange account to send the meeting request, changing the attendee's message format is sufficient to force the meeting request to go out in RTF format. For Internet accounts, however, the default in Outlook 2003 is to send meeting requests to Internet addresses as iCalendar items. Therefore, the meeting organizer will also need to make a change to Outlook's default settings or make a change for each meeting request.

To send all meeting requests as RTF

1. On the Tools menu, click **Options**, and then click the **Calendar Options** button.

2. Deselect the check box for **When sending meeting requests over the Internet, use iCalendar format**.

To send a single meeting request as RTF

1. Before sending the meeting request, click the Tools menu.

2. If **Send as iCalendar** is checked, click **Send as iCalendar** to turn that option off for the current meeting request.

Working with Document Workspace Sites from Outlook

When you send a file attachment, Outlook 2003 offers the option to send the file as a **shared attachment**, a file that can be accessed by multiple users through a Document Workspace site. If the Attachment Options pane doesn't automatically appear after you add the attachment, you can click the Attachment Options button to display it.

Outlook creates the Document Workspace site when you send the message, giving it the same name as the attached file, and it adds a link to the workspace site to the body of the message. If you attach more than one file, the Document Workspace site is created with the name of the first file that was attached to the message. The sender of the message is automatically added to the Administrator site group for the new Document Workspace site, while recipients of the message are added to the Contributor site group.

Recipients can open the file using either the attachment or the link in the body of the message. If they open the file with Microsoft Office Word 2003, Microsoft

Office Excel 2003, Microsoft Office PowerPoint 2003, or Microsoft Office Visio 2003, the Office application periodically will get automatic updates from the Document Workspace site showing changes that other workspace site members have made in the file. The Office application will also update the workspace site copy when the user saves the file so that changes are available to other users who might be working on the document. These updates apply to documents or single file Web pages (MHMTL) created with Word 2003, Excel 2003, or PowerPoint 2003; Visio 2003 documents; and XML files from Word 2003 or Excel 2003.

For more information on working with and configuring options for Document Workspace sites, see Chapter 19.

Managing Alerts

Outlook 2003 users can manage the e-mail alerts received from SharePoint sites by clicking Rules And Alerts on the Tools menu. If the user clicks New Alert or Alert Properties on the Manage Alerts tab and makes selections, Internet Explorer opens a browser window to the appropriate alert page on the SharePoint site. The user can also click Create Rule to build an Outlook rule that pops up a notification window, plays a sound, moves the alert e-mail message to a specified folder, or performs other actions on the alert message.

By default, users can manage alerts only for sites on the local intranet and sites in the Trusted Sites list in Internet Explorer. Administrators can manage this behavior with a registry entry or group policy, as discussed in the next section.

Managing Integration Features in Outlook

Most, if not all, of Outlook's integration features related to SharePoint Products and Technologies can be controlled with Windows registry entries, the deployment tools in the Microsoft Office 2003 Resource Kit, or group policies. The appropriate group policy templates (Office11.adm and Outlk11.adm) are included in the Office Resource Kit tools download or on the Office Resource Kit CD. Copy them to the \Winnt\Inf or \Windows\Inf folder on the domain controller so that you can add them to the templates available in the Group Policy Management Console. Chapter 18 in the Office 2003 Resource Kit has a "Managing Users' Configurations by Policy" section that describes how to install the policy template files.

Table 40-3 lists the key registry entries. Corresponding Office 2003 policies are available in the Group Policy Management Console under User Configuration /Administrative Templates/Microsoft Office 2003/Tools | Options | General | Service Options/Shared Workspace. Corresponding Outlook 2003 policies are listed under User Configuration/Administrative Templates/Microsoft Office Outlook 2003, under SharePoint Integration and Meeting Workspace.

All the registry values shown in Table 40-3 are in the HKEY_CURRENT_USER \Microsoft\Office\11.0 key.

Table 40-3   Outlook-Related SharePoint Registry Values

Key	Value	Type	Description
Common\DWS	PollingInterval	DWORD	Number of minutes between checks for updates to Document Workspace sites (default 10, minimum 1, maximum 999)
Common\Mail-Settings	DisableSharing-Options	DWORD	1 (or 0) = disable (or enable) the Shared Attachments option in Outlook e-mail messages
Common\Security \Trusted Alert Sources	All	DWORD	0 (or 1) = disallow (or allow) users to use Outlook to manage alerts from all SharePoint sites (default = 0)
Common\Security \Trusted Alert Sources	AllIntranet	DWORD	0 (or 1) = disallow (or allow) users to use Outlook to manage alerts from all SharePoint sites within Outlook (default = 0)
Common\Security \Trusted Alert Sources	AllTrusted	DWORD	0 (or 1) = disallow (or allow) users to use Outlook to manage alerts from all intranet (default = 1)
Meetings\Profile	EntryUI	DWORD	1 (or 0) = disable (or enable) the Meeting Workspaces button on Outlook meeting requests
Meetings\Profile	ServerUI	DWORD	2 = disable user entries to server list (publish default, disallow others)
Meetings\Profile	MRUInternal	String	Delimited list of up to five servers available for Meeting Workspace sites (See details in text that follows this table.)
Outlook\Preferences	DisallowSTS	DWORD	1 (or 0) = disable (or enable) the ability to link SharePoint contacts and events lists with Outlook
Outlook\Preferences	STSSyncInterval	DWORD	Number of minutes between updates of linked SharePoint contacts and events lists in Outlook (default 20, minimum 1, maximum 1430)

Table 40-3   Outlook-Related SharePoint Registry Values   *(continued)*

Key	Value	Type	Description
SharePointTracking\Name0	Name	String	Display name of SharePoint site to be displayed in the Select A Location list
SharePointTracking\Name0	URL	String	URL of SharePoint site to be displayed in the Select A Location list

The SharePointTracking\Name# keys and the ServerUI and MRUInternal values control what servers the user will see on the Select A Location drop-down list in the Meeting Workspace or Attachment Options task pane. The default behavior is for the drop-down list to show the following sites:

- My Site (if the user has made her personal SharePoint Portal Server site her default site).

- Sites listed in the MRUInternal value (only in the Meeting Workspace task pane).

- Up to five of the most recently used sites listed in the SharePointTracking\Name# keys.

- Up to five SharePoint sites that the user has recently visited. This list of sites comes from cookies stored when the user visits a site where they have the Create Subsite right.

- An entry for Other, which allows users to enter any other URL that points to a SharePoint site.

You can create additional SharePointTracking\Name# keys—for example, Name1 and Name2 (up to Name4) to add up to five sites to the initial user list.

For meeting requests, setting the Meetings\Profile\ServerUI value to 2 causes Outlook to ignore My Site, the SharePointTracking\Name# list of most recently used sites, and the list of most recently visited sites. Instead, users will see only the list of servers from the Meetings\Profile\MRUInternal value. Therefore, you must populate the MRUInternal value if you set ServerUI to 2.

In the Meetings\Profile\MRUInternal value, you can list up to five locations for creating Meeting Workspace sites, each location being a delimited list describing the server and, optionally, the template to be used to create the workspace site. Each location record contains six fields separated by the pipe (|) character:

- Server URL

- Server friendly name

- Language ID for the template (for example, 1033 for U.S. English)

- TemplateID value (defined in Table 40-4)

- TemplateName value (defined in Table 40-4)

- OrganizerName

All fields are required to be present, with a pipe separating each pair of locations and no carriage return or line-feed characters in the string. As a minimum, you should specify the server URL and friendly name for each location. If you don't want to specify a value for the template fields or OrganizerName, leave them blank but include the pipe delimiters. It's recommended that you create the list of servers in Notepad and then paste it into the policy or registry editor.

If the value for ServerUI is set to 2, the first location in the MRUInternal list will be the default location that the user sees when creating a new meeting workspace. The first MRUInternal location will also set the default template. If the user switches in the Meeting Workspace task pane to a different location from the MRUInternal list, Outlook doesn't change the selected template to match the template for that location. Therefore, specifying a template for any location other than the first one in the MRUInternal list has no effect.

This example sets three locations on the same intranet server. Note the lack of carriage returns or line feeds:

http://blackfall/workspaces|Basic Meeting |1033|Mps#0|Basic Meeting Workspace| |http://blackfall/sales/workspaces|Sales Meeting||| | |http://blackfall/hq/ workspaces|HQ Meeting | | | | |

Table 40-4   Meeting Workspace TemplateName and TemplateID Values

TemplateName	TemplateID
Basic Meeting Workspace	Mps#0
Blank Meeting Workspace	Mps#1
Decision Meeting Workspace	Mps#2
Social Meeting Workspace	Mps#3
Multipage Meeting Workspace	Mps#4

In addition to specifying the values in Table 40-4, you can also specify the name and ID for a custom Meeting Workspace template. Chapter 16, "Windows SharePoint Services Site Administration," describes how to create custom templates.

The OrganizerName is used to add an attendee to the workspace site who is marked as the organizer of the meeting but is not added to the list of workspace site users. In most cases, you'll probably leave the OrganizerName field blank.

Additional Outlook Integration Opportunities

Except for the display of attendee status in a Meeting Workspace site, the Outlook integration scenarios discussed in this chapter don't make any assumptions about what kind of mail server Outlook is connected to. Where Outlook connects to Microsoft Exchange Server 2003, additional integration is available through e-mail-enabled public folders and Web Parts that display Exchange mailbox data using Outlook Web Access.

Summary

Outlook 2003 offers ample integration with SharePoint Products and Technologies. Users can view SharePoint site pages as folder home pages and can link SharePoint contacts and events lists into read-only Outlook folders. When sending a message with an attachment or creating a meeting request, users can create related Document and Meeting Workspace sites.

Using group policies or Office Resource Kit deployment tools, administrators can control the lists of sites available to users creating Document Workspace and Meeting Workspace sites from within Outlook and manage other settings, including the interval for updating linked SharePoint contacts and events lists.

Part XI

Upgrading and Migrating to SharePoint Products and Technologies

Chapter 41

Integrating Exchange Server 2003 with SharePoint Products and Technologies

Although Microsoft SharePoint Products and Technologies do not require any particular mail server, the tightest integration is available with Microsoft Exchange Server 2003. Web Parts distributed with Microsoft Office SharePoint Portal Server 2003 can display a user's Inbox folder, Tasks folder, a list of upcoming appointments from the Calendar folder, or the contents of any other mailbox folder. An alternative technique is to use the Page Viewer Web Part to display any Exchange folder using the folder's Microsoft Office Outlook Web Access URL. Another approach available for Exchange 2003—and Exchange 2000 as well—is the automatic transfer of attachment files from an Exchange public folder into a Microsoft Windows SharePoint Services document library. Exchange content, of course, can also be included in SharePoint Portal Server indexes, as discussed in Chapter 22, "Managing External Content in Microsoft Office SharePoint Portal Server 2003."

Using the Exchange Web Parts

SharePoint Portal Server 2003 ships with four Web Parts that can display data from an Exchange 2003 mailbox, listed in Table 41-1. All four Exchange Web Parts are included in the default Web Part gallery, categorized as *Personal Web Parts*, because they allow users to connect to their own personal Exchange mailboxes.

Table 41-1   Exchange 2003 Web Parts

Name	Description	Web Part Definition File
My Calendar	Displays the Calendar folder from an Exchange 2003 mailbox	Owacalendar.dwp
My Inbox	Displays the Inbox folder from an Exchange 2003 mailbox	Owainbox.dwp
My Mail Folder	Displays any Exchange 2003 mailbox folder; enter the folder path in the format **My Folder /My Subfolder**	Owa.dwp
My Tasks	Displays the Tasks folder from an Exchange 2003 mailbox	Owatasks.dwp

The My Calendar Web Part, shown in Figure 41-1, appears in the Private view of the default My Site page and lists events and appointments from the user's Calendar folder in a format similar to one the user would see in the Outlook Today display in Microsoft Office Outlook 2003. Users can add the other Web Parts to the My Site page or to other personal site pages by clicking the Modify My Page link.

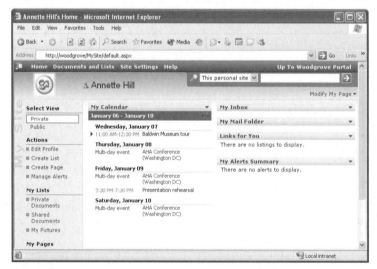

Figure 41-1   My Calendar Web Part displays appointments and events in a format similar to the Outlook Today page in Outlook 2003, regardless of the browser in use

Configuring the Exchange Web Parts

To display mailbox data, the user needs to configure each Exchange Web Part with the correct mail server URL, mailbox, and, for the My Mail Folder Web Part, the Exchange folder name. To configure any of these Web Parts, click the **open the tool pane** link in the Web Part and enter the information requested at the top of the tool pane, as shown in Figure 41-2.

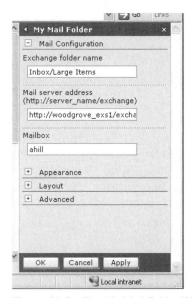

Figure 41-2   The My Mail Folder Web Part

Specify the server address in the Mail server address box; this address will generally be http://*servername*/exchange and is the same URL that the user would employ to access the mailbox from a browser using Outlook Web Access (OWA), the browser interface for Exchange. The Mailbox name is normally the same as the user's Windows login name. No additional information is required for the My Inbox Web Part.

For the My Mail Folder Web Part, however, the user must specify the Exchange folder name. If the desired folder is on the same level of the mailbox folder hierarchy as the Inbox, the name of the folder is sufficient. If the desired folder is a subfolder, the user must enter the path to the folder in the format My Folder/My Subfolder.

> **Note** The My Calendar and My Tasks Web Parts, like the My Mail Folder Web Part, have an option for an Exchange folder name. In fact, if you specify a folder path other than the default (*calendar* or *tasks*, respectively), either of those Web Parts will operate just like the My Mail Folder Web Part, displaying the desired mailbox folder. The reverse is also true: If you set the My Mail Folder Web Part to display a calendar or tasks folder, the items display in the same format that the My Calendar Web Part or My Tasks Web Part would use. In other words, the My Mail Folder Web Part is not limited to use just with mail folders.

Understanding the Two OWA Modes

For the My Inbox, My Tasks, and My Mailbox Folder Web Parts, how the Web Part displays the folder depends on the user's browser. Users of Microsoft Internet Explorer 5.0 or later will see the same layout as for the "premium" version of Outlook Web Access, which closely resembles the Outlook 2003 interface. The My Inbox control, for example, uses the Two-Line View display, which includes a column for setting the colored message flag. As shown in Figure 41-3, this display looks good in any Web Part zone.

Figure 41-3 My Inbox Web Part displays messages in a two-line view, like the default view in Outlook 2003

Users of other browsers will see the "basic" OWA layout, shown in Figure 41-4. Notice how the view does not resize its columns to fit entirely within a narrow zone. Therefore, users using a browser other than Internet Explorer 5.0 or later should be encouraged to use the My Inbox, My Tasks, and My Mailbox Folder Web Parts only in the Top or Bottom Web Part zones.

Figure 41-4   Other browsers, such as Mozilla 1.5 shown here, use a "basic" display

Displaying Exchange Data in a Page Viewer Web Part

The Exchange Web Parts are designed to show content from the user's Exchange mailbox. They cannot show content from Exchange public folders. To display public folder content, you can use the Page Viewer Web Part to display any Outlook Web Access page using the URL for that page. For example, the URL to display a month view of a top-level public folder named *Company Meetings* would be:

http:// *servername*/public/company%20meetings/?cmd= contents&view=monthly

Note that %20 replaces the space character in the folder name. The cmd=contents parameter specifies that only the contents of the folder should be displayed, not the folder navigation pane as well. The view=monthly parameter specifies that the complete current month should be displayed. Other possible values for the view parameter would be *weekly* or *daily* or the name of an existing saved view. The monthly, weekly, and daily values are case sensitive.

> **Tip**   Because of the width of the day, week, and month calendar view layouts, the wider Top and Bottom zones are probably the most suitable for displaying a calendar folder with the Page Viewer Web Part. However, using the default setting in which the Web Part adjusts its height to fit the zone might obscure the links at the top of the folder; these links allow the user to switch between the day, week, and month views. Instead, experiment with a fixed height to display those controls, as well as the link to create a new appointment.

Tracking messages sent to a distribution list, such as a company announcements list, is one practical example of using the Page Viewer Web Part with an Exchange folder. Public folders can have e-mail addresses. If you include a public folder among the members of a distribution list, all the messages sent to that list will appear in the folder and, in turn, can appear in a Page Viewer Web Part.

Another application would be to display Exchange mailbox data using OWA URLs for versions of Exchange earlier than Exchange 2003. (The Exchange Web Parts that ship with SharePoint Portal Server 2003 work only with Exchange 2003.)

Creating an E-Mail-Enabled Document Library

Windows SharePoint Services supports the concept of an **e-mail-enabled document library**, a document library linked with an Exchange 2000 or 2003 public folder so that files attached to messages in that public folder are automatically copied to a SharePoint library. Because Exchange public folders can be set up to allow e-mail submissions, this provides a mechanism for both internal and external users to submit documents to the SharePoint library without connecting to the document library site itself or even having permissions to add documents to it.

This feature uses the SharePoint Timer service, which periodically checks the public folder for new documents and copies them to the document library, creating a document for each attachment and generating a unique file name by adding numbers to the end of the file name if necessary. The service does not update, overwrite, or delete existing documents in the document library and sets only minimal field values for the document—the From address from the message, the subject line, and the date and the time the document was inserted in the document library. Any additional fields are left empty, even if they are required fields.

Setting up an e-mail-enabled document library requires configuration changes on the server running SharePoint Portal Server at the virtual server level, plus changes to the document library settings and the Exchange public folder settings.

Configuring the Exchange Public Folder

The Exchange administrator can create, mail-enable, and set permissions for a public folder using the Exchange System Manager tool using the following steps:

1. Expand the **Administrative Groups** hierarchy and the appropriate administrative group hierarchy to see the **Folders** hierarchy. Expand **Public Folders** to see the folder hierarchy.

2. Right-click the folder where you want to create a new public folder. Click **New**, and then click **Public Folder**. Give the folder a name, and then click **OK**.

3. In the folder hierarchy, right-click the folder, click **All Tasks**, and then click **Mail Enable**. Exchange creates SMTP and X.400 addresses from the folder name.

4. To manage permissions on the folder, right-click the folder and then click **Properties**. On the **Permissions** tab, click **Client permissions**. Add the Windows SharePoint Services application pool account(s) to the list of folder users with the Reviewer role or Read items permission. Alternatively, grant the Anonymous user the Read items permission. If you want non-authenticated users to be able to submit items to the public folder and thus to the document library, the Anonymous user also needs Create items permission. To manage which users can post to the folder, add the appropriate security group(s) as folder users with at least the Contributor role.

Tip   To change the e-mail address for a public folder, right-click the folder in the **Exchange System Manager** hierarchy and then click **Properties**. You can edit or add addresses on the **E-mail Addresses** tab.

Configuring Windows SharePoint Services

The first step toward enabling this feature is to configure the Windows SharePoint Services virtual server that hosts the document libraries you want to e-mail-enable. You must be a local server administrator or a member of the SharePoint administrators group to follow these steps.

1. Click **Start**, point to **All Programs**, point to **Administrative Tools**, and then click **SharePoint Central Administration**.

2. In the **Portal Site and Virtual Server Configuration** section, click **Configure virtual server settings**.

3. On the Virtual Server List page, click the link for the virtual server you want to configure.

4. On the Virtual Server Settings page, in the **Virtual Server Management** section, click **Virtual server general settings**.

5. In the **E-Mail Enabled Document Libraries** section (shown in Figure 41-5), under **Document libraries on this virtual server can accept e-mail attachments**, click **Yes**.

6. In the **Public folder server and root path** box, type the path to the public folder server, usually **http://*servername*/public**.

7. Under **Check for new e-mail in the public folder**, specify when public folders will be checked for attachments.

8. Click **OK**.

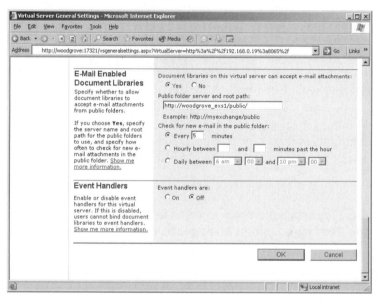

Figure 41-5 Configure a Windows SharePoint Services virtual server to monitor Exchange public folders for file attachments to be copied to document libraries

The default interval is hourly, at a random time during the hour. Using a random time means that each server running SharePoint Portal Server can check the Exchange public folders server at a different time during the hour, rather than all servers checking the public folders server at the same time.

Tip When you plan your SharePoint libraries, you should keep in mind that each SharePoint Portal Server virtual server can be linked to only one Exchange public folder server. If some document libraries need to be linked to folders on a different Exchange server, they will need to be in a different SharePoint virtual server.

Once e-mail-enabled document libraries have been enabled at the virtual server level, any SharePoint Portal Server administrator or any user with the Manage Lists Permissions right can link a document library with a public folder. To set up the link, follow these steps:

1. Navigate to the document library.

2. In the **Actions** list, click **Modify settings and columns**.

3. On the Customize document library name page, in the **General Settings** section, click **Change advanced settings**.

4. On the Document Library Advanced Settings (shown in Figure 41-6): Library name page, in the **E-Mail Settings** section, in the **Public folder address** box, type the path to the Exchange public folder you want to link to, such as **http: //*servername*/public/*myfolder*/*mysubfolder***.

5. Click **OK**.

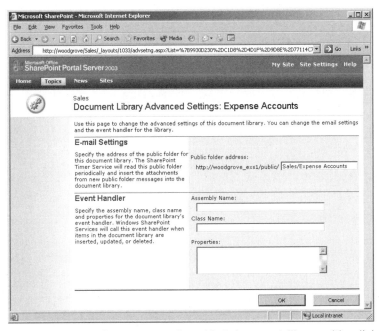

Figure 41-6   Configure an e-mail-enabled document library with a link to an Exchange public folder

Summary

With e-mail-enabled public folders, users can add documents to a SharePoint list as easily as they can send an e-mail message. At the same time, various Web Parts make it possible to view Exchange server folders in My Site or any other Web Part Page.

Chapter 42

Upgrading and Migrating to SharePoint Products and Technologies

If you have been using Microsoft SharePoint Portal Server 2001 and/or SharePoint Team Services from Microsoft, you probably have several portal sites you need to upgrade to Microsoft Office SharePoint Portal Server 2003 and websites that you need to move to new servers running Microsoft Windows SharePoint Services. This chapter details the approaches you might take and the tools you can use. It will also introduce the basic concepts of the technologies involved in these four products, which will allow you to formulate the extent of the task you are undertaking during the upgrade or migration process. The architecture between these sets of products has changed considerably; briefly, the previous versions of SharePoint Products and Technologies differ from the newer versions as follows:

- SharePoint Portal Server 2001 is based on **Web Parts** using Microsoft Digital Dashboard technology and stores data in the Microsoft **Web Storage System** (the same storage technology used by Microsoft Exchange Server). You can use tools such as a browser, My Network Places, Microsoft Office applications, and the Microsoft Office XP Development (MOD) Environment to access and customize it. You cannot install SharePoint Portal Server 2001 on a server farm.

■ SharePoint Team Services is based on Microsoft FrontPage 2002 Server Extensions and stores data in various locations on the file system, in the Windows registry, and in either Microsoft SQL Server Data Engine (MSDE) or Microsoft SQL Server databases. You can use tools such as a browser and FrontPage to access and customize it. SharePoint Team Services and SharePoint Portal Server 2001 are seen as complementary products that share no common technology other than that they can run on Microsoft Windows 2000 Server, which incorporates Microsoft Internet Information Server (IIS) 5.0. However, remember that you cannot install both SharePoint Team Services and SharePoint Portal Server 2001 on the same server.

■ Windows SharePoint Services is now an optional feature of the Microsoft Windows Server 2003 operating system and once installed runs as a Windows Server 2003 service. Windows SharePoint Services is based on a Web server rendering technology known as *Web Part Pages*, which uses Microsoft .NET Framework 1.1 and Microsoft ASP.NET, a customized version of FrontPage extensions, and either Windows MSDE (WMSDE) or SQL databases. You can use tools such as a browser, Web Folders, Microsoft Office applications, FrontPage 2003, and Microsoft Visual Studio .NET for access and customization purposes. Websites based on Windows SharePoint Services allow users to share information, collaborate with other users on documents, and create lists and Web Part pages. You can also use Windows SharePoint Services as a development platform to create collaboration applications and information-sharing applications.

■ Microsoft Office SharePoint Portal Server 2003 is built on top of Windows SharePoint Services; in fact, you cannot install SharePoint Portal Server 2003 without Windows SharePoint Services. A document management service is now part of Windows SharePoint Services, although a **backward-compatible document library**, based on the Web Storage System, can be installed with SharePoint Portal Server 2003. Like the earlier products, all websites are hosted on IIS; however, SharePoint Products and Technologies requires Windows Server 2003, which incorporates IIS 6.0. SharePoint Products and Technologies stores most of its data in the SQL server database, but for performance reasons, some base templates are stored in the file system. Once these templates are modified, they are stored in the SQL content database.

Note   Microsoft SQL Server is a separately licensed product that is not included with Windows SharePoint Services or SharePoint Portal Server 2003.

To migrate from an existing SharePoint Team Services installation or SharePoint Portal Server 2001 installation to a new SharePoint Products and Technologies 2003 installation, you need to understand the updated features and how the changes in the architecture affect your existing team and portal sites. You then need to plan your upgrade and migration process accordingly.

Planning is important to any upgrade or migration scenario. As well as understanding the updated features, you will need to identify the sites and the workspaces that are actively used and need to be migrated, and then identify the sites and the workspaces that are no longer used or are no longer required. In large installations, this analysis can reduce the number of sites you must migrate by as much as 25 percent. You can back up and retire the sites and workspaces that you do not migrate. When you plan your migration, you might want to restructure your new site(s), instead of just duplicating the old structure.

This chapter will introduce you to the tools you can use during the upgrade and migration process. You should refer to other chapters within this Resource Kit concerning the planning and installation of SharePoint Products and Technologies, and to the following related white papers:

- "Migrating from SharePoint Team Services and SharePoint Portal Server 2001 to Microsoft SharePoint Products and Technologies," by Michael Herman, Parallelspace Corporation, October 2003, which can be found at *http://www.microsoft .com/technet/prodtechnol/office/sps2003/deploy/spst2003.mspx.*

- "SharePoint Portal Server 2003 Advanced Migration Scenarios," by Michael Herman, Parallelspace Corporation, March 2004, which can be found at *http://www.microsoft .com/downloads/details.aspx?FamilyID=4925b907-0dd8-4be0-af9f- 02c8543f47c9&displaylang=en.*

- "Upgrading from an Evaluation Version to the Final Release of SharePoint Portal Server 2003," by Erik Heino, September 2003, which can be found at *http://www .microsoft.com/technet/prodtechnol/office/sps2003/deploy/upgreval.mspx.*

- "Converting Dashboard Web Parts to the Web Part Infrastructure for Microsoft SharePoint Products and Technologies," by Andrew Miller, Michael Herzfeld, and Scott Ruble, August 2003, which can be found at *http://msdn.microsoft .com/library/default.asp?url=/library/en-us/odc_sp2003_ta/html/sharepoint _north-windwebparts.asp.*

Migration Strategies

When you upgrade any software product, there are three possible strategies to consider.

- **In-place upgrade.** Install the new version on the same computer, on the same hard disk(s), and in the same directory as the previous version of the product, replacing the previous version of the product in a single step. This strategy is useful if you do not have another server available on which to install Windows Server 2003 and SharePoint Products and Technologies. The drawbacks with this strategy are that the server is unavailable during the upgrade, and you cannot compare or test the restored sites to the original sites to verify that the migration was successful. Also, during the operating system upgrade, the upgrade process will use the configuration and security settings of the previous Windows 2000 install. This will not be same as if you had chosen a clean installation of Windows Server 2003, which is a much more security-conscious installation. If you do choose this option, ensure that you refer to Chapter 6, "Security Architecture for SharePoint Products and Technologies," and to the Security Guidance Center for Windows Server 2003 at *http://www.microsoft.com /security/guidance/prodtech/WindowsServer2003.mspx.*

■ **Co-existence.** Install the new software product version on the same computer or on a different computer in such a way that the previous version of the product and the newly installed version of the product can both be used. This requires no additional hardware but is not recommended because there are coresidency issues to address. For SharePoint Products and Technologies, certain combinations of cross-version products and versions on the same computer are not supported. (See Chapter 3, "Installing Microsoft Office SharePoint Portal Server 2003.") Therefore, it is impossible to use the same machine co-existence strategy. If you wish to use this strategy, you will need additional hardware, and in most cases you will be using the following strategy, co-existence and migration.

■ **Co-existence and Migration.** Use a two-step process to support concurrent operation of the previous software version until the organization is ready to switch to the new software version and turn off the old version of the software product. Install the new software version in parallel with the previous version of the product, and run both solutions in parallel. During this time, migrate your users and their data from the previous version of the software to the new version. When the migration is complete, turn off and remove the previous version of the software. This strategy is beneficial because it allows you to keep original sites operational during the deployment of Windows SharePoint Services. It also allows you to verify that the migration was successful. However, it requires a greater number of servers to implement than the other two strategies.

When you migrate from SharePoint Portal Server 2001 to SharePoint Portal Server 2003, you can use the in-place upgrade, co-existence (additional hardware), and co-existence and migration strategies. Similarly, you can use all three strategies for SharePoint Team Services, but in reality the in-place upgrade is implemented as a migration progress, as is detailed in the next section of this chapter. Therefore, your SharePoint Team Services sites are likely to always be upgraded using the migration strategy, and I would recommend that you always migrate to a computer that has a clean install of Windows Server 2003 whenever possible. This will reduce the number of post-installation tasks concerning the configuration of the server, allow you to configure the hardware to suit the architecture of the new products, and reduce the risk that you have inherited settings that might affect your installation in the future. See Chapter 9, "Capacity Planning," for more information on capacity planning.

Upgrading a SharePoint Team Services Website to Windows SharePoint Services

If you want to move from SharePoint Team Services or FrontPage 2002 Server Extensions to Windows SharePoint Services, consider the following changes:

- The architecture has changed considerably. For example, you can now use Windows SharePoint Services in a server farm configuration. Also, all site content is now stored in the content databases instead of on the file system, and configuration data for a server or a server farm is stored in the configuration database. For more information about the new architecture, see Part 2, "SharePoint Products and Technologies Architecture."

- The security model has changed. For example, you can now grant Windows SharePoint Services administration rights to a specific domain group, in addition to the server's local Administrators group. For more information about the new security model, see Chapter 6, "Security Architecture for SharePoint Products and Technologies."

- There are many new features, some changed features, and some features that no longer exist in the new version. For more information about features included in Windows SharePoint Services, see Chapter 1, "Introduction to Microsoft SharePoint Products and Technologies."

In addition to these general changes, several specific issues should be considered when you upgrade your server to Windows SharePoint Services.

Microsoft SharePoint Products and Technologies no longer relies on role-based security for assigning rights and permissions to users. Instead, SharePoint Products and Technologies uses site groups and cross-site groups to assign rights and permissions to users. Site groups are custom security groups that apply to a specific website. Cross-site groups are custom security groups that apply to more than one website. Because the site group names and definitions changed between SharePoint Team Services and Windows SharePoint Services, the default site groups for your user accounts change when you upgrade. The new site group assignments attempt to preserve the meaning of the previous roles. Table 42-1 lists the roles in SharePoint Team Services and the new site group assignments that take effect when you upgrade to Windows SharePoint Services.

Table 42-1   Roles in SharePoint Team Services and the New Site Group Assignments

SharePoint Team Services Role Name	Windows SharePoint Services Site Group Membership after Upgrade
Administrator	Administrator
Advanced Author	Web Designer
Author	Contributor
Contributor	Reader
Browser	Reader

If you have a custom role that you created in SharePoint Team Services, a site group with the same name is created, and the Windows SharePoint Services rights that correspond to the SharePoint Team Services rights are assigned to the site group when you upgrade. In some cases, because of changes to how Windows SharePoint Services works, there is no corresponding right. Table 42-2 lists the rights mapping between SharePoint Team Services and Windows SharePoint Services.

Table 42-2   Rights Mapping Between SharePoint Team Services and Windows SharePoint Services

SharePoint Team Services Right Name	Windows SharePoint Services Rights
Author Lists	Add Items, Edit Items, and Delete Items
Author Pages	View Items and Add Items
Author Web Document Discussions	View Pages
Border Web	Apply Themes and Borders
Browse	View Pages
Close Web Document Discussions	View Pages
Configure Access	Manage Site Groups
Create Accounts	N/A
Design Lists	Manage Lists
Link Style Sheets	Apply Style Sheets
Manage Lists	Manage Lists
Manage Server Health	N/A
Manage Subweb	Create Subsites
Manage Usage Analysis	View Usage Data
Manage Web Document Discussions	N/A
Manage Web Subscriptions	N/A
Recalc Web	N/A
Set Source Control	N/A
Subscribe To Document	View Items

Table 42-2   Rights Mapping Between SharePoint Team Services and Windows SharePoint Services   *(continued)*

SharePoint Team Services Right Name	Windows SharePoint Services Rights
Theme Web	Apply Themes and Borders
View Lists	View Items
View Web Document Discussions	View Pages

For a complete list of the rights and site groups available in Windows SharePoint Services, see Chapter 6.

When you upgrade from SharePoint Team Services to Windows SharePoint Services, you can also specify whether to migrate the security settings for the site. Migrating security settings includes all the following elements:

- The list of user roles and associated rights

- The list of user accounts and role membership

- The anonymous access settings

- The setting for inherited or unique permissions for the site

Before you migrate a site, be sure that all of the settings are the way you want them to be in your destination site. Remember that if a user account cannot be verified in the domain, and you are not using Active Directory account creation mode, the account will not be restored. If you are running Windows SharePoint Services in Active Directory account creation mode, user accounts are automatically created in Active Directory directory services for the users that existed in the site before migration.

To migrate a site, you will use the SharePoint Migration Tool. The SharePoint Migration Tool, Smigrate.exe, is a command-line utility that is located in the Program Files\Common Files\Microsoft Shared\Web Server Extensions\60\Bin folder when Windows SharePoint Services is installed on a server, and the tool is used to back up SharePoint Team Services sites or Windows SharePoint Services sites and restore these backups to other servers running Windows SharePoint Services. This chapter will detail the use of the SharePoint Migration Tool and its parameters as part of the migration scenarios. For more information, see Chapter 30, "Default Tools to Customize Windows SharePoint Services." If you have not installed Windows SharePoint Services on a server, you can download the SharePoint Migration Tool from Microsoft Windows Update.

To find the SharePoint Migration tool on the Windows Update site, click Windows Update Catalog. Click Find updates for Microsoft Windows Operating Systems. In the Operating System list, click Windows Server 2003 family. In the Language list, click the language you need, and then click Search. The SharePoint Migration tool is available in the Recommended Updates, if it is not already installed.

Caution   If you are using the SharePoint Migration Tool to migrate and upgrade a site from SharePoint Team Services or FrontPage 2002 Server Extensions from Microsoft to Windows SharePoint Services, be aware that several features or types of customizations supported in these environments will not migrate properly or will not work in a migrated site. For a list of items that you must re-create or work around, see "Upgrade Considerations" in the Windows SharePoint Services Administrator's Guide. These are also available in Appendix B, "Upgrading SharePoint Team Services to Windows SharePoint Services" on the Companion CD-ROM. It is very important that you review this list. Of special note is that some characters are not supported in Windows SharePoint Services, such as /, \, :, *, ?, ", <, >, |, #, {, }, %, &, and ~, as well as tab characters and multiple periods.

If a file, a folder, or a URL name in your original site contains one of these characters, it is replaced with an underscore (_). Multiple periods are replaced with a single period. Additional digits might be appended to the file or folder name if there are conflicting renaming changes. If you have other applications that make reference to these objects, they could fail or display broken links. Also, remember that lists within Windows SharePoint Services have column restrictions. You will receive errors when you try to add too many columns to a list, and migrated content might be truncated or might fail to restore if the original list has more columns than the second version supports. In addition you should be aware that lists and document libraries will have a new creation date; that is, the creation modification dates for lists and document libraries within SharePoint Team Services are not preserved. Creation and modification dates for list items and documents should be preserved.

If you do not want to migrate user information to the new site, you would use the -x parameter with this tool. The new user accounts are created based on the users' e-mail addresses, so each user must have a unique e-mail address for the account creation to work correctly. If a user does not have an e-mail address in the old site, no account can be created for that user. Also, because only one account is created for each e-mail address, a shared e-mail address results in a merged user account that is given all of the rights that each original user had, and it is also listed as the user name for any items added to the site by any of the original users. If Windows SharePoint Services is installed using the Active Directory account creation mode, be sure that each existing user account has a unique e-mail address before migrating a site, and that you enter the full e-mail address (for example: *someone@example.com*).

If the site you are backing up or restoring is large, it can take quite a while to process. For example, a site with about 4.5 gigabytes (GB) of data can take up to three hours to back up. The same site can take up to three hours to restore because so many files must be uploaded to the new server. The more files included on a site, the longer the restore process will take. It might therefore be advisable with large websites to back up each individual subsite. You would then back up the remaining sites. The **SharePoint Migration Tool** includes a parameter (-e) to exclude subsites; therefore, to back up the remaining sites you could specify the virtual server and exclude the large websites, which you backed up individually. As a general performance guideline, you will have the best backup/restore performance when using separate computers for each task. An example of such a configuration is:

- One computer running the SharePoint Migration Tool (Smigrate.exe)

- One or more computers running as front-end Web servers

- One or more computers running as SQL Server back-end servers

There are two stages in upgrading from SharePoint Team Services or FrontPage 2002 Server Extensions to Microsoft Windows SharePoint Services:

- First you back up your existing websites using the Microsoft SharePoint Migration Tool. Then if you want to upgrade the server from SharePoint Team Services to Windows SharePoint Services, remove SharePoint Team Services or FrontPage 2002 Server Extensions from the virtual servers. During the backup process, you specify the URL for the website and the backup file to create. You can also specify the scope of the site migration (whether to migrate just the top-level website, or whether to migrate the top-level website and any subsites).

- Second you install Windows SharePoint Services on your server computer or to a new server and restore your websites to new locations on the existing server or to the same locations on a new server. During the restore process, you specify the new URL and the backup file from which to restore.

Step 1: Backing Up the SharePoint Team Services Websites

Use the SharePoint Migration Tool to back up the SharePoint Team Services websites into a single file or multiple files. See the discussion earlier in this chapter concerning backing up and restoring large websites. Complete the backup procedure, also known as the *export procedure*, as follows:

1. Verify that your SharePoint Team Services installation is at Microsoft Office XP Service Pack 2 (SP2) or later. If the administrator runs the `owsadm.exe -o` upgrade command after installing the service packs, the virtual server and the _vti_inf.html file version numbers will be updated. You can view these by using the Microsoft SharePoint Administrator; the version number of the extended virtual servers will be 5.0.2.4330 if SP 2 is installed, or display *http://virtualserver/_vti_inf.html* in a browser. Right-click the page, and then click **View** and look for the keyword

FPVersion=, as shown in Figure 42-1.[1] Alternatively, check the version number in **Add/Remove Programs**, where the version number will be 10.0.433.0 if Service Pack 2 is installed. If the service packs are not already installed on the server, install Microsoft Office XP Service Pack 1 (SP 1) and then SP 2. Service Packs can be obtained from TechNet CDs or from the Microsoft Office download site, *http://office.microsoft.com/ProductUpdates*, where you can use Office Update to install the service packs.

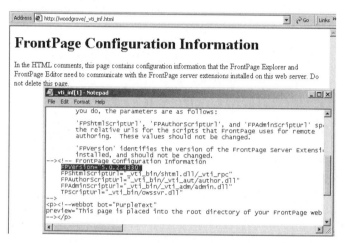

Figure 42-1   "FPVersion=" line indicates the version of the FrontPage Server Extension

2. If you do not have Office XP Service Pack 3 or higher installed, you will need to install the update to SharePoint Team Services, which is available from the Microsoft Download Center at *http://go.microsoft.com/fwlink/?LinkId=13275*. You might be prompted to reboot the system after the update is installed.

   If the appropriate Office XP Service Packs or the Ows1002.exe update for SharePoint Team Services are not installed on the SharePoint Team Services server, the server administration programs and the server extensions on the Web server are not compatible. Therefore, when you use Smigrate.exe to back up the SharePoint Team Service site you might receive an error message similar to the following:

   ```
   The server is too old to use with this administration program. Please consult
       the section in the Administration Guide on Migrating and Updating Web Sites
       for more information.
   ```

3. Set the original site(s) to read only. This can be achieved by clearing all but the **Browse**, **View Lists**, and **View Web Document Discussions** check boxes on the Set List of Available rights page within the **Microsoft SharePoint Administrator** website.

---

1. The values of FPVersion have the following meanings as to which FrontPage extension is installed: 6 = Windows SharePoint Services, 5 = FrontPage 2002 Server Extensions (Office XP) or SharePoint Services 1.0, 4 = FrontPage 2000 Server Extensions, and 3 = FrontPage 98 Server Extensions.

4. Increase page file size to at least 1 GB. Ensure that there is no group or local policy defined that deletes the page file on reboot; otherwise, you will see a huge increase in reboot times.

5. On a machine with Windows SharePoint Services installed, from a command prompt, navigate to the folder that contains the SharePoint Migration Tool and enter the following line of code:

```
smigrate -w http://STS_SERVER_NAME/STS_SITE_NAME -f c:\STS.fwp
```

While creating the backup file, the SharePoint Migration Tool creates temporary files in a folder at the same location where the backup file (*.fwp) is created. You should ensure that there is enough free space at the location where the backup file will be created to hold all of the data and the files from the original website, plus approximately 25 percent.

Step 2: Restoring the Windows SharePoint Team Services Website

The SharePoint Migration Tool will also be used to restore the site on a Windows SharePoint Services installation. The tool captures the content's author/editor metadata in the format *Domain/username* and not the account's security ID (SID). If the server cannot resolve the account, it will default to the account that is performing the migration; therefore, when restoring a site, it is often helpful to create an account specifically for this purpose. For example, if you create an account named "SharePoint Migration" and then use that account to restore a site, users will see "SharePoint Migration" as the author of list items for author accounts that could not be resolved during the migration process. If the SharePoint Team Services site used accounts from a domain that no longer exists or is unreachable, or if the site used local accounts and you have changed the name of the server, most of the contents will have the migration account as the author. You can either log on to Windows as the migration account or specify it using the -u and -pw options on the smigrate command line.

Note Some of the steps in this topic require changing settings in Microsoft Internet Information Services or Microsoft SQL Server. To complete the steps that use IIS, you must be logged on as a member of the Administrators group on the local computer, or you must be logged on using an account that is both a member of the SharePoint Administrators group (STS_WPG) and that has been granted permissions to administer IIS and is the identity that the Application Pool for the site is running under. To complete the steps that use SQL Server, you must be logged on using an account that is a member of the db_owner role in SQL Server. If SQL is installed on another machine, the account should be a network account.

You can migrate a site to a new virtual server, to a new top-level website on an existing virtual server, or to a subsite under an existing top-level website.

1. If you plan to complete an in-place upgrade—that is, you are going to use the same server that was running your SharePoint Team Services sites to run your Windows SharePoint Services site and the server is running Windows 2000 Server—remove SharePoint Team Services from all virtual servers that have been extended, as follows:

    a. Navigate to the Server Administration page. You can get to the Server Administration page by clicking **Start**, then clicking **All Programs**, **Administrative Tools**, and then clicking **Microsoft SharePoint Administrator**. Then, next to the virtual server you want to uninstall SharePoint Team Services from, click **Administration**.

    b. Click **Uninstall Microsoft SharePoint**.

    c. To perform a full uninstall, on the Uninstall Microsoft SharePoint page, next to Full Uninstall, select **Yes**.

    d. Click **Uninstall**. When you uninstall SharePoint Team Services, the virtual server remains, but in an un-extended status, and some content might be left on the file system in the virtual server directory. Because you have already backed up the websites, you can delete this content from the file system after you uninstall SharePoint Team Services and before you install Windows SharePoint Services. After you install Windows Share-Point Services you can restore the websites, and the content will be added to the content database.

    e. Once SharePoint Team Services is removed from all virtual servers, you should uninstall SharePoint Team Services from the server using the **Add/Remove Programs** feature. You might also consider uninstalling MSDE, if that was installed by SharePoint Team Services, first ensuring that no other applications are using that MSDE instance. Next, upgrade your server to Windows Server 2003. For more information about upgrading to Windows Server 2003, see the Windows Server 2003 documentation.

2. It is recommended that you uninstall FrontPage Server Extensions. These are automatically installed if you upgrade to Windows Server 2003 from a Windows 2000 Server that had FrontPage Server Extensions installed. If you want to run both FrontPage 2002 Server Extensions and Windows SharePoint Services, you must first remove FrontPage 2002 Server Extensions from the default website before installing Windows SharePoint Services. If the default site contains information that you wish to preserve, use the SharePoint Migration Tool to back up the data before removing FrontPage 2002 Server Extensions. To remove FrontPage Server Extensions, complete the following:

    a. Click **Start**, point to **All Programs**, then **Administrative Tools**, and click **Microsoft SharePoint Administrator**.

b. On the Server Administration page, click **Administration under Virtual Servers**.

c. Under **Administration**, click **Uninstall FrontPage Server Extensions**.

d. Restart IIS by entering this code on a command line:

```
iisreset /noforce ServerName
```

3. Install and enable ASP.NET. Enable IIS and set it to run in IIS 6.0 worker process isolation mode, and then install Windows SharePoint Services; for more information, see Chapter 2. If you receive the error message "Virtual Server Is Running FrontPage 2002 Server Extensions" when you run Windows SharePoint Services setup or when you try to extend the virtual server with Windows SharePoint Services, see Microsoft Knowledge Base article 823378.

4. Make sure the **Internet Explorer Enhanced Security mode** is not installed in Windows components. (Otherwise, you might have problems accessing the old STS sites.) To disable Enhanced Internet Explorer Security Mode, open **Control Panel**, click **Add or Remove Programs**, and then click **Add /Remove Windows Components** tab. Then in the window that opens, deselect the **Enhanced Internet Explorer Security** check box.

> **Note**   You have the option of leaving Enhanced Internet Explorer Security Mode enabled; however, you must add the server to your Trusted Sites list in Internet Explorer. In this scenario, whenever you open a Web Page, for example, to a Windows SharePoint Services website or an administration page, you will be prompted for your logon credentials

5. Disable all antivirus software before trying to migrate.

6. For IIS websites you are restoring to, use the IIS Manager to increase the website's **Connection time out** on the **Web Site** tab to **65000** seconds and on the **Directory Security** tab, under the **Authentication and access control**, click **Edit** and select **Enable anonymous access**. Turn on anonymous access only if you want to migrate anonymous access settings.

7. Click **Start**, point to **All Programs**, then **Administrative Tools**, and click **SharePoint Central Administrator**. On the SharePoint Central Administration page:

- Under **Component Configuration**, click **Configure full-text search** and disable full-text search before migrating, if the destination server is using a SQL Server 2000 database. This step can decrease amount of time required to restore by as much as 40 percent in some cases.

- Under **Component Configuration**, click **Manage quotas and locks** and ensure that the quota limit is large enough to ensure you can migrate the content.

- Under **Security Configuration**, click **Manage blocked file types** and delete the file types that you want to allow.

- Under the **Virtual Server Management**, click **Virtual server general settings** to set maximum upload file size and set the maximum number of alerts to be unlimited. By default, the maximum upload limit is set to 50 MB, which might not be enough to restore your site's content. However, uploading files larger than 50 MB might cause problems, depending on your available system resources. If you greatly increase the maximum file size and then attempt to upload a very large file, the upload might fail or the server might stop responding. The file size at which Windows SharePoint Services might stop responding depends on the hardware you are using and on usage patterns. For example, an installation that includes a front-end Web server with 512 MB of RAM and a back-end server with 1 GB of RAM might be able to handle files up to about 128 MB. In general, it is the amount of available memory that determines how large of a file can be uploaded—for a temporary solution, such as when you are running the SharePoint Migration Tool, you can set the maximum upload size to handle files about one-quarter of the size of the physical memory for your server.

8. Make sure the computer you use to run the SharePoint Migration Tool has sufficient disk space to temporarily store approximately 20 percent of the data and files from the original website. While the tool is restoring, this data is periodically saved in files in a directory in the Temporary Internet Files folder on the computer on which you are running the SharePoint Migration Tool. You can change the location of the Temporary Internet Files folder by clicking the **Settings** button on the **General** tab of Internet Options, which can be accessed through the Control Panel or through Internet Explorer.

9. Create a destination site collection, top-level website, or site, for example; go to the portal home page (if you have one) and click **Sites**; and then click **Create Site** under the **Actions** section. If you wish to create a stand-alone top-level Windows SharePoint Service site, click **Start**, point to **All Programs**, then **Administration Tools**, and click **SharePoint Central Administration**. Under the **Virtual Server Configuration** section, click **Create a top-level Web site**.

10. Give the new site a name and a URL, and define the properties, and then click **Create**.

11. When prompted for a template for the new site, close the Web browser window without selecting a template. You must create a blank site without

applying a site template or the restore operation will fail with the following error message:

```
ERROR:  2162776 Server error: A site template has already been applied to
    this site. Once a template has been applied, the site must be deleted and
    recreated in order to apply a different template.
```

12. To import the FWP file data, go back to the command window, and enter:

```
smigrate -r -w http://NEW_SITE_URL -f c:\STS.fwp
```

If you do not want to migrate user information to the new site, use the -x parameter.

The SharePoint Migration Tool will generate a number of messages. The tool automatically generates a log file for you that contains all of text that it sends to the screen. You can view the Smigrate.log file to see which items migrated successfully and which did not. The Smigrate.log file is stored in the %temp% directory for your user account. If a log file already exists from a previous backup or restore, a log file will be created using the next available name (such as *Smigrate_1.log*, *Smigrate_2.log*, and so on). These log files can be an audit trail of your migration process, as well as a troubleshooting aid.

The new site will now have the imported data of the old team site. If the old site had subsites, they were imported as well and are now available under the new site.

Review the messages that are displayed as a result of running the SharePoint Migration Tool. Pay particular attention to error messages such as invalid list templates, files that were not loaded due to your file blocking policies, files that could not be read, and user accounts that could not be added. In fact, search the log entries for the error messages with the following words and phrases: *cannot, could not, failure, server error, timed out, unable to*, and *the server sent a response*. By investigating such errors, you can confirm whether the migration was successful, and if not they will help you troubleshoot failures.

13. After you migrate a site to a server running Windows SharePoint Services in Active Directory account creation mode, you must reset the passwords for the new user accounts. When user accounts are created during site migration, no automatic e-mail messages are sent with the user name and passwords, so you must send the users their new logon information manually.

14. Review all sites that were migrated and customize them accordingly; for example, lists might have duplicate views, such as *All Items* and *All Items (v1)*. The latter view represents the view migrated from SharePoint Team services. You might wish to delete or rename one of these views. You might also wish to enable Windows SharePoint Services features, such as content approval or item-level permissions, or add the site to a portal site listing if you have SharePoint Portal Server 2003 installed.

15. Change the server settings to the configuration you want to use.

Upgrading to SharePoint Portal Server 2003

If you want to move from SharePoint Portal Server 2001 to SharePoint Portal Server 2003, consider the following changes:

- The architecture has changed considerably. For example, you can now use SharePoint Portal Server 2003 in a server farm configuration. Also, all site content is now stored in the content databases instead of in the Web Storage System, and configuration data for a server or server farm is stored in the configuration database. For more information about the new architecture, see Part 2, "SharePoint Products and Technologies Architecture."

- The security model has changed, not only concerning the security settings at the document library level, but also the ability to secure Web Parts. For more information about the new security model, see Chapter 6.

- There are many new features, some changed features, such as versioning, document profiling and metadata, and some features that no longer exist in the new version, such as approval routing if you do not install the backward-compatible document library. For more information about features included in SharePoint Portal Server 2003, see Chapter 1.

This section will detail the upgrade process, migrating Web Parts, and migrating document library content.

The upgrade process does provide you with certain advantages, such as the ability to link existing SharePoint Portal Server 2001 deployments into your new navigation hierarchy and continuing to use your digital dashboard applications on the SharePoint Portal Server 2001 machines. The upgrade process for a server running SharePoint Portal Server 2001 is similar to the upgrade process for a server running SharePoint Team Services. You will first have to decide how you wish to use the updated features. In most cases, the SQL Server content store is a better choice because the SQL Server content store provides fast database performance, manageability, scalability, and the familiar SQL Server administrator tools. However, if you wish to retain the ability of multiple document profiles per document library folder as well as the complex routing and approval workflow features of the document store from SharePoint Portal Server 2001, you will need to install the backward-compatible document library. Also, you will need to consider reviewing any application you have developed that integrates with SharePoint Portal Server 2001 and uses the Publishing and Knowledge Management Collaboration Data Objects (PKMCDO) interface to the Web Storage System.

If you decide that you wish to install the backward-compatible document library, to host the documents from your SharePoint Portal Server 2001 installation, you will need to run the in-place upgrade process. This process converts and retains the contents of the SharePoint Portal Server 2001 Web Storage System to the SharePoint Portal Server 2003 backward-compatible document library. If you do not wish to convert your Web Storage System, there are tools that enable you to export and then import documents from the Web Storage System to the SQL Server content database document library. For more information, see the section "Migrating SharePoint Portal Server 2001 Document Library Information to Windows SharePoint Services" later in this chapter.

If you decide that you do not need to convert the SharePoint Portal Server 2001 Web Storage System, you might still want to use the upgrade process because it will migrate your categories, keywords, and content sources. However, the upgrade process will not convert your dashboard site customization, your digital dashboard Web Parts, or Alerts. You will need to review your current Web Parts and your requirements for the deployment of SharePoint Portal Server 2003. For more information, see the section "Upgrading Web Parts to the Microsoft .NET Framework," later in this chapter. This section of the chapter will now detail the upgrade process.

Microsoft supports in-place upgrade to SharePoint Portal Server 2003 from the following versions of SharePoint Portal Server:

- SharePoint Portal Server 2001 Service Pack 2a (SP2a).

- Microsoft Office SharePoint Portal Server 2003 Beta 2 Technical Refresh.

- Microsoft Office SharePoint Portal Server 2003 Beta 2. If you are running SharePoint Portal Server 2003 Beta 2, you must first upgrade to SharePoint Portal Server 2003 Beta 2 Technical Refresh before you can upgrade to SharePoint Portal Server 2003. SharePoint Portal Server 2003 Beta 2 Technical Refresh is available for download from the Microsoft website at *http://www.microsoft.com/downloads/details.aspx? displaylang=en&familyid=3b6bc834-baeb-4d6b-8c57-58076b13e766.*

Note You must be running the release-to-manufacturing (RTM) version of Windows Server 2003 when you upgrade to SharePoint Portal Server 2003 Beta 2 Technical Refresh from SharePoint Portal Server 2003 Beta 2, or when you upgrade to the RTM version of SharePoint Portal Server 2003 from SharePoint Portal Server 2003 Beta 2 Technical Refresh.

- SharePoint Portal Server 2003 Evaluation version. Refer to the white paper mentioned earlier in this chapter, "Upgrading from an Evaluation Version to the Final Release of SharePoint Portal Server 2003."

The SharePoint Portal Server Upgrade Tool (Upgrade.exe) will automatically start when a SharePoint Portal Server CD is inserted into the CD-ROM drive on a SharePoint Portal Server 2001 computer. If the server is not at the correct level, a dialog box will be displayed as shown in Figure 42-2, and the upgrade process will not start.

Figure 42-2 Microsoft Office SharePoint Portal Server 2003 Upgrade warning message

During the upgrade, a SharePoint Portal Server 2003 portal site is built, and the documents from the SharePoint Portal Server 2001 document library (Web Storage System–based) are migrated to the SharePoint Portal Server 2003 backward-compatible document library. When the upgrade is complete, the server running SharePoint Portal Server 2003 contains the following components:

■ A backward-compatible document library that contains the documents previously stored in SharePoint Portal Server 2001 workspaces.

■ A SQL Server content store to support the upgraded portal site and to support creation of new SharePoint sites.

■ A SharePoint Portal Server 2003 portal site initialized with the categories and document links, content sources, site groups (formerly called *roles*), and keyword Best Bets from the SharePoint Portal Server 2001 workspaces. Workspaces are migrated to portal sites, and categories are migrated to Topic areas.

Before you start the in-place upgrade process, take note of the following points and make the necessary changes to your SharePoint Portal Server 2001 installation:

■ Make sure that existing category names contain 100 or fewer characters.

■ Check whether you have installed any third-party software such as backup programs and antivirus software. You should either remove them before the upgrade process or at least check with the vendor to see if these programs are also supported under Windows Server 2003 and SharePoint Portal Server 2003.

■ Review the "Upgrading from Microsoft SharePoint Portal Server 2001" topic in the SharePoint Portal Server 2003 Administrator's Guide online Help file.

■ Start the upgrade to SharePoint Portal Server 2003 *before* you upgrade the operating system to Windows Server 2003. You cannot export data from SharePoint Portal Server 2001 after the server is upgraded from Windows 2000 Server to Windows Server 2003.

■ After you upgrade to SharePoint Portal Server 2003, manually migrate any features that require manual migration. For more information, see the white paper "Migrating from SharePoint Team Services and SharePoint Portal Server 2001 to Microsoft SharePoint Products and Technologies," which was referenced at the start of this chapter.

Upgrading to SharePoint Portal Server 2003 consists of the following eight procedures, which are also documented in the white paper just mentioned:

1. Back up and restore the SharePoint Portal Server 2001 data to another computer that is running SharePoint Portal Server 2001. Check that both systems work.

2. Export the SharePoint Portal Server 2001 configuration information by running the Upgrade.exe program file, which is on the SharePoint Portal Server 2003 CD. You will need to specify a location. This can be a local drive or a network share. The upgrade process will create a directory named *$$_SharepointPortalV1Export-Data_$$*, in which will be a number of XML files with naming conventions such as *<workspacename>*_BestBetKeyWords, *<workspacename>*_Categories _$*<categoryname>*, *<workspacename>*_search*n*, *<workspacename>*_Security, and V1Export.XML, which contain the workspace details, categories, content sources, keywords, and Best Bets. V1Export.XML is a summary of your workspaces and contact names. You can edit these files if you do not wish to import a particular workspace or a category into your SharePoint Portal Server 2003 deployment.

3. Upgrade Windows 2000 Server to Windows Server 2003 and install ASP.NET. If you plan to rename the server, complete this change either before upgrading the computer to Windows Server 2003 or before you install ASP.NET.

4. Use the Upgrade.exe program a second time, which upgrades the SharePoint Portal Server 2001 document store to the SharePoint Portal Server 2003 backward-compatible document store.

5. Install SharePoint Portal Server 2003. Every SharePoint Portal Server 2003 installation includes a SQL Server content store. During the SharePoint Portal Server 2003 installation, the SQL Server content store is created to support the needs of the portal site and to support additional SharePoint sites created on the server. The original SharePoint Portal Server 2001 documents remain in the backward-compatible document store installed in procedure 4 of this list.

6. Import SharePoint Portal Server 2001 configuration information—that is, the categories, keywords, and content sources—into the new portal site by clicking **Site Settings** and then under the Portal Site Content section, clicking **Import Microsoft SharePoint Portal Server 2001 data** as shown in Figure 42-3.

7. The Import SharePoint Portal Server 2001 Data Web page is displayed as shown in Figure 42-4. Select the content type you wish to import, that is, *Areas*, *Listings and Best Bets*, and *Search*. Choose the workspace from which you wish to import the configuration details, and then click **OK**.

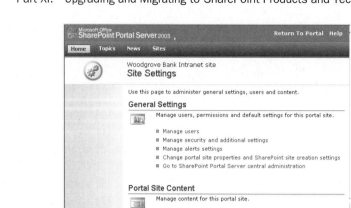

Figure 42-3   Site Settings: Import Microsoft SharePoint Portal Server 2001 data

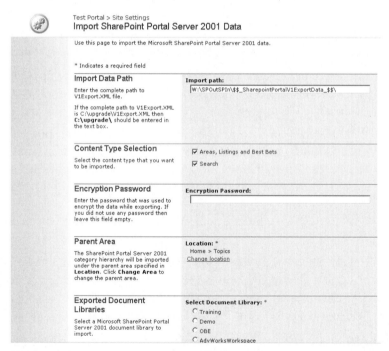

Figure 42-4   Import Microsoft SharePoint Portal Server 2001 Data Web page

A Web page is displayed to show the progress of the import operation. When the operation is complete, a summary Web page is displayed as shown in Figure 42-5.

Figure 42-5 Import SharePoint Portal Server 2001 operation completion summary page

8. Click **OK** and then check that the areas, listings, keyword Bests Bets, and content sources are configured as you would expect.

9. Convert dashboard Web Parts to the Web Part Infrastructure for Microsoft Products and Technologies.

10. Migrate documents and their associated descriptive information (*metadata*) from SharePoint Portal Server Web Storage System document libraries to the SQL content database document libraries.

If you just want to run the upgrade process so that you migrate just the configuration details, such as categories and content sources, complete procedure 2 of the preceding list and save the resulting XML file in a secure location where it will not be accidentally deleted; then follow the installation procedures as in Chapter 3, and, depending on your deployment scenario, Chapter 11, "Deploying a Single Server and a Small Server Farm," or Chapter 12, "Deploying Medium and Large Server Farms." Then complete procedure 6 of the preceding list.

When you import SharePoint Portal Server 2001 data to SharePoint Portal Server 2003 during an upgrade operation from SharePoint Portal Server 2001 to SharePoint Portal Server 2003, you might receive the following error message, where X is a number:

```
Successfully imported X out of X areas.
Error(s) occurred during the import. See logs for details.
```

Even though the error message indicates that all items are imported successfully, you might find that not all items are imported to SharePoint Portal Server 2003. When you view the log files, an entry indicates that the error that occurred is a result of a duplicate topic or category name. However, the actual name of the duplicate item is not specified in the entry. This problem might occur if one or more of the SharePoint Portal Server 2001 topics or one or more of the SharePoint Portal Server 2001 categories that you import to SharePoint Portal Server 2003 use the same name as one or more of the default topics or the default categories in SharePoint Portal Server 2003. Additionally, the duplicate item is not imported to SharePoint Portal Server 2003.

To work around this problem, in procedure 6 of the preceding list, change the name or the names of the duplicate SharePoint Portal Server 2001 categories or the duplicate SharePoint Portal Server 2001 topics in the .xml file that contains the data that you exported from SharePoint Portal Server 2001. To do so, open the .xml file, determine the name or the names of the duplicate topics or the duplicate categories, and then edit the .xml file to specify a unique name for each duplicate SharePoint Portal Server 2001 topic or category.

Upgrading Web Parts to the Microsoft .NET Framework

Web Parts were introduced as a part of Microsoft Digital Dashboard technology. The first version of the Web Part Development Kit provided the tools, documentation, and sample code that developers needed to build Web Parts for Microsoft Share-Point Portal Server 2001. SharePoint Team Services is an extension of Front Page Extensions and did not use Digital Dashboard Web Parts. However, now both Windows SharePoint Services and SharePoint Portal Server use the ASP.NET 1.1 Web Part infrastructure, which introduces several significant changes in the Web Part rendering model. Because of these changes, you will need to modify your dashboard Web Parts to run in the new Web Part infrastructure. Also, although the ASP.NET 1.1 Framework that supports Web Parts is the same in Windows SharePoint Services and SharePoint Portal Server 2003 so that any Web Part should work in either platform, if the Web Part is designed to use some specific functionality of SharePoint Portal Server, it would only run on a SharePoint Portal Server, unless you are using Web services to access the SharePoint Portal Server functionality.

Tip Web Parts are core to the next version of ASP.NET. In ASP.NET 2.0, currently known as *ASP.NET Whidbey*, Web Parts will not be limited to those websites based on Windows SharePoint Services, but will instead be the building blocks for dynamic websites. The new ASP.NET Web Part framework supports native user controls as well as a new System.Web.UI.WebControls .WebPart class and will work with either Windows or form authentication. The next versions of Windows SharePoint Services and SharePoint Portal Server will build on the ASP.NET 2.0 Web Part framework. Web Parts that you create with SharePoint Products and Technologies today will work with the next version of Windows SharePoint Services. Whidbey Web Part controls will work with ASP.NET Whidbey, with the next version of SharePoint Portal Server, and with the release of an update will work with the current version of Windows SharePoint Services. The information in this tip is based on pre-released information. You should check Microsoft's website for up-to-date information regarding ASP.NET 2.0 and the next versions of SharePoint Products and Technologies.

To convert a dashboard Web Part to the Web Part infrastructure, you must first create a new Web Part class. You can either choose an existing Web Part class or write a new Web Part class. If the ContentType property equals VBScript or Java-Script, you must write a new Web Part class and install it on the server. If the ContentType property in the legacy Web Part equals HTML or XML, you can use one of the built-in Web Parts, such as:

- Content Editor Web Part

- XML Web Part

- Page Viewer Web Part

- Image Web Part

Note   These Web Parts are sealed classes. You cannot derive new classes from them.

These four Web Parts are included in Windows SharePoint Services and Share-Point Portal Server 2003 and are described with the other built-in Web Parts in Chapter 31, "Working with Web Parts": If you have any of the following requirements, consider using the built-in Web Parts, before developing or converting your digital dashboard Web Parts.

- **Minimizing installation and deployment costs.**   Blank versions of the built-in Web Parts are available in the Web Part Gallery. For built-in Web Parts, you can customize and include prepopulated content that can be exported to the (.dwp) file. Each .dwp file is an XML file. The .dwp format for the Web Part infrastructure is similar to, but not the same as, the format that was used in dashboards. Administrators need to make only the .dwp file available to users. They do not need to install a separate dynamic-link library (DLL) and add it as a safe server control.

- **Minimizing maintenance costs.**   Customization to the Web Part is applied only to the .dwp file, so changes do not require you to recompile and reinstall the DLL.

- **Increasing portability for a Web Part.**   To share a Web Part, you can simply export and send the .dwp file to other users in an e-mail message. The other user must have the rights to load the Web Part, and the appropriate DLL must be installed and configured as safe on the website.

If the built-in Web Parts do not meet your needs, you can write a custom Web Part. Writing a custom Web Part requires a development tool such as Visual Studio .NET.

Custom Web Parts must derive from the Microsoft.SharePoint.WebPartPages.WebPart base class. For more information about how to create a Web Part, see Part 10, "Microsoft Office 2003 Integration with SharePoint Products and Technologies" and the SharePoint Products and Technologies SDK. You can write custom Web Parts for any of the following purposes:

- Creating custom properties and using the Web Part infrastructure to display them in the tool pane.

- Creating custom Tool Parts in the tool pane.

- Creating a base class for other Web Parts to extend. For example, to create a collection of Web Parts with similar features and functionality, create a custom base class from which multiple Web Parts can inherit. This reduces the overall cost of developing and testing subsequent Web Parts.

- Improving performance and scalability. A compiled custom Web Part runs faster than a script.

- Securing and controlling access to content within the Web Part. The built-in Web Parts allow any users with appropriate permissions to change content and alter Web Part functionality. With a custom Web Part, you can determine the content or properties to display to users, regardless of their permissions.

- Making your Web Part connectable by implementing one or more of the defined Web Part Connection interfaces. This allows the custom Web Part to provide or access data from other connectable Web Parts.

- Interacting with the object models that are exposed in SharePoint Products and Technologies. For example, you can create a custom Web Part to save documents to a Windows SharePoint Services document library.

- Controlling the cache for the Web Part by using built-in cache tools. For example, you can use these tools to specify when to read, write, or invalidate the Web Part cache.

- Benefiting from a rich development environment with debugging features that are provided by tools such as Visual Studio .NET.

- Implementing proprietary code without disclosing the source code.

- Controlling the implementation of the Web Part. For example, you can write a custom server-side Web Part that connects to a back-end database, or you can create a Web Part that is compatible with a broader range of Web browsers.

To successfully convert your dashboard Web Parts to the Web Part infrastructure, you must understand the changes to properties, namespace, resource handling, tokens, DDSC, and .dwp files that are described in the white paper "Converting Dashboard Web Parts to the Web Part Infrastructure for Microsoft SharePoint Products and Technologies," mentioned earlier in this chapter, and the SDKs.

Developing Dashboard Web Parts That Are Easy to Convert

As you continue to develop dashboard Web Parts for SharePoint Portal Server 2001, use the following recommendations to facilitate moving to the Web Part infrastructure.

- Keep the following general recommendations in mind:

    - Use Extensible Stylesheet Language Transformations (XSLT) instead of Extensible Stylesheet Language (XSL).[2]

    - Do not use deprecated DDSC objects, properties, or methods, for example the Item object and the LoadItem method.

    - Do not use deprecated base class properties, for example, ContentType and Content.

    - Do not use deprecated tokens, for example, _WPC_ and _LogonUserJS.

- Be aware of the caching behavior changes in the Web Parts architecture.

- Use .NET code as much as possible to reduce or eliminate server-side script code in your Web Parts. To do this, use one of the following methods.

Using a Web Service for Data Manipulation

To use a Web Service for data manipulation, design your dashboard Web Parts to separate the presentation code from the nonpresentation code. When you move to the Web Part infrastructure in Windows SharePoint Services and SharePoint Portal Server 2003, you can retain the Web Service and the custom XSLT data manipulation. However, you must use the Web Part base class or one of the built-in Web Parts in the Web Part infrastructure to rewrite the client-side script and the user interface.

Using an ASP.NET Page for Data Manipulation

This method represents a larger departure from the dashboard Web Parts programming model, but it presents far fewer migration challenges. To use an ASP.NET page for data manipulation, follow these steps:

1. Create an ASP.NET server control that contains as much nonpresentation code and as much presentation code as you want.

2. Embed this server control in an otherwise empty ASP.NET page, and set the margins for the page to zero.

3. Specify the ASP.NET page as the content link in your dashboard Web Part.

4. Configure the dashboard Web Part as "isolated." When you do this, the Web Part is rendered in an IFrame.

---

2. When Microsoft Internet Explorer 5.0 was released in 1998, the Microsoft XML Parser (MSXML) included an implementation of Extensible Stylesheet Language (XSL) that was based on a working draft. If you have any legacy XSL, you must convert this to XSLT compatible with the XSL transform engine in the .NET Framework. An xsl-xslt-converter is available from Microsoft's XML download page at *http://msdn.microsoft.com /downloads/list/xmlgeneral.asp*.

When you move to the Web Part infrastructure, you only have to modify the server control to inherit from the new Web Part base class.

Migrating SharePoint Portal Server 2001 Document Library Information to Windows SharePoint Services

The backward-compatible document library option is compatible with SharePoint Portal Server 2001 document approval and routing, and the support of multiple document profiles for each document library folder. With the backward-compatible document libraries, you can use a phased strategy to migrate to SharePoint Portal Server 2003; that is, first install the backward-compatible document library option and then according to your migration plan, move documents from the backward-compatible document library to document libraries in the SQL Server content store. You should note that the security settings on document libraries stored in the SQL Server content store are different from the security options you have on backward-compatible document libraries. You will need to take this into consideration, prior to migrating documents.

> **More Info**   See Chapter 6, "Security Architecture for SharePoint Products and Technologies."

To assist with this movement of documents, use the Microsoft Office SharePoint Portal Server 2003 Document Library Migration Tools. These are a set of utility programs developed by Microsoft for migrating documents and associated descriptive information (*metadata*) from SharePoint Portal Server Web Storage System–based document libraries—that is, from both SharePoint Portal Server 2001 document libraries as well as SharePoint Portal Server 2003 backward-compatible document libraries to the Microsoft SQL Server document libraries. The content exported by the tools can be imported into SharePoint Portal Server 2003 SQL Server document libraries that reside in a SharePoint Portal Server 2003 portal site, a team site, a My Site personal site, or a SharePoint Portal Server 2003 portal area.

The two document library migration tools developed by Microsoft are Spout.exe and Spin.exe. Spout.exe, the Document Library Export Tool, is a Microsoft Windows program that reads Web Storage System–based document libraries and exports (or outputs) the selected content as a collection of files in a format that is understood by the import program. Spin.exe, the Document Library Import Tool, is a Windows command-line program that reads the collection of files created by Spout.exe and adds the documents and associated descriptive information to a selected portal area, a portal site, a team site, or a personal website on the server running SharePoint Portal Server 2003.

The SharePoint Portal Server 2003 Document Library Tools and Documentation are available for download at *http://www.microsoft.com/downloads/details.aspx*. Download and save the file to a folder. Run the file, accepting the End User License

Agreement, and choose a folder to which to extract the three tool files: Spin.exe, Spout.exe, and Spinspouthelp.mht. You should reference the Help file for more information on the migration scenarios, frequently asked questions, and known issues with these tools.

You will need to run SPOut on a computer running one of these operating systems: Windows 2000 Service Pack 4, Windows Server 2003, or Windows XP. Microsoft .NET Framework 1.1 must be installed on the computer.

SPIn must be installed on the server to which the content will be migrated. In a Web farm configuration, SPIn must be run from a Web front-end server.

The tools may also be installed on other computers for the purpose of exporting content. You should only plan to complete the export and import processes when there is little activity on the two servers, mainly for performance reasons.

Using SPOut

To use SPOut, you must be a member of the Administrators group on the SharePoint Portal Server 2001 machine and be the workspace coordinator on the workspace concerned. Navigate to the folder that contains the SharePoint Portal Server 2003 Document Library Tools and double-click SPOut.exe. SPOut is a Windows forms application that consists of three tabs, as shown in Figure 42-6. This application is not localized and is only available in English. Directory browsing must be enabled on the IIS virtual server.

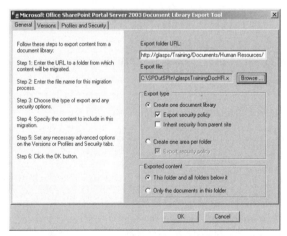

Figure 42-6   Microsoft Office SharePoint Portal Server 2003 Document Library Export Tool

Follow this procedure to export content from a document library:

On the General tab:

1. In the Export folder URL box, type the export folder for the "documents" folder (or a subfolder), such as **http://<*SPS2001server*>/<*workspace*>/Documents /<*documentLibrary*>/**. SPOut will be connecting to this folder as the user name you are running SPOut with. This user name must be a workspace coordinator for SPOut to complete the export process.

2. Click **Browse** to a select an export file folder where the XML manifest file and exported documents are to be written. The exported content must be written to a location that can be accessed from the target server running SharePoint Portal Server 2003, or the files must be copied to the target server before running Spin.exe. The folder must be on an NTFS-formatted file system, and if it is on a file share, it must allow an unlimited number of connections.

> **Security Alert** Ensure that you specify the appropriate security settings on the folder to which you export content. The security settings on the folder will control access to the content until it is imported into the target site and the content in the export folder is deleted.

3. If you are planning to import the content into a document library, do one of the following:

   ■ Select the **Export security policy** check box to map the Reader, Author, and Coordinator roles to site groups that already exist on the SharePoint Portal Server 2003 site. Alternatively, these roles can be mapped to new site groups specified on the **Profiles and Security** tab. The latter is the default, and the specific result depends on the options used during the import phase.

   or

   ■ Select the **Inherit security from parent site** check box to leave the existing security settings on the server running SharePoint Portal Server 2003 unchanged. All existing SharePoint site groups on the site are given default access to the document library.

   In the Export type section, select the export type based on how the exported content is to be imported by Spin.exe:

   ■ The documents from the Web Storage System–based document library folder are to be imported into a single document library, or

   ■ The documents from the Web Storage System–based document library folder are to be imported into a collection of SharePoint Portal Server 2003 portal areas (one source folder per portal area).

4. In the Exported content section, choose whether documents from the export folder URL folder and all subfolders are to be exported or whether only the documents in the export folder URL folder (and not the subfolders) are to be exported.

5. Set any necessary advance options on the **Versions** or **Profiles and Security** tabs.

- On the **Versions** tab, select whether you want to export multiple versions of the document or only one version per document. If you choose to **Export multiple versions per document**, do one of the following:

    1. Export only approved versions. These correspond to the versions of the documents with a major version number and zero as the value of the minor version number, such as 1.0, 2.0, 3.0, and they are converted to *simple versioning*: 1, 2, 3, and so on.

    or

    2. Maximizing. Version history information is converted to simple versioning, such that when imported to a website using SPIn, the version numbers 0.1, 0.2, 1.0, 1.1, and 2.0 become 1, 2, 3, 4, and 5.

    If you choose to **Export only one version per document**, you can limit the export to the:

    - **Most recent version**, or

    - **Most recently approved version**.

- On the **Profiles and Security** tab, select from the following document profile options:

    - **Merge properties from all profiles** (referenced in the documents to be exported) or

    - **Convert all documents to a single profile**. The profile can be selected from a list of available document profiles.

    In the **Role to site group conversion** section, either use the default names for the Reader, Author, and Coordinator site groups (based on the name of the top-level source folder):

    - sourcefoldername_readers

    - sourcefoldername_authors

    - sourcefoldername_coordinators

    or select the **Customize site group names for roles** check box, and enter the new site group names.

6. Verify that all options are set correctly. Click **OK** to begin the export of the documents and descriptive information to the specified folder. Carefully review the export settings in the confirmation dialog box before proceeding, especially warnings about security settings and the possibility of overwriting previously exported content.

Note Routing and approval workflow is not migrated.

An **Export Warning** dialog box will appear, as shown in Figure 42-7. Click **OK**.

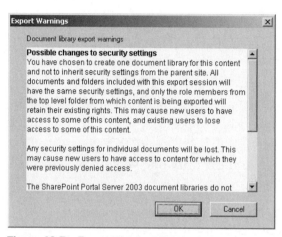

Figure 42-7 Export Warning dialog window

A progress report dialog box will be displayed. If the document library you have chosen to export from does not contain any subfolders, you will see the dialog box shown in Figure 42-8. You will also see this warning if directory browsing is not enabled on the "documents" folder; if this is the case, follow the instructions in the warning dialog box.

Figure 42-8 Server Configuration Warning

Once the export process is complete, read the **Most recent warnings**: text box in the **Progress Report** dialog window, shown in Figure 42-9, and then click Finish.

In the folder where you chose to place the XML manifest file, you will also see a new folder and two text files: an error and a log file. The folder contains subfolders, if you choose to export them and the exported files. The two text files will contain the Most Recent Warnings you read earlier, plus all other progress messages that occurred during the export process. You should check both these files, using a program such as Notepad.

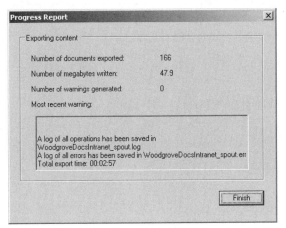

Figure 42-9   Progress Report dialog window

Using SPIn

SPIn is a command-line tool that must be run on the Web Server running the target SharePoint Portal Server 2003 machine. You must be a member of the Administrators group to use the tool. To import the documents and descriptive information created in the previous export procedure into a document library on a SharePoint site, open a command prompt, navigate to the folder where the migration tools are installed, and use the following command:

```
spin.exe <siteurl> <filename>.xml
```

In this code, *<siteurl>* is the URL of the SharePoint site where the imported documents are to be stored, and *<filename>* is the name of the manifest file. It is important that *<siteurl>* is the root URL for a SharePoint site and not, for example, the URL for a document library or another component of a site, or a subsite.

To import the documents and descriptive information created in the export procedure into a collection of SharePoint Portal Server 2003 portal areas, use the following command:

```
spin.exe <siteurl> <filename>.xml /area <areapath>
```

In this code, *<areapath>* is the URL of a top-level SharePoint Portal Server 2003 portal area where portal areas are to be created and the documents are to be stored. To use this format of the SPIn tool, you must have checked the Create one area per folder option in SPOut when you exported the documents; otherwise, you will receive the following error message:

```
Cannot import a folder (tree) exported as a document library into an area
    hierarchy. Remove the /area option and try again.
```

The import process will then fail. When the documents are imported, an area is created for each folder; a document library in that area is created with the same name as the area. The relevant documents are stored in this new document library, and links are placed in the Portal Listings list for the area, for each document in the document library. The SPIn output you will see on the command line will look similar to the following text:

```
W:\SPOutSPIn>spin http://intranet woodgrovedocsit.xml /area it

Validating .xml file. This might take several minutes.
The .xml file is valid.

Setting this registry key value will grant full permissions to the current user on
    the portal site.
Do you want to continue? [y/n] y
The registry value was set.
Disabling search schedule.
Verifying database access ...
Importing content.
Percentage completed: 100.00 %
Content was successfully imported.
Deleting registry key value.
Enabling search schedule.
Import Statistics:
Number of site groups created: 0
Number of areas created or modified: 4
Number of document libraries created or modified: 4
Number of folders created or modified: 0
Number of documents (not counting versions) imported: 16

Total time: 00:01:01
```

If the server running SharePoint Portal Server where you are running the SPIn tool is also an index server, the search component will be stopped. This is primarily for performance reasons. SPIn process creates a special registry value under *HKEY_LOCAL_MACHINE\SOFTWARE\Microsoft\Sharepoint Portal Server\FullControlSID* to ensure that the person who is running the import-job *always* has the right to access the imported files. This registry value is removed after the import job is finished.

In the folder where you execute SPIn, two SPIn-related text files will be created: an error file and a log file. You should review both these files. If SPIn could not resolve the accounts specified in the export XML files, it will default to the account that is performing the migration. This behavior is similar to the SharePoint Team Services migration tool. Therefore, when restoring a site, it is often helpful to create an account specifically for this purpose.

If you migrated SharePoint Portal Server 2001 categories into SharePoint Portal Server 2003 as portal areas, SPIn will detect this and use any categories in the document profiles information to link the imported documents into the appropriate areas.

Migration Tools

This chapter detailed a number of tools that you can use during your migration process. Table 42-3 summarizes these tools and others, together with their capabilities.

Table 42-3 Summary of Migration Tools

Tool	Source	Target	Scenarios
SPSIMEX.exe[*]	SharePoint Portal Server 2001	SharePoint Portal Server 2001	Migrating document content from portal site to portal site
SMIGRATE.exe	SharePoint Team Services and Windows SharePoint Services	Windows SharePoint Services	Site migration
STSADM.exe	Windows SharePoint Services	Windows SharePoint Services	Site backup
UPGRADE.exe	SharePoint Portal Server 2001	SharePoint Portal Server 2003	Moves portal workspaces with categories, content sources, keywords, Best Bets, document libraries, and security
Spout.exe	SharePoint Portal Server 2001 (Web Storage System) and SharePoint Portal Server 2003 (backward-compatible document library)	XML Intermediate file format	Folders, documents, and metadata
Spin.exe	XML Intermediate file format	SharePoint Portal Server 2003 (SQL Server content database)	Folders, documents, and metadata
Custom Extractors[†]	Various native systems	XML Intermediate Format	Folders, Documents, metadata, Lists, and Sites
Custom Importers	XML Intermediate Format	Windows SharePoint Services and SharePoint Portal Server 2003 (SQL Server content database)	Folders, Documents, metadata, Lists, and Sites

[*] Available from the *Microsoft SharePoint Portal Server 2001 Resource Kit*.

[†] The Custom Extractors and Importers tools were co-developed by Hewlett-Packard and Microsoft. These tools were not available at the time of writing this Resource Kit. They are distinct from SPIn/SPOut and focus on cross-product migration, such as Lotus QuickPlace, File system, and Exchange Public Folders. They will be available from Microsoft's MSDN site sometime in 2004, and you can extend the code or create your own extractors.

Summary

The chapter detailed how you might plan and implement a migration and an upgrade to SharePoint Products and Technologies, as follows:

- **SharePoint Team Services to Windows SharePoint Services.**   Both of these products might seem to have similar functionality, as well as a similar look and feel; therefore, you might find that you need little or no training for you or your users to use the new version. However, there are some significant differences between these two versions, and these were listed in this chapter, such as document management, content approval, and the use of the ASP.NET Framework that supports Web Parts. This is to become a Microsoft core technology in the next version of ASP.NET. Web Parts are the same in Windows SharePoint Services as they are in SharePoint Portal Server, so any Web Part should work in either platform, with certain exceptions. You can migrate SharePoint Team Services sites to Windows SharePoint Services websites by using the Smigrate.exe tool. This tool migrates all site content and security settings and can also be used to migrate sites between Windows SharePoint Services servers, site collections, and to different locations within a site collection's hierarchy.

- **SharePoint Portal Server 2001 to SharePoint Portal Server 2003.**   These two products use different technologies to store their content. You can use an upgrade strategy in which documents remain in the Web Storage System, known in SharePoint Portal Server 2003 as the backward-compatible document library. In this way, you can access these documents from the new portal, while maintaining the features of the previous version, such as approval routing and the ability to maintain multiple document profiles per document library. Using the backward-compatible document library with SharePoint Portal Server 2003, you can also maintain most of the PKMCDO application that you might have created. The upgrade program will also migrate categories and content sources to the new portal; however, digital dashboards are no longer supported and you might need to migrate to the newer ASP.NET Web Part Infrastructure rendering technology. Depending on the nature of your legacy Web Part, you might be able to use a built-in Web Part such as the Content Editor Web Part, the XML Web Part, the Page Viewer Web Part, or the Image Web Part, or you might have to write a custom Web Part. If you need to continue developing dashboard Web Parts, you need to design them to ease future conversion to the Web Part infrastructure.

Glossary

access control list (ACL)   A list of users or groups and their security permissions. Identifies who can update, modify, or delete an object on a computer or resource on the network.

Active Server Pages (ASP pages)   A technology that allows Web developers to combine scripts and HTML code to create dynamic Web content and Web-based applications.

administration port   The Internet Information Services (IIS) virtual server and port used for SharePoint Central Administration.

alert   A feature that notifies a user by e-mail when there is a change to an item, document, list, or document library on the website.

Anonymous authentication   An authentication method that provides access to users who do not have user accounts on the server computer.

anonymous user access   The ability to gain access to a Web server on which one does not have an account. Usually, anonymous users have more restricted access rights than users with accounts.

application pool   In Internet Information Services (IIS), a group of one or more URLs served by a worker process.

approval process   The process of reviewing a document before publishing it.

approval route   The path through which a document is approved.

approve   To accept a submitted item for publication.

approver   A user who has permission to approve or reject documents in a specified folder.

area   A classification for grouping content by user-defined criteria such as page contents, file types, or a similar distinction.

audience   A custom group used to target content to people based on membership within the group.

Authentication   The process of proving that a user is who he or she claims to be.

authorization   The process of determining what a user is permitted to do.

Basic authentication   Authentication protocol supported by most Web servers and browsers. Transmits the user name and password in clear text.

cache   A special memory subsystem in which frequently used data values are duplicated for quick access.

Certificate authentication   An authentication method that provides security for TCP/IP connections. Also known as Secure Sockets Layer (SSL).

character set   A group of alphabetic, numeric, and other characters that have some relationship in common. For example, the standard ASCII character set includes letters, numbers, symbols, and control codes that make up the ASCII code scheme. See also *code page*.

check in   To release the lock for editing and enable other users to view the updated file or check out the file.

check out   To lock a file while editing it to prevent others from overwriting or editing it inadvertently. Only the user who checks out a document can edit the document.

check-in form   The form that displays when a user checks in a document to a backward-compatible document library. The form contains a box for check-in comments, an option to publish a document, and a drop-down menu for selecting a document profile.

clear text   Unencrypted, non-machine-dependent ASCII text in readable form.

code page   An ordered set of characters in which a numeric index (code point) is associated with each character of a particular writing system. There are separate code pages for different writing systems, such as Western European and Cyrillic.

code point   A numeric value in Unicode or in a code page that corresponds to a character. For example, in the Western European code page, 132 is the code point for the character ä; however, in another code page, the code point 132 might correspond to a different character.

Common Gateway Interface (CGI)   A standard method of extending Web server functionality by executing programs or scripts on a Web server in response to Web browser requests, such as in form processing. Use of CGI can make a Web page more dynamic.

component settings database   A database that stores service information for each portal site in a deployment.

configuration database   The Microsoft SQL Server or MSDE database that contains the configuration information that applies across all servers in a deployment of SharePoint Products and Technologies, such as virtual server information.

configuration property   A property that allows an administrator to control Windows SharePoint Services settings.

connection type   The type of Web Part connection. For example, the Provide Row To connection type passes a row of data from one Web Part to another Web Part, and the Get Filter From connection type gets a value from one Web Part and filters the data in another Web Part based on that value.

content database   The Microsoft SQL Server, MSDE, or WMSDE database that contains the content for one or more SharePoint sites.

content index   The full-text index, pointer to the property store, and other data that describes content across content sources, scopes, and servers.

content source   A starting point for crawling a file system, database, or website.

crawl   To search content to include it in a content index.

cross-site group   A custom security group that applies to more than one website. A cross-site group can be assigned to a site group as if it were a single user.

customize   To change the layout, view, content, etc., for a group of users.

datasheet view   A view of a SharePoint list that allows you to modify multiple values.

dictionary   A defined list of values for a property.

Digest Access authentication   An authentication method that transmits user names and passwords in a secure format.

discussion server   A computer that stores discussion text and information about the location of the file being discussed.

discussion thread   In a discussion board or Web discussions, a series of messages or comments in which replies are nested under the message or comment instead of being arranged in chronological or alphabetical order.

document library   A folder where a collection of files is stored and where the files frequently use the same template. Each file in a library is associated with user-defined information that is displayed in the content listing for that library.

document profile   A set of properties applied to similar documents in the backward-compatible document library.

Document Workspace site   A website based on the Document Workspace template that workspace members use for discussing, editing, and working together on a document.

encryption   A method used to scramble the content of a file or data packet to make the data unreadable without the decryption key.

encryption key   A block of data that is used to encrypt or decrypt information.

encryption, 128-bit   A high level of encryption that uses a 128-bit key to scramble the contents of a file or data packet to make the data unreadable without the decryption key.

encryption, 40-bit   A low level of encryption that uses a 40-bit key to scramble the contents of a file or data packet to make the data unreadable without the decryption key.

enhanced folder   A folder in a backward-compatible document library that supports document management tasks such as check-in, check-out, versioning, approval, and publishing.

enterprise application   A back-end business application that SharePoint Portal Server 2003 connects to by using the application definition Web Part.

enterprise application integration   The process of bringing data or functions from an enterprise application together with data or functions from another enterprise application.

extend   To apply Windows SharePoint Services to a virtual server.

extranet   An external website for an organization; usually secured so that only authorized users can access it.

file allocation table (FAT)   A common format for file cataloging used by MS-DOS and Microsoft Windows operating systems to manage files on a hard disk; a physical method of storing and accessing files from a hard disk. The FAT contains a list of all files on the physical or logical drive.

File Transfer Protocol (FTP)   A protocol that is used to copy files to or from a Web server.

firewall   A security system that uses a proxy server outside of an organization's network to protect the network against external threats, such as malicious users or corrupt files.

FrontPage Server Extensions   A set of programs and scripts that support authoring in Microsoft Office FrontPage and that extend the functionality of a Web server.

full-text index   A resource that is compiled to enable full-text search of documents, document properties, and content that are stored outside the document library but are made available through content sources.

gallery   A collection of Web Parts, list templates, or site templates.

Highlight   A listing or document selected as the best recommendation for a specific portal area.

home page   The main page of a website. A home page usually has links to other pages, both inside and outside the site.

hyperlink   A colored and underlined block of text or a graphic that a user clicks to go to a file, a location in a file, an HTML page on the World Wide Web, or an HTML page on an intranet. Hyperlinks can also go to newsgroups and to Gopher, Telnet, and FTP sites.

IFilter   A component that can interpret a file format, such as the Microsoft Word document format, for the purpose of crawling the text content of files for inclusion in the full-text index.

index propagation   The process of distributing an index from a content index server to one or more Web servers for the purposes of providing search.

Integrated Windows authentication   An authentication method that encrypts user names and passwords in a multiple-transaction interaction between client and server. Also known as Windows NT Challenge/Response authentication.

Internet   The worldwide collection of networks and gateways that use the TCP/IP suite of protocols to communicate with one another. If you have access to the Internet, you can retrieve information from millions of sources, including schools, governments, businesses, and individuals.

Internet Information Services (IIS)   Software services from Microsoft that support website creation, configuration, management, and other Internet functions. Internet Information Services include Network News Transfer Protocol (NNTP), File Transfer Protocol (FTP), and Simple Mail Transfer Protocol (SMTP).

Internet Server Application Programming Interface (ISAPI)   A Web server application-development interface, developed by Process Software and Microsoft, that can be used in place of CGI.

intranet   A private network for an organization based on Internet protocols such as TCP/IP.

ISAPI   See *Internet Server Application Programming Interface.*

item   An entry in a list or portal area. An item can contain content or be a link to content stored elsewhere.

job server   A server that hosts shared jobs.

JScript   An object-based scripting language distantly and loosely related to Java. JScript code is inserted directly into an HTML page.

keyword   Metadata that facilitates effective search queries on content included in a full-text index.

keyword synonyms   Words that are identified as having the same or similar meaning as a specific keyword.

list   A website component that stores and displays information that users can add to by using their browsers. Requires a Web server that is running Windows SharePoint Services or SharePoint Portal Server 2003.

local administrators group   The group of users who have permission to perform administration tasks on the local server computer. The permissions for this group are set by using the administration tools for the operating system.

locale ID (LCID)   A 32-bit value defined by Microsoft Windows that identifies a particular language. The LCID consists of a language ID, a sort ID, and reserved bits. For example, the LCID for U.S. English is 1033, and the LCID for Japanese is 1041.

Meeting Workspace site   A website based on a Meeting Workspace site template that is used for planning, posting, and working together on meeting materials and following up after a meeting or series of meetings.

metadata   Data about data. For example, the metadata for a file can include the title, subject, author, and size of the file.

Microsoft SQL Server 2000 Desktop Engine (MSDE)   A data store based on Microsoft SQL Server technology, but designed and optimized for use on smaller computer systems, such as a single-user computer or a small workgroup server. Previously known as Microsoft Data Engine.

Microsoft SQL Server 2000 Desktop Engine (Windows) (WMSDE 2000)   A version of MSDE 2000 designed specifically for Windows SharePoint Services.

multihosting   The ability of a Web server to support more than one Internet address and more than one home page. Also called multihoming.

My Site   The name of a personal site created on a portal site.

network domain   A group of users in a network who share a common set of shared resources, such as server disk drives and printers. A large network may have several domains based on the needs of each set of users.

NTFS file system   An advanced file system designed for use specifically with Microsoft Windows NT and later operating systems. NTFS allows for stronger security and more flexible file management methods than FAT. See also *file allocation table*.

parallel approval   A type of approval route where a document is routed to multiple approvers at the same time.

personal site   A site, named "My Site," created by an individual on a portal site.

personal view   A view of a list, SharePoint document library, or Web Part Page that is available only to a particular user. The personal view of a Web Part Page uses a combination of shared property values and personalized property values. Changes made to a personal view apply only to the list, library, or page in that view and are therefore visible to that user only.

personalize   To change the layout, view, content, etc., for yourself but not for others.

personalized Web Part   A shared Web Part that has been modified by a user in personal view. The changes made to a personalized Web Part are visible only to the user who made the changes.

private Web Part   A Web Part added to a Web Part Page by a user who is working on the page in personal view. Private Web Parts are available only to the user who added or imported the Web Part.

property weighting   The ability to manipulate the rank of a search result by assigning more importance to particular property values. For example, a file that matches a search term in the title might rank higher than a file that matches the search term only in the text.

quiet installation   An installation started with the /q command-line option that runs without generating any user prompts. Also known as unattended installation.

quota   A value that limits the amount of storage or number of users for a website.

quota template   A predefined set of quotas to apply to a site or to all sites on a virtual server.

rank   The relevance of a file to a search query.

rank coercion   The ability to rank a file at the top of search results for a given search query.

remote host   A Web server on a separate server computer. A remote host is connected to other servers by a network connection.

rights   File-level and folder-level permissions that allow access to a website.

role   See *site group*.

scope   The range and depth of a search on the portal site.

scripting language   A programming language designed specifically for website programming. Examples include JScript and Microsoft Visual Basic Scripting Edition (VBScript).

Secure Sockets Layer (SSL)   A proposed open standard that was developed by Netscape Communications for establishing a secure communications channel to prevent the interception of critical information, such as credit card numbers.

serial approval   A type of approval route where a document is routed to one approver after another.

server farm   A central group of network servers maintained by an enterprise or an Internet service provider (ISP). A server farm provides a network with load balancing, scalability, and fault tolerance. In some configurations, multiple servers may appear to users as a single resource.

Setupsts.exe   The setup program for Windows SharePoint Services.

shared services   Portal services that are shared across server farms.

shared view   A view of a list, document library, or Web Part Page that every user with the appropriate permissions on a site can see. The shared view of a Web Part Page uses shared property values. Changes made to a shared view apply to the list, library, or page as it appears to all users.

shared Web Part   A Web Part added to a Web Part Page by a user who is working on the page in shared view. Shared Web Parts are available to all users of a Web Part Page who have the appropriate permissions.

single sign-on   An authentication process that permits a user to enter one name and password to access multiple applications.

site   A group of related Web pages that is hosted by an HTTP server on the World Wide Web or an intranet. The pages in a website typically cover one or more topics and are interconnected through links. Most websites have a home page as their starting point.

site collection   A set of websites on a virtual server that have the same owner and share administration settings. Each site collection contains a top-level website and can contain one or more subsites. There can be multiple site collections on each virtual server.

site group   A custom security group that applies to a specific website. Users are assigned to site groups to grant them permissions on a SharePoint site.

SMTP mail server   An e-mail server that uses the Simple Mail Transfer Protocol (SMTP). SMTP is a member of the TCP/IP suite of protocols that governs the exchange of electronic mail between message transfer agents.

Spotlight Site   A listing or document selected as the best recommendation in the Site Directory.

SQL Server computer   A computer running Microsoft SQL Server with a configured database.

static Web Part   A Web Part that is added to a Web page (.aspx file) and that is not in a Web Part zone.

subsite   A complete website stored in a named subdirectory of the top-level website. Each subsite can have administration, authoring, and browsing permissions that are independent from the top-level website and other subsites.

survey   A website component that presents users with a set of questions specified by the creator of the survey and collects user responses. Results are tallied in a graphical summary. A survey requires a Web server that is running Windows SharePoint Services or SharePoint Portal Server 2003.

Telnet   A protocol that enables an Internet user to log on to and enter commands on a remote computer linked to the Internet, as if the user were using a text-based terminal directly attached to that computer. Telnet is frequently used to gain remote access to UNIX Web servers.

tool pane   A task pane on a Web Part Page used to browse, search for, and import Web Parts from Web Part galleries, and to modify custom and common Web Part properties.

tool part   A control in the tool pane that allows users to set properties, execute commands, invoke wizards, and manipulate Web Parts on a Web Part Page.

Topic Assistant   A tool used to categorize content into areas automatically.

top-level website   The default, top-level site provided by a Web server or virtual server. To gain access to the top-level website, you supply the URL of the server without specifying a page name or subsite.

Uniform Resource Locator (URL)   An address that specifies a protocol (such as HTTP or FTP) and a location of an object, document, World Wide Web page, or other destination on the Internet or an intranet. For example: *http://www.microsoft.com/*.

usage analysis   Data collected to evaluate how a website is being used, such as visitor user names, number of visits to each page, and the types of Web browsers used.

user locale   A setting that determines formats and sort orders for date, time, currency, and so on. Also known as regional settings.

user profile   A collection of properties known about a person within a portal site and related data such as documents the person has written, teams the person belongs to, and links the person has shared.

vCard   The Internet standard for creating and sharing virtual business cards.

versioning   The process of creating a backup copy of a document or picture whenever a revision is saved to the library.

virtual server   A virtual computer that resides on an HTTP server but appears to the user as a separate HTTP server. Several virtual servers can reside on one computer, each capable of running its own programs and each with individualized access to input and peripheral devices. Each virtual server can have its own domain name and IP address.

Visual Basic Scripting Edition (VBScript)   A subset of the Microsoft Visual Basic for Applications programming language optimized for Web-related programming. As with Microsoft JScript, code for VBScript is embedded in HTML files.

Web address   The path to an object, document, file, page, or other destination. An address can be a URL (Web address) or a UNC path (network address) and can include a specific location within a file, such as a Word bookmark or an Excel cell range. Also known as address.

Web discussion   Comments that users attach to Web pages and documents. Known as Web discussions to differentiate them from discussion boards. Web discussions require a Web server that is running SharePoint Team Services or Windows SharePoint Services.

Web farm   See *server farm*.

Web Part   A modular unit of information that consists of a title bar, a frame, and content. Web Parts are the basic building blocks of a Web Part Page. A Web Part is the combination of a Web Part Description (.dwp) file and a Web Part assembly (.dll) file. All Web Parts are based on Web Custom Controls.

Web Part description (.dwp) file   An XML file that defines default property settings for installing a Web Part, including references to any other files required to run and display the part.

Web Part infrastructure   The programming architecture used to work with Web Parts and Web Part Pages.

Web Part Page   A special type of Web page that contains one or more Web Parts. A Web Part Page consolidates data, such as lists and charts, and Web content, such as text and images, into a dynamic information portal built around a common task or special interest.

Web Part zone   A container with a set of properties that can be configured to control the organization and format of Web Parts on a Web Part Page. Web Part zones can also be used to provide protection against changes to Web Parts.

Web server   A computer that hosts Web pages and responds to requests from browsers. URLs for files hosted on a Web server begin with http://. Also known as an HTTP server.

WMSDE   See *Microsoft SQL Server 2000 Desktop Engine (Windows)*.

word breaker   A search technology used to separate text into individual words for implementing search queries.

Index

What do you think of this book?
We want to hear from you!

Do you have a few minutes to participate in a brief online survey? Microsoft is interested in hearing your feedback about this publication so that we can continually improve our books and learning resources for you.

To participate in our survey, please visit:
www.microsoft.com/learning/booksurvey

And enter this book's ISBN, 0-7356-1881-X. As a thank-you to survey participants in the United States and Canada, each month we'll randomly select five respondents to win one of five $100 gift certificates from a leading online merchant.* At the conclusion of the survey, you can enter the drawing by providing your e-mail address, which will be used for prize notification *only*.

Thanks in advance for your input. Your opinion counts!

Sincerely,

Microsoft® Learning

Learn More. Go Further.

To see special offers on Microsoft Learning products for developers, IT professionals, and home and office users, visit: *www.microsoft.com/learning/offers*